American Places
DICTIONARY

American Places Dictionary

A Guide to 45,000 Populated Places, Natural Features, and Other Places in the United States

Covering States, Counties, Cities, Towns, Townships, Villages, and Boroughs, as well as Indian Reservations, Military Bases, and Major Geographical Features, the Entries Providing Description, Precise Location, and Name Origin Information, and Supplemented by Maps & Indexes

in Four Volumes

Volume One: Northeast

Connecticut	**Maryland**	**New York**
Delaware	**Massachusetts**	**Pennsylvania**
District of Columbia	**New Hampshire**	**Rhode Island**
Maine	**New Jersey**	**Vermont**

Edited by

Frank R. Abate

Omnigraphics, Inc.
Penobscot Building • Detroit, Michigan 48226

Editorial Staff

Frank R. Abate, *Editor*

Jacquelyn S. Goodwin, Katherine M. Isaacs, and Elizabeth J. Jewell, *Associate Editors*

Margaret Mary Missar, *Research*

Terri Finkeldey and Christine Kelley, *Editorial Assistants*

Additional Editorial Services provided by Sachem Publishing Associates, Inc., Guilford, CT
Data Processing and Typesetting: Weimer Graphics, Indianapolis, IN

Omnigraphics, Inc.

Eric Berger, *Vice President, Production*

Laurie Lanzen Harris, *Editorial Director*

Peter E. Ruffner, *Vice President, Administration*

James A. Sellgren, *Vice President, Operations & Finance*

Frederick G. Ruffner, Jr., *Publisher*

Library of Congress Cataloging-in-Publication Data

American places dictionary : a guide to 45,000 populated places, natural features, and other places in the United States . . . in four volumes / Frank R. Abate, editor.
   p.   cm.
   Includes indexes.
   Contents: v. 1. Northeast — v. 2. South — v. 3. Midwest — v. 4. West. Appendices & index.
   ISBN 1-55888-747-4 (lib. bdg. : alk. paper : set). — ISBN 1-55888-146-8 (lib. bdg. : alk. paper : v. 1). — ISBN 1-55888-147-6 (lib. bdg. : alk. paper : v. 2). — ISBN 1-55888-148-4 (lib. bdg. : alk. paper : v. 3). — ISBN 1-55888-149-2 (lib. bdg. : alk. paper : v. 4)
   1. United States—Gazetteers.   I. Abate, Frank R.
E154.A48   1994
917.3′003—dc20   93-12306
                                                                                          CIP

Grateful acknowledgment is made to Dr. Kelsie Harder for permission to use the name origin information from his book, *Illustrated Dictionary of Place Names: United States and Canada* (copyright © 1974 by Kelsie Harder).

Contents

Volume One: Northeast

(*Statewide Index at the end of each state section*)

Foreword:

Patterns and Practices in the Naming of American Places

Place names in the United States reflect the attitudes, ambitions, and desires of the namers, who themselves were uprooted from their homes in other countries or from their former homes in eastern states as they moved westward across the North American continent. That they found the land occupied already is also reflected in the Amerindian-derived names (names used by Native Americans) that dot the landscape. The southwestern areas—Texas, New Mexico, Arizona, and California—were settled by Spaniards, who also assigned names as did their English-speaking counterparts who were moving west. Primarily, however, the names now existing came from European languages, the namers being of European descent who sought new living conditions, more freedom, and more space to live out their dreams. From their point of view, they had a new land to settle and, hence, names to give. George R. Stewart, in his *Names on the Land,* wrote that "the names lay thickly over the land, and the Americans spoke them, great and little, easily and carelessly—Virginia, Susquehanna, Rio Grande, Deadman Creek, Sugarloaf Hill, Detroit, Wall Street—not thinking how they came to be."

And they did come to be. A good instance of the way naming occurred comes from the story of how **Hope**, county seat of Hempstead County, Arkansas, received its name. The name also is indicative of how names somehow interact historically, alluding to other names and other places. Hope appears to be an abstract name, symbolizing the thoughts of desire and expectation, placing faith in the future, all in all a good name. Established in 1874, the Arkansas city of Hope was named not necessarily in allegorical anticipation but for Hope Loughborough, daughter of James Loughborough, a director of the Cairo and Fulton Railroad. This is simple enough and a standard naming method, that of giving to a place the name of a loved one, such as a wife, daughter, sometimes a son, and many such names exist in the United States. But the former county seat of Hempstead County, **Washington**, named for George Washington, was called the "birthplace of Texas," because Stephen F. Austin resided there and held court before he went to Texas. James Bowie also lived in Washington, Arkansas, before he, too, went to Texas. Before leaving Bowie engaged a certain James Black to craft a special knife for him.

The citizens of Washington, however, would not cooperate with the railway officials, who took their revenge by building Hope and bypassing Washington. Hope became the county seat and the boyhood home of U.S. President Bill Clinton, while Washington became another hamlet. Intertwined here, with many meaningful connotations, are names that have become important for places. Hope is second only to **Union** as the abstract name most often used in the United States. **Austin** became the name for the capital of Texas and a county. Bowie went to his destiny at the Alamo, as well as being remembered for his Bowie knife and also by a county name in Texas.

Sometimes the bizarre occurs. **California**, the county seat of Moniteau County, Missouri, was to be established in 1834 as **Boonesborough**, for Daniel Boone, the frontiersman. But another **Boonesborough** existed in Missouri, so the name was not approved by postal officials, who often forced the alteration or wholesale change of place names before they could be made official. A man happened along who offered a jug of whiskey if the people would name the town for him. The offer was accepted. His name was California Wilson. An extreme case, no doubt, but indeed many honorific names were bestowed by town officials in recognition of the owner or purveyor of the land on which the town was first platted. **Lovewell**, Kansas, for instance, was named for Thomas Lovewell, who gave land for the railroad, a church, and a school. **Chardon**, Ohio, was named for Peter Chardon Brooks, who donated the site. Thomas Bell granted the land that became **Bellville, Texas**. **Phil Campbell**, Alabama, was named for the man who built a depot and railroad spur to the town in exchange for its being given his name.

Occasionally, town leaders will name the place for a wealthy person in hope of obtaining favors (money included). For instance, **Vanderbilt**, Tennessee, was named for Cornelius Vanderbilt, in the hope that this would persuade him and his family to live there during summer months. Vanderbilt chose Asheville, North Carolina, for that purpose, whereupon **Vanderbilt**, Tennessee, changed its name to **Ervin**, honoring Dr. J. N. Ervin, who had donated land for the courthouse. All along, the post office had been called **Erwin**, for Jesse B. Erwin, the first county-court clerk. When the town was incorporated, **Erwin** was made official, the excuse being that it was close enough to **Ervin**.

A close examination of the names in *American Places Dictionary* will reveal many patterns. It will also reveal psychological aspects of the minds of the namers and give insight into the character of the historical period in which the patterns occur. In the colonial years, from the time settlers began to arrive from Europe in the 17th century to the end of the Revolutionary War in 1783, place names indicated three distinct patterns: descriptive, those based on English royalty, and English transfer names. Also, a few religious names appeared (**Bethel, Canaan, Providence**), but the three larger patterns dominated.

The descriptive names always reflect the point of view of the namer, for what is now **Trout Brook** could just as easily have been **Birch Brook**. Descriptive names were attached especially to features, seldom to habitation places, unless a community developed around a feature, usually a spring or other watercourse, such as **Big Spring** and **Deep River**. The descriptive names were merely identifiers, serving the purpose of immediacy; some were actually translated from an Amerindian name.

English royalty names contributed many of the major names in the original colonies: **New York** (state and city) and **Albany** for James, Duke of York and Albany, later King James II of England; **Brunswick**, for one of the titles of the British royal house of Hanover; **Buckingham**, in reference to the title of George Villiers and later of his son; **Elizabeth** (New Jersey) for the wife of Sir George Carteret; **Cape Ann** (Massachusetts) for the wife of James I; **Annapolis** (Maryland) and **Anne Arundel County** (Virginia) for Anne Arundell, daughter of Lord Thomas Arundell of Wardour and wife of Cecilius Calvert, Lord Baltimore; **North Carolina, South Carolina, Cape Charles** (Virginia), **Charles River** (Massachusetts), **Charles City** (Virginia), and **Charles City County** (Virginia), for Charles I; **Charleston** and **Charleston County** (South Carolina) are named for Charles II. Such a list could go on for pages.

English county and town names used during these years show both nostalgia for the former homes of colonists and also the desire to perpetuate the names. Among the more well known transfers are **New England**, **Chester** (Connecticut, Massachusetts, Pennsylvania, and throughout the United States; at least forty other municipalities are named **Chester**), **Durham** (Connecticut, New Hampshire, New York, North Carolina, and nine other states), **Winchester** (Connecticut, Massachusetts, New Hampshire, Virginia, and twelve other states), **Kent** (Connecticut, Delaware, Florida, Maryland, New York, Rhode Island, and nine other states), **Norfolk** (Connecticut, Massachusetts, New York, Virginia, and three other states), **Dover** (Delaware, New Hampshire, New Jersey, North Carolina, Pennsylvania, and twenty other states), **New London** (Connecticut, New Hampshire, North Carolina, Pennsylvania, and six other states), **Plymouth** (Connecticut, Massachusetts, New Hampshire, Pennsylvania, Virginia, and seventeen other states), **Cumberland** (Maryland, Pennsylvania, Rhode Island, and seven other states), **Portland** (Connecticut, New York, Pennsylvania, and thirteen other states), **Essex** (Connecticut, Massachusetts, New York, and five other states), and **Bristol** (Connecticut, New York, New Hampshire, Rhode Island, and sixteen other states).

Other English place name transfers are not so well known, but still were quite popular. Examples include **Farmington** (Connecticut, Delaware, New Hampshire, New York, North Carolina, Pennsylvania, and sixteen other states), **Enfield** (Connecticut, New Hampshire, New York, North Carolina, and Illinois), **Glastonbury** (Connecticut), **Newington** (Connecticut, Georgia, and New Hampshire), **Torrington** (Connecticut), **Litchfield** (Connecticut, New York, New Hampshire, and seven other states), **Haddam** (Connecticut), **Killingworth** (from **Kenilworth;** Connecticut), **Guilford** (Connecticut, New York, and nine other states), **Derby** (Connecticut and three other states), and many more. **Brentford** (South Dakota) shows that the practice continued beyond colonial times. In some cases, particularly as Americans moved westward, the names were actually given in honor of the American town the pioneers had left behind, rather than for the original English name.

After the Revolutionary War, places began to be named for war heroes and leaders. This occurred especially in the new states being formed west of the Appalachian Mountains and were influenced strongly by the fervor of patriotism that swept through the former colonies. County names especially reflect this commemorative movement, with the major leaders all being so honored: (George) **Washington** (31 counties), (Benjamin) **Franklin** (23 counties), (Thomas) **Jefferson** (25 counties), (General Nathanael) **Greene** (17 counties), (Alexander) **Hamilton** (eight counties), (German-born French soldier Johann, Baron de Kalb, who fought with the Americans during the war) **DeKalb** (ten counties), (Patrick) **Henry** (ten counties), (James) **Madison** (20 counties), (General Richard) **Montgomery** (16 counties), (General Francis "The Swamp Fox") **Marion** (17 counties), (General Daniel) **Morgan** (9 counties), (Polish soldier Count Casimir, who also fought with the Americans) **Pulaski** (7 counties), (General Israel) **Putnam** (9 counties), and (General "Mad Anthony") **Wayne** (16 counties). The Marquis de **LaFayette**, French statesman and aide to Washington, is commemorated in 17 U.S. counties, and a host of cities and towns, some using only the **Fayette** portion of his name.

Names of other heroes from the American Revolution, now obscure, dot the maps of states: (soldier Anthony) **Bledsoe** (Tennessee), (Kentucky soldier and statesman John) **Adair** (Louisiana, Kentucky, Missouri), (Major General Ethan) **Allen** (Ohio), (soldier and U.S. Senator John) **Armstrong** (Pennsylvania), (soldier Nicholas) **Herkimer** (New York), (Sergeant William) **Jasper** (8 counties), (soldier and U.S. Representative Joseph) **McDowell** (North Carolina), (General Hugh)

Mercer (six counties), (soldier John) **Newton** (Georgia, Indiana), (one of the captors of British spy John Andre, soldier John) **Paulding** (Georgia, Oklahoma), (General Thomas) **Person** (North Carolina), and (soldier and U.S. Representative Andrew) **Pickins** (Alabama, Georgia, South Carolina) are examples.

Signers of the Declaration of Independence were among the most commemorated: (John) **Adams** (eight counties), (Carter) **Braxton** (Virginia), (Charles) **Carroll** (11 counties), (Benjamin) **Franklin** (23 counties), (Button) **Gwinnett** and (Lyman) **Hall** (Georgia), (John) **Hancock** (10 counties), (Benjamin) **Harrison** (West Virginia), (Samuel) **Huntington** (Indiana), (Thomas) **Jefferson** (25 counties), (Richard Henry) **Lee** (Georgia, Illinois), (Thomas) **McKean** (Pennsylvania), (Robert Hunter) **Morris** (New Jersey), (Thomas) **Nelson** (Virginia, Kentucky), (Benjamin) **Rush** (Indiana), (George) **Walton** (Georgia), and (George) **Wythe** (Virginia).

The same was true after the War of 1812, with counties being named for leaders and heroes, including (Andrew) **Jackson** (21 counties); (John) **Coffee** (Alabama, Tennessee); (Stephen F.) **Decatur** (five counties); (Oliver Hazard) **Perry** (10 counties); (Thomas) **McDonough** and (William, who also fought in the Black Hawk War of 1832) **McHenry** (Illinois); (James) **Lawrence** (11 counties); (Alexander) **Macomb** (Michigan); (Virgil) **McCracken**, (James) **Meade**, and (Alney) **McLean** (Kentucky); (William) **Moore** (Tennessee); and (Zebulon) **Pike** (10 counties).

In the so-called Military Tract of upstate New York, as noted by George R. Stewart in *Names on the Land*, many names from Greco-Roman history and culture were given by the state land commissioners. Though they themselves probably were not steeped in the classics, perhaps the influence of a name already assigned, **Seneca Lake** (itself of Amerindian origin, not classical, but converted into a classical name from Mohegan—with a Dutch spelling—**Sinneken**, or **Sinnegar**, or **Sennicky**), started the trend. Along with nearby **Troy, Seneca** seems to have been the catalyst to the naming of 23 townships on classical or literary models: **Lysander, Hannibal, Cato, Camillus, Cicero, Manlius, Marcellus, Aurelius, Romulus, Scipio, Sempronius, Tully, Fabius, Ovid, Homer, Solon, Hector, Ulysses, Virgil,** and **Cincinnatus.** After exhausting their store of classical names, they added the English literary greats, improvising with **Milton, Locke,** and **Dryden.** Once the precedent was set in New York, the custom of using classical or literary names became common and a pattern throughout the United States.

The use of suffixes in places has continued from the time of **Jamestown** to the present: **Elizabethtown, Youngstown,** and **Austintown,** plus the many **-towns** that were shortened to **-ton** (**Charles Town** to **Charleston**). The suffixes **-boro, -burg(h), -ville, -field,** and **-polis** yielded, among hundreds of others, **Hatboro** (Pennsylvania), **Pittsburgh** (Pennsylvania and elsewhere), **Bloomfield** (Illinois and elsewhere), and **Annapolis** (Maryland).

As befits a new country with a strong religious base, biblical names became common between the Revolutionary War and the Civil War, including **Bethel** (possibly the most popular biblical name), **Shiloh, Bethlehem, Corinth, Dothan, Ephrata, Jerusalem, Joseph, Mary, Salem, Zion,** and **Zoar,** along with many names assigned by the Church of Latter-Day Saints in Utah. In parts of the country already settled by Spanish speakers, the names of saints prevailed, many such names having been given by Spanish explorers for the saint's day, or day of naming: **San Luis Obispo, Santa Rosa, San Francisco, San Diego, San Gabriel, San Bernardino, San Juan, San Rafael,** and **Santa Barbara,** as well as many others in the western states. In Florida, **Saint Augustine** survives from the Spanish colonial era there, the oldest continuously inhabited settlement in the United States.

In the middle states and in Louisiana and in areas bordering Quebec in Canada, French names of saints survive, among them **St. Bernard Parish** (Louisiana), **Lake St. Catherine** (Vermont), **St. Croix County** (Wisconsin), **Ste. Genevieve County** (Missouri), and, probably the most famous French-derived name, **St. Lawrence River** (anglicized from **St. Laurent)**, given originally to a harbor by explorer Jacques Cartier on the saint's day, August 10, 1535, and then spread to the gulf, the river, and places along the river. But not much direct use of honorific saints' names occurred after the Revolutionary War, except humorously or facetiously. Some that are apparently saint's names actually have a more mundane explanation, such as **St. John** (Kansas) for John Pierce St. John, a prohibitionist; **St. James** (Missouri), probably for Thomas James, founder; and **St. George** (South Carolina), for James George, first settler.

The coming of the railroads in the mid-nineteenth century and the resulting explosion of new settlements dictated the need for many, many names, spread hastily and almost indiscriminately across the United States. The name origins of many of these towns are opaque, forgotten or buried in stored files of long discontinued railway offices. Railway officials, clerks, engineers, even some company presidents were entrusted with the practical necessity of naming stations along a line. Perhaps rough guidelines existed, but generally the namer was left to his or her devices, and these included names of superiors, female friends, male friends, family members, names from back East, foreign names, spelling deviations, back formations, blends, and personal whim. A few examples include **Mitchell** (Indiana), for a chief surveyor; **Conroe** (Texas), for a sawmill owner; **Crete** (Illinois) and **Corfu** (Washington), for the Mediterranean islands; **Creston** (Louisiana), for the highest point along the line; **Cressona** (Pennsylvania), for John Champman Cresson, president of a railroad; and **Depot** (Oregon), when inspiration ends.

After the Civil War **Lincoln** became the most popular name in the United States, commemorating the martyred president, although the giving of this honorific for Abraham Lincoln was far less common in the South. But **Lincoln**, for Benjamin Lincoln, commander of the American forces in the South during the Revolutionary War, does occur in southern states and several southern counties have his name. The continuing popularity of **Lincoln** is such that it still surpasses **Washington** as the name most often given to places needing a name, especially housing developments.

Names commemorating state and local politicians (legislators, state officials, and governors) represent a naming pattern of sizeable proportions. These names perpetuate the memory of the authors of bills, of friends in state legislatures, of those courted for political favors, and of self-aggrandizing legislators. A representative selection includes **Alexander County** (North Carolina), **Allen County** and **Anderson County** (Kansas), **Ashville** (Alabama), **Casey** and **Menard** (Illinois), **Morgan** (Utah), **Rabun** (Georgia), **Miller County** (Missouri), and **Pitkin** (Colorado).

Place names in the twentieth century generally were given by land developers and realtors, who are not apt to follow traditional patterns. Rather, they name to impress potential customers, the name somehow appealing to nostalgia, to Amerindian themes, to prestige, to love of nature, to snobbery, or to what is aesthetically pleasing. The names are self-consciously selected, sometimes invented. Examples of these types of names (typically with British connotations) would include **Cambridge Estates, Berkeley Grove, Essex Homes, Strathmore Village,** and **Brentwood-in-the-**

Pines. Nature names include **Tanglewood, Woodland Acres, Oak Manor, Seaside Shores, Sunset Hills, Cedar Farms**, and **Beechwood Lawns**. Amerindian names have strong appeal, but not necessarily to the Amerindians. Still, **Connetquot Park, Haccabauk Park, St. Regis Homes**, and **Winnesunk Gardens** indicate that such names have prestige value. Land development names strove to avoid the coarse, vulgar, or deviant; as a result, they have an innocence or blandness about them. This new wave of promotional naming has largely supplanted such older, unprepossessing examples as **Hog Hollow, Skunk Creek, Duck Pond.** Similarly, ethnic names that could possibly intimidate have given way to carefully sanitized ones.

Some influence in assigning place names was wielded by the U.S. Post Office Department, and also by the U.S. Board on Geographic Names, an interdepartmental agency composed of federal government officials. In the latter part of the nineteenth century, postal officials decided that names of places should be short, yielding the likes of **Ink** (Missouri), **Fry** (Texas), **Ono** and **Igo** (California), **Roy** (New Mexico), and **Ely** (Nevada). Some "original" names were changed by postal officials, either because the same name was already in use in the same state or out of bureaucratic propriety. One postal regulation stipulated that for "names consisting of more than one word, it is desirable to combine them into one word," resulting in **Mountpleasant, Boilingsprings, Bigprairie, Bigflat, Beaverdam, Bearcreek, Bonaire, Musselshell, Warmsprings, Plentywood, Forestgrove, Coscob, Glenlyon**, and **Polebridge**. Many have been changed back to two words, but many still exist unchanged. Apostrophes, with few exceptions—**Martha's Vineyard, D'hanis, O'brien**, and **O'Fallon**—have been eliminated through official guidelines. On the whole, however, the U.S. Board on Geographic Names has, at least in recent years, approved local preferences on names.

Names deriving from Amerindian languages have been popular since the earliest days of European settlement. The Amerindians had their own names (sometimes many, designating different locales along a single river) for geographical features, and many of these were used by the invaders, especially river names, such as **Potomac, Rappahanock, Susquehanna, Connecticut, Mohawk, Pomperaug, Naugatuck, Mystic**, and **Willimantic**. The names changed as they were filtered through the pronunciation and spellings of the English, French, or Dutch settlers, and were used without any consciousness of original meaning. Only later did an interest in the etymology of the place names develop, but by then the original meaning and pronunciation had been lost in so many instances that origins were either guessed at or romanticized. Still, the influence of Amerindian names led to several states having Amerindian-derived names, including two in the colonies—**Connecticut** and **Massachusetts**. The reasons why settlers retained and accepted Amerindian names are complicated. A practical reason was that the names were already there. Also, during the late eighteenth and early nineteenth centuries, Enlightenment and Romantic thinkers tended to idealize the Amerindians as "noble savages," symbolizing the goodness of natural life.

On the other hand, some Europeans looked upon the Amerindians as enemies and savages whose names should not be used for places. This attitude is shown in such states as **Kentucky**, which has few Amerindian-derived names. Whatever the reasons, the Europeans retained or gave Amerindian names to thousands of places, including the state name, **Indiana**. Such names as **Rockaway, Cherokee, Chickasaw, Apache, Ute, Creek, Iroquois, Minnewashka, Cathlamet, Catoctin, Edisto, Erie, Guyandot, Hassayampa, Manitou**, and **Winnebago** may only resemble the original names, but stand at least as commemoratives of the many Amerindian groups in the United States, all now woven into the country's fabric of names.

The geographical names in the United States have an unsurpassed variety. The ethnic mix of peoples has produced names not only from the four main linguistic sources (Amerindian, English, Spanish, and French) but also from the languages of immigrants who have settled throughout the fifty states. Germans, Swedes, Italians, Hungarians, Dutch, Russians, Polynesians, Japanese, Chinese, Czechs, Slovaks, Greeks, Norwegians, Danes, Hindus, and Middle Easterners have contributed to the named places, and their legacy appears on the pages of *American Places Dictionary*. Above all, the wonder is the assimilation of these names into acceptance in an expanse of land so varied and with peoples of such different national backgrounds. In this rich mix of names is the culture of a nation, its history, psychology, folklore, and perhaps its destiny.

Kelsie B. Harder
State University of
New York at Potsdam

October 1993

Introduction & How to Use This Book

American Places Dictionary (APD) provides comprehensive coverage of places throughout the United States that are the subject of frequent inquiry. Included among the 45,000 entries are:

Political Entities

- States

- Counties and County Equivalents

- Legally Incorporated Places: e.g., cities; towns in New England; etc.

- Unincorporated Places: e.g., townships and villages in some states; Census Designated Places (CDPs) in certain states; etc.

American Indian Reservations

Major U.S. Military Installations

Major U.S. Geographic Features: mountains and ranges, rivers, natural landmarks, etc.

This Introduction will first discuss the overall organization and contents of *APD*; then explain the entry presentation and information given at the state, county, and place levels; and finally touch on two major areas covered in *APD*: name origin information and the variety of government structures in the United States.

Organization of Entries by County

Each volume of *APD* covers the states of one region of the country, with each state presented alphabetically in its own section. In each state section entries appear *alphabetically by county*. This organization brings together entries that are closely related.

Unique Arrangement by County

There are few, if any, major reference books that present material by county. The county-by-county organization of APD was deliberately chosen to meet the needs of the many users who are interested in the local context. Within a county the places tend to be closely linked historically, culturally, and economically. The county-by-county organization of APD provides 3,141 county profiles covering the entire United States. This allows quick comparison and cross-study at the county level, and brings out clearly the interrelationship of entries. Thus population, land and water area, population density, historical background, and name origins can be easily compared. In metropolitan areas, suburbs and other communities are listed with their near neighbors.

State Indexes and National Index

For those needing alphabetical access to the populated places in a state, or all the populated places (and other entries) in the United States, both state indexes and a national index are provided. *State indexes*, including all places and counties listed alphabetically, are at the end of each state section. Volume Four contains a *national index*, covering all places and counties in the entire United States.

Coverage

Populated Places

Volumes One through Four of *APD* offer comprehensive coverage of populated places in the United States that have a functioning government, as well as many other inhabited places. No population limit or other arbitrary cutoff was applied to limit the coverage of *APD*. Every city, town or township, borough, or village was included—no matter its size—if it had legal incorporated status. In addition, thousands of unincorporated townships and other places also have entries. Such places are common in many states and, despite their lack of formal legal status, residents of them often say they are "from. . . ." Our editorial goal in *APD* was to cover U.S. populated places as comprehensively as possible while still giving a substantial amount of reliable data in each entry.

In some states selecting entries for comprehensive coverage presented difficulties, particularly for areas in the western U.S., where many vast tracts of inhabited land have no incorporated places. The editors of *APD* relied on baseline data from the U.S. Bureau of the Census, one of whose many tasks it is to keep track of all the inhabited places in the U.S. that have a functioning government and many less formally defined places that do not. As it is the purpose of the decennial censuses conducted by the Bureau to count all the inhabitants of the U.S., no inhabited area can be overlooked. Unincorporated places and districts must be given some status and name for purposes of the Census.

Another problem confronted the editors when it was discovered that some widely known places, such as La Jolla and Hollywood, California, were not incorporated cities and therefore had no census data from which to create an entry. For the fifty or so best-known of these unincorporated places, the editors placed a cross-reference in the county listing for the place, directing the reader to the incorporated place where data covering it was included. These unincorporated places also appear in the state and national indexes, with cross-references to the relevant entries.

Other Places and Features

In addition, other U.S. places that merit particular attention—American Indian reservations, major military installations, and major geographic features (see list of types below)—are each covered in separate Appendices in Volume Four. As many of these places are so vast that they cover all or parts of several counties, entering them in the state entries of Volumes One through

Four would have been impracticable. Stilltext, many of these places have important historical and cultural links to the populated places covered in Volumes One through Four, and are often referred to in the name origin or other information for populated places in *APD*. In addition, the American Indian reservations and military installations are themselves populated places.

Appendix A: American Indian Reservations

Appendix A of Volume Four has entries for each of the more than 300 American Indian reservations throughout the United States.

Appendix B: Military Installations

Appendix B of Volume Four has entries for more than 100 major U.S. military installations in the United States. In addition to the basic information given for each, the entries also note which facilities are scheduled to be affected by the 1993 recommendations of the Base Closure Commission.

Appendix C: Major Geographic Features

Appendix C of Volume Four has entries for more than 600 major geographic features across the United States. These include natural features on both land and water. In addition, some sizable features of human construction, such as dams and reservoirs, are also included. Many of these features are frequently referred to in written works, have historical significance, or are popular tourist spots. We have not included national parks as such, although some natural features found within national parks (e.g., Old Faithful, the geyser) do have entries.

The following types of major features are covered:

bays	deserts	oceans	seas
beaches	gaps	passes	sounds
canals	glaciers	peninsulas	trails
capes	gorges	plains	valleys
canyons	gulfs	plateaus	volcanoes
caves	islands	regions	waterfalls
currents	lakes	reservoirs	
dams	mountain ranges and peaks	rivers	

Contents of the Four Volumes

The complete *APD* is a four-volume set, organized as follows:

Entry Presentation and Information in *APD*

Entries for States

In each regional volume the states appear in alphabetic order, each in its own section. There is a section for each of the 50 states, plus a section for Washington, D.C., which appears in both Volume One (Northeast) and Volume Two (South).

Each state section opens with the state seal, followed by a one-page map showing the state and county boundaries and the names of neighboring states or provinces. Each map includes latitude and longitude references in the margins and a scale of miles and kilometers.

Opposite the map page is the state entry information and introductory information. Entries at the state level include the following basic information:

Population: in 1990 and 1980; 1990 rank among the 50 states; percent change from 1980 to 1990; projections for 1995 and 2000 (data from the U.S. Bureau of the Census).

Area: for land and water, in square miles; rank among the 50 states (data from the U.S. Bureau of the Census).

Coastline: number of miles of coastline, as applicable, as reported by the state and other sources.

Elevation: highest and lowest points (data from U.S. Geological Survey and other sources).
State capital: with county
Largest city: with population
Second largest city: with population
Largest county: with population

Housing: number of units, number occupied, percentage vacant (data from the U.S. Bureau of the Census).

Distribution of population by race and Hispanic origin: percentages for White, Black, Hispanic (may be of any race), Native American, Asian and Pacific islander, Other (data from the U.S. Bureau of the Census).

Admission date: with order of admission.

Location: descriptive, noting bordering states, provinces, and bodies of water.

Name Origin: concise account of state name origin.

State Symbols or Emblems: as given by state authorities.

State motto and nickname(s): as given by state authorities.

Telephone Area code(s): with indication of where used if multiple.

Time Zone(s): with indication of where used if multiple.

Abbreviations: both official postal and traditional.

Part of (region): the region or regions that the state is generally considered to be part of.

Following this standard presentation of basic data is a brief introductory essay. Generally, these essays follow a standard outline and include information on local government (counties and municipalities), settlement history and early development, and later history through the twentieth century. They close with a discussion of the state's boundaries, including any peculiarities or disputes with other states.

The state introduction closes with a list of all the counties and, for those states that have them, a list of all multi-county places. The multi-county places are municipalities or census designated places (CDPs) whose area lies within more than one county. Typically, multi-county places have a large portion in one county, with a smaller portion in a second county, often without any population residing there. For each multi-county place the population of the entire place and of each county portion is given. For further discussion of the multi-county places in the United States, see under "Counties" in the discussion below on **Hierarchy of Government in the United States**.

Entries for Counties or County Equivalents

Following the state introduction, each county appears alphabetically, followed by the populated places that are in that county. Each county has an entry that gives the following basic information:

Name
County Seat: with ZIP code
Population (1990 Census; 1980 Census)
Population density (per square mile)
Land area and water area (square miles)
Area code
Descriptive location
Background and establishment
Name origin

Entries for Places below the County Level

In compiling material for the populated places below the county level, which comprise the bulk of the entries in *APD*, the editorial policy was to include as much information as could be reliably reported for each data element in the entry. At minimum, entries in *APD* provide the following for each incorporated populated place below the county level:

Name
Status: city, town, township, etc.

Population (1990 Census)
Land area and water area (square miles)
Latitude and longitude
Population density (per square mile)
Area code (given with county entry)

For some unincorporated places, only name and some 1990 census data are given.

For larger places, particularly for those with a population above 10,000, the amount of data provided is greater, and normally also includes:

ZIP code
Population (1980 Census)

Aside from the statistical data, many entries also include:

Other Information: location, founder, dates of incorporation, etc.
Name Origin: as available; date of naming and previous names given whenever possible.

A typical "full" entry for a municipality in *APD* looks like this:

> **Worcester**   City
> **ZIP:** 01601   **Lat:** 42-16-10 N **Long:** 71-48-32 W
> **Pop:** 169,759 (1990); 161,799 (1980)   **Pop Density:** 4514.9
> **Land:** 37.6 sq. mi.; **Water:** 1.0 sq. mi.   **Elev:** 480 ft.
> In central MA, 15 mi. west of Boston. Second largest city in MA: settled 1673; incorporated as town 1722; as city 1848. Diverse industrial city: machinery and machine tools, fabricated metals, printed materials, and chemicals, plastics, and abrasives.
> **Name origin:** Either for the town of Worcester or for Worcestershire, the county in England in which it is located.

The various elements of an entry may be explained as follows:

Name: the full legal name for the place, or the common name for unincorporated places. In some cases the popular form of the name is given.

Status: (to the right of the name) the legal status of the incorporated place—e.g., City, Town, Township, Village, Borough—according to local use. The types of incorporated places in the state are discussed in each state introduction under the heading *Municipalities*. In the case of unincorporated places, status may be given as "populated place" if official or legal status could not be verified. Certain unincorporated places for which the U.S. Bureau of the Census reports population figures and other data, known as Census Designated Places, are identified as "CDP". *U.S. military installations with resident population* are identified as "Military Facility".

Population (1990 Census): the population reported by the U.S. Bureau of the Census for the decennial census of April 1, 1990. (1980 Census): the population reported by the U.S. Bureau of the Census for the decennial census of April 1, 1980, as corrected, for comparison with 1990. If the populated place is new since 1980 (or its boundaries changed between the 1980 and the 1990 censuses), 1980 data is not given.

Land area and water area (square miles): as provided by the U.S. Bureau of the Census.

Latitude and longitude: in degrees, minutes, and seconds; as provided by the U.S. Bureau of the Census.

Population density (per square mile): calculated by dividing the 1990 population by the land area in square miles.

Telephone Area code (given with county entry).

ZIP code: as reported by the U.S. Postal Service.

Other information: for state capitals, larger cities, county seats, commercial and industrial centers, and municipalities of historic or cultural significance, descriptive location and other background information are also provided. As often as possible, when reliable information could be obtained, incorporation dates of municipalities are also provided.

Name origin: given when reliable information could be obtained and verified.

Data given in *APD* for population (1990, 1980; 1995 and 2000 projections for states), for housing and population distribution (for states), and for latitude and longitude is from published reports or data files provided by the U.S. Bureau of the Census.

Land and water area measurement are from data files provided by the U.S. Bureau of the Census. The Bureau calculates area measurements by computer based on information from the TIGER geographic data base.

Water area measurements include all water, unlike previous Census measurements, which included only inland water. As a result, total water area reported, especially for coastal states, has increased from previous Census figures. Water area measurements from the 1990 Census include inland, coastal, Great Lakes (including Lake St. Clair), and territorial water (from the 3-mile limit to the shoreline or base lines that delimit inland and coastal waters).

Name Origin Information

This element of entry information was the greatest challenge to compile and remains an unfinished (perhaps never to be finished) task. Sources for the data are variable in quality and reliability, and are often very difficult to obtain. Many tend to deal with names within a state, county, or region, and it is typically difficult to acquire books or locally published material regarding name origins. Aside from the initial problem of acquiring or accessing any good source material, the information provided in the sources was often found to be incomplete, conflicting, or lacking in credibility.

"Onomastic Fact"

We have attempted to present *the reason a particular name was given to a place*, what Prof. Kelsie Harder (see "Foreword") has termed the "onomastic fact." Whenever possible, we have also indicated who gave the name and the date it was bestowed. Former names for a place, if known, are also indicated.

Occasionally the onomastic fact is easy to determine, well documented, and well known. More often the determination requires a study of history and biography, a sense for the settlement pattern within a state or region, and an understanding of the tenor of the times in which the naming was done. Some sensitivity for language and knowledge of naming practices also proves useful. For most of the name origins, we have relied upon Kelsie Harder's *Illustrated Dictionary of Place Names: United States and Canada* (1976).

What we have *not* done is to trace the etymology in terms of the linguistic roots of the names themselves. Such work is certainly legitimate and important, often fascinating, but is beyond the requirements of determining onomastic fact. We have been content with determining and presenting, as often as possible, when and why a place was named.

Borrowed Names

If the name was borrowed from another U.S. place, the entry indicates this. The onomastic fact for the eponymous place, if known, is given under its entry. If the place is not an entry in *APD* (e.g., a small river whose name is used for a populated place), we have attempted to give the onomastic fact, if known, within the name origin information for the populated place.

The editorial policy for name origins in *APD* was to present as much material as we could reliably offer, but to say nothing if reliable information could not be obtained. We were able to give such information for all states, counties, and a majority of the larger cities, as well as many smaller places, perhaps 10,000 entries overall. Thus many entries in *APD* lack name origin data. We hope that this feature can be augmented in subsequent editions of the book. We encourage users who have such information on a place, county, region, or state to notify the publisher. Please mail correspondence to:

> Editor, *American Places Dictionary*
> Omnigraphics, Inc.
> Penobscot Bldg.
> Detroit, MI 48226

Variability by Region

For some states name origin material is abundant and well researched. This generally reflects the interests of a local expert, or a set of experts over the years, who had access to good historical sources and who devoted prodigious amounts of research time and scholarly effort to producing publications of quality, knowing that their audience would likely be a small, albeit devoted one. For the names of counties and municipalities, the New England states have perhaps the best coverage of any single region, perhaps reflecting the relative simplicity or lack of complications for the names (many are of English origin), the existence of good historical records, and the geographic compactness of the region and its states. Other states have been blessed by the scholarship of particular researchers, so that the name origins and other information for places in Kentucky, Oregon, and California are generally better documented and widely available, thanks to the efforts of Robert Rennick, Lewis McArthur (father and son), and Erwin Gudde, to name but a notable few.

"American Indian" Names

This is an area fraught with controversy, even regarding the question of how to refer to these names. While recent developments have led some to favor such terms as *Amerindian* or *Native American* to refer to these names and the languages from which they originate, *APD* uses the more traditional forms *Indian* or *American Indian* when speaking in general of such names, or, whenever possible, notes a specific language or people.

Putting aside the issue of style, more critical to understanding the origin of names is the fact that American Indian languages have been less well documented and studied. Several reasons may be cited for this, including the fact that these languages were rarely recorded in writing by native speakers, so that records for them, if they exist, are generally sparse and very often second-hand, in the form of observations by Europeans or Americans. As a result, place names of American Indian origin generally have come down to us as if through a filter.

Another factor results from cultural differences regarding the use of names. As a rule, American Indian naming practices differed greatly from the tradition of the European cultures. Whereas the European explorers and settlers made a great issue of naming features and places and dutifully recording everything—as evidence of a claim, for convenience of future reference, and out of pride—it seems that American Indian cultures did not follow and in fact may have been opposed to the practice of systematically assigning names to particular places. Additionally, Indian naming seems to have been more localized, so that a river, for example, may have been referred to in several if not many ways along its entire course, each "name" reflecting local experience.

As Lewis L. McArthur notes in his Introduction to *Oregon Geographic Names,* Sixth Edition:

A good deal of nonsense has been written about the meaning of Indian names. The late Lewis A. McArthur knew many Indians. They eked out a living amidst hard circumstances and it seems improbable that Oregon Indians ever made up geographic names because of "moonlight filtering through trees," "sunshine dancing on the water," "rose petals floating on water" and "water rippling over pebbles." Competent researchers have found that most Indian names were based on much more practical and everyday matters.

What often can be said about an American place name is that it originates from an earlier Indian name or term. Beyond that the situation becomes much murkier. It has been the practice of *APD* to avoid speculation about names of American Indian origin. We have on occasion reported what is believed about certain names, but maintain that it is perilous to assert the original meaning of many American Indian names.

Hierarchy of Government in the United States

The organization of *APD* into state sections, county groupings, and entries for the individual places themselves repeats the pattern of government administration of the entire country below the federal level. This hierarchy of government starts at the state level, and at each level the entire territory of the United States is included in some administrative entity. Thus the "mosaic of governments" is complete at the state, county, and place levels. The primary reason for this bit of bureaucratic thoroughness is to ensure that all the U.S. population is included in each decennial census at every level, allowing for statistical integrity and (technically) equitable distribution of federal benefits at each level.

States

Most people are quite familiar with the state government level—50 states, plus the District of Columbia. This is the top level covered by *APD*, which has entries for each of these 51 entities.

Four of the states refer to themselves as commonwealths: Kentucky, Massachusetts, Pennsylvania, and Virginia.

There are no entries in *APD* for Puerto Rico or any territories or possessions of the United States.

Counties and County Equivalents

Below the state level are the counties or county equivalents, of which there are 3,141 in the entire United States. This total includes the District of Columbia government as a state and a county equivalent. If one considers Washington, D.C., also as a city, then the nation's capital is the only place that functions technically at all three government levels.

States without Counties or with County Equivalents

In certain states the county level of government is somewhat different from the "normal" pattern, as outlined for each state listed below.

In Louisiana, the parishes provide the equivalent of county government in other states.

In Connecticut and Rhode Island, county government has actually been abolished, but county boundaries still are used administratively, and counties are still recognized popularly.

In Maryland, the city of Baltimore is independent and serves as a county equivalent.

In Virginia, 41 independent cities serve as county equivalents; there are also 95 counties.

In Missouri, the city of St. Louis is an independent city and serves as a county equivalent.

In Nevada, Carson City is an independent city and serves as a county equivalent.

In Alaska there are no counties as such. Areas with some concentration of population are called boroughs and do provide government administration. Most of the territory of the state is included in large tracts called census areas, which have been designated by the U.S. Bureau of the Census.

In Hawaii alone among the states, all local government is at the county level. There are no incorporated municipalities. The four main islands—Oahu, Hawaii, Kauai, and Maui—are essentially each treated as counties. The island of Oahu and most of the smaller Hawaiian Islands are all governed by the consolidated government called the City and County of Honolulu. Also, a small part of Molokai Island is administered by the state Department of Health as Kalawao County, and is occupied by patients with Hansen's disease, or leprosy. This is the site of the noted leper colony ministered to by Father Joseph Damien (1840–89).

Two other variations on the standard county pattern, city-county consolidations and multi-county places, lead to the discussion of municipalities and other sub-county entities.

City-County Consolidations

A number of cities have consolidated their government with the county, and the two are largely functionally equivalent. These city-county consolidations are:

Anchorage, AK (city consolidated with Anchorage Borough)

Juneau, AK (city consolidated with Juneau Borough)

Sitka, AK (city consolidated with Sitka Borough)

San Francisco, CA (city consolidated with San Francisco County)

Denver, CO (city consolidated with Denver County)

Jacksonville, FL (city consolidated with Duval County, but the municipalities of Atlantic Beach, Baldwin, Jacksonville Beach, and Neptune Beach remain as separate entities in the county)

Columbus, GA (city consolidated with Muscogee County; Bibb City also consolidated with the county, but is a separate entity)

Honolulu, HI (city and county consolidated as the City and County of Honolulu)

Indianapolis, IN (city government consolidated with Marion County; the four suburbs of Beech Grove, Lawrence, Southport, and Speedway maintain independent status, and 13 other suburbs have quasi-independent status)

Lexington, KY (city consolidated with Fayette County as Lexington Fayette Urban County)

Baton Rouge, LA (city consolidated with East Baton Rouge Parish, but not coextensive)

Houma, LA (city consolidated with Terrebonne Parish, but not coextensive)

New Orleans, LA (city consolidated with Orleans Parish)

Nantucket, MA (town coextensive with Nantucket County; the whole of Nantucket Island)

Suffolk County, MA (government consolidated with city of Boston, but not coextensive)

Anaconda, MT (consolidated with Deer Lodge County as Anaconda-Deer Lodge County)

Butte, MT (consolidated with Silver Bow County as Butte-Silver Bow; Walkerville remains a separate municipality)

Yellowstone National Park, MT (administered by the National Park Service, but considered as a county equivalent)

Philadelphia, PA (city consolidated with Philadelphia County)

Lynchburg, TN (consolidated with Moore County as Lynchburg, Moore County)

Nashville, TN (city consolidated with Davidson County; six suburban cities continue as separate municipalities for certain purposes)

Multi-County Places

As noted above, a number of municipalities in the United States cover an area that is in more than one county. Typically, multi-county places have a large portion in one county, with a smaller portion in a second county, often without any population residing in the second county. The total number of multi-county places in the United States is 923, broken down as follows:

2-county places: 855
3-county places: 60
4-county places: 5*
5-county places: 3**
  * Broomfield, CO; Allentown, GA; Barrington Hills, IL; Kansas City, MO; High Point, NC
 ** New York, NY (its five boroughs are county equivalents); Oklahoma City, OK; Dallas, TX

Municipalities and Other Sub-county Entities

Owing to the diverse and varied settlement of the United States (and to the diverse and varied nature of its settlers), no two states treat their sub-county populated places in exactly the same way administratively. In different regions of the nation, government below the county level is represented by cities, towns, villages, townships, boroughs, and other administrative entities.

In the western and southern states particularly many populated areas are not administered by any government below the county level. These places are not cities or towns, but often have established popular names, even if they lack legal boundaries.

Taken as a whole, the variety of local governments and other populated districts reflects the long and varied history of settlement in the United States. But the situation also means a complicated burden for the federal agencies, such as the U.S. Bureau of the Census, that have to deal with this patchwork of local administration or, in some cases, lack thereof. Two common problems encountered at the sub-county level are discussed here to illustrate the kinds of unexpected peculiarities that arise in compiling entries for these places.

"Same Name, Same County" (Entries with Asterisks)

Frequently in *APD* there will be two entries for places in a single county, that will have the same name. This may seem puzzling, but reflects the fact that, in many states, local government or administrative units may overlap or divide certain functions. In states where land was surveyed into townships prior to much of the subsequent settlement, the township pattern was established before incorporated places were in existence or even necessary. As townships became settled, centers of population desired corporate status and legal standing as a government. Depending on the state, the incorporated place might be called a town, village, borough, or city. Frequently, places that were incorporated as towns would develop and grow to the point where they would want to become cities, often gaining thereby a greater amount of autonomy under state law. But as the incorporated places—cities, towns, villages, or whatever—became established, the original township pattern usually remained. Very often, the incorporated area might be only part (the most densely settled part) of a township. Also very often, the township name was adopted by the new incorporated place. The result usually is two places with the same name in the same county. Examples include Chevy Chase, MD; Farmington, NH; Grosse Pointe, MI; Green Bay, WI.

Our policy for this situation has been to retain both places if they are recognized by the state as incorporated. Naturally, they will come together alphabetically as entries within their county. One of the two entries, normally the one of lesser administrative function (and often smaller population), will appear second and be marked with an asterisk.

The Differing Use of *Borough* in Five States

One example of variation among the states can be seen in the use of the term *borough* in conjunction with other terms for municipalities in five states. Each has populated places called boroughs, but they differ greatly in function and relationship to other administrative units.

Alaska: the 16 boroughs are actually county equivalents; three are governmentally consolidated with cities (Anchorage, Juneau, Sitka).

Connecticut: the 11 boroughs are incorporated places; but are actually part of a town and not entirely independent. The borough of Naugatuck is coextensive with the town of the same name.

New Jersey: the 252 boroughs function as municipalities. New Jersey's cities, towns, townships, and villages are other types of municipalities.

New York: the five boroughs that make up New York City—Manhattan, Brooklyn, the Bronx, Queens, and Staten Island—function as parts of the city and county equivalents. Manhattan is coextensive with New York County, Brooklyn is coextensive with Kings County, and Staten Island is coextensive with Richmond County. Borough and county names are the same for the Bronx and Queens.

Pennsylvania: the 966 boroughs function as municipalities, along with 55 cities and one town. Pennsylvania also has 1,549 townships, which are similar in character to townships in New England (see below).

In *APD* we have attempted to present as much sub-county administrative detail as possible for populated places. As a result, many places that might normally be thought of as a single city or town may have two (or more) entries in *APD*. In the introductions for the individual states some of the nature of each state's municipalities is noted.

In the following paragraphs we shall attempt to suggest something of the complexity of the local administrative hierarchy that must be taken into account in any comprehensive treatment of U.S. populated places nationwide.

Minor Civil Divisions (MCDs) in 28 States

In 28 states the sub-county entities are functioning local governments or other sub-county administrative entities, broadly referred to as minor civil divisions (MCDs). In these states the U.S. Bureau of the Census tracks population totals within these established local boundaries. The names and relationships of the sub-county populated places in these 28 states varies regionally and from state to state.

In the Northeast (the six New England states, New York, New Jersey, and Pennsylvania), counties are generally divided into towns or townships. Typically, these are much more important administratively than the counties (hence, the vestigial counties of Connecticut and Rhode Island, noted above). Towns in the Northeast are typically incorporated, legal entities, and in most of these states there are very few areas that lie outside the boundaries of some town or township (except for some incorporated cities). In northern New England some sparsely inhabited or uninhabited districts provide sub-county boundaries. These areas are called plantations, gores, grants, unorganized territory (in northern Maine), or locations and purchases (in New Hampshire).

In the six Great Lakes states (Ohio, Michigan, Indiana, Illinois, Wisconsin, and Minnesota) and six other central states (Iowa, Kansas, Missouri, Nebraska, North Dakota, and South Dakota) the division into townships (called *towns* in Wisconsin) is the typical pattern. Compared to the Northeast, however, the townships in most of these states are generally of considerably less administrative importance than the counties. The towns or townships of the central states may or may not be incorporated, and less often have the authority to levy taxes or otherwise carry on the governmental functions of their counterparts in the Northeast. The exception is Wisconsin, where the towns function in a manner very similar to New England towns.

In North Carolina and Arkansas townships and unorganized territories provide sub-county boundaries where there are no incorporated places such as cities.

In some so-called "MCD states," the Census Bureau tracks population within the boundaries of other existing administrative districts, which vary in designation by state; these are listed as "Populated Places" in *APD*.

Census County Divisions (CCDs) in 21 States

In 21 states the U.S. Bureau of the Census, in cooperation with state and local officials, has established statistical entities below the county level for states that do not have MCDs or where MCDs are not adequate for reporting sub-county statistics. These statistical entities are called Census County Divisions (CCDs). The 21 "CCD states" are primarily in the South and the West, where, except for the incorporated places, much of the area below the county level is unincorporated. CCDs were created solely for statistical purposes, and are not normally used or referred to by the resident population. They have no legal functions and are not units of government. CCDs do have names, however, based on a place, county, or well-known local name. The Census County Divisions exist to maintain statistical integrity—and a complete "mosaic" at the sub-county level.

The 21 CCD states are as follows:

Alabama	Georgia	New Mexico	Utah
Arizona	Hawaii	Oklahoma	Washington
California	Idaho	Oregon	Wyoming
Colorado	Kentucky	South Carolina	
Delaware	Montana	Tennessee	
Florida	Nevada	Texas	

Census Subareas in Alaska

In Alaska the Census Bureau and the state delineated census subareas as statistical subdivisions of the county equivalent boroughs and census areas.

Census Designated Places (CDPs)

Another statistical entity used by the Census Bureau is called the Census Designated Place (CDP). CDPs, delineated in 49 states, are densely settled concentrations of population that are identifiable by name, but are not legally incorporated places. Like CCDs, their names are generally reflective of local usage, but they have no legal status.

In *APD* we have included entries for CDPs where they provide additional detail and do not cause potential confusion because of close similarity of the CDP name with an actual municipality within the same county. One state in which they are particularly noticeable is Hawaii, where there are no legally incorporated places besides the City and County of Honolulu. All other populated places in Hawaii that are entries are based on CDPs.

Conclusion

The melting pot that has become the United States of America reveals itself in many facets of our culture, not the least of which are historical settlement patterns, the place names given to settlements, and the diverse systems of organization and administration. As we delve deeper into why the United States, or the individual states, were set up as they were, we see more and more diversity. Establishing order in the midst of the state-by-state variation, as the Bureau of the Census has done with minor civil divisions and census county divisions (and census areas in Alaska), is a necessary task of government.

* * * * *

Acknowledgments

The compilation of *American Places Dictionary* would not have been possible without the vision, inspiration, and diligence of many individuals and organizations. Foremost among all those who had a role in the work is Fred Ruffner, publisher and president of Omnigraphics, Inc., who conceived of the project originally and whose support for it was unwavering despite unforeseen delays and setbacks. Other key personnel at Omnigraphics included Laurie Harris, editorial director; Jim Sellgren, operations; Jane Steele, promotion; and Eric Berger, production manager. The concern for quality that they exhibited, as well as their patience with the editor, are much appreciated.

Assisting the editorial process in all its details was Chuck Lacy of Weimer Graphics, Indianapolis, Indiana, who met the formidable challenge of the data processing and typesetting with exceptional skill and efficiency. Mr. Lacy helped conceive and implement the procedures to process, consolidate, sort, and typeset a massive body of data. The quality and efficiency of his work were never compromised by the demands imposed by editorial and publishing specifications.

We also wish to recognize the assistance provided by a number of specialists in federal agencies, including especially, at the Bureau of the Census, Marie Pees, of the Population Division; Don Hirschfeld (retired) and Joel Miller, of the Geography Division; and, at the National Institute of Standards and Technology, Henry Tom. These highly skilled, dedicated, and profoundly knowledgeable professionals promptly and ably responded to our many inquiries into the vagaries of U.S. populated places. Their work, and that of others like them in various federal agencies, is indispensable to the creation of place name reference tools.

Officials in state and local government nationwide, far too numerous to mention, assisted throughout the editorial process, sometimes answering single, focused inquiries, often sending enormously important publications and other data from their files. This state-specific information was vital to our work, especially given the complexity and variation across the United States in the way government and administration function below the federal level.

While the invaluable contributions of each of the individuals mentioned cannot be overemphasized, we must add that the responsibility for any errors or omissions in *American Places Dictionary* rests solely with the editor.

We encourage users of this dictionary to send suggestions on how the work might be improved, expanded, or made more accessible in subsequent editions.

Editor, *American Places Dictionary*
Omnigraphics, Inc.
Penobscot Bldg.
Detroit, MI, 48226

Frank R. Abate
Editor

Old Saybrook, Connecticut
April 1994

Editor's Miscellany:

American Places and American Names—
Curiosities and Peculiarities

In the course of compiling and editing *American Places Dictionary* the editorial staff came upon many fascinating tidbits and facts about the United States. Collectively, this grab-bag of trivia, history, odd names, and other surprises lacks a coherent theme, and while the material seemed inappropriate for the Introduction, we could not resist the opportunity to present what we found. Hence, this brief miscellany, a collection of unrelated details that we felt should not go unrecorded.

This brief list reveals the variety of items included here and serves as a handy summary:

I.   Early U.S. Capitals
II. Geopolitical Peculiarities
III. Unusual Official State Symbols
IV. Historical Development and Changes in Counties
V.   Some Out-of-the-Ordinary Place Names
VI. First Name/Last Name Places

I. Early U.S. Capitals

In the earliest years of U.S. history there was no permanent federal capital. This situation lasted from the signing of the Declaration of Independence in 1776 until 1800, when the federal government settled into the newly established Washington, D.C. The different meeting places of the Continental Congress, the Congress of the Confederation (authorized under the Articles of Confederation), and later the U.S. Congress (under the U.S. Constitution, from March 4, 1789) in these years, a total of eight different cities in four states, are listed below, with the span of first and last meeting dates in each place:

Philadelphia:	September 5, 1774 to December 12, 1776
Baltimore:	December 20, 1776 to March 4, 1777
Philadelphia:	March 5, 1777 to September 18, 1777
Lancaster, PA:	September 27, 1777 (one day only)
York, PA:	September 30, 1777 to June 27, 1778
Philadelphia:	July 2, 1778 to June 21, 1783
Princeton, NJ:	June 30, 1783 to November 4, 1783
Annapolis, MD:	November 26, 1783 to June 3, 1784
Trenton, NJ:	November 1, 1784 to December 24, 1784

New York City: January 11, 1785 to August 12, 1790
Philadelphia: December 6, 1790 to May 14, 1800

II. Geopolitical Peculiarities

The following section describes a number of instances of geopolitical peculiarities across the U.S. Some of these unusual or unique border patterns are rather obvious on a map of the United States, while others are quite hard to find except on very detailed maps. Several different kinds of situations are described, some affecting several states and others peculiar to a single state.

Panhandles and Other Border Extensions

The following states have panhandles or border extensions of some sort. A panhandle is generally defined as a projecting, relatively narrow strip of land that is surrounded by the territory of other states or a water boundary, but is not a peninsula.

Alabama	Missouri
Alaska	New Mexico
Florida	Oklahoma
Idaho	Pennsylvania
Maryland	Texas
Mississippi	West Virginia

Two "classic" panhandles are those of Oklahoma and Florida, projecting as long narrow strips to the west in each case, and truly resembling panhandles when viewed on a map. The panhandle of **Oklahoma** was ceded to the U.S. by Texas before Texas was admitted to the Union. It was part of Oklahoma Territory by 1890, called the Public Land Strip, sometimes referred to as "No Man's Land." **Florida's** panhandle, the area west of the Apalachicola River, was part of the original Spanish province that extended west to the Mississippi River. When Spain ceded Florida to Great Britain in 1763, the territory was divided into West Florida and East Florida along the river. West Florida was later reduced in extent as western portions to the Mississippi River became part of Louisiana, Mississippi, and Alabama.

The other commonly referred to panhandle, that of **Texas**, was created when the state sold a portion of its original northwest territory to the federal government in 1850. The new boundary lines of northwest Texas were set by survey, and left a distinctive broad panhandle that projects northward.

The panhandle of **Alaska**, extending southeast from the 141st meridian, is a remnant of the boundaries established by Great Britain and Russia in a convention of 1825. The territory, including this panhandle, was purchased by the United States from Russia in 1867, and the United States consistently maintained claim to the region despite objection over the years from Canada. The dispute was settled by an international tribunal in 1903.

West Virginia is the only state to have two panhandles, one extending north between Ohio and Pennsylvania near Wheeling, the other east, bordering Virginia to the south and Maryland to the north.

Western **Maryland**, from Hagerstown west, extends like a panhandle between West Virginia and Pennsylvania. In addition, Maryland is also cut by Chesapeake Bay, so that to the east there is a portion on the Delmarva Peninsula (see below) that is separated from the rest of the state. This region of the state is called the Eastern Shore.

Missouri has a distinctive portion at its southeast corner that is called the "bootheel" because of its shape. It lies below the line of 36 degrees, 30 minutes north latitude that marks the rest of Missouri's southern border. The eastern border of the bootheel is the Mississippi River, and the western the St. Francis River. This portion became a part of Missouri on its admission to statehood. Prominent landowner J. Hardeman Walker, founder of Caruthersville, an important town in the region, was influential in having this addition become part of the state.

The panhandle of **Idaho** is the result of a reduction to the original Idaho territory prior to statehood in 1890. This narrow area, lying between Idaho's western border with Washington and the Bitterroot Range of the Rockies, was left when land to the east of the Bitterroot Range was made part of the Territory of Montana in 1864.

The extreme southwestern corner of **New Mexico**, extending below its long southern boundary with Texas at 32 degrees north latitude, was an addition made to the original territory of 1850. The land was acquired from Mexico in the Gadsden Purchase of 1853, negotiated for the United States by James Gadsden, who wanted to ensure a good route for a southern railroad to the Pacific. The bulk of the Gadsden Purchase became part of the Territory of Arizona (1863) along its southern border with Mexico.

While they are not truly panhandles, Pennsylvania, Alabama, and Mississippi each have narrow projections that give the states access to water. The "Erie Triangle" of **Pennsylvania**, once a part of New York but ceded to the federal government in 1781, was purchased from the U.S. by Pennsylvania on March 3, 1792, to give the state a broader land access to Lake Erie. The purchase price was $151,640.25, and the deed was signed by George Washington. **Alabama** and **Mississippi** each have projections to the Gulf of Mexico that are a part of what was once called West Florida, originally part of the Spanish province of Florida. The land, to the west of the Perdido River, was occupied by the United States in 1812, and eventually was added to the territories of Alabama and Mississippi.

The Four Corners: Utah, Colorado, New Mexico, Arizona

One corner of each of these four states, each of which has very regular, straight borders, meets at a point referred to as the Four Corners. The point is the intersection of 37 degrees north latitude and 109 degrees, 2 minutes west longitude. The longitude is exactly 32 degrees west of Washington, D.C. The spot is marked by a prominent boundary monument, and is the only point in the U.S. common to four states.

Portions of Land Separated from the Rest of the State along Rivers

In a number of places, particularly along major rivers such as the Mississippi and Missouri, small portions of certain states are separated from the rest of the state owing to changes over the years in the course of the rivers. Natural events such as floods and earthquakes bring about these changes in river channels. The situation arises when two states have fixed their border along the channel of a river. Whenever the river changes course, an area of land that was once on one side of the river is left on the other. There are many such places along the southern course of the Mississippi River to the Gulf of Mexico, affecting, on the eastern banks, Kentucky, Tennessee, and Mississippi, and on the western banks Missouri, Arkansas, and Louisiana.

Kentucky–Missouri–Tennessee at New Madrid

A small portion of extreme southwestern Kentucky lies isolated from the rest of the state along the course of the Mississippi River near New Madrid, Missouri. This is the result of a change in the course of the river caused by the noted earthquake of 1811, whose epicenter was at New Madrid. From this part of Kentucky one can cross by land into Tennessee or by river to Missouri, but must pass through one of these two states to get to the rest of Kentucky.

Iowa–Nebraska at Omaha

A small portion of Iowa is separated from the rest of the state near Omaha, Nebraska. The border between the states is the Missouri River. When the river changed course in 1877, moving to its present channel, it isolated a portion of what had been on the eastern bank, also leaving a small lake, Carter Lake, as a remnant of the former channel. This small portion on the western bank of the Missouri is still part of Iowa.

Delmarva Peninsula

This peninsula extends between Chesapeake Bay to the west and Delaware Bay and the Atlantic Ocean to the east. It is divided among three states, Delaware, Maryland, and Virginia, hence the name, a combination of the first syllables of the first two states with the standard abbreviation letters for Virginia. The extreme southern portion of the peninsula has been a part of Virginia since colonial days, although it is totally separated from the rest of the state. The exact border with Maryland was a source of controversy from colonial times until 1972, when both states finally agreed on a well-defined boundary.

Going *South* from the United States into Canada—Detroit to Windsor

Owing to the natural course of the Detroit River, which forms the international boundary between southeastern Michigan and the Canadian province of Ontario, travelers crossing the border from Detroit into Canada, using either the Ambassador Bridge or the Detroit-Windsor tunnel under the river, are actually going nearly due south. Excepting in Alaska, this is the only instance of a major border crossing between the two countries where one travels south to reach Canada.

The Notch in the Connecticut–Massachusetts Border

The generally straight west-east border line between Connecticut and Massachusetts is broken by a notch north of Hartford, Connecticut. The Massachusetts town of Southwick extends into this notch; hence it is sometimes referred to as the "Southwick jog." In Connecticut it is sometimes referred to as the "Suffield gap," as it lies between the towns of Suffield and Granby. The area within the notch became part of Massachusetts in 1803 by ruling of a survey commission formed by both states. The commission determined that Massachusetts had lost territory owing to errors in the previous surveys that had set the straight-line border between the states. The notch was intended to compensate Massachusetts with an area equivalent to that lost.

Arc-of-a-Circle Border between Delaware and Pennsylvania

Most of Delaware's short northern border with Pennsylvania is the arc of a circle, the center of which is some 12 miles to the south at New Castle, Delaware. This unusual boundary line was fixed by a survey authorized in 1701 by William Penn. It is the only instance of such a border shape in the United States.

Michigan's Upper Peninsula

A portion of the state of Michigan shares a border with Wisconsin but is not connected to the rest of the state. Michigan's Upper Peninsula separates Lake Michigan from Lake Superior and extends to the Canadian province of Ontario at Sault Ste. Marie and to the Lower Peninsula of the state at the Straits of Mackinac and the entrance to Lake Huron. It was not a part of the original Michigan Territory organized in 1805, but was added as part of an extension of Michigan Territory in 1818. Wisconsin Territory was created in 1836 from the western portion of this extension, but the Upper Peninsula was retained by Michigan upon its admission to statehood in 1837. Subsequent disputes over the exact border line with Wisconsin raged for many years, finally being settled in 1948 after U.S. Supreme Court intervention and approval of the U.S. Congress.

Portion of Minnesota North of the 49th Parallel—The "Northwest Angle"

Minnesota's Lake of the Woods County includes an area of about 124 square miles, called the Northwest Angle, that is non-contiguous with the rest of the state. This area can only be reached from the rest of Minnesota by boat or by traveling through or over part of Canada (Manitoba or Ontario). Excepting Alaska, it is the northernmost tract of the United States, wholly above the forty-ninth parallel. This area became part of the United States because inaccurate maps were used during treaty negotiations with the British in 1783 and 1818. In 1917 the International Joint Commission between the United States and Canada described the situation as a "politico-geographical curiosity of a boundary."

Portion of New Hampshire North of the Forty-Fifth Parallel—Pittsburg, N.H.

This small portion of northern New Hampshire extends north of 45 degrees north latitude, which is the general line for the international boundary between the Canadian province of Quebec and the U.S. states of New York and Vermont. The area above the forty-fifth parallel was disputed for many years by New Hampshire and Canada. In 1829 the settlers in the region organized an independent republic known as the Indian Stream Territory. This government was in effect until New Hampshire took control in 1835. The area is now the town of Pittsburg, N.H., the largest town (in area) in the state, population 901 (in 1990).

III. Unusual Official State Symbols (by state)

Each state introduction provides a complete list of official state symbols. Some of the more unusual ones are listed here.

Alaska
    sport: dog mushing (sled-dog
        racing)
Arizona
    neckwear: bola tie
Connecticut
    hero: Nathan Hale
    ship: Nautilus (first nuclear
        submarine)
Idaho
    horse: Appaloosa
Maryland
    sport: jousting
Massachusetts
    bean: baked navy bean
        (Boston baked beans)
    cat: tabby
    heroine: Deborah Samson
    horse: Morgan
    muffin: corn

Michigan
    soil: Kalkaska soil series
Minnesota
    muffin: blueberry
Missouri
    musical instrument: fiddle
New Mexico
    cookie: biscochito
    vegetables: frijol (pinto bean)
        and chile (pepper)
Ohio
    rock song: "Hang On Sloopy"
Pennsylvania
    flagship: Niagara (U.S. Brig)
Vermont
    horse: Morgan
Wisconsin
    dog: American water spaniel
    soil: Antigo silt loam

IV. Historical Development and Changes in Counties

The counties of the U.S. today appear fairly stable and unchanging. In fact, from the 1950 Census through 1993 the total number of counties in the U.S. increased only from 3,112 to 3,143, a net gain of 31, or about one percent. But this apparent stability does not reflect the historical development and increase in counties over the decades from the founding of the nation, especially in the states east of the Rockies. The story is an exceedingly complicated one geographically, as large areas were broken up to form new, more compact entities. The number of counties in a state proliferated as the state was settled by pioneers or by residents seeking open land or new horizons. Very often, as previously unsettled territory was reached, it became inconvenient for the residents to make the journey to the county seat to register births, deaths, and marriages, or to file a suit or make a claim in court. In agricultural, pre-industrial America, any day away from the livestock on the farm was a serious inconvenience, and more than a day nearly impossible to arrange or too costly to bear. The farmers' need to be within a day's ride of the county seat was frequently the reason for the formation of new counties, with county seats nearer the newer settlers

V. Some Out-of-the-Ordinary Place Names

The following list is highly selective, and reflects only a sampling of what struck us as most noteworthy.

Aubbeenaubbee, IN
Bee Branch, MO
Beisizl, ND
Coffee Springs, AL
Correctionville, IA

Dismal, NC
Dog Ear, SD
Dry Prong, LA
East and West Chillisquaque,
PA

East Loony, MO
Fair Play, MO
Farr West, UT
Flippin, AR
Funks Grove, IL

Gun Barrel City, TX
Haymow, NE
Humansville, MO
Kaaawa, HI
Magnetic Springs, OH
Mule Barn, OK
Nanty-Glo, PA
New Diggins, WI
Nodaway, IA
Oil Trough, AR
Omphghent, IL

One Road, SD
Oolagah, OK
Pecan Gap, TX
Pe Ell, WA
Quewhiffle, NC
Roasting Ear, AR
Skedee, OK
Sleepy Eye, MN
Snee Oosh, WA
Sni-A-Bar, MO
Snow Shoe, PA

Sopchoppy, FL
Sublimity, OR
Teec Nos Pos, AZ
Tightwad, MO
Turnback, MO
Tywappity, MO
Uncertain, TX
Weeki Wachee, FL
What Cheer, IA
White Eyes, OH

VI. First Name/Last Name Municipalities (by state)

The pattern of the following place names suggests a person's name, and in some cases that is clearly behind the origin of the name. In any case, these are distinctive.

Alabama:
  Phil Campbell
Arkansas:
  Ben Lomond
  Lou Norris
  Reed Keathly
  Joe Burleson
California:
  Ben Lomond
Florida:
  Mary Esther
  Anna Maria
  Jan Phyl Village

Georgia:
  Warner Robins
Indiana:
  Dick Johnson
Louisiana:
  Jean Lafitte
Missouri:
  Jim Henry
Oklahoma:
  John Day
  Gene Autry
Pennsylvania:
  Jim Thorpe

  Henry Clay
  Glen Campbell
Texas:
  Robert Lee
  Tom Bean
  Seth Ward
  George West
Virginia:
  Jack Jonett
  Samuel Miller
  Patrick Henry
West Virginia:
  Jane Lew

Selected Bibliography

In addition to the sources listed below, the editors consulted various printed sources issued by state and local governments, government assoications, etc., including "blue books" or state government manuals, state and municipal directories, and informational brochures.

The *Flying the Colors* series, published by Clements Research II of Dallas, TX (published from 1987 to 1991) was also consulted for the following states: AL, AZ, CA, CT, FL, GA, IL, IN, IA, KS, KY, MA, MI, MO, NH, NJ, NY, NC, PA, SC, TX, VA, WA, WI.

Abate, Frank R., ed. *Omni Gazetteer of the United States of America*, 11 vols. Detroit: Omnigraphics, 1991.

Adams, James N., compiler, and Keller, William E. *Illinois Place Names*. Springfield: Illinois State Historical Society, 1989.

Andriot, Jay, compiler. *Township Atlas of the United States*. McLean, VA: Documents Index, 1991.

Baker, Ronald L., and Carmony, Marvin. *Indiana Place Names*. Bloomington: Indiana University Press, 1975.

Barnes, Will C. *Arizona Place Names*. Tucson: University of Arizona Press, 1988.

Beck, Warren A., and Haase, Ynez D. *Historical Atlas of California*. Norman: University of Oklahoma Press, 1974.

—. *Historical Atlas of New Mexico*. Norman: University of Oklahoma Press, 1969.

Bentley, Elizabeth Petty. *County Courthouse Book*. Baltimore: Genealogical Publishing Co., 1990.

Bloid, John T. *Gazetteer of the State of Michigan*. New York: Arno Press, 1975 (reprint).

Bloodworth, Bertha E. and Morris, Alton C. *Places in the Sun*. Gainesville: University Presses of Florida, 1978.

Boone, Lalia. *Idaho Place Names: A Geographical Dictionary*. Moscow, ID: University of Idaho Press, 1988.

Browning, Peter. *Place Names of the Sierra Nevada, from Abbot to Zumwalt*.

—. *Yosemite Place Names: The Historic Background of Geographic Names in Yosemite National Park*. Lafayette, CA: Great West Books, 1988.

Carlson, Helen S. *Nevada Place Names: A Geographical Dictionary*. Reno: University of Nevada Press, 1974.

Cheney, Roberta Carkeek. *Names on the Face of Montana: The Story of Montana's Place Names*. Missoula, MT: Mountain Press, 1983.

Chernow, Barbara A., and Vallasi, George A., eds. *Columbia Encyclopedia*, 5th ed. New York: Columbia University Press, 1993.

Confederation of American Indians, compilers. *Indian Reservations: A State and Federal Handbook*. Jefferson, NC: McFarland, 1986.

Coulet du Gard, Rene, and Western, Dominique C. *Handbook of American Counties, Parishes and Independent Cities.* Newark, DE: Editions des Deux Mondes, 1981.

Dean, Ernie. *Arkansas Place Names.* Branson, MO: Ozarks Mountaineer, 1986.

Espenshade, A. Howry. *Pennsylvania Place Names.* Harrisburg: Evangelical Press, 1925.

Evinger, William R. *Directory of Military Bases in the U.S.* Phoenix, AZ: Oryx Press, 1991.

Fitzpatrick, Lilian L. *Nebraska Place Names.* Lincoln: University of Nebraska Press, 1960.

Foscue, Virginia O. *Place Names in Alabama.* Tuscaloosa: University of Alabama Press, 1989.

Fullerton, Ralph O. *Place Names of Tennessee.* Nashville: Tennessee Division of Geology, 1974.

Gannett, Henry. *Geographic Dictionary of Connecticut and Rhode Island.* Baltimore: Genealogical Publishing, 1978 (reprint).

—. *Origin of Certain Place Names in the United States*, 2nd ed. Williamstown, MA: Corner House, 1978 (reprint).

Gard, Robert, and Sorden, L.G. *Romance of Wisconsin Placenames.* Minocqua, WI: Heartland Press, 1988.

Gudde, Erwin G. *California Place Names: The Origin and Etymology of Current Geographical Names.* Berkeley: University of California Press, 1949.

Hagemann, James. *Heritage of Virginia: The Story of Place Names in the Old Dominion.* West Chester, PA: Whitford Press, 1986.

Halverson, F. Douglas, compiler. *County Histories of the United States Giving Present Name, Date Formed, Parent County, and County Seat.* (unpublished manuscript, n.d.)

Hanson, Gerald T., and Moneyhon, Carl H. *Historical Atlas of Arkansas.* Norman: University of Oklahoma Press, 1989.

Harder, Kelsie B., ed. *Illustrated Dictionary of Place Names, United States and Canada.* New York: Facts On File, 1985.

Harris, William H., and Levey, Judith S., eds. *New Columbia Encyclopedia.* New York: Columbia University Press, 1975.

Hart, James D. *Companion to California.* New York: Oxford University Press, 1978.

Heck, L.W.; Wraight, A.J.; Orth, D.J.; Carter, J.R.; Van Winkle, L.G.; and Hazen, Janet. *Delaware Place Names.* Geological Survey and Coast & Geodetic Survey, 1966.

Hitchman, Robert. *Place Names of Washington.* Washington State Historical Society, 1985.

Hunt, Elmer Munson. *New Hampshire Town Names and Whence They Came.* Peterborough, NH: Noone House, 1970.

Indian Service Population and Labor Force Estimates. U.S. Dept. of the Interior, Bureau of Indian Affairs (report), 1991.

Kaminkow, Marion J. *Maryland A to Z: A Topographical Dictionary.* Baltimore: Magna Carta Book Co., 1985.

Kane, Joseph Nathan. *American Counties,* 4th ed. Metuchen, NJ: Scarecrow Press, 1983.

Kenny, Hamill. *Placenames of Maryland: Their Origin and Meaning.* Baltimore: Museum and Library of Maryland History, Maryland Historical Society, 1984.

Krakow, Kenneth K. *Georgia Place-Names.* Macon, GA: Winship Press, 1975.

Lekisch, Barbara. *Tahoe Place Names: The Origin and History of Names in the Lake Tahoe Basin.* Lafayette, CA: Great West Books, 1988.

McArthur, Lewis A. *Oregon Geographic Names*, 6th ed. Oregon Historical Society Press, 1992.

McCoy, Sondra Van Meter, and Hults, Jan. *1001 Kansas Place Names.* University Press of Kansas, 1989.

Morris, Allen. *Florida Place Names.* Coral Gables: University of Miami, 1974.

Morris, John W.; Goins, Charles R.; and McReynolds, Edwin C. *Historical Atlas of Oklahoma.* Norman: University of Oklahoma Press, 1969.

National Gazetteer of the United States of America, United States Concise. U.S. Geological Survey in cooperation with U.S. Board on Geographic Names, 1990.

Neuffer, Claude Henry. *Names in South Carolina: Vols. I-XII, 1954-1965.* University of South Carolina, 1967.

Neuffer, Claude and Irene. *Correct Mispronunciations of Some South Carolina Names.* Columbia: University of South Carolina, 1983.

Origin of New Jersey Place Names. Reprinted by NJ Public Library Commission, Trenton, 1945.

Orth, Donald J. *Dictionary of Alaska Place Names.* U.S. Geological Survey, Dept. of the Interior, 1967.

Paisano, Edna; Greendeer-Lee, Joan; Cowles, June; and Carroll, Debbie. *American Indian and Alaska Native Areas.* Population Division, Bureau of Census, 1990.

Palmer, T.S., ed. *Place Names of the Death Valley Region in California and Nevada.* Morongo Valley, CA: Sagebrush Press, 1980.

Palmetto Place Names. South Carolina Education Association, n.d.

Payne, Roger L. *Place Names of the Outer Banks.* Washington, NC: Thomas A. Williams, 1985.

Pearce, T.M., ed. *New Mexico Place Names: A Geographical Dictionary.* University of New Mexico Press, 1965.

Perkey, Elton A. *Perkey's Nebraska Place Names.* Lincoln: Nebraska State Historical Society, 1982.

Phillips, James W. *Washington State Place Names.* Seattle: University of Washington Press, 1971.

Powell William S. *North Carolina Gazetteer: A Dictionary of Tar Heel Places.* Chapel Hill: University of North Carolina Press, 1968.

Pukui, Mary Kawena, and Elbert, Samuel H. *Hawaiian Dictionary: Hawaiian-English, English-Hawaiian*, rev. ed. Honolulu: University of Hawaii Press, 1986.

Pukui, Mary Kawena; Elbert, Samuel H.; and Mookini, Esther T. *Place Names of Hawaii.* Honolulu: University of Hawaii Press, 1974.

Quimby, Myron J. *Scratch Ankle, U.S.A.: American Place Names and their Derivation.* New York: A.S. Barnes, 1969.

Rafferty, Milton D. *Historical Atlas of Missouri.* Norman: University of Oklahoma Press, 1982.

Ramsey, Robert L. *Our Storehouse of Missouri Place Names.* Columbia: University of Missouri Press, 1973.

Read, William A. *Florida Place-names of Indian Origin and Seminole Personal Names.* Baton Rouge: Louisiana State University, 1934.

Rennick, Robert M. *Kentucky Place Names.* University Press of Kentucky, 1984.

Rippley, La Verne J., and Schmeissner, Rainer H. *German Place Names in Minnesota (Deutsche Ortsnamen in Minnesota).* Northfield, MN: St. Olaf College, 1989.

Romig, Walter. *Michigan Place Names: The History of the Founding and the Naming of More than Five Thousand Past and Present Michigan Communities*. Detroit: Wayne State University Press, 1986.

Rydjord, John. *Indian Place-Names: Their Origin, Evolution, and Meanings, Collected in Kansas from the Siouan, Algonquian, Shoshonean, Caddoan, Iroquoian, and Other Tongues*. Norman: University of Oklahoma Press, 1968.

—. *Kansas Place-Names*. Norman: University of Oklahoma Press, 1972.

Savela, Judith A., ed. *Michigan Municipalities*. Sterling Heights Public Library, MI, 1989.

Scott, James W., and De Lorme, Roland L. *Historical Atlas of Washington*. Norman: University of Oklahoma Press, 1988.

Seltzer, Leon E., ed. *Columbia Lippincott Gazetteer of the World*. New York: Columbia University Press, 1952.

Shirk, George H. *Oklahoma Place Names*, 2nd ed. Norman: University of Oklahoma Press, 1965.

Sixth Report of the United States Geographic Board, 1890 to 1932. U.S. Government Printing Office; reprinted by Gale Research, 1967.

Sneve, Virginia Driving Hawk, ed. *South Dakota Geographic Names*. Sioux Falls, SD: Brevet Press, 1973.

Snyder, John P. *The Story of New Jersey's Civil Boundaries, 1606-1968*. Trenton: Bureau of Geology and Topography, 1969.

Socolofsky, Homer E., and Self, Huber. *Historical Atlas of Kansas*, 2nd ed. Norman: University of Oklahoma Press, 1972.

Stephens, A. Ray, and Holmes, William M. *Historical Atlas of Texas*. Norman: University of Oklahoma Press, 1989.

Stewart, George R. *American Place-Names: A Concise and Selective Dictionary for the Continental United States of America*. New York: Oxford University Press, 1970.

—. *Names on the Land: A Historical Account of Place-Naming in the United States*. Boston: Houghton Mifflin, 1967.

Swift, Esther Munroe. *Vermont Place-Names*. Brattleboro: Stephen Greene Press, 1977.

Tarpley, Fred. *1001 Texas Place Names*. Austin: University of Texas Press, 1980.

—. *Place Names of Northeast Texas*. Commerce, TX: East Texas State University, 1969.

Tilden, Freeman; revised and expanded by Paul Schullery. *National Parks: The Classic Book on the National Parks, National Monuments, & Historic Sites*. New York: Alfred A. Knopf, 1986.

Upham, Warren. *Minnesota Geographic Names: Their Origin and Historic Significance*. St. Paul: Minnesota Historical Society, 1969.

Urbanek, Mae. *Wyoming Place Names*. Missoula, MT: Mountain Press, 1988.

Van Cott, John W. *Utah Place Names: A Comprehensive Guide to the Origins of Geographic Names*. Salt Lake City: University of Utah Press, 1990.

Van Zandt, Franklin K. *Boundaries of the United States and the Several States*. Geological Survey, U.S. Dept. of the Interior, 1976.

Vermont Year Book. Chester, VT: The National Survey, 1992.

Vogel, Virgil J. *Indian Names in Michigan*. Ann Arbor: University of Michigan Press, 1986.

—. *Iowa Place Names of Indian Origin*. Iowa City: University of Iowa Press, 1983.

Walker, Henry P., and Bufkin, Don. *Historical Atlas of Arizona.* Norman: University of Oklahoma Press, 1979.

Warmsley, Arthur J. *Connecticut Post Offices and Postmarks.* Portland, CT (private publication), 1977.

Webster's New Geographical Dictionary. Springfield, MA: Merriam-Webster, 1988.

Worldmark Encyclopedia of the States, 2nd ed. New York: John Wiley & Sons, 1986.

Who Was Who in America: Historical Volume 1607-1896, rev. ed. Chicago: Marquis Who's Who, 1967

Wick, Doulgas A. *North Dakota Place Names.* Hedemarken Collectibles, 1988.

Connecticut

CONNECTICUT

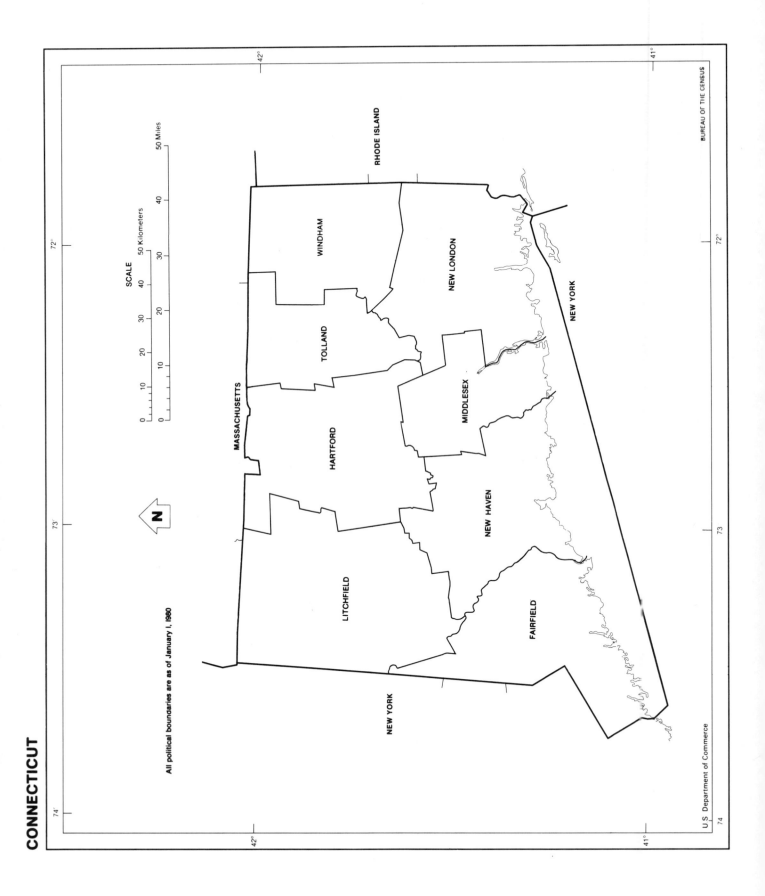

All political boundaries are as of January I, 1980

N

SCALE

50 Miles

50 Kilometers

MASSACHUSETTS

RHODE ISLAND

WINDHAM

TOLLAND

HARTFORD

NEW LONDON

LITCHFIELD

MIDDLESEX

NEW HAVEN

FAIRFIELD

NEW YORK

NEW YORK

U.S. Department of Commerce

Connecticut

Population: 3,287,116 (1990); 3,107,576 (1980)
Population rank (1990): 27
Percent population change (1980-1990): 5.8
Population projection: 3,363,000 (1995);
3,432,000 (2000)

Area: total 5,544 sq. mi.; 4,845 sq. mi. land, 698 sq.
mi. water. Coastline 253 mi.
Area rank: 48
Highest elevation: 2,380 ft., south slope of Mt. Frissell
Lowest point: sea level along Long Island Sound

State capital: Hartford (Hartford County)
Largest city: Bridgeport (141,686)
Second largest city: Hartford (139,739)
Largest county: Hartford (851,783)

Total housing units: 1,320,850
No. of occupied housing units: 1,230,479
Vacant housing units (%): 6.8
**Distribution of population by race and
  Hispanic origin (%):**
  White: 87.0
  Black: 8.3
  Hispanic (any race): 6.5
  Native American: 0.2
  Asian/Pacific: 1.5
  Other: 2.9

Admission date: January 9, 1788 (5th state)

Location: In the northeastern United States, bordering
New York, Massachusetts, Rhode Island, and Long
Island Sound. One of the thirteen original English
colonies.

Name Origin: For the Connecticut River, which bisects the state, flowing south from the Massachusetts
border into Long Island Sound.

State animal: sperm whale *(Physeter catodon)*
State bird: American robin *(Turdus migratorius)*
State flower: mountain laurel *(Kalmia latifolia)*
State hero: Nathan Hale
State insect: praying mantis *(Mantis religiosa)*
State mineral: garnet
State ship: SS Nautilus (first nuclear submarine)
State song: "Yankee Doodle"
State tree: white oak *(Quercus alba)*
State motto: *Qui Transtulit Sustinet* (Latin 'He Who
  Transplanted Still Sustains')
State nickname: The Constitution State; The Nutmeg
  State; Land of Steady Habits; Blue Law State

Area code: 203

Time zone: Eastern
Abbreviations: CT (postal); Conn. (traditional)
Part of (region): New England

Local Government

Counties

The eight counties of Connecticut are popularly recognized, although county government was abolished by the
state legislature effective October 1, 1960. Town and city
governments provide local-level administration. The former counties are used as state court districts, and state
superior courts are based in the former county seats.

Municipalities

The entire area of Connecticut is within one or another of
169 towns. Some of these are coextensive with the 21
Connecticut cities; in these, city government, in effect,
replaces the town authority. Most of the towns remain as
independent government entities. There are also 11 boroughs, each a local administrative unit within one of the
towns.

Settlement History and Early Development

The region was first populated by Indians; archeological
evidence suggests habitation as long as 10,000 years ago.
By the beginning of the seventeenth century there were at
least sixteen tribes, among them the Nehantic, Podunk,
Nipmuck, and Wappinger, all part of the Algonquian
Confederation. The warlike Pequots settled along the
coast near the Thames River, which divides the present-
day cities of New London and Groton. Mohawk raiding
parties from the west prevented tribes who lived in the
Connecticut River Valley from moving into what are now
the west and northwestern parts of the state. Fear of these
two tribes induced other Indians to befriend the English
settlers when they began arriving in the 1630s.

The first recorded European exploration in what is now
Connecticut was by Dutch explorer Adriaen Block. In
1614 he sailed up the Connecticut River (which he named
the Versche) probably as far as the Enfield Rapids, claiming the area for Holland. Dutch colonists never settled in
Connecticut, but in 1633 did build a fort called the *House
of Hope* near present-day Hartford. In the same year
English Puritans (some 20,000 of whom arrived between
1630 and 1642), established their first settlement near
what is now Windsor, followed shortly by others in Hartford, New London, Saybrook, and Wethersfield. Hartford, Wethersfield, and Windsor united to form the Connecticut Colony (also known as the River Colony) in
1636. In 1638, wealthy Puritans established New Haven
as an independent colony.

English colonization soon became a threat to Pequot supremacy in the area of the Thames River, which led to the Pequot War of 1637. The main battle was fought near Mystic. John Mason led the English, who were aided by Narragansett and Mohegan warriors led by Uncas, chief of the Mohegans. More than 500 Pequots were killed, the rest driven away or sold into slavery.

Many early English settlers came to the Colony from Massachusetts in search of religious and political freedom. The most famous was Congregationalist minister Thomas Hooker, the chief founder of Hartford, who preached that government should be based on the will of the people. The Connecticut Colony, applying his principle, adopted the Fundamental Orders in 1639. Some historians believe this to have been the first written constitution, hence Connecticut's nickname "Constitution State." The U.S. Constitution may have been modeled in part on the Fundamental Orders.

By 1660 Connecticut Colony included Fairfield, Farmington, Middletown, New London, Norwalk, Saybrook, and Stratford. In 1662, King Charles II of England granted the colony a tract of land 73 miles wide, extending west from Narragansett Bay in present-day Rhode Island to the Pacific Ocean, including the New Haven Colony. The latter, after initial objection, united with the Connecticut Colony in 1665 for economic reasons and for fear of incorporation into Anglican New York.

Prior to the Revolutionary War, Connecticut functioned as an independent republic. Its autonomy was threatened in 1687 by Sir Edmund Andros, governor of the Dominion of New England, an appointee of England's King James II. Andros went to Hartford and demanded the surrender of Connecticut's 1662 charter. Legend has it that the charter was saved by being hidden in an oak tree. The tree, known as the Charter Oak, was a revered landmark; it fell during a great storm in 1856.

The American Revolution

Possibly because of its Puritan background and historic independence, Connecticut was a patriot stronghold during the American Revolution. About 3,600 Connecticut men went to Massachusetts at the outbreak of the Revolution in 1775. On June 14, 1776, the colonists passed a resolution favoring independence, and on July 9, 1778, ratified the Articles of Confederation, the forerunner of the U.S. Constitution. Her most famous patriot was Nathan Hale, executed by the British as a spy in 1776, whose dying words became famous: "I only regret that I have but one life to lose for my country." Governor Jonathan Trumbull was a trusted friend and adviser of General George Washington, who called him "Brother Jonathan." The British came to use the term as a derisive nickname for Americans. Later Brother Jonathan evolved into a comic character in plays who symbolized the Yankee virtues of common sense, simplicity, honesty, and forthrightness.

In addition to sending troops, Connecticut privateers captured more than 500 British merchant vessels, and its small navy captured about 40 enemy ships. Connecticut also produced arms and gunpowder for the American cause, thus earning it the unofficial nickname of "arsenal

of the nation." On January 9, 1788, Connecticut became the fifth state to ratify the Constitution.

The Civil War and Industrial Development

Connecticut had been anti-slavery since the early years of independence, and when the Civil War broke out about 55,000 of her men joined the Union forces. The Colt and Winchester companies produced rifles and revolvers for the Union army, and other Connecticut industries produced uniforms, buttons, blankets, and boots, signaling its development as a thriving industrial state. Other key industries, some started during the early 1700s, included clockmaking, shipbuilding, silversmithing, and brass and tinware. Canny Yankee peddlers gained a reputation as shrewd tradesmen who could even sell wooden nutmegs, giving rise to another state nickname.

Several noted inventors from Connecticut contributed to the state's industrial growth. Eli Whitney, inventor of the cotton gin, was perhaps more influential as the father of mass-production manufacturing. In Hamden in 1800, Whitney developed machine tools to make interchangeable gun parts in quantity. In 1808, Eli Terry of East Hartford first mass-produced clocks. In 1810, Rodney Hanks and his nephew, Horatio, built the first silk mill in the nation at Mansfield. In 1836, Hartford's Samuel Colt invented and patented the first successful repeating pistol. Elias Howe of Hartford invented the first practical sewing machine in 1843. Charles Goodyear of New Haven developed and patented vulcanization of rubber in 1844.

Abundant waterpower from its rivers, capital provided by banks and insurance companies, and a good transportation network, including railroads and steamships that could easily reach East Coast markets contributed to Connecticut's development. The state capital Hartford is known as the "insurance capital" of the nation, and is the home of several major insurance firms. Connecticut's first insurance company was formed in 1795 in Norwich to provide fire insurance. Marine insurance companies were established in Hartford and in major port cities between 1797 and 1805.

State Boundaries

The royal charter of 1622 for Connecticut Colony established its north and south boundaries as Massachusetts and Long Island Sound. A dispute with Massachusetts in 1803, however, required a settlement that created the "Southwick jog," the small portion of the town of Southwick, Mass. that juts into north-central Connecticut. The east and west boundaries were disputed for years by Connecticut, Massachusetts, Rhode Island, New York, and Pennsylvania. The most serious disagreement was with New York, who claimed the whole area from the Delaware Bay to the Connecticut River. In 1683 the boundary was set 20 miles east of and parallel to the Hudson River, but the exact line was not established until Connecticut, New York, and the U.S. Congress agreed to it in 1881. Connecticut ceded to the federal government all the land beyond her western border in 1786, keeping only the Western Reserve, a tract of land in northeastern Ohio. This land was sold to the Connecticut Land Company in 1800 and eventually developed as a part of the Northwest Territory. The present Connecticut-Rhode Island border was established by two commissions, one in 1840 and the other in 1888.

Connecticut Counties

Fairfield	Middlesex	Tolland
Hartford	New Haven	Windham
Litchfield	New London	

American Places Dictionary

Fairfield County
Former County Seat: Bridgeport (ZIP: 06601)

Pop: 827,645 (1990); 807,143 (1980)   **Pop Density:** 1322.4
Land: 625.9 sq. mi.; **Water:** 211.2 sq. mi.   **Area Code:** 203

In southwestern CT, bordered on the west by NY and on the south by Long Island Sound. Original county, organized May 10, 1666.
Name origin: Descriptive of the area.

Bethel   Town
ZIP: 06801   **Lat:** 41-22-27 N **Long:** 73-23-43 W
Pop: 17,541 (1990); 16,004 (1980)   **Pop Density:** 1044.1
Land: 16.8 sq. mi.; **Water:** 0.1 sq. mi.

In southwestern CT, 20 mi. north of Norwalk. Settled soon after 1685; incorporated 1855.
Name origin: For the biblical town (from the Hebrew for 'house of God').

Bridgeport   City
ZIP: 06601   **Lat:** 41-11-10 N **Long:** 73-11-46 W
Pop: 141,686 (1990); 142,546 (1980)   **Pop Density:** 8855.4
Land: 16.0 sq. mi.; **Water:** 3.4 sq. mi.

In southwestern CT on Long Island Sound, 15 mi. southwest of New Haven. County seat; settled 1639; town incorporated 1821; city chartered 1836. Once an important manufacturing center and resort town.
Name origin: For the first drawbridge built over the Poquonock River, in the center of the city. Previous names include Pequonnock, New Fairfield, Stratfield, and Fairfield Village.

Brookfield   Town
ZIP: 06804   **Lat:** 41-28-06 N **Long:** 73-23-32 W
Pop: 14,113 (1990); 12,872 (1980)   **Pop Density:** 712.8
Land: 19.8 sq. mi.; **Water:** 0.6 sq. mi.

In southwestern CT, 18 mi. west-southwest of Waterbury. Incorporated 1788.
Name origin: For Rev. Thomas Brooks, the town's first pastor. Previous names include Quabaug, Whisconier, Pocono, Newbury, and West Farms.

Danbury   City
ZIP: 06810   **Lat:** 41-24-07 N **Long:** 73-28-17 W
Pop: 65,585 (1990); 60,470 (1980)   **Pop Density:** 1557.8
Land: 42.1 sq. mi.; **Water:** 2.2 sq. mi.   **Elev:** 378 ft.

In southwestern CT, 20 mi. northwest of Bridgeport. Settled 1685; incorporated 1889. Once noted as a center of hat-making.
Name origin: For Danbury, England. Called Swampfield or Swamfield by early settlers.

Darien   Town
ZIP: 06820   **Lat:** 41-03-04 N **Long:** 73-28-46 W
Pop: 18,196 (1990); 18,892 (1980)   **Pop Density:** 1410.5
Land: 12.9 sq. mi.; **Water:** 10.6 sq. mi.

In southwestern CT on Long Island Sound, 5 mi. northeast of Stamford. Residential town. A center for the colonial shipping industry. Settled after 1700; incorporated 1820.
Name origin: For the Isthmus of Darien (now the Isthmus of Panama), for one or more reasons: a local shipowner of influence made his fortune trading on the isthmus; Scottish settlers commemorated an expedition to the isthmus; a land form in the area suggested the isthmus.

Easton   Town
ZIP: 06612   **Lat:** 41-15-56 N **Long:** 73-18-05 W
Pop: 6,303 (1990); 5,962 (1980)   **Pop Density:** 230.0
Land: 27.4 sq. mi.; **Water:** 1.2 sq. mi.

In southwestern CT, 5 mi. northwest of Bridgeport. Incorporated as North Fairfield in 1762, and as part of Weston in 1787.
Name origin: Former North Fairfield parish was divided from Weston in 1845 and called Easton, for its location relative to Weston.

Fairfield   Town
ZIP: 06430   **Lat:** 41-10-32 N **Long:** 73-16-20 W
Pop: 53,418 (1990); 54,849 (1980)   **Pop Density:** 1780.6
Land: 30.0 sq. mi.; **Water:** 1.3 sq. mi.

In southwestern CT on Long Island Sound, adjacent to Bridgeport. Settled 1639. Site of Fairfield University.
Name origin: Named by Roger Ludlow, either for the surrounding area or for Fairfield, Kent, England. Previous Indian name Uncowaye.

Georgetown   CDP
          Lat: 41-14-50 N **Long:** 73-26-00 W
Pop: 1,694 (1990); 362 (1980)   **Pop Density:** 605.0
Land: 2.8 sq. mi.; **Water:** 0.0 sq. mi.

Greenwich   Town
ZIP: 06830   **Lat:** 41-02-20 N **Long:** 73-36-50 W
Pop: 58,441 (1990); 59,578 (1980)   **Pop Density:** 1220.1
Land: 47.9 sq. mi.; **Water:** 28.8 sq. mi.

In southwestern CT on Long Island Sound near New York border, 5 mi. southwest of Stamford. Settled 1540. Residential commuter town in New York metropolitan area.
Name origin: For Greenwich, England. Indian names included Patuquapaen and Sicascock.

Monroe   Town
ZIP: 06468   **Lat:** 41-20-09 N **Long:** 73-13-34 W
Pop: 16,896 (1990); 14,010 (1980)   **Pop Density:** 647.4
Land: 26.1 sq. mi.; **Water:** 0.2 sq. mi.

In southwestern Connecticut on Housatonic River, 10 mi. north of Bridgeport. Settled 1720; incorporated 1823.
Name origin: For Pres. James Monroe (1758–1831). Previous names include Flat Rock and Huntington.

New Canaan   Town
ZIP: 06840   **Lat:** 41-09-36 N **Long:** 73-30-04 W
Pop: 17,864 (1990); 17,931 (1980)   **Pop Density:** 808.3
Land: 22.1 sq. mi.; **Water:** 0.4 sq. mi.

In southwestern CT, 5 mi. northwest of Norwalk. Canaan Parish established 1731; town incorporated 1801.
Name origin: For the name of the biblical promised land. Named "New" Canaan upon incorporation to avoid confusion with Canaan in northwestern CT.

New Fairfield
Town
ZIP: 06810   **Lat:** 41-28-57 N **Long:** 73-29-20 W
Pop: 12,911 (1990); 11,260 (1980)   **Pop Density:** 629.8
Land: 20.5 sq. mi.; **Water:** 4.6 sq. mi.

In southwestern CT. Settled 1729; incorporated 1740.

Name origin: For the town of Fairfield, from which the early settlers came.

Newtown
Borough
                       Lat: 41-24-47 N **Long:** 73-18-57 W
Pop: 1,800 (1990); 2,022 (1980)   **Pop Density:** 720.0
Land: 2.5 sq. mi.; **Water:** 0.0 sq. mi.

*Newtown
Town
ZIP: 06470   **Lat:** 41-23-54 N **Long:** 73-17-37 W
Pop: 20,779 (1990); 19,107 (1980)   **Pop Density:** 359.5
Land: 57.8 sq. mi.; **Water:** 1.3 sq. mi.

In southwestern CT near Housatonic River, 8 mi. east of Danbury. Incorporated 1711. Includes borough of Newtown.

Name origin: Settled from nearby town of Stratford, incorporated as New Town. Previously called Pootatuck and Quanneapague by the Indians.

Norwalk
City
ZIP: 06850   **Lat:** 41-05-38 N **Long:** 73-25-12 W
Pop: 78,331 (1990); 77,767 (1980)   **Pop Density:** 3435.6
Land: 22.8 sq. mi.; **Water:** 13.5 sq. mi.

In southwestern CT on Long Island Sound, midway between Stamford and Bridgeport. Settled and incorporated 1651.

Name origin: Two theories: When purchased from Indians, boundary was to extend northward from the sea one day's walk. May also have come from a Siwanay Indian word meaning 'point of land.'

Redding
Town
ZIP: 06896   **Lat:** 41-18-15 N **Long:** 73-23-35 W
Pop: 7,927 (1990); 7,272 (1980)   **Pop Density:** 251.7
Land: 31.5 sq. mi.; **Water:** 0.6 sq. mi.

In southwestern CT. Established around 1717; incorporated 1767.

Name origin: Named Reading for Col. John Read, the original patentee. Over time, the pronunciation varied; present spelling became official upon incorporation.

Ridgefield
Town
ZIP: 06877   **Lat:** 41-18-18 N **Long:** 73-30-07 W
Pop: 20,919 (1990); 20,120 (1980)   **Pop Density:** 608.1
Land: 34.4 sq. mi.; **Water:** 0.5 sq. mi.

In southwestern CT on New York border, 10 mi. northeast of Norwalk. Incorporated 1709. Site of Revolutionary War battle in April 1777.

Name origin: Named in 1709, by general assembly, for the area's high ridges. Called Caudatowa ('high land') by the Indians.

Shelton
City
ZIP: 06484   **Lat:** 41-18-14 N **Long:** 73-08-18 W
Pop: 35,418 (1990); 31,314 (1980)   **Pop Density:** 1157.5
Land: 30.6 sq. mi.; **Water:** 1.4 sq. mi.

In southern CT on Housatonic River, 8 mi. west of New Haven. Incorporated 1915. Coextensive with town (incorporated 1789).

Name origin: Named in 1919 by the general assembly, for Edward N. Shelton, industrialist and promoter of the Derby-Shelton dam (built 1870). Previously named Huntington. Indians called the area Quorum.

Sherman
Town
ZIP: 06784   **Lat:** 41-34-46 N **Long:** 73-29-46 W
Pop: 2,809 (1990); 2,281 (1980)   **Pop Density:** 128.9
Land: 21.8 sq. mi.; **Water:** 1.6 sq. mi.

In western CT. Incorporated 1802.

Name origin: For Roger Sherman (1721–93), signer of the Declaration of Independence, Articles of Confederation, and U.S. Constitution. Originally called Upper Seven Miles, part of New Fairfield.

Stamford
City
ZIP: 06901   **Lat:** 41-05-48 N **Long:** 73-33-09 W
Pop: 108,056 (1990); 102,453 (1980)   **Pop Density:** 2866.2
Land: 37.7 sq. mi.; **Water:** 5.0 sq. mi.

In southwestern CT on Long Island Sound, 25 mi. southwest of Bridgeport. Important commercial and corporate center. Settled 1641; city incorporated 1893; town and city consolidated 1947.

Name origin: Probably named in 1642 for Stamford, England. Earlier called Rippowam, from the Sinanoy Indian word for 'cliff of rocks.'

Stratford
Town
ZIP: 06497   **Lat:** 41-12-15 N **Long:** 73-07-48 W
Pop: 49,389 (1990); 50,541 (1980)   **Pop Density:** 2806.2
Land: 17.6 sq. mi.; **Water:** 2.3 sq. mi.

In southwestern CT on Long Island Sound and Housatonic River, directly east of Bridgeport. Settled 1639.

Name origin: Probably for Stratford-on-Avon, England.

Trumbull
Town
ZIP: 06611   **Lat:** 41-15-29 N **Long:** 73-12-26 W
Pop: 32,016 (1990); 32,989 (1980)   **Pop Density:** 1374.1
Land: 23.3 sq. mi.; **Water:** 0.2 sq. mi.

In southwestern CT, 3 mi. north of Bridgeport. Incorporated October 1797.

Name origin: For Jonathan Trumbull (1710–1785), governor of CT during the Revolutionary War. Before incorporation known as Unity and North Stratford.

Weston
Town
ZIP: 06880   **Lat:** 41-13-31 N **Long:** 73-22-15 W
Pop: 8,648 (1990); 8,284 (1980)   **Pop Density:** 436.8
Land: 19.8 sq. mi.; **Water:** 0.9 sq. mi.

In southwestern CT, 10 mi. northwest of Bridgeport. Incorporated 1787.

Name origin: For its being the western town or settlement of Fairfield. Previously called Aspetuck by the Indians.

Westport
Town
ZIP: 06880   **Lat:** 41-07-23 N **Long:** 73-20-51 W
Pop: 24,410 (1990); 25,290 (1980)   **Pop Density:** 1220.5
Land: 20.0 sq. mi.; **Water:** 13.3 sq. mi.

In southwestern CT on Long Island Sound at mouth of Naugatuck River, 4 mi. northeast of Norwalk. Settled 1648; incorporated 1835. Once a part of Weston, Norwalk, and Fairfield.

Name origin: For having been Fairfield's western port. Previously called Saugatuck.

Wilton
Town
ZIP: 06897   **Lat:** 41-12-04 N **Long:** 73-26-16 W
Pop: 15,989 (1990); 15,351 (1980)   **Pop Density:** 592.2
Land: 27.0 sq. mi.; **Water:** 0.4 sq. mi.

In southwestern CT, 5 mi. northeast of Norwalk. Settled 1706; incorporated May 2, 1802.

Name origin: For either the town of Wilton or Wilton Parish, England.

Hartford County
Former County Seat: Hartford (ZIP: 06101)

Pop: 851,783 (1990); 807,766 (1980)   **Pop Density:** 1158.1
Land: 735.5 sq. mi.; **Water:** 15.1 sq. mi.   **Area Code:** 203
In north-central CT. Original county, organized May 10, 1666.
Name origin: For Hertford or Hertfordshire, England. Spelling reflects English pronunciation.

Avon   Town
ZIP: 06001   **Lat:** 41-47-40 N **Long:** 72-51-30 W
Pop: 13,937 (1990); 11,201 (1980)   **Pop Density:** 603.3
Land: 23.1 sq. mi.; **Water:** 0.4 sq. mi.   **Elev:** 202 ft.
In northern CT, 5 mi. west of Hartford.
Name origin: Named in 1830 for the Avon River in England.

Berlin   Town
ZIP: 06037   **Lat:** 41-36-50 N **Long:** 72-46-23 W
Pop: 16,787 (1990); 15,121 (1980)   **Pop Density:** 633.5
Land: 26.5 sq. mi.; **Water:** 0.6 sq. mi.
In central CT, 10 mi. south-southwest of Hartford. Settled in the 1660s.
Name origin: Incorporated and named in 1785 for the city in Germany. Earlier names include Great Swamp, Kensington, Worthington, and Farmington.

Bloomfield   Town
ZIP: 06002   **Lat:** 41-50-39 N **Long:** 72-44-30 W
Pop: 19,483 (1990); 18,608 (1980)   **Pop Density:** 749.3
Land: 26.0 sq. mi.; **Water:** 0.2 sq. mi.
In northern CT, 5 mi. north-northwest of Hartford. Incorporated 1835.
Name origin: Probably from a nearby orchard settled by freeman William Blumfield (or Bloomfield). Previously known as Wintonbury, as inhabitants came from the towns of Windsor, Farmington, and Simsbury.

Blue Hills   CDP
Lat: 41-48-46 N **Long:** 72-41-53 W
Pop: 3,206 (1990)   **Pop Density:** 2914.5
Land: 1.1 sq. mi.; **Water:** 0.0 sq. mi.

Bristol   City
ZIP: 06010   **Lat:** 41-40-52 N **Long:** 72-56-27 W
Pop: 60,640 (1990); 57,370 (1980)   **Pop Density:** 2288.3
Land: 26.5 sq. mi.; **Water:** 0.3 sq. mi.
In northern CT, 15 mi. southwest of Hartford. Settled 1727; town incorporated 1785; city in 1911.
Name origin: Named in 1785, probably for Bristol, England.

Broad Brook   CDP
ZIP: 06016   **Lat:** 41-54-32 N **Long:** 72-32-39 W
Pop: 3,585 (1990)   **Pop Density:** 607.6
Land: 5.9 sq. mi.; **Water:** 0.0 sq. mi.

Burlington   Town
ZIP: 06085   **Lat:** 41-45-31 N **Long:** 72-57-29 W
Pop: 7,026 (1990); 5,660 (1980)   **Pop Density:** 235.8
Land: 29.8 sq. mi.; **Water:** 0.6 sq. mi.
In northern CT, 15 mi. west of Hartford. Settled 1721; incorporated 1806.
Name origin: For Richard Boyle (1695–1753), 3d Earl of Burlington or from pronunciation of Bridlington, England. Known earlier as West Woods or West Britain.

Canton   Town
ZIP: 06019   **Lat:** 41-51-42 N **Long:** 72-54-34 W
Pop: 8,268 (1990); 7,635 (1980)   **Pop Density:** 336.1
Land: 24.6 sq. mi.; **Water:** 0.5 sq. mi.
In northern CT. Settled 1737; incorporated 1806.
Name origin: Probably named for Canton, China, due to a growing interest in trade with that country. Called Suffrage or West Simsbury prior to 1806.

Canton Valley   CDP
Lat: 41-50-02 N **Long** 72-53-31 W
Pop: 1,563 (1990); 1,680 (1980)   **Pop Density:** 868.3
Land: 1.8 sq. mi.; **Water:** 0.0 sq. mi.

Collinsville   CDP
ZIP: 06022   **Lat:** 41-49-09 N **Long** 72-55-22 W
Pop: 2,591 (1990); 2,555 (1980)   **Pop Density:** 835.8
Land: 3.1 sq. mi.; **Water:** 0.4 sq. mi.

East Granby   Town
ZIP: 06026   **Lat:** 41-56-48 N **Long** 72-44-30 W
Pop: 4,302 (1990); 4,102 (1980)   **Pop Density:** 245.8
Land: 17.5 sq. mi.; **Water:** 0.1 sq. mi.
In northern CT. Settled 1664; incorporated 1858.
Name origin: For its location on the east side of Granby.

East Hartford   Town
ZIP: 06128   **Lat:** 41-45-40 N **Long** 72-36-57 W
Pop: 50,452 (1990); 52,563 (1980)   **Pop Density:** 2802.9
Land: 18.0 sq. mi.; **Water:** 0.8 sq. mi.
In northern CT, across the Connecticut River from Hartford. Settled c. 1650 as part of Hartford; incorporated 1783. Industrial town.
Name origin: For the parent city. Indians called the area Podunk.

East Windsor   Town
ZIP: 06088   **Lat:** 41-54-13 N **Long** 72-33-52 W
Pop: 10,081 (1990); 8,925 (1980)   **Pop Density:** 383.3
Land: 26.3 sq. mi.; **Water:** 0.5 sq. mi.
In northern CT on Connecticut River. Incorporated May 2, 1768.
Name origin: For having been the part of Windsor located east of the Connecticut River. Known earlier as Windsor Farms.

Enfield   Town
ZIP: 06082   **Lat:** 41-59-01 N **Long** 72-33-22 W
Pop: 45,532 (1990); 42,695 (1980)   **Pop Density:** 1363.2
Land: 33.4 sq. mi.; **Water:** 0.8 sq. mi.   **Elev:** 154 ft.
In northern CT on Connecticut River near Massachusetts border, 15 mi. north of Hartford. Settled 1681 as part of Massachusetts; annexed to Connecticut 1749. Town includes Thompsonville.
Name origin: Named in 1683 for Enfield, Middlesex, England. Previously named Freshwater.

Farmington
Town
ZIP: 06032   **Lat:** 41-43-39 N **Long:** 72-50-27 W
Pop: 20,608 (1990); 16,407 (1980)   **Pop Density:** 733.4
Land: 28.1 sq. mi.; **Water:** 0.7 sq. mi.

In northern CT on Farmington River, 7 mi. southwest of Hartford. Settled 1640; incorporated 1645. Seven towns have been formed from its original area: Avon, Berlin, Bristol, Burlington, New Britain, Plainville, and Southington.

Name origin: For either Farmington, England, or its status as an agricultural community. Previously known as Tunxis for the Tunxis Indians.

Glastonbury
Town
ZIP: 06033   **Lat:** 41-41-12 N **Long:** 72-32-43 W
Pop: 27,901 (1990); 24,327 (1980)   **Pop Density:** 542.8
Land: 51.4 sq. mi.; **Water:** 0.9 sq. mi.

In northern CT, 5 mi. southeast of Hartford. Settled 1650; incorporated 1690.

Name origin: Name changed in 1692 from Naubuc to Glassenbury, for Glastonbury, England. Present spelling accepted by town vote in 1870.

Granby
Town
ZIP: 06035   **Lat:** 41-57-43 N **Long:** 72-50-23 W
Pop: 9,369 (1990); 7,956 (1980)   **Pop Density:** 230.2
Land: 40.7 sq. mi.; **Water:** 0.1 sq. mi.

In northern CT on Massachusetts border.

Name origin: Named in 1786 for John Manners, Marquess of Granby (1721–1770). Formerly the Salmon Brook section of Simsbury.

Hartford
City
ZIP: 06101   **Lat:** 41-45-56 N **Long:** 72-41-01 W
Pop: 139,739 (1990); 136,392 (1980)   **Pop Density:** 8077.4
Land: 17.3 sq. mi.; **Water:** 0.7 sq. mi.

In northern CT on Connecticut River, 35 mi. northeast of New Haven. State capital and county seat. Town of Hartford (incorporated 1794) consolidated with city in 1896. Home of the first constitution of the Connecticut Colony, the Fundamental Orders (1639), one of the first written constitutions. Industrial and commercial center; a major insurance center of the United States.

Name origin: Named by the General Court in 1636 for Hertford, England, birthplace of one of the settlement's ministers. Indian name Suckiaug. First English settlement by Thomas Hooker from Newtown (later Cambridge), Massachusetts was called Newtown.

Hartland
Town
ZIP: 06027   **Lat:** 42-00-18 N **Long:** 72-56-55 W
Pop: 1,866 (1990); 1,416 (1980)   **Pop Density:** 56.5
Land: 33.0 sq. mi.; **Water:** 1.5 sq. mi.

In northern Connecticut. Incorporated 1761.

Name origin: Either a shortening of Hartford Land because it was owned by men from Hartford, or for Hartland, Devonshire, England.

Hazardville
CDP
ZIP: 06082   **Lat:** 41-59-12 N **Long:** 72-31-46 W
Pop: 5,179 (1990); 5,436 (1980)   **Pop Density:** 1785.9
Land: 2.9 sq. mi.; **Water:** 0.0 sq. mi.

Kensington
CDP
ZIP: 06037   **Lat:** 41-37-42 N **Long:** 72-46-16 W
Pop: 8,306 (1990); 7,502 (1980)   **Pop Density:** 1567.2
Land: 5.3 sq. mi.; **Water:** 0.2 sq. mi.

Manchester
Town
ZIP: 06040   **Lat:** 41-46-31 N **Long:** 72-31-28 W
Pop: 51,618 (1990); 49,761 (1980)   **Pop Density:** 1890.8
Land: 27.3 sq. mi.; **Water:** 0.4 sq. mi.

In northern CT, 6 mi. east of Hartford. Settled 1673; incorporated 1823.

Name origin: For Manchester, England (the "Cotton City"), because of the town's once-important silk and cotton industry. Previously known as Five Mile Tract, then as the parish of Orford or Charlotte.

Marlborough
Town
ZIP: 06447   **Lat:** 41-38-07 N **Long:** 72-27-16 W
Pop: 5,535 (1990); 4,746 (1980)   **Pop Density:** 237.6
Land: 23.3 sq. mi.; **Water:** 0.1 sq. mi.

In central CT.

Name origin: Named in 1747, for either the Duke of Marlborough or the town of Marlborough, MA.

New Britain
City
ZIP: 06050   **Lat:** 41-40-30 N **Long:** 72-47-16 W
Pop: 75,491 (1990); 73,840 (1980)   **Pop Density:** 5676.0
Land: 13.3 sq. mi.; **Water:** 0.1 sq. mi.

In central CT, 10 mi. southwest of Hartford. Incorporated 1870; city and town coextensive.

Name origin: Laid out and named in 1754 by Col. Isaac Lee in honor of Great Britain.

Newington
Town
ZIP: 06111   **Lat:** 41-41-14 N **Long:** 72-43-50 W
Pop: 29,208 (1990); 28,841 (1980)   **Pop Density:** 2212.7
Land: 13.2 sq. mi.; **Water:** 0.0 sq. mi.

In northern CT, 5 mi. southwest of Hartford. Settled 1670; incorporated July 10, 1871.

Name origin: Probably for Newington, England. Previous names included Pipestave Swamp, Cow Plain, West Farms, and New Meadow Town.

North Granby
CDP
ZIP: 06060   **Lat:** 42-01-04 N **Long:** 72-50-37 W
Pop: 1,455 (1990)   **Pop Density:** 173.2
Land: 8.4 sq. mi.; **Water:** 0.0 sq. mi.

Plainville
Town
ZIP: 06062   **Lat:** 41-40-29 N **Long:** 72-51-27 W
Pop: 17,392 (1990); 16,401 (1980)   **Pop Density:** 1793.0
Land: 9.7 sq. mi.; **Water:** 0.1 sq. mi.   **Elev:** 191 ft.

In central CT, west of New Britain.

Name origin: Named 1829, for its level topography. Previously called Great Plain or the Great Plain of Farmington.

Rocky Hill
Town
ZIP: 06067   **Lat:** 41-39-26 N **Long:** 72-39-37 W
Pop: 16,554 (1990); 14,559 (1980)   **Pop Density:** 1226.2
Land: 13.5 sq. mi.; **Water:** 0.3 sq. mi.

In northern CT, 5 mi. south of Hartford. Settled 1650; incorporated 1843.

Name origin: For Rocky, or Shipman Hill, the area's most prominent feature. Earlier names included Lexington Parish and Stepney Parish.

Salmon Brook
CDP
Lat: 41-57-23 N **Long:** 72-47-45 W
Pop: 2,185 (1990)   **Pop Density:** 728.3
Land: 3.0 sq. mi.; **Water:** 0.0 sq. mi.

Sherwood Manor
CDP
ZIP: 06082   Lat: 42-00-47 N Long: 72-33-53 W
Pop: 6,357 (1990); 6,303 (1980)   Pop Density: 2050.6
Land: 3.1 sq. mi.; Water: 0.0 sq. mi.

Simsbury
Town
ZIP: 06070   Lat: 41-52-13 N Long: 72-49-32 W
Pop: 22,023 (1990); 21,161 (1980)   Pop Density: 649.6
Land: 33.9 sq. mi.; Water: 0.4 sq. mi.   Elev: 181 ft.

In northern CT on Farmington River, 8 mi. northwest of Hartford. Incorporated 1670.

Name origin: Named in 1670 by general assembly, either for "Sim" Wolcott or Symondsbury (or Simonsbury), Dorsetshire, England. Called Massacoe by the Indians.

Southington
Town
ZIP: 06489   Lat: 41-36-18 N Long: 72-52-46 W
Pop: 38,518 (1990); 36,879 (1980)   Pop Density: 1069.9
Land: 36.0 sq. mi.; Water: 0.6 sq. mi.

In central CT, 5 mi. southwest of New Britain. Settled 1698; incorporated 1779.

Name origin: A contraction of South Farmington; it was once a part of Farmington.

South Windsor
Town
ZIP: 06074   Lat: 41-49-56 N Long: 72-34-12 W
Pop: 22,090 (1990); 17,198 (1980)   Pop Density: 788.9
Land: 28.0 sq. mi.; Water: 0.7 sq. mi.

In northern CT, 5 mi. northeast of Hartford. Settled 1636; incorporated 1845.

Name origin: For its parent city of Windsor. Previously called Nowashe by the Indians, Nowaas by the Dutch, and Wapping, from either Wapping, England, or the Algonquian word for 'east land.'

Southwood Acres
CDP
ZIP: 06082   Lat: 41-57-45 N Long: 72-34-19 W
Pop: 8,963 (1990); 9,779 (1980)   Pop Density: 2186.1
Land: 4.1 sq. mi.; Water: 0.0 sq. mi.

Suffield
Town
ZIP: 06078   Lat: 42-00-00 N Long: 72-40-53 W
Pop: 11,427 (1990); 9,294 (1980)   Pop Density: 270.8
Land: 42.2 sq. mi.; Water: 0.7 sq. mi.

On Massachusetts border in northern CT. Settled 1670.

Name origin: Owing to a surveying error, originally part of Massachusetts and called Southfield as that state's southernmost town. It became a part of CT in 1749. Present spelling reflects pronunciation.

Tariffville
CDP
ZIP: 06081   Lat: 41-54-29 N Long: 72-46-02 W
Pop: 1,477 (1990); 1,324 (1980)   Pop Density: 2461.7
Land: 0.6 sq. mi.; Water: 0.0 sq. mi.

Terramuggus
CDP
Lat: 41-38-05 N Long: 72-28-15 W
Pop: 1,044 (1990)   Pop Density: 870.0
Land: 1.2 sq. mi.; Water: 0.1 sq. mi.

Thompsonville
CDP
Lat: 41-59-26 N Long: 72-35-46 W
Pop: 8,458 (1990)   Pop Density: 3844.5
Land: 2.2 sq. mi.; Water: 0.2 sq. mi.

Weatogue
CDP
ZIP: 06089   Lat: 41-50-36 N Long: 72-49-44 W
Pop: 2,521 (1990); 2,249 (1980)   Pop Density: 840.3
Land: 3.0 sq. mi.; Water: 0.0 sq. mi.

West Hartford
Town
ZIP: 06127   Lat: 41-46-03 N Long: 72-45-15 W
Pop: 60,110 (1990); 61,301 (1980)   Pop Density: 2732.3
Land: 22.0 sq. mi.; Water: 0.4 sq. mi.

In northern CT, adjacent to Hartford. Residential suburb of Hartford. Birthplace of lexicographer Noah Webster (1758–1843). Settled in 1670s; incorporated 1854.

Name origin: Created from a tract of land divided from Hartford. Named in 1806 for the parent city.

West Simsbury
CDP
ZIP: 06092   Lat: 41-52-24 N Long: 72-50-39 W
Pop: 2,149 (1990); 2,140 (1980)   Pop Density: 488.4
Land: 4.4 sq. mi.; Water: 0.0 sq. mi.

Wethersfield
Town
ZIP: 06109   Lat: 41-42-04 N Long: 72-40-12 W
Pop: 25,651 (1990); 26,013 (1980)   Pop Density: 2068.6
Land: 12.4 sq. mi.; Water: 0.7 sq. mi.

In central CT on Connecticut River, 2 mi. south of Hartford. Settled 1634; incorporated 1636. Oldest town settlement in CT.

Name origin: Named in 1637 for Wethersfield, England. Earlier known as Watertown. Wongunk Indians called the area Pyquaug.

Windsor
Town
ZIP: 06095   Lat: 41-52-01 N Long: 72-40-16 W
Pop: 27,817 (1990); 25,204 (1980)   Pop Density: 939.8
Land: 29.6 sq. mi.; Water: 1.4 sq. mi.

In northern CT on Connecticut River, 5 mi. north of Hartford. Settled 1635 by Massachusetts Bay colonists.

Name origin: Named in 1637 by the General Court for Windsor, England. Previously known as Dorchester.

Windsor Locks
Town
ZIP: 06096   Lat: 41-55-33 N Long: 72-39-28 W
Pop: 12,358 (1990); 12,190 (1980)   Pop Density: 1373.1
Land: 9.0 sq. mi.; Water: 0.3 sq. mi.

In northern CT on Connecticut River, 10 mi. north of Hartford. Settled early 1660s; incorporated 1854. Site of Bradley International Airport.

Name origin: Once the Pine Meadow district of Windsor, with locks along its canal to the Connecticut River. Name proposed by Alfred Smith, president of the Enfield Falls Canal Co.

Litchfield County
Former County Seat: Litchfield (ZIP: 06759)

Pop: 174,092 (1990); 156,769 (1980)　　　　　　**Pop Density:** 189.2
Land: 920.0 sq. mi.; **Water:** 24.6 sq. mi.　　　　　**Area Code:** 203

In northeastern CT, bordered on the west by NY and on the north by MA; organized Oct 14, 1751 from Hartford and Fairfield counties.
Name origin: For the town in England, in Hampshire County.

Bantam
Borough
ZIP: 06750　　　　**Lat:** 41-43-24 N **Long:** 73-14-37 W
Pop: 757 (1990); 860 (1980)　　**Pop Density:** 757.0
Land: 1.0 sq. mi.; **Water:** 0.0 sq. mi.

In northwestern CT. Part of town of Litchfield.
Name origin: From the Potatuck Indian name for the area.

Barkhamsted
Town
ZIP: 06063　　　　**Lat:** 41-55-45 N **Long:** 72-58-21 W
Pop: 3,369 (1990); 2,935 (1980)　　**Pop Density:** 93.1
Land: 36.2 sq. mi.; **Water:** 2.6 sq. mi.

In northwestern CT. Settled early 1700s.
Name origin: For Berkhampstead, England. The spelling was subsequently changed to conform to pronunciation.

Bethlehem
Town
ZIP: 06751　　　　**Lat:** 41-38-20 N **Long:** 73-12-32 W
Pop: 3,071 (1990); 2,573 (1980)　　**Pop Density:** 158.3
Land: 19.4 sq. mi.; **Water:** 0.3 sq. mi.

In western CT. Settled 1734; incorporated 1787.
Name origin: Named in 1739, probably after the biblical Bethlehem of Judea, since the area nearby was then known as Judea. The name was formerly spelled Bethlem for many years.

Bridgewater
Town
ZIP: 06752　　　　**Lat:** 41-31-33 N **Long:** 73-21-40 W
Pop: 1,654 (1990); 1,563 (1980)　　**Pop Density:** 102.1
Land: 16.2 sq. mi.; **Water:** 1.0 sq. mi.

In western CT. Incorporated 1856.
Name origin: Named in 1803 for a bridge across the Housatonic River. Previously known by various names, including New Milford Neck, Shepaug Neck, and the Neck.

Canaan
Town
ZIP: 06018　　　　**Lat:** 41-57-42 N **Long:** 73-18-32 W
Pop: 1,057 (1990); 1,002 (1980)　　**Pop Density:** 32.0
Land: 33.0 sq. mi.; **Water:** 0.3 sq. mi.

In northwestern CT. Established 1738.
Name origin: For the biblical name of the promised land of the Israelites.

Colebrook
Town
ZIP: 06021　　　　**Lat:** 42-00-05 N **Long:** 73-05-05 W
Pop: 1,365 (1990); 1,221 (1980)　　**Pop Density:** 43.3
Land: 31.5 sq. mi.; **Water:** 1.4 sq. mi.

In northwestern CT. Settled in the 1760s.
Name origin: Named for Colebrooke, Devonshire, England.

Cornwall
Town
ZIP: 06796　　　　**Lat:** 41-50-42 N **Long:** 73-19-55 W
Pop: 1,414 (1990); 1,288 (1980)　　**Pop Density:** 30.7
Land: 46.0 sq. mi.; **Water:** 0.3 sq. mi.

In northwestern CT. Incorporated 1740.
Name origin: Named in 1738 for Cornwall, England.

Goshen
Town
ZIP: 06756　　　　**Lat:** 41-51-04 N **Long:** 73-14-10 W
Pop: 2,329 (1990); 1,706 (1980)　　**Pop Density:** 53.3
Land: 43.7 sq. mi.; **Water:** 1.5 sq. mi.

In northwestern CT. Incorporated 1739.
Name origin: Named May, 1738 for Goshen in ancient Egypt, the biblical land occupied by the Israelites in Egypt.

Harwinton
Town
ZIP: 06790　　　　**Lat:** 41-45-15 N **Long:** 73-03-26 W
Pop: 5,228 (1990); 4,889 (1980)　　**Pop Density:** 169.7
Land: 30.8 sq. mi.; **Water:** 0.3 sq. mi.

In northwestern CT. Incorporated October 1737.
Name origin: Originally owned by proprietors from Hartford and Windsor, its name derives from the first three letters of the names of each of the two towns, plus -*ton*.

Kent
Town
ZIP: 06757　　　　**Lat:** 41-43-53 N **Long:** 73-27-10 W
Pop: 2,918 (1990); 2,505 (1980)　　**Pop Density:** 60.2
Land: 48.5 sq. mi.; **Water:** 1.1 sq. mi.

In western CT. Incorporated 1739.
Name origin: For Kent, England. The early Indian name was Scatacook.

Litchfield
Town
ZIP: 06759　　　　**Lat:** 41-44-28 N **Long:** 73-11-34 W
Pop: 8,365 (1990); 7,605 (1980)　　**Pop Density:** 149.1
Land: 56.1 sq. mi.; **Water:** 0.7 sq. mi.

In northwestern CT. Village designated as county seat in 1751. Includes boroughs of Bantam and Litchfield.
Name origin: For the cathedral city of Lichfield, Staffordshire, England. Before white settlement in 1720, the Indians called the place Bantam. The first English settlers called it New Bantam.

*Litchfield
Borough
ZIP: 06759　　　　**Lat:** 41-44-40 N **Long:** 73-11-24 W
Pop: 1,378 (1990); 1,489 (1980)　　**Pop Density:** 984.3
Land: 1.4 sq. mi.; **Water:** 0.0 sq. mi.　　**Elev:** 1086 ft.

Morris
Town
ZIP: 06763　　　　**Lat:** 41-41-37 N **Long:** 73-12-39 W
Pop: 2,039 (1990); 1,899 (1980)　　**Pop Density:** 118.5
Land: 17.2 sq. mi.; **Water:** 1.5 sq. mi.

In western CT. Settled in the 1720s, then called South Farms. Incorporated 1859.
Name origin: For James Morris (1752–1820), captain in the Revolutionary War, selectman, state legislator, and founder of the Morris Academy (1790–1888).

New Hartford
ZIP: 06057   **Lat:** 41-50-28 N   Town
Long: 73-00-17 W
Pop: 5,769 (1990); 4,884 (1980)   **Pop Density:** 155.9
Land: 37.0 sq. mi.; **Water:** 1.1 sq. mi.

In northwestern CT. Originally part of the Western Lands allotted to Hartford. Settled 1734; incorporated 1738.
Name origin: From its parent town.

New Milford
ZIP: 06776   **Lat:** 41-36-29 N   Town
Long: 73-25-27 W
Pop: 23,629 (1990); 19,420 (1980)   **Pop Density:** 383.6
Land: 61.6 sq. mi.; **Water:** 2.1 sq. mi.

In western CT on Housatonic River, 20 mi. west of Waterbury. Settled 1707; incorporated 1712.
Name origin: Named and organized in 1703 by a land company from Milford. Previously called Weantinock by the Potatuck Indians.

New Preston
CDP
Lat: 41-40-54 N   **Long:** 73-21-15 W
Pop: 1,217 (1990); 1,209 (1980)   **Pop Density:** 164.5
Land: 7.4 sq. mi.; **Water:** 0.5 sq. mi.

Norfolk
ZIP: 06058   **Lat:** 41-59-00 N   Town
Long: 73-11-48 W
Pop: 2,060 (1990); 2,156 (1980)   **Pop Density:** 45.5
Land: 45.3 sq. mi.; **Water:** 1.1 sq. mi.

In northwestern CT. Settled 1744; incorporated 1758.
Name origin: Named for Norfolk, England.

North Canaan
ZIP: 06018   **Lat:** 42-01-20 N   Town
Long: 73-17-28 W
Pop: 3,284 (1990); 3,185 (1980)   **Pop Density:** 168.4
Land: 19.5 sq. mi.; **Water:** 0.0 sq. mi.

In northwestern corner of CT. Incorporated May 28, 1858.
Name origin: For its relation to Canaan, of which it originally was a part.

Oakville
ZIP: 06795   **Lat:** 41-35-31 N   CDP
Long: 73-05-09 W
Pop: 8,741 (1990); 8,737 (1980)   **Pop Density:** 2731.6
Land: 3.2 sq. mi.; **Water:** 0.0 sq. mi.

Plymouth
ZIP: 06782   **Lat:** 41-39-58 N   Town
Long: 73-01-37 W
Pop: 11,822 (1990); 10,732 (1980)   **Pop Density:** 544.8
Land: 21.7 sq. mi.; **Water:** 0.6 sq. mi.

In central CT, 5 mi. north of Waterbury. Settled 1728; incorporated 1795.
Name origin: Named in 1795 by Henry Cook, the first settler, for his great-grandfather, a pilgrim at Plymouth, MA. Originally called Northbury.

Roxbury
ZIP: 06783   **Lat:** 41-33-07 N   Town
Long: 73-18-10 W
Pop: 1,825 (1990); 1,468 (1980)   **Pop Density:** 69.7
Land: 26.2 sq. mi.; **Water:** 0.1 sq. mi.

In western CT. Settled 1713; incorporated 1796.
Name origin: Named Roxbury in 1743, probably for the surrounding rocky area. Earlier names included Rucum and Rocum. The Indian name was *Shepaug*, 'rocky river.'

Salisbury
ZIP: 06068   **Lat:** 41-59-05 N   Town
Long: 73-25-21 W
Pop: 4,090 (1990); 3,896 (1980)   **Pop Density:** 71.4
Land: 57.3 sq. mi.; **Water:** 2.8 sq. mi.

In northwestern corner of CT. Incorporated 1741.
Name origin: For either Salisbury, England, or for an early resident.

Sharon
ZIP: 06069   **Lat:** 41-51-37 N   Town
Long: 73-26-56 W
Pop: 2,928 (1990); 2,623 (1980)   **Pop Density:** 49.9
Land: 58.7 sq. mi.; **Water:** 0.9 sq. mi.

In northwestern corner of CT. Incorporated 1739.
Name origin: First named New Sharon, after the fertile coastal plain of the Bible. Called Sharon after incorporation.

Terryville
CDP
ZIP: 06786   **Lat:** 41-40-44 N   **Long:** 73-00-27 W
Pop: 5,426 (1990); 5,234 (1980)   **Pop Density:** 1937.9
Land: 2.8 sq. mi.; **Water:** 0.0 sq. mi.

Thomaston
ZIP: 06787   **Lat:** 41-40-15 N   Town
Long: 73-04-58 W
Pop: 6,947 (1990); 6,276 (1980)   **Pop Density:** 578.9
Land: 12.0 sq. mi.; **Water:** 0.2 sq. mi.

In western CT. Incorporated July 6, 1875.
Name origin: For the Thomas family, well-known clock manufacturers of the town. Previously part of Northbury, Watertown, and Plymouth; once called Plymouth Hollow.

Torrington
City
ZIP: 06790   **Lat:** 41-50-05 N   **Long:** 73-07-45 W
Pop: 33,687 (1990); 30,987 (1980)   **Pop Density:** 846.4
Land: 39.8 sq. mi.; **Water:** 0.6 sq. mi.

In northwestern CT, 20 mi. northwest of Waterbury. Town incorporated 1740; coextensive with city (incorporated 1923).
Name origin: For Torrington, Devonshire, England. Earlier called Wolcottville, after the Wolcott family, builders of a woolen mill.

Warren
ZIP: 06753   **Lat:** 41-44-11 N   Town
Long: 73-20-33 W
Pop: 1,226 (1990); 1,027 (1980)   **Pop Density:** 46.6
Land: 26.3 sq. mi.; **Water:** 1.2 sq. mi.

In northwestern CT. Settled 1737; incorporated 1786.
Name origin: For Gen. Joseph Warren (1741–75) of Revolutionary War fame.

Washington
ZIP: 06793   **Lat:** 41-39-11 N   Town
Long: 73-19-08 W
Pop: 3,905 (1990); 3,657 (1980)   **Pop Density:** 102.2
Land: 38.2 sq. mi.; **Water:** 0.5 sq. mi.

In northwestern CT. Settled 1734; incorporated 1779.
Name origin: For George Washington (1732–99). Prior to incorporation, eastern section called Judea, western section called New Preston.

Watertown
ZIP: 06795   **Lat:** 41-36-54 N   Town
Long: 73-07-02 W
Pop: 20,456 (1990); 19,489 (1980)   **Pop Density:** 700.5
Land: 29.2 sq. mi.; **Water:** 0.4 sq. mi.

In south-central CT on Naugatuck River, 3 mi. northwest of Waterbury. Settled 1684; incorporated 1780.
Name origin: From its parent city of Waterbury. Previously called Westbury.

Winchester   Town
ZIP: 06098   **Lat:** 41-55-30 N **Long:** 73-06-13 W
Pop: 11,524 (1990); 10,841 (1980)   **Pop Density:** 356.8
Land: 32.3 sq. mi.; **Water:** 1.6 sq. mi.

In northwestern CT, 7 mi. north of Torrington. Incorporated May 1771. Includes former city of Winsted.

Name origin: Named in 1733 for Winchester, England.

Winsted   CDP
ZIP: 06098   **Lat:** 41-55-37 N **Long:** 73-04-00 W
Pop: 8,254 (1990); 8,092 (1980)   **Pop Density:** 1756.2
Land: 4.7 sq. mi.; **Water:** 0.2 sq. mi.   **Elev:** 713 ft.

Formerly a city, now part of town of Winchester.

Name origin: A combination of elements from Winchester and Barkhamsted. Name used in 1778 for the establishment of the Ecclesiastical Society of Winsted.

Woodbury   Town
ZIP: 06798   **Lat:** 41-33-43 N **Long:** 73-12-36 W
Pop: 8,131 (1990); 6,942 (1980)   **Pop Density:** 222.8
Land: 36.5 sq. mi.; **Water:** 0.3 sq. mi.

In western CT. Established 1674.

Name origin: Named for its wooded location. The Indian name for the region of which Woodbury is a part was Pomperaug.

Middlesex County
Former County Seat: Middletown (ZIP: 06457)

Pop: 143,196 (1990); 129,017 (1980)   **Pop Density:** 387.8
Land: 369.3 sq. mi.; **Water:** 69.8 sq. mi.   **Area Code:** 203

In south-central CT, east of New Haven, with Long Island Sound to the south and the Connecticut River to the east; organized May 2, 1785 (prior to statehood) from Hartford, New London, and New Haven counties.

Name origin: For a former county in southeast England.

Chester   Town
ZIP: 06412   **Lat:** 41-24-07 N **Long:** 72-28-59 W
Pop: 3,417 (1990); 3,068 (1980)   **Pop Density:** 213.6
Land: 16.0 sq. mi.; **Water:** 0.8 sq. mi.

In southern CT. Originally part of the colony of Saybrook, which split into several towns. Land known as Pataconk in Indian deeds of the 1660s. Incorporated 1836.

Name origin: Named around 1740 by Abraham Waterhouse for his ancestors' hometown of Chester, England.

Clinton   Town
ZIP: 06413   **Lat:** 41-17-40 N **Long:** 72-31-40 W
Pop: 12,767 (1990); 11,195 (1980)   **Pop Density:** 783.3
Land: 16.3 sq. mi.; **Water:** 2.8 sq. mi.

In southern CT on Long Island Sound and Hammonasset River, 23 mi. east of New Haven. Settled 1663; incorporated 1838.

Name origin: For either Gov. DeWitt Clinton (1769–1828) of New York or Clinton Abbey in England.

Cromwell   Town
ZIP: 06416   **Lat:** 41-36-35 N **Long:** 72-39-49 W
Pop: 12,286 (1990); 10,265 (1980)   **Pop Density:** 990.8
Land: 12.4 sq. mi.; **Water:** 0.5 sq. mi.

In central CT on Connecticut River, 10 mi. south of Hartford. Settled 1650; incorporated 1851.

Name origin: For Oliver Cromwell (1599–1658), Lord Protector of England, or for the *Oliver Cromwell,* a steamboat constructed here in 1823.

Deep River   Town
ZIP: 06417   **Lat:** 41-22-03 N **Long:** 72-27-51 W
Pop: 4,332 (1990); 3,994 (1980)   **Pop Density:** 318.5
Land: 13.6 sq. mi.; **Water:** 0.6 sq. mi.

In southern CT on the Connecticut River. Originally part of the colony of Saybrook, which eventually split into several towns.

Name origin: Named for the river that flows through the town. Formerly called Saybrook; to avoid confusion with the nearby town of Old Saybrook, renamed Deep River in 1947.

Durham   Town
ZIP: 06422   **Lat:** 41-27-37 N **Long:** 72-40-56 W
Pop: 5,732 (1990); 5,143 (1980)   **Pop Density:** 242.9
Land: 23.6 sq. mi.; **Water:** 0.2 sq. mi.

In southern CT, 5 mi. south of Middletown.

Name origin: Named in 1704 for Durham, England, ancestral home of Col. James Wadsworth, a prominent settler. The Indians called this place Coginchaug or Cockingchaug, meaning 'long swamp.'

East Haddam   Town
ZIP: 06423   **Lat:** 41-28-30 N **Long:** 72-23-31 W
Pop: 6,676 (1990); 5,621 (1980)   **Pop Density:** 122.9
Land: 54.3 sq. mi.; **Water:** 2.2 sq. mi.

In southern CT on the Connecticut River. Settled 1685; incorporated 1734.

Name origin: For its proximity to Haddam, on the eastern side of the Connecticut and Salmon rivers. Incorporated in 1734.

East Hampton   Town
ZIP: 06424   **Lat:** 41-34-04 N **Long:** 72-30-22 W
Pop: 10,428 (1990); 8,572 (1980)   **Pop Density:** 292.9
Land: 35.6 sq. mi.; **Water:** 1.2 sq. mi.

In southern CT. Settled 1710.

Name origin: Named East Hampton in 1746, but incorporated in 1767 as Chatham, honoring Earl of Chatham in England for his support of the colony. In 1915 the Connecticut legislature approved the restoration of the older name, presumed to be an adaptation of Eastham, MA, the town from which many settlers came.

Essex
Town

ZIP: 06426   **Lat:** 41-21-06 N   **Long:** 72-25-00 W
Pop: 5,904 (1990); 5,078 (1980)   **Pop Density:** 567.7
Land: 10.4 sq. mi.; **Water:** 1.5 sq. mi.

In southern CT on the Connecticut River. Originally part of the colony of Saybrook, which eventually split into several towns. Became borough 1820; incorporated 1852.

Name origin: For Essex, England, former home of some early settlers. Originally called Potopaug by local Indians.

Fenwick
Borough

ZIP: 06475   **Lat:** 41-16-16 N   **Long:** 72-21-19 W
Pop: 89 (1990); 41 (1980)   **Pop Density:** 222.5
Land: 0.4 sq. mi.; **Water:** 0.0 sq. mi.

In southern CT on Long Island Sound. A borough of Old Saybrook.

Haddam
Town

ZIP: 06438   **Lat:** 41-27-57 N   **Long:** 72-32-41 W
Pop: 6,769 (1990); 6,383 (1980)   **Pop Density:** 153.8
Land: 44.0 sq. mi.; **Water:** 2.3 sq. mi.

In southern CT on Connecticut River.

Name origin: The estates owned by Connecticut's first governor John Haynes at Great Haddam suggested the name for the town. Officially named in Oct. 1668 for Little Haddam, Hertfordshire, England.

Higganum
CDP

ZIP: 06441   **Lat:** 41-29-28 N   **Long:** 72-33-28 W
Pop: 1,692 (1990); 1,660 (1980)   **Pop Density:** 319.2
Land: 5.3 sq. mi.; **Water:** 0.2 sq. mi.

Killingworth
Town

ZIP: 06419   **Lat:** 41-22-49 N   **Long:** 72-34-36 W
Pop: 4,814 (1990); 3,976 (1980)   **Pop Density:** 136.4
Land: 35.3 sq. mi.; **Water:** 0.5 sq. mi.

In southern CT. Setting for *The Birds of Killingworth* by Henry Wadsworth Longfellow (1807–82).

Name origin: Named Kenilworth in 1667 for the English birthplace of pioneer Edward Griswold. The pronunciation varied, and the name was finally set down by the town clerk in 1707 as Killingworth. Originally called Hammonasset, together with Clinton to the south.

Lake Pocotopaug
CDP

Lat: 41-35-33 N   **Long:** 72-30-40 W
Pop: 3,029 (1990); 2,137 (1980)   **Pop Density:** 1121.9
Land: 2.7 sq. mi.; **Water:** 0.8 sq. mi.

Middlefield
Town

ZIP: 06455   **Lat:** 41-31-02 N   **Long:** 72-42-45 W
Pop: 3,925 (1990); 3,796 (1980)   **Pop Density:** 309.1
Land: 12.7 sq. mi.; **Water:** 0.6 sq. mi.

In central CT. Settled about 1700; chartered 1871.

Name origin: Named and organized in 1744 as Middlefield Parish of Middletown. It no doubt took its name from the parent town.

Middletown
City

ZIP: 06457   **Lat:** 41-32-54 N   **Long:** 72-39-15 W
Pop: 42,762 (1990); 39,040 (1980)   **Pop Density:** 1045.5
Land: 40.9 sq. mi.; **Water:** 1.4 sq. mi.

In central CT on Connecticut River, 15 mi. south of Hartford. County seat; settled 1650; town incorporated 1651, city in 1784. Site of Wesleyan University (1831).

Name origin: For its location halfway between Saybrook and Windsor. Known as Mattabesett by the Wangunk Indians.

Moodus
CDP

ZIP: 06469   **Lat:** 41-30-14 N   **Long:** 72-27-00 W
Pop: 1,170 (1990); 1,179 (1980)   **Pop Density:** 403.4
Land: 2.9 sq. mi.; **Water:** 0.0 sq. mi.

Old Saybrook
Town

ZIP: 06475   **Lat:** 41-17-37 N   **Long:** 72-22-58 W
Pop: 9,552 (1990); 9,287 (1980)   **Pop Density:** 636.8
Land: 15.0 sq. mi.; **Water:** 6.6 sq. mi.

In southern CT on Long Island Sound, at the mouth of the Connecticut River. Founded as Saybrook colony in 1635; incorporated 1854. Original site of Yale University (1701) before its removal to New Haven (1716). Includes borough of Fenwick.

Name origin: Said to be for Lord Say and Sele and Lord Brooke, English sponsors of the colony, although the earlier Dutch name for the site, Zeebrugge, should be noted. "Old" in the name denotes the fact that the town was the site of the earliest habitation in Saybrook colony.

Portland
Town

ZIP: 06480   **Lat:** 41-35-56 N   **Long:** 72-35-28 W
Pop: 8,418 (1990); 8,383 (1980)   **Pop Density:** 359.7
Land: 23.4 sq. mi.; **Water:** 1.5 sq. mi.

In southern CT, across the Connecticut River from Middletown. Noted site of brownstone quarries. Settled 1690; incorporated 1841.

Name origin: For Portland, Dorsetshire, England, also noted for its stone quarries. Previously known by the names Wangunk (for the Indian tribe who lived in the area, whose name means 'big bend' in the river), East Middletown, and Chatham.

Westbrook
Town

ZIP: 06498   **Lat:** 41-17-45 N   **Long:** 72-27-52 W
Pop: 5,414 (1990); 5,216 (1980)   **Pop Density:** 344.8
Land: 15.7 sq. mi.; **Water:** 5.7 sq. mi.

In southern CT on Long Island Sound, 5 mi. west of the mouth of Connecticut River. Settled 1648; incorporated (as Third or West Parish) 1724, as Westbrook in 1840. Originally part of Saybrook colony.

Name origin: Renamed Westbrook in 1810, shortened from its earlier name, the Saybrook West Ecclesiastical Society. Indian name Pochoug.

> ## New Haven County
> ### Former County Seat: New Haven (ZIP: 06501)
>
> **Pop:** 804,219 (1990); 761,325 (1980)   **Pop Density:** 1327.6
> **Land:** 605.8 sq. mi.; **Water:** 256.3 sq. mi.   **Area Code:** 203
> In south-central CT on Long Island Sound, south of Hartford. Original county, organized May 10, 1666.
> **Name origin:** For the colonial settlement at New Haven.

Ansonia   City
ZIP: 06401   **Lat:** 41-20-36 N **Long:** 73-04-08 W
Pop: 18,403 (1990); 19,039 (1980)   **Pop Density:** 3067.2
Land: 6.0 sq. mi.; **Water:** 0.2 sq. mi.

In southern CT, on Naugatuck River, 10 mi. west-northwest of New Haven. Settled 1654 as Uptown Derby; incorporated 1889.

Name origin: For Anson G. Phelps, founding father and prominent businessman.

Beacon Falls   Town
ZIP: 06403   **Lat:** 41-26-19 N **Long:** 73-03-22 W
Pop: 5,083 (1990); 3,995 (1980)   **Pop Density:** 518.7
Land: 9.8 sq. mi.; **Water:** 0.1 sq. mi.

In southern CT, 10 mi. south of Waterbury. Incorporated June 30, 1871.

Name origin: Named in 1856 for the falls in Beacon Brook. The brook took its name from nearby Beacon Hill.

Bethany   Town
ZIP: 06524   **Lat:** 41-25-32 N **Long:** 72-59-35 W
Pop: 4,608 (1990); 4,330 (1980)   **Pop Density:** 219.4
Land: 21.0 sq. mi.; **Water:** 0.4 sq. mi.   **Elev:** 520 ft.

In southern CT. Established as a parish 1762. Incorporated 1832.

Name origin: For the biblical town near Jerusalem.

Branford   Town
ZIP: 06405   **Lat:** 41-16-39 N **Long:** 72-48-00 W
Pop: 27,603 (1990); 23,363 (1980)   **Pop Density:** 1254.7
Land: 22.0 sq. mi.; **Water:** 6.0 sq. mi.

In southern CT on Long Island Sound, 5 mi. east of New Haven. Settled 1644; incorporated 1930.

Name origin: For Brentford, England. Called Totokett by the Indians.

Cheshire   Town
ZIP: 06410   **Lat:** 41-30-44 N **Long:** 72-54-14 W
Pop: 25,684 (1990); 21,788 (1980)   **Pop Density:** 780.7
Land: 32.9 sq. mi.; **Water:** 0.5 sq. mi.

In southern CT, 10 mi. northeast of New Haven. Settled 1695; incorporated 1780. Site of Cheshire Academy (founded 1794).

Name origin: For Cheshire, England.

Derby   City
ZIP: 06418   **Lat:** 41-19-36 N **Long:** 73-04-58 W
Pop: 12,199 (1990); 12,346 (1980)   **Pop Density:** 2439.8
Land: 5.0 sq. mi.; **Water:** 0.4 sq. mi.

In southern CT at confluence of Housatonic and Naugatuck rivers, 10 mi. west of New Haven. Settled 1642; incorporated as a city 1893.

Name origin: For Derby, England, former home of early settlers. Indian names included Paugasset and Paugasuck.

East Haven   Town
ZIP: 06512   **Lat:** 41-17-44 N **Long:** 72-51-46 W
Pop: 26,144 (1990); 25,028 (1980)   **Pop Density:** 2125.5
Land: 12.3 sq. mi.; **Water:** 1.2 sq. mi.

In southern CT on Long Island Sound, across the Quinnipiac River from New Haven. Settled 1639; incorporated as a town 1785. Became separate from New Haven in 1707.

Name origin: Known as the East Village of New Haven until 1707.

Guilford   Town
ZIP: 06437   **Lat:** 41-19-41 N **Long:** 72-41-48 W
Pop: 19,848 (1990); 17,375 (1980)   **Pop Density:** 420.5
Land: 47.2 sq. mi.; **Water:** 2.6 sq. mi.

In southern CT on Long Island Sound, 18 mi. east of New Haven. Settled 1639. Site of Henry Whitfield House, oldest stone house in U.S.

Name origin: For Guilford, Surrey, England, hometown of early settlers. Called Memunkatucket by Indians.

Hamden   Town
ZIP: 06514   **Lat:** 41-23-51 N **Long:** 72-55-19 W
Pop: 52,434 (1990); 51,071 (1980)   **Pop Density:** 1598.6
Land: 32.8 sq. mi.; **Water:** 0.5 sq. mi.

In southern CT, directly north of New Haven. Incorporated 1786.

Name origin: Named in 1786 for John Hampden, an English statesman (1594–1643).

Heritage Village   CDP
          Lat: 41-29-08 N **Long:** 73-14-17 W
Pop: 3,623 (1990)   **Pop Density:** 1575.2
Land: 2.3 sq. mi.; **Water:** 0.0 sq. mi.

Madison   Town
ZIP: 06443   **Lat:** 41-20-15 N **Long:** 72-37-47 W
Pop: 15,485 (1990); 14,031 (1980)   **Pop Density:** 427.8
Land: 36.2 sq. mi.; **Water:** 0.6 sq. mi.   **Elev:** 22 ft.

In southern CT on Long Island Sound and Hammonasset River, 20 mi. east of New Haven. Settled 1650; incorporated 1826.

Name origin: Named in 1826 for Pres. James Madison (1751–1836). Originally part of Guilford, previously named East Guilford.

Meriden   City
ZIP: 06450   **Lat:** 41-32-11 N **Long:** 72-47-42 W
Pop: 59,479 (1990); 57,118 (1980)   **Pop Density:** 2509.7
Land: 23.7 sq. mi.; **Water:** 0.4 sq. mi.

In southern CT, 15 mi. northeast of New Haven. Settled 1661; town incorporated 1806; city in 1867. Town of Meriden consolidated with city of Meriden 1922.

Name origin: Possibly for Meriden, England. Called Merideen in an Indian deed of 1664. Various names, prior to present one, include Moridan and Merredan.

Middlebury
Town
ZIP: 06762 **Lat:** 41-31-39 N **Long:** 73-07-26 W
Pop: 6,145 (1990); 5,995 (1980) **Pop Density:** 345.2
Land: 17.8 sq. mi.; **Water:** 0.7 sq. mi.

In western CT, west of Waterbury. Settled 1702. Organized 1790 from an area called West Farms and portions of Woodbury and Southbury.

Name origin: For its location within the triangle formed by Waterbury, Woodbury, and Southbury.

Milford
City
ZIP: 06460 **Lat:** 41-13-34 N **Long:** 73-03-45 W
Pop: 49,938 (1990); 49,101 (1980) **Pop Density:** 2209.6
Land: 22.6 sq. mi.; **Water:** 2.2 sq. mi.

In southern CT on Long Island Sound and Housatonic River, 8 mi. southwest of New Haven. County seat; settled 1639; incorporated as city 1959. Includes Woodmont Borough.

Name origin: Possibly for Milford Haven, Pembroke, Wales, or for William Fowler's local mill (c. 1640), or for Milford, Surrey, England.

Naugatuck
Town, Borough
ZIP: 06770 **Lat:** 41-29-22 N **Long:** 73-03-07 W
Pop: 30,625 (1990); 26,456 (1980) **Pop Density:** 1867.4
Land: 16.4 sq. mi.; **Water:** 0.1 sq. mi.

In southern CT on Naugatuck River, 5 mi. south of Waterbury. Settled 1702; incorporated 1895. Town and borough are coextensive.

Name origin: Algonquian 'lone tree,' for a tree near the site of the settlement. Name used as first element in Naugahyde, a trademark for a synthetic upholstery material, in recognition of the town's importance in the rubber and plastics industries.

New Haven
City
ZIP: 06501 **Lat:** 41-18-36 N **Long:** 72-55-26 W
Pop: 130,474 (1990); 126,109 (1980) **Pop Density:** 6903.4
Land: 18.9 sq. mi.; **Water:** 1.4 sq. mi.

In southern CT on Long Island Sound and Quinnipiac River, 35 mi. southwest of Hartford. County seat; settled 1638; incorporated as a city 1784. Joint state capital (with Hartford) 1701–1873. Home of Eli Whitney (1765–1825) and Samuel F. B. Morse (1791–1872). Site of Yale University (moved from Old Saybrook 1716). The town consolidated with the city in 1895.

Name origin: Seen as a new place of refuge by first Puritan settlers who arrived from London via Boston. Previously called Quinnipiac.

North Branford
Town
ZIP: 06471 **Lat:** 41-21-25 N **Long:** 72-46-07 W
Pop: 12,996 (1990); 11,554 (1980) **Pop Density:** 521.9
Land: 24.9 sq. mi.; **Water:** 1.7 sq. mi.

In southern CT, 5 mi. northeast of New Haven. Settled in the 1690s; incorporated 1831. Was first an ecclesiastical society and part of Branford, became a separate town in 1831.

Name origin: From the parent town. Earlier known as North Farms and Northford. Indian name Totoket.

North Haven
Town
ZIP: 06473 **Lat:** 41-22-54 N **Long:** 72-51-32 W
Pop: 22,247 (1990); 22,080 (1980) **Pop Density:** 1069.6
Land: 20.8 sq. mi.; **Water:** 0.3 sq. mi.

In southern CT on Quinnipiac River, 5 mi. north of New Haven. Settled 1670; incorporated 1786.

Name origin: Was part of New Haven as the North East Ecclesiastical Society of New Haven until separated in 1786.

Orange
Town
ZIP: 06477 **Lat:** 41-16-46 N **Long:** 73-01-33 W
Pop: 12,830 (1990); 13,237 (1980) **Pop Density:** 745.9
Land: 17.2 sq. mi.; **Water:** 0.2 sq. mi.

In southern CT, 5 mi. west of New Haven. Settled 1700; incorporated May 28, 1822.

Name origin: For King William III of England (1650–1702), the Prince of Orange. Earlier known as Bryan's Farms.

Oxford
Town
ZIP: 06478 **Lat:** 41-25-48 N **Long:** 73-08-06 W
Pop: 8,685 (1990); 6,634 (1980) **Pop Density:** 264.0
Land: 32.9 sq. mi.; **Water:** 0.5 sq. mi.

In southern CT. Originally part of Derby; incorporated as separate town in 1798.

Name origin: Probably named by John Twitchell, who came from Oxford, Massachusetts. The Indians called this place Manchaug.

Prospect
Town
ZIP: 06712 **Lat:** 41-29-58 N **Long:** 72-58-33 W
Pop: 7,775 (1990); 6,807 (1980) **Pop Density:** 543.7
Land: 14.3 sq. mi.; **Water:** 0.2 sq. mi. **Elev:** 852 ft.

In southern CT, 5 mi. southeast of Waterbury. Settled 1712; incorporated May 1827.

Name origin: For the view afforded by the town's elevation.

Seymour
Town
ZIP: 06483 **Lat:** 41-23-02 N **Long:** 73-05-14 W
Pop: 14,288 (1990); 13,434 (1980) **Pop Density:** 978.6
Land: 14.6 sq. mi.; **Water:** 0.4 sq. mi.

In southern CT on Naugatuck River, 8 mi. northeast of New Haven. Incorporated 1850. Site of first successful woolen mill in U.S.

Name origin: Named in 1850 for then Governor Thomas H. Seymour. In 1650 an Indian village at the site was known as Nawcatock.

Southbury
Town
ZIP: 06488 **Lat:** 41-28-24 N **Long:** 73-14-04 W
Pop: 15,818 (1990); 14,156 (1980) **Pop Density:** 404.6
Land: 39.1 sq. mi.; **Water:** 0.9 sq. mi.

In western CT, 10 mi. southwest of Waterbury. Settled 1673; incorporated 1787.

Name origin: Named in 1731 for its being the southern part of Woodbury, the town from which it later divided. Previously known as South Purchase. Called Potatuck by the Indians.

Wallingford
Town
ZIP: 06492 **Lat:** 41-27-23 N **Long:** 72-48-16 W
Pop: 40,822 (1990); 37,274 (1980) **Pop Density:** 1046.7
Land: 39.0 sq. mi.; **Water:** 0.9 sq. mi.

In southern CT on Quinnipiac River, midway between New Haven and Meriden.

Name origin: Laid out and named in 1670 for Wallingford, Berkshire, England. Called New Haven Village by first settlers. Known to the Indians as Coginchaug.

Waterbury
City

ZIP: 06701   **Lat:** 41-33-30 N **Long:** 73-02-14 W
Pop: 108,961 (1990); 103,266 (1980)   **Pop Density:** 3809.8
Land: 28.6 sq. mi.; **Water:** 0.4 sq. mi.

In south-central CT on Naugatuck River, 20 mi. northwest of New Haven. County seat; settled 1674; incorporated 1686.

Name origin: Named in 1686 for the area's many rivers, ponds, and swamps. Called Mattatuck by the Indians.

West Haven
City

ZIP: 06516   **Lat:** 41-16-26 N **Long:** 72-58-05 W
Pop: 54,021 (1990); 53,184 (1980)   **Pop Density:** 5001.9
Land: 10.8 sq. mi.; **Water:** 0.2 sq. mi.

In southern CT on Long Island Sound and West River, directly west of New Haven. Settled 1648; incorporated as part of Orange 1822, as a separate town in 1921, and as a city in 1961.

Name origin: Known for many years as the West Farms of New Haven.

Wolcott
Town

ZIP: 06716   **Lat:** 41-36-04 N **Long:** 72-58-31 W
Pop: 13,700 (1990); 13,008 (1980)   **Pop Density:** 671.6
Land: 20.4 sq. mi.; **Water:** 0.7 sq. mi.

In south central CT, northeast of Waterbury. Incorporated May 12, 1796.

Name origin: For Gov. Oliver Wolcott, who cast the deciding vote in the General Assembly in the act to incorporate the town, which was to be called Farmingbury.

Woodbridge
Town

ZIP: 06525   **Lat:** 41-21-14 N **Long:** 73-00-43 W
Pop: 7,924 (1990); 7,761 (1980)   **Pop Density:** 421.5
Land: 18.8 sq. mi.; **Water:** 0.4 sq. mi.

In southern CT, northwest of New Haven.

Name origin: Founded in 1738 as the Parish of Amity. Named in 1784 for Rev. Benjamin Woodbridge, the town's first minister from 1742 to 1785.

Woodmont
Borough

ZIP: 06460   **Lat:** 41-13-27 N **Long:** 72-59-33 W
Pop: 1,770 (1990); 1,797 (1980)   **Pop Density:** 5900.0
Land: 0.3 sq. mi.; **Water:** 0.9 sq. mi.

A borough, part of city of Milford.

New London County
Former County Seat: New London (ZIP: 06320)

Pop: 254,957 (1990); 238,409 (1980)   **Pop Density:** 382.8
Land: 666.1 sq. mi.; **Water:** 105.6 sq. mi.   **Area Code:** 203

In southeastern CT on Long Island Sound and east of the Connecticut River. Original county, organized May 10, 1666.

Name origin: For the city in England.

Bozrah
Town

ZIP: 06334   **Lat:** 41-32-40 N **Long:** 72-10-33 W
Pop: 2,297 (1990); 2,135 (1980)   **Pop Density:** 114.8
Land: 20.0 sq. mi.; **Water:** 0.3 sq. mi.

In southeastern CT.

Name origin: Named in 1786 or earlier, from a name used of several towns in the Bible. Known as Norwich Farms in the early 1700s.

Colchester
Town

ZIP: 06415   **Lat:** 41-33-30 N **Long:** 72-21-09 W
Pop: 10,980 (1990); 7,761 (1980)   **Pop Density:** 223.6
Land: 49.1 sq. mi.; **Water:** 0.7 sq. mi.

In east central CT. Chartered in 1698. Includes borough of Colchester (not coextensive).

Name origin: For Colchester, England, from which ancestors of early settler Nathaniel Foote had come.

*Colchester
Borough

ZIP: 06415   **Lat:** 41-34-26 N **Long:** 72-19-55 W
Pop: 3,212 (1990); 3,190 (1980)   **Pop Density:** 1396.5
Land: 2.3 sq. mi.; **Water:** 0.0 sq. mi.

East Lyme
Town

ZIP: 06333   **Lat:** 41-21-10 N **Long:** 72-13-48 W
Pop: 15,340 (1990); 13,870 (1980)   **Pop Density:** 451.2
Land: 34.0 sq. mi.; **Water:** 7.9 sq. mi.

In southeastern CT, west of New London. Originally the eastern part of the town of Lyme, separately incorporated 1839.

Name origin: Once home of the Nehantic Indians, hence the name of the Niantic district in the town. See also Lyme.

Franklin
Town

ZIP: 06254   **Lat:** 41-37-11 N **Long:** 72-08-34 W
Pop: 1,810 (1990); 1,592 (1980)   **Pop Density:** 92.8
Land: 19.5 sq. mi.; **Water:** 0.1 sq. mi.

In eastern CT. Incorporated 1786.

Name origin: For Benjamin Franklin (1706–90). Before incorporation, known as West Farms.

Griswold
Town

ZIP: 06351   **Lat:** 41-35-04 N **Long:** 71-55-17 W
Pop: 10,384 (1990); 8,967 (1980)   **Pop Density:** 296.7
Land: 35.0 sq. mi.; **Water:** 2.1 sq. mi.

In southeastern CT on Quinebaug River, 20 mi. northeast of New London. Settled 1690; incorporated 1815. Includes borough of Jewett City.

Name origin: For Gov. Roger Griswold (1762–1812).

Groton
City

ZIP: 06340   **Lat:** 41-20-44 N **Long:** 72-01-49 W
Pop: 45,144 (1990); 41,062 (1980)   **Pop Density:** 1442.3
Land: 31.3 sq. mi.; **Water:** 13.9 sq. mi.

In southeastern corner of CT on Long Island Sound, across Thames River from New London. Site of the U.S. Navy's principal East Coast submarine base. Settled 1646; incorporated 1705. Includes city and town of Groton (not coextensive).

Name origin: Named in the 1660s probably by settler and future governor Fitz-John Winthrop, whose family owned the county seat of Groton in Suffolk, England. Known by the Indians as Poquonnock.

*Groton   Town
ZIP: 06340   **Lat:** 41-19-38 N **Long:** 72-04-18 W
Pop: 9,837 (1990); 10,086 (1980)   **Pop Density:** 3074.1
Land: 3.2 sq. mi.; **Water:** 3.5 sq. mi.

Jewett City   Borough
ZIP: 06351   **Lat:** 41-36-21 N **Long:** 71-58-54 W
Pop: 3,349 (1990); 3,294 (1980)   **Pop Density:** 4784.3
Land: 0.7 sq. mi.; **Water:** 0.0 sq. mi.

Name origin: For Eliezer Jewett, who opened a sawmill on the Pachaug River in 1771. Formerly called Pachaug City, later the area was known as Jewett's City.

Lebanon   Town
ZIP: 06249   **Lat:** 41-37-57 N **Long:** 72-14-25 W
Pop: 6,041 (1990); 4,762 (1980)   **Pop Density:** 111.7
Land: 54.1 sq. mi.; **Water:** 1.1 sq. mi.

In eastern CT.

Name origin: Named by a Mr. Fitch because the landscape resembled the "cedars of Lebanon." Early Indian names include Poquechannug, Pomakuk, and Poquedamseg.

Ledyard   Town
ZIP: 06339   **Lat:** 41-26-23 N **Long:** 72-00-56 W
Pop: 14,913 (1990); 13,735 (1980)   **Pop Density:** 391.4
Land: 38.1 sq. mi.; **Water:** 1.9 sq. mi.

In southeastern CT, 5 mi. northeast of New London. Settled 1653 as part of New London; incorporated 1836.

Name origin: For Col. William Ledyard, defender to the death of Fort Griswold at Ledyard during the Revolutionary War.

Lisbon   Town
ZIP: 06351   **Lat:** 41-36-14 N **Long:** 72-00-43 W
Pop: 3,790 (1990); 3,279 (1980)   **Pop Density:** 232.5
Land: 16.3 sq. mi.; **Water:** 0.4 sq. mi.

In eastern CT. Settled 1687; incorporated 1786. Once part of Norwich.

Name origin: From the fact that merchants Hezekiah and Jabez Perkins traded from Norwich with Lisbon, Portugal.

Lyme   Town
ZIP: 06371   **Lat:** 41-23-51 N **Long:** 72-20-49 W
Pop: 1,949 (1990); 1,822 (1980)   **Pop Density:** 61.1
Land: 31.9 sq. mi.; **Water:** 2.6 sq. mi.

In southeastern CT. Settled 1664. Broke from Saybrook colony in the "Loving Parting" of February 13, 1665, became separate community of East Saybrook. Gave its name to Lyme disease, a tick-borne viral condition that was first identified and described in the area.

Name origin: Renamed Lyme in 1667, for Lyme Regis, Dorsetshire, England.

Montville   Town
ZIP: 06353   **Lat:** 41-27-50 N **Long:** 72-09-21 W
Pop: 16,673 (1990); 16,455 (1980)   **Pop Density:** 397.0
Land: 42.0 sq. mi.; **Water:** 2.1 sq. mi.

In southeastern CT near Thames River, 10 mi. northwest of

New London. Settled 1670; incorporated 1786. Prior to white settlement, inhabited by Mohegan Indians.

Name origin: French 'hill town,' descriptive of the town's setting.

Mystic   CDP
ZIP: 06355   **Lat:** 41-21-26 N **Long:** 71-57-08 W
Pop: 2,618 (1990); 2,333 (1980)   **Pop Density:** 872.7
Land: 3.0 sq. mi.; **Water:** 0.4 sq. mi.

Postal district; west part is in Groton, east part is in Stonington, separated by Mystic River.

New London   City
ZIP: 06320   **Lat:** 41-19-46 N **Long:** 72-05-42 W
Pop: 28,540 (1990); 28,842 (1980)   **Pop Density:** 5189.1
Land: 5.5 sq. mi.; **Water:** 5.2 sq. mi.

In southeastern CT on Long Island Sound at mouth of Thames River, across from Groton, 45 mi. east of New Haven. County seat; founded 1646; incorporated as a city in 1784. Home of U.S. Coast Guard Academy, Connecticut College (1911).

Name origin: For London, England. Called Pequot by early settlers after 1637 defeat of Pequots. Indian names included Nameaug and Towawog.

Niantic   CDP
ZIP: 06357   **Lat:** 41-19-22 N **Long:** 72-11-39 W
Pop: 3,048 (1990); 3,151 (1980)   **Pop Density:** 2032.0
Land: 1.5 sq. mi.; **Water:** 2.1 sq. mi.

North Stonington   Town
ZIP: 06359   **Lat:** 41-28-10 N **Long:** 71-52-18 W
Pop: 4,884 (1990); 4,219 (1980)   **Pop Density:** 89.9
Land: 54.3 sq. mi.; **Water:** 0.7 sq. mi.

In southeastern corner of CT. Incorporated 1307.

Name origin: Called Mashentuxet by the Indians. Named North Stonington in 1724, as it was the north region of the society of Stonington. At one time known as Milltown.

Norwich   City; Town
ZIP: 06360   **Lat:** 41-33-00 N **Long:** 72-05-16 W
Pop: 37,391 (1990); 38,074 (1980)   **Pop Density:** 1321.2
Land: 28.3 sq. mi.; **Water:** 1.1 sq. mi.

In southeastern CT at confluence of Shetucket, Thames, and Yantic rivers, 10 mi. north of New London. Settled 1659; incorporated 1784. City and town are coextensive.

Name origin: For Norwich, England.

Old Lyme   Town
ZIP: 06371   **Lat:** 41-19-02 N **Long:** 72-18-12 W
Pop: 6,535 (1990); 6,159 (1980)   **Pop Density:** 282.9
Land: 23.1 sq. mi.; **Water:** 5.7 sq. mi.

In southeastern CT on Long Island Sound at the mouth of the Connecticut River. Settled in 1640s. Separated from Saybrook colony in 1665 as part of the community of Lyme.

Name origin: Formerly known as South Lyme, its name was changed to Old Lyme in 1857 (in imitation of Old Saybrook, across the river) when Lyme was divided into four towns. Lyme is probably for Lyme Regis, Dorsetshire, England.

Pawcatuck   CDP
ZIP: 06379   **Lat:** 41-22-32 N **Long:** 71-51-10 W
Pop: 5,289 (1990); 5,216 (1980)   **Pop Density:** 1429.5
Land: 3.7 sq. mi.; **Water:** 0.0 sq. mi.

Poquonock Bridge   CDP
                       Lat: 41-20-56 N **Long:** 72-01-41 W
Pop: 2,770 (1990); 2,549 (1980)   **Pop Density:** 1846.7
Land: 1.5 sq. mi.; **Water:** 0.1 sq. mi.

Preston
Town
ZIP: 06365   **Lat:** 41-31-11 N **Long:** 72-00-22 W
Pop: 5,006 (1990); 4,644 (1980)   **Pop Density:** 162.0
Land: 30.9 sq. mi.; **Water:** 0.9 sq. mi.

In southeastern CT, 5 mi. north of Norwich. Incorporated 1687.

Name origin: Named for Preston, England, home of Thomas Parke, an early settler.

Salem
Town
ZIP: 06420   **Lat:** 41-28-59 N **Long:** 72-16-01 W
Pop: 3,310 (1990); 2,335 (1980)   **Pop Density:** 114.1
Land: 29.0 sq. mi.; **Water:** 0.8 sq. mi.

In southeastern CT. Settled about 1700; incorporated 1819.

Name origin: Named in 1725 by landowner Samuel Brown for his former home of Salem, Massachusetts. Area called Paugwonk by Indians.

Sprague
Town
ZIP: 06330   **Lat:** 41-37-25 N **Long:** 72-04-32 W
Pop: 3,008 (1990); 2,996 (1980)   **Pop Density:** 227.9
Land: 13.2 sq. mi.; **Water:** 0.6 sq. mi.

In eastern CT, north of Norwich. Incorporated May 1861.

Name origin: For William Sprague of Rhode Island, who laid out the manufacturing center of town. Earlier known as the Hanover Society.

Stonington
Borough
ZIP: 06378   **Lat:** 41-20-01 N **Long:** 71-54-16 W
Pop: 1,100 (1990); 1,228 (1980)   **Pop Density:** 3666.7
Land: 0.3 sq. mi.; **Water:** 0.4 sq. mi.

In southeastern CT, 12 mi. east of New London. Settled 1649; incorporated 1801. Fishing village on Long Island Sound, part of the town of Stonington.

*Stonington
Town
ZIP: 06378   **Lat:** 41-21-54 N **Long:** 71-54-25 W
Pop: 16,919 (1990); 16,220 (1980)   **Pop Density:** 437.2
Land: 38.7 sq. mi.; **Water:** 11.3 sq. mi.

In southeastern CT, 8 mi. east of Groton. Settled 1649. Includes borough of Stonington (not coextensive).

Name origin: Named in 1666 for the many stones in the area. Previously called Mistick.

Uncasville-Oxoboxo Valley
CDP
Lat: 41-26-37 N **Long:** 72-07-28 W
Pop: 2,975 (1990); 1,240 (1980)   **Pop Density:** 691.9
Land: 4.3 sq. mi.; **Water:** 0.2 sq. mi.

Voluntown
Town
ZIP: 06384   **Lat:** 41-34-55 N **Long:** 71-49-55 W
Pop: 2,113 (1990); 1,637 (1980)   **Pop Density:** 54.2
Land: 39.0 sq. mi.; **Water:** 0.8 sq. mi.

In southeastern CT, on RI border. Incorporated May 21, 1721.

Name origin: So named because most of the town was settled by volunteers granted land after the Narragansett Indian War (1675–76).

Waterford
Town
ZIP: 06385   **Lat:** 41-20-59 N **Long:** 72-08-50 W
Pop: 17,930 (1990); 17,843 (1980)   **Pop Density:** 546.6
Land: 32.8 sq. mi.; **Water:** 11.6 sq. mi.

In southeastern CT on Long Island Sound, adjoining New London. Settled 1651; incorporated 1801.

Name origin: Suggested by Isaac Rogers, descriptive of the town's location on Long Island Sound.

Tolland County
Former County Seat: Rockville (ZIP: 06066)

Pop: 128,699 (1990); 114,823 (1980)   **Pop Density:** 313.8
Land: 410.1 sq. mi.; **Water:** 7.0 sq. mi.   **Area Code:** 203

In north-central CT, east of Hartford; organized Oct 17, 1785 (prior to statehood) from Windham County.

Name origin: For the town in western England, in Somerset County.

Andover
Town
ZIP: 06232   **Lat:** 41-43-58 N **Long:** 72-22-30 W
Pop: 2,540 (1990); 2,144 (1980)   **Pop Density:** 163.9
Land: 15.5 sq. mi.; **Water:** 0.2 sq. mi.

In central CT. First settled 1713; incorporated 1848.

Name origin: Named either for Andover, MA, or Andover, England.

Bolton
Town
ZIP: 06043   **Lat:** 41-45-50 N **Long:** 72-26-16 W
Pop: 4,575 (1990); 3,951 (1980)   **Pop Density:** 317.7
Land: 14.4 sq. mi.; **Water:** 0.3 sq. mi.

In northern CT. Incorporated 1720.

Name origin: Named in October 1720, possibly for Bolton, England, or for Charles Powlett (1661–1722), 2d Duke of Bolton, or another of the dukes in that line.

Columbia
Town
ZIP: 06237   **Lat:** 41-41-27 N **Long:** 72-18-28 W
Pop: 4,510 (1990); 3,386 (1980)   **Pop Density:** 210.7
Land: 21.4 sq. mi.; **Water:** 0.6 sq. mi.

In east central CT. Settled in early 1700s; incorporated 1804.

Name origin: From the poetic name for the United States.

Coventry
Town
ZIP: 06238   **Lat:** 41-47-03 N **Long:** 72-20-21 W
Pop: 10,063 (1990); 8,895 (1980)   **Pop Density:** 266.9
Land: 37.7 sq. mi.; **Water:** 0.6 sq. mi.

In east central CT. Settled 1709.

Name origin: Named in 1711 for Coventry, England.

Coventry Lake
CDP
Lat: 41-46-20 N **Long:** 72-19-58 W
Pop: 2,895 (1990)   **Pop Density:** 998.3
Land: 2.9 sq. mi.; **Water:** 0.6 sq. mi.

Crystal Lake
CDP
Lat: 41-56-00 N **Long:** 72-22-30 W
Pop: 1,175 (1990) **Pop Density:** 150.6
Land: 7.8 sq. mi.; **Water:** 0.3 sq. mi.

Ellington
Town
ZIP: 06029 **Lat:** 41-54-46 N **Long:** 72-27-00 W
Pop: 11,197 (1990); 9,711 (1980) **Pop Density:** 328.4
Land: 34.1 sq. mi.; **Water:** 0.6 sq. mi.
In northern CT, 12 mi. northeast of Hartford. Settled 1717; incorporated 1786.
Name origin: For either Ellington, England, or the town's L-shape (a long, narrow strip projects eastward). Known earlier as Great Swamp, Great Marsh, and Windsor Goshen. Indian name Weaxskashuck.

Hebron
Town
ZIP: 06248 **Lat:** 41-39-10 N **Long:** 72-23-21 W
Pop: 7,079 (1990); 5,453 (1980) **Pop Density:** 191.8
Land: 36.9 sq. mi.; **Water:** 0.4 sq. mi.
In northern CT, 15 mi. southeast of Hartford. Incorporated 1708.
Name origin: Named in 1707 for the biblical city.

Mansfield
Town
ZIP: 06250 **Lat:** 41-47-17 N **Long:** 72-13-46 W
Pop: 21,103 (1990); 20,634 (1980) **Pop Density:** 474.2
Land: 44.5 sq. mi.; **Water:** 1.0 sq. mi.
In northern CT on Willimantic River, 20 mi. east of Hartford. Incorporated May 1703.
Name origin: For either Maj. Moses Mansfield, a prominent landowner, or Lord Mansfield, one of the original patentees. Earlier known as Pond Place, a part of Windham. Known to the Indians as Naubesatuck.

Rockville
CDP
ZIP: 06066 **Lat:** 41-52-00 N **Long:** 07-22-70 W
Pop: See Vernon
Land: 18.8 sq. mi.; **Water:** 0.4 sq. mi.
In central CT, 13 mi. east of Hartford. Incorporated as city Jan 1889; consolidated with town of Vernon Jul 1, 1965; now post office of Vernon. County seat.

Somers
Town
ZIP: 06071 **Lat:** 41-59-44 N **Long:** 72-27-13 W
Pop: 9,108 (1990); 8,473 (1980) **Pop Density:** 321.8
Land: 28.3 sq. mi.; **Water:** 0.1 sq. mi. **Elev:** 272 ft.
In northern CT, east of Enfield. Settled 1706; incorporated 1734.
Name origin: For Lord John Somers of England (1651–1716).

Stafford
Town
ZIP: 06076 **Lat:** 41-59-38 N **Long:** 72-18-45 W
Pop: 11,091 (1990); 9,268 (1980) **Pop Density:** 191.2
Land: 58.0 sq. mi.; **Water:** 0.8 sq. mi. **Elev:** 591 ft.
In northern CT, on MA border. Includes borough of Stafford Springs.
Name origin: For Stafford, England.

Stafford Springs
Borough
ZIP: 06076 **Lat:** 41-57-14 N **Long:** 72-18-34 W
Pop: 4,100 (1990); 3,392 (1980) **Pop Density:** 1708.3
Land: 2.4 sq. mi.; **Water:** 0.0 sq. mi. **Elev:** 479 ft.
A borough of the town of Stafford.
Name origin: For its once-popular mineral springs; part of the town of Stafford.

Storrs
CDP
ZIP: 06268 **Lat:** 41-48-21 N **Long:** 72-15-24 W
Pop: 12,198 (1990); 11,394 (1980) **Pop Density:** 2033.0
Land: 6.0 sq. mi.; **Water:** 0.0 sq. mi.
Part of Mansfield. Site of the main campus of the University of Connecticut.

Tolland
Town
ZIP: 06084 **Lat:** 41-52-36 N **Long:** 72-22-06 W
Pop: 11,001 (1990); 9,694 (1980) **Pop Density:** 277.1
Land: 39.7 sq. mi.; **Water:** 0.6 sq. mi.
In northern CT, 20 mi. northeast of Hartford. Settled 1713; incorporated 1715.
Name origin: For Tolland, England.

Union
Town
ZIP: 06076 **Lat:** 41-59-17 N **Long:** 72-09-43 W
Pop: 612 (1990); 546 (1980) **Pop Density:** 21.3
Land: 28.7 sq. mi.; **Water:** 1.1 sq. mi.
In northwestern CT, on MA border.
Name origin: Opened for settlement in 1727 under the name Union Lands or Union Right.

Vernon
Town
ZIP: 06066 **Lat:** 41-50-12 N **Long:** 72-27-39 W
Pop: 29,841 (1990); 27,974 (1980) **Pop Density:** 1685.9
Land: 17.7 sq. mi.; **Water:** 0.3 sq. mi.
In northern CT, 10 mi. northeast of Hartford. Settled 1716; incorporated 1808. Includes former city of Rockville.
Name origin: Probably for Mount Vernon, Virginia home of George Washington (1732–99).

Willington
Town
ZIP: 06279 **Lat:** 41-53-07 N **Long:** 72-15-43 W
Pop: 5,979 (1990); 4,694 (1980) **Pop Density:** 179.5
Land: 33.3 sq. mi.; **Water:** 0.2 sq. mi.
In northern CT. Incorporated 1727.
Name origin: First English settlers in 1720 named it Wellington for Wellington, England. Incorporated as Willington.

Windham County
Former County Seat: Putnam (ZIP: 06260)

Pop: 102,525 (1990); 92,312 (1980)   **Pop Density:** 199.9
Land: 512.8 sq. mi.; **Water:** 8.7 sq. mi.   **Area Code:** 203

In northeastern CT, bordered on the east by RI and on the north by MA; organized May 12, 1726 from Hartford and New London counties.
Name origin: For Wymondham, Norfolk, England; spelling reflects pronunciation.

Ashford   Town
ZIP: 06278   **Lat:** 41-53-10 N **Long:** 72-10-24 W
Pop: 3,765 (1990); 3,221 (1980)   **Pop Density:** 97.0
Land: 38.8 sq. mi.; **Water:** 0.7 sq. mi.

In northeastern corner of CT.
Name origin: Named in Oct. 1710 for either Ashford, Kent, England, or many ash trees in the area.

Brooklyn   Town
ZIP: 06234   **Lat:** 41-47-16 N **Long:** 71-57-22 W
Pop: 6,681 (1990); 5,691 (1980)   **Pop Density:** 230.4
Land: 29.0 sq. mi.; **Water:** 0.2 sq. mi.

In northeastern CT.
Name origin: Named the Society of Brooklyn, or Brookline, in 1752. Formerly called Mortlake.

Canterbury   Town
ZIP: 06331   **Lat:** 41-41-49 N **Long:** 72-00-12 W
Pop: 4,467 (1990); 3,426 (1980)   **Pop Density:** 112.0
Land: 39.9 sq. mi.; **Water:** 0.3 sq. mi.

In eastern CT. Incorporated 1703.
Name origin: For Canterbury, England.

Chaplin   Town
ZIP: 06235   **Lat:** 41-47-30 N **Long:** 72-07-37 W
Pop: 2,048 (1990); 1,793 (1980)   **Pop Density:** 105.6
Land: 19.4 sq. mi.; **Water:** 0.1 sq. mi.

In northeastern CT. Incorporated 1822.
Name origin: Named the Society of Chaplin in 1809 for Deacon Benjamin Chaplin, the town's first settler, whose will had provided for the local Congregational Church.

Danielson   Borough
ZIP: 06239   **Lat:** 41-48-34 N **Long:** 71-53-14 W
Pop: 4,441 (1990); 4,553 (1980)   **Pop Density:** 4037.3
Land: 1.1 sq. mi.; **Water:** 0.1 sq. mi.   **Elev:** 236 ft.

A borough of Killingly.

East Brooklyn   CDP
ZIP: 06239   **Lat:** 41-47-20 N **Long:** 71-53-49 W
Pop: 1,481 (1990); 1,251 (1980)   **Pop Density:** 1057.9
Land: 1.4 sq. mi.; **Water:** 0.0 sq. mi.

Eastford   Town
ZIP: 06242   **Lat:** 41-53-37 N **Long:** 72-05-50 W
Pop: 1,314 (1990); 1,028 (1980)   **Pop Density:** 45.5
Land: 28.9 sq. mi.; **Water:** 0.3 sq. mi.

In northeastern CT. Formed from Ashford 1777; incorporated 1847.
Name origin: For its status as Ashford's east parish.

Hampton   Town
ZIP: 06247   **Lat:** 41-47-12 N **Long:** 72-03-32 W
Pop: 1,578 (1990); 1,322 (1980)   **Pop Density:** 63.1
Land: 25.0 sq. mi.; **Water:** 0.5 sq. mi.

In northeastern CT. Incorporated 1786.
Name origin: For the parish of Hampton in Middlesex County, England. Previously called Canada, Kennedy, and Windham Village.

Killingly   Town
ZIP: 06239   **Lat:** 41-49-53 N **Long:** 71-51-02 W
Pop: 15,889 (1990); 14,519 (1980)   **Pop Density:** 327.6
Land: 48.5 sq. mi.; **Water:** 1.5 sq. mi.

On RI border in northeastern CT on Quinebaug River. Settled 1700; incorporated May 1708. Includes borough of Danielson.
Name origin: Named by Connecticut Gov. Gurdon Saltonstall in 1708 for Killanslie, England, site of Gov. Saltonstall's ancestral manor. Formerly spelled Kellingly. Earlier called Aspinock.

Moosup   CDP
ZIP: 06354   **Lat:** 41-43-03 N **Long:** 71-52-26 W
Pop: 3,289 (1990); 3,308 (1980)   **Pop Density:** 1430.0
Land: 2.3 sq. mi.; **Water:** 0.0 sq. mi.

North Grosvenor Dale   CDP
               Lat: 41-59-01 N **Long:** 71-54-13 W
Pop: 1,705 (1990); 1,856 (1980)   **Pop Density:** 741.3
Land: 2.3 sq. mi.; **Water:** 0.0 sq. mi.

Plainfield   Town
ZIP: 06374   **Lat:** 41-42-02 N **Long:** 71-53-43 W
Pop: 14,363 (1990); 12,774 (1980)   **Pop Density:** 339.6
Land: 42.3 sq. mi.; **Water:** 0.8 sq. mi.   **Elev:** 203 ft.

In northeastern CT on Quinebaug River, 25 mi. northeast of New London. Settled 1689; incorporated 1699.
Name origin: Named in 1699 by the governor for its level topography along the Quinebaug.

Pomfret   Town
ZIP: 06258   **Lat:** 41-51-48 N **Long:** 71-59-03 W
Pop: 3,102 (1990); 2,775 (1980)   **Pop Density:** 77.0
Land: 40.3 sq. mi.; **Water:** 0.3 sq. mi.

In northeastern CT. Incorporated 1713.
Name origin: For Pontefract, Yorkshire, England, respelling reflecting pronunciation. Land acquired in 1686 in the Mashamoquet Purchase of 15,100 acres from James Fitch, who had acquired it from Owaneco, an Indian sachem.

Putnam   Town
ZIP: 06260   **Lat:** 41-54-22 N **Long:** 71-52-15 W
Pop: 9,031 (1990); 8,580 (1980)   **Pop Density:** 444.9
Land: 20.3 sq. mi.; **Water:** 0.1 sq. mi.

In northeastern CT on RI border. County seat; incorporated

1855. Includes the former city of Putnam, consolidated with the town in 1983.

Name origin: For Gen. Israel Putnam (1718–90), Revolutionary War figure. Area originally known as Aspinock.

Quinebaug
CDP
ZIP: 06262   **Lat:** 42-00-32 N **Long:** 71-56-13 W
Pop: 1,031 (1990); 1,088 (1980)   **Pop Density:** 234.3
Land: 4.4 sq. mi.; **Water:** 0.2 sq. mi.

Scotland
Town
ZIP: 06264   **Lat:** 41-42-00 N **Long:** 72-05-00 W
Pop: 1,215 (1990); 1,072 (1980)   **Pop Density:** 65.3
Land: 18.6 sq. mi.; **Water:** 0.0 sq. mi.

In eastern CT. Incorporated 1857.

Name origin: Settled by Scotsman Isaac Magoon around 1700 and named for his native country.

Sterling
Town
ZIP: 06377   **Lat:** 41-42-08 N **Long:** 71-49-01 W
Pop: 2,357 (1990); 1,791 (1980)   **Pop Density:** 86.7
Land: 27.2 sq. mi.; **Water:** 0.1 sq. mi.

In eastern CT on RI border. Incorporated May 8, 1794.

Name origin: For Dr. John Sterling, a resident of the town, who promised to donate a public library but failed to make good on his promise.

Thompson
Town
ZIP: 06277   **Lat:** 41-59-04 N **Long:** 71-52-41 W
Pop: 8,668 (1990); 8,141 (1980)   **Pop Density:** 184.8
Land: 46.9 sq. mi.; **Water:** 1.7 sq. mi.

In northeastern corner of CT. Settled 1693; incorporated 1785.

Name origin: Named in 1728 for its chief land owner, Sir Robert Thompson, of Middlesex, England. Area called Quinnatisset by the Nipmac Indians.

Wauregan
CDP
    Lat: 41-45-09 N **Long:** 71-54-41 W
Pop: 1,079 (1990)   **Pop Density:** 1198.9
Land: 0.9 sq. mi.; **Water:** 0.0 sq. mi.

Willimantic
CDP
ZIP: 06226   **Lat:** 41-42-56 N **Long:** 72-13-04 W
Pop: 14,746 (1990); 14,652 (1980)   **Pop Density:** 3351.4
Land: 4.4 sq. mi.; **Water:** 0.1 sq. mi.

In northeastern CT on Natachaug and Willimantic rivers, 25 mi. east of Hartford. Formerly a city (incorporated 1893), but no longer incorporated; consolidated with the town of Windham as a service district.

Name origin: From an Indian word meaning 'good lookout' or 'good cedar swamps.'

Windham
Town
ZIP: 06280   **Lat:** 41-42-39 N **Long:** 72-10-02 W
Pop: 22,039 (1990); 21,062 (1980)   **Pop Density:** 813.2
Land: 27.1 sq. mi.; **Water:** 0.9 sq. mi.

In northeastern CT, 20 mi. east of Hartford. Includes Willimantic, formerly a city, now a service district. Settled 1675; incorporated May 12, 1692. Consolidation with Willimantic July 1, 1983.

Name origin: For Wymondham, Norfolkshire, England, home of early settlers (spelling reflects pronunciation).

Woodstock
Town
ZIP: 06281   **Lat:** 41-57-55 N **Long** 72-01-21 W
Pop: 6,008 (1990); 5,117 (1980)   **Pop Density:** 99.3
Land: 60.5 sq. mi.; **Water:** 1.3 sq. mi.

In northeastern CT, on MA border.

Name origin: For Woodstock, England; named by Judge Samuel Sewall in 1690.

Index to Places and Counties in Connecticut

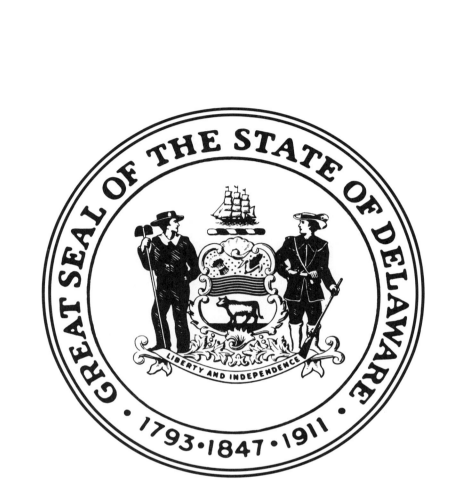

GREAT SEAL OF THE STATE OF DELAWARE

LIBERTY AND INDEPENDENCE

1793·1847·1911

Delaware

DELAWARE

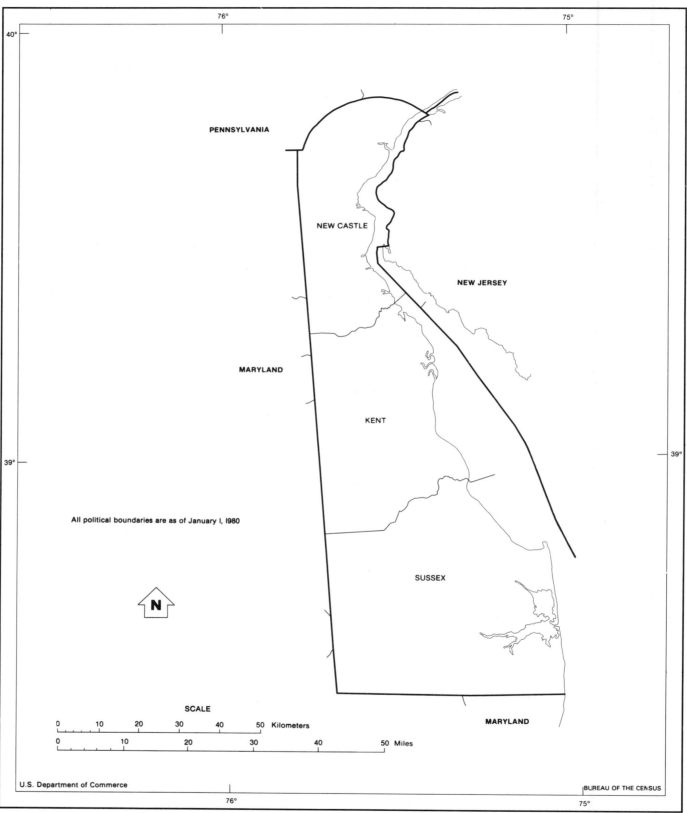

PENNSYLVANIA

NEW CASTLE

NEW JERSEY

MARYLAND

KENT

All political boundaries are as of January I, 1980

N

SUSSEX

MARYLAND

SCALE

0   10   20   30   40   50   Kilometers

0   10   20   30   40   50   Miles

U.S. Department of Commerce

BUREAU OF THE CENSUS

40°   76°   75°   40°

39°   39°

76°   75°

Delaware

Population: 666,168 (1990); 594,338 (1980)
Population rank: 46
Percent population change (1980-1990): 12.1
Population projection: 723,000 (1995);
  760,000 (2000)

Area: total 2,489 sq. mi.; 1,955 sq. mi. land, 535 sq.
  mi. water. Coastline 28 mi.
Area rank: 49
Highest elevation: 442 ft. on Ebright Rd. on northern
  border of New Castle County
Lowest point: sea level along the Atlantic coast

State capital: Dover (Kent County)
Largest city: Wilmington (71,529)
Second largest city: Dover (27,630)
Largest county: New Castle (441,946)

Total housing units: 289,919
No. of occupied housing units: 247,497
Vacant housing units (%): 14.6
Distribution of population by race and
  Hispanic origin (%):
  White: 80.3
  Black: 16.9
  Hispanic (any race): 2.4
  Native American: 0.3
  Asian/Pacific: 1.4
  Other: 1.1

Admission date: December 7, 1787 (1st state)

Location: On the central Atlantic coast of the United
States, bordering Maryland, Pennsylvania, New
Jersey, and Delaware Bay. One of the thirteen original
English colonies.

Name Origin: For Delaware Bay, named by Capt.
Samuel Argall, who discovered it in 1610, for Thomas
West, Lord De La Warr (1577-1618), first British governor of the colony of Virginia. The river, Indian tribe
(also called Lenni Lenape), colony, and state are
named for the bay.

State bird: Blue Hen chicken
State fish: weakfish (*Cynoscion regalis*)
State flower: peach blossom (*Prunus persica*)
State insect: ladybug (*Hippodamia convergens*)
State rock: sillimanite
State song: "Our Delaware"
State tree: American holly (*Ilex opaca*)
State motto: Liberty and Independence
State nickname: The First State; The Diamond State; The
  Blue Hen State

Area code: 302
Time zone: Eastern
Abbreviations: DE (postal), Del. (traditional)
Part of (region): Middle Atlantic

Local Government

Counties:

Delaware has 3 counties, which are divided into areas
called *hundreds*, the old name (of obscure origin) for the
administrative division of an English county. The hundreds have no government but still serve as a basis for
property and zoning.

Municipalities:

Other forms of local government include 10 cities (4 of
which are incorporated), 44 towns, and 3 villages. Delaware is the only state in the U.S. in which the legislature
can change the state constitution without the approval of
the voters.

Settlement History and Early Development

For 10,000 years before the first Europeans arrived, two
tribes of Algonquian Indians inhabited the area. The Delaware (or Lenni Lenape) lived along the banks of the
Delaware River in the north, and the Nanticoke lived
along the Nanticoke River in the southwest. Spanish and
Portuguese ships may have explored the region in the
sixteenth century. Englishman Henry Hudson sailed into
Delaware Bay in 1609 on his exploration for the Dutch to
find a trade route to the Far East; he left and sailed
northward. Capt. Samuel Argall of the Virginia colony
entered the bay in 1610 while escaping a storm; he named
it for Lord De La Warr, the governor of Virginia. In 1631
the Dutch established the colony of Zwaanendael ('valley
of swans') at present-day Lewes, but troubles with the
Indians led to the massacre of the settlers and its destruc-
tion.

In 1638 the Swedes established the first permanent settlement in present-day Wilmington. The first expedition,
two ships under the leadership of Peter Minuit, landed
about March 29, 1638. They settled at "The Rocks" on
the Christina River, and built Fort Christina; the fort and
river were both named for the Queen of Sweden. In 1651
they seized the Dutch Fort Casmir at what is now New
Castle. The Colony of New Sweden lasted until the autumn of 1655 when Peter Stuyvesant, sailing south from
New Amsterdam (present-day New York), captured the
Swedish forts with his Dutch fleet, and established the
Colony of New Netherlands. Fort Casmir became the
principal settlement of the Zuidt ('South') River (as opposed to the Hudson or North River). When the number
of settlers necessitated a new town, New Amstel (now
New Castle) was founded.

From 1681 until 1701 present-day Delaware was a territory of the Province of Pennsylvania, and referred to as the Three Lower Counties, for their location down the Delaware River from Philadelphia (see Pennsylvania). In 1701 the counties were allowed to separate and set up their own legislature, which first met in 1704. However, they technically remained under the proprietary government of William Penn until a constitutional convention at New Castle in August 1776 established "Delaware State."

The American Revolution and Statehood

On July 2, 1776, Delaware joined with other American colonies at the Second Continental Congress in Philadelphia and voted for independence from Britain. In August Delaware officially became a state, and sent troops to fight in the Revolutionary War. The men of Capt. Jonathan Caldwell's company from Kent County took along Blue Hen gamecocks, which were noted for their fighting. When not in battle, the men held cockfights the notoriety of which spread throughout the Continental Army. Caldwell's men fought so valorously that they were given the nickname "Blue Hen's Chickens." On December 7, 1787, Delaware became the first state to ratify the U.S. Constitution, hence one of its nicknames.

The Civil War

During the Civil War Delaware fought on the side of the Union, despite being a slave state. Because of her location between the North and South, she had strong ties with both the Union and the Confederacy, and many of her citizens sympathized with the latter. Abraham Lincoln's Emancipation Proclamation (1863) did not affect slave states that had remained loyal to the Union, so as a result Delaware's slaves were not freed until 1865, when the Thirteenth Amendment to the U.S. Constitution abolished all slavery in the U.S.

Business and Industry

During and after the Revolutionary War, Delaware was the center of the flour-milling industry. In 1802 Eleuthere Irenee du Pont established a gunpowder mill on the Brandywine Creek, near Wilmington, and began what developed into the Du Pont Corporation, Delaware's giant chemical concern. In 1838 a railroad was completed that ran through Wilmington, connecting Philadelphia and Baltimore. It played a major role in the industrial development of the northern part of the state, and, because farmers could now get their crops to larger markets more rapidly, increased the value of the southern farmlands.

During the early 1900s Delaware improved its education, public welfare, and roads, but the Depression of the 1930s affected many in the state. However after World War II, during which Delaware's factories and mills produced military supplies, and up into the 1960s, the economy grew rapidly. The Delaware Memorial Bridge, which opened in 1951, connected the state with New Jersey and brought many giant corporations into Delaware. Delaware's business laws make it easier and less expensive to incorporate there than in many other states; as a result, many large U.S. firms are among the 173,000 companies incorporated in Delaware, including thousands that do most of their business outside the state. During the 1980s Delaware's economy improved, despite a recession in the early years of the decade that halted growth elsewhere.

State Boundaries

Delaware's present boundaries are substantially the same as those of September 10, 1776, when she became a state. Most of its border with Pennsylvania is the arc of a circle whose center is at New Castle, the only instance of such a border shape in the U.S. The state forms the northeastern corner of the Delmarva Peninsula (between Chesapeake Bay, Delaware Bay, and the Atlantic), which it shares with Maryland and Virginia. (*See also* Pennsylvania and New Jersey.)

Delaware Counties

Kent   New Castle   Sussex

Multi-County Places

The following Delaware places are in more than one county. Given here is the total population for each multi-county place, and the names of the counties it is in.

Milford, pop. 6,040; Sussex (3,564), Kent (2,476)
Smyrna, pop. 5,231; Kent (5,231), New Castle (0)

> ## Kent County
> ### County Seat: Dover (ZIP: 19901)
>
> **Pop:** 110,993 (1990); 98,219 (1980)　　　　　**Pop Density:** 187.9
> **Land:** 590.7 sq. mi.; **Water:** 209.5 sq. mi.　　　**Area Code:** 302
>
> In central DE; organized as St. Jones County in 1680 from Horre Kill District, which was organized in 1664; name changed in 1682.
> **Name origin:** For the county in England.

Bowers
Town
Lat: 39-03-37 N **Long:** 75-24-00 W
Pop: 179 (1990); 198 (1980)　　　**Pop Density:** 596.7
Land: 0.3 sq. mi.; **Water:** 0.0 sq. mi.

In east-central DE where the St. Jones and Murderkill rivers empty into Delaware Bay.
Name origin: Also known as Bowers Beach. Originally known as Reeds Landing.

Camden
Town
ZIP: 19934　　　　**Lat:** 39-06-45 N **Long:** 75-32-58 W
Pop: 1,899 (1990); 1,757 (1980)　　**Pop Density:** 1186.9
Land: 1.6 sq. mi.; **Water:** 0.0 sq. mi.　　**Elev:** 40 ft.

In central DE.
Name origin: Named in the early 19th century. Known in the 18th century as Mifflin's Cross Roads and Piccadilly.

Cheswold
Town
ZIP: 19936　　　　**Lat:** 39-12-59 N **Long:** 75-35-04 W
Pop: 321 (1990); 269 (1980)　　　**Pop Density:** 802.5
Land: 0.4 sq. mi.; **Water:** 0.0 sq. mi.　　**Elev:** 44 ft.

In central DE.
Name origin: Originally Leipsic Station, name changed to Moorton in 1861 for postmaster James S. Moore. Renamed in 1888 to avoid confusion with the post office in Morton, PA.

Clayton
Town
ZIP: 19938　　　　**Lat:** 39-17-33 N **Long:** 75-37-59 W
Pop: 1,163 (1990); 1,216 (1980)　　**Pop Density:** 2326.0
Land: 0.5 sq. mi.; **Water:** 0.0 sq. mi.

In central DE.
Name origin: Named in 1877 for Sen. John M. Clayton (1796–1856), a promoter of the Delaware Railroad. Originally known as Smyrna Station and Jimtown.

Dover
City
ZIP: 19901　　　　**Lat:** 39-09-31 N **Long:** 75-31-02 W
Pop: 27,630 (1990); 23,512 (1980)　　**Pop Density:** 1297.2
Land: 21.3 sq. mi.; **Water:** 0.3 sq. mi.　　**Elev:** 36 ft.

In central DE on St. Jones River, south of Wilmington. County seat; founded 1717; state capital since 1777; incorporated as a town in 1829, as a city in 1929. Site of Dover Air Force Base. Diverse manufacturing (canning, food processing, latex products) and farming city (poultry, soybeans, corn, potatoes).
Name origin: Named in 1683 by William Penn (1644–1718) for the English Channel port of Dover, Kent, England.

Farmington
Town
ZIP: 19942　　　　**Lat:** 38-52-14 N **Long:** 75-34-46 W
Pop: 122 (1990); 141 (1980)　　　**Pop Density:** 1220.0
Land: 0.1 sq. mi.; **Water:** 0.0 sq. mi.　　**Elev:** 63 ft.

In south-central DE.
Name origin: Previously called Flatiron.

Felton
Town
ZIP: 19943　　　　**Lat:** 39-00-32 N **Long:** 75-34-40 W
Pop: 683 (1990); 547 (1980)　　　**Pop Density:** 1707.5
Land: 0.4 sq. mi.; **Water:** 0.0 sq. mi.

In central DE.
Name origin: Originally known as Felton Station.

Frederica
Town
ZIP: 19946　　　　**Lat:** 39-00-31 N **Long:** 75-27-53 W
Pop: 761 (1990); 864 (1980)　　　**Pop Density:** 951.3
Land: 0.8 sq. mi.; **Water:** 0.0 sq. mi.

In east-central DE on the Murderkill River, 10 mi. south of Dover.
Name origin: Originally known as Indian Point, Johnnycake Landing, and Frederica Landing.

Harrington
City
ZIP: 19952　　　　**Lat:** 38-55-21 N **Long:** 75-34-20 W
Pop: 2,311 (1990); 2,405 (1980)　　**Pop Density:** 1650.7
Land: 1.4 sq. mi.; **Water:** 0.0 sq. mi.

In central DE.
Name origin: Named in 1859 for State Chancellor Samuel M. Harrington. Previously called Clark's Corner.

Hartly
Town
ZIP: 19953　　　　**Lat:** 39-10-06 N **Long:** 75-42-47 W
Pop: 107 (1990); 106 (1980)　　　**Pop Density:** 1070.0
Land: 0.1 sq. mi.; **Water:** 0.0 sq. mi.　　**Elev:** 71 ft.

In west-central DE.
Name origin: Previously called Arthurville, Arthursville, Butterpot, Butterpat, Davisville.

Highland Acres
CDP
Lat: 39-07-02 N **Long:** 75-31-23 W
Pop: 3,151 (1990); 2,994 (1980)　　**Pop Density:** 1969.4
Land: 1.6 sq. mi.; **Water:** 0.0 sq. mi.

Houston
Town
ZIP: 19954　　　　**Lat:** 38-55-00 N **Long:** 75-30-16 W
Pop: 487 (1990); 357 (1980)　　　**Pop Density:** 1217.5
Land: 0.4 sq. mi.; **Water:** 0.0 sq. mi.

In south-central DE.
Name origin: Named in 1854 for Judge John W. Houston. Previously called Houston Station and Killens Crossroad.

Kent Acres
CDP
Lat: 39-07-59 N **Long:** 75-31-07 W
Pop: 1,807 (1990); 1,590 (1980)　　**Pop Density:** 1807.0
Land: 1.0 sq. mi.; **Water:** 0.0 sq. mi.

Kenton
Town
Lat: 39-13-37 N **Long:** 75-39-57 W
Pop: 232 (1990); 243 (1980)　　　**Pop Density:** 1160.0
Land: 0.2 sq. mi.; **Water:** 0.0 sq. mi.

In central DE.
Name origin: Named by the legislature in 1806. Originally

known in the 18th century first as Lewis Cross Roads and later as Grogtown.

Leipsic
Town
Lat: 39-14-35 N **Long:** 75-31-01 W
Pop: 236 (1990); 228 (1980)   **Pop Density:** 786.7
Land: 0.3 sq. mi.; **Water:** 0.0 sq. mi.
In central DE on Leipsic River, 6 mi. north of Dover.
Name origin: Named in 1814 for Leipzig, Germany. Previously called Fast Landing.

Little Creek
Town
ZIP: 19961   **Lat:** 39-09-54 N **Long:** 75-26-55 W
Pop: 167 (1990); 230 (1980)   **Pop Density:** 1670.0
Land: 0.1 sq. mi.; **Water:** 0.0 sq. mi.   **Elev:** 10 ft.
In east-central DE.
Name origin: For Little Creek, a nearby stream; shortened form of Little Creek Landing. Previously called Bayview.

Magnolia
Town
ZIP: 19962   **Lat:** 39-04-11 N **Long:** 75-28-36 W
Pop: 211 (1990); 197 (1980)   **Pop Density:** 1055.0
Land: 0.2 sq. mi.; **Water:** 0.0 sq. mi.
In central DE.
Name origin: Originally known as White House.

Milford
City
ZIP: 19963   **Lat:** 38-55-26 N **Long:** 75-26-13 W
Pop: 2,476 (1990); 2,147 (1980)   **Pop Density:** 952.3
Land: 2.6 sq. mi.; **Water:** 0.0 sq. mi.   **Elev:** 21 ft.
In south-central DE on Mispillion River, 18 mi. south of Dover, crossed by the Kent-Sussex county line. Part of the town is also in Sussex County.
Name origin: Probably for nearby Milford Mill Pond, now known as Silver Lake.

Rising Sun-Lebanon
CDP
Lat: 39-06-04 N **Long:** 75-30-23 W
Pop: 2,177 (1990)   **Pop Density:** 604.7
Land: 3.6 sq. mi.; **Water:** 0.0 sq. mi.

Riverview
CDP
Lat: 39-01-44 N **Long:** 75-31-11 W
Pop: 1,138 (1990)   **Pop Density:** 316.1
Land: 3.6 sq. mi.; **Water:** 0.1 sq. mi.

Rodney Village
CDP
Lat: 39-07-34 N **Long:** 75-32-12 W
Pop: 1,745 (1990); 1,753 (1980)   **Pop Density:** 2492.9
Land: 0.7 sq. mi.; **Water:** 0.0 sq. mi.

Smyrna
Town
ZIP: 19977   **Lat:** 39-17-41 N **Long:** 75-36-27 W
Pop: 5,231 (1990); 4,750 (1980)   **Pop Density:** 1868.2
Land: 2.8 sq. mi.; **Water:** 0.1 sq. mi.   **Elev:** 36 ft.
In north-central DE on the Smyrna River, 10 mi. north of Dover, crossed by the Kent-New Castle county line. Part of the town is also in New Castle County.
Name origin: Named in 1806 for the Turkish seaport. Originally known as Duck Creek or Duck Creek Cross Roads.

Viola
Town
ZIP: 19979   **Lat:** 39-02-31 N **Long:** 75-34-19 W
Pop: 153 (1990); 167 (1980)   **Pop Density:** 765.0
Land: 0.2 sq. mi.; **Water:** 0.0 sq. mi.   **Elev:** 60 ft.
In central DE.
Name origin: Previously called Golden Thicket and Canterbury Station.

Woodside
Town
ZIP: 19980   **Lat:** 39-04-13 N **Long:** 75-34-06 W
Pop: 140 (1990); 248 (1980)   **Pop Density:** 700.0
Land: 0.2 sq. mi.; **Water:** 0.0 sq. mi.   **Elev:** 61 ft.
In central DE.
Name origin: Named in 1869 (changed from Fredonia). Previously called Burnt House Crossroad.

Wyoming
Town
ZIP: 19934   **Lat:** 39-07-00 N **Long:** 75-33-38 W
Pop: 977 (1990); 960 (1980)   **Pop Density:** 1395.7
Land: 0.7 sq. mi.; **Water:** 0.0 sq. mi.
In central DE.
Name origin: For the Wyoming Valley of PA home of the town's first minister. Previously called West Camden and Camden Station.

New Castle County
County Seat: Wilmington (ZIP: 19736)

Pop: 441,946 (1990); 398,115 (1980)   **Pop Density:** 1036.7
Land: 426.3 sq. mi.; **Water:** 67.2 sq. mi.   **Area Code:** 302
In northern DE; original county; organized 1673.
Name origin: Col. Richard Nicolls, in Oct. 1664, renamed the former Swedish-Dutch settlement of New Amstel to honor William Cavendish (1592–1676), Duke of Newcastle.

Arden
Village
ZIP: 19803   **Lat:** 39-48-37 N **Long:** 75-29-22 W
Pop: 477 (1990); 516 (1980)   **Pop Density:** 1590.0
Land: 0.3 sq. mi.; **Water:** 0.0 sq. mi.   **Elev:** 250 ft.
In northeastern DE.
Name origin: Possibly for the Forest of Arden in Shakespeare's *As You Like It*. Originally known as Ardentown.

Ardencroft
Village
Lat: 39-48-14 N **Long:** 75-29-12 W
Pop: 282 (1990); 267 (1980)   **Pop Density:** 2820.0
Land: 0.1 sq. mi.; **Water:** 0.0 sq. mi.
In northeastern DE.
Name origin: For the nearby village of Arden

Ardentown
Village
ZIP: 19810   **Lat:** 39-48-32 N **Long:** 75-28-54 W
Pop: 325 (1990); 307 (1980)   **Pop Density:** 1625.0
Land: 0.2 sq. mi.; **Water:** 0.0 sq. mi.   **Elev:** 250 ft.
In northeastern DE; a suburb of Wilmington.
Name origin: Probably from the nearby village of Arden.

Bellefonte
Village
          Lat: 39-45-58 N **Long:** 75-29-53 W
Pop: 1,243 (1990); 1,279 (1980)   **Pop Density:** 6215.0
Land: 0.2 sq. mi.; **Water:** 0.0 sq. mi.
In northeastern DE on the Delaware River.
Name origin: From the French for 'beautiful fountain.'

Brookside
CDP
ZIP: 19713   **Lat:** 39-40-04 N **Long:** 75-42-57 W
Pop: 15,307 (1990); 15,255 (1980)   **Pop Density:** 3924.9
Land: 3.9 sq. mi.; **Water:** 0.0 sq. mi.

Claymont
CDP
ZIP: 19703   **Lat:** 39-48-10 N **Long:** 75-27-33 W
Pop: 9,800 (1990); 10,022 (1980)   **Pop Density:** 4666.7
Land: 2.1 sq. mi.; **Water:** 0.0 sq. mi.

Delaware City
City
          Lat: 39-34-31 N **Long:** 75-36-01 W
Pop: 1,682 (1990); 1,858 (1980)   **Pop Density:** 1401.7
Land: 1.2 sq. mi.; **Water:** 0.1 sq. mi.
In northern DE.
Name origin: Named in 1826 by William L. Newbold. Previously called Newbold's Wharf.

Edgemoor
CDP
ZIP: 19802   **Lat:** 39-45-20 N **Long:** 75-30-28 W
Pop: 5,853 (1990); 7,397 (1980)   **Pop Density:** 3251.7
Land: 1.8 sq. mi.; **Water:** 0.0 sq. mi.

Elsmere
Town
ZIP: 19805   **Lat:** 39-44-16 N **Long:** 75-35-41 W
Pop: 5,935 (1990); 6,493 (1980)   **Pop Density:** 5935.0
Land: 1.0 sq. mi.; **Water:** 0.0 sq. mi.   **Elev:** 80 ft.
In northern DE at the junction of the Reading and B & O railroads.

Middletown
Town
ZIP: 19709   **Lat:** 39-27-04 N **Long:** 75-42-52 W
Pop: 3,834 (1990); 2,946 (1980)   **Pop Density:** 1127.6
Land: 3.4 sq. mi.; **Water:** 0.0 sq. mi.   **Elev:** 66 ft.
In northern DE.
Name origin: Probably for its location between Wilmington and Dover.

Newark
City
ZIP: 19711   **Lat:** 39-40-35 N **Long:** 75-45-27 W
Pop: 25,098 (1990); 6 (1980)   **Pop Density:** 2918.4
Land: 8.6 sq. mi.; **Water:** 0.0 sq. mi.
In northwestern DE, 15 mi. southwest of Wilmington, near the Maryland border. Site of the University of Delaware.
Name origin: From New Worke, name of a tract of land settled on by Valentine Hollingsworth, a Quaker, who in 1688 gave a piece of this land for a meeting house.

New Castle
City
          Lat: 39-39-59 N **Long:** 75-34-13 W
Pop: 4,837 (1990); 4,907 (1980)   **Pop Density:** 2198.6
Land: 2.2 sq. mi.; **Water:** 0.1 sq. mi.
In northeastern DE on the Delaware River.
Name origin: Named by the British in 1664. Previous Dutch name was Niew Amstel, for the river in Amsterdam. Originally an Indian village at the site was named Tamakonck (possibly meaning 'place of the beaver'); next settled by the Dutch and called Santhoeck ('Sand Point'). Under Swedish rule (1654–55) called Quinamkot and Fort Trefalldigheet (Fort Trinity); recovered by the Dutch in 1655, and named Niew Amstel in 1657.

Newport
Town
ZIP: 19804   **Lat:** 39-42-47 N **Long:** 75-36-25 W
Pop: 1,240 (1990); 1,167 (1980)   **Pop Density:** 3100.0
Land: 0.4 sq. mi.; **Water:** 0.0 sq. mi.   **Elev:** 35 ft.
In northern DE on Christina River, 4 mi. southwest of Wilmington.
Name origin: Previously called Newport Ayre.

Odessa
Town
          Lat: 39-27-22 N **Long:** 75-39-36 W
Pop: 303 (1990); 384 (1980)   **Pop Density:** 757.5
Land: 0.4 sq. mi.; **Water:** 0.0 sq. mi.
In north-central DE.
Name origin: Named in 1855 for Odessa, Ukraine. Previously an Indian village called Appoquinini and Cantwell's Bridge, for Edmund Cantwell, the first sheriff and owner of an Appoquinimink River toll bridge.

Pike Creek
CDP
          Lat: 39-43-51 N **Long:** 75-42-16 W
Pop: 10,163 (1990)   **Pop Density:** 3387.7
Land: 3.0 sq. mi.; **Water:** 0.0 sq. mi.

Smyrna
Town
          Lat: 39-18-33 N **Long:** 75-36-26 W
Pop: 0 (1990)
Land: 0.03 sq. mi.; **Water:** 0.0 sq. mi.
In north-central DE on the Smyrna River, 10 mi. north of Dover, crossed by the Kent-New Castle county line. Part of the town is also in Kent County.
Name origin: Named in 1806 for the Turkish seaport. Originally known as Duck Creek or Duck Creek Cross Roads.

Stanton
CDP
ZIP: 19804   **Lat:** 39-43-05 N **Long:** 75-39-05 W
Pop: 5,028 (1990); 5,495 (1980)   **Pop Density:** 4190.0
Land: 1.2 sq. mi.; **Water:** 0.0 sq. mi.

Talleyville
CDP
ZIP: 19803   **Lat:** 39-48-36 N **Long:** 75-33-01 W
Pop: 6,346 (1990); 6,880 (1980)   **Pop Density:** 2115.3
Land: 3.0 sq. mi.; **Water:** 0.0 sq. mi.

Townsend
Town
ZIP: 19734   **Lat:** 39-23-38 N **Long:** 75-41-34 W
Pop: 322 (1990); 386 (1980)   **Pop Density:** 1610.0
Land: 0.2 sq. mi.; **Water:** 0.0 sq. mi.
In north-central DE.
Name origin: Named in 1855 for Samuel Townsend, a local landowner. Originally known as Charleytown.

Wilmington
City
ZIP: 19736   **Lat:** 39-44-08 N **Long:** 75-31-47 W
Pop: 71,529 (1990); 70,195 (1980)   **Pop Density:** 6623.1
Land: 10.8 sq. mi.; **Water:** 6.2 sq. mi.   **Elev:** 100 ft.
County seat and largest city in DE, across the Delaware River from New Jersey. Called the "Chemical Capital of the World"; international headquarters of Du Pont (E.I. du Pont de Nemours and Company). City's river port is connected to the Atlantic Ocean by Delaware Bay.
Name origin: Named in 1739 for Spenser Compton, Earl of

Wilmington (c. 1673–1743), member of the Privy Council, a patron of colonial administrators, and a friend of William Penn (1644–1718). Previously called Willingtown (1730s) by English settlers, for local property owner Thomas Willing. Site of first Swedish settlement, Fort Christina, in 1638.

Wilmington Manor CDP
ZIP: 19720 **Lat:** 39-41-07 N **Long:** 75-35-05 W
Pop: 8,568 (1990); 9,233 (1980) **Pop Density:** 5040.0
Land: 1.7 sq. mi.; **Water:** 0.0 sq. mi.

Sussex County
County Seat: Georgetown (ZIP: 19947)

Pop: 113,229 (1990); 98,004 (1980) **Pop Density:** 120.8
Land: 937.7 sq. mi.; **Water:** 258.0 sq. mi. **Area Code:** 302

In southern DE; organized as Deale County in 1680 from Horre Kill District, which was organized in 1664; name changed in 1682.
Name origin: For the county in England.

Bethany Beach Town
ZIP: 19930 **Lat:** 38-32-16 N **Long:** 75-03-55 W
Pop: 326 (1990); 330 (1980) **Pop Density:** 296.4
Land: 1.1 sq. mi.; **Water:** 0.0 sq. mi. **Elev:** 10 ft.
In southeast DE on Atlantic coast.
Name origin: Probably named for the biblical village.

Bethel Town
ZIP: 19931 **Lat:** 38-34-12 N **Long:** 75-37-11 W
Pop: 178 (1990); 197 (1980) **Pop Density:** 445.0
Land: 0.4 sq. mi.; **Water:** 0.0 sq. mi.

Blades Town
ZIP: 19973 **Lat:** 38-38-04 N **Long:** 75-36-33 W
Pop: 834 (1990); 664 (1980) **Pop Density:** 2780.0
Land: 0.3 sq. mi.; **Water:** 0.0 sq. mi.
In southwestern DE on Nanticoke River across from Seaford.

Bridgeville Town
ZIP: 19933 **Lat:** 38-44-36 N **Long:** 75-36-08 W
Pop: 1,210 (1990); 1,238 (1980) **Pop Density:** 1728.6
Land: 0.7 sq. mi.; **Water:** 0.0 sq. mi. **Elev:** 47 ft.
In southwestern DE, 8 mi. north of Seaford.

Dagsboro Town
ZIP: 19939 **Lat:** 38-32-51 N **Long:** 75-14-51 W
Pop: 398 (1990); 344 (1980) **Pop Density:** 331.7
Land: 1.2 sq. mi.; **Water:** 0.0 sq. mi.
In southeastern DE.
Name origin: For Gen. John Dagworthy, a British officer in the French and Indian War. Originally known as Blackfoot, Dagsbury, and Dagsborough.

Delmar Town
ZIP: 19940 **Lat:** 38-27-31 N **Long:** 75-34-12 W
Pop: 962 (1990); 948 (1980) **Pop Density:** 1924.0
Land: 0.5 sq. mi.; **Water:** 0.0 sq. mi. **Elev:** 55 ft.
In southwestern DE on the MD border. Founded 1859 as the southern terminus of the Eastern Shore Railroad.
Name origin: From its border location, taking the first three letters of each state.

Dewey Beach Town
ZIP: 19971 **Lat:** 38-41-43 N **Long:** 75-04-36 W
Pop: 204 (1990) **Pop Density:** 680.0
Land: 0.3 sq. mi.; **Water:** 0.0 sq. mi. **Elev:** 7 ft.
In southeastern DE on Atlantic coast.

Ellendale Town
ZIP: 19941 **Lat:** 38-48-25 N **Long:** 75-25-27 W
Pop: 313 (1990); 361 (1980) **Pop Density:** 1043.3
Land: 0.3 sq. mi.; **Water:** 0.0 sq. mi.
In south-central DE.
Name origin: Named by Dr. John S. Prettyman for his wife, Ellen.

Fenwick Island Town
Lat: 38-27-38 N **Long:** 75-03-13 W
Pop: 186 (1990); 114 (1980) **Pop Density:** 620.0
Land: 0.3 sq. mi.; **Water:** 0.1 sq. mi.
In southeastern DE on Atlantic coast. Now a peninsula, but formerly an island.
Name origin: Earlier names include Fenwicks Island, False Cape, Assawoman Beach, Phenix Island, Hinlopen Cape, and Hinloopen Cape.

Frankford Town
ZIP: 19945 **Lat:** 38-31-20 N **Long:** 75-13-58 W
Pop: 591 (1990); 686 (1980) **Pop Density:** 844.3
Land: 0.7 sq. mi.; **Water:** 0.0 sq. mi. **Elev:** 30 ft.
In southeastern DE.
Name origin: Originally known as Gum's Store.

Georgetown Town
ZIP: 19947 **Lat:** 38-41-26 N **Long:** 75-23-09 W
Pop: 3,732 (1990); 1,710 (1980) **Pop Density:** 1555.0
Land: 2.4 sq. mi.; **Water:** 0.0 sq. mi. **Elev:** 52 ft.
In south-central DE. County seat; laid out 1791 to replace Lewes as county seat.
Name origin: For George Mitchell, who supervised the town's location.

Greenwood Town
Lat: 38-48-26 N **Long:** 75-35-31 W
Pop: 578 (1990); 578 (1980) **Pop Density:** 825.7
Land: 0.7 sq. mi.; **Water:** 0.0 sq. mi.

Henlopen Acres Town
ZIP: 19971 **Lat:** 38-43-32 N **Long:** 75-05-09 W
Pop: 107 (1990); 176 (1980) **Pop Density:** 356.7
Land: 0.3 sq. mi.; **Water:** 0.0 sq. mi. **Elev:** 10 ft.
In southeastern DE on Atlantic coast.
Name origin: Probably for a Dutch town or a prominent Netherlander.

Laurel　　　　　　　　　　　　　　　　Town
ZIP: 19956　　　　　**Lat:** 38-33-17 N **Long:** 75-34-23 W
Pop: 3,226 (1990); 3,052 (1980)　　**Pop Density:** 2304.3
Land: 1.4 sq. mi.; **Water:** 0.1 sq. mi.

In southwestern DE on Broad Creek.

Name origin: Probably for Laurel River, former name of Broad Creek.

Lewes　　　　　　　　　　　　　　　　City
ZIP: 19958　　　　　**Lat:** 38-46-49 N **Long:** 75-08-59 W
Pop: 2,295 (1990); 2,197 (1980)　　**Pop Density:** 637.5
Land: 3.6 sq. mi.; **Water:** 0.6 sq. mi.

In southeastern DE on Delaware Bay. Site of the state's first Dutch settlement.

Name origin: For Lewes, Sussex, England. Previously called Zwaanendael, Dutch for 'Valley of Swans.'

Long Neck　　　　　　　　　　　　　CDP
　　　　　　　　　Lat: 38-37-12 N **Long:** 75-09-03 W
Pop: 886 (1990)　　　　**Pop Density:** 443.0
Land: 2.0 sq. mi.; **Water:** 0.0 sq. mi.

Milford　　　　　　　　　　　　　　　City
ZIP: 19963　　　　　**Lat:** 38-54-11 N **Long:** 75-25-46 W
Pop: 3,564 (1990); 3,209 (1980)　　**Pop Density:** 1549.6
Land: 2.3 sq. mi.; **Water:** 0.0 sq. mi.　　**Elev:** 21 ft.

In south-central DE on Mispillion River, 18 mi. south of Dover, crossed by the Kent-Sussex county line. Part of the town is also in Kent County.

Name origin: Probably for nearby Milford Mill Pond, now known as Silver Lake.

Millsboro　　　　　　　　　　　　　Town
ZIP: 19966　　　　　**Lat:** 38-35-06 N **Long:** 75-17-30 W
Pop: 1,643 (1990); 1,233 (1980)　　**Pop Density:** 966.5
Land: 1.7 sq. mi.; **Water:** 0.2 sq. mi.　　**Elev:** 26 ft.

In southern DE on Indian River.

Name origin: Previously called Millsborough, Rock Hole, and Washington.

Millville　　　　　　　　　　　　　Town
ZIP: 19967　　　　　**Lat:** 38-32-42 N **Long:** 75-06-44 W
Pop: 206 (1990); 178 (1980)　　**Pop Density:** 515.0
Land: 0.4 sq. mi.; **Water:** 0.0 sq. mi.　　**Elev:** 12 ft.

In southeastern DE, 3.5 mi. west of Bethany Beach.

Milton　　　　　　　　　　　　　　Town
ZIP: 19968　　　　　**Lat:** 38-46-43 N **Long:** 75-18-47 W
Pop: 1,417 (1990); 1,359 (1980)　　**Pop Density:** 1574.4
Land: 0.9 sq. mi.; **Water:** 0.0 sq. mi.

In southeastern DE on Broadkill River.

Name origin: Previously called Clowes, Osbornes Landing, Conwells Landing, Upper Landing, Head of Broadkiln, Broadkill, and Sockumtown.

Ocean View　　　　　　　　　　　Town
ZIP: 19970　　　　　**Lat:** 38-32-42 N **Long:** 75-05-33 W
Pop: 606 (1990); 495 (1980)　　**Pop Density:** 550.9
Land: 1.1 sq. mi.; **Water:** 0.0 sq. mi.　　**Elev:** 14 ft.

In southeastern DE on Indian River Bay.

Name origin: Originally known as Halls Store.

Rehoboth Beach　　　　　　　　　City
ZIP: 19971　　　　　**Lat:** 38-43-02 N **Long:** 75-04-51 W
Pop: 1,234 (1990); 1,730 (1980)　　**Pop Density:** 1028.3
Land: 1.2 sq. mi.; **Water:** 0.5 sq. mi.

In southeastern DE on Atlantic coast. Noted ocean resort.

Name origin: The beach took its name from nearby Rehoboth Bay. Rehoboth is the name of Isaac's well (Genesis 26:22).

Seaford　　　　　　　　　　　　　　City
ZIP: 19973　　　　　**Lat:** 38-38-56 N **Long:** 75-36-59 W
Pop: 5,689 (1990); 5,256 (1980)　　**Pop Density:** 1723.9
Land: 3.3 sq. mi.; **Water:** 0.0 sq. mi.　　**Elev:** 29 ft.

In southwestern DE on Nanticoke River, 15 mi. west of Georgetown. Founded 1799.

Name origin: Previously called Seford and Hooper's Landing.

Selbyville　　　　　　　　　　　　Town
ZIP: 19944　　　　　**Lat:** 38-27-29 N **Long:** 75-13-26 W
Pop: 1,335 (1990); 1,251 (1980)　　**Pop Density:** 1026.9
Land: 1.3 sq. mi.; **Water:** 0.0 sq. mi.　　**Elev:** 32 ft.

In southeastern DE near Maryland border.

Name origin: For town's first postmaster, Josiah Selby.

Slaughter Beach　　　　　　　　　Town
ZIP: 19963　　　　　**Lat:** 38-54-44 N **Long:** 75-18-15 W
Pop: 114 (1990); 121 (1980)　　**Pop Density:** 87.7
Land: 1.3 sq. mi.; **Water:** 0.0 sq. mi.　　**Elev:** 5 ft.

In southern DE on Delaware Bay, 15 mi. northeast of Georgetown. Resort community.

Name origin: For William Slaughter, postmaster (1833).

South Bethany　　　　　　　　　　Town
　　　　　　　　　Lat: 38-30-58 N **Long:** 75-03-30 W
Pop: 148 (1990); 115 (1980)　　**Pop Density:** 296.0
Land: 0.5 sq. mi.; **Water:** 0.0 sq. mi.

In southeastern DE on Atlantic coast.

Name origin: For its location south of Bethany Beach.

Index to Places and Counties in Delaware

District of Columbia

DISTRICT OF COLUMBIA

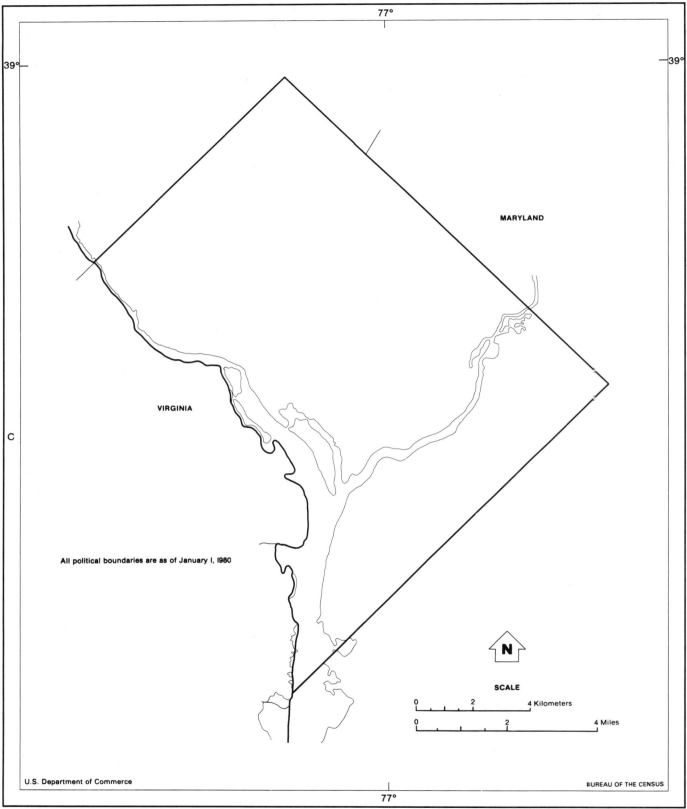

77°

39°

39°

MARYLAND

VIRGINIA

C

All political boundaries are as of January I, 1980

N

SCALE

0   2   4 Kilometers

0   2   4 Miles

District of Columbia (Washington, D.C.)

Population: 606,900 (1990); 638,333 (1980)
Percent population change (1980-1990): -4.9
Population projection: 590,000 (1995); 586,000 (2000)

Area: total 68 sq. mi.; 61 sq. mi. land, 7 sq. mi. water
Highest elevation: 420-30 ft., Fort Reno
Lowest point: slightly above sea level along the Potomac River

Total housing units: 278,489
No. of occupied housing units: 249,634
Vacant housing units (%): 10.4
Distribution of population by race and
  Hispanic origin (%):
  White: 29.6
  Black: 65.8
  Hispanic (any race): 5.4
  Native American: 0.2
  Asian/Pacific: 1.8
  Other: 2.5

It became the capital of the United States on December 1, 1800.

Location: In the eastern United States between Maryland and Virginia, on the eastern shore of the Potomac River. The district is coextensive with the city of Washington.

Name Origin: From *Columbia*, a name commonly applied to the United States in the late eighteenth century, derived from the surname of Christopher Columbus.

Bird: wood thrush *(Hylocichla mustelina)*
Flower: American beauty rose
Tree: scarlet oak *(Quercus coccinea)*

Motto: *Justitia omnibus* (Latin 'Justice for all')

Area code: 202
Time zone: Eastern
Abbreviations: DC (postal); D.C. (traditional)
Part of (region): Middle Atlantic

District Government

The city of Washington, which is coextensive with the District of Columbia, is the only U.S. city not part of a state. While ultimately under congressional jurisdiction, as set out in Article 1, section 8 of the U.S. Constitution, the District was granted home rule in 1973 and has since had an elected mayor and city council. In Congress the District is represented by a delegate in the House of Representatives. This delegate was non-voting until 1993, when the House acted to give all Congressional delegates a vote in the Committee of the Whole. A lawsuit on this action is pending. Statehood for the District has been proposed numerous times but has not passed either as an amendment to the Constitution or as an act of Congress. In 1990 two "shadow" senators and one "shadow" representative were elected to lobby for statehood.

History

Washington is one of the few cities in the world that was designed before being built. The U.S. Constitution provided for a tract of land to be set aside for the seat of federal government. The site was chosen by George Washington in January 1791 and the land formally ceded by Maryland and Virginia. He immediately hired Pierre Charles l'Enfant, a French military engineer who had served in the Continental Army during the Revolutionary War, to draw up plans for the city. However, it was Andrew Ellicott who produced the final map.

Three commissioners were appointed to oversee the construction. Work was delayed by lack of financing and difficulties in acquiring building materials. Construction on the major public buildings was far from finished when Congress moved to the District in 1800. On May 3, 1802, the city of Washington was incorporated, with an elected council and a mayor appointed by the president.

In 1871 the District government was changed to the Territorial form with an appointed governor and elected bicameral Legislature. The territorial government was abolished in 1874 and replaced again with a three-commissioner system. The three commissioners were appointed by the president, one commissioner coming from the Army Corps of Engineers. In 1967 the president reorganized the District government, appointing a Mayor-Commissioner and a nine-member council. In 1973 the District government was again changed, allowing for the election of a mayor and council.

Development

In August 1814 the British landed and burned the Capitol, the President's House, and other public buildings. They were rebuilt within five years, but for a long time the city remained rude, rough, muddy, and, in summer's humidity, very unhealthy. After several years of agitation, the Virginia portion of the district, today the city of Alexandria and Arlington County, VA, was returned to Virginia in 1846.

After the Civil War, Union soldiers, workers, and former slaves poured in, almost doubling the population by 1870. The flourishing city ignored some aspects of the plan of L'Enfant. In 1901 the Senate appointed a committee to design a plan for Washington's growth, and since 1902 the McMillan Commission plan has been a guide to the city's development. The city continued to grow with each World War. The postwar years saw expansion of the suburban Maryland and Virginia population at the expense of the center city. The 1980s saw extensive downtown redevelopment.

Maine

MAINE

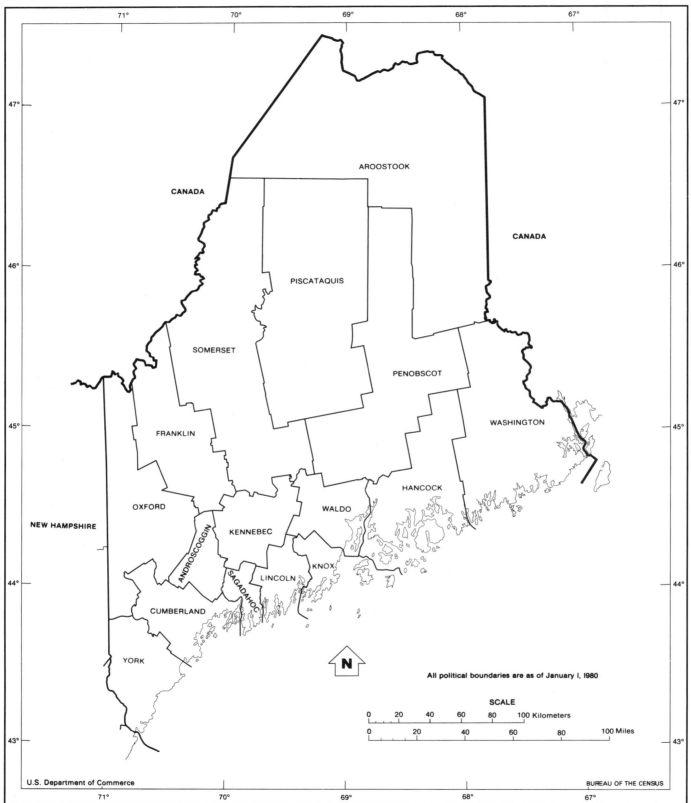

NEW HAMPSHIRE

CANADA

CANADA

AROOSTOOK

PISCATAQUIS

SOMERSET

PENOBSCOT

FRANKLIN

WASHINGTON

OXFORD

HANCOCK

WALDO

KENNEBEC

ANDROSCOGGIN

KNOX

SAGADAHOC

LINCOLN

CUMBERLAND

YORK

N

All political boundaries are as of January 1, 1980

SCALE

0   20   40   60   80   100 Kilometers

0   20   40   60   80   100 Miles

U.S. Department of Commerce

BUREAU OF THE CENSUS

Maine

Population: 1,227,928 (1990); 1,124,660 (1980)
Population rank: 38
Percent population change (1980-1990): 9.2
Population projection: 1,301,000 (1995);
1,359,000 (2000)

Area: total 35,387 sq. mi.; 30,865 sq. mi. land, 4,523
sq. mi. water. General outline of coastline is 228
mi.; total coastline, including bays, islands, and in-
lets 3,500 mi.
Area rank: 39
Highest elevation: 5,268 ft., Mount Katahdin
Lowest point: sea level along Atlantic Ocean

State capital: Augusta (Kennebec County)
Largest city: Portland (64,358)
Second largest city: Lewiston (39,757)
Largest county: Cumberland (243,135)

Total housing units: 587,045
No. of occupied housing units: 465,312
Vacant housing units (%): 20.7
Distribution of population by race and
Hispanic origin (%):
White: 98.4
Black: 0.4
Hispanic (any race): 0.6
Native American: 0.5
Asian/Pacific: 0.5
Other: 0.1

Admission date: March 15, 1820 (23rd state)

Location: In extreme northeastern United States on
the Atlantic coast, bordering New Hampshire and the
Canadian provinces of Quebec and New Brunswick.
The easternmost point in the U.S. is at West Quoddy
Head.

Name Origin: For the former province of Maine in
western France. Also reflects an older reference to the
mainland as distinct from the offshore islands. French
explorers in the sixteenth century referred to the area
west of the Kennebec River as "Maine" and the area
to the east as "Acadie."

State animal: moose *(Alces alces)*
State bird: chickadee *(Parus atricapillus)*
State fish: landlocked salmon *(Salmo salar)*
State flower: white pine cone and tassel *(Pinus strobus)*
State insect: honeybee *(Apis mellifera)*
State mineral: tourmaline
State song: "State of Maine Song"
State tree: eastern white pine *(Pinus strobus)*
State motto: *Dirigo* (Latin 'I direct')

State nickname: The Pine Tree State

Area code: 207
Time zone: Eastern
Abbreviation: ME (postal); Me. (traditional)
Part of (region): New England

Local Government

Counties:
Maine has 16 counties.

Municipalities:
There are 22 cities, each with home rule, and 471 towns
and plantations (small incorporated areas). The towns are
similar to those in other parts of New England; there may
be several communities within them, but they are all
under a single town government. The plantations are
headed by a board of assessors and are governed much
the same as the towns.

Settlement History and Early Development

The Paleolithic Red Paint people, so-called for the red
ocher found in their graves, occupied what is now Maine
from 3000 to 1000 B.C. Later came the Algonquian
Abnaki (or Wabanaki) Indians, most of whom died in
intertribal wars and an epidemic of smallpox. Those that
remained lived peacefully with the white settlers. In
1980, the U.S. government agreed to pay $81.5 million to
the Passamaquoddy and Penobscot Indians for the land
seized by the U.S. between the end of the eighteenthth
and beginning of the nineteenth centuries.

Many historians believe Leif Ericson probably visited
what is now the Maine coast about 1000. Other historians
believe John Cabot reached Maine in 1498. However, the
first documented European contact was by Giovanni da
Verrazano during his exploration of 1524, followed in
1604 by French explorers including Samuel de Champlain, who named Mount Desert (French *Ile de Monts
Deserts* 'island of bald mountains'), the largest island off
the coast of Maine. The French established a permanent
colony on an island in the St. Croix River in 1604 near
present-day Calais, and the English established Popham
Plantation in 1607 on the peninsula of Sabino at the
mouth of the Kennebec River (present-day Hunnewell
Point). Both failed, but by 1630 there were English settlements at nearly a dozen spots along the coast and on
several islands.

In 1622 Sir Ferdinando Gorges and Capt. John Mason
received the first grant of Maine lands from the Council
for New England (also called the Plymouth Company).
Gorges was a wealthy Englishman who headed the Council, an English joint-stock company that received and

made royal grants of New England territory. The tract covered the territory between the Merrimack River (in what is now New Hampshire and Massachusetts) and the Kennebec River, and extended back to Canadian rivers and lakes. It was called the Province of Maine and included present-day New Hampshire and the western part of Maine. In 1629 they divided the land at the Piscataqua River, and Gorges received the part east of the river, which he called Maine. He established the first government in Maine in 1636, and made Gorgeana (now York) the first chartered English city in what is now the U.S.

After Gorges's death in 1647, Kittery, Wells, and York united under a new government. Between 1652-58 they and the citizens of Casco Bay, Kennebunk, Saco, and Scarborough agreed to make Maine part of the Massachusetts Bay Colony. The latter bought the rights to Maine from the Gorges heirs in 1677, and a royal charter in 1691 declared Maine a district of Massachusetts.

French claims to Maine and most of the rest of North America were ended by the Treaty of Paris in 1763 at the conclusion of the French and Indian Wars (1689-1763).

The American Revolution

Hundreds of Maine patriots fought in the Revolutionary War (1775-83). The first naval encounter of the war was fought off the coast of Machias in June 1775, during which a group of Maine patriots captured the British armed schooner *Margaretta*.

Statehood

By 1785 Maine colonists began talking of separation from Massachusetts, but there was no overwhelming vote for statehood until an 1819 referendum. Maine joined the Union as the twenty-third state on March 15, 1820 under the Missouri Compromise of 1820. The Compromise was an act of Congress by which Maine was admitted as a free state to balance the admission of Missouri as a slave state. Further, no slavery was to be allowed in the territory of the Louisiana Purchase north of latitude 36 36 N, with the exception of Missouri.

Business and Industry

Prior to the Civil War, Maine's economy was based on fishing, trading, and exploitation of the forests, especially for shipbuilding and white-pine masts. After the war textile and leather industries blossomed, and farming increased, especially Maine potatoes. Toward the end of the nineteenth century hydroelectric power was developed on the rivers, which attracted many new industries. In the early twentieth century the paper and pulp industry expanded greatly. Potatoes are still an important cash crop, especially in Aroostook County. Today, tourism and winter sports contribute significantly to the state's economy, although these businesses have generated concern within the state about protecting the environment and Maine's natural resources.

State Boundaries

Maine ceased being governed by Massachusetts upon becoming a state on March 15, 1820. The north and east boundaries of Maine with Canada were fixed as they presently exist by the 1842 Webster-Ashburton Treaty between Great Britain and the U.S. The western boundary was disputed by Maine and New Hampshire from 1740 until it was finally fixed in 1929 by A.T. Fowler of the U.S. Geological Survey.

Maine Counties

Androscoggin	Hancock	Oxford	Somerset
Aroostook	Kennebec	Penobscot	Waldo
Cumberland	Knox	Piscataquis	Washington
Franklin	Lincoln	Sagadahoc	York

Androscoggin County
County Seat: Auburn (ZIP: 04210)

Pop: 105,259 (1990); 99,509 (1980)　　　　　　**Pop Density:** 223.8
Land: 470.3 sq. mi.; **Water:** 27.0 sq. mi.　　　　**Area Code:** 207

In southern ME, southwest of Augusta; organized Mar 18, 1854 from Cumberland, Oxford, and Kennebec counties.

Name origin: For the river, from an Abnaki Indian name meaning either 'place where fish are cured,' 'fishing place for alewives,' or 'fish spearing.'

Auburn　　　　　　　　　　　　　　　　City
ZIP: 04210　　　　**Lat:** 44-05-03 N **Long:** 70-14-58 W
Pop: 24,309 (1990); 23,128 (1980)　　**Pop Density:** 406.5
Land: 59.8 sq. mi.; **Water:** 6.0 sq. mi.

In southwestern ME on the Androscoggin River, 30 mi. north of Portland. Incorporated as a town in 1842; as a city in 1869.

Name origin: For the Yorkshire village of Auburn, called "Sweet Auburn" in the popular 1770 poem, "The Deserted Village" by Oliver Goldsmith's (1730–74).

Durham　　　　　　　　　　　　　　Town
　　　　　　　　　　Lat: 43-57-50 N **Long:** 70-07-17 W
Pop: 2,842 (1990); 2,074 (1980)　　**Pop Density:** 74.6
Land: 38.1 sq. mi.; **Water:** 0.6 sq. mi.

Incorporated 1789.

Name origin: For the former home in England of prominent landowner Col. Royal.

Greene　　　　　　　　　　　　　　Town
ZIP: 04236　　　　**Lat:** 44-11-23 N **Long:** 70-08-39 W
Pop: 3,661 (1990); 3,037 (1980)　　**Pop Density:** 113.0
Land: 32.4 sq. mi.; **Water:** 2.9 sq. mi.

Incorporated 1788.

Name origin: For Gen. Nathanael Greene (1742–86), hero of the Revolutionary War.

Leeds　　　　　　　　　　　　　　　Town
ZIP: 04263　　　　**Lat:** 44-17-29 N **Long:** 70-08-01 W
Pop: 1,669 (1990); 1,463 (1980)　　**Pop Density:** 41.3
Land: 40.4 sq. mi.; **Water:** 3.1 sq. mi.

Incorporated 1801.

Name origin: For Leeds, England, former home of the first settlers.

Lewiston　　　　　　　　　　　　　　City
ZIP: 04240　　　　**Lat:** 44-05-21 N **Long:** 70-10-20 W
Pop: 39,757 (1990); 40,481 (1980)　　**Pop Density:** 1165.9
Land: 34.1 sq. mi.; **Water:** 1.1 sq. mi.　　**Elev:** 121 ft.

In southwestern ME on the Androscoggin River, 30 mi. north of Portland. Settled 1770; became a city 1861. Second largest city in ME; diverse manufacturing city: textiles, footwear, electrical equipment, fabricated metals.

Name origin: For Lewis Falls, which was named for an Indian called Lewis who drowned in the city's falls.

Lisbon　　　　　　　　　　　　　　Town
ZIP: 04250　　　　**Lat:** 44-01-40 N **Long:** 70-05-38 W
Pop: 9,457 (1990); 8,769 (1980)　　**Pop Density:** 400.7
Land: 23.6 sq. mi.; **Water:** 0.6 sq. mi.

In southwestern ME, 8 mi. southeast of Lewiston. Incorporated 1799.

Name origin: For Lisbon, Portugal, following an early American practice of naming Maine's towns after European cities.

Lisbon Falls　　　　　　　　　　　　CDP
ZIP: 04252　　　　**Lat:** 44-00-29 N **Long:** 70-03-28 W
Pop: 4,674 (1990); 4,370 (1980)　　**Pop Density:** 1230.0
Land: 3.8 sq. mi.; **Water:** 0.1 sq. mi.

Livermore　　　　　　　　　　　　　Town
ZIP: 04253　　　　**Lat:** 44-24-32 N **Long:** 70-12-41 W
Pop: 1,950 (1990); 1,826 (1980)　　**Pop Density:** 51.7
Land: 37.7 sq. mi.; **Water:** 1.7 sq. mi.

Incorporated 1795.

Name origin: For the town's first settler, Deacon Elijah Livermore.

Livermore Falls　　　　　　　　　　Town
ZIP: 04254　　　　**Lat:** 44-26-05 N **Long:** 70-09-06 W
Pop: 3,455 (1990); 3,572 (1980)　　**Pop Density:** 175.4
Land: 19.7 sq. mi.; **Water:** 0.7 sq. mi.

Incorporated 1843.

Name origin: See Livermore.

Mechanic Falls　　　　　　　　　　Town
ZIP: 04256　　　　**Lat:** 44-05-51 N **Long:** 70-24-25 W
Pop: 2,919 (1990); 2,616 (1980)　　**Pop Density:** 263.0
Land: 11.1 sq. mi.; **Water:** 0.0 sq. mi.　　**Elev:** 304 ft.

Incorporated 1893.

Name origin: For early local industry, whose mechanical mills depended on the falls for water power.

Minot　　　　　　　　　　　　　　　Town
ZIP: 04258　　　　**Lat:** 44-09-17 N **Long:** 70-20-01 W
Pop: 1,664 (1990); 1,631 (1980)　　**Pop Density:** 55.8
Land: 29.8 sq. mi.; **Water:** 0.1 sq. mi.

Incorporated 1802.

Name origin: For Judge Minot, an early member of the general court of MA.

Poland　　　　　　　　　　　　　　Town
ZIP: 04273　　　　**Lat:** 44-02-56 N **Long:** 70-23-28 W
Pop: 4,342 (1990); 3,578 (1980)　　**Pop Density:** 102.6
Land: 42.3 sq. mi.; **Water:** 4.9 sq. mi.

Incorporated 1795.

Name origin: For an old hymn or for the country in Europe.

Sabattus　　　　　　　　　　　　　Town
ZIP: 04280　　　　**Lat:** 44-05-22 N **Long:** 70-04-13 W
Pop: 3,696 (1990); 3,081 (1980)　　**Pop Density:** 144.9
Land: 25.5 sq. mi.; **Water:** 1.1 sq. mi.

In southwestern ME.

Name origin: For Sabattus Pond, which extends north from the town center. It was named for the Anasagunticook Chief Sabattus, who was killed in the area. Sabattus may be based on the French for St. Jean Baptiste.

Turner
ZIP: 04282   **Lat:** 44-16-00 N   **Long:** 70-14-46 W
Pop: 4,315 (1990); 3,539 (1980)   **Pop Density:** 72.4
Land: 59.6 sq. mi.; **Water:** 3.1 sq. mi.
Incorporated 1786.
Name origin: For the Rev. Charles Turner, resident in the area before 1786 and a Massachusetts state senator.

Town

Wales
Lat: 44-09-43 N   **Long:** 70-02-55 W
Pop: 1,223 (1990); 862 (1980)   **Pop Density:** 75.0
Land: 16.3 sq. mi.; **Water:** 1.0 sq. mi.
Incorporated 1816.
Name origin: For Wales in Great Britain.

Town

Aroostook County
County Seat: Houlton (ZIP: 04730)

Pop: 86,936 (1990); 91,344 (1980)   **Pop Density:** 13.0
Land: 6671.9 sq. mi.; **Water:** 157.2 sq. mi.   **Area Code:** 207
In northern ME, bordered on west and northwest by Quebec, Canada, and on the northeast and east by New Brunswick, Canada. Organized Mar 16, 1839 from Washington and Penobscot counties.
Name origin: For the Aroostook River, which runs through the county; from Micmac Indian 'clear river.'

Allagash
Lat: 47-05-02 N   **Long:** 69-06-04 W
Pop: 359 (1990); 448 (1980)   **Pop Density:** 2.8
Land: 128.5 sq. mi.; **Water:** 2.8 sq. mi.   **Elev:** 620 ft.
Name origin: From Abnaki term meaning 'bark cabin.'

Town

Amity
Lat: 45-54-50 N   **Long:** 67-51-33 W
Pop: 186 (1990); 168 (1980)   **Pop Density:** 4.4
Land: 42.1 sq. mi.; **Water:** 0.0 sq. mi.
Incorporated 1836.
Name origin: Recalls the friendship of the early settlers.

Town

Ashland
Lat: 46-39-21 N   **Long:** 68-21-46 W
Pop: 1,542 (1990); 1,865 (1980)   **Pop Density:** 19.1
Land: 80.6 sq. mi.; **Water:** 1.1 sq. mi.
Incorporated 1862.
Name origin: For the former home of American statesman Henry Clay (1777–1852) of KY.

Town

Bancroft
Lat: 45-41-09 N   **Long:** 67-58-34 W
Pop: 66 (1990); 61 (1980)   **Pop Density:** 1.6
Land: 40.0 sq. mi.; **Water:** 0.6 sq. mi.
Incorporated 1889.
Name origin: For historian George Bancroft (1800–91), whose brother was town historian.

Town

Blaine
Lat: 46-29-05 N   **Long:** 67-50-54 W
Pop: 784 (1990); 922 (1980)   **Pop Density:** 42.4
Land: 18.5 sq. mi.; **Water:** 0.1 sq. mi.
Incorporated 1874.
Name origin: For one-time presidential candidate, James G. Blaine (1830–93).

Town

Bridgewater
ZIP: 04735   **Lat:** 46-25-05 N   **Long:** 67-51-02 W
Pop: 647 (1990); 742 (1980)   **Pop Density:** 16.7
Land: 38.8 sq. mi.; **Water:** 0.2 sq. mi.
Incorporated 1858.
Name origin: For Bridgewater, MA.

Town

Caribou
ZIP: 04736   **Lat:** 46-52-00 N   **Long:** 67-59-26 W
Pop: 9,415 (1990); 9,916 (1980)   **Pop Density:** 118.7
Land: 79.3 sq. mi.; **Water:** 0.9 sq. mi.   **Elev:** 442 ft.
In northern ME, 13 mi. north of Presque Island. Incorporated 1859.
Name origin: Named in 1829 for the area's once-abundant caribou population.

City

Cary
Lat: 45-59-26 N   **Long:** 67-50-15 W
Pop: 235 (1990); 229 (1980)   **Pop Density:** 12.4
Land: 19.0 sq. mi.; **Water:** 0.0 sq. mi.
Name origin: For Shepard Cary, once a leading lumberman of the county.

Plantation

Castle Hill
Lat: 46-41-58 N   **Long:** 68-13-38 W
Pop: 449 (1990); 509 (1980)   **Pop Density:** 12.6
Land: 35.7 sq. mi.; **Water:** 0.5 sq. mi.
Incorporated 1903.

Town

Caswell
Lat: 47-00-55 N   **Long:** 67-51-56 W
Pop: 408 (1990); 586 (1980)   **Pop Density:** 9.8
Land: 41.5 sq. mi.; **Water:** 0.3 sq. mi.
Name origin: For the Caswell family, who owned the first farm in the area.

Plantation

Central Aroostook (unorganized)
Lat: 46-22-51 N   **Long:** 68-11-18 W
Pop: 53 (1990); 16 (1980)   **Pop Density:** 0.1
Land: 534.6 sq. mi.; **Water:** 10.4 sq. mi.

Pop. Place

Chapman
Town
Lat: 46-37-52 N **Long:** 68-06-37 W
Pop: 422 (1990); 406 (1980)   **Pop Density:** 11.0
Land: 38.4 sq. mi.; **Water:** 0.4 sq. mi.
Incorporated 1915.
Name origin: For the original surveyor, Chris Chapman, who carved his name on the town's corner posts.

Connor (unorganized)
Pop. Place
Lat: 47-00-37 N **Long:** 67-59-24 W
Pop: 468 (1990); 574 (1980)   **Pop Density:** 11.9
Land: 39.4 sq. mi.; **Water:** 0.1 sq. mi.

Crystal
Town
Lat: 46-00-02 N **Long:** 68-21-55 W
Pop: 303 (1990); 349 (1980)   **Pop Density:** 7.6
Land: 40.1 sq. mi.; **Water:** 0.0 sq. mi.
Incorporated 1901.

Cyr
Pop. Place
Lat: 47-05-11 N **Long:** 67-59-13 W
Pop: 142 (1990); 147 (1980)   **Pop Density:** 3.7
Land: 38.4 sq. mi.; **Water:** 0.0 sq. mi.

Dyer Brook
Town
Lat: 46-04-27 N **Long:** 68-13-11 W
Pop: 243 (1990); 275 (1980)   **Pop Density:** 6.3
Land: 38.5 sq. mi.; **Water:** 0.0 sq. mi.
Incorporated 1891.

E (Plantation of)
Pop. Place
Lat: 46-28-39 N **Long:** 67-59-19 W
Pop: 64 (1990); 55 (1980)   **Pop Density:** 3.0
Land: 21.4 sq. mi.; **Water:** 0.0 sq. mi.

Eagle Lake
Town
Lat: 47-03-42 N **Long:** 68-37-25 W
Pop: 942 (1990); 1,019 (1980)   **Pop Density:** 25.3
Land: 37.2 sq. mi.; **Water:** 2.1 sq. mi.
Incorporated 1911.
Name origin: Named 1839 by Maj. Hastings Strickland after the nearby lake where bald eagles were sighted.

Easton
Town
ZIP: 04740   **Lat:** 46-38-55 N **Long:** 67-51-28 W
Pop: 1,291 (1990); 1,305 (1980)   **Pop Density:** 33.4
Land: 38.7 sq. mi.; **Water:** 0.2 sq. mi.
Incorporated 1864.
Name origin: For its location on the eastern boundary of Aroostock County and of ME.

Fort Fairfield
Town
ZIP: 04742   **Lat:** 46-46-28 N **Long:** 67-51-02 W
Pop: 3,998 (1990); 4,376 (1980)   **Pop Density:** 52.2
Land: 76.6 sq. mi.; **Water:** 1.7 sq. mi.
Incorporated 1858.
Name origin: Site of a fort named in honor of John Fairfield, an early governor of ME.

Fort Kent
Town
ZIP: 04743   **Lat:** 47-14-22 N **Long:** 68-33-38 W
Pop: 4,268 (1990); 4,826 (1980)   **Pop Density:** 78.7
Land: 54.2 sq. mi.; **Water:** 1.2 sq. mi.
Incorporated 1869.
Name origin: Site of a fort named for Edward Kent, an early governor of ME.

Frenchville
Town
Lat: 47-16-35 N **Long:** 68-23-41 W
Pop: 1,338 (1990); 1,450 (1980)   **Pop Density:** 46.8
Land: 28.6 sq. mi.; **Water:** 0.6 sq. mi.
Incorporated 1869.
Name origin: For the large French-Canadian population.

Garfield
Plantation
Lat: 46-36-24 N **Long:** 68-30-26 W
Pop: 102 (1990); 107 (1980)   **Pop Density:** 2.7
Land: 38.2 sq. mi.; **Water:** 0.3 sq. mi.
Name origin: For James Garfield (1831–81), 20th president of the U.S. (1881).

Glenwood
Pop. Place
Lat: 45-48-28 N **Long:** 68-06-01 W
Pop: 8 (1990); 7 (1980)   **Pop Density:** 0.2
Land: 38.2 sq. mi.; **Water:** 1.3 sq. mi.

Grand Isle
Town
ZIP: 04746   **Lat:** 47-15-22 N **Long:** 68-07-45 W
Pop: 558 (1990); 719 (1980)   **Pop Density:** 16.3
Land: 34.3 sq. mi.; **Water:** 0.9 sq. mi.
Incorporated 1869.
Name origin: For a large island in the St. John River.

Hamlin
Plantation
Lat: 47-05-27 N **Long:** 67-52-41 W
Pop: 204 (1990); 340 (1980)   **Pop Density:** 8.8
Land: 23.3 sq. mi.; **Water:** 0.8 sq. mi.
Name origin: For Hannibal Hamlin of ME (1809–1891), U.S. vice president under Abraham Lincoln (1809–65).

Hammond
Plantation
Lat: 46-14-11 N **Long:** 67-57-27 W
Pop: 93 (1990); 73 (1980)   **Pop Density:** 2.4
Land: 38.9 sq. mi.; **Water:** 0.1 sq. mi.
Name origin: Probably for an early settler.

Haynesville
Town
ZIP: 04446   **Lat:** 45-49-03 N **Long:** 67-58-44 W
Pop: 243 (1990); 169 (1980)   **Pop Density:** 5.9
Land: 41.0 sq. mi.; **Water:** 0.5 sq. mi.
Incorporated 1876.
Name origin: Named in 1835 for a local storekeeper, Alvin Haynes.

Hersey
Town
Lat: 46-04-44 N **Long:** 68-22-16 W
Pop: 69 (1990); 67 (1980)   **Pop Density:** 1.7
Land: 39.8 sq. mi.; **Water:** 0.2 sq. mi.
Incorporated 1873.
Name origin: For Gen. Samuel Hersey, 1894 prohibition candidate for governor of ME.

Hodgdon
Town
Lat: 46-03-07 N **Long:** 67-50-52 W
Pop: 1,257 (1990); 1,084 (1980)   **Pop Density:** 31.7
Land: 39.7 sq. mi.; **Water:** 0.1 sq. mi.
Incorporated 1832.
Name origin: For prominent landowner, John Hodgdon.

Houlton
Town
ZIP: 04730   Lat: 46-08-25 N Long: 67-50-38 W
Pop: 6,613 (1990); 6,766 (1980)   Pop Density: 180.2
Land: 36.7 sq. mi.; Water: 0.0 sq. mi.

In northern ME, 22 mi. north of Grand Lake. Incorporated 1831.

Name origin: For Joseph Houlton, a local landowner, who settled in the area c. 1810.

Island Falls
Town
ZIP: 04747   Lat: 45-59-40 N Long: 68-14-13 W
Pop: 897 (1990); 981 (1980)   Pop Density: 25.0
Land: 35.9 sq. mi.; Water: 4.6 sq. mi.

Incorporated 1872.

Name origin: For local topography.

Limestone
Town
ZIP: 04750   Lat: 46-54-25 N Long: 67-51-47 W
Pop: 9,922 (1990); 8,719 (1980)   Pop Density: 245.6
Land: 40.4 sq. mi.; Water: 0.3 sq. mi.

In northeastern ME, 18 mi. north-northeast of Presque Isle. Incorporated 1869.

Name origin: For the town's limestone deposits.

Linneus
Town
Lat: 46-02-58 N Long: 67-58-13 W
Pop: 810 (1990); 752 (1980)   Pop Density: 18.2
Land: 44.6 sq. mi.; Water: 1.3 sq. mi.

Incorporated 1836.

Name origin: Honors Swedish botanist Linnaeus (1707–78), in recognition of the fact that land in the area was granted to Harvard in 1804 to endow a chair in botany.

Littleton
Town
Lat: 46-13-53 N Long: 67-50-37 W
Pop: 956 (1990); 1,009 (1980)   Pop Density: 24.9
Land: 38.4 sq. mi.; Water: 0.2 sq. mi.

Incorporated 1856.

Loring Air Force Base
Military facility
ZIP: 04751   Lat: 46-56-25 N Long: 67-53-41 W
Pop: 7,829 (1990); 6,572 (1980)   Pop Density: 966.5
Land: 8.1 sq. mi.; Water: 0.0 sq. mi.

Ludlow
Town
Lat: 46-09-34 N Long: 67-58-38 W
Pop: 430 (1990); 403 (1980)   Pop Density: 19.5
Land: 22.0 sq. mi.; Water: 0.0 sq. mi.

Incorporated 1864.

Macwahoc
Plantation
Lat: 45-38-28 N Long: 68-14-39 W
Pop: 114 (1990); 126 (1980)   Pop Density: 3.9
Land: 29.3 sq. mi.; Water: 0.2 sq. mi.

Name origin: From Abnaki term meaning 'wet ground.'

Madawaska
Town
ZIP: 04756   Lat: 47-17-41 N Long: 68-15-01 W
Pop: 4,803 (1990); 5,282 (1980)   Pop Density: 86.2
Land: 55.7 sq. mi.; Water: 0.8 sq. mi.

In northern tip of ME, 17 mi. east-northeast of Fort Kent. Incorporated 1869.

Name origin: For the nearby river of the same name; its name is from a Micmac term probably meaning 'having reeds at its outlet.'

Mapleton
Town
ZIP: 04757   Lat: 46-42-03 N Long: 58-06-59 W
Pop: 1,853 (1990); 1,895 (1980)   Pop Density: 54.5
Land: 34.0 sq. mi.; Water: 0.4 sq. mi.

Incorporated 1880.

Name origin: For its maple trees.

Mars Hill
Town
ZIP: 04758   Lat: 46-33-34 N Long: 67-51-07 W
Pop: 1,760 (1990); 1,892 (1980)   Pop Density: 50.1
Land: 35.1 sq. mi.; Water: 0.1 sq. mi.

Named 1790; incorporated 1867.

Name origin: From a verse in the Bible that mentions a Mars Hill where Paul preached, suggested when read by a chaplain to a survey crew working the area.

Masardis
Town
Lat: 46-30-56 N Long: 68-21-52 W
Pop: 305 (1990); 328 (1980)   Pop Density: 7.9
Land: 38.7 sq. mi.; Water: 1.2 sq. mi.

Incorporated 1839.

Name origin: From Abnaki term probably meaning 'place of white clay.'

Merrill
Town
Lat: 46-09-50 N Long: 68-13-58 W
Pop: 296 (1990); 285 (1980)   Pop Density: 7.9
Land: 37.6 sq. mi.; Water: 0.0 sq. mi.

Incorporated 1911.

Name origin: For Capt. William Merrill, a landowner in the region c. 1840.

Monticello
Town
ZIP: 04760   Lat: 46-19-43 N Long: 67-50-51 W
Pop: 872 (1990); 950 (1980)   Pop Density: 22.8
Land: 38.2 sq. mi.; Water: 0.2 sq. mi.

Incorporated 1846.

Name origin: For the Virginia home and estate of Pres. Thomas Jefferson (1743–1826).

Moro
Pop. Place
Lat: 46-09-54 N Long: 68-22-23 W
Pop: 38 (1990); 30 (1980)   Pop Density: 1.1
Land: 35.6 sq. mi.; Water: 1.1 sq. mi.

Nashville
Pop. Place
Lat: 46-41-57 N Long: 68-29-50 W
Pop: 43 (1990); 48 (1980)   Pop Density: 1.2
Land: 35.1 sq. mi.; Water: 0.4 sq. mi.

New Canada
Town
Lat: 47-07-06 N Long: 68-30-16 W
Pop: 253 (1990); 269 (1980)   Pop Density: 7.1
Land: 35.8 sq. mi.; Water: 0.6 sq. mi.

Name origin: For the many French-Canadians settlers; it lies very near the Canadian border.

New Limerick
Town
Lat: 46-07-04 N Long: 67-57-58 W
Pop: 524 (1990); 513 (1980)   Pop Density: 28.3
Land: 18.5 sq. mi.; Water: 1.0 sq. mi.

Incorporated 1837.

Name origin: For Limerick, Ireland, former home of many early settlers.

New Sweden   Town
ZIP: 04762   **Lat:** 46-58-31 N   **Long:** 68-07-00 W
Pop: 715 (1990); 737 (1980)   **Pop Density:** 20.6
Land: 34.7 sq. mi.; **Water:** 0.0 sq. mi.
Incorporated 1895.
Name origin: Named by early Swedish settlers.

Northwest Aroostook
(unorganized)   Pop. Place
         Lat: 46-50-56 N   **Long:** 69-11-56 W
Pop: 45 (1990); 101 (1980)   **Pop Density:** 0.0
Land: 2629.2 sq. mi.; **Water:** 39.7 sq. mi.

Oakfield   Town
ZIP: 04763   **Lat:** 46-04-59 N   **Long:** 68-05-05 W
Pop: 846 (1990); 847 (1980)   **Pop Density:** 24.0
Land: 35.3 sq. mi.; **Water:** 0.8 sq. mi.
Incorporated 1897.
Name origin: Named in 1866 by the oldest resident, James Timonsy, for the nearby oak trees and fields.

Orient   Town
ZIP: 04471   **Lat:** 45-49-24 N   **Long:** 67-51-24 W
Pop: 157 (1990); 97 (1980)   **Pop Density:** 4.4
Land: 35.8 sq. mi.; **Water:** 2.1 sq. mi.
Incorporated 1856.
Name origin: For its location on the eastern boundary of ME with New Brunswick, Canada.

Oxbow   Plantation
         Lat: 46-25-22 N   **Long:** 68-30-42 W
Pop: 69 (1990); 84 (1980)   **Pop Density:** 1.8
Land: 37.8 sq. mi.; **Water:** 0.5 sq. mi.
Incorporated 1870.
Name origin: For its situation near an oxbow on the Aroostook River.

Perham   Town
         Lat: 46-53-00 N   **Long:** 68-15-20 W
Pop: 395 (1990); 437 (1980)   **Pop Density:** 10.8
Land: 36.5 sq. mi.; **Water:** 0.1 sq. mi.
Incorporated 1897.
Name origin: For Sidney Perham, an early governor of ME.

Portage Lake   Town
         Lat: 46-47-16 N   **Long:** 68-29-40 W
Pop: 445 (1990); 562 (1980)   **Pop Density:** 14.5
Land: 30.7 sq. mi.; **Water:** 3.8 sq. mi.
Incorporated 1909. Also called Portage.
Name origin: For the lake; portage is necessary south of the lake to the Aroostook River to eventually reach the Atlantic.

Presque Isle   City
ZIP: 04769   **Lat:** 46-41-09 N   **Long:** 67-59-14 W
Pop: 10,550 (1990); 11,172 (1980)   **Pop Density:** 139.4
Land: 75.7 sq. mi.; **Water:** 1.8 sq. mi.   **Elev:** 446 ft.
In northern ME, 40 mi. north of Houlton. Incorporated as a town 1859; as a city 1939.
Name origin: For a peninsula on the Presque Isle Stream that bisects the city; from a French term meaning 'almost an island.'

Reed   Pop. Place
         Lat: 45-41-43 N   **Long:** 68-07-06 W
Pop: 296 (1990); 274 (1980)   **Pop Density:** 5.0
Land: 59.4 sq. mi.; **Water:** 0.2 sq. mi.

Saint Agatha   Town
         Lat: 47-14-06 N   **Long:** 68-19-11 W
Pop: 919 (1990); 1,035 (1980)   **Pop Density:** 31.2
Land: 29.5 sq. mi.; **Water:** 5.4 sq. mi.
Incorporated 1899.
Name origin: For the local St. Agatha Church.

Saint Francis   Plantation
         Lat: 47-08-50 N   **Long:** 68-53-10 W
Pop: 683 (1990); 839 (1980)   **Pop Density:** 22.9
Land: 29.8 sq. mi.; **Water:** 0.6 sq. mi.
Name origin: Probably for St. Francis of Assisi (c. 1181–1226).

Saint John (Plantation of)   Pop. Place
         Lat: 47-09-03 N   **Long:** 68-45-59 W
Pop: 274 (1990); 322 (1980)   **Pop Density:** 5.4
Land: 50.3 sq. mi.; **Water:** 1.5 sq. mi.

Sherman   Town
         Lat: 45-53-40 N   **Long:** 68-21-33 W
Pop: 1,027 (1990); 1,021 (1980)   **Pop Density:** 25.5
Land: 40.3 sq. mi.; **Water:** 0.5 sq. mi.
Incorporated 1862.
Name origin: For Sen. John Sherman (1823–1900) of OH, noted statesman, financier, and abolitionist.

Smyrna   Town
         Lat: 46-09-55 N   **Long:** 68-05-38 W
Pop: 378 (1990); 354 (1980)   **Pop Density:** 10.7
Land: 35.2 sq. mi.; **Water:** 0.1 sq. mi.
Name origin: For the ancient city of Smyrna, Turkey.

South Aroostook (unorganized)   Pop. Place
         Lat: 45-49-32 N   **Long:** 68-12-49 W
Pop: 404 (1990); 261 (1980)   **Pop Density:** 1.1
Land: 357.3 sq. mi.; **Water:** 11.4 sq. mi.

Square Lake (unorganized)   Pop. Place
         Lat: 46-59-45 N   **Long:** 68-21-25 W
Pop: 564 (1990); 604 (1980)   **Pop Density:** 1.5
Land: 383.2 sq. mi.; **Water:** 31.8 sq. mi.

Stockholm   Town
ZIP: 04783   **Lat:** 47-04-08 N   **Long:** 68-07-26 W
Pop: 286 (1990); 319 (1980)   **Pop Density:** 8.3
Land: 34.6 sq. mi.; **Water:** 0.1 sq. mi.
Incorporated 1911.
Name origin: Named by Swedish immigrants for Stockholm, Sweden.

Van Buren   Town
ZIP: 04785   **Lat:** 47-10-52 N   **Long:** 68-00-23 W
Pop: 3,045 (1990); 3,557 (1980)   **Pop Density:** 89.8
Land: 33.9 sq. mi.; **Water:** 1.2 sq. mi.
Incorporated 1881.
Name origin: For Martin Van Buren (1782–1862), president of the U.S. during the Aroostook War.

Wade   Town
         Lat: 46-47-37 N   **Long:** 68-14-57 W
Pop: 243 (1990); 285 (1980)   **Pop Density:** 6.7
Land: 36.1 sq. mi.; **Water:** 0.3 sq. mi.
Incorporated 1913.

Wallagrass
Town
Lat: 47-08-47 N Long: 68-37-39 W
Pop: 582 (1990); 653 (1980)   Pop Density: 14.6
Land: 39.8 sq. mi.; Water: 0.7 sq. mi.
Name origin: For Wallagrass Lake, to its west; its name is either from an Abnaki term meaning 'shallow' or a Micmac term meaning 'good river.'

Washburn
Town
ZIP: 04786   Lat: 46-47-41 N Long: 68-06-39 W
Pop: 1,880 (1990); 2,028 (1980)   Pop Density: 55.0
Land: 34.2 sq. mi.; Water: 0.7 sq. mi.
Incorporated 1861.
Name origin: For Israel Washburn, one-time governor of ME.

Westfield
Town
ZIP: 04787   Lat: 46-32-53 N Long: 67-58-02 W
Pop: 589 (1990); 647 (1980)   Pop Density: 14.6
Land: 40.3 sq. mi.; Water: 0.0 sq. mi.
Incorporated 1863.
Name origin: For Westfield, MA.

Westmanland
Plantation
Lat: 46-57-59 N Long: 68-14-23 W
Pop: 72 (1990); 53 (1980)   Pop Density: 2.0
Land: 35.7 sq. mi.; Water: 0.9 sq. mi.
Name origin: Named, with anglicization, by Swedish settlers for the Vastmanland district in Sweden.

Weston
Town
Lat: 45-43-22 N Long: 67-51-53 W
Pop: 207 (1990); 155 (1980)   Pop Density: 6.8
Land: 30.5 sq. mi.; Water: 9.9 sq. mi.
Incorporated 1835.
Name origin: For the surveyor who laid out the town in 1835.

Winterville
Plantation
Lat: 46-58-09 N Long: 68-37-49 W
Pop: 217 (1990); 235 (1980)   Pop Density: 6.1
Land: 35.7 sq. mi.; Water: 3.4 sq. mi.
Name origin: Possibly for the severe winters characteristic of the area.

Woodland
Town
Lat: 46-52-39 N Long: 68-06-43 W
Pop: 1,402 (1990); 1,369 (1980)   Pop Density: 39.7
Land: 35.3 sq. mi.; Water: 0.0 sq. mi.
Incorporated 1880.
Name origin: For the woods in the area.

Cumberland County
County Seat: Portland (ZIP: 04101)

Pop: 243,135 (1990); 215,789 (1980)   Pop Density: 291.0
Land: 835.6 sq. mi.; Water: 381.4 sq. mi.   Area Code: 207
In southern ME, south of Lewiston; organized May 28, 1760 (prior to statehood) from York County.
Name origin: For William Augustus, Duke of Cumberland (1721–65), British general and second son of King George II (1683–1760).

Baldwin
Town
Lat: 43-50-28 N Long: 70-42-45 W
Pop: 1,219 (1990); 1,140 (1980)   Pop Density: 34.5
Land: 35.3 sq. mi.; Water: 1.0 sq. mi.
Incorporated 1802.
Name origin: For Loammi Baldwin, an early settler.

Bridgton
Town
ZIP: 04009   Lat: 44-02-21 N Long: 70-44-06 W
Pop: 4,307 (1990); 3,528 (1980)   Pop Density: 75.2
Land: 57.3 sq. mi.; Water: 10.4 sq. mi.
Incorporated 1794.
Name origin: For Moody Bridges, an early landowner.

Brunswick
Town
ZIP: 04011   Lat: 43-53-45 N Long: 69-58-37 W
Pop: 20,906 (1990); 17,366 (1980)   Pop Density: 446.7
Land: 46.8 sq. mi.; Water: 7.9 sq. mi.
In southwestern ME, 23 mi. northeast of Portland. Incorporated 1738.
Name origin: Named by early settlers for the Brunswick area of Germany.

Brunswick Station
Military facility
Lat: 43-53-46 N Long: 69-55-53 W
Pop: 1,829 (1990); 1,533 (1980)   Pop Density: 481.3
Land: 3.8 sq. mi.; Water: 0.0 sq. mi.

Cape Elizabeth
Town
ZIP: 04107   Lat: 43-33-37 N Long: 70-12-38 W
Pop: 8,854 (1990); 7,838 (1980)   Pop Density: 598.2
Land: 14.8 sq. mi.; Water: 43.7 sq. mi.
In western coastal ME, 7 mi. south of Portland. Incorporated 1765.
Name origin: For the cape on the Atlantic below Casco Bay, itself named for Princess Elizabeth, eldest daughter of King James I (1566–1625) of England.

Casco
Town
ZIP: 04015   Lat: 43-57-58 N Long: 70-30-49 W
Pop: 3,018 (1990); 2,243 (1980)   Pop Density: 96.4
Land: 31.3 sq. mi.; Water: 5.2 sq. mi.
In southwestern ME near Sebago Lake. Incorporated 1841.
Name origin: For Casco Bay, itself named from an Algonquian term probably meaning 'muddy' in reference to mud flats along the bay.

Cumberland
Town
ZIP: 04021   Lat: 43-45-21 N Long: 70-11-22 W
Pop: 5,836 (1990); 5,284 (1980)   Pop Density: 223.6
Land: 26.1 sq. mi.; Water: 20.2 sq. mi.

In southwestern coastal ME, 14 mi. north-northwest of Portland. Incorporated 1821.

Name origin: For William Augustus, Duke of Cumberland (1721–65), son of King George II of Great Britain (1683–1760).

Falmouth
Town
ZIP: 04105   Lat: 43-44-24 N Long: 70-16-42 W
Pop: 7,610 (1990); 6,853 (1980)   Pop Density: 257.1
Land: 29.6 sq. mi.; Water: 7.8 sq. mi.

In southwestern coastal ME, 6 mi. north of Portland. Incorporated 1658.

Name origin: For Falmouth, England.

Freeport
Town
ZIP: 04032   Lat: 43-50-39 N Long: 70-06-01 W
Pop: 6,905 (1990); 5,863 (1980)   Pop Density: 199.0
Land: 34.7 sq. mi.; Water: 11.8 sq. mi.

In southwestern coastal ME, 16 mi. north-northeast of Portland. Incorporated 1789.

Name origin: Probably for the accessibility of the town harbor, but perhaps also alluding to Sir Anthony Freeport, a character in a play by Joseph Addison (1672–1719).

Gorham
Town
ZIP: 04038   Lat: 43-41-56 N Long: 70-27-34 W
Pop: 11,856 (1990); 10,101 (1980)   Pop Density: 234.3
Land: 50.6 sq. mi.; Water: 0.6 sq. mi.

In southwestern coastal ME, 10 mi. west of Portland. Incorporated 1764.

Name origin: For Capt. John Gorham, who served in King Philip's War.

Gray
Town
ZIP: 04039   Lat: 43-52-55 N Long: 70-21-21 W
Pop: 5,904 (1990); 4,344 (1980)   Pop Density: 136.4
Land: 43.3 sq. mi.; Water: 2.7 sq. mi.

Incorporated 1778.

Name origin: For Thomas Gray, an early landowner from MA.

Harpswell
Town
ZIP: 04079   Lat: 43-46-23 N Long: 69-58-18 W
Pop: 5,012 (1990); 3,796 (1980)   Pop Density: 207.1
Land: 24.2 sq. mi.; Water: 53.6 sq. mi.

Incorporated 1758.

Name origin: Named by the pioneer Denning family for Harpswell, England.

Harrison
Town
ZIP: 04040   Lat: 44-06-07 N Long: 70-38-07 W
Pop: 1,951 (1990); 1,667 (1980)   Pop Density: 59.1
Land: 33.0 sq. mi.; Water: 0.8 sq. mi.

Incorporated 1805.

Name origin: For Harrison Gray Otis, one of the early landowners.

Little Falls-South Windham
CDP
Lat: 43-44-07 N Long: 70-25-33 W
Pop: 1,715 (1990); 686 (1980)   Pop Density: 635.2
Land: 2.7 sq. mi.; Water: 0.1 sq. mi.

Naples
Town
ZIP: 04055   Lat: 43-58-20 N Long: 70-36-41 W
Pop: 2,860 (1990); 1,833 (1980)   Pop Density: 89.9
Land: 31.8 sq. mi.; Water: 5.4 sq. mi.

Incorporated 1834.

Name origin: For Naples, Italy.

New Gloucester
Town
ZIP: 04260   Lat: 43-57-26 N Long: 70-17-43 W
Pop: 3,916 (1990); 3,180 (1980)   Pop Density: 83.1
Land: 47.1 sq. mi.; Water: 0.7 sq. mi.

Incorporated 1774.

Name origin: For Gloucester, MA, former home of early settlers.

North Windham
CDP
Lat: 43-49-17 N Long: 70-25-47 W
Pop: 4,077 (1990); 5,492 (1980)   Pop Density: 582.4
Land: 7.0 sq. mi.; Water: 0.3 sq. mi.

North Yarmouth
Town
Lat: 43-51-09 N Long: 70-14-07 W
Pop: 2,429 (1990); 1,919 (1980)   Pop Density: 114.6
Land: 21.2 sq. mi.; Water: 0.2 sq. mi.

Incorporated 1680.

Name origin: Named by early settlers to distinguish it from Yarmouth, MA.

Portland
City
ZIP: 04101   Lat: 43-40-01 N Long: 70-12-25 W
Pop: 64,358 (1990); 61,572 (1980)   Pop Density: 2847.7
Land: 22.6 sq. mi.; Water: 40.5 sq. mi.

In southwestern ME, a seaport city on Casco Bay. Founded 1632; incorporated as a town in 1786; as a city in 1832. State capital 1820–32. Largest city in ME, a chief Atlantic coast port, closer to Europe than any other major port in the U.S.; an important industrial and commercial center.

Name origin: For the English city in Dorsetshire. Previously called Machigonne and Falmouth.

Pownal
Town
ZIP: 04069   Lat: 43-53-54 N Long: 70-10-46 W
Pop: 1,262 (1990); 1,189 (1980)   Pop Density: 55.1
Land: 22.9 sq. mi.; Water: 0.0 sq. mi.

Incorporated 1808.

Name origin: For Thomas Pownal, one-time governor of MA.

Raymond
Town
ZIP: 04071   Lat: 43-55-10 N Long: 70-28-01 W
Pop: 3,311 (1990); 2,251 (1980)   Pop Density: 99.4
Land: 33.3 sq. mi.; Water: 13.0 sq. mi.

Incorporated 1804.

Name origin: For Capt. William Raymond, who served in early Indian wars.

Scarborough
Town
ZIP: 04074   Lat: 43-34-54 N Long: 70-21-40 W
Pop: 12,518 (1990); 11,347 (1980)   Pop Density: 262.4
Land: 47.7 sq. mi.; Water: 7.6 sq. mi.

In southwestern ME, 7 mi. south of Portland. Incorporated 1658.

Name origin: For Scarborough, Yorkshire, England.

Sebago
Town
Lat: 43-53-39 N Long: 70-40-10 W
Pop: 1,259 (1990); 974 (1980)   Pop Density: 38.4
Land: 32.8 sq. mi.; Water: 13.3 sq. mi.
Incorporated 1826.
Name origin: For Sebago Lake, to its east; its name is from an Abnaki term probably meaning 'big lake.'

South Portland
City
ZIP: 04106   Lat: 43-37-58 N Long: 70-17-07 W
Pop: 23,163 (1990); 22,712 (1980)   Pop Density: 1946.5
Land: 11.9 sq. mi.; Water: 2.3 sq. mi.
A suburb of Portland, to its southeast.

Standish
Town
ZIP: 04084   Lat: 43-47-29 N Long: 70-34-29 W
Pop: 7,678 (1990); 5,946 (1980)   Pop Density: 127.1
Land: 60.4 sq. mi.; Water: 24.9 sq. mi.
Incorporated 1786.
Name origin: For Miles Standish (1584?–1656), military leader of the Plymouth colony in Massachusetts.

Westbrook
City
ZIP: 04092   Lat: 43-41-38 N Long: 70-21-14 W
Pop: 16,121 (1990); 14,976 (1980)   Pop Density: 953.9
Land: 16.9 sq. mi.; Water: 0.2 sq. mi.
In southwestern ME, 7 mi. west of Portland. Incorporated as town 1814; as city 1889.
Name origin: For Col. Thomas Westbrook.

Windham
Town
ZIP: 04062   Lat: 43-47-50 N Long: 70-24-18 W
Pop: 13,020 (1990); 11,282 (1980)   Pop Density: 278.8
Land: 46.7 sq. mi.; Water: 3.6 sq. mi.
In southwestern ME, 15 mi. northwest of Portland. Incorporated 1762.
Name origin: For Wymondham, Norfolk, England; American spelling reflects the English pronunciation.

Yarmouth
Town
ZIP: 04096   Lat: 43-47-15 N Long: 70-09-37 W
Pop: 7,862 (1990); 6,585 (1980)   Pop Density: 591.1
Land: 13.3 sq. mi.; Water: 9.4 sq. mi.
In southwestern ME, 10 mi. north of Portland. Incorporated 1849.
Name origin: For Yarmouth, England.

Franklin County
County Seat: Farmington (ZIP: 04938)

Pop: 29,008 (1990); 27,447 (1980)   Pop Density: 17.1
Land: 1698.0 sq. mi.; Water: 46.5 sq. mi.   Area Code: 207
On northwestern border of ME, northwest of Augusta; organized Mar 20, 1838 from Cumberland County.
Name origin: For Benjamin Franklin (1706–90), U.S. patriot, diplomat, and statesman.

Avon
Town
Lat: 44-46-08 N Long: 70-18-49 W
Pop: 559 (1990); 475 (1980)   Pop Density: 13.5
Land: 41.3 sq. mi.; Water: 0.2 sq. mi.
Incorporated 1802.
Name origin: For the Avon River in England.

Carrabassett Valley
Town
Lat: 45-03-58 N Long: 70-16-25 W
Pop: 325 (1990); 107 (1980)   Pop Density: 4.2
Land: 77.4 sq. mi.; Water: 0.1 sq. mi.
In western ME.
Name origin: For the valley. Carrabassett is from an Abnaki term probably meaning 'place of small moose' or 'place of sturgeon.'

Carthage
Town
Lat: 44-37-17 N Long: 70-25-14 W
Pop: 458 (1990); 438 (1980)   Pop Density: 13.8
Land: 33.2 sq. mi.; Water: 0.1 sq. mi.
Incorporated 1826.
Name origin: For the ancient city of Carthage in northern Africa.

Chesterville
Town
Lat: 44-33-11 N Long: 70-05-22 W
Pop: 1,012 (1990); 869 (1980)   Pop Density: 27.7
Land: 36.5 sq. mi.; Water: 1.2 sq. mi.
Incorporated 1802.
Name origin: For either Chester, NH, or the hymn "Chester."

Chisholm
CDP
Lat: 44-29-32 N Long: 70-11-35 W
Pop: 1,653 (1990); 1,796 (1980)   Pop Density: 751.4
Land: 2.2 sq. mi.; Water: 0.0 sq. mi.

Coplin
Pop. Place
Lat: 45-05-00 N Long: 70-28-07 W
Pop: 120 (1990); 111 (1980)   Pop Density: 3.6
Land: 33.1 sq. mi.; Water: 0.0 sq. mi.

Dallas
Plantation
Lat: 45-00-11 N Long: 70-34-37 W
Pop: 161 (1990); 146 (1980)   Pop Density: 4.1
Land: 39.0 sq. mi.; Water: 1.4 sq. mi.
In western ME.
Name origin: Probably for George M. Dallas (1792–1864), vice president of the U.S. under James Polk (1845–49).

East Central Franklin (unorganized)
Pop. Place
Lat: 44-58-43 N **Long:** 70-16-46 W
Pop: 459 (1990); 2 (1980) **Pop Density:** 3.6
Land: 128.8 sq. mi.; **Water:** 0.1 sq. mi.

Eustis
Town
ZIP: 04936 **Lat:** 45-10-21 N **Long:** 70-29-22 W
Pop: 616 (1990); 582 (1980) **Pop Density:** 15.8
Land: 39.1 sq. mi.; **Water:** 2.2 sq. mi.
Incorporated 1871.
Name origin: For Charles L. Eustis, who owned part of the township.

Farmington
Town
ZIP: 04938 **Lat:** 44-40-36 N **Long:** 70-08-28 W
Pop: 7,436 (1990); 6,730 (1980) **Pop Density:** 133.3
Land: 55.8 sq. mi.; **Water:** 0.2 sq. mi.
In western ME, 26 mi. west-northwest of Waterville. Incorporated 1794.
Name origin: For the good farming in the region.

Industry
Town
Lat: 44-45-40 N **Long:** 70-03-20 W
Pop: 685 (1990); 563 (1980) **Pop Density:** 22.8
Land: 30.0 sq. mi.; **Water:** 1.2 sq. mi.
Incorporated 1803.
Name origin: Named by the wife of the Rev. J. Thompson for the character of the town's people.

Jay
Town
ZIP: 04239 **Lat:** 44-32-05 N **Long:** 70-13-03 W
Pop: 5,080 (1990); 5,080 (1980) **Pop Density:** 104.7
Land: 48.5 sq. mi.; **Water:** 0.8 sq. mi.
In western ME, 28 mi. north of Lewiston. Incorporated as a town 1795; as a city 1861.
Name origin: For John Jay (1745–1829), first Chief Justice of the U.S.

Kingfield
Town
ZIP: 04947 **Lat:** 45-00-04 N **Long:** 70-10-53 W
Pop: 1,114 (1990); 1,083 (1980) **Pop Density:** 25.7
Land: 43.4 sq. mi.; **Water:** 0.2 sq. mi.
Incorporated 1816.
Name origin: For William King, first governor of ME.

Madrid
Town
Lat: 44-53-50 N **Long:** 70-25-59 W
Pop: 178 (1990); 178 (1980) **Pop Density:** 4.3
Land: 41.7 sq. mi.; **Water:** 0.1 sq. mi.
Incorporated 1836.
Name origin: For Madrid, Spain.

New Sharon
Town
ZIP: 04955 **Lat:** 44-38-27 N **Long:** 70-00-24 W
Pop: 1,175 (1990); 969 (1980) **Pop Density:** 25.5
Land: 46.0 sq. mi.; **Water:** 0.6 sq. mi.
Incorporated 1794.
Name origin: For Sharon, MA, former home of the town's first settlers.

New Vineyard
Town
ZIP: 04956 **Lat:** 44-48-28 N **Long:** 70-07-06 W
Pop: 661 (1990); 607 (1980) **Pop Density:** 18.3
Land: 36.1 sq. mi.; **Water:** 0.5 sq. mi.
Incorporated 1802.
Name origin: For Martha's Vineyard in MA, the former home of settlers.

North Franklin (unorganized)
Pop. Place
Lat: 45-18-54 N **Long:** 70-37-42 W
Pop: 21 (1990); 28 (1980) **Pop Density:** 0.04
Land: 499.4 sq. mi.; **Water:** 8.7 sq. mi.

Phillips
Town
ZIP: 04966 **Lat:** 44-50-25 N **Long:** 70-22-22 W
Pop: 1,148 (1990); 1,092 (1980) **Pop Density:** 22.6
Land: 50.9 sq. mi.; **Water:** 0.2 sq. mi.
Incorporated 1812.
Name origin: For Jonathan Phillips of Boston, an early pioneer.

Rangeley
Town
ZIP: 04970 **Lat:** 44-58-40 N **Long:** 70-43-39 W
Pop: 1,063 (1990); 1,023 (1980) **Pop Density:** 25.6
Land: 41.6 sq. mi.; **Water:** 14.1 sq. mi.
Name origin: For Squire Rangeley of Yorkshire, England, who bought the area in 1825.

*Rangeley
Plantation
Lat: 44-53-41 N **Long:** 70-43-32 W
Pop: 103 (1990); 69 (1980) **Pop Density:** 2.5
Land: 40.7 sq. mi.; **Water:** 6.7 sq. mi.
Incorporated 1855.
Name origin: See Rangeley (Town).

Sandy River
Pop. Place
Lat: 44-53-46 N **Long:** 70-33-26 W
Pop: 64 (1990); 50 (1980) **Pop Density:** 1.9
Land: 34.1 sq. mi.; **Water:** 1.2 sq. mi.

South Franklin (unorganized)
Pop. Place
Lat: 44-40-04 N **Long:** 70-21-06 W
Pop: 56 (1990); 48 (1980) **Pop Density:** 4.5
Land: 12.4 sq. mi.; **Water:** 0.0 sq. mi.

Strong
Town
ZIP: 04983 **Lat:** 44-47-18 N **Long:** 70-12-03 W
Pop: 1,217 (1990); 1,506 (1980) **Pop Density:** 42.7
Land: 28.5 sq. mi.; **Water:** 0.5 sq. mi.
Incorporated 1801.
Name origin: For Caleb Strong, the governor of MA who signed the town's incorporation papers.

Temple
Town
ZIP: 04984 **Lat:** 44-41-50 N **Long:** 70-17-16 W
Pop: 560 (1990); 518 (1980) **Pop Density:** 15.7
Land: 35.6 sq. mi.; **Water:** 0.2 sq. mi.
Incorporated 1803.
Name origin: For Temple, NH, former home of the first settlers.

Weld
Town
ZIP: 04285 **Lat:** 44-41-54 N **Long:** 70-26-59 W
Pop: 430 (1990); 435 (1980) **Pop Density:** 7.2
Land: 59.6 sq. mi.; **Water:** 3.4 sq. mi.
Incorporated 1816.
Name origin: For Benjamin Weld, an early settler and landowner.

West Central Franklin (unorganized)
Pop. Place
Lat: 44-48-34 N **Long:** 70-37-33 W
Pop: 2 (1980)   **Pop Density:** 0.02
Land: 104.0 sq. mi.; **Water:** 0.7 sq. mi.

Wilton
Town
ZIP: 04294   **Lat:** 44-36-58 N **Long:** 70-14-36 W
Pop: 4,242 (1990); 4,382 (1980)   **Pop Density:** 102.7
Land: 41.3 sq. mi.; **Water:** 1.6 sq. mi.
Incorporated 1803.
Name origin: For Wilton, NH, home of Abraham Butterfield,

who offered to pay for the town's incorporaticn if the citizens would name it for him.

Wyman (unorganized)
Pop. Place
Lat: 45-08-15 N **Long:** 70-21-35 W
Pop: 65 (1990); 7 (1980)   **Pop Density:** 3.2
Land: 20.1 sq. mi.; **Water:** 0.1 sq. mi.

Hancock County
County Seat: Ellsworth (ZIP: 04605)

Pop: 46,948 (1990); 41,781 (1980)   **Pop Density:** 29.5
Land: 1589.1 sq. mi.; **Water:** 762.1 sq. mi.   **Area Code:** 207
In eastern ME, on the Atlantic coast; organized Jun 25,1789 (prior to statehood) from Lincoln County.
Name origin: For John Hancock (1737–93), president of the Continental Congress (1775–77), noted signer of the Declaration of Independence, and governor of MA (1780–85; 1787–93).

Amherst
Town
Lat: 44-51-37 N **Long:** 68-24-16 W
Pop: 226 (1990); 203 (1980)   **Pop Density:** 5.8
Land: 39.0 sq. mi.; **Water:** 0.3 sq. mi.
Incorporated 1831.
Name origin: For Amherst, MA.

Aurora
Town
ZIP: 04408   **Lat:** 44-52-10 N **Long:** 68-15-45 W
Pop: 82 (1990); 110 (1980)   **Pop Density:** 2.2
Land: 37.3 sq. mi.; **Water:** 1.5 sq. mi.
In southeastern ME. Incorporated 1831.
Name origin: Named by Rev. Sylvester Williams for the goddess of dawn.

Bar Harbor
Town
ZIP: 04609   **Lat:** 44-22-29 N **Long:** 68-15-36 W
Pop: 4,443 (1990); 4,124 (1980)   **Pop Density:** 105.3
Land: 42.2 sq. mi.; **Water:** 28.2 sq. mi.
In eastern coastal ME on Mount Desert Island. Incorporated 1796.
Name origin: For Bar Island, a narrow strip of land that partly blocks the harbor.

Blue Hill
Town
ZIP: 04614   **Lat:** 44-24-15 N **Long:** 68-34-06 W
Pop: 1,941 (1990); 1,644 (1980)   **Pop Density:** 31.1
Land: 62.5 sq. mi.; **Water:** 24.1 sq. mi.
In east-central coastal ME. Incorporated 1789.
Name origin: For Blue Hill Bay on the Atlantic coast. Its name probably derives from the appearance of the hills on the mainland when viewed from the bay.

Brooklin
Town
ZIP: 04616   **Lat:** 44-15-26 N **Long:** 68-32-40 W
Pop: 785 (1990); 619 (1980)   **Pop Density:** 43.6
Land: 18.0 sq. mi.; **Water:** 23.2 sq. mi.
Incorporated 1849.
Name origin: Descriptive name referring to a brook that is the boundary to adjacent Sedgwick.

Brooksville
Town
ZIP: 04617   **Lat:** 44-21-15 N **Long:** 68-45-39 W
Pop: 760 (1990); 753 (1980)   **Pop Density:** 24.4
Land: 31.1 sq. mi.; **Water:** 19.6 sq. mi.
In east-central coastal ME. Incorporated 1817.
Name origin: For MA governor John Brooks (1752–1825).

Bucksport
Town
ZIP: 04416   **Lat:** 44-38-32 N **Long:** 68-44-55 W
Pop: 4,825 (1990); 4,345 (1980)   **Pop Density:** 93.5
Land: 51.6 sq. mi.; **Water:** 4.9 sq. mi.
In east-central coastal ME on the Penobscot River. Incorporated 1792.
Name origin: For its founder, Col. Jonathan Buck, who built a mill nearby in 1764.

Castine
Town
Lat: 44-24-32 N **Long:** 68-48-55 W
Pop: 1,161 (1990); 1,304 (1980)   **Pop Density:** 150.8
Land: 7.7 sq. mi.; **Water:** 12.2 sq. mi.
In eastern coastal ME, on a promontory enclosing Belfast Bay. Incorporated 1796.
Name origin: For Baron Vincent de St. Castine, an early resident (1667–97).

Central Hancock (unorganized)
Pop. Place
Lat: 44-36-30 N **Long:** 68-21-00 W
Pop: 138 (1990); 124 (1980)   **Pop Density:** 9.1
Land: 15.2 sq. mi.; **Water:** 0.8 sq. mi.

Cranberry Isles
Town
Lat: 44-13-17 N **Long:** 68-12-19 W
Pop: 189 (1990); 198 (1980)   **Pop Density:** 59.1
Land: 3.2 sq. mi.; **Water:** 39.2 sq. mi.
On a small island just south of Mt. Desert Island, eastern coastal ME. Incorporated 1830.
Name origin: For its numerous cranberry patches.

Dedham
Town
Lat: 44-41-14 N **Long:** 68-35-14 W
Pop: 1,229 (1990); 841 (1980)   **Pop Density:** 31.3
Land: 39.3 sq. mi.; **Water:** 5.0 sq. mi.
Incorporated 1837.
Name origin: For Dedham, MA, former home of Reubon Gregg, an early settler.

Deer Isle
Town
ZIP: 04627   **Lat:** 44-13-43 N **Long:** 68-42-45 W
Pop: 1,829 (1990); 1,492 (1980)   **Pop Density:** 59.2
Land: 30.9 sq. mi.; **Water:** 92.8 sq. mi.
Incorporated 1789.
Name origin: For the area's once large deer population.

Eastbrook
Town
Lat: 44-41-29 N **Long:** 68-13-52 W
Pop: 289 (1990); 262 (1980)   **Pop Density:** 8.7
Land: 33.3 sq. mi.; **Water:** 4.3 sq. mi.
Incorporated 1837.
Name origin: For the fact that drainage of the southern half of the town flows into the East Branch Union River.

East Hancock (unorganized)
Pop. Place
Lat: 44-56-56 N **Long:** 68-08-32 W
Pop: 40 (1990); 44 (1980)   **Pop Density:** 0.1
Land: 444.4 sq. mi.; **Water:** 36.9 sq. mi.

Ellsworth
City
ZIP: 04605   **Lat:** 44-35-08 N **Long:** 68-29-46 W
Pop: 5,975 (1990); 5,179 (1980)   **Pop Density:** 75.3
Land: 79.3 sq. mi.; **Water:** 14.6 sq. mi.
In southeastern ME, 27 mi. southeast of Bangor. Incorporated as town 1800; as city 1869.
Name origin: For Oliver Ellsworth, a delegate to the Constitutional Convention from MA.

Franklin
Town
ZIP: 04634   **Lat:** 44-36-09 N **Long:** 68-14-00 W
Pop: 1,141 (1990); 979 (1980)   **Pop Density:** 31.3
Land: 36.5 sq. mi.; **Water:** 5.0 sq. mi.
Incorporated 1825.
Name origin: For Benjamin Franklin (1706–90), American patriot and statesman.

Frenchboro
Town
ZIP: 04635   **Lat:** 44-07-41 N **Long:** 68-15-47 W
Pop: 44 (1990); 43 (1980)   **Pop Density:** 9.2
Land: 4.8 sq. mi.; **Water:** 89.7 sq. mi.
On Long Island, a small island off the Maine coast south of Mt. Desert Island.
Name origin: Probably for early French explorers or settlers.

Gouldsboro
Town
ZIP: 04607   **Lat:** 44-25-37 N **Long:** 68-02-32 W
Pop: 1,986 (1990); 1,574 (1980)   **Pop Density:** 43.1
Land: 46.1 sq. mi.; **Water:** 54.7 sq. mi.
Incorporated 1789.

Great Pond
Plantation
Lat: 44-57-50 N **Long:** 68-18-43 W
Pop: 59 (1990); 45 (1980)   **Pop Density:** 1.6
Land: 36.9 sq. mi.; **Water:** 2.1 sq. mi.
In southeastern coastal ME.
Name origin: For Great Pond, within the borders of the plantation.

Hancock
Town
ZIP: 04640   **Lat:** 44-31-28 N **Long:** 68-17-00 W
Pop: 1,757 (1990); 1,409 (1980)   **Pop Density:** 58.6
Land: 30.0 sq. mi.; **Water:** 8.8 sq. mi.
Incorporated 1828.
Name origin: For John Hancock (1737–93), a governor of MA and noted signer of the Declaration of Independence.

Lamoine
Town
Lat: 44-29-22 N **Long:** 68-18-34 W
Pop: 1,311 (1990); 953 (1980)   **Pop Density:** 73.2
Land: 17.9 sq. mi.; **Water:** 7.2 sq. mi.
Incorporated 1870.
Name origin: For an early French settler named DeLamoine.

Mariaville
Town
Lat: 44-44-47 N **Long:** 68-23-22 W
Pop: 270 (1990); 168 (1980)   **Pop Density:** 6.9
Land: 39.0 sq. mi.; **Water:** 8.2 sq. mi.
Incorporated 1836.
Name origin: For Maria Matilda, the daughter of land baron William Bingham.

Mount Desert
Town
ZIP: 04660   **Lat:** 44-19-58 N **Long:** 68-19-41 W
Pop: 1,899 (1990); 2,063 (1980)   **Pop Density:** 51.5
Land: 36.9 sq. mi.; **Water:** 18.3 sq. mi.
Incorporated 1789.
Name origin: For the island; it was named 'island of bare mountains' in 1604 by French explorer Samuel de Champlain (c. 1567–1635) for its several treeless low peaks visible for some distance at sea.

Orland
Town
ZIP: 04472   **Lat:** 44-34-33 N **Long:** 68-40-04 W
Pop: 1,805 (1990); 1,645 (1980)   **Pop Density:** 38.5
Land: 46.9 sq. mi.; **Water:** 5.6 sq. mi.
Incorporated 1800.
Name origin: Supposedly named by settler Joseph Gross in 1764 for the oar he found on the banks of a nearby river.

Osborn
Town
Lat: 44-46-01 N **Long:** 68-14-48 W
Pop: 72 (1990); 47 (1980)   **Pop Density:** 2.0
Land: 35.6 sq. mi.; **Water:** 2.8 sq. mi.

Otis
Town
Lat: 44-42-26 N **Long:** 68-28-04 W
Pop: 355 (1990); 307 (1980)   **Pop Density:** 14.3
Land: 24.9 sq. mi.; **Water:** 3.8 sq. mi.
Incorporated 1835.

Penobscot
Town
ZIP: 04476   **Lat:** 44-28-46 N **Long:** 68-43-15 W
Pop: 1,131 (1990); 1,104 (1980)   **Pop Density:** 28.3
Land: 40.0 sq. mi.; **Water:** 6.9 sq. mi.
Incorporated 1787.
Name origin: For the river. The town is at the mouth of the Penobscot.

Sedgwick Town
ZIP: 04676 Lat: 44-19-43 N Long: 68-39-13 W
Pop: 905 (1990); 795 (1980) Pop Density: 33.5
Land: 27.0 sq. mi.; Water: 4.5 sq. mi.
Incorporated 1788.
Name origin: For Maj. Robert Sedgwick of Charlestown, MA, a soldier in the French and Indian Wars.

Sorrento Town
ZIP: 04677 Lat: 44-28-23 N Long: 68-10-52 W
Pop: 295 (1990); 276 (1980) Pop Density: 73.8
Land: 4.0 sq. mi.; Water: 10.9 sq. mi.
Incorporated 1895.
Name origin: Either for Sorrento, near Naples, Italy, or for a Mr. Soren who founded a summer resort.

Southwest Harbor Town
ZIP: 04656 Lat: 44-15-40 N Long: 68-19-05 W
Pop: 1,952 (1990); 1,855 (1980) Pop Density: 144.6
Land: 13.5 sq. mi.; Water: 9.1 sq. mi.
Incorporated 1905.
Name origin: For its location relative to the other harbors on Mt. Desert Island.

Stonington Town
ZIP: 04681 Lat: 44-09-33 N Long: 68-38-34 W
Pop: 1,252 (1990); 1,273 (1980) Pop Density: 127.8
Land: 9.8 sq. mi.; Water: 28.0 sq. mi.
Incorporated 1897.
Name origin: For the area's good granite quarries.

Sullivan Town
Lat: 44-32-08 N Long: 68-08-44 W
Pop: 1,118 (1990); 967 (1980) Pop Density: 42.0
Land: 26.6 sq. mi.; Water: 3.0 sq. mi.
Incorporated 1789.
Name origin: For Daniel Sullivan, an early settler.

Surry Town
ZIP: 04684 Lat: 44-29-38 N Long: 68-30-49 W
Pop: 1,004 (1990); 894 (1980) Pop Density: 27.0
Land: 37.2 sq. mi.; Water: 14.1 sq. mi.
Incorporated 1803.
Name origin: For Surry, England.

Swans Island Town
Lat: 44-06-32 N Long 68-28-03 W
Pop: 348 (1990); 337 (1980) Pop Density: 24.9
Land: 14.0 sq. mi.; Water: 68.4 sq. mi.
South of Mt. Desert Island, protecting Blue Hill Bay. Incorporated 1897.
Name origin: For Englishman James Swan, an 18th-century land speculator in ME.

Tremont Town
Lat: 44-16-00 N Long 68-24-58 W
Pop: 1,324 (1990); 1,222 (1980) Pop Density: 78.3
Land: 16.9 sq. mi.; Water: 35.5 sq. mi.
Incorporated 1848.
Name origin: For the tree-covered mountains in the area.

Trenton Town
Lat: 44-26-01 N Long: 68-23-46 W
Pop: 1,060 (1990); 718 (1980) Pop Density: 58.2
Land: 18.2 sq. mi.; Water: 10.3 sq. mi.
Incorporated 1789.
Name origin: For the Battle of Trenton fought during the Revolutionary War.

Verona Town
Lat: 44-31-36 N Long: 68-46-40 W
Pop: 515 (1990); 559 (1980) Pop Density: 83.1
Land: 6.2 sq. mi.; Water: 2.5 sq. mi.
Incorporated 1861.
Name origin: For Verona, Italy.

Waltham Town
Lat: 44-41-26 N Long: 68-20-07 W
Pop: 276 (1990); 186 (1980) Pop Density: 9.3
Land: 29.7 sq. mi.; Water: 3.3 sq. mi.
Incorporated 1833.
Name origin: For Waltham, MA.

Winter Harbor Town
ZIP: 04693 Lat: 44-20-33 N Long: 68-04-13 W
Pop: 1,157 (1990); 1,120 (1980) Pop Density: 80.3
Land: 14.4 sq. mi.; Water: 51.3 sq. mi.
Incorporated 1895.
Name origin: For the harbor, which does not freeze in the winter.

Kennebec County
County Seat: Augusta (ZIP: 04330)

Pop: 115,904 (1990); 109,889 (1980) Pop Density: 133.6
Land: 867.5 sq. mi.; Water: 83.8 sq. mi. Area Code: 207
In south-central ME, southwest of Bangor; organized Feb 20, 1799 (prior to statehood) from Lincoln County.
Name origin: For part of the Kennebec River; from an Abnaki Indian word probably meaning 'long, quiet water.'

Albion Town
ZIP: 04910 Lat: 44-30-48 N Long: 69-26-07 W
Pop: 1,736 (1990); 1,551 (1980) Pop Density: 44.6
Land: 38.9 sq. mi.; Water: 0.6 sq. mi.
Incorporated 1804.
Name origin: For Britain's literary name.

Augusta City
ZIP: 04330 Lat: 44-19-50 N Long: 69-43-46 W
Pop: 21,325 (1990); 21,819 (1980) Pop Density: 384.9
Land: 55.4 sq. mi.; Water: 2.9 sq. mi.
In southwestern ME on the Kennebec River, 25 mi. north-

east of Lewiston. Incorporated as a town in 1797; as a city in 1849; became state capital 1831.

Name origin: For Pamela Augusta Dearborn, the daughter of Revolutionary War general, Harry Dearborn.

Belgrade   Town
ZIP: 04917   **Lat:** 44-29-17 N **Long:** 69-50-56 W
Pop: 2,375 (1990); 2,043 (1980)   **Pop Density:** 54.8
Land: 43.3 sq. mi.; **Water:** 14.7 sq. mi.

Incorporated 1796.

Name origin: For Belgrade, Yugoslavia.

Benton   Town
              Lat: 44-35-27 N **Long:** 69-31-05 W
Pop: 2,312 (1990); 2,188 (1980)   **Pop Density:** 81.4
Land: 28.4 sq. mi.; **Water:** 0.6 sq. mi.

Incorporated 1842.

Name origin: For Thomas Hart Benton (1782–1858), a prominent Democrat and congressman.

Chelsea   Town
              Lat: 44-15-41 N **Long:** 69-43-09 W
Pop: 2,497 (1990); 2,522 (1980)   **Pop Density:** 127.4
Land: 19.6 sq. mi.; **Water:** 0.4 sq. mi.

In south-central ME, 5 mi. south of Augusta. Incorporated 1850.

Name origin: For Chelsea, MA.

China   Town
              Lat: 44-24-48 N **Long:** 69-32-09 W
Pop: 3,713 (1990); 2,918 (1980)   **Pop Density:** 74.4
Land: 49.9 sq. mi.; **Water:** 6.9 sq. mi.

Incorporated 1796.

Name origin: Named in 1818 for a hymn popular with the townspeople.

Clinton   Town
ZIP: 04927   **Lat:** 44-39-33 N **Long:** 69-31-51 W
Pop: 3,332 (1990); 2,696 (1980)   **Pop Density:** 75.9
Land: 43.9 sq. mi.; **Water:** 0.9 sq. mi.

Incorporated 1795.

Name origin: For DeWitt Clinton (1769–1828), NY statesman and promoter of the Erie Canal.

Farmingdale   Town
              Lat: 44-15-27 N **Long:** 69-49-39 W
Pop: 2,918 (1990); 2,535 (1980)   **Pop Density:** 258.2
Land: 11.3 sq. mi.; **Water:** 0.4 sq. mi.

Incorporated 1852.

Name origin: For the many farms in the vicinity.

Fayette   Town
              Lat: 44-26-23 N **Long:** 70-03-47 W
Pop: 855 (1990); 812 (1980)   **Pop Density:** 29.4
Land: 29.1 sq. mi.; **Water:** 2.9 sq. mi.

Incorporated 1795.

Name origin: For the Marquis de Lafayette (1757–1834), French soldier and Revolutionary War hero.

Gardiner   City
ZIP: 04345   **Lat:** 44-11-26 N **Long:** 69-47-21 W
Pop: 6,746 (1990); 6,485 (1980)   **Pop Density:** 429.7
Land: 15.7 sq. mi.; **Water:** 0.9 sq. mi.   **Elev:** 122 ft.

In southwestern ME, 8 mi. south of Augusta. Incorporated as a town 1803; as a city 1850.

Name origin: For an early landowner, Dr. Sylvester Gardiner.

Hallowell   City
ZIP: 04347   **Lat:** 44-17-38 N **Long:** 69-48-52 W
Pop: 2,534 (1990); 2,502 (1980)   **Pop Density:** 429.5
Land: 5.9 sq. mi.; **Water:** 0.2 sq. mi.

Incorporated as a town 1771; as a city 1850.

Name origin: For Benjamin Hallowell, a prominent landowner, who received large tracts in the Kennebec patent.

Litchfield   Town
ZIP: 04350   **Lat:** 44-09-28 N **Long:** 69-56-23 W
Pop: 2,650 (1990); 1,954 (1980)   **Pop Density:** 70.9
Land: 37.4 sq. mi.; **Water:** 2.3 sq. mi.

Incorporated 1795.

Name origin: For the town in England.

Manchester   Town
ZIP: 04351   **Lat:** 44-19-31 N **Long:** 69-51-29 W
Pop: 2,099 (1990); 1,949 (1980)   **Pop Density:** 99.5
Land: 21.1 sq. mi.; **Water:** 1.2 sq. mi.

Incorporated 1850.

Name origin: For Manchester, MA, former home of the town's first settlers.

Monmouth   Town
ZIP: 04259   **Lat:** 44-14-20 N **Long:** 70-00-44 W
Pop: 3,353 (1990); 2,888 (1980)   **Pop Density:** 98.3
Land: 34.1 sq. mi.; **Water:** 4.9 sq. mi.

Incorporated 1792.

Name origin: Named by Gen. Henry Dearborn (1751–1829) for the Battle of Monmouth in the Revolutionary War.

Mount Vernon   Town
ZIP: 04352   **Lat:** 44-27-57 N **Long:** 69-57-40 W
Pop: 1,362 (1990); 1,021 (1980)   **Pop Density:** 35.9
Land: 37.9 sq. mi.; **Water:** 4.9 sq. mi.

Incorporated 1792.

Name origin: For the Virginia estate of Pres. George Washington (1732–99).

Oakland   Town
ZIP: 04963   **Lat:** 44-33-36 N **Long:** 69-43-49 W
Pop: 5,595 (1990); 5,162 (1980)   **Pop Density:** 217.7
Land: 25.7 sq. mi.; **Water:** 2.5 sq. mi.

In southwestern ME, 5 mi. west of Waterville. Incorporated 1873.

Name origin: For the area's oak trees.

Pittston   Town
              Lat: 44-10-52 N **Long:** 69-42-06 W
Pop: 2,444 (1990); 2,267 (1980)   **Pop Density:** 75.9
Land: 32.2 sq. mi.; **Water:** 1.2 sq. mi.

Incorporated 1779.

Name origin: For the family of John Pitt, who were instrumental in settling the area.

Randolph   Town
              Lat: 44-14-09 N **Long:** 69-45-08 W
Pop: 1,949 (1990); 1,834 (1980)   **Pop Density:** 928.1
Land: 2.1 sq. mi.; **Water:** 0.1 sq. mi.

Incorporated 1887.

Name origin: For Randolph, MA.

Readfield
Town
ZIP: 04355   **Lat:** 44-22-55 N   **Long:** 69-57-05 W
Pop: 2,033 (1990); 1,943 (1980)   **Pop Density:** 69.6
Land: 29.2 sq. mi.; **Water:** 1.9 sq. mi.
Incorporated 1791.
Name origin: Supposedly for Peter Norton, who was an avid reader.

Rome
Town
       Lat: 44-34-18 N   **Long:** 69-53-05 W
Pop: 758 (1990); 627 (1980)   **Pop Density:** 29.8
Land: 25.4 sq. mi.; **Water:** 6.3 sq. mi.
Incorporated 1804.
Name origin: For Rome, Italy.

Sidney
Town
       Lat: 44-26-29 N   **Long:** 69-45-20 W
Pop: 2,593 (1990); 2,052 (1980)   **Pop Density:** 61.4
Land: 42.2 sq. mi.; **Water:** 3.3 sq. mi.
Incorporated 1792.
Name origin: For English author Sir Philip Sidney (1554–86).

Unity (unorganized)
Pop. Place
       Lat: 44-37-44 N   **Long:** 69-25-44 W
Pop: 36 (1990); 37 (1980)   **Pop Density:** 3.5
Land: 10.4 sq. mi.; **Water:** 0.0 sq. mi.

Vassalborough
Town
ZIP: 04989   **Lat:** 44-25-38 N   **Long:** 69-39-01 W
Pop: 3,679 (1990); 3,410 (1980)   **Pop Density:** 83.0
Land: 44.3 sq. mi.; **Water:** 3.5 sq. mi.
Incorporated 1771.
Name origin: Either for Florentine Vassall of London, an original proprietor of the Plymouth colony, or for William Vassal, a prominent MA citizen.

Vienna
Town
ZIP: 04360   **Lat:** 44-33-16 N   **Long:** 70-00-08 W
Pop: 417 (1990); 454 (1980)   **Pop Density:** 17.2
Land: 24.2 sq. mi.; **Water:** 1.2 sq. mi.
Incorporated 1802.
Name origin: For Vienna, Austria.

Waterville
City
ZIP: 04901   **Lat:** 44-32-44 N   **Long:** 69-39-40 W
Pop: 17,173 (1990); 17,779 (1980)   **Pop Density:** 1262.7
Land: 13.6 sq. mi.; **Water:** 0.5 sq. mi.
In southwestern ME on the Kennebec River, 18 mi. north of Augusta. Incorporated as a town in 1802; as a city in 1883.
Name origin: For the city's location on the Kennebec River.

Wayne
Town
ZIP: 04284   **Lat:** 44-20-36 N   **Long:** 70-04-07 W
Pop: 1,029 (1990); 680 (1980)   **Pop Density:** 53.3
Land: 19.3 sq. mi.; **Water:** 6.4 sq. mi.
Incorporated 1798.
Name origin: For Gen. "Mad Anthony" Wayne (1745–96), a Revolutionary War hero.

West Gardiner
Town
       Lat: 44-13-25 N   **Long:** 69-52-30 W
Pop: 2,531 (1990); 2,113 (1980)   **Pop Density:** 102.9
Land: 24.6 sq. mi.; **Water:** 2.4 sq. mi.
Incorporated 1850.
Name origin: For its location due west of the city of Gardiner.

Windsor
Town
ZIP: 04363   **Lat:** 44-19-01 N   **Long:** 69-34-22 W
Pop: 1,895 (1990); 1,702 (1980)   **Pop Density:** 54.6
Land: 34.7 sq. mi.; **Water:** 0.9 sq. mi.
Incorporated 1809.
Name origin: For the English royal house.

Winslow
Town
ZIP: 04901   **Lat:** 44-31-23 N   **Long:** 69-34-45 W
Pop: 7,997 (1990); 8,057 (1980)   **Pop Density:** 216.7
Land: 36.9 sq. mi.; **Water:** 1.9 sq. mi.
In southwestern ME, a suburb southeast of Waterville. Incorporated 1771.
Name origin: For Gen. John Winslow, who helped construct Fort Halifax.

Winthrop
Town
ZIP: 04364   **Lat:** 44-19-03 N   **Long:** 69-57-50 W
Pop: 5,968 (1990); 5,889 (1980)   **Pop Density:** 191.9
Land: 31.1 sq. mi.; **Water:** 6.9 sq. mi.
In southwestern ME, 10 mi. west of Augusta. Incorporated 1771.
Name origin: For John Winthrop (1588–1649), first colonial governor of MA.

Knox County
County Seat: Rockland (ZIP: 04841)

Pop: 36,310 (1990); 32,941 (1980)   **Pop Density:** 99.3
Land: 365.6 sq. mi.; **Water:** 776.5 sq. mi.   **Area Code:** 207
On Atlantic coast of ME, east of Augusta; organized Mar 9, 1860 from Lincoln and Waldo counties.
Name origin: For Gen. Henry Knox (1750–1806), officer in the Revolutionary War, and first U.S. secretary of war (1785–95).

Appleton   Town
          Lat: 44-18-03 N **Long:** 69-15-47 W
Pop: 1,069 (1990); 818 (1980)   **Pop Density:** 32.7
Land: 32.7 sq. mi.; **Water:** 0.8 sq. mi.
Incorporated 1829.
Name origin: For Samuel Appleton, an early settler.

Camden   Town
ZIP: 04843   **Lat:** 44-13-34 N **Long:** 69-04-46 W
Pop: 5,060 (1990); 4,584 (1980)   **Pop Density:** 284.3
Land: 17.8 sq. mi.; **Water:** 7.5 sq. mi.
Incorporated 1791.
Name origin: For Charles Pratt (1714–94), Earl of Camden.

Criehaven (unorganized)   Pop. Place
          Lat: 43-48-09 N **Long:** 68-53-36 W
Pop: 5 (1980)   **Pop Density:** 7.1
Land: 0.7 sq. mi.; **Water:** 131.1 sq. mi.

Cushing   Town
ZIP: 04563   **Lat:** 44-00-36 N **Long:** 69-15-32 W
Pop: 988 (1990); 795 (1980)   **Pop Density:** 50.9
Land: 19.4 sq. mi.; **Water:** 6.7 sq. mi.
Incorporated 1789.
Name origin: For Thomas Cushing, one-time lieutenant governor of MA.

Friendship   Town
ZIP: 04547   **Lat:** 43-58-09 N **Long:** 69-20-40 W
Pop: 1,099 (1990); 1,000 (1980)   **Pop Density:** 78.5
Land: 14.0 sq. mi.; **Water:** 17.0 sq. mi.
Incorporated 1807.
Name origin: For the friendliness of the town's citizens.

Hope   Town
          Lat: 44-15-19 N **Long:** 69-11-18 W
Pop: 1,017 (1990); 730 (1980)   **Pop Density:** 46.4
Land: 21.9 sq. mi.; **Water:** 2.0 sq. mi.
Incorporated 1804.
Name origin: For its perception as a "land of hope," considered so by early settlers.

Isle au Haut   Town
          Lat: 44-00-32 N **Long:** 68-34-26 W
Pop: 46 (1990); 57 (1980)   **Pop Density:** 3.6
Land: 12.7 sq. mi.; **Water:** 96.9 sq. mi.
On the island of the same name off the ME coast near Penobscot Bay. Incorporated 1874.
Name origin: Named by French explorer Samuel de Champlain (c. 1567–1635) from the French term meaning 'high island.'

Matinicus Isle   Plantation
          Lat: 43-53-18 N **Long:** 68-54-12 W
Pop: 67 (1990); 66 (1980)   **Pop Density:** 41.9
Land: 1.6 sq. mi.; **Water:** 104.9 sq. mi.
On Matinicus Island off the coast of ME.

North Haven   Town
ZIP: 04853   **Lat:** 44-09-33 N **Long:** 68-53-29 W
Pop: 332 (1990); 373 (1980)   **Pop Density:** 28.6
Land: 11.6 sq. mi.; **Water:** 70.9 sq. mi.
Incorporated 1846.
Name origin: Descriptively named by the early settlers.

Owls Head   Town
ZIP: 04854   **Lat:** 44-04-09 N **Long:** 69-04-19 W
Pop: 1,574 (1990); 1,633 (1980)   **Pop Density:** 176.9
Land: 8.9 sq. mi.; **Water:** 10.7 sq. mi.
Incorporated 1921.
Name origin: Named 1759 by MA Gov. Thomas Pownall (1722–1805) for the shape of the promontory at the southern end of Penobscot Bay, where the town is situated.

Rockland   City
ZIP: 04841   **Lat:** 44-07-24 N **Long:** 69-07-52 W
Pop: 7,972 (1990); 7,919 (1980)   **Pop Density:** 618.0
Land: 12.9 sq. mi.; **Water:** 2.2 sq. mi.   **Elev:** 35 ft.
In southern ME, 37 mi. east-southeast of Augusta. Incorporated as a town in 1848; as a city in 1853.
Name origin: For its limestone quarries.

Rockport   Town
ZIP: 04856   **Lat:** 44-10-10 N **Long:** 69-05-35 W
Pop: 2,854 (1990); 2,749 (1980)   **Pop Density:** 128.6
Land: 22.2 sq. mi.; **Water:** 12.4 sq. mi.
Incorporated 1891.
Name origin: For the port's rocky terrain.

Saint George   Town
          Lat: 43-54-32 N **Long:** 69-14-01 W
Pop: 2,261 (1990); 1,948 (1980)   **Pop Density:** 90.1
Land: 25.1 sq. mi.; **Water:** 132.9 sq. mi.
Incorporated 1803.
Name origin: Named in 1605 by English captain George Weymouth for St. George, the patron saint of England.

South Thomaston   Town
ZIP: 04858   **Lat:** 44-02-16 N **Long:** 69-08-06 W
Pop: 1,227 (1990); 1,064 (1980)   **Pop Density:** 107.6
Land: 11.4 sq. mi.; **Water:** 6.5 sq. mi.
Two miles southeast of Thomaston. Incorporated 1848.

Thomaston
ZIP: 04861   **Lat:** 44-05-34 N   **Long:** 69-10-23 W
Pop: 3,306 (1990); 2,900 (1980)   **Pop Density:** 303.3
Land: 10.9 sq. mi.; **Water:** 0.6 sq. mi.

Incorporated 1777.

Name origin: For Maj. Gen. Jon Thomas, an officer in the Revolutionary War.

Union
ZIP: 04862   **Lat:** 44-13-03 N   **Long:** 69-17-20 W
Pop: 1,989 (1990); 1,569 (1980)   **Pop Density:** 62.0
Land: 32.1 sq. mi.; **Water:** 2.4 sq. mi.

Incorporated 1786.

Name origin: For the political union formed to incorporate the town.

Vinalhaven
ZIP: 04863   **Lat:** 44-02-01 N   **Long:** 68-54-09 W
Pop: 1,072 (1990); 1,211 (1980)   **Pop Density:** 42.4
Land: 25.3 sq. mi.; **Water:** 167.5 sq. mi.

On the island of the same name in Penobscot Bay. Incorporated 1789.

Name origin: For John Vinal, a Boston merchant who assisted the first settlers in getting clear title to the land.

Warren
ZIP: 04864   **Lat:** 44-07-44 N   **Long:** 69-14-48 W
Pop: 3,192 (1990); 2,566 (1980)   **Pop Density:** 68.9
Land: 46.3 sq. mi.; **Water:** 2.3 sq. mi.

Incorporated 1776.

Name origin: For Gen. Joseph Warren (1741–75), who fell in the Battle of Bunker Hill.

Washington
ZIP: 04574   **Lat:** 44-16-31 N   **Long:** 69-23-32 W
Pop: 1,185 (1990); 954 (1980)   **Pop Density:** 31.2
Land: 38.0 sq. mi.; **Water:** 1.2 sq. mi.

Incorporated 1811.

Name origin: For Gen. George Washington.

Lincoln County
County Seat: Wiscasset (ZIP: 04578)

Pop: 30,357 (1990); 25,691 (1980)   **Pop Density:** 66.6
Land: 455.6 sq. mi.; **Water:** 244.4 sq. mi.   **Area Code:** 207

On Atlantic coast of ME, south of Augusta; organized May 28, 1760 (prior to statehood) from York County.

Name origin: For either Enoch Lincoln (1788–1829), governor of ME (1827–29), or for Gen. Benjamin Lincoln (1733–1810), officer in the Revolutionary War, U.S. secretary of war (1781–83), and lt. gov. of MA (1788).

Alna
ZIP: 04535   **Lat:** 44-05-22 N   **Long:** 69-38-35 W
Pop: 571 (1990); 425 (1980)   **Pop Density:** 27.3
Land: 20.9 sq. mi.; **Water:** 0.5 sq. mi.

Incorporated 1794.

Name origin: From *alnus,* the Latin term meaning 'alder tree.'

Boothbay
ZIP: 04537   **Lat:** 43-50-30 N   **Long:** 69-36-24 W
Pop: 2,648 (1990); 2,308 (1980)   **Pop Density:** 119.8
Land: 22.1 sq. mi.; **Water:** 24.0 sq. mi.

Incorporated 1764.

Name origin: Named in 1764 for the bay, which was supposedly named after a local agent, testifying before a legislative committee in charge of names, described the bay as "snug as a booth."

Boothbay Harbor
           Lat: 43-50-58 N   **Long:** 69-38-03 W
Pop: 2,347 (1990); 2,207 (1980)   **Pop Density:** 404.7
Land: 5.8 sq. mi.; **Water:** 3.5 sq. mi.

Incorporated 1889.

Name origin: See Boothbay.

Bremen
           Lat: 43-58-07 N   **Long:** 69-25-29 W
Pop: 674 (1990); 598 (1980)   **Pop Density:** 37.2
Land: 18.1 sq. mi.; **Water:** 24.8 sq. mi.

Incorporated 1828.

Name origin: For Bremen, Germany.

Bristol
ZIP: 04539   **Lat:** 43-55-17 N   **Long:** 69-29-35 W
Pop: 2,326 (1990); 2,095 (1980)   **Pop Density:** 68.6
Land: 33.9 sq. mi.; **Water:** 13.1 sq. mi.

Incorporated 1765.

Name origin: For Bristol, England, reflecting the origin of many early settlers.

Damariscotta
ZIP: 04543   **Lat:** 44-01-53 N   **Long:** 69-29-46 W
Pop: 1,811 (1990); 1,493 (1980)   **Pop Density:** 146.0
Land: 12.4 sq. mi.; **Water:** 2.2 sq. mi.

Incorporated 1847.

Name origin: From Abnaki term probably meaning 'plenty of fish.'

Dresden
ZIP: 04342   **Lat:** 44-04-44 N **Long:** 69-44-22 W   Town
Pop: 1,332 (1990); 998 (1980)   **Pop Density:** 44.3
Land: 30.1 sq. mi.; **Water:** 3.0 sq. mi.
Incorporated 1794.
Name origin: For the city in Germany.

Edgecomb
Lat: 43-58-21 N **Long:** 69-37-06 W   Town
Pop: 993 (1990); 841 (1980)   **Pop Density:** 54.9
Land: 18.1 sq. mi.; **Water:** 2.7 sq. mi.
Incorporated 1774.
Name origin: For Lord Edgecomb, a friend of the American colonies before the Revolutionary War.

Hibberts Gore
Lat: 44-19-30 N **Long:** 69-25-38 W   Pop. Place
Pop: 1 (1990); 2 (1980)   **Pop Density:** 1.3
Land: 0.8 sq. mi.; **Water:** 0.0 sq. mi.

Jefferson
ZIP: 04348   **Lat:** 44-11-16 N **Long:** 69-30-26 W   Town
Pop: 2,111 (1990); 1,616 (1980)   **Pop Density:** 40.1
Land: 52.7 sq. mi.; **Water:** 6.0 sq. mi.
Incorporated 1807.
Name origin: For Thomas Jefferson (1743–1826), third president of the U.S.

Monhegan
Lat: 43-46-43 N **Long:** 69-18-41 W   Pop. Place
Pop: 88 (1990); 109 (1980)   **Pop Density:** 97.8
Land: 0.9 sq. mi.; **Water:** 3.7 sq. mi.

Newcastle
ZIP: 04553   **Lat:** 44-02-48 N **Long:** 69-34-18 W   Town
Pop: 1,538 (1990); 1,227 (1980)   **Pop Density:** 53.0
Land: 29.0 sq. mi.; **Water:** 3.6 sq. mi.
Incorporated 1753.

Nobleboro
ZIP: 04555   **Lat:** 44-06-06 N **Long:** 69-28-31 W   Town
Pop: 1,455 (1990); 1,154 (1980)   **Pop Density:** 76.6
Land: 19.0 sq. mi.; **Water:** 4.3 sq. mi.
Incorporated 1788.

Somerville
Lat: 44-17-18 N **Long:** 69-29-09 W   Town
Pop: 458 (1990); 377 (1980)   **Pop Density:** 20.9
Land: 21.9 sq. mi.; **Water:** 0.9 sq. mi.

South Bristol
ZIP: 04568   **Lat:** 43-53-56 N **Long:** 69-33-34 W   Town
Pop: 825 (1990); 800 (1980)   **Pop Density:** 62.5
Land: 13.2 sq. mi.; **Water:** 10.5 sq. mi.
Name origin: For its location on an island south of Bristol.

Southport
Lat: 43-49-22 N **Long:** 69-40-01 W   Town
Pop: 645 (1990); 598 (1980)   **Pop Density:** 119.4
Land: 5.4 sq. mi.; **Water:** 8.5 sq. mi.
Incorporated 1842.
Name origin: For Southport Island, on which it is situated.

Waldoboro
ZIP: 04572   **Lat:** 44-06-22 N **Long:** 69-22-20 W   Town
Pop: 4,601 (1990); 3,985 (1980)   **Pop Density:** 64.5
Land: 71.3 sq. mi.; **Water:** 7.6 sq. mi.
Incorporated 1772.
Name origin: For Samuel Waldo (1695–1759), Boston-born merchant and land speculator who acquired vast land holdings in what was later to become ME.

Westport
Lat: 43-54-20 N **Long:** 69-42-00 W   Town
Pop: 663 (1990); 420 (1980)   **Pop Density:** 76.2
Land: 8.7 sq. mi.; **Water:** 5.5 sq. mi.
Incorporated 1828.

Whitefield
ZIP: 04362   **Lat:** 44-12-43 N **Long:** 69-36-58 W   Town
Pop: 1,931 (1990); 1,606 (1980)   **Pop Density:** 41.3
Land: 46.8 sq. mi.; **Water:** 0.7 sq. mi.
Incorporated 1809.
Name origin: For George Whitefield, a minister from England.

Wiscasset
ZIP: 04578   **Lat:** 44-00-53 N **Long:** 69-41-19 W   Town
Pop: 3,339 (1990); 2,832 (1980)   **Pop Density:** 135.7
Land: 24.6 sq. mi.; **Water:** 3.1 sq. mi.
Incorporated 1802.
Name origin: From an Abnaki term probably meaning 'at the hidden outlet.'

Oxford County
County Seat: South Paris (ZIP: 04281)

Pop: 52,602 (1990); 49,043 (1980)   **Pop Density:** 25.3
Land: 2078.2 sq. mi.; **Water:** 97.3 sq. mi.   **Area Code:** 207
On western border of ME and NH, west of Lewiston; organized Mar 4, 1805 (prior to statehood) from York and Cumberland counties.
Name origin: For Oxford, MA; named by David Leonard, an early settler who came from there.

Andover   Town
ZIP: 04216   **Lat:** 44-37-15 N   **Long:** 70-45-12 W
Pop: 953 (1990); 850 (1980)   **Pop Density:** 16.6
Land: 57.4 sq. mi.; **Water:** 0.0 sq. mi.
Incorporated 1804.
Name origin: For Andover, MA.

Bethel   Town
ZIP: 04217   **Lat:** 44-25-07 N   **Long:** 70-45-57 W
Pop: 2,329 (1990); 2,340 (1980)   **Pop Density:** 35.9
Land: 64.8 sq. mi.; **Water:** 1.1 sq. mi.
Incorporated 1796.
Name origin: For a biblical town.

Brownfield   Town
ZIP: 04010   **Lat:** 43-56-06 N   **Long:** 70-55-11 W
Pop: 1,034 (1990); 767 (1980)   **Pop Density:** 23.0
Land: 44.9 sq. mi.; **Water:** 1.3 sq. mi.
In western ME on NH border. Incorporated 1802.
Name origin: For Capt. Henry Brown, who saw service in the French and Indian War.

Buckfield   Town
ZIP: 04220   **Lat:** 44-17-10 N   **Long:** 70-22-06 W
Pop: 1,566 (1990); 1,333 (1980)   **Pop Density:** 41.5
Land: 37.7 sq. mi.; **Water:** 0.2 sq. mi.
Incorporated 1793.
Name origin: For Abijah Buck, an early settler.

Byron   Town
Lat: 44-44-01 N   **Long:** 70-39-34 W
Pop: 111 (1990); 114 (1980)   **Pop Density:** 2.1
Land: 51.8 sq. mi.; **Water:** 0.7 sq. mi.
Incorporated 1833.
Name origin: For the English poet George Gordon, Lord Byron (1788–1824).

Canton   Town
ZIP: 04221   **Lat:** 44-28-16 N   **Long:** 70-18-02 W
Pop: 951 (1990); 831 (1980)   **Pop Density:** 32.9
Land: 28.9 sq. mi.; **Water:** 1.3 sq. mi.
Incorporated 1821.
Name origin: For Canton, MA.

Denmark   Town
ZIP: 04022   **Lat:** 43-58-44 N   **Long:** 70-48-25 W
Pop: 855 (1990); 672 (1980)   **Pop Density:** 19.1
Land: 44.8 sq. mi.; **Water:** 3.5 sq. mi.
Incorporated 1807.
Name origin: Probably for the country of Denmark.

Dixfield   Town
ZIP: 04224   **Lat:** 44-32-23 N   **Long:** 70-23-01 W
Pop: 2,574 (1990); 2,389 (1980)   **Pop Density:** 62.5
Land: 41.2 sq. mi.; **Water:** 0.4 sq. mi.
Incorporated 1803.
Name origin: For Dr. Elijah Dix, who agreed to build the town a library if they would name the community for him; the town got its library.

Fryeburg   Town
ZIP: 04037   **Lat:** 44-03-07 N   **Long:** 70-56-12 W
Pop: 2,968 (1990); 2,715 (1980)   **Pop Density:** 50.6
Land: 58.6 sq. mi.; **Water:** 7.6 sq. mi.
Incorporated 1777.
Name origin: For the original area landowner Capt. Joseph Frye.

Gilead   Town
Lat: 44-23-56 N   **Long:** 70-56-58 W
Pop: 204 (1990); 191 (1980)   **Pop Density:** 10.7
Land: 19.1 sq. mi.; **Water:** 0.6 sq. mi.
Incorporated 1804.
Name origin: For the biblical balm of Gilead.

Greenwood   Town
Lat: 44-19-51 N   **Long:** 70-40-44 W
Pop: 689 (1990); 653 (1980)   **Pop Density:** 16.5
Land: 41.8 sq. mi.; **Water:** 1.3 sq. mi.
Incorporated 1816.
Name origin: For Alexander Greenwood, the area's early surveyor.

Hanover   Town
ZIP: 04237   **Lat:** 44-29-33 N   **Long:** 70-44-09 W
Pop: 272 (1990); 256 (1980)   **Pop Density:** 38.9
Land: 7.0 sq. mi.; **Water:** 0.5 sq. mi.
Incorporated 1843.
Name origin: For the province in Germany from which the town's pioneers had come.

Hartford   Town
Lat: 44-22-23 N   **Long:** 70-19-57 W
Pop: 722 (1990); 480 (1980)   **Pop Density:** 16.4
Land: 43.9 sq. mi.; **Water:** 1.2 sq. mi.
Incorporated 1798.
Name origin: For Hartford, CT.

Hebron   Town
ZIP: 04238   **Lat:** 44-12-31 N   **Long:** 70-23-14 W
Pop: 878 (1990); 665 (1980)   **Pop Density:** 39.2
Land: 22.4 sq. mi.; **Water:** 0.1 sq. mi.
Incorporated 1792.
Name origin: For the biblical place, possibly chosen by the Hebron Baptist Society in 1791.

Hiram   Town
ZIP: 04041   **Lat:** 43-52-17 N **Long:** 70-50-03 W
Pop: 1,260 (1990); 1,067 (1980)   **Pop Density:** 33.6
Land: 37.5 sq. mi.; **Water:** 1.3 sq. mi.
Incorporated 1814.
Name origin: For the biblical King Hiram of Tyre.

Lincoln   Plantation
            Lat: 44-56-42 N **Long:** 70-59-48 W
Pop: 38 (1990); 50 (1980)   **Pop Density:** 1.2
Land: 32.5 sq. mi.; **Water:** 4.4 sq. mi.
On western border with NH.
Name origin: For Enoch Lincoln (1788–1829), sixth governor of ME.

Lovell   Town
ZIP: 04051   **Lat:** 44-11-35 N **Long:** 70-53-09 W
Pop: 888 (1990); 767 (1980)   **Pop Density:** 20.6
Land: 43.2 sq. mi.; **Water:** 4.7 sq. mi.
Incorporated 1837.
Name origin: For Capt. Lovell, an Indian fighter killed in the 1720s.

Magalloway   Plantation
            Lat: 44-51-29 N **Long:** 70-58-49 W
Pop: 45 (1990); 79 (1980)   **Pop Density:** 0.9
Land: 48.4 sq. mi.; **Water:** 5.8 sq. mi.
In western ME.
Name origin: For Malecite term probably meaning 'many caribou.'

Mexico   Town
ZIP: 04257   **Lat:** 44-35-10 N **Long:** 70-30-47 W
Pop: 3,344 (1990); 3,698 (1980)   **Pop Density:** 141.7
Land: 23.6 sq. mi.; **Water:** 0.2 sq. mi.
Incorporated 1818.
Name origin: For Mexico, which was rebelling against Spain in 1818 when the town was incorporated.

Milton (unorganized)   Pop. Place
            Lat: 44-27-27 N **Long:** 70-36-06 W
Pop: 128 (1990); 123 (1980)   **Pop Density:** 8.7
Land: 14.7 sq. mi.; **Water:** 0.0 sq. mi.

Newry   Town
ZIP: 04261   **Lat:** 44-31-10 N **Long:** 70-49-28 W
Pop: 316 (1990); 235 (1980)   **Pop Density:** 5.1
Land: 61.4 sq. mi.; **Water:** 0.0 sq. mi.
Incorporated 1805.
Name origin: For Newry, County Down, Ireland.

North Oxford (unorganized)   Pop. Place
            Lat: 44-54-28 N **Long:** 70-55-06 W
Pop: 11 (1990); 37 (1980)   **Pop Density:** 0.0
Land: 509.7 sq. mi.; **Water:** 36.6 sq. mi.

Norway   Town
ZIP: 04268   **Lat:** 44-13-44 N **Long:** 70-36-41 W
Pop: 4,754 (1990); 4,042 (1980)   **Pop Density:** 105.4
Land: 45.1 sq. mi.; **Water:** 2.4 sq. mi.
Incorporated 1797.
Name origin: From *norage,* an Indian term probably meaning 'falls'; a legislative clerk "corrected" the spelling to Norway; the towns of Sweden and Denmark are nearby.

Otisfield   Town
            Lat: 44-05-25 N **Long:** 70-32-58 W
Pop: 1,136 (1990); 897 (1980)   **Pop Density:** 28.4
Land: 40.0 sq. mi.; **Water:** 4.3 sq. mi.
Incorporated 1798.
Name origin: Probably for an early settler named Otis.

Oxford   Town
ZIP: 04270   **Lat:** 44-08-42 N **Long:** 70-28-23 W
Pop: 3,705 (1990); 3,143 (1980)   **Pop Density:** 95.7
Land: 38.7 sq. mi.; **Water:** 3.1 sq. mi.
Incorporated 1829.

Paris   Town
ZIP: 04271   **Lat:** 44-14-50 N **Long:** 70-29-29 W
Pop: 4,492 (1990); 4,168 (1980)   **Pop Density:** 110.1
Land: 40.8 sq. mi.; **Water:** 0.2 sq. mi.
Incorporated 1793.
Name origin: Either for Paris, France, or possibly for Alfon Paris, a leading Democrat who helped in ME's separation from MA.

Peru   Town
ZIP: 04290   **Lat:** 44-28-29 N **Long:** 70-27-41 W
Pop: 1,541 (1990); 1,564 (1980)   **Pop Density:** 32.9
Land: 46.9 sq. mi.; **Water:** 0.9 sq. mi.
Incorporated 1821.
Name origin: For Peru in South America, which attained its independence in 1821, the same year that the town was incorporated.

Porter   Town
ZIP: 04068   **Lat:** 43-49-48 N **Long:** 70-56-09 W
Pop: 1,301 (1990); 1,222 (1980)   **Pop Density:** 41.3
Land: 31.5 sq. mi.; **Water:** 1.4 sq. mi.
Incorporated 1807.
Name origin: For leading citizen, Dr. Aaron Porter, who owned much of the land.

Roxbury   Town
ZIP: 04275   **Lat:** 44-38-33 N **Long:** 70-35-49 W
Pop: 437 (1990); 373 (1980)   **Pop Density:** 10.2
Land: 42.9 sq. mi.; **Water:** 1.2 sq. mi.
Incorporated 1835.
Name origin: For Roxbury, MA.

Rumford   Town
ZIP: 04276   **Lat:** 44-31-18 N **Long:** 70-37-45 W
Pop: 7,078 (1990); 8,240 (1980)   **Pop Density:** 102.9
Land: 68.8 sq. mi.; **Water:** 1.2 sq. mi.
Incorporated 1800.
Name origin: For Sir Benjamin Thompson (1753–1814), Count of Rumford.

South Oxford (unorganized)   Pop. Place
            Lat: 44-19-57 N **Long:** 70-50-46 W
Pop: 455 (1990); 348 (1980)   **Pop Density:** 4.8
Land: 95.0 sq. mi.; **Water:** 0.7 sq. mi.

South Paris   CDP
ZIP: 04281   **Lat:** 44-13-08 N **Long:** 70-30-49 W
Pop: 2,320 (1990); 2,128 (1980)   **Pop Density:** 594.9
Land: 3.9 sq. mi.; **Water:** 0.1 sq. mi.

Stoneham
Town
Lat: 44-15-58 N **Long:** 70-53-56 W
Pop: 224 (1990); 204 (1980)   **Pop Density:** 6.3
Land: 35.7 sq. mi.; **Water:** 1.0 sq. mi.
Incorporated 1834.

Stow
Town
Lat: 44-11-54 N **Long:** 70-58-31 W
Pop: 283 (1990); 186 (1980)   **Pop Density:** 11.6
Land: 24.4 sq. mi.; **Water:** 0.1 sq. mi.
Incorporated 1833.
Name origin: For Stow, MA.

Sumner
Town
Lat: 44-21-52 N **Long:** 70-27-12 W
Pop: 761 (1990); 613 (1980)   **Pop Density:** 17.2
Land: 44.2 sq. mi.; **Water:** 0.6 sq. mi.
Incorporated 1798.
Name origin: For Increase Sumner, an early governor of MA.

Sweden
Town
Lat: 44-07-23 N **Long:** 70-48-59 W
Pop: 222 (1990); 163 (1980)   **Pop Density:** 7.7
Land: 28.8 sq. mi.; **Water:** 0.9 sq. mi.
Incorporated 1813.
Name origin: For the country in Europe.

Upton
Town
Lat: 44-43-44 N **Long:** 70-59-18 W
Pop: 70 (1990); 65 (1980)   **Pop Density:** 1.8
Land: 39.8 sq. mi.; **Water:** 2.2 sq. mi.
Incorporated 1860.
Name origin: For Upton, MA.

Waterford
Town
ZIP: 04088   Lat: 44-11-41 N **Long:** 70-43-27 W
Pop: 1,299 (1990); 951 (1980)   **Pop Density:** 25.7
Land: 50.5 sq. mi.; **Water:** 2.6 sq. mi.
Incorporated 1797.
Name origin: For the area's many ponds, lakes, and streams.

West Paris
Town
ZIP: 04289   Lat: 44-19-30 N **Long:** 70-31-30 W
Pop: 1,514 (1990); 1,390 (1980)   **Pop Density:** 62.6
Land: 24.2 sq. mi.; **Water:** 0.2 sq. mi.
Name origin: For its location northwest of the town of Paris.

Woodstock
Town
Lat: 44-23-14 N **Long:** 70-35-12 W
Pop: 1,194 (1990); 1,087 (1980)   **Pop Density:** 26.1
Land: 45.7 sq. mi.; **Water:** 1.1 sq. mi.
Incorporated 1815.

Penobscot County
County Seat: Bangor (ZIP: 04401)

Pop: 146,601 (1990); 137,015 (1980)   **Pop Density:** 43.2
Land: 3396.0 sq. mi.; **Water:** 160.4 sq. mi.   **Area Code:** 207
In east-central ME; organized Feb 15, 1816 (prior to statehood) from Hancock County.
Name origin: For the Penobscot River, which flows through the county; from an Indian word *penobskeag* 'rocky place' or 'river of rocks.'

Alton
Town
Lat: 45-02-47 N **Long:** 68-46-14 W
Pop: 771 (1990); 468 (1980)   **Pop Density:** 18.2
Land: 42.4 sq. mi.; **Water:** 0.4 sq. mi.   **Elev:** 170 ft.
Incorporated 1844.
Name origin: For Alton, Southampton, England.

Argyle (unorganized)
Pop. Place
Lat: 45-04-50 N **Long:** 68-42-21 W
Pop: 202 (1990); 225 (1980)   **Pop Density:** 7.6
Land: 26.7 sq. mi.; **Water:** 0.0 sq. mi.

Bangor
City
ZIP: 04401   Lat: 44-49-55 N **Long:** 68-47-15 W
Pop: 33,181 (1990); 31,643 (1980)   **Pop Density:** 961.8
Land: 34.5 sq. mi.; **Water:** 0.3 sq. mi.   **Elev:** 158 ft.
In south-central ME on the Penobscot River, 60 mi. northeast of Augusta. Settled 1769; incorporated as a town 1790, as a city 1834. Trade and distribution center for the area; produces electronic components, lumber equipment, metal products, paper, shoes.
Name origin: For the church hymn "Bangor"; name given by Rev. Seth Noble. May also be for the cities in Wales and Northern Ireland. Previously called Kendus Keag Plantation.

Bradford
Town
ZIP: 04410   Lat: 45-05-17 N **Long:** 68-54-37 W
Pop: 1,103 (1990); 888 (1980)   **Pop Density:** 26.7
Land: 41.3 sq. mi.; **Water:** 0.0 sq. mi.
Incorporated 1831.
Name origin: For Bradford, MA.

Bradley
Town
Lat: 44-53-24 N **Long:** 68-36-16 W
Pop: 1,136 (1990); 1,149 (1980)   **Pop Density:** 22.9
Land: 49.6 sq. mi.; **Water:** 1.2 sq. mi.
Incorporated 1835.
Name origin: For Bradley Blackman, an early settler and prominent citizen.

Brewer
City
ZIP: 04412   Lat: 44-46-43 N **Long:** 68-43-55 W
Pop: 9,021 (1990); 9,017 (1980)   **Pop Density:** 597.4
Land: 15.1 sq. mi.; **Water:** 0.5 sq. mi.
In east-central ME on Penobscot River opposite Bangor. Incorporated 1812.
Name origin: For Col. John Brewer, an early settler from MA.

Burlington
Town
ZIP: 04417   Lat: 45-16-07 N Long: 68-22-19 W
Pop: 360 (1990); 322 (1980)   Pop Density: 6.7
Land: 53.8 sq. mi.; **Water:** 2.4 sq. mi.
Incorporated 1832.
Name origin: For Burlington, MA.

Carmel
Town
ZIP: 04419   Lat: 44-48-07 N Long: 69-02-14 W
Pop: 1,906 (1990); 1,695 (1980)   Pop Density: 52.2
Land: 36.5 sq. mi.; **Water:** 0.5 sq. mi.
In central ME, 12 mi. west of Bangor. Incorporated 1811.
Name origin: Named by the town's first settler, the Rev. Paul Ruggles, for the biblical prophet Elijah's experience on Mount Carmel.

Carroll
Plantation
Lat: 45-24-29 N Long: 68-03-18 W
Pop: 185 (1990); 175 (1980)   Pop Density: 4.2
Land: 44.2 sq. mi.; **Water:** 0.2 sq. mi.
In eastern ME. Incorporated 1845.
Name origin: For Daniel Carroll, a signer of the U.S. Constitution.

Charleston
Town
ZIP: 04422   Lat: 45-04-20 N Long: 69-02-19 W
Pop: 1,187 (1990); 1,037 (1980)   Pop Density: 29.5
Land: 40.2 sq. mi.; **Water:** 0.0 sq. mi.
Incorporated 1811.

Chester
Town
Lat: 45-26-12 N Long: 68-29-13 W
Pop: 442 (1990); 434 (1980)   Pop Density: 13.7
Land: 32.2 sq. mi.; **Water:** 0.0 sq. mi.
In east-central ME on the Penobscot River. Incorporated 1834.
Name origin: For Chester, NH, former home of Samuel Chesley, an early settler.

Clifton
Town
Lat: 44-48-55 N Long: 68-30-56 W
Pop: 607 (1990); 462 (1980)   Pop Density: 17.6
Land: 34.4 sq. mi.; **Water:** 1.4 sq. mi.
Incorporated 1848.
Name origin: For the topography of the area.

Corinna
Town
ZIP: 04928   Lat: 44-56-44 N Long: 69-15-24 W
Pop: 2,196 (1990); 1,887 (1980)   Pop Density: 56.7
Land: 38.7 sq. mi.; **Water:** 0.8 sq. mi.
Incorporated 1816.
Name origin: For the daughter of the first landowner, Dr. John Warren.

Corinth
Town
Lat: 44-58-47 N Long: 69-00-28 W
Pop: 2,177 (1990); 1,711 (1980)   Pop Density: 54.2
Land: 40.2 sq. mi.; **Water:** 0.0 sq. mi.
Incorporated 1811.
Name origin: For the ancient Greek city.

Dexter
Town
ZIP: 04930   Lat: 45-02-23 N Long: 69-16-47 W
Pop: 4,419 (1990); 4,286 (1980)   Pop Density: 125.5
Land: 35.2 sq. mi.; **Water:** 2.0 sq. mi.
Incorporated 1816.
Name origin: For Samuel Dexter, unsuccessful Democratic candidate for governor of MA in 1816.

Dixmont
Town
ZIP: 04932   Lat: 44-41-08 N Long: 69-07-52 W
Pop: 1,007 (1990); 812 (1980)   Pop Density: 27.7
Land: 36.3 sq. mi.; **Water:** 0.1 sq. mi.
Incorporated 1807.
Name origin: For Dr. Elijah Dix, a large landowner.

Drew
Plantation
Lat: 45-34-29 N Long: 68-05-29 W
Pop: 43 (1990); 57 (1980)   Pop Density: 1.1
Land: 37.6 sq. mi.; **Water:** 1.2 sq. mi.
In east-central ME.
Name origin: Probably for an early settler.

East Central Penobscot (unorganized)
Pop. Place
Lat: 45-08-30 N Long: 68-24-06 W
Pop: 12 (1990)   Pop Density: 0.2
Land: 76.7 sq. mi.; **Water:** 1.3 sq. mi.

East Millinocket
Town
ZIP: 04430   Lat: 45-39-01 N Long: 68-35-04 W
Pop: 2,166 (1990)   Pop Density: 305.1
Land: 7.1 sq. mi.; **Water:** 0.8 sq. mi.
Incorporated 1907.
Name origin: For its location east of Millinocket; paper mill engineers marked their blueprints "east of Millinocket," and the "of" was later dropped.

Eddington
Town
Lat: 44-49-47 N Long: 68-37-08 W
Pop: 1,947 (1990)   Pop Density: 77.6
Land: 25.1 sq. mi.; **Water:** 1.4 sq. mi.
Incorporated 1811.
Name origin: For Col. Jonathan Eddy, a soldier from MA.

Edinburg
Town
Lat: 45-10-34 N Long: 68-41-27 W
Pop: 107 (1990)   Pop Density: 3.0
Land: 35.1 sq. mi.; **Water:** 0.0 sq. mi.
Incorporated 1835.
Name origin: Named by John Bennoch, local road builder, for Edinburgh, Scotland.

Enfield
Town
ZIP: 04433   Lat: 45-15-56 N Long: 68-35-39 W
Pop: 1,476 (1990)   Pop Density: 52.9
Land: 27.9 sq. mi.; **Water:** 5.3 sq. mi.
Incorporated 1835.
Name origin: Believed to be for Enfield, England.

Etna
Town
ZIP: 04434   Lat: 44-47-13 N Long: 69-08-00 W
Pop: 977 (1990)   Pop Density: 40.0
Land: 24.4 sq. mi.; **Water:** 0.2 sq. mi.
Incorporated 1820.
Name origin: Named by Benjamin Friend for Mt. Etna in Sicily.

Exeter
Town

ZIP: 04435 Lat: 44-57-58 N Long: 69-08-29 W
Pop: 937 (1990) Pop Density: 24.4
Land: 38.4 sq. mi.; Water: 0.0 sq. mi.
Incorporated 1811.
Name origin: For Exeter, NH, former home of early settlers.

Garland
Town

Lat: 45-02-55 N Long: 69-09-37 W
Pop: 1,064 (1990) Pop Density: 28.1
Land: 37.8 sq. mi.; Water: 0.3 sq. mi.
Incorporated 1811.
Name origin: For Joseph Garland, the first settler, who arrived in 1802.

Glenburn
Town

Lat: 44-54-55 N Long: 68-51-19 W
Pop: 3,198 (1990) Pop Density: 117.6
Land: 27.2 sq. mi.; Water: 2.1 sq. mi.
Incorporated 1822.
Name origin: From the Scottish term for a small stream in a narrow valley.

Greenbush
Town

Lat: 45-04-53 N Long: 68-35-34 W
Pop: 1,309 (1990) Pop Density: 29.9
Land: 43.8 sq. mi.; Water: 0.3 sq. mi.
Incorporated 1834.
Name origin: Descriptively named for greenery in the area.

Greenfield
Town

Lat: 45-01-23 N Long: 68-26-47 W
Pop: 267 (1990) Pop Density: 7.1
Land: 37.8 sq. mi.; Water: 0.0 sq. mi.
Incorporated 1831.
Name origin: Probably for Greenfield, MA, the former home of early settlers.

Hampden
Town

ZIP: 04444 Lat: 44-43-32 N Long: 68-53-25 W
Pop: 5,974 (1990) Pop Density: 156.8
Land: 38.1 sq. mi.; Water: 0.9 sq. mi.
In east-central ME, 7 mi. south of Bangor. Incorporated 1794.
Name origin: For John Hampden, a 17-century English patriot.

Hermon
Town

Lat: 44-49-08 N Long: 68-54-56 W
Pop: 3,755 (1990) Pop Density: 104.6
Land: 35.9 sq. mi.; Water: 0.9 sq. mi.
Incorporated 1814.
Name origin: Named by the original settlers for the biblical Mt. Hermon.

Holden
Town

Lat: 44-45-39 N Long: 68-40-24 W
Pop: 2,952 (1990) Pop Density: 95.5
Land: 30.9 sq. mi.; Water: 1.2 sq. mi.
Incorporated 1852.
Name origin: For either Holden, MA, or a Dr. Holden.

Howland
Town

ZIP: 04448 Lat: 45-15-41 N Long: 68-42-16 W
Pop: 1,435 (1990) Pop Density: 41.5
Land: 34.6 sq. mi.; Water: 0.7 sq. mi.
Incorporated 1826.
Name origin: For Mayflower pioneer, John Howland.

Hudson
Town

ZIP: 04449 Lat: 44-59-58 N Long: 68-53-05 W
Pop: 1,048 (1990) Pop Density: 27.7
Land: 37.8 sq. mi.; Water: 2.4 sq. mi.
Incorporated 1825.
Name origin: For Hudson, MA.

Kenduskeag
Town

ZIP: 04450 Lat: 44-55-11 N Long: 68-55-51 W
Pop: 1,234 (1990) Pop Density: 73.5
Land: 16.8 sq. mi.; Water: 0.0 sq. mi.
Incorporated 1852.
Name origin: For the stream of the same name which flows through the town; its name is from an Abnaki term probably meaning 'eel weir place,' that is, 'place where eels are caught.'

Kingman (unorganized)
Pop. Place

Lat: 45-35-13 N Long: 68-12-19 W
Pop: 246 (1990) Pop Density: 9.8
Land: 25.0 sq. mi.; Water: 0.4 sq. mi.

Lagrange
Town

ZIP: 04453 Lat: 45-09-59 N Long: 68-48-33 W
Pop: 557 (1990) Pop Density: 11.3
Land: 49.4 sq. mi.; Water: 0.1 sq. mi.
Incorporated 1832.
Name origin: For "LaGrange" the estate of the Marquis De Lafayette (1757–1834).

Lakeville
Town

Lat: 45-18-32 N Long: 68-06-37 W
Pop: 45 (1990) Pop Density: 0.8
Land: 58.1 sq. mi.; Water: 7.2 sq. mi.
Name origin: For its location in lake country.

Lee
Town

ZIP: 04455 Lat: 45-22-14 N Long: 68-17-49 W
Pop: 832 (1990) Pop Density: 21.6
Land: 38.6 sq. mi.; Water: 1.1 sq. mi.
Incorporated 1832.
Name origin: For an early settler, Stephen Lee.

Levant
Town

ZIP: 04456 Lat: 44-53-16 N Long: 68-59-12 W
Pop: 1,627 (1990) Pop Density: 54.2
Land: 30.0 sq. mi.; Water: 0.0 sq. mi.
Incorporated 1813.
Name origin: For the former home of French settlers from the Levant plateau in Nova Scotia.

Lincoln
Town

ZIP: 04457 Lat: 45-20-50 N Long: 68-27-50 W
Pop: 5,587 (1990) Pop Density: 82.3
Land: 67.9 sq. mi.; Water: 6.9 sq. mi.
In east-central ME, 42 mi. north of Bangor.
Name origin: For Enoch Lincoln (1788–1829), sixth governor of ME.

Lowell
Town
Lat: 45-13-10 N Long: 68-29-45 W
Pop: 267 (1990) **Pop Density:** 7.0
Land: 38.2 sq. mi.; **Water:** 1.9 sq. mi.
Incorporated 1800.

Mattawamkeag
Town
ZIP: 04459 Lat: 45-33-01 N Long: 68-18-45 W
Pop: 830 (1990) **Pop Density:** 22.2
Land: 37.4 sq. mi.; **Water:** 0.4 sq. mi.
Incorporated 1860.
Name origin: From Abnaki term probably meaning 'fishing place beyond the gravel bar.'

Maxfield
Town
Lat: 45-18-08 N Long: 68-45-52 W
Pop: 86 (1990) **Pop Density:** 4.5
Land: 19.1 sq. mi.; **Water:** 0.3 sq. mi.
Incorporated 1824.
Name origin: For the second settler, Joseph McIntosh, whose farm became known as "Mac's field," hence the present spelling.

Medway
Town
ZIP: 04460 Lat: 45-37-18 N Long: 68-29-58 W
Pop: 1,922 (1990) **Pop Density:** 46.9
Land: 41.0 sq. mi.; **Water:** 0.8 sq. mi.
Incorporated 1875.
Name origin: For the town's location midway between Bangor and the county's north boundary.

Milford
Town
ZIP: 04461 Lat: 44-59-41 N Long: 68-34-18 W
Pop: 2,884 (1990) **Pop Density:** 63.2
Land: 45.6 sq. mi.; **Water:** 0.2 sq. mi.
Incorporated 1833.
Name origin: For Milford, MA, former home of early settlers.

Millinocket
Town
ZIP: 04462 Lat: 45-38-52 N Long: 68-42-13 W
Pop: 6,956 (1990) **Pop Density:** 638.2
Land: 10.9 sq. mi.; **Water:** 1.1 sq. mi. **Elev:** 358 ft.
In east-central ME, 54 mi. southwest of Houlton. Incorporated 1901.
Name origin: From Abnaki term probably meaning 'this place is admirable.'

Mount Chase
Town
Lat: 46-05-01 N Long: 68-30-24 W
Pop: 254 (1990) **Pop Density:** 7.0
Land: 36.3 sq. mi.; **Water:** 1.1 sq. mi.
Incorporated 1864.
Name origin: For a Maine forest agent, who searched for timber thieves in the area.

Newburgh
Town
Lat: 44-42-24 N Long: 69-01-01 W
Pop: 1,317 (1990) **Pop Density:** 42.6
Land: 30.9 sq. mi.; **Water:** 0.1 sq. mi.
Incorporated 1819.
Name origin: Named by early settlers for its status as a "new town."

Newport
Town
ZIP: 04953 Lat: 44-51-32 N Long: 69-13-45 W
Pop: 3,036 (1990) **Pop Density:** 102.9
Land: 29.5 sq. mi.; **Water:** 7.5 sq. mi.
Incorporated 1814.
Name origin: For an Indian portage between the Penobscot and Sebasticook rivers called 'new portage.'

North Penobscot (unorganized)
Pop. Place
Lat: 45-52-49 N Long: 68-40-51 W
Pop: 403 (1990) **Pop Density:** 0.4
Land: 1068.8 sq. mi.; **Water:** 68.5 sq. mi.

Old Town
City
ZIP: 04468 Lat: 44-57-12 N Long: 68-44-11 W
Pop: 8,317 (1990); 8,422 (1980) **Pop Density:** 217.2
Land: 38.3 sq. mi.; **Water:** 4.4 sq. mi. **Elev:** 108 ft.
In east-central ME, 11 mi. north-northeast of Bangor. Incorporated as town 1841; as city 1891.
Name origin: For its continuous occupation since 1669.

Orono
Town
ZIP: 04473 Lat: 44-52-57 N Long: 68-42-13 W
Pop: 10,573 (1990) **Pop Density:** 580.9
Land: 18.2 sq. mi.; **Water:** 1.6 sq. mi. **Elev:** 132 ft.
In east-central ME, 8 mi. north-northeast of Bangor. Incorporated 1806. Site of the main campus of the University of Maine.
Name origin: For Chief Joseph Orono of the Penobscot tribe.

Orrington
Town
ZIP: 04474 Lat: 44-43-30 N Long: 68-46-48 W
Pop: 3,309 (1990) **Pop Density:** 130.3
Land: 25.4 sq. mi.; **Water:** 2.1 sq. mi.
Incorporated 1788.
Name origin: Named by Parson Noble through his misspelling of "Orangetown" on the town's incorporation papers, or chosen by an agent of the MA general courts.

Passadumkeag
Town
ZIP: 04475 Lat: 45-11-00 N Long: 68-35-25 W
Pop: 428 (1990) **Pop Density:** 18.7
Land: 22.9 sq. mi.; **Water:** 0.2 sq. mi.
Incorporated 1835.
Name origin: From an Abnaki term probably meaning 'rapids over gravel beds.'

Patten
Town
ZIP: 04765 Lat: 45-59-10 N Long: 68-29-06 W
Pop: 1,256 (1990) **Pop Density:** 32.7
Land: 38.4 sq. mi.; **Water:** 0.1 sq. mi.
Incorporated 1841.
Name origin: For early settler Amos Patten, who purchased the township in 1830.

Penobscot Indian Island Reservation
Pop. Place
Lat: 45-12-00 N Long: 68-37-11 W
Pop: 476 (1990) **Pop Density:** 61.0
Land: 7.8 sq. mi.; **Water:** 12.9 sq. mi.

Plymouth
Town
ZIP: 04969 Lat: 44-46-53 N Long: 69-13-19 W
Pop: 1,152 (1990) **Pop Density:** 38.5
Land: 29.9 sq. mi.; **Water:** 1.3 sq. mi.
Incorporated 1826.
Name origin: For Plymouth, MA.

Prentiss

Plantation
Lat: 45-30-01 N Long: 68-04-26 W
Pop: 245 (1990) **Pop Density:** 6.4
Land: 38.4 sq. mi.; **Water:** 0.0 sq. mi.
Incorporated 1858.
Name origin: For prominent landowner, Henry E. Prentiss.

Seboeis

Plantation
Lat: 45-22-56 N Long: 68-45-00 W
Pop: 40 (1990) **Pop Density:** 1.0
Land: 40.0 sq. mi.; **Water:** 1.7 sq. mi.
Name origin: For the Seboeis Stream, which bisects the area. From an Abnaki term probably meaning 'little stream.'

Springfield

Town
ZIP: 04487 Lat: 45-23-34 N Long: 68-09-32 W
Pop: 406 (1990) **Pop Density:** 10.6
Land: 38.4 sq. mi.; **Water:** 0.0 sq. mi.
Incorporated 1834.

Stacyville

Town
Lat: 45-54-26 N Long: 68-29-37 W
Pop: 480 (1990) **Pop Density:** 12.0
Land: 39.9 sq. mi.; **Water:** 0.0 sq. mi.

Stetson

Town
ZIP: 04488 Lat: 44-52-58 N Long: 69-06-42 W
Pop: 847 (1990) **Pop Density:** 24.3
Land: 34.9 sq. mi.; **Water:** 1.7 sq. mi.
Incorporated 1831.
Name origin: For early landowner, Amasa Stetson of Dedham, MA.

Veazie

Town
Lat: 44-50-08 N Long: 68-42-57 W
Pop: 1,633 (1990) **Pop Density:** 563.1
Land: 2.9 sq. mi.; **Water:** 0.2 sq. mi.
Incorporated 1853.
Name origin: For Samuel Veazie, a local businessman.

Webster

Pop. Place
Lat: 45-28-33 N Long: 68-11-51 W
Pop: 95 (1990) **Pop Density:** 2.6
Land: 36.8 sq. mi.; **Water:** 0.1 sq. mi.
Incorporated 1840.

Winn

Town
ZIP: 04495 Lat: 45-27-14 N Long: 68-20-06 W
Pop: 479 (1990) **Pop Density:** 10.9
Land: 44.1 sq. mi.; **Water:** 0.1 sq. mi.
Incorporated 1857.
Name origin: For John M. Winn, who owned much of the land.

Woodville

Town
Lat: 45-31-28 N Long: 68-26-05 W
Pop: 215 (1990) **Pop Density:** 5.0
Land: 42.9 sq. mi.; **Water:** 0.0 sq. mi.
Incorporated 1895.
Name origin: Named by the Benjamin Stanwood family for the local woods.

Piscataquis County
County Seat: Dover-Foxcroft (ZIP: 04426)

Pop: 18,653 (1990); 17,634 (1980) **Pop Density:** 4.7
Land: 3966.5 sq. mi.; **Water:** 411.2 sq. mi. **Area Code:** 207
In central ME, north of Bangor; organized 1838 from Penobscot and Somerset counties.
Name origin: For the Piscataquis River, which runs through it; from an Abnaki Indian word probably meaning 'divided tidal river.'

Abbot

Town
Lat: 45-10-47 N Long: 69-28-05 W
Pop: 677 (1990) **Pop Density:** 19.5
Land: 34.7 sq. mi.; **Water:** 0.8 sq. mi.
Incorporated 1827.
Name origin: For Professor John Abbot, treasurer of Bowdoin College.

Atkinson

Town
Lat: 45-09-24 N Long: 69-03-39 W
Pop: 332 (1990) **Pop Density:** 8.6
Land: 38.7 sq. mi.; **Water:** 0.0 sq. mi.
Incorporated 1819.
Name origin: For Judge Atkinson, who owned a great deal of land in this area.

Beaver Cove

Town
Lat: 45-32-58 N Long: 69-28-30 W
Pop: 104 (1990) **Pop Density:** 3.3
Land: 31.7 sq. mi.; **Water:** 0.9 sq. mi.
In north-central ME.
Name origin: For the large beaver population once in the area.

Blanchard (unorganized)

Pop. Place
Lat: 45-14-57 N Long: 69-38-26 W
Pop: 78 (1990) **Pop Density:** 1.8
Land: 44.3 sq. mi.; **Water:** 0.7 sq. mi.

Bowerbank

Town
Lat: 45-18-50 N Long: 69-15-25 W
Pop: 72 (1990) **Pop Density:** 1.7
Land: 41.7 sq. mi.; **Water:** 5.6 sq. mi.
Incorporated 1839.
Name origin: For a London merchant, the second owner of the township's land.

Brownville
ZIP: 04414   **Lat:** 45-21-46 N   **Long:** 69-00-03 W   Town
Pop: 1,506 (1990)   **Pop Density:** 33.9
Land: 44.4 sq. mi.; **Water:** 0.3 sq. mi.
Incorporated 1824.
Name origin: For Francis Brown, an early settler, who built a mill here in 1812.

Dover-Foxcroft
ZIP: 04426   **Lat:** 45-11-03 N   **Long:** 69-12-13 W   Town
Pop: 4,657 (1990)   **Pop Density:** 68.3
Land: 68.2 sq. mi.; **Water:** 3.0 sq. mi.   **Elev:** 356 ft.
Dover incorporated 1822; Foxcroft incorporated 1812; became one town 1922.

Greenville
ZIP: 04441   **Lat:** 45-27-48 N   **Long:** 69-33-14 W   Town
Pop: 1,884 (1990)   **Pop Density:** 44.3
Land: 42.5 sq. mi.; **Water:** 3.9 sq. mi.
Incorporated 1836.

Guilford
ZIP: 04443   **Lat:** 45-12-31 N   **Long:** 69-20-28 W   Town
Pop: 1,710 (1990)   **Pop Density:** 48.9
Land: 35.0 sq. mi.; **Water:** 0.7 sq. mi.
Incorporated 1816.
Name origin: For Moses Guilford Law, the first child born in the town.

Kingsbury
                 Plantation
Lat: 45-09-00 N   **Long:** 69-35-52 W
Pop: 13 (1990)   **Pop Density:** 0.3
Land: 44.1 sq. mi.; **Water:** 0.5 sq. mi.
Incorporated 1836.
Name origin: For Judge Sanford Kingsbury, a prominent landowner.

Lake View
                 Pop. Place
Lat: 45-21-45 N   **Long:** 68-53-21 W
Pop: 23 (1990)   **Pop Density:** 0.6
Land: 41.5 sq. mi.; **Water:** 11.7 sq. mi.
Name origin: For its view of Schoodic Lake.

Medford
                 Town
Lat: 45-16-59 N   **Long:** 68-51-07 W
Pop: 194 (1990)   **Pop Density:** 4.6
Land: 42.4 sq. mi.; **Water:** 0.7 sq. mi.
Incorporated 1824.
Name origin: For the "middle ford" of the Piscataquis River, where the town lies.

Milo
ZIP: 04463   **Lat:** 45-15-27 N   **Long:** 68-59-01 W   Town
Pop: 2,600 (1990)   **Pop Density:** 79.3
Land: 32.8 sq. mi.; **Water:** 0.7 sq. mi.
Incorporated 1823.
Name origin: Named by early settler, Theophilus Sargent, for the classical Greek athlete, Milo of Croton (6th century B.C.).

Monson
ZIP: 04464   **Lat:** 45-17-10 N   **Long:** 69-30-22 W   Town
Pop: 744 (1990)   **Pop Density:** 15.8
Land: 47.1 sq. mi.; **Water:** 2.2 sq. mi.
Incorporated 1822.
Name origin: For Monson, MA, because the land on which the town was built was owned by the Hebron Society from there.

Northeast Piscataquis (unorganized)
                 Pop. Place
Lat: 45-54-36 N   **Long:** 69-05-15 W
Pop: 218 (1990)   **Pop Density:** 0.1
Land: 1710.7 sq. mi.; **Water:** 109.9 sq. mi.

Northwest Piscataquis (unorganized)
                 Pop. Place
Lat: 46-03-55 N   **Long:** 69-29-30 W
Pop: 141 (1990)   **Pop Density:** 0.1
Land: 1372.5 sq. mi.; **Water:** 259.6 sq. mi.

Parkman
                 Town
Lat: 45-06-43 N   **Long:** 69-26-55 W
Pop: 790 (1990)   **Pop Density:** 17.4
Land: 45.5 sq. mi.; **Water:** 0.7 sq. mi.
Incorporated 1822.
Name origin: For Samuel Parkman, an early settler.

Sangerville
ZIP: 04479   **Lat:** 45-07-26 N   **Long:** 69-18-39 W   Town
Pop: 1,398 (1990)   **Pop Density:** 36.3
Land: 38.5 sq. mi.; **Water:** 1.2 sq. mi.
Incorporated 1814.
Name origin: For Col. Calvin Sanger of Sherborn, MA, who owned land in the area.

Sebec
                 Town
Lat: 45-14-31 N   **Long:** 69-06-25 W
Pop: 554 (1990)   **Pop Density:** 15.0
Land: 37.0 sq. mi.; **Water:** 1.0 sq. mi.
Incorporated 1812.
Name origin: For Sebec Lake, to its west; from an Abnaki term probably meaning 'much water.'

Shirley
                 Town
Lat: 45-20-51 N   **Long:** 69-37-53 W
Pop: 271 (1990)   **Pop Density:** 5.1
Land: 52.9 sq. mi.; **Water:** 0.9 sq. mi.
Incorporated 1834.
Name origin: For Shirley, MA, home of Joseph Kelsey, a representative to the legislature.

Southeast Piscataquis (unorganized)
                 Pop. Place
Lat: 45-10-34 N   **Long:** 68-55-41 W
Pop: 247 (1990)   **Pop Density:** 6.7
Land: 36.7 sq. mi.; **Water:** 1.8 sq. mi.

Wellington
                 Town
Lat: 45-04-42 N   **Long:** 69-34-08 W
Pop: 270 (1990)   **Pop Density:** 6.8
Land: 39.9 sq. mi.; **Water:** 0.0 sq. mi.
Incorporated 1828.
Name origin: For Arthur Wellesley the Duke of Wellington (1769–1852), hero of the Napoleonic Wars.

Willimantic
                 Town
Lat: 45-18-26 N   **Long:** 69-22-39 W
Pop: 170 (1990)   **Pop Density:** 3.9
Land: 43.5 sq. mi.; **Water:** 4.6 sq. mi.
Incorporated 1881.
Name origin: For the Willimantic (Connecticut) Thread Company, which had a factory in the town in the 1880s.

Sagadahoc County
County Seat: Bath (ZIP: 04530)

Pop: 33,535 (1990); 28,795 (1980)   **Pop Density:** 132.0
Land: 254.0 sq. mi.; **Water:** 116.3 sq. mi.   **Area Code:** 207

On Atlantic coast of ME, east of Portland; organized Apr 4, 1854 from Lincoln County.

Name origin: From an Abnaki Indian word probably meaning 'land of the mouth,' or 'mouth of the river,' for its location at the confluence of the Androscoggin and Kennebec rivers where they meet the Atlantic.

Arrowsic
Town
Lat: 43-51-52 N **Long:** 69-47-18 W
Pop: 498 (1990)   **Pop Density:** 63.8
Land: 7.8 sq. mi.; **Water:** 3.0 sq. mi.
In west-central coastal ME. Incorporated 1841.
Name origin: From Abnaki term probably meaning 'place of obstruction.'

Bath
City
ZIP: 04530   **Lat:** 43-56-17 N **Long:** 69-50-14 W
Pop: 9,799 (1990); 10,246 (1980) **Pop Density:** 1076.8
Land: 9.1 sq. mi.; **Water:** 4.1 sq. mi.   **Elev:** 79 ft.
In coastal ME near the mouth of the Kennebec River and the Atlantic Ocean, 28 mi. northeast of Portland. Incorporated as a town in 1781; as a city 1848. Formerly an important shipbuilding center.
Name origin: Named by Col. Dummer Sewall for Bath, England.

Bowdoin
Town
Lat: 44-03-38 N **Long:** 69-58-03 W
Pop: 2,207 (1990)   **Pop Density:** 50.7
Land: 43.5 sq. mi.; **Water:** 0.2 sq. mi.
In western coastal ME. Incorporated 1788.
Name origin: For James Bowdoin, governor of MA (1785–86).

Bowdoinham
Town
ZIP: 04008   **Lat:** 44-01-53 N **Long:** 69-52-00 W
Pop: 2,192 (1990)   **Pop Density:** 63.7
Land: 34.4 sq. mi.; **Water:** 4.7 sq. mi.
In western coastal ME. Incorporated 1762.
Name origin: For Dr. Peter Bowdoin, an early landholder.

Georgetown
Town
ZIP: 04548   **Lat:** 43-48-47 N **Long:** 69-44-48 W
Pop: 914 (1990)   **Pop Density:** 48.9
Land: 18.7 sq. mi.; **Water:** 13.1 sq. mi.
Incorporated 1716.
Name origin: For either England's King George I (1660–1727), or nearby Fort St. George.

Perkins (unorganized)
Pop. Place
Lat: 44-02-46 N **Long:** 69-48-07 W
Pop: 6 (1990)   **Pop Density:** 2.7
Land: 2.2 sq. mi.; **Water:** 1.5 sq. mi.

Phippsburg
Town
ZIP: 04567   **Lat:** 43-46-42 N **Long:** 69-49-41 W
Pop: 1,815 (1990)   **Pop Density:** 62.8
Land: 28.9 sq. mi.; **Water:** 15.0 sq. mi.
Incorporated 1814.
Name origin: For Sir William Phipps, governor of MA in 1692.

Richmond
Town
ZIP: 04357   **Lat:** 44-07-27 N **Long:** 69-49-36 W
Pop: 3,072 (1990)   **Pop Density:** 101.1
Land: 30.4 sq. mi.; **Water:** 1.2 sq. mi.
Incorporated 1823.
Name origin: For Fort Richmond, named for the Duke of Richmond and built in 1719.

Topsham
Town
ZIP: 04086   **Lat:** 43-57-47 N **Long:** 69-57-33 W
Pop: 8,746 (1990)   **Pop Density:** 273.3
Land: 32.0 sq. mi.; **Water:** 3.4 sq. mi.
In southern ME at the mouth of the Androscoggin River. Incorporated 1762.
Name origin: For Topsham, England, the former home of settlers.

West Bath
Town
Lat: 43-52-29 N **Long:** 69-51-34 W
Pop: 1,716 (1990)   **Pop Density:** 145.4
Land: 11.8 sq. mi.; **Water:** 3.2 sq. mi.
Incorporated 1844.

Woolwich
Town
ZIP: 04579   **Lat:** 43-57-57 N **Long:** 69-45-57 W
Pop: 2,570 (1990)   **Pop Density:** 73.2
Land: 35.1 sq. mi.; **Water:** 6.6 sq. mi.
Incorporated 1759.
Name origin: For Woolwich, England.

Somerset County
County Seat: Skowhegan (ZIP: 04976)

Pop: 49,767 (1990); 45,049 (1980)   **Pop Density:** 12.7
Land: 3926.8 sq. mi.; **Water:** 168.9 sq. mi.   **Area Code:** 207
In west-central ME and north to the border with Quebec, Canada; organized Mar 1, 1809 (prior to statehood) from Kennebec County.
Name origin: For Somerset county in England.

Anson
ZIP: 04911   **Lat:** 44-48-38 N **Long:** 69-56-21 W
Pop: 2,382 (1990)   **Pop Density:** 50.1
Land: 47.5 sq. mi.; **Water:** 0.9 sq. mi.
In west-central ME. Incorporated 1798.
Name origin: For an Englishman, Lord George Anson.

Athens   Town
ZIP: 04912   **Lat:** 44-56-44 N **Long:** 69-39-43 W
Pop: 897 (1990)   **Pop Density:** 20.6
Land: 43.5 sq. mi.; **Water:** 0.0 sq. mi.
In west-central ME. Incorporated 1804.
Name origin: For the capital city of Greece.

Bingham   Town
ZIP: 04920   **Lat:** 45-02-15 N **Long:** 69-49-01 W
Pop: 1,230 (1990)   **Pop Density:** 35.5
Land: 34.6 sq. mi.; **Water:** 0.4 sq. mi.
In west-central ME. Incorporated 1812.
Name origin: For William Bingham, who owned great tracts of land in the area at one time.

Brighton   Pop. Place
                    Lat: 45-02-52 N **Long:** 69-41-34 W
Pop: 94 (1990)   **Pop Density:** 2.4
Land: 39.3 sq. mi.; **Water:** 0.7 sq. mi.

Cambridge   Town
ZIP: 04923   **Lat:** 45-01-53 N **Long:** 69-27-00 W
Pop: 490 (1990)   **Pop Density:** 25.3
Land: 19.4 sq. mi.; **Water:** 0.1 sq. mi.
In west-central ME. Incorporated 1834.
Name origin: Named in 1834 for the university town in England.

Canaan   Town
ZIP: 04924   **Lat:** 44-46-42 N **Long:** 69-32-42 W
Pop: 1,636 (1990)   **Pop Density:** 39.8
Land: 41.1 sq. mi.; **Water:** 1.0 sq. mi.
In west-central ME. Incorporated 1788.
Name origin: For biblical Canaan, because the town's people considered their area as bountiful as the promised land.

Caratunk   Plantation
ZIP: 04925   **Lat:** 45-12-52 N **Long:** 69-52-59 W
Pop: 98 (1990)   **Pop Density:** 1.9
Land: 52.3 sq. mi.; **Water:** 3.0 sq. mi.
In western ME.
Name origin: From Abnaki term probably meaning 'crooked stream.'

Central Somerset (unorganized)   Pop. Place
                    Lat: 45-01-01 N **Long:** 70-00-12 W
Pop: 289 (1990)   **Pop Density:** 3.8
Land: 76.7 sq. mi.; **Water:** 1.1 sq. mi.

Cornville   Town
                    Lat: 44-51-42 N **Long:** 69-40-19 W
Pop: 1,008 (1990)   **Pop Density:** 24.9
Land: 40.5 sq. mi.; **Water:** 0.2 sq. mi.
In west-central ME. Incorporated 1798.
Name origin: For the abundant local Indian corn.

Dennistown   Plantation
                    Lat: 45-41-06 N **Long:** 70-21-03 W
Pop: 32 (1990)   **Pop Density:** 0.8
Land: 38.8 sq. mi.; **Water:** 1.8 sq. mi.   **Elev:** 1367 ft.
In western ME.
Name origin: Probably for an early settler.

Detroit   Town
ZIP: 04929   **Lat:** 44-46-13 N **Long:** 69-18-09 W
Pop: 751 (1990)   **Pop Density:** 37.0
Land: 20.3 sq. mi.; **Water:** 0.2 sq. mi.
Incorporated 1838.
Name origin: From the French for 'of the strait,' referring to the straits of the Sebasticook River.

Embden   Town
                    Lat: 44-55-11 N **Long:** 69-55-58 W
Pop: 659 (1990)   **Pop Density:** 16.4
Land: 40.1 sq. mi.; **Water:** 3.9 sq. mi.
Incorporated 1804.
Name origin: For Emden, Germany; spelling variation.

Fairfield   Town
ZIP: 04937   **Lat:** 44-38-13 N **Long:** 69-40-12 W
Pop: 6,718 (1990)   **Pop Density:** 124.9
Land: 53.8 sq. mi.; **Water:** 0.9 sq. mi.
In western ME, 4 mi. north of Waterville. Incorporated 1788.
Name origin: For the town's beautiful surroundings.

Harmony   Town
ZIP: 04942   **Lat:** 44-58-37 N **Long:** 69-32-44 W
Pop: 838 (1990)   **Pop Density:** 21.6
Land: 38.8 sq. mi.; **Water:** 1.7 sq. mi.
Incorporated 1804.
Name origin: For the good feeling among the early settlers, as described by the wife of Deacon John Moses.

Hartland   Town
ZIP: 04943   **Lat:** 44-53-17 N **Long:** 69-30-38 W
Pop: 1,806 (1990)   **Pop Density:** 48.7
Land: 37.1 sq. mi.; **Water:** 5.8 sq. mi.
Incorporated 1820.
Name origin: For either the large deer herds or its position in the "heart" of the county.

Highland
Plantation
Lat: 45-05-41 N **Long:** 70-04-29 W
Pop: 38 (1990) **Pop Density:** 0.9
Land: 42.0 sq. mi.; **Water:** 0.0 sq. mi.
Name origin: For the hilly topography of the area.

Jackman
Town
ZIP: 04945 **Lat:** 45-36-44 N **Long:** 70-12-31 W
Pop: 920 (1990) **Pop Density:** 22.4
Land: 41.0 sq. mi.; **Water:** 1.2 sq. mi.
Name origin: For a family of early settlers.

Madison
Town
ZIP: 04950 **Lat:** 44-49-35 N **Long:** 69-47-52 W
Pop: 4,725 (1990) **Pop Density:** 91.2
Land: 51.8 sq. mi.; **Water:** 2.8 sq. mi.
Incorporated 1804.
Name origin: For the Madison Bridge over the Kennebec River, which was named for James Madison (1751–1836), 4th president of the U.S.

Mercer
Town
Lat: 44-40-10 N **Long:** 69-54-23 W
Pop: 593 (1990) **Pop Density:** 22.2
Land: 26.7 sq. mi.; **Water:** 0.7 sq. mi.
Incorporated 1804.
Name origin: For Revolutionary War hero, Brig. Gen. Hugh Mercer.

Moose River
Town
Lat: 45-41-56 N **Long:** 70-13-14 W
Pop: 233 (1990) **Pop Density:** 5.7
Land: 40.6 sq. mi.; **Water:** 0.5 sq. mi.
Name origin: For the large moose population in the area.

Moscow
Town
Lat: 45-06-58 N **Long:** 69-52-28 W
Pop: 608 (1990) **Pop Density:** 13.3
Land: 45.8 sq. mi.; **Water:** 2.4 sq. mi.
Incorporated 1816.
Name origin: For Moscow, Russia, because the town was surveyed in 1812, the year the Russians repulsed Napoleon (1769–1821).

New Portland
Town
ZIP: 04954 **Lat:** 44-54-15 N **Long:** 70-03-55 W
Pop: 789 (1990) **Pop Density:** 18.2
Land: 43.4 sq. mi.; **Water:** 0.3 sq. mi.
Incorporated 1808.
Name origin: Named by early settlers for Portland, ME; they had resettled after Indian raids on Falmouth, near Portland.

Norridgewock
Town
ZIP: 04957 **Lat:** 44-43-34 N **Long:** 69-48-47 W
Pop: 3,105 (1990) **Pop Density:** 62.3
Land: 49.8 sq. mi.; **Water:** 1.3 sq. mi.
Incorporated 1788.
Name origin: From an Abnaki term probably referring to a waterfall.

Northeast Somerset (unorganized)
Pop. Place
Lat: 45-29-28 N **Long:** 69-52-20 W
Pop: 377 (1990) **Pop Density:** 0.8
Land: 485.3 sq. mi.; **Water:** 35.8 sq. mi.

Northwest Somerset (unorganized)
Pop. Place
Lat: 45-22-32 N **Long:** 70-17-15 W
Pop: 8 (1990) **Pop Density:** 0.0
Land: 657.1 sq. mi.; **Water:** 51.5 sq. mi.

Palmyra
Town
Lat: 44-50-45 N **Long:** 69-22-05 W
Pop: 1,867 (1990) **Pop Density:** 46.4
Land: 40.2 sq. mi.; **Water:** 1.3 sq. mi.
Incorporated 1807.
Name origin: For the daughter of the pioneer Warren family.

Pittsfield
Town
ZIP: 04967 **Lat:** 44-46-12 N **Long:** 69-26-05 W
Pop: 4,190 (1990) **Pop Density:** 86.9
Land: 48.2 sq. mi.; **Water:** 0.5 sq. mi.
Incorporated 1819.
Name origin: For landowner, William Pitts of Boston.

Pleasant Ridge
Pop. Place
Lat: 45-06-37 N **Long:** 69-59-15 W
Pop: 91 (1990) **Pop Density:** 4.1
Land: 22.0 sq. mi.; **Water:** 2.1 sq. mi.

Ripley
Town
Lat: 45-00-34 N **Long:** 69-23-03 W
Pop: 445 (1990) **Pop Density:** 18.2
Land: 24.5 sq. mi.; **Water:** 0.4 sq. mi.
Incorporated 1816.
Name origin: For Gen. Eleazer Ripley, an officer in the War of 1812.

Saint Albans
Town
Lat: 44-55-38 N **Long** 69-23-16 W
Pop: 1,724 (1990) **Pop Density:** 38.4
Land: 44.9 sq. mi.; **Water:** 2.3 sq. mi.
Incorporated 1814.
Name origin: For St. Albans, England.

Seboomook Lake (unorganized)
Pop. Place
Lat: 46-06-25 N **Long** 69-59-48 W
Pop: 19 (1990) **Pop Density:** 0.0
Land: 1401.1 sq. mi.; **Water:** 33.7 sq. mi.

Skowhegan
Town
ZIP: 04976 **Lat:** 44-45-22 N **Long** 69-40-04 W
Pop: 8,725 (1990) **Pop Density:** 147.9
Land: 59.0 sq. mi.; **Water:** 1.6 sq. mi.
In western ME, 15 mi. north-northwest of Waterville. Incorporated 1823.
Name origin: From an Abnaki term probably meaning 'place of waiting,' referring to the nearby falls on the Kennebec River where Indians waited to catch salmon.

Smithfield
Town
Lat: 44-38-39 N **Long:** 69-48-52 W
Pop: 865 (1990) **Pop Density:** 43.5
Land: 19.9 sq. mi.; **Water:** 4.8 sq. mi.
Incorporated 1840.
Name origin: For the Rev. Henry Smith, an early settler.

Solon
Town
ZIP: 04979 **Lat:** 44-56-25 N **Long** 69-48-29 W
Pop: 916 (1990) **Pop Density:** 23.0
Land: 39.9 sq. mi.; **Water:** 1.1 sq. mi.
Incorporated 1809.
Name origin: For Solon (c. 630–c. 560 B.C.), lawgiver and sage of ancient Greece.

Starks
Town
Lat: 44-44-13 N Long: 69-57-16 W
Pop: 508 (1990)   **Pop Density:** 16.2
Land: 31.4 sq. mi.; **Water:** 0.5 sq. mi.
Incorporated 1795.
Name origin: For Gen. John Stark (1728–1822), hero of the Revolutionary War.

The Forks
Plantation
Lat: 45-15-57 N Long: 69-54-55 W
Pop: 30 (1990)   **Pop Density:** 0.8
Land: 39.6 sq. mi.; **Water:** 1.8 sq. mi.
Name origin: For the nearby confluence of the Dead River and the Kennebec River.

West Forks
Plantation
Lat: 45-24-05 N Long: 70-00-57 W
Pop: 63 (1990)   **Pop Density:** 1.3
Land: 48.9 sq. mi.; **Water:** 0.5 sq. mi.
In western ME.
Name origin: For its location northwest of The Forks.

Waldo County
County Seat: Belfast (ZIP: 04915)

Pop: 33,018 (1990); 28,414 (1980)   **Pop Density:** 45.2
Land: 729.8 sq. mi.; **Water:** 123.0 sq. mi.   **Area Code:** 207
On central Atlantic coast of ME, southwest of Bangor; organized Feb 7, 1827 from Hancock County.
Name origin: For Gen. Samuel Waldo (1695–1759), an officer in the French and Indian Wars, and promoter of settlement in the area that became Maine.

Belfast
City
ZIP: 04915   **Lat:** 44-25-32 N **Long:** 69-01-36 W
Pop: 6,355 (1990); 6,243 (1980)   **Pop Density:** 186.9
Land: 34.0 sq. mi.; **Water:** 4.3 sq. mi.   **Elev:** 103 ft.
In central coastal ME, 30 mi. south-southwest of Bangor. Incorporated as a town 1773; as a city 1853.
Name origin: Named in 1770 for the home city of many Irish immigrants.

Belmont
Town
Lat: 44-22-37 N Long: 69-07-04 W
Pop: 652 (1990)   **Pop Density:** 47.9
Land: 13.6 sq. mi.; **Water:** 0.6 sq. mi.
Incorporated 1814.
Name origin: Named by George Watson, one of the town's founding fathers, from the French for 'beautiful mountain.'

Brooks
Town
ZIP: 04921   **Lat:** 44-32-17 N **Long:** 69-07-28 W
Pop: 900 (1990)   **Pop Density:** 36.9
Land: 24.4 sq. mi.; **Water:** 0.7 sq. mi.
Incorporated 1816.
Name origin: For MA governor John Brooks (1752–1825).

Burnham
Town
ZIP: 04922   **Lat:** 44-41-05 N **Long:** 69-22-29 W
Pop: 961 (1990)   **Pop Density:** 24.7
Land: 38.9 sq. mi.; **Water:** 2.2 sq. mi.
In central southern ME. Incorporated 1824.
Name origin: For a Dr. Burnham, a settler in the early 1800s.

Frankfort
Town
ZIP: 04438   **Lat:** 44-35-35 N **Long:** 68-55-11 W
Pop: 1,020 (1990)   **Pop Density:** 41.5
Land: 24.6 sq. mi.; **Water:** 1.3 sq. mi.
Incorporated 1789.
Name origin: For either the original home of many early German settlers, or as a compliment to Count Henri Luther from Frankfurt, who held large land tracts in the area.

Freedom
Town
ZIP: 04941   **Lat:** 44-30-19 N **Long:** 69-20-30 W
Pop: 593 (1990)   **Pop Density:** 27.6
Land: 21.5 sq. mi.; **Water:** 0.7 sq. mi.
Incorporated 1813.
Name origin: Named during the War of 1812 by citizens determined to retain their freedom.

Islesboro
Town
ZIP: 04848   **Lat:** 44-17-14 N **Long:** 68-55-24 W
Pop: 579 (1990)   **Pop Density:** 40.5
Land: 14.3 sq. mi.; **Water:** 54.7 sq. mi.
On an island of the same name in Penobscot Bay. Incorporated 1788.
Name origin: For the town's island location.

Jackson
Town
Lat: 44-36-33 N Long: 69-08-58 W
Pop: 415 (1990)   **Pop Density:** 16.5
Land: 25.2 sq. mi.; **Water:** 0.1 sq. mi.
Incorporated 1818.
Name origin: For Gen. Henry Jackson, Revolutionary War hero.

Knox
Town
Lat: 44-31-01 N Long: 69-12-50 W
Pop: 681 (1990)   **Pop Density:** 23.4
Land: 29.1 sq. mi.; **Water:** 0.2 sq. mi.
Incorporated 1819.
Name origin: For Gen. Henry Knox (1750–1806), a commander in the American Revolution, who settled in ME after the war.

Liberty
Town
ZIP: 04949   Lat: 44-21-37 N   Long: 69-20-17 W
Pop: 790 (1990)   Pop Density: 30.5
Land: 25.9 sq. mi.; Water: 2.4 sq. mi.
Incorporated 1827.
Name origin: For the townspeople's love of freedom.

Lincolnville
Town
ZIP: 04849   Lat: 44-17-34 N   Long: 69-04-05 W
Pop: 1,809 (1990)   Pop Density: 48.4
Land: 37.4 sq. mi.; Water: 6.4 sq. mi.
Incorporated 1802.
Name origin: For Gen. Benjamin Lincoln, a prominent land-owner.

Monroe
Town
ZIP: 04951   Lat: 44-35-58 N   Long: 69-02-45 W
Pop: 802 (1990)   Pop Density: 20.7
Land: 38.8 sq. mi.; Water: 0.2 sq. mi.
On the Atlantic coast of ME. Incorporated 1818.
Name origin: For James Monroe (1758–1831), 5th president of the U.S.

Montville
Town
Lat: 44-26-13 N   Long: 69-16-51 W
Pop: 877 (1990)   Pop Density: 20.6
Land: 42.6 sq. mi.; Water: 0.5 sq. mi.
Incorporated 1807.
Name origin: From French term meaning 'mountain town.'

Morrill
Town
ZIP: 04952   Lat: 44-25-41 N   Long: 69-10-19 W
Pop: 644 (1990)   Pop Density: 38.8
Land: 16.6 sq. mi.; Water: 0.5 sq. mi.
Incorporated 1855.
Name origin: For Anson Peaslee Morrill, governor of ME (1855–58).

Northport
Town
Lat: 44-21-19 N   Long: 68-59-27 W
Pop: 1,201 (1990)   Pop Density: 50.7
Land: 23.7 sq. mi.; Water: 10.8 sq. mi.
Incorporated 1796.
Name origin: Named by early settlers for its location north of Ducktrap Harbor.

Palermo
Town
ZIP: 04354   Lat: 44-23-48 N   Long: 69-25-32 W
Pop: 1,021 (1990)   Pop Density: 25.1
Land: 40.6 sq. mi.; Water: 3.0 sq. mi.
Incorporated 1804.
Name origin: For Palermo, Sicily, following a popular early 18th-century practice of naming towns after European cities.

Prospect
Town
Lat: 44-33-28 N   Long: 68-51-53 W
Pop: 542 (1990)   Pop Density: 29.9
Land: 18.1 sq. mi.; Water: 2.2 sq. mi.
Incorporated 1794.
Name origin: For its beautiful view of the Penobscot River and Bay.

Searsmont
Town
ZIP: 04973   Lat: 44-21-39 N   Long: 59-11-38 W
Pop: 938 (1990)   Pop Density: 24.8
Land: 37.8 sq. mi.; Water: 1.4 sq. mi.
Incorporated 1814.
Name origin: For local landowner David Sears, who held much of the original grant..

Searsport
Town
ZIP: 04974   Lat: 44-28-26 N   Long: 68-55-45 W
Pop: 2,603 (1990)   Pop Density: 91.0
Land: 28.6 sq. mi.; Water: 14.3 sq. mi.
Incorporated 1845.
Name origin: See Searsmont.

Stockton Springs
Town
ZIP: 04981   Lat: 44-29-25 N   Long: 68-50-38 W
Pop: 1,383 (1990)   Pop Density: 70.6
Land: 19.6 sq. mi.; Water: 10.3 sq. mi.
Incorporated 1857.
Name origin: Named by N. G. Hichborn for Stockton, a seaport town in England, and for local springs.

Swanville
Town
Lat: 44-30-56 N   Long: 69-00-37 W
Pop: 1,130 (1990)   Pop Density: 57.1
Land: 19.8 sq. mi.; Water: 1.9 sq. mi.
Incorporated 1818.
Name origin: For a number of area families having the surname Swan.

Thorndike
Town
ZIP: 04986   Lat: 44-35-46 N   Long: 69-14-03 W
Pop: 702 (1990)   Pop Density: 27.7
Land: 25.3 sq. mi.; Water: 0.0 sq. mi.
Incorporated 1819.
Name origin: For Israel Thorndike, one of the early landowners.

Troy
Town
ZIP: 04987   Lat: 44-40-30 N   Long: 69-15-18 W
Pop: 802 (1990)   Pop Density: 23.0
Land: 34.8 sq. mi.; Water: 0.7 sq. mi.
Incorporated 1827.
Name origin: For the ancient city in Asia Minor immortalized by the poet Homer (9th–8th? century B.C.).

Unity
Town
ZIP: 04988   Lat: 44-35-36 N   Long: 69-19-56 W
Pop: 1,817 (1990)   Pop Density: 45.9
Land: 39.6 sq. mi.; Water: 2.3 sq. mi.
Incorporated 1804.
Name origin: For the democratic political unity at the township's founding.

Waldo
Town
Lat: 44-27-46 N   Long: 69-05-38 W
Pop: 626 (1990)   Pop Density: 32.3
Land: 19.4 sq. mi.; Water: 0.0 sq. mi.
Incorporated 1845.
Name origin: For Samuel Waldo (1695–1759), Boston-born merchant and land speculator who acquired vast land holdings in what was later to become ME.

Winterport
ZIP: 04496   Town
Lat: 44-40-01 N   **Long:** 68-54-43 W
Pop: 3,175 (1990)   **Pop Density:** 89.2
Land: 35.6 sq. mi.; **Water:** 1.5 sq. mi.
On the Penobscot River between Bangor and Bucksport.
Incorporated 1860.

Washington County
County Seat: Machias (ZIP: 04654)

Pop: 35,308 (1990); 34,963 (1980)   **Pop Density:** 13.7
Land: 2568.6 sq. mi.; **Water:** 686.6 sq. mi.   **Area Code:** 207
On Atlantic coast in extreme eastern ME, east of Bangor; organized Jun 25, 1789
(prior to statehood) from Lincoln County.
Name origin: For George Washington (1732–99), American patriot and first U.S.
president.

Addison
ZIP: 04606   Town
Lat: 44-30-49 N   **Long:** 67-42-29 W
Pop: 1,114 (1990)   **Pop Density:** 26.3
Land: 42.4 sq. mi.; **Water:** 54.9 sq. mi.
In eastern coastal ME. Incorporated 1797.
Name origin: For Joseph Addison (1672–1719), English author.

Alexander
Town
Lat: 45-05-13 N   **Long:** 67-28-39 W
Pop: 478 (1990)   **Pop Density:** 12.1
Land: 39.6 sq. mi.; **Water:** 5.5 sq. mi.
In southeastern ME. Incorporated 1825.
Name origin: For Alexander Baring, Lord Ashburton (1774–
1848), who with Daniel Webster (1782–1852) settled the
dispute over Maine's northeastern boundary.

Baileyville
Town
Lat: 45-10-58 N   **Long:** 67-26-35 W
Pop: 2,031 (1990)   **Pop Density:** 55.6
Land: 36.5 sq. mi.; **Water:** 4.6 sq. mi.
In southeastern ME on St. Croix River. Incorporated 1826.
Name origin: For either early settler Thomas Bailey or two
Bailey brothers who were local landowners.

Baring
Plantation
Lat: 45-05-30 N   **Long:** 67-18-29 W
Pop: 275 (1990)   **Pop Density:** 13.2
Land: 20.9 sq. mi.; **Water:** 3.2 sq. mi.
In southeastern ME on the St. Croix River. Incorporated
1825.
Name origin: For Alexander Baring, Lord Ashburton (1774–
1848), who with Daniel Webster (1782–1852) settled the
dispute over Maine's northeastern boundary.

Beals
Town
Lat: 44-27-23 N   **Long:** 67-36-29 W
Pop: 667 (1990)   **Pop Density:** 117.0
Land: 5.7 sq. mi.; **Water:** 41.8 sq. mi.
Along eastern coastal ME on Great Wass Island. Incorporated 1925.
Name origin: For the first settler in the area, Manwaring
Beal.

Beddington
Town
Lat: 44-49-02 N   **Long:** 68-00-39 W
Pop: 43 (1990)   **Pop Density:** 1.2
Land: 34.8 sq. mi.; **Water:** 3.3 sq. mi.
In southeastern ME. Incorporated 1833.
Name origin: For Beddington, England.

Calais
ZIP: 04619   City
Lat: 45-08-01 N   **Long:** 67-12-32 W
Pop: 3,963 (1990); 4,262 (1980)   **Pop Density:** 116.6
Land: 34.0 sq. mi.; **Water:** 6.0 sq. mi.   **Elev:** 19 ft.
In eastern coastal ME near the mouth of the St. Croix River.
Incorporated as a town in 1809; as a city in 1850.
Name origin: For Calais, France, probably to commemorate
French assistance in the Revolutionary War.

Centerville
Town
Lat: 44-45-53 N   **Long:** 67-37-12 W
Pop: 30 (1990)   **Pop Density:** 0.7
Land: 41.9 sq. mi.; **Water:** 1.1 sq. mi.
In eastern coastal ME. Incorporated 1842.
Name origin: For its location in the center of the county.

Charlotte
Town
Lat: 45-00-45 N   **Long:** 67-16-09 W
Pop: 271 (1990)   **Pop Density:** 8.7
Land: 31.3 sq. mi.; **Water:** 2.8 sq. mi.
In eastern coastal ME. Incorporated 1825.
Name origin: Named in 1821 for the wife of settler David
Blanchard.

Cherryfield
ZIP: 04622   Town
Lat: 44-37-57 N   **Long:** 67-56-53 W
Pop: 1,183 (1990)   **Pop Density:** 27.1
Land: 43.7 sq. mi.; **Water:** 0.5 sq. mi.
In eastern coastal ME. Incorporated 1816.
Name origin: For a cherry orchard or field of wild cherry.

Codyville
Plantation
Lat: 45-28-08 N   **Long:** 67-39-53 W
Pop: 35 (1990)   **Pop Density:** 0.6
Land: 54.8 sq. mi.; **Water:** 0.2 sq. mi.
In southeastern ME.
Name origin: For an early settler.

Columbia
Town

Lat: 44-40-16 N Long: 67-48-38 W
Pop: 437 (1990)   Pop Density: 12.1
Land: 36.0 sq. mi.; Water: 0.3 sq. mi.

In eastern coastal ME. Incorporated 1796.

Name origin: A designation commemorating Christopher Columbus (1451–1506).

Columbia Falls
Town

ZIP: 04623   Lat: 44-40-22 N Long: 67-42-49 W
Pop: 552 (1990)   Pop Density: 22.5
Land: 24.5 sq. mi.; Water: 0.1 sq. mi.

In eastern coastal ME. Incorporated 1863.

Cooper
Town

Lat: 45-00-14 N Long: 67-25-59 W
Pop: 124 (1990)   Pop Density: 4.0
Land: 31.1 sq. mi.; Water: 1.8 sq. mi.

In southeastern ME. Incorporated 1822.

Name origin: For Gen. John Cooper, a landowner and one-time sheriff of the county.

Crawford
Town

Lat: 45-02-00 N Long: 67-34-49 W
Pop: 89 (1990)   Pop Density: 2.6
Land: 34.6 sq. mi.; Water: 3.1 sq. mi.

In southeastern ME. Incorporated 1826.

Name origin: For William Harris Crawford (1772–1834), former secretary of the treasury.

Cutler
Town

ZIP: 04626   Lat: 44-38-08 N Long: 67-13-47 W
Pop: 779 (1990)   Pop Density: 16.6
Land: 47.0 sq. mi.; Water: 69.3 sq. mi.

Incorporated 1826.

Name origin: For Joseph Cutler of MA, an early settler.

Danforth
Town

ZIP: 04424   Lat: 45-37-24 N Long: 67-50-46 W
Pop: 710 (1990)   Pop Density: 13.1
Land: 54.4 sq. mi.; Water: 6.5 sq. mi.

Incorporated 1860.

Name origin: For an early landowner.

Deblois
Town

Lat: 44-43-32 N Long: 67-59-24 W
Pop: 73 (1990)   Pop Density: 2.2
Land: 33.4 sq. mi.; Water: 0.2 sq. mi.

Incorporated 1852.

Name origin: For T. A. Deblois, president of the Bank of Portland, which owned much of the town.

Dennysville
Town

ZIP: 04628   Lat: 44-56-50 N Long: 67-14-46 W
Pop: 355 (1990)   Pop Density: 24.0
Land: 14.8 sq. mi.; Water: 0.4 sq. mi.

Incorporated 1816.

Name origin: For either an Indian, John Denny, or Nicholas Denys, pioneer historian and lieutenant governor of Acadia.

East Central Washington (unorganized)
Pop. Place

Lat: 44-51-39 N Long: 67-19-36 W
Pop: 661 (1990)   Pop Density: 3.2
Land: 208.0 sq. mi.; Water: 44.6 sq. mi.

East Machias
Town

ZIP: 04630   Lat: 44-46-19 N Long: 67-25-15 W
Pop: 1,218 (1990)   Pop Density: 34.6
Land: 35.2 sq. mi.; Water: 4.8 sq. mi.

Incorporated 1826.

Name origin: For its location east of the town of Machias.

Eastport
City

ZIP: 04631   Lat: 44-55-08 N Long: 67-00-43 W
Pop: 1,965 (1990); 1,982 (1980)   Pop Density: 531.1
Land: 3.7 sq. mi.; Water: 8.4 sq. mi.

At the eastern tip of ME, facing Campobello Island, New Brunswick, Canada. Incorporated as a town in 1798; as a city 1873.

Name origin: Named by Capt. Wopley Yeaton for its location.

Grand Lake Stream
Plantation

Lat: 45-13-46 N Long: 67-43-42 W
Pop: 174 (1990)   Pop Density: 3.9
Land: 44.2 sq. mi.; Water: 4.5 sq. mi.

In southeastern corner of coastal ME.

Name origin: For the stream that flows through the area from nearby Grand Lake.

Harrington
Town

ZIP: 04643   Lat: 44-31-16 N Long: 67-47-45 W
Pop: 893 (1990)   Pop Density: 42.1
Land: 21.2 sq. mi.; Water: 31.7 sq. mi.

In southeastern coastal ME. Incorporated 1797.

Name origin: Named by the original English surveyor for a British noble, and kept by the first settlers when the town was incorporated.

Jonesboro
Town

ZIP: 04648   Lat: 44-39-57 N Long: 67-34-58 W
Pop: 585 (1990)   Pop Density: 15.9
Land: 36.7 sq. mi.; Water: 1.8 sq. mi.

Incorporated 1809.

Name origin: For John Coffin Jones, who received a large land grant in the area in 1789.

Jonesport
Town

ZIP: 04649   Lat: 44-33-17 N Long: 67-30-53 W
Pop: 1,525 (1990)   Pop Density: 53.5
Land: 28.5 sq. mi.; Water: 72.2 sq. mi.

Originally a part of Jonesboro. Incorporated 1832.

Name origin: See Jonesboro.

Lubec
Town

ZIP: 04652   Lat: 44-49-46 N Long: 67-01-17 W
Pop: 1,853 (1990)   Pop Density: 55.6
Land: 33.3 sq. mi.; Water: 45.6 sq. mi.

Incorporated 1811.

Name origin: Named by an early German settler for Lubeck, Germany; spelling variation.

Machias
Town

ZIP: 04654   Lat: 44-41-03 N Long: 67-27-47 W
Pop: 2,569 (1990)   Pop Density: 184.8
Land: 13.9 sq. mi.; Water: 0.9 sq. mi.

Incorporated 1784.

Name origin: From Abnaki term probably meaning 'bad little falls.'

Machiasport   Town
ZIP: 04655   **Lat:** 44-37-14 N **Long:** 67-23-04 W
Pop: 1,166 (1990)   **Pop Density:** 54.7
Land: 21.3 sq. mi.; **Water:** 40.9 sq. mi.
Incorporated 1826.
Name origin: The port for Machias.

Marshfield   Town
                    Lat: 44-46-31 N **Long:** 67-30-27 W
Pop: 461 (1990)   **Pop Density:** 27.1
Land: 17.0 sq. mi.; **Water:** 0.6 sq. mi.
Incorporated 1846.
Name origin: For the town's marshlands.

Meddybemps   Town
ZIP: 04657   **Lat:** 45-02-46 N **Long:** 67-21-19 W
Pop: 133 (1990)   **Pop Density:** 9.9
Land: 13.4 sq. mi.; **Water:** 3.4 sq. mi.
Incorporated 1841.
Name origin: From a Passamaquodoy-Abnaki term probably meaning 'plenty of fish.'

Milbridge   Town
ZIP: 04658   **Lat:** 44-28-54 N **Long:** 67-51-37 W
Pop: 1,305 (1990)   **Pop Density:** 54.1
Land: 24.1 sq. mi.; **Water:** 33.3 sq. mi.
Incorporated 1848.
Name origin: For a mill and bridge built in the town in the 1830s by a Mr. Gordiner.

Northfield   Town
                    Lat: 44-49-05 N **Long:** 67-36-47 W
Pop: 99 (1990)   **Pop Density:** 2.3
Land: 43.7 sq. mi.; **Water:** 2.3 sq. mi.
Incorporated 1838.
Name origin: For the large fields north of the town of Machias.

North Washington (unorganized)   Pop. Place
                    Lat: 45-10-48 N **Long:** 67-48-54 W
Pop: 496 (1990)   **Pop Density:** 0.6
Land: 886.1 sq. mi.; **Water:** 93.6 sq. mi.

Passamaquoddy Indian Township Reservation
                                        Pop. Place
                    Lat: 45-15-32 N **Long:** 67-36-28 W
Pop: 617 (1990)   **Pop Density:** 16.5
Land: 37.5 sq. mi.; **Water:** 6.0 sq. mi.

Passamaquoddy Pleasant Point Reservation
                                        Pop. Place
                    Lat: 44-57-48 N **Long:** 67-03-20 W
Pop: 572 (1990)   **Pop Density:** 715.0
Land: 0.8 sq. mi.; **Water:** 0.1 sq. mi.

Pembroke   Town
ZIP: 04666   **Lat:** 44-56-32 N **Long:** 67-10-19 W
Pop: 852 (1990)   **Pop Density:** 31.1
Land: 27.4 sq. mi.; **Water:** 7.8 sq. mi.
Incorporated 1832.
Name origin: Named for Pembroke in Wales by Jerry Burgin, an early settler.

Perry   Town
ZIP: 04667   **Lat:** 44-58-56 N **Long:** 67-06-05 W
Pop: 758 (1990)   **Pop Density:** 26.0
Land: 29.1 sq. mi.; **Water:** 13.0 sq. mi.
Incorporated 1818.
Name origin: For Oliver H. Perry (1785–1819), naval hero in the War of 1812.

Princeton   Town
ZIP: 04668   **Lat:** 45-11-21 N **Long:** 67-33-08 W
Pop: 973 (1990)   **Pop Density:** 26.3
Land: 37.0 sq. mi.; **Water:** 5.2 sq. mi.
Incorporated 1832.
Name origin: For Princeton, MA, the former home of the original settler, Ebenezer Rolfe.

Robbinston   Town
ZIP: 04671   **Lat:** 45-04-23 N **Long:** 67-09-00 W
Pop: 495 (1990)   **Pop Density:** 17.6
Land: 28.2 sq. mi.; **Water:** 5.5 sq. mi.
Incorporated 1811.
Name origin: For the Robbins brothers, who were the original land grantees.

Roque Bluffs   Town
                    Lat: 44-37-24 N **Long:** 67-28-18 W
Pop: 234 (1990)   **Pop Density:** 21.9
Land: 10.7 sq. mi.; **Water:** 8.9 sq. mi.
Incorporated 1891.
Name origin: Named by H. P. Garner for nearby Roque Island in Englishman Bay.

Steuben   Town
ZIP: 04680   **Lat:** 44-27-46 N **Long:** 67-55-49 W
Pop: 1,084 (1990)   **Pop Density:** 25.2
Land: 43.0 sq. mi.; **Water:** 31.8 sq. mi.
Incorporated 1795.
Name origin: For Baron von Steuben (1730–94), the German officer who helped the American cause during the Revolutionary War.

Talmadge   Town
                    Lat: 45-20-30 N **Long:** 67-46-32 W
Pop: 62 (1990)   **Pop Density:** 1.6
Land: 37.7 sq. mi.; **Water:** 1.2 sq. mi.
Incorporated 1875.
Name origin: For Benjamin Talmadge, who purchased the town's land in 1804.

Topsfield   Town
ZIP: 04490   **Lat:** 45-27-13 N **Long:** 67-47-58 W
Pop: 235 (1990)   **Pop Density:** 4.6
Land: 50.7 sq. mi.; **Water:** 4.4 sq. mi.
Incorporated 1838.
Name origin: For Topsfield, MA, the former home of first settler, Nehemiah Kindsland.

Vanceboro   Town
                    Lat: 45-33-57 N **Long:** 67-28-17 W
Pop: 201 (1990)   **Pop Density:** 9.9
Land: 20.4 sq. mi.; **Water:** 2.2 sq. mi.
On the St. Croix River along the border with New Brunswick, Canada. Incorporated 1874.
Name origin: For William Vance, a prominent landowner in nearby Baring.

Waite
Town
Lat: 45-21-42 N **Long:** 67-37-21 W
Pop: 119 (1990)   **Pop Density:** 2.8
Land: 43.1 sq. mi.; **Water:** 0.1 sq. mi.
Incorporated 1876.
Name origin: For Benjamin Waite, a lumberman from nearby Calais.

Wesley
Town
Lat: 44-55-42 N **Long:** 67-38-53 W
Pop: 146 (1990)   **Pop Density:** 2.9
Land: 50.1 sq. mi.; **Water:** 0.8 sq. mi.
Incorporated 1833.
Name origin: For John Wesley (1703–91), founder of Methodism.

Whiting
Town
Lat: 44-45-10 N **Long:** 67-14-46 W
Pop: 407 (1990)   **Pop Density:** 8.7
Land: 46.8 sq. mi.; **Water:** 5.3 sq. mi.
Incorporated 1825.
Name origin: For Timothy Whiting, an early settler.

Whitneyville
Town
Lat: 44-43-29 N **Long:** 67-31-16 W
Pop: 241 (1990)   **Pop Density:** 16.9
Land: 14.3 sq. mi.; **Water:** 0.3 sq. mi.
Incorporated 1845.
Name origin: For Col. Joseph Whitney, who built a dam on the river and established a mill.

Woodland
CDP
ZIP: 04694   **Lat:** 45-09-33 N **Long:** 67-24-42 W
Pop: 1,287 (1990); 1,363 (1980)   **Pop Density:** 1287.0
Land: 1.0 sq. mi.; **Water:** 0.3 sq. mi.

York County
County Seat: Alfred (ZIP: 04002)

Pop: 164,587 (1990); 139,739 (1980)   **Pop Density:** 166.1
Land: 991.0 sq. mi.; **Water:** 280.5 sq. mi.   **Area Code:** 207
At southwestern tip of ME along Atlantic coast and NH border, southwest of Portland; original county (formerly Yorkshire County, MA), organized Nov 20, 1652 (prior to statehood).
Name origin: For James, Duke of York and Albany (1633–1701), later James II of England.

Acton
Town
ZIP: 04001   **Lat:** 43-32-01 N **Long:** 70-54-57 W
Pop: 1,727 (1990)   **Pop Density:** 45.7
Land: 37.8 sq. mi.; **Water:** 3.4 sq. mi.
In southwestern ME near NH border. Incorporated 1830.
Name origin: For a town in England.

Alfred
Town
ZIP: 04002   **Lat:** 43-28-55 N **Long:** 70-44-17 W
Pop: 2,238 (1990)   **Pop Density:** 82.3
Land: 27.2 sq. mi.; **Water:** 0.7 sq. mi.
Incorporated 1794.
Name origin: For Alfred the Great, 9th-century king of England.

Arundel
Town
Lat: 43-26-25 N **Long:** 70-31-40 W
Pop: 2,669 (1990)   **Pop Density:** 111.7
Land: 23.9 sq. mi.; **Water:** 0.0 sq. mi.
Incorporated 1718.

Berwick
Town
ZIP: 03901   **Lat:** 43-18-19 N **Long:** 70-50-45 W
Pop: 5,995 (1990)   **Pop Density:** 161.6
Land: 37.1 sq. mi.; **Water:** 0.5 sq. mi.
Incorporated 1713.
Name origin: For Berwick, Dorsetshire, England.

Biddeford
City
ZIP: 04005   **Lat:** 43-27-55 N **Long:** 70-26-36 W
Pop: 20,710 (1990); 19,638 (1980)   **Pop Density:** 690.3
Land: 30.0 sq. mi.; **Water:** 4.5 sq. mi.
In western coastal ME on the Saco River opposite Saco. Settled 1630; incorporated as a town 1718; as a city 1855.
Name origin: Named by early settlers for Bideford, Devonshire, England. Previously called Winter Harbour.

Buxton
Town
ZIP: 04093   **Lat:** 43-38-53 N **Long:** 70-32-08 W
Pop: 6,494 (1990)   **Pop Density:** 160.3
Land: 40.5 sq. mi.; **Water:** 0.7 sq. mi.
In southwestern ME, 15 mi. west of Portland. Incorporated 1762.
Name origin: Named by an English pioneer settler for a city in England.

Cape Neddick
CDP
ZIP: 03902   **Lat:** 43-10-12 N **Long:** 70-37-09 W
Pop: 2,193 (1990)   **Pop Density:** 592.7
Land: 3.7 sq. mi.; **Water:** 1.2 sq. mi.

Cornish
Town
ZIP: 04020   **Lat:** 43-46-07 N **Long:** 70-49-13 W
Pop: 1,178 (1990)   **Pop Density:** 53.3
Land: 22.1 sq. mi.; **Water:** 0.2 sq. mi.
Incorporated 1794.
Name origin: For the county of Cornwall in England.

Dayton

Town
Lat: 43-32-59 N **Long:** 70-34-32 W
Pop: 1,197 (1990)   **Pop Density:** 66.9
Land: 17.9 sq. mi.; **Water:** 0.5 sq. mi.
Incorporated 1854.
Name origin: For Jonathan Dayton, youngest member of the Constitutional Convention and speaker of the House of Representatives.

Eliot

Town
ZIP: 03903   Lat: 43-08-49 N **Long:** 70-47-22 W
Pop: 5,329 (1990)   **Pop Density:** 270.5
Land: 19.7 sq. mi.; **Water:** 1.6 sq. mi.
Incorporated 1810.
Name origin: For Robert Eliot, a member of the provincial council of NH in colonial days.

Hollis

Town
Lat: 43-37-37 N **Long:** 70-37-47 W
Pop: 3,573 (1990)   **Pop Density:** 111.7
Land: 32.0 sq. mi.; **Water:** 0.9 sq. mi.
Name origin: For the Duke of Newcastle, whose family name was Hollis.

Kennebunk

Town
ZIP: 04043   Lat: 43-24-00 N **Long:** 70-34-24 W
Pop: 8,004 (1990)   **Pop Density:** 228.0
Land: 35.1 sq. mi.; **Water:** 0.4 sq. mi.
In southwestern ME, 8 mi. south of Biddeford. Incorporated 1820.
Name origin: From Abnaki term probably meaning 'long sandbar.'

Kennebunkport

Town
ZIP: 04014   Lat: 43-23-54 N **Long:** 70-27-04 W
Pop: 3,356 (1990)   **Pop Density:** 162.9
Land: 20.6 sq. mi.; **Water:** 1.4 sq. mi.
On the coast of ME. Site of vacation retreat of U.S. President George Bush, at Walkers Point. Incorporated 1821.
Name origin: For Kennebunk.

Kittery

Town
ZIP: 03904   Lat: 43-06-03 N **Long:** 70-42-51 W
Pop: 9,372 (1990)   **Pop Density:** 526.5
Land: 17.8 sq. mi.; **Water:** 3.2 sq. mi.
At the southwestern tip of ME, across the bay from Portsmouth, NH. Incorporated 1647.
Name origin: For the Kittery Court manor in Kingsweare, Devon, England.

Kittery Point

CDP
ZIP: 03905   Lat: 43-05-04 N **Long:** 70-41-58 W
Pop: 1,093 (1990); 1,260 (1980)   **Pop Density:** 575.3
Land: 1.9 sq. mi.; **Water:** 0.7 sq. mi.

Lebanon

Town
Lat: 43-24-15 N **Long:** 70-54-34 W
Pop: 4,263 (1990)   **Pop Density:** 77.9
Land: 54.7 sq. mi.; **Water:** 1.1 sq. mi.
Incorporated 1767.
Name origin: Named by the first settlers for the biblical land.

Limerick

Town
ZIP: 04048   Lat: 43-41-12 N **Long:** 70-47-24 W
Pop: 1,688 (1990)   **Pop Density:** 62.3
Land: 27.1 sq. mi.; **Water:** 1.1 sq. mi.
Incorporated 1787.
Name origin: For Limerick, Ireland, former home of pioneer James Sullivan, who named the town in 1787.

Limington

Town
ZIP: 04049   Lat: 43-44-01 N **Long:** 70-42-11 W
Pop: 2,796 (1990)   **Pop Density:** 66.6
Land: 42.0 sq. mi.; **Water:** 1.3 sq. mi.
Incorporated 1792.
Name origin: For Lymington in Hampshire, England.

Lyman

Town
Lat: 43-29-58 N **Long:** 70-38-31 W
Pop: 3,390 (1990)   **Pop Density:** 87.1
Land: 38.9 sq. mi.; **Water:** 1.5 sq. mi.
Incorporated 1777.
Name origin: For Theodore Lyman, a successful Boston merchant who was born here.

Newfield

Town
ZIP: 04056   Lat: 43-38-32 N **Long:** 70-54-37 W
Pop: 1,042 (1990)   **Pop Density:** 32.3
Land: 32.3 sq. mi.; **Water:** 1.2 sq. mi.
Incorporated 1794.

North Berwick

Town
ZIP: 03906   Lat: 43-20-37 N **Long:** 70-46-21 W
Pop: 3,793 (1990)   **Pop Density:** 99.0
Land: 38.3 sq. mi.; **Water:** 0.1 sq. mi.
Incorporated 1831.
Name origin: For Berwick, Dorsetshire, England.

Ogunquit

Town
ZIP: 03907   Lat: 43-15-19 N **Long:** 70-36-39 W
Pop: 974 (1990)   **Pop Density:** 237.6
Land: 4.1 sq. mi.; **Water:** 0.2 sq. mi.
Name origin: From an Algonquian term, perhaps referring to a coastal lagoon hemmed by sand dunes.

Old Orchard Beach

Town
ZIP: 04063   Lat: 43-31-36 N **Long:** 70-23-40 W
Pop: 7,789 (1990)   **Pop Density:** 1052.6
Land: 7.4 sq. mi.; **Water:** 0.1 sq. mi.
Incorporated 1883. The beach, a popular tourist spot, features one of the longest stretches of hard-packed sand on the Atlantic coast.
Name origin: For the beach, which derives its name from a nearby orchard planted by Thomas Rogers in 1638.

Parsonsfield

Town
Lat: 43-44-05 N **Long:** 70-55-07 W
Pop: 1,472 (1990)   **Pop Density:** 24.9
Land: 59.0 sq. mi.; **Water:** 1.1 sq. mi.
Incorporated 1785.
Name origin: For Thomas Parsons, an early landowner.

Saco
City
ZIP: 04072   **Lat:** 43-32-13 N   **Long:** 70-27-16 W
Pop: 15,181 (1990); 12,921 (1980)   **Pop Density:** 394.3
Land: 38.5 sq. mi.; **Water:** 0.9 sq. mi.

In southwestern ME, near the mouth of the Saco River at Saco Bay. Incorporated as a town in 1653; as a city in 1867.
Name origin: From an Abnaki term probably meaning 'flowing out' or 'the outlet of the river.'

Sanford
Town
ZIP: 04073   **Lat:** 43-25-26 N   **Long:** 70-45-32 W
Pop: 20,463 (1990)   **Pop Density:** 428.1
Land: 47.8 sq. mi.; **Water:** 0.9 sq. mi.

In southwestern ME, 15 mi. west of Biddeford. Incorporated 1768.
Name origin: For the children of early settler, John Sanford.

Shapleigh
Town
ZIP: 04076   **Lat:** 43-33-09 N   **Long:** 70-50-20 W
Pop: 1,911 (1990)   **Pop Density:** 49.4
Land: 38.7 sq. mi.; **Water:** 2.4 sq. mi.

Incorporated 1785.
Name origin: For Nicholas Shapleigh, an Englishman who was a major landowner at Kittery Point.

South Berwick
Town
ZIP: 03908   **Lat:** 43-14-32 N   **Long:** 70-44-45 W
Pop: 5,877 (1990)   **Pop Density:** 182.5
Land: 32.2 sq. mi.; **Water:** 0.5 sq. mi.

Incorporated 1814.
Name origin: For its location south of Berwick on the Salmon Falls River.

South Eliot
CDP
Lat: 43-07-38 N   **Long:** 70-47-53 W
Pop: 3,112 (1990); 1,681 (1980)   **Pop Density:** 432.2
Land: 7.2 sq. mi.; **Water:** 0.4 sq. mi.

South Sanford
CDP
Lat: 43-24-06 N   **Long:** 70-42-54 W
Pop: 3,929 (1990)   **Pop Density:** 172.3
Land: 22.8 sq. mi.; **Water:** 0.7 sq. mi.

Springvale
CDP
ZIP: 04083   **Lat:** 43-28-01 N   **Long:** 70-48-11 W
Pop: 3,542 (1990); 2,940 (1980)   **Pop Density:** 1106.9
Land: 3.2 sq. mi.; **Water:** 0.1 sq. mi.

Waterboro
Town
ZIP: 04087   **Lat:** 43-35-06 N   **Long:** 70-44-09 W
Pop: 4,510 (1990)   **Pop Density:** 81.3
Land: 55.5 sq. mi.; **Water:** 1.8 sq. mi.

Incorporated 1787.

Wells
Town
ZIP: 04090   **Lat:** 43-19-39 N   **Long:** 70-37-33 W
Pop: 7,778 (1990)   **Pop Density:** 134.8
Land: 57.7 sq. mi.; **Water:** 0.5 sq. mi.

Incorporated 1653.
Name origin: For Wells in England.

York
Town
ZIP: 03909   **Lat:** 43-11-10 N   **Long:** 70-40-04 W
Pop: 9,818 (1990)   **Pop Density:** 178.8
Land: 54.9 sq. mi.; **Water:** 2.8 sq. mi.

In southwestern ME on the Atlantic Ocean, 24 mi. south-southwest of Biddeford. Incorporated 1652.
Name origin: For James, Duke of York and Albany (1633–1701), later King James II of England.

York Harbor
CDP
Lat: 43-08-32 N   **Long:** 70-38-51 W
Pop: 2,555 (1990)   **Pop Density:** 798.4
Land: 3.2 sq. mi.; **Water:** 0.3 sq. mi.

Index to Places and Counties in Maine

Maryland

MARYLAND

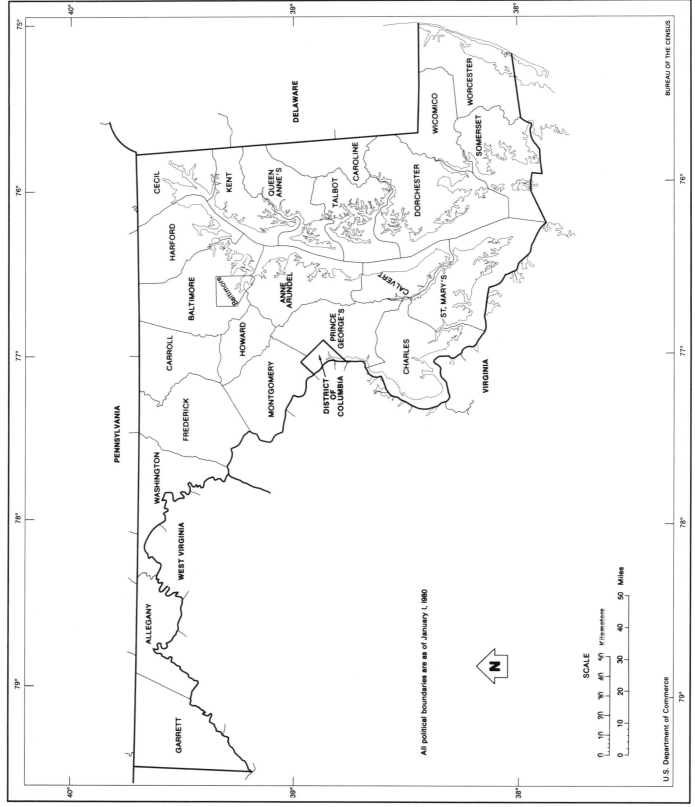

PENNSYLVANIA

GARRETT

ALLEGANY

WEST VIRGINIA

WASHINGTON

FREDERICK

CARROLL

MONTGOMERY

HOWARD

BALTIMORE

Baltimore

HARFORD

CECIL

KENT

QUEEN
ANNE'S

ANNE
ARUNDEL

DISTRICT
OF
COLUMBIA

PRINCE
GEORGE'S

CHARLES

CALVERT

ST. MARY'S

TALBOT

CAROLINE

DELAWARE

DORCHESTER

WICOMICO

SOMERSET

WORCESTER

VIRGINIA

All political boundaries are as of January 1, 1980

N

SCALE

Miles

Kilometers

0   10   20   30   40   50

0   10   20   30   40   50

U.S. Department of Commerce

BUREAU OF THE CENSUS

75°

76°

77°

78°

79°

40°

39°

38°

Maryland

Population: 4,781,468 (1990); 4,216,975 (1980)
Population rank (1990): 19
Percent population change (1980-1990): 13.4
Population projection: 5,090,000 (1995);
5,370,000 (2000)

Area: total 12,407 sq. mi.; 9,775 sq. mi. land, 2,633 sq.
mi. water. Coastline is 31 mi.; including Chesapeake
Bay, Potomac and other rivers: 3,190 mi.
Area rank: 42
Highest elevation: 3,360 ft., Backbone Mountain
Lowest point: sea level along the coasts

State capital: Annapolis (Anne Arundel County)
Largest city: Baltimore (736,014)
Second largest city: Rockville (44,835)
Largest county: Baltimore City (736,014)

Total housing units: 1,891,917
No. of occupied housing units: 1,748,991
Vacant housing units (%): 7.6
**Distribution of population by race and
  Hispanic origin (%):**
  White: 71.0
  Black: 24.9
  Hispanic (any race): 2.6
  Native American: 0.3
  Asian/Pacific: 2.9
  Other: 0.9

Admission date: April 28, 1788 (7th state)

Location: On the central Atlantic coast of the United
States, bordering Virginia, West Virginia, Pennsylva-
nia, and Delaware, and divided by Chesapeake Bay.
One of the thirteen original English colonies.

Name Origin: For Queen Henrietta Maria (1609–99),
wife of Charles I of England. It has been suggested, but
not documented, that the Roman Catholic founders
were not averse to its being considered "the land of
(the Virgin) Mary."

State bird: Baltimore oriole *(Icterus galbula)*
State boat: skipjack
State crustacean: Maryland blue crab *(Callinectes
  sapidus)*
State dog: Chesapeake Bay retriever
State fish: rockfish or striped bass *(Roccus saxatilis)*
State flower: black-eyed Susan *(Rudbeckie hirta)*
State fossil shell: Ecphora quadricostata
State insect: Baltimore checkerspot butterfly *(Euphydryas
  phaeton)*
State sport: jousting
State song: "Maryland, My Maryland"

State summer theater: Olney Theatre (Montgomery
County)
State theater: Center Stage (Baltimore)
State tree: white oak *(Quercus alba)*
State motto: *Fatti maschii, parole femine* (Latin 'Manly
deeds, womanly words')
State nickname: The Old Line State; Free State
Area codes: 301 (northwest and Washington, D.C. sub-
urbs), 410 (Baltimore area and rest of state)
Time zone: Eastern
Abbreviations: MD (postal) and Md. (traditional)
Part of (region): Middle Atlantic

Local Government

Counties

Maryland has 23 counties and one independent city, Baltimore. Eight are charter counties governed by a county
executive and county council. Eleven are governed by
county commissioners, and four have home rule with
commissioners who have additional powers. The independent city of Baltimore is the only city in Maryland not
contained within a county; it provides the same services
as a county but is governed by a mayor and city council.

Municipalities

There are 152 incorporated cities and towns; all of the
former have adopted home rule. All of the other settled
areas within a county are under the jurisdiction of county
government.

Settlement History and Early Development

Many historians believe Indians lived and farmed in permanent settlements in the area of present-day Maryland
hundreds of years before the arrival of the Europeans.
Early explorers found Susquehannock and a number of
Algonquian tribes: the Choptank, Nanticoke, Patuxent,
Portobago, and Wicomico. Most dispersed in the early
years of European colonization.

While the Spaniards were the first Europeans to explore
the Maryland region in the 1520s, it was the English who
first settled the area. In 1608, Capt. John Smith of Jamestown, Virginia sailed north up Chesapeake Bay and produced a map of the area that was used for years. In 1631,
William Claiborne, also of Virginia, opened a trading
post on Kent Island in the bay; this was the first colonial
settlement in present-day Maryland.

It is George Calvert, though, whose name is most connected to the founding of Maryland. In 1624 he became a
Roman Catholic. Since only Anglicans were allowed to
hold public office in England, he resigned as British secretary of state. As a reward for his services, King James I
gave him two large Irish estates and a peerage with the

title of Baron of Baltimore. In 1632, King Charles I granted him land north of the Potomac River, which included present day Maryland, Delaware, a large part of Pennsylvania, and the valley between the two branches of the Potomac. On his death in 1632, his son, Cecil, the second Baron Baltimore (usually called Lord Baltimore) inherited this area.

Colonial Times

In 1634 Leonard Calvert, half-brother of Cecil, accompanied by some 250 colonists, including many Roman Catholics and two Jesuit priests, sailed to America on the *Ark* and the *Dove*. They arrived at St. Clements Island on the Potomac River. Two days later Calvert bought a site from the Indians, named it St. Marys City (Maryland's first capital), and assumed the governorship of the colony.

In 1649 the colonial assembly approved Lord Baltimore's draft of a law granting religious freedom to all Christians, and shortly thereafter a band of Puritans came from Virginia.

William Claiborne's settlement on Kent Island was part of Maryland colony, but he refused to recognize Lord Baltimore's authority. In 1654 he led a band of Puritans who overthrew Baltimore's government, exiled Governor Calvert to Virginia, and ruled the colony for four years. In 1657 Oliver Cromwell recognized Lord Baltimore's charter, and Claiborne returned Maryland to him the following year.

Cecil Calvert died in 1675 and was succeeded by Charles Calvert, 3rd Baron Baltimore and the next lord proprietary of the colony. While Charles upheld the religious freedoms previously established, the Protestants disliked having a Roman Catholic governor. In 1689 the Protestant Association seized control of the government and demanded that England assume the government, which they did, and in 1692 the Church of England became the established religion in the colony. Charles Calvert's heir, Benedict Leonard Calvert, 4th Baron Baltimore, gained back full proprietary rights but only because he had become a Protestant. In 1718 Roman Catholics lost the right to vote in Maryland. Calvert's heirs ruled until the Revolutionary War.

The Revolutionary War

The colonists in Maryland, like those in the other colonies, resisted the imposition of severe taxes by England. They supported the ban on trade with Great Britain voted on at the First Continental Congress in 1774. On July 2, 1776 at the Second Continental Congress they voted for independence. Maryland's first state constitution was adopted November 8, 1776. In December of that year the Continental Congress moved to Baltimore and stayed until March of the following year; it moved to Annapolis from November 1783 to June 1784. These cities were thus among the eight that served as the U.S. capital before Washington, D.C.

Maryland sent troops and Baltimore's industries built ships and cannons for the patriots, but little fighting took place on her soil. During the war the Continental Congress formed a U.S. government under the Articles of Confederation, which Maryland refused to ratify until

other states dropped their claims to land that would later become the Northwest Territory. Maryland signed on March 1, 1781, and in that same year ceded land (along with Virginia) to Congress for the District of Columbia, site of the new federal capital. On April 28, 1788 Maryland became the seventh state to ratify the U.S. Constitution.

The War of 1812 and "The Star-Spangled Banner"

This war did not spare Maryland as the Revolutionary War had. In 1813, British forces raided towns and farms along Chesapeake Bay. In 1814 they sailed up the Patuxent River and defeated the Americans on August 24. The same day they burned the capitol and other government buildings in Washington, D.C. On September 12 they attacked Fort McHenry in Baltimore, but American forces saved the city and the British were driven from Maryland. During the bombardment of the fort, Francis Scott Key, who was imprisoned on a British warship, was inspired to write the words of "The Star-Spangled Banner," which became the national anthem of the United States (officially so designated in March 1931).

The Civil War

Maryland was a slave state, and her people were divided in their loyalties between Union and secession. The fate of the federal capital in Washington, D.C. depended on whether Maryland joined the Union. Virginia had already joined the Confederacy and if Maryland followed, Washington would be surrounded by Confederate territory. On April 29, 1861, Maryland rejected a bill of secession, but many Marylanders fought with the Confederacy.

Of the many battles fought in the state, the major one was the Battle of Antietam or Sharpsburg, which the Union won but at enormous cost to both sides. In 1863 Gen. Robert E. Lee led his Confederate troops through Maryland on his way to Gettysburg, Pennsylvania. In 1864, Confederate Gen. Jubal Early and his troops crossed into Maryland, ravaged the Hagerstown area and threatened Baltimore before being driven back.

In 1864 Maryland adopted a constitution that abolished slavery but placed harsh penalties on Confederate supporters. In 1867 a less severe constitution was adopted; the same basic constitution is still in effect, as amended.

Business and Industry

Tobacco was until recently the staple crop of most of Maryland, and during the early eighteenth century more and more slave labor was used. German immigrants moved into western Maryland where wheat became the primary crop. Baltimore had an excellent port and the city grew in size and importance with the increased export of crops and development of commerce and shipbuilding. It was one of the largest and most important U.S. cities throughout the nineteenth century.

The Baltimore and Ohio Railroad, the Chesapeake and Ohio Canal, and Chesapeake and Delaware Canal all provided commercial links between Baltimore, the Ohio Valley, and the West. In 1830, Peter Cooper built the first coal-burning American steam locomotive, the *Tom*

Thumb. The first ocean-going iron steamship built in the U.S., the *De Rosset*, was completed in Baltimore in 1839.

After the Civil War, Baltimore played a major role in rebuilding the South. Industry gradually replaced agriculture, especially shipbuilding, steelmaking, and the manufacture of clothing and shoes. The expansion of the shipyards and factories occurred in response to the nation's needs during the two world wars. Improved transportation systems after World War II brought many more people into the state. Today, Maryland is a national center for space research, development, and production. Baltimore, which had fallen into decline, has been revitalized by projects during the past few decades designed to develop and renovate both the downtown area and the harbor facilities.

State Boundaries

The various Maryland-Virginia land and riparian borders were disputed from 1638 until their final resolution in 1972. The Maryland-West Virginia boundary was confirmed by the U.S. Supreme Court May 27, 1912. See the Pennsylvania section for details on the Maryland-Pennsylvania-Delaware border.

Maryland Counties

Allegany	Charles	Prince George's
Anne Arundel	Dorchester	Queen Anne's
Baltimore (city)	Frederick	St. Mary's
Baltimore	Garrett	Somerset
Calvert	Harford	Talbot
Caroline	Howard	Washington
Carroll	Kent	Wicomico
Cecil	Montgomery	Worcester

Multi-County Places

The following Maryland places are in more than one county. Given here is the total population for each multi-county place, and the names of the counties it is in.

Adelphi, pop. 13,524; Prince George's (13,524), Montgomery (0)
Calverton, pop. 12,046; Montgomery (7,585), Prince George's (4,461)
Charlotte Hall, pop. 1,992; St. Mary's (1,376), Charles (616)
Hampstead, pop. 2,608; Carroll (2,608), Baltimore (0)
Hillandale, pop. 10,318; Montgomery (8,151), Prince George's (2,167)
Jessup, pop. 6,537; Anne Arundel (5,324), Howard (1,213)
Langley Park, pop. 17,474; Prince George's (14,345), Montgomery (3,129)
Millington, pop. 409; Kent (375), Queen Anne's (34)
Mount Airy, pop. 3,730; Carroll (2,233), Frederick (1,497)
Queen Anne, pop. 250; Queen Anne's (140), Talbot (110)
Takoma Park, pop. 16,700; Montgomery (11,544), Prince George's (5,156)
Templeville, pop. 66; Queen Anne's (44), Caroline (22)

Allegany County
County Seat: Cumberland (ZIP: 21502)

Pop: 74,946 (1990); 80,548 (1980)   **Pop Density:** 176.2
Land: 425.3 sq. mi.; **Water:** 4.4 sq. mi.   **Area Code:** 301

On northwestern border of panhandle of MD; organized Dec 25, 1789 from Washington County.

Name origin: For the Allegheny Mountains (using a variant spelling), which cross through the county.

Barton   Town
ZIP: 21521   **Lat:** 39-31-57 N **Long:** 79-01-01 W
Pop: 530 (1990); 617 (1980)   **Pop Density:** 2650.0
Land: 0.2 sq. mi.; **Water:** 0.0 sq. mi.   **Elev:** 1251 ft.
Founded by coal developer Andrew Shaw. Incorporated 1900.
Name origin: For Barton, England, birthplace of Andrew Shaw's father.

Cresaptown-Bel Air   CDP
          Lat: 39-35-17 N **Long:** 78-51-31 W
Pop: 4,586 (1990); 83 (1980)   **Pop Density:** 619.7
Land: 7.4 sq. mi.; **Water:** 0.0 sq. mi.

Cumberland   City
ZIP: 21502   **Lat:** 39-39-03 N **Long:** 78-45-49 W
Pop: 23,706 (1990); 11,155 (1980)   **Pop Density:** 2856.1
Land: 8.3 sq. mi.; **Water:** 0.0 sq. mi.
In northwestern MD on the Potomac River. Founded 1754 by Thomas Beall; incorporated 1815. Starting point of the old National Road and of the Chesapeake & Ohio Canal, important in early U.S. westward expansion.
Name origin: For George II's son, William Augustus (1721–1765), Duke of Cumberland.

Frostburg   City
ZIP: 21532   **Lat:** 39-38-59 N **Long:** 78-55-44 W
Pop: 8,075 (1990); 566 (1980)   **Pop Density:** 2883.9
Land: 2.8 sq. mi.; **Water:** 0.0 sq. mi.   **Elev:** 2075 ft.
Incorporated 1839.
Name origin: For the Frosts, who ran a tavern in the area in 1812.

La Vale   CDP
          Lat: 39-39-48 N **Long:** 78-49-07 W
Pop: 4,694 (1990); 58 (1980)   **Pop Density:** 579.5
Land: 8.1 sq. mi.; **Water:** 0.0 sq. mi.

Lonaconing   Town
ZIP: 21539   **Lat:** 39-33-54 N **Long:** 78-58-47 W
Pop: 1,122 (1990); 1,420 (1980)   **Pop Density:** 2805.0
Land: 0.4 sq. mi.; **Water:** 0.0 sq. mi.
Incorporated 1890.
Name origin: From Algonquian term perhaps meaning 'where there is a beautiful summit.'

Luke   Town
ZIP: 21540   **Lat:** 39-28-32 N **Long:** 79-03-37 W
Pop: 184 (1990); 329 (1980)   **Pop Density:** 613.3
Land: 0.3 sq. mi.; **Water:** 0.0 sq. mi.
Incorporated 1922.
Name origin: For the Luke family, who emigrated to the area from Scotland in the 1850s.

Midland   Town
ZIP: 21542   **Lat:** 39-35-23 N **Long:** 78-56-56 W
Pop: 574 (1990); 601 (1980)   **Pop Density:** 2870.0
Land: 0.2 sq. mi.; **Water:** 0.0 sq. mi.   **Elev:** 1694 ft.
Incorporated 1900; established 1902.
Name origin: For the Midlands region of England.

Westernport   Town
ZIP: 21540   **Lat:** 39-29-19 N **Long:** 79-02-32 W
Pop: 2,454 (1990); 2,706 (1980)   **Pop Density:** 2726.7
Land: 0.9 sq. mi.; **Water:** 0.0 sq. mi.
In western MD. Incorporated 1858.
Name origin: The westernmost coal-loading port on the Potomac during the coal-mining days in the George's Creek Valley.

Anne Arundel County
County Seat: Annapolis (ZIP: 21401)

Pop: 427,239 (1990); 370,775 (1980)   **Pop Density:** 1027.1
Land: 416.0 sq. mi.; **Water:** 172.0 sq. mi.   **Area Code:** 410
In east-central MD, south of Baltimore; original county, organized 1650.
Name origin: For Anne Arundel, daughter of Lord Thomas Arundell of Wardour and wife of Cecilius Calvert, Lord Baltimore (1605–75).

Annapolis   City
ZIP: 21401   **Lat:** 38-58-17 N **Long:** 76-30-10 W
Pop: 33,187 (1990); 31,740 (1980)   **Pop Density:** 5267.8
Land: 6.3 sq. mi.; **Water:** 0.9 sq. mi.
On Severn River, inlet of the Chesapeake Bay, 23 mi. southeast of Baltimore. Founded c. 1650. Made state capital in 1694. Incorporated 1708. Served as the U.S. national capital, Nov 26, 1783 to Aug 13, 1784. Site of U.S. Naval Academy.
Name origin: For Queen Anne of England. Previously called Providence and Anne Arundel Town.

Arden-on-the-Severn   CDP
          Lat: 39-04-11 N **Long:** 76-35-41 W
Pop: 2,427 (1990); 2,303 (1980)   **Pop Density:** 1516.9
Land: 1.6 sq. mi.; **Water:** 0.3 sq. mi.

Arnold   CDP
ZIP: 21012   **Lat:** 39-02-33 N **Long:** 76-29-57 W
Pop: 20,261 (1990); 12,285 (1980)   **Pop Density:** 1876.0
Land: 10.8 sq. mi.; **Water:** 2.6 sq. mi.

Brooklyn Park   CDP
ZIP: 21225   **Lat:** 39-13-01 N **Long:** 76-36-37 W
Pop: 10,987 (1990); 11,508 (1980)   **Pop Density:** 3788.6
Land: 2.9 sq. mi.; **Water:** 0.0 sq. mi.

Cape St. Claire   CDP
ZIP: 21401   **Lat:** 39-02-39 N **Long:** 76-26-45 W
Pop: 7,878 (1990); 6,022 (1980)   **Pop Density:** 3939.0
Land: 2.0 sq. mi.; **Water:** 0.6 sq. mi.

Crofton   CDP
ZIP: 21114   **Lat:** 39-00-39 N **Long:** 76-41-14 W
Pop: 12,781 (1990); 12,009 (1980)   **Pop Density:** 2556.2
Land: 5.0 sq. mi.; **Water:** 0.0 sq. mi.

Crownsville   CDP
ZIP: 21032   **Lat:** 39-01-00 N **Long:** 76-35-43 W
Pop: 1,514 (1990)   **Pop Density:** 270.4
Land: 5.6 sq. mi.; **Water:** 0.0 sq. mi.

Deale   CDP
ZIP: 20751   **Lat:** 38-47-35 N **Long:** 76-32-47 W
Pop: 4,151 (1990); 3,008 (1980)   **Pop Density:** 965.3
Land: 4.3 sq. mi.; **Water:** 0.2 sq. mi.

Ferndale   CDP
ZIP: 21061   **Lat:** 39-11-11 N **Long:** 76-38-03 W
Pop: 16,355 (1990); 14,314 (1980)   **Pop Density:** 4088.8
Land: 4.0 sq. mi.; **Water:** 0.0 sq. mi.

Fort Meade   Military facility
ZIP: 20755   **Lat:** 39-06-29 N **Long:** 76-44-31 W
Pop: 12,509 (1990); 14,083 (1980)   **Pop Density:** 1895.3
Land: 6.6 sq. mi.; **Water:** 0.0 sq. mi.

Glen Burnie   CDP
ZIP: 21061   **Lat:** 39-09-58 N **Long:** 76-36-08 W
Pop: 37,305 (1990); 21,684 (1980)   **Pop Density:** 3032.9
Land: 12.3 sq. mi.; **Water:** 0.7 sq. mi.

Green Haven   CDP
ZIP: 21122   **Lat:** 39-08-12 N **Long:** 76-32-24 W
Pop: 14,416 (1990); 6,577 (1980)   **Pop Density:** 4505.0
Land: 3.2 sq. mi.; **Water:** 0.2 sq. mi.

Herald Harbor   CDP
ZIP: 21032   **Lat:** 39-03-01 N **Long:** 76-34-27 W
Pop: 1,707 (1990); 1,266 (1980)   **Pop Density:** 1138.0
Land: 1.5 sq. mi.; **Water:** 0.6 sq. mi.

Highland Beach   Town
ZIP: 21403   **Lat:** 38-55-54 N **Long:** 76-28-00 W
Pop: 102 (1990); 8 (1980)   **Pop Density:** 1020.0
Land: 0.1 sq. mi.; **Water:** 0.0 sq. mi.
Incorporated 1922.
Name origin: Descriptively named for land overlooking the shore of Chesapeake Bay.

Hillsmere Shores   CDP
          Lat: 38-55-54 N **Long:** 76-29-49 W
Pop: 3,321 (1990); 2,972 (1980)   **Pop Density:** 2554.6
Land: 1.3 sq. mi.; **Water:** 0.6 sq. mi.

Jessup   CDP
ZIP: 20794   **Lat:** 39-08-22 N **Long:** 76-46-06 W
Pop: 5,324 (1990); 3,586 (1980)   **Pop Density:** 1521.1
Land: 3.5 sq. mi.; **Water:** 0.0 sq. mi.
Part of the town is in Howard County.

Lake Shore   CDP
ZIP: 21122   **Lat:** 39-05-51 N **Long:** 76-29-08 W
Pop: 13,269 (1990); 10,181 (1980)   **Pop Density:** 1300.9
Land: 10.2 sq. mi.; **Water:** 4.4 sq. mi.

Linthicum   CDP
ZIP: 21090   **Lat:** 39-12-19 N **Long:** 76-39-57 W
Pop: 7,547 (1990); 7,457 (1980)   **Pop Density:** 1796.9
Land: 4.2 sq. mi.; **Water:** 0.0 sq. mi.

Londontowne   CDP
ZIP: 21037   **Lat:** 38-56-08 N **Long:** 76-33-28 W
Pop: 6,992 (1990); 6,052 (1980)   **Pop Density:** 2330.7
Land: 3.0 sq. mi.; **Water:** 0.8 sq. mi.

Maryland City   CDP
ZIP: 20724   **Lat:** 39-05-38 N **Long:** 76-49-27 W
Pop: 6,813 (1990); 6,949 (1980)   **Pop Density:** 2620.4
Land: 2.6 sq. mi.; **Water:** 0.0 sq. mi.

Mayo   CDP
ZIP: 21037   **Lat:** 38-53-30 N **Long:** 76-30-01 W
Pop: 2,537 (1990); 2,795 (1980)   **Pop Density:** 1014.8
Land: 2.5 sq. mi.; **Water:** 2.1 sq. mi.

Naval Academy   Military facility
ZIP: 21402   **Lat:** 38-59-08 N **Long:** 76-29-20 W
Pop: 5,420 (1990); 5,367 (1980)   **Pop Density:** 9033.3
Land: 0.6 sq. mi.; **Water:** 0.3 sq. mi.

Odenton   CDP
ZIP: 21113   **Lat:** 39-03-40 N **Long:** 76-41-44 W
Pop: 12,833 (1990); 13,270 (1980)   **Pop Density:** 957.7
Land: 13.4 sq. mi.; **Water:** 0.0 sq. mi.

Parole   CDP
ZIP: 21401   **Lat:** 38-59-02 N **Long:** 76-33-11 W
Pop: 10,054 (1990); 3,377 (1980)   **Pop Density:** 976.1
Land: 10.3 sq. mi.; **Water:** 1.7 sq. mi.

Pasadena   CDP
ZIP: 21122   **Lat:** 39-06-43 N **Long:** 76-33-08 W
Pop: 10,012 (1990); 7,439 (1980)   **Pop Density:** 1353.0
Land: 7.4 sq. mi.; **Water:** 0.3 sq. mi.

Pumphrey   CDP
ZIP: 21227   **Lat:** 39-13-04 N **Long:** 76-38-34 W
Pop: 5,483 (1990); 5,666 (1980)   **Pop Density:** 2193.2
Land: 2.5 sq. mi.; **Water:** 0.1 sq. mi.

Riva   CDP
ZIP: 21140   **Lat:** 38-56-45 N **Long:** 76-35-22 W
Pop: 3,438 (1990); 1,109 (1980)   **Pop Density:** 1375.2
Land: 2.5 sq. mi.; **Water:** 0.4 sq. mi.

Riviera Beach   CDP
ZIP: 21122   **Lat:** 39-09-38 N **Long:** 76-31-24 W
Pop: 11,376 (1990); 8,812 (1980)   **Pop Density:** 4740.0
Land: 2.4 sq. mi.; **Water:** 0.6 sq. mi.

Selby-on-the-Bay   CDP
                       Lat: 38-54-57 N **Long:** 76-31-21 W
Pop: 3,101 (1990); 3,125 (1980)   **Pop Density:** 969.1
Land: 3.2 sq. mi.; **Water:** 1.5 sq. mi.

Severn   CDP
ZIP: 21144   **Lat:** 39-08-06 N **Long:** 76-41-29 W
Pop: 24,499 (1990); 20,147 (1980)   **Pop Density:** 1870.2
Land: 13.1 sq. mi.; **Water:** 0.0 sq. mi.

Severna Park   CDP
ZIP: 21146   **Lat:** 39-04-55 N **Long** 76-34-21 W
Pop: 25,879 (1990); 21,253 (1980)   **Pop Density:** 2006.1
Land: 12.9 sq. mi.; **Water:** 2.6 sq. mi.

Shady Side   CDP
ZIP: 20764   **Lat:** 38-49-48 N **Long** 76-31-28 W
Pop: 4,107 (1990); 2,877 (1980)   **Pop Density:** 562.6
Land: 7.3 sq. mi.; **Water:** 0.6 sq. mi.

South Gate   CDP
ZIP: 21061   **Lat:** 39-07-44 N **Long** 76-37-33 W
Pop: 27,564 (1990); 16,892 (1980)   **Pop Density:** 4375.2
Land: 6.3 sq. mi.; **Water:** 0.0 sq. mi.

Baltimore (city)

ZIP: 21201   **Lat:** 39-18-02 N **Long:** 76-36-38 W
Pop: 736,014 (1990); 786,741 (1980)   **Pop Density:** 9109.1
Land: 80.8 sq. mi.; **Water:** 11.3 sq. mi.   **Area Code:** 410

In northern MD on Patapsco River, upper Chesapeake Bay, 41 mi. northeast of Washington. Founded 1729; incorporated 1796. Distinct from and independent of Baltimore County since 1851, with the same political power as a county. Major East Coast port. Headquarters of McCormick & Co, world's largest producer of spices and seasonings. Other industries include steel, chemicals, and manufacture of radar and other electronic equipment. Site of Johns Hopkins University. Site of Fort McHenry, whose bombardment by the British in 1814 inspired Francis Scott Key (1779–1843) to write The Star-Spangled Banner.

Name origin: For the barony of Baltimore in Ireland, source of the hereditary title Lord Baltimore of the Calvert family, proprietors of the colony of MD.

Baltimore County
County Seat: Towson (ZIP: 21204)

Pop: 692,134 (1990); 655,615 (1980)   **Pop Density:** 1156.3
Land: 598.6 sq. mi.; **Water:** 83.5 sq. mi.   **Area Code:** 410

On central northern border of MD, north of Annapolis; original county, legal origin not known, but was in existence by Jan 12, 1659. Baltimore City was made independent of the county in 1851.

Name origin: For the barony of Baltimore in Ireland, source of the hereditary title Lord Baltimore of the Calvert family, proprietors of the colony of MD.

Arbutus   CDP
ZIP: 21227   **Lat:** 39-14-33 N **Long:** 76-41-32 W
Pop: 19,750 (1990); 20,163 (1980)   **Pop Density:** 3038.5
Land: 6.5 sq. mi.; **Water:** 0.0 sq. mi.

Bowleys Quarters   CDP
                     Lat: 39-18-44 N **Long:** 76-22-56 W
Pop: 5,595 (1990)   **Pop Density:** 1748.4
Land: 3.2 sq. mi.; **Water:** 2.9 sq. mi.

Carney   CDP
ZIP: 21234   **Lat:** 39-24-15 N **Long:** 76-31-21 W
Pop: 25,578 (1990); 13,090 (1980)   **Pop Density:** 3654.0
Land: 7.0 sq. mi.; **Water:** 0.0 sq. mi.

Catonsville   CDP
ZIP: 21228   **Lat:** 39-15-52 N **Long:** 76-44-29 W
Pop: 35,233 (1990); 33,208 (1980)   **Pop Density:** 2516.6
Land: 14.0 sq. mi.; **Water:** 0.0 sq. mi.

Cockeysville   CDP
ZIP: 21030   **Lat:** 39-28-40 N **Long:** 76-37-54 W
Pop: 18,668 (1990); 17,013 (1980)   **Pop Density:** 1666.8
Land: 11.2 sq. mi.; **Water:** 0.1 sq. mi.

Dundalk   CDP
ZIP: 21222   **Lat:** 39-16-06 N **Long:** 76-29-50 W
Pop: 65,800 (1990); 60,467 (1980)   **Pop Density:** 4947.4
Land: 13.3 sq. mi.; **Water:** 4.1 sq. mi.

Edgemere   CDP
ZIP: 21221   **Lat:** 39-13-22 N **Long:** 76-27-34 W
Pop: 9,226 (1990); 9,078 (1980)   **Pop Density:** 854.3
Land: 10.8 sq. mi.; **Water:** 9.7 sq. mi.

Essex   CDP
ZIP: 21221   **Lat:** 39-18-09 N **Long:** 76-26-45 W
Pop: 40,872 (1990); 39,614 (1980)   **Pop Density:** 4302.3
Land: 9.5 sq. mi.; **Water:** 2.4 sq. mi.

Garrison   CDP
ZIP: 21117   **Lat:** 39-24-04 N **Long:** 76-44-57 W
Pop: 5,045 (1990)   **Pop Density:** 1627.4
Land: 3.1 sq. mi.; **Water:** 0.0 sq. mi.

Hampstead   Town
ZIP: 21074   **Lat:** 39-35-27 N **Long:** 76-50-05 W
Land: 0.003 sq. mi.; **Water:** 0.0 sq. mi.

Established 1786; incorporated 1888. Part of the town is also in Carroll County.
Name origin: For Hampstead, England.

Hampton   CDP
                     Lat: 39-25-05 N **Long:** 76-34-21 W
Pop: 4,926 (1990); 5,220 (1980)   **Pop Density:** 864.2
Land: 5.7 sq. mi.; **Water:** 0.0 sq. mi.

Kingsville   CDP
ZIP: 21087   **Lat:** 39-26-56 N **Long:** 76-25-06 W
Pop: 3,550 (1990); 2,824 (1980)   **Pop Density:** 351.5
Land: 10.1 sq. mi.; **Water:** 0.0 sq. mi.

Lansdowne-Baltimore Highlands   CDP
ZIP: 21227   **Lat:** 39-14-11 N **Long:** 76-39-16 W
Pop: 15,509 (1990); 16,759 (1980)   **Pop Density:** 3782.7
Land: 4.1 sq. mi.; **Water:** 0.2 sq. mi.

Lochearn   CDP
ZIP: 21207   **Lat:** 39-20-50 N **Long:** 76-43-50 W
Pop: 25,240 (1990); 15,934 (1980)   **Pop Density:** 4507.1
Land: 5.6 sq. mi.; **Water:** 0.0 sq. mi.

Lutherville-Timonium   CDP
ZIP: 21093   **Lat:** 39-26-26 N **Long:** 76-36-44 W
Pop: 16,442 (1990); 15,543 (1980)   **Pop Density:** 2221.9
Land: 7.4 sq. mi.; **Water:** 0.0 sq. mi.

Mays Chapel   CDP
ZIP: 21093   **Lat:** 39-25-58 N **Long:** 76-38-58 W
Pop: 10,132 (1990); 5,213 (1980)   **Pop Density:** 2666.3
Land: 3.8 sq. mi.; **Water:** 0.0 sq. mi.

Middle River   CDP
ZIP: 21220   **Lat:** 39-20-02 N **Long:** 76-26-02 W
Pop: 24,616 (1990); 26,756 (1980)   **Pop Density:** 3155.9
Land: 7.8 sq. mi.; **Water:** 0.7 sq. mi.

Milford Mill   CDP
ZIP: 21207   **Lat:** 39-20-51 N **Long:** 76-46-12 W
Pop: 22,547 (1990); 20,354 (1980)   **Pop Density:** 3221.0
Land: 7.0 sq. mi.; **Water:** 0.0 sq. mi.

Overlea   CDP
ZIP: 21206   **Lat:** 39-21-48 N **Long:** 76-31-04 W
Pop: 12,137 (1990); 12,965 (1980)   **Pop Density:** 3915.2
Land: 3.1 sq. mi.; **Water:** 0.0 sq. mi.

Owings Mills   CDP
ZIP: 21117   **Lat:** 39-24-40 N **Long:** 76-47-35 W
Pop: 9,474 (1990); 9,526 (1980)   **Pop Density:** 986.9
Land: 9.6 sq. mi.; **Water:** 0.0 sq. mi.

Parkville   CDP
ZIP: 21234   **Lat:** 39-23-02 N **Long:** 76-33-06 W
Pop: 31,617 (1990); 29,937 (1980)   **Pop Density:** 7527.9
Land: 4.2 sq. mi.; **Water:** 0.0 sq. mi.

Perry Hall   CDP
ZIP: 21128   **Lat:** 39-24-23 N **Long:** 76-28-43 W
Pop: 22,723 (1990); 13,455 (1980)   **Pop Density:** 3246.1
Land: 7.0 sq. mi.; **Water:** 0.0 sq. mi.

Pikesville   CDP
ZIP: 21208   **Lat:** 39-23-28 N **Long:** 76-42-02 W
Pop: 24,815 (1990); 22,555 (1980)   **Pop Density:** 2067.9
Land: 12.0 sq. mi.; **Water:** 0.0 sq. mi.

Randallstown
CDP
ZIP: 21133   Lat: 39-22-18 N Long: 76-48-07 W
Pop: 26,277 (1990); 25,927 (1980)   Pop Density: 2551.2
Land: 10.3 sq. mi.; Water: 0.0 sq. mi.

Reisterstown
CDP
ZIP: 21136   Lat: 39-27-24 N Long: 76-48-53 W
Pop: 19,314 (1990); 19,385 (1980)   Pop Density: 3862.8
Land: 5.0 sq. mi.; Water: 0.0 sq. mi.

Rosedale
CDP
ZIP: 21237   Lat: 39-19-39 N Long: 76-30-30 W
Pop: 18,703 (1990); 15,680 (1980)   Pop Density: 2750.4
Land: 6.8 sq. mi.; Water: 0.3 sq. mi.

Rossville
CDP
ZIP: 21237   Lat: 39-21-17 N Long: 76-28-51 W
Pop: 9,492 (1990)   Pop Density: 1757.8
Land: 5.4 sq. mi.; Water: 0.0 sq. mi.

Towson
CDP
ZIP: 21204   Lat: 39-23-42 N Long 76-37-16 W
Pop: 49,445 (1990); 2,782 (1980)   Pop Density: 3531.8
Land: 14.0 sq. mi.; Water: 0.1 sq. mi.
Suburb of Baltimore, 8 mi. north of the central downtown area.
Name origin: For the Towson family, who ran an inn here. Formerly called Towsontown

White Marsh
CDP
ZIP: 21162   Lat: 39-23-00 N Long 76-27-31 W
Pop: 8,183 (1990)   Pop Density: 1544.0
Land: 5.3 sq. mi.; Water: 0.0 sq. mi.

Woodlawn
CDP
Lat: 39-18-24 N Long 76-44-52 W
Pop: 32,907 (1990)   Pop Density: 3427.8
Land: 9.6 sq. mi.; Water: 0.0 sq. mi.

Calvert County
County Seat: Prince Frederick (ZIP: 20678)

Pop: 51,372 (1990); 34,638 (1980)   Pop Density: 238.7
Land: 215.2 sq. mi.; Water: 129.9 sq. mi.   Area Code: 410

In south-central MD, south of Annapolis; original county, organized as Patuxent County in 1654; name changed in 1658.
Name origin: For the family name of the Lords Baltimore, proprietors of MD.

Calvert Beach-Long Beach
CDP
Lat: 38-27-39 N Long: 76-28-41 W
Pop: 1,728 (1990)   Pop Density: 640.0
Land: 2.7 sq. mi.; Water: 0.0 sq. mi.

Chesapeake Beach
Town
ZIP: 20732   Lat: 38-41-14 N Long: 76-32-09 W
Pop: 2,403 (1990); 1,408 (1980)   Pop Density: 1264.7
Land: 1.9 sq. mi.; Water: 1.1 sq. mi.
Incorporated 1886.
Name origin: For its location on Chesapeake Bay.

Chesapeake Ranch Estates
CDP
Lat: 38-21-20 N Long: 76-24-57 W
Pop: 5,423 (1990)   Pop Density: 686.5
Land: 7.9 sq. mi.; Water: 0.3 sq. mi.

North Beach
Town
ZIP: 20714   Lat: 38-42-31 N Long 76-32-04 W
Pop: 1,173 (1990); 1,504 (1980)   Pop Density: 3910.0
Land: 0.3 sq. mi.; Water: 0.0 sq. mi.
Incorporated 1910.
Name origin: A northward extension of Chesapeake Beach.

Prince Frederick
CDP
ZIP: 20678   Lat: 38-32-54 N Long 76-35-20 W
Pop: 1,885 (1990); 1,805 (1980)   Pop Density: 273.2
Land: 6.9 sq. mi.; Water: 0.0 sq. mi.

Caroline County
County Seat: Denton (ZIP: 21629)

Pop: 27,035 (1990); 23,143 (1980)　　　　**Pop Density:** 84.4
Land: 320.2 sq. mi.; **Water:** 5.9 sq. mi.　　　**Area Code:** 410

On eastern border of MD, southwest of Dover, DE; organized Jun 15, 1773 (prior to statehood) from Dorchester and Queen Anne's counties.

Name origin: For Caroline Calvert Eden, sister of Frederick Calvert, 6th Baron Baltimore and the last proprietor of MD.

Denton
Town
ZIP: 21629　　　**Lat:** 38-52-56 N **Long:** 75-49-20 W
Pop: 2,977 (1990); 1,927 (1980)　　**Pop Density:** 1294.3
Land: 2.3 sq. mi.; **Water:** 0.1 sq. mi.

Incorporated 1802.

Name origin: Formerly called Pig Town, then Edenton in honor of Sir Robert Eden, the last royal governor of MD; the initial letter was dropped during the Revolutionary War.

Federalsburg
Town
ZIP: 21632　　　**Lat:** 38-41-27 N **Long:** 75-46-25 W
Pop: 2,365 (1990); 1,952 (1980)　　**Pop Density:** 1182.5
Land: 2.0 sq. mi.; **Water:** 0.1 sq. mi.

Established 1789; incorporated 1823.

Name origin: For the Federalist party convention held here in 1812.

Goldsboro
Town
ZIP: 21636　　　**Lat:** 39-02-07 N **Long:** 75-47-14 W
Pop: 185 (1990); 188 (1980)　　**Pop Density:** 925.0
Land: 0.2 sq. mi.; **Water:** 0.0 sq. mi.

Incorporated 1906.

Name origin: For 1870s landowner, Dr. G. W. Goldsborough. Previously called Oldtown.

Greensboro
Town
ZIP: 21639　　　**Lat:** 38-58-34 N **Long:** 75-48-24 W
Pop: 1,441 (1990); 1,253 (1980)　　**Pop Density:** 2058.6
Land: 0.7 sq. mi.; **Water:** 0.0 sq. mi.

Founded 1732; incorporated 1826.

Name origin: For a local farmer. Previously called Choptank Bridge.

Henderson
Town
ZIP: 21640　　　**Lat:** 39-04-29 N **Long:** 75-46-01 W
Pop: 66 (1990); 156 (1980)　　**Pop Density:** 660.0
Land: 0.1 sq. mi.; **Water:** 0.0 sq. mi.

Settled 1850s; incorporated 1949.

Name origin: For a local family. Previously called Mellville's Crossroads.

Hillsboro
Town
ZIP: 21641　　　**Lat:** 38-54-58 N **Long:** 75-56-30 W
Pop: 164 (1990); 180 (1980)　　**Pop Density:** 1640.0
Land: 0.1 sq. mi.; **Water:** 0.0 sq. mi.　　**Elev:** 47 ft.

Incorporated 1853.

Name origin: Descriptively named by early settlers.

Marydel
Town
ZIP: 21649　　　**Lat:** 39-06-50 N **Long:** 75-44-54 W
Pop: 143 (1990); 152 (1980)　　**Pop Density:** 1430.0
Land: 0.1 sq. mi.; **Water:** 0.0 sq. mi.

On the north-south border with DE. Incorporated 1929.

Name origin: A blend of the names Maryland and Delaware, for its location on the border. See also Delmar (Wicomico County).

Preston
Town
ZIP: 21655　　　**Lat:** 38-42-38 N **Long:** 75-54-31 W
Pop: 437 (1990); 498 (1980)　　**Pop Density:** 728.3
Land: 0.6 sq. mi.; **Water:** 0.0 sq. mi.

Incorporated 1892.

Name origin: Named in 1856 for prominent Baltimore lawyer Alexander Preston.

Ridgely
Town
ZIP: 21660　　　**Lat:** 38-56-51 N **Long:** 75-53-07 W
Pop: 1,034 (1990); 933 (1980)　　**Pop Density:** 940.0
Land: 1.1 sq. mi.; **Water:** 0.0 sq. mi.　　**Elev:** 70 ft.

Incorporated 1896.

Name origin: For the Rev. Greenbury W. Ridgely, who was a law partner of Henry Clay.

Templeville
Town
ZIP: 21670　　　**Lat:** 39-08-05 N **Long:** 75-46-04 W
Pop: 22 (1990); 36 (1980)　　**Pop Density:** 440.0
Land: 0.05 sq. mi.; **Water:** 0.0 sq. mi.

Incorporated 1865. Part of the town is in Queen Anne's County.

Name origin: For the prominent local Temple family. One of its members was a governor of Delaware.

Carroll County
County Seat: Westminster (ZIP: 21157)

Pop: 123,372 (1990); 96,356 (1980)   **Pop Density:** 274.7
Land: 449.2 sq. mi.; **Water:** 3.3 sq. mi.   **Area Code:** 410

On central northern border of MD, northwest of Baltimore; organized Jun 19, 1836 from Baltimore and Frederick counties.

Name origin: For Charles Carroll (1737–1832), signer of the Declaration of Independence, U.S. senator from MD, and founder of the Baltimore and Ohio Railroad.

Eldersburg   CDP
ZIP: 21784   **Lat:** 39-24-30 N **Long:** 76-56-35 W
Pop: 9,720 (1990); 4,959 (1980)   **Pop Density:** 1157.1
Land: 8.4 sq. mi.; **Water:** 0.0 sq. mi.

Hampstead   Town
ZIP: 21074   **Lat:** 39-37-06 N **Long:** 76-51-20 W
Pop: 2,608 (1990); 1,293 (1980)   **Pop Density:** 1133.9
Land: 2.3 sq. mi.; **Water:** 0.0 sq. mi.

Established 1786; incorporated 1888. Part of the town is also in Baltimore County.

Name origin: For Hampstead, England.

Manchester   Town
ZIP: 21088   **Lat:** 39-39-30 N **Long:** 76-53-26 W
Pop: 2,810 (1990); 1,830 (1980)   **Pop Density:** 1478.9
Land: 1.9 sq. mi.; **Water:** 0.0 sq. mi.

Founded 1790s by Capt. Richard Richards. Incorporated 1833.

Name origin: For Manchester, England.

Mount Airy   Town
ZIP: 21771   **Lat:** 39-22-15 N **Long:** 77-09-10 W
Pop: 2,233 (1990); 1,910 (1980)   **Pop Density:** 1488.7
Land: 1.5 sq. mi.; **Water:** 0.0 sq. mi.   **Elev:** 764 ft.

Incorporated 1894. Part of the town is in Frederick County.

Name origin: For its location on Parr's Ridge, maximum elevation 887 feet.

New Windsor   Town
ZIP: 21776   **Lat:** 39-32-38 N **Long:** 77-06-06 W
Pop: 757 (1990); 799 (1980)   **Pop Density:** 1514.0
Land: 0.5 sq. mi.; **Water:** 0.0 sq. mi.

Incorporated 1843.

Name origin: Named in 1816 for Windsor, England. Previously called Sulphur Springs.

Oakland   CDP
Lat: 39-24-44 N **Long:** 76-54-06 W
Pop: 2,078 (1990); 2,242 (1980)   **Pop Density:** 629.7
Land: 3.3 sq. mi.; **Water:** 0.0 sq. mi.

Sykesville   Town
ZIP: 21784   **Lat:** 39-22-12 N **Long:** 76-58-31 W
Pop: 2,303 (1990); 1,712 (1980)   **Pop Density:** 1771.5
Land: 1.3 sq. mi.; **Water:** 0.0 sq. mi.

Incorporated 1904.

Name origin: For English businessman James Sykes, who established several mills in the area.

Taneytown   City
ZIP: 21787   **Lat:** 39-39-18 N **Long:** 77-10-07 W
Pop: 3,695 (1990); 2,618 (1980)   **Pop Density:** 1478.0
Land: 2.5 sq. mi.; **Water:** 0.0 sq. mi.   **Elev:** 524 ft.

Incorporated 1836.

Name origin: For the prominent local Taney family, who reached the area in the 1660s.

Union Bridge   Town
ZIP: 21791   **Lat:** 39-34-05 N **Long:** 77-10-34 W
Pop: 910 (1990); 927 (1980)   **Pop Density:** 1516.7
Land: 0.6 sq. mi.; **Water:** 0.0 sq. mi.

Incorporated 1872.

Name origin: Named in 1810 for the bridge over Little Pipe Creek that united two small villages.

Westminster   City
ZIP: 21157   **Lat:** 39-34-43 N **Long:** 77-00-27 W
Pop: 13,068 (1990); 8,808 (1980)   **Pop Density:** 2376.0
Land: 5.5 sq. mi.; **Water:** 0.0 sq. mi.   **Elev:** 717 ft.

In northern MD, 31 mi. northwest of Baltimore. Founded 1764 by William Winchester; incorporated 1818.

Name origin: For Westminster, a borough of London, England. Called Winchester, after its founder, until 1768.

Westminster South   CDP
Lat: 39-32-53 N **Long:** 76-58-56 W
Pop: 4,284 (1990)   **Pop Density:** 1044.9
Land: 4.1 sq. mi.; **Water:** 0.0 sq. mi.

Cecil County
County Seat: Elkton (ZIP: 21921)

Pop: 71,347 (1990); 60,430 (1980)   **Pop Density:** 204.9
Land: 348.2 sq. mi.; **Water:** 69.7 sq. mi.   **Area Code:** 410

On northeastern border of MD, west of Wilmington, DE; organized 1674 from Baltimore and Kent counties.

Name origin: For Cecilius Calvert, 2nd Lord Baltimore (1605–75), founder and first proprietor of the colony of MD, though he never visited it.

Cecilton   Town
ZIP: 21913   **Lat:** 39-24-10 N **Long:** 75-52-11 W
Pop: 489 (1990); 508 (1980)   **Pop Density:** 1222.5
Land: 0.4 sq. mi.; **Water:** 0.0 sq. mi.   **Elev:** 79 ft.
Incorporated 1864.
Name origin: For Cecilius Calvert (1605–75), second Lord Baltimore.

Charlestown   Town
ZIP: 21914   **Lat:** 39-34-30 N **Long:** 75-58-45 W
Pop: 578 (1990); 720 (1980)   **Pop Density:** 722.5
Land: 0.8 sq. mi.; **Water:** 0.3 sq. mi.
Incorporated 1742.
Name origin: For Charles, the fifth Lord Baltimore.

Chesapeake City   Town
ZIP: 21915   **Lat:** 39-31-46 N **Long:** 75-48-38 W
Pop: 735 (1990); 899 (1980)   **Pop Density:** 1470.0
Land: 0.5 sq. mi.; **Water:** 0.1 sq. mi.
Founded 1804; incorporated 1849.
Name origin: For Chesapeake Bay.

Elkton   Town
ZIP: 21921   **Lat:** 39-36-12 N **Long:** 75-49-14 W
Pop: 9,073 (1990); 6,468 (1980)   **Pop Density:** 1120.1
Land: 8.1 sq. mi.; **Water:** 0.2 sq. mi.
County seat. Incorporated 1821.
Name origin: For its location at the head of the Elk River.

North East   Town
ZIP: 21901   **Lat:** 39-36-00 N **Long:** 75-56-32 W
Pop: 1,913 (1990); 1,469 (1980)   **Pop Density:** 2125.6
Land: 0.9 sq. mi.; **Water:** 0.0 sq. mi.   **Elev:** 10 ft.
Established 1716; incorporated 1849.
Name origin: For its location at the head of the Northeast River.

Perryville   Town
ZIP: 21903   **Lat:** 39-34-15 N **Long:** 76-04-07 W
Pop: 2,456 (1990); 2,018 (1980)   **Pop Density:** 1116.4
Land: 2.2 sq. mi.; **Water:** 0.0 sq. mi.
Incorporated 1882.
Name origin: For Capt. Richard Perry, who purchased the land in 1710.

Port Deposit   Town
ZIP: 21904   **Lat:** 39-36-12 N **Long:** 76-06-56 W
Pop: 685 (1990); 664 (1980)   **Pop Density:** 1712.5
Land: 0.4 sq. mi.; **Water:** 0.0 sq. mi.
Incorporated 1824.
Name origin: Named in 1812 for its function as a port of deposit for the lumber trade.

Rising Sun   Town
ZIP: 21911   **Lat:** 39-41-53 N **Long:** 76-03-38 W
Pop: 1,263 (1990); 1,160 (1980)   **Pop Density:** 1403.3
Land: 0.9 sq. mi.; **Water:** 0.0 sq. mi.   **Elev:** 388 ft.
Incorporated 1860.
Name origin: For an early tavern with a rising sun on its shingle.

Charles County
County Seat: La Plata (ZIP: 20646)

Pop: 101,154 (1990); 72,751 (1980)   **Pop Density:** 219.4
Land: 461.1 sq. mi.; **Water:** 182.2 sq. mi.   **Area Code:** 301

In southwestern MD, south of Alexandria, VA; original county, organized 1658.

Name origin: For Charles Calvert, 3rd Baron Baltimore (1637–1715), second proprietor of the colony of MD; the son of Cecilius Calvert (1605–75) and Anne Arundell.

Bryans Road   CDP
ZIP: 20616   **Lat:** 38-37-54 N **Long:** 77-04-46 W
Pop: 3,809 (1990); 3,739 (1980)   **Pop Density:** 656.7
Land: 5.8 sq. mi.; **Water:** 0.0 sq. mi.

Charlotte Hall   CDP
          Lat: 38-30-07 N **Long:** 76-47-29 W
Pop: 616 (1990); 535 (1980)   **Pop Density:** 212.4
Land: 2.9 sq. mi.; **Water:** 0.0 sq. mi.
Part of the town is also in St. Mary's County.

Hughesville   CDP
ZIP: 20637   **Lat:** 38-32-19 N **Long:** 76-47-01 W
Pop: 1,319 (1990); 504 (1980)   **Pop Density:** 122.1
Land: 10.8 sq. mi.; **Water:** 0.0 sq. mi.

Indian Head — Town
ZIP: 20640   Lat: 38-35-54 N   Long: 77-09-28 W
Pop: 3,531 (1990); 1,381 (1980)   Pop Density: 3210.0
Land: 1.1 sq. mi.; Water: 0.0 sq. mi.

Incorporated 1920.

Name origin: For nearby Indian Head, a high, wooded point along the Potomac River.

La Plata — Town
ZIP: 20646   Lat: 38-32-02 N   Long: 76-58-13 W
Pop: 5,841 (1990); 2,481 (1980)   Pop Density: 1192.0
Land: 4.9 sq. mi.; Water: 0.0 sq. mi.

Incorporated 1888.

Name origin: Named in 1873 for the Chapman farm, Le Plateau. This name was shortened to La Plata.

Marbury — CDP
ZIP: 20658   Lat: 38-33-21 N   Long: 77-09-30 W
Pop: 1,244 (1990); 1,189 (1980)   Pop Density: 296.2
Land: 4.2 sq. mi.; Water: 0.0 sq. mi.

Port Tobacco Village — Town
ZIP: 20677   Lat: 38-30-40 N   Long: 77-01-13 W
Pop: 36 (1990); 40 (1980)   Pop Density: 180.0
Land: 0.2 sq. mi.; Water: 0.0 sq. mi.

Incorporated 1888.

Name origin: For its location on Port Tobacco Creek. Once a thriving tobacco port, its name is also apt because an Algonquian village, Potobac, was on this site when Captain John Smith (c. 1580–1631) came upon it in 1608.

Potomac Heights — CDP
Lat: 38-36-27 N   Long: 77-07-21 W
Pop: 1,524 (1990); 2,456 (1980)   Pop Density: 461.8
Land: 3.3 sq. mi.; Water: 0.2 sq. mi.

St. Charles — CDP
ZIP: 20601   Lat: 38-36-20 N   Long: 76-55-23 W
Pop: 28,717 (1990); 13,921 (1980)   Pop Density: 2610.6
Land: 11.0 sq. mi.; Water: 0.1 sq. mi.

In southern MD, 30 mi. south of Washington, D.C.

Waldorf — CDP
ZIP: 20601   Lat: 38-38-30 N   Long: 76-54-16 W
Pop: 15,058 (1990); 4,952 (1980)   Pop Density: 1024.4
Land: 14.7 sq. mi.; Water: 0.0 sq. mi.

White Plains — CDP
ZIP: 20695   Lat: 38-35-39 N   Long: 76-58-35 W
Pop: 3,560 (1990); 4 (1980)   Pop Density: 304.3
Land: 11.7 sq. mi.; Water: 0.0 sq. mi.

Dorchester County
County Seat: Cambridge (ZIP: 21613)

Pop: 30,236 (1990); 30,623 (1980)   Pop Density: 54.2
Land: 557.6 sq. mi.; Water: 425.4 sq. mi.   Area Code: 410

In south-central MD, west of Salisbury; original county whose legal origin is unknown, but it was in existence by Feb 16, 1668/69.

Name origin: For Richard Sackville II, 5th Earl of Dorset (1622–77), friend of the Calvert family.

Brookview — Town
ZIP: 21659   Lat: 38-34-27 N   Long: 75-47-42 W
Pop: 64 (1990); 78 (1980)   Pop Density: 1600.0
Land: 0.04 sq. mi.; Water: 0.0 sq. mi.

Incorporated 1953.

Name origin: Descriptively named by early settlers for the view.

Cambridge — City
ZIP: 21613   Lat: 38-33-42 N   Long: 76-04-40 W
Pop: 11,514 (1990); 11,703 (1980)   Pop Density: 1744.5
Land: 6.6 sq. mi.; Water: 1.1 sq. mi.

In southeastern MD on the Eastern Shore of Chesapeake Bay, 40 mi. northwest of Salisbury. Established 1684; incorporated 1793.

Name origin: For Cambridge, Cambridgeshire, England.

Church Creek — Town
ZIP: 21622   Lat: 38-30-19 N   Long: 76-09-17 W
Pop: 113 (1990); 124 (1980)   Pop Density: 376.7
Land: 0.3 sq. mi.; Water: 0.0 sq. mi.

Incorporated 1867.

Name origin: Descriptively named for a small creek, once the site of a Roman Catholic church.

East New Market — Town
ZIP: 21631   Lat: 38-35-56 N   Long: 75-55-25 W
Pop: 153 (1990); 230 (1980)   Pop Density: 765.0
Land: 0.2 sq. mi.; Water: 0.0 sq. mi.

Founded 1803; incorporated 1832.

Name origin: Originally called New Market, but "East" was added in 1827 to avoid confusion with New Market in Frederick County.

Eldorado — Town
ZIP: 21659   Lat: 38-34-56 N   Long: 75-47-26 W
Pop: 49 (1990); 93 (1980)   Pop Density: 490.0
Land: 0.1 sq. mi.; Water: 0.0 sq. mi.   Elev: 9 ft.

Incorporated 1947.

Name origin: From the name of a farm in the area.

Galestown — Town
ZIP: 19973   Lat: 38-33-43 N   Long: 75-43-00 W
Pop: 123 (1990); 142 (1980)   Pop Density: 615.0
Land: 0.2 sq. mi.; Water: 0.0 sq. mi.

Incorporated 1951.

Name origin: For 18th-century pioneer, George Gale.

Hurlock   Town
ZIP: 21643   **Lat:** 38-37-44 N **Long:** 75-52-15 W
Pop: 1,706 (1990); 1,690 (1980)   **Pop Density:** 812.4
Land: 2.1 sq. mi.; **Water:** 0.0 sq. mi.
Incorporated 1892.

Name origin: For early merchant, John M. Hurlock, who
built the first store in the area in 1869.

Secretary   Town
ZIP: 21664   **Lat:** 38-36-26 N **Long:** 75-56-50 W
Pop: 528 (1990); 487 (1980)   **Pop Density:** 1760.0
Land: 0.3 sq. mi.; **Water:** 0.0 sq. mi.
Incorporated 1900.

Name origin: For Henry Sewell, who erected a house here in
1662 and was secretary of the colony under Gov. Charles
Calvert.

Vienna   Town
ZIP: 21869   **Lat:** 38-29-06 N **Long:** 75-49-38 W
Pop: 264 (1990); 300 (1980)   **Pop Density:** 1320.0
Land: 0.2 sq. mi.; **Water:** 0.0 sq. mi.
Incorporated 1833.

Name origin: Perhaps shortened and altered from Vin-
nacokasimmon, name of a chief of the Nanticoke Indians
about 1677.

Frederick County
County Seat: Frederick (ZIP: 21701)

Pop: 150,208 (1990); 114,792 (1980)   **Pop Density:** 226.6
Land: 662.9 sq. mi.; **Water:** 4.5 sq. mi.   **Area Code:** 301

On northwestern border of MD, southeast of Hagerstown; organized Jun 10, 1748
from Baltimore and Prince George's counties.

Name origin: For Frederick Calvert, 6th Baron Baltimore (1731–71), fifth and last
proprietor of the colony of MD.

Ballenger Creek   CDP
                       Lat: 39-22-20 N **Long:** 77-26-08 W
Pop: 5,546 (1990)   **Pop Density:** 990.4
Land: 5.6 sq. mi.; **Water:** 0.0 sq. mi.

Braddock Heights   CDP
                       Lat: 39-24-51 N **Long:** 77-30-26 W
Pop: 4,778 (1990); 1,054 (1980)   **Pop Density:** 628.7
Land: 7.6 sq. mi.; **Water:** 0.0 sq. mi.

Brunswick   Town
ZIP: 21716   **Lat:** 39-18-58 N **Long:** 77-37-23 W
Pop: 5,117 (1990); 4,572 (1980)   **Pop Density:** 2436.7
Land: 2.1 sq. mi.; **Water:** 0.0 sq. mi.   **Elev:** 247 ft.
Incorporated 1890.

Name origin: Named by early German settlers for Brunswick,
Germany.

Burkittsville   Town
ZIP: 21718   **Lat:** 39-23-28 N **Long:** 77-37-38 W
Pop: 194 (1990); 202 (1980)   **Pop Density:** 485.0
Land: 0.4 sq. mi.; **Water:** 0.0 sq. mi.
Founded 1829; incorporated 1894.

Name origin: For settler Henry Burkitt.

Clover Hill   CDP
                       Lat: 39-27-26 N **Long:** 77-25-47 W
Pop: 2,823 (1990); 2 (1980)   **Pop Density:** 2171.5
Land: 1.3 sq. mi.; **Water:** 0.0 sq. mi.

Discovery-Spring Garden   CDP
                       Lat: 39-27-37 N **Long:** 77-21-38 W
Pop: 2,443 (1990); 2,328 (1980)   **Pop Density:** 2443.0
Land: 1.0 sq. mi.; **Water:** 0.0 sq. mi.

Emmitsburg   Town
ZIP: 21727   **Lat:** 39-42-16 N **Long:** 77-19-32 W
Pop: 1,688 (1990); 1,552 (1980)   **Pop Density:** 1406.7
Land: 1.2 sq. mi.; **Water:** 0.0 sq. mi.   **Elev:** 449 ft.
Laid out 1785 by Samuel Emmit. Incorporated 1824.

Name origin: For Irish emigrant, Samuel Emmit, its founder.

Frederick   City
ZIP: 21701   **Lat:** 39-25-41 N **Long:** 77-25-00 W
Pop: 40,148 (1990); 28,086 (1980)   **Pop Density:** 2205.9
Land: 18.2 sq. mi.; **Water:** 0.0 sq. mi.   **Elev:** 290 ft.
In western MD, 25 mi. southeast of Hagerstown. Laid out
1745. Incorporated 1816.

Name origin: For the sixth Lord Baltimore, Frederick Calvert
(1731–1771).

Green Valley   CDP
ZIP: 21771   **Lat:** 39-20-36 N **Long:** 77-14-42 W
Pop: 9,424 (1990); 906 (1980)   **Pop Density:** 457.5
Land: 20.6 sq. mi.; **Water:** 0.0 sq. mi.

Linganore-Bartonsville   CDP
                       Lat: 39-24-30 N **Long:** 77-19-26 W
Pop: 4,079 (1990)   **Pop Density:** 263.2
Land: 15.5 sq. mi.; **Water:** 0.3 sq. mi.

Middletown   Town
ZIP: 21769   **Lat:** 39-26-32 N **Long:** 77-32-39 W
Pop: 1,834 (1990); 1,748 (1980)   **Pop Density:** 1834.0
Land: 1.0 sq. mi.; **Water:** 0.0 sq. mi.   **Elev:** 547 ft.
Incorporated 1833.

Mount Airy   Town
ZIP: 21771   **Lat:** 39-22-24 N **Long:** 77-10-21 W
Pop: 1,497 (1990); 540 (1980)   **Pop Density:** 1151.5
Land: 1.3 sq. mi.; **Water:** 0.0 sq. mi.   **Elev:** 764 ft.
Incorporated 1894. Part of the town is in Carroll County.

Name origin: For its location on Parr's Ridge, maximum
elevation 887 feet.

Myersville
Town
ZIP: 21773   **Lat:** 39-30-22 N **Long:** 77-33-54 W
Pop: 464 (1990); 432 (1980)   **Pop Density:** 773.3
Land: 0.6 sq. mi.; **Water:** 0.0 sq. mi.   **Elev:** 669 ft.
Incorporated 1904.
Name origin: For pioneer James Stottlemyer, who settled in the area in 1742. The last part of his name later became the town's name.

New Market
Town
ZIP: 21774   **Lat:** 39-23-02 N **Long:** 77-16-27 W
Pop: 328 (1990); 306 (1980)   **Pop Density:** 546.7
Land: 0.6 sq. mi.; **Water:** 0.0 sq. mi.   **Elev:** 551 ft.
Incorporated 1878.
Name origin: Named by early settlers for New Market, England.

Rosemont
Town
ZIP: 21758   **Lat:** 39-20-05 N **Long:** 77-37-16 W
Pop: 256 (1990); 305 (1980)   **Pop Density:** 426.7
Land: 0.6 sq. mi.; **Water:** 0.0 sq. mi.
Incorporated 1953.
Name origin: A pleasant-sounding name given by its developers.

Thurmont
Town
ZIP: 21788   **Lat:** 39-37-25 N **Long:** 77-24-34 W
Pop: 3,398 (1990); 2,934 (1980)   **Pop Density:** 1359.2
Land: 2.5 sq. mi.; **Water:** 0.0 sq. mi.   **Elev:** 523 ft.
Founded 1751; incorporated as Mechanicstown 1831; as Thurmont 1894.
Name origin: For a prominent local family.

Walkersville
Town
ZIP: 21793   **Lat:** 39-29-04 N **Long:** 77-21-11 W
Pop: 4,145 (1990); 2,212 (1980)   **Pop Density:** 1036.3
Land: 4.0 sq. mi.; **Water:** 0.0 sq. mi.   **Elev:** 320 ft.
Incorporated 1892.
Name origin: For the Walkers, early Scottish settlers in the area.

Woodsboro
Town
ZIP: 21798   **Lat:** 39-31-55 N **Long:** 77-18-39 W
Pop: 513 (1990); 506 (1980)   **Pop Density:** 1026.0
Land: 0.5 sq. mi.; **Water:** 0.0 sq. mi.
Incorporated 1836.
Name origin: For Joseph Wood, an early settler, who laid out the town in 1786.

Garrett County
County Seat: Oakland (ZIP: 21550)

Pop: 28,138 (1990); 26,490 (1980)   **Pop Density:** 43.4
Land: 648.1 sq. mi.; **Water:** 7.9 sq. mi.   **Area Code:** 301
On northwestern border of the panhandle of MD, west of Cumberland; organized Apr 1, 1872 from Allegany County; the last county to be formed in MD.
Name origin: For John Work Garrett (1820–84), president of the Baltimore and Ohio railroad (1858–84).

Accident
Town
ZIP: 21520   **Lat:** 39-37-37 N **Long:** 79-19-15 W
Pop: 349 (1990); 246 (1980)   **Pop Density:** 698.0
Land: 0.5 sq. mi.; **Water:** 0.0 sq. mi.   **Elev:** 2395 ft.
Incorporated 1916.
Name origin: For the first two surveyors in the 1770s, who surveyed and claimed the same piece of land.

Deer Park
Town
ZIP: 21550   **Lat:** 39-25-24 N **Long:** 79-19-36 W
Pop: 419 (1990); 478 (1980)   **Pop Density:** 419.0
Land: 1.0 sq. mi.; **Water:** 0.0 sq. mi.

Friendsville
Town
ZIP: 21531   **Lat:** 39-39-46 N **Long:** 79-24-18 W
Pop: 577 (1990); 511 (1980)   **Pop Density:** 641.1
Land: 0.9 sq. mi.; **Water:** 0.0 sq. mi.   **Elev:** 1497 ft.
Incorporated 1902.
Name origin: For the area's first settler, John Friend.

Grantsville
Town
ZIP: 21536   **Lat:** 39-41-47 N **Long:** 79-09-25 W
Pop: 505 (1990); 498 (1980)   **Pop Density:** 1683.3
Land: 0.3 sq. mi.; **Water:** 0.0 sq. mi.   **Elev:** 2300 ft.
Incorporated 1864.
Name origin: For settler Daniel Grant, who came to the area in 1785.

Kitzmiller
Town
Lat: 39-23-16 N **Long:** 07-91-05 W
Pop: 275 (1990); 390 (1980)   **Pop Density:** 780.0
Land: 0.5 sq. mi.; **Water:** 0.0 sq. mi.
Settled early 1800s; incorporated 1906.
Name origin: For Ebenezer Kitzmiller, who ran a sawmill nearby.

Kitzmillerville
Town
ZIP: 21538   **Lat:** 39-23-21 N **Long:** 79-11-01 W
Pop: 275 (1990); 387 (1980)   **Pop Density:** 916.7
Land: 0.3 sq. mi.; **Water:** 0.0 sq. mi.

Loch Lynn Heights
Town
ZIP: 21550   **Lat:** 39-23-28 N **Long:** 79-22-23 W
Pop: 461 (1990); 503 (1980)   **Pop Density:** 1536.7
Land: 0.3 sq. mi.; **Water:** 0.0 sq. mi.   **Elev:** 2438 ft.
Incorporated 1896.
Name origin: Named in 1894 for settler David Lynn, with the addition of the Scottish word for lake.

Mountain Lake Park
Town
ZIP: 21550   **Lat:** 39-24-13 N **Long:** 79-22-45 W
Pop: 1,938 (1990); 385 (1980)   **Pop Density:** 1292.0
Land: 1.5 sq. mi.; **Water:** 0.1 sq. mi.
Incorporated 1931.
Name origin: Descriptively named by the town's developers for a nearby summer resort lake.

Oakland
Town
ZIP: 21550   **Lat:** 39-24-49 N **Long:** 79-24-28 W
Pop: 1,741 (1990); 825 (1980)   **Pop Density:** 1024.1
Land: 1.7 sq. mi.; **Water:** 0.0 sq. mi.   **Elev:** 2384 ft.
Incorporated 1862.

Name origin: For the abundance of oak trees.

Harford County
County Seat: Bel Air (ZIP: 21014)

Pop: 182,132 (1990); 145,930 (1980)   **Pop Density:** 413.6
Land: 440.4 sq. mi.; **Water:** 86.4 sq. mi.   **Area Code:** 410

On northern border of MD, northeast of Baltimore; organized 1773 (prior to statehood) from Baltimore County.

Name origin: For Henry Harford (c. 1759–1834), an illegitimate son of Frederick Calvert (1731–71), 6th Lord Baltimore, and the last proprietor of the colony of MD.

Aberdeen
Town
ZIP: 21001   **Lat:** 39-30-42 N **Long:** 76-10-21 W
Pop: 13,087 (1990); 11,533 (1980)   **Pop Density:** 2469.2
Land: 5.3 sq. mi.; **Water:** 0.0 sq. mi.   **Elev:** 83 ft.

In northeastern MD, 35 mi. northeast of Baltimore. Incorporated 1892.

Name origin: Named by the first postmaster, a Mr. Winston of Aberdeen, Scotland.

Aberdeen Proving Ground
Military facility
ZIP: 21005   **Lat:** 39-28-20 N **Long:** 76-07-47 W
Pop: 5,267 (1990); 5,722 (1980)   **Pop Density:** 483.2
Land: 10.9 sq. mi.; **Water:** 0.6 sq. mi.

Bel Air
Town
ZIP: 21014   **Lat:** 39-32-04 N **Long:** 76-20-48 W
Pop: 8,860 (1990); 7,814 (1980)   **Pop Density:** 3407.7
Land: 2.6 sq. mi.; **Water:** 0.0 sq. mi.

In northeastern MD, 25 mi. northeast of Baltimore. Incorporated 1874.

Name origin: From French term meaning 'fine air.'

Bel Air North
CDP
ZIP: 21050   **Lat:** 39-33-12 N **Long:** 76-22-25 W
Pop: 14,880 (1990); 5,043 (1980)   **Pop Density:** 907.3
Land: 16.4 sq. mi.; **Water:** 0.0 sq. mi.

Bel Air South
CDP
ZIP: 21015   **Lat:** 39-30-14 N **Long:** 76-19-05 W
Pop: 26,421 (1990); 3,033 (1980)   **Pop Density:** 1672.2
Land: 15.8 sq. mi.; **Water:** 0.0 sq. mi.

Edgewood
Military facility
ZIP: 21040   **Lat:** 39-25-13 N **Long:** 76-17-57 W
Pop: 23,903 (1990); 19,455 (1980)   **Pop Density:** 1327.9
Land: 18.0 sq. mi.; **Water:** 0.1 sq. mi.

Fallston
CDP
ZIP: 21047   **Lat:** 39-31-15 N **Long:** 76-25-35 W
Pop: 5,730 (1990); 4,948 (1980)   **Pop Density:** 658.6
Land: 8.7 sq. mi.; **Water:** 0.0 sq. mi.

Havre de Grace
City
ZIP: 21078   **Lat:** 39-32-49 N **Long:** 76-05-56 W
Pop: 8,952 (1990); 8,763 (1980)   **Pop Density:** 2712.7
Land: 3.3 sq. mi.; **Water:** 1.4 sq. mi.

Settled 1659; incorporated 1785.

Name origin: French 'harbor of mercy'; name said to have been suggested by Marquis de Lafayette (1757–1834), French-born Revolutionary War hero. Previously called Lower Ferry.

Jarrettsville
CDP
ZIP: 21084   **Lat:** 39-36-13 N **Long:** 76-28-21 W
Pop: 2,148 (1990); 1,485 (1980)   **Pop Density:** 311.3
Land: 6.9 sq. mi.; **Water:** 0.0 sq. mi.

Joppatowne
CDP
ZIP: 21610   **Lat:** 39-24-55 N **Long:** 76-21-15 W
Pop: 11,084 (1990); 11,348 (1980)   **Pop Density:** 1630.0
Land: 6.8 sq. mi.; **Water:** 0.5 sq. mi.   **Elev:** 15 ft.

Unincorporated district, 10 mi. northeast of Baltimore.

Name origin: For the former town of Joppa, three miles south of the present village, once the seat of Baltimore County.

Perryman
CDP
          Lat: 39-28-11 N **Long:** 76-12-20 W
Pop: 2,160 (1990); 1,819 (1980)   **Pop Density:** 480.0
Land: 4.5 sq. mi.; **Water:** 0.0 sq. mi.

Pleasant Hills
CDP
          Lat: 39-29-13 N **Long:** 76-23-42 W
Pop: 2,591 (1990); 2,790 (1980)   **Pop Density:** 588.9
Land: 4.4 sq. mi.; **Water:** 0.0 sq. mi.

Howard County
County Seat: Ellicott City (ZIP: 21043)

Pop: 187,328 (1990); 118,572 (1980)   **Pop Density:** 742.8
Land: 252.2 sq. mi.; **Water:** 1.4 sq. mi.   **Area Code:** 410

In north-central MD, west of Baltimore; organized as Howard District in 1838 from Anne Arundel County; formed as county May 13, 1851.

Name origin: For John Eager Howard (1752–1827), member of the Continental Congress (1784–88), MD governor (1788–91), and U.S. senator (1796–1803).

Columbia   CDP
ZIP: 21029   **Lat:** 39-12-10 N **Long:** 76-51-28 W
Pop: 75,883 (1990); 21,413 (1980)   **Pop Density:** 3270.8
Land: 23.2 sq. mi.; **Water:** 0.1 sq. mi.

Elkridge   CDP
          Lat: 39-12-06 N **Long:** 76-45-01 W
Pop: 12,953 (1990)   **Pop Density:** 1639.6
Land: 7.9 sq. mi.; **Water:** 0.0 sq. mi.

Ellicott City   CDP
ZIP: 21043   **Lat:** 39-16-19 N **Long:** 76-50-04 W
Pop: 41,396 (1990); 21,784 (1980)   **Pop Density:** 1289.6
Land: 32.1 sq. mi.; **Water:** 0.0 sq. mi.

Jessup   CDP
          Lat: 39-10-17 N **Long:** 76-46-48 W
Pop: 1,213 (1990); 702 (1980)   **Pop Density:** 1732.9
Land: 0.7 sq. mi.; **Water:** 0.0 sq. mi.

Part of the town is in Anne Arundel County.

North Laurel   CDP
ZIP: 21784   **Lat:** 39-08-20 N **Long:** 76-52-15 W
Pop: 15,008 (1990); 6,093 (1980)   **Pop Density:** 1471.4
Land: 10.2 sq. mi.; **Water:** 0.3 sq. mi.

Savage-Guilford   CDP
          Lat: 39-08-56 N **Long:** 76-49-40 W
Pop: 9,669 (1990); 2,928 (1980)   **Pop Density:** 1933.8
Land: 5.0 sq. mi.; **Water:** 0.0 sq. mi.

Kent County
County Seat: Chestertown (ZIP: 21620)

Pop: 17,842 (1990); 16,695 (1980)   **Pop Density:** 63.8
Land: 279.4 sq. mi.; **Water:** 134.9 sq. mi.   **Area Code:** 410

On northeastern border of MD, northwest of Dover, MD; original county, organized Dec 16, 1642.

Name origin: For the county in England.

Betterton   Town
ZIP: 21610   **Lat:** 39-22-01 N **Long:** 76-04-21 W
Pop: 360 (1990); 356 (1980)   **Pop Density:** 400.0
Land: 0.9 sq. mi.; **Water:** 0.0 sq. mi.   **Elev:** 330 ft.
Incorporated 1906.

Name origin: Named descriptively by its first settlers.

Chestertown   Town
ZIP: 21620   **Lat:** 39-13-09 N **Long:** 76-04-13 W
Pop: 4,005 (1990); 3,300 (1980)   **Pop Density:** 1602.0
Land: 2.5 sq. mi.; **Water:** 0.2 sq. mi.
Established 1708; incorporated 1805.

Name origin: For its location on the Chester River.

Galena   Town
ZIP: 21635   **Lat:** 39-20-35 N **Long:** 75-52-44 W
Pop: 324 (1990); 374 (1980)   **Pop Density:** 1080.0
Land: 0.3 sq. mi.; **Water:** 0.0 sq. mi.
Incorporated 1858.

Name origin: For small deposit of galena, a lead ore (lead sulfide) mined in the area in the early 1800s.

Millington   Town
ZIP: 21651   **Lat:** 39-15-33 N **Long:** 75-50-20 W
Pop: 375 (1990); 512 (1980)   **Pop Density:** 1875.0
Land: 0.2 sq. mi.; **Water:** 0.0 sq. mi.   **Elev:** 27 ft.
Incorporated 1890. Part of the town is in Queen Anne's County.

Name origin: Named in 1827 for early settler Richard Millington.

Rock Hall   Town
ZIP: 21661   **Lat:** 39-08-25 N **Long:** 76-14-27 W
Pop: 1,584 (1990); 1,511 (1980)   **Pop Density:** 1218.5
Land: 1.3 sq. mi.; **Water:** 0.2 sq. mi.   **Elev:** 25 ft.
Incorporated 1908.

Name origin: For a colonial mansion made of local white sandstone, built nearby in 1812.

Montgomery County
County Seat: Rockville (ZIP: 20850)

Pop: 757,027 (1990); 579,053 (1980)   **Pop Density:** 1530.7
Land: 494.6 sq. mi.; **Water:** 11.6 sq. mi.   **Area Code:** 301
On central western border of MD, north of Washington, D.C.; organized Sep 6, 1776 (prior to statehood) from Frederick County.
Name origin: For Gen. Richard Montgomery (1736–75), an officer in the Revolutionary War.

Adelphi   CDP
Lat: 39-00-40 N **Long:** 76-58-38 W
Land: 0.0004 sq. mi.; **Water:** 0.0 sq. mi.
Part of the town is also in Prince George's County.

Ashton-Sandy Springs   CDP
Lat: 39-08-58 N **Long:** 77-00-45 W
Pop: 3,092 (1990)   **Pop Density:** 406.8
Land: 7.6 sq. mi.; **Water:** 0.0 sq. mi.

Aspen Hill   CDP
ZIP: 20906   **Lat:** 39-05-31 N **Long:** 77-04-44 W
Pop: 45,494 (1990)   **Pop Density:** 4332.8
Land: 10.5 sq. mi.; **Water:** 0.1 sq. mi.

Barnesville   Town
ZIP: 20838   **Lat:** 39-13-11 N **Long:** 77-22-52 W
Pop: 170 (1990); 141 (1980)   **Pop Density:** 340.0
Land: 0.5 sq. mi.; **Water:** 0.0 sq. mi.
Incorporated 1888.
Name origin: For an early settler family, the Barnes, who came to MD in 1678.

Bethesda   CDP
ZIP: 20817   **Lat:** 38-59-23 N **Long:** 77-07-13 W
Pop: 62,936 (1990); 62,736 (1980)   **Pop Density:** 4252.4
Land: 14.8 sq. mi.; **Water:** 0.0 sq. mi.   **Elev:** 303 ft.
Unincorporated residential district, 7 mi. northwest of downtown Washington, D.C. Home of the National Institutes of Health, the Naval Medical Center, and the National Library of Medicine.
Name origin: Biblical name (see John 5 in King James version) of a healing pool in Jerusalem; Hebrew name means 'house of mercy.' Named in 1820 by early settlers who built the Presbyterian church. During the Civil War it was called Darcy's Store for local store owner and postmaster William Darcy.

Brookeville   Town
ZIP: 20833   **Lat:** 39-10-35 N **Long:** 77-03-26 W
Pop: 54 (1990); 120 (1980)   **Pop Density:** 270.0
Land: 0.2 sq. mi.; **Water:** 0.0 sq. mi.
Incorporated 1808.
Name origin: For early surveyor James Brooke.

Burtonsville   CDP
ZIP: 20866   **Lat:** 39-06-40 N **Long:** 76-55-55 W
Pop: 5,853 (1990); 2,046 (1980)   **Pop Density:** 750.4
Land: 7.8 sq. mi.; **Water:** 0.2 sq. mi.

Cabin John-Brookmont   CDP
ZIP: 20816   **Lat:** 38-58-02 N **Long:** 77-08-51 W
Pop: 5,341 (1990); 5,135 (1980)   **Pop Density:** 2054.2
Land: 2.6 sq. mi.; **Water:** 1.0 sq. mi.

Calverton   CDP
ZIP: 20705   **Lat:** 39-03-21 N **Long:** 76-57-20 W
Pop: 7,585 (1990)   **Pop Density:** 2370.3
Land: 3.2 sq. mi.; **Water:** 0.0 sq. mi.
Part of the town is also in Prince George's County.

Chevy Chase   Town
ZIP: 20815   **Lat:** 38-58-49 N **Long:** 77-05-02 W
Pop: 2,675 (1990)   **Pop Density:** 5350.0
Land: 0.5 sq. mi.; **Water:** 0.0 sq. mi.
Incorporated as a town 1918.
Name origin: For Chevy Chase Village.

*Chevy Chase   CDP
ZIP: 20815   **Lat:** 38-59-41 N **Long:** 77-04-23 W
Pop: 8,559 (1990); 12,232 (1980)   **Pop Density:** 3291.9
Land: 2.6 sq. mi.; **Water:** 0.0 sq. mi.

Chevy Chase Section Five   Village
ZIP: 20813   **Lat:** 38-58-58 N **Long:** 77-04-30 W
Pop: 632 (1990)   **Pop Density:** 6320.0
Land: 0.1 sq. mi.; **Water:** 0.0 sq. mi.
Incorporated Jun 25, 1982.
Name origin: For Chevy Chase Village.

Chevy Chase Section Three   Village
ZIP: 20813   **Lat:** 38-58-10 N **Long:** 77-04-45 W
Pop: 2,078 (1990); 2,118 (1980)   **Pop Density:** 5195.0
Land: 0.4 sq. mi.; **Water:** 0.0 sq. mi.
Incorporated Jun 24, 1982.
Name origin: For Chevy Chase Village.

Chevy Chase Village   Town
ZIP: 20813   **Lat:** 38-58-44 N **Long:** 77-04-28 W
Pop: 749 (1990)   **Pop Density:** 7490.0
Land: 0.1 sq. mi.; **Water:** 0.0 sq. mi.
Incorporated 1910. The other "Chevy Chase" communities developed later.
Name origin: From an old English ballad.

Cloverly   CDP
ZIP: 20904   **Lat:** 39-06-10 N **Long:** 76-58-35 W
Pop: 7,904 (1990); 5,153 (1980)   **Pop Density:** 2026.7
Land: 3.9 sq. mi.; **Water:** 0.0 sq. mi.

Colesville   CDP
ZIP: 20904   **Lat:** 39-05-17 N **Long:** 77-00-25 W
Pop: 18,819 (1990); 14,359 (1980)   **Pop Density:** 2045.5
Land: 9.2 sq. mi.; **Water:** 0.0 sq. mi.

Damascus   CDP
ZIP: 20872   **Lat:** 39-16-39 N **Long:** 77-12-17 W
Pop: 9,817 (1990); 4,129 (1980)   **Pop Density:** 1033.4
Land: 9.5 sq. mi.; **Water:** 0.0 sq. mi.

Fairland
CDP
ZIP: 20904 **Lat:** 39-04-55 N **Long:** 76-57-05 W
Pop: 19,828 (1990); 5,154 (1980) **Pop Density:** 3965.6
Land: 5.0 sq. mi.; **Water:** 0.0 sq. mi.

Gaithersburg
City
ZIP: 20877 **Lat:** 39-08-28 N **Long:** 77-12-59 W
Pop: 39,542 (1990); 26,424 (1980) **Pop Density:** 4345.3
Land: 9.1 sq. mi.; **Water:** 0.1 sq. mi. **Elev:** 508 ft.

In western MD, 21 mi. northwest of Washington. Founded 1802; incorporated 1878.

Name origin: For Benjamin Gaither, who built the first house. Previously called Forest Grove.

Garrett Park
Town
ZIP: 20896 **Lat:** 39-02-10 N **Long:** 77-05-40 W
Pop: 884 (1990); 1,178 (1980) **Pop Density:** 2946.7
Land: 0.3 sq. mi.; **Water:** 0.0 sq. mi. **Elev:** 314 ft.

Incorporated 1898.

Name origin: For John Garrett, then president of the Baltimore and Ohio Railroads.

Germantown
CDP
ZIP: 20874 **Lat:** 39-10-41 N **Long:** 77-15-38 W
Pop: 41,145 (1990); 1,408 (1980) **Pop Density:** 3845.3
Land: 10.7 sq. mi.; **Water:** 0.3 sq. mi.

Glen Echo
Town
ZIP: 20812 **Lat:** 38-58-02 N **Long:** 77-08-26 W
Pop: 234 (1990); 229 (1980) **Pop Density:** 2340.0
Land: 0.1 sq. mi.; **Water:** 0.0 sq. mi.

Incorporated 1904.

Name origin: Named by settlers for the scenic, hilly area.

Hillandale
CDP
ZIP: 20903 **Lat:** 39-01-05 N **Long:** 76-58-45 W
Pop: 8,151 (1990); 7,251 (1980) **Pop Density:** 6270.0
Land: 1.3 sq. mi.; **Water:** 0.0 sq. mi.

Part of the town is also in Prince George's County.

Kensington
Town
ZIP: 20895 **Lat:** 39-01-33 N **Long:** 77-04-23 W
Pop: 1,713 (1990); 1,822 (1980) **Pop Density:** 3426.0
Land: 0.5 sq. mi.; **Water:** 0.0 sq. mi.

Incorporated 1894.

Name origin: Named by settlers for the district in London.

Langley Park
CDP
Lat: 38-59-51 N **Long:** 76-59-23 W
Pop: 3,129 (1990); 2,924 (1980) **Pop Density:** 15645.0
Land: 0.2 sq. mi.; **Water:** 0.0 sq. mi.

Part of the town is in Prince George's County.

Laytonsville
Town
ZIP: 20879 **Lat:** 39-12-34 N **Long:** 77-08-29 W
Pop: 248 (1990); 195 (1980) **Pop Density:** 248.0
Land: 1.0 sq. mi.; **Water:** 0.0 sq. mi. **Elev:** 609 ft.

Incorporated 1892.

Name origin: For settler John Layton. Previously called Goshen Mills.

Martin's Additions
Village
ZIP: 20815 **Lat:** 38-58-42 N **Long:** 77-04-10 W
Pop: 846 (1990) **Pop Density:** 8460.0
Land: 0.1 sq. mi.; **Water:** 0.0 sq. mi.

Incorporated Mar 19, 1985.

Montgomery Village
CDP
ZIP: 20879 **Lat:** 39-10-52 N **Long:** 77-11-37 W
Pop: 32,315 (1990); 18,725 (1980) **Pop Density:** 4971.5
Land: 6.5 sq. mi.; **Water:** 0.0 sq. mi.

North Bethesda
CDP
ZIP: 20895 **Lat:** 39-02-40 N **Long:** 77-07-08 W
Pop: 29,656 (1990); 22,671 (1980) **Pop Density:** 4007.6
Land: 7.4 sq. mi.; **Water:** 0.0 sq. mi.

North Kensington
CDP
ZIP: 20902 **Lat:** 39-02-22 N **Long:** 77-04-18 W
Pop: 8,607 (1990); 9,039 (1980) **Pop Density:** 5738.0
Land: 1.5 sq. mi.; **Water:** 0.0 sq. mi.

North Potomac
CDP
ZIP: 20878 **Lat:** 39-05-47 N **Long:** 77-14-41 W
Pop: 18,456 (1990) **Pop Density:** 3076.0
Land: 6.0 sq. mi.; **Water:** 0.0 sq. mi.

Olney
CDP
ZIP: 20832 **Lat:** 39-08-57 N **Long:** 77-04-56 W
Pop: 23,019 (1990); 13,026 (1980) **Pop Density:** 2529.6
Land: 9.1 sq. mi.; **Water:** 0.0 sq. mi.

Poolesville
Town
ZIP: 20837 **Lat:** 39-08-41 N **Long:** 77-24-36 W
Pop: 3,796 (1990); 3,428 (1980) **Pop Density:** 1084.6
Land: 3.5 sq. mi.; **Water:** 0.0 sq. mi.

Incorporated 1867.

Name origin: Named in 1793 for Joseph Poole, the son of the original settler.

Potomac
CDP
ZIP: 20851 **Lat:** 39-01-32 N **Long:** 77-11-51 W
Pop: 45,634 (1990); 13,209 (1980) **Pop Density:** 1435.0
Land: 31.8 sq. mi.; **Water:** 1.6 sq. mi.

Redland
CDP
ZIP: 20855 **Lat:** 39-07-53 N **Long:** 77-09-00 W
Pop: 16,145 (1990); 231 (1980) **Pop Density:** 2339.9
Land: 6.9 sq. mi.; **Water:** 0.1 sq. mi.

Rockville
City
ZIP: 20850 **Lat:** 39-04-52 N **Long:** 77-09-14 W
Pop: 44,835 (1990); 43,811 (1980) **Pop Density:** 3705.4
Land: 12.1 sq. mi.; **Water:** 0.0 sq. mi. **Elev:** 451 ft.

In central MD, 16 mi. northwest of Washington. Incorporated 1860.

Name origin: Named in 1803 for the lovely Rock Creek nearby. Previously called Hungerford's Tavern, Montgomery Courthouse, and Williamsburg.

Rossmoor
CDP
Lat: 39-06-13 N **Long:** 77-04-16 W
Pop: 6,182 (1990) **Pop Density:** 5620.0
Land: 1.1 sq. mi.; **Water:** 0.0 sq. mi.

Silver Spring
CDP
ZIP: 20901 **Lat:** 39-00-49 N **Long:** 77-01-26 W
Pop: 76,046 (1990); 72,893 (1980) **Pop Density:** 6233.3
Land: 12.2 sq. mi.; **Water:** 0.0 sq. mi.

Large suburban district and commercial center immediately north of Washington, D.C.

Name origin: For the white sand or mica produced by a spring on the former Blair estate, reflecting sunlight through the water.

Somerset   Town
ZIP: 20813   **Lat:** 38-57-56 N **Long:** 77-05-43 W
Pop: 993 (1990); 1,101 (1980)   **Pop Density:** 3310.0
Land: 0.3 sq. mi.; **Water:** 0.0 sq. mi.
Incorporated 1906.
Name origin: For the county in England.

South Kensington   CDP
ZIP: 20895   **Lat:** 39-01-07 N **Long:** 77-04-49 W
Pop: 8,777 (1990); 9,344 (1980)   **Pop Density:** 3657.1
Land: 2.4 sq. mi.; **Water:** 0.0 sq. mi.

Takoma Park   City
ZIP: 20912   **Lat:** 38-58-51 N **Long:** 77-00-26 W
Pop: 11,544 (1990); 11,331 (1980)   **Pop Density:** 9620.0
Land: 1.2 sq. mi.; **Water:** 0.0 sq. mi.
In central MD, 6 mi. north of Washington. Founded 1883; incorporated 1890. Part of the town is also in Prince George's County.
Name origin: Named by 1880s real estate developer Benjamin Gilbert for Mt. Tacoma in Washington, but with spelling change. Previously called Brightwood.

Washington Grove   Town
ZIP: 20880   **Lat:** 39-08-28 N **Long:** 77-10-29 W
Pop: 434 (1990); 527 (1980)   **Pop Density:** 1446.7
Land: 0.3 sq. mi.; **Water:** 0.0 sq. mi.
Incorporated 1937.
Name origin: Named by its settlers for nearby Washington, D.C.

Wheaton-Glenmont   CDP
ZIP: 20902   **Lat:** 39-03-25 N **Long:** 77-03-08 W
Pop: 53,720 (1990); 48,598 (1980)   **Pop Density:** 5266.7
Land: 10.2 sq. mi.; **Water:** 0.0 sq. mi.

White Oak   CDP
ZIP: 20901   **Lat:** 39-02-31 N **Long:** 76-59-18 W
Pop: 18,671 (1990); 13,700 (1980)   **Pop Density:** 3734.2
Land: 5.0 sq. mi.; **Water:** 0.0 sq. mi.

Prince George's County
County Seat: Upper Marlboro (ZIP: 20772)

Pop: 729,268 (1990); 665,071 (1980)   **Pop Density:** 1499.3
Land: 486.4 sq. mi.; **Water:** 13.0 sq. mi.   **Area Code:** 301
In central MD, east of Washington, D.C.; organized May 20, 1695 from Charles and Calvert counties.
Name origin: For Prince George of Denmark (1653–1708), husband of Queen Anne of England (1665–1714).

Accokeek   CDP
ZIP: 20607   **Lat:** 38-40-33 N **Long:** 77-00-58 W
Pop: 4,477 (1990); 3,894 (1980)   **Pop Density:** 199.9
Land: 22.4 sq. mi.; **Water:** 1.0 sq. mi.

Adelphi   CDP
ZIP: 20783   **Lat:** 39-00-06 N **Long:** 76-57-55 W
Pop: 13,524 (1990); 9,497 (1980)   **Pop Density:** 4508.0
Land: 3.0 sq. mi.; **Water:** 0.0 sq. mi.
Part of the town is also in Montgomery County.

Andrews Air Force Base   Military facility
ZIP: 20331   **Lat:** 38-48-12 N **Long:** 76-52-18 W
Pop: 10,228 (1990); 10,064 (1980)   **Pop Density:** 1504.1
Land: 6.8 sq. mi.; **Water:** 0.0 sq. mi.

Beltsville   CDP
ZIP: 20705   **Lat:** 39-02-12 N **Long:** 76-55-24 W
Pop: 14,476 (1990); 12,760 (1980)   **Pop Density:** 2193.3
Land: 6.6 sq. mi.; **Water:** 0.0 sq. mi.

Berwyn Heights   Town
ZIP: 20740   **Lat:** 38-59-31 N **Long:** 76-54-43 W
Pop: 2,952 (1990); 3,135 (1980)   **Pop Density:** 4920.0
Land: 0.6 sq. mi.; **Water:** 0.0 sq. mi.   **Elev:** 100 ft.
Founded 1883; incorporated 1896.
Name origin: For the Berwyn Mountains in Wales.

Bladensburg   Town
ZIP: 20710   **Lat:** 38-56-37 N **Long:** 76-55-34 W
Pop: 8,064 (1990); 7,689 (1980)   **Pop Density:** 8064.0
Land: 1.0 sq. mi.; **Water:** 0.0 sq. mi.   **Elev:** 45 ft.
Founded 1742; incorporated 1854.
Name origin: For Thomas Bladen, the governor of MD in 1742.

Bowie   City
ZIP: 20715   **Lat:** 38-57-34 N **Long:** 76-44-15 W
Pop: 37,589 (1990); 19,786 (1980)   **Pop Density:** 2913.9
Land: 12.9 sq. mi.; **Water:** 0.0 sq. mi.
In western MD, 20 mi. northeast of Washington. Founded 1870; incorporated 1882.
Name origin: For Oden Bowie, the thirty-seventh governor of MD. Previously called Huntington City.

Brandywine   CDP
ZIP: 20613   **Lat:** 38-41-54 N **Long:** 76-51-15 W
Pop: 1,406 (1990); 1,319 (1980)   **Pop Density:** 327.0
Land: 4.3 sq. mi.; **Water:** 0.0 sq. mi.

Brentwood   Town
ZIP: 20722   **Lat:** 38-56-36 N **Long:** 76-57-25 W
Pop: 3,005 (1990); 2,988 (1980)   **Pop Density:** 7512.5
Land: 0.4 sq. mi.; **Water:** 0.0 sq. mi.
Incorporated 1912.
Name origin: For pioneer family, the Brents.

Calverton   CDP
Lat: 39-03-40 N Long: 76-55-52 W
Pop: 4,461 (1990)   **Pop Density:** 2788.1
Land: 1.6 sq. mi.; **Water:** 0.0 sq. mi.
Part of the town is also in Montgomery County.

Camp Springs   CDP
ZIP: 20748   Lat: 38-48-12 N Long: 76-55-14 W
Pop: 16,392 (1990); 10,312 (1980)   **Pop Density:** 2276.7
Land: 7.2 sq. mi.; **Water:** 0.0 sq. mi.

Capitol Heights   Town
ZIP: 20743   Lat: 38-52-40 N Long: 76-54-29 W
Pop: 3,633 (1990); 3,271 (1980)   **Pop Density:** 5190.0
Land: 0.7 sq. mi.; **Water:** 0.0 sq. mi.   **Elev:** 109 ft.
Incorporated 1910.
Name origin: Descriptively named as the town is slightly elevated and near Washington, D. C.

Carmody Hills-Pepper Mill Village   CDP
Lat: 38-53-36 N Long: 76-53-18 W
Pop: 4,815 (1990); 5,571 (1980)   **Pop Density:** 6878.6
Land: 0.7 sq. mi.; **Water:** 0.0 sq. mi.

Cheverly   Town
ZIP: 20785   Lat: 38-55-32 N Long: 76-54-49 W
Pop: 6,023 (1990); 5,508 (1980)   **Pop Density:** 4633.1
Land: 1.3 sq. mi.; **Water:** 0.0 sq. mi.
Incorporated 1931.
Name origin: For the village of Cheveley in England.

Chillum   CDP
ZIP: 20783   Lat: 38-58-05 N Long: 76-58-40 W
Pop: 31,309 (1990); 32,775 (1980)   **Pop Density:** 7636.3
Land: 4.1 sq. mi.; **Water:** 0.0 sq. mi.

Clinton   CDP
ZIP: 20735   Lat: 38-45-49 N Long: 76-53-44 W
Pop: 19,987 (1990); 16,438 (1980)   **Pop Density:** 1867.9
Land: 10.7 sq. mi.; **Water:** 0.0 sq. mi.

College Park   City
ZIP: 20740   Lat: 38-59-45 N Long: 76-56-05 W
Pop: 21,927 (1990); 1,230 (1980)   **Pop Density:** 4060.6
Land: 5.4 sq. mi.; **Water:** 0.0 sq. mi.
Nine mi. northeast of Washington, D.C. Incorporated 1945. Site of the main campus of the University of Maryland.
Name origin: For Maryland Agricultural College, established 1807 (now the University of Maryland).

Colmar Manor   Town
ZIP: 20722   Lat: 38-55-49 N Long: 76-56-36 W
Pop: 1,249 (1990); 1,286 (1980)   **Pop Density:** 3122.5
Land: 0.4 sq. mi.; **Water:** 0.1 sq. mi.
Incorporated 1927.

Coral Hills   CDP
ZIP: 20743   Lat: 38-52-17 N Long: 76-55-24 W
Pop: 11,032 (1990); 4,855 (1980)   **Pop Density:** 7354.7
Land: 1.5 sq. mi.; **Water:** 0.0 sq. mi.

Cottage City   Town
ZIP: 20722   Lat: 38-56-11 N Long: 76-56-59 W
Pop: 1,236 (1990); 1,122 (1980)   **Pop Density:** 6180.0
Land: 0.2 sq. mi.; **Water:** 0.0 sq. mi.
Developed around 1920; incorporated 1924.
Name origin: For one-story cottages that were put up by an early developer.

District Heights   City
ZIP: 20747   Lat: 38-51-27 N Long: 07-65-32 W
Pop: 6,950 (1980)   **Pop Density:** 3021.7
Land: 2.3 sq. mi.; **Water:** 0.1 sq. mi.
A suburb of Washington, D.C. Incorporated 1936.
Name origin: For its 280–foot elevation and its location near Washington, D.C.

Dodge Park   CDP
Lat: 38-55-52 N Long: 76-52-53 W
Pop: 4,842 (1990); 5,275 (1980)   **Pop Density:** 6052.5
Land: 0.8 sq. mi.; **Water:** 0.0 sq. mi.

Eagle Harbor   Town
ZIP: 20608   Lat: 38-33-58 N Long: 76-41-13 W
Pop: 38 (1990); 45 (1980)   **Pop Density:** 380.0
Land: 0.1 sq. mi.; **Water:** 0.0 sq. mi.
Incorporated 1929.
Name origin: For the eagles in the vicinity and its location on the Patuxent River.

East Riverdale   CDP
ZIP: 20737   Lat: 38-57-38 N Long: 76-54-37 W
Pop: 14,187 (1990); 4,015 (1980)   **Pop Density:** 8345.3
Land: 1.7 sq. mi.; **Water:** 0.0 sq. mi.

Edmonston   Town
ZIP: 20781   Lat: 38-57-00 N Long: 76-56-00 W
Pop: 851 (1990)   **Pop Density:** 2127.5
Land: 0.4 sq. mi.; **Water:** 0.0 sq. mi.
Incorporated 1924.
Name origin: For the Edmonston family, prominent early settlers.

Fairmount Heights   Town
ZIP: 20743   Lat: 38-54-05 N Long: 76-54-53 W
Pop: 1,238 (1990); 1,616 (1980)   **Pop Density:** 4126.7
Land: 0.3 sq. mi.; **Water:** 0.0 sq. mi.
Suburb of Washington, D.C. Incorporated 1935.
Name origin: Pleasant-sounding name given by early settlers; the elevation is not great.

Forest Heights   Town
ZIP: 20745   Lat: 38-48-36 N Long: 76-59-55 W
Pop: 2,859 (1990); 2,999 (1980)   **Pop Density:** 5718.0
Land: 0.5 sq. mi.; **Water:** 0.0 sq. mi.
Incorporated 1949.
Name origin: Named in 1941 for its location on a hillside above the Potomac River.

Forestville   CDP
ZIP: 20747   Lat: 38-50-58 N Long: 76-52-29 W
Pop: 16,731 (1990); 16,161 (1980)   **Pop Density:** 3718.0
Land: 4.5 sq. mi.; **Water:** 0.0 sq. mi.

Fort Washington   CDP
ZIP: 20744   Lat: 38-44-07 N Long: 77-00-11 W
Pop: 24,032 (1990)   **Pop Density:** 1767.1
Land: 13.6 sq. mi.; **Water:** 0.4 sq. mi.

Friendly   CDP
ZIP: 20744   Lat: 38-45-23 N Long: 76-57-56 W
Pop: 9,028 (1990); 6,159 (1980)   **Pop Density:** 1327.6
Land: 6.8 sq. mi.; **Water:** 0.0 sq. mi.

Glenarden   Town
ZIP: 20801   **Lat:** 38-55-50 N **Long:** 76-51-46 W
Pop: 5,025 (1990); 3,173 (1980)   **Pop Density:** 6281.3
Land: 0.8 sq. mi.; **Water:** 0.0 sq. mi.   **Elev:** 110 ft.
Incorporated 1939.
Name origin: From a euphonious term meaning 'forest valley.'

Glenn Dale   CDP
ZIP: 20769   **Lat:** 38-59-12 N **Long:** 76-48-03 W
Pop: 9,689 (1990); 277 (1980)   **Pop Density:** 1181.6
Land: 8.2 sq. mi.; **Water:** 0.0 sq. mi.

Goddard   Military facility
                        Lat: 38-59-22 N **Long:** 76-51-13 W
Pop: 4,576 (1990); 934 (1980)   **Pop Density:** 1906.7
Land: 2.4 sq. mi.; **Water:** 0.0 sq. mi.

Greater Upper Marlboro   CDP
                        Lat: 38-49-49 N **Long:** 76-45-09 W
Pop: 11,528 (1990)   **Pop Density:** 309.9
Land: 37.2 sq. mi.; **Water:** 0.3 sq. mi.

Greenbelt   City
ZIP: 20770   **Lat:** 38-59-41 N **Long:** 76-53-08 W
Pop: 21,096 (1990); 17,332 (1980) **Pop Density:** 3575.6
Land: 5.9 sq. mi.; **Water:** 0.0 sq. mi.   **Elev:** 180 ft.
In south-central MD, 10 mi. east of Washington. Incorporated 1937.
Name origin: For its surrounding ring of parkland.

Hillandale   CDP
ZIP: 20903   **Lat:** 39-01-26 N **Long:** 76-57-39 W
Pop: 2,167 (1990); 406 (1980)   **Pop Density:** 3095.7
Land: 0.7 sq. mi.; **Water:** 0.0 sq. mi.
Part of the town is also in Montgomery County.

Hillcrest Heights   CDP
ZIP: 20748   **Lat:** 38-50-11 N **Long:** 76-57-50 W
Pop: 17,136 (1990); 10,502 (1980) **Pop Density:** 7140.0
Land: 2.4 sq. mi.; **Water:** 0.0 sq. mi.

Hyattsville   City
ZIP: 20780   **Lat:** 38-57-33 N **Long:** 76-57-12 W
Pop: 13,864 (1990); 12,523 (1980) **Pop Density:** 6601.9
Land: 2.1 sq. mi.; **Water:** 0.0 sq. mi.
In south-central MD, 6 mi. northeast of Washington. Incorporated 1886.
Name origin: For pioneer Christopher Clarke Hyatt, who settled in the area in 1845.

Kentland   CDP
ZIP: 20785   **Lat:** 38-55-05 N **Long:** 76-53-38 W
Pop: 7,967 (1990); 8,596 (1980)   **Pop Density:** 4686.5
Land: 1.7 sq. mi.; **Water:** 0.0 sq. mi.

Kettering   CDP
ZIP: 20772   **Lat:** 38-53-24 N **Long:** 76-47-08 W
Pop: 9,901 (1990); 4,278 (1980)   **Pop Density:** 1800.2
Land: 5.5 sq. mi.; **Water:** 0.0 sq. mi.

Landover   CDP
ZIP: 20784   **Lat:** 38-56-10 N **Long:** 76-54-05 W
Pop: 5,052 (1990); 5,374 (1980)   **Pop Density:** 6315.0
Land: 0.8 sq. mi.; **Water:** 0.0 sq. mi.

Landover Hills   Town
ZIP: 20784   **Lat:** 38-56-35 N **Long:** 76-53-28 W
Pop: 2,074 (1990); 1,428 (1980)   **Pop Density:** 6913.3
Land: 0.3 sq. mi.; **Water:** 0.0 sq. mi.
Incorporated 1945.
Name origin: For the Welsh city of Llandovery.

Langley Park   CDP
ZIP: 20783   **Lat:** 38-59-22 N **Long:** 76-58-39 W
Pop: 14,345 (1990); 11,114 (1980) **Pop Density:** 17931.3
Land: 0.8 sq. mi.; **Water:** 0.0 sq. mi.
Part of the town is also in Montgomery county.

Lanham-Seabrook   CDP
ZIP: 20706   **Lat:** 38-58-00 N **Long:** 76-50-38 W
Pop: 16,792 (1990); 3,153 (1980)   **Pop Density:** 3229.2
Land: 5.2 sq. mi.; **Water:** 0.0 sq. mi.

Largo   CDP
ZIP: 20772   **Lat:** 38-52-46 N **Long:** 76-49-48 W
Pop: 9,475 (1990); 5,557 (1980)   **Pop Density:** 3158.3
Land: 3.0 sq. mi.; **Water:** 0.0 sq. mi.

Laurel   City
ZIP: 20707   **Lat:** 39-05-51 N **Long:** 76-51-30 W
Pop: 19,438 (1990); 12,103 (1980) **Pop Density:** 6074.4
Land: 3.2 sq. mi.; **Water:** 0.0 sq. mi.
In south-central MD, 17 mi. north-northeast of Washington. Founded 1658; incorporated 1870.
Name origin: For the abundant laurel trees of the colonial era. Previously called Laurel Factory.

Marlow Heights   CDP
ZIP: 20748   **Lat:** 38-49-28 N **Long:** 76-56-58 W
Pop: 5,885 (1990); 3,465 (1980)   **Pop Density:** 2802.4
Land: 2.1 sq. mi.; **Water:** 0.0 sq. mi.

Marlton   CDP
ZIP: 20772   **Lat:** 38-45-29 N **Long:** 76-47-23 W
Pop: 5,523 (1990)   **Pop Density:** 920.5
Land: 6.0 sq. mi.; **Water:** 0.0 sq. mi.

Mitchellville   CDP
ZIP: 20717   **Lat:** 38-55-45 N **Long:** 76-49-23 W
Pop: 12,593 (1990)   **Pop Density:** 1166.0
Land: 10.8 sq. mi.; **Water:** 0.1 sq. mi.

Morningside   Town
ZIP: 20746   **Lat:** 38-49-45 N **Long:** 76-53-26 W
Pop: 930 (1990); 1,395 (1980)   **Pop Density:** 3100.0
Land: 0.3 sq. mi.; **Water:** 0.0 sq. mi.
Developed 1940s; incorporated 1949.
Name origin: Chosen by the developers for its sound.

Mount Rainier   City
ZIP: 20712   **Lat:** 38-56-29 N **Long:** 76-57-50 W
Pop: 7,954 (1990); 7,361 (1980)   **Pop Density:** 11362.9
Land: 0.7 sq. mi.; **Water:** 0.0 sq. mi.
Incorporated 1910.
Name origin: Named by several army officers from the Seattle area for Mt. Rainier in WA.

New Carrollton   City
ZIP: 20784   **Lat:** 38-57-58 N **Long:** 76-52-37 W
Pop: 12,002 (1990); 12,632 (1980) **Pop Density:** 8001.3
Land: 1.5 sq. mi.; **Water:** 0.0 sq. mi.
In south-central MD, 9 mi. northeast of Washington. Incorporated 1953.
Name origin: For pioneer Charles Carroll, who owned large

tracts of land in colonial MD. Previously called Carrollton; "New" added after post office opened in 1965 to avoid confusion with the former Carrollton in Carroll County.

North Brentwood — Town
ZIP: 20722   Lat: 38-56-42 N   Long: 76-57-03 W
Pop: 512 (1990); 580 (1980)   Pop Density: 5120.0
Land: 0.1 sq. mi.; Water: 0.0 sq. mi.

Settled after World War I by commuters from Washington, D.C. Incorporated 1924.

Name origin: For the Brent family, early settlers.

Oxon Hill-Glassmanor — CDP
ZIP: 20745   Lat: 38-47-47 N   Long: 76-58-30 W
Pop: 35,794 (1990); 474 (1980)   Pop Density: 4067.5
Land: 8.8 sq. mi.; Water: 0.0 sq. mi.

Palmer Park — CDP
ZIP: 20785   Lat: 38-55-05 N   Long: 76-52-20 W
Pop: 7,019 (1990); 7,986 (1980)   Pop Density: 10027.1
Land: 0.7 sq. mi.; Water: 0.0 sq. mi.

Riverdale — Town
ZIP: 20737   Lat: 38-57-51 N   Long: 76-55-39 W
Pop: 5,185 (1990); 3,449 (1980)   Pop Density: 3240.6
Land: 1.6 sq. mi.; Water: 0.0 sq. mi.

Incorporated 1920.

Name origin: Named c. 1800 for its location on the upper reaches of the Anacostia River.

Rosaryville — CDP
ZIP: 20772   Lat: 38-46-33 N   Long: 76-50-04 W
Pop: 8,976 (1990)   Pop Density: 645.8
Land: 13.9 sq. mi.; Water: 0.0 sq. mi.

Seat Pleasant — City
ZIP: 20743   Lat: 38-53-42 N   Long: 76-54-09 W
Pop: 5,359 (1990); 5,217 (1980)   Pop Density: 7655.7
Land: 0.7 sq. mi.; Water: 0.0 sq. mi.

Incorporated 1931.

Name origin: Previously called Chesapeake Junction; name changed in 1906 to a more pleasant-sounding name.

South Laurel — CDP
ZIP: 20708   Lat: 39-04-10 N   Long: 76-51-01 W
Pop: 18,591 (1990); 18,034 (1980)   Pop Density: 4534.4
Land: 4.1 sq. mi.; Water: 0.0 sq. mi.

Suitland-Silver Hill — CDP
ZIP: 20746   Lat: 38-50-43 N   Long: 76-55-22 W
Pop: 35,111 (1990); 32,164 (1980)   Pop Density: 5319.8
Land: 6.6 sq. mi.; Water: 0.0 sq. mi.

A suburb of Washington, D.C., immediately southeast of the District. Suitland is the site of the home office of the U.S. Bureau of the Census.

Takoma Park — City
ZIP: 20912   Lat: 38-58-53 N   Long: 76-59-34 W
Pop: 5,156 (1990); 4,900 (1980)   Pop Density: 6445.0
Land: 0.8 sq. mi.; Water: 0.0 sq. mi.

In central MD, 6 mi. north of Washington. Founded 1883; incorporated 1890. Part of the town is in Montgomery County.

Name origin: Named by 1880s real estate developer Benjamin Gilbert for Mt. Tacoma in Washington, but with spelling change. Previously called Brightwood.

Temple Hills — CDP
ZIP: 20748   Lat: 38-48-35 N   Long 76-56-55 W
Pop: 6,865 (1990); 508 (1980)   Pop Density: 4903.6
Land: 1.4 sq. mi.; Water: 0.0 sq. mi.

University Park — Town
ZIP: 20784   Lat: 38-58-16 N   Long 76-56-37 W
Pop: 2,243 (1990); 2,508 (1980)   Pop Density: 4486.0
Land: 0.5 sq. mi.; Water: 0.0 sq. mi.

Incorporated 1936.

Name origin: For its location near College Park.

Upper Marlboro — Town
ZIP: 20772   Lat: 38-49-03 N   Long 76-45-19 W
Pop: 745 (1990); 828 (1980)   Pop Density: 1862.5
Land: 0.4 sq. mi.; Water: 0.0 sq. mi.

Settled 1704; incorporated 1870.

Name origin: For John Churchill (1650–1722), first Duke of Marlborough, great English military hero. "Upper" is to distinguish it from Lower Marlboro in Calvert County. Spelled Marlborough until 1893.

Walker Mill — CDP
ZIP: 20743   Lat: 38-52-31 N   Long 76-53-19 W
Pop: 10,920 (1990); 5,063 (1980)   Pop Density: 3412.5
Land: 3.2 sq. mi.; Water: 0.0 sq. mi.

West Laurel — CDP
Lat: 39-06-03 N   Long 76-53-59 W
Pop: 4,151 (1990)   Pop Density: 1012.4
Land: 4.1 sq. mi.; Water: 0.1 sq. mi.

Woodlawn — CDP
ZIP: 20784   Lat: 38-56-57 N   Long 76-53-53 W
Pop: 5,329 (1990); 4,747 (1980)   Pop Density: 4440.8
Land: 1.2 sq. mi.; Water: 0.0 sq. mi.

Woodmore — CDP
Lat: 38-56-05 N   Long 76-46-30 W
Pop: 2,874 (1990)   Pop Density: 219.4
Land: 13.1 sq. mi.; Water: 0.1 sq. mi.

Queen Anne's County
County Seat: Centreville (ZIP: 21617)

Pop: 33,953 (1990); 25,508 (1980)   **Pop Density:** 91.2
Land: 372.2 sq. mi.; **Water:** 137.6 sq. mi.   **Area Code:** 410

On eastern border of MD, west of Dover, DE; organized 1706 from Talbot County.
Name origin: For Anne (1665–1714), queen of Great Britain and Ireland (1702–14).

Barclay (Merrickton)   Town
ZIP: 21607   **Lat:** 39-08-37 N **Long:** 75-51-51 W
Pop: 170 (1990); 132 (1980)   **Pop Density:** 566.7
Land: 0.3 sq. mi.; **Water:** 0.0 sq. mi.

Centreville   Town
ZIP: 21617   **Lat:** 39-02-36 N **Long:** 76-03-55 W
Pop: 2,097 (1990); 2,018 (1980)   **Pop Density:** 1310.6
Land: 1.6 sq. mi.; **Water:** 0.0 sq. mi.
Founded 1792; incorporated 1794.
Name origin: For its location within the county.

Church Hill   Town
ZIP: 21623   **Lat:** 39-08-36 N **Long:** 75-58-50 W
Pop: 481 (1990); 319 (1980)   **Pop Density:** 1202.5
Land: 0.4 sq. mi.; **Water:** 0.0 sq. mi.
Founded 1802; incorporated 1876.
Name origin: Descriptively named, as it was the site of several churches.

Grasonville   CDP
ZIP: 21638   **Lat:** 38-57-28 N **Long:** 76-11-39 W
Pop: 2,439 (1990); 1,910 (1980)   **Pop Density:** 399.8
Land: 6.1 sq. mi.; **Water:** 0.0 sq. mi.

Kingstown   CDP
                       Lat: 39-12-22 N **Long:** 76-02-53 W
Pop: 1,660 (1990); 1,192 (1980)   **Pop Density:** 830.0
Land: 2.0 sq. mi.; **Water:** 0.3 sq. mi.

Millington   Town
ZIP: 21651   **Lat:** 39-15-11 N **Long:** 75-50-30 W
Pop: 34 (1990); 34 (1980)   **Pop Density:** 340.0
Land: 0.1 sq. mi.; **Water:** 0.0 sq. mi.   **Elev:** 27 ft.
Incorporated 1890. Part of the town is in Kent County.
Name origin: Named in 1827 for early settler Richard Millington.

Queen Anne   Town
ZIP: 21657   **Lat:** 38-55-12 N **Long:** 75-57-16 W
Pop: 140 (1990); 131 (1980)   **Pop Density:** 1400.0
Land: 0.1 sq. mi.; **Water:** 0.0 sq. mi.   **Elev:** 39 ft.
Incorporated 1953. Part of the town is in Talbot County.
Name origin: See Queen Anne's County above.

Queenstown   Town
ZIP: 21658   **Lat:** 38-59-23 N **Long:** 76-09-21 W
Pop: 453 (1990); 491 (1980)   **Pop Density:** 1132.5
Land: 0.4 sq. mi.; **Water:** 0.0 sq. mi.
Incorporated 1892.
Name origin: First county seat and so named for the county.

Stevensville   CDP
ZIP: 21666   **Lat:** 38-59-38 N **Long:** 76-18-32 W
Pop: 1,862 (1990)   **Pop Density:** 642.1
Land: 2.9 sq. mi.; **Water:** 0.0 sq. mi.

Stevensville South   CDP
                       Lat: 38-57-36 N **Long:** 76-19-45 W
Pop: 1,751 (1990)   **Pop Density:** 473.2
Land: 3.7 sq. mi.; **Water:** 0.0 sq. mi.

Sudlersville   Town
ZIP: 21668   **Lat:** 39-11-10 N **Long:** 75-51-30 W
Pop: 428 (1990); 443 (1980)   **Pop Density:** 1426.7
Land: 0.3 sq. mi.; **Water:** 0.0 sq. mi.   **Elev:** 67 ft.
Incorporated 1870.
Name origin: Site of the Sadler family estate in the 1690s; name changed when a railroad station was established in the 1860s.

Templeville   Town
ZIP: 21670   **Lat:** 39-08-10 N **Long:** 75-46-07 W
Pop: 44 (1990); 60 (1980)   **Pop Density:** 1466.7
Land: 0.03 sq. mi.; **Water:** 0.0 sq. mi.
Incorporated 1865. Part of the town is in Caroline County.
Name origin: For the prominent local Temple family. One of its members was a governor of Delaware.

St. Mary's County
County Seat: Leonardtown (ZIP: 20650)

Pop: 75,974 (1990); 59,895 (1980)   **Pop Density:** 210.3
Land: 361.3 sq. mi.; **Water:** 403.2 sq. mi.   **Area Code:** 301

On southern border of MD, bounded by the Potomac River on the west, the Patuxent River on the east, and Chesapeake Bay on the south; the first original county, organized 1637.

Name origin: For Mary, the mother of Jesus Christ. The ships *Ark* and *Dove*, carrying colonists, landed on St. Clement's Island on Mar 25, 1634, the Feast of the Annunciation of Mary.

California   CDP
ZIP: 20619   **Lat:** 38-17-46 N **Long:** 76-29-46 W
Pop: 7,626 (1990); 5,770 (1980)   **Pop Density:** 591.2
Land: 12.9 sq. mi.; **Water:** 1.9 sq. mi.

Charlotte Hall   CDP
ZIP: 20622   **Lat:** 38-27-58 N **Long:** 76-47-34 W
Pop: 1,376 (1990); 1,013 (1980)   **Pop Density:** 269.8
Land: 5.1 sq. mi.; **Water:** 0.0 sq. mi.

Part of the town is also in Charles County.

Golden Beach   CDP
Lat: 38-29-14 N **Long:** 76-41-35 W
Pop: 2,944 (1990); 2,098 (1980)   **Pop Density:** 1132.3
Land: 2.6 sq. mi.; **Water:** 0.8 sq. mi.

Leonardtown   Town
ZIP: 20650   **Lat:** 38-17-58 N **Long** 76-38-30 W
Pop: 1,475 (1990); 1,448 (1980)   **Pop Density:** 546.3
Land: 2.7 sq. mi.; **Water:** 0.0 sq. mi.   **Elev:** 87 ft.

Established 1690s; incorporated 1858.

Name origin: Named in 1733 for the fourth Lord Baltimore, Benedict Leonard Calvert.

Lexington Park   CDP
ZIP: 20653   **Lat:** 38-15-37 N **Long** 76-26-45 W
Pop: 9,943 (1990); 10,361 (1980)   **Pop Density:** 1242.9
Land: 8.0 sq. mi.; **Water:** 0.1 sq. mi.

Residential development in southern MD, near the mouth of the Patuxent River. Nearby is the Patuxent River Naval Air Test Center.

Name origin: Formerly called Jarboesville.

Somerset County
County Seat: Princess Anne (ZIP: 21853)

Pop: 23,440 (1990); 19,188 (1980)   **Pop Density:** 71.6
Land: 327.2 sq. mi.; **Water:** 283.6 sq. mi.   **Area Code:** 410

On southern border of MD, southwest of Salisbury; original county; organized Aug 22, 1666.

Name origin: For Mary Somerset, sister-in-law of Cecilius Calvert (1605–75), 2nd Lord Baltimore.

Crisfield   City
ZIP: 21817   **Lat:** 37-58-37 N **Long:** 75-51-33 W
Pop: 2,880 (1990); 2,776 (1980)   **Pop Density:** 1800.0
Land: 1.6 sq. mi.; **Water:** 1.4 sq. mi.   **Elev:** 4 ft.

Incorporated 1872.

Name origin: For nineteenth-century railroad developer John Crisfield.

Lawsonia   CDP
Lat: 37-57-26 N **Long:** 75-50-31 W
Pop: 1,326 (1990); 289 (1980)   **Pop Density:** 207.2
Land: 6.4 sq. mi.; **Water:** 0.0 sq. mi.

Princess Anne   Town
ZIP: 21853   **Lat:** 38-12-15 N **Long:** 75-41-43 W
Pop: 1,666 (1990); 498 (1980)   **Pop Density:** 1514.5
Land: 1.1 sq. mi.; **Water:** 0.0 sq. mi.

Laid out 1733; incorporated 1894.

Name origin: For Princess Anne, the daughter of King George II

Talbot County
County Seat: Easton (ZIP: 21601)

Pop: 30,549 (1990); 25,604 (1980)   **Pop Density:** 113.5
Land: 269.2 sq. mi.; **Water:** 207.6 sq. mi.   **Area Code:** 410

In east-central MD, southeast of Annapolis; in existence by Feb 18, 1661/62, organized from Kent County.

Name origin: For Grace Talbot, daughter of George Calvert (1580?–1632), 1st Lord Baltimore, and sister of Cecilius Calvert, first proprietor of the colony of MD.

Easton   Town
ZIP: 21601   **Lat:** 38-46-28 N **Long:** 76-04-11 W
Pop: 9,372 (1990); 7,536 (1980)   **Pop Density:** 1186.3
Land: 7.9 sq. mi.; **Water:** 0.1 sq. mi.   **Elev:** 38 ft.
Established 1700s; incorporated 1790.
Name origin: For Easton, Somersetshire, England.

Oxford   Town
ZIP: 21654   **Lat:** 38-41-21 N **Long:** 76-10-14 W
Pop: 699 (1990); 754 (1980)   **Pop Density:** 1747.5
Land: 0.4 sq. mi.; **Water:** 0.2 sq. mi.
Settled 1635; incorporated 1852.
Name origin: Named in 1702 for England's great university town. Previously called Thread Haven.

Queen Anne   Town
ZIP: 21657   **Lat:** 38-55-05 N **Long:** 75-57-12 W
Pop: 110 (1990); 128 (1980)   **Pop Density:** 1100.0
Land: 0.1 sq. mi.; **Water:** 0.0 sq. mi.   **Elev:** 39 ft.
Incorporated 1953. Part of the town is in Queen Anne's County.
Name origin: For Anne, queen of England 1702–1714.

St. Michaels   Town
         Lat: 38-47-18 N **Long:** 76-13-20 W
Pop: 1,301 (1990); 1,301 (1980)   **Pop Density:** 1858.6
Land: 0.7 sq. mi.; **Water:** 0.1 sq. mi.
Incorporated 1804.
Name origin: For St. Michaels Church, which was built here in 1690.

Trappe   Town
ZIP: 21673   **Lat:** 38-39-35 N **Long:** 76-03-30 W
Pop: 974 (1990); 739 (1980)   **Pop Density:** 1217.5
Land: 0.8 sq. mi.; **Water:** 0.0 sq. mi.
Incorporated 1827.
Name origin: Several theories: former site of a Trappist monastery; from a former tavern "The Partridge Trap"; site in colonial days of a wolf trap.

Washington County
County Seat: Hagerstown (ZIP: 21740)

Pop: 121,393 (1990); 113,086 (1980)   **Pop Density:** 265.0
Land: 458.2 sq. mi.; **Water:** 9.4 sq. mi.   **Area Code:** 301

On central northern border of MD; organized Sep 6, 1776 from Frederick County.
Name origin: For George Washington (1732–99), American patriot and first U.S. president.

Boonsboro   Town
ZIP: 21713   **Lat:** 39-30-34 N **Long:** 77-39-20 W
Pop: 2,445 (1990); 1,908 (1980)   **Pop Density:** 2222.7
Land: 1.1 sq. mi.; **Water:** 0.0 sq. mi.
Incorporated 1831.
Name origin: For pioneers George and William Boone, who settled here in 1774.

Bridgeport   CDP
         Lat: 39-38-27 N **Long:** 77-40-23 W
Pop: 2,702 (1990); 3,626 (1980)   **Pop Density:** 965.0
Land: 2.8 sq. mi.; **Water:** 0.0 sq. mi.

Clear Spring   Town
ZIP: 21722   **Lat:** 39-39-21 N **Long:** 77-55-51 W
Pop: 415 (1990); 477 (1980)   **Pop Density:** 4150.0
Land: 0.1 sq. mi.; **Water:** 0.0 sq. mi.
Established 1821; incorporated 1836.
Name origin: For an adjacent spring.

Fort Ritchie   Military facility
         Lat: 39-42-01 N **Long:** 77-30-13 W
Pop: 1,249 (1990); 1,754 (1980)   **Pop Density:** 1249.0
Land: 1.0 sq. mi.; **Water:** 0.0 sq. mi.

Funkstown   Town
ZIP: 21734   **Lat:** 39-36-29 N **Long:** 77-42-28 W
Pop: 1,136 (1990); 1,103 (1980)   **Pop Density:** 3786.7
Land: 0.3 sq. mi.; **Water:** 0.0 sq. mi.
Incorporated 1840.
Name origin: For Henry Funk, who was granted land in the area in 1754.

Hagerstown   City
ZIP: 21740   **Lat:** 39-38-16 N **Long:** 77-43-09 W
Pop: 35,445 (1990); 9,250 (1980)   **Pop Density:** 3580.3
Land: 9.9 sq. mi.; **Water:** 0.0 sq. mi.
In western MD, 70 mi. west-northwest of Baltimore. Origi-

nally settled after c. 1740; town laid out by Hager in 1762. Incorporated Dec 1813.

Name origin: Named by settler Capt. Jonathan Hager (1714–1775). First called Elizabethtown, after Hager's wife.

Halfway   CDP
ZIP: 21740   Lat: 39-36-47 N Long: 77-46-14 W
Pop: 8,873 (1990); 245 (1980)   Pop Density: 1971.8
Land: 4.5 sq. mi.; Water: 0.0 sq. mi.

Hancock   Town
ZIP: 21750   Lat: 39-42-10 N Long: 78-10-25 W
Pop: 1,926 (1990); 1,887 (1980)   Pop Density: 713.3
Land: 2.7 sq. mi.; Water: 0.0 sq. mi.   Elev: 448 ft.
Incorporated 1853.

Name origin: For pioneer Joseph Hancock, who settled here in 1749.

Keedysville   Town
ZIP: 21756   Lat: 39-29-13 N Long: 77-41-57 W
Pop: 464 (1990); 476 (1980)   Pop Density: 662.9
Land: 0.7 sq. mi.; Water: 0.0 sq. mi.   Elev: 404 ft.
Incorporated 1872.

Name origin: Named in 1860s for the many Keedy family members in the area. Previously called Centerville.

Long Meadow   CDP
ZIP: 21784   Lat: 39-41-10 N Long: 77-42-44 W
Pop: 5,594 (1990)   Pop Density: 887.9
Land: 6.3 sq. mi.; Water: 0.0 sq. mi.

Mount Aetna   CDP
                    Lat: 39-36-39 N Long: 77-40-15 W
Pop: 3,608 (1990)   Pop Density: 859.0
Land: 4.2 sq. mi.; Water: 0.0 sq. mi.

Sharpsburg   Town
ZIP: 21782   Lat: 39-27-27 N Long: 77-44-59 W
Pop: 659 (1990); 721 (1980)   Pop Density: 3295.0
Land: 0.2 sq. mi.; Water: 0.0 sq. mi.   Elev: 413 ft.
Laid out 1763. Incorporated 1832. Site of the Battle of Sharpsburg or Antietam, bloodiest battle of the Civil War (more than 20,000 killed).

Name origin: For Horatio Sharpe, MD colonial governor 1753–69. See also Sharptown (Wicomico County).

Smithsburg   Town
ZIP: 21783   Lat: 39-39-31 N Long: 77-34-40 W
Pop: 1,221 (1990); 833 (1980)   Pop Density: 1356.7
Land: 0.9 sq. mi.; Water: 0.0 sq. mi.
Founded early 1800s; incorporated 1841.

Name origin: For founder Christopher Smith (1750–1821).

Williamsport   Town
ZIP: 21795   Lat: 39-35-46 N Long: 77-49-07 W
Pop: 2,103 (1990); 2,153 (1980)   Pop Density: 1911.8
Land: 1.1 sq. mi.; Water: 0.0 sq. mi.
Founded 1787. Incorporated 1823.

Name origin: For its founder Otto Holland Williams (1747–94), Revolutionary War general.

Wicomico County
County Seat: Salisbury (ZIP: 21801)

Pop: 74,339 (1990); 64,540 (1980)   Pop Density: 197.1
Land: 377.2 sq. mi.; Water: 22.6 sq. mi.   Area Code: 410

In southeastern MD, north of Princess Anne; organized Aug 17, 1867 from Somerset and Worcester counties.

Name origin: For the Wicomico River, which flows through it. Possibly for a Nanticoke Indian village near its banks named *wicko-mekee,* possibly 'where houses are being built,' or 'pleasant place of dwelling.'

Delmar   Town
ZIP: 21875   Lat: 38-27-09 N Long: 75-34-29 W
Pop: 1,430 (1990); 1,232 (1980)   Pop Density: 3575.0
Land: 0.4 sq. mi.; Water: 0.0 sq. mi.   Elev: 55 ft.
On the DE border, 10 mi. north of Salisbury. Established 1859; incorporated 1888.

Name origin: A blend of the first syllables of Delaware and Maryland, for its location on the border. See also Marydel (Caroline County).

Fruitland   City
ZIP: 21826   Lat: 38-19-18 N Long: 75-37-34 W
Pop: 3,511 (1990)   Pop Density: 1003.1
Land: 3.5 sq. mi.; Water: 0.0 sq. mi.   Elev: 39 ft.
Incorporated 1947.

Name origin: Chosen in 1873 by a poll of the residents for its local farm produce.

Hebron   Town
ZIP: 21830   Lat: 38-25-03 N Long: 75-41-16 W
Pop: 665 (1990); 714 (1980)   Pop Density: 1662.5
Land: 0.4 sq. mi.; Water: 0.0 sq. mi.   Elev: 43 ft.
Incorporated 1931.

Name origin: Named by pioneer settlers for the biblical city of Hebron.

Mardela Springs   Town
ZIP: 21837   Lat: 38-27-29 N Long: 75-45-23 W
Pop: 360 (1990); 320 (1980)   Pop Density: 900.0
Land: 0.4 sq. mi.; Water: 0.0 sq. mi.
Incorporated 1906.

Pittsville   Town
ZIP: 21850   Lat: 38-23-36 N Long: 75-24-47 W
Pop: 602 (1990); 519 (1980)   Pop Density: 860.0
Land: 0.7 sq. mi.; Water: 0.0 sq. mi.
Incorporated 1906.

Name origin: For Dr. H. R. Pitts, who was president of a small railroad in the area in the 1860s.

Salisbury
City

ZIP: 21801   **Lat:** 38-22-18 N **Long:** 75-35-20 W
Pop: 20,592 (1990); 4,629 (1980)   **Pop Density:** 1999.2
Land: 10.3 sq. mi.; **Water:** 0.4 sq. mi.

In southeastern MD on the Delmarva Peninsula. Important center of the Eastern Shore region. Founded 1732; incorporated as a town 1811; as a city 1854.

Name origin: For Salisbury, Wiltshire, England.

Sharptown
Town

ZIP: 21861   **Lat:** 38-32-21 N **Long:** 75-43-12 W
Pop: 609 (1990); 654 (1980)   **Pop Density:** 1522.5
Land: 0.4 sq. mi.; **Water:** 0.0 sq. mi.

Incorporated 1874.

Name origin: For Horatio Sharpe, MD colonial governor 1753–69. See also Sharpsburg (Washington County).

Willards
Town

ZIP: 21874   **Lat:** 38-23-30 N **Long:** 75-20-59 W
Pop: 708 (1990); 540 (1980)   **Pop Density:** 708.0
Land: 1.0 sq. mi.; **Water:** 0.0 sq. mi.

Incorporated 1906.

Name origin: For Willards Thompson, executive of the railroad that once served the town.

Worcester County
County Seat: Snow Hill (ZIP: 21863)

Pop: 35,028 (1990); 30,889 (1980)   **Pop Density:** 74.0
Land: 473.2 sq. mi.; **Water:** 221.5 sq. mi.   **Area Code:** 410

On southeastern border of MD, on Atlantic Ocean; organized Oct 29, 1742 from Somerset County.

Name origin: For Edward Somerset, Earl of Worcester (c.1601–67), son-in-law of George Calvert (1580?–1632).

Berlin
Town

ZIP: 21811   **Lat:** 38-19-30 N **Long:** 75-13-05 W
Pop: 2,616 (1990); 2,162 (1980)   **Pop Density:** 1308.0
Land: 2.0 sq. mi.; **Water:** 0.0 sq. mi.   **Elev:** 45 ft.

Incorporated 1868.

Name origin: Said to be a combination of the English name Burleigh (its former name) and Inn.

Ocean City
Town

ZIP: 21842   **Lat:** 38-22-46 N **Long:** 75-02-11 W
Pop: 5,146 (1990); 4,946 (1980)   **Pop Density:** 1118.7
Land: 4.6 sq. mi.; **Water:** 31.8 sq. mi.   **Elev:** 8 ft.

Founded 1875; incorporated 1880.

Name origin: For its location on the Atlantic; MD's only town on the ocean.

Ocean Pines
CDP

                    Lat: 38-22-59 N **Long:** 75-08-58 W
Pop: 4,251 (1990)   **Pop Density:** 644.1
Land: 6.6 sq. mi.; **Water:** 2.6 sq. mi.

Pocomoke City
City

ZIP: 21851   **Lat:** 38-04-01 N **Long:** 75-33-42 W
Pop: 3,922 (1990); 3,558 (1980)   **Pop Density:** 1782.7
Land: 2.2 sq. mi.; **Water:** 0.2 sq. mi.

Incorporated as New Town 1865; as Pocomoke City 1878.

Name origin: For its location on the Pocomoke River; Pocomoke is from an Algonquian term probably meaning 'broken ground.'

Snow Hill
Town

ZIP: 21863   **Lat:** 38-10-23 N **Long:** 75-23-29 W
Pop: 2,217 (1990); 2,192 (1980)   **Pop Density:** 1705.4
Land: 1.3 sq. mi.; **Water:** 0.0 sq. mi.   **Elev:** 21 ft.

Settled 1642. First county courthouse built in 1742. Incorporated 1812.

Name origin: Named by settlers from the Snow Hill district of London.

West Ocean City
CDP

ZIP: 21842   **Lat:** 38-20-43 N **Long:** 75-06-34 W
Pop: 1,928 (1990)   **Pop Density:** 459.0
Land: 4.2 sq. mi.; **Water:** 2.7 sq. mi.

Index to Places and Counties in Maryland

Massachusetts

MASSACHUSETTS

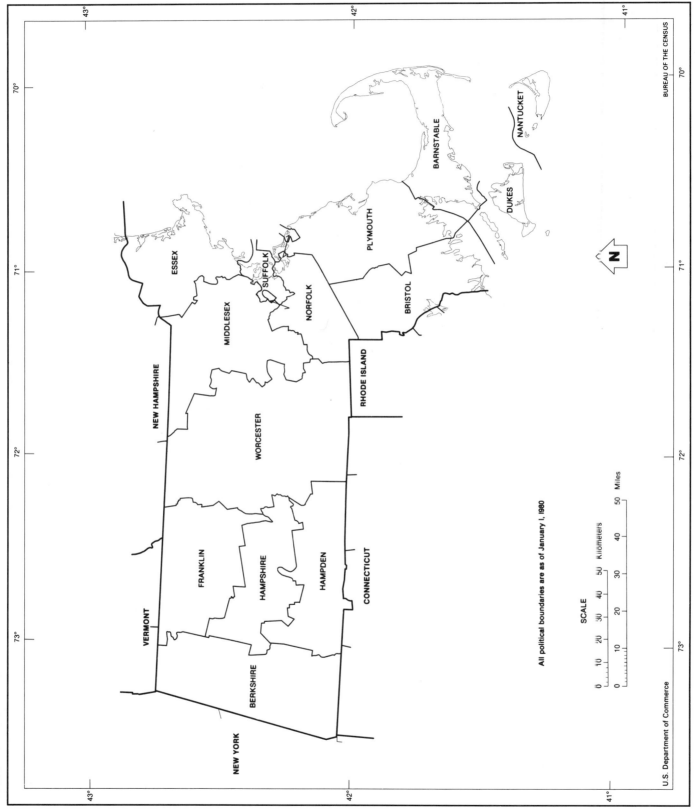

N

SCALE

Miles
0   10   20   30   40   50

0   10   20   30   40   50   Kilometers

All political boundaries are as of January 1, 1980

U.S. Department of Commerce

BUREAU OF THE CENSUS

NANTUCKET

DUKES

BARNSTABLE

PLYMOUTH

BRISTOL

NORFOLK

SUFFOLK

ESSEX

MIDDLESEX

WORCESTER

RHODE ISLAND

NEW HAMPSHIRE

VERMONT

FRANKLIN

HAMPSHIRE

HAMPDEN

BERKSHIRE

NEW YORK

CONNECTICUT

Massachusetts

Population: 6,016,425 (1990); 5,737,037 (1980)
Population rank (1990): 13
Percent population change (1980-1990): 4.9
Population projection: 5,939,000 (1995); 5,959,000 (2000)

Area: total 10,555 sq. mi.; 7,838 sq. mi. land, 2,717 sq. mi. water. Coastline 192 mi.
Area rank: 44
Highest elevation: 3,491 ft., Mount Greylock
Lowest point: sea level along Atlantic Ocean

State capital: Boston (Suffolk County)
Largest city: Boston (574,283)
Second largest city: Worcester (169,759)
Largest county: Middlesex (1,398,468)

Total housing units: 2,472,711
No. of occupied housing units: 2,247,110
Vacant housing units (%): 9.1
Distribution of population by race and Hispanic origin (%):
White: 89.8
Black: 5.0
Hispanic (any race): 4.8
Native American: 0.2
Asian/Pacific: 2.4
Other: 2.6

Admission date: February 6, 1788 (6th state)

Location: In the northeastern United States on the Atlantic coast, bordering Rhode Island, Connecticut, New York, Vermont, and New Hampshire. One of the thirteen original English colonies.

Name Origin: From Algonquian (Natick) Indian *massa* 'great,' and *chuset* or *wachuset* 'hill,' probably referring to the present Blue Hills near Boston. Massachusetts Bay was named first.

State bean: baked navy bean
State beverage: cranberry juice
State bird: chickadee *(Parus atricapillus)*
State building and monument stone: granite
State cat: tabby cat
State ceremonial march: "The Road to Boston"
State dog: Boston terrier
State explorer rock: Dighton Rock
State fish: cod *(Gadus morhua)*
State flower: mayflower (also called ground laurel or trailing arbutus; *Epigaea repens)*
State folk dance: square dance
State folk song: "Massachusetts"
State fossil: theropod dinosaur tracks

State gem: rhodonite
State heroine: Deborah Samson
State historical rock: Plymouth Rock
State horse: Morgan horse
State insect: ladybug *(Hippodamia convergens)*
State marine mammal: right whale
State mineral: babingtonite
State muffin: corn muffin
State patriotic song: "Massachusetts (Because of You Our Land is Free)"
State poem: "Blue Hills of Massachusetts"
State rock: Roxbury pudding stone (Roxbury conglomerate)
State shell: New England neptune *(Neptuna decemcostata)*
State song: "All Hail to Massachusetts"
State tree: American elm *(Ulmus americana)*
State motto: *Ense petit placidam sub libertate quietem* (Latin 'By the sword we seek peace, but peace only under liberty')
State nickname: The (Old) Bay State; the Old Colony State; the Puritan State; the Baked Bean State

Area codes: 413 (Springfield and western MA), 508 (Worcester area and east), 617 (Boston and immediate environs)
Time zone: Eastern
Abbreviations: MA (postal), Mass. (traditional)
Part of (region): New England

Local Government

Counties:

The Commonwealth of Massachusetts (the state's official title) has 14 counties. The county seat is called a *shire* town, from the old English term for county. In some cases there is more than one shire town.

Municipalities:

All territory within Massachusetts is in one of the 39 chartered cities or 312 incorporated towns. As elsewhere in New England, a town may consist of several villages and rural areas, all governed by the town as a single unit. Massachusetts cities and towns all have home rule.

Settlement History and Early Development

Historians believe Indians were farming in present-day Massachusetts about 10,000 B.C. When the Pilgrims arrived in 1620 they found five main Algonquian tribes: Nauset, Wampanoag, Massachuset, Nipmuc, and Pocumtuc.

Among the earliest European explorers of the area were Vikings led by Leif Ericson about 1000; John Cabot, Italian-born explorer serving England, in 1498, and Bartholomew Gosnold, an Englishman, in 1602. English claims to this region are based on the discovery of mainland North America by Cabot. By the early sixteenth century fishermen from England, France, Portugal, and Spain were fishing off the coast, and by mid-century they were going ashore to process and pack their catch. During the next 50 years, fur trading with the Indians was established.

The Pilgrims arrived aboard the *Mayflower* on September 16, 1620 in what is now Provincetown harbor. They established the first permanent English settlement in present-day Massachusetts in an abandoned Wampanoag village they named Plymouth. There they set up a democratic government based on majority rule, in accordance with the terms of the Mayflower Compact.

About half of the Pilgrims died during the first winter from cold and lack of food. The following spring friendly Indians gave them seeds and taught them how to plant corn, squash, and beans. This, combined with what they could hunt, gather, and harvest from the sea, gave them enough food to last through the next winter. They celebrated the first Thanksgiving Day in 1621 in gratitude for this plenty.

In 1629 King Charles I of England granted a group of Puritans a charter to settle and govern an English colony in the Massachusetts Bay area. In 1630 about 1000 of them, led by John Winthrop, a country gentleman with some legal training, joined a settlement that had been previously established in Salem. They left soon after and settled near present-day Boston. Harvard College was founded in 1636 to provide future leaders for the community. By 1640 Massachusetts Bay Colony had about 20,000 settlers.

The colony established political freedom and representative government, but in fact the Puritans did not permit the practice of any other religion. Some settlers such as Roger Williams (a minister who called for greater religious freedom) and Anne Hutchinson (leader of the antinomians) were convicted of heresy and banished. The Salem witchcraft trials of 1642 resulted in the execution of 19 people. Others left of their own accord, moving westward and settling towns in what are now other New England states.

In 1660 the Stuarts were restored to the English throne and began to exert stricter control over the colony. Massachusetts Bay Colony resisted all such attempts and, as a result, lost its charter in 1684. It became a part of the Dominion of New England under the administration of Sir Edmund Andros, a royal appointee. In 1691 King William and Queen Mary granted a new charter, which merged Massachusetts Bay, the colony of (New) Plymouth, the province of Maine, the territory called Acadia or Nova Scotia, and the island of Martha's Vineyard. It was called Massachusetts Bay and became a Royal Province under a governor appointed by the Crown.

Clashes between the colonists and Indians ended with King Philip's War of 1675-76. Metacom, better known as King Philip, was the chief of the Wampanoags. His father, Massasoit, had been a good friend to the colonists, but King Philip feared them. The English, afraid King Philip

would successfully bring together various tribes in a military alliance, attacked first. Using Christian Indians as auxiliaries, they decimated the Indians, killing some 3,000, including King Philip, who was killed by one of the auxiliaries.

Precursors of Revolution

During the end of the 17th and beginning of the eighteenth century, Massachusetts' population expanded and her maritime trade grew, especially with Caribbean ports. Boston became known as "the Market Town of the West Indies." During these years (1688-1763), Britain and France were fighting on the European continent and over their rival colonial interests in North America in the French and Indian Wars. Massachusetts gave considerable aid to Britain but continued to trade with the enemy. After the war's conclusion the colony refused to pay a fixed share of the wars' expenses, which had left Britain in debt. The severe taxes then levied on the colonists caused more protests and defiance until the Stamp Act of 1765 produced the famous cry "no taxation without representation."

The Boston Massacre of March 5, 1770, during which British soldiers stationed in Boston fired into a mob of jeering colonists, killing several, added fuel to the unrest. In 1773, the Tea Act was answered by the Boston Tea Party, in which Bostonians dressed as Indians dumped the cargoes of three East India Company ships into Boston Harbor to prevent their taxation. England retaliated by closing the Port of Boston in 1774 and with other "Intolerable Acts." The colonists called a Continental Congress that ordered a general boycott of British goods. Both sides began arming.

The American Revolution

On April 18, 1775, British troops marched towards Concord to seize supplies of gunpowder hidden there by the colonists. That evening Paul Revere, William Dawes, and Dr. Samuel Prescott rode through the countryside warning everyone that the British were coming. The signal in the steeple of the Old North Church in Boston was to be one lantern if the British attack were by land, two lanterns if by sea. The next morning American minutemen (members of the militia who were in constant readiness for instant action) engaged the British at Lexington and Concord, firing the "shot heard round the world."

Most of the early fighting of the Revolutionary War took place in Massachusetts, including the Battle of Bunker Hill. The British were driven from Boston in the spring of 1776, and thereafter the colony had no foreign troops within its borders. The war moved southward but Massachusetts soldiers remained active throughout the war and her ships caused heavy damage to British merchant ships.

The Constitution of Massachusetts was drafted mainly by John Adams and ratified by the people on June 15, 1780. It is the oldest written Constitution in the world still in effect. On February 6, 1788, Massachusetts ratified the U.S. Constitution and became the sixth state in the Union. She ratified it on condition that certain amendments for individual rights be added, and indeed the Bill of Rights went into effect December 15, 1791.

Intellectual Activity and Social Activism

The early nineteenth century was marked by great intellectual and literary development. Novelists Nathaniel Hawthorne, Louisa May Alcott, Horatio Alger, and Henry James lived in Massachusetts, especially around Boston, as did poets Henry Wadsworth Longfellow, John Greenleaf Whittier, Oliver Wendell Holmes, Sr., James Russell Lowell, and Emily Dickinson. Ralph Waldo Emerson, Henry David Thoreau, and their followers in Concord became the center of Transcendentalist philosophy. Horace Mann, the Secretary of the Massachusetts Board of Education, campaigned so strongly for universal education that he became known as the "Father of the Common School." Mary Lyon founded Mount Holyoke, the first women's college, in 1837. Dorothea L. Dix crusaded for the mentally disturbed. Clara Barton founded the American Red Cross. Utopian communities, such as Brook Farm in West Roxbury, were formed by idealists. Women's rights advocates included Lucy Stone, Abigail Kelley Foster, Margaret Fuller, and Susan Brownell Anthony.

The Boston area became (and remains) a center of higher education, with prestigious institutions including Harvard, Radcliffe, Massachusetts Institute of Technology, Boston University, Boston College, Tufts, Wellesley, as well as the Berklee School of Music and the New England Conservatory.

The Civil War

The Abolitionist movement had its start in Boston and included William Lloyd Garrison, Wendell Phillips, and Lydia Maria Child. Prominent men and women formed the "underground railway" to help slaves escape to Canada. When the war began, Massachusetts strongly supported the Union. More than 125,000 Massachusetts men joined the Union army and another 20,000 joined the navy. They also formed the first African-American regiment. Shipbuilders in the state built and equipped many Union ships.

Business and Industry

The Embargo Act of 1807 and the War of 1812 both forced Massachusetts to manufacture, not import, the goods she needed, encouraging the start of the American Industrial Revolution in the mills and factories of Massachusetts and Rhode Island. In 1814, Francis Cabot Lowell built a large-scale textile factory (one of the first factories in America) in Waltham. Others soon followed, as did smaller textile mills. In Springfield and Watertown federal armories made the state a leader in metalworking. Shoes and leather goods were produced in Lynn, and shipbuilding and the whaling industry flourished in New Bedford. By the 1850s, steam engines and clipper ships were both being built in the state.

The economic opportunities attracted immigrants from Great Britain and all parts of Europe. Meanwhile, local farmers could not compete with the cheaper goods brought in from the western states by the railroads in 1840, and agriculture declined. Many farmers chose to move to the industrial towns for better employment and opportunities. Between 1860 and 1900, Massachusetts changed from an agrarian society to an urbanized commonwealth.

The influx of immigrants throughout the latter half of the nineteenth century and the first half of the twentieth created a workforce in Massachusetts that often found itself at odds with Yankee businessowners and leaders, leading to strikes by textile workers in 1912 and the Boston police in 1919.

During the 1920s, competition from the southern and western states caused the textile and shoe industries to fade, but other industries continued to prosper. World War II brought a boom in factory and shipyard production of war materials, but again in the 1950s and 1960s shoe and textile manufacturing declined.

In 1959 the U.S. Navy launched its first nuclear surface ship, the cruiser *Long Beach,* at Quincy, and in 1960 a nuclear power plant began operations in Rowe. Today, the state remains a center for military research and development, and during the 1980s had one of the lowest unemployment rates in the nation. Massachusetts draws on a highly educated workforce for its electronics, computer, and defense industries; these in turn have spurred growth in service industries, including banking, insurance, and health care. Recession in the late 1980s and early 1990s has blunted the enthusiasm and phenomenal growth of the 1980s, but the state's strong educational base promises a road to recovery and stability.

State Boundaries

The Commonwealth of Massachusetts includes the islands of Martha's Vineyard and Nantucket, as well as the smaller Elizabeth Islands, all in the Atlantic. The present northern boundary was set in 1741. On April 19, 1785, Massachusetts ceded to the U.S. all of its land west of the present western boundary with New York. The east-west Massachusetts-Rhode Island boundary was disputed for more than 200 years, twice before the U.S. Supreme Court. Both states finally agreed on their present border in May 1899. Massachusetts and Connecticut had a minor contretemps in 1803 that was resolved by the "Southwick jog," the small portion of the town of Southwick, Massachusetts that juts into north-central Connecticut. Their present-day border was fixed in 1905. The Massachusetts-New York border was also controversial but was finally set and approved by Massachusetts on May 8, 1901, and by New York on June 9, 1910. Nova Scotia, which had been part of Massachusetts since the 1691 charter, remained in the possession of England at the end of the Revolutionary War. Massachusetts ceased governing the province of Maine when the latter became a state on March 15, 1820.

Massachusetts Counties

Barnstable	Dukes	Hampden	Nantucket	Suffolk
Berkshire	Essex	Hampshire	Norfolk	Worcester
Bristol	Franklin	Middlesex	Plymouth	

Multi-County Places

The following Massachusetts places are in more than one county. Given here is the total population for each multi-county place, and the names of the counties it is in.

Bondsville, pop. 1,992; Hampden (1,744), Hampshire (248)
Fort Devens, pop. 8,973; Worcester (7,667), Middlesex (1,306)

Barnstable County
County Seat: Barnstable (ZIP: 02630)

Pop: 186,605 (1990); 147,925 (1980)   **Pop Density:** 471.5
Land: 395.8 sq. mi.; **Water:** 909.8 sq. mi.   **Area Code:** 508
Coextensive with Cape Cod, in southeastern MA; organized Jun 2, 1685 from Old Plymouth Colony.
Name origin: For Barnstaple, Devonshire, England. Original meaning was 'Bearda's staple or post,' or 'post to which a warship was moored.' Folk etymology changed it to -*stable*.

Barnstable   Town
ZIP: 02630   **Lat:** 41-40-05 N **Long:** 70-21-15 W
Pop: 40,949 (1990); 30,898 (1980)   **Pop Density:** 681.3
Land: 60.1 sq. mi.; **Water:** 16.2 sq. mi.

In southeastern MA on north shore of Cape Cod, 65 mi. southeast of Boston.
Name origin: For Barnstable, Devonshire, England.

Bourne   Town
ZIP: 02559   **Lat:** 41-43-07 N **Long:** 70-35-37 W
Pop: 16,064 (1990); 13,874 (1980)   **Pop Density:** 392.8
Land: 40.9 sq. mi.; **Water:** 11.9 sq. mi.

In southeastern MA on Cape Cod Canal, 14 mi. west of Barnstable.
Name origin: For its most early prominent citizen, Jonathan Bourne. Originally called Monument Village.

Brewster   Town
ZIP: 02631   **Lat:** 41-44-41 N **Long:** 70-04-11 W
Pop: 8,440 (1990); 5,226 (1980)   **Pop Density:** 367.0
Land: 23.0 sq. mi.; **Water:** 2.5 sq. mi.

Buzzards Bay   CDP
Lat: 41-45-18 N **Long:** 70-36-53 W
Pop: 3,250 (1990); 3,375 (1980)   **Pop Density:** 1625.0
Land: 2.0 sq. mi.; **Water:** 1.0 sq. mi.

Centerville   CDP
ZIP: 02632   **Lat:** 41-39-12 N **Long:** 70-20-39 W
Pop: 9,190 (1990); 3,640 (1980)   **Pop Density:** 1178.2
Land: 7.8 sq. mi.; **Water:** 4.2 sq. mi.

Chatham   Town
ZIP: 02633   **Lat:** 41-40-28 N **Long:** 69-58-34 W
Pop: 6,579 (1990); 6,071 (1980)   **Pop Density:** 401.2
Land: 16.4 sq. mi.; **Water:** 7.9 sq. mi.

In southeastern MA on the Atlantic coast of Cape Cod. Incorporated 1712.

Cotuit   CDP
ZIP: 02635   **Lat:** 41-37-13 N **Long:** 70-26-24 W
Pop: 2,364 (1990)   **Pop Density:** 482.4
Land: 4.9 sq. mi.; **Water:** 1.0 sq. mi.

Dennis   Town
ZIP: 02638   **Lat:** 41-42-22 N **Long:** 70-09-55 W
Pop: 13,864 (1990); 12,360 (1980)   **Pop Density:** 673.0
Land: 20.6 sq. mi.; **Water:** 1.6 sq. mi.

In southeastern MA on Cape Cod, 5 mi. northeast of Barnstable. Settled 1639.
Name origin: For the Rev. Josiah Dennis, pastor of the first meeting house.

Dennis Port   CDP
ZIP: 02639   **Lat:** 41-40-11 N **Long:** 70-08-21 W
Pop: 2,775 (1990); 2,570 (1980)   **Pop Density:** 895.2
Land: 3.1 sq. mi.; **Water:** 0.2 sq. mi.

East Dennis   CDP
ZIP: 02641   **Lat:** 41-44-24 N **Long:** 70-09-27 W
Pop: 2,584 (1990)   **Pop Density:** 538.3
Land: 4.8 sq. mi.; **Water:** 0.1 sq. mi.

East Falmouth   CDP
ZIP: 02536   **Lat:** 41-33-51 N **Long:** 70-33-29 W
Pop: 5,577 (1990); 5,181 (1980)   **Pop Density:** 1032.8
Land: 5.4 sq. mi.; **Water:** 2.7 sq. mi.

Eastham   Town
ZIP: 02642   **Lat:** 41-50-15 N **Long:** 69-59-18 W
Pop: 4,462 (1990); 3,472 (1980)   **Pop Density:** 318.7
Land: 14.0 sq. mi.; **Water:** 13.3 sq. mi.

In southeastern MA, just south of Cape Cod. Settled 1644; incorporated 1651.

East Harwich   CDP
ZIP: 02645   **Lat:** 41-42-27 N **Long:** 70-01-50 W
Pop: 3,828 (1990)   **Pop Density:** 461.2
Land: 8.3 sq. mi.; **Water:** 0.7 sq. mi.

East Sandwich   CDP
ZIP: 02537   **Lat:** 41-44-18 N **Long:** 70-26-04 W
Pop: 3,171 (1990)   **Pop Density:** 428.5
Land: 7.4 sq. mi.; **Water:** 0.0 sq. mi.

Falmouth   Town
ZIP: 02540   **Lat:** 41-35-42 N **Long:** 70-35-47 W
Pop: 27,960 (1990); 23,640 (1980)   **Pop Density:** 631.2
Land: 44.3 sq. mi.; **Water:** 10.2 sq. mi.

In southeastern MA near Buzzards Bay, 15 mi. southeast of New Bedford. Settled c. 1660.
Name origin: For Falmouth, Cornwall, England.

Harwich   Town
ZIP: 02645   **Lat:** 41-41-00 N **Long:** 70-04-11 W
Pop: 10,275 (1990); 8,971 (1980)   **Pop Density:** 489.3
Land: 21.0 sq. mi.; **Water:** 12.1 sq. mi.

In southeastern MA, 10 mi. east of Barnstable. Settled 1670.
Name origin: For Harwich, Essex, England, which Queen Elizabeth called "happy-go-lucky Harwich."

Harwich Port   CDP
ZIP: 02646   **Lat:** 41-40-11 N **Long:** 70-03-53 W
Pop: 1,742 (1990)   **Pop Density:** 670.0
Land: 2.6 sq. mi.; **Water:** 0.8 sq. mi.

Hyannis   CDP
ZIP: 02601   **Lat:** 41-39-10 N **Long:** 70-17-44 W
Pop: 14,120 (1990); 9,118 (1980)   **Pop Density:** 1440.8
Land: 9.8 sq. mi.; **Water:** 3.4 sq. mi.

Marstons Mills · CDP
ZIP: 02648   **Lat:** 41-40-24 N **Long:** 70-24-29 W
Pop: 8,017 (1990)   **Pop Density:** 593.9
Land: 13.5 sq. mi.; **Water:** 1.0 sq. mi.

Mashpee · Town
ZIP: 02649   **Lat:** 41-37-02 N **Long:** 70-29-22 W
Pop: 7,884 (1990); 3,700 (1980)   **Pop Density:** 335.5
Land: 23.5 sq. mi.; **Water:** 3.8 sq. mi.

In southeastern MA in an area with picturesque ponds, groves, streams, and stretches of woodland. Settled 1660.
Name origin: From an Indian term probably meaning 'standing water.'

Monument Beach · CDP
ZIP: 02553   **Lat:** 41-43-09 N **Long:** 70-36-35 W
Pop: 1,842 (1990)   **Pop Density:** 921.0
Land: 2.0 sq. mi.; **Water:** 0.8 sq. mi.

North Eastham · CDP
ZIP: 02651   **Lat:** 41-50-31 N **Long:** 70-01-24 W
Pop: 1,570 (1990); 1,318 (1980)   **Pop Density:** 461.8
Land: 3.4 sq. mi.; **Water:** 8.6 sq. mi.

North Falmouth · CDP
     Lat: 41-38-28 N **Long:** 70-37-55 W
Pop: 2,625 (1990)   **Pop Density:** 656.3
Land: 4.0 sq. mi.; **Water:** 2.7 sq. mi.

Northwest Harwich · CDP
     Lat: 41-41-24 N **Long:** 70-06-20 W
Pop: 3,037 (1990)   **Pop Density:** 374.9
Land: 8.1 sq. mi.; **Water:** 1.5 sq. mi.

Orleans · Town
ZIP: 02653   **Lat:** 41-45-58 N **Long:** 69-58-04 W
Pop: 5,838 (1990); 5,306 (1980)   **Pop Density:** 414.0
Land: 14.1 sq. mi.; **Water:** 6.9 sq. mi.

In southeastern MA on an inlet of the Atlantic Ocean, 20 mi. northeast of Barnstable. Settled 1693; incorporated 1797. The settlers were engaged in shipping, shell fisheries, and salt works. Windmills and surf mills were used to pump sea water for the latter into vats on the shore.
Name origin: Presumably for Louis Phillippe, duke of Orleans, who visited New England in 1797.

Osterville · CDP
ZIP: 02655   **Lat:** 41-37-30 N **Long:** 70-23-16 W
Pop: 2,911 (1990); 1,799 (1980)   **Pop Density:** 501.9
Land: 5.8 sq. mi.; **Water:** 2.7 sq. mi.

Pocasset · CDP
ZIP: 02559   **Lat:** 41-41-28 N **Long:** 70-38-14 W
Pop: 2,756 (1990)   **Pop Density:** 725.3
Land: 3.8 sq. mi.; **Water:** 6.1 sq. mi.

Provincetown · Town
ZIP: 02657   **Lat:** 42-03-26 N **Long:** 70-11-33 W
Pop: 3,561 (1990); 3,536 (1980)   **Pop Density:** 367.1
Land: 9.7 sq. mi.; **Water:** 7.8 sq. mi.   **Elev:** 11 ft.

In southeastern MA, on the northern tip of Cape Cod. Settled 1700; incorporated 1727.

Sagamore · CDP
ZIP: 02561   **Lat:** 41-46-59 N **Long:** 70-32-03 W
Pop: 2,589 (1990); 1,152 (1980)   **Pop Density:** 761.5
Land: 3.4 sq. mi.; **Water:** 0.2 sq. mi.

Sandwich · Town
ZIP: 02563   **Lat:** 41-42-54 N **Long:** 70-29-07 W
Pop: 15,489 (1990); 8,727 (1980)   **Pop Density:** 360.2
Land: 43.0 sq. mi.; **Water:** 1.3 sq. mi.

In southeastern MA, south of Cape Cod. Settled 1637; incorporated 1639.
Name origin: For Sandwich, Kent, England.

South Dennis · CDP
ZIP: 02660   **Lat:** 41-42-15 N **Long:** 70-09-21 W
Pop: 3,559 (1990)   **Pop Density:** 790.9
Land: 4.5 sq. mi.; **Water:** 0.2 sq. mi.

South Yarmouth · CDP
ZIP: 02664   **Lat:** 41-40-12 N **Long:** 70-12-02 W
Pop: 10,358 (1990); 7,525 (1980)   **Pop Density:** 1479.7
Land: 7.0 sq. mi.; **Water:** 0.8 sq. mi.

Teaticket · CDP
ZIP: 02536   **Lat:** 41-33-30 N **Long:** 70-35-15 W
Pop: 1,856 (1990)   **Pop Density:** 1687.3
Land: 1.1 sq. mi.; **Water:** 0.6 sq. mi.

Truro · Town
ZIP: 02666   **Lat:** 42-00-48 N **Long:** 70-04-19 W
Pop: 1,573 (1990); 1,486 (1980)   **Pop Density:** 74.5
Land: 21.1 sq. mi.; **Water:** 5.3 sq. mi.

In southeastern, MA, on what is called the wrist of the bended arm of Cape Cod. Settled 1700.

Wellfleet · Town
ZIP: 02667   **Lat:** 41-55-02 N **Long:** 70-01-31 W
Pop: 2,493 (1990); 2,209 (1980)   **Pop Density:** 125.9
Land: 19.8 sq. mi.; **Water:** 15.5 sq. mi.

In southeastern MA. Settled 1724; incorporated 1763.

West Barnstable · CDP
ZIP: 02668   **Lat:** 41-42-23 N **Long** 70-22-23 W
Pop: 1,508 (1990)   **Pop Density:** 232.0
Land: 6.5 sq. mi.; **Water:** 0.2 sq. mi.

West Chatham · CDP
ZIP: 02669   **Lat:** 41-40-50 N **Long** 69-59-35 W
Pop: 1,504 (1990); 1,398 (1980)   **Pop Density:** 501.3
Land: 3.0 sq. mi.; **Water:** 0.4 sq. mi.

West Dennis · CDP
ZIP: 02670   **Lat:** 41-40-00 N **Long** 70-10-02 W
Pop: 2,307 (1990); 2,023 (1980)   **Pop Density:** 678.5
Land: 3.4 sq. mi.; **Water:** 0.9 sq. mi.

West Falmouth · CDP
ZIP: 02574   **Lat:** 41-36-04 N **Long** 70-38-24 W
Pop: 1,752 (1990)   **Pop Density:** 547.5
Land: 3.2 sq. mi.; **Water:** 1.2 sq. mi.

West Yarmouth · CDP
ZIP: 02673   **Lat:** 41-38-49 N **Long** 70-14-53 W
Pop: 5,409 (1990); 3,852 (1980)   **Pop Density:** 807.3
Land: 6.7 sq. mi.; **Water:** 2.4 sq. mi.

Yarmouth · Town
ZIP: 02675   **Lat:** 41-40-33 N **Long** 70-13-34 W
Pop: 21,174 (1990); 18,449 (1980)   **Pop Density:** 871.4
Land: 24.3 sq. mi.; **Water:** 4.0 sq. mi.

In southeastern MA, 5 mi. east of Barnstable. Settled 1639.
Name origin: For Yarmouth, Norfolk, England.

Yarmouth Port
CDP
ZIP: 02601   **Lat:** 41-42-34 N **Long:** 70-13-43 W
Pop: 4,271 (1990); 2,490 (1980)   **Pop Density:** 711.8
Land: 6.0 sq. mi.; **Water:** 0.4 sq. mi.

Berkshire County
County Seat: Pittsfield (ZIP: 01201)

Pop: 139,352 (1990); 145,110 (1980)   **Pop Density:** 149.6
Land: 931.4 sq. mi.; **Water:** 14.9 sq. mi.   **Area Code:** 413

On western border of MA, bordered on north by VT, by NY on west, and by CT on south; organized April 21, 1761 from Hampshire County.
Name origin: For the county in England.

Adams
Town
ZIP: 01220   **Lat:** 42-37-39 N **Long:** 73-07-09 W
Pop: 9,445 (1990); 10,381 (1980)   **Pop Density:** 412.4
Land: 22.9 sq. mi.; **Water:** 0.0 sq. mi.

In northwestern MA. Settled 1762.
Name origin: For Revolutionary War propagandist Samuel Adams (1722–1803).

Alford
Town
ZIP: 01230   **Lat:** 42-15-06 N **Long:** 73-25-23 W
Pop: 418 (1990); 394 (1980)   **Pop Density:** 36.0
Land: 11.6 sq. mi.; **Water:** 0.0 sq. mi.

In southwestern MA. Settled c. 1740.
Name origin: For John Alford, founder of the Alford professorship of moral philosophy at Harvard University.

Becket
Town
ZIP: 01223   **Lat:** 42-17-15 N **Long:** 73-04-35 W
Pop: 1,481 (1990); 1,339 (1980)   **Pop Density:** 32.0
Land: 46.3 sq. mi.; **Water:** 1.5 sq. mi.

In western MA, 15 mi. southeast of Pittsfield.

Cheshire
Town
ZIP: 01225   **Lat:** 42-34-03 N **Long:** 73-08-55 W
Pop: 3,479 (1990); 3,124 (1980)   **Pop Density:** 129.3
Land: 26.9 sq. mi.; **Water:** 0.6 sq. mi.

In northwestern MA on the Hoosic River, northeast of Pittsfield. Settled 1766.

Clarksburg
Town
Lat: 42-43-15 N **Long:** 73-06-19 W
Pop: 1,745 (1990); 1,871 (1980)   **Pop Density:** 136.3
Land: 12.8 sq. mi.; **Water:** 0.1 sq. mi.

Dalton
Town
ZIP: 01226   **Lat:** 42-28-59 N **Long:** 73-09-08 W
Pop: 7,155 (1990); 6,797 (1980)   **Pop Density:** 328.2
Land: 21.8 sq. mi.; **Water:** 0.0 sq. mi.

In western MA, 5 mi. northeast of Pittsfield.

Egremont
Town
ZIP: 01230   **Lat:** 42-10-07 N **Long:** 73-26-07 W
Pop: 1,229 (1990); 1,311 (1980)   **Pop Density:** 65.4
Land: 18.8 sq. mi.; **Water:** 0.1 sq. mi.

Florida
Town
Lat: 42-40-44 N **Long:** 73-00-57 W
Pop: 742 (1990); 730 (1980)   **Pop Density:** 30.4
Land: 24.4 sq. mi.; **Water:** 0.2 sq. mi.

In northern MA, 125 mi. northwest of Boston. Settled 1783.

Great Barrington
Town
ZIP: 01230   **Lat:** 42-12-24 N **Long:** 73-20-38 W
Pop: 7,725 (1990); 7,405 (1980)   **Pop Density:** 170.9
Land: 45.2 sq. mi.; **Water:** 0.5 sq. mi.

Hancock
Town
Lat: 42-31-27 N **Long:** 73-19-25 W
Pop: 628 (1990); 643 (1980)   **Pop Density:** 17.6
Land: 35.7 sq. mi.; **Water:** 0.0 sq. mi.

Hinsdale
Town
ZIP: 01235   **Lat:** 42-26-07 N **Long:** 73-06-49 W
Pop: 1,959 (1990); 1,707 (1980)   **Pop Density:** 94.2
Land: 20.8 sq. mi.; **Water:** 0.9 sq. mi.

In west-central MA, 10 mi. southeast of Pittsfield. Settled 1763.
Name origin: For Rev. Theodore Hinsdale, who founded a church here in 1795.

Housatonic
CDP
ZIP: 01236   **Lat:** 42-15-01 N **Long:** 73-21-45 W
Pop: 1,184 (1990); 1,314 (1980)   **Pop Density:** 1315.6
Land: 0.9 sq. mi.; **Water:** 0.1 sq. mi.

Lanesborough
Town
ZIP: 01237   **Lat:** 42-31-44 N **Long:** 73-14-28 W
Pop: 3,032 (1990); 3,131 (1980)   **Pop Density:** 104.2
Land: 29.1 sq. mi.; **Water:** 0.7 sq. mi.

In northwestern MA, 5 mi. north of Pittsfield. Settled 1753.
Name origin: For the Irish Countess of Lanesborough, a court favorite and a friend of the then governor of MA. Originally known as New Framingham.

Lee
Town
ZIP: 01238   **Lat:** 42-17-57 N **Long:** 73-13-59 W
Pop: 5,849 (1990); 6,247 (1980)   **Pop Density:** 221.6
Land: 26.4 sq. mi.; **Water:** 0.6 sq. mi.

In western MA, 10 mi. south of Pittsfield. Settled 1760; incorporated 1777.
Name origin: For Gen. Charles Lee (1731–82), later notorious for his treasonous acts against his country.

Lenox
Town
ZIP: 01240   **Lat:** 42-22-18 N **Long:** 73-16-40 W
Pop: 5,069 (1990); 6,523 (1980)   **Pop Density:** 239.1
Land: 21.2 sq. mi.; **Water:** 0.3 sq. mi.

In western MA, 5 mi. south of Pittsfield. Settled 1750.
Name origin: For Charles Lennox, Duke of Richmond (1735–1806), a defender of colonial rights.

Monterey   Town
ZIP: 01245   **Lat:** 42-11-07 N   **Long:** 73-13-33 W
Pop: 805 (1990); 818 (1980)   **Pop Density:** 30.4
Land: 26.5 sq. mi.; **Water:** 0.8 sq. mi.

In western MA. Settled 1739; incorporated 1847. Formerly a district of Tyringham.
Name origin: For the American victory in the Mexican War.

Mount Washington   Town
ZIP: 01258   **Lat:** 42-05-46 N   **Long:** 73-27-45 W
Pop: 135 (1990); 93 (1980)   **Pop Density:** 6.1
Land: 22.2 sq. mi.; **Water:** 0.1 sq. mi.

New Ashford   Town
             Lat: 42-36-25 N   **Long:** 73-13-32 W
Pop: 192 (1990); 159 (1980)   **Pop Density:** 14.2
Land: 13.5 sq. mi.; **Water:** 0.0 sq. mi.

New Marlborough   Town
ZIP: 01230   **Lat:** 42-05-57 N   **Long:** 73-14-20 W
Pop: 1,240 (1990); 1,160 (1980)   **Pop Density:** 26.3
Land: 47.2 sq. mi.; **Water:** 0.7 sq. mi.

North Adams   City
ZIP: 01247   **Lat:** 42-41-12 N   **Long:** 73-06-49 W
Pop: 16,797 (1990); 18,063 (1980)   **Pop Density:** 823.4
Land: 20.4 sq. mi.; **Water:** 0.1 sq. mi.   **Elev:** 707 ft.

In northwestern MA. Settled c. 1767.

Otis   Town
ZIP: 01253   **Lat:** 42-12-26 N   **Long:** 73-04-41 W
Pop: 1,073 (1990); 963 (1980)   **Pop Density:** 30.0
Land: 35.8 sq. mi.; **Water:** 2.2 sq. mi.   **Elev:** 1,240 ft.

In northwestern MA. Settled 1735; incorporated 1778.
Name origin: For Harrison Gray Otis (1765–1848), then Speaker of the House of Representatives.

Peru   Town
             Lat: 42-26-15 N   **Long:** 73-02-48 W
Pop: 779 (1990); 633 (1980)   **Pop Density:** 30.1
Land: 25.9 sq. mi.; **Water:** 0.1 sq. mi.   **Elev:** 2,295 ft.

In northeastern MA on the summit of the Green Mountain range; the highest village in MA. Settled 1767; incorporated 1771.
Name origin: Named 1806 by Rev. John Leland because of its location. Originally called Patridgefield.

Pittsfield   City
ZIP: 01201   **Lat:** 42-27-06 N   **Long:** 73-15-39 W
Pop: 48,622 (1990); 51,974 (1980)   **Pop Density:** 1194.6
Land: 40.7 sq. mi.; **Water:** 1.6 sq. mi.   **Elev:** 1039 ft.

In western MA on the Housatonic River, 40 mi. west-north-west of Springfield. Settled 1752; incorporated as town 1761; as city 1889.

Richmond   Town
ZIP: 01254   **Lat:** 42-23-23 N   **Long:** 73-21-24 W
Pop: 1,677 (1990); 1,659 (1980)   **Pop Density:** 88.3
Land: 19.0 sq. mi.; **Water:** 0.3 sq. mi.

In northwestern MA. Settled 1760.
Name origin: Named in 1785 for Charles Lennox, Duke of

Richmond (1735–1806) and defender of colonial rights. Formerly called Yokumtown and Richmont.

Sandisfield   Town
ZIP: 01255   **Lat:** 42-06-17 N   **Long:** 73-07-46 W
Pop: 667 (1990); 720 (1980)   **Pop Density:** 12.8
Land: 52.3 sq. mi.; **Water:** 0.7 sq. mi.

Savoy   Town
ZIP: 01256   **Lat:** 42-35-36 N   **Long:** 73-01-01 W
Pop: 634 (1990); 644 (1980)   **Pop Density:** 17.7
Land: 35.9 sq. mi.; **Water:** 0.1 sq. mi.

In western MA.

Sheffield   Town
ZIP: 01257   **Lat:** 42-06-11 N   **Long:** 73-21-39 W
Pop: 2,910 (1990); 2,743 (1980)   **Pop Density:** 60.5
Land: 48.1 sq. mi.; **Water:** 0.4 sq. mi.

In the southwestern corner of MA, 25 mi. southwest of Pittsfield. Settled 1726; incorporated 1733.

Stockbridge   Town
             Lat: 42-18-12 N   **Long:** 73-19-31 W
Pop: 2,408 (1990); 2,328 (1980)   **Pop Density:** 105.2
Land: 22.9 sq. mi.; **Water:** 0.8 sq. mi.

In western MA near NY state line. Settled 1734.
Name origin: For an English municipality.

Tyringham   Town
             Lat: 42-14-36 N   **Long:** 73-12-04 W
Pop: 369 (1990); 344 (1980)   **Pop Density:** 19.7
Land: 18.7 sq. mi.; **Water:** 0.2 sq. mi.

Washington   Town
ZIP: 01223   **Lat:** 42-21-59 N   **Long:** 73-09-23 W
Pop: 615 (1990); 587 (1980)   **Pop Density:** 16.3
Land: 37.8 sq. mi.; **Water:** 0.9 sq. mi.

West Stockbridge   Town
             Lat: 42-18-48 N   **Long:** 73-23-23 W
Pop: 1,483 (1990); 1,280 (1980)   **Pop Density:** 80.2
Land: 18.5 sq. mi.; **Water:** 0.2 sq. mi.

In northwestern MA. Settled 1766; incorporated 1775.

Williamstown   Town
ZIP: 01267   **Lat:** 42-41-11 N   **Long:** 73-13-50 W
Pop: 8,220 (1990); 8,741 (1980)   **Pop Density:** 175.3
Land: 46.9 sq. mi.; **Water:** 0.0 sq. mi.

In western MA, 20 mi. north of Pittsfield. Settled 1749; incorporated 1765.
Name origin: For Col. Ephraim Williams, who was killed in the French and Indian War.

Windsor   Town
ZIP: 01270   **Lat:** 42-30-32 N   **Long:** 73-02-38 W
Pop: 770 (1990); 598 (1980)   **Pop Density:** 22.0
Land: 35.0 sq. mi.; **Water:** 0.1 sq. mi.

In northwestern MA, 10 mi. northeast of Pittsfield. Settled 1767.

Bristol County
County Seat: Taunton (ZIP: 02780)

Pop: 506,325 (1990); 474,641 (1980)   **Pop Density:** 910.6
Land: 556.0 sq. mi.; **Water:** 135.2 sq. mi.   **Area Code:** 508

On southwestern border of MA with RI; organized Jun 2, 1685 from Old Plymouth Colony.

Name origin: For Bristol, Gloucestershire and Somerset, England.

Acushnet   Town
ZIP: 02743   **Lat:** 41-42-40 N **Long:** 70-53-50 W
Pop: 9,554 (1990); 8,704 (1980)   **Pop Density:** 516.4
Land: 18.5 sq. mi.; **Water:** 0.5 sq. mi.

Name origin: From an Indian term probably meaning 'bathing place.'

Attleboro   City
ZIP: 02703   **Lat:** 41-55-50 N **Long:** 71-17-44 W
Pop: 38,383 (1990); 34,196 (1980)   **Pop Density:** 1395.7
Land: 27.5 sq. mi.; **Water:** 0.8 sq. mi.   **Elev:** 138 ft.

In southeastern MA, 10 mi north of Providence, RI.

Name origin: For Attleborough, Norfolk, England. Spelling changed in 1914 upon establishment of city government.

Berkley   Town
          Lat: 41-50-25 N **Long:** 71-04-44 W
Pop: 4,237 (1990); 2,731 (1980)   **Pop Density:** 256.8
Land: 16.5 sq. mi.; **Water:** 0.8 sq. mi.

In southeastern MA, 8 mi. north of Fall River.

Bliss Corner   CDP
          Lat: 41-36-18 N **Long:** 70-56-34 W
Pop: 4,908 (1990)   **Pop Density:** 2454.0
Land: 2.0 sq. mi.; **Water:** 0.0 sq. mi.

Dartmouth   Town
ZIP: 02714   **Lat:** 41-36-42 N **Long:** 70-59-53 W
Pop: 27,244 (1990); 23,966 (1980)   **Pop Density:** 443.0
Land: 61.5 sq. mi.; **Water:** 2.4 sq. mi.

In southeastern MA, 6 mi. southwest of New Bedford. Settled 1650; incorporated 1664.

Name origin: For the port city of Dartmouth, Devonshire, England.

Dighton   Town
ZIP: 02715   **Lat:** 41-50-21 N **Long:** 71-09-07 W
Pop: 5,631 (1990); 5,352 (1980)   **Pop Density:** 251.4
Land: 22.4 sq. mi.; **Water:** 0.5 sq. mi.

In southeastern MA, 10 mi. north of Fall River. Settled 1678.

Easton   Town
ZIP: 02334   **Lat:** 42-02-11 N **Long:** 71-06-56 W
Pop: 19,807 (1990); 16,623 (1980)   **Pop Density:** 697.4
Land: 28.4 sq. mi.; **Water:** 0.7 sq. mi.

In southeastern MA, 5 mi. southwest of Brockton. Settled 1694; incorporated 1725.

Fairhaven   Town
ZIP: 02719   **Lat:** 41-38-09 N **Long:** 70-52-25 W
Pop: 16,132 (1990); 15,759 (1980)   **Pop Density:** 1301.0
Land: 12.4 sq. mi.; **Water:** 1.7 sq. mi.

In southeastern MA on Buzzards Bay across the harbor from New Bedford. Settled 1660; incorporated 1812.

Name origin: For its harbor on Buzzards Bay at the mouth of the Acushnet River.

Fall River   City
ZIP: 02720   **Lat:** 41-42-52 N **Long:** 71-06-18 W
Pop: 92,703 (1990); 92,574 (1980)   **Pop Density:** 2990.4
Land: 31.0 sq. mi.; **Water:** 7.2 sq. mi.   **Elev:** 200 ft.

In southeastern MA at the mouth of the Taunton River, 10 mi. northwest of New Bedford. Settled 1656; incorporated 1803.

Name origin: Named in 1834 for the English translation of the Indian term *quequechan* probably meaning 'falling water', for the Quequechan River, which runs through the city and gives power to its mills.

Freetown   Town
ZIP: 02702   **Lat:** 41-46-06 N **Long:** 71-01-17 W
Pop: 8,522 (1990); 7,058 (1980)   **Pop Density:** 232.8
Land: 36.6 sq. mi.; **Water:** 1.7 sq. mi.

Mansfield   Town
ZIP: 02048   **Lat:** 42-00-51 N **Long:** 71-13-10 W
Pop: 16,568 (1990); 13,453 (1980)   **Pop Density:** 808.2
Land: 20.5 sq. mi.; **Water:** 0.3 sq. mi.

In southeastern MA, southwest of Brockton. Settled 1659. Occupies the site of an Indian winter camping ground.

Name origin: For Lord Mansfield.

New Bedford   City
ZIP: 02740   **Lat:** 41-39-40 N **Long:** 70-56-17 W
Pop: 99,922 (1990); 98,478 (1980)   **Pop Density:** 4971.2
Land: 20.1 sq. mi.; **Water:** 3.9 sq. mi.   **Elev:** 50 ft.

In southeastern MA on New Bedford Harbor, 48 mi. south of Boston. Settled 1640; chartered as city 1847.

Name origin: Named by Joseph Russell, known as the "Father of New Bedford," for the Duke of Bedford. Previously called Bedford Village.

North Attleborough   Town
ZIP: 02760   **Lat:** 41-58-17 N **Long:** 71-20-05 W
Pop: 25,038 (1990); 21,095 (1980)   **Pop Density:** 1346.1
Land: 18.6 sq. mi.; **Water:** 0.4 sq. mi.

In southeastern MA. Settled 1669.

North Seekonk   CDP
ZIP: 02771   **Lat:** 41-53-21 N **Long:** 71-19-50 W
Pop: 2,635 (1990)   **Pop Density:** 2026.9
Land: 1.3 sq. mi.; **Water:** 0.0 sq. mi.

North Westport   CDP
ZIP: 02790   **Lat:** 41-39-37 N **Long:** 71-05-20 W
Pop: 4,697 (1990)   **Pop Density:** 903.3
Land: 5.2 sq. mi.; **Water:** 1.0 sq. mi.

Norton
Town
ZIP: 02766 **Lat:** 41-57-55 N **Long:** 71-11-06 W
Pop: 14,265 (1990); 12,690 (1980) **Pop Density:** 497.0
Land: 28.7 sq. mi.; **Water:** 1.1 sq. mi.

In southeastern MA, 10 mi. southwest of Brockton. Settled 1669.
Name origin: For Norton, England.

Ocean Grove
CDP
Lat: 41-43-43 N **Long:** 71-12-35 W
Pop: 3,169 (1990) **Pop Density:** 4527.1
Land: 0.7 sq. mi.; **Water:** 0.2 sq. mi.

Raynham
Town
ZIP: 02767 **Lat:** 41-55-54 N **Long:** 71-02-37 W
Pop: 9,867 (1990); 9,085 (1980) **Pop Density:** 481.3
Land: 20.5 sq. mi.; **Water:** 0.4 sq. mi. **Elev:** 51 ft.

In southeastern MA, 10 mi. southwest of Brockton. Settled 1652; incorporated 1731.
Name origin: For Lord Townshend of Rainham, England.

Rehoboth
Town
ZIP: 02769 **Lat:** 41-50-49 N **Long:** 71-14-49 W
Pop: 8,656 (1990); 7,570 (1980) **Pop Density:** 186.2
Land: 46.5 sq. mi.; **Water:** 0.3 sq. mi.

In southeastern MA, 10 mi. northwest of Fall River. Settled 1636.

Seekonk
Town
ZIP: 02771 **Lat:** 41-50-07 N **Long:** 71-19-07 W
Pop: 13,046 (1990); 12,269 (1980) **Pop Density:** 712.9
Land: 18.3 sq. mi.; **Water:** 0.1 sq. mi.

In southeastern MA, 10 mi. northwest of Fall River. Settled 1636; incorporated 1812.
Name origin: From the Indian term probably meaning 'black goose', indicating an abundance of these birds prior to the coming of the white men.

Smith Mills
CDP
Lat: 41-38-22 N **Long:** 70-59-40 W
Pop: 4,593 (1990) **Pop Density:** 977.2
Land: 4.7 sq. mi.; **Water:** 0.1 sq. mi.

Somerset
Town
ZIP: 02725 **Lat:** 41-44-21 N **Long:** 71-09-32 W
Pop: 17,655 (1990); 18,813 (1980) **Pop Density:** 2179.6
Land: 8.1 sq. mi.; **Water:** 3.9 sq. mi.

In southeastern MA, 5 mi. north of Fall River. Settled 1677; incorporated 1790.
Name origin: For Somerset, Somersetshire, England.

Swansea
Town
ZIP: 02777 **Lat:** 41-45-32 N **Long:** 71-12-54 W
Pop: 15,411 (1990); 15,461 (1980) **Pop Density:** 667.1
Land: 23.1 sq. mi.; **Water:** 2.5 sq. mi.

In southeastern MA, 5 mi. northeast of Fall River. Settled 1632; incorporated 1668.
Name origin: For Swansea, Glamorganshire, Wales.

Taunton
City
ZIP: 02780 **Lat:** 41-54-10 N **Long:** 71-05-35 W
Pop: 49,832 (1990); 45,001 (1980) **Pop Density:** 1069.4
Land: 46.6 sq. mi.; **Water:** 1.4 sq. mi. **Elev:** 30 ft.

In southeastern MA on Taunton River, 15 mi. north of Fall River. Settled 1638.
Name origin: For Taunton, Somersetshire, England.

Westport
Town
ZIP: 02790 **Lat:** 41-34-23 N **Long:** 71-04-54 W
Pop: 13,852 (1990); 13,763 (1980) **Pop Density:** 276.5
Land: 50.1 sq. mi.; **Water:** 14.3 sq. mi.

In southeastern MA, 10 mi. west of New Bedford.
Name origin: For being created from western part of Dartmouth and for its closeness to the coast.

Dukes County
County Seat: Edgartown (ZIP: 02539)

Pop: 11,639 (1990); 8,942 (1980) **Pop Density:** 112.1
Land: 103.8 sq. mi.; **Water:** 387.2 sq. mi. **Area Code:** 617

Southeast of New Bedford; includes islands of Martha's Vineyard, Chappaquiddick, Elizabeth, and Noman's Land. Organized Jun 22, 1695 from Martha's Vineyard.
Name origin: For James II (1633–1701), Duke of York and Albany, administrator of the colonies at the time of naming.

Chilmark
Town
ZIP: 02535 **Lat:** 41-22-07 N **Long:** 70-44-31 W
Pop: 650 (1990); 489 (1980) **Pop Density:** 34.0
Land: 19.1 sq. mi.; **Water:** 15.6 sq. mi.

On the western end of Martha's Vineyard.

Edgartown
Town
ZIP: 02539 **Lat:** 41-22-56 N **Long:** 70-31-54 W
Pop: 3,062 (1990); 2,204 (1980) **Pop Density:** 113.4
Land: 27.0 sq. mi.; **Water:** 7.7 sq. mi.

Settled 1642; incorporated 1671.
Name origin: For Edgar, son of James II (1633–1701). Originally called Nunnepog, from the Indian term probably meaning 'fresh pond.'

Gay Head
Town
ZIP: 02535 **Lat:** 41-22-45 N **Long:** 70-50-17 W
Pop: 201 (1990); 220 (1980) **Pop Density:** 37.2
Land: 5.4 sq. mi.; **Water:** 35.4 sq. mi.

Gosnold
Town
Lat: 41-26-03 N **Long:** 70-51-14 W
Pop: 98 (1990); 63 (1980) **Pop Density:** 7.4
Land: 13.3 sq. mi.; **Water:** 118.9 sq. mi.

Oak Bluffs
Town
ZIP: 02557 **Lat:** 41-26-11 N **Long:** 70-35-06 W
Pop: 2,804 (1990); 1,984 (1980) **Pop Density:** 378.9
Land: 7.4 sq. mi.; **Water:** 1.3 sq. mi.

On Martha's Vineyard, MA, in the northeastern section of

the island. Settled 1642; incorporated 1880. Population increases greatly in the summer.

Name origin: The Algonquin Indians called it *ogkeshkuppe* probably meaning 'damp thicket.'

Tisbury
                                                        Town
Lat: 41-27-11 N **Long:** 70-36-49 W
Pop: 3,120 (1990); 2,972 (1980)   **Pop Density:** 472.7
Land: 6.6 sq. mi.; **Water:** 1.5 sq. mi.

Vineyard Haven
                                                        CDP
Lat: 41-27-21 N **Long:** 70-36-20 W
Pop: 1,762 (1990); 1,704 (1980)   **Pop Density:** 1468.3
Land: 1.2 sq. mi.; **Water:** 0.3 sq. mi.

West Tisbury
                                                        Town
ZIP: 02575   **Lat:** 41-24-50 N **Long:** 70-39-55 W
Pop: 1,704 (1990); 1,010 (1980)   **Pop Density:** 68.2
Land: 25.0 sq. mi.; **Water:** 8.7 sq. mi.

On Martha's Vineyard Island in southeastern MA. Settled 1669.

Name origin: For the English birthplace of Gov. Thomas Mayhew (1593–1682). Originally called Tackhum-Min-Eyi of Takemmy, from Indian term probably meaning 'the place where one goes to grind corn.'

Essex County
County Seat: Salem (ZIP: 01970)

Pop: 670,080 (1990); 633,688 (1980)   **Pop Density:** 1345.4
Land: 498.1 sq. mi.; **Water:** 330.6 sq. mi.   **Area Code:** 617

On northeastern border of MA, north of Boston; original county, organized May 10, 1643.

Name origin: For the county of Essex, England.

Amesbury
                                                        Town
ZIP: 01913   **Lat:** 42-51-15 N **Long:** 70-56-44 W
Pop: 14,997 (1990); 13,971 (1980)   **Pop Density:** 1209.4
Land: 12.4 sq. mi.; **Water:** 1.2 sq. mi.

In northeastern MA on the Merrimack River, 25 mi. northeast of Lowell. The northernmost town in MA. Settled 1645; incorporated 1668.

Name origin: For Amesbury, Wilkshire, England. The town was formed from Salisbury, and the English Amesbury is near Salisbury in England.

Andover
                                                        Town
ZIP: 01810   **Lat:** 42-38-45 N **Long:** 71-09-58 W
Pop: 29,151 (1990); 26,370 (1980)   **Pop Density:** 940.4
Land: 31.0 sq. mi.; **Water:** 1.1 sq. mi.

In northeastern MA, 9 mi. east of Lowell. Settled 1642.

Name origin: For Andover, Hampshire, England, former home of early settlers.

Beverly
                                                        City
ZIP: 01915   **Lat:** 42-33-27 N **Long:** 70-50-25 W
Pop: 38,195 (1990); 37,655 (1980)   **Pop Density:** 2480.2
Land: 15.4 sq. mi.; **Water:** 7.3 sq. mi.   **Elev:** 26 ft.

In northeastern MA, 15 mi. northeast of Boston.

Name origin: For Beverley, county seat, East Riding, Yorkshire, England.

Boxford
                                                        Town
ZIP: 01921   **Lat:** 42-40-44 N **Long:** 71-01-04 W
Pop: 6,266 (1990); 5,374 (1980)   **Pop Density:** 261.1
Land: 24.0 sq. mi.; **Water:** 0.6 sq. mi.

Danvers
                                                        Town
ZIP: 01923   **Lat:** 42-34-18 N **Long:** 70-57-04 W
Pop: 24,174 (1990); 24,100 (1980)   **Pop Density:** 1817.6
Land: 13.3 sq. mi.; **Water:** 0.8 sq. mi.

In northeastern MA, 15 mi. northeast of Boston.

Name origin: For the Danvers Osborn family of NY. Previously called Salem Village.

Essex
                                                        Town
ZIP: 01929   **Lat:** 42-37-57 N **Long:** 70-46-47 W
Pop: 3,260 (1990); 2,998 (1980)   **Pop Density:** 229.6
Land: 14.2 sq. mi.; **Water:** 1.8 sq. mi.

In northeastern MA, 20 mi. northeast of Boston. Settled 1634.

Name origin: For Essex, England.

Georgetown
                                                        Town
ZIP: 01833   **Lat:** 42-43-22 N **Long:** 70-59-09 W
Pop: 6,384 (1990); 5,687 (1980)   **Pop Density:** 494.9
Land: 12.9 sq. mi.; **Water:** 0.2 sq. mi.

In northeastern MA. Settled 1639; incorporated 1838.

Gloucester
                                                        City
ZIP: 01930   **Lat:** 42-37-54 N **Long:** 70-41-00 W
Pop: 28,716 (1990); 27,768 (1980)   **Pop Density:** 1104.5
Land: 26.0 sq. mi.; **Water:** 15.5 sq. mi.   **Elev:** 50 ft.

In northeastern MA on the Granite peninsula of Cape Ann, 30 mi. northeast of Boston. Settled 1623; incorporated as town 1642.

Name origin: For Gloucester, Gloucestershire, England.

Groveland
                                                        Town
ZIP: 01834   **Lat:** 42-45-26 N **Long:** 71-00-57 W
Pop: 5,214 (1990); 5,040 (1980)   **Pop Density:** 585.8
Land: 8.9 sq. mi.; **Water:** 0.5 sq. mi.

Hamilton
                                                        Town
ZIP: 01936   **Lat:** 42-37-34 N **Long:** 70-51-25 W
Pop: 7,280 (1990); 6,960 (1980)   **Pop Density:** 498.6
Land: 14.6 sq. mi.; **Water:** 0.3 sq. mi.

Haverhill
                                                        City
ZIP: 01830   **Lat:** 42-47-03 N **Long:** 71-05-10 W
Pop: 51,418 (1990); 46,865 (1980)   **Pop Density:** 1544.1
Land: 33.3 sq. mi.; **Water:** 2.3 sq. mi.   **Elev:** 27 ft.

In northeastern MA on Merrimack River, 15 mi northeast of Lowell. Settled 1640.

Name origin: Named in 1640 by the Rev. John Ward for the quiet market town of Haverhill, Essex, England. Previously named Pentucket.

Ipswich Town
ZIP: 01938   **Lat:** 42-41-08 N **Long:** 70-49-49 W
Pop: 11,873 (1990); 11,158 (1980)   **Pop Density:** 364.2
Land: 32.6 sq. mi.; **Water:** 9.5 sq. mi.

In northeastern MA, 24 mi. east of Lowell. Settled 1633.
Name origin: For Ipswich, Suffolk, England. Previously called Agawam and Deperion, an Indian term possibly for 'fishing station.'

Lawrence City
ZIP: 01840   **Lat:** 42-41-59 N **Long:** 71-09-43 W
Pop: 70,207 (1990); 63,175 (1980)   **Pop Density:** 10029.6
Land: 7.0 sq. mi.; **Water:** 0.5 sq. mi.   **Elev:** 50 ft.

In northeastern MA on the Merrimack River, 10 mi. northeast of Lowell. Settled 1655; incorporated as town 1847, as city 1853
Name origin: For founder Lawrence Abbott (1792–1855).

Lynn City
ZIP: 01901   **Lat:** 42-28-27 N **Long:** 70-57-45 W
Pop: 81,245 (1990); 78,471 (1980)   **Pop Density:** 7522.7
Land: 10.8 sq. mi.; **Water:** 2.7 sq. mi.   **Elev:** 30 ft.

In northeastern MA on Lynn Harbor, 10 mi. northeast of Boston. Settled 1629; incorporated as town 1631, as city 1850.
Name origin: Named in 1637 for King's Lynn in Norfolk County, England. Previously called Saugus.

Lynnfield Town
ZIP: 01940   **Lat:** 42-32-08 N **Long:** 71-02-25 W
Pop: 11,274 (1990); 11,267 (1980)   **Pop Density:** 1116.2
Land: 10.1 sq. mi.; **Water:** 0.3 sq. mi.

In northeastern MA, 10 mi. northeast of Boston. Settled 1638–39.
Name origin: For Lynn Regis, or King's Lynn, Norfolk, England.

Manchester Town
ZIP: 01944   **Lat:** 42-33-39 N **Long:** 70-45-46 W
Pop: 5,286 (1990); 5,424 (1980)   **Pop Density:** 677.7
Land: 7.8 sq. mi.; **Water:** 10.4 sq. mi.

In northeastern MA on the Atlantic Ocean, 20 mi. northeast of Boston. Settled 1626–27; incorporated 1645.

Marblehead Town
ZIP: 01945   **Lat:** 42-29-38 N **Long:** 70-50-10 W
Pop: 19,971 (1990); 20,126 (1980)   **Pop Density:** 4438.0
Land: 4.5 sq. mi.; **Water:** 15.1 sq. mi.

In northeastern MA on Atlantic Ocean, 14 mi. northeast of Boston. Settled 1629 as a plantation of Salem.
Name origin: Named by first settlers who mistook deposits of gray granite for marble.

Merrimac Town
ZIP: 01860   **Lat:** 42-50-12 N **Long:** 71-00-38 W
Pop: 5,166 (1990); 4,451 (1980)   **Pop Density:** 607.8
Land: 8.5 sq. mi.; **Water:** 0.3 sq. mi.

In northeastern MA, northeast of Lowell. Settled 1638.
Name origin: Named Swift Waters by the Indians.

Methuen Town
ZIP: 01844   **Lat:** 42-44-02 N **Long:** 71-11-23 W
Pop: 39,990 (1990); 36,701 (1980)   **Pop Density:** 1785.3
Land: 22.4 sq. mi.; **Water:** 0.7 sq. mi.

In northeastern MA, 10 mi. northeast of Lowell. Settled 1642. Formerly part of Haverhill.
Name origin: For Lord Paul Methuen (1672–1757).

Middleton Town
ZIP: 01949   **Lat:** 42-36-10 N **Long:** 71-01-13 W
Pop: 4,921 (1990); 4,135 (1980)   **Pop Density:** 351.5
Land: 14.0 sq. mi.; **Water:** 0.5 sq. mi.

In northeastern MA, 15 mi. southeast of Lowell. Settled 1659.

Nahant Town
     Lat: 42-25-08 N **Long:** 70-54-48 W
Pop: 3,828 (1990); 3,947 (1980)   **Pop Density:** 3190.0
Land: 1.2 sq. mi.; **Water:** 14.2 sq. mi.

In northeastern MA.

Newbury Town
ZIP: 01950   **Lat:** 42-46-17 N **Long:** 70-52-32 W
Pop: 5,623 (1990); 4,529 (1980)   **Pop Density:** 232.4
Land: 24.2 sq. mi.; **Water:** 2.2 sq. mi.

In northeastern MA. Settled and incorporated 1635.

Newburyport Town
ZIP: 01950   **Lat:** 42-48-53 N **Long:** 70-53-22 W
Pop: 16,317 (1990); 15,900 (1980)   **Pop Density:** 1942.5
Land: 8.4 sq. mi.; **Water:** 2.2 sq. mi.   **Elev:** 37 ft.

In northeastern MA at the mouth of the Merrimack River, 25 mi. northeast of Lowell. Settled 1635; incorporated 1764.
Name origin: For Newbury, Berkshire, England, or as the port for Newbury.

North Andover Town
ZIP: 01845   **Lat:** 42-40-27 N **Long:** 71-05-12 W
Pop: 22,792 (1990); 20,129 (1980)   **Pop Density:** 853.6
Land: 26.7 sq. mi.; **Water:** 1.2 sq. mi.

In northeastern MA, 8 mi. northeast of Lowell.

Peabody City
ZIP: 01960   **Lat:** 42-31-58 N **Long:** 70-58-13 W
Pop: 47,039 (1990); 45,976 (1980)   **Pop Density:** 2868.2
Land: 16.4 sq. mi.; **Water:** 0.5 sq. mi.   **Elev:** 17 ft.

In northeastern MA. Incorporated 1916.
Name origin: Named 1868 for financier George Peabody (1795–1869). Previously called South Danvers.

Rockport Town
ZIP: 01966   **Lat:** 42-39-20 N **Long** 70-36-17 W
Pop: 7,482 (1990); 6,345 (1980)   **Pop Density:** 1053.8
Land: 7.1 sq. mi.; **Water:** 10.5 sq. mi.

In eastern MA on the Granite peninsula of Cape Ann. Settled 1690; incorporated 1840.

Rowley Town
ZIP: 01969   **Lat:** 42-43-15 N **Long** 70-53-18 W
Pop: 4,452 (1990); 3,867 (1980)   **Pop Density:** 238.1
Land: 18.7 sq. mi.; **Water:** 1.9 sq. mi.

In northeastern MA, 5 mi. north of Ipswich. Settled 1638; incorporated 1639.

Salem   City
ZIP: 01970   **Lat:** 42-31-35 N **Long:** 70-52-10 W
Pop: 38,091 (1990); 38,220 (1980)   **Pop Density:** 4702.6
Land: 8.1 sq. mi.; **Water:** 10.0 sq. mi.   **Elev:** 9 ft.

In northeastern MA on the Atlantic Ocean, 15 mi. northeast of Boston. Settled 1626.

Name origin: Named by early settlers from the Hebrew term meaning 'city of peace.'

Salisbury   Town
ZIP: 01950   **Lat:** 42-50-36 N **Long:** 70-51-40 W
Pop: 6,882 (1990); 5,973 (1980)   **Pop Density:** 446.9
Land: 15.4 sq. mi.; **Water:** 2.4 sq. mi.

In northeastern MA. Settled 1638; incorporated 1640.

Saugus   Town
ZIP: 01906   **Lat:** 42-28-02 N **Long:** 71-00-55 W
Pop: 25,549 (1990); 24,746 (1980)   **Pop Density:** 2322.6
Land: 11.0 sq. mi.; **Water:** 0.8 sq. mi.

In northeastern MA not far from Massachusetts Bay, 10 mi. north-northeast of Boston. Settled 1630; incorporated 1815.

Name origin: For the Saugus River that runs through town.

Swampscott   Town
ZIP: 01907   **Lat:** 42-27-59 N **Long:** 70-53-32 W
Pop: 13,650 (1990); 13,837 (1980)   **Pop Density:** 4550.0
Land: 3.0 sq. mi.; **Water:** 3.7 sq. mi.

In northeastern MA on Massachusetts Bay, 10 mi. northeast of Boston. Settled 1629.

Name origin: From Algonquian term *muski-ompsk-up* possibly meaning 'at the red rocks' or 'broken waters.'

Topsfield   Town
ZIP: 01983   **Lat:** 42-38-08 N **Long:** 70-56-40 W
Pop: 5,754 (1990); 5,709 (1980)   **Pop Density:** 453.1
Land: 12.7 sq. mi.; **Water:** 0.2 sq. mi.

In northeastern MA, 20 mi. east of Boston. Settled c. 1635.

Wenham   Town
ZIP: 01984   **Lat:** 42-36-01 N **Long:** 70-53-02 W
Pop: 4,212 (1990); 3,897 (1980)   **Pop Density:** 547.0
Land: 7.7 sq. mi.; **Water:** 0.4 sq. mi.

Formerly a part of Salem.

West Newbury   Town
ZIP: 01985   **Lat:** 42-47-26 N **Long:** 70-58-24 W
Pop: 3,421 (1990); 2,861 (1980)   **Pop Density:** 253.4
Land: 13.5 sq. mi.; **Water:** 1.1 sq. mi.

In northeastern MA, 20 mi. northeast of Lowell. Settled 1635; incorporated 1819.

Franklin County
County Seat: Greenfield (ZIP: 01301)

Pop: 70,092 (1990); 64,317 (1980)   **Pop Density:** 99.8
Land: 702.1 sq. mi.; **Water:** 22.7 sq. mi.   **Area Code:** 413

On northern border of MA, north of Northampton; organized Jun 24, 1811 from Hampshire County.

Name origin: For Benjamin Franklin (1706–90), U.S. patriot, diplomat, and statesman.

Ashfield   Town
ZIP: 01330   **Lat:** 42-31-15 N **Long:** 72-48-22 W
Pop: 1,715 (1990); 1,458 (1980)   **Pop Density:** 42.6
Land: 40.3 sq. mi.; **Water:** 0.1 sq. mi.

In northwestern MA. Settled 1743.

Bernardston   Town
ZIP: 01337   **Lat:** 42-41-37 N **Long:** 72-32-56 W
Pop: 2,048 (1990); 1,750 (1980)   **Pop Density:** 87.5
Land: 23.4 sq. mi.; **Water:** 0.0 sq. mi.

In northwestern MA, near the VT border. Settled 1738; incorporated 1762.

Name origin: For Sir Francis Bernard, provincial governor of MA (1760–69).

Buckland   Town
ZIP: 01338   **Lat:** 42-35-31 N **Long:** 72-47-22 W
Pop: 1,928 (1990); 1,864 (1980)   **Pop Density:** 98.4
Land: 19.6 sq. mi.; **Water:** 0.2 sq. mi.

Charlemont   Town
                        Lat: 42-38-08 N **Long:** 72-52-08 W
Pop: 1,249 (1990); 1,149 (1980)   **Pop Density:** 47.9
Land: 26.1 sq. mi.; **Water:** 0.3 sq. mi.

In northwestern MA, 15 mi. west of Greenfield. Settled c. 1742.

Colrain   Town
ZIP: 01340   **Lat:** 42-40-41 N **Long:** 72-43-14 W
Pop: 1,757 (1990); 1,552 (1980)   **Pop Density:** 40.5
Land: 43.4 sq. mi.; **Water:** 0.1 sq. mi.

In northwestern MA. Settled 1735 by Scotch-Irish from northern Ireland.

Name origin: Probably for Lord Coleraine, an Irish peer.

Conway   Town
ZIP: 01341   **Lat:** 42-30-30 N **Long:** 72-42-25 W
Pop: 1,529 (1990); 1,213 (1980)   **Pop Density:** 40.6
Land: 37.7 sq. mi.; **Water:** 0.1 sq. mi.

Settled 1762.

Name origin: For Gen. Henry Conway (1721–95), a member of the British ministry, popular in the colonies after he secured repeal of the Stamp Act in 1766.

Deerfield   Town
ZIP: 01342   **Lat:** 42-31-27 N **Long:** 72-36-41 W
Pop: 5,018 (1990); 4,517 (1980)   **Pop Density:** 155.4
Land: 32.3 sq. mi.; **Water:** 1.1 sq. mi.

Erving Town
ZIP: 01344 Lat: 42-36-33 N Long: 72-25-24 W
Pop: 1,372 (1990); 1,326 (1980) Pop Density: 98.7
Land: 13.9 sq. mi.; Water: 0.5 sq. mi.

In northern MA, 10 mi. northeast of Greenfield and 85 mi. northwest of Boston. Settled 1801.

Name origin: For John Erving of Boston, to whom the town land was sold in 1752.

Gill Town
Lat: 42-37-46 N Long: 72-30-24 W
Pop: 1,583 (1990); 1,259 (1980) Pop Density: 113.1
Land: 14.0 sq. mi.; Water: 0.8 sq. mi.

Greenfield Town
ZIP: 01301 Lat: 42-36-51 N Long: 72-35-53 W
Pop: 18,666 (1990); 18,436 (1980) Pop Density: 860.2
Land: 21.7 sq. mi.; Water: 0.2 sq. mi.

In northwestern MA on Connecticut River, 35 mi. north of Springfield.

Name origin: For the Green River.

Hawley Town
Lat: 42-35-32 N Long: 72-54-29 W
Pop: 317 (1990); 280 (1980) Pop Density: 10.3
Land: 30.9 sq. mi.; Water: 0.0 sq. mi.

Heath Town
Lat: 42-41-48 N Long: 72-49-33 W
Pop: 716 (1990); 482 (1980) Pop Density: 28.8
Land: 24.9 sq. mi.; Water: 0.0 sq. mi.

Leverett Town
ZIP: 01054 Lat: 42-28-12 N Long: 72-29-11 W
Pop: 1,785 (1990); 1,471 (1980) Pop Density: 78.3
Land: 22.8 sq. mi.; Water: 0.1 sq. mi.

In northwestern MA, 10 mi. southeast of Greenfield. Settled 1713.

Leyden Town
Lat: 42-41-33 N Long: 72-37-35 W
Pop: 662 (1990); 498 (1980) Pop Density: 36.8
Land: 18.0 sq. mi.; Water: 0.0 sq. mi.

Millers Falls CDP
Lat: 42-34-47 N Long: 72-29-34 W
Pop: 1,084 (1990); 549 (1980) Pop Density: 1204.4
Land: 0.9 sq. mi.; Water: 0.0 sq. mi.

Monroe Town
Lat: 42-43-20 N Long: 72-58-52 W
Pop: 115 (1990); 179 (1980) Pop Density: 10.7
Land: 10.7 sq. mi.; Water: 0.1 sq. mi.

Montague Town
ZIP: 01351 Lat: 42-33-17 N Long: 72-31-02 W
Pop: 8,316 (1990); 8,011 (1980) Pop Density: 273.6
Land: 30.4 sq. mi.; Water: 1.0 sq. mi.

In western MA.

New Salem Town
Lat: 42-27-07 N Long: 72-19-11 W
Pop: 802 (1990); 688 (1980) Pop Density: 17.8
Land: 45.0 sq. mi.; Water: 13.7 sq. mi.

Settled 1737; incorporated 1753.

Name origin: For Salem because the original proprietors were residents of that town.

Northfield Town
ZIP: 01354 Lat: 42-40-42 N Long: 72-26-43 W
Pop: 2,838 (1990); 2,386 (1980) Pop Density: 82.5
Land: 34.4 sq. mi.; Water: 0.9 sq. mi.

Name origin: For its northern situation in the county.

Orange Town
ZIP: 01364 Lat: 42-36-40 N Long: 72-17-43 W
Pop: 7,312 (1990); 6,844 (1980) Pop Density: 206.6
Land: 35.4 sq. mi.; Water: 0.6 sq. mi.

In northern MA, 15 mi. east of Greenfield. Settled c. 1746; incorporated 1810. On the banks of a rapid river, the town became a manufacturing center.

Name origin: For William, prince of Orange.

Rowe Town
ZIP: 01367 Lat: 42-42-03 N Long: 72-54-49 W
Pop: 378 (1990); 336 (1980) Pop Density: 16.0
Land: 23.6 sq. mi.; Water: 0.5 sq. mi.

Shelburne Town
ZIP: 01370 Lat: 42-36-11 N Long: 72-41-24 W
Pop: 2,012 (1990); 2,002 (1980) Pop Density: 86.4
Land: 23.3 sq. mi.; Water: 0.2 sq. mi.

In northwestern MA. Settled 1756.

Name origin: Named in 1760 for William Petty (1737–1805) the 2d Earl of Shelburne. Formerly called Deerfield Pasture, Deerfield Northwest, and Shelburne Falls.

Shelburne Falls CDP
ZIP: 01370 Lat: 42-36-12 N Long: 72-44-34 W
Pop: 1,996 (1990); 1,017 (1980) Pop Density: 798.4
Land: 2.5 sq. mi.; Water: 0.1 sq. mi.

Shutesbury Town
ZIP: 01072 Lat: 42-26-57 N Long: 72-25-27 W
Pop: 1,561 (1990); 1,049 (1980) Pop Density: 58.7
Land: 26.6 sq. mi.; Water: 0.6 sq. mi.

In central MA, west of the Quabbin Reservoir. Settled 1735; incorporated 1761.

Name origin: For Samuel Shute, one-time governor of the Bay Colony. Originally called Roadtown.

South Deerfield CDP
ZIP: 01373 Lat: 42-28-47 N Long: 72-35-24 W
Pop: 1,906 (1990); 1,926 (1980) Pop Density: 614.8
Land: 3.1 sq. mi.; Water: 0.1 sq. mi.

Sunderland Town
ZIP: 01375 Lat: 42-28-13 N Long: 72-33-20 W
Pop: 3,399 (1990); 2,929 (1980) Pop Density: 236.0
Land: 14.4 sq. mi.; Water: 0.4 sq. mi.

In central MA on the Connecticut River, 10 mi. southeast of Greenfield. Settled 1713.

Turners Falls CDP
Lat: 42-35-45 N Long: 72-33-28 W
Pop: 4,731 (1990); 4,711 (1980) Pop Density: 2365.5
Land: 2.0 sq. mi.; Water: 0.3 sq. mi.

Warwick Town
Lat: 42-40-30 N Long: 72-20-27 W
Pop: 740 (1990); 603 (1980) Pop Density: 19.8
Land: 37.3 sq. mi.; Water: 0.3 sq. mi.

Wendell
Town
ZIP: 01379   **Lat:** 42-33-19 N **Long:** 72-24-45 W
Pop: 899 (1990); 694 (1980)   **Pop Density:** 28.1
Land: 32.0 sq. mi.; **Water:** 0.2 sq. mi.

In northwestern MA, 10 mi. southeast of Greenfield. Settled 1754.
Name origin: For Judge Oliver Wendell of Boston.

Whately
Town
ZIP: 01373   **Lat:** 42-26-15 N **Long:** 72-38-52 W
Pop: 1,375 (1990); 1,341 (1980)   **Pop Density:** 68.1
Land: 20.2 sq. mi.; **Water:** 0.5 sq. mi.

In northwestern MA, 10 mi. south of Greenfield. Settled 1672.
Name origin: Named by Gov. Hutchinson for Thomas Whately of England.

Hampden County
County Seat: Springfield (ZIP: 01101)

Pop: 456,310 (1990); 443,018 (1980)   **Pop Density:** 737.7
Land: 618.5 sq. mi.; **Water:** 15.7 sq. mi.   **Area Code:** 413

On southern border of MA, south of Northampton; organized Feb 25, 1812 from Hampshire County.
Name origin: For John Hampden (1594–1643), English statesman influential in the establishment of Puritan colonies in North America.

Agawam
Town
ZIP: 01001   **Lat:** 42-04-01 N **Long:** 72-39-03 W
Pop: 27,323 (1990); 26,271 (1980)   **Pop Density:** 1177.7
Land: 23.2 sq. mi.; **Water:** 1.0 sq. mi.

In southeast central MA, bounded on the north by the Agawam River, 5 mi. southwest of Springfield. Settled 1635; incorporated 1855.
Name origin: For the river, which is from an Indian term *agaam* probably meaning 'crooked river.'

Blandford
Town
ZIP: 01008   **Lat:** 42-11-09 N **Long:** 72-57-11 W
Pop: 1,187 (1990); 1,038 (1980)   **Pop Density:** 23.0
Land: 51.7 sq. mi.; **Water:** 1.8 sq. mi.

In southwestern MA, 20 mi. west of Springfield. Incorporated 1741.
Name origin: Named on incorporation by then colonial governor William Shirley (1694–1771) for the ship that brought him from England.

Bondsville
CDP
Lat: 42-12-11 N **Long:** 72-20-18 W
Pop: 1,744 (1990); 1,743 (1980)   **Pop Density:** 581.3
Land: 3.0 sq. mi.; **Water:** 0.0 sq. mi.

Part of the town is also in Hampshire County.

Brimfield
Town
ZIP: 01010   **Lat:** 42-07-47 N **Long:** 72-12-20 W
Pop: 3,001 (1990); 2,318 (1980)   **Pop Density:** 86.2
Land: 34.8 sq. mi.; **Water:** 0.4 sq. mi.

Chester
Town
ZIP: 01011   **Lat:** 42-17-43 N **Long:** 72-56-28 W
Pop: 1,280 (1990); 1,123 (1980)   **Pop Density:** 34.9
Land: 36.7 sq. mi.; **Water:** 0.4 sq. mi.

In western MA, 20 mi. southeast of Pittsfield. Settled 1760; incorporated 1765.

Chicopee
City
ZIP: 01013   **Lat:** 42-10-33 N **Long:** 72-34-23 W
Pop: 56,632 (1990); 55,112 (1980)   **Pop Density:** 2473.0
Land: 22.9 sq. mi.; **Water:** 1.0 sq. mi.   **Elev:** 200 ft.

In southwestern MA on the Connecticut River, 4 mi. north of Springfield. Town incorporated 1848; city government 1890.
Name origin: For the Chicopee River, from an Indian term probably meaning 'swift water.'

East Longmeadow
Town
ZIP: 01028   **Lat:** 42-03-34 N **Long:** 72-30-00 W
Pop: 13,367 (1990); 12,905 (1980)   **Pop Density:** 1028.2
Land: 13.0 sq. mi.; **Water:** 0.0 sq. mi.

In south-central MA, 6 mi. southeast of Springfield.

Granville
Town
ZIP: 01034   **Lat:** 42-04-49 N **Long:** 72-54-41 W
Pop: 1,403 (1990); 1,204 (1980)   **Pop Density:** 33.2
Land: 42.2 sq. mi.; **Water:** 0.7 sq. mi.

Hampden
Town
ZIP: 01036   **Lat:** 42-03-45 N **Long:** 72-24-56 W
Pop: 4,709 (1990); 4,745 (1980)   **Pop Density:** 240.3
Land: 19.6 sq. mi.; **Water:** 0.0 sq. mi.

Holland
Town
Lat: 42-03-44 N **Long:** 72-10-02 W
Pop: 2,185 (1990); 1,589 (1980)   **Pop Density:** 176.2
Land: 12.4 sq. mi.; **Water:** 0.7 sq. mi.

Holyoke
City
ZIP: 01040   **Lat:** 42-12-48 N **Long:** 72-38-32 W
Pop: 43,704 (1990); 44,678 (1980)   **Pop Density:** 2051.8
Land: 21.3 sq. mi.; **Water:** 1.5 sq. mi.   **Elev:** 200 ft.

In southwestern MA on the Connecticut River, 10 mi. north of Springfield. Settled 1745.
Name origin: For Rev. Edward Holyoke, president of Harvard (1737–69) or Eliezur Holyoke, an early settler and explorer. Previously called Springfield.

Longmeadow
Town
ZIP: 01106   **Lat:** 42-02-51 N **Long:** 72-34-12 W
Pop: 15,467 (1990); 16,301 (1980)   **Pop Density:** 1718.6
Land: 9.0 sq. mi.; **Water:** 0.5 sq. mi.

In southwestern MA on Connecticut River, just south of Springfield. Settled 1644. Purchased from the Indians 1636.
Name origin: For its surroundings.

Ludlow
Town
ZIP: 01056 **Lat:** 42-11-30 N **Long:** 72-27-35 W
Pop: 18,820 (1990); 18,150 (1980) **Pop Density:** 694.5
Land: 27.1 sq. mi.; **Water:** 1.1 sq. mi.

In southwestern MA, 5 mi. northeast of Springfield. Settled 1751. Part of Springfield until 1775.
Name origin: For Ludlow, Shropshire, England. Originally called Stony Hill.

Monson
Town
ZIP: 01057 **Lat:** 42-05-25 N **Long:** 72-19-27 W
Pop: 7,776 (1990); 7,315 (1980) **Pop Density:** 175.5
Land: 44.3 sq. mi.; **Water:** 0.5 sq. mi.

In southern MA, 20 mi. east of Springfield.

Montgomery
Town
Lat: 42-12-42 N **Long:** 72-49-05 W
Pop: 759 (1990); 637 (1980) **Pop Density:** 50.3
Land: 15.1 sq. mi.; **Water:** 0.1 sq. mi.

Palmer
Town
ZIP: 01069 **Lat:** 42-11-34 N **Long:** 72-18-43 W
Pop: 12,054 (1990); 11,389 (1980) **Pop Density:** 382.7
Land: 31.5 sq. mi.; **Water:** 0.5 sq. mi.

In southwestern MA, northeast of Springfield.

Russell
Town
ZIP: 01071 **Lat:** 42-09-56 N **Long:** 72-51-19 W
Pop: 1,594 (1990); 1,570 (1980) **Pop Density:** 90.6
Land: 17.6 sq. mi.; **Water:** 0.3 sq. mi.

In southwestern MA. Settled 1782.

Southwick
Town
ZIP: 01077 **Lat:** 42-03-14 N **Long:** 72-46-38 W
Pop: 7,667 (1990); 7,382 (1980) **Pop Density:** 247.3
Land: 31.0 sq. mi.; **Water:** 0.7 sq. mi.

In southern MA. Settled 1770.
Name origin: For an English village.

Springfield
City
ZIP: 01101 **Lat:** 42-06-54 N **Long:** 72-32-20 W
Pop: 156,983 (1990); 152,319 (1980) **Pop Density:** 4890.4
Land: 32.1 sq. mi.; **Water:** 1.1 sq. mi. **Elev:** 70 ft.

In southwestern MA on Connecticut River, 5 mi. north of CT border. Incorporated 1641. Springfield armory was first federal U.S. armory. First military musket produced in 1795; Springfield rifle and M1 rifle both developed here. Diverse commercial and industrial city.
Name origin: For Springfield, Essex, England. Previously called Agawam.

Three Rivers
CDP
ZIP: 01080 **Lat:** 42-10-49 N **Long:** 72-22-17 W
Pop: 3,006 (1990); 3,322 (1980) **Pop Density:** 939.4
Land: 3.2 sq. mi.; **Water:** 0.2 sq. mi.

Tolland
Town
Lat: 42-05-37 N **Long:** 73-00-36 W
Pop: 289 (1990); 235 (1980) **Pop Density:** 9.1
Land: 31.6 sq. mi.; **Water:** 1.1 sq. mi.

Wales
Town
ZIP: 01081 **Lat:** 42-04-00 N **Long:** 72-13-44 W
Pop: 1,566 (1990); 1,177 (1980) **Pop Density:** 99.1
Land: 15.8 sq. mi.; **Water:** 0.2 sq. mi.

In southwestern MA, 20 mi. southeast of Springfield. Settled 1726.
Name origin: For James Lawrence Wales in 1828, in acknowledgement of a $2,000 legacy. Originally called South Brimfield.

Westfield
City
ZIP: 01085 **Lat:** 42-08-20 N **Long:** 72-45-21 W
Pop: 38,372 (1990); 36,465 (1980) **Pop Density:** 823.4
Land: 46.6 sq. mi.; **Water:** 0.7 sq. mi. **Elev:** 140 ft.

In southwestern MA on Westfield River, 10 mi. west of Springfield. Founded 1660; incorporated 1669; chartered as city 1920.
Name origin: For being formed from the western part of Springfield.

West Springfield
Town
ZIP: 01089 **Lat:** 42-07-23 N **Long:** 72-39-10 W
Pop: 27,537 (1990); 27,042 (1980) **Pop Density:** 1639.1
Land: 16.8 sq. mi.; **Water:** 0.8 sq. mi.

In southwestern MA on Connecticut River, across from Springfield. Settled 1660.

Wilbraham
Town
ZIP: 01095 **Lat:** 42-07-39 N **Long:** 72-25-53 W
Pop: 12,635 (1990); 12,053 (1980) **Pop Density:** 569.1
Land: 22.2 sq. mi.; **Water:** 0.2 sq. mi.

In southwestern MA, 10 mi. east of Springfield.
Name origin: For town of Wilbraham, England, or for Viscount Wilbraham, a royalist.

Hampshire County
County Seat: Northampton (ZIP: 01060)

Pop: 146,568 (1990); 138,813 (1980)   **Pop Density:** 277.1
Land: 529.0 sq. mi.; **Water:** 16.4 sq. mi.   **Area Code:** 413
In west-central MA, north of Springfield; organized May 7, 1662 from Middlesex County.
Name origin: Named by Capt. John Mason (1586–1635) for the county of Hampshire, England.

Amherst   Town
ZIP: 01002   **Lat:** 42-21-52 N **Long:** 72-30-25 W
Pop: 35,228 (1990); 33,229 (1980)   **Pop Density:** 1271.8
Land: 27.7 sq. mi.; **Water:** 0.1 sq. mi.

In western MA, 20 mi. north of Springfield. Site of Amherst College and the University of Massachusetts. Birthplace of poet Emily Dickinson (1830–86).
Name origin: For Lord Jeffrey Amherst (1717–97), a British general in the French and Indian War.

Belchertown   Town
ZIP: 01007   **Lat:** 42-16-47 N **Long:** 72-24-02 W
Pop: 10,579 (1990); 8,339 (1980)   **Pop Density:** 200.7
Land: 52.7 sq. mi.; **Water:** 2.6 sq. mi.

In western MA, 15 mi. north of Springfield. Settled 1731.
Name origin: For Jonathan Belcher (1682–1757) colonial governor of MA and NH (1730–41).

Bondsville   CDP
                        Lat: 42-12-47 N **Long:** 72-21-27 W
Pop: 248 (1990); 163 (1980)   **Pop Density:** 496.0
Land: 0.5 sq. mi.; **Water:** 0.0 sq. mi.

Part of the town is also in Hampden County.

Chesterfield   Town
ZIP: 01012   **Lat:** 42-23-20 N **Long:** 72-50-41 W
Pop: 1,048 (1990); 1,000 (1980)   **Pop Density:** 33.7
Land: 31.1 sq. mi.; **Water:** 0.2 sq. mi.

In western MA, 12 mi. west of Northampton. Settled 1760.
Name origin: For the Earl of Chesterfield. Originally called New Hingham.

Cummington   Town
ZIP: 01026   **Lat:** 42-27-43 N **Long:** 72-55-12 W
Pop: 785 (1990); 657 (1980)   **Pop Density:** 34.0
Land: 23.1 sq. mi.; **Water:** 0.0 sq. mi.

Easthampton   Town
ZIP: 01027   **Lat:** 42-15-51 N **Long:** 72-40-19 W
Pop: 15,537 (1990); 15,580 (1980)   **Pop Density:** 1159.5
Land: 13.4 sq. mi.; **Water:** 0.2 sq. mi.

In west-central MA, 14 mi. north-northwest of Springfield. Settled 1664.
Name origin: For location east of Northampton and Southampton.

Goshen   Town
ZIP: 01032   **Lat:** 42-26-48 N **Long:** 72-48-18 W
Pop: 830 (1990); 651 (1980)   **Pop Density:** 47.7
Land: 17.4 sq. mi.; **Water:** 0.3 sq. mi.

Granby   Town
ZIP: 01033   **Lat:** 42-15-44 N **Long:** 72-30-10 W
Pop: 5,565 (1990); 5,380 (1980)   **Pop Density:** 199.5
Land: 27.9 sq. mi.; **Water:** 0.2 sq. mi.

Hadley   Town
ZIP: 01035   **Lat:** 42-21-30 N **Long:** 72-34-09 W
Pop: 4,231 (1990); 4,125 (1980)   **Pop Density:** 181.6
Land: 23.3 sq. mi.; **Water:** 1.4 sq. mi.

Hatfield   Town Hampshire County
ZIP: 01038   **Lat:** 42-23-18 N **Long:** 72-37-28 W
Pop: 3,184 (1990); 3,045 (1980)   **Pop Density:** 199.0
Land: 16.0 sq. mi.; **Water:** 0.8 sq. mi.

In western MA, on the Connecticut River.

Huntington   Town
ZIP: 01050   **Lat:** 42-16-51 N **Long:** 72-51-32 W
Pop: 1,987 (1990); 1,804 (1980)   **Pop Density:** 74.7
Land: 26.6 sq. mi.; **Water:** 0.3 sq. mi.

In western MA. Settled 1769.
Name origin: For Charles F. Huntington. Originally called Norwich.

Middlefield   Town
                        Lat: 42-20-52 N **Long:** 73-00-41 W
Pop: 392 (1990); 385 (1980)   **Pop Density:** 16.2
Land: 24.2 sq. mi.; **Water:** 0.0 sq. mi.

North Amherst   CDP
ZIP: 01059   **Lat:** 42-24-33 N **Long:** 72-31-18 W
Pop: 6,239 (1990); 5,616 (1980)   **Pop Density:** 2971.0
Land: 2.1 sq. mi.; **Water:** 0.0 sq. mi.

Northampton   City
ZIP: 01060   **Lat:** 42-19-37 N **Long:** 72-40-30 W
Pop: 29,289 (1990); 29,286 (1980)   **Pop Density:** 849.0
Land: 34.5 sq. mi.; **Water:** 1.1 sq. mi.   **Elev:** 140 ft.

In western MA on the Connecticut River, 15 mi. north of Springfield. Settled 1654.
Name origin: For Northampton or Northamptonshire, England, or for its location at the time of settlement as the town farthest north on the Connecticut River.

Pelham   Town
                        Lat: 42-23-11 N **Long:** 72-24-52 W
Pop: 1,373 (1990); 1,112 (1980)   **Pop Density:** 54.7
Land: 25.1 sq. mi.; **Water:** 1.4 sq. mi.   **Elev:** 800 ft.

In central MA. Settled 1738; incorporated 1743.
Name origin: For Lord Pelham, then traveling in the colony.

Plainfield   Town
ZIP: 01070   **Lat:** 42-31-02 N **Long:** 72-55-33 W
Pop: 571 (1990); 425 (1980)   **Pop Density:** 27.1
Land: 21.1 sq. mi.; **Water:** 0.2 sq. mi.

South Amherst   CDP
ZIP: 01002   **Lat:** 42-20-19 N **Long:** 72-31-00 W
Pop: 5,053 (1990); 4,861 (1980)   **Pop Density:** 1203.1
Land: 4.2 sq. mi.; **Water:** 0.0 sq. mi.

Southampton
Town
ZIP: 01073   **Lat:** 42-13-35 N **Long:** 72-44-33 W
Pop: 4,478 (1990); 4,137 (1980)   **Pop Density:** 158.8
Land: 28.2 sq. mi.; **Water:** 0.9 sq. mi.

In west-central MA, 10 mi. northwest of Springfield. Settled 1732; incorporated 1775.
Name origin: For Southampton, England.

South Hadley
Town
ZIP: 01075   **Lat:** 42-15-20 N **Long:** 72-34-49 W
Pop: 16,685 (1990); 16,399 (1980)   **Pop Density:** 942.7
Land: 17.7 sq. mi.; **Water:** 0.7 sq. mi.

In western MA, north of Springfield. Settled 1659.

Ware
Town
ZIP: 01082   **Lat:** 42-17-09 N **Long:** 72-16-41 W
Pop: 9,808 (1990); 8,953 (1980)   **Pop Density:** 285.1
Land: 34.4 sq. mi.; **Water:** 5.6 sq. mi.

In western MA, 20 mi. east-northeast of Springfield. Settled 1717.
Name origin: Formerly called Nenameseck, from an Indian term probably meaning 'fishing weir.'

Westhampton
Town
    Lat: 42-18-16 N **Long:** 72-46-42 W
Pop: 1,327 (1990); 1,137 (1980)   **Pop Density:** 49.0
Land: 27.1 sq. mi.; **Water:** 0.2 sq. mi.

Williamsburg
Town
ZIP: 01096   **Lat:** 42-23-56 N **Long:** 72-43-50 W
Pop: 2,515 (1990); 2,237 (1980)   **Pop Density:** 98.2
Land: 25.6 sq. mi.; **Water:** 0.1 sq. mi.

In west-central MA. Settled 1735.

Worthington
Town
ZIP: 01098   **Lat:** 42-23-45 N **Long:** 72-56-37 W
Pop: 1,156 (1990); 932 (1980)   **Pop Density:** 36.0
Land: 32.1 sq. mi.; **Water:** 0.0 sq. mi.

Middlesex County
County Seat: Cambridge (ZIP: 02138)

Pop: 1,398,470 (1990); 1,367,030 (1980)   **Pop Density:** 1698.1
Land: 823.5 sq. mi.; **Water:** 24.1 sq. mi.   **Area Code:** 508

In northern MA, west and northwest of Boston; bounded on north by NH and on the south by Massachusetts Bay. Original county, organized May 10, 1643.
Name origin: For an ancient county in England, most of which became part of Greater London in 1965.

Acton
Town
ZIP: 01720   **Lat:** 42-28-58 N **Long:** 71-26-24 W
Pop: 17,872 (1990); 17,544 (1980)   **Pop Density:** 893.6
Land: 20.0 sq. mi.; **Water:** 0.3 sq. mi.

In northeastern MA, 11 mi. south-southeast of Lowell.
Name origin: Probably for Acton, Middlesex, England.

Arlington
Town
ZIP: 02174   **Lat:** 42-25-06 N **Long:** 71-09-51 W
Pop: 44,630 (1990); 48,219 (1980)   **Pop Density:** 8582.7
Land: 5.2 sq. mi.; **Water:** 0.3 sq. mi.

In northeastern MA, 5 mi. northwest of Boston.
Name origin: Formerly West Cambridge; name changed in 1867.

Ashby
Town
ZIP: 01431   **Lat:** 42-40-38 N **Long:** 71-49-13 W
Pop: 2,717 (1990); 2,311 (1980)   **Pop Density:** 114.2
Land: 23.8 sq. mi.; **Water:** 0.4 sq. mi.

In north-central MA, 8 mi. north of Fitchburg, bordering on Rindge, NH.

Ashland
Town
ZIP: 01721   **Lat:** 42-15-28 N **Long:** 71-28-00 W
Pop: 12,066 (1990); 9,165 (1980)   **Pop Density:** 973.1
Land: 12.4 sq. mi.; **Water:** 0.5 sq. mi.

In northeastern MA, 18 mi. east of Worcester. Incorporated 1846.

Ayer
Town
ZIP: 01432   **Lat:** 42-33-50 N **Long:** 71-34-19 W
Pop: 6,871 (1990); 6,993 (1980)   **Pop Density:** 763.4
Land: 9.0 sq. mi.; **Water:** 0.6 sq. mi.

In east-central MA, 12 mi. east of Fitchburg. Adjacent to Fort Devens.

Bedford
Town
ZIP: 01730   **Lat:** 42-29-45 N **Long:** 71-16-40 W
Pop: 12,996 (1990); 13,067 (1980)   **Pop Density:** 948.6
Land: 13.7 sq. mi.; **Water:** 0.1 sq. mi.

In northeastern MA, 10 mi. south of Lowell.
Name origin: For Bedford, Bedfordshire, England.

Belmont
Town
ZIP: 02178   **Lat:** 42-23-47 N **Long:** 71-10-48 W
Pop: 24,720 (1990); 26,100 (1980)   **Pop Density:** 5259.6
Land: 4.7 sq. mi.; **Water:** 0.0 sq. mi.

In northeastern MA, 8 mi. west-northwest of Boston.
Name origin: French for 'beautiful mountain.'

Billerica
Town
ZIP: 01821   **Lat:** 42-33-28 N **Long:** 71-16-09 W
Pop: 37,609 (1990); 36,727 (1980)   **Pop Density:** 1452.1
Land: 25.9 sq. mi.; **Water:** 0.5 sq. mi.

In northeastern MA, 5 mi. south of Lowell. Settled 1637; incorporated 1655.
Name origin: For Billericay, Essex, England. Formerly called Shawshin.

Boxborough
Town
Lat: 42-29-29 N **Long:** 71-31-09 W
Pop: 3,343 (1990); 3,126 (1980)   **Pop Density:** 321.4
Land: 10.4 sq. mi.; **Water:** 0.0 sq. mi.

Burlington
Town
ZIP: 01803   **Lat:** 42-30-11 N **Long:** 71-12-07 W
Pop: 23,302 (1990); 23,486 (1980)   **Pop Density:** 1974.7
Land: 11.8 sq. mi.; **Water:** 0.1 sq. mi.

In northeastern MA, 10 mi. south-southeast of Lowell.

Name origin: Possibly an altered version of Bridlington, Yorkshire, England. The spelling reflects one pronunciation of the English name.

Cambridge
City
ZIP: 02138   **Lat:** 42-22-32 N **Long:** 71-07-07 W
Pop: 95,802 (1990); 95,322 (1980)   **Pop Density:** 14969.1
Land: 6.4 sq. mi.; **Water:** 0.7 sq. mi.   **Elev:** 30 ft.

In eastern MA, across the Charles River from Boston. Settled 1630; incorporated as a town 1636; city government established 1846. Home of Harvard/Radcliffe and Massachusetts Institute of Technology (MIT).

Name origin: Following a bequest by John Harvard (1607–38) for a college, the General Court of the MA Bay Colony ruled in 1638 that "Newetowne shall henceforward be called Cambridge," for the old English university town.

Carlisle
Town
ZIP: 01741   **Lat:** 42-31-42 N **Long:** 71-21-04 W
Pop: 4,333 (1990); 3,306 (1980)   **Pop Density:** 281.4
Land: 15.4 sq. mi.; **Water:** 0.2 sq. mi.

In northeastern MA, 20 mi. northwest of Boston. Settled 1650.

Name origin: For the Scottish birthplace of James Adams, who, banished by Oliver Cromwell (1599–1658) for political offenses, became the first settler of the district.

Chelmsford
Town
ZIP: 01824   **Lat:** 42-35-59 N **Long:** 71-22-03 W
Pop: 32,383 (1990); 31,174 (1980)   **Pop Density:** 1426.6
Land: 22.7 sq. mi.; **Water:** 0.5 sq. mi.

In northeastern MA, 5 mi. southeast of Lowell. Settled 1633 by residents of Concord and Woburn.

Name origin: For Chelmsford, Essex, England.

Cochituate
CDP
ZIP: 01778   **Lat:** 42-19-44 N **Long:** 71-21-38 W
Pop: 6,046 (1990); 62 (1980)   **Pop Density:** 1634.1
Land: 3.7 sq. mi.; **Water:** 0.3 sq. mi.

Concord
Town
ZIP: 01742   **Lat:** 42-27-40 N **Long:** 71-21-53 W
Pop: 17,076 (1990); 16,293 (1980)   **Pop Density:** 685.8
Land: 24.9 sq. mi.; **Water:** 1.0 sq. mi.

In northern MA where the Sudbury and Assabet join to form the Concord River, south of Lowell. Incorporated 1635. Concord minutemen fired "the shot heard 'round the world,'" beginning the American Revolutionary War.

Name origin: For harmony with the Indians that remained after white settlers purchased land from them.

Dracut
Town
ZIP: 01826   **Lat:** 42-40-57 N **Long:** 71-18-03 W
Pop: 25,594 (1990); 21,249 (1980)   **Pop Density:** 1224.6
Land: 20.9 sq. mi.; **Water:** 0.5 sq. mi.

In northeastern MA, 3 mi. north of Lowell, 27 mi. north of Boston.

Name origin: For Draycott, Derbyshire, England.

Dunstable
Town
ZIP: 01827   **Lat:** 42-40-36 N **Long:** 71-30-04 W
Pop: 2,236 (1990); 1,671 (1980)   **Pop Density:** 135.5
Land: 16.5 sq. mi.; **Water:** 0.2 sq. mi.

East Pepperell
CDP
ZIP: 01463   **Lat:** 42-40-00 N **Long:** 71-33-52 W
Pop: 2,296 (1990); 2,212 (1980)   **Pop Density:** 1640.0
Land: 1.4 sq. mi.; **Water:** 0.0 sq. mi.

Everett
City
ZIP: 02149   **Lat:** 42-24-23 N **Long:** 71-03-16 W
Pop: 35,701 (1990); 37,195 (1980)   **Pop Density:** 10500.3
Land: 3.4 sq. mi.; **Water:** 0.3 sq. mi.   **Elev:** 10 ft.

In northeastern MA, 5 mi. north of Boston. Settled 1649.

Name origin: For orator, statesman, and scholar Edward Everett (1794–1865).

Fort Devens
Military facility
ZIP: 01433   **Lat:** 42-32-58 N **Long:** 71-36-53 W
Pop: 1,306 (1990); 710 (1980)   **Pop Density:** 1004.6
Land: 1.3 sq. mi.; **Water:** 0.0 sq. mi.

Part of the facility is also in Worcester County.

Framingham
Town
ZIP: 01701   **Lat:** 42-18-21 N **Long:** 71-26-16 W
Pop: 64,989 (1990); 65,113 (1980)   **Pop Density:** 2589.2
Land: 25.1 sq. mi.; **Water:** 1.3 sq. mi.

In northeastern MA, 20 mi. southwest of Boston. Settled 1650.

Name origin: For Framingham, Suffolk, England.

Groton
Town
ZIP: 01450   **Lat:** 42-36-42 N **Long:** 71-33-53 W
Pop: 7,511 (1990); 6,154 (1980)   **Pop Density:** 229.0
Land: 32.8 sq. mi.; **Water:** 0.9 sq. mi.

Holliston
Town
ZIP: 01746   **Lat:** 42-12-09 N **Long:** 71-26-50 W
Pop: 12,926 (1990); 12,622 (1980)   **Pop Density:** 691.2
Land: 18.7 sq. mi.; **Water:** 0.3 sq. mi.

In eastern MA, 20 mi. southeast of Worcester. Settled c. 1659.

Name origin: For Thomas Hollis, an early benefactor of Harvard College.

Hopkinton
Town
ZIP: 01748   **Lat:** 42-13-30 N **Long:** 71-32-09 W
Pop: 9,191 (1990); 7,114 (1980)   **Pop Density:** 345.5
Land: 26.6 sq. mi.; **Water:** 1.6 sq. mi.

In eastern MA, 30 mi. southwest of Boston.

Hudson
Town
ZIP: 01749   **Lat:** 42-23-16 N **Long:** 71-32-52 W
Pop: 17,233 (1990); 16,408 (1980)   **Pop Density:** 1498.5
Land: 11.5 sq. mi.; **Water:** 0.3 sq. mi.

In northeastern MA, 16 mi. northeast of Worcester.

Name origin: For minister Charles Hudson (1795–1881). Previously called Hones Mills and Feltonville.

Lexington
Town
ZIP: 02173   **Lat:** 42-26-44 N **Long:** 71-13-53 W
Pop: 28,974 (1990); 29,479 (1980)   **Pop Density:** 1766.7
Land: 16.4 sq. mi.; **Water:** 0.1 sq. mi.

In northeastern MA, 10 mi. northwest of Boston. Settled 1642.

Name origin: For Laxton, Nottinghamshire, England.

Lincoln
Town
ZIP: 01773   Lat: 42-25-33 N Long: 71-18-39 W
Pop: 7,666 (1990); 7,098 (1980)   Pop Density: 532.4
Land: 14.4 sq. mi.; Water: 0.6 sq. mi.

Once a part of Concord, Lexingon, and Weston.

Littleton
Town
ZIP: 01460   Lat: 42-32-08 N Long: 71-29-22 W
Pop: 7,051 (1990); 6,970 (1980)   Pop Density: 424.8
Land: 16.6 sq. mi.; Water: 0.9 sq. mi.

In northeastern MA, 10 mi. southwest of Lowell. Granted 1714.

Name origin: For George Littleton, a member of the British parliament. Also called by its Indian name, Nashobah.

Lowell
City
ZIP: 01850   Lat: 42-38-19 N Long: 71-19-19 W
Pop: 103,439 (1990); 92,418 (1980)   Pop Density: 7495.6
Land: 13.8 sq. mi.; Water: 0.8 sq. mi.   Elev: 102 ft.

In northeastern MA on Merrimack River at Pawtucket Falls, 25 mi. northwest of Boston. Settled 1653; incorporated as town 1826, as city 1836. First planned industrial community in U.S.; formerly noted for textile manufacturing. Headquarters of Wang Computer Co.

Name origin: For Francis Cabot Lowell (1775–1817), American textile manufacturer.

Malden
City
ZIP: 02148   Lat: 42-25-49 N Long: 71-03-30 W
Pop: 53,884 (1990); 53,386 (1980)   Pop Density: 10565.5
Land: 5.1 sq. mi.; Water: 0.0 sq. mi.   Elev: 13 ft.

In northeastern MA, 5 mi. north of Boston. Settled 1640; incorporated 1649; chartered as city 1881.

Name origin: For Maldon, Essex, England.

Marlborough
City
ZIP: 01752   Lat: 42-20-59 N Long: 71-32-51 W
Pop: 31,813 (1990); 30,617 (1980)   Pop Density: 1507.7
Land: 21.1 sq. mi.; Water: 1.1 sq. mi.   Elev: 450 ft.

Maynard
Town
ZIP: 01754   Lat: 42-25-32 N Long: 71-27-25 W
Pop: 10,325 (1990); 9,590 (1980)   Pop Density: 1985.6
Land: 5.2 sq. mi.; Water: 0.1 sq. mi.

In northeastern MA, 15 mi. southwest of Lowell. Settled 1638.

Name origin: For Amory Maynard (1804–90), founder of the original textile mill, out of which grew American Woolen Company.

Medford
City
ZIP: 02155   Lat: 42-25-20 N Long: 71-06-31 W
Pop: 57,407 (1990); 58,076 (1980)   Pop Density: 7087.3
Land: 8.1 sq. mi.; Water: 0.5 sq. mi.   Elev: 14 ft.

In northeastern MA, 6 mi. north of Boston.

Name origin: For an English place name, 'the middle ford.'

Melrose
City
ZIP: 02176   Lat: 42-27-17 N Long: 71-03-32 W
Pop: 28,150 (1990); 30,055 (1980)   Pop Density: 5989.4
Land: 4.7 sq. mi.; Water: 0.1 sq. mi.   Elev: 133 ft.

In northeastern MA, 5 mi. north of Boston. Settled 1629.

Name origin: For Melrose, Roxburghshire, Scotland. Formerly a part of Malden, this district was known locally as the North End of North Malden.

Natick
Town
ZIP: 01760   Lat: 42-17-06 N Long: 71-21-04 W
Pop: 30,510 (1990); 29,461 (1980)   Pop Density: 2020.5
Land: 15.1 sq. mi.; Water: 1.0 sq. mi.

In northeastern MA, 16 mi. west-southwest of Boston. Founded 1651 by John Eliot, author of an Indian Bible.

Name origin: For a local Indian tribe, whose name possibly meant 'a place of hills', 'a clear place', or 'my land.'

Newton
City
ZIP: 02158   Lat: 42-19-53 N Long: 71-12-25 W
Pop: 82,585 (1990); 83,622 (1980)   Pop Density: 4562.7
Land: 18.1 sq. mi.; Water: 0.2 sq. mi.   Elev: 100 ft.

In northeastern MA, 5 mi. west of Boston. Settled 1639; incorporated 1691. Originally part of Cambridge. Fig Newtons cookies first manufactured here in the Kennedy Biscuit Works.

Name origin: A "new town" when it separated from Cambridge and became independent.

North Reading
Town
ZIP: 01864   Lat: 42-34-52 N Long: 71-05-23 W
Pop: 12,002 (1990); 11,455 (1980)   Pop Density: 902.4
Land: 13.3 sq. mi.; Water: 0.3 sq. mi.

In northeastern MA, 11 mi. southeast of Lowell.

Pepperell
Town
ZIP: 01463   Lat: 42-40-12 N Long: 71-36-18 W
Pop: 10,098 (1990); 8,061 (1980)   Pop Density: 446.8
Land: 22.6 sq. mi.; Water: 0.6 sq. mi.

In northeastern MA, 10 mi. northeast of Fitchburg. Settled 1720; incorporated 1753.

Name origin: For Sir William Pepperell (1696–1759), a hero of the Battle of Louisburg.

Pinehurst
CDP
ZIP: 01866   Lat: 42-32-03 N Long: 71-14-10 W
Pop: 6,614 (1990); 6,588 (1980)   Pop Density: 2066.9
Land: 3.2 sq. mi.; Water: 0.0 sq. mi.

Reading
Town
ZIP: 01867   Lat: 42-32-08 N Long: 71-06-25 W
Pop: 22,539 (1990); 22,678 (1980)   Pop Density: 2276.7
Land: 9.9 sq. mi.; Water: 0.0 sq. mi.

In northeastern MA, 10 mi. north of Boston. Settled 1639; incorporated 1644.

Name origin: For Reading, Berkshire, England.

Sherborn
Town
ZIP: 01770   Lat: 42-13-51 N Long: 71-22-21 W
Pop: 3,989 (1990); 4,049 (1980)   Pop Density: 249.3
Land: 16.0 sq. mi.; Water: 0.2 sq. mi.

Shirley
Town
ZIP: 01464   Lat: 42-34-19 N Long: 71-38-58 W
Pop: 6,118 (1990); 5,124 (1980)   Pop Density: 387.2
Land: 15.8 sq. mi.; Water: 0.1 sq. mi.

In northeastern MA, 5 mi. southeast of Fitchburg. Settled 1720; incorporated 1753.

Somerville
City
ZIP: 02143   Lat: 42-23-25 N Long: 71-06-06 W
Pop: 76,210 (1990); 77,372 (1980)   Pop Density: 18587.8
Land: 4.1 sq. mi.; Water: 0.1 sq. mi.   Elev: 12 ft.

In northeastern MA, 5 mi. northwest of Boston. Settled 1630; incorporated as town 1842; as city 1871.

Name origin: For naval hero, Capt. Richard Somers (1778–1804).

Stoneham
Town
ZIP: 02180 **Lat:** 42-28-26 N **Long:** 71-05-53 W
Pop: 22,203 (1990); 21,424 (1980) **Pop Density:** 3639.8
Land: 6.1 sq. mi.; **Water:** 0.6 sq. mi.

In northeastern MA, 10 mi. north of Boston. Settled 1645; incorporated 1725.

Name origin: Previously called Charlestown End.

Stow
Town
ZIP: 01775 **Lat:** 42-25-45 N **Long:** 71-30-45 W
Pop: 5,328 (1990); 5,144 (1980) **Pop Density:** 302.7
Land: 17.6 sq. mi.; **Water:** 0.5 sq. mi.

In northeastern MA, 20 mi. northwest of Boston. Settled 1658.

Sudbury
Town
ZIP: 01776 **Lat:** 42-22-57 N **Long:** 71-25-27 W
Pop: 14,358 (1990); 14,027 (1980) **Pop Density:** 588.4
Land: 24.4 sq. mi.; **Water:** 0.3 sq. mi.

In northeastern MA on the Sudbury River, 20 mi. west of Boston. Settled 1638.

Name origin: For Sudbury, Suffolk, England.

Tewksbury
Town
ZIP: 01876 **Lat:** 42-36-38 N **Long:** 71-13-47 W
Pop: 27,266 (1990); 24,635 (1980) **Pop Density:** 1317.2
Land: 20.7 sq. mi.; **Water:** 0.3 sq. mi.

In northeastern MA, 5 mi. southeast of Lowell. Settled 1637; incorporated 1734.

Name origin: For Tewkesbury, Gloucestershire, England. Previously an Indian village called Wamesitt.

Townsend
Town
ZIP: 01469 **Lat:** 42-39-59 N **Long:** 71-42-41 W
Pop: 8,496 (1990); 7,201 (1980) **Pop Density:** 258.2
Land: 32.9 sq. mi.; **Water:** 0.2 sq. mi.

Tyngsborough
Town
ZIP: 01879 **Lat:** 42-40-03 N **Long:** 71-25-49 W
Pop: 8,642 (1990); 5,683 (1980) **Pop Density:** 514.4
Land: 16.8 sq. mi.; **Water:** 1.2 sq. mi.

In northeastern MA on the Merrimack River, 10 mi. northwest of Lowell. Settled 1661.

Name origin: For the Tyng family, whose coat of arms became its official seal.

Wakefield
Town
ZIP: 01880 **Lat:** 42-30-16 N **Long:** 71-03-59 W
Pop: 24,825 (1990); 24,895 (1980) **Pop Density:** 3310.0
Land: 7.5 sq. mi.; **Water:** 0.4 sq. mi.

In northeastern MA, 11 mi. north of Boston.

Name origin: For local businessman Cyrus Wakefield (1811–73). Previously called Reading and South Reading.

Waltham
City
ZIP: 02154 **Lat:** 42-23-16 N **Long:** 71-14-31 W
Pop: 57,878 (1990); 58,200 (1980) **Pop Density:** 4557.3
Land: 12.7 sq. mi.; **Water:** 0.9 sq. mi. **Elev:** 50 ft.

In northeastern MA on the Charles River, 10 mi. west of Boston. Settled 1634; incorporated as town 1738; as city 1884.

Name origin: For Waltham Abbey, Essex, England, from a term meaning 'forest home.'

Watertown
Town
ZIP: 02172 **Lat:** 42-22-10 N **Long:** 71-10-39 W
Pop: 33,284 (1990); 34,384 (1980) **Pop Density:** 8118.0
Land: 4.1 sq. mi.; **Water:** 0.1 sq. mi.

In northeastern MA on Charles River, 5 mi. west of Boston. Settled 1630.

Name origin: For being so well watered.

Wayland
Town
ZIP: 01778 **Lat:** 42-21-36 N **Long:** 71-21-34 W
Pop: 11,874 (1990); 12,170 (1980) **Pop Density:** 781.2
Land: 15.2 sq. mi.; **Water:** 0.7 sq. mi.

In northeastern MA, 15 mi. west of Boston. Settled 1638; incorporated 1835.

Name origin: For Francis Wayland, clergyman and president of Brown University (1827–55).

West Concord
CDP
ZIP: 01742 **Lat:** 42-27-05 N **Long:** 71-24-12 W
Pop: 5,761 (1990); 5,331 (1980) **Pop Density:** 1694.4
Land: 3.4 sq. mi.; **Water:** 0.2 sq. mi.

Westford
Town
ZIP: 01886 **Lat:** 42-35-12 N **Long:** 71-26-26 W
Pop: 16,392 (1990); 13,434 (1980) **Pop Density:** 535.7
Land: 30.6 sq. mi.; **Water:** 0.7 sq. mi.

In northeastern MA, 10 mi. southwest of Lowell.

Name origin: For being the western precinct of Chelmsford.

Weston
Town
ZIP: 02193 **Lat:** 42-21-38 N **Long:** 71-18-09 W
Pop: 10,200 (1990); 11,169 (1980) **Pop Density:** 600.0
Land: 17.0 sq. mi.; **Water:** 0.3 sq. mi.

In northeastern MA, 10 mi. west of Boston.

Name origin: For western part of Watertown or one of two Westons in England.

Wilmington
Town
ZIP: 01887 **Lat:** 42-33-33 N **Long:** 71-09-59 W
Pop: 17,651 (1990); 17,471 (1980) **Pop Density:** 1032.2
Land: 17.1 sq. mi.; **Water:** 0.1 sq. mi.

In northeastern MA, 10 mi. southeast of Lowell. Settled 1639; incorporated 1730.

Name origin: For Spencer Compton Wilmington (c. 1673–1743), a member of the British Privy Council.

Winchester
Town
ZIP: 01890 **Lat:** 42-27-06 N **Long:** 71-08-48 W
Pop: 20,267 (1990); 20,701 (1980) **Pop Density:** 3377.8
Land: 6.0 sq. mi.; **Water:** 0.3 sq. mi.

In northeastern MA, 10 mi. northwest of Boston.

Name origin: For Col. William P. Winchester (1801–50).

Woburn
City
ZIP: 01801 **Lat:** 42-29-07 N **Long:** 71-09-18 W
Pop: 35,943 (1990); 36,626 (1980) **Pop Density:** 2830.2
Land: 12.7 sq. mi.; **Water:** 0.2 sq. mi. **Elev:** 100 ft.

In northeastern MA, 10 mi. north-northwest of Boston. Settled 1640; incorporated as town 1642; as city 1888.

Name origin: For Woburn, Bedfordshire, England.

Nantucket County and City
County Seat: Nantucket (ZIP: 02554)

Pop: 6,012 (1990); 5,087 (1980)   **Pop Density:** 125.8
Land: 47.8 sq. mi.; **Water:** 255.5 sq. mi.   **Area Code:** 508

Coextensive with Nantucket Island, south of Cape Cod, MA; original county, organized Jun 22, 1695.

Name origin: From an Indian word of uncertain meaning. An early map marks the island as *Natocok*, which may mean 'far away.' Others suggest the root *Nantuck* means 'the sandy, sterile soil tempted no one.'

Nantucket   Town
ZIP: 02554   **Lat:** 41-17-25 N **Long:** 70-06-52 W
Pop: 6,012 (1990); 5,087 (1980)   **Pop Density:** 125.8
Land: 47.8 sq. mi.; **Water:** 35.0 sq. mi.
On Nantucket Island, MA, near the harbor. Settled 1641; incorporated 1687. Population includes all communities on island.

Name origin: From an Indian, Nanticut.

Norfolk County
County Seat: Dedham (ZIP: 02026)

Pop: 616,087 (1990); 606,587 (1980)   **Pop Density:** 1541.7
Land: 399.6 sq. mi.; **Water:** 44.4 sq. mi.   **Area Code:** 617

In eastern MA, south of Boston; organized Mar 26, 1793 from Suffolk County.

Name origin: For the county in England.

Avon   Town
ZIP: 02322   **Lat:** 42-07-28 N **Long:** 71-02-56 W
Pop: 4,558 (1990); 5,026 (1980)   **Pop Density:** 1035.9
Land: 4.4 sq. mi.; **Water:** 0.2 sq. mi.
In eastern MA. Settled before 1700.

Name origin: Suggested by the town schoolmaster to commemorate the birthplace of William Shakespeare (1564–1616).

Bellingham   Town
ZIP: 02019   **Lat:** 42-04-37 N **Long:** 71-28-29 W
Pop: 14,877 (1990); 14,300 (1980)   **Pop Density:** 804.2
Land: 18.5 sq. mi.; **Water:** 0.5 sq. mi.
In eastern MA, 20 mi. southeast of Worcester. Settled 1713.

Name origin: For Richard Bellingham (c. 1592–1672), colonial governor of MA (1641; 1654; 1665–72).

Braintree   Town
ZIP: 02184   **Lat:** 42-12-09 N **Long:** 71-00-12 W
Pop: 33,836 (1990); 36,337 (1980)   **Pop Density:** 2434.2
Land: 13.9 sq. mi.; **Water:** 0.6 sq. mi.
In eastern MA, 8 mi. south of Boston.

Name origin: For Braintree, Norfolk, England.

Brookline   Town
ZIP: 02146   **Lat:** 42-19-23 N **Long:** 71-08-32 W
Pop: 54,718 (1990); 55,062 (1980)   **Pop Density:** 8046.8
Land: 6.8 sq. mi.; **Water:** 0.0 sq. mi.
In eastern MA, 5 mi. west-southwest of Boston. Incorporated 1705.

Name origin: Named by Judge Samuel Sewall (1652–1730) for the brook that marked the back border of his estate. Formerly called Muddy River Hamlet.

Canton   Town
ZIP: 02021   **Lat:** 42-10-38 N **Long:** 71-07-40 W
Pop: 18,530 (1990); 18,182 (1980)   **Pop Density:** 980.4
Land: 18.9 sq. mi.; **Water:** 0.6 sq. mi.
In eastern MA, 15 mi. southwest of Boston. Settled 1630.

Name origin: For Canton, China, which was a port of call for Boston ships.

Cohasset   Town
ZIP: 02025   **Lat:** 42-17-29 N **Long:** 70-46-44 W
Pop: 7,075 (1990); 7,174 (1980)   **Pop Density:** 714.6
Land: 9.9 sq. mi.; **Water:** 21.6 sq. mi.
Incorporated 1775; formerly part of Hingham.

Name origin: From an Indian term *coinohasset* probably meaning 'rocky place.'

Dedham   Town
ZIP: 02026   **Lat:** 42-14-47 N **Long:** 71-10-45 W
Pop: 23,782 (1990); 25,298 (1980)   **Pop Density:** 2265.0
Land: 10.5 sq. mi.; **Water:** 0.2 sq. mi.
In eastern MA on the Charles River, 10 mi. southwest of Boston. Settled 1635.

Name origin: For Dedham, Essex, England.

Dover   Town
ZIP: 02030   **Lat:** 42-14-15 N **Long:** 71-17-11 W
Pop: 4,915 (1990); 4,703 (1980)   **Pop Density:** 321.2
Land: 15.3 sq. mi.; **Water:** 0.1 sq. mi.
In southeastern MA.

Foxborough   Town
ZIP: 02035   **Lat:** 42-03-50 N **Long:** 71-14-46 W
Pop: 14,637 (1990); 14,148 (1980)   **Pop Density:** 728.2
Land: 20.1 sq. mi.; **Water:** 0.8 sq. mi.

In eastern MA, 10 mi. west of Brockton. Settled 1704.

Name origin: For Charles James Fox (1749–1806), British champion of the American colonies.

Franklin   Town
ZIP: 02038   **Lat:** 42-05-10 N **Long:** 71-24-39 W
Pop: 22,095 (1990); 18,217 (1980)   **Pop Density:** 827.5
Land: 26.7 sq. mi.; **Water:** 0.3 sq. mi.

In southern MA, 20 mi. west of Brockton. Settled 1660.

Name origin: For statesman, scholar, and humanist Benjamin Franklin (1706–90). He was not insensible to the honor, and, after wavering for some time between presenting a church bell or a collection of books to his municipal namesake, he decided in favor of the books because it is said he considered sense more essential than sound.

Holbrook   Town
ZIP: 02343   **Lat:** 42-08-52 N **Long:** 71-00-25 W
Pop: 11,041 (1990); 11,140 (1980)   **Pop Density:** 1492.0
Land: 7.4 sq. mi.; **Water:** 0.1 sq. mi.

In eastern MA, 5 mi. north of Brockton. Settled 1710.

Name origin: For boot and shoe manufacturer and banker Elisha Niles Holbrook.

Medfield   Town
ZIP: 02052   **Lat:** 42-11-04 N **Long:** 71-18-19 W
Pop: 10,531 (1990); 10,220 (1980)   **Pop Density:** 726.3
Land: 14.5 sq. mi.; **Water:** 0.1 sq. mi.

In eastern MA, 15 mi. southwest of Boston. Settled and incorporated 1651.

Medway   Town
ZIP: 02053   **Lat:** 42-09-05 N **Long:** 71-25-46 W
Pop: 9,931 (1990); 8,447 (1980)   **Pop Density:** 863.6
Land: 11.5 sq. mi.; **Water:** 0.1 sq. mi.

In eastern MA, 20 mi. southwest of Boston. Settled 1657.

Millis   Town
ZIP: 02054   **Lat:** 42-10-07 N **Long:** 71-21-47 W
Pop: 7,613 (1990); 6,908 (1980)   **Pop Density:** 624.0
Land: 12.2 sq. mi.; **Water:** 0.1 sq. mi.

Milton   Town
ZIP: 02186   **Lat:** 42-14-35 N **Long:** 71-04-59 W
Pop: 25,725 (1990); 25,860 (1980)   **Pop Density:** 1978.8
Land: 13.0 sq. mi.; **Water:** 0.2 sq. mi.

In eastern MA, 5 mi. south of Boston. Settled 1636; incorporated 1662.

Name origin: Originally called Uncataquisset, an Indian term probably for 'head of tidewater.'

Needham   Town
ZIP: 02192   **Lat:** 42-16-50 N **Long:** 71-14-27 W
Pop: 27,557 (1990); 27,901 (1980)   **Pop Density:** 2187.1
Land: 12.6 sq. mi.; **Water:** 0.1 sq. mi.

In eastern MA, 12 mi. west-southwest of Boston.

Name origin: For Needham, Norfolk, England.

Norfolk   Town
ZIP: 02056   **Lat:** 42-07-14 N **Long:** 71-19-44 W
Pop: 9,270 (1990); 6,363 (1980)   **Pop Density:** 626.4
Land: 14.8 sq. mi.; **Water:** 0.4 sq. mi.

In eastern MA, 21 mi. southwest of Boston.

Norwood   Town
ZIP: 02062   **Lat:** 42-11-06 N **Long:** 71-11-42 W
Pop: 28,700 (1990); 29,711 (1980)   **Pop Density:** 2733.3
Land: 10.5 sq. mi.; **Water:** 0.1 sq. mi.

In eastern MA, 11 mi. southwest of Boston. Settled 1678.

Name origin: For Norwood, England.

Plainville   Town
ZIP: 02762   **Lat:** 42-00-33 N **Long:** 71-20-11 W
Pop: 6,871 (1990); 5,857 (1980)   **Pop Density:** 619.0
Land: 11.1 sq. mi.; **Water:** 0.5 sq. mi.   **Elev:** 207 ft.

In southeastern MA, 30 mi. southeast of Boston. Settled 1661; incorporated 1905.

Quincy   City
ZIP: 02169   **Lat:** 42-15-40 N **Long:** 71-00-25 W
Pop: 84,985 (1990); 84,743 (1980)   **Pop Density:** 5058.6
Land: 16.8 sq. mi.; **Water:** 10.1 sq. mi.   **Elev:** 20 ft.

In eastern MA, 10 mi. south of Boston. Settled 1625 by Thomas Morton. Birthplace of Pres. John Adams.

Name origin: For Col. John Quincy, an eminent citizen who had occupied nearby Mount Wollaston. Formerly called Mount Wollaston, Merry Mount, and Braintree.

Randolph   Town
ZIP: 02368   **Lat:** 42-10-30 N **Long:** 71-03-15 W
Pop: 30,093 (1990); 28,218 (1980)   **Pop Density:** 2979.5
Land: 10.1 sq. mi.; **Water:** 0.4 sq. mi.

In eastern MA, 5 mi. north of Brockton. Settled c. 1718.

Name origin: For Peyton Randolph (1721–75), first president of the Continental Congress.

Sharon   Town
ZIP: 02067   **Lat:** 42-06-25 N **Long:** 71-10-57 W
Pop: 15,517 (1990); 13,601 (1980)   **Pop Density:** 666.0
Land: 23.3 sq. mi.; **Water:** 0.9 sq. mi.

In southeastern MA, 10 mi. west-northwest of Brockton. Settled 1650; incorporated 1765.

Name origin: Formerly called Massapoag, from the Indian term probably meaning 'great waters,' and Stoughtonham.

Stoughton   Town
ZIP: 02072   **Lat:** 42-07-07 N **Long:** 71-06-06 W
Pop: 26,777 (1990); 26,710 (1980)   **Pop Density:** 1673.6
Land: 16.0 sq. mi.; **Water:** 0.2 sq. mi.

In southeastern MA, 6 mi. northwest of Brockton and 20 mi. south of Boston. Settled 1713; incorporated 1743.

Name origin: For William Stoughton (1631–1701), lieutenant-governor of MA.

Walpole   Town
ZIP: 02081   **Lat:** 42-08-45 N **Long:** 71-15-17 W
Pop: 20,212 (1990); 18,859 (1980)   **Pop Density:** 986.0
Land: 20.5 sq. mi.; **Water:** 0.5 sq. mi.

In eastern MA, 20 mi. southwest of Boston. Settled 1659.

Name origin: For English statesman Sir Robert Walpole (1676–1745).

Wellesley   Town
ZIP: 02181   **Lat:** 42-18-16 N **Long:** 71-17-12 W
Pop: 26,615 (1990); 27,209 (1980)   **Pop Density:** 2609.3
Land: 10.2 sq. mi.; **Water:** 0.3 sq. mi.

In eastern MA, 10 mi. west-southwest of Boston. Site of Wellesley College.

Name origin: For the estate of banker Horatio H. Hunnewell (1810–1902), which was named for maiden name of his wife, Isabelle Pratt Welles.

Westwood
Town
ZIP: 02090   **Lat:** 42-13-04 N   **Long:** 71-12-24 W
Pop: 12,557 (1990); 13,212 (1980)   **Pop Density:** 1141.5
Land: 11.0 sq. mi.; **Water:** 0.1 sq. mi.

In eastern MA, 10 mi. southwest of Boston. Settled 1640;
incorporated 1897.

Weymouth
Town
ZIP: 02188   **Lat:** 42-12-22 N   **Long:** 70-56-42 W
Pop: 54,063 (1990); 55,601 (1980)   **Pop Density:** 3180.2
Land: 17.0 sq. mi.; **Water:** 4.6 sq. mi.

In eastern MA, 10 mi. southeast of Boston. Settled 1630;
incorporated 1635.

Name origin: For Weymouth, Dorsetshire, England.

Wrentham
Town
ZIP: 02093   **Lat:** 42-02-51 N   **Long:** 71-21-18 W
Pop: 9,006 (1990); 7,580 (1980)   **Pop Density:** 405.7
Land: 22.2 sq. mi.; **Water:** 0.7 sq. mi.

Plymouth County
County Seat: Plymouth (ZIP: 02360)

Pop: 435,276 (1990); 405,437 (1980)   **Pop Density:** 658.9
Land: 660.6 sq. mi.; **Water:** 432.9 sq. mi.   **Area Code:** 617

In southeastern MA, northeast of New Bedford; organized Jun 2, 1685 from Old
Plymouth Colony.

Name origin: For Plymouth, Devonshire, England, from which the *Mayflower* sailed
for America.

Abington
Town
ZIP: 02351   **Lat:** 42-07-02 N   **Long:** 70-57-32 W
Pop: 13,817 (1990); 13,517 (1980)   **Pop Density:** 1395.7
Land: 9.9 sq. mi.; **Water:** 0.2 sq. mi.

In southeastern MA, 5 mi. northeast of Brockton.

Name origin: For Great and Little Abington, Cambridgeshire, England, or for Lord Abington (1653–99), friend of
MA Gov. Dudley.

Bridgewater
Town
ZIP: 02324   **Lat:** 41-58-12 N   **Long:** 70-58-44 W
Pop: 21,249 (1990); 17,202 (1980)   **Pop Density:** 772.7
Land: 27.5 sq. mi.; **Water:** 0.7 sq. mi.

In southeastern MA, 8 mi. south of Brockton.

Name origin: For Bridgewater, Somersetshire, England.

Brockton
City
ZIP: 02401   **Lat:** 42-04-52 N   **Long:** 71-01-31 W
Pop: 92,788 (1990); 95,172 (1980)   **Pop Density:** 4315.7
Land: 21.5 sq. mi.; **Water:** 0.1 sq. mi.   **Elev:** 112 ft.

In southeastern MA, 20 mi. south of Boston. Lands were
deeded in 1649 by the Indians to Miles Standish (1584?–
1656) and John Alden (1599?–1687) for about $30. Settled
1700; town incorporated 1821; city established 1881.

Name origin: Named in 1874. Originally called North
Bridgewater.

Carver
Town
ZIP: 02330   **Lat:** 41-52-37 N   **Long:** 70-45-23 W
Pop: 10,590 (1990); 6,988 (1980)   **Pop Density:** 281.6
Land: 37.6 sq. mi.; **Water:** 2.3 sq. mi.

In southeastern MA, 8 mi. south-southwest of Plymouth and
38 mi. southeast of Boston.

Name origin: For the first governor of Plymouth colony.

Duxbury
Town
ZIP: 02332   **Lat:** 42-02-39 N   **Long:** 70-41-23 W
Pop: 13,895 (1990); 11,807 (1980)   **Pop Density:** 583.8
Land: 23.8 sq. mi.; **Water:** 13.9 sq. mi.

In southeastern MA on Plymouth Bay, 20 m . southeast of
Brockton.

Name origin: For Duxbury Hall, family seat in England of
Miles Standish (c. 1584–1656).

East Bridgewater
Town
ZIP: 02333   **Lat:** 42-02-13 N   **Long:** 70-56-29 W
Pop: 11,104 (1990); 9,945 (1980)   **Pop Density:** 645.6
Land: 17.2 sq. mi.; **Water:** 0.3 sq. mi.

In southeastern MA, 5 mi. southeast of Brockton. Settled
1649; incorporated 1823.

Green Harbor-Cedar Crest
CDP
     Lat: 42-04-29 N   **Long:** 70-39-35 W
Pop: 2,205 (1990); 2,002 (1980)   **Pop Density:** 1225.0
Land: 1.8 sq. mi.; **Water:** 0.2 sq. mi.

Halifax
Town
ZIP: 02338   **Lat:** 41-59-26 N   **Long:** 70-51-53 W
Pop: 6,526 (1990); 5,513 (1980)   **Pop Density:** 410.4
Land: 15.9 sq. mi.; **Water:** 1.5 sq. mi.

Hanover
Town
ZIP: 02339   **Lat:** 42-07-22 N   **Long:** 70-51-26 W
Pop: 11,912 (1990); 11,358 (1980)   **Pop Density:** 763.6
Land: 15.6 sq. mi.; **Water:** 0.1 sq. mi.

In southeastern MA, 11 mi. east of Brockton.

Name origin: For George I (1660–1727).

Hanson
Town

ZIP: 02341   **Lat:** 42-03-14 N **Long:** 70-52-30 W
Pop: 9,028 (1990); 8,617 (1980)   **Pop Density:** 601.9
Land: 15.0 sq. mi.; **Water:** 0.7 sq. mi.

In southeastern MA, 8 mi. southeast of Brockton. Settled 1632.

Name origin: For Alexander Conte Hanson, a patriot assaulted by a Baltimore mob in 1812 for criticizing the federal administration.

Hingham
Town

ZIP: 02043   **Lat:** 42-13-12 N **Long:** 70-53-10 W
Pop: 19,821 (1990); 20,339 (1980)   **Pop Density:** 880.9
Land: 22.5 sq. mi.; **Water:** 2.6 sq. mi.

In southeastern MA, 10 mi. southeast of Boston. Settled 1633.

Name origin: For Hingham, Norfolk, England, the former English home of most of its settlers. Previously called Barecove Common.

Hull
Town

ZIP: 02045   **Lat:** 42-18-10 N **Long:** 70-52-59 W
Pop: 10,466 (1990); 9,714 (1980)   **Pop Density:** 3488.7
Land: 3.0 sq. mi.; **Water:** 25.2 sq. mi.

Kingston
Town

ZIP: 02364   **Lat:** 41-58-54 N **Long:** 70-44-48 W
Pop: 9,045 (1990); 7,362 (1980)   **Pop Density:** 488.9
Land: 18.5 sq. mi.; **Water:** 1.9 sq. mi.

In southeastern MA. Formerly a part of Plymouth.

Name origin: Formerly called Jones' River Parish in 1717.

Lakeville
Town

ZIP: 02346   **Lat:** 41-50-05 N **Long:** 70-57-36 W
Pop: 7,785 (1990); 5,931 (1980)   **Pop Density:** 260.4
Land: 29.9 sq. mi.; **Water:** 6.2 sq. mi.

Marion
Town

ZIP: 02738   **Lat:** 41-41-50 N **Long:** 70-44-35 W
Pop: 4,496 (1990); 3,932 (1980)   **Pop Density:** 307.9
Land: 14.6 sq. mi.; **Water:** 12.1 sq. mi.

In southeastern MA on Buzzards Bay, northeast of New Bedford. Settled 1679.

Name origin: For Gen. Francis Marion (1732?–95), southern Revolutionary War hero.

Marshfield
Town

ZIP: 02050   **Lat:** 42-06-50 N **Long:** 70-42-36 W
Pop: 21,531 (1990); 20,916 (1980)   **Pop Density:** 755.5
Land: 28.5 sq. mi.; **Water:** 3.3 sq. mi.

In southeastern MA, 15 mi. east of Brockton. Settled 1632.

Marshfield Hills
CDP

Lat: 42-09-01 N **Long:** 70-43-47 W
Pop: 2,201 (1990); 2,308 (1980)   **Pop Density:** 489.1
Land: 4.5 sq. mi.; **Water:** 0.4 sq. mi.

Mattapoisett
Town

ZIP: 02739   **Lat:** 41-39-34 N **Long:** 70-48-43 W
Pop: 5,850 (1990); 5,597 (1980)   **Pop Density:** 354.5
Land: 16.5 sq. mi.; **Water:** 6.8 sq. mi.

In southeastern MA on Buzzards Bay, 5 mi. northeast of New Bedford. Settled 1750.

Name origin: From an Indian term probably meaning 'place of rest.'

Middleborough
Town

ZIP: 02346   **Lat:** 41-52-51 N **Long:** 70-52-45 W
Pop: 17,867 (1990); 16,404 (1980)   **Pop Density:** 256.7
Land: 69.6 sq. mi.; **Water:** 2.7 sq. mi.

In southeastern MA, 15 mi. south of Brockton. Settled 1660.

Name origin: For Middlesborough, Yorkshire, England. Originally known to the Indians as Nemasket.

North Lakeville
CDP

Lat: 41-51-27 N **Long:** 70-56-33 W
Pop: 2,048 (1990)   **Pop Density:** 401.6
Land: 5.1 sq. mi.; **Water:** 0.1 sq. mi.

North Pembroke
CDP

ZIP: 02358   **Lat:** 42-05-46 N **Long:** 70-46-58 W
Pop: 2,485 (1990); 2,215 (1980)   **Pop Density:** 564.8
Land: 4.4 sq. mi.; **Water:** 0.0 sq. mi.

North Plymouth
CDP

Lat: 41-58-40 N **Long:** 70-40-57 W
Pop: 3,450 (1990); 3,250 (1980)   **Pop Density:** 2653.8
Land: 1.3 sq. mi.; **Water:** 2.2 sq. mi.

North Scituate
CDP

Lat: 42-12-43 N **Long:** 70-46-01 W
Pop: 4,891 (1990); 5,221 (1980)   **Pop Density:** 1254.1
Land: 3.9 sq. mi.; **Water:** 0.0 sq. mi.

Norwell
Town

ZIP: 02061   **Lat:** 42-09-46 N **Long:** 70-48-57 W
Pop: 9,279 (1990); 9,182 (1980)   **Pop Density:** 444.0
Land: 20.9 sq. mi.; **Water:** 0.3 sq. mi.

Ocean Bluff-Brant Rock
CDP

Lat: 42-06-09 N **Long:** 70-39-31 W
Pop: 4,541 (1990); 4,055 (1980)   **Pop Density:** 2162.4
Land: 2.1 sq. mi.; **Water:** 2.3 sq. mi.

Onset
CDP

ZIP: 02558   **Lat:** 41-44-51 N **Long:** 70-40-03 W
Pop: 1,461 (1990); 1,493 (1980)   **Pop Density:** 1328.2
Land: 1.1 sq. mi.; **Water:** 0.2 sq. mi.

Pembroke
Town

ZIP: 02359   **Lat:** 42-03-55 N **Long:** 70-48-17 W
Pop: 14,544 (1990); 13,487 (1980)   **Pop Density:** 667.2
Land: 21.8 sq. mi.; **Water:** 1.6 sq. mi.

In southeastern MA, 10 mi. east of Brockton. Settled 1650; incorporated 1712.

Name origin: Possibly for one of the several earls of Pembroke.

Plymouth
Town

ZIP: 02360   **Lat:** 41-53-43 N **Long:** 70-37-02 W
Pop: 45,608 (1990); 35,913 (1980)   **Pop Density:** 472.6
Land: 96.5 sq. mi.; **Water:** 37.5 sq. mi.

In eastern MA on Plymouth Bay, 20 mi. southeast of Brockton. Landing place of the Pilgrims.

Name origin: For Plymouth, Devonshire, England, the place where the Pilgrims had been hospitably entertained before their journey to America.

Plympton
Town

ZIP: 02367   **Lat:** 41-57-31 N **Long:** 70-48-26 W
Pop: 2,384 (1990); 1,974 (1980)   **Pop Density:** 161.1
Land: 14.8 sq. mi.; **Water:** 0.4 sq. mi.   **Elev:** 79 ft.

In southeastern MA. Settled 1662; incorporated 1707.

Name origin: For Plympton, a borough near Plymouth, England, because of its geographic propinquity to Plymouth.

Rochester Town
ZIP: 02770 Lat: 41-45-38 N Long: 70-50-20 W
Pop: 3,921 (1990); 3,205 (1980) Pop Density: 115.7
Land: 33.9 sq. mi.; Water: 2.5 sq. mi.

In eastern MA. Settled 1638; incorporated 1686.

Name origin: For the English home of some of its settlers. Originally called Sippician.

Rockland Town
ZIP: 02370 Lat: 42-07-48 N Long: 70-54-39 W
Pop: 16,123 (1990); 15,695 (1980) Pop Density: 1612.3
Land: 10.0 sq. mi.; Water: 0.1 sq. mi.

In southeastern MA, 6 mi. east-northeast of Brockton. Settled 1673; incorporated 1874.

Scituate Town
ZIP: 02066 Lat: 42-12-18 N Long: 70-44-50 W
Pop: 16,786 (1990); 17,317 (1980) Pop Density: 975.9
Land: 17.2 sq. mi.; Water: 14.6 sq. mi.

In southeastern MA on Atlantic Ocean, 15 mi. east-northeast of Brockton.

South Duxbury CDP
Lat: 42-01-00 N Long: 70-41-25 W
Pop: 3,017 (1990); 2,985 (1980) Pop Density: 1005.7
Land: 3.0 sq. mi.; Water: 1.5 sq. mi.

Wareham Town
ZIP: 02571 Lat: 41-45-42 N Long: 70-42-00 W
Pop: 19,232 (1990); 18,457 (1980) Pop Density: 537.2
Land: 35.8 sq. mi.; Water: 10.5 sq. mi.

In southeastern MA, 15 mi. east-northeast of New Bedford. Settled 1678; incorporated 1739.

Name origin: For Wareham, Dorsetshire, England.

West Bridgewater Town
ZIP: 02379 Lat: 42-01-11 N Long: 71-01-37 W
Pop: 6,389 (1990); 6,359 (1980) Pop Density: 406.9
Land: 15.7 sq. mi.; Water: 0.1 sq. mi.

In eastern MA, 5 mi. south of Brockton. Settled 1651.

West Wareham CDP
ZIP: 02576 Lat: 41-47-23 N Long: 70-45-23 W
Pop: 2,059 (1990); 1,837 (1980) Pop Density: 556.5
Land: 3.7 sq. mi.; Water: 0.1 sq. mi.

Weweantic CDP
Lat: 41-44-06 N Long: 70-43-56 W
Pop: 1,812 (1990) Pop Density: 1393.8
Land: 1.3 sq. mi.; Water: 0.5 sq. mi.

White Island Shores CDP
Lat: 41-47-37 N Long: 70-38-20 W
Pop: 1,827 (1990) Pop Density: 1522.5
Land: 1.2 sq. mi.; Water: 0.1 sq. mi.

Whitman Town
ZIP: 02382 Lat: 42-04-46 N Long: 70-56-30 W
Pop: 13,240 (1990); 13,534 (1980) Pop Density: 1891.4
Land: 7.0 sq. mi.; Water: 0.0 sq. mi.

In southeastern MA, 5 mi. east of Brockton. Settled 1670.

Name origin: For Augustus Whitman. Formerly called Little Comfort and South Abington.

Suffolk County
County Seat: Boston

Pop: 663,906 (1990); 650,142 (1980) Pop Density: 11345.2
Land: 58.5 sq. mi.; Water: 61.6 sq. mi. Area Code: 617

In eastern MA, on Massachusetts Bay; original county, organized May 10, 1643.

Name origin: For the county in England.

Boston City
ZIP: 02101 Lat: 42-20-09 N Long: 71-01-04 W
Pop: 574,283 (1990); 562,994 (1980) Pop Density: 11865.4
Land: 48.4 sq. mi.; Water: 41.2 sq. mi. Elev: 20 ft.

In eastern MA on Atlantic coast and Massachusetts Bay. Settled 1625; town incorporated Sep 7, 1630; city government established Feb 23, 1822. State capital and largest city in New England. Nicknamed *the Hub (of the Universe)* and *Athens of America* for its cultural richness; home to many libraries, museums, colleges, and universities. Birthplace of the American Revolution; called *Cradle of Liberty*. An important financial, industrial, and transportation center. Also includes the following unincorporated places: Charlestown, Dorchester, Jamaica Plain, Mattapan, and Roxbury.

Name origin: Named in 1630 for Boston, Lincolnshire, England, former home of most of its early Puritan leaders. Formerly called Shawmut and Tremont or Trimountain.

Charlestown *See* **Boston**

Chelsea City
ZIP: 02150 Lat: 42-23-45 N Long: 71-02-00 W
Pop: 28,710 (1990); 25,431 (1980) Pop Density: 13050.0
Land: 2.2 sq. mi.; Water: 0.3 sq. mi. Elev: 10 ft.

In eastern MA, 5 mi. northeast of Boston.

Name origin: For the residential section of London on the north bank of the Thames. Previously called Winnisimmet.

Dorchestser *See* **Boston**

Jamaica Plain *See* **Boston**

Mattapan *See* **Boston**

Revere City
ZIP: 02151 Lat: 42-25-05 N Long: 70-59-32 W
Pop: 42,786 (1990); 42,423 (1980) Pop Density: 7251.9
Land: 5.9 sq. mi.; Water: 4.1 sq. mi. Elev: 20 ft.

In eastern MA, 5 mi. northeast of Boston. Settled 1630; incorporated 1914.

Name origin: For Paul Revere (1735–1818).

Roxbury *See* **Boston**

Winthrop Town
ZIP: 02152 Lat: 42-22-51 N Long: 70-58-07 W
Pop: 18,127 (1990); 19,294 (1980) Pop Density: 9063.5
Land: 2.0 sq. mi.; Water: 6.3 sq. mi.

In eastern MA, 5 mi. east-northeast of Boston.

Name origin: For John Winthrop (1588–1649), 1st governor of Massachusetts Bay Colony.

Worcester County
County Seat: Worcester (ZIP: 01601)

Pop: 709,705 (1990); 646,352 (1980) Pop Density: 469.0
Land: 1513.2 sq. mi.; Water: 65.9 sq. mi. Area Code: 508

In central MA, having its northern border with NH, its southern border with CT; organized Apr 2, 1731 from Middlesex and Suffolk counties.

Name origin: For either the town of Worcester or the county of Worcestershire, both in England.

Ashburnham Town
ZIP: 01430 Lat: 42-39-29 N Long: 71-55-43 W
Pop: 5,433 (1990); 4,075 (1980) Pop Density: 140.4
Land: 38.7 sq. mi.; Water: 2.3 sq. mi.

In north-central MA. Settled 1736.

Athol Town
ZIP: 01331 Lat: 42-35-00 N Long: 72-13-00 W
Pop: 11,451 (1990); 10,634 (1980) Pop Density: 351.3
Land: 32.6 sq. mi.; Water: 0.8 sq. mi.

In central MA, 20 mi. west of Fitchburg. Settled 1735.

Name origin: Named by John Murray, one of the leading proprietors, who thought that the scenery resembled that near Blair Castle, home of the Scottish Duke of Atholl.

Auburn Town
ZIP: 01501 Lat: 42-11-43 N Long: 71-50-42 W
Pop: 15,005 (1990); 14,845 (1980) Pop Density: 974.4
Land: 15.4 sq. mi.; Water: 1.0 sq. mi.

In central MA, 6 mi. south-southwest of Worcester.

Name origin: For Auburn, Yorkshire, England. Previously called Ward.

Baldwinville CDP
ZIP: 01436 Lat: 42-36-22 N Long: 72-04-33 W
Pop: 1,795 (1990); 1,709 (1980) Pop Density: 690.4
Land: 2.6 sq. mi.; Water: 0.0 sq. mi.

Barre Town
ZIP: 01005 Lat: 42-25-07 N Long: 72-06-25 W
Pop: 4,546 (1990); 4,102 (1980) Pop Density: 102.6
Land: 44.3 sq. mi.; Water: 0.3 sq. mi.

In central MA, 60 mi. southwest of Boston. Settled 1720.

Berlin Town
Lat: 42-23-09 N Long: 71-38-00 W
Pop: 2,293 (1990); 2,215 (1980) Pop Density: 177.8
Land: 12.9 sq. mi.; Water: 0.2 sq. mi.

In east-central MA, 10 mi. east of Worcester.

Blackstone Town
ZIP: 01504 Lat: 42-02-22 N Long: 71-31-43 W
Pop: 8,023 (1990); 6,570 (1980) Pop Density: 736.1
Land: 10.9 sq. mi.; Water: 0.3 sq. mi.

In south-central MA on RI border north of Woonsocket. Settled 1662.

Name origin: For the Rev. William Blackstone (1595–1675), an Episcopal clergyman, the first white settler on the banks of the local river, also named for him.

Bolton Town
ZIP: 01740 Lat: 42-26-01 N Long: 71-36-23 W
Pop: 3,134 (1990); 2,530 (1980) Pop Density: 157.5
Land: 19.9 sq. mi.; Water: 0.1 sq. mi.

In central MA, 10 mi. northeast of Worcester.

Boylston Town
ZIP: 01505 Lat: 42-21-34 N Long: 71-43-25 W
Pop: 3,517 (1990); 3,470 (1980) Pop Density: 219.8
Land: 16.0 sq. mi.; Water: 3.6 sq. mi.

Brookfield CDP
ZIP: 01506 Lat: 42-11-43 N Long: 72-06-12 W
Pop: 2,968 (1990); 2,397 (1980) Pop Density: 191.5
Land: 15.5 sq. mi.; Water: 1.1 sq. mi.

Name origin: Originally called Quabaug.

Charlton Town
ZIP: 01507 Lat: 42-08-06 N Long: 71-58-12 W
Pop: 9,576 (1990); 6,719 (1980) Pop Density: 224.3
Land: 42.7 sq. mi.; Water: 1.2 sq. mi.

In central MA, 12 mi. southwest of Worcester.

Clinton Town
ZIP: 01510 Lat: 42-24-44 N Long: 71-41-21 W
Pop: 13,222 (1990); 12,771 (1980) Pop Density: 2319.6
Land: 5.7 sq. mi.; Water: 1.6 sq. mi.

In north-central MA, 10 mi. northeast of Worcester. Settled 1654; incorporated 1850.

Name origin: For NY legislator DeWitt Clinton (1769–1828).

Cordaville CDP
Lat: 42-16-18 N Long: 71-31-18 W
Pop: 1,530 (1990); 1,384 (1980) Pop Density: 850.0
Land: 1.8 sq. mi.; Water: 0.0 sq. mi.

Douglas
Town
ZIP: 01516   Lat: 42-03-01 N **Long:** 71-45-17 W
Pop: 5,438 (1990); 3,730 (1980)   **Pop Density:** 149.4
Land: 36.4 sq. mi.; **Water:** 1.3 sq. mi.

Dudley
Town
ZIP: 01571   Lat: 42-03-21 N **Long:** 71-56-15 W
Pop: 9,540 (1990); 8,717 (1980)   **Pop Density:** 452.1
Land: 21.1 sq. mi.; **Water:** 1.0 sq. mi.
Name origin: For Paul and William Dudley, who were among the first proprietors.

East Brookfield
Town
ZIP: 01515   Lat: 42-12-04 N **Long:** 72-02-53 W
Pop: 2,033 (1990); 1,955 (1980)   **Pop Density:** 207.4
Land: 9.8 sq. mi.; **Water:** 0.5 sq. mi.
In central MA. Settled 1664. One of the youngest towns in the state.

East Douglas
CDP
ZIP: 01516   Lat: 42-04-30 N **Long:** 71-42-45 W
Pop: 1,945 (1990); 1,683 (1980)   **Pop Density:** 572.1
Land: 3.4 sq. mi.; **Water:** 0.1 sq. mi.

Fiskdale
CDP
ZIP: 01518   Lat: 42-07-27 N **Long:** 72-06-38 W
Pop: 2,189 (1990); 1,859 (1980)   **Pop Density:** 684.1
Land: 3.2 sq. mi.; **Water:** 0.1 sq. mi.

Fitchburg
City
ZIP: 01420   Lat: 42-35-21 N **Long:** 71-48-55 W
Pop: 41,194 (1990); 39,580 (1980)   **Pop Density:** 1481.8
Land: 27.8 sq. mi.; **Water:** 0.3 sq. mi.   **Elev:** 482 ft.
Settled 1740; chartered as a city in 1872.
Name origin: For early settler John Fitch (1707/08–95).

Fort Devens
Military facility
ZIP: 01433   Lat: 42-32-01 N **Long:** 71-37-08 W
Pop: 7,667 (1990); 8,118 (1980)   **Pop Density:** 1965.9
Land: 3.9 sq. mi.; **Water:** 0.1 sq. mi.
Part of the facility is also in Middlesex County.

Gardner
City
ZIP: 01440   Lat: 42-35-02 N **Long:** 71-59-10 W
Pop: 20,125 (1990); 17,900 (1980)   **Pop Density:** 906.5
Land: 22.2 sq. mi.; **Water:** 0.8 sq. mi.   **Elev:** 1100 ft.
In north-central MA, 10 mi. west of Fitchburg. Settled 1764.
Name origin: For Col. Thomas Gardner (1724–75) of Cambridge, who fell in the Battle of Bunker Hill.

Grafton
Town
ZIP: 01519   Lat: 42-12-22 N **Long:** 71-41-08 W
Pop: 13,035 (1990); 11,238 (1980)   **Pop Density:** 574.2
Land: 22.7 sq. mi.; **Water:** 0.5 sq. mi.
In central MA, 5 mi. east-southeast of Worcester.
Name origin: For Charles Fitzroy, 2d Duke of Grafton (1683–1722), a member of the Privy Council.

Hardwick
Town
     Lat: 42-21-12 N **Long:** 72-13-06 W
Pop: 2,385 (1990); 2,272 (1980)   **Pop Density:** 61.8
Land: 38.6 sq. mi.; **Water:** 2.2 sq. mi.
In central MA. Settled 1737. Purchased in 1686 from the Nipmuck Indians by eight Roxbury residents.
Name origin: Probably for Philip York, first Lord Hardwick. Originally called Lambstown.

Harvard
Town
ZIP: 01451   Lat: 42-30-21 N **Long** 71-35-21 W
Pop: 12,329 (1990); 12,170 (1980)   **Pop Density:** 467.0
Land: 26.4 sq. mi.; **Water:** 0.6 sq. mi.
In central MA, 10 mi. southeast of Fitchburg. Settled 1704.
Name origin: For John Harvard (1607–38), first patron of Harvard University.

Holden
Town
ZIP: 01520   Lat: 42-21-20 N **Long** 71-51-43 W
Pop: 14,628 (1990); 13,336 (1980)   **Pop Density:** 417.9
Land: 35.0 sq. mi.; **Water:** 1.2 sq. mi.
In central MA, 10 mi. northwest of Worcester. Settled 1723.
Name origin: For Samuel Holden, a London merchant whose philanthropies aided the colonies.

Hopedale
Town
ZIP: 01747   Lat: 42-07-25 N **Long** 71-32-07 W
Pop: 5,666 (1990); 3,905 (1980)   **Pop Density:** 1089.6
Land: 5.2 sq. mi.; **Water:** 0.2 sq. mi.

Hubbardston
Town
ZIP: 01452   Lat: 42-29-08 N **Long** 72-00-01 W
Pop: 2,797 (1990); 1,797 (1980)   **Pop Density:** 68.2
Land: 41.0 sq. mi.; **Water:** 0.9 sq. mi.

Lancaster
Town
ZIP: 01523   Lat: 42-28-44 N **Long** 71-40-54 W
Pop: 6,661 (1990); 6,334 (1980)   **Pop Density:** 240.5
Land: 27.7 sq. mi.; **Water:** 0.5 sq. mi.
In central MA, 34 mi. northwest of Boston.

Leicester
Town
ZIP: 01524   Lat: 42-14-14 N **Long** 71-54-47 W
Pop: 10,191 (1990); 9,446 (1980)   **Pop Density:** 435.5
Land: 23.4 sq. mi.; **Water:** 1.3 sq. mi.
In central MA, 5 mi. west of Worcester. Settled 1713; incorporated 1722.
Name origin: For Leicester, Leicestershire, England.

Leominster
City
ZIP: 01453   Lat: 42-31-08 N **Long:** 71-46-19 W
Pop: 38,145 (1990); 34,508 (1980)   **Pop Density:** 1319.9
Land: 28.9 sq. mi.; **Water:** 0.9 sq. mi.   **Elev:** 400 ft.
In central MA, 5 mi. southeast of Fitchburg. Settled 1653. Part of Lancaster until 1740; chartered as city 1915.
Name origin: For Leominster, Herefordshire, England.

Lunenburg
Town
ZIP: 01462   Lat: 42-35-34 N **Long:** 71-42-58 W
Pop: 9,117 (1990); 8,405 (1980)   **Pop Density:** 345.3
Land: 26.4 sq. mi.; **Water:** 1.3 sq. mi.
In northern MA, 5 mi. east of Fitchburg. Settled 1721. Originally a part of Turkey Hills.

Mendon
Town
ZIP: 01756   Lat: 42-05-13 N **Long:** 71-33-08 W
Pop: 4,010 (1990); 3,108 (1980)   **Pop Density:** 221.5
Land: 18.1 sq. mi.; **Water:** 0.2 sq. mi.
In southern MA, 15 mi. southeast of Worcester. Settled 1660.
Name origin: For Mendon, England. Originally called Quinshepauge.

Milford
Town
ZIP: 01757 **Lat:** 42-09-31 N **Long:** 71-31-01 W
Pop: 25,355 (1990); 23,390 (1980) **Pop Density:** 1736.6
Land: 14.6 sq. mi.; **Water:** 0.3 sq. mi.

In eastern MA, 15 mi. southeast of Worcester. Settled 1662.
Name origin: For a mill by a river crossing.

Millbury
Town
ZIP: 01527 **Lat:** 42-11-15 N **Long:** 71-46-37 W
Pop: 12,228 (1990); 11,808 (1980) **Pop Density:** 778.9
Land: 15.7 sq. mi.; **Water:** 0.5 sq. mi.

In central MA, 5 mi. south of Worcester. Settled 1716.
Name origin: For mill or mills in area.

Millville
Town
Lat: 42-02-10 N **Long:** 71-34-42 W
Pop: 2,236 (1990); 1,693 (1980) **Pop Density:** 456.3
Land: 4.9 sq. mi.; **Water:** 0.1 sq. mi.

In southern MA, southeast of Worcester. Settled 1662; incorporated 1916.

New Braintree
Town
ZIP: 01531 **Lat:** 42-19-02 N **Long:** 72-07-36 W
Pop: 881 (1990); 671 (1980) **Pop Density:** 42.6
Land: 20.7 sq. mi.; **Water:** 0.2 sq. mi.

Northborough
Town
ZIP: 01532 **Lat:** 42-19-20 N **Long:** 71-38-50 W
Pop: 11,929 (1990); 10,568 (1980) **Pop Density:** 644.8
Land: 18.5 sq. mi.; **Water:** 0.2 sq. mi.

In central MA, 10 mi. northeast of Worcester. Incorporated 1775. Originally part of Marlborough.
Name origin: For the fact that it used to be the north precinct of Marlborough.

Northbridge
Town
ZIP: 01534 **Lat:** 42-07-53 N **Long:** 71-39-10 W
Pop: 13,371 (1990); 12,246 (1980) **Pop Density:** 777.4
Land: 17.2 sq. mi.; **Water:** 0.9 sq. mi.

In central MA.
Name origin: For the fact that it used to be the northern section of Uxbridge. Originally called Whitinsville, for Paul Whitin, who opened a cotton textile factory here.

North Brookfield
Town
ZIP: 01535 **Lat:** 42-16-05 N **Long:** 72-04-48 W
Pop: 4,708 (1990); 4,150 (1980) **Pop Density:** 223.1
Land: 21.1 sq. mi.; **Water:** 0.7 sq. mi.

Incorporated 1812.
Name origin: For the fact that it was the northern parish of Brookfield.

Oakham
Town
ZIP: 01068 **Lat:** 42-20-50 N **Long:** 72-02-48 W
Pop: 1,503 (1990); 994 (1980) **Pop Density:** 71.2
Land: 21.1 sq. mi.; **Water:** 0.4 sq. mi.

In central MA. Once a part of Rutland.
Name origin: Originally called Rutland West Wing.

Oxford
Town
ZIP: 01540 **Lat:** 42-07-44 N **Long:** 71-52-03 W
Pop: 12,588 (1990); 11,680 (1980) **Pop Density:** 473.2
Land: 26.6 sq. mi.; **Water:** 0.9 sq. mi.

In south-central MA, 10 mi. southwest of Worcester. Settled 1687 on land purchased from the Nipmucks in 1681. Early French Huguenot settlements were not successful; the first permanent settlement was by the English in 1713. Incorporated 1693.
Name origin: For Oxford, England.

Paxton
Town
Lat: 42-18-58 N **Long:** 71-56-10 W
Pop: 4,047 (1990); 3,762 (1980) **Pop Density:** 275.3
Land: 14.7 sq. mi.; **Water:** 0.7 sq. mi.

Petersham
Town
ZIP: 01366 **Lat:** 42-26-44 N **Long:** 72-13-01 W
Pop: 1,131 (1990); 1,024 (1980) **Pop Density:** 20.9
Land: 54.2 sq. mi.; **Water:** 14.1 sq. mi.

In central MA. Settled 1733; incorporated 1754.
Name origin: For Petersham, Surrey, England. Formerly called Nichewaug and Volunteers Town.

Phillipston
Town
Lat: 42-33-02 N **Long:** 72-08-03 W
Pop: 1,485 (1990); 953 (1980) **Pop Density:** 61.1
Land: 24.3 sq. mi.; **Water:** 0.4 sq. mi. **Elev:** 914 ft.

In central MA. Settled 1751; incorporated 1814.
Name origin: For William Phillips, in tribute to his 12 successive terms as lieutenant-governor of MA.

Princeton
Town
ZIP: 01541 **Lat:** 42-27-15 N **Long:** 71-52-52 W
Pop: 3,189 (1990); 2,425 (1980) **Pop Density:** 90.1
Land: 35.4 sq. mi.; **Water:** 0.4 sq. mi. **Elev:** 949 ft.

In central MA, 15 mi. northwest of Worcester. Settled 1743; incorporated 1771.
Name origin: Named 1718 for the Rev. Thomas Prince, associate pastor of Old South Church in Boston.

Royalston
Town
Lat: 42-40-32 N **Long:** 72-11-17 W
Pop: 1,147 (1990); 955 (1980) **Pop Density:** 27.4
Land: 41.9 sq. mi.; **Water:** 0.6 sq. mi.

In northern MA. Settled 1762.

Rutland
Town
ZIP: 01543 **Lat:** 42-22-53 N **Long:** 71-57-59 W
Pop: 4,936 (1990); 4,334 (1980) **Pop Density:** 139.8
Land: 35.3 sq. mi.; **Water:** 1.1 sq. mi.

In central MA, 10 mi. northwest of Worcester. Settled 1716; incorporated 1722.

Shrewsbury
Town
ZIP: 01545 **Lat:** 42-17-00 N **Long:** 71-42-57 W
Pop: 24,146 (1990); 22,674 (1980) **Pop Density:** 1166.5
Land: 20.7 sq. mi.; **Water:** 0.9 sq. mi.

In central MA, 5 mi. east–northeast of Worcester. Settled 1722.
Name origin: For Charles Talbot (1660–1718), Duke of Shrewsbury.

South Ashburnham
CDP
ZIP: 01772 **Lat:** 42-36-36 N **Long:** 71-56-22 W
Pop: 1,110 (1990); 1,123 (1980) **Pop Density:** 336.4
Land: 3.3 sq. mi.; **Water:** 0.0 sq. mi.

Southborough
Town
ZIP: 01772 **Lat:** 42-17-58 N **Long:** 71-31-56 W
Pop: 6,628 (1990); 6,193 (1980) **Pop Density:** 470.1
Land: 14.1 sq. mi.; **Water:** 1.5 sq. mi.

In central MA, 15 mi. east of Westboro.

Southbridge
Town
ZIP: 01550   **Lat:** 42-03-35 N **Long:** 72-02-01 W
Pop: 17,816 (1990); 16,665 (1980)   **Pop Density:** 882.0
Land: 20.2 sq. mi.; **Water:** 0.5 sq. mi.

In central MA, 15 mi. southwest of Worcester. Incorporated 1816.

Name origin: For being formed from the southern part of Sturbridge.

South Lancaster
CDP
Lat: 42-26-09 N **Long:** 71-41-36 W
Pop: 1,772 (1990); 2,329 (1980)   **Pop Density:** 1363.1
Land: 1.3 sq. mi.; **Water:** 0.0 sq. mi.

Spencer
Town
ZIP: 01562   **Lat:** 42-14-49 N **Long:** 71-59-33 W
Pop: 11,645 (1990); 10,774 (1980)   **Pop Density:** 355.0
Land: 32.8 sq. mi.; **Water:** 1.2 sq. mi.

In central MA, 11 mi. west of Worcester. Settled 1721.

Name origin: For Lieutenant-Governor Spencer Phipps (1685–1757), instrumental in securing the town's district status.

Sterling
Town
ZIP: 01564   **Lat:** 42-26-36 N **Long:** 71-46-10 W
Pop: 6,481 (1990); 5,440 (1980)   **Pop Density:** 212.5
Land: 30.5 sq. mi.; **Water:** 1.1 sq. mi.

In central MA, 10 mi. south of Fitchburg. Settled 1720.

Name origin: For Lord Stirling.

Sturbridge
Town
ZIP: 01566   **Lat:** 42-06-30 N **Long:** 72-05-33 W
Pop: 7,775 (1990); 5,976 (1980)   **Pop Density:** 207.9
Land: 37.4 sq. mi.; **Water:** 1.5 sq. mi.

In central MA, 20 mi. southwest of Worcester. Settled 1729; incorporated 1738.

Sutton
Town
ZIP: 01590   **Lat:** 42-07-51 N **Long:** 71-45-06 W
Pop: 6,824 (1990); 5,855 (1980)   **Pop Density:** 210.6
Land: 32.4 sq. mi.; **Water:** 1.6 sq. mi.

In southern MA, 10 mi. southeast of Worcester. Settled 1716.

Templeton
Town
ZIP: 01468   **Lat:** 42-34-06 N **Long:** 72-04-23 W
Pop: 6,438 (1990); 6,070 (1980)   **Pop Density:** 201.2
Land: 32.0 sq. mi.; **Water:** 0.4 sq. mi.

In central MA, 15 mi. west of Fitchburg. Settled 1751.

Upton
Town
Lat: 42-10-32 N **Long:** 71-36-15 W
Pop: 4,677 (1990); 3,886 (1980)   **Pop Density:** 217.5
Land: 21.5 sq. mi.; **Water:** 0.2 sq. mi.

In central MA, 15 mi. southeast of Worcester. Settled 1728; incorporated 1735.

Name origin: For a village in Worcestershire, England.

Uxbridge
Town
ZIP: 01569   **Lat:** 42-03-40 N **Long:** 71-38-41 W
Pop: 10,415 (1990); 8,374 (1980)   **Pop Density:** 353.1
Land: 29.5 sq. mi.; **Water:** 0.8 sq. mi.

In southern MA, 15 mi. southeast of Worcester. Settled 1662; incorporated 1727.

Name origin: Formerly called Wacantuck.

Warren
Town
Lat: 42-11-53 N **Long:** 72-12-03 W
Pop: 4,437 (1990); 3,777 (1980)   **Pop Density:** 161.3
Land: 27.5 sq. mi.; **Water:** 0.1 sq. mi.

Webster
Town
ZIP: 01570   **Lat:** 42-03-17 N **Long:** 71-51-12 W
Pop: 16,196 (1990); 14,480 (1980)   **Pop Density:** 1295.7
Land: 12.5 sq. mi.; **Water:** 2.0 sq. mi.

In south-central MA near CT-MA state line, 16 mi. south of Worcester. Settled 1713.

Name origin: For Daniel Webster (1782–1852).

Westborough
Town
ZIP: 01581   **Lat:** 42-16-05 N **Long:** 71-36-51 W
Pop: 14,133 (1990); 13,619 (1980)   **Pop Density:** 689.4
Land: 20.5 sq. mi.; **Water:** 1.1 sq. mi.

In central MA, 10 mi. north of Worcester.

Name origin: For being formed from western part of Marlborough.

West Boylston
Town
ZIP: 01583   **Lat:** 42-22-11 N **Long:** 71-47-05 W
Pop: 6,611 (1990); 6,204 (1980)   **Pop Density:** 512.5
Land: 12.9 sq. mi.; **Water:** 0.9 sq. mi.

In central MA, 5 mi. north of Worcester. Settled 1642.

West Brookfield
Town
ZIP: 01585   **Lat:** 42-15-13 N **Long:** 72-09-39 W
Pop: 3,532 (1990); 3,026 (1980)   **Pop Density:** 172.3
Land: 20.5 sq. mi.; **Water:** 0.6 sq. mi.

Westminster
Town
ZIP: 01473   **Lat:** 42-33-14 N **Long:** 71-54-22 W
Pop: 6,191 (1990); 5,139 (1980)   **Pop Density:** 174.4
Land: 35.5 sq. mi.; **Water:** 1.8 sq. mi.

In north-central MA, 5 mi. southwest of Fitchburg. Settled 1737; incorporated 1759.

Whitinsville
CDP
ZIP: 01588   **Lat:** 42-06-44 N **Long:** 71-40-16 W
Pop: 5,639 (1990); 5,379 (1980)   **Pop Density:** 1566.4
Land: 3.6 sq. mi.; **Water:** 0.4 sq. mi.

Winchendon
Town
ZIP: 01475   **Lat:** 42-40-05 N **Long:** 72-03-19 W
Pop: 8,805 (1990); 7,019 (1980)   **Pop Density:** 203.3
Land: 43.3 sq. mi.; **Water:** 0.8 sq. mi.

In north-central MA, 15 mi. northwest of Fitchburg. Settled 1753.

Name origin: For an old English town. Originally called Ipswich Canada. Also known as "Toy Town."

Worcester
City
ZIP: 01601   **Lat:** 42-16-10 N **Long:** 71-48-32 W
Pop: 169,759 (1990); 161,799 (1980)   **Pop Density:** 4514.9
Land: 37.6 sq. mi.; **Water:** 1.0 sq. mi.   **Elev:** 480 ft.

In central MA, 15 mi. west of Boston. Second largest city in MA: settled 1673; incorporated as town 1722; as city 1848. Diverse industrial city: machinery and machine tools, fabricated metals, printed materials, and chemicals, plastics, and abrasives.

Name origin: Either for the town of Worcester or for Worcestershire, the county in England in which it is located.

Index to Places and Counties in Massachusetts

New Hampshire

NEW HAMPSHIRE

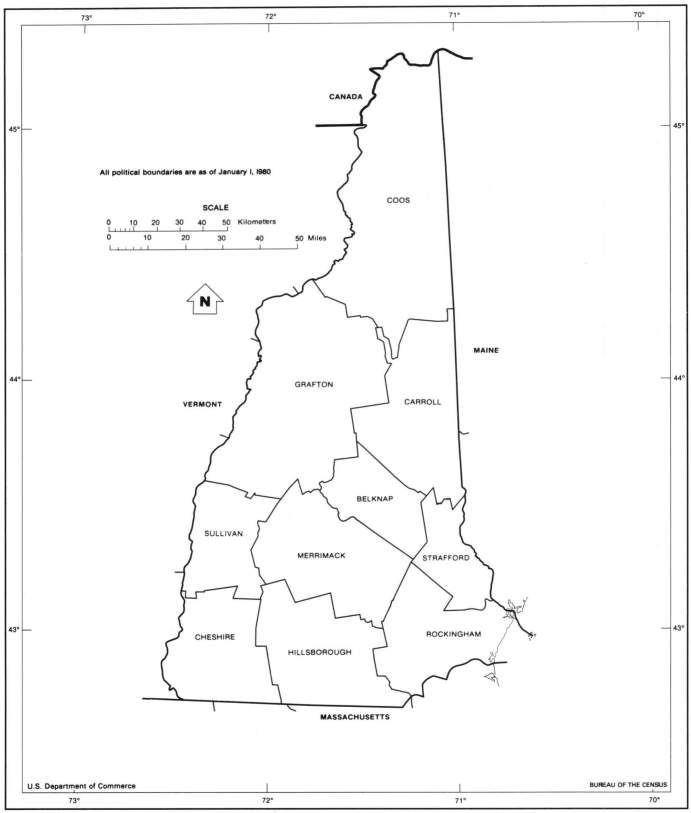

CANADA

73° 72° 71° 70°

45°

All political boundaries are as of January I, 1980

SCALE

0 10 20 30 40 50 Kilometers
0 10 20 30 40 50 Miles

N

COOS

MAINE

44°

VERMONT

GRAFTON

CARROLL

BELKNAP

SULLIVAN

MERRIMACK

STRAFFORD

43°

CHESHIRE

HILLSBOROUGH

ROCKINGHAM

MASSACHUSETTS

73° 72° 71° 70°

New Hampshire

Population: 1,109,252 (1990); 920,610 (1980)
Population rank (1990): 40
Percent population change (19801990): 20.5
Population projection: 1,270,000 (1995); 1,373,000 (2000)

Area: total 9,351 sq. mi.; 8,969 sq. mi. land, 382 sq. mi. water. Coastline 13 mi.
Area rank: 46
Highest elevation: 6,288, Mount Washington (Coos County)
Lowest point: sea level on Atlantic coast

State capital: Concord (Merrimack County)
Largest city: Manchester (99,567)
Second largest city: Nashua (79,662)
Largest county: Hillsborough (336,073)

Total housing units: 503,904
No. of occupied housing units: 411,186
Vacant housing units (%): 18.4
Distribution of population by race and Hispanic origin (%):
White: 98.0
Black: 0.6
Hispanic (any race): 1.0
Native American: 0.2
Asian/Pacific: 0.8
Other: 0.3

Admission date: June 21, 1788 (9th state)

Location: In the northeastern United States, with a small portion along the Atlantic, bordering Massachusetts, Vermont, the Canadian province of Quebec, and Maine. The three southernmost Isles of Shoals off the Atlantic coast also belong to New Hampshire. One of the thirteen original English colonies.

Name Origin: For the county of Hampshire, England. Named by Capt. John Mason (1586–1635), who received a grant to a portion of the territory later occupied by the colony and state. He had been governor of Portsmouth in Hampshire, England.

State bird: purple finch (*Carpodacus purpureus*)
State flower: purple lilac (*Syringa vulgaris*)
State insect: ladybug (*Hippodamia convergens*)
State song: "Old New Hampshire"
State tree: white birch (*Betula pendula*)

State motto: Live Free or Die
State nickname: The Granite State

Area code: 603

Time zone: Eastern
Abbreviations: NH (postal) and N.H. (traditional)
Part of (region): New England

Local Government

Counties:

New Hampshire has 10 counties, but their government is secondary to the governments of cities and towns. The county delegation appropriates funds and rules on other fiscal matters but may not make ordinances or laws for the county. Every state representative is automatically a member of the county delegation. Most government services are provided by the cities and towns. Hillsborough County has Nashua and Manchester as county seats, with the county courthouse in the former.

Municipalities:

There are 13 incorporated cities governed by a mayor and council. The 221 towns are nicknamed "little republics" because they are almost completely self-governed by town meetings. Once a year each town (two-thirds of which have populations of less than 2,500) holds a town meeting at which the citizens approve the budget, elect the town officials, and vote for each item on that year's warrant. If adopted, this is the guide for the town's actions for the next twelve months.

Settlement History and Early Development

There is evidence of human habitation in the region of present-day New Hampshire dating back 10,000 years. The earliest European colonists found two branches of Algonquian Indians: Abenaki and Pennacook. The former included the Ossipee and Pequawket tribes; the Pennacook included the Amoskeag, Nashua, Piscataqua, Souhegan, and Squamscot.

In 1603 Martin Pring of England sailed up the Piscataqua River and may have landed at Portsmouth. In 1605 French explorer Samuel de Champlain landed on the coast, and in 1614, Capt. John Smith explored the Isles of Shoals, naming them Smith's Islands. At about the same time, English fishermen were spending summers on New England's coasts, drying their catch on the Isles of Shoals.

England's Council for New England granted land in present-day New Hampshire to David Thomson about 1620. He and his followers arrived in 1623 and established the first English settlement at Odiorne's Point (part of present-day Rye). In 1622 the Council gave John Mason and Sir Ferdinando Gorges a tract of land comprising present-day New Hampshire and Maine. They divided the land in 1629 and Mason received the part between the Merrimack and Piscataqua rivers, which he named New

Hampshire after his former home. In 1641 New Hampshire was made part of Massachusetts, but in 1680 King Charles II made it a separate colony again and appointed John Cutt as the first "President" or provincial governor.

Colonial Life

Throughout the eighteenth century settlers spread out up the Merrimack and Connecticut river valleys. They made their living by fishing, farming, cutting and sawing timber, shipbuilding, and coastal and overseas trade. Portsmouth became a thriving port, but Boston, because of its location relative to markets (and other factors), developed into the main New England trading center.

Revolutionary War and Statehood

The British restrictive laws and severe taxes affected New Hampshire as well as the other colonies. On December 14, 1774, in one of the first armed actions by the colonists against the British, John Sullivan led a band of New Hampshire men and seized military supplies from a fort on the island of New Castle, off Portsmouth.

Hundreds of New Hampshire minutemen joined with Massachusetts when war broke out there in 1775, but it was the only one of the original colonies in which no actual fighting occurred.

New Hampshire was the first colony to establish an independent government, which it did on January 5, 1776, six months before the Declaration of Independence. On July 9, 1778 it ratified the Articles of Confederation, and on June 21, 1788 New Hampshire became the ninth state to ratify the U.S. Constitution.

The Civil War

The Civil War was fought far from New Hampshire, but about 34,000 of her men served in the Union army, and the Portsmouth Naval Shipyard built ships used to blockade Confederate ports.

Business and Industry

Until the mid nineteenth century, New Hampshire was primarily an agricultural state. However, Portsmouth had become a leading clipper-ship port in the early 1800s, and the first railroad opened in 1838. During the 1850s, woolen and hosiery mills and factories that made boots, shoes, machine tools, and wood products were started in Manchester and along the Merrimack River, taking advantage of water power.

After the Civil War, New Hampshire's industries began to grow by leaps and bounds. Thousands of European and French-Canadian immigrants arrived to fill the demand for workers. At the same time, many of the farmers who could not compete with the produce coming in from the fertile Midwest left to claim free land in the West.

Industry continued to grow until the 1920s and 1930s when competition from southern states forced the decline of the cotton and woolen textile industries. Leather and shoe manufacturing became the state's leading industries until after World War II, when Italian imports caused a sharp decline. This loss was more than compensated for by the rapid expansion of New Hampshire's electronics industry, which today is a major source of the state's economic base. In some respects, southern New Hampshire has become an extension of the Boston metropolitan area, as both businesses and residents of Massachusetts are attracted to New Hampshire's less-congested urban areas and lower state taxes.

State Boundaries

Disputes over the New Hampshire-Massachusetts border, ongoing for more than 150 years, were finally settled in 1901. The New Hampshire-Vermont border runs along the Connecticut River. The New Hampshire-Maine border was finally fixed in 1929 by A.T. Fowler of the U.S. Geological Survey.

New Hampshire Counties

Belknap	Hillsborough
Carroll	Merrimack
Cheshire	Rockingham
Coos	Strafford
Grafton	Sullivan

Multi-County Places

The following New Hampshire place is in more than one county. Given here is the total population and the names of the counties it is in.

Tilton-Northfield, pop. 3,081; Belknap (1,557), Merrimack (1,524)

> ## Belknap County
> ### County Seat: Laconia (ZIP: 03247)
>
> **Pop:** 49,216 (1990); 42,884 (1980)   **Pop Density:** 122.6
> **Land:** 401.3 sq. mi.; **Water:** 67.3 sq. mi.   **Area Code:** 603
>
> In east-central NH, north of Concord; organized Dec 22, 1840 from Strafford County.
>
> **Name origin:** For Jeremy Belknap (1744–98), clergyman and historian, author of *History of New Hampshire* (1784–92) and *American Biography* (1794–98).

Alton   Town
ZIP: 03809   **Lat:** 43-29-24 N **Long:** 71-14-50 W
Pop: 3,286 (1990); 2,440 (1980)   **Pop Density:** 52.1
Land: 63.1 sq. mi.; **Water:** 19.1 sq. mi.

Incorporated 1796.

Name origin: For the Alton family, prominent early landowners. Before incorporation called New Durham Gore.

Barnstead   Town
ZIP: 03218   **Lat:** 43-21-04 N **Long:** 71-15-32 W
Pop: 3,100 (1990); 2,292 (1980)   **Pop Density:** 74.0
Land: 41.9 sq. mi.; **Water:** 2.1 sq. mi.

Granted 1727.

Name origin: From the first syllable of Barnstable on Cape Cod and the last of Hampstead, Long Island, former homes of early settlers.

Belmont   Town
ZIP: 03220   **Lat:** 43-28-25 N **Long:** 71-28-48 W
Pop: 5,796 (1990); 4,026 (1980)   **Pop Density:** 189.4
Land: 30.6 sq. mi.; **Water:** 1.7 sq. mi.

Chartered 1727. Incorporated 1859.

Name origin: Incorporated as Upper Gilmanton. Renamed Belmont in 1869, honoring financier August Belmont of NY.

Center Harbor   Town
ZIP: 03226   **Lat:** 43-42-12 N **Long:** 71-30-35 W
Pop: 996 (1990); 808 (1980)   **Pop Density:** 74.3
Land: 13.4 sq. mi.; **Water:** 3.1 sq. mi.

Incorporated 1797.

Name origin: Either for its location between Meredith and Moultonborough harbors on Lake Winnipesaukee, or for the locally prominent Senter (also spelled Center) family.

Gilford   Town
ZIP: 03246   **Lat:** 43-33-16 N **Long:** 71-22-28 W
Pop: 5,867 (1990); 4,841 (1980)   **Pop Density:** 150.4
Land: 39.0 sq. mi.; **Water:** 14.9 sq. mi.

Name origin: Commemorating the Revolutionary War battle at Guilford Court House, North Carolina, in 1781, with altered spelling. Name given in 1812, proposed by resident Lemuel B. Mason, who fought in the battle.

Gilmanton   Town
ZIP: 03237   **Lat:** 43-25-47 N **Long:** 71-21-54 W
Pop: 2,609 (1990); 1,941 (1980)   **Pop Density:** 45.7
Land: 57.1 sq. mi.; **Water:** 2.0 sq. mi.

Granted by Lieutenant-Governor John Wentworth in 1727.
Name origin: For the Gilman family, many of whom received grants and settled in the town from MA. Originally Gilmantown.

Laconia   City
ZIP: 03246   **Lat:** 43-34-10 N **Long:** 71-28-49 W
Pop: 15,743 (1990); 15,575 (1980)   **Pop Density:** 775.5
Land: 20.3 sq. mi.; **Water:** 6.3 sq. mi.

In central NH, 23 mi. north of Concord. Settled 1761; incorporated as a town in 1855, as a city in 1893.

Name origin: For a region of ancient Greece. Originally called Meredith Bridge.

Meredith   Town
ZIP: 03253   **Lat:** 43-38-07 N **Long:** 71-30-18 W
Pop: 4,837 (1990); 4,646 (1980)   **Pop Density:** 120.3
Land: 40.2 sq. mi.; **Water:** 13.9 sq. mi.

Chartered 1748; regranted 1768.

Name origin: For Sir William Meredith, British parliamentarian and friend of NH Gov. Benning Wentworth (1696–1770); named 1768. Previously called Palmer's Town and New Salem.

New Hampton   Town
ZIP: 03256   **Lat:** 43-37-24 N **Long:** 71-38-00 W
Pop: 1,606 (1990); 1,249 (1980)   **Pop Density:** 43.8
Land: 36.7 sq. mi.; **Water:** 1.5 sq. mi.

Granted 1765.

Name origin: For Hampton, NH, from which early settlers had come; named 1777. Previously called Moultonborough Addition.

Sanbornton   Town
ZIP: 03269   **Lat:** 43-31-46 N **Long:** 71-36-03 W
Pop: 2,136 (1990); 1,679 (1980)   **Pop Density:** 45.0
Land: 47.5 sq. mi.; **Water:** 2.2 sq. mi.

Granted 1748; incorporated 1770.

Name origin: For John Sanborn, a friend of NH Gov. Benning Wentworth (1696–1770). Several Sanborns were among the early settlers. Originally named Sanborntown.

Tilton   Town
ZIP: 03276   **Lat:** 43-27-57 N **Long:** 71-34-10 W
Pop: 3,240 (1990); 3,387 (1980)   **Pop Density:** 284.2
Land: 11.4 sq. mi.; **Water:** 0.6 sq. mi.

Separated from Sanbornton in 1869.

Name origin: Named in 1869 by resident Charles Tilton, whose grandfather Nathaniel was an early settler. Previously called Sanburton Bridge and Bridge Village.

Carroll County
County Seat: Ossipee (ZIP: 03864)

Pop: 35,410 (1990); 27,931 (1980)   **Pop Density:** 37.9
Land: 933.9 sq. mi.; **Water:** 58.4 sq. mi.   **Area Code:** 603

On central eastern border of NH, north of Laconia; organized Dec 22, 1840 from Strafford, Coos, and Grafton counties.

Name origin: For Charles Carroll (1737–1832), signer of the Declaration of Independence, U.S. senator from MD, and founder of the Baltimore and Ohio Railroad.

Albany   Town
Lat: 43-57-42 N **Long:** 71-16-31 W
Pop: 536 (1990); 383 (1980)   **Pop Density:** 7.2
Land: 74.8 sq. mi.; **Water:** 0.3 sq. mi.

Chartered 1766; incorporated 1833.

Name origin: For Albany, NY, apparently in recognition of the opening of the railroad from New York City to Albany in 1833. Previously called Burton.

Bartlett   Town
ZIP: 03812   **Lat:** 44-04-46 N **Long:** 71-14-39 W
Pop: 2,290 (1990); 1,566 (1980)   **Pop Density:** 30.6
Land: 74.9 sq. mi.; **Water:** 0.0 sq. mi.

Name origin: For Dr. Josiah Bartlett (1729–95), NH governor and signer of the Declaration of Independence. Named 1790.

Brookfield   Town
Lat: 43-33-42 N **Long:** 71-05-10 W
Pop: 518 (1990); 385 (1980)   **Pop Density:** 22.6
Land: 22.9 sq. mi.; **Water:** 0.4 sq. mi.

Settled 1726. Incorporated 1794.

Name origin: For Brookfield, MA, former home of early settlers.

Chatham   Town
Lat: 44-09-27 N **Long:** 71-03-14 W
Pop: 268 (1990); 189 (1980)   **Pop Density:** 4.7
Land: 56.7 sq. mi.; **Water:** 0.5 sq. mi.

Granted 1767; regranted 1770.

Name origin: For William Pitt, first Earl of Chatham (1708–78), English supporter of colonial interests.

Conway   Town
ZIP: 03818   **Lat:** 44-00-21 N **Long:** 71-04-18 W
Pop: 7,940 (1990); 7,158 (1980)   **Pop Density:** 113.9
Land: 69.7 sq. mi.; **Water:** 2.1 sq. mi.

Name origin: For Englishman Henry Seymour Conway (1721–1793), who supported colonial interests prior to the American Revolution. Named in 1765 by Gov. Benning Wentworth (1696–1770).

Eaton   Town
Lat: 43-54-25 N **Long:** 71-02-51 W
Pop: 362 (1990); 256 (1980)   **Pop Density:** 14.8
Land: 24.4 sq. mi.; **Water:** 1.2 sq. mi.

Granted by Governor Benning Wentworth (1696–1770) in 1760.

Name origin: For Gov. Theophilus Eaton of CT (d. 1658), who was married to Anne Lloyd. The Lloyds were friends of the NH Wentworths.

Effingham   Town
Lat: 43-44-41 N **Long:** 71-02-43 W
Pop: 941 (1990); 599 (1980)   **Pop Density:** 24.4
Land: 38.5 sq. mi.; **Water:** 1.1 sq. mi.

Granted by Governor Benning Wentworth (1596–1770) in 1749; incorporated 1778.

Name origin: For the English Earls of Effingham, of the Howard family, related to the NH Wentworths by marriage.

Freedom   Town
ZIP: 03836   **Lat:** 43-49-28 N **Long:** 71-04-10 W
Pop: 935 (1990); 720 (1980)   **Pop Density:** 27.0
Land: 34.6 sq. mi.; **Water:** 3.3 sq. mi.

Incorporated 1831.

Name origin: In recognition of its separation and independence from North Effingham in 1831.

Hale's Location   Pop. Place
Lat: 44-02-18 N **Long:** 71-10-16 W
Pop: 0 (1990); 2 (1980)
Land: 2.4 sq. mi.; **Water:** 0.0 sq. mi.

Hart's Location   Town
Lat: 44-07-58 N **Long:** 71-21-46 W
Pop: 36 (1990); 27 (1980)   **Pop Density:** 1.9
Land: 19.0 sq. mi.; **Water:** 0.0 sq. mi.

Jackson   Town
ZIP: 03846   **Lat:** 44-11-12 N **Long:** 71-11-46 W
Pop: 678 (1990); 642 (1980)   **Pop Density:** 10.1
Land: 66.9 sq. mi.; **Water:** 0.0 sq. mi.

Granted 1771.

Name origin: Originally called New Madbury, then renamed Adams in 1800 to honor U.S. president John Adams (1735–1826). Renamed again in 1829 to honor newly inaugurated Pres. Andrew Jackson (1767–1845) through the influence of NH Gov. Benjamin Pierce, a staunch Jackson supporter.

Madison   Town
ZIP: 03849   **Lat:** 43-54-02 N **Long:** 71-09-17 W
Pop: 1,704 (1990); 1,051 (1980)   **Pop Density:** 44.0
Land: 38.7 sq. mi.; **Water:** 2.2 sq. mi.

Incorporated 1852.

Name origin: For James Madison (1751–1836), fourth U.S. president.

Moultonborough   Town
ZIP: 03254   **Lat:** 43-43-45 N **Long:** 71-22-33 W
Pop: 2,956 (1990); 2,206 (1980)   **Pop Density:** 49.4
Land: 59.8 sq. mi.; **Water:** 14.7 sq. mi.

Chartered 1763.

Name origin: For the Moulton family, among the original grantees.

North Conway
CDP
ZIP: 03860   **Lat:** 44-03-13 N **Long:** 71-07-36 W
Pop: 2,032 (1990); 2,104 (1980)   **Pop Density:** 534.7
Land: 3.8 sq. mi.; **Water:** 0.0 sq. mi.

Ossipee
Town
ZIP: 03864   **Lat:** 43-43-58 N **Long:** 71-09-02 W
Pop: 3,309 (1990); 2,465 (1980)   **Pop Density:** 46.5
Land: 71.2 sq. mi.; **Water:** 4.4 sq. mi.

Name origin: Named in 1785 for the Ossipee Indians, an Algonquian tribe who occupied the area. Previously called Wigwam Village and New Garden.

Sandwich
Town
                Lat: 43-50-20 N **Long:** 71-26-38 W
Pop: 1,066 (1990); 905 (1980)   **Pop Density:** 11.8
Land: 90.6 sq. mi.; **Water:** 2.9 sq. mi.

In east-central NH, north of Lake Winnipesaukee. Chartered 1763; incorporated 1770.

Name origin: For Sandwich, Kent, England.

Tamworth
Town
ZIP: 03886   **Lat:** 43-51-17 N **Long:** 71-16-28 W
Pop: 2,165 (1990); 1,672 (1980)   **Pop Density:** 36.1
Land: 59.9 sq. mi.; **Water:** 0.8 sq. mi.

Granted 1766.

Name origin: For British naval officer Adm. Washington Shirley, Viscount Tamworth, a friend of NH Gov. Benning Wentworth (1696–1770).

Tuftonboro
Town
                Lat: 43-40-42 N **Long:** 71-15-58 W
Pop: 1,842 (1990); 1,500 (1980)   **Pop Density:** 44.8
Land: 41.1 sq. mi.; **Water:** 8.9 sq. mi.

Incorporated 1795.

Name origin: Named 1750 for John Tufton Mason, who had owned all the town land.

Wakefield
Town
                Lat: 43-35-39 N **Long:** 71-00-36 W
Pop: 3,057 (1990); 2,237 (1980)   **Pop Density:** 77.8
Land: 39.3 sq. mi.; **Water:** 5.3 sq. mi.

Name origin: For the English ancestral home, in Yorkshire, of NH Gov. John Wentworth (1737–1820); named 1774.

Wolfeboro
Town
ZIP: 03894   **Lat:** 43-36-54 N **Long:** 71-10-10 W
Pop: 4,807 (1990); 3,968 (1980)   **Pop Density:** 99.5
Land: 48.3 sq. mi.; **Water:** 10.2 sq. mi.

Granted 1759.

Name origin: For British Gen. James Wolfe (1727–59), victor over the French at Quebec in 1759. Under his leadership NH colonial recruits had fought at Louisburg in 1758.

Cheshire County
County Seat: Keene (ZIP: 03431)

Pop: 70,121 (1990); 62,116 (1980)   **Pop Density:** 99.1
Land: 707.5 sq. mi.; **Water:** 21.7 sq. mi.   **Area Code:** 603

In southwestern corner of NH, west of Manchester; original county, organized Apr 29, 1769.

Name origin: For Cheshire county in England, site of one of the estates of the Wentworths; named by NH Gov. John Wentworth (1737–1820) on its establishment.

Alstead
Town
ZIP: 03602   **Lat:** 43-07-13 N **Long:** 72-18-27 W
Pop: 1,721 (1990); 1,461 (1980)   **Pop Density:** 44.2
Land: 38.9 sq. mi.; **Water:** 0.5 sq. mi.

Established 1735.

Name origin: For early German encyclopedia compiler Johann Heinrich Alsted (1588–1638), whose work had influenced NH Gov. Benning Wentworth (1696–1770) during his studies at Harvard. Name adopted in 1763. Previously called Number Four and Newton.

Chesterfield
Town
ZIP: 03443   **Lat:** 42-53-25 N **Long:** 72-27-20 W
Pop: 3,112 (1990); 2,561 (1980)   **Pop Density:** 68.2
Land: 45.6 sq. mi.; **Water:** 2.0 sq. mi.

Incorporated 1752.

Name origin: For Philip Stanhope (1694–1773), fourth Earl of Chesterfield, an English supporter of the colonies.

Dublin
Town
                Lat: 42-53-47 N **Long:** 72-04-11 W
Pop: 1,474 (1990); 1,303 (1980)   **Pop Density:** 52.6
Land: 28.0 sq. mi.; **Water:** 1.1 sq. mi.

Granted 1749; incorporated 1771.
Name origin: For Dublin, Ireland.

Fitzwilliam
Town
                Lat: 42-45-34 N **Long:** 72-09-03 W
Pop: 2,011 (1990); 1,795 (1980)   **Pop Density:** 58.1
Land: 34.6 sq. mi.; **Water:** 1.4 sq. mi.

Granted 1773.

Name origin: For William, fourth Earl Fitzwilliam, English cousin of NH Gov. Wentworth.

Gilsum
Town
ZIP: 03448   **Lat:** 43-02-25 N **Long:** 72-15-49 W
Pop: 745 (1990); 652 (1980)   **Pop Density:** 44.6
Land: 16.7 sq. mi.; **Water:** 0.0 sq. mi.

Granted 1752. Rechartered 1763.

Name origin: For the first syllables of the names of two founding families. Capt. Samuel Gilbert was a prominent early settler. His daughter, Elizabeth, married Clement Sumner, a relative of Benjamin Sumner, who was issued the charter of 1863.

Harrisville
Town
Lat: 42-56-38 N **Long:** 72-05-39 W
Pop: 981 (1990); 860 (1980) **Pop Density:** 52.5
Land: 18.7 sq. mi.; **Water:** 1.5 sq. mi.
Settled 1760.
Name origin: For the locally prominent Harris family; named in 1870. Previously called Twitchellville.

Hinsdale
Town
ZIP: 03451 **Lat:** 42-48-45 N **Long:** 72-30-19 W
Pop: 3,936 (1990); 3,631 (1980) **Pop Density:** 190.1
Land: 20.7 sq. mi.; **Water:** 2.1 sq. mi.
Incorporated 1753.
Name origin: For NH pioneer Ebenezer Hinsdale.

Jaffrey
Town
ZIP: 03452 **Lat:** 42-49-43 N **Long:** 72-03-37 W
Pop: 5,361 (1990); 4,349 (1980) **Pop Density:** 140.0
Land: 38.3 sq. mi.; **Water:** 1.7 sq. mi.
Granted 1736. Incorporated 1773.
Name origin: For George Jaffrey, a prominent citizen of Portsmouth and grant holder of town land.

Keene
City
ZIP: 03431 **Lat:** 42-57-00 N **Long:** 72-17-50 W
Pop: 22,430 (1990); 21,449 (1980) **Pop Density:** 601.3
Land: 37.3 sq. mi.; **Water:** 0.3 sq. mi. **Elev:** 486 ft.
In southwestern NH on the Ashuelot River, 39 mi. west of Manchester. Granted 1735; settled 1750; incorporated 1873.
Name origin: For Sir Benjamin Keene (1697–1757) of England, a businessman and diplomat.

Marlborough
Town
ZIP: 03455 **Lat:** 42-53-23 N **Long:** 72-10-54 W
Pop: 1,927 (1990); 1,846 (1980) **Pop Density:** 94.5
Land: 20.4 sq. mi.; **Water:** 0.2 sq. mi.
Incorporated 1776.
Name origin: For Marlborough, MA, former home of early settlers.

Marlow
Town
ZIP: 03456 **Lat:** 43-07-45 N **Long:** 72-12-51 W
Pop: 650 (1990); 542 (1980) **Pop Density:** 25.0
Land: 26.0 sq. mi.; **Water:** 0.5 sq. mi.
Name origin: For English scholar and playwright Christopher Marlowe (1564–93). Formerly called Addison.

Nelson
Town
Lat: 42-59-54 N **Long:** 72-07-21 W
Pop: 535 (1990); 442 (1980) **Pop Density:** 24.4
Land: 21.9 sq. mi.; **Water:** 1.4 sq. mi.
Laid out for settlement 1752.
Name origin: For British naval hero Lord Horatio Nelson (1758–1805); named 1814. Previously called Monadnock No. 6 and Packersfield.

Richmond
Town
Lat: 42-45-43 N **Long:** 72-16-07 W
Pop: 877 (1990); 518 (1980) **Pop Density:** 23.3
Land: 37.6 sq. mi.; **Water:** 0.2 sq. mi.
Settled 1735 after a grant by MA Gov. Jonathan Belcher (1682–1757) to descendants of veterans of the war with Canada in 1690. Incorporated by NH 1752.
Name origin: For Charles Lennox (1672–1723), Duke of Richmond, a friend of NH Gov. Benning Wentworth (1696–1770); named 1752. Previously called Sylvester Canada, one of the "Canada" towns.

Rindge
Town
ZIP: 03461 **Lat:** 42-45-01 N **Long:** 72-00-35 W
Pop: 4,941 (1990); 3,375 (1980) **Pop Density:** 132.8
Land: 37.2 sq. mi.; **Water:** 2.8 sq. mi.
Granted 1736; incorporated 1768.
Name origin: For Capt. Daniel Rindge, who had settled his family there from Rowley, MA. Previously called Monadnock No. 1.

Roxbury
Town
Lat: 42-57-22 N **Long:** 72-11-36 W
Pop: 248 (1990); 190 (1980) **Pop Density:** 20.8
Land: 11.9 sq. mi.; **Water:** 0.3 sq. mi.
Incorporated 1812.
Name origin: For Roxbury, now a section of Boston, MA, then a village that early settlers had come from.

Stoddard
Town
ZIP: 03464 **Lat:** 43-04-33 N **Long:** 72-07-04 W
Pop: 622 (1990); 482 (1980) **Pop Density:** 12.2
Land: 50.9 sq. mi.; **Water:** 2.1 sq. mi.
Granted 1752; incorporated 1774.
Name origin: For Col. Sampson Stoddard, a surveyor and early landowner in the region. Name given in 1774 by NH Gov. John Wentworth (1737–1820). Previously called Monadnock No. 7 and Limerick.

Sullivan
Town
Lat: 43-01-13 N **Long:** 72-12-51 W
Pop: 706 (1990); 585 (1980) **Pop Density:** 38.2
Land: 18.5 sq. mi.; **Water:** 0.2 sq. mi.
Incorporated 1787.
Name origin: For Revolutionary War Gen. John Sullivan (1740–95).

Surry
Town
Lat: 43-01-20 N **Long:** 72-19-29 W
Pop: 667 (1990); 656 (1980) **Pop Density:** 42.8
Land: 15.6 sq. mi.; **Water:** 0.3 sq. mi.
Chartered 1769.
Name origin: For Charles Howard, Earl of Surrey (1720–86); named by NH Gov. John Wentworth (1737–1820).

Swanzey
Town
ZIP: 03431 **Lat:** 42-52-13 N **Long:** 72-18-00 W
Pop: 6,236 (1990); 5,183 (1980) **Pop Density:** 138.6
Land: 45.0 sq. mi.; **Water:** 0.4 sq. mi.
Chartered 1753.
Name origin: For Swansea, MA, with spelling change. Name bestowed on charter by Gov. Benning Wentworth (1696–1770) in 1753, at the suggestion of Gov. Brenton of RI, who owned land in NH and was a major landowner in Swansea, MA, as well.

Troy
Town
ZIP: 03465 **Lat:** 42-49-44 N **Long:** 72-11-26 W
Pop: 2,097 (1990); 2,131 (1980) **Pop Density:** 120.5
Land: 17.4 sq. mi.; **Water:** 0.2 sq. mi.
Separated from Marlborough in 1815; incorporated 1816.
Name origin: For Troy, NY, at the suggestion of Capt. Benjamin Mann, a close friend of NH Gov. Gilman. Mann's daughter Betsy was married to Samuel Wilson (1766–1854), a prominent citizen of Troy, NY, recognized as the original "Uncle Sam."

Walpole
Town
Lat: 43-04-51 N **Long:** 72-24-32 W
Pop: 3,210 (1990); 3,188 (1980)   **Pop Density:** 90.2
Land: 35.6 sq. mi.; **Water:** 1.1 sq. mi.

Settled 1736; granted 1752; regranted 1761.

Name origin: For Sir Robert Walpole (1676–1745), British statesman, an associate of NH Gov. Benning Wentworth (1696–1770); named 1761. Previously called Bellowstown.

Westmoreland
Town
ZIP: 03467   **Lat:** 42-58-15 N **Long:** 72-25-32 W
Pop: 1,596 (1990); 1,452 (1980)   **Pop Density:** 44.5
Land: 35.9 sq. mi.; **Water:** 1.0 sq. mi.

Established 1735; granted 1752.

Name origin: For John Fane, seventh Earl of Westmoreland, a relative of NH Gov. Benning Wentworth (1696–1770); named 1752.

West Swanzey
CDP
Lat: 42-52-14 N **Long:** 72-19-20 W
Pop: 1,055 (1990); 1,022 (1980)   **Pop Density:** 405.8
Land: 2.6 sq. mi.; **Water:** 0.0 sq. mi.

Winchester
Town
ZIP: 03470   **Lat:** 42-47-09 N **Long:** 72-24-07 W
Pop: 4,038 (1990); 3,465 (1980)   **Pop Density:** 73.6
Land: 54.9 sq. mi.; **Water:** 0.6 sq. mi.

Settled 1733; incorporated 1753.

Name origin: For Charles Paulet, Marquess of Winchester; named in his honor by NH Gov. Benning Wentworth (1696–1770). Previously known as Arlington.

Coos County
County Seat: Lancaster (ZIP: 03584)

Pop: 34,828 (1990); 35,147 (1980)   **Pop Density:** 19.3
Land: 1800.6 sq. mi.; **Water:** 31.1 sq. mi.   **Area Code:** 603

In northern NH; organized Dec 24, 1803 from Grafton County.

Name origin: From the Pennacook Indian word *cohos* 'pine tree' or 'place where pines grow.'

Atkinson and Gilmanton Academy Grant
Pop. Place
Lat: 44-58-16 N **Long:** 71-07-52 W
Pop: 0 (1990)
Land: 19.7 sq. mi.; **Water:** 0.0 sq. mi.

Beans Grant
Pop. Place
Lat: 44-13-33 N **Long:** 71-22-55 W
Pop: 0 (1990)
Land: 9.7 sq. mi.; **Water:** 0.0 sq. mi.

Beans Purchase
Pop. Place
Lat: 44-17-51 N **Long:** 71-04-46 W
Pop: 0 (1990)
Land: 65.3 sq. mi.; **Water:** 0.0 sq. mi.

Berlin
City
ZIP: 03570   **Lat:** 44-29-22 N **Long:** 71-15-18 W
Pop: 11,824 (1990); 13,084 (1980)   **Pop Density:** 191.6
Land: 61.7 sq. mi.; **Water:** 0.7 sq. mi.   **Elev:** 1010 ft.

In northern NH in the White Mountains region, at the confluence of Dead and Androscoggin rivers, 16 mi. south of Umbagoy Lake.

Name origin: For Berlin, Germany.

Cambridge
Township
Lat: 44-39-35 N **Long:** 71-06-33 W
Pop: 0 (1990); 5 (1980)
Land: 50.8 sq. mi.; **Water:** 0.6 sq. mi.

Carroll
Town
Lat: 44-18-20 N **Long:** 71-29-39 W
Pop: 528 (1990); 647 (1980)   **Pop Density:** 10.5
Land: 50.2 sq. mi.; **Water:** 0.0 sq. mi.

Chartered 1772 as Bretton Woods. Site of the Bretton Woods conference in July 1944, which led to the creation of the International Monetary Fund.

Name origin: For Charles Carroll (1737–1832) of Carrollton, MD, signer of the Declaration of Independence. Called Bretton Woods from 1772; renamed 1832.

Chandlers Purchase
Pop. Place
Lat: 44-15-51 N **Long:** 71-21-35 W
Pop: 0 (1990)
Land: 2.1 sq. mi.; **Water:** 0.0 sq. mi.

Clarksville
Town
Lat: 45-00-59 N **Long:** 71-18-31 W
Pop: 232 (1990); 262 (1980)   **Pop Density:** 3.9
Land: 60.2 sq. mi.; **Water:** 1.9 sq. mi.

Incorporated 1853. Once part of a tract granted to Dartmouth College.

Name origin: For early developer Benjamin Clark of Boston.

Colebrook
Town
ZIP: 03576   **Lat:** 44-53-45 N **Long:** 71-24-33 W
Pop: 2,444 (1990); 2,459 (1980)   **Pop Density:** 59.6
Land: 41.0 sq. mi.; **Water:** 0.0 sq. mi.

Granted 1762; regranted 1770. Incorporated 1896.

Name origin: For Sir George Colebrooke, chairman of the East India Company; named 1770. Original name Dryden for English author John Dryden (1631–1700).

Columbia
Town
ZIP: 03576   **Lat:** 44-50-43 N **Long:** 71-28-04 W
Pop: 661 (1990); 673 (1980)   **Pop Density:** 10.9
Land: 60.9 sq. mi.; **Water:** 0.1 sq. mi.   **Elev:** 1014 ft.

Originally chartered 1762; regranted in 1770.

Name origin: Honoring Christopher Columbus (1451–1506) in 1811 during a period of national pride preceding the War of 1812. Name suggested by Gov. John Langdon (1741–1819). Called Preston upon incorporation for Richard Graham, Viscount Preston of Scotland. Renamed Cockburntown in 1770 for Sir James Cockburn.

Crawfords Purchase
Pop. Place
Lat: 44-15-17 N Long: 71-23-46 W
Pop: 0 (1990)
Land: 8.2 sq. mi.; **Water:** 0.0 sq. mi.

Cutts Grant
Pop. Place
Lat: 44-13-42 N Long: 71-18-38 W
Pop: 0 (1990)
Land: 11.4 sq. mi.; **Water:** 0.0 sq. mi.

Dalton
Town
Lat: 44-22-56 N Long: 71-41-04 W
Pop: 827 (1990); 672 (1980)   **Pop Density:** 30.1
Land: 27.5 sq. mi.; **Water:** 0.8 sq. mi.
Name origin: Named in 1784 for Tristram Dalton, noted New England merchant.

Dixs Grant
Pop. Place
Lat: 44-55-57 N Long: 71-11-27 W
Pop: 0 (1990)
Land: 20.2 sq. mi.; **Water:** 0.0 sq. mi.

Dixville
Township
ZIP: 03576   Lat: 44-52-12 N Long: 71-15-44 W
Pop: 50 (1990); 36 (1980)   **Pop Density:** 1.0
Land: 48.9 sq. mi.; **Water:** 0.1 sq. mi.
An unincorporated community.
Name origin: For Col. Timothy Dix, a major landowner in the area.

Dixville Notch
Pop. Place
ZIP: 03576
Part of Dixville Township. Noted as the first place in the U.S. from which vote totals are reported in presidential elections.
Name origin: A part of Dixville Township near a notch or gap in the mountains.

Dummer
Town
Lat: 44-40-17 N Long: 71-15-10 W
Pop: 327 (1990); 390 (1980)   **Pop Density:** 6.8
Land: 47.8 sq. mi.; **Water:** 1.3 sq. mi.
Granted 1773; incorporated 1848.
Name origin: For Gov. William Dummer (1677–1761) of MA, noted for settling a peace treaty with the Indians.

Errol
Town
ZIP: 03579   Lat: 44-46-49 N Long: 71-07-53 W
Pop: 292 (1990); 313 (1980)   **Pop Density:** 4.8
Land: 61.0 sq. mi.; **Water:** 8.6 sq. mi.
Chartered 1774; incorporated 1836.
Name origin: For James Hay, fifteenth Earl of Erroll in Scotland, as proposed by Gov. John Wentworth (1737–1820).

Ervings Location
Pop. Place
Lat: 44-47-44 N Long: 71-20-42 W
Pop: 0 (1990)
Land: 3.7 sq. mi.; **Water:** 0.0 sq. mi.

Gorham
Town
ZIP: 03581   Lat: 44-23-51 N Long: 71-12-13 W
Pop: 3,173 (1990); 3,322 (1980)   **Pop Density:** 99.5
Land: 31.9 sq. mi.; **Water:** 0.4 sq. mi.
Chartered 1770; incorporated 1836.
Name origin: Proposed in 1836 by resident Sylvester Davis, formerly of Gorham, ME, and a relative of the Gorham family, who founded the ME town.

Greens Grant
Pop. Place
Lat: 44-18-18 N Long: 71-13-15 W
Pop: 0 (1990)
Land: 3.7 sq. mi.; **Water:** 0.0 sq. mi.

Groveton
CDP
ZIP: 03582   Lat: 44-35-57 N Long: 71-31-05 W
Pop: 1,255 (1990); 1,389 (1980)   **Pop Density:** 896.4
Land: 1.4 sq. mi.; **Water:** 0.0 sq. mi.

Hadleys Purchase
Pop. Place
Lat: 44-06-01 N Long: 71-19-44 W
Pop: 0 (1990)
Land: 7.4 sq. mi.; **Water:** 0.0 sq. mi.

Jefferson
Town
ZIP: 03583   Lat: 44-23-33 N Long: 71-28-15 W
Pop: 965 (1990); 803 (1980)   **Pop Density:** 19.2
Land: 50.2 sq. mi.; **Water:** 0.2 sq. mi.
Granted 1765.
Name origin: Originally called Dartmouth; name changed in 1796 to honor Thomas Jefferson (1743–1826) before his presidency at the instigation of Col. Joseph Whipple, who greatly developed the town and was an ardent Jefferson supporter.

Kilkenny
Township
Lat: 44-29-42 N Long: 71-23-34 W
Pop: 0 (1990)
Land: 25.6 sq. mi.; **Water:** 0.0 sq. mi.

Lancaster
Town
ZIP: 03584   Lat: 44-28-31 N Long: 71-32-54 W
Pop: 3,522 (1990); 3,401 (1980)   **Pop Density:** 70.3
Land: 50.1 sq. mi.; **Water:** 1.2 sq. mi.
Granted 1763; county seat 1803.
Name origin: For Lancaster, MA, home of early settler Joseph Wilder.

Low and Burbanks Grant
Pop. Place
Lat: 44-19-00 N Long: 71-20-30 W
Pop: 0 (1990); 1 (1980)
Land: 26.1 sq. mi.; **Water:** 0.0 sq. mi.

Martins Location
Pop. Place
Lat: 44-19-38 N Long: 71-13-00 W
Pop: 0 (1990)
Land: 3.8 sq. mi.; **Water:** 0.0 sq. mi.

Milan
Town
ZIP: 03588   Lat: 44-33-46 N Long: 71-13-31 W
Pop: 1,295 (1990); 1,013 (1980)   **Pop Density:** 21.0
Land: 61.7 sq. mi.; **Water:** 0.5 sq. mi.
Chartered 1771.
Name origin: Named in 1824 at the order of NH Gov. Levi Woodbury (1789–1851) to honor Milan Harris of Harrisville, NH, a friend of the governor from a noted family in the wool-milling industry. Originally called Paulsbourg after Paul Wentworth, cousin of Gov. John Wentworth (1737–1820).

Millsfield
Township
Lat: 44-48-07 N Long: 71-16-33 W
Pop: 21 (1990); 7 (1980)   **Pop Density:** 0.5
Land: 45.0 sq. mi.; **Water:** 0.3 sq. mi.

Northumberland
Town
Lat: 44-33-56 N Long: 71-31-21 W
Pop: 2,492 (1990); 2,520 (1980)   Pop Density: 68.8
Land: 36.2 sq. mi.; Water: 0.8 sq. mi.
Settled in the 1750s. Includes unincorporated town of Groveton.
Name origin: For Hugh Smithson (1715–86), Earl Percy and first Duke of Northumberland, a supporter of colonial interests. Named 1771 at the suggestion of NH Gov. John Wentworth (1737–1820). Previously called Stonington.

Odell
Township
Lat: 44-44-51 N Long: 71-22-49 W
Pop: 0 (1990)
Land: 44.5 sq. mi.; Water: 0.7 sq. mi.

Pinkhams Grant
Pop. Place
Lat: 44-15-56 N Long: 71-14-52 W
Pop: 11 (1990); 30 (1980)   Pop Density: 2.9
Land: 3.8 sq. mi.; Water: 0.0 sq. mi.

Pittsburg
Town
ZIP: 03592   Lat: 45-08-55 N Long: 71-13-53 W
Pop: 901 (1990); 780 (1980)   Pop Density: 3.2
Land: 282.3 sq. mi.; Water: 9.1 sq. mi.
Largest town in area in NH, and the furthest north. Borders on Maine and Quebec, Canada, and, along the 45th parallel, the point at which NH, VT, and Quebec meet. Within its area are the lakes that are the source of the Connecticut River. As Indian Stream Republic for about four years from 1832, citizens claimed it an independent republic with a constitution. Incorporated as a town in NH in 1840.
Name origin: Named in 1840 to honor English statesman William Pitt. Previously called Indian Stream Territory.

Randolph
Town
Lat: 44-24-00 N Long: 71-19-18 W
Pop: 371 (1990); 274 (1980)   Pop Density: 7.9
Land: 47.1 sq. mi.; Water: 0.0 sq. mi.
Chartered 1772.
Name origin: Named 1824 for Sen. John Randolph (1773–1833) of VA. Originally called Durand.

Sargents Purchase
Pop. Place
Lat: 44-15-04 N Long: 71-18-29 W
Pop: 0 (1990); 1 (1980)
Land: 25.9 sq. mi.; Water: 0.0 sq. mi.

Second College Grant
Pop. Place
Lat: 44-54-03 N Long: 71-07-28 W
Pop: 0 (1990); 2 (1980)
Land: 41.6 sq. mi.; Water: 0.0 sq. mi.

Shelburne
Town
Lat: 44-23-50 N Long: 71-04-31 W
Pop: 437 (1990); 318 (1980)   Pop Density: 9.1
Land: 47.9 sq. mi.; Water: 0.9 sq. mi.
Chartered 1769; incorporated 1820.
Name origin: For William Fitzmaurice, Earl of Shelburne (1737–1805), a staunch ally of the colonies in the days before the Revolutionary War.

Stark
Town
Lat: 44-36-02 N Long: 71-24-23 W
Pop: 518 (1990); 470 (1980)   Pop Density: 8.8
Land: 59.1 sq. mi.; Water: 0.5 sq. mi.
Granted 1774.
Name origin: Named in 1832 for NH Revolutionary War hero Gen. John Stark (1728–1822). Originally called Percy in 1774.

Stewartstown
Town
Lat: 44-57-41 N Long: 71-24-26 W
Pop: 1,048 (1990); 943 (1980)   Pop Density: 22.6
Land: 46.4 sq. mi.; Water: 0.4 sq. mi.
Granted 1770; incorporated 1799.
Name origin: For Sir John Stuart, Lord Bute, who was influential at the Court of King George III (1738–1820). Spelling adopted on incorporation, reflecting a Scottish spelling form.

Stratford
Town
Lat: 44-44-21 N Long: 71-31-50 W
Pop: 927 (1990); 989 (1980)   Pop Density: 11.6
Land: 79.9 sq. mi.; Water: 0.1 sq. mi.
Granted 1762.
Name origin: Named in 1773 by early settlers for Stratford, CT.

Success
Township
Lat: 44-31-37 N Long: 71-04-48 W
Pop: 0 (1990)
Land: 58.8 sq. mi.; Water: 0.5 sq. mi.

Thompson and Meserves Purchase
Pop. Place
Lat: 44-18-17 N Long: 71-17-26 W
Pop: 0 (1990); 2 (1980)
Land: 18.5 sq. mi.; Water: 0.0 sq. mi.

Wentworth (or Wentworth Location)
Town
Lat: 44-50-22 N Long: 71-08-06 W
Pop: 53 (1990); 49 (1980)   Pop Density: 2.8
Land: 18.8 sq. mi.; Water: 0.7 sq. mi.
Incorporated 1881.
Name origin: For the Wentworth family, prominent in colonial NH.

Whitefield
Town
ZIP: 03598   Lat: 44-22-30 N Long: 71-35-22 W
Pop: 1,909 (1990); 1,681 (1980)   Pop Density: 55.7
Land: 34.3 sq. mi.; Water: 0.4 sq. mi.
Granted July 4, 1774, the last town chartered under the English provincial government. Incorporated 1804.
Name origin: For the English evangelist, George Whitefield.

Grafton County
County Seat: Woodsville (ZIP: 03785)

Pop: 74,929 (1990); 65,806 (1980)   **Pop Density:** 43.7
Land: 1713.5 sq. mi.; **Water:** 36.8 sq. mi. **Area Code:** 603

On central western border of NH; original county, organized Apr 29, 1769.

Name origin: For Augustus Henry Fitzroy (1735–1811), 3rd Duke of Grafton, an English parliamentarian who supported American colonial interests.

Alexandria
Town
Lat: 43-36-57 N **Long:** 71-49-43 W
Pop: 1,190 (1990); 706 (1980) **Pop Density:** 27.7
Land: 43.0 sq. mi.; **Water:** 0.1 sq. mi.

Granted 1753.

Name origin: For Alexandria, VA, starting point of the French and Indian War.

Ashland
Town
ZIP: 03217 **Lat:** 43-43-07 N **Long:** 71-37-49 W
Pop: 1,915 (1990); 1,807 (1980) **Pop Density:** 169.5
Land: 11.3 sq. mi.; **Water:** 0.5 sq. mi.

Incorporated 1868.

Name origin: For the KY estate of Henry Clay (1777–1852).

Bath
Town
ZIP: 03740 **Lat:** 44-10-53 N **Long:** 71-59-13 W
Pop: 784 (1990); 761 (1980) **Pop Density:** 20.5
Land: 38.2 sq. mi.; **Water:** 0.5 sq. mi.

Chartered 1761.

Name origin: For English statesman William Pulteney, first Earl of Bath (1684–1764).

Benton
Town
Lat: 44-03-16 N **Long:** 71-53-24 W
Pop: 330 (1990); 333 (1980) **Pop Density:** 6.8
Land: 48.2 sq. mi.; **Water:** 0.2 sq. mi.

Granted 1764; incorporated 1840.

Name origin: For Thomas Hart Benton (1782–1858), U.S. senator from MO; so named on incorporation at the suggestion of Gov. Isaac Hill, a friend of Benton's. Originally called Coventry.

Bethlehem
Town
ZIP: 03574 **Lat:** 44-15-25 N **Long:** 71-35-08 W
Pop: 2,033 (1990); 1,784 (1980) **Pop Density:** 22.4
Land: 90.9 sq. mi.; **Water:** 0.1 sq. mi.

Incorporated Dec 27, 1799.

Name origin: For the biblical town, birthplace of Jesus Christ.

Bridgewater
Town
Lat: 43-40-34 N **Long:** 71-41-23 W
Pop: 796 (1990); 606 (1980) **Pop Density:** 37.4
Land: 21.3 sq. mi.; **Water:** 0.2 sq. mi.

Incorporated 1788.

Name origin: For Bridgewater, MA, former home of founding families.

Bristol
Town
ZIP: 03222 **Lat:** 43-37-26 N **Long:** 71-44-04 W
Pop: 2,537 (1990); 2,198 (1980) **Pop Density:** 146.6
Land: 17.3 sq. mi.; **Water:** 4.9 sq. mi.

Incorporated 1819.

Name origin: For Bristol, England, because the town had a fine sand useful in making ceramics similar to the variety made there.

Campton
Town
Lat: 43-49-37 N **Long:** 71-38-52 W
Pop: 2,377 (1990); 1,694 (1980) **Pop Density:** 45.8
Land: 51.9 sq. mi.; **Water:** 0.6 sq. mi.

Granted 1761.

Name origin: Named by Gov. Benning Wentworth (1696–1770) for his business friend Spencer Compton (1673?–1743), Earl of Wilmington. Its spelling was changed later.

Canaan
Town
ZIP: 03741 **Lat:** 43-40-33 N **Long** 72-02-49 W
Pop: 3,045 (1990); 2,456 (1980) **Pop Density:** 57.2
Land: 53.2 sq. mi.; **Water:** 1.8 sq. mi.

Chartered 1761.

Name origin: For Canaan, CT.

Dorchester
Town
Lat: 43-46-02 N **Long:** 71-59-36 W
Pop: 392 (1990); 244 (1980) **Pop Density:** 8.8
Land: 44.7 sq. mi.; **Water:** 0.5 sq. mi.

Established 1761.

Name origin: For Dorchester, England.

Easton
Town
Lat: 44-07-24 N **Long:** 71-48-04 W
Pop: 223 (1990); 124 (1980) **Pop Density:** 7.1
Land: 31.2 sq. mi.; **Water:** 0.0 sq. mi.

Incorporated 1867.

Name origin: A corruption and respelling based on its previous names, Eastern Landaff and Eastern.

Ellsworth
Town
Lat: 43-54-52 N **Long:** 71-46-16 W
Pop: 74 (1990); 53 (1980) **Pop Density:** 3.5
Land: 21.4 sq. mi.; **Water:** 0.1 sq. mi.

Granted 1769; incorporated 1802.

Name origin: Given on incorporation for Chief Justice Oliver Ellsworth (1745–1807) of CT, who negotiated the treaty with France that led to the Louisiana Purchase. Until 1802 called Trecothick for Barlow Trecothick, Lord Mayor of London.

Enfield
Town
ZIP: 03748 **Lat:** 43-35-46 N **Long:** 72-06-59 W
Pop: 3,979 (1990); 3,175 (1980) **Pop Density:** 98.7
Land: 40.3 sq. mi.; **Water:** 2.8 sq. mi.

Name origin: For Enfield, CT, the former home of settlers. Originally called Relhan.

Franconia   Town
ZIP: 03580   **Lat:** 44-09-38 N   **Long:** 71-39-33 W
Pop: 811 (1990); 743 (1980)   **Pop Density:** 12.3
Land: 65.9 sq. mi.; **Water:** 0.1 sq. mi.
Granted 1764.
Name origin: Named in 1782 for the Franconian Alps in Germany.

Grafton   Town
ZIP: 03240   **Lat:** 43-34-23 N   **Long:** 71-58-28 W
Pop: 923 (1990); 739 (1980)   **Pop Density:** 22.1
Land: 41.8 sq. mi.; **Water:** 0.8 sq. mi.
Chartered 1761.
Name origin: For Augustus Henry Fitzroy (1735–1811), Duke of Grafton.

Groton   Town
Lat: 43-44-27 N   **Long:** 71-51-23 W
Pop: 318 (1990); 255 (1980)   **Pop Density:** 7.8
Land: 40.8 sq. mi.; **Water:** 0.0 sq. mi.
Settled after the Revolutionary War.
Name origin: For Groton, MA.

Hanover   Town
ZIP: 03755   **Lat:** 43-43-10 N   **Long:** 72-11-38 W
Pop: 9,212 (1990); 9,119 (1980)   **Pop Density:** 187.6
Land: 49.1 sq. mi.; **Water:** 1.1 sq. mi.
Established 1761.
Name origin: For Hanover parish in eastern CT.

Haverhill   Town
ZIP: 03765   **Lat:** 44-04-36 N   **Long:** 71-59-49 W
Pop: 4,164 (1990); 3,445 (1980)   **Pop Density:** 81.5
Land: 51.1 sq. mi.; **Water:** 1.3 sq. mi.
Granted 1763; county seat 1773.
Name origin: For Haverhill, MA, former home of early settlers.

Hebron   Town
ZIP: 03241   **Lat:** 43-41-31 N   **Long:** 71-47-23 W
Pop: 386 (1990); 349 (1980)   **Pop Density:** 23.0
Land: 16.8 sq. mi.; **Water:** 2.1 sq. mi.
Originally part of Groton.
Name origin: Named by early settlers for Hebron, CT.

Holderness   Town
Lat: 43-44-41 N   **Long:** 71-35-58 W
Pop: 1,694 (1990); 1,586 (1980)   **Pop Density:** 55.5
Land: 30.5 sq. mi.; **Water:** 5.3 sq. mi.
Granted in 1751.
Name origin: For Robert Darcy, 4th Earl of Holderness, to whom it was granted.

Landaff   Town
Lat: 44-09-04 N   **Long:** 71-52-32 W
Pop: 350 (1990); 266 (1980)   **Pop Density:** 12.3
Land: 28.4 sq. mi.; **Water:** 0.1 sq. mi.
Granted 1764; incorporated 1774.
Name origin: For the Bishop of Llandaff, a bishopric in Cardiff, Wales. The bishop was chaplain to King George III (1738–1820). Welsh "Ll" was simplified.

Lebanon   City
ZIP: 03766   **Lat:** 43-38-06 N   **Long:** 72-15-15 W
Pop: 12,183 (1990); 11,134 (1980)   **Pop Density:** 301.6
Land: 40.4 sq. mi.; **Water:** 1.0 sq. mi.   **Elev:** 595 ft.
In western NH, 20 mi. north of Claremont. Established 1761; incorporated 1957.
Name origin: Named by early settlers for Lebanon, CT.

Lincoln   Town
ZIP: 03251   **Lat:** 44-05-37 N   **Long:** 71-34-40 W
Pop: 1,229 (1990); 1,313 (1980)   **Pop Density:** 9.4
Land: 130.7 sq. mi.; **Water:** 0.2 sq. mi.
Name origin: Named in 1764 for Henry Clinton, 9th Earl of Lincoln.

Lisbon   Town
ZIP: 03585   **Lat:** 44-14-40 N   **Long:** 71-51-55 W
Pop: 1,664 (1990); 1,517 (1980)   **Pop Density:** 62.8
Land: 26.5 sq. mi.; **Water:** 0.2 sq. mi.
Granted 1763.
Name origin: Named in 1824 for Lisbon, Portugal.

Littleton   Town
ZIP: 03561   **Lat:** 44-19-23 N   **Long:** 71-48-23 W
Pop: 5,827 (1990); 5,558 (1980)   **Pop Density:** 116.1
Land: 50.2 sq. mi.; **Water:** 3.9 sq. mi.
Granted 1770.
Name origin: Named in 1784 for Col. Moses Little, a Revolutionary War officer.

Livermore   Town
Lat: 44-01-05 N   **Long:** 71-27-11 W
Pop: 0 (1990)
Land: 63.6 sq. mi.; **Water:** 0.2 sq. mi.

Lyman   Town
Lat: 44-16-01 N   **Long:** 71-56-19 W
Pop: 388 (1990); 281 (1980)   **Pop Density:** 13.6
Land: 28.5 sq. mi.; **Water:** 0.3 sq. mi.
Granted 1761.
Name origin: For English general Phineas Lyman.

Lyme   Town
ZIP: 03768   **Lat:** 43-47-58 N   **Long:** 72-06-58 W
Pop: 1,496 (1990); 1,289 (1980)   **Pop Density:** 27.8
Land: 53.9 sq. mi.; **Water:** 1.1 sq. mi.
Chartered 1761.
Name origin: For Lyme Regis in England.

Monroe   Town
ZIP: 03771   **Lat:** 44-17-55 N   **Long:** 72-00-41 W
Pop: 746 (1990); 619 (1980)   **Pop Density:** 33.3
Land: 22.4 sq. mi.; **Water:** 1.5 sq. mi.
Incorporated 1854.
Name origin: For James Monroe (1758–1831), fifth U.S. president.

Orange   Town
Lat: 43-39-05 N   **Long:** 71-56-42 W
Pop: 237 (1990); 197 (1980)   **Pop Density:** 10.2
Land: 23.2 sq. mi.; **Water:** 0.0 sq. mi.
Granted 1769.
Name origin: For the nearby deposits of orange-yellow ochre. Originally called Cardigan.

Orford
Town
ZIP: 03777   **Lat:** 43-54-01 N   **Long:** 72-04-15 W
Pop: 1,008 (1990); 928 (1980)   **Pop Density:** 21.6
Land: 46.7 sq. mi.; **Water:** 1.4 sq. mi.
Chartered 1761.
Name origin: For Robert Walpole (1676–1745), Earl of Orford.

Piermont
Town
ZIP: 03779   **Lat:** 43-59-06 N   **Long:** 72-01-24 W
Pop: 624 (1990); 507 (1980)   **Pop Density:** 16.2
Land: 38.5 sq. mi.; **Water:** 1.3 sq. mi.
Name origin: Named in 1764 for the Piedmont in the Italian Alps; the spelling was changed to Piermont, but the original idea was to compare the natural beauty of the two areas.

Plymouth
Town
ZIP: 03264   **Lat:** 43-44-32 N   **Long:** 71-43-02 W
Pop: 5,811 (1990); 5,094 (1980)   **Pop Density:** 205.3
Land: 28.3 sq. mi.; **Water:** 0.3 sq. mi.
Granted 1763.
Name origin: For Plymouth, MA.

Rumney
Town
ZIP: 03266   **Lat:** 43-49-28 N   **Long:** 71-48-40 W
Pop: 1,446 (1990); 1,212 (1980)   **Pop Density:** 34.5
Land: 41.9 sq. mi.; **Water:** 0.6 sq. mi.
Granted 1761.
Name origin: For Robert Marsham, 2nd Baron of Rumney.

Sugar Hill
Town
     Lat: 44-13-17 N   **Long:** 71-48-04 W
Pop: 464 (1990); 397 (1980)   **Pop Density:** 27.1
Land: 17.1 sq. mi.; **Water:** 0.1 sq. mi.
NH's youngest town. Incorporated 1962.
Name origin: For a large grove of sugar maples.

Thornton
Town
     Lat: 43-55-25 N   **Long:** 71-37-55 W
Pop: 1,505 (1990); 952 (1980)   **Pop Density:** 29.9
Land: 50.4 sq. mi.; **Water:** 0.4 sq. mi.
Established 1763.
Name origin: For NH surgeon Dr. Matthew Thornton

(1714?–1803), later a signer of the Declaration of Independence.

Warren
Town
ZIP: 03279   **Lat:** 43-57-03 N   **Long:** 71-53-22 W
Pop: 820 (1990); 650 (1980)   **Pop Density:** 16.8
Land: 48.7 sq. mi.; **Water:** 0.4 sq. mi.
Granted 1764.
Name origin: For Adm. Sir Peter Warren, best known for his role in the capture of the French fortress of Louisburg in 1745.

Waterville Valley
Town
     Lat: 43-54-49 N   **Long:** 71-27-16 W
Pop: 151 (1990); 180 (1980)   **Pop Density:** 2.3
Land: 64.9 sq. mi.; **Water:** 0.0 sq. mi.
Settled 1760s; incorporated 1829.
Name origin: Originally called Waterville for its location between the Mad and Swift rivers; "Valley" was added to the name in 1967.

Wentworth
Town
ZIP: 03282   **Lat:** 43-51-38 N   **Long:** 71-55-55 W
Pop: 630 (1990); 527 (1980)   **Pop Density:** 15.1
Land: 41.7 sq. mi.; **Water:** 0.3 sq. mi.
Chartered 1766.
Name origin: For colonial governors John (1737–1820) and Benning (1696–1770) Wentworth.

Woodstock
Town
     Lat: 43-58-40 N   **Long:** 71-44-09 W
Pop: 1,167 (1990); 1,008 (1980)   **Pop Density:** 19.9
Land: 58.7 sq. mi.; **Water:** 0.5 sq. mi.
Established 1763.
Name origin: For Woodstock, England. Originally called Pegline.

Woodsville
CDP
ZIP: 03785   **Lat:** 44-08-43 N   **Long:** 72-01-44 W
Pop: 1,122 (1990); 1,195 (1980)   **Pop Density:** 1246.7
Land: 0.9 sq. mi.; **Water:** 0.0 sq. mi.

Hillsborough County
County Seat: Nashua (ZIP: 03060)

Pop: 336,073 (1990); 276,608 (1980)   **Pop Density:** 383.4
Land: 876.5 sq. mi.; **Water:** 15.8 sq. mi.   **Area Code:** 603
On central southern border of NH, south of Concord; original county, organized Apr 29, 1769.
Name origin: For Wills Hill (1718–93), 1st Earl of Hillsborough, English secretary of state for the colonies (1768–72). Also spelled _Hillsboro_. Some also note that one of the original grantees of land was Col. John Hill of MA.

Amherst
Town
ZIP: 03031   **Lat:** 42-52-08 N   **Long:** 71-36-16 W
Pop: 9,068 (1990); 8,243 (1980)   **Pop Density:** 264.4
Land: 34.3 sq. mi.; **Water:** 0.5 sq. mi.
Granted 1728.
Name origin: For Lord Jeffrey Amherst (1717–97), British commander in the French and Indian War.

Antrim
Town
ZIP: 03440   **Lat:** 43-03-15 N   **Long:** 71-59-20 W
Pop: 2,360 (1990); 2,208 (1980)   **Pop Density:** 66.1
Land: 35.7 sq. mi.; **Water:** 0.8 sq. mi.
Incorporated 1777.
Name origin: For early settler Phillip Riley's former home in Country Antrim, Ireland.

Bedford   Town
ZIP: 03110   **Lat:** 42-56-23 N **Long:** 71-32-00 W
Pop: 12,563 (1990); 9,481 (1980)   **Pop Density:** 383.0
Land: 32.8 sq. mi.; **Water:** 0.3 sq. mi.

In southern NH, 4 mi. southwest of Manchester. Granted 1730; incorporated 1750.

Name origin: Named in 1732 for Lord John Russell (1710–71), 4th Duke of Bedford.

Bennington   Town
Lat: 43-00-39 N **Long:** 71-54-41 W
Pop: 1,236 (1990); 890 (1980)   **Pop Density:** 111.4
Land: 11.1 sq. mi.; **Water:** 0.3 sq. mi.

Chartered 1749.

Name origin: Named in 1842 to commemorate the Aug 14, 1777, Revolutionary War battle at Bennington, VT.

Brookline   Town
ZIP: 03033   **Lat:** 42-44-41 N **Long:** 71-40-30 W
Pop: 2,410 (1990); 1,766 (1980)   **Pop Density:** 121.7
Land: 19.8 sq. mi.; **Water:** 0.4 sq. mi.

Founded 1769; reincorporated as Brookline 1798.

Name origin: For Brookline, MA, former home of landowner Benjamin Shattuck. Originally called West Hollis.

Deering   Town
Lat: 43-04-25 N **Long:** 71-50-56 W
Pop: 1,707 (1990); 1,041 (1980)   **Pop Density:** 55.4
Land: 30.8 sq. mi.; **Water:** 0.7 sq. mi.

Name origin: For the family name of the wife of NH colonial governor John Wentworth (1737–1820).

East Merrimack   CDP
Lat: 42-52-04 N **Long:** 71-29-02 W
Pop: 3,656 (1990); 2,052 (1980)   **Pop Density:** 1218.7
Land: 3.0 sq. mi.; **Water:** 0.3 sq. mi.

Francestown   Town
ZIP: 03043   **Lat:** 42-59-54 N **Long:** 71-48-51 W
Pop: 1,217 (1990); 830 (1980)   **Pop Density:** 40.3
Land: 30.2 sq. mi.; **Water:** 0.5 sq. mi.

Incorporated 1772.

Name origin: Named in 1772 for Frances Deering Wentworth, wife of royal governor John Wentworth (1737–1820).

Goffstown   Town
ZIP: 03045   **Lat:** 43-01-03 N **Long:** 71-34-12 W
Pop: 14,621 (1990); 11,315 (1980)   **Pop Density:** 396.2
Land: 36.9 sq. mi.; **Water:** 0.6 sq. mi.

In southern NH, 4 mi. west-northwest of Manchester. Chartered 1748 by the NH provincial government.

Name origin: Named for Col. John Goffe, who was among the first settlers.

Greenfield   Town
ZIP: 03047   **Lat:** 42-56-08 N **Long:** 71-52-22 W
Pop: 1,519 (1990); 972 (1980)   **Pop Density:** 59.6
Land: 25.5 sq. mi.; **Water:** 0.6 sq. mi.

Settled 1753.

Name origin: For the town's location between hills on fertile, level ground.

Greenville   Town
ZIP: 03048   **Lat:** 42-45-33 N **Long:** 71-47-57 W
Pop: 2,231 (1990); 1,988 (1980)   **Pop Density:** 323.3
Land: 6.9 sq. mi.; **Water:** 0.0 sq. mi.

Incorporated 1872.

Name origin: For the area's fertile agriculture.

Hancock   Town
ZIP: 03449   **Lat:** 42-58-24 N **Long:** 71-59-35 W
Pop: 1,604 (1990); 1,193 (1980)   **Pop Density:** 53.5
Land: 30.0 sq. mi.; **Water:** 1.2 sq. mi.

Settled 1764.

Name origin: Named in 1779 for Revolutionary War patriot John Hancock (1737–93), who owned land in the town. Previously had been part of a tract called "Society land."

Hillsborough   Town
ZIP: 03244   **Lat:** 43-08-46 N **Long:** 71-57-10 W
Pop: 4,498 (1990); 3,437 (1980)   **Pop Density:** 103.2
Land: 43.6 sq. mi.; **Water:** 1.0 sq. mi.

Granted 1735. Founded as a defensive outpost against Indian attacks.

Name origin: Named in 1748 for Will Hills, Earl of Hillsborough.

Hollis   Town
ZIP: 03049   **Lat:** 42-45-25 N **Long:** 71-35-05 W
Pop: 5,705 (1990); 4,679 (1980)   **Pop Density:** 180.0
Land: 31.7 sq. mi.; **Water:** 0.6 sq. mi.

Incorporated 1746 by Gov. Benning Wentworth (1696–1770).

Name origin: For the noted English Hollis family, relatives by marriage with the NH Wentworths.

Hudson   Town
ZIP: 03051   **Lat:** 42-45-59 N **Long:** 71-24-20 W
Pop: 19,530 (1990); 14,022 (1980)   **Pop Density:** 690.1
Land: 28.3 sq. mi.; **Water:** 0.8 sq. mi.

In southern NH on the Merrimack River, across from Nashua. Founded 1741.

Name origin: For the Hudson River. Previously called Nottingham.

Litchfield   Town
ZIP: 03051   **Lat:** 42-50-21 N **Long:** 71-27-35 W
Pop: 5,516 (1990); 4,150 (1980)   **Pop Density:** 365.3
Land: 15.1 sq. mi.; **Water:** 0.4 sq. mi.

Name origin: Named in 1749 for George Henry Lee, Earl of Litchfield. Formerly called Naticook and Brenton.

Lyndeborough   Town
ZIP: 03082   **Lat:** 42-54-13 N **Long:** 71-46-43 W
Pop: 1,294 (1990); 1,070 (1980)   **Pop Density:** 41.9
Land: 30.9 sq. mi.; **Water:** 0.1 sq. mi.

Settled 1735.

Name origin: For lawyer Benjamin Lynde.

Manchester   City
ZIP: 03101   **Lat:** 42-59-00 N **Long:** 71-26-41 W
Pop: 99,567 (1990); 90,936 (1980)   **Pop Density:** 3017.2
Land: 33.0 sq. mi.; **Water:** 1.9 sq. mi.

In southern NH on the Merrimack River, 17 mi. north of MA. Settled 1722; granted by Governor Benning Wentworth (1696–1770) 1751; incorporated as city 1846. Chief manufacturing and financial center of the state.

Name origin: For the English industrial city, Manchester, as suggested by Samuel Blodgett (1724–1807), a local merchant who was impressed by the canals in the English city and built one in NH. Originally called (Old) Derryfield.

Mason
Town

Lat: 42-44-55 N **Long:** 71-45-17 W
Pop: 1,212 (1990); 792 (1980) **Pop Density:** 50.7
Land: 23.9 sq. mi.; **Water:** 0.1 sq. mi.

Granted 1749.

Name origin: For NH's founder, Capt. John Mason, who sent over a group of colonists and founded the first settlements in 1631.

Merrimack
Town

ZIP: 03054 **Lat:** 42-51-19 N **Long:** 71-31-08 W
Pop: 22,156 (1990); 15,406 (1980) **Pop Density:** 679.6
Land: 32.6 sq. mi.; **Water:** 0.8 sq. mi.

In southern NH, near Nashua. Founded 1722.

Name origin: Named in 1746 for its location on the Merrimack River. Previously called Naticook.

Milford
Town

ZIP: 03055 **Lat:** 42-49-07 N **Long:** 71-40-24 W
Pop: 11,795 (1990); 8,685 (1980) **Pop Density:** 468.1
Land: 25.2 sq. mi.; **Water:** 0.1 sq. mi.

In southern NH, 10 mi. west-northwest of Nashua. Incorporated 1794.

Name origin: For Milford, Hampshire, England.

Mont Vernon
Town

ZIP: 03057 **Lat:** 42-53-57 N **Long:** 71-40-51 W
Pop: 1,812 (1990); 1,444 (1980) **Pop Density:** 107.9
Land: 16.8 sq. mi.; **Water:** 0.1 sq. mi.

Name origin: Named in 1803 for the VA estate of George Washington (1732–99), with spelling change. George had died only four years before, and his wife, Martha, the previous year.

Nashua
City

ZIP: 03060 **Lat:** 42-44-54 N **Long:** 71-29-30 W
Pop: 79,662 (1990); 67,865 (1980) **Pop Density:** 2578.1
Land: 30.9 sq. mi.; **Water:** 0.9 sq. mi. **Elev:** 169 ft.

In southern NH on the Merrimack River, 14 mi. south of Manchester. Incorporated 1853.

Name origin: For the Nashua River, which itself is named for the Nashaway Indians, whose name is said to mean 'beautiful river with pebbly bottom.' Originally called Dunstable.

New Boston
Town

ZIP: 03070 **Lat:** 42-58-37 N **Long:** 71-41-18 W
Pop: 3,214 (1990); 1,928 (1980) **Pop Density:** 75.1
Land: 42.8 sq. mi.; **Water:** 0.4 sq. mi.

Settled 1736; incorporated 1763.

Name origin: For Boston, MA.

New Ipswich
Town

ZIP: 03071 **Lat:** 42-44-35 N **Long:** 71-52-24 W
Pop: 4,014 (1990); 2,433 (1980) **Pop Density:** 122.4
Land: 32.8 sq. mi.; **Water:** 0.3 sq. mi.

Granted 1735; incorporated 1762.

Name origin: For Ipswich, MA.

Pelham
Town

ZIP: 03076 **Lat:** 42-43-56 N **Long:** 71-19-27 W
Pop: 9,408 (1990); 8,090 (1980) **Pop Density:** 356.4
Land: 26.4 sq. mi.; **Water:** 0.5 sq. mi.

Incorporated 1746.

Name origin: For Henry Pelham (1696–1754), then prime minister of England.

Peterborough
Town

ZIP: 03458 **Lat:** 42-53-21 N **Long:** 71-56-28 W
Pop: 5,239 (1990); 4,895 (1980) **Pop Density:** 139.0
Land: 37.7 sq. mi.; **Water:** 0.4 sq. mi.

Name origin: Named in 1738 for Charles Mordaunt (1658–1735), noted English admiral and 3rd Earl of Peterborough.

Pinardville
CDP

Lat: 43-00-04 N **Long:** 71-30-50 W
Pop: 4,654 (1990) **Pop Density:** 2908.8
Land: 1.6 sq. mi.; **Water:** 0.1 sq. mi.

Sharon
Town

Lat: 42-48-17 N **Long:** 71-56-33 W
Pop: 299 (1990); 184 (1980) **Pop Density:** 20.5
Land: 14.6 sq. mi.; **Water:** 0.0 sq. mi.

Founded 1738.

Name origin: Named in 1791 for Sharon, CT. Originally known as Suptown.

Temple
Town

ZIP: 03084 **Lat:** 42-49-38 N **Long:** 71-50-48 W
Pop: 1,194 (1990); 692 (1980) **Pop Density:** 51.5
Land: 23.2 sq. mi.; **Water:** 0.2 sq. mi.

Incorporated 1768.

Name origin: For NH's last royal lieutenant governor, John Temple.

Weare
Town

ZIP: 03281 **Lat:** 43-04-51 N **Long:** 71-43-25 W
Pop: 6,193 (1990); 3,232 (1980) **Pop Density:** 105.1
Land: 58.9 sq. mi.; **Water:** 1.0 sq. mi.

Incorporated 1764.

Name origin: For pioneer settler and first town clerk, Col. Meshech Weare.

Wilton
Town

ZIP: 03086 **Lat:** 42-49-49 N **Long:** 71-46-31 W
Pop: 3,122 (1990); 2,669 (1980) **Pop Density:** 121.0
Land: 25.8 sq. mi.; **Water:** 0.1 sq. mi.

Established 1730s as a site for defense against Indian raids.

Name origin: Named by Gov. Benning Wentworth (1696–1770) for a friend, English sculptor Sir Joseph Wilton.

Windsor
Town

Lat: 43-06-49 N **Long:** 72-00-56 W
Pop: 107 (1990); 72 (1980) **Pop Density:** 12.9
Land: 8.3 sq. mi.; **Water:** 0.3 sq. mi.

Incorporated 1798.

Name origin: For Windsor, CT, former home of early settlers.

Merrimack County
County Seat: Concord (ZIP: 03301)

Pop: 120,005 (1990); 98,302 (1980)   **Pop Density:** 128.4
Land: 934.5 sq. mi.; **Water:** 22.0 sq. mi.   **Area Code:** 603

In south-central NH, north of Manchester; organized Jul 1, 1823 from Rockingham and Hillsborough counties.

Name origin: For the Merrimack River, which bisects the county.

Allenstown   Town
Lat: 43-08-10 N **Long:** 71-23-25 W
Pop: 4,649 (1990); 4,398 (1980)   **Pop Density:** 226.8
Land: 20.5 sq. mi.; **Water:** 0.1 sq. mi.

Granted 1721; incorporated 1831.

Name origin: Named in 1721 for MA Gov. Samuel Allen.

Andover   Town
ZIP: 03216   **Lat:** 43-27-00 N **Long:** 71-47-39 W
Pop: 1,883 (1990); 1,587 (1980)   **Pop Density:** 46.5
Land: 40.5 sq. mi.; **Water:** 0.9 sq. mi.

Incorporated 1779.

Name origin: Named in 1799 by Dr. Anthony Emery for Andover, MA.

Boscawen   Town
Lat: 43-19-27 N **Long:** 71-39-25 W
Pop: 3,586 (1990); 3,435 (1980)   **Pop Density:** 145.2
Land: 24.7 sq. mi.; **Water:** 0.7 sq. mi.

Granted 1732.

Name origin: Named in 1761 for English admiral Edward Boscawen (1711–61), whose squadron captured the French fortress of Louisburg in Nova Scotia in 1758.

Bow   Town
ZIP: 03301   **Lat:** 43-08-00 N **Long:** 71-31-54 W
Pop: 5,500 (1990); 4,015 (1980)   **Pop Density:** 195.7
Land: 28.1 sq. mi.; **Water:** 0.4 sq. mi.

Granted 1727.

Name origin: Either for the bend in the Merrimack River along its eastern border, and possibly also honoring the English town of Bow near Exeter.

Bradford   Town
ZIP: 03221   **Lat:** 43-14-16 N **Long:** 71-58-07 W
Pop: 1,405 (1990); 1,115 (1980)   **Pop Density:** 39.8
Land: 35.3 sq. mi.; **Water:** 0.7 sq. mi.

Granted 1771.

Name origin: For Bradford, MA.

Canterbury   Town
ZIP: 03224   **Lat:** 43-21-01 N **Long:** 71-32-53 W
Pop: 1,687 (1990); 1,410 (1980)   **Pop Density:** 38.5
Land: 43.8 sq. mi.; **Water:** 0.8 sq. mi.

Founded 1727; incorporated 1741.

Name origin: For William Wake (1657–1737), Archbishop of Canterbury.

Chichester   Town
Lat: 43-14-57 N **Long:** 71-24-00 W
Pop: 1,942 (1990); 1,492 (1980)   **Pop Density:** 92.0
Land: 21.1 sq. mi.; **Water:** 0.1 sq. mi.

Founded 1724.

Name origin: For Thomas Holles, Earl of Chichester.

Concord   City
ZIP: 03301   **Lat:** 43-13-53 N **Long:** 71-33-36 W
Pop: 36,006 (1990); 30,400 (1980)   **Pop Density:** 560.0
Land: 64.3 sq. mi.; **Water:** 3.2 sq. mi.   **Elev:** 288 ft.

In south-central NH on the Merrimack River, 14 mi. north of Manchester. Capital of NH officially since 1808. Settled 1727; incorporated 1733 by MA; 1765 by NH. Became a town 1784; incorporated as a city 1853.

Name origin: For the peaceful resolution of a boundary dispute in colonial times. Name adopted 1765.

Contoocook   CDP
ZIP: 03229   **Lat:** 43-13-24 N **Long:** 71-42-54 W
Pop: 1,334 (1990); 1,499 (1980)   **Pop Density:** 580.0
Land: 2.3 sq. mi.; **Water:** 0.1 sq. mi.

Danbury   Town
ZIP: 03230   **Lat:** 43-31-36 N **Long:** 71-51-58 W
Pop: 881 (1990); 680 (1980)   **Pop Density:** 23.6
Land: 37.4 sq. mi.; **Water:** 0.3 sq. mi.

Incorporated 1795.

Name origin: For Danbury, England.

Dunbarton   Town
Lat: 43-05-53 N **Long:** 71-36-19 W
Pop: 1,759 (1990); 1,174 (1980)   **Pop Density:** 56.9
Land: 30.9 sq. mi.; **Water:** 0.5 sq. mi.

Granted 1735; incorporated 1765.

Name origin: For Dunbartonshire, on the River Clyde in Scotland.

Epsom   Town
ZIP: 03234   **Lat:** 43-13-20 N **Long:** 71-20-08 W
Pop: 3,591 (1990); 2,743 (1980)   **Pop Density:** 105.0
Land: 34.2 sq. mi.; **Water:** 0.2 sq. mi.

Established 1727.

Name origin: For Epsom, the town in England.

Franklin   City
ZIP: 03235   **Lat:** 43-27-04 N **Long:** 71-40-06 W
Pop: 8,304 (1990); 7,901 (1980)   **Pop Density:** 300.9
Land: 27.6 sq. mi.; **Water:** 1.6 sq. mi.   **Elev:** 335 ft.

Incorporated as a town in 1828, as a city in 1895.

Name origin: For U.S. patriot Benjamin Franklin (1706–90).

Henniker   Town
ZIP: 03242   **Lat:** 43-10-24 N **Long:** 71-49-16 W
Pop: 4,151 (1990); 3,246 (1980)   **Pop Density:** 94.1
Land: 44.1 sq. mi.; **Water:** 0.7 sq. mi.

Name origin: Named in 1768 by Gov. Wentworth for London merchant Sir John Henniker.

Hill
Town

ZIP: 03243 **Lat:** 43-31-39 N **Long:** 71-46-00 W
Pop: 814 (1990); 736 (1980) **Pop Density:** 30.5
Land: 26.7 sq. mi.; **Water:** 0.2 sq. mi.

Incorporated 1753.

Name origin: For NH Gov. Isaac Hill. Originally called Chester.

Hooksett
Town

ZIP: 03106 **Lat:** 43-03-53 N **Long:** 71-26-30 W
Pop: 8,767 (1990); 7,303 (1980) **Pop Density:** 242.2
Land: 36.2 sq. mi.; **Water:** 1.1 sq. mi.

Name origin: For the hook-shaped bend nearby in the Merrimack River.

Hopkinton
Town

Lat: 43-11-41 N **Long:** 71-41-33 W
Pop: 4,806 (1990); 3,861 (1980) **Pop Density:** 111.0
Land: 43.3 sq. mi.; **Water:** 1.8 sq. mi.

Granted 1735.

Name origin: For Hopkinton, MA, the former home of settlers.

Loudon
Town

Lat: 43-19-00 N **Long:** 71-26-22 W
Pop: 4,114 (1990); 2,454 (1980) **Pop Density:** 87.9
Land: 46.8 sq. mi.; **Water:** 0.7 sq. mi.

Chartered 1773.

Name origin: Shortened from the title of John Campbell, 4th Earl of Loudoun.

Newbury
Town

Lat: 43-18-41 N **Long:** 72-01-34 W
Pop: 1,347 (1990); 961 (1980) **Pop Density:** 37.6
Land: 35.8 sq. mi.; **Water:** 2.3 sq. mi.

Settled 1753; incorporated 1837.

Name origin: For Newbury, MA. Originally called Dantzic.

New London
Town

ZIP: 03257 **Lat:** 43-25-03 N **Long:** 71-59-30 W
Pop: 3,180 (1990); 2,935 (1980) **Pop Density:** 141.3
Land: 22.5 sq. mi.; **Water:** 3.1 sq. mi.

Founded 1753; incorporated 1779.

Name origin: Originally called Heidelberg (also spelled Heidlebourg and Hiddleburg). Name changed to New Londonderry on incorporation by settlers from Londonderry, NH, then shortened.

Northfield
Town

Lat: 43-24-43 N **Long:** 71-34-11 W
Pop: 4,263 (1990); 3,051 (1980) **Pop Density:** 148.0
Land: 28.8 sq. mi.; **Water:** 0.3 sq. mi.

Established 1780.

Name origin: Originally called North Hill.

Pembroke
Town

ZIP: 03275 **Lat:** 43-11-00 N **Long:** 71-26-52 W
Pop: 6,561 (1990); 4,861 (1980) **Pop Density:** 287.8
Land: 22.8 sq. mi.; **Water:** 0.2 sq. mi.

Granted 1728; incorporated 1759.

Name origin: For Henry Herbert, 9th Earl of Wiliam Pembroke.

Pittsfield
Town

ZIP: 03263 **Lat:** 43-17-59 N **Long:** 71-18-43 W
Pop: 3,701 (1990); 2,889 (1980) **Pop Density:** 156.8
Land: 23.6 sq. mi.; **Water:** 0.3 sq. mi.

Incorporated 1782.

Name origin: For William Pitt, English statesman and friend to the colonies in the years before the Revolutionary War.

Salisbury
Town

ZIP: 03268 **Lat:** 43-22-33 N **Long:** 71-45-46 W
Pop: 1,061 (1990); 781 (1980) **Pop Density:** 26.5
Land: 40.0 sq. mi.; **Water:** 0.3 sq. mi.

Granted 1736; incorporated 1768.

Name origin: For Salisbury, MA. Previously known as Baker's Town, for explorer Thomas Baker, and also Gerrishtown, after an early settler.

South Hooksett
CDP

Lat: 43-02-05 N **Long:** 71-25-21 W
Pop: 3,638 (1990) **Pop Density:** 686.4
Land: 5.3 sq. mi.; **Water:** 0.0 sq. mi.

Suncook
CDP

ZIP: 03275 **Lat:** 43-08-19 N **Long:** 71-27-07 W
Pop: 5,214 (1990); 1,931 (1980) **Pop Density:** 1448.3
Land: 3.6 sq. mi.; **Water:** 0.1 sq. mi.

Sutton
Town

Lat: 43-20-48 N **Long:** 71-56-05 W
Pop: 1,457 (1990); 1,091 (1980) **Pop Density:** 34.4
Land: 42.3 sq. mi.; **Water:** 0.8 sq. mi.

Settled 1748; incorporated 1784.

Name origin: For Sutton, MA.

Warner
Town

ZIP: 03278 **Lat:** 43-16-54 N **Long:** 71-49-42 W
Pop: 2,250 (1990); 1,963 (1980) **Pop Density:** 40.4
Land: 55.7 sq. mi.; **Water:** 0.2 sq. mi.

Incorporated 1774; one of last NH towns established under English rule.

Name origin: Named 1774 for a prominent Portsmouth citizen.

Webster
Town

Lat: 43-18-23 N **Long:** 71-42-56 W
Pop: 1,405 (1990); 1,095 (1980) **Pop Density:** 50.4
Land: 27.9 sq. mi.; **Water:** 0.7 sq. mi.

Incorporated 1860.

Name origin: For New Hampshire-born lawyer, orator, and statesman Daniel Webster (1782–1852).

Wilmot
Town

Lat: 43-27-12 N **Long:** 71-55-13 W
Pop: 935 (1990); 725 (1980) **Pop Density:** 31.7
Land: 29.5 sq. mi.; **Water:** 0.2 sq. mi.

Settled 1807.

Name origin: For Dr. James Wilmot, an English clergyman and friend to the colonies in the days before the Revolutionary War.

Rockingham County
County Seat: Exeter (ZIP: 03833)

Pop: 245,845 (1990); 190,345 (1980)   **Pop Density:** 353.6
Land: 695.2 sq. mi.; **Water:** 98.8 sq. mi.   **Area Code:** 603

On southeastern border of NH, southeast of Concord; original county, organized Apr 29, 1769.

Name origin: For Charles Watson-Wentworth, Marquess of Rockingham (1730–82), British statesman, prime minister, and cousin of the NH Wentworths, largely responsible for repeal of the Stamp Act.

Atkinson   Town
ZIP: 03811   **Lat:** 42-50-10 N **Long:** 71-09-46 W
Pop: 5,188 (1990); 4,397 (1980)   **Pop Density:** 467.4
Land: 11.1 sq. mi.; **Water:** 0.1 sq. mi.

Founded 1767.

Name origin: For Col. Theodore Atkinson, whose farmland comprised a significant proportion of the town.

Auburn   Town
ZIP: 03032   **Lat:** 42-59-48 N **Long:** 71-20-32 W
Pop: 4,085 (1990); 2,883 (1980)   **Pop Density:** 162.1
Land: 25.2 sq. mi.; **Water:** 3.5 sq. mi.

Incorporated 1845.

Name origin: For Auburn in Yorkshire, England; the name was popularized in the first line of "The Deserted Village" (1770) by Oliver Goldsmith (1730–74). Originally called Chester Woods.

Brentwood   Town
    Lat: 42-59-22 N **Long:** 71-02-51 W
Pop: 2,590 (1990); 2,004 (1980)   **Pop Density:** 154.2
Land: 16.8 sq. mi.; **Water:** 0.2 sq. mi.

Name origin: For Brentwood, England.

Candia   Town
ZIP: 03034   **Lat:** 43-03-17 N **Long:** 71-18-29 W
Pop: 3,557 (1990); 2,989 (1980)   **Pop Density:** 117.4
Land: 30.3 sq. mi.; **Water:** 0.2 sq. mi.

Name origin: Named in 1763 by Gov. Benning Wentworth (1696–1770) for Candia, largest city on the Greek island of Crete and former name for Crete.

Chester   Town
ZIP: 03036   **Lat:** 42-57-58 N **Long:** 71-15-01 W
Pop: 2,691 (1990); 2,006 (1980)   **Pop Density:** 103.9
Land: 25.9 sq. mi.; **Water:** 0.1 sq. mi.

Granted 1722.

Danville   Town
ZIP: 03819   **Lat:** 42-55-48 N **Long:** 71-07-16 W
Pop: 2,534 (1990); 1,318 (1980)   **Pop Density:** 216.6
Land: 11.7 sq. mi.; **Water:** 0.2 sq. mi.

Settled 1694; incorporated 1836.

Name origin: For several early settlers whose Christian name was Daniel.

Deerfield   Town
ZIP: 03037   **Lat:** 43-08-07 N **Long:** 71-15-19 W
Pop: 3,124 (1990); 1,979 (1980)   **Pop Density:** 61.4
Land: 50.9 sq. mi.; **Water:** 1.3 sq. mi.

Granted 1774; incorporated 1766.

Name origin: Named by early settlers for Deerfield, MA.

Derry   Town
ZIP: 03038   **Lat:** 42-53-12 N **Long:** 71-16-52 W
Pop: 29,603 (1990); 18,875 (1980)   **Pop Density:** 826.9
Land: 35.8 sq. mi.; **Water:** 0.9 sq. mi.

In southeastern NH, 9 mi. southeast of Manchester. Incorporated 1827.

Name origin: For Londonderry, also called Derry, in Northern Ireland.

East Kingston   Town
ZIP: 03827   **Lat:** 42-55-23 N **Long:** 71-00-31 W
Pop: 1,352 (1990); 1,135 (1980)   **Pop Density:** 135.2
Land: 10.0 sq. mi.; **Water:** 0.1 sq. mi.

Established 1738.

Name origin: For Kingston, of which it was originally a part.

Epping   Town
ZIP: 03042   **Lat:** 43-02-49 N **Long:** 71-04-42 W
Pop: 5,162 (1990); 3,460 (1980)   **Pop Density:** 198.5
Land: 26.0 sq. mi.; **Water:** 0.2 sq. mi.

Chartered 1741.

Name origin: Named by MA governor Jonathan Belcher (1682–1757) for Epping Forest, a park-suburb of London.

Exeter   Town
ZIP: 03833   **Lat:** 42-59-20 N **Long:** 70-57-43 W
Pop: 12,481 (1990); 11,024 (1980)   **Pop Density:** 636.8
Land: 19.6 sq. mi.; **Water:** 0.4 sq. mi.

In southeastern NH, 11 mi. west-southwest of Portsmouth. Settled 1638. Capital of NH for several years from 1775. Site of Phillips Exeter Academy (1781).

Name origin: Named by the Rev. John Wheelwright for Exeter, Devonshire, England.

Fremont   Town
ZIP: 03044   **Lat:** 42-59-33 N **Long:** 71-07-20 W
Pop: 2,576 (1990); 1,333 (1980)   **Pop Density:** 149.8
Land: 17.2 sq. mi.; **Water:** 0.3 sq. mi.

Settled 1764.

Name origin: Named in 1854 for Republican Presidential hopeful John C. Frémont (1813–90). Originally called Poplin.

Greenland   Town
ZIP: 03840   **Lat:** 43-02-17 N **Long:** 70-50-51 W
Pop: 2,768 (1990); 2,129 (1980)   **Pop Density:** 263.6
Land: 10.5 sq. mi.; **Water:** 2.8 sq. mi.

Settled 1638. One of the earliest towns in NH.

Name origin: For pioneer Henry Greenland.

Hampstead
Town
ZIP: 03841   **Lat:** 42-53-01 N **Long:** 71-10-07 W
Pop: 6,732 (1990); 3,785 (1980)   **Pop Density:** 498.7
Land: 13.5 sq. mi.; **Water:** 0.5 sq. mi.

Established 1739.

Hampton
Town
ZIP: 03842   **Lat:** 42-56-21 N **Long:** 70-50-05 W
Pop: 12,278 (1990); 10,493 (1980)   **Pop Density:** 944.5
Land: 13.0 sq. mi.; **Water:** 1.5 sq. mi.

Chartered 1635; incorporated 1639.

Name origin: For Hampton, England.

Hampton Falls
Town
ZIP: 03844   **Lat:** 42-55-25 N **Long:** 70-53-13 W
Pop: 1,503 (1990); 1,372 (1980)   **Pop Density:** 123.2
Land: 12.2 sq. mi.; **Water:** 0.3 sq. mi.

Originally part of Hampton. Granted 1726.

Name origin: For its location near Hampton and at the falls on the Taylor River.

Kensington
Town
     Lat: 42-55-50 N **Long:** 70-56-45 W
Pop: 1,631 (1990); 1,322 (1980)   **Pop Density:** 135.9
Land: 12.0 sq. mi.; **Water:** 0.0 sq. mi.

Granted 1730s.

Name origin: For Edward Rich, Earl of Holland and Baron Kensington.

Kingston
Town
ZIP: 03848   **Lat:** 42-54-45 N **Long:** 71-03-59 W
Pop: 5,591 (1990); 4,111 (1980)   **Pop Density:** 283.8
Land: 19.7 sq. mi.; **Water:** 1.2 sq. mi.

Established 1694.

Name origin: For Kingston, MA.

Londonderry
Town
ZIP: 03053   **Lat:** 42-52-56 N **Long:** 71-23-09 W
Pop: 19,781 (1990); 13,598 (1980)   **Pop Density:** 473.2
Land: 41.8 sq. mi.; **Water:** 0.1 sq. mi.

In southeastern NH, 9 mi. southeast of Manchester.

Name origin: Named in 1722 by emigrants for their former home, Londonderry, in northern Ireland. Previously called Derry.

New Castle
Town
     Lat: 43-03-46 N **Long:** 70-42-55 W
Pop: 840 (1990); 936 (1980)   **Pop Density:** 1050.0
Land: 0.8 sq. mi.; **Water:** 1.6 sq. mi.

Incorporated 1693.

Name origin: For Fort William and Mary, built to defend settlers from Indian attacks and known as "the Castle."

Newfields
Town
     Lat: 43-02-22 N **Long:** 70-58-05 W
Pop: 888 (1990); 817 (1980)   **Pop Density:** 126.9
Land: 7.0 sq. mi.; **Water:** 0.2 sq. mi.

Originally part of Exeter. Incorporated 1895.

Name origin: Named in 1895 for the meadows adjacent to the Squamscott River.

Newington
Town
     Lat: 43-05-51 N **Long:** 70-50-07 W
Pop: 990 (1990); 716 (1980)   **Pop Density:** 119.3
Land: 8.3 sq. mi.; **Water:** 4.1 sq. mi.

Chartered 1714.

Name origin: For the town of Newington, England.

Newmarket
Town
ZIP: 03857   **Lat:** 43-04-08 N **Long** 70-57-04 W
Pop: 7,157 (1990); 4,290 (1980)   **Pop Density:** 568.0
Land: 12.6 sq. mi.; **Water:** 1.6 sq. mi.

Granted 1737.

Name origin: For Newmarket, County Suffolk, England.

Newton
Town
ZIP: 03858   **Lat:** 42-51-54 N **Long** 71-02-39 W
Pop: 3,473 (1990); 3,068 (1980)   **Pop Density:** 350.8
Land: 9.9 sq. mi.; **Water:** 0.2 sq. mi.

Incorporated 1749.

Name origin: Named in 1846. Previously called Newtown.

North Hampton
Town
ZIP: 03862   **Lat:** 42-58-39 N **Long:** 70-49-51 W
Pop: 3,637 (1990); 3,425 (1980)   **Pop Density:** 261.7
Land: 13.9 sq. mi.; **Water:** 0.5 sq. mi.

First a part of Hampton. Settled 1639; granted 1742.

Name origin: For its location north of Hampton.

Northwood
Town
ZIP: 03261   **Lat:** 43-12-49 N **Long:** 71-12-45 W
Pop: 3,124 (1990); 2,175 (1980)   **Pop Density:** 111.6
Land: 28.0 sq. mi.; **Water:** 2.1 sq. mi.

Settled 1763.

Nottingham
Town
ZIP: 03290   **Lat:** 43-06-59 N **Long:** 71-07-17 W
Pop: 2,939 (1990); 1,952 (1980)   **Pop Density:** 63.2
Land: 46.5 sq. mi.; **Water:** 1.9 sq. mi.

Established 1722.

Name origin: For Daniel Finch, 2nd Earl of Nottingham.

Plaistow
Town
ZIP: 03865   **Lat:** 42-50-26 N **Long:** 71-05-45 W
Pop: 7,316 (1990); 5,609 (1980)   **Pop Density:** 690.2
Land: 10.6 sq. mi.; **Water:** 0.0 sq. mi.

Name origin: Named in 1749 for a plaistow, an open space near a village center where sports or games are played.

Portsmouth
City
ZIP: 03801   **Lat:** 43-03-24 N **Long:** 70-46-55 W
Pop: 25,925 (1990); 26,254 (1980)   **Pop Density:** 1661.9
Land: 15.6 sq. mi.; **Water:** 1.2 sq. mi.   **Elev:** 21 ft.

In southeastern NH on the Atlantic Ocean at the mouth of the Piscataqua River. One of NH's original settlements, 1630. Chief seaport of NH, site of Portsmouth Naval Shipyard, and a commercial center for the area. Became the capital in 1679. City incorporated 1849.

Name origin: Named by NH founder, Capt. John Mason, for Portsmouth, England. Originally called Strawbery Banke.

Raymond
Town
ZIP: 03077   **Lat:** 43-01-52 N **Long:** 71-11-53 W
Pop: 8,713 (1990); 5,453 (1980)   **Pop Density:** 302.5
Land: 28.8 sq. mi.; **Water:** 0.8 sq. mi.

Name origin: Named in 1764 for Capt. William Raymond of Beverly, MA, who received land in the area for military services against the French in Canada.

Rye
Town
ZIP: 03870   **Lat:** 43-00-31 N **Long:** 70-44-16 W
Pop: 4,612 (1990); 4,508 (1980)   **Pop Density:** 366.0
Land: 12.6 sq. mi.; **Water:** 22.9 sq. mi.

Established 1623, the first settlement in NH. Incorporated 1726.

Name origin: For the English port town of Rye.

Salem
Town
ZIP: 03079   **Lat:** 42-47-26 N **Long:** 71-13-19 W
Pop: 25,746 (1990); 24,124 (1980)   **Pop Density:** 1042.3
Land: 24.7 sq. mi.; **Water:** 1.2 sq. mi.

In southeastern NH, 11 mi. east of Nashua. Incorporated 1750. Originally part of Methuen.
Name origin: Named in 1741 for Salem, MA. Originally known as Haverhill.

Sandown
Town
ZIP: 03873   **Lat:** 42-56-03 N **Long:** 71-11-01 W
Pop: 4,060 (1990); 2,057 (1980)   **Pop Density:** 292.1
Land: 13.9 sq. mi.; **Water:** 0.5 sq. mi.

Incorporated 1756.
Name origin: For the English resort on the Isle of Wight.

Seabrook
Town
ZIP: 03874   **Lat:** 42-53-13 N **Long:** 70-51-41 W
Pop: 6,503 (1990); 5,917 (1980)   **Pop Density:** 730.7
Land: 8.9 sq. mi.; **Water:** 0.8 sq. mi.

Incorporated 1768.
Name origin: For the nearby Seabrook River, which flows into the Atlantic Ocean.

South Hampton
Town
Lat: 42-53-12 N **Long:** 70-58-13 W
Pop: 740 (1990); 660 (1980)   **Pop Density:** 93.7
Land: 7.9 sq. mi.; **Water:** 0.1 sq. mi.

Chartered 1742. One of the original Hampton border towns.
Name origin: For Hampton, England.

Stratham
Town
ZIP: 03885   **Lat:** 43-00-56 N **Long:** 70-54-08 W
Pop: 4,955 (1990); 2,507 (1980)   **Pop Density:** 328.1
Land: 15.1 sq. mi.; **Water:** 0.4 sq. mi.

Incorporated 1716.
Name origin: For Streatham, a district near London, England, with spelling change.

Windham
Town
ZIP: 03087   **Lat:** 42-48-20 N **Long:** 71-17-55 W
Pop: 9,000 (1990); 5,664 (1980)   **Pop Density:** 335.8
Land: 26.8 sq. mi.; **Water:** 1.1 sq. mi.

Incorporated Feb 12, 1741.
Name origin: For Sir Charles Windham, Earl of Egremont.

Strafford County
County Seat: Dover (ZIP: 03820)

Pop: 104,233 (1990); 85,408 (1980)   **Pop Density:** 282.6
Land: 368.8 sq. mi.; **Water:** 15.1 sq. mi.   **Area Code:** 603

On southeastern border of NH, north of Portsmouth; original county, organized Apr 29, 1769.
Name origin: For William Wentworth (1722–91), 4th Earl of Strafford, cousin of John Wentworth (1737–1820), governor of NH at the time of its establishment.

Barrington
Town
ZIP: 03825   **Lat:** 43-12-54 N **Long:** 71-02-20 W
Pop: 6,164 (1990); 4,404 (1980)   **Pop Density:** 132.3
Land: 46.6 sq. mi.; **Water:** 1.9 sq. mi.

Settled 1718.
Name origin: For Samuel Shute of Barrington Hall, governor of Massachusetts Bay and New Hampshire colonies (1716–27).

Dover
City
ZIP: 03820   **Lat:** 43-11-23 N **Long:** 70-53-00 W
Pop: 25,042 (1990); 22,377 (1980)   **Pop Density:** 937.9
Land: 26.7 sq. mi.; **Water:** 2.3 sq. mi.

In southeastern NH, 10 mi. north-northwest of Portsmouth. Settled 1623; incorporated 1641.
Name origin: For English soldier and lawyer Robert Dover (1575–1641).

Durham
Town
ZIP: 03824   **Lat:** 43-07-01 N **Long:** 70-55-08 W
Pop: 11,818 (1990); 10,652 (1980)   **Pop Density:** 527.6
Land: 22.4 sq. mi.; **Water:** 2.4 sq. mi.

In southeastern NH, 4 mi. south-southwest of Dover. Settled 1635; incorporated 1732.
Name origin: For the 17th-century English Bishop of Durham, Richard Barnes (1532–87), known as the "Puritan Bishop."

Farmington
Town
ZIP: 03835   **Lat:** 43-21-19 N **Long:** 71-04-05 W
Pop: 5,739 (1990); 4,630 (1980)   **Pop Density:** 154.3
Land: 37.2 sq. mi.; **Water:** 0.3 sq. mi.

Name origin: For the area's many fertile farms.

Lee
Town
Lat: 43-07-10 N **Long:** 71-00-30 W
Pop: 3,729 (1990); 2,111 (1980)   **Pop Density:** 187.4
Land: 19.9 sq. mi.; **Water:** 0.2 sq. mi.

Established 1766.
Name origin: For English general Charles Lee, an officer during the French and Indian War.

Madbury
Town
Lat: 43-10-42 N **Long:** 70-56-23 W
Pop: 1,404 (1990); 987 (1980)   **Pop Density:** 120.0
Land: 11.7 sq. mi.; **Water:** 0.6 sq. mi.

Granted 1768.
Name origin: Named by Sir Francis Champernowne (who came to America in the 1640s) for his farm, Madbury, in England.

Middleton
Town

Lat: 43-28-56 N **Long:** 71-04-17 W
Pop: 1,183 (1990); 734 (1980) **Pop Density:** 65.4
Land: 18.1 sq. mi.; **Water:** 0.4 sq. mi.

Chartered 1749.

Name origin: For Sir Charles Middleton, a British naval officer.

Milton
Town

Lat: 43-27-09 N **Long:** 71-00-49 W
Pop: 3,691 (1990); 2,438 (1980) **Pop Density:** 111.5
Land: 33.1 sq. mi.; **Water:** 1.2 sq. mi.

Incorporated 1802.

Name origin: For its being the site of early water mills on the Salmon Falls River.

New Durham
Town

ZIP: 03855 **Lat:** 43-28-00 N **Long:** 71-08-10 W
Pop: 1,974 (1990); 1,183 (1980) **Pop Density:** 47.3
Land: 41.7 sq. mi.; **Water:** 2.5 sq. mi.

Granted 1749; incorporated 1762.

Name origin: Named by settlers from Durham, NH.

Rochester
City

ZIP: 03867 **Lat:** 43-18-03 N **Long:** 70-58-44 W
Pop: 26,630 (1990); 21,560 (1980) **Pop Density:** 589.2
Land: 45.2 sq. mi.; **Water:** 0.6 sq. mi.

In southeastern NH, 8 mi. north-northwest of Dover. Founded 1600s; incorporated as town 1722; as city 1891.

Name origin: For Lawrence Hyde (1641–1711), Earl of Rochester.

Rollinsford
Town

ZIP: 03869 **Lat:** 43-13-15 N **Long:** 70-50-35 W
Pop: 2,645 (1990); 2,319 (1980) **Pop Density:** 362.3
Land: 7.3 sq. mi.; **Water:** 0.2 sq. mi.

Name origin: Named in 1849 for Edward Rollins (1824–89), a prominent local druggist and banker who became a noted politician.

Somersworth
City

ZIP: 03878 **Lat:** 43-15-20 N **Long:** 70-53-03 W
Pop: 11,249 (1990); 10,350 (1980) **Pop Density:** 1147.9
Land: 9.8 sq. mi.; **Water:** 0.2 sq. mi. **Elev:** 204 ft.

In southeastern NH on Salmon Falls, 4 mi. north of Dover. Incorporated as a town 1754, as a city 1893.

Name origin: Named by the Rev. John Pike, probably for *summer* plus the suffix -*worth* because he spent his summers preaching here.

Strafford
Town

ZIP: 03884 **Lat:** 43-16-42 N **Long:** 71-08-53 W
Pop: 2,965 (1990); 1,663 (1980) **Pop Density:** 60.3
Land: 49.2 sq. mi.; **Water:** 2.2 sq. mi.

Established 1769; incorporated 1820.

Name origin: For the county.

Sullivan County
County Seat: Newport (ZIP: 03773)

Pop: 38,592 (1990); 36,063 (1980) **Pop Density:** 71.8
Land: 537.4 sq. mi.; **Water:** 14.5 sq. mi. **Area Code:** 603

On southwestern border of NH, north of Keene; organized Jul 5, 1827 from Cheshire County.

Name origin: For Gen. John Sullivan (1740–95), officer in the Revolutionary War, member of the Continental Congress, chief executive of NH (1786–87), and governor (1789).

Acworth
Town

ZIP: 03601 **Lat:** 43-13-08 N **Long:** 72-17-08 W
Pop: 776 (1990); 590 (1980) **Pop Density:** 19.9
Land: 38.9 sq. mi.; **Water:** 0.2 sq. mi.

Incorporated 1772.

Name origin: Named in 1766 for Sir Jacob Acworth, a British admiral associated with the West Indies trade.

Charlestown
Town

ZIP: 03603 **Lat:** 43-14-57 N **Long:** 72-23-26 W
Pop: 4,630 (1990); 4,417 (1980) **Pop Density:** 129.3
Land: 35.8 sq. mi.; **Water:** 2.2 sq. mi.

Name origin: Named in 1753 for British admiral Sir Charles Knowles.

Claremont
City

ZIP: 03743 **Lat:** 43-22-41 N **Long:** 72-20-20 W
Pop: 13,902 (1990); 14,557 (1980) **Pop Density:** 322.6
Land: 43.1 sq. mi.; **Water:** 1.0 sq. mi. **Elev:** 561 ft.

Incorporated as a city 1947.

Name origin: For John Holles, 1st Earl of Clare (1564–1637), whose home was known as Claremont Castle. He was an ancestor by marriage of NH colonial governor Benning Wentworth (1696–1770).

Cornish
Town

Lat: 43-28-42 N **Long:** 72-19-00 W
Pop: 1,659 (1990); 1,390 (1980) **Pop Density:** 39.4
Land: 42.1 sq. mi.; **Water:** 0.7 sq. mi.

Founded 1763 as a supply depot for the Royal Navy.

Name origin: For British Adm. Sir Samuel Cornish.

Croydon
Town
Lat: 43-26-33 N **Long:** 72-11-46 W
Pop: 627 (1990); 457 (1980)   **Pop Density:** 16.9
Land: 37.1 sq. mi.; **Water:** 0.8 sq. mi.
Chartered 1763.
Name origin: For the suburb of Croydon in London, England.

Goshen
Town
ZIP: 03752   **Lat:** 43-17-57 N **Long:** 72-06-26 W
Pop: 742 (1990); 549 (1980)   **Pop Density:** 33.0
Land: 22.5 sq. mi.; **Water:** 0.1 sq. mi.
Incorporated 1791.
Name origin: Named by settlers for Goshen, CT, where they had relatives.

Grantham
Town
ZIP: 03753   **Lat:** 43-31-11 N **Long:** 72-09-16 W
Pop: 1,247 (1990); 704 (1980)   **Pop Density:** 46.5
Land: 26.8 sq. mi.; **Water:** 0.9 sq. mi.
Incorporated 1761.
Name origin: For English diplomat Thomas Robinson, Baron of Grantham.

Langdon
Town
Lat: 43-10-03 N **Long:** 72-22-48 W
Pop: 580 (1990); 437 (1980)   **Pop Density:** 35.6
Land: 16.3 sq. mi.; **Water:** 0.1 sq. mi.
Incorporated 1787.
Name origin: For NH's second governor, John Langdon (1741–1819).

Lempster
Town
ZIP: 03606   **Lat:** 43-13-26 N **Long:** 72-11-01 W
Pop: 947 (1990); 637 (1980)   **Pop Density:** 29.3
Land: 32.3 sq. mi.; **Water:** 0.4 sq. mi.
Granted 1735.
Name origin: Named in 1761 to honor Sir Thomas Farmer of Lempster.

Newport
Town
ZIP: 03773   **Lat:** 43-22-05 N **Long:** 72-11-59 W
Pop: 6,110 (1990); 6,229 (1980)   **Pop Density:** 140.1
Land: 43.6 sq. mi.; **Water:** 0.1 sq. mi.
Incorporated 1761.
Name origin: For English soldier and statesman, Henry Newport, Earl of Bradford.

Plainfield
Town
ZIP: 03781   **Lat:** 43-33-51 N **Long:** 72-16-45 W
Pop: 2,056 (1990); 1,749 (1980)   **Pop Density:** 39.4
Land: 52.2 sq. mi.; **Water:** 0.7 sq. mi.
Founded 1761 at the beginning of the reign of King George III (1738–1820).
Name origin: For Plainfield, CT.

Springfield
Town
Lat: 43-29-32 N **Long:** 72-02-13 W
Pop: 788 (1990); 532 (1980)   **Pop Density:** 18.2
Land: 43.3 sq. mi.; **Water:** 0.9 sq. mi.
Granted 1769 by Gov. John Wentworth (1737–1820); incorporated 1794.
Name origin: Named in 1794. Previously known as Protectworth.

Sunapee
Town
ZIP: 03782   **Lat:** 43-23-25 N **Long:** 72-05-35 W
Pop: 2,559 (1990); 2,312 (1980)   **Pop Density:** 121.3
Land: 21.1 sq. mi.; **Water:** 4.1 sq. mi.
Founded 1768; incorporated 1850.
Name origin: For nearby Sunapee Lake, from an Algonquian term probably meaning 'goose lake.'

Unity
Town
Lat: 43-17-52 N **Long:** 72-16-25 W
Pop: 1,341 (1990); 1,092 (1980)   **Pop Density:** 36.3
Land: 36.9 sq. mi.; **Water:** 0.2 sq. mi.
Founded 1753.
Name origin: Commemorating the settlement of a legal dispute over ownership of the grant.

Washington
Town
Lat: 43-10-55 N **Long:** 72-05-07 W
Pop: 628 (1990); 411 (1980)   **Pop Density:** 13.8
Land: 45.4 sq. mi.; **Water:** 2.2 sq. mi.
Incorporated 1776.
Name origin: For then-General George Washington (1732–99).

Index to Places and Counties in New Hampshire

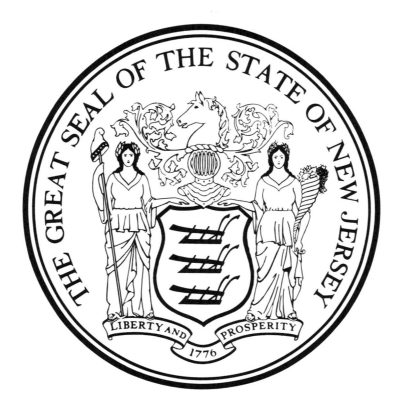

New Jersey

NEW JERSEY

SUSSEX

PASSAIC

WARREN

MORRIS

BERGEN

NEW YORK

ESSEX

HUDSON

UNION

SOMERSET

HUNTERDON

PENNSYLVANIA

MIDDLESEX

MERCER

MONMOUTH

BURLINGTON

OCEAN

CAMDEN

GLOUCESTER

SALEM

ATLANTIC

DELAWARE

CUMBERLAND

CAPE MAY

N

76°   75°   74°

41°   41°

40°   40°

39°   39°

SCALE

0 10 20 30 40 50 Kilometers

0 10 20 30 40 50 Miles

All political boundaries are as of January 1, 1980

U.S. Department of Commerce   BUREAU OF THE CENSUS

76°   75°   74°

New Jersey

Population: 7,730,188 (1990); 7,364,823 (1980)
Population rank (1990): 9
Percent population change (1980-1990): 5.0
Population projection: 8,062,000 (1995);
  8,238,000 (2000)

Area: total 8,722 sq. mi.; 7,419 sq. mi. land, 1,303 sq.
  mi. water. Coastline 166 mi.
Area rank: 47
Highest elevation: 1,803 ft at High Point in northern
  Sussex County
Lowest point: sea level on the Atlantic coast

State capital: Trenton (Mercer County)
Largest city: Newark (275,221)
Second largest city: Jersey City (228,537)
Largest county: Bergen (825,380)

Total housing units: 3,075,310
No. of occupied housing units: 2,794,711
Vacant housing units (%): 9.1
Distribution of population by race and
  Hispanic origin (%):
  White: 79.3
  Black: 13.4
  Hispanic (any race): 9.6
  Native American: 0.2
  Asian/Pacific: 3.5
  Other: 3.6

Admission date: December 18, 1787 (3rd state).

Location: In the northeastern United States on the
Atlantic coast, bordering New York, Pennsylvania,
and the Delaware River. One of the thirteen original
English colonies.

Name Origin: For the island of Jersey in the English
Channel. Probably named by James, Duke of York, for
his friend, Sir George Carteret, who was born on
Jersey and was its principal royal defender during the
English Commonwealth.

State animal: horse
State bird: eastern goldfinch
State flower: purple violet
State insect: honeybee *(Apis mellifera)*
State memorial tree: dogwood *(Cornus florida)*
State tree: red oak *(Quercus rubra)*

State motto: Liberty and Prosperity
State nickname: The Garden State

Area codes: 201 (Newark), 609 (Trenton), 908 (New
  Brunswick)

Time zone: Eastern
Abbreviations: NJ (postal) N.J. (traditional)
Part of (region): Middle Atlantic; Northeast

Local Government

Counties

New Jersey has 21 counties. The governing body of each
is called the Board of Chosen Freeholders (New Jersey is
the only state to use this name), which derives from early
state history when only landowners (freeholders) could
vote and hold office, and those elected to office were
"chosen."

Municipalities

In New Jersey, "municipalities" applies equally to the 53
cities, 256 boroughs, 234 townships, 21 towns, and 3
villages. They are each chartered corporations under state
law and choose their own form of government. Townships are usually rural regions, but many encompass large
urban areas.

Settlement History and Early Development

The Delaware (also called Lenni Lenape) Indians arrived
in the upland and coastal areas between the Hudson and
Delaware rivers, what is now New Jersey, about 6,000
years ago. They were peaceful, hospitable farmer-hunters,
but European colonization of the land ultimately led to
the demise or departure of the Indians.

Giovanni da Verrazano sailed into present-day Newark
Bay in 1524 but did not stay. Henry Hudson, an Englishman exploring for the Dutch, sailed on the *Half Moon*
into Sandy Hook Bay in late summer of 1609 and established a Dutch claim in the New World. He was followed
by the Dutch explorer Cornelius Mey who sailed the
Delaware River in 1614 (Cape May was later named for
him). Dutch traders arrived in present-day Hudson
County in northern New Jersey by 1618. Traders and
settlers from Sweden arrived in southern New Jersey in
1638, and began moving westward toward the Delaware
in 1639. The Colony of New Sweden lasted from 1643 to
1655, when the Dutch forced them out, fearing their
competition in the fur trade. In 1660 New Jersey's first
permanent settlement, called Bergen (now part of Jersey
City), was founded by the Dutch.

In March 1664 King Charles II granted the area from the
Connecticut River to the Delaware River, including various islands and a large part of Maine, to his brother
James, the Duke of York. This "Duke's Grant," the largest territorial gift ever given by the English crown, included most of the Dutch possessions in the New World.
The duke in turn gave the land between the Hudson and

Delaware rivers, which he named New Jersey, to two friends, Lord John Berkeley and Sir George Carteret. Berkeley and Carteret became proprietors, owning the land and having the right to govern the people. On August 18, 1664, the English sailed four ships into the harbor of New Amsterdam (present-day New York City) and ordered the Dutch to surrender, which they did eleven days later.

In 1674 Edward Byllynge and a group of Quakers bought Berkeley's share and two years later the colony was divided into two sections: East Jersey and West Jersey, the capitals of which were Perth Amboy and Burlington, respectively. West Jersey was the first Quaker colony in America. Carteret owned East Jersey, which had been settled primarily by Puritans from Long Island and New England, until his death in 1680; two years later the Twenty-Four Proprietors, another Quaker group, bought it. In the 1690s many colonists rioted over land ownership and payment of rent to the proprietors. In 1702 the owners relinquished their claims and Queen Anne united East and West Jersey but placed them under New York rule. New Jersey did not get its own government until 1738 when Lewis Morris became the first royally appointed colonial governor. William Franklin, illegitimate son of Benjamin Franklin, served as governor from 1763 until 1776.

The American Revolution and Statehood

New Jersey served as a pathway between the cities of New York and Philadelphia and hence had more roads than any other colony. After the American Revolution began in 1775 in Massachusetts, the colony's pivotal location between these two important cities made it strategically critical. New Jersey voted for the Declaration of Independence in June 1776; thereafter almost one hundred engagements took place there, earning New Jersey the nickname *Cockpit of the Revolution.*

New Jersey adopted its first constitution on July 2, 1776. On November 16, 1778, New Jersey ratified the Articles of Confederation. It officially became the third state on December 18, 1787, when it ratified the U.S. Constitution. Princeton served as the nation's capital from June 30 to November 4, 1783, and Trenton from November 1 to December 24, 1784. The New Jersey delegates to the Constitutional Convention of 1787 proposed the New Jersey Plan, which recommended that the thirteen colonies should become a federation with equal representation in one national legislative body. The plan influenced the establishment of the U.S. Senate.

Civil War

The Civil War bitterly divided New Jersey. The Democrats believed the war was a "Black Republican" affair. Industrialists in Newark and Trenton were afraid their trade with the South would suffer, while the Cape May tourist industry feared the loss of Virginian vacationers. The state sent its full quota of troops into battle, however, and New Jersey factories provided munitions and other equipment for the Union army. Still, in 1864 New Jersey was only one of three states that voted against the reelection of Abraham Lincoln. At the end of the war the 13th, 14th, and 15th Amendments to the U.S. Constitution, which outlawed slavery, established due process and equal protection, and gave blacks the right to vote, were bitterly opposed in New Jersey.

Business and Commerce

New Jersey was one of the first great industrial states, beginning as early as 1792 when Paterson was established as a textile center and later became known for the manufacture of locomotives and silk production. In the first half of the nineteenth century many new railroads and canals were built. The 90-mile long Morris Canal connected northern New Jersey with the coalfields of Pennsylvania. The new energy source freed industry from dependence on waterpower and helped the dyeing and weaving mills of Paterson to prosper. Newark benefited the most and became the state's first incorporated city in 1836. The Delaware and Raritan Canal connected Bordentown and New Brunswick and helped those two cities and Trenton to flourish.

The railroads expanded the transportation system, but caused the decline of the canals. The Hudson County waterfront (across the Hudson River from New York City) was the eastern terminus for most of the nation's railway systems and became the most important railroad area in the U.S. Today the freight yards remain among the largest in the world. Rail lines also carried tourists to the Jersey shore, still an important source of state income. Thousands of immigrants from Europe were attracted to the factories in New Jersey, and by 1910 more than half the people in the state were either immigrants or first-generation Americans.

Thomas A. Edison helped develop motion pictures while working at Menlo Park and West Orange, and at the beginning of the twentieth century Fort Lee was actually the center of the new motion picture industry. During World War I, New Jersey became the leading shipbuilding state in the U.S. During and after World War II the electronics and chemical industries expanded rapidly; military bases such as Ft. Dix have also been important to the state's economy. In 1977 gambling casinos were opened in Atlantic City, but the income generated by the influx of visitors to the glittering hotel-casinos facing the boardwalk has not led to general revitalization. The 1980s saw tremendous growth and prosperity, followed by a lingering recession into the early 1990s. However, the state can look to its strong industrial base, proximity to major markets, and wealthy and well-educated workforce for recovery.

State Boundaries

The Delaware River forms the New Jersey-Pennsylvania border. The islands between the falls of Trenton and the Delaware line were apportioned to New Jersey and Pennsylvania according to which state they lay nearest. The middle of Delaware Bay forms the New Jersey-Delaware border. The northern New Jersey border with New York was stated in the royal grant to Berkeley and Carteret, and accepted by both colonies in 1772. In 1834 New Jersey and New York agreed that Staten Island would remain part of New York, and the boundary between the two states was set at the midpoint between the Hudson River, the Arthur Kill, and the Kill Van Kull. Bedloes and Ellis islands, however, although on the New Jersey side of the boundary, are officially part of New York.

New Jersey Counties

Atlantic	Essex	Middlesex	Salem
Bergen	Gloucester	Monmouth	Somerset
Burlington	Hudson	Morris	Sussex
Camden	Hunterdon	Ocean	Union
Cape May	Mercer	Passaic	Warren
Cumberland			

Atlantic County
County Seat: Mays Landing (ZIP: 08330)

Pop: 224,327 (1990); 194,119 (1980)   **Pop Density:** 399.8
Land: 561.2 sq. mi.; **Water:** 110.3 sq. mi.   **Area Code:** 609

In southern NJ on Atlantic coast, east of Vineland; organized Feb 7, 1837 from Gloucester County.
Name origin: For the Atlantic Ocean.

Absecon
City
ZIP: 08201   **Lat:** 39-25-30 N **Long:** 74-29-44 W
Pop: 7,298 (1990); 6,859 (1980)   **Pop Density:** 1280.4
Land: 5.7 sq. mi.; **Water:** 1.2 sq. mi.   **Elev:** 25 ft.

In southeastern NJ on the Atlantic Ocean, 5 mi. northwest of Atlantic City. Replaced Absecon Town Mar 24, 1902.

Name origin: For the Absegami tribe, whose name probably means 'place of the swans.'

Atlantic City
City
ZIP: 08401   **Lat:** 39-22-39 N **Long:** 74-27-05 W
Pop: 37,986 (1990); 40,199 (1980)   **Pop Density:** 3361.6
Land: 11.3 sq. mi.; **Water:** 6.0 sq. mi.   **Elev:** 8 ft.

An island in southeastern NJ on the Atlantic Ocean, 60 mi. southeast of Philadelphia. Beach resort famed for its boardwalk, rolling chairs, amusement pier, salt water taffy, Miss America pageant, and casino gambling. Incorporated as a city Mar 3, 1854.

Name origin: For the Atlantic Ocean. Formerly called Absecon Beach.

Brigantine
City
ZIP: 08203   **Lat:** 39-24-48 N **Long:** 74-22-47 W
Pop: 11,354 (1990); 8,318 (1980)   **Pop Density:** 1774.1
Land: 6.4 sq. mi.; **Water:** 3.4 sq. mi.   **Elev:** 6 ft.

In southeastern NJ on the Atlantic coast, northeast of Atlantic City. Replaced East Atlantic City and part of Galloway Township Mar 6, 1924.

Name origin: For a ship, the *Brigantine*, which was wrecked c. 1710 in this area.

Buena
Borough
ZIP: 08310   **Lat:** 39-31-40 N **Long:** 74-56-41 W
Pop: 4,441 (1990); 3,642 (1980)   **Pop Density:** 584.3
Land: 7.6 sq. mi.; **Water:** 0.0 sq. mi.   **Elev:** 108 ft.
Reincorporated May 18, 1949.

Name origin: A contraction for the Battle of Buena Vista during the Mexican War.

Buena Vista
Township
ZIP: 08360   **Lat:** 39-30-43 N **Long:** 74-53-34 W
Pop: 7,655 (1990); 6,959 (1980)   **Pop Density:** 184.9
Land: 41.4 sq. mi.; **Water:** 0.1 sq. mi.
Formed Mar 5, 1867.

Collings Lakes
CDP
Lat: 39-35-40 N **Long:** 74-52-59 W
Pop: 2,046 (1990); 2,093 (1980)   **Pop Density:** 2922.9
Land: 0.7 sq. mi.; **Water:** 0.0 sq. mi.

Corbin City
City
Lat: 39-18-04 N **Long:** 74-42-38 W
Pop: 412 (1990); 254 (1980)   **Pop Density:** 52.2
Land: 7.9 sq. mi.; **Water:** 1.1 sq. mi.   **Elev:** 13 ft.
Formed Mar 11, 1922.

Egg Harbor
Township
ZIP: 08221   **Lat:** 39-22-47 N **Long:** 74-36-47 W
Pop: 24,544 (1990); 19,381 (1980)   **Pop Density:** 364.7
Land: 67.3 sq. mi.; **Water:** 7.6 sq. mi.

In southeastern NJ, 17 mi. northwest of Atlantic City. Incorporated Feb 21, 1798.

Name origin: For the gull's eggs found there, a source of food for early settlers.

Egg Harbor City
City
ZIP: 08215   **Lat:** 39-33-51 N **Long:** 74-35-46 W
Pop: 4,583 (1990); 4,618 (1980)   **Pop Density:** 412.9
Land: 11.1 sq. mi.; **Water:** 0.4 sq. mi.

Formed Jun 14, 1858; reincorporated Feb 13, 1868.

Name origin: For its proximity to Great Egg Harbor Bay to the south and Little Egg Harbor Bay to the northeast. A proposed canal to connect it with Gloucester Furnace and the Mullica River to the northeast would have allowed access to Great Bay and Little Egg Harbor, but it was never built.

Elwood-Magnolia
CDP
Lat: 39-34-22 N **Long:** 74-43-06 W
Pop: 1,487 (1990); 1,538 (1980)   **Pop Density:** 450.6
Land: 3.3 sq. mi.; **Water:** 0.0 sq. mi.

Estell Manor
City
ZIP: 08319   **Lat:** 39-21-15 N **Long:** 74-46-25 W
Pop: 1,404 (1990); 848 (1980)   **Pop Density:** 26.2
Land: 53.6 sq. mi.; **Water:** 1.3 sq. mi.

Folsom
Borough
ZIP: 08037   **Lat:** 39-35-31 N **Long:** 74-50-51 W
Pop: 2,181 (1990); 1,892 (1980)   **Pop Density:** 262.8
Land: 8.3 sq. mi.; **Water:** 0.2 sq. mi.   **Elev:** 90 ft.
Formed May 23, 1906.

Name origin: For Frances Folsom, wife of U.S. president Grover Cleveland (1837–1908).

Galloway
Township
ZIP: 08213   **Lat:** 39-29-34 N **Long:** 74-28-48 W
Pop: 23,330 (1990); 12,176 (1980)   **Pop Density:** 258.1
Land: 90.4 sq. mi.; **Water:** 24.3 sq. mi.

Incorporated Feb 21, 1798.

Hamilton
Township
ZIP: 08330   **Lat:** 39-29-49 N **Long:** 74-45-06 W
Pop: 16,012 (1990); 9,499 (1980)   **Pop Density:** 143.9
Land: 111.3 sq. mi.; **Water:** 1.7 sq. mi.
Formed Apr 11, 1842.

Name origin: Named in 1842 for Alexander Hamilton. Originally known as the Crossroads in Nottingham Township and Nottingham Square.

Hammonton
Town
ZIP: 08037   **Lat:** 39-39-17 N **Long:** 74-46-20 W
Pop: 12,208 (1990); 12,298 (1980)   **Pop Density:** 295.6
Land: 41.3 sq. mi.; **Water:** 0.2 sq. mi.   **Elev:** 100 ft.

In southeastern NJ, 27 mi. southeast of Camden. Formed Mar 5, 1866.

Name origin: For John Hammond Coffin, the owner of a glassworks in the area during the early to mid-1800s.

Linwood
City
ZIP: 08221   **Lat:** 39-20-31 N **Long:** 74-34-13 W
Pop: 6,866 (1990); 6,144 (1980)   **Pop Density:** 1806.8
Land: 3.8 sq. mi.; **Water:** 0.3 sq. mi.   **Elev:** 28 ft.

In southeastern NJ. Replaced Linwood Borough Apr 27, 1931.

Longport
Borough
ZIP: 08403   **Lat:** 39-18-42 N **Long:** 74-31-31 W
Pop: 1,224 (1990); 1,249 (1980)   **Pop Density:** 3060.0
Land: 0.4 sq. mi.; **Water:** 1.2 sq. mi.   **Elev:** 6 ft.

Formed Mar 7, 1898.

Name origin: For John Long, landowner.

Margate City
City
ZIP: 08402   **Lat:** 39-19-50 N **Long:** 74-30-26 W
Pop: 8,431 (1990); 9,179 (1980)   **Pop Density:** 6022.1
Land: 1.4 sq. mi.; **Water:** 0.2 sq. mi.   **Elev:** 8 ft.

Replaced South Atlantic City Apr 20, 1909.

Name origin: For Margate, England.

Mays Landing
CDP
ZIP: 08330   **Lat:** 39-27-10 N **Long:** 74-43-27 W
Pop: 2,090 (1990); 2,054 (1980)   **Pop Density:** 1229.4
Land: 1.7 sq. mi.; **Water:** 0.2 sq. mi.

Mullica
Township
ZIP: 08217   **Lat:** 39-35-43 N **Long:** 74-40-49 W
Pop: 5,896 (1990); 5,243 (1980)   **Pop Density:** 104.2
Land: 56.6 sq. mi.; **Water:** 0.4 sq. mi.

Formed Mar 13, 1838.

Name origin: For Eric Mullica, Swedish pioneer.

Northfield
City
ZIP: 08225   **Lat:** 39-22-23 N **Long:** 74-33-17 W
Pop: 7,305 (1990); 7,795 (1980)   **Pop Density:** 2087.1
Land: 3.5 sq. mi.; **Water:** 0.0 sq. mi.   **Elev:** 33 ft.

Formed Mar 21, 1905.

Pleasantville
City
ZIP: 08232   **Lat:** 39-23-25 N **Long:** 74-31-07 W
Pop: 16,027 (1990); 13,435 (1980)   **Pop Density:** 2763.3
Land: 5.8 sq. mi.; **Water:** 1.5 sq. mi.   **Elev:** 22 ft.

In southeastern NJ, 5 mi. northwest of Atlantic City. Incorporated Mar 14, 1925.

Name origin: Named by Dr. Daniel Ingersoll for the surroundings.

Pomona
CDP
Lat: 39-28-10 N **Long:** 74-33-06 W
Pop: 2,624 (1990); 2,358 (1980)   **Pop Density:** 937.1
Land: 2.8 sq. mi.; **Water:** 0.0 sq. mi.

Port Republic
City
ZIP: 08241   **Lat:** 39-32-16 N **Long:** 74-29-13 W
Pop: 992 (1990); 837 (1980)   **Pop Density:** 128.8
Land: 7.7 sq. mi.; **Water:** 1.1 sq. mi.   **Elev:** 17 ft.

Formed Mar 1, 1905.

Name origin: For the U.S. Republic.

Somers Point
City
ZIP: 08244   **Lat:** 39-19-02 N **Long:** 74-36-24 W
Pop: 11,216 (1990); 10,330 (1980)   **Pop Density:** 2804.0
Land: 4.0 sq. mi.; **Water:** 1.1 sq. mi.   **Elev:** 27 ft.

In southeastern NJ on Great Egg Harbor, 10 mi. southwest of Atlantic City. Formed Apr 9, 1902.

Name origin: For landowner John Somers.

Ventnor City
City
ZIP: 08406   **Lat:** 39-20-30 N **Long:** 74-28-59 W
Pop: 11,005 (1990); 11,704 (1980)   **Pop Density:** 5240.5
Land: 2.1 sq. mi.; **Water:** 1.4 sq. mi.   **Elev:** 12 ft.

In southeastern NJ on the Atlantic Ocean, 3 mi. southwest of Atlantic City. Formed Mar 17, 1903.

Name origin: For Ventnor, England.

Weymouth
Township
ZIP: 08317   **Lat:** 39-25-10 N **Long:** 74-47-51 W
Pop: 1,957 (1990); 1,260 (1980)   **Pop Density:** 160.4
Land: 12.2 sq. mi.; **Water:** 0.4 sq. mi.

Incorporated Feb 21, 1798.

Name origin: For Weymouth, England.

Bergen County
County Seat: Hackensack (ZIP: 07601)

Pop: 825,380 (1990); 845,385 (1980)   **Pop Density:** 3524.2
Land: 234.2 sq. mi.; **Water:** 12.6 sq. mi.   **Area Code:** 201

In northeastern NJ bordering on NY, north of Jersey City; original county, organized Mar 7, 1683.

Name origin: Named by early Dutch settlers for the town of Bergen-op-zoom, North Brabant, Netherlands.

Allendale   Borough
ZIP: 07401   **Lat:** 41-01-59 N **Long:** 74-07-58 W
Pop: 5,900 (1990); 5,901 (1980)   **Pop Density:** 1903.2
Land: 3.1 sq. mi.; **Water:** 0.0 sq. mi.   **Elev:** 375 ft.

In northeastern NJ, 10 mi. north of Paterson. Formed Nov 10, 1894.

Name origin: For Col. Wm. C. Allen, a surveyor for the Erie Railroad.

Alpine   Borough
ZIP: 07620   **Lat:** 40-57-28 N **Long:** 73-55-13 W
Pop: 1,716 (1990); 1,549 (1980)   **Pop Density:** 268.1
Land: 6.4 sq. mi.; **Water:** 2.8 sq. mi.   **Elev:** 450 ft.

Formed Apr 8, 1903.

Name origin: For the Alps, the European mountain range.

Bergenfield   Borough
ZIP: 07621   **Lat:** 40-55-26 N **Long:** 73-59-54 W
Pop: 24,458 (1990); 25,568 (1980)   **Pop Density:** 8433.8
Land: 2.9 sq. mi.; **Water:** 0.0 sq. mi.   **Elev:** 93 ft.

In northeastern NJ, 9 mi. east of Paterson. Formed Jun 26, 1894.

Name origin: For either Bergen-op-zoom, Holland or Bergen, Norway.

Bogota   Borough
ZIP: 07603   **Lat:** 40-52-31 N **Long:** 74-01-45 W
Pop: 7,824 (1990); 8,344 (1980)   **Pop Density:** 9780.0
Land: 0.8 sq. mi.; **Water:** 0.1 sq. mi.   **Elev:** 100 ft.

In northeastern NJ. Formed Nov 17, 1894.

Name origin: Said to be for the Bogert family, early settlers, with spelling alteration.

Carlstadt   Borough
ZIP: 07072   **Lat:** 40-49-28 N **Long:** 74-03-50 W
Pop: 5,510 (1990); 6,166 (1980)   **Pop Density:** 1377.5
Land: 4.0 sq. mi.; **Water:** 0.3 sq. mi.   **Elev:** 187 ft.

Replaced Carlstadt Village Jun 28, 1894.

Name origin: German word meaning 'Carl's town,' for Dr. Carl Klein, leader of the German immigrants who bought the land from the Americans. Formerly called Tailor Town, for the many inhabitants who worked for NY tailors.

Cliffside Park   Borough
ZIP: 07010   **Lat:** 40-49-17 N **Long:** 73-59-18 W
Pop: 20,393 (1990); 21,464 (1980)   **Pop Density:** 20393.0
Land: 1.0 sq. mi.; **Water:** 0.0 sq. mi.

In northeastern NJ on the Hudson River, across from New York City, 10 mi. northeast of Jersey City. Formed Jan 16, 1895.

Name origin: For its location on the Palisades, the cliffs lining the western side of the river.

Closter   Borough
ZIP: 07624   **Lat:** 40-58-21 N **Long:** 73-57-37 W
Pop: 8,094 (1990); 8,164 (1980)   **Pop Density:** 2529.4
Land: 3.2 sq. mi.; **Water:** 0.1 sq. mi.   **Elev:** 62 ft.

Formed Jan 1, 1904.

Name origin: For Frederick Closter, an early settler.

Cresskill   Borough
ZIP: 07626   **Lat:** 40-56-23 N **Long:** 73-57-32 W
Pop: 7,558 (1990); 7,609 (1980)   **Pop Density:** 3599.0
Land: 2.1 sq. mi.; **Water:** 0.0 sq. mi.   **Elev:** 86 ft.

Formed May 11, 1894.

Name origin: For a place where watercress grew. From Dutch *kill* meaning 'channel, creek.'

Demarest   Borough
ZIP: 07627   **Lat:** 40-57-22 N **Long:** 73-57-27 W
Pop: 4,800 (1990); 4,963 (1980)   **Pop Density:** 2285.7
Land: 2.1 sq. mi.; **Water:** 0.0 sq. mi.   **Elev:** 50 ft.

In northeastern NJ, 15 mi. northeast of Paterson. Formed Apr 8, 1903.

Name origin: For the Demarest family, early settlers.

Dumont   Borough
ZIP: 07628   **Lat:** 40-56-43 N **Long** 73-59-33 W
Pop: 17,187 (1990); 18,334 (1980)   **Pop Density:** 8593.5
Land: 2.0 sq. mi.; **Water:** 0.0 sq. mi.   **Elev:** 104 ft.

In northeastern NJ, 9 mi. east of Paterson. Replaced Schraalenburgh Borough Jun 13, 1898.

Name origin: For Dumont Clark, the first mayor.

East Rutherford   Borough
ZIP: 07073   **Lat:** 40-49-02 N **Long** 74-05-03 W
Pop: 7,902 (1990); 7,849 (1980)   **Pop Density:** 2079.5
Land: 3.8 sq. mi.; **Water:** 0.3 sq. mi.   **Elev:** 60 ft.

In northeastern NJ, north of Newark. Separated from Rutherford only by the tracks of the Erie Railroad. Replaced Boiling Springs Township Mar 28, 1894.

Name origin: For its location.

Edgewater   Borough
ZIP: 07020   **Lat:** 40-49-17 N **Long** 73-58-42 W
Pop: 5,001 (1990); 4,628 (1980)   **Pop Density:** 6251.3
Land: 0.8 sq. mi.; **Water:** 1.6 sq. mi.

Replaced Undercliff Borough Nov 8, 1899.

Name origin: For its location along the Hudson River.

Elmwood Park   Borough
ZIP: 07407   **Lat:** 40-54-16 N **Long** 74-07-11 W
Pop: 17,623 (1990); 18,377 (1980)   **Pop Density:** 6527.0
Land: 2.7 sq. mi.; **Water:** 0.1 sq. mi.   **Elev:** 59 ft.

In northeastern NJ, southeast of Paterson. Replaced East Paterson Borough Jan 1, 1973.

Name origin: Originally called East Paterson.

Emerson
Borough
ZIP: 07630   **Lat:** 40-58-29 N **Long:** 74-01-25 W
Pop: 6,930 (1990); 7,793 (1980)   **Pop Density:** 3150.0
Land: 2.2 sq. mi.; **Water:** 0.2 sq. mi.   **Elev:** 50 ft.
Replaced Etna Borough Nov 8, 1899.
Name origin: For author Ralph Waldo Emerson (1803–82).

Englewood
City
ZIP: 07631   **Lat:** 40-53-32 N **Long:** 73-58-27 W
Pop: 24,850 (1990); 23,701 (1980)   **Pop Density:** 5071.4
Land: 4.9 sq. mi.; **Water:** 0.0 sq. mi.   **Elev:** 44 ft.
In northeastern NJ west of the Hudson River, 10 mi. east of Paterson. Formed Mar 17, 1899.

Englewood Cliffs
Borough
ZIP: 07632   **Lat:** 40-53-01 N **Long:** 73-56-51 W
Pop: 5,634 (1990); 5,698 (1980)   **Pop Density:** 2682.9
Land: 2.1 sq. mi.; **Water:** 1.3 sq. mi.   **Elev:** 350 ft.
Formed May 10, 1895.
Name origin: For its position atop the Palisades along the west bank of the Hudson River.

Fair Lawn
Borough
ZIP: 07410   **Lat:** 40-56-09 N **Long:** 74-07-04 W
Pop: 30,548 (1990); 32,229 (1980)   **Pop Density:** 5874.6
Land: 5.2 sq. mi.; **Water:** 0.1 sq. mi.   **Elev:** 100 ft.
In northeastern NJ, 3 mi. northeast of Paterson. Formed Mar 6, 1924.
Name origin: For the Ackerson estate.

Fairview
Borough
ZIP: 07022   **Lat:** 40-49-02 N **Long:** 74-00-05 W
Pop: 10,733 (1990); 10,519 (1980)   **Pop Density:** 13416.3
Land: 0.8 sq. mi.; **Water:** 0.0 sq. mi.   **Elev:** 238 ft.
In northeastern NJ, 7 mi. north of Jersey City. Formed Dec 19, 1894.
Name origin: For the view across the Hackensack River valley.

Fort Lee
Borough
ZIP: 07024   **Lat:** 40-51-01 N **Long:** 73-58-16 W
Pop: 31,997 (1990); 32,449 (1980)   **Pop Density:** 12798.8
Land: 2.5 sq. mi.; **Water:** 0.3 sq. mi.   **Elev:** 313 ft.
In northeastern NJ on the Hudson River, 10 mi. northeast of Jersey City. Replaced Ridgefield Township Mar 29, 1904.
Name origin: For the Revolutionary War fort, which was named for Maj. Gen. Charles Lee.

Franklin Lakes
Borough
ZIP: 07417   **Lat:** 41-00-24 N **Long:** 74-12-28 W
Pop: 9,873 (1990); 8,769 (1980)   **Pop Density:** 1039.3
Land: 9.5 sq. mi.; **Water:** 0.4 sq. mi.   **Elev:** 390 ft.
Formed Mar 11, 1922.
Name origin: For William Franklin, last royal governor of NJ.

Garfield
Borough
ZIP: 07026   **Lat:** 40-52-47 N **Long:** 74-06-30 W
Pop: 26,727 (1990); 26,803 (1980)   **Pop Density:** 12727.1
Land: 2.1 sq. mi.; **Water:** 0.1 sq. mi.   **Elev:** 36 ft.
In northeastern NJ on the Passaic River, 5 mi. southeast of Paterson. Replaced Garfield Borough Apr 19, 1917.
Name origin: For James A. Garfield (1831–81), twentieth U.S. president.

Glen Rock
Borough
ZIP: 07452   **Lat:** 40-57-32 N **Long:** 74-07-31 W
Pop: 10,883 (1990); 11,497 (1980)   **Pop Density:** 4030.7
Land: 2.7 sq. mi.; **Water:** 0.0 sq. mi.   **Elev:** 90 ft.
In northeastern NJ, 4 mi. northeast of Paterson. Formed Sep 14, 1894.
Name origin: For a ridge in a glen formed by Toney's Brook.

Hackensack
City
ZIP: 07601   **Lat:** 40-53-21 N **Long:** 74-02-46 W
Pop: 37,049 (1990); 36,039 (1980)   **Pop Density:** 9036.3
Land: 4.1 sq. mi.; **Water:** 0.2 sq. mi.   **Elev:** 22 ft.
In northeastern NJ on the Hackensack River, 7 mi. southeast of Paterson. Replaced Hackensack Commission and New Barbadoes Township Nov 21, 1921.
Name origin: From an Indian tribal name of uncertain meaning.

Harrington Park
Borough
ZIP: 07640   **Lat:** 40-59-21 N **Long:** 73-58-48 W
Pop: 4,623 (1990); 4,532 (1980)   **Pop Density:** 2433.2
Land: 1.9 sq. mi.; **Water:** 0.2 sq. mi.   **Elev:** 62 ft.
In northeastern NJ. Formed Mar 29, 1904.
Name origin: For the Harring family, early settlers.

Hasbrouck Heights
Borough
ZIP: 07604   **Lat:** 40-51-38 N **Long:** 74-04-27 W
Pop: 11,488 (1990); 12,166 (1980)   **Pop Density:** 7658.7
Land: 1.5 sq. mi.; **Water:** 0.0 sq. mi.   **Elev:** 130 ft.
In northeastern NJ, 7 mi. southeast of Paterson. Founded 1685; formed Aug 2, 1894.
Name origin: For a Dutch colonist.

Haworth
Borough
ZIP: 07641   **Lat:** 40-57-42 N **Long:** 73-59-55 W
Pop: 3,384 (1990); 3,509 (1980)   **Pop Density:** 1692.0
Land: 2.0 sq. mi.; **Water:** 0.4 sq. mi.   **Elev:** 90 ft.
Formed Feb 24, 1904.
Name origin: For Haworth, England.

Hillsdale
Borough
ZIP: 07642   **Lat:** 41-00-29 N **Long:** 74-02-37 W
Pop: 9,750 (1990); 10,495 (1980)   **Pop Density:** 3250.0
Land: 3.0 sq. mi.; **Water:** 0.0 sq. mi.   **Elev:** 83 ft.
In northeastern NJ, 9 mi. northeast of Paterson. Replaced Hillsdale Township Mar 2, 1923.
Name origin: For its location in a dale among the hills.

Ho-Ho-Kus
Borough
     Lat: 40-59-58 N **Long:** 74-05-49 W
Pop: 3,935 (1990); 4,129 (1980)   **Pop Density:** 2314.7
Land: 1.7 sq. mi.; **Water:** 0.0 sq. mi.   **Elev:** 113 ft.
In northeastern NJ, northeast of Paterson. Replaced Orvil Borough Oct 12, 1908.
Name origin: From *Mehohokus*, a Chihohokies Indian word probably meaning 'red cedar.' Originally called Hoppertown for an early settler.

Leonia
Borough
ZIP: 07605   **Lat:** 40-51-47 N **Long:** 73-59-29 W
Pop: 8,365 (1990); 8,027 (1980)   **Pop Density:** 5576.7
Land: 1.5 sq. mi.; **Water:** 0.1 sq. mi.   **Elev:** 100 ft.
Formed Dec 6, 1894.
Name origin: Name coined from Fort Lee.

Little Ferry
Borough
ZIP: 07643   **Lat:** 40-50-44 N **Long:** 74-02-22 W
Pop: 9,989 (1990); 9,399 (1980)   **Pop Density:** 6659.3
Land: 1.5 sq. mi.; **Water:** 0.2 sq. mi.   **Elev:** 9 ft.
Formed Sep 20, 1894.

Name origin: For a colonial ferry across the Hackensack River.

Lodi
Borough
ZIP: 07644   **Lat:** 40-52-44 N **Long:** 74-04-52 W
Pop: 22,355 (1990); 23,956 (1980)   **Pop Density:** 9719.6
Land: 2.3 sq. mi.; **Water:** 0.0 sq. mi.   **Elev:** 43 ft.
In northeastern NJ, 5 mi. southeast of Paterson. Formed Dec 22, 1894.

Name origin: For the Bridge of Lodi in northern Italy, site of victory of Napoleon (1769–1821) over the Austrians in 1796.

Lyndhurst
Township
ZIP: 07071   **Lat:** 40-47-48 N **Long:** 74-06-48 W
Pop: 18,262 (1990); 20,326 (1980)   **Pop Density:** 3970.0
Land: 4.6 sq. mi.; **Water:** 0.3 sq. mi.
Replaced Union Township May 15, 1917.

Name origin: For Lord Lyndhurst, a frequent visitor to a local landowner. Originally called New Barbados Neck by an early settler from Barbados.

Mahwah
Township
ZIP: 07430   **Lat:** 41-04-51 N **Long:** 74-11-13 W
Pop: 17,905 (1990); 12,127 (1980)   **Pop Density:** 691.3
Land: 25.9 sq. mi.; **Water:** 0.3 sq. mi.
Replaced Hohokus Township Nov 7, 1944.

Name origin: From an Indian term perhaps meaning 'meeting place.'

Maywood
Borough
ZIP: 07607   **Lat:** 40-54-10 N **Long:** 74-03-49 W
Pop: 9,473 (1990); 9,895 (1980)   **Pop Density:** 7286.9
Land: 1.3 sq. mi.; **Water:** 0.0 sq. mi.   **Elev:** 94 ft.
Formed Jun 30, 1894.

Midland Park
Borough
ZIP: 07432   **Lat:** 40-59-41 N **Long:** 74-08-31 W
Pop: 7,047 (1990); 7,381 (1980)   **Pop Density:** 4404.4
Land: 1.6 sq. mi.; **Water:** 0.0 sq. mi.   **Elev:** 350 ft.
Formed Sep 6, 1894.

Name origin: For its location "amid the Bergen hills."

Montvale
Borough
ZIP: 07645   **Lat:** 41-03-07 N **Long:** 74-02-56 W
Pop: 6,946 (1990); 7,318 (1980)   **Pop Density:** 1736.5
Land: 4.0 sq. mi.; **Water:** 0.0 sq. mi.   **Elev:** 310 ft.
Formed Aug 31, 1894.

Name origin: Descriptive of the topography.

Moonachie
Borough
ZIP: 07074   **Lat:** 40-50-32 N **Long:** 74-03-33 W
Pop: 2,817 (1990); 2,706 (1980)   **Pop Density:** 1657.1
Land: 1.7 sq. mi.; **Water:** 0.0 sq. mi.   **Elev:** 5 ft.
Formed Apr 11, 1910.

Name origin: For an Iroquois chief.

New Milford
Borough
ZIP: 07646   **Lat:** 40-56-02 N **Long:** 74-01-11 W
Pop: 15,990 (1990); 16,876 (1980)   **Pop Density:** 6952.2
Land: 2.3 sq. mi.; **Water:** 0.0 sq. mi.   **Elev:** 33 ft.
In northeastern NJ, 8 mi. northeast of Paterson. Replaced Palisades Township Mar 11, 1922.

Name origin: For Milford, PA.

North Arlington
Borough
ZIP: 07031   **Lat:** 40-47-24 N **Long:** 74-07-37 W
Pop: 13,790 (1990); 16,587 (1980)   **Pop Density:** 5303.8
Land: 2.6 sq. mi.; **Water:** 0.0 sq. mi.   **Elev:** 122 ft.
In northeastern NJ on the Passaic River, 4 mi. north of Newark. Formed Mar 11, 1896.

Northvale
Borough
ZIP: 07647   **Lat:** 41-00-35 N **Long:** 73-57-00 W
Pop: 4,563 (1990); 5,046 (1980)   **Pop Density:** 3510.0
Land: 1.3 sq. mi.; **Water:** 0.0 sq. mi.   **Elev:** 50 ft.
Replaced Harrington Township Mar 15, 1916.

Norwood
Borough
ZIP: 07648   **Lat:** 40-59-38 N **Long:** 73-57-06 W
Pop: 4,858 (1990); 4,413 (1980)   **Pop Density:** 1735.0
Land: 2.8 sq. mi.; **Water:** 0.0 sq. mi.   **Elev:** 50 ft.
Formed Mar 14, 1905.

Name origin: For its location in the north woods of the county.

Oakland
Borough
ZIP: 07436   **Lat:** 41-01-52 N **Long:** 74-14-25 W
Pop: 11,997 (1990); 13,443 (1980)   **Pop Density:** 1395.0
Land: 8.6 sq. mi.; **Water:** 0.1 sq. mi.   **Elev:** 220 ft.
In northeastern NJ, northwest of Paterson. Formed Apr 8, 1902.

Name origin: For white oak trees native to the area.

Old Tappan
Borough
ZIP: 07675   **Lat:** 41-00-58 N **Long:** 73-58-58 W
Pop: 4,254 (1990); 4,168 (1980)   **Pop Density:** 1329.4
Land: 3.2 sq. mi.; **Water:** 0.8 sq. mi.   **Elev:** 80 ft.
Formed Oct 18, 1894.

Name origin: From an Indian tribal name perhaps meaning 'cold stream.'

Oradell
Borough
ZIP: 07649   **Lat:** 40-57-18 N **Long:** 74-01-51 W
Pop: 8,024 (1990); 8,658 (1980)   **Pop Density:** 3343.3
Land: 2.4 sq. mi.; **Water:** 0.1 sq. mi.   **Elev:** 91 ft.
Replaced Delford Borough Nov 12, 1920.

Name origin: From Latin term *ora* meaning 'edge,' combined with *dell*.

Palisades Park
Borough
ZIP: 07650   **Lat:** 40-50-49 N **Long:** 73-59-50 W
Pop: 14,536 (1990); 13,732 (1980)   **Pop Density:** 12113.3
Land: 1.2 sq. mi.; **Water:** 0.1 sq. mi.   **Elev:** 100 ft.
Formed Mar 22, 1899.

Name origin: For its location on the Palisades along the western bank of the Hudson River.

Paramus
Borough
ZIP: 07652   **Lat:** 40-56-42 N **Long:** 74-04-17 W
Pop: 25,067 (1990); 26,474 (1980)   **Pop Density:** 2387.3
Land: 10.5 sq. mi.; **Water:** 0.0 sq. mi.   **Elev:** 56 ft.
Formed Mar 2, 1922.

Name origin: From an Algonquian term probably meaning 'turkey river,' their name for the Saddle River.

Park Ridge
Borough
ZIP: 07656   **Lat:** 41-02-08 N **Long:** 74-02-29 W
Pop: 8,102 (1990); 8,515 (1980)   **Pop Density:** 3116.2
Land: 2.6 sq. mi.; **Water:** 0.0 sq. mi.   **Elev:** 250 ft.
Formed May 15, 1894.
Name origin: For its location.

Ramsey
Borough
ZIP: 07446   **Lat:** 41-03-33 N **Long:** 74-08-47 W
Pop: 13,228 (1990); 12,899 (1980)   **Pop Density:** 2405.1
Land: 5.5 sq. mi.; **Water:** 0.0 sq. mi.   **Elev:** 330 ft.
In northeastern NJ, 9 mi. north of Paterson. Formed Mar 10, 1908.
Name origin: For either Peter Ramsey, a local landowner, or for a Ramsey who owned a tavern in the area in the 1700s.

Ridgefield
Borough
ZIP: 07657   **Lat:** 40-49-53 N **Long:** 74-00-56 W
Pop: 9,996 (1990); 10,294 (1980)   **Pop Density:** 3844.6
Land: 2.6 sq. mi.; **Water:** 0.3 sq. mi.   **Elev:** 70 ft.
Formed May 26, 1892.
Name origin: For gently undulating ridges found in the region.

Ridgefield Park
Village
ZIP: 07660   **Lat:** 40-51-16 N **Long:** 74-01-13 W
Pop: 12,454 (1990); 12,738 (1980)   **Pop Density:** 7325.9
Land: 1.7 sq. mi.; **Water:** 0.2 sq. mi.   **Elev:** 100 ft.
In northeastern NJ, 8 mi. southeast of Paterson. Formed Jun 15, 1892.
Name origin: For Ridgefield, NJ.

Ridgewood
Village
ZIP: 07450   **Lat:** 40-58-51 N **Long:** 74-06-50 W
Pop: 24,152 (1990); 25,208 (1980)   **Pop Density:** 4164.1
Land: 5.8 sq. mi.; **Water:** 0.0 sq. mi.   **Elev:** 144 ft.
In northeastern NJ, 5 mi. northeast of Paterson. Replaced Ridgewood Township Nov 20, 1894.
Name origin: Descriptive of its location and terrain.

River Edge
Borough
ZIP: 07661   **Lat:** 40-55-37 N **Long:** 74-02-24 W
Pop: 10,603 (1990); 11,111 (1980)   **Pop Density:** 5580.5
Land: 1.9 sq. mi.; **Water:** 0.0 sq. mi.   **Elev:** 90 ft.
In northeastern NJ, 4 mi. north of Hackensack. Replaced Riverside Borough Dec 1, 1930.
Name origin: For its location on the Hackensack River.

River Vale
Township
ZIP: 07675   **Lat:** 41-00-49 N **Long:** 74-00-25 W
Pop: 9,410 (1990); 9,489 (1980)   **Pop Density:** 2295.1
Land: 4.1 sq. mi.; **Water:** 0.2 sq. mi.
Formed Apr 30, 1906.
Name origin: For its location on the Hackensack River.

Rochelle Park
Township
ZIP: 07662   **Lat:** 40-54-23 N **Long:** 74-04-42 W
Pop: 5,587 (1990); 5,603 (1980)   **Pop Density:** 5587.0
Land: 1.0 sq. mi.; **Water:** 0.0 sq. mi.
Replaced Midland Township Nov 5, 1929.
Name origin: For La Rochelle, France.

Rockleigh
Borough
ZIP: 07647   **Lat:** 41-00-07 N **Long:** 73-56-07 W
Pop: 270 (1990); 192 (1980)   **Pop Density:** 270.0
Land: 1.0 sq. mi.; **Water:** 0.0 sq. mi.   **Elev:** 50 ft.
Formed Mar 13, 1923.
Name origin: For the VA estate of Robert L. Tait, the borough's first mayor.

Rutherford
Borough
ZIP: 07070   **Lat:** 40-49-11 N **Long:** 74-06-25 W
Pop: 17,790 (1990); 19,068 (1980)   **Pop Density:** 6353.6
Land: 2.8 sq. mi.; **Water:** 0.1 sq. mi.   **Elev:** 100 ft.
In northeastern NJ, 7 mi. southeast of Paterson. Formed Sep 21, 1881.
Name origin: For John Rutherford, son of a retired British officer but an active patriot and personal friend of George Washington (1732–99).

Saddle Brook
Township
ZIP: 07662   **Lat:** 40-54-15 N **Long:** 74-05-43 W
Pop: 13,296 (1990); 14,084 (1980)   **Pop Density:** 4924.4
Land: 2.7 sq. mi.; **Water:** 0.0 sq. mi.
In northeastern NJ, east of Paterson. Replaced Saddle River Township Nov 8, 1955.
Name origin: For the brook, meaning of name is unknown.

Saddle River
Borough
ZIP: 07458   **Lat:** 41-01-34 N **Long:** 74-05-56 W
Pop: 2,950 (1990); 2,763 (1980)   **Pop Density:** 590.0
Land: 5.0 sq. mi.; **Water:** 0.0 sq. mi.   **Elev:** 143 ft.
Formed Nov 22, 1894.
Name origin: For a stream and valley in Argyleshire, Scotland; meaning of name is unknown.

South Hackensack
Township
     Lat: 40-51-27 N **Long:** 74-02-57 W
Pop: 2,106 (1990); 2,229 (1980)   **Pop Density:** 3008.6
Land: 0.7 sq. mi.; **Water:** 0.0 sq. mi.
Replaced Lodi Township Nov 15, 1935.

Teaneck
Township
ZIP: 07666   **Lat:** 40-53-22 N **Long:** 74-00-43 W
Pop: 37,825 (1990); 39,007 (1980)   **Pop Density:** 6200.8
Land: 6.1 sq. mi.; **Water:** 0.2 sq. mi.
In northeastern NJ, 8 mi. east of Paterson. Formed Feb 19, 1895.
Name origin: From a local Dutch family name, Teneyck or Ten Eyck, possibly meaning 'on a neck' of land.

Tenafly
Borough
ZIP: 07670   **Lat:** 40-55-01 N **Long:** 73-57-18 W
Pop: 13,326 (1990); 13,552 (1980)   **Pop Density:** 2897.0
Land: 4.6 sq. mi.; **Water:** 0.6 sq. mi.   **Elev:** 52 ft.
In northeastern NJ, 11 mi. east of Paterson. Formed Jan 24, 1894.
Name origin: From Dutch *thyne* or *tuin* and *vly* meaning 'garden meadow.'

Teterboro
Borough
ZIP: 07608   **Lat:** 40-51-12 N **Long:** 74-03-38 W
Pop: 22 (1990); 19 (1980)   **Pop Density:** 20.0
Land: 1.1 sq. mi.; **Water:** 0.0 sq. mi.   **Elev:** 5 ft.
Formed Mar 26, 1917.

Upper Saddle River
Borough
ZIP: 07458   **Lat:** 41-03-48 N **Long:** 74-06-01 W
Pop: 7,198 (1990); 7,958 (1980)   **Pop Density:** 1358.1
Land: 5.3 sq. mi.; **Water:** 0.0 sq. mi.   **Elev:** 220 ft.
Formed Nov 22, 1894.
Name origin: For its location north of Saddle River Township.

Waldwick
Borough
ZIP: 07463   **Lat:** 41-00-46 N **Long:** 74-07-30 W
Pop: 9,757 (1990); 10,802 (1980)   **Pop Density:** 4646.2
Land: 2.1 sq. mi.; **Water:** 0.0 sq. mi.   **Elev:** 228 ft.
In northeastern NJ, 7 mi. north of Paterson. Replaced Orvil Township Apr 7, 1919.
Name origin: From an Anglo-Saxon term meaning 'village in a grove.'

Wallington
Borough
ZIP: 07057   **Lat:** 40-51-11 N **Long:** 74-06-24 W
Pop: 10,828 (1990); 10,741 (1980)   **Pop Density:** 10828.0
Land: 1.0 sq. mi.; **Water:** 0.0 sq. mi.   **Elev:** 30 ft.
In northeastern NJ on the Passaic River, 6 mi. southeast of Paterson. Formed Jan 2, 1895.
Name origin: For Walling Jackobs.

Washington
Township
ZIP: 07675   **Lat:** 40-59-20 N **Long:** 74-03-54 W
Pop: 9,245 (1990); 9,550 (1980)   **Pop Density:** 3187.9
Land: 2.9 sq. mi.; **Water:** 0.0 sq. mi.

Westwood
Borough
ZIP: 07675   **Lat:** 40-59-18 N **Long:** 74-01-52 W
Pop: 10,446 (1990); 10,714 (1980)   **Pop Density:** 4541.7
Land: 2.3 sq. mi.; **Water:** 0.0 sq. mi.   **Elev:** 75 ft.
In northeastern NJ, 9 mi. northeast of Paterson. Formed May 9, 1894.

Woodcliff Lake
Borough
ZIP: 07675   **Lat:** 41-01-32 N **Long:** 74-03-40 W
Pop: 5,303 (1990); 5,644 (1980)   **Pop Density:** 1607.0
Land: 3.3 sq. mi.; **Water:** 0.2 sq. mi.   **Elev:** 249 ft.
Replaced Woodcliff Borough Mar 1, 1910.
Name origin: For its location on a lake in the woods at the base of a cliff.

Wood-Ridge
Borough
ZIP: 07075   **Lat:** 40-51-01 N **Long:** 74-05-15 W
Pop: 7,506 (1990); 7,929 (1980)   **Pop Density:** 6823.6
Land: 1.1 sq. mi.; **Water:** 0.0 sq. mi.   **Elev:** 170 ft.
Formed Dec 6, 1894.

Wyckoff
Township
ZIP: 07481   **Lat:** 40-59-52 N **Long:** 74-09-59 W
Pop: 15,372 (1990); 15,500 (1980)   **Pop Density:** 2329.1
Land: 6.6 sq. mi.; **Water:** 0.0 sq. mi.
In northeastern NJ, 7 mi. north of Paterson. Replaced Franklin Township Nov 2, 1926.
Name origin: For Wicaugh, Malpas, England, with spelling alteration.

Burlington County
County Seat: Mount Holly (ZIP: 08060)

Pop: 395,066 (1990); 362,542 (1980)   **Pop Density:** 490.9
Land: 804.8 sq. mi.; **Water:** 14.7 sq. mi.   **Area Code:** 609
In central NJ, east of Philadelphia; original county, organized May 17, 1694.
Name origin: For Bridlington, Yorkshire, England. The alternate spelling reflects the pronunciation used in England.

Bass River
Township
Lat: 39-39-27 N **Long:** 74-26-59 W
Pop: 1,580 (1990); 1,344 (1980)   **Pop Density:** 20.8
Land: 75.9 sq. mi.; **Water:** 2.4 sq. mi.
Formed Mar 30, 1864.
Name origin: For its location on the river.

Beverly
City
ZIP: 08010   **Lat:** 40-03-52 N **Long:** 74-55-18 W
Pop: 2,973 (1990); 2,919 (1980)   **Pop Density:** 4955.0
Land: 0.6 sq. mi.; **Water:** 0.2 sq. mi.   **Elev:** 28 ft.
Replaced Beverly Borough Apr 13, 1857.
Name origin: For Beverly, England.

Bordentown
City
ZIP: 08505   **Lat:** 40-08-54 N **Long:** 74-42-34 W
Pop: 4,341 (1990); 4,441 (1980)   **Pop Density:** 4823.3
Land: 0.9 sq. mi.; **Water:** 0.0 sq. mi.   **Elev:** 40 ft.
Replaced Bordentown Borough Apr 3, 1867.
Name origin: For founder Joseph Borden.

*Bordentown
Township
ZIP: 08505   **Lat:** 40-08-19 N **Long:** 74-42-35 W
Pop: 7,683 (1990); 7,170 (1980)   **Pop Density:** 903.9
Land: 8.5 sq. mi.; **Water:** 0.8 sq. mi.
Formed Mar 8, 1852.

Brown Mills
CDP
ZIP: 08015   **Lat:** 39-58-24 N **Long:** 74-34-04 W
Pop: 11,429 (1990); 10,568 (1980)   **Pop Density:** 2156.4
Land: 5.3 sq. mi.; **Water:** 0.2 sq. mi.

*Burlington
City
ZIP: 08016   **Lat:** 40-04-42 N **Long:** 74-51-10 W
Pop: 9,835 (1990); 10,246 (1980)   **Pop Density:** 3278.3
Land: 3.0 sq. mi.; **Water:** 0.7 sq. mi.   **Elev:** 10 ft.
In southern NJ on the Delaware River, 11 mi. southwest of Trenton. Not included in the township. Incorporated Oct 1693.
Name origin: A corruption of Bridlington. Also previously called New Beverly.

*Burlington   Township
ZIP: 08016   **Lat:** 40-03-54 N **Long:** 74-50-25 W
Pop: 12,454 (1990); 11,527 (1980)   **Pop Density:** 922.5
Land: 13.5 sq. mi.; **Water:** 0.5 sq. mi.
Incorporated Feb 21, 1798.

Chesterfield   Township
ZIP: 08505   **Lat:** 40-07-18 N **Long:** 74-39-19 W
Pop: 5,152 (1990); 3,867 (1980)   **Pop Density:** 238.5
Land: 21.6 sq. mi.; **Water:** 0.1 sq. mi.
Incorporated Feb 21, 1798.

Cinnaminson   Township
ZIP: 08077   **Lat:** 39-59-59 N **Long:** 74-59-29 W
Pop: 14,583 (1990); 16,072 (1980)   **Pop Density:** 1918.8
Land: 7.6 sq. mi.; **Water:** 0.5 sq. mi.
Formed Mar 15, 1860.
Name origin: From Algonquian, possibly meaning 'stone island' or 'stone tree,' e.g., the sugar maple (for its hard wood).

Country Lake Estates   CDP
Lat: 39-56-55 N **Long:** 74-32-27 W
Pop: 4,492 (1990); 3,739 (1980)   **Pop Density:** 4083.6
Land: 1.1 sq. mi.; **Water:** 0.3 sq. mi.

Delanco   Township
Lat: 40-02-57 N **Long:** 74-56-56 W
Pop: 3,316 (1990); 3,730 (1980)   **Pop Density:** 1326.4
Land: 2.5 sq. mi.; **Water:** 0.9 sq. mi.
Replaced Beverly Township Dec 20, 1926.
Name origin: A coined word from its location on the Delaware River and Rancocas Creek.

Delran   Township
ZIP: 08075   **Lat:** 40-00-49 N **Long:** 74-56-55 W
Pop: 13,178 (1990); 14,811 (1980)   **Pop Density:** 1996.7
Land: 6.6 sq. mi.; **Water:** 0.6 sq. mi.
Formed Feb 12, 1880.
Name origin: Probably a coined word for its location near the Delaware River and Rancocas Creek.

Eastampton   Township
Lat: 40-00-02 N **Long:** 74-45-28 W
Pop: 4,962 (1990); 3,814 (1980)   **Pop Density:** 870.5
Land: 5.7 sq. mi.; **Water:** 0.1 sq. mi.
Formed Feb 11, 1880.

Edgewater Park   Township
ZIP: 08010   **Lat:** 40-03-16 N **Long:** 74-54-44 W
Pop: 8,388 (1990); 9,273 (1980)   **Pop Density:** 2892.4
Land: 2.9 sq. mi.; **Water:** 0.1 sq. mi.
Formed Feb 26, 1924.

Evesham   Township
ZIP: 08053   **Lat:** 39-51-21 N **Long:** 74-53-36 W
Pop: 35,309 (1990); 21,508 (1980)   **Pop Density:** 1196.9
Land: 29.5 sq. mi.; **Water:** 0.2 sq. mi.
Incorporated Feb 21, 1798.
Name origin: For Evesham, England.

Fieldsboro   Borough
ZIP: 08505   **Lat:** 40-08-10 N **Long:** 74-43-47 W
Pop: 579 (1990); 597 (1980)   **Pop Density:** 1930.0
Land: 0.3 sq. mi.; **Water:** 0.0 sq. mi.   **Elev:** 67 ft.
Formed Mar 7, 1850; reincorporated 1872.
Name origin: For the Field family.

Florence   Township
ZIP: 08518   **Lat:** 40-05-52 N **Long:** 74-47-39 W
Pop: 10,266 (1990); 9,084 (1980)   **Pop Density:** 1058.4
Land: 9.7 sq. mi.; **Water:** 0.4 sq. mi.
Formed Mar 7, 1872.
Name origin: For Florence, Italy.

Fort Dix   Military facility
ZIP: 08640   **Lat:** 40-00-17 N **Long:** 74-36-47 W
Pop: 10,205 (1990)   **Pop Density:** 911.2
Land: 11.2 sq. mi.; **Water:** 0.1 sq. mi.

Hainesport   Township
Lat: 39-58-40 N **Long:** 74-50-07 W
Pop: 3,249 (1990); 3,236 (1980)   **Pop Density:** 499.8
Land: 6.5 sq. mi.; **Water:** 0.2 sq. mi.
Formed Mar 12, 1924.
Name origin: For Barclay Haines, an early resident.

Leisuretowne   CDP
Lat: 39-54-03 N **Long:** 74-42-16 W
Pop: 2,552 (1990); 2,375 (1980)   **Pop Density:** 1417.8
Land: 1.8 sq. mi.; **Water:** 0.0 sq. mi.

Lumberton   Township
ZIP: 08048   **Lat:** 39-57-15 N **Long:** 74-48-16 W
Pop: 6,705 (1990); 5,236 (1980)   **Pop Density:** 519.8
Land: 12.9 sq. mi.; **Water:** 0.2 sq. mi.
Formed Mar 14, 1860.
Name origin: For a colonial lumber industry.

Mansfield   Township
Lat: 40-04-57 N **Long:** 74-42-51 W
Pop: 3,874 (1990); 2,523 (1980)   **Pop Density:** 178.5
Land: 21.7 sq. mi.; **Water:** 0.1 sq. mi.
Incorporated Feb 21, 1798.
Name origin: For Mansfield, England.

Maple Shade   Township
ZIP: 08052   **Lat:** 39-57-04 N **Long:** 74-59-44 W
Pop: 19,211 (1990); 20,525 (1980)   **Pop Density:** 5055.5
Land: 3.8 sq. mi.; **Water:** 0.0 sq. mi.
In southeastern NJ, 7 mi. east of Camden. Replaced Chester Township Nov 6, 1945.

Marlton   CDP
ZIP: 08053   **Lat:** 39-54-05 N **Long:** 74-55-45 W
Pop: 10,228 (1990); 9,411 (1980)   **Pop Density:** 3196.3
Land: 3.2 sq. mi.; **Water:** 0.0 sq. mi.

McGuire Air Force Base   Military facility
ZIP: 08641   **Lat:** 40-02-28 N **Long:** 74-35-03 W
Pop: 7,580 (1990); 2,538 (1980)   **Pop Density:** 3609.5
Land: 2.1 sq. mi.; **Water:** 0.0 sq. mi.

Medford   Township
ZIP: 08055   **Lat:** 39-51-43 N **Long:** 74-49-27 W
Pop: 20,526 (1990); 17,622 (1980)   **Pop Density:** 522.3
Land: 39.3 sq. mi.; **Water:** 0.5 sq. mi.
Founded before 1759; formed Mar 1, 1847.
Name origin: Named in 1828 by Mark Reeve for Medford, MA.

Medford Lakes
Borough
Lat: 39-51-33 N **Long:** 74-48-20 W
Pop: 4,462 (1990); 4,958 (1980) **Pop Density:** 3718.3
Land: 1.2 sq. mi.; **Water:** 0.1 sq. mi. **Elev:** 80 ft.
Formed May 17, 1939.
Name origin: For the local lake, which was named for Medford, MA.

Moorestown
Township
ZIP: 08057 **Lat:** 39-58-46 N **Long:** 74-56-29 W
Pop: 16,116 (1990); 15,596 (1980) **Pop Density:** 1088.9
Land: 14.8 sq. mi.; **Water:** 0.2 sq. mi.
In south-central NJ, 9 mi. east of Camden. Formed Mar 11, 1922.
Name origin: For poet Thomas Moore (1779–1852).

Mount Holly
Township
ZIP: 08060 **Lat:** 39-59-42 N **Long:** 74-47-12 W
Pop: 10,639 (1990); 10,818 (1980) **Pop Density:** 3668.6
Land: 2.9 sq. mi.; **Water:** 0.0 sq. mi.
In south-central NJ, 16 mi. south of Trenton. Settled 1676. County seat 1796. Replaced Northampton Township Nov 6, 1931.
Name origin: For a hill covered with holly trees.

Mount Laurel
Township
ZIP: 08054 **Lat:** 39-56-59 N **Long:** 74-54-25 W
Pop: 30,270 (1990); 17,614 (1980) **Pop Density:** 1388.5
Land: 21.8 sq. mi.; **Water:** 0.1 sq. mi.
Formed Mar 7, 1872.
Name origin: For a hill covered with laurel bushes.

New Hanover
Township
ZIP: 08511 **Lat:** 40-00-54 N **Long:** 74-34-27 W
Pop: 9,546 (1990); 14,258 (1980) **Pop Density:** 428.1
Land: 22.3 sq. mi.; **Water:** 0.1 sq. mi.
Incorporated Feb 21, 1798.

North Hanover
Township
ZIP: 08562 **Lat:** 40-04-51 N **Long:** 74-35-09 W
Pop: 9,994 (1990); 9,050 (1980) **Pop Density:** 584.4
Land: 17.1 sq. mi.; **Water:** 0.0 sq. mi.
Formed Apr 12, 1905.

Palmyra
Borough
ZIP: 08065 **Lat:** 40-00-07 N **Long:** 75-02-05 W
Pop: 7,056 (1990); 7,085 (1980) **Pop Density:** 3528.0
Land: 2.0 sq. mi.; **Water:** 0.4 sq. mi. **Elev:** 18 ft.
Replaced Palmyra Township Feb 20, 1923.
Name origin: For Palmyra, Syria, which means 'palm trees.'

Pemberton
Township
ZIP: 08068 **Lat:** 39-57-26 N **Long:** 74-36-05 W
Pop: 31,342 (1990); 29,720 (1980) **Pop Density:** 507.2
Land: 61.8 sq. mi.; **Water:** 0.8 sq. mi.
Formed Mar 10, 1846.

*Pemberton
Borough
ZIP: 08068 **Lat:** 39-58-17 N **Long:** 74-41-10 W
Pop: 1,367 (1990); 1,198 (1980) **Pop Density:** 2278.3
Land: 0.6 sq. mi.; **Water:** 0.0 sq. mi. **Elev:** 60 ft.
Formed Dec 15, 1826.
Name origin: For landowner James Pemberton.

Pemberton Heights
CDP
Lat: 39-57-27 N **Long:** 74-40-41 W
Pop: 2,941 (1990); 3,150 (1980) **Pop Density:** 3267.8
Land: 0.9 sq. mi.; **Water:** 0.0 sq. mi.

Presidential Lakes Estates
CDP
Lat: 39-54-49 N **Long:** 74-33-53 W
Pop: 2,450 (1990); 2,607 (1980) **Pop Density:** 2450.0
Land: 1.0 sq. mi.; **Water:** 0.0 sq. mi.

Ramblewood
CDP
ZIP: 08054 **Lat:** 39-55-53 N **Long:** 74-57-11 W
Pop: 6,181 (1990); 6,475 (1980) **Pop Density:** 1817.9
Land: 3.4 sq. mi.; **Water:** 0.0 sq. mi.

Riverside
Township
ZIP: 08075 **Lat:** 40-02-07 N **Long:** 74-57-21 W
Pop: 7,974 (1990); 7,941 (1980) **Pop Density:** 5316.0
Land: 1.5 sq. mi.; **Water:** 0.1 sq. mi.
Formed Feb 20, 1895.
Name origin: For its location on the Delaware River.

Riverton
Borough
ZIP: 08077 **Lat:** 40-00-42 N **Long:** 75-00-53 W
Pop: 2,775 (1990); 3,068 (1980) **Pop Density:** 3964.3
Land: 0.7 sq. mi.; **Water:** 0.3 sq. mi. **Elev:** 17 ft.
Formed Dec 18, 1893.
Name origin: For its proximity to the Delaware River.

Shamong
Township
ZIP: 08088 **Lat:** 39-46-12 N **Long:** 74-43-18 W
Pop: 5,765 (1990); 4,537 (1980) **Pop Density:** 128.7
Land: 44.8 sq. mi.; **Water:** 0.2 sq. mi.
Formed Feb 19, 1852.
Name origin: From an Indian term possibly meaning 'horn place.'

Southampton
Township
ZIP: 08088 **Lat:** 39-54-52 N **Long:** 74-42-58 W
Pop: 10,202 (1990); 8,808 (1980) **Pop Density:** 231.3
Land: 44.1 sq. mi.; **Water:** 0.1 sq. mi.
Replaced Coaxen Township Apr 1, 1845.

Springfield
Township
Lat: 40-02-24 N **Long:** 74-42-32 W
Pop: 3,028 (1990); 2,691 (1980) **Pop Density:** 100.9
Land: 30.0 sq. mi.; **Water:** 0.0 sq. mi.
Incorporated Feb 21, 1798.
Name origin: For the abundant springs and brooks in the area.

Tabernacle
Township
ZIP: 08088 **Lat:** 39-49-19 N **Long:** 74-39-01 W
Pop: 7,360 (1990); 6,236 (1980) **Pop Density:** 148.7
Land: 49.5 sq. mi.; **Water:** 0.1 sq. mi.
Formed Mar 22, 1901.
Name origin: For a tabernacle built for David and John Brainerd, Indian missionaries.

Washington
Township
Lat: 39-41-01 N **Long:** 74-34-24 W
Pop: 805 (1990); 808 (1980) **Pop Density:** 8.0
Land: 100.1 sq. mi.; **Water:** 2.7 sq. mi.
Formed Nov 19, 1802.
Name origin: For George Washington (1732–99), first U.S. president.

Westampton
Township
ZIP: 08073 **Lat:** 40-01-00 N **Long:** 74-49-03 W
Pop: 6,004 (1990); 3,383 (1980) **Pop Density:** 545.8
Land: 11.0 sq. mi.; **Water:** 0.1 sq. mi.
Formed Mar 6, 1850.

Willingboro　　　　　　　　　　Township
ZIP: 08046　　　　**Lat:** 40-01-37 N **Long:** 74-53-14 W
Pop: 36,291 (1990); 39,912 (1980)　　**Pop Density:** 4713.1
Land: 7.7 sq. mi.; **Water:** 0.3 sq. mi.

In southern NJ, northeast of Camden. Incorporated as Willingborough Feb 21, 1798; replaced Levittown Township Nov 12, 1963.

Woodland　　　　　　　　　　Township
　　　　　　Lat: 39-50-27 N **Long:** 74-31-05 W
Pop: 2,063 (1990); 2,285 (1980)　　**Pop Density:** 21.5
Land: 95.9 sq. mi.; **Water:** 0.4 sq. mi.

Formed Mar 7, 1866.

Wrightstown　　　　　　　　　　Borough
ZIP: 08562　　　　**Lat:** 40-01-38 N **Long:** 74-37-51 W
Pop: 3,843 (1990); 3,031 (1980)　　**Pop Density:** 2260.6
Land: 1.7 sq. mi.; **Water:** 0.0 sq. mi.　　**Elev:** 185 ft.

Formed Mar 4, 1866.

Name origin: For John Wright, donor of a street site.

Camden County
County Seat: Camden (ZIP: 08103)

Pop: 502,824 (1990); 471,650 (1980)　　**Pop Density:** 2261.6
Land: 222.3 sq. mi.; **Water:** 5.3 sq. mi.　　**Area Code:** 609

On central western border of NJ, east of Philadelphia; organized Mar 13, 1844 from Gloucester County.

Name origin: For the city of Camden.

Audubon　　　　　　　　　　Borough
ZIP: 08106　　　　**Lat:** 39-53-22 N **Long:** 75-04-21 W
Pop: 9,205 (1990); 9,533 (1980)　　**Pop Density:** 6136.7
Land: 1.5 sq. mi.; **Water:** 0.0 sq. mi.　　**Elev:** 60 ft.

In southwestern NJ, 5 mi. southeast of Camden. Formed Mar 13, 1905.

Name origin: For John James Audubon (1785–1851), naturalist and founder of the Audubon Society.

Audubon Park　　　　　　　　　　Borough
ZIP: 08106　　　　**Lat:** 39-53-45 N **Long:** 75-05-19 W
Pop: 1,150 (1990); 1,274 (1980)　　**Pop Density:** 11500.0
Land: 0.1 sq. mi.; **Water:** 0.0 sq. mi.

Formed Jul 3, 1947.

Barrington　　　　　　　　　　Borough
ZIP: 08007　　　　**Lat:** 39-52-13 N **Long:** 75-03-10 W
Pop: 6,774 (1990); 7,418 (1980)　　**Pop Density:** 4233.8
Land: 1.6 sq. mi.; **Water:** 0.0 sq. mi.　　**Elev:** 81 ft.

In southwestern NJ, 5 mi. southeast of Camden. Formed Mar 27, 1917.

Bellmawr　　　　　　　　　　Borough
ZIP: 08031　　　　**Lat:** 39-51-57 N **Long:** 75-05-41 W
Pop: 12,603 (1990); 13,721 (1980)　　**Pop Density:** 4201.0
Land: 3.0 sq. mi.; **Water:** 0.1 sq. mi.　　**Elev:** 70 ft.

In southwestern NJ, 5 mi. south of Camden. Formed Mar 23, 1926.

Name origin: For horse breeder Ernest C. Bell; *mawr* added for euphony. Originally called Heddings for a church built in 1865; present name adopted when a post office was established.

Berlin　　　　　　　　　　Borough
ZIP: 08009　　　　**Lat:** 39-47-38 N **Long:** 74-56-16 W
Pop: 5,672 (1990); 5,786 (1980)　　**Pop Density:** 1575.6
Land: 3.6 sq. mi.; **Water:** 0.0 sq. mi.　　**Elev:** 155 ft.

In southwestern NJ, 15 mi. southeast of Camden. Formed Mar 29, 1927.

Name origin: For Berlin, Germany. Formerly called Long-a-

Coming by impatient passengers because the stagecoach was usually late arriving here for the dinner stop. Present name adopted when a post office was established.

*Berlin　　　　　　　　　　Township
ZIP: 08009　　　　**Lat:** 39-48-08 N **Long:** 74-55-29 W
Pop: 5,466 (1990); 5,348 (1980)　　**Pop Density:** 1708.1
Land: 3.2 sq. mi.; **Water:** 0.0 sq. mi.

Formed Apr 11, 1910.

Blackwood　　　　　　　　　　CDP
ZIP: 08012　　　　**Lat:** 39-47-54 N **Long:** 75-03-46 W
Pop: 5,120 (1990); 5,219 (1980)　　**Pop Density:** 3938.5
Land: 1.3 sq. mi.; **Water:** 0.0 sq. mi.

Brooklawn　　　　　　　　　　Borough
ZIP: 08030　　　　**Lat:** 39-52-41 N **Long:** 75-07-17 W
Pop: 1,805 (1990); 2,133 (1980)　　**Pop Density:** 3610.0
Land: 0.5 sq. mi.; **Water:** 0.1 sq. mi.　　**Elev:** 24 ft.

A suburb of Camden in southwestern NJ. Formed Mar 11, 1924; reincorporated Mar 23, 1926.

Name origin: Descriptive: bounded on the west by the Delaware River, on the north by Little Timber Creek, and on the south by Big Timber Creek.

Camden　　　　　　　　　　City
ZIP: 08101　　　　**Lat:** 39-56-09 N **Long:** 75-06-30 W
Pop: 87,492 (1990); 84,910 (1980)　　**Pop Density:** 9942.3
Land: 8.8 sq. mi.; **Water:** 1.6 sq. mi.　　**Elev:** 33 ft.

In southwestern NJ on the Delaware River across from Philadelphia. Manufacturing includes licorice extract, fabricated metal products. Site of Rutgers State University of NJ. Formed Feb 13, 1828; reincorporated Mar 11, 1850.

Name origin: For Charles Pratt (1714–94), the first Earl of Camden, who supported the colonies during their disputes with England.

Cherry Hill
Township
ZIP: 08002 **Lat:** 39-54-08 N **Long:** 74-59-45 W
Pop: 69,348 (1990); 68,785 (1980) **Pop Density:** 2853.8
Land: 24.3 sq. mi.; **Water:** 0.1 sq. mi.

In west-central NJ, an eastern suburb of Camden. Replaced Delaware Township Nov 7, 1961.

Name origin: For a path lined with cherry trees that led to an old farm on a hill.

Chesilhurst
Borough
ZIP: 08089 **Lat:** 39-43-55 N **Long:** 74-52-47 W
Pop: 1,526 (1990); 1,590 (1980) **Pop Density:** 897.6
Land: 1.7 sq. mi.; **Water:** 0.0 sq. mi. **Elev:** 178 ft.
Formed Nov 26, 1887.

Name origin: A coined name; origin unknown.

Clementon
Borough
ZIP: 08021 **Lat:** 39-48-15 N **Long:** 74-59-08 W
Pop: 5,601 (1990); 5,764 (1980) **Pop Density:** 2947.9
Land: 1.9 sq. mi.; **Water:** 0.1 sq. mi. **Elev:** 96 ft.

In southwestern NJ, southeast of Camden. Formed Feb 13, 1925.

Name origin: For industrialist Samuel Clements.

Collingswood
Borough
ZIP: 08108 **Lat:** 39-54-58 N **Long:** 75-04-30 W
Pop: 15,289 (1990); 15,838 (1980) **Pop Density:** 8493.9
Land: 1.8 sq. mi.; **Water:** 0.1 sq. mi. **Elev:** 20 ft.

In southwestern NJ, 3 mi. southeast of Camden. Formed May 22, 1888; reincorporated Mar 15, 1911.

Name origin: For the mother of Edward Collings Knight. Originally called Newton.

Gibbsboro
Borough
ZIP: 08026 **Lat:** 39-50-00 N **Long:** 74-57-59 W
Pop: 2,383 (1990); 2,510 (1980) **Pop Density:** 1083.2
Land: 2.2 sq. mi.; **Water:** 0.0 sq. mi. **Elev:** 122 ft.
Formed Mar 8, 1924.

Glendora
CDP
ZIP: 08029 **Lat:** 39-50-25 N **Long:** 75-04-08 W
Pop: 5,201 (1990); 5,632 (1980) **Pop Density:** 4728.2
Land: 1.1 sq. mi.; **Water:** 0.0 sq. mi.

Gloucester
Township
ZIP: 08012 **Lat:** 39-47-33 N **Long:** 75-02-06 W
Pop: 53,797 (1990); 45,156 (1980) **Pop Density:** 2318.8
Land: 23.2 sq. mi.; **Water:** 0.1 sq. mi.
Incorporated Feb 21, 1798.

Gloucester City
City
ZIP: 08030 **Lat:** 39-53-32 N **Long:** 75-07-04 W
Pop: 12,649 (1990); 13,121 (1980) **Pop Density:** 5749.5
Land: 2.2 sq. mi.; **Water:** 0.6 sq. mi.

In southwestern NJ on Delaware River, 3 mi. south of Camden. Replaced Union Township Feb 25, 1868.

Name origin: Probably for Henry, Duke of Gloucester (1639–60), son of King Charles I of England.

Haddon
Township
ZIP: 08108 **Lat:** 39-54-21 N **Long:** 75-03-46 W
Pop: 14,837 (1990); 15,875 (1980) **Pop Density:** 5495.2
Land: 2.7 sq. mi.; **Water:** 0.1 sq. mi.

In southwestern NJ, southeast of Camden. Formed Feb 23, 1865.

Name origin: Probably for Elizabeth Haddon.

Haddonfield
Borough
ZIP: 08033 **Lat:** 39-53-41 N **Long:** 75-02-04 W
Pop: 11,628 (1990); 12,337 (1980) **Pop Density:** 4152.9
Land: 2.8 sq. mi.; **Water:** 0.0 sq. mi. **Elev:** 81 ft.

In southwestern NJ, 10 mi. west of Camden. Founded 1710 by Elizabeth Haddon, a Quaker, who was sent over from England by her father, who had no sons, to develop 400 acres of land. Within a year the young woman had started her colony, erected a home, and married John Estaugh, a Quaker missionary, because she had the courage to propose to him. Henry Wadsworth Longfellow (1807–82) tells the story of the romance with the "Theologian's Tale" in *Tales of a Wayside Inn*. Formed Apr 6, 1875.

Name origin: For founder Elizabeth Haddon.

Haddon Heights
Borough
ZIP: 08035 **Lat:** 39-52-43 N **Long:** 75-03-57 W
Pop: 7,860 (1990); 8,361 (1980) **Pop Density:** 4912.5
Land: 1.6 sq. mi.; **Water:** 0.0 sq. mi. **Elev:** 60 ft.
Formed Mar 2, 1904.

Hi-Nella
Borough
ZIP: 08083 **Lat:** 39-50-06 N **Long:** 75-01-19 W
Pop: 1,045 (1990); 1,250 (1980) **Pop Density:** 5225.0
Land: 0.2 sq. mi.; **Water:** 0.0 sq. mi.
Formed Apr 23, 1929.

Name origin: For an Indian village formerly on the site, the name meaning 'high rolling knoll.'

Laurel Springs
Borough
ZIP: 08021 **Lat:** 39-49-12 N **Long:** 75-00-21 W
Pop: 2,341 (1990); 2,249 (1980) **Pop Density:** 4682.0
Land: 0.5 sq. mi.; **Water:** 0.0 sq. mi. **Elev:** 82 ft.
Formed Apr 2, 1913.

Name origin: For its medicinal springs in a grove of laurels.

Lawnside
Borough
ZIP: 08045 **Lat:** 39-51-56 N **Long:** 75-01-50 W
Pop: 2,841 (1990); 3,042 (1980) **Pop Density:** 2029.3
Land: 1.4 sq. mi.; **Water:** 0.0 sq. mi. **Elev:** 110 ft.

Founded during 19th-century antislavery agitation. One of the first black-owned boroughs in NJ and one of the few in the U.S. Formed Mar 24, 1926.

Name origin: For the lawn beside the railroad station.

Lindenwold
Borough
ZIP: 08021 **Lat:** 39-48-57 N **Long:** 74-59-24 W
Pop: 18,734 (1990); 18,196 (1980) **Pop Density:** 4803.6
Land: 3.9 sq. mi.; **Water:** 0.0 sq. mi. **Elev:** 90 ft.

In southwestern NJ, 12 mi. southeast of Camden. Formed Apr 23, 1929.

Name origin: For the linden trees and the open, hilly countryside.

Magnolia
Borough
ZIP: 08049 **Lat:** 39-51-19 N **Long:** 75-02-10 W
Pop: 4,861 (1990); 4,881 (1980) **Pop Density:** 4861.0
Land: 1.0 sq. mi.; **Water:** 0.0 sq. mi. **Elev:** 79 ft.
Formed Apr 14, 1915.

Name origin: For the magnolia trees in the area. Called Greenland in Civil War days for the greenish tinge of the soil.

Merchantville
Borough
ZIP: 08109 **Lat:** 39-56-59 N **Long:** 75-03-02 W
Pop: 4,095 (1990); 3,972 (1980) **Pop Density:** 6825.0
Land: 0.6 sq. mi.; **Water:** 0.0 sq. mi. **Elev:** 80 ft.
Formed Mar 3, 1874.

Mount Ephraim
Borough
ZIP: 08059   Lat: 39-52-51 N Long: 75-05-30 W
Pop: 4,517 (1990); 4,863 (1980)   Pop Density: 5018.9
Land: 0.9 sq. mi.; Water: 0.0 sq. mi.

Oaklyn
Borough
ZIP: 08107   Lat: 39-54-07 N Long: 75-04-50 W
Pop: 4,430 (1990); 4,223 (1980)   Pop Density: 7383.3
Land: 0.6 sq. mi.; Water: 0.1 sq. mi.   Elev: 20 ft.
In southwestern NJ. Formed Mar 13, 1905.

Pennsauken
Township
ZIP: 08110   Lat: 39-57-49 N Long: 75-03-22 W
Pop: 34,738 (1990); 33,775 (1980)   Pop Density: 3308.4
Land: 10.5 sq. mi.; Water: 1.7 sq. mi.
In southwestern NJ, east of Camden. Formed Feb 18, 1892.
Name origin: For William Penn and the Indian term *sauk* probably meaning 'water inlet or outlet.'

Pine Hill
Borough
ZIP: 08021   Lat: 39-47-11 N Long: 74-59-09 W
Pop: 9,854 (1990); 8,684 (1980)   Pop Density: 2526.7
Land: 3.9 sq. mi.; Water: 0.0 sq. mi.   Elev: 170 ft.
Formed Apr 23, 1929.
Name origin: For its terrain and wood cover.

Pine Valley
Borough
ZIP: 08021   Lat: 39-47-18 N Long: 74-58-20 W
Pop: 19 (1990); 23 (1980)   Pop Density: 19.0
Land: 1.0 sq. mi.; Water: 0.0 sq. mi.   Elev: 164 ft.
Formed Apr 23, 1929.

Runnemede
Borough
ZIP: 08078   Lat: 39-51-05 N Long: 75-04-30 W
Pop: 9,042 (1990); 9,461 (1980)   Pop Density: 4305.7
Land: 2.1 sq. mi.; Water: 0.0 sq. mi.   Elev: 132 ft.
In southwestern NJ, south of Camden City. Formed Mar 23, 1926.
Name origin: For Runnymeade, England, the meadow near London where King John (1167–1216) signed the Magna Carta; with spelling variation.

Somerdale
Borough
ZIP: 08083   Lat: 39-50-43 N Long: 75-01-22 W
Pop: 5,440 (1990); 5,900 (1980)   Pop Density: 3885.7
Land: 1.4 sq. mi.; Water: 0.0 sq. mi.   Elev: 83 ft.
Formed Apr 23, 1929.

Stratford
Borough
ZIP: 08084   Lat: 39-49-41 N Long: 75-00-54 W
Pop: 7,614 (1990); 8,005 (1980)   Pop Density: 4758.8
Land: 1.6 sq. mi.; Water: 0.0 sq. mi.   Elev: 70 ft.
Formed Feb 13, 1925.
Name origin: For Stratford-upon-Avon, England.

Tavistock
Borough
ZIP: 08033   Lat: 39-52-30 N Long: 75-01-42 W
Pop: 35 (1990); 9 (1980)   Pop Density: 116.7
Land: 0.3 sq. mi.; Water: 0.0 sq. mi.   Elev: 40 ft.
Formed Feb 16, 1921.
Name origin: For the English estate of John Gill, an early settler.

Voorhees
Township
ZIP: 08043   Lat: 39-50-48 N Long: 74-57-16 W
Pop: 24,559 (1990); 12,919 (1980)   Pop Density: 2117.2
Land: 11.6 sq. mi.; Water: 0.0 sq. mi.
Formed Mar 1, 1899.
Name origin: For the Van Voor Hees family, Dutch settlers.

Waterford
Township
ZIP: 08089   Lat: 39-44-05 N Long: 74-49-10 W
Pop: 10,940 (1990); 8,126 (1980)   Pop Density: 302.2
Land: 36.2 sq. mi.; Water: 0.1 sq. mi.
Incorporated Feb 21, 1798.
Name origin: For Waterford, England.

Winslow
Township
ZIP: 08004   Lat: 39-42-06 N Long: 74-54-20 W
Pop: 30,087 (1990); 20,034 (1980)   Pop Density: 521.4
Land: 57.7 sq. mi.; Water: 0.4 sq. mi.
Formed Mar 8, 1845.
Name origin: For the Winslow glassworks.

Woodlynne
Borough
ZIP: 08107   Lat: 39-54-58 N Long: 75-05-44 W
Pop: 2,547 (1990); 2,578 (1980)   Pop Density: 12735.0
Land: 0.2 sq. mi.; Water: 0.0 sq. mi.
Borough Hall stands on the site of Mark Newbie's Bank, said to have been the first bank of issue in America. Formed Mar 19, 1901.
Name origin: For linden trees.

Cape May County
County Seat: Cape May Court House (ZIP: 08210)

Pop: 95,089 (1990); 82,266 (1980)   **Pop Density:** 372.6
Land: 255.2 sq. mi.; **Water:** 365.1 sq. mi.   **Area Code:** 609

On southern tip of NJ, south of Atlantic City; organized Nov 12, 1692 from Cumberland County.

Name origin: For the cape, whose name commemorates Cornelis Jacobsen Mey, Dutch captain who explored the Atlantic coast of North America from Long Island to Cape May in 1612–14.

Avalon   Borough
ZIP: 08202   **Lat:** 39-05-29 N **Long:** 74-44-13 W
Pop: 1,809 (1990); 2,162 (1980)   **Pop Density:** 430.7
Land: 4.2 sq. mi.; **Water:** 0.7 sq. mi.   **Elev:** 6 ft.

Formed Apr 18, 1892; reincorporated Mar 6, 1896; reincorporated May 4, 1897.
Name origin: For an island in Celtic mythology.

Cape May   City
ZIP: 08204   **Lat:** 38-56-24 N **Long:** 74-54-19 W
Pop: 4,668 (1990); 4,853 (1980)   **Pop Density:** 1867.2
Land: 2.5 sq. mi.; **Water:** 0.3 sq. mi.   **Elev:** 10 ft.

At the southernmost point of NJ, on a peninsula bordered on the east by the Atlantic Ocean and on the west by Delaware Bay. Replaced Cape Island City Mar 9, 1869; reincorporated 1875.
Name origin: For explorer Cornelius Jacobsen Mey, who explored the area in 1612–14.

Cape May Court House   CDP
ZIP: 08210   **Lat:** 39-04-47 N **Long:** 74-49-26 W
Pop: 4,426 (1990); 3,597 (1980)   **Pop Density:** 491.8
Land: 9.0 sq. mi.; **Water:** 0.1 sq. mi.

Cape May Point   Borough
ZIP: 08212   **Lat:** 38-56-12 N **Long:** 74-57-56 W
Pop: 248 (1990); 255 (1980)   **Pop Density:** 826.7
Land: 0.3 sq. mi.; **Water:** 0.0 sq. mi.

Formed Apr 19, 1878; reincorporated Aug 19, 1891; reincorporated Apr 6, 1908.

Dennis   Township
                       Lat: 39-11-53 N **Long:** 74-49-06 W
Pop: 5,574 (1990); 3,989 (1980)   **Pop Density:** 90.8
Land: 61.4 sq. mi.; **Water:** 2.9 sq. mi.

Formed Mar 1, 1827.

Erma   CDP
ZIP: 08204   **Lat:** 38-59-54 N **Long:** 74-53-41 W
Pop: 2,045 (1990); 1,774 (1980)   **Pop Density:** 601.5
Land: 3.4 sq. mi.; **Water:** 0.0 sq. mi.

Lower   Township
ZIP: 08204   **Lat:** 38-58-43 N **Long:** 74-54-26 W
Pop: 20,820 (1990); 17,105 (1980)   **Pop Density:** 738.3
Land: 28.2 sq. mi.; **Water:** 2.8 sq. mi.

Formed Apr 2, 1723; incorporated Feb 21, 1798.
Name origin: For its location in the lowest part of the county.

Middle   Township
ZIP: 08210   **Lat:** 39-05-10 N **Long:** 74-50-10 W
Pop: 14,771 (1990); 11,373 (1980)   **Pop Density:** 207.2
Land: 71.3 sq. mi.; **Water:** 11.8 sq. mi.

Formed Apr 2, 1723; incorporated Feb 21, 1798.
Name origin: For its location in the center of the county.

North Cape May   CDP
                       Lat: 38-58-34 N **Long:** 74-57-06 W
Pop: 3,574 (1990); 4,029 (1980)   **Pop Density:** 2552.9
Land: 1.4 sq. mi.; **Water:** 0.1 sq. mi.

North Wildwood   City
ZIP: 08260   **Lat:** 39-00-15 N **Long:** 74-47-59 W
Pop: 5,017 (1990); 4,714 (1980)   **Pop Density:** 2787.2
Land: 1.8 sq. mi.; **Water:** 0.4 sq. mi.   **Elev:** 6 ft.

Replaced North Wildwood Borough Apr 30, 1917; reincorporated Mar 8, 1924.

Ocean City   City
ZIP: 08226   **Lat:** 39-16-10 N **Long:** 74-36-12 W
Pop: 15,512 (1990); 13,949 (1980)   **Pop Density:** 2248.1
Land: 6.9 sq. mi.; **Water:** 4.1 sq. mi.   **Elev:** 6 ft.

In southern NJ, 10 mi. southwest of Atlantic City. Replaced Ocean City Borough Mar 25, 1897.
Name origin: For its location on the Atlantic Ocean.

Rio Grande   CDP
ZIP: 08242   **Lat:** 39-01-19 N **Long:** 74-52-39 W
Pop: 2,505 (1990); 2,016 (1980)   **Pop Density:** 1043.8
Land: 2.4 sq. mi.; **Water:** 0.0 sq. mi.

Sea Isle City   City
ZIP: 08243   **Lat:** 39-09-08 N **Long:** 74-41-52 W
Pop: 2,692 (1990); 2,644 (1980)   **Pop Density:** 1223.6
Land: 2.2 sq. mi.; **Water:** 0.3 sq. mi.   **Elev:** 6 ft.

Replaced Sea Isle City Borough Apr 20, 1907.
Name origin: For its location on the island reef bordering Barnegat Bay.

Stone Harbor   Borough
ZIP: 08247   **Lat:** 39-02-38 N **Long:** 74-46-04 W
Pop: 1,025 (1990); 1,187 (1980)   **Pop Density:** 732.1
Land: 1.4 sq. mi.; **Water:** 0.6 sq. mi.   **Elev:** 10 ft.

Formed Apr 3, 1914.
Name origin: Descriptive.

Upper   Township
ZIP: 08250   **Lat:** 39-15-26 N **Long:** 74-43-38 W
Pop: 10,681 (1990); 6,713 (1980)   **Pop Density:** 169.0
Land: 63.2 sq. mi.; **Water:** 5.7 sq. mi.

Formed Apr 2, 1723; incorporated Feb 21, 1798.
Name origin: The northernmost township in the county.

Villas   CDP
ZIP: 08251   **Lat:** 39-00-56 N **Long:** 74-56-12 W
Pop: 8,136 (1990); 5,909 (1980)   **Pop Density:** 2034.0
Land: 4.0 sq. mi.; **Water:** 0.0 sq. mi.

West Cape May   Borough
ZIP: 08204　　**Lat:** 38-56-29 N　**Long:** 74-56-16 W
Pop: 1,026 (1990); 1,091 (1980)　**Pop Density:** 855.0
Land: 1.2 sq. mi.; **Water:** 0.0 sq. mi.　　**Elev:** 6 ft.

Formed Apr 17, 1884; reincorporated Apr 11, 1890; reincorporated May 4, 1897.

Name origin: For its location west of Cape May Township.

West Wildwood   Borough
ZIP: 08260　　**Lat:** 39-00-00 N　**Long:** 74-49-27 W
Pop: 453 (1990); 360 (1980)　**Pop Density:** 1510.0
Land: 0.3 sq. mi.; **Water:** 0.1 sq. mi.　　**Elev:** 10 ft.

Formed Apr 21, 1920.

Name origin: For its location west of Wildwood Township.

Whitesboro-Burleigh   CDP
Lat: 39-02-45 N　**Long:** 74-51-56 W
Pop: 2,080 (1990); 1,583 (1980)　**Pop Density:** 452.2
Land: 4.6 sq. mi.; **Water:** 0.0 sq. mi.

Wildwood   City
ZIP: 08260　　**Lat:** 38-59-19 N　**Long:** 74-49-12 W
Pop: 4,484 (1990); 4,913 (1980)　**Pop Density:** 3449.2
Land: 1.3 sq. mi.; **Water:** 0.1 sq. mi.　　**Elev:** 8 ft.

Replaced Wildwood and Holly Beach city boroughs Jan 1, 1912.

Wildwood Crest   Borough
ZIP: 08260　　**Lat:** 38-58-20 N　**Long:** 74-50-19 W
Pop: 3,631 (1990); 4,149 (1980)　**Pop Density:** 3025.8
Land: 1.2 sq. mi.; **Water:** 0.2 sq. mi.　　**Elev:** 9 ft.

Formed Apr 6, 1910.

Woodbine   Borough
ZIP: 08270　　**Lat:** 39-13-40 N　**Long:** 74-48-30 W
Pop: 2,678 (1990); 2,809 (1980)　**Pop Density:** 334.8
Land: 8.0 sq. mi.; **Water:** 0.0 sq. mi.　　**Elev:** 40 ft.

Formed Mar 3, 1903.

Name origin: For a woody vine, probably honeysuckle or Virginia creeper, abundant in the area.

Cumberland County
County Seat: Bridgeton (ZIP: 08302)

Pop: 138,053 (1990); 132,866 (1980)　　**Pop Density:** 282.1
Land: 489.3 sq. mi.; **Water:** 187.3 sq. mi.　　**Area Code:** 609

In southern NJ, on Delaware Bay; organized Jan 19, 1748 from Salem County.

Name origin: For William Augustus, Duke of Cumberland (1721–65), British general and second son of King George II (1683–1760).

Bridgeton   City
ZIP: 08302　　**Lat:** 39-25-39 N　**Long:** 75-13-41 W
Pop: 18,942 (1990); 18,795 (1980)　**Pop Density:** 3055.2
Land: 6.2 sq. mi.; **Water:** 0.2 sq. mi.　　**Elev:** 40 ft.

In southwestern NJ, 10 mi. north of the mouth of the Delaware River. Replaced Bridgeton and Cohansey townships Mar 1, 1865.

Name origin: A contraction of Bridge Town. Also previously called Cohansy Bridge (for a bridge built across Cohansey Creek c. 1716).

Commercial   Township
ZIP: 08349　　**Lat:** 39-16-24 N　**Long:** 75-02-30 W
Pop: 5,026 (1990); 4,674 (1980)　**Pop Density:** 154.6
Land: 32.5 sq. mi.; **Water:** 2.0 sq. mi.

Formed Feb 27, 1874.

Name origin: For the shellfish industry.

Deerfield   Township
Lat: 39-28-01 N　**Long:** 75-08-27 W
Pop: 2,933 (1990); 2,523 (1980)　**Pop Density:** 174.6
Land: 16.8 sq. mi.; **Water:** 0.0 sq. mi.

Formed Jan 19, 1748; incorporated Feb 21, 1798.

Name origin: For Deerfield, MA.

Downe   Township
Lat: 39-16-10 N　**Long:** 75-08-00 W
Pop: 1,702 (1990); 1,803 (1980)　**Pop Density:** 33.5
Land: 50.8 sq. mi.; **Water:** 3.5 sq. mi.

Formed Sep 26, 1772; incorporated Feb 21, 1798.

Fairfield   Township
ZIP: 08320　　**Lat:** 39-22-10 N　**Long:** 75-14-42 W
Pop: 5,699 (1990); 5,693 (1980)　**Pop Density:** 134.7
Land: 42.3 sq. mi.; **Water:** 1.5 sq. mi.

Formed May 12, 1697; incorporated Feb 21, 1798.

Name origin: For Fairfield, CT.

Fairton   CDP
Lat: 39-22-40 N　**Long:** 75-12-53 W
Pop: 1,359 (1990); 1,107 (1980)　**Pop Density:** 485.4
Land: 2.8 sq. mi.; **Water:** 0.1 sq. mi.

Greenwich   Township
Lat: 39-23-39 N　**Long:** 75-22-11 W
Pop: 911 (1990); 973 (1980)　**Pop Density:** 50.1
Land: 18.2 sq. mi.; **Water:** 0.7 sq. mi.

Formed Jan 19, 1748; incorporated Feb 21, 1798.

Name origin: For Greenwich, England.

Hopewell   Township
Lat: 39-26-04 N　**Long:** 75-16-38 W
Pop: 4,215 (1990); 4,365 (1980)　**Pop Density:** 141.0
Land: 29.9 sq. mi.; **Water:** 0.9 sq. mi.

Formed Jan 19, 1748; incorporated Feb 21, 1798.

Lawrence   Township
Lat: 39-20-01 N　**Long:** 75-11-23 W
Pop: 2,433 (1990); 2,116 (1980)　**Pop Density:** 64.9
Land: 37.5 sq. mi.; **Water:** 1.0 sq. mi.

Formed Feb 17, 1885.

Name origin: For Capt. James Lawrence (1781–1813), commander of the U.S.S. *Chesapeake* during the War of 1812, famous for saying, "Don't give up the ship."

Maurice River
Township
ZIP: 08327   Lat: 39-18-03 N Long: 74-56-26 W
Pop: 6,648 (1990); 4,577 (1980)   Pop Density: 71.2
Land: 93.4 sq. mi.; Water: 2.3 sq. mi.

Formed Jan 19, 1748; incorporated Feb 21, 1798.

Name origin: For the river, itself named for a ship, *Prince Maurice*, burned by Indians; the ship, in turn, named for Prince Maurice (1567–1625) of Orange and Nassau.

Millville
City
ZIP: 08332   Lat: 39-23-24 N Long: 75-03-16 W
Pop: 25,992 (1990); 24,815 (1980)   Pop Density: 613.0
Land: 42.4 sq. mi.; Water: 2.2 sq. mi.   Elev: 37 ft.

In southwestern NJ on the Maurice River, 10 mi. southeast of Bridgeton. Replaced Millville Township Mar 1, 1866.

Name origin: For being founded as a mill town. Formerly called Shingle Landing, Maurice River Bridge, and The Bridge.

Port Norris
CDP
ZIP: 08349   Lat: 39-14-52 N Long: 75-02-28 W
Pop: 1,701 (1990); 1,730 (1980)   Pop Density: 265.8
Land: 6.4 sq. mi.; Water: 0.5 sq. mi.

Rosenhayn
CDP
Lat: 39-28-43 N Long: 75-08-11 W
Pop: 1,053 (1990)   Pop Density: 390.0
Land: 2.7 sq. mi.; Water: 0.0 sq. mi.

Seabrook Farms
CDP
Lat: 39-30-03 N Long: 75-13-05 W
Pop: 1,457 (1990); 1,411 (1980)   Pop Density: 728.5
Land: 2.0 sq. mi.; Water: 0.0 sq. mi.

Shiloh
Borough
ZIP: 08353   Lat: 39-27-28 N Long: 75-17-52 W
Pop: 408 (1990); 604 (1980)   Pop Density: 340.0
Land: 1.2 sq. mi.; Water: 0.0 sq. mi.   Elev: 118 ft.

Founded 1705 by Seventh-Day Baptists fleeing persecution in England. Formed Apr 9, 1929.

Name origin: In 1771, when moving an old frame church, they reached here at sundown on a Friday. Work ceased and religious services were begun. Their pastor used as his text "The Ark of the Lord resteth at Shiloh." Originally known as Cohansey, for an Indian chief.

Stow Creek
Township
Lat: 39-27-08 N Long: 75-20-54 W
Pop: 1,437 (1990); 1,365 (1980)   Pop Density: 78.1
Land: 18.4 sq. mi.; Water: 0.4 sq. mi.

Formed Jan 19, 1748; incorporated Feb 21, 1798.

Upper Deerfield
Township
ZIP: 08313   Lat: 39-29-29 N Long: 75-12-55 W
Pop: 6,927 (1990); 6,810 (1980)   Pop Density: 222.7
Land: 31.1 sq. mi.; Water: 0.1 sq. mi.

Formed Feb 23, 1922.

Name origin: For its location north and west of Deerfield Township.

Vineland
City
ZIP: 08360   Lat: 39-27-53 N Long: 74-59-50 W
Pop: 54,780 (1990); 53,753 (1980)   Pop Density: 797.4
Land: 68.7 sq. mi.; Water: 0.3 sq. mi.   Elev: 106 ft.

In south-central NJ, 11 mi. northeast of Bridgeton. Replaced Landis Township and Vineland Borough Jul 1, 1952.

Name origin: For vineyards developed there in the 19th century.

Essex County
County Seat: Newark (ZIP: 07102)

Pop: 778,206 (1990); 851,304 (1980)   Pop Density: 6162.0
Land: 126.3 sq. mi.; Water: 3.3 sq. mi.   Area Code: 201

In northeastern NJ, west of New York City; original county, organized Mar 7, 1683.
Name origin: For the county of Essex, England.

Belleville
Township
ZIP: 07109   Lat: 40-47-41 N Long: 74-09-45 W
Pop: 34,213 (1990); 35,367 (1980)   Pop Density: 10367.6
Land: 3.3 sq. mi.; Water: 0.1 sq. mi.

In northeastern NJ on the steep banks of the Passaic River, 4 mi. north of Newark. Replaced Belleville Township Nov 16, 1910.

Name origin: French for 'beautiful city.'

Bloomfield
Township
ZIP: 07003   Lat: 40-48-38 N Long: 74-11-12 W
Pop: 45,061 (1990); 47,792 (1980)   Pop Density: 8502.1
Land: 5.3 sq. mi.; Water: 0.0 sq. mi.

In northeastern NJ, 4 mi. northwest of Newark. Replaced Bloomfield Township Feb 26, 1900.

Name origin: Named in 1796 by townspeople for Joseph Bloomfield, Revolutionary War general and later governor (1810–12). Originally called Wardsesson.

Caldwell Township
Borough
ZIP: 07004   Lat: 40-50-18 N Long: 74-16-40 W
Pop: 7,549 (1990); 7,624 (1980)   Pop Density: 6290.8
Land: 1.2 sq. mi.; Water: 0.0 sq. mi.

Formed Feb 10, 1892.

Name origin: For the Rev. James Caldwell, a "fighting parson" during the Revolutionary War.

Cedar Grove
Township
ZIP: 07009   Lat: 40-51-21 N Long: 74-13-46 W
Pop: 12,053 (1990); 12,600 (1980)   Pop Density: 2869.8
Land: 4.2 sq. mi.; Water: 0.1 sq. mi.

In northeastern NJ, 6 mi. southwest of Paterson. Replaced Verona Township Apr 9, 1908.

Name origin: For stands of cedar trees.

East Orange
City
ZIP: 07017   **Lat:** 40-45-57 N **Long:** 74-12-43 W
Pop: 73,552 (1990); 77,690 (1980)   **Pop Density:** 18859.5
Land: 3.9 sq. mi.; **Water:** 0.0 sq. mi.   **Elev:** 166 ft.

In northeastern NJ, 4 mi. northwest of Newark. Largest of "The Oranges." Replaced East Orange Township Dec 9, 1899.

Name origin: For the European ruling family of Orange-Nassau.

Essex Fells
Borough & Township
ZIP: 07021   **Lat:** 40-49-38 N **Long:** 74-16-52 W
Pop: 2,139 (1990); 2,320 (1980)   **Pop Density:** 1527.9
Land: 1.4 sq. mi.; **Water:** 0.0 sq. mi.

Formed Mar 31, 1902.

Name origin: For John Fells.

Fairfield
Township
ZIP: 07101   **Lat:** 40-53-00 N **Long:** 74-18-22 W
Pop: 7,615 (1990)   **Pop Density:** 725.2
Land: 10.5 sq. mi.; **Water:** 0.0 sq. mi.   **Elev:** 180 ft.

Became Fairfield Borough Jun 8, 1964; reincorporated as township in 1973.

Name origin: For the rich soil.

Glen Ridge Township
Borough
ZIP: 07028   **Lat:** 40-48-11 N **Long:** 74-12-18 W
Pop: 7,076 (1990)   **Pop Density:** 5443.1
Land: 1.3 sq. mi.; **Water:** 0.0 sq. mi.

Formed Feb 13, 1895.

Name origin: For a ridge in a glen formed by Toney's Brook.

Irvington
Township
ZIP: 07111   **Lat:** 40-43-28 N **Long:** 74-13-57 W
Pop: 61,018 (1990); 61,540 (1980)   **Pop Density:** 21040.7
Land: 2.9 sq. mi.; **Water:** 0.0 sq. mi.   **Elev:** 217 ft.

In northeastern NJ, 3 mi. southwest of Newark. Formed Mar 2, 1898.

Name origin: For author Washington Irving (1783–1859).

Livingston
Township
ZIP: 07039   **Lat:** 40-47-08 N **Long:** 74-19-46 W
Pop: 26,609 (1990)   **Pop Density:** 1914.3
Land: 13.9 sq. mi.; **Water:** 0.2 sq. mi.

In northeastern NJ, 5 mi. west of Newark. Formed Feb 5, 1813.

Name origin: For William Livingston (1723–90), NJ's Revolutionary War governor and one of the signers of the Constitution.

Maplewood
Township
ZIP: 07040   **Lat:** 40-43-59 N **Long:** 74-16-18 W
Pop: 21,652 (1990)   **Pop Density:** 5551.8
Land: 3.9 sq. mi.; **Water:** 0.0 sq. mi.

In northeastern NJ, 6 mi. west of Newark. Replaced South Orange Township Nov 7, 1922.

Millburn
Township
ZIP: 07041   **Lat:** 40-44-25 N **Long:** 74-19-28 W
Pop: 18,630 (1990)   **Pop Density:** 1981.9
Land: 9.4 sq. mi.; **Water:** 0.5 sq. mi.

In northeastern NJ. Formed Mar 20, 1857.

Name origin: For a creek (burn) that supplied power for paper and other mills.

Montclair
Township
ZIP: 07042   **Lat:** 40-49-28 N **Long:** 74-12-41 W
Pop: 37,729 (1990); 38,340 (1980)   **Pop Density:** 5988.7
Land: 6.3 sq. mi.; **Water:** 0.0 sq. mi.

In northeastern NJ, 6 mi. northwest of Newark. Replaced Montclair Township Feb 24, 1894.

Name origin: From French meaning 'bright mountain.'

Newark
City
ZIP: 07101   **Lat:** 40-43-26 N **Long:** 74-10-23 W
Pop: 275,221 (1990); 329,248 (1980) **Pop Density:** 11563.9
Land: 23.8 sq. mi.; **Water:** 2.2 sq. mi.   **Elev:** 95 ft.

In northeastern NJ on the Passaic River and Newark Bay, 9 mi. west of New York City. Manufacturing: drugs and chemicals; electric equipment; insurance; large port; site of Newark International Airport. Replaced Newark Township Apr 11, 1836.

Name origin: From the biblical "New Ark." The belief that it was from Newark-on-Trent, the supposed English home of the Rev. Abraham Pierson, pastor of the first church, has been disproved.

North Caldwell
Township
ZIP: 07006   **Lat:** 40-51-48 N **Long:** 74-15-32 W
Pop: 6,706 (1990); 6,880 (1980)   **Pop Density:** 2235.3
Land: 3.0 sq. mi.; **Water:** 0.0 sq. mi.   **Elev:** 400 ft.

Formed Mar 31, 1898.

Nutley
Township
ZIP: 07110   **Lat:** 40-49-07 N **Long:** 74-09-25 W
Pop: 27,099 (1990); 28,980 (1980)   **Pop Density:** 7970.3
Land: 3.4 sq. mi.; **Water:** 0.1 sq. mi.

In northeastern NJ, 6 mi. north of Newark. Replaced Franklin Township Mar 5, 1902.

Name origin: For a resident's estate.

Orange
Township
ZIP: 07050   **Lat:** 40-46-05 N **Long:** 74-14-11 W
Pop: 29,925 (1990)   **Pop Density:** 13602.3
Land: 2.2 sq. mi.; **Water:** 0.0 sq. mi.

Settled 1678. Replaced Orange Town Apr 3, 1872.

Name origin: Probably for William (1689–1702), prince of Orange, who became King William III of England. Originally called Mountain Plantations.

Roseland
Borough
ZIP: 07068   **Lat:** 40-49-19 N **Long:** 74-18-30 W
Pop: 4,847 (1990); 5,330 (1980)   **Pop Density:** 1346.4
Land: 3.6 sq. mi.; **Water:** 0.0 sq. mi.   **Elev:** 356 ft.

Formed Mar 10, 1908.

Name origin: Named Roslyn (reason unknown) and became Roseland through mispronunciation.

South Orange Village
Township
ZIP: 07079   **Lat:** 40-44-56 N **Long:** 74-15-41 W
Pop: 16,390 (1990)   **Pop Density:** 5651.7
Land: 2.9 sq. mi.; **Water:** 0.0 sq. mi.   **Elev:** 220 ft.

In northeastern NJ, 5 mi. west of Newark. Formed May 4, 1869.

Verona
Borough
ZIP: 07044   **Lat:** 40-49-56 N **Long:** 74-14-33 W
Pop: 13,597 (1990)   **Pop Density:** 4856.1
Land: 2.8 sq. mi.; **Water:** 0.0 sq. mi.

In northeastern NJ, 7 mi. southwest of Paterson. Formed Apr 18, 1907.

Name origin: For Verona, Italy.

West Caldwell
Borough & Township
ZIP: 07006 **Lat:** 40-50-59 N **Long:** 74-17-54 W
Pop: 10,422 (1990); 11,430 (1980) **Pop Density:** 2084.4
Land: 5.0 sq. mi.; **Water:** 0.0 sq. mi.

In northeastern NJ, 9 mi. southwest of Paterson. Formed Feb 24, 1904.

Name origin: For its location to the west and north of Caldwell.

West Orange
Township
ZIP: 07052 **Lat:** 40-47-34 N **Long:** 74-15-48 W
Pop: 39,103 (1990); 41,150 (1980) **Pop Density:** 3231.7
Land: 12.1 sq. mi.; **Water:** 0.1 sq. mi.

In northeastern NJ, 5 mi. northwest of Newark. Replaced West Orange Township Feb 28, 1900.

Name origin: For its location west of Orange Township.

Gloucester County
County Seat: Woodbury (ZIP: 08096)

Pop: 230,082 (1990); 199,917 (1980) **Pop Density:** 708.2
Land: 324.9 sq. mi.; **Water:** 12.1 sq. mi. **Area Code:** 609

In southwestern NJ, southeast of Philadelphia; original county, organized May 26, 1686.

Name origin: For Henry, Duke of Gloucester (1639–60), third son of Charles I (1600–49), king of England.

Beckett
CDP
Lat: 39-45-13 N **Long:** 75-21-28 W
Pop: 3,815 (1990) **Pop Density:** 2119.4
Land: 1.8 sq. mi.; **Water:** 0.1 sq. mi.

Clayton
Borough
ZIP: 08312 **Lat:** 39-39-32 N **Long:** 75-04-58 W
Pop: 6,155 (1990); 6,013 (1980) **Pop Density:** 854.9
Land: 7.2 sq. mi.; **Water:** 0.2 sq. mi. **Elev:** 135 ft.
Incorporated Mar 8, 1924.

Deptford
Township
ZIP: 08096 **Lat:** 39-48-56 N **Long:** 75-07-10 W
Pop: 24,137 (1990) **Pop Density:** 1379.3
Land: 17.5 sq. mi.; **Water:** 0.1 sq. mi.
Formed Jun 1, 1695; incorporated Feb 21, 1798.
Name origin: For Deptford, England.

East Greenwich
Township
ZIP: 08020 **Lat:** 39-47-31 N **Long:** 75-14-14 W
Pop: 5,258 (1990) **Pop Density:** 355.3
Land: 14.8 sq. mi.; **Water:** 0.2 sq. mi.
Formed Feb 10, 1881.
Name origin: Possibly for its location east of Greenwich Township (Cumberland Co.).

Elk
Township
Lat: 39-39-43 N **Long:** 75-09-34 W
Pop: 3,806 (1990) **Pop Density:** 194.2
Land: 19.6 sq. mi.; **Water:** 0.1 sq. mi.
Formed Apr 17, 1891.
Name origin: A former hunting area for elk.

Franklin
Township
ZIP: 08322 **Lat:** 39-35-35 N **Long:** 75-01-06 W
Pop: 14,482 (1990) **Pop Density:** 258.6
Land: 56.0 sq. mi.; **Water:** 0.4 sq. mi.

Gibbstown
CDP
ZIP: 08027 **Lat:** 39-49-27 N **Long:** 75-16-47 W
Pop: 3,902 (1990) **Pop Density:** 2438.8
Land: 1.6 sq. mi.; **Water:** 0.0 sq. mi.

Glassboro
Borough
ZIP: 08028 **Lat:** 39-42-04 N **Long:** 75-06-47 W
Pop: 15,614 (1990); 14,574 (1980) **Pop Density:** 1697.2
Land: 9.2 sq. mi.; **Water:** 0.0 sq. mi. **Elev:** 144 ft.
In southwestern NJ, 17 mi. south of Camden. Replaced Glassboro Township Mar 8, 1920.
Name origin: For its early glass industry.

Greenwich
Township
ZIP: 08027 **Lat:** 39-49-41 N **Long:** 75-17-27 W
Pop: 5,102 (1990) **Pop Density:** 548.6
Land: 9.3 sq. mi.; **Water:** 2.7 sq. mi.
Formed Mar 1, 1695; incorporated Feb 21, 1798.

Harrison
Township
Lat: 39-43-27 N **Long:** 75-12-15 W
Pop: 4,715 (1990) **Pop Density:** 245.6
Land: 19.2 sq. mi.; **Water:** 0.0 sq. mi.
In southwestern NJ. Replaced Spicer Township Apr 1, 1845.
Name origin: For William Henry Harrison (1773–1841), ninth U.S. president.

Logan
Township
ZIP: 08014 **Lat:** 39-47-31 N **Long:** 75-21-20 W
Pop: 5,147 (1990) **Pop Density:** 225.7
Land: 22.8 sq. mi.; **Water:** 4.1 sq. mi.
Replaced West Woolwich Township Mar 6, 1878.
Name origin: For Gen. John Alexander Logan (1826–86), Union officer in the Civil War.

Mantua
Township
ZIP: 08051 **Lat:** 39-45-43 N **Long:** 75-10-20 W
Pop: 10,074 (1990) **Pop Density:** 633.6
Land: 15.9 sq. mi.; **Water:** 0.0 sq. mi.
Formed Feb 23, 1853.
Name origin: For the Mantua Indians.

Monroe
Township
ZIP: 08094 **Lat:** 39-39-35 N **Long:** 74-58-26 W
Pop: 26,703 (1990) **Pop Density:** 573.0
Land: 46.6 sq. mi.; **Water:** 0.4 sq. mi.
Formed Mar 3, 1859.
Name origin: Probably for James Monroe (1758–1831), fifth U.S. president.

Mullica Hill　　　　　　　　CDP
ZIP: 08062　　Lat: 39-44-10 N　Long: 75-13-28 W
Pop: 1,117 (1990); 1,050 (1980)　Pop Density: 930.8
Land: 1.2 sq. mi.; Water: 0.0 sq. mi.

National Park　　　　　　　Borough
ZIP: 08063　　Lat: 39-52-04 N　Long: 75-11-10 W
Pop: 3,413 (1990); 3,552 (1980)　Pop Density: 3413.0
Land: 1.0 sq. mi.; Water: 0.4 sq. mi.　Elev: 20 ft.
Formed Apr 15, 1902.
Name origin: For Red Bank Battlefield National Park.

Newfield　　　　　　　　Borough
ZIP: 08344　　Lat: 39-32-57 N　Long: 75-01-07 W
Pop: 1,592 (1990); 1,563 (1980)　Pop Density: 936.5
Land: 1.7 sq. mi.; Water: 0.0 sq. mi.　Elev: 120 ft.
Formed Mar 8, 1924.
Name origin: Named descriptively for a new town.

Oak Valley　　　　　　　CDP
ZIP: 08090　　Lat: 39-48-21 N　Long: 75-09-32 W
Pop: 4,055 (1990)　　Pop Density: 5792.9
Land: 0.7 sq. mi.; Water: 0.0 sq. mi.

Paulsboro　　　　　　　Borough
ZIP: 08066　　Lat: 39-50-23 N　Long: 75-14-25 W
Pop: 6,577 (1990); 6,944 (1980)　Pop Density: 3288.5
Land: 2.0 sq. mi.; Water: 0.7 sq. mi.　Elev: 12 ft.
Settled 1681. Formed Mar 2, 1904.
Name origin: For Phillip Paul, settler who arrived in 1685.

Pitman　　　　　　　　Borough
ZIP: 08071　　Lat: 39-43-59 N　Long: 75-07-51 W
Pop: 9,365 (1990); 9,744 (1980)　Pop Density: 4071.7
Land: 2.3 sq. mi.; Water: 0.0 sq. mi.　Elev: 132 ft.
Formed May 24, 1905.
Name origin: For the Rev. Charles Pitman.

South Harrison　　　　　Township
　　　　Lat: 39-41-49 N　Long: 75-15-22 W
Pop: 1,919 (1990)　　Pop Density: 121.5
Land: 15.8 sq. mi.; Water: 0.0 sq. mi.
Formed Mar 2, 1883.

Swedesboro　　　　　　Borough
ZIP: 08085　　Lat: 39-44-45 N　Long: 75-18-46 W
Pop: 2,024 (1990); 2,031 (1980)　Pop Density: 2891.4
Land: 0.7 sq. mi.; Water: 0.0 sq. mi.　Elev: 68 ft.
Formed Apr 9, 1902.
Name origin: For its Swedish settlers.

Turnersville　　　　　　CDP
　　　　Lat: 39-45-55 N　Long: 75-03-43 W
Pop: 3,843 (1990)　　Pop Density: 2562.0
Land: 1.5 sq. mi.; Water: 0.0 sq. mi.

Victory Lakes　　　　　CDP
　　　　Lat: 39-37-58 N　Long: 74-57-59 W
Pop: 2,160 (1990)　　Pop Density: 900.0
Land: 2.4 sq. mi.; Water: 0.1 sq. mi.

Washington　　　　　　Township
ZIP: 08080　　Lat: 39-44-44 N　Long: 75-04-18 W
Pop: 41,960 (1990)　　Pop Density: 1960.7
Land: 21.4 sq. mi.; Water: 0.1 sq. mi.
Formed Feb 17, 1836.
Name origin: For George Washington (1732–99), first U.S. president.

Wenonah　　　　　　　Borough
ZIP: 08090　　Lat: 39-47-30 N　Long: 75-08-54 W
Pop: 2,331 (1990); 2,303 (1980)　Pop Density: 2331.0
Land: 1.0 sq. mi.; Water: 0.0 sq. mi.　Elev: 60 ft.
Formed Mar 10, 1883.
Name origin: For the mother of Hiawatha.

West Deptford　　　　　Township
ZIP: 08086　　Lat: 39-50-30 N　Long: 75-11-09 W
Pop: 19,380 (1990)　　Pop Density: 1218.9
Land: 15.9 sq. mi.; Water: 1.9 sq. mi.
Formed Mar 1, 1871.
Name origin: For its location west of Deptford Township.

Westville　　　　　　　Borough
ZIP: 08093　　Lat: 39-52-11 N　Long: 75-07-47 W
Pop: 4,573 (1990); 4,786 (1980)　Pop Density: 4573.0
Land: 1.0 sq. mi.; Water: 0.4 sq. mi.　Elev: 16 ft.
Formed Apr 7, 1914; reincorporated Mar 8, 1924.
Name origin: For Thomas West.

Williamstown　　　　　CDP
ZIP: 08094　　Lat: 39-41-08 N　Long: 74-59-01 W
Pop: 10,891 (1990); 5,768 (1980)　Pop Density: 1756.6
Land: 6.2 sq. mi.; Water: 0.0 sq. mi.

Woodbury　　　　　　　City
ZIP: 08096　　Lat: 39-50-14 N　Long: 75-09-12 W
Pop: 10,904 (1990); 10,353 (1980)　Pop Density: 5192.4
Land: 2.1 sq. mi.; Water: 0.0 sq. mi.　Elev: 57 ft.
In southwestern NJ, 8 mi. south of Camden. County seat. Replaced Woodbury Borough Jan 2, 1871.
Name origin: For settler John Wood.

Woodbury Heights　　　Borough
ZIP: 08097　　Lat: 39-48-58 N　Long: 75-09-03 W
Pop: 3,392 (1990); 3,460 (1980)　Pop Density: 2826.7
Land: 1.2 sq. mi.; Water: 0.0 sq. mi.　Elev: 74 ft.
Formed Apr 6, 1915.

Woolwich　　　　　　　Township
　　　　Lat: 39-44-33 N　Long: 75-19-07 W
Pop: 1,459 (1990)　　Pop Density: 69.8
Land: 20.9 sq. mi.; Water: 0.2 sq. mi.
Formed Mar 7, 1767; incorporated Feb 21, 1798.
Name origin: For Woolwich, England.

Hudson County
County Seat: Jersey City (ZIP: 07306)

Pop: 553,099 (1990); 556,972 (1980)

Pop Density: 11855.3

Land: 46.7 sq. mi.; **Water:** 15.6 sq. mi.

Area Code: 201

In northeastern NJ, across the Hudson River from New York City; organized Feb 22, 1840 from Bergen County.

Name origin: For the Hudson River.

Bayonne
City

ZIP: 07002 **Lat:** 40-39-53 N **Long:** 74-06-37 W

Pop: 61,444 (1990); 65,047 (1980) **Pop Density:** 10972.1

Land: 5.6 sq. mi.; **Water:** 5.5 sq. mi. **Elev:** 49 ft.

In northeastern NJ on a peninsula that separates Upper New York Bay from Newark Bay. Replaced Bayonne Township Mar 10, 1869.

Name origin: For Bayonne, France.

East Newark
Borough

ZIP: 07029 **Lat:** 40-45-01 N **Long:** 74-09-47 W

Pop: 2,157 (1990); 1,923 (1980) **Pop Density:** 21570.0

Land: 0.1 sq. mi.; **Water:** 0.0 sq. mi.

Formed Jul 3, 1895.

Name origin: For its location east of the city.

Guttenberg
Town

ZIP: 07093 **Lat:** 40-47-33 N **Long:** 74-00-17 W

Pop: 8,268 (1990); 7,340 (1980) **Pop Density:** 41340.0

Land: 0.2 sq. mi.; **Water:** 0.0 sq. mi. **Elev:** 240 ft.

Formed Mar 9, 1859.

Name origin: A German term meaning 'good mountain,' with spelling variation.

Harrison
Township

ZIP: 07029 **Lat:** 40-44-36 N **Long:** 74-09-12 W

Pop: 13,425 (1990); 12,242 (1980) **Pop Density:** 11187.5

Land: 1.2 sq. mi.; **Water:** 0.1 sq. mi. **Elev:** 30 ft.

In northeastern NJ on the Passaic River, opposite Newark. Settled 1673; replaced Harrison Township Mar 25, 1869; reincorporated 1872.

Name origin: For William Henry Harrison (1773–1841), ninth U.S. president.

Hoboken
City

ZIP: 07030 **Lat:** 40-44-33 N **Long:** 74-01-43 W

Pop: 33,397 (1990); 42,460 (1980) **Pop Density:** 25690.0

Land: 1.3 sq. mi.; **Water:** 0.7 sq. mi. **Elev:** 5 ft.

In northeastern NJ on the Hudson River, 2 mi. north of Jersey City and opposite New York City. Replaced Hoboken township Mar 28, 1855.

Name origin: From either the Delaware Indian territory of Hobocan Hackingh, 'land of the tobacco pipe,' or the name of a village in northern Belgium, near the Dutch border.

Jersey City
City

ZIP: 07301 **Lat:** 40-42-40 N **Long:** 74-03-53 W

Pop: 228,537 (1990); 223,532 (1980) **Pop Density:** 15338.1

Land: 14.9 sq. mi.; **Water:** 6.2 sq. mi. **Elev:** 83 ft.

In northeastern NJ on the Hudson River and Upper New York Bay, across from New York City. Settled c. 1629; formed Jan 28, 1820; reincorporated Jan 23, 1829; reincorporated Feb 22, 1838; reincorporated 1871. Major seaport; industries: clothing, electrical equipment, chemicals; and

transportation center of the New York City metropolitan area.

Name origin: For the state.

Kearny
Town

ZIP: 07029 **Lat:** 40-45-04 N **Long:** 74-07-10 W

Pop: 34,874 (1990); 35,735 (1980) **Pop Density:** 3832.3

Land: 9.1 sq. mi.; **Water:** 1.0 sq. mi. **Elev:** 125 ft.

In northeastern NJ between the Passaic and Hackensack rivers at the head of Newark Bay, just northeast of Newark. Replaced Kearny Township Jan 19, 1899.

Name origin: For Maj. Gen. Philip Kearny, cavalry officer, whose permanent residence was here.

North Bergen
Township

ZIP: 07047 **Lat:** 40-47-33 N **Long:** 74-01-32 W

Pop: 48,414 (1990) **Pop Density:** 9310.4

Land: 5.2 sq. mi.; **Water:** 0.4 sq. mi.

Formed Apr 10, 1843.

Secaucus
Town

ZIP: 07094 **Lat:** 40-46-52 N **Long:** 74-03-53 W

Pop: 14,061 (1990); 13,719 (1980) **Pop Density:** 2383.2

Land: 5.9 sq. mi.; **Water:** 0.6 sq. mi. **Elev:** 12 ft.

In northeastern NJ, 5 mi. northwest of Jersey City. Replaced Secaucus Borough Jun 7, 1917.

Name origin: From an Indian term perhaps meaning 'black snake.'

Union City
City

ZIP: 07087 **Lat:** 40-46-01 N **Long:** 74-01-56 W

Pop: 58,012 (1990); 55,593 (1980) **Pop Density:** 44624.6

Land: 1.3 sq. mi.; **Water:** 0.0 sq. mi. **Elev:** 175 ft.

In northeastern NJ on the Hudson River, 3 m. north of and adjoining Jersey City. Replaced Union and West Hoboken towns Jan 1, 1925.

Weehawken
Township

ZIP: 07087 **Lat:** 40-46-07 N **Long:** 74-01-07 W

Pop: 12,385 (1990) **Pop Density:** 13761.1

Land: 0.9 sq. mi.; **Water:** 0.7 sq. mi.

In northeastern NJ on the Hudson River opposite New York City, 5 mi. north of Jersey City. Formed Mar 15, 1859.

Name origin: From an Indian term perhaps meaning 'place of gulls.'

West New York
Town

ZIP: 07093 **Lat:** 40-47-09 N **Long:** 74-00-35 W

Pop: 38,125 (1990); 39,194 (1980) **Pop Density:** 38125.0

Land: 1.0 sq. mi.; **Water:** 0.3 sq. mi. **Elev:** 185 ft.

In northeastern NJ on the Hudson River, 4 mi. north of Jersey City. Replaced Union Township Jul 8, 1898.

Name origin: For its location west of New York City.

Hunterdon County
County Seat: Flemington (ZIP: 08822)

Pop: 107,776 (1990); 87,361 (1980) **Pop Density:** 250.6
Land: 430.1 sq. mi.; **Water:** 7.8 sq. mi. **Area Code:** 201

In central NJ along the Delaware River, northwest of Trenton; organized Mar 13, 1714 from Burlington County.

Name origin: For Robert Hunter (? –1734), colonial governor of New York and East and West Jersey (1710–19).

Alexandria
Township
Lat: 40-35-20 N **Long:** 75-01-59 W
Pop: 3,594 (1990) **Pop Density:** 130.2
Land: 27.6 sq. mi.; **Water:** 0.1 sq. mi.
Formed Mar 5, 1765; incorporated Feb 21, 1798.
Name origin: For James Alexander, secretary of the Province of NJ.

Annandale
CDP
ZIP: 08801 **Lat:** 40-38-42 N **Long:** 74-53-28 W
Pop: 1,074 (1990); 1,040 (1980) **Pop Density:** 767.1
Land: 1.4 sq. mi.; **Water:** 0.0 sq. mi.

Bethlehem
Township
Lat: 40-39-59 N **Long:** 75-00-32 W
Pop: 3,104 (1990) **Pop Density:** 149.2
Land: 20.8 sq. mi.; **Water:** 0.0 sq. mi.
Incorporated Feb 21, 1798.
Name origin: For the birthplace of Jesus.

Bloomsbury
Borough
ZIP: 08804 **Lat:** 40-39-10 N **Long:** 75-05-08 W
Pop: 890 (1990); 864 (1980) **Pop Density:** 988.9
Land: 0.9 sq. mi.; **Water:** 0.0 sq. mi. **Elev:** 333 ft.
Formed Mar 30, 1905.

Califon
Borough
ZIP: 07830 **Lat:** 40-43-09 N **Long:** 74-50-12 W
Pop: 1,073 (1990); 1,023 (1980) **Pop Density:** 1073.0
Land: 1.0 sq. mi.; **Water:** 0.0 sq. mi. **Elev:** 471 ft.
Formed Apr 2, 1918.
Name origin: For the state of California.

Clinton
Town
ZIP: 08809 **Lat:** 40-38-07 N **Long:** 74-54-44 W
Pop: 2,054 (1990); 1,910 (1980) **Pop Density:** 1467.1
Land: 1.4 sq. mi.; **Water:** 0.0 sq. mi. **Elev:** 195 ft.
Formed Apr 5, 1865.
Name origin: For DeWitt Clinton (1769–1828), governor of NY.

*Clinton
Township
ZIP: 08809 **Lat:** 40-38-14 N **Long:** 74-51-16 W
Pop: 10,816 (1990) **Pop Density:** 358.1
Land: 30.2 sq. mi.; **Water:** 3.9 sq. mi.
Formed Apr 12, 1841.

Delaware
Township
Lat: 40-26-33 N **Long:** 74-57-27 W
Pop: 4,512 (1990) **Pop Density:** 123.6
Land: 36.5 sq. mi.; **Water:** 0.3 sq. mi.
Formed Apr 2, 1838.
Name origin: For its location near the river.

East Amwell
Township
ZIP: 08551 **Lat:** 40-26-05 N **Long:** 74-49-23 W
Pop: 4,332 (1990) **Pop Density:** 151.5
Land: 28.6 sq. mi.; **Water:** 0.0 sq. mi.
Formed Apr 6, 1846.
Name origin: For the Amwell district in England.

Flemington
Borough
ZIP: 08822 **Lat:** 40-30-32 N **Long:** 74-51-37 W
Pop: 4,047 (1990); 4,132 (1980) **Pop Density:** 3679.1
Land: 1.1 sq. mi.; **Water:** 0.0 sq. mi. **Elev:** 179 ft.
In northwestern NJ about 10 mi. east of the Delaware River. Philip Kase is generally credited as being the town's first settler. Replaced Flemington Village Apr 7, 1910; incorporation confirmed Apr 27, 1931.
Name origin: For Samuel Fleming, an early settler.

Franklin
Township
Lat: 40-34-00 N **Long:** 74-55-53 W
Pop: 2,851 (1990) **Pop Density:** 124.5
Land: 22.9 sq. mi.; **Water:** 0.0 sq. mi.
Formed Apr 7, 1845.

Frenchtown
Borough
ZIP: 08825 **Lat:** 40-31-32 N **Long:** 75-03-22 W
Pop: 1,528 (1990); 1,573 (1980) **Pop Density:** 1175.4
Land: 1.3 sq. mi.; **Water:** 0.1 sq. mi. **Elev:** 161 ft.
In northwestern NJ on the Delaware River. Formed Apr 4, 1867.
Name origin: For fugitives from the French Revolution who settled in the area.

Glen Gardner
Borough
ZIP: 08826 **Lat:** 40-41-56 N **Long:** 74-56-28 W
Pop: 1,665 (1990); 834 (1980) **Pop Density:** 1040.6
Land: 1.6 sq. mi.; **Water:** 0.0 sq. mi. **Elev:** 405 ft.
Formed Mar 26, 1919.

Hampton
Borough
ZIP: 08827 **Lat:** 40-42-31 N **Long:** 74-58-03 W
Pop: 1,515 (1990); 1,614 (1980) **Pop Density:** 1010.0
Land: 1.5 sq. mi.; **Water:** 0.0 sq. mi. **Elev:** 500 ft.
Replaced Junction Borough Feb 11, 1909.
Name origin: For Jonathan Hampton, donor of church land.

High Bridge
Borough
ZIP: 08829 **Lat:** 40-40-06 N **Long:** 74-53-44 W
Pop: 3,886 (1990); 3,435 (1980) **Pop Density:** 1619.2
Land: 2.4 sq. mi.; **Water:** 0.0 sq. mi. **Elev:** 332 ft.
Formed Feb 19, 1898.
Name origin: A bridge through the Musconetcong Mountains leading to an ironworks.

Holland
Township
Lat: 40-35-43 N Long: 75-07-31 W
Pop: 4,892 (1990) Pop Density: 206.4
Land: 23.7 sq. mi.; Water: 0.4 sq. mi.
Formed Apr 13, 1874.
Name origin: For the former home of many early settlers.

Kingwood
Township
Lat: 40-29-13 N Long: 75-00-55 W
Pop: 3,325 (1990) Pop Density: 93.9
Land: 35.4 sq. mi.; Water: 0.6 sq. mi.
Formed 1749; incorporated Feb 21, 1798.

Lambertville
City
ZIP: 08530 Lat: 40-22-04 N Long: 74-56-35 W
Pop: 3,927 (1990); 4,044 (1980) Pop Density: 3570.0
Land: 1.1 sq. mi.; Water: 0.1 sq. mi. Elev: 71 ft.
Replaced Lamberville Town Mar 26, 1872.
Name origin: For John Lambert, U.S. senator from NJ (1809-15), who opened the first post office shortly after the War of 1812. Formerly called Coryel's Ferry and George-town.

Lebanon
Borough
ZIP: 08833 Lat: 40-38-38 N Long: 74-50-06 W
Pop: 1,036 (1990); 820 (1980) Pop Density: 1151.1
Land: 0.9 sq. mi.; Water: 0.0 sq. mi. Elev: 296 ft.
Formed Mar 26, 1926.
Name origin: For Mt. Lebanon in Palestine.

*Lebanon
Township
ZIP: 08833 Lat: 40-43-34 N Long: 74-53-41 W
Pop: 5,679 (1990) Pop Density: 179.1
Land: 31.7 sq. mi.; Water: 0.0 sq. mi.
Incorporated Feb 21, 1798.

Milford
Borough
ZIP: 08848 Lat: 40-34-05 N Long: 75-05-24 W
Pop: 1,273 (1990); 1,368 (1980) Pop Density: 1060.8
Land: 1.2 sq. mi.; Water: 0.1 sq. mi. Elev: 300 ft.
Formed Apr 15, 1911; incorporation confirmed Mar 13, 1925.
Name origin: Possibly for a mill located at a ford across the Delaware River.

Raritan
Township
ZIP: 08822 Lat: 40-30-17 N Long: 74-52-08 W
Pop: 15,616 (1990) Pop Density: 412.0
Land: 37.9 sq. mi.; Water: 0.0 sq. mi.
In north-central NJ, 11 mi. northwest of New Brunswick. Formed Apr 2, 1838.
Name origin: For the river, itself named for a Delaware Indian tribal name whose meaning is uncertain.

Readington
Township
ZIP: 08870 Lat: 40-35-01 N Long: 74-46-56 W
Pop: 13,400 (1990) Pop Density: 281.5
Land: 47.6 sq. mi.; Water: 0.1 sq. mi.
Formed Jul 15, 1730; incorporated Feb 21, 1798.
Name origin: For John Reading, NJ governor (1747; 1757-58).

Stockton
Borough
ZIP: 08559 Lat: 40-24-19 N Long: 74-58-38 W
Pop: 629 (1990); 643 (1980) Pop Density: 1258.0
Land: 0.5 sq. mi.; Water: 0.1 sq. mi. Elev: 80 ft.
Formed Apr 14, 1898.
Name origin: For the Stockton family.

Tewksbury
Township
Lat: 40-42-00 N Long: 74-46-47 W
Pop: 4,803 (1990) Pop Density: 152.0
Land: 31.6 sq. mi.; Water: 0.0 sq. mi.
Incorporated Feb 21, 1798.

Union
Township
ZIP: 08802 Lat: 40-38-04 N Long: 74-58-06 W
Pop: 5,078 (1990) Pop Density: 267.3
Land: 19.0 sq. mi.; Water: 1.6 sq. mi.
Formed Feb 17, 1853.
Name origin: For the union of several communities.

West Amwell
Township
ZIP: 08530 Lat: 40-22-47 N Long: 74-53-59 W
Pop: 2,251 (1990) Pop Density: 103.7
Land: 21.7 sq. mi.; Water: 0.2 sq. mi.
Formed Apr 6, 1846.

White House Station
CDP
ZIP: 08889 Lat: 40-36-58 N Long: 74-46-20 W
Pop: 1,287 (1990) Pop Density: 990.0
Land: 1.3 sq. mi.; Water: 0.0 sq. mi.

Mercer County
County Seat: Trenton (ZIP: 08650)

Pop: 325,824 (1990); 307,863 (1980) **Pop Density:** 1442.0
Land: 226.0 sq. mi.; **Water:** 2.9 sq. mi. **Area Code:** 609

In central NJ along the Delaware River, northeast of Philadelphia; organized Feb 22, 1838 from Hunterdon and Middlesex counties.

Name origin: For Gen. Hugh Mercer (1721–77), Revolutionary War officer and physician.

East Windsor
Township
ZIP: 08520 **Lat:** 40-15-32 N **Long:** 74-32-03 W
Pop: 22,353 (1990) **Pop Density:** 1423.8
Land: 15.7 sq. mi.; **Water:** 0.0 sq. mi.

Formed Feb 9, 1797; incorporated Feb 21, 1798.

Name origin: For Windsor, England.

Ewing
Township
ZIP: 08618 **Lat:** 40-15-55 N **Long:** 74-48-04 W
Pop: 34,185 (1990) **Pop Density:** 2234.3
Land: 15.3 sq. mi.; **Water:** 0.3 sq. mi.

In west-central NJ, northwest of Trenton. Formed Feb 22, 1834.

Name origin: For Charles Ewing, a NJ chief justice.

Hamilton
Township
ZIP: 08619 **Lat:** 40-12-21 N **Long:** 74-40-28 W
Pop: 86,553 (1990) **Pop Density:** 2196.8
Land: 39.4 sq. mi.; **Water:** 0.9 sq. mi.

In west-central NJ, east of Trenton. Formed Feb 5, 1813.

Hightstown
Borough
ZIP: 08520 **Lat:** 40-16-04 N **Long:** 74-31-31 W
Pop: 5,126 (1990); 4,581 (1980) **Pop Density:** 4271.7
Land: 1.2 sq. mi.; **Water:** 0.0 sq. mi. **Elev:** 84 ft.

Founded 1721; formed Mar 5, 1853. In 1834 it became a station on the Camden & Amboy Railroad, the first railroad built in NJ.

Name origin: For John Hight, an early landowner and miller.

Hopewell
Borough
ZIP: 08525 **Lat:** 40-23-20 N **Long:** 74-45-51 W
Pop: 1,968 (1990); 2,001 (1980) **Pop Density:** 2811.4
Land: 0.7 sq. mi.; **Water:** 0.0 sq. mi. **Elev:** 200 ft.

Formed Apr 14, 1891; reincorporated Mar 6, 1924.

Name origin: For the ship *Hopewell*, which brought many settlers to America.

*Hopewell
Township
ZIP: 08525 **Lat:** 40-20-34 N **Long:** 74-48-25 W
Pop: 11,590 (1990) **Pop Density:** 199.5
Land: 58.1 sq. mi.; **Water:** 0.5 sq. mi.

In west-central NJ, 13 mi. north of Trenton. Formed Feb 20, 1700; incorporated by royal charter Mar 1, 1755; incorporated Feb 21, 1798.

Lawrence
Township
ZIP: 08638 **Lat:** 40-17-46 N **Long:** 74-43-31 W
Pop: 25,787 (1990) **Pop Density:** 1166.8
Land: 22.1 sq. mi.; **Water:** 0.0 sq. mi.

Replaced Maidenhead Township Jan 24, 1816.

Name origin: For Capt. James Lawrence (1781–1813), commander of the U.S.S. *Chesapeake* during the War of 1812, famous for saying "Don't give up the ship."

Lawrenceville
CDP
Lat: 40-18-05 N **Long:** 74-43-48 W
Pop: 6,446 (1990) **Pop Density:** 1401.3
Land: 4.6 sq. mi.; **Water:** 0.0 sq. mi.

Mercerville-Hamilton Square
CDP
ZIP: 08619 **Lat:** 40-13-50 N **Long:** 74-40-18 W
Pop: 26,873 (1990); 25,446 (1980) **Pop Density:** 3490.0
Land: 7.7 sq. mi.; **Water:** 0.0 sq. mi.

Pennington
Borough
ZIP: 08534 **Lat:** 40-19-35 N **Long:** 74-47-31 W
Pop: 2,537 (1990); 2,109 (1980) **Pop Density:** 2537.0
Land: 1.0 sq. mi.; **Water:** 0.0 sq. mi. **Elev:** 211 ft.

Formed Jan 31, 1890.

Name origin: A corruption of its previous derisive nickname, Penny Town, so called because of its insignificant size. Originally called Queenstown, for England's Queen Anne.

Princeton
Borough
ZIP: 08540 **Lat:** 40-21-00 N **Long:** 74-39-34 W
Pop: 12,016 (1990); 12,035 (1980) **Pop Density:** 6675.6
Land: 1.8 sq. mi.; **Water:** 0.0 sq. mi. **Elev:** 215 ft.

In western NJ, 11 mi. northeast of Trenton. Formed Feb 11, 1813; reincorporated Nov 27, 1822.

Name origin: For the Prince of Orange and Nassau, later King William III of England. Originally called Prince's Town. Site of Princeton University.

*Princeton
Township
ZIP: 08540 **Lat:** 40-21-19 N **Long:** 74-40-19 W
Pop: 13,198 (1990) **Pop Density:** 804.8
Land: 16.4 sq. mi.; **Water:** 0.2 sq. mi.

Formed Apr 9, 1838.

Princeton Junction
CDP
ZIP: 08550 **Lat:** 40-19-13 N **Long:** 74-37-25 W
Pop: 2,362 (1990); 2,419 (1980) **Pop Density:** 1243.2
Land: 1.9 sq. mi.; **Water:** 0.0 sq. mi.

Princeton North
CDP
Lat: 40-21-40 N **Long:** 74-38-53 W
Pop: 4,386 (1990); 4,814 (1980) **Pop Density:** 2741.3
Land: 1.6 sq. mi.; **Water:** 0.0 sq. mi.

Trenton
City
ZIP: 08601 **Lat:** 40-13-24 N **Long:** 74-45-51 W
Pop: 88,675 (1990); 92,124 (1980) **Pop Density:** 11516.2
Land: 7.7 sq. mi.; **Water:** 0.5 sq. mi. **Elev:** 54 ft.

On the western NJ border with PA, on the Delaware River, 28 mi. northeast of Philadelphia. State capital since 1790; incorporated as a city 1792. Industries include electrical goods, fabricated metal products, rubber products, printing, and publishing.

Name origin: For William Trent, founder. Originally called Trent's Town.

Twin Rivers — CDP
ZIP: 08520   **Lat:** 40-15-50 N **Long:** 74-29-33 W
Pop: 7,715 (1990); 7,742 (1980)   **Pop Density:** 5934.6
Land: 1.3 sq. mi.; **Water:** 0.0 sq. mi.

Washington — Township
ZIP: 08691   **Lat:** 40-13-25 N **Long:** 74-35-42 W
Pop: 5,815 (1990)   **Pop Density:** 283.7
Land: 20.5 sq. mi.; **Water:** 0.0 sq. mi.
Formed Mar 1, 1860.
Name origin: For George Washington (1732–99), first U.S. president.

West Windsor — Township
ZIP: 08520   **Lat:** 40-17-23 N **Long:** 74-37-24 W
Pop: 16,021 (1990)   **Pop Density:** 616.2
Land: 26.0 sq. mi.; **Water:** 0.3 sq. mi.
Formed Feb 9, 1797; incorporated Feb 21, 1798.

White Horse — CDP
ZIP: 08610   **Lat:** 40-11-27 N **Long:** 74-42-16 W
Pop: 9,397 (1990); 10,098 (1980)   **Pop Density:** 2936.6
Land: 3.2 sq. mi.; **Water:** 0.1 sq. mi.

Yardville-Groveville — CDP
ZIP: 08620   **Lat:** 40-10-52 N **Long:** 74-40-03 W
Pop: 9,248 (1990); 9,414 (1980)   **Pop Density:** 2720.0
Land: 3.4 sq. mi.; **Water:** 0.0 sq. mi.

Middlesex County
County Seat: New Brunswick (ZIP: 08901)

Pop: 671,780 (1990); 595,893 (1980)   **Pop Density:** 2162.6
Land: 310.6 sq. mi.; **Water:** 12.0 sq. mi.   **Area Code:** 201
In northern NJ, southwest of Newark; original county, organized Mar 1, 1683.
Name origin: For the ancient county in England (most of which is now part of Greater London).

Avenel — CDP
ZIP: 07001   **Lat:** 40-34-56 N **Long:** 74-16-25 W
Pop: 15,504 (1990)   **Pop Density:** 4560.0
Land: 3.4 sq. mi.; **Water:** 0.0 sq. mi.

Carteret — Borough
ZIP: 07008   **Lat:** 40-35-00 N **Long:** 74-13-43 W
Pop: 19,025 (1990); 20,598 (1980)   **Pop Density:** 4323.9
Land: 4.4 sq. mi.; **Water:** 0.6 sq. mi.   **Elev:** 16 ft.
In central NJ, 6 mi. northeast of Perth Amboy near Staten Island, NY. Replaced Roosevelt Borough Nov 7, 1922.
Name origin: For the first English governor, Philip Carteret (1639–82).

Clearbrook Park — CDP
Lat: 40-18-34 N **Long:** 74-27-54 W
Pop: 2,853 (1990)   **Pop Density:** 3170.0
Land: 0.9 sq. mi.; **Water:** 0.0 sq. mi.

Colonia — CDP
ZIP: 07067   **Lat:** 40-35-33 N **Long:** 74-18-56 W
Pop: 18,238 (1990)   **Pop Density:** 4676.4
Land: 3.9 sq. mi.; **Water:** 0.0 sq. mi.

Concordia — CDP
Lat: 40-18-39 N **Long:** 74-26-55 W
Pop: 2,683 (1990)   **Pop Density:** 2439.1
Land: 1.1 sq. mi.; **Water:** 0.0 sq. mi.

Cranbury — Township
Lat: 40-18-31 N **Long:** 74-31-09 W
Pop: 2,500 (1990)   **Pop Density:** 186.6
Land: 13.4 sq. mi.; **Water:** 0.0 sq. mi.
Formed Mar 7, 1872.
Name origin: For the abundant wild cranberries that grow locally, with spelling variation.

Dayton — CDP
ZIP: 08810   **Lat:** 40-22-57 N **Long:** 74-30-36 W
Pop: 4,321 (1990)   **Pop Density:** 2057.6
Land: 2.1 sq. mi.; **Water:** 0.0 sq. mi.

Dunellen — Borough
ZIP: 08812   **Lat:** 40-35-21 N **Long:** 74-27-55 W
Pop: 6,528 (1990); 6,593 (1980)   **Pop Density:** 6528.0
Land: 1.0 sq. mi.; **Water:** 0.0 sq. mi.   **Elev:** 60 ft.
In central NJ, 9 mi. northeast of New Brunswick. Established 1868. Formed Oct 28, 1887; incorporation confirmed Apr 15, 1914.
Name origin: For Ellen Betts, a friend of Central Railroad of New Jersey president De Forest, plus the prefix "dun" because he liked its sound.

East Brunswick — Township
ZIP: 08816   **Lat:** 40-25-39 N **Long:** 74-24-59 W
Pop: 43,548 (1990)   **Pop Density:** 1979.5
Land: 22.0 sq. mi.; **Water:** 0.4 sq. mi.
Formed Feb 28, 1860.

Edison — Township
ZIP: 08817   **Lat:** 40-31-43 N **Long:** 74-22-09 W
Pop: 88,680 (1990)   **Pop Density:** 2936.4
Land: 30.2 sq. mi.; **Water:** 0.5 sq. mi.
In central NJ, southwest of Elizabeth. Replaced Raritan Township Nov 10, 1954.
Name origin: For Thomas Alva Edison (1847–1931), inventor and resident.

Fords — CDP
ZIP: 08863   **Lat:** 40-32-31 N **Long:** 74-18-44 W
Pop: 14,392 (1990)   **Pop Density:** 5535.4
Land: 2.6 sq. mi.; **Water:** 0.0 sq. mi.

Heathcote — CDP
Lat: 40-23-18 N **Long:** 74-34-34 W
Pop: 3,112 (1990)   **Pop Density:** 1196.9
Land: 2.6 sq. mi.; **Water:** 0.0 sq. mi.

Helmetta   Borough
ZIP: 08828   **Lat:** 40-22-35 N **Long:** 74-25-27 W
Pop: 1,211 (1990); 955 (1980)   **Pop Density:** 1513.8
Land: 0.8 sq. mi.; **Water:** 0.1 sq. mi.   **Elev:** 44 ft.
Formed Mar 20, 1888.

Name origin: For Etta Helme, daughter of a snuff factory owner. Name transposed for euphony.

Highland Park   Borough
ZIP: 08904   **Lat:** 40-30-01 N **Long:** 74-25-42 W
Pop: 13,279 (1990); 13,396 (1980) **Pop Density:** 7377.2
Land: 1.8 sq. mi.; **Water:** 0.0 sq. mi.   **Elev:** 74 ft.
In central NJ on the Raritan River, 2 mi. east of New Brunswick. An Indian village was on the townsite in 1675. Formed Mar 15, 1905.

Name origin: Originally called Raritan Falls.

Iselin   CDP
ZIP: 08830   **Lat:** 40-34-12 N **Long:** 74-19-00 W
Pop: 16,141 (1990)   **Pop Density:** 5206.8
Land: 3.1 sq. mi.; **Water:** 0.0 sq. mi.

Jamesburg   Borough
ZIP: 08831   **Lat:** 40-20-56 N **Long:** 74-26-24 W
Pop: 5,294 (1990); 4,114 (1980)   **Pop Density:** 6617.5
Land: 0.8 sq. mi.; **Water:** 0.0 sq. mi.   **Elev:** 65 ft.
Formed Mar 19, 1887; incorporation confirmed Apr 15, 1915.

Name origin: For James Buckelew, miller and stagecoach owner.

Kendall Park   CDP
ZIP: 08824   **Lat:** 40-24-48 N **Long:** 74-33-45 W
Pop: 7,127 (1990); 7,419 (1980)   **Pop Density:** 1926.2
Land: 3.7 sq. mi.; **Water:** 0.0 sq. mi.

Kingston   CDP
                       Lat: 40-22-30 N **Long:** 74-36-29 W
Pop: 1,047 (1990)   **Pop Density:** 2094.0
Land: 0.5 sq. mi.; **Water:** 0.0 sq. mi.

Laurence Harbor   CDP
ZIP: 08879   **Lat:** 40-26-52 N **Long:** 74-14-58 W
Pop: 6,361 (1990); 6,737 (1980)   **Pop Density:** 2271.8
Land: 2.8 sq. mi.; **Water:** 0.0 sq. mi.

Madison Park   CDP
ZIP: 08859   **Lat:** 40-26-46 N **Long:** 74-17-42 W
Pop: 7,490 (1990); 7,447 (1980)   **Pop Density:** 4681.3
Land: 1.6 sq. mi.; **Water:** 0.0 sq. mi.

Metuchen   Borough
ZIP: 08840   **Lat:** 40-32-30 N **Long:** 74-21-48 W
Pop: 12,804 (1990); 13,762 (1980) **Pop Density:** 4742.2
Land: 2.7 sq. mi.; **Water:** 0.0 sq. mi.   **Elev:** 117 ft.
In central NJ, 5 mi. northwest of Perth Amboy. Formed Mar 20, 1900.

Name origin: For the Indian chief Matochshoning, who lived in the area in the 1600s.

Middlesex   Borough
ZIP: 08846   **Lat:** 40-34-25 N **Long:** 74-30-07 W
Pop: 13,055 (1990); 13,480 (1980) **Pop Density:** 3730.0
Land: 3.5 sq. mi.; **Water:** 0.0 sq. mi.   **Elev:** 61 ft.
In north-central NJ, 6 mi. north of New Brunswick. Formed Apr 9, 1913.

Name origin: For Middlesex, England.

Milltown   Borough
ZIP: 08850   **Lat:** 40-27-00 N **Long:** 74-26-04 W
Pop: 6,968 (1990); 7,136 (1980)   **Pop Density:** 4355.0
Land: 1.6 sq. mi.; **Water:** 0.0 sq. mi.   **Elev:** 60 ft.
Formed Jan 29, 1889; incorporated May 2, 1896.

Name origin: For early gristmills.

Monmouth Junction   CDP
ZIP: 08852   **Lat:** 40-22-48 N **Long:** 74-32-42 W
Pop: 1,570 (1990); 2,579 (1980)   **Pop Density:** 1046.7
Land: 1.5 sq. mi.; **Water:** 0.0 sq. mi.

Monroe   Township
ZIP: 08520   **Lat:** 40-19-06 N **Long:** 74-25-45 W
Pop: 22,255 (1990)   **Pop Density:** 527.4
Land: 42.2 sq. mi.; **Water:** 0.1 sq. mi.
Formed Apr 9, 1838.

Name origin: For James Monroe (1758–1831), fifth U.S. president.

New Brunswick   City
ZIP: 08901   **Lat:** 40-29-11 N **Long:** 74-26-42 W
Pop: 41,711 (1990); 41,442 (1980) **Pop Density:** 8021.3
Land: 5.2 sq. mi.; **Water:** 0.5 sq. mi.   **Elev:** 80 ft.
In central NJ at the head of navigation on the Raritan River, 9 mi. west of Perth Amboy. Formed Dec 30, 1730. Reincorporated Sep 1, 1784; Feb 23, 1801; May 14, 1838; May 13, 1844; Apr 4, 1845; and Feb 20, 1849.

Name origin: For the Duke of Brunswick, another title of King George I of England.

North Brunswick   Township
ZIP: 08902   **Lat:** 40-26-54 N **Long:** 74-28-39 W
Pop: 31,287 (1990)   **Pop Density:** 2607.3
Land: 12.0 sq. mi.; **Water:** 0.2 sq. mi.
Incorporated Feb 21, 1798.

Old Bridge   Township
ZIP: 08857   **Lat:** 40-24-12 N **Long:** 74-18-33 W
Pop: 56,475 (1990)   **Pop Density:** 1486.2
Land: 38.0 sq. mi.; **Water:** 2.5 sq. mi.
Replaced Madison Township Nov 17, 1975.

Name origin: For a bridge existing either in ruins or in memory.

Perth Amboy   City
ZIP: 08861   **Lat:** 40-31-12 N **Long:** 74-16-19 W
Pop: 41,967 (1990); 38,951 (1980) **Pop Density:** 8743.1
Land: 4.8 sq. mi.; **Water:** 1.2 sq. mi.   **Elev:** 65 ft.
In north-central NJ on Raritan Bay at the mouth of the Raritan River, 17 mi. southwest of Newark. The oldest incorporated city in NJ, with a charter granted Aug 4, 1718; reincorporated Apr 8, 1844.

Name origin: For the Scottish Earl of Perth who in 1685 permitted the immigration of 200 oppressed Scots. *Amboy* from Algonquin *ombage*, which possibly means 'large level piece of ground' or 'something hollowed out.'

Piscataway   Township
ZIP: 08854   **Lat:** 40-32-51 N **Long:** 74-27-47 W
Pop: 47,089 (1990)   **Pop Density:** 2504.7
Land: 18.8 sq. mi.; **Water:** 0.2 sq. mi.
Formed Oct 31, 1693; incorporated Feb 21, 1798.

Name origin: From an Indian word perhaps meaning 'divided river,' possibly for the confluence of the Green and Bound brooks.

Plainsboro
Township
ZIP: 08536   **Lat:** 40-20-05 N **Long:** 74-35-29 W
Pop: 14,213 (1990)   **Pop Density:** 1184.4
Land: 12.0 sq. mi.; **Water:** 0.2 sq. mi.
Formed Apr 1, 1919.

Port Reading
CDP
ZIP: 07064   **Lat:** 40-33-52 N **Long:** 74-14-49 W
Pop: 3,977 (1990)   **Pop Density:** 1729.1
Land: 2.3 sq. mi.; **Water:** 0.6 sq. mi.

Rossmoor
CDP
     Lat: 40-20-11 N **Long:** 74-28-25 W
Pop: 3,231 (1990)   **Pop Density:** 3590.0
Land: 0.9 sq. mi.; **Water:** 0.0 sq. mi.

Sayreville
Borough
ZIP: 08872   **Lat:** 40-27-56 N **Long:** 74-19-19 W
Pop: 34,986 (1990); 29,969 (1980)   **Pop Density:** 2173.0
Land: 16.1 sq. mi.; **Water:** 2.6 sq. mi.   **Elev:** 41 ft.
In central NJ on Raritan Bay inlet, 5 mi. southeast of New Brunswick. Replaced Sayreville Township Apr 2, 1919.
Name origin: For James F. Sayre, Jr., founder of Sayer and Fisher Brick Company, which at that time was one of the largest brick manufacturers in the world.

Sewaren
CDP
ZIP: 07077   **Lat:** 40-33-03 N **Long:** 74-15-39 W
Pop: 2,569 (1990)   **Pop Density:** 2569.0
Land: 1.0 sq. mi.; **Water:** 0.0 sq. mi.

Society Hill
CDP
     Lat: 40-32-02 N **Long:** 74-27-29 W
Pop: 3,577 (1990)   **Pop Density:** 2555.0
Land: 1.4 sq. mi.; **Water:** 0.0 sq. mi.

South Amboy
City
ZIP: 08879   **Lat:** 40-29-07 N **Long:** 74-16-38 W
Pop: 7,863 (1990); 8,322 (1980)   **Pop Density:** 4914.4
Land: 1.6 sq. mi.; **Water:** 1.2 sq. mi.   **Elev:** 99 ft.
Replaced South Amboy borough Apr 11, 1908.
Name origin: From Algonquian *omboge*, which possibly means 'large level piece of ground' or 'something hollowed out.'

South Brunswick
Township
ZIP: 08852   **Lat:** 40-22-57 N **Long:** 74-31-35 W
Pop: 25,792 (1990)   **Pop Density:** 629.1
Land: 41.0 sq. mi.; **Water:** 0.1 sq. mi.
Incorporated Feb 21, 1798.

South Plainfield
Borough
ZIP: 07080   **Lat:** 40-34-31 N **Long:** 74-24-54 W
Pop: 20,489 (1990); 20,521 (1980)   **Pop Density:** 2439.2
Land: 8.4 sq. mi.; **Water:** 0.0 sq. mi.   **Elev:** 67 ft.
In central NJ, 6 mi. northeast of New Brunswick. Formed Mar 10, 1926.

South River
Borough
ZIP: 08882   **Lat:** 40-26-42 N **Long:** 74-22-42 W
Pop: 13,692 (1990); 14,361 (1980)   **Pop Density:** 4890.0
Land: 2.8 sq. mi.; **Water:** 0.1 sq. mi.   **Elev:** 80 ft.
In central NJ, 6 mi. southeast of New Brunswick. Formed Feb 28, 1898.
Name origin: For a tributary of the Raritan River.

Spotswood
Borough
ZIP: 08884   **Lat:** 40-23-38 N **Long:** 74-23-25 W
Pop: 7,983 (1990); 7,840 (1980)   **Pop Density:** 3470.9
Land: 2.3 sq. mi.; **Water:** 0.2 sq. mi.   **Elev:** 31 ft.
Formed Apr 15, 1908.
Name origin: For Spottiswoode, Scotland, with spelling alteration.

Woodbridge
Township
ZIP: 07095   **Lat:** 40-33-38 N **Long:** 74-17-37 W
Pop: 93,086 (1990)   **Pop Density:** 4047.2
Land: 23.0 sq. mi.; **Water:** 1.2 sq. mi.
In central NJ, 4 mi. north of Perth Amboy. Settled 1665 by Puritans from Massachusetts Bay and NH. Formed Jun 1, 1669; reincorporated Oct 31, 1693; incorporated Feb 21, 1798.
Name origin: For the Rev. John Woodbridge, leader of settlers from MA.

Monmouth County
County Seat: Freehold (ZIP: 07728)

Pop: 553,124 (1990); 503,173 (1980)　　　**Pop Density:** 1172.2
Land: 471.9 sq. mi.; **Water:** 193.5 sq. mi.　　　**Area Code:** 201

In central NJ on Lower New York Bay and the Atlantic Ocean, south of Jersey City; original county, organized Mar 7, 1683.
Name origin: For Monmouthshire, a county in England.

Aberdeen　　　　　　　　　　　Township
ZIP: 07747　　　**Lat:** 40-25-52 N **Long:** 74-13-30 W
Pop: 17,038 (1990)　　　**Pop Density:** 3042.5
Land: 5.6 sq. mi.; **Water:** 2.2 sq. mi.
Replaced Matawan Township Nov 9, 1977.
Name origin: Possibly for the city in Scotland.

Allenhurst　　　　　　　　　　Borough
ZIP: 07711　　　**Lat:** 40-14-09 N **Long:** 74-00-08 W
Pop: 759 (1990); 912 (1980)　　　**Pop Density:** 2530.0
Land: 0.3 sq. mi.; **Water:** 0.0 sq. mi.　　　**Elev:** 24 ft.
In east-central NJ on the Atlantic Ocean. Formed Apr 26, 1897.
Name origin: For Abner Allen, an early resident.

Allentown　　　　　　　　　　Borough
ZIP: 08501　　　**Lat:** 40-10-32 N **Long:** 74-35-12 W
Pop: 1,828 (1990); 1,962 (1980)　　　**Pop Density:** 3046.7
Land: 0.6 sq. mi.; **Water:** 0.0 sq. mi.　　　**Elev:** 82 ft.
In east-central NJ on the Atlantic Ocean. Formed Jan 29, 1889.
Name origin: For Nathan Allen, son-in-law of early settler Robert Burnet.

Asbury Park　　　　　　　　　　　City
ZIP: 07712　　　**Lat:** 40-13-23 N **Long:** 74-00-41 W
Pop: 16,799 (1990); 17,015 (1980)　　**Pop Density:** 11999.3
Land: 1.4 sq. mi.; **Water:** 0.2 sq. mi.　　　**Elev:** 21 ft.
In northeast-central NJ on the Atlantic coast, 25 mi. southeast of Perth Amboy. Replaced Asbury Park Borough Mar 25, 1897.
Name origin: For Francis Asbury, the first Methodist bishop in America.

Atlantic Highlands　　　　　　　Borough
ZIP: 07716　　　**Lat:** 40-25-15 N **Long:** 74-00-58 W
Pop: 4,629 (1990); 4,950 (1980)　　　**Pop Density:** 3857.5
Land: 1.2 sq. mi.; **Water:** 3.3 sq. mi.　　　**Elev:** 26 ft.
Formed Feb 28, 1887; reincorporated Sep 1, 1891.
Name origin: For its headlands and location at the mouth of Sandy Hook Bay on the Atlantic Ocean.

Avon-by-the-Sea　　　　　　　　Borough
　　　　　　　　　Lat: 40-11-27 N **Long:** 74-00-54 W
Pop: 2,165 (1990); 2,337 (1980)　　　**Pop Density:** 5412.5
Land: 0.4 sq. mi.; **Water:** 0.1 sq. mi.　　　**Elev:** 22 ft.
In east-central NJ on the Atlantic coast. Formed Mar 23, 1900.
Name origin: For Avon, England.

Belmar　　　　　　　　　　　　Borough
ZIP: 07719　　　**Lat:** 40-10-49 N **Long:** 74-01-31 W
Pop: 5,877 (1990); 6,771 (1980)　　　**Pop Density:** 5877.0
Land: 1.0 sq. mi.; **Water:** 0.7 sq. mi.　　　**Elev:** 19 ft.
Replaced City of Belmar Borough Nov 20, 1890.
Name origin: Contraction of Italian *bello mare* meaning 'beautiful sea.'

Bradley Beach　　　　　　　　　Borough
ZIP: 07720　　　**Lat:** 40-12-06 N **Long:** 74-00-43 W
Pop: 4,475 (1990); 4,772 (1980)　　　**Pop Density:** 7458.3
Land: 0.6 sq. mi.; **Water:** 0.0 sq. mi.　　　**Elev:** 20 ft.
Formed Mar 13, 1893; incorporation confirmed Mar 13, 1925.
Name origin: For founder James A. Bradley and its location on the Atlantic Ocean.

Brielle　　　　　　　　　　　　Borough
ZIP: 08730　　　**Lat:** 40-06-16 N **Long:** 74-03-46 W
Pop: 4,406 (1990); 4,068 (1980)　　　**Pop Density:** 2447.8
Land: 1.8 sq. mi.; **Water:** 0.6 sq. mi.　　　**Elev:** 30 ft.
Formed Apr 10, 1919.
Name origin: For a commune in Holland.

Cliffwood Beach　　　　　　　　　　CDP
ZIP: 07735　　　**Lat:** 40-26-33 N **Long:** 74-13-04 W
Pop: 3,543 (1990)　　　**Pop Density:** 3936.7
Land: 0.9 sq. mi.; **Water:** 0.0 sq. mi.

Colts Neck　　　　　　　　　　Township
ZIP: 07722　　　**Lat:** 40-17-31 N **Long:** 74-10-06 W
Pop: 8,559 (1990)　　　**Pop Density:** 272.6
Land: 31.4 sq. mi.; **Water:** 0.7 sq. mi.
Replaced Atlantic Township Nov 6, 1962.
Name origin: According to legend a colt of the renowned race horse, Old Fashioned, fell and broke its neck here, a well known breeding place for race horses. Originally called Caul's Neck for an early settler.

Deal　　　　　　　　　　　　　Borough
ZIP: 07723　　　**Lat:** 40-14-59 N **Long:** 73-59-50 W
Pop: 1,179 (1990); 1,952 (1980)　　　**Pop Density:** 982.5
Land: 1.2 sq. mi.; **Water:** 0.1 sq. mi.
Formed Mar 7, 1898.
Name origin: For Deal, Kent, England.

East Freehold　　　　　　　　　　　CDP
ZIP: 07728　　　**Lat:** 40-16-07 N **Long:** 74-14-25 W
Pop: 3,842 (1990); 2,984 (1980)　　　**Pop Density:** 1280.7
Land: 3.0 sq. mi.; **Water:** 0.0 sq. mi.

Eatontown
Borough
ZIP: 07724   Lat: 40-17-29 N Long: 74-03-18 W
Pop: 13,800 (1990); 12,703 (1980)   Pop Density: 2339.0
Land: 5.9 sq. mi.; Water: 0.0 sq. mi.   Elev: 46 ft.
In eastern NJ, 5 mi. northwest of Asbury Park. Replaced Eatontown Township Mar 8, 1926.
Name origin: For Thomas Eaton, who came here from RI before 1685.

Englishtown
Borough
ZIP: 07726   Lat: 40-17-47 N Long: 74-21-38 W
Pop: 1,268 (1990); 976 (1980)   Pop Density: 2113.3
Land: 0.6 sq. mi.; Water: 0.0 sq. mi.   Elev: 70 ft.
Formed Jan 4, 1888.
Name origin: For James English, in whose house Gen. Washington (1732–99) spent the night of June 27, 1778, before the Battle of Monmouth.

Fair Haven
Borough
ZIP: 07701   Lat: 40-21-37 N Long: 74-02-16 W
Pop: 5,270 (1990); 5,679 (1980)   Pop Density: 3100.0
Land: 1.7 sq. mi.; Water: 0.0 sq. mi.   Elev: 40 ft.
Formed Mar 28, 1912.
Name origin: From a remark made by a ship's captain.

Fairview
CDP
Lat: 40-21-55 N Long: 74-04-52 W
Pop: 3,853 (1990)   Pop Density: 2963.8
Land: 1.3 sq. mi.; Water: 0.0 sq. mi.

Farmingdale
Borough
ZIP: 07727   Lat: 40-11-54 N Long: 74-10-17 W
Pop: 1,462 (1990); 1,348 (1980)   Pop Density: 2924.0
Land: 0.5 sq. mi.; Water: 0.0 sq. mi.   Elev: 79 ft.
Formed Apr 8, 1903.
Name origin: For its location in the center of a farming district.

Freehold
Borough
ZIP: 07728   Lat: 40-15-31 N Long: 74-16-32 W
Pop: 10,742 (1990); 10,020 (1980)   Pop Density: 5371.0
Land: 2.0 sq. mi.; Water: 0.0 sq. mi.   Elev: 178 ft.
In eastern NJ, 18 mi. south of Perth Amboy. Formed Apr 15, 1919.
Name origin: Originally known as Monmouth Court House, for Monmouthshire, England, and Monmouth county. Named by postal authorities to avoid confusion with county name.

*Freehold
Township
ZIP: 07728   Lat: 40-13-27 N Long: 74-17-56 W
Pop: 24,710 (1990)   Pop Density: 641.8
Land: 38.5 sq. mi.; Water: 0.1 sq. mi.
Formed Oct 31, 1693; incorporated Feb 21, 1798.

Hazlet
Township
ZIP: 07730   Lat: 40-25-35 N Long: 74-10-16 W
Pop: 21,976 (1990)   Pop Density: 3924.3
Land: 5.6 sq. mi.; Water: 0.0 sq. mi.
Replaced Raritan Township Nov 28, 1967.
Name origin: For an early settler.

Highlands
Borough
ZIP: 07732   Lat: 40-24-15 N Long: 73-59-27 W
Pop: 4,849 (1990); 5,187 (1980)   Pop Density: 6061.3
Land: 0.8 sq. mi.; Water: 0.6 sq. mi.   Elev: 10 ft.
A fishing village and summer resort in northeastern NJ near the Atlantic Ocean. Formed Mar 22, 1900.
Name origin: For its location on a bluff overlooking Sandy Hook Bay. Formerly called Parkertown.

Holmdel
Township
ZIP: 07733   Lat: 40-22-28 N Long: 74-10-24 W
Pop: 11,532 (1990)   Pop Density: 644.2
Land: 17.9 sq. mi.; Water: 0.1 sq. mi.
Formed Feb 23, 1857.
Name origin: For the Holmes family, leading landowners and descendants of the Rev. Obadiah Holmes, who came from England in 1638 and became pastor of the Baptist Church at Newport, RI, in 1676.

Howell
Township
ZIP: 07731   Lat: 40-10-53 N Long: 74-11-30 W
Pop: 38,987 (1990)   Pop Density: 640.2
Land: 60.9 sq. mi.; Water: 0.1 sq. mi.
Formed Feb 23, 1801.
Name origin: For Richard Howell, NJ governor (1792–1801).

Interlaken
Borough
ZIP: 07712   Lat: 40-14-03 N Long: 74-00-57 W
Pop: 910 (1990); 1,037 (1980)   Pop Density: 2275.0
Land: 0.4 sq. mi.; Water: 0.0 sq. mi.   Elev: 21 ft.
Formed Mar 11, 1922.
Name origin: For Interlaken, Switzerland, because of its location between the two arms of Deal Lake.

Keansburg
Borough
ZIP: 07734   Lat: 40-28-01 N Long: 74-09-42 W
Pop: 11,069 (1990); 10,613 (1980)   Pop Density: 10062.7
Land: 1.1 sq. mi.; Water: 15.8 sq. mi.   Elev: 13 ft.
In eastern NJ on Raritan Bay. Formed Mar 26, 1917.
Name origin: For John Kean, U.S. senator (1899–1911).

Keyport
Borough
ZIP: 07735   Lat: 40-25-55 N Long: 74-12-05 W
Pop: 7,586 (1990); 7,413 (1980)   Pop Density: 5418.6
Land: 1.4 sq. mi.; Water: 0.0 sq. mi.   Elev: 36 ft.
Replaced Keyport Town Apr 2, 1908.
Name origin: For its natural harbor, which made it a boat-building center. Indian name was Chingarora.

Leonardo
CDP
ZIP: 07737   Lat: 40-25-09 N Long: 74-03-38 W
Pop: 3,788 (1990)   Pop Density: 6313.3
Land: 0.6 sq. mi.; Water: 0.0 sq. mi.

Lincroft
CDP
ZIP: 07738   Lat: 40-20-29 N Long: 74-07-30 W
Pop: 6,193 (1990)   Pop Density: 1317.7
Land: 4.7 sq. mi.; Water: 0.0 sq. mi.

Little Silver
Borough
ZIP: 07739   Lat: 40-20-05 N Long: 74-02-05 W
Pop: 5,721 (1990); 5,548 (1980)   Pop Density: 2043.2
Land: 2.8 sq. mi.; Water: 0.6 sq. mi.   Elev: 38 ft.
Formed Mar 19, 1923.
Name origin: For either a payment to Indians or for the appearance of the quiet waters of the Shrewsbury River.

Loch Arbour
Borough
ZIP: 07711   **Lat:** 40-13-54 N **Long:** 74-00-04 W
Pop: 380 (1990); 369 (1980)   **Pop Density:** 3800.0
Land: 0.1 sq. mi.; **Water:** 0.0 sq. mi.   **Elev:** 24 ft.
Formed Apr 23, 1957.
Name origin: For Lochaber, Scotland, with spelling variation.

Long Branch
City
ZIP: 07740   **Lat:** 40-17-48 N **Long:** 73-59-21 W
Pop: 28,658 (1990); 29,819 (1980)   **Pop Density:** 5511.2
Land: 5.2 sq. mi.; **Water:** 1.0 sq. mi.   **Elev:** 19 ft.
In east-central NJ along the coast, 21 mi. southeast of Perth Amboy. Replaced Long Branch Commission Apr 8, 1903; incorporated as city 1902; incorporation confirmed 1903; reincorporated Mar 29, 1904.
Name origin: For the long branch of the Shrewsbury River.

Manalapan
Township
ZIP: 07726   **Lat:** 40-16-54 N **Long:** 74-20-44 W
Pop: 26,716 (1990)   **Pop Density:** 873.1
Land: 30.6 sq. mi.; **Water:** 0.0 sq. mi.
Formed Mar 9, 1848.
Name origin: From an Indian term possibly meaning 'within a covered swamp' or 'edible roots.'

Manasquan
Borough
ZIP: 08736   **Lat:** 40-06-46 N **Long:** 74-02-13 W
Pop: 5,369 (1990); 5,354 (1980)   **Pop Density:** 3835.0
Land: 1.4 sq. mi.; **Water:** 1.2 sq. mi.   **Elev:** 28 ft.
In eastern NJ on the Manasquan River. Formed Dec 30, 1887.
Name origin: For the river.

Marlboro
Township
ZIP: 07746   **Lat:** 40-20-33 N **Long:** 74-15-33 W
Pop: 27,974 (1990)   **Pop Density:** 914.2
Land: 30.6 sq. mi.; **Water:** 0.0 sq. mi.
In east-central NJ. Formed Feb 17, 1848.
Name origin: For marl beds, a source of fertilizer.

Matawan
Borough
ZIP: 07747   **Lat:** 40-24-44 N **Long:** 74-14-16 W
Pop: 9,270 (1990); 8,837 (1980)   **Pop Density:** 4030.4
Land: 2.3 sq. mi.; **Water:** 0.1 sq. mi.   **Elev:** 55 ft.
Formed Jun 28, 1895.
Name origin: From an Algonquian term probably meaning 'where two rivers come together.'

Middletown
Township
ZIP: 07748   **Lat:** 40-24-17 N **Long:** 74-04-28 W
Pop: 68,183 (1990)   **Pop Density:** 1659.0
Land: 41.1 sq. mi.; **Water:** 18.3 sq. mi.
Formed Oct 31, 1693; incorporated Feb 21, 1798.

Millstone
Township
ZIP: 08510   **Lat:** 40-12-40 N **Long:** 74-25-56 W
Pop: 5,069 (1990)   **Pop Density:** 137.7
Land: 36.8 sq. mi.; **Water:** 0.4 sq. mi.
Formed Feb 28, 1844.
Name origin: Possibly for a millstone that dropped into the river.

Monmouth Beach
Borough
ZIP: 07750   **Lat:** 40-20-09 N **Long:** 73-59-10 W
Pop: 3,303 (1990); 3,318 (1980)   **Pop Density:** 3002.7
Land: 1.1 sq. mi.; **Water:** 0.9 sq. mi.   **Elev:** 9 ft.
Formed Mar 9, 1906.

Neptune
Township
ZIP: 07753   **Lat:** 40-12-37 N **Long:** 74-03-17 W
Pop: 28,148 (1990)   **Pop Density:** 3432.7
Land: 8.2 sq. mi.; **Water:** 0.5 sq. mi.
In east-central NJ, northwest of Neptune City. Formed Feb 26, 1879.

Neptune City
Borough
ZIP: 07753   **Lat:** 40-12-02 N **Long:** 74-01-59 W
Pop: 4,997 (1990); 5,276 (1980)   **Pop Density:** 5552.2
Land: 0.9 sq. mi.; **Water:** 0.0 sq. mi.
Formed Oct 4, 1881.
Name origin: For the Roman god of the sea.

North Middletown
CDP
ZIP: 07734   **Lat:** 40-26-22 N **Long:** 74-07-09 W
Pop: 3,160 (1990)   **Pop Density:** 6320.0
Land: 0.5 sq. mi.; **Water:** 0.0 sq. mi.

Oakhurst
CDP
ZIP: 07755   **Lat:** 40-15-42 N **Long:** 74-01-37 W
Pop: 4,130 (1990)   **Pop Density:** 2581.3
Land: 1.6 sq. mi.; **Water:** 0.0 sq. mi.

Ocean
Township
ZIP: 07755   **Lat:** 40-15-06 N **Long:** 74-02-22 W
Pop: 25,058 (1990)   **Pop Density:** 2278.0
Land: 11.0 sq. mi.; **Water:** 0.1 sq. mi.
Formed Feb 24, 1849.
Name origin: For its location on the Atlantic Ocean.

Ocean Grove
CDP
ZIP: 07756   **Lat:** 40-12-42 N **Long:** 74-00-34 W
Pop: 4,818 (1990)   **Pop Density:** 16060.0
Land: 0.3 sq. mi.; **Water:** 0.0 sq. mi.

Oceanport
Borough
ZIP: 07757   **Lat:** 40-18-53 N **Long:** 74-01-13 W
Pop: 6,146 (1990); 5,888 (1980)   **Pop Density:** 1920.6
Land: 3.2 sq. mi.; **Water:** 0.6 sq. mi.   **Elev:** 24 ft.
Formed Apr 6, 1920.

Port Monmouth
CDP
ZIP: 07758   **Lat:** 40-25-55 N **Long:** 74-06-04 W
Pop: 3,558 (1990)   **Pop Density:** 2736.9
Land: 1.3 sq. mi.; **Water:** 0.0 sq. mi.

Red Bank
Borough
ZIP: 07701   **Lat:** 40-20-50 N **Long:** 74-04-02 W
Pop: 10,636 (1990); 12,031 (1980)   **Pop Density:** 5908.9
Land: 1.8 sq. mi.; **Water:** 0.4 sq. mi.   **Elev:** 39 ft.
In eastern NJ on the Navesink River, 15 mi. southeast of Perth Amboy. Replaced Red Bank Town Mar 10, 1908.
Name origin: For the clay banks along the Navesink River.

Robertsville
CDP
ZIP: 07746   **Lat:** 40-20-25 N **Long:** 74-17-50 W
Pop: 9,841 (1990); 8,461 (1980)   **Pop Density:** 1668.0
Land: 5.9 sq. mi.; **Water:** 0.0 sq. mi.

Roosevelt
Borough
Lat: 40-13-16 N Long: 74-28-27 W
Pop: 884 (1990); 835 (1980) **Pop Density:** 442.0
Land: 2.0 sq. mi.; **Water:** 0.0 sq. mi. **Elev:** 152 ft.
Replaced Jersey Homesteads Borough Nov 9, 1945.
Name origin: For Theodore Roosevelt (1858–1919), twenty-sixth U.S. president.

Rumson
Borough
ZIP: 07760 Lat: 40-21-45 N Long: 74-00-13 W
Pop: 6,701 (1990); 7,623 (1980) **Pop Density:** 1288.7
Land: 5.2 sq. mi.; **Water:** 2.0 sq. mi. **Elev:** 40 ft.
Formed May 15, 1907.
Name origin: From Algonquian, a shortened form of *Navaarumsunk*, meaning uncertain. Or possibly an Indian chief named Alumson.

Sea Bright
Borough
ZIP: 07760 Lat: 40-21-43 N Long: 73-58-31 W
Pop: 1,693 (1990); 1,812 (1980) **Pop Density:** 2821.7
Land: 0.6 sq. mi.; **Water:** 0.5 sq. mi. **Elev:** 10 ft.
In eastern NJ. Formed Mar 21, 1889; reincorporated Mar 10, 1897.
Name origin: For Sea Bright, England.

Sea Girt
Borough
ZIP: 08750 Lat: 40-07-45 N Long: 74-02-04 W
Pop: 2,099 (1990); 2,650 (1980) **Pop Density:** 1908.2
Land: 1.1 sq. mi.; **Water:** 0.4 sq. mi. **Elev:** 19 ft.
Formed Mar 29, 1917.
Name origin: For the estate of Comm. Robert F. Stockton (1795–1866).

Shark River Hills
CDP
Lat: 40-11-37 N Long: 74-02-53 W
Pop: 4,228 (1990) **Pop Density:** 5285.0
Land: 0.8 sq. mi.; **Water:** 0.0 sq. mi.

Shrewsbury
Borough
ZIP: 07702 Lat: 40-19-35 N Long: 74-03-35 W
Pop: 3,096 (1990); 2,962 (1980) **Pop Density:** 1407.3
Land: 2.2 sq. mi.; **Water:** 0.0 sq. mi. **Elev:** 133 ft.
Formed Mar 22, 1926.
Name origin: For Shrewsbury, England.

*Shrewsbury
Township
Lat: 40-18-43 N Long: 74-04-20 W
Pop: 1,098 (1990) **Pop Density:** 10980.0
Land: 0.1 sq. mi.; **Water:** 0.0 sq. mi.
Formed Oct 31, 1693; incorporated Feb 21, 1798.

South Belmar
Borough
ZIP: 07719 Lat: 40-10-12 N Long: 74-01-34 W
Pop: 1,482 (1990); 1,566 (1980) **Pop Density:** 7410.0
Land: 0.2 sq. mi.; **Water:** 0.0 sq. mi.
Formed Mar 12, 1924.

Spring Lake
Borough
ZIP: 07762 Lat: 40-09-09 N Long: 74-01-38 W
Pop: 3,499 (1990); 4,215 (1980) **Pop Density:** 2691.5
Land: 1.3 sq. mi.; **Water:** 0.4 sq. mi. **Elev:** 25 ft.
Formed Mar 14, 1892.
Name origin: For a local fresh water stream.

Spring Lake Heights
Borough
ZIP: 07762 Lat: 40-09-07 N Long: 74-02-32 W
Pop: 5,341 (1990); 5,424 (1980) **Pop Density:** 4108.5
Land: 1.3 sq. mi.; **Water:** 0.0 sq. mi. **Elev:** 54 ft.
Formed Mar 19, 1927.

Strathmore
CDP
ZIP: 07747 Lat: 40-24-09 N Long: 74-13-07 W
Pop: 7,060 (1990) **Pop Density:** 3922.2
Land: 1.8 sq. mi.; **Water:** 0.0 sq. mi.

Tinton Falls
Borough
ZIP: 07724 Lat: 40-16-20 N Long: 74-05-21 W
Pop: 12,361 (1990); 7,740 (1980) **Pop Density:** 792.4
Land: 15.6 sq. mi.; **Water:** 0.0 sq. mi.
Replaced New Shrewsbury Borough Nov 6, 1975.
Name origin: A corruption of Tintern Manor, owned by Col. Lewis Morris, located near falls in the Swimming River.

Union Beach
Borough
ZIP: 07735 Lat: 40-26-50 N Long: 74-10-08 W
Pop: 6,156 (1990); 6,354 (1980) **Pop Density:** 3240.0
Land: 1.9 sq. mi.; **Water:** 0.1 sq. mi. **Elev:** 9 ft.
Formed Mar 16, 1925.

Upper Freehold
Township
ZIP: 08501 Lat: 40-09-26 N Long: 74-31-27 W
Pop: 3,277 (1990) **Pop Density:** 69.9
Land: 46.9 sq. mi.; **Water:** 0.3 sq. mi.
Formed 1731; incorporated Feb 21, 1798.

Wall
Borough
ZIP: 08736 Lat: 40-10-01 N Long: 74-05-53 W
Pop: 20,244 (1990) **Pop Density:** 661.6
Land: 30.6 sq. mi.; **Water:** 0.8 sq. mi.
In eastern NJ. Formed Mar 7, 1851.
Name origin: For Ganet D. Wall, U.S. senator from NJ (1835–41).

Wanamassa
CDP
Lat: 40-14-12 N Long: 74-01-45 W
Pop: 4,530 (1990) **Pop Density:** 4118.2
Land: 1.1 sq. mi.; **Water:** 0.0 sq. mi.

West Belmar
CDP
ZIP: 07719 Lat: 40-10-12 N Long: 74-02-14 W
Pop: 2,498 (1990) **Pop Density:** 4996.0
Land: 0.5 sq. mi.; **Water:** 0.0 sq. mi.

West Freehold
CDP
ZIP: 07728 Lat: 40-13-58 N Long: 74-17-43 W
Pop: 11,166 (1990); 9,929 (1980) **Pop Density:** 1892.5
Land: 5.9 sq. mi.; **Water:** 0.0 sq. mi.

West Long Branch
Borough
ZIP: 07764 Lat: 40-17-23 N Long: 74-01-05 W
Pop: 7,690 (1990); 7,380 (1980) **Pop Density:** 2651.7
Land: 2.9 sq. mi.; **Water:** 0.0 sq. mi. **Elev:** 20 ft.
Formed Apr 7, 1908.
Name origin: For its location west of Long Branch Township.

Yorketown
CDP
ZIP: 07726 Lat: 40-18-27 N Long: 74-20-16 W
Pop: 6,313 (1990); 5,330 (1980) **Pop Density:** 2630.4
Land: 2.4 sq. mi.; **Water:** 0.0 sq. mi.

Morris County
County Seat: Morristown (ZIP: 07960)

Pop: 421,353 (1990); 407,630 (1980) Pop Density: 898.3
Land: 469.1 sq. mi.; Water: 12.3 sq. mi. Area Code: 201

In north-central NJ, west of Newark; organized Mar 15, 1739 from Hunterdon County.
Name origin: For Lewis Morris (1671–1746), chief justice of the superior court of NY and NJ (1692) and first governor of the colony of NJ (1738–46).

Boonton
Town
ZIP: 07005 Lat: 40-54-14 N Long: 74-24-19 W
Pop: 8,343 (1990); 8,620 (1980) Pop Density: 3476.2
Land: 2.4 sq. mi.; Water: 0.1 sq. mi. Elev: 431 ft.
Settled 1762. Formed Mar 16, 1866; reincorporated Mar 18, 1867.
Name origin: For Thomas Boone, governor (1760–61), with spelling alteration.

*Boonton
Township
ZIP: 07005 Lat: 40-55-42 N Long: 74-25-33 W
Pop: 3,566 (1990) Pop Density: 414.7
Land: 8.6 sq. mi.; Water: 0.2 sq. mi.
Formed Apr 11, 1867.

Budd Lake
CDP
ZIP: 07828 Lat: 40-52-23 N Long: 74-44-13 W
Pop: 7,272 (1990); 6,523 (1980) Pop Density: 1232.5
Land: 5.9 sq. mi.; Water: 0.6 sq. mi.

Butler
Borough
ZIP: 07405 Lat: 40-59-57 N Long: 74-20-48 W
Pop: 7,392 (1990); 7,616 (1980) Pop Density: 3520.0
Land: 2.1 sq. mi.; Water: 0.0 sq. mi. Elev: 480 ft.
Formed Mar 13, 1901.
Name origin: For an early landowner.

Chatham
Township
ZIP: 07928 Lat: 40-43-42 N Long: 74-25-23 W
Pop: 9,361 (1990) Pop Density: 1006.6
Land: 9.3 sq. mi.; Water: 0.0 sq. mi.
Formed Feb 12, 1806.

*Chatham
Borough
ZIP: 07928 Lat: 40-44-25 N Long: 74-23-00 W
Pop: 8,007 (1990); 8,537 (1980) Pop Density: 3336.2
Land: 2.4 sq. mi.; Water: 0.0 sq. mi. Elev: 244 ft.
In northern NJ, 5 mi. southeast of Morristown; 10 mi. west of Newark. Replaced Chatham Village Mar 1, 1897.
Name origin: For the Earl of Chatham, who supported the colonists.

Chester
Township
ZIP: 07930 Lat: 40-46-44 N Long: 74-41-04 W
Pop: 5,958 (1990) Pop Density: 203.3
Land: 29.3 sq. mi.; Water: 0.0 sq. mi.
Formed Apr 1, 1799.

*Chester
Borough
ZIP: 07930 Lat: 40-47-09 N Long: 74-41-35 W
Pop: 1,214 (1990); 1,433 (1980) Pop Density: 809.3
Land: 1.5 sq. mi.; Water: 0.0 sq. mi. Elev: 846 ft.
Formed Apr 3, 1930.
Name origin: For Chestershire, England.

Denville
Township
ZIP: 07834 Lat: 40-53-19 N Long: 74-29-20 W
Pop: 13,812 (1990) Pop Density: 1141.5
Land: 12.1 sq. mi.; Water: 0.5 sq. mi.
In northern NJ, on the northeastern side of Indian Lake. Formed Apr 14, 1913.
Name origin: A combination of *Den* for Daniel Denton, a landowner, and *ville*.

Dover
Town
ZIP: 07801 Lat: 40-53-09 N Long: 74-33-34 W
Pop: 15,115 (1990); 14,681 (1980) Pop Density: 5598.1
Land: 2.7 sq. mi.; Water: 0.0 sq. mi. Elev: 800 ft.
In northern NJ, 8 mi. northwest of Morristown. Formed Apr 1, 1869.
Name origin: For Dover, NH.

East Hanover
Township
ZIP: 07936 Lat: 40-49-11 N Long: 74-21-54 W
Pop: 9,926 (1990) Pop Density: 1210.5
Land: 8.2 sq. mi.; Water: 0.0 sq. mi.
Formed Mar 12, 1928.

Florham Park
Borough
ZIP: 07932 Lat: 40-46-39 N Long: 74-23-48 W
Pop: 8,521 (1990); 9,359 (1980) Pop Density: 1151.5
Land: 7.4 sq. mi.; Water: 0.0 sq. mi. Elev: 240 ft.
In northern NJ, 4 mi. east of Morristown. Formed Mar 9, 1899.
Name origin: A contraction of *Flor*ence and *Ham*ilton Twombly whose mansion is now part of Fairleigh Dickinson University.

Hanover
Township
ZIP: 07981 Lat: 40-49-08 N Long: 74-25-49 W
Pop: 11,538 (1990) Pop Density: 1078.3
Land: 10.7 sq. mi.; Water: 0.0 sq. mi.
Incorporated Feb 21, 1798.

Harding
Township
Lat: 40-44-44 N Long: 74-29-51 W
Pop: 3,640 (1990) Pop Density: 178.4
Land: 20.4 sq. mi.; Water: 0.0 sq. mi.
Formed Sep 1, 1922.

Jefferson
Township
ZIP: 07849 Lat: 41-00-09 N Long: 74-33-02 W
Pop: 17,825 (1990) Pop Density: 438.0
Land: 40.7 sq. mi.; Water: 2.4 sq. mi.
Formed Feb 11, 1804.
Name origin: For Thomas Jefferson (1743–1826), third U.S. president.

Kinnelon
Borough
ZIP: 07405 Lat: 40-59-05 N Long: 74-23-12 W
Pop: 8,470 (1990); 7,770 (1980) Pop Density: 460.3
Land: 18.4 sq. mi.; Water: 0.9 sq. mi. Elev: 700 ft.
Formed Feb 20, 1922.
Name origin: For founder Francis S. Kinney.

Lake Telemark
CDP
 Lat: 40-57-40 N Long: 74-29-48 W
Pop: 1,121 (1990); 1,216 (1980) Pop Density: 509.5
Land: 2.2 sq. mi.; Water: 0.0 sq. mi.

Lincoln Park
Borough
ZIP: 07035 Lat: 40-55-26 N Long: 74-18-14 W
Pop: 10,978 (1990); 8,806 (1980) Pop Density: 1638.5
Land: 6.7 sq. mi.; Water: 0.2 sq. mi.
In northern NJ, 7 mi. west of Paterson. Formed Mar 11, 1922; reincorporated Feb 26, 1925.
Name origin: For Abraham Lincoln (1809–65), sixteenth U.S. president.

Long Valley
CDP
ZIP: 07853 Lat: 40-47-07 N Long: 74-46-06 W
Pop: 1,744 (1990); 1,682 (1980) Pop Density: 405.6
Land: 4.3 sq. mi.; Water: 0.0 sq. mi.

Madison
Borough
ZIP: 07940 Lat: 40-45-30 N Long: 74-25-02 W
Pop: 15,850 (1990); 15,357 (1980) Pop Density: 3773.8
Land: 4.2 sq. mi.; Water: 0.0 sq. mi. Elev: 261 ft.
In northern NJ, west of Newark, 4 mi. southeast of Morristown. Formed Dec 27, 1889.
Name origin: For James Madison (1751–1836), fifth U.S. president.

Mendham
Borough
ZIP: 07945 Lat: 40-46-01 N Long: 74-35-53 W
Pop: 4,890 (1990); 4,899 (1980) Pop Density: 815.0
Land: 6.0 sq. mi.; Water: 0.0 sq. mi. Elev: 618 ft.
Formed May 15, 1906.
Name origin: For Myndham, England, with spelling alteration.

*Mendham
Township
ZIP: 07945 Lat: 40-46-50 N Long: 74-34-59 W
Pop: 4,537 (1990) Pop Density: 253.5
Land: 17.9 sq. mi.; Water: 0.1 sq. mi.
Formed Mar 29, 1749; incorporated Feb 21, 1798.

Mine Hill
Township
 Lat: 40-52-45 N Long: 74-36-02 W
Pop: 3,333 (1990) Pop Density: 1111.0
Land: 3.0 sq. mi.; Water: 0.0 sq. mi.
Formed Mar 2, 1923.
Name origin: For iron mines in the nearby hills.

Montville
Township
ZIP: 07045 Lat: 40-54-51 N Long: 74-21-42 W
Pop: 15,600 (1990) Pop Density: 825.4
Land: 18.9 sq. mi.; Water: 0.3 sq. mi.
Formed Apr 11, 1867.
Name origin: For the mountainous terrain of its location.

Morris
Township
ZIP: 07961 Lat: 40-47-44 N Long: 74-29-39 W
Pop: 19,952 (1990) Pop Density: 1262.8
Land: 15.8 sq. mi.; Water: 0.1 sq. mi.
Formed Mar 25, 1740; incorporated Feb 21, 1798.
Name origin: For Lewis Morris, first governor of NJ (1738–46).

Morris Plains
Borough
ZIP: 07950 Lat: 40-50-09 N Long: 74-28-53 W
Pop: 5,219 (1990); 5,305 (1980) Pop Density: 2007.3
Land: 2.6 sq. mi.; Water: 0.0 sq. mi. Elev: 399 ft.
Formed Mar 15, 1926.
Name origin: For Lewis Morris, first governor of NJ (1738–46).

Morristown
Town
ZIP: 07960 Lat: 40-47-48 N Long: 74-28-39 W
Pop: 16,189 (1990); 16,614 (1980) Pop Density: 5582.4
Land: 2.9 sq. mi.; Water: 0.1 sq. mi. Elev: 327 ft.
In northern NJ, 17 mi. northwest of Newark. Laid out 1739. Formed Apr 6, 1865.
Name origin: For Lewis Morris, first governor of NJ (1738–46).

Mountain Lakes
Borough
ZIP: 07046 Lat: 40-53-30 N Long: 74-26-26 W
Pop: 3,847 (1990); 4,153 (1980) Pop Density: 1424.8
Land: 2.7 sq. mi.; Water: 0.2 sq. mi. Elev: 513 ft.
Formed Mar 3, 1924.
Name origin: Descriptive.

Mount Arlington
Borough
ZIP: 07856 Lat: 40-55-10 N Long: 74-38-25 W
Pop: 3,630 (1990); 4,251 (1980) Pop Density: 1728.6
Land: 2.1 sq. mi.; Water: 0.7 sq. mi. Elev: 1000 ft.
Formed Nov 3, 1890.
Name origin: For Henry Bennet (1618–85), Earl of Arlington.

Mount Olive
Township
ZIP: 07828 Lat: 40-52-02 N Long: 74-44-26 W
Pop: 21,282 (1990) Pop Density: 700.1
Land: 30.4 sq. mi.; Water: 0.7 sq. mi.
Formed Mar 22, 1871.
Name origin: For Benjamin Olive, donor of land for a church.

Netcong
Borough
ZIP: 07857 Lat: 40-53-56 N Long: 74-42-04 W
Pop: 3,311 (1990); 3,557 (1980) Pop Density: 4138.8
Land: 0.8 sq. mi.; Water: 0.1 sq. mi. Elev: 882 ft.
Formed Oct 23, 1894.
Name origin: For the last two syllables of the Algonquian word *Musconetcong* probably meaning 'rapid stream.'

Parsippany-Troy Hills
Township
ZIP: 07054 Lat: 40-51-33 N Long: 74-25-25 W
Pop: 48,478 (1990) Pop Density: 2028.4
Land: 23.9 sq. mi.; Water: 1.5 sq. mi.
In northern NJ, 6 mi. northeast of Morristown. Formed Mar 12, 1928.
Name origin: From an Indian tribal name; Troy for the ancient city in Asia Minor.

Passaic
Township
ZIP: 07946　　Lat: 40-40-44 N　Long: 74-29-07 W
Pop: 7,826 (1990)　　Pop Density: 646.8
Land: 12.1 sq. mi.; Water: 0.0 sq. mi.
Formed Mar 23, 1866.

Pequannock
Township
ZIP: 07440　　Lat: 40-57-47 N　Long: 74-18-13 W
Pop: 12,844 (1990)　　Pop Density: 1834.9
Land: 7.0 sq. mi.; Water: 0.1 sq. mi.
In northern NJ, 7 mi. west of Paterson. Formed Mar 25, 1740; incorporated Feb 21, 1798.
Name origin: From Algonquian 'land made clear for cultivation.'

Randolph
Township
ZIP: 07869　　Lat: 40-50-40 N　Long: 74-34-51 W
Pop: 19,974 (1990)　　Pop Density: 951.1
Land: 21.0 sq. mi.; Water: 0.1 sq. mi.
Formed Jan 1, 1806.
Name origin: For Benjamin Randolph, a Revolutionary War–era settler and businessman.

Riverdale
Borough
ZIP: 07457　　Lat: 40-59-42 N　Long: 74-18-49 W
Pop: 2,370 (1990); 2,530 (1980)　Pop Density: 1128.6
Land: 2.1 sq. mi.; Water: 0.0 sq. mi.　　Elev: 232 ft.
Formed Mar 12, 1923.
Name origin: For its location in the Pequannock River valley. Riverdale-Pompton is its railroad name.

Rockaway
Township
ZIP: 07866　　Lat: 40-57-37 N　Long: 74-29-56 W
Pop: 19,572 (1990)　　Pop Density: 463.8
Land: 42.2 sq. mi.; Water: 3.2 sq. mi.
In northern NJ, 8 mi. north of Morristown.

*Rockaway
Borough
ZIP: 07866　　Lat: 40-53-48 N　Long: 74-30-53 W
Pop: 6,243 (1990); 6,852 (1980)　Pop Density: 2972.9
Land: 2.1 sq. mi.; Water: 0.0 sq. mi.　　Elev: 534 ft.
Formed Jun 19, 1894.
Name origin: For the river, itself named for the Indian term *rechouwakie* possibly meaning 'place of sands.'

Roxbury
Township
ZIP: 07876　　Lat: 40-52-50 N　Long: 74-39-17 W
Pop: 20,429 (1990)　　Pop Density: 954.6
Land: 21.4 sq. mi.; Water: 0.5 sq. mi.
Formed Dec 24, 1740; incorporated Feb 21, 1798.
Name origin: Possibly for Roxburgh County, Scotland.

Succasunna-Kenvil
CDP
ZIP: 07876　　Lat: 40-51-19 N　Long: 74-39-10 W
Pop: 11,781 (1990); 10,931 (1980)　Pop Density: 1785.0
Land: 6.6 sq. mi.; Water: 0.1 sq. mi.

Victory Gardens
Borough
Lat: 40-52-34 N　Long: 74-32-39 W
Pop: 1,314 (1990); 1,043 (1980)　Pop Density: 13140.0
Land: 0.1 sq. mi.; Water: 0.0 sq. mi.　　Elev: 660 ft.
Formed Jun 20, 1951.

Washington
Township
ZIP: 07853　　Lat: 40-47-14 N　Long: 74-47-39 W
Pop: 15,592 (1990)　　Pop Density: 348.0
Land: 44.8 sq. mi.; Water: 0.0 sq. mi.
Formed Apr 2, 1798; incorporated Feb 21, 1798.
Name origin: For George Washington (1732–99), first U.S. president.

Wharton
Borough
ZIP: 07885　　Lat: 40-53-58 N　Long: 74-34-56 W
Pop: 5,405 (1990); 5,485 (1980)　Pop Density: 2456.8
Land: 2.2 sq. mi.; Water: 0.0 sq. mi.　　Elev: 660 ft.
Replaced Port Oram Borough Apr 16, 1902.
Name origin: For Wharton Steel Company.

White Meadow Lake
CDP
ZIP: 07866　　Lat: 40-55-24 N　Long: 74-30-39 W
Pop: 8,002 (1990); 8,429 (1980)　Pop Density: 1951.7
Land: 4.1 sq. mi.; Water: 0.5 sq. mi.

Ocean County
County Seat: Toms River (ZIP: 08753)

Pop: 433,203 (1990); 346,038 (1980)　　Pop Density: 680.8
Land: 636.3 sq. mi.; Water: 279.6 sq. mi.　　Area Code: 908
In central NJ, north of Atlantic City; organized Feb 15, 1850 from Monmouth County.
Name origin: For its location on the Atlantic coast.

Barnegat
Township
ZIP: 08005　　Lat: 39-46-06 N　Long: 74-16-48 W
Pop: 12,235 (1990)　　Pop Density: 364.1
Land: 33.6 sq. mi.; Water: 6.1 sq. mi.
In eastern NJ on the Atlantic coast. Replaced Union Township Dec 6, 1976.
Name origin: From *barendegat*, a Dutch term meaning 'breaker's inlet.'

Barnegat Light
Borough
ZIP: 08006　　Lat: 39-45-06 N　Long: 74-06-40 W
Pop: 675 (1990); 619 (1980)　　Pop Density: 964.3
Land: 0.7 sq. mi.; Water: 0.1 sq. mi.　　Elev: 10 ft.
Replaced Barnegat City Borough Nov 2, 1948.

Bay Head   Borough
ZIP: 08742   Lat: 40-04-12 N Long: 74-02-55 W
Pop: 1,226 (1990); 1,340 (1980)   Pop Density: 2043.3
Land: 0.6 sq. mi.; Water: 0.1 sq. mi.   Elev: 9 ft.
In eastern NJ on the Atlantic coast. Formed Jun 15, 1886.
Name origin: For its location at the head of Barnegat Bay.

Beach Haven   Borough
ZIP: 08008   Lat: 39-33-50 N Long: 74-14-43 W
Pop: 1,475 (1990); 1,714 (1980)   Pop Density: 1475.0
Land: 1.0 sq. mi.; Water: 1.3 sq. mi.   Elev: 10 ft.
Formed Nov 11, 1890.
Name origin: For its location just north of Beach Haven Inlet.

Beach Haven West   CDP
ZIP: 08050   Lat: 39-40-12 N Long: 74-14-00 W
Pop: 4,237 (1990); 3,020 (1980)   Pop Density: 2118.5
Land: 2.0 sq. mi.; Water: 0.1 sq. mi.

Beachwood   Borough
ZIP: 08722   Lat: 39-55-38 N Long: 74-12-09 W
Pop: 9,324 (1990); 7,687 (1980)   Pop Density: 3330.0
Land: 2.8 sq. mi.; Water: 0.0 sq. mi.   Elev: 40 ft.
In eastern NJ on the Toms River. Formed Mar 22, 1917.
Name origin: For its location as the former terminal of a wooden railway that ran from charcoal-burning pits at Lakehurst to Toms River.

Berkeley   Township
ZIP: 08721   Lat: 39-54-57 N Long: 74-11-01 W
Pop: 37,319 (1990)   Pop Density: 869.9
Land: 42.9 sq. mi.; Water: 12.9 sq. mi.

Brick   Township
ZIP: 08723-24   Lat: 40-03-27 N Long: 74-06-36 W
Pop: 66,473 (1990)   Pop Density: 2527.5
Land: 26.3 sq. mi.; Water: 6.0 sq. mi.
Formed Feb 15, 1850.
Name origin: For resident Joseph W. Brick.

Cedar Glen Lakes   CDP
                    Lat: 39-57-07 N Long: 74-24-00 W
Pop: 1,611 (1990); 1,987 (1980)   Pop Density: 2301.4
Land: 0.7 sq. mi.; Water: 0.0 sq. mi.

Cedar Glen West   CDP
                    Lat: 40-02-36 N Long: 74-17-15 W
Pop: 1,396 (1990)   Pop Density: 1269.1
Land: 1.1 sq. mi.; Water: 0.0 sq. mi.

Crestwood Village   CDP
ZIP: 08759   Lat: 39-57-25 N Long: 74-21-18 W
Pop: 8,030 (1990); 7,965 (1980)   Pop Density: 2059.0
Land: 3.9 sq. mi.; Water: 0.0 sq. mi.

Dover   Township
ZIP: 08753   Lat: 39-59-22 N Long: 74-10-01 W
Pop: 76,371 (1990)   Pop Density: 1858.2
Land: 41.1 sq. mi.; Water: 11.9 sq. mi.
Formed Mar 1, 1768; incorporated Feb 21, 1798.
Name origin: For Dover, England.

Eagleswood   Township
                    Lat: 39-39-09 N Long: 74-17-32 W
Pop: 1,476 (1990)   Pop Density: 90.0
Land: 16.4 sq. mi.; Water: 2.5 sq. mi.
Formed Mar 17, 1874.

Forked River   CDP
ZIP: 08731   Lat: 39-48-49 N Long: 74-08-50 W
Pop: 4,243 (1990)   Pop Density: 1631.9
Land: 2.6 sq. mi.; Water: 7.4 sq. mi.

Gilford Park   CDP
ZIP: 08753   Lat: 39-57-14 N Long 74-07-48 W
Pop: 8,668 (1990); 6,528 (1980)   Pop Density: 3940.0
Land: 2.2 sq. mi.; Water: 0.4 sq. mi.

Harvey Cedars   Borough
ZIP: 08008   Lat: 39-41-58 N Long 74-08-31 W
Pop: 362 (1990); 363 (1980)   Pop Density: 603.3
Land: 0.6 sq. mi.; Water: 0.6 sq. mi.   Elev: 9 ft.
The oldest settlement on Long Beach Island on Barnegat Bay. It drew whalers from Long Island and New England soon after the War of 1812. Formed Dec 13, 1894.

Holiday City-Berkeley   CDP
ZIP: 08753   Lat: 39-57-34 N Long 74-16-39 W
Pop: 14,293 (1990); 9,019 (1980)   Pop Density: 2464.3
Land: 5.8 sq. mi.; Water: 0.0 sq. mi.

Holiday City-Dover   CDP
                    Lat: 40-01-16 N Long 74-10-01 W
Pop: 2,391 (1990)   Pop Density: 2173.6
Land: 1.1 sq. mi.; Water: 0.1 sq. mi.

Holiday City South   CDP
                    Lat: 39-56-55 N Long 74-14-11 W
Pop: 5,452 (1990)   Pop Density: 2869.5
Land: 1.9 sq. mi.; Water: 0.0 sq. mi.

Holiday Heights   CDP
                    Lat: 39-56-44 N Long 74-15-15 W
Pop: 703 (1990)   Pop Density: 468.7
Land: 1.5 sq. mi.; Water: 0.0 sq. mi.

Island Heights   Borough
ZIP: 08732   Lat: 39-56-32 N Long 74-08-58 W
Pop: 1,470 (1990); 1,575 (1980)   Pop Density: 2450.0
Land: 0.6 sq. mi.; Water: 0.5 sq. mi.   Elev: 30 ft.
Formed May 6, 1887.
Name origin: For its topography overlooking the Toms River.

Jackson   Township
ZIP: 08527   Lat: 40-06-06 N Long: 74-21-33 W
Pop: 33,233 (1990)   Pop Density: 332.0
Land: 100.1 sq. mi.; Water: 0.8 sq. mi.
Formed Mar 6, 1844.
Name origin: For Andrew Jackson (1767–1845), seventh U.S. president.

Lacey   Township
ZIP: 08731   Lat: 39-51-24 N Long: 74-16-04 W
Pop: 22,141 (1990)   Pop Density: 263.6
Land: 84.0 sq. mi.; Water: 14.5 sq. mi.
Formed Mar 23, 1871.
Name origin: Probably for Gen. John Lacey, officer in the American Revolution.

Lakehurst   Borough
ZIP: 08733   Lat: 40-00-46 N Long: 74-19-14 W
Pop: 3,078 (1990); 2,908 (1980)   Pop Density: 3420.0
Land: 0.9 sq. mi.; Water: 0.1 sq. mi.   Elev: 72 ft.
Formed Apr 7, 1921.
Name origin: For its location near two lakes and a pine thicket.

Lakewood　　　　　　　　　　　Township
ZIP: 08701　　　　　　Lat: 40-04-47 N　Long: 74-12-14 W
Pop: 45,048 (1990)　　　　　Pop Density: 1816.5
Land: 24.8 sq. mi.; Water: 0.3 sq. mi.

In eastern NJ, 14 mi. southwest of Asbury Park. Formed Mar 23, 1892.

Name origin: For its location near two lakes and pine woods.

Lavallette　　　　　　　　　　　Borough
ZIP: 08735　　　　　　Lat: 39-58-08 N　Long: 74-04-20 W
Pop: 2,299 (1990); 2,072 (1980)　　Pop Density: 2873.8
Land: 0.8 sq. mi.; Water: 0.1 sq. mi.　　　　Elev: 5 ft.

Formed Dec 21, 1887.

Name origin: For Adm. Elie A. F. Lavallette of the U.S. Navy, officer in the War of 1812.

Leisure Knoll　　　　　　　　　　CDP
　　　　　　　　　　Lat: 40-01-08 N　Long: 74-17-33 W
Pop: 2,707 (1990)　　　　　Pop Density: 3007.8
Land: 0.9 sq. mi.; Water: 0.0 sq. mi.

Leisure Village　　　　　　　　　CDP
　　　　　　　　　　Lat: 40-02-41 N　Long: 74-10-56 W
Pop: 4,295 (1990)　　　　　Pop Density: 3579.2
Land: 1.2 sq. mi.; Water: 0.1 sq. mi.

Leisure Village East　　　　　　　CDP
　　　　　　　　　　Lat: 40-02-29 N　Long: 74-10-02 W
Pop: 1,989 (1990)　　　　　Pop Density: 1326.0
Land: 1.5 sq. mi.; Water: 0.0 sq. mi.

Leisure Village West-Pine Lake Park　　CDP
　　　　　　　　　　Lat: 40-00-13 N　Long: 74-15-59 W
Pop: 10,139 (1990)　　　　　Pop Density: 2668.2
Land: 3.8 sq. mi.; Water: 0.0 sq. mi.

Little Egg Harbor　　　　　　　Township
ZIP: 08087　　　　　　Lat: 39-35-55 N　Long: 74-21-03 W
Pop: 13,333 (1990)　　　　　Pop Density: 271.5
Land: 49.1 sq. mi.; Water: 24.1 sq. mi.

Formed Feb 13, 1740; incorporated Feb 21, 1798.

Name origin: For Little Egg Harbor Bay, along whose shores gulls' eggs could be found.

Long Beach　　　　　　　　　Township
　　　　　　　　　　Lat: 39-38-19 N　Long: 74-11-54 W
Pop: 3,407 (1990)　　　　　Pop Density: 642.8
Land: 5.3 sq. mi.; Water: 16.7 sq. mi.

Formed Mar 23, 1899.

Name origin: For the strip of beach bounding Barnegat Bay on Long Beach Island.

Manahawkin　　　　　　　　　CDP
ZIP: 08050　　　　　　Lat: 39-41-44 N　Long: 74-15-14 W
Pop: 1,594 (1990); 1,469 (1980)　　Pop Density: 1062.7
Land: 1.5 sq. mi.; Water: 0.1 sq. mi.

Manchester　　　　　　　　　Township
ZIP: 08759　　　　　　Lat: 39-57-52 N　Long: 74-22-21 W
Pop: 35,976 (1990)　　　　　Pop Density: 435.5
Land: 82.6 sq. mi.; Water: 0.3 sq. mi.

Formed Apr 6, 1865.

Name origin: For Manchester, England

Mantoloking　　　　　　　　　Borough
ZIP: 08738　　　　　　Lat: 40-02-42 N　Long: 74-02-58 W
Pop: 334 (1990); 433 (1980)　　Pop Density: 835.0
Land: 0.4 sq. mi.; Water: 0.2 sq. mi.

Formed Apr 10, 1911.

Name origin: For an Indian sub-tribe whose name probably meant 'sand place.'

Mystic Island　　　　　　　　　CDP
ZIP: 08087　　　　　　Lat: 39-33-56 N　Long: 74-22-59 W
Pop: 7,400 (1990); 4,929 (1980)　　Pop Density: 961.0
Land: 7.7 sq. mi.; Water: 0.2 sq. mi.

New Egypt　　　　　　　　　CDP
ZIP: 08533　　　　　　Lat: 40-03-50 N　Long: 74-31-54 W
Pop: 2,327 (1990); 2,111 (1980)　　Pop Density: 775.7
Land: 3.0 sq. mi.; Water: 0.0 sq. mi.

North Beach Haven　　　　　　　CDP
ZIP: 08008　　　　　　Lat: 39-36-00 N　Long: 74-12-42 W
Pop: 2,413 (1990); 2,652 (1980)　　Pop Density: 1340.6
Land: 1.8 sq. mi.; Water: 0.0 sq. mi.

Ocean　　　　　　　　　　　Township
ZIP: 08758　　　　　　Lat: 39-47-27 N　Long: 74-13-04 W
Pop: 5,416 (1990)　　　　　Pop Density: 260.4
Land: 20.8 sq. mi.; Water: 11.2 sq. mi.

Formed Apr 13, 1876.

Name origin: For its location on the Atlantic Ocean.

Ocean Acres　　　　　　　　　CDP
ZIP: 08050　　　　　　Lat: 39-44-35 N　Long: 74-16-52 W
Pop: 5,587 (1990); 137 (1980)　　Pop Density: 946.9
Land: 5.9 sq. mi.; Water: 0.1 sq. mi.

Ocean Gate　　　　　　　　　Borough
ZIP: 08740　　　　　　Lat: 39-55-34 N　Long: 74-08-06 W
Pop: 2,078 (1990); 1,385 (1980)　　Pop Density: 5195.0
Land: 0.4 sq. mi.; Water: 0.0 sq. mi.　　　　Elev: 7 ft.

Formed Feb 28, 1918.

Name origin: For its location on the Atlantic Ocean.

Pine Beach　　　　　　　　　Borough
ZIP: 08741　　　　　　Lat: 39-56-07 N　Long: 74-10-12 W
Pop: 1,954 (1990); 1,796 (1980)　　Pop Density: 3256.7
Land: 0.6 sq. mi.; Water: 0.0 sq. mi.　　　　Elev: 20 ft.

Formed Feb 26, 1925.

Name origin: Descriptive of the location.

Pine Ridge at Crestwood　　　　　CDP
　　　　　　　　　　Lat: 39-57-16 N　Long: 74-18-56 W
Pop: 2,372 (1990)　　　　　Pop Density: 1395.3
Land: 1.7 sq. mi.; Water: 0.0 sq. mi.

Pleasant Plains　　　　　　　　CDP
　　　　　　　　　　Lat: 39-59-49 N　Long: 74-13-08 W
Pop: 2,577 (1990)　　　　　Pop Density: 1982.3
Land: 1.3 sq. mi.; Water: 0.0 sq. mi.

Plumsted　　　　　　　　　Township
ZIP: 08533　　　　　　Lat: 40-02-44 N　Long: 74-29-05 W
Pop: 6,005 (1990)　　　　　Pop Density: 150.1
Land: 40.0 sq. mi.; Water: 0.2 sq. mi.

Formed Mar 11, 1845.

Name origin: For Clement Plumstead, an early proprietor.

Point Pleasant
Borough
ZIP: 08742 **Lat:** 40-04-42 N **Long:** 74-04-15 W
Pop: 18,177 (1990); 17,747 (1980) **Pop Density:** 5193.4
Land: 3.5 sq. mi.; **Water:** 0.6 sq. mi. **Elev:** 16 ft.

In eastern NJ, 10 mi. south of Asbury Park. Formed Apr 21, 1920.

Name origin: For its location on the Atlantic Ocean and Manasquan Inlet.

Point Pleasant Beach
Borough
ZIP: 08742 **Lat:** 40-05-33 N **Long:** 74-02-44 W
Pop: 5,112 (1990); 5,415 (1980) **Pop Density:** 3651.4
Land: 1.4 sq. mi.; **Water:** 0.3 sq. mi. **Elev:** 10 ft.

Formed May 18, 1886.

Seaside Heights
Borough
ZIP: 08751 **Lat:** 39-56-35 N **Long:** 74-04-35 W
Pop: 2,366 (1990); 1,802 (1980) **Pop Density:** 4732.0
Land: 0.5 sq. mi.; **Water:** 0.0 sq. mi. **Elev:** 7 ft.

Formed Feb 26, 1913.

Name origin: For its location on a bluff on Island Beach, the island reef bordering Barnegat Bay.

Seaside Park
Borough
ZIP: 08752 **Lat:** 39-55-32 N **Long:** 74-04-44 W
Pop: 1,871 (1990); 1,795 (1980) **Pop Density:** 2672.9
Land: 0.7 sq. mi.; **Water:** 0.1 sq. mi. **Elev:** 6 ft.

Formed Mar 3, 1898.

Name origin: For its location on Long Beach, the island reef bordering Barnegat Bay.

Ship Bottom
Borough
ZIP: 08008 **Lat:** 39-38-42 N **Long:** 74-10-59 W
Pop: 1,352 (1990); 1,427 (1980) **Pop Density:** 1931.4
Land: 0.7 sq. mi.; **Water:** 0.3 sq. mi. **Elev:** 10 ft.

Replaced Ship Bottom-Beach Arlington Borough 1947.

Name origin: One tradition is that in 1817 Capt. Stephen Willits during a storm came upon a ship aground, bottom up. His men heard tapping inside and chopped a hole with an axe. Out stepped a beautiful young girl, whom they carried to shore, where she thanked them in a strange tongue, sank to her knees, and drew the sign of the cross on the sand. She was sent to New York and was never heard of again. Another tradition, dated 1846, is similar except the girl stayed in the village, married locally, and is referred to as the ancestor of a Sandy Hook pilot.

Silver Ridge
CDP
Lat: 39-57-39 N **Long:** 74-14-10 W
Pop: 1,138 (1990) **Pop Density:** 2845.0
Land: 0.4 sq. mi.; **Water:** 0.0 sq. mi.

Silverton
CDP
ZIP: 08753 **Lat:** 40-00-28 N **Long:** 74-07-18 W
Pop: 9,175 (1990); 7,236 (1980) **Pop Density:** 3989.1
Land: 2.3 sq. mi.; **Water:** 2.1 sq. mi.

South Toms River
Borough
ZIP: 08753 **Lat:** 39-56-26 N **Long:** 74-12-34 W
Pop: 3,869 (1990); 3,954 (1980) **Pop Density:** 3517.3
Land: 1.1 sq. mi.; **Water:** 0.1 sq. mi. **Elev:** 31 ft.

In eastern NJ. Formed Mar 28, 1927.

Stafford
Township
ZIP: 08050 **Lat:** 39-42-12 N **Long:** 74-15-46 W
Pop: 13,325 (1990) **Pop Density:** 279.9
Land: 47.6 sq. mi.; **Water:** 8.3 sq. mi.

Formed Mar 3, 1750; incorporated Feb 21, 1798.

Name origin: For Staffordshire, England.

Surf City
Borough
ZIP: 08008 **Lat:** 39-39-44 N **Long:** 74-10-08 W
Pop: 1,375 (1990); 1,571 (1980) **Pop Density:** 1964.3
Land: 0.7 sq. mi.; **Water:** 0.2 sq. mi. **Elev:** 10 ft.

In eastern NJ on Long Beach Island, a barrier reef bordering Barnegat Bay. Replaced Long Beach City Borough May 26, 1899.

Toms River
CDP
ZIP: 08753 **Lat:** 39-57-16 N **Long:** 74-11-03 W
Pop: 7,524 (1990); 7,465 (1980) **Pop Density:** 2893.8
Land: 2.6 sq. mi.; **Water:** 0.3 sq. mi.

Tuckerton
Borough
ZIP: 08087 **Lat:** 39-35-52 N **Long:** 74-19-46 W
Pop: 3,048 (1990); 2,472 (1980) **Pop Density:** 823.8
Land: 3.7 sq. mi.; **Water:** 0.1 sq. mi. **Elev:** 23 ft.

In eastern NJ on the Atlantic coast. Formed Feb 18, 1901.

Name origin: For Ebenezer Tucker, a resident.

Waretown
CDP
ZIP: 08758 **Lat:** 39-47-22 N **Long:** 74-11-37 W
Pop: 1,283 (1990); 1,175 (1980) **Pop Density:** 1166.4
Land: 1.1 sq. mi.; **Water:** 0.0 sq. mi.

Passaic County
County Seat: Paterson (ZIP: 07505)

Pop: 453,060 (1990); 447,585 (1980)   **Pop Density:** 2448.3
Land: 185.1 sq. mi.; **Water:** 12.0 sq. mi.   **Area Code:** 201

In northern NJ on the NY border, northwest of Newark; organized Feb 7, 1837 from Bergen and Sussex counties.

Name origin: For the Passaic River; its name is from a Delaware Indian term *passaic* or *passajeek*, variously translated as 'peace' or 'valley.'

Bloomingdale   Borough
ZIP: 07403   **Lat:** 41-01-36 N **Long:** 74-20-04 W
Pop: 7,530 (1990); 7,867 (1980)   **Pop Density:** 855.7
Land: 8.8 sq. mi.; **Water:** 0.4 sq. mi.   **Elev:** 280 ft.
Formed Feb 23, 1918.

Name origin: Descriptive of its location in a valley of the Pequannock River.

Clifton   City
ZIP: 07011   **Lat:** 40-51-50 N **Long:** 74-09-27 W
Pop: 71,742 (1990); 74,388 (1980)   **Pop Density:** 6348.8
Land: 11.3 sq. mi.; **Water:** 0.1 sq. mi.   **Elev:** 233 ft.

In northern NJ, northwest of Passaic. Replaced Acquackanonk Township Apr 26, 1917.

Name origin: Descriptive of the western part of the city.

Haledon   Borough
ZIP: 07508   **Lat:** 40-56-12 N **Long:** 74-11-20 W
Pop: 6,951 (1990); 6,607 (1980)   **Pop Density:** 5792.5
Land: 1.2 sq. mi.; **Water:** 0.0 sq. mi.   **Elev:** 300 ft.
Replaced Manchester Township Apr 8, 1908.

Name origin: For Haledon, England.

Hawthorne   Borough
ZIP: 07506   **Lat:** 40-57-24 N **Long:** 74-09-32 W
Pop: 17,084 (1990); 18,200 (1980)   **Pop Density:** 5024.7
Land: 3.4 sq. mi.; **Water:** 0.0 sq. mi.   **Elev:** 100 ft.

In northern NJ, 2 mi. northeast of Paterson. Formed Mar 24, 1898.

Name origin: For novelist Nathaniel Hawthorne (1804–64).

Little Falls   Township
ZIP: 07424   **Lat:** 40-52-31 N **Long:** 74-13-06 W
Pop: 11,294 (1990)   **Pop Density:** 4033.6
Land: 2.8 sq. mi.; **Water:** 0.1 sq. mi.

In northern NJ on the Passaic River, 5 mi. southwest of Paterson. Formed Apr 2, 1868.

Name origin: For the lesser falls of the Passaic River.

North Haledon   Borough
ZIP: 07508   **Lat:** 40-57-42 N **Long:** 74-11-10 W
Pop: 7,987 (1990); 8,177 (1980)   **Pop Density:** 2349.1
Land: 3.4 sq. mi.; **Water:** 0.0 sq. mi.   **Elev:** 250 ft.
Formed Mar 20, 1901.

Passaic   City
ZIP: 07055   **Lat:** 40-51-26 N **Long:** 74-07-45 W
Pop: 58,041 (1990); 52,463 (1980)   **Pop Density:** 18722.9
Land: 3.1 sq. mi.; **Water:** 0.1 sq. mi.   **Elev:** 115 ft.

In northern NJ on the Passaic River, 4 mi. south of Paterson. Settled by the Dutch. Replaced Passaic Village Apr 2, 1873.

Name origin: For the river.

Paterson   City
ZIP: 07501   **Lat:** 40-54-52 N **Long:** 74-09-48 W
Pop: 140,891 (1990); 137,970 (1980)   **Pop Density:** 16772.7
Land: 8.4 sq. mi.; **Water:** 0.3 sq. mi.   **Elev:** 70 ft.

In northern NJ on the Passaic River, 14 mi. north of Newark. Replaced Paterson Township Apr 14, 1851; reincorporated Mar 14, 1861; reincorporated Mar 23, 1871.

Name origin: For William Paterson (1745–1806), U.S. senator (1789–90), governor (1790–93), and associate justice of the U.S. Supreme Court (1793–1806).

Pompton Lakes   Borough
ZIP: 07442   **Lat:** 41-00-10 N **Long:** 74-17-09 W
Pop: 10,539 (1990); 10,660 (1980)   **Pop Density:** 3513.0
Land: 3.0 sq. mi.; **Water:** 0.2 sq. mi.   **Elev:** 220 ft.

In northern NJ, 9 mi. northwest of Paterson. Formed Feb 26, 1895.

Prospect Park   Borough
ZIP: 07508   **Lat:** 40-56-13 N **Long:** 74-10-21 W
Pop: 5,053 (1990); 5,142 (1980)   **Pop Density:** 10106.0
Land: 0.5 sq. mi.; **Water:** 0.0 sq. mi.   **Elev:** 250 ft.
Formed Mar 13, 1901.

Name origin: For a section of Brooklyn, NY.

Ringwood   Borough
ZIP: 07456   **Lat:** 41-06-41 N **Long:** 74-16-29 W
Pop: 12,623 (1990); 12,625 (1980)   **Pop Density:** 504.9
Land: 25.0 sq. mi.; **Water:** 3.0 sq. mi.   **Elev:** 470 ft.

In northeastern NJ, 17 mi. northwest of Paterson. Founded 1760s. Formed Feb 23, 1918.

Name origin: For the mountainous terrain "ringed with woods."

Totowa   Borough
ZIP: 07512   **Lat:** 40-54-17 N **Long:** 74-13-19 W
Pop: 10,177 (1990); 11,448 (1980)   **Pop Density:** 2544.3
Land: 4.0 sq. mi.; **Water:** 0.1 sq. mi.   **Elev:** 200 ft.

In northern NJ, 3 mi. west of Paterson. Formed Mar 15, 1898.

Name origin: From a Dutch translation of an Algonquian term probably meaning 'between a river and mountain.'

Wanaque   Borough
ZIP: 07465   **Lat:** 41-02-35 N **Long:** 74-17-26 W
Pop: 9,711 (1990); 10,025 (1980)   **Pop Density:** 1213.9
Land: 8.0 sq. mi.; **Water:** 1.2 sq. mi.   **Elev:** 240 ft.

In northern NJ, 10 mi. northwest of Paterson. Formed Feb 23, 1918.

Name origin: From an Indian term possibly meaning 'place where the sassafras tree grows.'

Wayne
Township
ZIP: 07470   **Lat:** 40-56-45 N   **Long:** 74-14-43 W
Pop: 47,025 (1990)   **Pop Density:** 1975.8
Land: 23.8 sq. mi.; **Water:** 1.4 sq. mi.

In northern NJ, 6 mi. west of Paterson. Formed Apr 12, 1847.

Name origin: For Gen. "Mad" Anthony Wayne (1745–96) of the Revolutionary War.

West Milford
Township
ZIP: 07480   **Lat:** 41-06-22 N   **Long:** 74-23-46 W
Pop: 25,430 (1990)   **Pop Density:** 337.3
Land: 75.4 sq. mi.; **Water:** 5.0 sq. mi.

Formed Mar 10, 1834.

Name origin: For Milford, CT.

West Paterson
Borough
ZIP: 07424   **Lat:** 40-53-20 N   **Long:** 74-11-44 W
Pop: 10,982 (1990); 11,293 (1980)   **Pop Density:** 3660.7
Land: 3.0 sq. mi.; **Water:** 0.1 sq. mi.   **Elev:** 330 ft.

In northern NJ, a southwestern suburb of Paterson. Formed Mar 25, 1914.

Salem County
County Seat: Salem City (ZIP: 08079)

Pop: 65,294 (1990); 64,676 (1980)   **Pop Density:** 193.3
Land: 337.8 sq. mi.; **Water:** 34.7 sq. mi.   **Area Code:** 609

In southwestern NJ along Delaware River, east of Wilmington, DE; original county, organized May 17, 1694.

Name origin: Anglicization of Hebrew *shalom* 'peace.'

Alloway
Township
Lat: 39-33-30 N   **Long:** 75-19-08 W
Pop: 2,795 (1990)   **Pop Density:** 85.2
Land: 32.8 sq. mi.; **Water:** 0.3 sq. mi.

Replaced Upper Alloways Creek Township Feb 21, 1884.

Name origin: For Aloes Alloway, an Indian chief.

Carneys Point
Township
ZIP: 08069   **Lat:** 39-41-47 N   **Long:** 75-26-42 W
Pop: 8,443 (1990)   **Pop Density:** 482.5
Land: 17.5 sq. mi.; **Water:** 0.3 sq. mi.   **Elev:** 19 ft.

In southwestern NJ, 6 mi. northeast of Perth Amboy. Replaced Upper Penns Neck Township Nov 10, 1976.

Name origin: For Thomas Carney, the original owner of the land.

Elmer
Borough
ZIP: 08318   **Lat:** 39-35-28 N   **Long:** 75-10-25 W
Pop: 1,571 (1990); 1,569 (1980)   **Pop Density:** 1745.6
Land: 0.9 sq. mi.; **Water:** 0.0 sq. mi.   **Elev:** 118 ft.

Formed Jan 28, 1893.

Name origin: For L. Q. C. Elmer, a NJ Supreme Court justice.

Elsinboro
Township
Lat: 39-32-00 N   **Long:** 75-29-52 W
Pop: 1,170 (1990)   **Pop Density:** 95.1
Land: 12.3 sq. mi.; **Water:** 1.1 sq. mi.

Incorporated Feb 21, 1798.

Name origin: For Fort Elfsborg, Sweden. Spelling probably reflects pronunciation.

Lower Alloways Creek
Township
Lat: 39-26-56 N   **Long:** 75-27-35 W
Pop: 1,858 (1990)   **Pop Density:** 39.7
Land: 46.8 sq. mi.; **Water:** 25.8 sq. mi.

Formed Jun 17, 1767; incorporated Feb 21, 1798.

Mannington
Township
Lat: 39-37-20 N   **Long:** 75-25-01 W
Pop: 1,693 (1990)   **Pop Density:** 48.6
Land: 34.8 sq. mi.; **Water:** 3.6 sq. mi.

Incorporated Feb 21, 1798.

Oldmans
Township
Lat: 39-44-24 N   **Long:** 75-24-46 W
Pop: 1,683 (1990)   **Pop Density:** 84.6
Land: 19.9 sq. mi.; **Water:** 0.3 sq. mi.

Formed Feb 7, 1881.

Name origin: A corruption of *Alderman's.*

Olivet
CDP
Lat: 39-32-22 N   **Long:** 75-10-30 W
Pop: 1,315 (1990)   **Pop Density:** 526.0
Land: 2.5 sq. mi.; **Water:** 0.2 sq. mi.

Penns Grove
Borough
ZIP: 08069   **Lat:** 39-43-35 N   **Long:** 75-28-09 W
Pop: 5,228 (1990); 5,760 (1980)   **Pop Density:** 5808.9
Land: 0.9 sq. mi.; **Water:** 0.0 sq. mi.   **Elev:** 12 ft.

Formed Mar 8, 1894.

Name origin: For William Penn (1644–1718), founder of PA.

Pennsville
Township
ZIP: 08070   **Lat:** 39-37-38 N   **Long:** 75-30-15 W
Pop: 13,794 (1990)   **Pop Density:** 597.1
Land: 23.1 sq. mi.; **Water:** 1.7 sq. mi.

Replaced Lower Penns Neck Township Nov 2, 1965.

Name origin: For William Penn (1644–1718), founder of PA.

Pilesgrove
Township
Lat: 39-39-02 N   **Long:** 75-18-59 W
Pop: 3,250 (1990)   **Pop Density:** 93.1
Land: 34.9 sq. mi.; **Water:** 0.1 sq. mi.

Incorporated Feb 21, 1798.

Name origin: For Thomas Pyle, with spelling variation.

Pittsgrove
Township
ZIP: 08318   **Lat:** 39-32-18 N **Long:** 75-07-49 W
Pop: 8,121 (1990)   **Pop Density:** 178.9
Land: 45.4 sq. mi.; **Water:** 0.7 sq. mi.
Formed Dec 6, 1769; incorporated Feb 21, 1798.
Name origin: For William Pitt.

Quinton
Township
Lat: 39-31-47 N **Long:** 75-22-49 W
Pop: 2,511 (1990)   **Pop Density:** 103.8
Land: 24.2 sq. mi.; **Water:** 0.4 sq. mi.
Formed Feb 18, 1873.
Name origin: For Tobias Quinton, an early settler.

Salem
City
ZIP: 08079   **Lat:** 39-34-04 N **Long:** 75-28-23 W
Pop: 6,883 (1990); 6,959 (1980)   **Pop Density:** 2647.3
Land: 2.6 sq. mi.; **Water:** 0.2 sq. mi.   **Elev:** 19 ft.
Replaced Salem Township Feb 25, 1858.
Name origin: From the Hebrew word meaning 'peace'; or possibly for the biblical city identified with Jerusalem.

Upper Pittsgrove
Township
Lat: 39-36-41 N **Long:** 75-12-39 W
Pop: 3,140 (1990)   **Pop Density:** 78.1
Land: 40.2 sq. mi.; **Water:** 0.1 sq. mi.
Formed Mar 10, 1846.
Name origin: For its location north and west of Pittsgrove Township.

Woodstown
Borough
ZIP: 08098   **Lat:** 39-39-03 N **Long:** 75-19-30 W
Pop: 3,154 (1990); 3,250 (1980)   **Pop Density:** 1971.3
Land: 1.6 sq. mi.; **Water:** 0.0 sq. mi.   **Elev:** 47 ft.
Formed Jul 26, 1882; incorporation confirmed Mar 3, 1925.
Name origin: For Jackanias Wood, an early settler .

Somerset County
County Seat: Somerville (ZIP: 08876)

Pop: 240,279 (1990); 203,129 (1980)   **Pop Density:** 788.5
Land: 304.7 sq. mi.; **Water:** 0.3 sq. mi.   **Area Code:** 201
In north-central NJ, southwest of Newark; organized May 14, 1688 from Middlesex County.
Name origin: For Somersetshire, the county in England.

Bedminster
Township
ZIP: 07921   **Lat:** 40-40-16 N **Long:** 74-40-56 W
Pop: 7,086 (1990)   **Pop Density:** 267.4
Land: 26.5 sq. mi.; **Water:** 0.0 sq. mi.
Formed Apr 4, 1749; incorporated Feb 21, 1798.
Name origin: For Bedminster, England.

Bernards
Township
ZIP: 07920   **Lat:** 40-40-24 N **Long:** 74-34-09 W
Pop: 17,199 (1990)   **Pop Density:** 716.6
Land: 24.0 sq. mi.; **Water:** 0.0 sq. mi.
In north-central NJ, 8 mi. southwest of Morristown. Formed May 24, 1760; incorporated Feb 21, 1798.
Name origin: For Francis Bernard, governor of NJ (1758–60).

Bernardsville
Borough
ZIP: 07924   **Lat:** 40-43-50 N **Long:** 74-35-34 W
Pop: 6,597 (1990); 6,715 (1980)   **Pop Density:** 511.4
Land: 12.9 sq. mi.; **Water:** 0.0 sq. mi.   **Elev:** 400 ft.
Formed Mar 6, 1924.
Name origin: For Francis Bernard, governor of NJ (1758–60). Formerly part of Bernards Township and originally called Vealtown for the Vealtown Tavern used by Revolutionary War soldiers traveling to and from Morristown.

Bound Brook
Borough
ZIP: 08805   **Lat:** 40-34-03 N **Long:** 74-32-15 W
Pop: 9,487 (1990); 9,710 (1980)   **Pop Density:** 5580.6
Land: 1.7 sq. mi.; **Water:** 0.0 sq. mi.   **Elev:** 48 ft.
Replaced Bound Brook Town Feb 11, 1891.
Name origin: Named for the boundary in an Indian deed.

Branchburg
Township
ZIP: 08876   **Lat:** 40-33-36 N **Long:** 74-42-50 W
Pop: 10,888 (1990)   **Pop Density:** 536.4
Land: 20.3 sq. mi.; **Water:** 0.0 sq. mi.
Formed Apr 5, 1845.
Name origin: For its location at the junction of the north and south branches of the Raritan River.

Bridgewater
Township
ZIP: 08807   **Lat:** 40-35-29 N **Long:** 74-36-35 W
Pop: 32,509 (1990)   **Pop Density:** 1003.4
Land: 32.4 sq. mi.; **Water:** 0.1 sq. mi.
Formed Apr 4, 1749; incorporated Feb 21, 1798.
Name origin: For Bridgewater, England.

Far Hills
Borough
ZIP: 07931   **Lat:** 40-41-25 N **Long:** 74-37-19 W
Pop: 657 (1990); 677 (1980)   **Pop Density:** 134.1
Land: 4.9 sq. mi.; **Water:** 0.1 sq. mi.   **Elev:** 140 ft.
Formed Apr 7, 1921.
Name origin: For the hilly terrain surrounded by the Ramapo Mountains.

Franklin
Township
ZIP: 08873   **Lat:** 40-28-21 N **Long:** 74-32-48 W
Pop: 42,780 (1990)   **Pop Density:** 914.1
Land: 46.8 sq. mi.; **Water:** 0.1 sq. mi.
Incorporated Feb 21, 1798.

Green Brook
Township
Lat: 40-36-15 N Long: 74-28-59 W
Pop: 4,460 (1990) **Pop Density:** 969.6
Land: 4.6 sq. mi.; **Water:** 0.0 sq. mi.
Replaced North Plainfield Township Nov 8, 1932.

Hills
Township
Lat: 40-29-59 N Long: 74-40-38 W
Pop: 28,808 (1990) **Pop Density:** 526.7
Land: 54.7 sq. mi.; **Water:** 0.1 sq. mi.
Formed Sep 12, 1771; incorporated Feb 21, 1798.

Manville
Borough
ZIP: 08835 Lat: 40-32-29 N Long: 74-35-21 W
Pop: 10,567 (1990); 11,278 (1980) **Pop Density:** 4226.8
Land: 2.5 sq. mi.; **Water:** 0.0 sq. mi. **Elev:** 60 ft.
In northern NJ, 9 mi. northwest of New Brunswick. Formed Apr 1, 1929.
Name origin: For the Johns-Manville Corporation, a leading asbestos products company.

Millstone
Borough
ZIP: 08876 Lat: 40-29-57 N Long: 74-35-28 W
Pop: 450 (1990); 530 (1980) **Pop Density:** 642.9
Land: 0.7 sq. mi.; **Water:** 0.0 sq. mi. **Elev:** 60 ft.
Formed May 14, 1894; reincorporated Mar 12, 1928.
Name origin: For the stone found there, considered to be suitable for milling.

Montgomery
Township
ZIP: 08558 Lat: 40-25-45 N Long: 74-40-55 W
Pop: 9,612 (1990) **Pop Density:** 294.8
Land: 32.6 sq. mi.; **Water:** 0.0 sq. mi.
Incorporated Feb 21, 1798.
Name origin: Probably for Gen. Richard Montgomery (1736–75), hero of the American Revolution.

North Plainfield
Borough
ZIP: 07060 Lat: 40-37-16 N Long: 74-26-24 W
Pop: 18,820 (1990); 19,108 (1980) **Pop Density:** 6721.4
Land: 2.8 sq. mi.; **Water:** 0.0 sq. mi. **Elev:** 100 ft.
In northern NJ, 9 mi. west of New Brunswick. Formed Jun 9, 1885; reincorporated Apr 15, 1914.

Peapack and Gladstone
Borough
Lat: 40-42-55 N Long: 74-39-26 W
Pop: 2,111 (1990); 2,038 (1980) **Pop Density:** 364.0
Land: 5.8 sq. mi.; **Water:** 0.0 sq. mi.
Formed Mar 28, 1912.
Name origin: From an Indian term possibly meaning 'water roots'; and for William Gladstone, prime minister of England four times between 1868 and 1894.

Raritan
Borough
ZIP: 08869 Lat: 40-34-19 N Long: 74-38-30 W
Pop: 5,798 (1990); 6,128 (1980) **Pop Density:** 2899.0
Land: 2.0 sq. mi.; **Water:** 0.0 sq. mi. **Elev:** 76 ft.
Formed May 12, 1948.
Name origin: For the Raritan River, itself named for a Delaware Indian tribal name whose meaning is uncertain.

Rocky Hill
Borough
ZIP: 08553 Lat: 40-24-01 N Long: 74-38-21 W
Pop: 693 (1990); 717 (1980) **Pop Density:** 990.0
Land: 0.7 sq. mi.; **Water:** 0.0 sq. mi.
Formed Dec 18, 1889.
Name origin: Descriptive of the terrain.

Somerset
CDP
ZIP: 08873 Lat: 40-29-51 N Long: 74-29-20 W
Pop: 22,070 (1990); 21,731 (1980) **Pop Density:** 4164.2
Land: 5.3 sq. mi.; **Water:** 0.0 sq. mi.

Somerville
Borough
ZIP: 08876 Lat: 40-34-12 N Long: 74-36-37 W
Pop: 11,632 (1990); 11,973 (1980) **Pop Density:** 4846.7
Land: 2.4 sq. mi.; **Water:** 0.0 sq. mi. **Elev:** 54 ft.
In north-central NJ, 10 mi. northwest of New Brunswick. Replaced Somerville Town Apr 16, 1909.
Name origin: For Somersetshire, England.

South Bound Brook
Borough
ZIP: 08880 Lat: 40-33-14 N Long: 74-31-41 W
Pop: 4,185 (1990); 4,331 (1980) **Pop Density:** 5231.3
Land: 0.8 sq. mi.; **Water:** 0.0 sq. mi.
Replaced South Bound Brook Town Apr 11, 1907.

Warren
Township
ZIP: 07059 Lat: 40-38-10 N Long: 74-31-10 W
Pop: 10,830 (1990) **Pop Density:** 549.7
Land: 19.7 sq. mi.; **Water:** 0.0 sq. mi.
Formed Mar 5, 1806.
Name origin: For Gen. Joseph Warren (1741–75), officer in the American Revolution.

Watchung
Borough
ZIP: 07060 Lat: 40-38-37 N Long: 74-26-15 W
Pop: 5,110 (1990); 5,290 (1980) **Pop Density:** 851.7
Land: 6.0 sq. mi.; **Water:** 0.0 sq. mi. **Elev:** 181 ft.
Formed Mar 23, 1926.
Name origin: From an Indian term possibly meaning 'hill.'

Sussex County
County Seat: Newton (ZIP: 07860)

Pop: 130,943 (1990); 116,119 (1980)   **Pop Density:** 251.2
Land: 521.2 sq. mi.; **Water:** 14.7 sq. mi.   **Area Code:** 201

In northwestern NJ on border with PA and NY, northwest of Newark; organized May 16, 1753 from Morris County.

Name origin: For the county of Sussex, England.

Andover
Township
ZIP: 07821   Lat: 41-01-25 N **Long:** 74-43-37 W
Pop: 5,438 (1990)   **Pop Density:** 270.5
Land: 20.1 sq. mi.; **Water:** 0.6 sq. mi.
Formed Apr 11, 1864.

*Andover
Borough
ZIP: 07821   Lat: 40-59-09 N **Long:** 74-44-33 W
Pop: 700 (1990); 892 (1980)   **Pop Density:** 388.9
Land: 1.8 sq. mi.; **Water:** 0.0 sq. mi.   **Elev:** 646 ft.
Formed Mar 25, 1904. Borough not coextensive with the township.

Name origin: For Andover Mine, part of a tract of 11,000 acres obtained from the heirs of William Penn.

Branchville
Borough
ZIP: 07826   Lat: 41-08-47 N **Long:** 74-44-58 W
Pop: 851 (1990); 870 (1980)   **Pop Density:** 1418.3
Land: 0.6 sq. mi.; **Water:** 0.0 sq. mi.   **Elev:** 800 ft.
Formed Mar 9, 1898.

Name origin: For its location on the main branch of Paulins Kill (from the Dutch *kill* meaning 'creek,' 'stream,' or 'river').

Byram
Township
ZIP: 07821   Lat: 40-57-21 N **Long:** 74-42-53 W
Pop: 8,048 (1990)   **Pop Density:** 385.1
Land: 20.9 sq. mi.; **Water:** 1.1 sq. mi.
Formed Apr 9, 1798; incorporated Feb 21, 1798.

Name origin: For the Byram family.

Crandon Lakes
CDP
Lat: 41-07-27 N **Long:** 74-50-25 W
Pop: 1,177 (1990); 576 (1980)   **Pop Density:** 470.8
Land: 2.5 sq. mi.; **Water:** 0.1 sq. mi.

Frankford
Township
ZIP: 07826   Lat: 41-09-32 N **Long:** 74-44-24 W
Pop: 5,114 (1990)   **Pop Density:** 150.0
Land: 34.1 sq. mi.; **Water:** 1.3 sq. mi.
Formed Apr 10, 1797; incorporated Feb 21, 1798.

Franklin
Borough
ZIP: 07416   Lat: 41-06-37 N **Long:** 74-35-23 W
Pop: 4,977 (1990); 4,486 (1980)   **Pop Density:** 1106.0
Land: 4.5 sq. mi.; **Water:** 0.1 sq. mi.   **Elev:** 621 ft.
In northern NJ, 10 mi. northeast of Newton. Formed Jan 27, 1820.

Name origin: For Benjamin Franklin (1706–90), U.S. patriot, diplomat, and statesman.

Fredon
Township
ZIP: 07860   Lat: 41-01-57 N **Long:** 74-48-56 W
Pop: 2,763 (1990)   **Pop Density:** 156.1
Land: 17.7 sq. mi.; **Water:** 0.2 sq. mi.
Formed Feb 24, 1904.

Green
Township
Lat: 40-58-39 N **Long:** 74-48-13 W
Pop: 2,709 (1990)   **Pop Density:** 168.3
Land: 16.1 sq. mi.; **Water:** 0.1 sq. mi.
Formed Dec 27, 1824.

Hamburg
Borough
ZIP: 07419   Lat: 41-08-55 N **Long:** 74-34-29 W
Pop: 2,566 (1990); 1,832 (1980)   **Pop Density:** 2138.3
Land: 1.2 sq. mi.; **Water:** 0.0 sq. mi.   **Elev:** 453 ft.
Formed Mar 19, 1920.

Name origin: For Hamburg, Germany.

Hampton
Township
Lat: 41-06-29 N **Long:** 74-47-00 W
Pop: 4,438 (1990)   **Pop Density:** 180.4
Land: 24.6 sq. mi.; **Water:** 0.7 sq. mi.
Formed Apr 11, 1864.

Hardyston
Township
ZIP: 07460   Lat: 41-07-07 N **Long:** 74-33-19 W
Pop: 5,275 (1990)   **Pop Density:** 163.8
Land: 32.2 sq. mi.; **Water:** 0.5 sq. mi.
Formed Feb 25, 1762; incorporated Feb 21, 1798.

Highland Lakes
CDP
Lat: 41-10-35 N **Long:** 74-27-25 W
Pop: 4,550 (1990); 2,888 (1980)   **Pop Density:** 989.1
Land: 4.6 sq. mi.; **Water:** 1.0 sq. mi.

Hopatcong
Borough
ZIP: 07843   Lat: 40-57-21 N **Long:** 74-39-27 W
Pop: 15,586 (1990); 15,531 (1980)   **Pop Density:** 1429.9
Land: 10.9 sq. mi.; **Water:** 1.4 sq. mi.   **Elev:** 1000 ft.
In northern NJ, 14 mi. northwest of Morristown. Replaced Brooklyn Borough Mar 22, 1901.

Name origin: An Indian word possibly meaning 'hill above a body of still water having an outlet.'

Lafayette
Township
ZIP: 07848   Lat: 41-07-04 N **Long:** 74-40-27 W
Pop: 1,902 (1990)   **Pop Density:** 105.7
Land: 18.0 sq. mi.; **Water:** 0.0 sq. mi.
Formed Apr 14, 1845.

Name origin: For the Marquis de Lafayette (1757–1834), who fought with the Americans during the Revolutionary War.

Lake Mohawk
CDP
ZIP: 07871   Lat: 41-01-06 N **Long:** 74-39-37 W
Pop: 8,930 (1990); 668 (1980)   **Pop Density:** 1786.0
Land: 5.0 sq. mi.; **Water:** 1.2 sq. mi.

Montague
Township
Lat: 41-17-50 N **Long:** 74-43-21 W
Pop: 2,832 (1990)   **Pop Density:** 64.4
Land: 44.0 sq. mi.; **Water:** 1.3 sq. mi.
Formed Mar 26, 1759; incorporated Feb 21, 1798.
Name origin: For George Montagu, Duke of Manchester, supporter of the American colonies; with spelling alteration.

Newton
Town
ZIP: 07860   **Lat:** 41-03-17 N **Long:** 74-45-13 W
Pop: 7,521 (1990); 7,748 (1980)   **Pop Density:** 2426.1
Land: 3.1 sq. mi.; **Water:** 0.0 sq. mi.   **Elev:** 608 ft.
In northern NJ. Formed Apr 11, 1864.
Name origin: For being a "new town." The Indians called it *Chinchewunska* probably meaning 'side hill town.'

Ogdensburg
Borough
ZIP: 07439   **Lat:** 41-04-30 N **Long:** 74-35-52 W
Pop: 2,722 (1990); 2,737 (1980)   **Pop Density:** 1183.5
Land: 2.3 sq. mi.; **Water:** 0.0 sq. mi.   **Elev:** 693 ft.
Formed Feb 26, 1914.
Name origin: For Robert Ogden, distiller and mine owner.

Sandyston
Township
Lat: 41-12-52 N **Long:** 74-48-20 W
Pop: 1,732 (1990)   **Pop Density:** 40.7
Land: 42.6 sq. mi.; **Water:** 0.7 sq. mi.
Formed Feb 26, 1762; incorporated Feb 21, 1798.

Sparta
Township
ZIP: 07871   **Lat:** 41-02-44 N **Long:** 74-37-37 W
Pop: 15,157 (1990)   **Pop Density:** 405.3
Land: 37.4 sq. mi.; **Water:** 1.8 sq. mi.
Formed Apr 14, 1845.
Name origin: For the ancient Greek state.

Stanhope
Borough
ZIP: 07874   **Lat:** 40-54-46 N **Long:** 74-42-10 W
Pop: 3,393 (1990); 3,638 (1980)   **Pop Density:** 1785.8
Land: 1.9 sq. mi.; **Water:** 0.3 sq. mi.   **Elev:** 882 ft.
Formed Mar 24, 1904.

Stillwater
Township
Lat: 41-04-38 N **Long:** 74-52-17 W
Pop: 4,253 (1990)   **Pop Density:** 156.4
Land: 27.2 sq. mi.; **Water:** 1.3 sq. mi.
Formed Dec 27, 1824.
Name origin: Possibly for the small pond nearby, or the Paulins Kill.

Sussex
Borough
ZIP: 07461   **Lat:** 41-12-35 N **Long:** 74-36-30 W
Pop: 2,201 (1990); 2,418 (1980)   **Pop Density:** 3668.3
Land: 0.6 sq. mi.; **Water:** 0.0 sq. mi.   **Elev:** 464 ft.
Replaced Deckertown Borough Mar 2, 1902.
Name origin: For Sussex, England.

Vernon
Township
ZIP: 07462   **Lat:** 41-11-50 N **Long:** 74-28-58 W
Pop: 21,211 (1990)   **Pop Density:** 310.6
Land: 68.3 sq. mi.; **Water:** 2.1 sq. mi.
Formed Apr 8, 1793; incorporated Feb 21, 1798.
Name origin: For Edward Vernon, English admiral.

Vernon Valley
CDP
Lat: 41-14-12 N **Long:** 74-29-15 W
Pop: 1,696 (1990); 1,169 (1980)   **Pop Density:** 770.9
Land: 2.2 sq. mi.; **Water:** 0.0 sq. mi.

Walpack
Township
Lat: 41-07-31 N **Long:** 74-54-45 W
Pop: 67 (1990)   **Pop Density:** 2.8
Land: 24.0 sq. mi.; **Water:** 0.6 sq. mi.
Incorporated Feb 21, 1798.
Name origin: For *walpekat*, an Indian term possibly meaning 'very deep water.'

Wantage
Township
ZIP: 07461   **Lat:** 41-14-26 N **Long:** 74-37-34 W
Pop: 9,487 (1990)   **Pop Density:** 141.4
Land: 67.1 sq. mi.; **Water:** 0.4 sq. mi.
Formed May 30, 1754; incorporated Feb 21, 1798.
Name origin: For Wantage, England.

Union County
County Seat: Elizabeth (ZIP: 07207)

Pop: 493,819 (1990); 504,094 (1980)   **Pop Density:** 4781.0
Land: 103.3 sq. mi.; **Water:** 2.2 sq. mi.   **Area Code:** 201
In northeastern NJ, south of Newark; organized Mar 19, 1857 from Essex County.
Name origin: As an expression of belief in the federal union of the states; also in the hope that citizens of Elizabeth and Newark would settle their differences.

Berkeley Heights
Township
ZIP: 07922   **Lat:** 40-40-31 N **Long:** 74-25-30 W
Pop: 11,980 (1990)   **Pop Density:** 1901.6
Land: 6.3 sq. mi.; **Water:** 0.0 sq. mi.
Replaced New Providence Township Nov 6, 1951.
Name origin: For Lord John Berkeley, a proprietor.

Clark
Township
ZIP: 07066   **Lat:** 40-37-15 N **Long:** 74-18-41 W
Pop: 14,629 (1990)   **Pop Density:** 3402.1
Land: 4.3 sq. mi.; **Water:** 0.1 sq. mi.
In northeastern NJ, southwest of Elizabeth. Formed Mar 23, 1864.
Name origin: For Abraham Clark (1726–94), a signer of the Declaration of Independence.

Cranford   Township
ZIP: 07016   **Lat:** 40-39-22 N **Long:** 74-18-14 W
Pop: 22,633 (1990)   **Pop Density:** 4715.2
Land: 4.8 sq. mi.; **Water:** 0.0 sq. mi.

In northeastern NJ, 5 mi. west of Elizabeth. Formed Mar 14, 1871.

Name origin: For the Crane family, with spelling alteration.

Elizabeth   City
ZIP: 07201   **Lat:** 40-39-58 N **Long:** 74-11-38 W
Pop: 110,002 (1990); 106,201 (1980)   **Pop Density:** 8943.3
Land: 12.3 sq. mi.; **Water:** 1.4 sq. mi.   **Elev:** 38 ft.

In northeastern NJ on Newark Bay, 5 mi. south of Newark. Oldest English settlement in the state. Industries: bedding, chemicals, clothing, industrial machinery. Replaced Elizabeth borough and township Mar 13, 1855.

Name origin: Named by Philip Carteret (1639–82), the first English governor of NJ, for the wife of his cousin, Sir George Carteret (c.1610–80), a proprietor. Originally Elizabethtown.

Fanwood   Borough
ZIP: 07023   **Lat:** 40-38-30 N **Long:** 74-23-08 W
Pop: 7,115 (1990); 7,767 (1980)   **Pop Density:** 5473.1
Land: 1.3 sq. mi.; **Water:** 0.0 sq. mi.   **Elev:** 157 ft.
Formed Oct 2, 1895.

Name origin: Contraction of Fannie Wood, author and daughter of a Jersey Central Railroad official.

Garwood   Borough
ZIP: 07027   **Lat:** 40-39-04 N **Long:** 74-19-26 W
Pop: 4,227 (1990); 4,752 (1980)   **Pop Density:** 6038.6
Land: 0.7 sq. mi.; **Water:** 0.0 sq. mi.   **Elev:** 100 ft.
Formed Mar 19, 1903.

Hillside   Township
ZIP: 07205   **Lat:** 40-41-46 N **Long:** 74-13-48 W
Pop: 21,044 (1990)   **Pop Density:** 7794.1
Land: 2.7 sq. mi.; **Water:** 0.0 sq. mi.

In northeastern NJ, 2 mi. north of Elizabeth. Formed Apr 3, 1913.

Name origin: For its location in the Watchung Mountains.

Kenilworth   Borough
ZIP: 07033   **Lat:** 40-40-44 N **Long:** 74-17-20 W
Pop: 7,574 (1990); 8,221 (1980)   **Pop Density:** 3606.7
Land: 2.1 sq. mi.; **Water:** 0.0 sq. mi.   **Elev:** 91 ft.
Formed May 13, 1907.

Name origin: For Kenilworth Castle, England.

Linden   City
ZIP: 07036   **Lat:** 40-37-30 N **Long:** 74-14-18 W
Pop: 36,701 (1990); 37,836 (1980)   **Pop Density:** 3398.2
Land: 10.8 sq. mi.; **Water:** 0.4 sq. mi.   **Elev:** 10 ft.

In northeastern NJ, 4 mi. southwest of Elizabeth. Replaced Linden township and borough Jan 1, 1925.

Name origin: For linden trees brought from Germany by early settlers.

Mountainside   Borough
ZIP: 07092   **Lat:** 40-40-50 N **Long:** 74-21-39 W
Pop: 6,657 (1990); 7,118 (1980)   **Pop Density:** 1664.3
Land: 4.0 sq. mi.; **Water:** 0.0 sq. mi.   **Elev:** 142 ft.
Formed Sep 25, 1895.

Name origin: For its location in wooded hills.

New Providence   Borough
ZIP: 07974   **Lat:** 40-42-01 N **Long:** 74-24-12 W
Pop: 11,439 (1990); 12,426 (1980)   **Pop Density:** 3091.6
Land: 3.7 sq. mi.; **Water:** 0.0 sq. mi.   **Elev:** 220 ft.
Formed Mar 14, 1899.

Name origin: For a congregation's escape from injury when a church gallery fell on them. Formerly called Turkey.

Plainfield   City
ZIP: 07060   **Lat:** 40-36-54 N **Long:** 74-24-59 W
Pop: 46,567 (1990); 45,555 (1980)   **Pop Density:** 7761.2
Land: 6.0 sq. mi.; **Water:** 0.0 sq. mi.   **Elev:** 110 ft.

In northeastern NJ, 11 mi. southwest of Elizabeth. Formed Apr 21, 1869.

Name origin: For a resident's estate.

Rahway   City
ZIP: 07065   **Lat:** 40-36-25 N **Long:** 74-16-53 W
Pop: 25,325 (1990); 26,723 (1980)   **Pop Density:** 6331.3
Land: 4.0 sq. mi.; **Water:** 0.0 sq. mi.   **Elev:** 20 ft.

In northeastern NJ on the Rahway River, 5 mi. southwest of Elizabeth. Formed Apr 19, 1858; reincorporated 1859.

Name origin: For the river, itself named from *rechouwakie* meaning 'place of sands.'

Roselle   Borough
ZIP: 07203   **Lat:** 40-39-07 N **Long:** 74-15-38 W
Pop: 20,314 (1990); 20,641 (1980)   **Pop Density:** 7813.1
Land: 2.6 sq. mi.; **Water:** 0.0 sq. mi.   **Elev:** 78 ft.

In northeastern NJ, 2 mi. west of Elizabeth. Formed Dec 20, 1894.

Name origin: For John C. Rose, developer.

Roselle Park   Borough
ZIP: 07204   **Lat:** 40-39-56 N **Long:** 74-16-01 W
Pop: 12,805 (1990); 13,377 (1980)   **Pop Density:** 10670.8
Land: 1.2 sq. mi.; **Water:** 0.0 sq. mi.   **Elev:** 85 ft.

In northeastern NJ, 3 mi. west of Elizabeth and adjoining Roselle. Formed Mar 22, 1901.

Scotch Plains   Township
ZIP: 07076   **Lat:** 40-37-59 N **Long:** 74-22-24 W
Pop: 21,160 (1990)   **Pop Density:** 2325.3
Land: 9.1 sq. mi.; **Water:** 0.0 sq. mi.

In northeastern NJ, west of Elizabeth. Settled 1684 by Scottish Presbyterian and Quaker immigrants who refused to swear allegiance to the British crown. Replaced Fanwood Township Mar 29, 1917.

Name origin: For the Scottish settlers, led by George Scott.

Springfield   Township
ZIP: 07081   **Lat:** 40-41-58 N **Long:** 74-19-30 W
Pop: 13,420 (1990)   **Pop Density:** 2580.8
Land: 5.2 sq. mi.; **Water:** 0.0 sq. mi.

In northeastern NJ, 6 mi. northwest of Elizabeth. Formed Apr 14, 1794; incorporated Feb 21, 1798.

Name origin: For its abundant springs and brooks.

Summit   City
ZIP: 07901   **Lat:** 40-42-53 N **Long:** 74-21-55 W
Pop: 19,757 (1990); 21,071 (1980)   **Pop Density:** 3238.9
Land: 6.1 sq. mi.; **Water:** 0.0 sq. mi.   **Elev:** 388 ft.

In northeastern NJ, 10 mi. west of Newark. Replaced Summit Township Mar 8, 1899.

Name origin: For its location in the Watchung Mountains.

Union   Township
ZIP: 07083   **Lat:** 40-41-43 N **Long:** 74-16-11 W
Pop: 50,024 (1990)   **Pop Density:** 5497.1
Land: 9.1 sq. mi.; **Water:** 0.0 sq. mi.
In northeastern NJ, 5 mi. northwest of Elizabeth. Formed
Nov 23, 1808.
Name origin: For the union of several communities.

Westfield   Town
ZIP: 07090   **Lat:** 40-39-05 N **Long:** 74-20-39 W
Pop: 28,870 (1990); 30,447 (1980)   **Pop Density:** 4309.0
Land: 6.7 sq. mi.; **Water:** 0.0 sq. mi.   **Elev:** 126 ft.
Replaced Westfield Township Mar 4, 1903.
Name origin: For an undeveloped section called "the west
fields."

Winfield   Township
                          Lat: 40-38-08 N **Long:** 74-17-23 W
Pop: 1,576 (1990)   **Pop Density:** 7880.0
Land: 0.2 sq. mi.; **Water:** 0.0 sq. mi.
Formed Aug 6, 1941.

Warren County
County Seat: Belvidere (ZIP: 07823)

Pop: 91,607 (1990); 84,429 (1980)   **Pop Density:** 255.9
Land: 357.9 sq. mi.; **Water:** 4.9 sq. mi.   **Area Code:** 201
On northwestern border of NJ, east of Easton, PA; organized Nov 20, 1824 from
Sussex County.
Name origin: For Joseph Warren (1741–75), the Revolutionary War patriot and
member of the Continental Congress who dispatched Paul Revere (1735–1818) on
his famous ride.

Allamuchy   Township
                          Lat: 40-55-13 N **Long:** 74-50-03 W
Pop: 3,484 (1990)   **Pop Density:** 170.0
Land: 20.5 sq. mi.; **Water:** 0.2 sq. mi.
Formed Apr 4, 1873.
Name origin: For an Indian term possibly meaning 'place
within the hills.'

Alpha   Borough
ZIP: 08865   **Lat:** 40-39-35 N **Long:** 75-09-26 W
Pop: 2,530 (1990); 2,644 (1980)   **Pop Density:** 1488.2
Land: 1.7 sq. mi.; **Water:** 0.0 sq. mi.   **Elev:** 299 ft.
In northwestern NJ, 5 mi. southeast of Phillipsburg. Formed
Apr 27, 1911.
Name origin: For the Alpha Cement Works.

Beattyestown   CDP
                          Lat: 40-49-09 N **Long:** 74-51-19 W
Pop: 3,966 (1990)   **Pop Density:** 1322.0
Land: 3.0 sq. mi.; **Water:** 0.0 sq. mi.

Belvidere   Town
ZIP: 07823   **Lat:** 40-49-40 N **Long:** 75-04-23 W
Pop: 2,669 (1990); 2,475 (1980)   **Pop Density:** 2053.1
Land: 1.3 sq. mi.; **Water:** 0.0 sq. mi.   **Elev:** 257 ft.
Formed Apr 7, 1845.
Name origin: Italian for 'beautiful to see,' with spelling alter-
ation.

Blairstown   Township
ZIP: 07825   **Lat:** 40-58-53 N **Long:** 75-00-00 W
Pop: 5,331 (1990)   **Pop Density:** 172.0
Land: 31.0 sq. mi.; **Water:** 0.8 sq. mi.
Formed Apr 14, 1845.
Name origin: For John I. Blair, financier and town benefac-
tor. Previously called Gravel Hill.

Brass Castle   CDP
                          Lat: 40-45-38 N **Long:** 75-00-43 W
Pop: 1,419 (1990)   **Pop Density:** 489.3
Land: 2.9 sq. mi.; **Water:** 0.0 sq. mi.

Franklin   Township
                          Lat: 40-42-45 N **Long:** 75-02-30 W
Pop: 2,404 (1990)   **Pop Density:** 100.2
Land: 24.0 sq. mi.; **Water:** 0.0 sq. mi.
Formed Apr 8, 1839.

Frelinghuysen   Township
                          Lat: 40-57-42 N **Long:** 74-53-48 W
Pop: 1,779 (1990)   **Pop Density:** 77.3
Land: 23.0 sq. mi.; **Water:** 0.1 sq. mi.
Formed Mar 7, 1848.
Name origin: For the Freylinghuysen family.

Great Meadows-Vienna   CDP
                          Lat: 40-52-14 N **Long:** 74-53-23 W
Pop: 1,108 (1990)   **Pop Density:** 263.8
Land: 4.2 sq. mi.; **Water:** 0.0 sq. mi.

Greenwich   Township
                          Lat: 40-40-46 N **Long:** 75-06-36 W
Pop: 1,899 (1990)   **Pop Density:** 179.2
Land: 10.6 sq. mi.; **Water:** 0.0 sq. mi.
Incorporated Feb 21, 1798.

Hackettstown   Town
ZIP: 07840   **Lat:** 40-51-13 N **Long:** 74-49-31 W
Pop: 8,120 (1990); 8,850 (1980)   **Pop Density:** 2194.6
Land: 3.7 sq. mi.; **Water:** 0.0 sq. mi.   **Elev:** 571 ft.
Formed Mar 9, 1853.
Name origin: For Samuel Hackett, largest landowner in the
district. Originally called Helm's Mills and Musconetcong.

Hardwick
Township
Lat: 41-01-23 N **Long:** 74-55-57 W
Pop: 1,235 (1990)   **Pop Density:** 70.2
Land: 17.6 sq. mi.; **Water:** 0.2 sq. mi.
Formed Jan 22, 1750; incorporated Feb 21, 1798.

Harmony
Township
Lat: 40-44-55 N **Long:** 75-07-22 W
Pop: 2,653 (1990)   **Pop Density:** 111.5
Land: 23.8 sq. mi.; **Water:** 0.3 sq. mi.
Formed Apr 8, 1839.

Hope
Township
Lat: 40-54-42 N **Long:** 74-58-58 W
Pop: 1,719 (1990)   **Pop Density:** 92.9
Land: 18.5 sq. mi.; **Water:** 0.2 sq. mi.
Settled 1774 by Moravian colonists from Bethlehem, PA. Formed Apr 8, 1839.
Name origin: Named by settlers for "hope of immortality."

Independence
Township
Lat: 40-52-47 N **Long:** 74-52-38 W
Pop: 3,940 (1990)   **Pop Density:** 199.0
Land: 19.8 sq. mi.; **Water:** 0.0 sq. mi.
Formed Nov 11, 1782; incorporated Feb 21, 1798.
Name origin: For its independence from England.

Knowlton
Township
Lat: 40-56-00 N **Long:** 75-03-55 W
Pop: 2,543 (1990)   **Pop Density:** 102.5
Land: 24.8 sq. mi.; **Water:** 0.5 sq. mi.
Formed Feb 23, 1763; incorporated Feb 21, 1798.

Liberty
Township
Lat: 40-52-09 N **Long:** 74-57-10 W
Pop: 2,493 (1990)   **Pop Density:** 211.3
Land: 11.8 sq. mi.; **Water:** 0.2 sq. mi.
Formed Mar 25, 1926.
Name origin: For its separation from Hope Township.

Lopatcong
Township
ZIP: 08865   **Lat:** 40-42-28 N **Long:** 75-09-22 W
Pop: 5,052 (1990)   **Pop Density:** 711.5
Land: 7.1 sq. mi.; **Water:** 0.1 sq. mi.
Replaced Phillipsburg Township Mar 18, 1863.
Name origin: An Indian term possibly meaning 'winter watering-place of deer.'

Mansfield
Township
ZIP: 07863   **Lat:** 40-48-31 N **Long:** 74-54-35 W
Pop: 7,154 (1990)   **Pop Density:** 239.3
Land: 29.9 sq. mi.; **Water:** 0.0 sq. mi.
Formed May 30, 1754; incorporated Feb 21, 1798.

Oxford
Township
ZIP: 07863   **Lat:** 40-48-37 N **Long:** 74-59-48 W
Pop: 1,790 (1990)   **Pop Density:** 303.4
Land: 5.9 sq. mi.; **Water:** 0.1 sq. mi.
Formed May 30, 1754; incorporated Feb 21, 1798.
Name origin: For settler John Axford, with spelling alteration.

Pahaquarry
Township
Lat: 41-01-56 N **Long:** 75-02-12 W
Pop: 20 (1990)   **Pop Density:** 1.0
Land: 19.4 sq. mi.; **Water:** 1.2 sq. mi.
Formed Dec 27, 1824.
Name origin: From an Indian term meaning possibly 'end of two mountains with stream between.'

Phillipsburg
Town
ZIP: 08865   **Lat:** 40-41-19 N **Long:** 75-10-58 W
Pop: 15,757 (1990); 16,647 (1980)   **Pop Density:** 4924.1
Land: 3.2 sq. mi.; **Water:** 0.1 sq. mi.   **Elev:** 314 ft.
In north-central NJ on the Delaware River, opposite Easton, PA. Site of an Indian village called Chintewink. Formed Mar 8, 1861.
Name origin: For settler William Phillips.

Pohatcong
Township
Lat: 40-38-19 N **Long:** 75-09-40 W
Pop: 3,591 (1990)   **Pop Density:** 270.0
Land: 13.3 sq. mi.; **Water:** 0.3 sq. mi.
Formed Jan 1, 1882.
Name origin: For the Pohatcong River, itself named for an Indian term possibly meaning 'stream outlet.'

Washington
Borough
ZIP: 07882   **Lat:** 40-45-33 N **Long:** 74-58-58 W
Pop: 6,474 (1990); 6,429 (1980)   **Pop Density:** 3237.0
Land: 2.0 sq. mi.; **Water:** 0.0 sq. mi.   **Elev:** 463 ft.
In northwestern NJ. Formed Feb 20, 1868.
Name origin: For George Washington (1732–99), first U.S. president.

*Washington
Township
ZIP: 07882   **Lat:** 40-44-58 N **Long:** 74-58-56 W
Pop: 5,367 (1990)   **Pop Density:** 304.9
Land: 17.6 sq. mi.; **Water:** 0.0 sq. mi.
In northwestern NJ, 12 mi. northeast of Phillipsburg. Formed Apr 13, 1840.
Name origin: For George Washington (1732–99), first U.S. president.

White
Township
Lat: 40-49-25 N **Long:** 75-02-46 W
Pop: 3,603 (1990)   **Pop Density:** 131.5
Land: 27.4 sq. mi.; **Water:** 0.4 sq. mi.
Formed Apr 9, 1913.
Name origin: For the White family, early settlers.

Index to Places and Counties in New Jersey

New York

NEW YORK

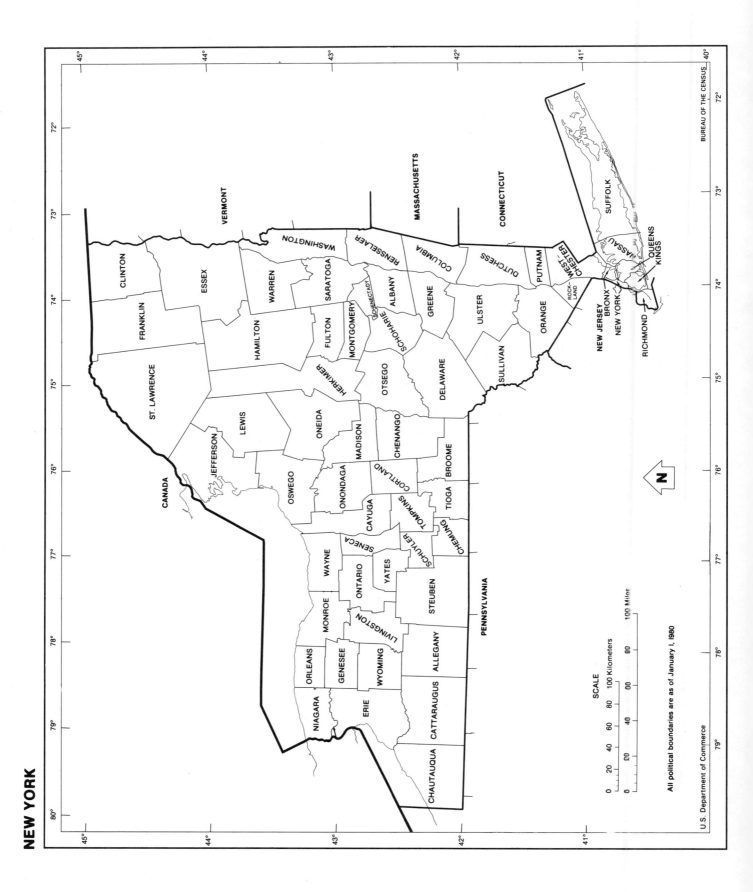

CANADA

VERMONT

MASSACHUSETTS

CONNECTICUT

NEW JERSEY

PENNSYLVANIA

CLINTON

FRANKLIN

ST. LAWRENCE

ESSEX

WARREN

WASHINGTON

HAMILTON

SARATOGA

FULTON

MONTGOMERY

SCHENECTADY

RENSSELAER

SCHOHARIE

ALBANY

GREENE

COLUMBIA

DUTCHESS

PUTNAM

WESTCHESTER

ROCKLAND

ORANGE

ULSTER

SULLIVAN

DELAWARE

OTSEGO

HERKIMER

LEWIS

JEFFERSON

ONEIDA

MADISON

CHENANGO

OSWEGO

ONONDAGA

CORTLAND

BROOME

TIOGA

CAYUGA

TOMPKINS

CHEMUNG

SENECA

SCHUYLER

WAYNE

ONTARIO

YATES

STEUBEN

MONROE

LIVINGSTON

ORLEANS

GENESEE

WYOMING

ALLEGANY

NIAGARA

ERIE

CATTARAUGUS

CHAUTAUQUA

SUFFOLK

NASSAU

QUEENS

KINGS

BRONX

NEW YORK

RICHMOND

N

SCALE

100 Miles

0   20   40   60   80   100 Kilometers

All political boundaries are as of January 1, 1980

U.S. Department of Commerce

BUREAU OF THE CENSUS

New York

Population: 17,990,455 (1990); 17,558,072 (1980)
Population rank (1990): 2
Percent population change (1980-1990): 2.5
Population projection: 17,727,000 (1995);
  17,563,000 (2000)

Area: total 54,475 sq. mi.; 47,224 sq. mi. land, 7,251
  sq. mi. water. Coastline 127 mi.
Area rank: 27
Highest elevation: 5,344 ft., Mount Marcy
Lowest point: sea level on Atlantic coast

State capital: Albany (Albany County)
Largest city: New York (7,322,564)
Second largest city: Buffalo (328,123)
Largest county: Kings (2,300,664)

Total housing units: 7,226,891
No. of occupied housing units: 6,639,322
Vacant housing units (%): 8.1
Distribution of population by race and
  Hispanic origin (%):
  White: 74.4
  Black: 15.9
  Hispanic (any race): 12.3
  Native American: 0.3
  Asian/Pacific: 3.9
  Other: 5.5

Admission date: July 26, 1788 (11th state).

Location: In the northeastern United States, bordering New Jersey, Pennsylvania, Lake Erie and Lake Ontario, the Canadian provinces of Ontario and Quebec, Vermont, Massachusetts, and Connecticut, with Atlantic coast along Long Island. One of the thirteen original English colonies.

Name Origin: For James, Duke of York and Albany (1633-1701), later King James II of England.

State animal: beaver (Castor canadensis)
State beverage: milk
State bird: bluebird (Sialia sialis)
State fish: brook or speckled trout (Salvelinus fontinalis)
State flower: rose
State fossil: prehistoric crab (Eurypterus remipes)
State fruit: apple (Malus sylvestris)
State gem: garnet
State song: "I Love New York"
State tree: sugar maple (Acer saccharum)

State motto: Excelsior (Latin 'Ever upward')
State nickname: The Empire State; Excelsior State

Area codes: 212 (Manhattan and the Bronx), 315 (Syracuse and northwestern NY), 516 (Long Island: Nassau & Suffolk counties), 518 (Albany and northeastern NY), 607 (Binghamton and south-central NY), 716 (Buffalo and southwestern NY), 718 (Brooklyn, Queens, and Staten Island)
Time zone: Eastern
Part of (region): Middle Atlantic; Northeast

Local Government

Counties

New York has 62 counties, including the five that are the boroughs of New York City.

Municipalities

There are 62 cities, 928 towns, and 554 villages in the state. All cities are within a county with the exception of New York City, which is made up of five counties, one coextensive with each borough. A group of people within a town may incorporate as a village and elect their own government. However, they remain part of the town and must pay taxes to both jurisdictions.

Settlement History and Early Development

Archaeologists have determined that much of the area now known as New York State has been inhabited about 10,000 years. The Mound Builders (Indians who buried their dead in large mounds) were still there after 1000, but by that time the Algonquian family of Indians controlled much of the state: the Delaware (Lenni Lenape), Mahican, Wappinger, Montauk, and Munsee. In the early part of the fourteenth century the Iroquois (League of Five Nations), including the Cayuga, Mohawk, Oneida, Onondaga, and Seneca tribes, moved in from the north and west and controlled much of upstate New York. In 1715 the Tuscarora became the sixth nation to join the League. The Iroquois kept peace among themselves but warred on other tribes. During most of the eighteenth century they skillfully balanced competing French and British interests.

Italian explorer Giovanni da Verrazano, in the service of France, was the first European known to have entered New York Harbor, on April 17, 1524. Samuel de Champlain explored the St. Lawrence River in 1603 giving France claim to the northern part of what is now New York. Henry Hudson, an Englishman sailing for the Dutch, entered New York Bay and sailed up the river (later to be named for him) to Albany. Based on this voyage, the Dutch claimed the area that is present-day New York, New Jersey, Delaware, and part of Connecticut, and named the colony New Netherland. The first permanent Dutch settlement was founded near Albany in

1624. In 1626, Peter Minuit bought Manhattan Island from the Indians for a reputed $24 worth of goods and founded New Amsterdam.

English colonists from Massachusetts and Connecticut moved to Long Island and for a long time cooperated with the Dutch. However, King Charles II of England granted a charter for all of this territory to his brother James, the Duke of York, and in 1664 the English sent warships and demanded that Peter Stuyvesant surrender New Amsterdam. His colonists did not want to fight and he was forced to comply. The territory was renamed New York and remained an English colony for the next 112 years, except for a period in 1673 when Dutch rule was briefly restored.

In 1669 the French began further exploration of northern New York. In 1731 they built a fortress on Lake Champlain and prepared to claim northern New York for themselves. New York became a battleground for the decades of conflict that began between England and France in 1689, known in America as the French and Indian Wars. The Treaty of Paris that ended these wars in 1763 ceded all territory east of the Mississippi to England, except for New Orleans, ending most of France's claims in America. The Iroquois, whose power was weakened during the wars, signed treaties granting large areas of their land to the New York colony.

The American Revolution and Statehood

British restrictive laws and taxes angered many New Yorkers as well as those in the other colonies, but the settlers were deeply divided: during and after the Revolutionary War more than 30,000 British loyalists left the state. During the war, which began in Massachusetts in 1775, nearly one-third of the battles took place in New York territory.

On July 9, 1776, New York approved the Declaration of Independence, and on April 20, 1777, adopted its first constitution. On February 6, 1778 New York became the second state to ratify the Articles of Confederation; on July 26, 1788, it became the eleventh state to ratify the U.S. Constitution. New York City served as the first national capital under the U.S. Constitution from January 11, 1785, to August 12, 1790, and on April 30, 1789, George Washington was inaugurated there as the first U.S. president.

Development after the American Revolution

The Iroquois, who had sided with the British during the Revolutionary War, were defeated by Washington's troops and their territory left in ruin; most fled to Canada. This opened the way for European settlers to move westward into the fertile Mohawk and Genesee valleys. Much of the fighting in the War of 1812 between the U.S. and England took place near the New York-Canada border. At war's end, many of those who fought there returned to settle, joined by flocks of migrants from New England. The census of 1810 showed that New York had surpassed Virginia to become the most populous state in the country, a position it retained until 1970, when it was surpassed by California.

Through the efforts of Governor DeWitt Clinton, the

construction of the Erie Canal began in 1817. Upon its completion in 1825, vessels could sail from the Atlantic Ocean to the Great Lakes, which greatly expanded trade: by 1831 50% of U.S. imports and 27% of its exports passed through New York. The canal also connected New York City and Buffalo, which reduced transportation costs so that products from New York's expanding factories (which developed all along the canal's route) could be shipped to western markets and farm produce from the west could be shipped east. The canal towns of Utica, Syracuse, and Rochester benefited greatly. During the 1840s the first of several large groups of European immigrants arrived in New York.

New York had become the leading commercial center in the U.S. by the mid-1820s, especially in textiles and dairy products. During the same period, culture flourished. New York City was a center of literary activity as early as the 1820s, and was the nation's theatrical capital by the 1840s. Slavery was legally abolished on July 4, 1827, and in 1848 the first women's rights convention in the U.S. was held in Seneca Falls.

The Civil War

New Yorkers were strong supporters of the Union cause, but many strongly objected to the military draft. Beginning on July 11, 1863, mobs rioted for four days in New York City, burning and robbing the homes of abolitionists and lynching blacks. The rioting did not end until troops from the battlefield were called in. An estimated 1,000 people were killed or wounded in the riots and more than $1.5 million worth of property destroyed. Despite this, New York provided more soldiers, materiel, and financial support to the Union war effort than any other state. New York was far from any battlefields, and in fact, its businesses thrived because of the war.

Business and Industry

The decades after the Civil War, called the Gilded Age (c. 1870-98), was an era of extraordinary growth, primarily due to the development of railroads, which took hold in the 1850s and expanded dramatically after 1867 when Cornelius Vanderbilt took over the New York Central Railroad. New industries were begun that are still household names: Standard Oil, formed by John D. Rockefeller in 1882, Westinghouse Electric in 1886, General Electric (originally Edison Electric) in 1889, and Eastman Kodak in 1892. New York City, the state's major port and later the largest in the U.S., also became the nation's financial capital and leading cultural center.

The Great Depression in the 1920s and 1930s hit New York hard, and it wasn't until World War II, when New York became the center of the U.S. defense industry, that growth started again, especially in the fields of agriculture, banking, insurance, and manufacturing. Many manufacturing plants in New York closed during the early 1970s, a decade that also saw New York City facing an enormous debt and fearing bankruptcy. After great prosperity through most of the 1980s, in recent years New York has weathered the recession of the late 1980s and early 1990s to remain a world leader in such areas as printing and publishing, fashion and apparel, banking, securities, communications, electronics manufacturing, and various service industries.

State Boundaries

New York's eastern border with Vermont, Massachusetts, and Connecticut was formed and agreed to in 1791. Its northern border with Canada was fixed by the peace treaty in 1783, which was accepted and confirmed by the treaty of 1842. The New York-New Jersey border was fixed in the 1664 grant to Berkeley and Carteret and was ratified by both states and confirmed by Congress on June 28, 1834 (see also New Jersey). The New York-Pennsylvania border was confirmed by Congressional act on August 19, 1890.

The legislatures of New York and New Jersey created a Port of New York District in 1921 to systematically develop the transportation and terminal facilities in the area. Three commissioners from each state constitute a Port Authority of New York and New Jersey that plans tunnels, bridges, and railways, which, when approved by both states, are constructed and administered under the Authority's supervision. The District includes near its borders parts or all of the cities of Paterson, Summit, Plainfield, New Brunswick, and Sandy Hook, New Jersey; and Rockaway Beach, Jamaica, Rye, and White Plains, New York, an area of about 1,540 square miles.

Counties

Albany	Dutchess	Madison	Otsego	Steuben
Allegany	Erie	Monroe	Putnam	Suffolk
Bronx	Essex	Montgomery	Queens	Sullivan
Broome	Franklin	Nassau	Rensselaer	Tioga
Cattaraugus	Fulton	New York	Richmond	Tompkins
Cayuga	Genesee	Niagara	Rockland	Ulster
Chautauqua	Greene	Oneida	St. Lawrence	Warren
Chemung	Hamilton	Onondaga	Saratoga	Washington
Chenango	Herkimer	Ontario	Schenectady	Wayne
Clinton	Jefferson	Orange	Schoharie	Westchester
Columbia	Kings	Orleans	Schuyler	Wyoming
Cortland	Lewis	Oswego	Seneca	Yates
Delaware	Livingston			

Multi-County Places

The following places are in more than one county. Given here is the total population for each multi-county place, and the names of the counties it is in.

Almond, pop. 458; Allegany (442), Steuben (16)
Attica, pop. 2,630; Wyoming (2,622), Genesee (8)
Brewerton, pop. 2,954; Onondaga (2,127), Oswego (827)
Bridgeport, pop. 2,107; Onondaga (1,651), Madison (456)
Deposit, pop. 1,936; Delaware (999), Broome (937)
Dolgeville, pop. 2,452; Herkimer (2,344), Fulton (108)
Earlville, pop. 883; Madison (542), Chenango (341)
Geneva, pop. 14,143; Ontario (14,143), Seneca (0)
Gowanda, pop. 2,901; Cattaraugus (2,016), Erie (885)
Keeseville, pop. 1,854; Clinton (972), Essex (882)
Lake Luzerne-Hadley, pop. 2,042; Warren (1,165), Saratoga (877)
New York, pop. 7,322,564; Kings (2,300,664), Queens (1,951,598), New York (1,487,536), Bronx (1,203,789), Richmond (378,977)
Peach Lake, pop. 1,499; Putnam (960), Westchester (539)
Rushville, pop. 609; Yates (408), Ontario (201)
Saranac Lake, pop. 5,377; Franklin (4,012), Essex (1,365)

Albany County
County Seat: Albany (ZIP: 12207)

Pop: 292,594 (1990); 285,909 (1980)   **Pop Density:** 558.6
Land: 523.8 sq. mi.; **Water:** 9.7 sq. mi.   **Area Code:** 518

In east-central NY, southeast of Schenectady; original county, organized Nov 1, 1683.

Name origin: For James Stuart, Duke of York and Albany (1633–1701), who later became James II, king of England.

Albany   City
ZIP: 12201   **Lat:** 42-39-56 N **Long:** 73-47-56 W
Pop: 101,082 (1990); 101,727 (1980)   **Pop Density:** 4723.5
Land: 21.4 sq. mi.; **Water:** 0.5 sq. mi.

In central-eastern NY on the Hudson River, 150 mi. north of New York City. State capital since 1797. Leading transportation center, industrial city (brass and iron castings, drugs and medicines) and shipping port (the Hudson River has been dredged so ocean ships can sail the 150 miles from the Atlantic Ocean to Albany). Nicknamed "Cradle of the Union" because Benjamin Franklin (1706–90) presented the first formal proposal to unite the American Colonies, the Plan of Union, to the Albany Congress in 1754.

Name origin: For James, Duke of York and Albany (1633–1701), later King James II of England.

Altamont   Village
ZIP: 12009   **Lat:** 42-42-18 N **Long:** 74-02-10 W
Pop: 1,519 (1990); 1,292 (1980)   **Pop Density:** 1380.9
Land: 1.1 sq. mi.; **Water:** 0.0 sq. mi.   **Elev:** 451 ft.

In eastern NY, 8 mi. west of Albany.

Name origin: Adapted from Italian *alta monte* meaning 'high mountain.'

Berne   Town
ZIP: 12023   **Lat:** 42-35-30 N **Long:** 74-07-11 W
Pop: 3,053 (1990); 2,532 (1980)   **Pop Density:** 47.6
Land: 64.1 sq. mi.; **Water:** 0.6 sq. mi.
Settled 1750.

Name origin: French spelling for the Swiss capital city.

Bethlehem   Town
ZIP: 12054   **Lat:** 42-35-21 N **Long:** 73-49-26 W
Pop: 27,552 (1990); 24,296 (1980)   **Pop Density:** 564.6
Land: 48.8 sq. mi.; **Water:** 0.8 sq. mi.

Name origin: For the birthplace of Jesus Christ.

Coeymans   Town
ZIP: 12045   **Lat:** 42-29-42 N **Long:** 73-52-58 W
Pop: 8,158 (1990); 7,896 (1980)   **Pop Density:** 162.5
Land: 50.2 sq. mi.; **Water:** 2.9 sq. mi.

Name origin: For Dutch settler Barent Coeymans.

Cohoes   City
ZIP: 12047   **Lat:** 42-46-21 N **Long:** 73-42-30 W
Pop: 16,825 (1990); 18,144 (1980)   **Pop Density:** 4547.3
Land: 3.7 sq. mi.; **Water:** 0.5 sq. mi.

In eastern NY at the confluence of the Mohawk and Hudson rivers, 10 mi. north of Albany.

Name origin: An Indian term possibly meaning 'pine tree.'

Colonie   Town
ZIP: 12212   **Lat:** 42-44-18 N **Long:** 73-47-09 W
Pop: 76,494 (1990); 74,593 (1980)   **Pop Density:** 1363.5
Land: 56.1 sq. mi.; **Water:** 1.8 sq. mi.

*Colonie   Village
ZIP: 12212   **Lat:** 42-43-14 N **Long:** 73-50-04 W
Pop: 8,019 (1990); 8,869 (1980)   **Pop Density:** 2358.5
Land: 3.4 sq. mi.; **Water:** 0.0 sq. mi.

In eastern NY, northwest of Albany. Not coextensive with the town of the same name.

Name origin: For an early settlement.

Delmar   CDP
ZIP: 12054   **Lat:** 42-37-27 N **Long:** 73-50-00 W
Pop: 8,360 (1990); 8,423 (1980)   **Pop Density:** 1944.2
Land: 4.3 sq. mi.; **Water:** 0.0 sq. mi.

Green Island   Village
ZIP: 12183   **Lat:** 42-44-51 N **Long:** 73-41-33 W
Pop: 2,490 (1990); 2,696 (1980)   **Pop Density:** 3557.1
Land: 0.7 sq. mi.; **Water:** 0.2 sq. mi.

Guilderland   Town
ZIP: 12084   **Lat:** 42-42-20 N **Long:** 73-57-48 W
Pop: 28,764 (1990); 26,515 (1980)   **Pop Density:** 493.4
Land: 58.3 sq. mi.; **Water:** 0.7 sq. mi.

Name origin: For the province in the Netherlands.

Knox   Town
    Lat: 42-40-26 N **Long:** 74-06-55 W
Pop: 2,661 (1990); 2,471 (1980)   **Pop Density:** 64.1
Land: 41.5 sq. mi.; **Water:** 0.1 sq. mi.

Name origin: For Gen. Henry Knox (1750–1806), Revolutionary War hero and first U.S. secretary of war.

Latham   CDP
ZIP: 12110   **Lat:** 42-44-42 N **Long:** 73-44-48 W
Pop: 10,131 (1990); 11,182 (1980)   **Pop Density:** 2110.6
Land: 4.8 sq. mi.; **Water:** 0.0 sq. mi.

Loudonville   CDP
ZIP: 12211   **Lat:** 42-42-26 N **Long:** 73-45-58 W
Pop: 10,822 (1990); 11,480 (1980)   **Pop Density:** 2164.4
Land: 5.0 sq. mi.; **Water:** 0.0 sq. mi.

Menands   Village
ZIP: 12204   **Lat:** 42-41-28 N **Long:** 73-43-43 W
Pop: 4,333 (1990); 4,012 (1980)   **Pop Density:** 1354.1
Land: 3.2 sq. mi.; **Water:** 0.2 sq. mi.

New Scotland   Town
ZIP: 12159   **Lat:** 42-36-14 N **Long:** 73-56-24 W
Pop: 9,139 (1990); 8,976 (1980)   **Pop Density:** 157.3
Land: 58.1 sq. mi.; **Water:** 0.3 sq. mi.

Ravena   Village
ZIP: 12143   **Lat:** 42-28-35 N **Long:** 73-48-44 W
Pop: 3,547 (1990); 3,091 (1980)   **Pop Density:** 2728.5
Land: 1.3 sq. mi.; **Water:** 0.0 sq. mi.   **Elev:** 182 ft.

In eastern NY on the west bank of the Hudson River, 11 mi. south of Albany.

Name origin: For the Italian city, with a spelling variation.

Rensselaerville Town
ZIP: 12147   Lat: 42-28-36 N Long: 74-10-43 W
Pop: 1,990 (1990); 1,780 (1980)   Pop Density: 32.3
Land: 61.7 sq. mi.; Water: 0.4 sq. mi.

Roessleville CDP
ZIP: 12205   Lat: 42-41-58 N Long: 73-48-13 W
Pop: 10,753 (1990); 11,685 (1980)   Pop Density: 3707.9
Land: 2.9 sq. mi.; Water: 0.0 sq. mi.

Voorheesville Village
ZIP: 12186   Lat: 42-38-47 N Long: 73-55-59 W
Pop: 3,225 (1990); 3,320 (1980)   Pop Density: 1040.3
Land: 3.1 sq. mi.; Water: 0.0 sq. mi.   Elev: 332 ft.
Name origin: For Walker and Gamelin Voorhees.

Watervliet City
ZIP: 12189   Lat: 42-43-29 N Long: 73-42-27 W
Pop: 11,061 (1990); 11,354 (1980)   Pop Density: 8508.5
Land: 1.3 sq. mi.; Water: 0.2 sq. mi.
In eastern NY on Hudson River, 6 mi. north of Albany.
Name origin: From Dutch meaning 'water-brook.'

Westerlo Town
ZIP: 12055   Lat: 42-29-02 N Long: 74-02-32 W
Pop: 3,325 (1990); 2,929 (1980)   Pop Density: 57.4
Land: 57.9 sq. mi.; Water: 0.7 sq. mi.

Westmere CDP
ZIP: 12203   Lat: 42-41-15 N Long: 73-52-29 W
Pop: 6,750 (1990); 6,881 (1980)   Pop Density: 2109.4
Land: 3.2 sq. mi.; Water: 0.0 sq. mi.

Allegany County
County Seat: Belmont (ZIP: 14813)

Pop: 50,470 (1990); 51,742 (1980)   Pop Density: 49.0
Land: 1030.3 sq. mi.; Water: 4.2 sq. mi.   Area Code: 716

In southwestern NY, southeast of Buffalo; organized Apr 7, 1806 from Genesee County.
Name origin: For the Allegheny River, with a variant spelling.

Alfred Town
ZIP: 14802   Lat: 42-14-36 N Long: 77-47-27 W
Pop: 5,791 (1990); 6,191 (1980)   Pop Density: 183.8
Land: 31.5 sq. mi.; Water: 0.1 sq. mi.

*Alfred Village
ZIP: 14802   Lat: 42-15-14 N Long: 77-47-23 W
Pop: 4,559 (1990); 4,967 (1980)   Pop Density: 3799.2
Land: 1.2 sq. mi.; Water: 0.0 sq. mi.   Elev: 1762 ft.
In southwestern NY, 10 mi. southwest of Hornell. Not coextensive with the town of the same name.
Name origin: For an early settler.

Allen Town
                   Lat: 42-23-10 N Long: 78-00-59 W
Pop: 406 (1990); 486 (1980)   Pop Density: 11.2
Land: 36.4 sq. mi.; Water: 0.2 sq. mi.

Alma Town
ZIP: 14708   Lat: 42-02-50 N Long: 78-01-05 W
Pop: 846 (1990); 920 (1980)   Pop Density: 23.2
Land: 36.5 sq. mi.; Water: 0.1 sq. mi.
In southwestern NY, just north of the PA border.
Name origin: From the Latin term meaning 'nourishing.'

Almond Town
ZIP: 14804   Lat: 42-20-36 N Long: 77-47-00 W
Pop: 1,640 (1990); 1,671 (1980)   Pop Density: 35.8
Land: 45.8 sq. mi.; Water: 0.0 sq. mi.
Not coextensive with the village of the same name.

*Almond Village
ZIP: 14804   Lat: 42-19-08 N Long: 77-44-22 W
Pop: 442 (1990); 529 (1980)   Pop Density: 884.0
Land: 0.5 sq. mi.; Water: 0.0 sq. mi.
A small part of the village is also in Steuben County. Not coextensive with the town of the same name.

Amity Town
                   Lat: 42-13-07 N Long: 78-01-12 W
Pop: 2,255 (1990); 2,272 (1980)   Pop Density: 65.4
Land: 34.5 sq. mi.; Water: 0.1 sq. mi.

Andover Town
ZIP: 14806   Lat: 42-09-14 N Long: 77-48-28 W
Pop: 1,981 (1990); 1,956 (1980)   Pop Density: 50.2
Land: 39.5 sq. mi.; Water: 0.0 sq. mi.

*Andover Village
ZIP: 14806   Lat: 42-09-25 N Long: 77-47-47 W
Pop: 1,125 (1990); 1,120 (1980)   Pop Density: 1125.0
Land: 1.0 sq. mi.; Water: 0.0 sq. mi.   Elev: 1665 ft.
Not coextensive with the town of the same name.
Name origin: For the city in England.

Angelica Town
ZIP: 14709   Lat: 42-18-16 N Long: 78-00-54 W
Pop: 1,446 (1990); 1,438 (1980)   Pop Density: 39.6
Land: 36.5 sq. mi.; Water: 0.0 sq. mi.

*Angelica Village
ZIP: 14709   Lat: 42-18-15 N Long: 78-01-15 W
Pop: 963 (1990); 982 (1980)   Pop Density: 458.6
Land: 2.1 sq. mi.; Water: 0.0 sq. mi.
Not coextensive with the town of the same name.

Belfast Town
ZIP: 14711   Lat: 42-17-55 N Long: 78-07-40 W
Pop: 1,539 (1990); 1,495 (1980)   Pop Density: 42.5
Land: 36.2 sq. mi.; Water: 0.3 sq. mi.
Name origin: For Belfast, Northern Ireland.

Belmont Village
ZIP: 14813   Lat: 42-13-20 N Long: 78-02-00 W
Pop: 1,006 (1990); 1,024 (1980)   Pop Density: 1006.0
Land: 1.0 sq. mi.; Water: 0.0 sq. mi.   Elev: 1418 ft.
Name origin: For financier and sportsman August Belmont (1816–90).

Birdsall
Town
Lat: 42-23-38 N **Long:** 77-53-30 W
Pop: 232 (1990); 257 (1980)   **Pop Density:** 6.4
Land: 36.0 sq. mi.; **Water:** 0.1 sq. mi.

Bolivar
Town
ZIP: 14715   **Lat:** 42-02-49 N **Long:** 78-07-54 W
Pop: 2,361 (1990); 2,496 (1980)   **Pop Density:** 65.8
Land: 35.9 sq. mi.; **Water:** 0.0 sq. mi.

*Bolivar
Village
ZIP: 14715   **Lat:** 42-04-12 N **Long:** 78-10-00 W
Pop: 1,261 (1990); 1,345 (1980)   **Pop Density:** 1576.3
Land: 0.8 sq. mi.; **Water:** 0.0 sq. mi.
Not coextensive with the town of the same name.
Name origin: For South American liberator Simon Bolívar (1783–1830).

Burns
Town
Lat: 42-26-10 N **Long:** 77-46-50 W
Pop: 1,299 (1990); 1,211 (1980)   **Pop Density:** 47.8
Land: 27.2 sq. mi.; **Water:** 0.0 sq. mi.

Canaseraga
Village
ZIP: 14822   **Lat:** 42-27-50 N **Long:** 77-46-36 W
Pop: 684 (1990); 700 (1980)   **Pop Density:** 526.2
Land: 1.3 sq. mi.; **Water:** 0.0 sq. mi.

Caneadea
Town
ZIP: 14717   **Lat:** 42-23-45 N **Long:** 78-07-55 W
Pop: 2,551 (1990); 2,421 (1980)   **Pop Density:** 71.9
Land: 35.5 sq. mi.; **Water:** 0.8 sq. mi.
Name origin: An Indian term possibly meaning 'where heaven meets earth.'

Centerville
Town
Lat: 42-28-48 N **Long:** 78-14-55 W
Pop: 678 (1990); 696 (1980)   **Pop Density:** 19.2
Land: 35.4 sq. mi.; **Water:** 0.0 sq. mi.

Clarksville
Town
Lat: 42-07-34 N **Long:** 78-14-42 W
Pop: 1,041 (1990); 938 (1980)   **Pop Density:** 28.7
Land: 36.3 sq. mi.; **Water:** 0.0 sq. mi.

Cuba
Town
ZIP: 14727   **Lat:** 42-13-20 N **Long:** 78-15-01 W
Pop: 3,401 (1990); 3,428 (1980)   **Pop Density:** 96.9
Land: 35.1 sq. mi.; **Water:** 0.7 sq. mi.

*Cuba
Village
ZIP: 14727   **Lat:** 42-13-06 N **Long:** 78-16-34 W
Pop: 1,690 (1990); 1,739 (1980)   **Pop Density:** 1207.1
Land: 1.4 sq. mi.; **Water:** 0.0 sq. mi.   **Elev:** 1500 ft.
Not coextensive with the town of the same name.

Fillmore
Village
ZIP: 14735   **Lat:** 42-28-04 N **Long:** 78-06-47 W
Pop: 455 (1990); 563 (1980)   **Pop Density:** 1137.5
Land: 0.4 sq. mi.; **Water:** 0.0 sq. mi.   **Elev:** 1213 ft.

Friendship
Town
ZIP: 14739   **Lat:** 42-13-10 N **Long:** 78-07-55 W
Pop: 2,185 (1990); 2,164 (1980)   **Pop Density:** 60.4
Land: 36.2 sq. mi.; **Water:** 0.0 sq. mi.

Genesee
Town
Lat: 42-02-25 N **Long:** 78-14-49 W
Pop: 1,672 (1990); 1,787 (1980)   **Pop Density:** 46.1
Land: 36.3 sq. mi.; **Water:** 0.0 sq. mi.

Granger
Town
Lat: 42-28-36 N **Long:** 78-00-41 W
Pop: 515 (1990); 508 (1980)   **Pop Density:** 16.1
Land: 32.0 sq. mi.; **Water:** 0.0 sq. mi.

Grove
Town
Lat: 42-28-10 N **Long:** 77-53-39 W
Pop: 479 (1990); 497 (1980)   **Pop Density:** 14.3
Land: 33.5 sq. mi.; **Water:** 0.2 sq. mi.

Hume
Town
Lat: 42-29-00 N **Long:** 78-07-16 W
Pop: 1,970 (1990); 2,040 (1980)   **Pop Density:** 52.0
Land: 37.9 sq. mi.; **Water:** 0.4 sq. mi.
Name origin: For an early settler.

Independence
Town
Lat: 42-03-11 N **Long:** 77-47-10 W
Pop: 1,026 (1990); 1,138 (1980)   **Pop Density:** 29.7
Land: 34.5 sq. mi.; **Water:** 0.0 sq. mi.

New Hudson
Town
Lat: 42-18-14 N **Long:** 78-15-01 W
Pop: 715 (1990); 669 (1980)   **Pop Density:** 19.7
Land: 36.3 sq. mi.; **Water:** 0.1 sq. mi.

Oil Springs Reservation
Pop. Place
Lat: 42-13-45 N **Long:** 78-18-12 W
Pop: 2 (1990); 2 (1980)   **Pop Density:** 3.3
Land: 0.6 sq. mi.; **Water:** 0.0 sq. mi.

Richburg
Village
ZIP: 14774   **Lat:** 42-05-23 N **Long:** 78-09-21 W
Pop: 494 (1990); 139 (1980)   **Pop Density:** 548.9
Land: 0.9 sq. mi.; **Water:** 0.0 sq. mi.   **Elev:** 1655 ft.

Rushford
Town
ZIP: 14777   **Lat:** 42-23-30 N **Long:** 78-15-05 W
Pop: 1,176 (1990); 1,125 (1980)   **Pop Density:** 33.2
Land: 35.4 sq. mi.; **Water:** 0.8 sq. mi.

Scio
Town
ZIP: 14880   **Lat:** 42-08-51 N **Long:** 78-00-29 W
Pop: 1,965 (1990); 1,971 (1980)   **Pop Density:** 55.8
Land: 35.2 sq. mi.; **Water:** 0.0 sq. mi.

Stannards
CDP
Lat: 42-04-43 N **Long:** 77-54-46 W
Pop: 1,028 (1990); 526 (1980)   **Pop Density:** 367.1
Land: 2.8 sq. mi.; **Water:** 0.0 sq. mi.

Ward
Town
Lat: 42-13-39 N **Long:** 77-54-03 W
Pop: 334 (1990); 362 (1980)   **Pop Density:** 11.4
Land: 29.2 sq. mi.; **Water:** 0.0 sq. mi.

Wellsville
Town
ZIP: 14895   **Lat:** 42-07-18 N **Long:** 77-55-18 W
Pop: 8,116 (1990); 8,658 (1980)   **Pop Density:** 221.1
Land: 36.7 sq. mi.; **Water:** 0.0 sq. mi.

*Wellsville
Village
ZIP: 14895   **Lat:** 42-07-15 N **Long:** 77-56-50 W
Pop: 5,241 (1990); 5,769 (1980)   **Pop Density:** 2278.7
Land: 2.3 sq. mi.; **Water:** 0.0 sq. mi.   **Elev:** 1517 ft.
In southwestern NY. Settled 1795. Not coextensive with the town of the same name.
Name origin: For Gardiner Wells, early settler and chief land-owner.

West Almond
Town
Lat: 42-18-08 N Long: 77-53-50 W
Pop: 277 (1990); 357 (1980)   Pop Density: 7.7
Land: 36.0 sq. mi.; Water: 0.0 sq. mi.

Willing
Town
Lat: 42-02-20 N Long: 77-53-47 W
Pop: 1,428 (1990); 1,451 (1980)   Pop Density: 39.3
Land: 36.3 sq. mi.; Water: 0.0 sq. mi.

Wirt
Town
Lat: 42-08-09 N Long: 78-07-38 W
Pop: 1,143 (1990); 1,137 (1980)   Pop Density: 31.8
Land: 35.9 sq. mi.; Water: 0.1 sq. mi.

Bronx County and Borough
County Seat: Bronx (ZIP: 10451)

Pop: 1,203,789 (1990); 1,168,972 (1980)   Pop Density: 28661.6
Land: 42.0 sq. mi.; Water: 15.4 sq. mi.   Area Code: 718

Established Apr 19, 1912 from New York County. The county is coterminous with the borough of the Bronx, part of New York City. The only borough of New York City that is not on an island.

Name origin: For Jonas Bronck or Bronk (? –1643), the first European settler north of the Harlem River. His farm was called "Broncksland." The borough is usually called "The Bronx."

Broome County
County Seat: Binghamton (ZIP: 13902)

Pop: 212,160 (1990); 213,648 (1980)   Pop Density: 300.1
Land: 706.9 sq. mi.; Water: 8.6 sq. mi.   Area Code: 607

On central southern border of NY, southeast of Ithaca; organized Mar 28, 1806 from Tioga County.

Name origin: For John Broome (1738–1810), member of the NY constitutional convention (1777) and lieutenant governor (1804–10).

Barker
Town
ZIP: 13746   Lat: 42-17-05 N Long: 75-54-59 W
Pop: 2,714 (1990); 2,244 (1980)   Pop Density: 65.6
Land: 41.4 sq. mi.; Water: 0.5 sq. mi.

Binghamton
City
ZIP: 13901   Lat: 42-06-05 N Long: 75-54-34 W
Pop: 53,008 (1990); 55,860 (1980)   Pop Density: 5096.9
Land: 10.4 sq. mi.; Water: 0.6 sq. mi.

In south-central NY at the confluence of the Chenango and Susquehana rivers, 65 mi. south of Syracuse. Not coextensive with the town of the same name. Site of a major campus of the State University of New York.

Name origin: For Philadelphia merchant William Bingham (1752–1804).

*Binghamton
Town
ZIP: 13902   Lat: 42-02-51 N Long: 75-55-17 W
Pop: 5,006 (1990); 5,007 (1980)   Pop Density: 196.3
Land: 25.5 sq. mi.; Water: 0.0 sq. mi.

Chenango
Town
ZIP: 13745   Lat: 42-11-45 N Long: 75-54-04 W
Pop: 12,310 (1990); 12,233 (1980)   Pop Density: 362.1
Land: 34.0 sq. mi.; Water: 0.3 sq. mi.

Colesville
Town
ZIP: 13787   Lat: 42-10-13 N Long: 75-39-58 W
Pop: 5,590 (1990); 4,965 (1980)   Pop Density: 71.2
Land: 78.5 sq. mi.; Water: 0.7 sq. mi.

Conklin
Town
ZIP: 13748   Lat: 42-02-26 N Long: 75-50-08 W
Pop: 6,265 (1990); 6,204 (1980)   Pop Density: 255.7
Land: 24.5 sq. mi.; Water: 0.4 sq. mi.

Deposit
Village
ZIP: 13754   Lat: 42-03-47 N Long: 75-25-43 W
Pop: 937 (1990); 1,017 (1980)   Pop Density: 1338.6
Land: 0.7 sq. mi.; Water: 0.0 sq. mi.   Elev: 991 ft.

Part of the town is in Delaware County.

Dickinson
Town
ZIP: 13905   Lat: 42-07-44 N Long: 75-54-31 W
Pop: 5,486 (1990); 5,594 (1980)   Pop Density: 1142.9
Land: 4.8 sq. mi.; Water: 0.1 sq. mi.

Endicott
Village
ZIP: 13760   Lat: 42-05-52 N Long: 76-03-49 W
Pop: 13,531 (1990); 14,457 (1980)   Pop Density: 4364.8
Land: 3.1 sq. mi.; Water: 0.0 sq. mi.

In southern NY on the Susquehana River, 8 mi. west of Binghamton.

Endwell
CDP
ZIP: 13760   Lat: 42-07-02 N Long: 76-01-23 W
Pop: 12,602 (1990); 13,745 (1980)   Pop Density: 3405.9
Land: 3.7 sq. mi.; Water: 0.1 sq. mi.

Fenton
Town
ZIP: 13833   Lat: 42-12-27 N Long: 75-48-10 W
Pop: 7,236 (1990); 7,400 (1980)   Pop Density: 219.9
Land: 32.9 sq. mi.; Water: 0.5 sq. mi.

Johnson City
Village
ZIP: 13790   Lat: 42-07-24 N Long: 75-57-42 W
Pop: 16,890 (1990); 17,126 (1980)   Pop Density: 3838.6
Land: 4.4 sq. mi.; Water: 0.1 sq. mi.

In southern NY, 3 mi. west of Binghamton.

Name origin: For George F. Johnson and the Endicott-Johnson Corporation; the town was built by the company.

Kirkwood
Town
ZIP: 13795   Lat: 42-05-30 N Long: 75-48-31 W
Pop: 6,096 (1990); 5,834 (1980)   Pop Density: 196.6
Land: 31.0 sq. mi.; Water: 0.3 sq. mi.

Name origin: For an early settler.

Lisle
Town
ZIP: 13797   Lat: 42-21-34 N Long: 76-03-08 W
Pop: 2,486 (1990); 2,039 (1980)   Pop Density: 53.0
Land: 46.9 sq. mi.; Water: 0.1 sq. mi.

*Lisle
Village
ZIP: 13797   Lat: 42-21-02 N Long: 76-00-13 W
Pop: 361 (1990); 357 (1980)   Pop Density: 401.1
Land: 0.9 sq. mi.; Water: 0.0 sq. mi.   Elev: 975 ft.

Not coextensive with the town of the same name.

Maine
Town
ZIP: 13802   Lat: 42-11-46 N Long: 76-01-51 W
Pop: 5,576 (1990); 5,262 (1980)   Pop Density: 122.0
Land: 45.7 sq. mi.; Water: 0.0 sq. mi.

Name origin: For the state.

Nanticoke
Town
ZIP: 13802   Lat: 42-17-05 N Long: 76-01-30 W
Pop: 1,846 (1990); 1,425 (1980)   Pop Density: 76.0
Land: 24.3 sq. mi.; Water: 0.0 sq. mi.

Port Dickinson
Village
ZIP: 13901   Lat: 42-08-11 N Long: 75-53-31 W
Pop: 1,785 (1990); 1,974 (1980)   Pop Density: 2975.0
Land: 0.6 sq. mi.; Water: 0.1 sq. mi.

Sanford
Town
ZIP: 13754   Lat: 42-05-33 N Long: 75-28-47 W
Pop: 2,576 (1990); 2,635 (1980)   Pop Density: 28.6
Land: 90.1 sq. mi.; Water: 0.9 sq. mi.

Triangle
Town
Lat: 42-22-36 N Long: 75-55-10 W
Pop: 3,006 (1990); 2,618 (1980)   Pop Density: 78.9
Land: 38.1 sq. mi.; Water: 1.7 sq. mi.

Union
Town
ZIP: 13760   Lat: 42-07-35 N Long: 76-02-00 W
Pop: 59,786 (1990); 61,179 (1980)   Pop Density: 1698.5
Land: 35.2 sq. mi.; Water: 0.7 sq. mi.

Vestal
Town
ZIP: 13850-51   Lat: 42-03-05 N Long: 76-01-40 W
Pop: 26,733 (1990); 27,238 (1980)   Pop Density: 512.1
Land: 52.2 sq. mi.; Water: 0.5 sq. mi.

Whitney Point
Village
ZIP: 13862   Lat: 42-19-53 N Long: 75-58-04 W
Pop: 1,054 (1990); 1,093 (1980)   Pop Density: 1054.0
Land: 1.0 sq. mi.; Water: 0.1 sq. mi.

Windsor
Town
ZIP: 13865   Lat: 42-03-22 N Long: 75-39-58 W
Pop: 6,440 (1990); 5,911 (1980)   Pop Density: 70.4
Land: 91.5 sq. mi.; Water: 1.3 sq. mi.

*Windsor
Village
ZIP: 13865   Lat: 42-04-37 N Long: 75-38-27 W
Pop: 1,051 (1990); 1,155 (1980)   Pop Density: 955.5
Land: 1.1 sq. mi.; Water: 0.1 sq. mi.

Not coextensive with the town of the same name.

Name origin: For either the castle in England or the borough in which it is located.

Cattaraugus County
County Seat: Little Valley (ZIP: 14755)

Pop: 84,234 (1990); 85,697 (1980)   **Pop Density:** 64.3
Land: 1309.9 sq. mi.; **Water:** 12.4 sq. mi.   **Area Code:** 716

On southwestern border of NY, south of Buffalo; organized Mar 11, 1808 from Genesee County.

Name origin: For the Cattaraugus Creek, which forms its northern border; probably from Seneca 'bad smelling shore.'

Allegany
Town
ZIP: 14706   **Lat:** 42-05-15 N **Long:** 78-30-43 W
Pop: 8,327 (1990); 8,619 (1980)   **Pop Density:** 117.0
Land: 71.2 sq. mi.; **Water:** 0.5 sq. mi.

*Allegany
Village
ZIP: 14706   **Lat:** 42-05-24 N **Long:** 78-29-29 W
Pop: 1,980 (1990); 2,078 (1980)   **Pop Density:** 2828.6
Land: 0.7 sq. mi.; **Water:** 0.0 sq. mi.

In southeastern NY on the Allegany River. Not coextensive with the town of the same name.
Name origin: For the river.

Allegany Reservation
Pop. Place
Lat: 42-06-26 N **Long:** 78-47-28 W
Pop: 1,143 (1990); 1,243 (1980)   **Pop Density:** 31.4
Land: 36.4 sq. mi.; **Water:** 7.5 sq. mi.

Ashford
Town
Lat: 42-26-23 N **Long:** 78-38-40 W
Pop: 2,162 (1990); 1,922 (1980)   **Pop Density:** 42.1
Land: 51.3 sq. mi.; **Water:** 0.1 sq. mi.

Carrollton
Town
Lat: 42-03-03 N **Long:** 78-38-14 W
Pop: 1,555 (1990); 1,566 (1980)   **Pop Density:** 36.8
Land: 42.3 sq. mi.; **Water:** 0.0 sq. mi.

Cattaraugus
Village
ZIP: 14719   **Lat:** 42-19-46 N **Long:** 78-52-04 W
Pop: 1,100 (1990); 1,200 (1980)   **Pop Density:** 1000.0
Land: 1.1 sq. mi.; **Water:** 0.0 sq. mi.   **Elev:** 1383 ft.

Cattaraugus Reservation
Pop. Place
Lat: 42-31-23 N **Long:** 78-59-54 W
Pop: 359 (1990); 352 (1980)   **Pop Density:** 61.9
Land: 5.8 sq. mi.; **Water:** 0.2 sq. mi.

Coldspring
Town
Lat: 42-04-51 N **Long:** 78-53-41 W
Pop: 732 (1990); 708 (1980)   **Pop Density:** 14.2
Land: 51.5 sq. mi.; **Water:** 0.5 sq. mi.

Conewango
Town
Lat: 42-12-24 N **Long:** 78-59-52 W
Pop: 1,702 (1990); 1,578 (1980)   **Pop Density:** 47.0
Land: 36.2 sq. mi.; **Water:** 0.0 sq. mi.

Dayton
Town
ZIP: 14041   **Lat:** 42-23-48 N **Long:** 79-00-04 W
Pop: 1,915 (1990); 1,981 (1980)   **Pop Density:** 53.5
Land: 35.8 sq. mi.; **Water:** 0.3 sq. mi.

Delevan
Village
ZIP: 14042   **Lat:** 42-29-27 N **Long:** 78-28-45 W
Pop: 1,214 (1990); 1,113 (1980)   **Pop Density:** 1214.0
Land: 1.0 sq. mi.; **Water:** 0.0 sq. mi.

East Otto
Town
ZIP: 14729   **Lat:** 42-24-00 N **Long:** 78-44-57 W
Pop: 1,003 (1990); 942 (1980)   **Pop Density:** 24.3
Land: 41.2 sq. mi.; **Water:** 0.2 sq. mi.

East Randolph
Village
ZIP: 14730   **Lat:** 42-10-13 N **Long:** 78-57-02 W
Pop: 629 (1990); 248 (1980)   **Pop Density:** 571.8
Land: 1.1 sq. mi.; **Water:** 0.0 sq. mi.

Ellicottville
Town
ZIP: 14731   **Lat:** 42-19-01 N **Long:** 78-38-35 W
Pop: 1,607 (1990); 1,677 (1980)   **Pop Density:** 35.6
Land: 45.1 sq. mi.; **Water:** 0.1 sq. mi.

*Ellicottville
Village
ZIP: 14731   **Lat:** 42-16-29 N **Long:** 78-40-21 W
Pop: 513 (1990); 713 (1980)   **Pop Density:** 641.3
Land: 0.8 sq. mi.; **Water:** 0.0 sq. mi.   **Elev:** 1549 ft.

Not coextensive with the town of the same name.
Name origin: For Joseph Ellicott, Holland Land Company surveyor.

Farmersville
Town
ZIP: 14060   **Lat:** 42-23-05 N **Long:** 78-22-45 W
Pop: 869 (1990); 978 (1980)   **Pop Density:** 18.2
Land: 47.8 sq. mi.; **Water:** 0.2 sq. mi.

Franklinville
Town
ZIP: 14737   **Lat:** 42-18-25 N **Long:** 78-29-57 W
Pop: 2,968 (1990); 3,102 (1980)   **Pop Density:** 57.3
Land: 51.8 sq. mi.; **Water:** 0.2 sq. mi.

*Franklinville
Village
ZIP: 14737   **Lat:** 42-20-06 N **Long:** 78-27-23 W
Pop: 1,739 (1990); 1,887 (1980)   **Pop Density:** 1580.9
Land: 1.1 sq. mi.; **Water:** 0.0 sq. mi.

Not coextensive with the town of the same name.
Name origin: For Benjamin Franklin (1706–90), U.S. patriot, diplomat, and statesman.

Freedom
Town
ZIP: 14065   **Lat:** 42-28-47 N **Long:** 78-22-47 W
Pop: 2,018 (1990); 1,840 (1980)   **Pop Density:** 50.1
Land: 40.3 sq. mi.; **Water:** 0.3 sq. mi.

Gowanda
Village
ZIP: 14070   **Lat:** 42-27-27 N **Long:** 78-56-02 W
Pop: 2,016 (1990); 1,864 (1980)   **Pop Density:** 2016.0
Land: 1.0 sq. mi.; **Water:** 0.0 sq. mi.

Not coextensive with the town of the same name. Part of the town is also in Erie County.
Name origin: From an Indian term probably meaning 'surrounded by a hill.'

Great Valley Town
ZIP: 14741 **Lat:** 42-11-58 N **Long:** 78-38-54 W
Pop: 2,090 (1990); 2,014 (1980) **Pop Density:** 41.6
Land: 50.2 sq. mi.; **Water:** 0.0 sq. mi.

Hinsdale Town
ZIP: 14743 **Lat:** 42-10-02 N **Long:** 78-23-11 W
Pop: 2,095 (1990); 2,182 (1980) **Pop Density:** 54.0
Land: 38.8 sq. mi.; **Water:** 0.0 sq. mi.

Humphrey Town
ZIP: 14741 **Lat:** 42-12-41 N **Long:** 78-31-18 W
Pop: 580 (1990); 529 (1980) **Pop Density:** 15.8
Land: 36.6 sq. mi.; **Water:** 0.0 sq. mi.

Ischua Town
Lat: 42-13-31 N **Long:** 78-23-07 W
Pop: 847 (1990); 775 (1980) **Pop Density:** 26.1
Land: 32.4 sq. mi.; **Water:** 0.0 sq. mi.
Name origin: For its location along Ischua Creek.

Leon Town
Lat: 42-18-01 N **Long:** 79-00-11 W
Pop: 1,245 (1990); 1,055 (1980) **Pop Density:** 34.3
Land: 36.3 sq. mi.; **Water:** 0.0 sq. mi.

Lime Lake-Machias CDP
Lat: 42-25-42 N **Long:** 78-28-56 W
Pop: 1,269 (1990); 1,191 (1980) **Pop Density:** 384.5
Land: 3.3 sq. mi.; **Water:** 0.4 sq. mi.

Limestone Village
ZIP: 14753 **Lat:** 42-01-26 N **Long:** 78-37-51 W
Pop: 459 (1990); 466 (1980) **Pop Density:** 286.9
Land: 1.6 sq. mi.; **Water:** 0.0 sq. mi. **Elev:** 1407 ft.

Little Valley Town
ZIP: 14755 **Lat:** 42-13-35 N **Long:** 78-45-40 W
Pop: 1,881 (1990); 1,830 (1980) **Pop Density:** 62.9
Land: 29.9 sq. mi.; **Water:** 0.0 sq. mi.

*Little Valley Village
ZIP: 14755 **Lat:** 42-14-57 N **Long:** 78-47-57 W
Pop: 1,188 (1990); 1,203 (1980) **Pop Density:** 1188.0
Land: 1.0 sq. mi.; **Water:** 0.0 sq. mi. **Elev:** 1594 ft.
Not coextensive with the town of the same name.

Lyndon Town
Lat: 42-18-06 N **Long:** 78-21-56 W
Pop: 503 (1990); 610 (1980) **Pop Density:** 15.2
Land: 33.2 sq. mi.; **Water:** 0.1 sq. mi.

Machias Town
ZIP: 14101 **Lat:** 42-23-55 N **Long:** 78-31-40 W
Pop: 2,338 (1990); 2,058 (1980) **Pop Density:** 57.6
Land: 40.6 sq. mi.; **Water:** 0.5 sq. mi.

Mansfield Town
Lat: 42-18-10 N **Long:** 78-45-36 W
Pop: 724 (1990); 784 (1980) **Pop Density:** 18.3
Land: 39.6 sq. mi.; **Water:** 0.0 sq. mi.

Napoli Town
Lat: 42-12-59 N **Long:** 78-53-03 W
Pop: 1,102 (1990); 886 (1980) **Pop Density:** 30.3
Land: 36.4 sq. mi.; **Water:** 0.1 sq. mi.

New Albion Town
Lat: 42-18-38 N **Long:** 78-53-27 W
Pop: 1,978 (1990); 2,156 (1980) **Pop Density:** 54.3
Land: 36.4 sq. mi.; **Water:** 0.1 sq. mi.

Oil Springs Reservation Pop. Place
Lat: 42-13-59 N **Long:** 78-18-51 W
Pop: 3 (1990); 4 (1980) **Pop Density:** 7.5
Land: 0.4 sq. mi.; **Water:** 0.0 sq. mi.

Olean City
ZIP: 14760 **Lat:** 42-04-55 N **Long:** 78-25-56 W
Pop: 16,946 (1990); 18,207 (1980) **Pop Density:** 2872.2
Land: 5.9 sq. mi.; **Water:** 0.2 sq. mi. **Elev:** 1451 ft.
In southwestern NY on the Allegheny River, about five mi.
north of the PA border, east of Jamestown. Not coextensive
with the town of the same name.
Name origin: For Olean Shepard, the first white child born in
the town.

*Olean Town
ZIP: 14760 **Lat:** 42-03-35 N **Long:** 78-25-30 W
Pop: 1,999 (1990); 2,130 (1980) **Pop Density:** 67.5
Land: 29.6 sq. mi.; **Water:** 0.1 sq. mi.

Otto Town
Lat: 42-24-00 N **Long:** 78-50-38 W
Pop: 777 (1990); 828 (1980) **Pop Density:** 24.1
Land: 32.2 sq. mi.; **Water:** 0.1 sq. mi.

Perrysburg Town
ZIP: 14129 **Lat:** 42-28-08 N **Long:** 79-00-39 W
Pop: 1,838 (1990); 2,180 (1980) **Pop Density:** 64.5
Land: 28.5 sq. mi.; **Water:** 0.0 sq. mi.

*Perrysburg Village
ZIP: 14129 **Lat:** 42-27-34 N **Long:** 79-00-05 W
Pop: 404 (1990); 405 (1980) **Pop Density:** 404.0
Land: 1.0 sq. mi.; **Water:** 0.0 sq. mi.
Not coextensive with the town of the same name.

Persia Town
Lat: 42-23-19 N **Long:** 78-55-34 W
Pop: 2,530 (1990); 2,442 (1980) **Pop Density:** 121.1
Land: 20.9 sq. mi.; **Water:** 0.1 sq. mi.
Name origin: For the former name of Iran.

Portville Town
ZIP: 14770 **Lat:** 42-03-31 N **Long:** 78-21-11 W
Pop: 4,397 (1990); 4,486 (1980) **Pop Density:** 123.5
Land: 35.6 sq. mi.; **Water:** 0.4 sq. mi.

*Portville Village
ZIP: 14770 **Lat:** 42-02-08 N **Long:** 78-20-20 W
Pop: 1,040 (1990); 1,136 (1980) **Pop Density:** 1733.3
Land: 0.6 sq. mi.; **Water:** 0.0 sq. mi.
Not coextensive with the town of the same name.

Randolph Town
ZIP: 14772 **Lat:** 42-07-41 N **Long:** 79-00-03 W
Pop: 2,613 (1990); 2,593 (1980) **Pop Density:** 72.2
Land: 36.2 sq. mi.; **Water:** 0.1 sq. mi.

*Randolph Village
ZIP: 14772 **Lat:** 42-09-44 N **Long:** 78-58-47 W
Pop: 1,298 (1990); 1,398 (1980) **Pop Density:** 393.3
Land: 3.3 sq. mi.; **Water:** 0.0 sq. mi. **Elev:** 1278 ft.
Not coextensive with the town of the same name.
Name origin: For a prominent colonial citizen.

Red House Town
Lat: 42-03-16 N **Long:** 78-44-57 W
Pop: 159 (1990); 110 (1980) **Pop Density:** 2.9
Land: 55.7 sq. mi.; **Water:** 0.2 sq. mi.

St. Bonaventure　　　　　　　　　　　CDP
Lat: 42-04-48 N **Long:** 78-28-30 W
Pop: 2,397 (1990); 2,587 (1980)　　　**Pop Density:** 1198.5
Land: 2.0 sq. mi.; **Water:** 0.1 sq. mi.

Salamanca　　　　　　　　　　　　　City
ZIP: 14779　　　　**Lat:** 42-09-51 N **Long:** 78-43-21 W
Pop: 6,566 (1990); 6,890 (1980)　　　**Pop Density:** 1094.3
Land: 6.0 sq. mi.; **Water:** 0.0 sq. mi.　　**Elev:** 1392 ft.
Name origin: Named by grateful citizens for the Duke of Salamanca, who provided capital for the Atlantic and Great Western railroad company, which built shops and yards here.

*Salamanca　　　　　　　　　　　Town
ZIP: 14779　　　　**Lat:** 42-10-10 N **Long:** 78-45-11 W
Pop: 477 (1990); 608 (1980)　　　**Pop Density:** 26.2
Land: 18.2 sq. mi.; **Water:** 0.0 sq. mi.

South Dayton　　　　　　　　　　Village
ZIP: 14138　　　　**Lat:** 42-21-45 N **Long:** 79-03-07 W
Pop: 601 (1990); 661 (1980)　　　**Pop Density:** 601.0
Land: 1.0 sq. mi.; **Water:** 0.0 sq. mi.　　**Elev:** 1303 ft.

South Valley　　　　　　　　　　　Town
Lat: 42-02-07 N **Long:** 79-00-00 W
Pop: 281 (1990); 212 (1980)　　　**Pop Density:** 7.6
Land: 36.9 sq. mi.; **Water:** 0.2 sq. mi.

Weston Mills　　　　　　　　　　　CDP
Lat: 42-04-33 N **Long:** 78-22-22 W
Pop: 1,750 (1990); 717 (1980)　　　**Pop Density:** 261.2
Land: 6.7 sq. mi.; **Water:** 0.1 sq. mi.

Yorkshire　　　　　　　　　　　　Town
Lat: 42-29-18 N **Long:** 78-31-00 W
Pop: 3,905 (1990); 3,620 (1980)　　　**Pop Density:** 105.5
Land: 37.0 sq. mi.; **Water:** 0.1 sq. mi.
In southwestern NY, 37 mi. southwest of Buffalo.
Name origin: For the county in England.

Cayuga County
County Seat: Auburn (ZIP: 13021)

Pop: 82,313 (1990); 79,894 (1980)　　　**Pop Density:** 118.7
Land: 693.3 sq. mi.; **Water:** 85.7 sq. mi.　　**Area Code:** 315
On central northern border of NY, east of Rochester; organized Mar 8, 1799 from Onondaga County.
Name origin: For the Cayuga Indians, one of the Five Nations of the Iroquois.

Auburn　　　　　　　　　　　　　City
ZIP: 13021　　　　**Lat:** 42-55-59 N **Long:** 76-34-08 W
Pop: 31,258 (1990); 32,548 (1980)　　　**Pop Density:** 3721.2
Land: 8.4 sq. mi.; **Water:** 0.0 sq. mi.
In central NY on the end of Lake Owasco, 25 mi. west-southwest of Syracuse.
Name origin: From the village named in the first line of Oliver Goldsmith's (1730–74) poem "The Deserted Village" (1770).

Aurelius　　　　　　　　　　　　Town
Lat: 42-55-34 N **Long:** 76-40-03 W
Pop: 2,913 (1990); 2,920 (1980)　　　**Pop Density:** 96.1
Land: 30.3 sq. mi.; **Water:** 1.7 sq. mi.

Aurora　　　　　　　　　　　　Village
ZIP: 13026　　　　**Lat:** 42-45-07 N **Long:** 76-41-55 W
Pop: 687 (1990); 926 (1980)　　　**Pop Density:** 687.0
Land: 1.0 sq. mi.; **Water:** 0.0 sq. mi.

Brutus　　　　　　　　　　　　　Town
ZIP: 13166　　　　**Lat:** 43-02-43 N **Long:** 76-32-48 W
Pop: 5,013 (1990); 4,212 (1980)　　　**Pop Density:** 226.8
Land: 22.1 sq. mi.; **Water:** 0.4 sq. mi.

Cato　　　　　　　　　　　　　　Town
ZIP: 13033　　　　**Lat:** 43-07-29 N **Long:** 76-32-19 W
Pop: 2,452 (1990); 2,139 (1980)　　　**Pop Density:** 73.0
Land: 33.6 sq. mi.; **Water:** 2.6 sq. mi.

*Cato　　　　　　　　　　　　Village
ZIP: 13033　　　　**Lat:** 43-10-04 N **Long:** 76-34-20 W
Pop: 581 (1990); 144 (1980)　　　**Pop Density:** 581.0
Land: 1.0 sq. mi.; **Water:** 0.0 sq. mi.
Not coextensive with the town of the same name.
Name origin: For the Roman republican hero.

Cayuga　　　　　　　　　　　　Village
ZIP: 13034　　　　**Lat:** 42-55-10 N **Long:** 76-43-42 W
Pop: 556 (1990); 604 (1980)　　　**Pop Density:** 926.7
Land: 0.6 sq. mi.; **Water:** 0.4 sq. mi.

Conquest　　　　　　　　　　　　Town
ZIP: 13140　　　　**Lat:** 43-07-01 N **Long:** 76-38-59 W
Pop: 1,859 (1990); 1,628 (1980)　　　**Pop Density:** 52.8
Land: 35.2 sq. mi.; **Water:** 1.1 sq. mi.

Fair Haven　　　　　　　　　　Village
ZIP: 13156　　　　**Lat:** 43-19-32 N **Long:** 76-42-08 W
Pop: 895 (1990); 976 (1980)　　　**Pop Density:** 497.2
Land: 1.8 sq. mi.; **Water:** 1.2 sq. mi.

Fleming　　　　　　　　　　　　Town
Lat: 42-52-15 N **Long:** 76-34-57 W
Pop: 2,644 (1990); 2,394 (1980)　　　**Pop Density:** 121.3
Land: 21.8 sq. mi.; **Water:** 2.4 sq. mi.

Genoa　　　　　　　　　　　　　Town
ZIP: 13071　　　　**Lat:** 42-39-13 N **Long:** 76-34-21 W
Pop: 1,868 (1990); 1,921 (1980)　　　**Pop Density:** 47.1
Land: 39.7 sq. mi.; **Water:** 3.5 sq. mi.
Name origin: For Genoa, Italy.

Ira
Town
Lat: 43-12-35 N **Long:** 76-32-52 W
Pop: 1,990 (1990); 1,869 (1980) **Pop Density:** 57.2
Land: 34.8 sq. mi.; **Water:** 0.1 sq. mi.

Ledyard
Town
ZIP: 13026 **Lat:** 42-44-36 N **Long:** 76-40-29 W
Pop: 1,737 (1990); 1,869 (1980) **Pop Density:** 47.9
Land: 36.3 sq. mi.; **Water:** 12.3 sq. mi.

Locke
Town
ZIP: 13092 **Lat:** 42-39-21 N **Long:** 76-25-07 W
Pop: 1,917 (1990); 1,751 (1980) **Pop Density:** 78.6
Land: 24.4 sq. mi.; **Water:** 0.0 sq. mi.
Name origin: For John Locke (1632–1704), English philosopher.

Melrose Park
CDP
Lat: 42-54-08 N **Long:** 76-31-41 W
Pop: 2,091 (1990) **Pop Density:** 565.1
Land: 3.7 sq. mi.; **Water:** 0.6 sq. mi.

Ment
Town
Lat: 43-02-24 N **Long:** 76-38-01 W
Pop: 2,453 (1990); 2,441 (1980) **Pop Density:** 144.3
Land: 17.0 sq. mi.; **Water:** 0.1 sq. mi.

Meridian
Village
ZIP: 13113 **Lat:** 43-09-48 N **Long:** 76-32-07 W
Pop: 351 (1990); 344 (1980) **Pop Density:** 501.4
Land: 0.7 sq. mi.; **Water:** 0.0 sq. mi. **Elev:** 455 ft.

Montezuma
Town
Lat: 43-00-54 N **Long:** 76-41-45 W
Pop: 1,280 (1990); 1,125 (1980) **Pop Density:** 69.6
Land: 18.4 sq. mi.; **Water:** 0.4 sq. mi.
Name origin: For one of the Aztec Indian kings.

Moravia
Town
ZIP: 13118 **Lat:** 42-45-04 N **Long:** 76-25-03 W
Pop: 3,871 (1990); 2,640 (1980) **Pop Density:** 133.5
Land: 29.0 sq. mi.; **Water:** 0.7 sq. mi.

*Moravia
Village
ZIP: 13118 **Lat:** 42-42-43 N **Long:** 76-25-21 W
Pop: 1,559 (1990); 1,582 (1980) **Pop Density:** 917.1
Land: 1.7 sq. mi.; **Water:** 0.0 sq. mi.
Not coextensive with the town of the same name.

Niles
Town
Lat: 42-48-29 N **Long:** 76-24-17 W
Pop: 1,194 (1990); 1,115 (1980) **Pop Density:** 30.5
Land: 39.1 sq. mi.; **Water:** 4.3 sq. mi.

Owasco
Town
Lat: 42-53-27 N **Long:** 76-29-34 W
Pop: 3,490 (1990); 3,612 (1980) **Pop Density:** 167.0
Land: 20.9 sq. mi.; **Water:** 2.5 sq. mi.
Name origin: From an Indian term possibly meaning 'at the bridge.'

Port Byron
Village
ZIP: 13140 **Lat:** 43-02-12 N **Long** 76-37-32 W
Pop: 1,359 (1990); 1,400 (1980) **Pop Density:** 1359.0
Land: 1.0 sq. mi.; **Water:** 0.0 sq. mi.

Scipio
Town
ZIP: 13147 **Lat:** 42-47-44 N **Long** 76-33-40 W
Pop: 1,517 (1990); 1,471 (1980) **Pop Density:** 41.3
Land: 36.7 sq. mi.; **Water:** 2.7 sq. mi.

Sempronius
Town
ZIP: 13118 **Lat:** 42-44-45 N **Long** 76-19-18 W
Pop: 802 (1990); 733 (1980) **Pop Density:** 27.3
Land: 29.4 sq. mi.; **Water:** 0.3 sq. mi.
Name origin: For Roman military leader.

Sennett
Town
Lat: 42-58-01 N **Long** 76-30-41 W
Pop: 2,913 (1990); 2,561 (1980) **Pop Density:** 101.1
Land: 28.8 sq. mi.; **Water:** 0.0 sq. mi.

Springport
Town
ZIP: 13160 **Lat:** 42-51-29 N **Long** 76-40-45 W
Pop: 2,198 (1990); 2,210 (1980) **Pop Density:** 102.2
Land: 21.5 sq. mi.; **Water:** 5.3 sq. mi.

Sterling
Town
ZIP: 13156 **Lat:** 43-19-01 N **Long** 76-39-28 W
Pop: 3,285 (1990); 3,301 (1980) **Pop Density:** 72.0
Land: 45.6 sq. mi.; **Water:** 1.5 sq. mi.

Summerhill
Town
ZIP: 13092 **Lat:** 42-39-32 N **Long** 76-19-14 W
Pop: 1,017 (1990); 850 (1980) **Pop Density:** 39.3
Land: 25.9 sq. mi.; **Water:** 0.1 sq. mi.

Throop
Town
Lat: 42-58-46 N **Long** 76-36-36 W
Pop: 1,792 (1990); 1,797 (1980) **Pop Density:** 95.8
Land: 18.7 sq. mi.; **Water:** 0.0 sq. mi.

Union Springs
Village
ZIP: 13160 **Lat:** 42-50-42 N **Long** 76-41-35 W
Pop: 1,142 (1990); 1,201 (1980) **Pop Density:** 634.4
Land: 1.8 sq. mi.; **Water:** 0.0 sq. mi.
Name origin: For the numerous sulphur and salt springs in the vicinity.

Venice
Town
ZIP: 13147 **Lat:** 42-42-55 N **Long** 76-32-49 W
Pop: 1,315 (1990); 1,268 (1980) **Pop Density:** 32.0
Land: 41.1 sq. mi.; **Water:** 0.2 sq. mi.
Name origin: For the city in Italy.

Victory
Town
Lat: 43-12-35 N **Long** 76-38-56 W
Pop: 1,535 (1990); 1,519 (1980) **Pop Density:** 44.6
Land: 34.4 sq. mi.; **Water:** 0.0 sq. mi.

Weedsport
Village
ZIP: 13166 **Lat:** 43-02-49 N **Long** 76-33-52 W
Pop: 1,996 (1990); 1,952 (1980) **Pop Density:** 1996.0
Land: 1.0 sq. mi.; **Water:** 0.0 sq. mi.

Chautauqua County
County Seat: Mayville (ZIP: 14757)

Pop: 141,895 (1990); 146,925 (1980)   **Pop Density:** 133.6
Land: 1062.1 sq. mi.; **Water:** 438.0 sq. mi.   **Area Code:** 716

In southwestern corner of NY, southwest of Buffalo; organized Mar 11, 1808 from Genesee County.

Name origin: For Lake Chautauqua, which is in the middle of the county; its name is a contraction of Seneca Indian words of uncertain origin and meaning; possibly 'where the fish was taken out.'

Arkwright   Town
                          Lat: 42-23-16 N **Long:** 79-14-33 W
Pop: 1,040 (1990); 980 (1980)   **Pop Density:** 29.1
Land: 35.7 sq. mi.; **Water:** 0.1 sq. mi.

Bemus Point   Village
ZIP: 14712   **Lat:** 42-09-48 N **Long:** 79-23-28 W
Pop: 383 (1990); 444 (1980)   **Pop Density:** 957.5
Land: 0.4 sq. mi.; **Water:** 0.0 sq. mi.

Brocton   Village
ZIP: 14716   **Lat:** 42-23-21 N **Long:** 79-26-32 W
Pop: 1,387 (1990); 1,416 (1980)   **Pop Density:** 815.9
Land: 1.7 sq. mi.; **Water:** 0.0 sq. mi.

Busti   Town
ZIP: 14701   **Lat:** 42-02-27 N **Long:** 79-19-06 W
Pop: 8,050 (1990); 8,728 (1980)   **Pop Density:** 168.4
Land: 47.8 sq. mi.; **Water:** 2.7 sq. mi.

Carroll   Town
                          Lat: 42-02-13 N **Long:** 79-07-19 W
Pop: 3,539 (1990); 3,579 (1980)   **Pop Density:** 105.6
Land: 33.5 sq. mi.; **Water:** 0.0 sq. mi.

Cassadaga   Village
ZIP: 14718   **Lat:** 42-20-27 N **Long:** 79-19-01 W
Pop: 768 (1990); 821 (1980)   **Pop Density:** 853.3
Land: 0.9 sq. mi.; **Water:** 0.2 sq. mi.   **Elev:** 1316 ft.

Cattaraugus Reservation   Pop. Place
                          Lat: 42-32-32 N **Long:** 79-04-58 W
Pop: 30 (1990); 14 (1980)   **Pop Density:** 11.5
Land: 2.6 sq. mi.; **Water:** 0.1 sq. mi.

Celoron   Village
ZIP: 14720   **Lat:** 42-06-17 N **Long:** 79-16-33 W
Pop: 1,232 (1990); 1,405 (1980)   **Pop Density:** 1760.0
Land: 0.7 sq. mi.; **Water:** 0.0 sq. mi.

Charlotte   Town
                          Lat: 42-18-21 N **Long:** 79-14-13 W
Pop: 1,528 (1990); 1,494 (1980)   **Pop Density:** 41.9
Land: 36.5 sq. mi.; **Water:** 0.0 sq. mi.

Chautauqua   Town
                          Lat: 42-14-26 N **Long:** 79-30-06 W
Pop: 4,554 (1990); 4,728 (1980)   **Pop Density:** 67.8
Land: 67.2 sq. mi.; **Water:** 7.0 sq. mi.
In southwestern NY on Chautauqua Lake.
Name origin: For Lake Chautauqua.

Cherry Creek   Town
ZIP: 14723   **Lat:** 42-18-12 N **Long:** 79-07-18 W
Pop: 1,064 (1990); 1,227 (1980)   **Pop Density:** 29.1
Land: 36.6 sq. mi.; **Water:** 0.0 sq. mi.

*Cherry Creek   Village
ZIP: 14723   **Lat:** 42-17-42 N **Long:** 79-06-05 W
Pop: 539 (1990); 677 (1980)   **Pop Density:** 385.0
Land: 1.4 sq. mi.; **Water:** 0.0 sq. mi.   **Elev:** 1306 ft.
Not coextensive with the town of the same name.

Clymer   Town
ZIP: 14724   **Lat:** 42-02-06 N **Long:** 79-35-18 W
Pop: 1,474 (1990); 1,484 (1980)   **Pop Density:** 40.8
Land: 36.1 sq. mi.; **Water:** 0.0 sq. mi.

Dunkirk   City
ZIP: 14048   **Lat:** 42-33-55 N **Long:** 79-19-26 W
Pop: 13,989 (1990); 15,310 (1980)   **Pop Density:** 3108.7
Land: 4.5 sq. mi.; **Water:** 36.6 sq. mi.   **Elev:** 598 ft.
In southwestern NY on Lake Erie, 35 mi. southwest of Buffalo. Not coextensive with the town of the same name.
Name origin: For the French channel port.

*Dunkirk   Town
                          Lat: 42-28-19 N **Long:** 79-19-19 W
Pop: 1,482 (1990); 1,584 (1980)   **Pop Density:** 239.0
Land: 6.2 sq. mi.; **Water:** 0.1 sq. mi.

Ellery   Town
                          Lat: 42-11-03 N **Long:** 79-21-37 W
Pop: 4,534 (1990); 4,617 (1980)   **Pop Density:** 95.3
Land: 47.6 sq. mi.; **Water:** 7.4 sq. mi.

Ellicott   Town
ZIP: 14733   **Lat:** 42-07-50 N **Long:** 79-14-25 W
Pop: 9,455 (1990); 9,979 (1980)   **Pop Density:** 309.0
Land: 30.6 sq. mi.; **Water:** 0.6 sq. mi.

Ellington   Town
                          Lat: 42-12-50 N **Long:** 79-07-07 W
Pop: 1,615 (1990); 1,690 (1980)   **Pop Density:** 44.1
Land: 36.6 sq. mi.; **Water:** 0.0 sq. mi.

Falconer   Village
ZIP: 14733   **Lat:** 42-07-08 N **Long:** 79-11-50 W
Pop: 2,653 (1990); 2,778 (1980)   **Pop Density:** 2411.8
Land: 1.1 sq. mi.; **Water:** 0.0 sq. mi.   **Elev:** 1262 ft.

Forestville   Village
ZIP: 14062   **Lat:** 42-28-07 N **Long:** 79-10-29 W
Pop: 738 (1990); 804 (1980)   **Pop Density:** 738.0
Land: 1.0 sq. mi.; **Water:** 0.0 sq. mi.   **Elev:** 928 ft.

Fredonia   Village
ZIP: 14063   **Lat:** 42-26-25 N **Long:** 79-19-54 W
Pop: 10,436 (1990); 11,126 (1980)   **Pop Density:** 2006.9
Land: 5.2 sq. mi.; **Water:** 0.0 sq. mi.   **Elev:** 728 ft.
In southwestern NY near Lake Erie, 23 mi. north of Jamestown.
Name origin: Coined by Dr. Samuel Latham Mitchill shortly

after 1800, from English *freedom* with a Latin ending, to connote 'a place of freedom.'

French Creek
Town
Lat: 42-02-43 N **Long:** 79-41-57 W
Pop: 916 (1990); 878 (1980)   **Pop Density:** 25.3
Land: 36.2 sq. mi.; **Water:** 0.0 sq. mi.

Frewsburg
CDP
ZIP: 14738   **Lat:** 42-03-25 N **Long:** 79-09-40 W
Pop: 1,817 (1990); 1,908 (1980)   **Pop Density:** 1009.4
Land: 1.8 sq. mi.; **Water:** 0.0 sq. mi.

Gerry
Town
ZIP: 14740   **Lat:** 42-12-30 N **Long:** 79-13-26 W
Pop: 2,147 (1990); 2,022 (1980)   **Pop Density:** 59.3
Land: 36.2 sq. mi.; **Water:** 0.0 sq. mi.

Hanover
Town
ZIP: 14136   **Lat:** 42-29-36 N **Long:** 79-07-30 W
Pop: 7,380 (1990); 7,876 (1980)   **Pop Density:** 149.7
Land: 49.3 sq. mi.; **Water:** 0.2 sq. mi.

Harmony
Town
Lat: 42-02-00 N **Long:** 79-27-32 W
Pop: 2,177 (1990); 2,121 (1980)   **Pop Density:** 47.8
Land: 45.5 sq. mi.; **Water:** 0.1 sq. mi.

Jamestown
City
ZIP: 14701   **Lat:** 42-05-50 N **Long:** 79-14-10 W
Pop: 34,681 (1990); 35,775 (1980)   **Pop Density:** 3896.7
Land: 8.9 sq. mi.; **Water:** 0.1 sq. mi.

In southwestern NY at the south end of Chautauqua Lake, 57 mi. southwest of Buffalo.

Name origin: For Jamestown, VA, the first English settlement in North America.

Jamestown West
CDP
Lat: 42-05-21 N **Long:** 79-16-43 W
Pop: 2,633 (1990); 2,680 (1980)   **Pop Density:** 1012.7
Land: 2.6 sq. mi.; **Water:** 0.0 sq. mi.

Kiantone
Town
Lat: 42-01-58 N **Long:** 79-12-23 W
Pop: 1,322 (1990); 1,443 (1980)   **Pop Density:** 71.5
Land: 18.5 sq. mi.; **Water:** 0.1 sq. mi.

Lakewood
Village
ZIP: 14750   **Lat:** 42-06-00 N **Long:** 79-19-11 W
Pop: 3,564 (1990); 3,941 (1980)   **Pop Density:** 1782.0
Land: 2.0 sq. mi.; **Water:** 0.0 sq. mi.   **Elev:** 1329 ft.

In southwestern NY at the southern end of Chautauqua Lake, 5 mi. west of Jamestown.

Name origin: For its descriptive connotations.

Mayville
Village
ZIP: 14757   **Lat:** 42-15-10 N **Long:** 79-30-08 W
Pop: 1,636 (1990); 1,626 (1980)   **Pop Density:** 861.1
Land: 1.9 sq. mi.; **Water:** 0.0 sq. mi.   **Elev:** 1468 ft.

Mina
Town
Lat: 42-07-57 N **Long:** 79-42-44 W
Pop: 1,129 (1990); 1,245 (1980)   **Pop Density:** 31.4
Land: 35.9 sq. mi.; **Water:** 0.4 sq. mi.

North Harmony
Town
Lat: 42-08-17 N **Long:** 79-27-13 W
Pop: 2,301 (1990); 2,263 (1980)   **Pop Density:** 54.5
Land: 42.2 sq. mi.; **Water:** 2.9 sq. mi.

Panama
Village
ZIP: 14767   **Lat:** 42-04-30 N **Long:** 79-29-10 W
Pop: 468 (1990); 511 (1980)   **Pop Density:** 212.7
Land: 2.2 sq. mi.; **Water:** 0.0 sq. mi.   **Elev:** 1550 ft.

Poland
Town
Lat: 42-07-45 N **Long:** 79-07-17 W
Pop: 2,604 (1990); 2,639 (1980)   **Pop Density:** 71.0
Land: 36.7 sq. mi.; **Water:** 0.1 sq. mi.

Pomfret
Town
ZIP: 14063   **Lat:** 42-24-15 N **Long:** 79-21-22 W
Pop: 14,224 (1990); 14,992 (1980)   **Pop Density:** 324.0
Land: 43.9 sq. mi.; **Water:** 0.4 sq. mi.

Portland
Town
ZIP: 14769   **Lat:** 42-22-28 N **Long:** 79-28-08 W
Pop: 4,832 (1990); 4,433 (1980)   **Pop Density:** 140.9
Land: 34.3 sq. mi.; **Water:** 6.1 sq. mi.

Ripley
Town
ZIP: 14775   **Lat:** 42-14-24 N **Long:** 79-41-34 W
Pop: 2,967 (1990); 3,229 (1980)   **Pop Density:** 60.7
Land: 48.9 sq. mi.; **Water:** 5.6 sq. mi.

Name origin: For an early settler.

Sheridan
Town
Lat: 42-29-09 N **Long:** 79-14-16 W
Pop: 2,582 (1990); 2,659 (1980)   **Pop Density:** 69.2
Land: 37.3 sq. mi.; **Water:** 0.0 sq. mi.

Name origin: For Gen. Philip Sheridan (1831–88), commander of Union forces during the Civil War.

Sherman
Town
ZIP: 14781   **Lat:** 42-08-05 N **Long:** 79-35-28 W
Pop: 1,505 (1990); 1,490 (1980)   **Pop Density:** 41.5
Land: 36.3 sq. mi.; **Water:** 0.1 sq. mi.

*Sherman
Village
ZIP: 14781   **Lat:** 42-09-36 N **Long:** 79-35-41 W
Pop: 694 (1990); 775 (1980)   **Pop Density:** 867.5
Land: 0.8 sq. mi.; **Water:** 0.0 sq. mi.   **Elev:** 1539 ft.

Not coextensive with the town of the same name.

Silver Creek
Village
ZIP: 14136   **Lat:** 42-32-36 N **Long:** 79-10-07 W
Pop: 2,927 (1990); 3,088 (1980)   **Pop Density:** 2660.9
Land: 1.1 sq. mi.; **Water:** 0.0 sq. mi.

In southwestern NY on Lake Erie, 28 mi. south of Buffalo.

Name origin: For Silver Creek, which flows through it.

Sinclairville
Village
ZIP: 14782   **Lat:** 42-15-51 N **Long:** 79-15-29 W
Pop: 708 (1990); 596 (1980)   **Pop Density:** 442.5
Land: 1.6 sq. mi.; **Water:** 0.0 sq. mi.

Stockton
Town
ZIP: 14784   **Lat:** 42-17-50 N **Long:** 79-21-28 W
Pop: 2,515 (1990); 2,331 (1980)   **Pop Density:** 53.2
Land: 47.3 sq. mi.; **Water:** 0.3 sq. mi.

Villenova
Town
Lat: 42-23-39 N **Long:** 79-07-03 W
Pop: 1,065 (1990); 1,061 (1980)   **Pop Density:** 29.5
Land: 36.1 sq. mi.; **Water:** 0.1 sq. mi.

Westfield
Town
ZIP: 14787   **Lat:** 42-17-09 N **Long:** 79-36-07 W
Pop: 5,194 (1990); 5,054 (1980)   **Pop Density:** 110.0
Land: 47.2 sq. mi.; **Water:** 5.6 sq. mi.

*Westfield   Village
ZIP: 14787   **Lat:** 42-19-19 N **Long:** 79-34-33 W
Pop: 3,451 (1990); 3,446 (1980)   **Pop Density:** 908.2
Land: 3.8 sq. mi.; **Water:** 0.0 sq. mi.   **Elev:** 754 ft.

Not coextensive with the town of the same name.

Chemung County
County Seat: Elmira (ZIP: 14902)

Pop: 95,195 (1990); 97,656 (1980)   **Pop Density:** 233.2
Land: 408.2 sq. mi.; **Water:** 2.6 sq. mi.   **Area Code:** 607

On central southern border of NY, southwest of Syracuse; organized Mar 29, 1836 from Tioga County.

Name origin: For a former Seneca village near the town of Chemung. The name means 'big horn.'

Ashland   Town
          Lat: 42-01-40 N **Long:** 76-44-49 W
Pop: 1,966 (1990); 1,967 (1980)   **Pop Density:** 138.5
Land: 14.2 sq. mi ; **Water:** 0.4 sq. mi.

Baldwin   Town
          Lat: 42-05-53 N **Long:** 76-39-39 W
Pop: 829 (1990); 892 (1980)   **Pop Density:** 32.1
Land: 25.8 sq. mi.; **Water:** 0.0 sq. mi.

Big Flats   Town
ZIP: 14814   **Lat:** 42-08-19 N **Long:** 76-54-50 W
Pop: 7,596 (1990); 7,649 (1980)   **Pop Density:** 170.7
Land: 44.5 sq. mi.; **Water:** 0.6 sq. mi.

In southern NY, a suburb of Elmira just north of the PA border.

Name origin: For its location at flatlands along the Chemung River.

Catlin   Town
          Lat: 42-14-39 N **Long:** 76-54-00 W
Pop: 2,626 (1990); 2,719 (1980)   **Pop Density:** 69.1
Land: 38.0 sq. mi.; **Water:** 0.0 sq. mi.

Chemung   Town
ZIP: 14825   **Lat:** 42-02-47 N **Long:** 76-37-11 W
Pop: 2,540 (1990); 2,436 (1980)   **Pop Density:** 51.4
Land: 49.4 sq. mi.; **Water:** 0.6 sq. mi.

Name origin: From the Iroquoian term meaning 'big horn.'

Elmira   City
ZIP: 14901   **Lat:** 42-05-35 N **Long:** 76-48-36 W
Pop: 33,724 (1990); 35,327 (1980)   **Pop Density:** 4619.7
Land: 7.3 sq. mi.; **Water:** 0.3 sq. mi.   **Elev:** 873 ft.

In south-central NY on the Chemung River, 48 mi. west of Binghamton. Not coextensive with the town of the same name.

Name origin: For Elmira Teall, daughter of an early settler.

*Elmira   Town
ZIP: 14902   **Lat:** 42-05-40 N **Long:** 76-46-45 W
Pop: 7,440 (1990); 7,635 (1980)   **Pop Density:** 333.6
Land: 22.3 sq. mi.; **Water:** 0.3 sq. mi.

Elmira Heights   Village
ZIP: 14903   **Lat:** 42-07-34 N **Long:** 76-49-35 W
Pop: 4,359 (1990); 1,009 (1980)   **Pop Density:** 3962.7
Land: 1.1 sq. mi.; **Water:** 0.0 sq. mi.

Erin   Town
ZIP: 14838   **Lat:** 42-11-06 N **Long:** 76-40-24 W
Pop: 2,002 (1990); 2,037 (1980)   **Pop Density:** 45.2
Land: 44.3 sq. mi.; **Water:** 0.2 sq. mi.

Horseheads   Town
ZIP: 14845   **Lat:** 42-10-06 N **Long:** 76-47-49 W
Pop: 19,926 (1990); 20,238 (1980)   **Pop Density:** 555.0
Land: 35.9 sq. mi.; **Water:** 0.1 sq. mi.

*Horseheads   Village
ZIP: 14845   **Lat:** 42-10-10 N **Long:** 76-49-47 W
Pop: 6,802 (1990); 7,348 (1980)   **Pop Density:** 1744.1
Land: 3.9 sq. mi.; **Water:** 0.0 sq. mi.   **Elev:** 898 ft.

In southwestern NY, 5 mi. north of Elmira. Not coextensive with the town of the same name.

Name origin: Origin of the name is unclear: either because of horse skulls discovered in the area by early settlers, thought to be remains of pack horses destroyed in an expedition against the Iroquois; or for an incident in the American Revolution when some soldiers killed their horses for food and left their heads piled up.

Horseheads North   CDP
          Lat: 42-11-31 N **Long:** 76-48-32 W
Pop: 3,003 (1990); 3,081 (1980)   **Pop Density:** 1305.7
Land: 2.3 sq. mi.; **Water:** 0.0 sq. mi.

Millport   Village
ZIP: 14864   **Lat:** 42-16-03 N **Long:** 76-50-11 W
Pop: 342 (1990); 440 (1980)   **Pop Density:** 855.0
Land: 0.4 sq. mi.; **Water:** 0.0 sq. mi.

Southport   Town
ZIP: 14904   **Lat:** 42-02-21 N **Long:** 76-52-47 W
Pop: 11,571 (1990); 11,586 (1980)   **Pop Density:** 248.8
Land: 46.5 sq. mi.; **Water:** 0.3 sq. mi.

In southern NY near the PA state line, 2 mi. south of Elmira near the Chemung River.

Van Etten   Town
ZIP: 14889   **Lat:** 42-12-32 N **Long:** 76-35-01 W
Pop: 1,507 (1990); 1,519 (1980)   **Pop Density:** 36.2
Land: 41.6 sq. mi.; **Water:** 0.0 sq. mi.

*Van Etten   Village
ZIP: 14889   **Lat:** 42-11-53 N **Long:** 76-33-16 W
Pop: 552 (1990); 559 (1980)   **Pop Density:** 613.3
Land: 0.9 sq. mi.; **Water:** 0.0 sq. mi.

Not coextensive with the town of the same name.

Veteran Town
Lat: 42-14-59 N Long: 76-47-17 W
Pop: 3,468 (1990); 3,651 (1980) Pop Density: 90.3
Land: 38.4 sq. mi.; Water: 0.1 sq. mi.

Wellsburg Village
ZIP: 14894 Lat: 42-00-46 N Long: 76-43-46 W
Pop: 617 (1990); 647 (1980) Pop Density: 1028.3
Land: 0.6 sq. mi.; Water: 0.0 sq. mi. Elev: 824 ft.

West Elmira CDP
ZIP: 14905 Lat: 42-05-22 N Long: 76-51-02 W
Pop: 5,218 (1990); 5,485 (1980) Pop Density: 1739.3
Land: 3.0 sq. mi.; Water: 0.1 sq. mi.

Chenango County
County Seat: Norwich (ZIP: 13815)

Pop: 51,768 (1990); 49,344 (1980) Pop Density: 57.9
Land: 894.4 sq. mi.; Water: 4.3 sq. mi. Area Code: 607

In south-central NY, southeast of Ithaca; organized Mar 15, 1798 from Herkimer and Tioga counties.

Name origin: From an Onondaga Indian word probably meaning 'bull thistle.'

Afton Town
ZIP: 13730 Lat: 42-13-39 N Long: 75-31-29 W
Pop: 2,972 (1990); 2,728 (1980) Pop Density: 64.7
Land: 45.9 sq. mi.; Water: 0.6 sq. mi.

*Afton Village
ZIP: 13730 Lat: 42-13-44 N Long: 75-31-30 W
Pop: 838 (1990); 982 (1980) Pop Density: 558.7
Land: 1.5 sq. mi.; Water: 0.1 sq. mi.
Not coextensive with the town of the same name.
Name origin: For the Afton River in Scotland or the poem and song, "Flow Gently, Sweet Afton," by Robert Burns (1759–96), about the river.

Bainbridge Town
ZIP: 13733 Lat: 42-17-46 N Long: 75-28-37 W
Pop: 3,445 (1990); 3,331 (1980) Pop Density: 100.4
Land: 34.3 sq. mi.; Water: 0.4 sq. mi.

*Bainbridge Village
ZIP: 13733 Lat: 42-17-45 N Long: 75-28-49 W
Pop: 1,550 (1990); 1,603 (1980) Pop Density: 1291.7
Land: 1.2 sq. mi.; Water: 0.0 sq. mi. Elev: 1006 ft.
In southern NY on the Susquehanna River. Not coextensive with the town of the same name.
Name origin: For U.S. naval hero William Bainbridge (1774–1833).

Columbus Town
ZIP: 13411 Lat: 42-41-45 N Long: 75-21-39 W
Pop: 869 (1990); 802 (1980) Pop Density: 23.2
Land: 37.4 sq. mi.; Water: 0.1 sq. mi.

Coventry Town
ZIP: 13778 Lat: 42-18-09 N Long: 75-37-46 W
Pop: 1,517 (1990); 1,271 (1980) Pop Density: 31.1
Land: 48.7 sq. mi.; Water: 0.1 sq. mi.

Earlville Village
ZIP: 13332 Lat: 42-44-08 N Long: 75-32-15 W
Pop: 341 (1990); 363 (1980) Pop Density: 568.3
Land: 0.6 sq. mi.; Water: 0.0 sq. mi. Elev: 1100 ft.
Part of the town is in Madison County.

German Town
Lat: 42-29-45 N Long: 75-49-34 W
Pop: 311 (1990); 250 (1980) Pop Density: 11.0
Land: 28.4 sq. mi.; Water: 0.0 sq. mi.

Greene Town
ZIP: 13778 Lat: 42-19-17 N Long: 75-46-20 W
Pop: 6,053 (1990); 5,729 (1980) Pop Density: 80.6
Land: 75.1 sq. mi.; Water: 0.5 sq. mi.

*Greene Village
ZIP: 13778 Lat: 42-19-47 N Long: 75-46-13 W
Pop: 1,812 (1990); 1,747 (1980) Pop Density: 1812.0
Land: 1.0 sq. mi.; Water: 0.0 sq. mi. Elev: 924 ft.
Not coextensive with the town of the same name.

Guilford Town
ZIP: 13780 Lat: 42-23-53 N Long: 75-27-21 W
Pop: 2,875 (1990); 2,442 (1980) Pop Density: 46.6
Land: 61.7 sq. mi.; Water: 0.2 sq. mi.

Lincklaen Town
Lat: 42-41-12 N Long: 75-50-34 W
Pop: 486 (1990); 473 (1980) Pop Density: 18.5
Land: 26.3 sq. mi.; Water: 0.0 sq. mi.

McDonough Town
ZIP: 13801 Lat: 42-30-13 N Long: 75-43-33 W
Pop: 809 (1990); 796 (1980) Pop Density: 20.7
Land: 39.1 sq. mi.; Water: 0.5 sq. mi.

New Berlin Town
ZIP: 13411 Lat: 42-34-46 N Long: 75-23-53 W
Pop: 3,046 (1990); 3,025 (1980) Pop Density: 65.6
Land: 46.4 sq. mi.; Water: 0.3 sq. mi.

*New Berlin Village
ZIP: 13411 Lat: 42-37-26 N Long: 75-20-08 W
Pop: 1,220 (1990); 1,392 (1980) Pop Density: 1109.1
Land: 1.1 sq. mi.; Water: 0.0 sq. mi.
Not coextensive with the town of the same name.

North Norwich Town
Lat: 42-36-47 N Long: 75-29-44 W
Pop: 1,998 (1990); 1,687 (1980) Pop Density: 70.9
Land: 28.2 sq. mi.; Water: 0.0 sq. mi.

Norwich   City
ZIP: 13815   **Lat:** 42-32-05 N **Long:** 75-31-25 W
Pop: 7,613 (1990); 8,082 (1980)   **Pop Density:** 3806.5
Land: 2.0 sq. mi.; **Water:** 0.0 sq. mi.   **Elev:** 1015 ft.
In south-central NY, 36 mi. north-northeast of Binghamton.
Not coextensive with the town of the same name.
Name origin: For the city in England.

*Norwich   Town
ZIP: 13815   **Lat:** 42-30-28 N **Long:** 75-29-17 W
Pop: 4,084 (1990); 4,042 (1980)   **Pop Density:** 97.0
Land: 42.1 sq. mi.; **Water:** 0.1 sq. mi.

Otselic   Town
                        Lat: 42-41-03 N **Long:** 75-44-22 W
Pop: 990 (1990); 955 (1980)   **Pop Density:** 26.1
Land: 38.0 sq. mi.; **Water:** 0.0 sq. mi.

Oxford   Town
ZIP: 13830   **Lat:** 42-24-21 N **Long:** 75-35-31 W
Pop: 4,075 (1990); 3,961 (1980)   **Pop Density:** 67.8
Land: 60.1 sq. mi.; **Water:** 0.3 sq. mi.

*Oxford   Village
ZIP: 13830   **Lat:** 42-26-26 N **Long:** 75-35-46 W
Pop: 1,738 (1990); 1,765 (1980)   **Pop Density:** 965.6
Land: 1.8 sq. mi.; **Water:** 0.0 sq. mi.   **Elev:** 973 ft.
Not coextensive with the town of the same name.

Pharsalia   Town
                        Lat: 42-35-53 N **Long:** 75-44-09 W
Pop: 735 (1990); 606 (1980)   **Pop Density:** 18.9
Land: 38.8 sq. mi ; **Water:** 0.3 sq. mi.

Pitcher   Town
ZIP: 13136   **Lat:** 42-35-43 N **Long:** 75-50-21 W
Pop: 751 (1990); 735 (1980)   **Pop Density:** 26.4
Land: 28.5 sq. mi.; **Water:** 0.0 sq. mi.

Plymouth   Town
ZIP: 13832   **Lat:** 42-35-57 N **Long:** 75-36-41 W
Pop: 1,704 (1990); 1,515 (1980)   **Pop Density:** 40.4
Land: 42.2 sq. mi.; **Water:** 0.2 sq. mi.
Name origin: For the town in MA.

Preston   Town
ZIP: 13830   **Lat:** 42-30-11 N **Long:** 75-36-39 W
Pop: 1,100 (1990); 941 (1980)   **Pop Density:** 31.5
Land: 34.9 sq. mi.; **Water:** 0.2 sq. mi.

Sherburne   Town
ZIP: 13460   **Lat:** 42-41-35 N **Long:** 75-29-07 W
Pop: 3,903 (1990); 3,657 (1980)   **Pop Density:** 89.5
Land: 43.6 sq. mi.; **Water:** 0.0 sq. mi.

*Sherburne   Village
ZIP: 13460   **Lat:** 42-40-49 N **Long:** 75-29-51 W
Pop: 1,531 (1990); 1,561 (1980)   **Pop Density:** 1020.7
Land: 1.5 sq. mi.; **Water:** 0.0 sq. mi.   **Elev:** 1055 ft.
Not coextensive with the town of the same name.

Smithville   Town
ZIP: 13778   **Lat:** 42-24-46 N **Long:** 75-45-55 W
Pop: 1,167 (1990); 1,174 (1980)   **Pop Density:** 23.1
Land: 50.5 sq. mi.; **Water:** 0.4 sq. mi.

Smyrna   Town
ZIP: 13464   **Lat:** 42-41-15 N **Long:** 75-36-57 W
Pop: 1,265 (1990); 1,142 (1980)   **Pop Density:** 30.0
Land: 42.1 sq. mi.; **Water:** 0.1 sq. mi.

*Smyrna   Village
ZIP: 13464   **Lat:** 42-41-09 N **Long:** 75-34-03 W
Pop: 211 (1990); 225 (1980)   **Pop Density:** 1055.0
Land: 0.2 sq. mi.; **Water:** 0.0 sq. mi.
Not coextensive with the town of the same name.

Clinton County
County Seat: Plattsburgh (ZIP: 12901)

Pop: 85,969 (1990); 80,750 (1980)   **Pop Density:** 82.7
Land: 1039.4 sq. mi.; **Water:** 78.3 sq. mi.   **Area Code:** 518
In northeastern corner of NY, northwest of Burlington, VT; organized Mar 7, 1788
(prior to statehood) from Washington County.
Name origin: For George Clinton (1739–1812), first governor of NY (1777–95).

Altona   Town
ZIP: 12910   **Lat:** 44-51-05 N **Long:** 73-39-56 W
Pop: 2,775 (1990); 2,077 (1980)   **Pop Density:** 27.5
Land: 101.0 sq. mi.; **Water:** 0.3 sq. mi.

Au Sable   Town
                        Lat: 44-31-07 N **Long:** 73-31-34 W
Pop: 2,870 (1990); 2,792 (1980)   **Pop Density:** 73.4
Land: 39.1 sq. mi.; **Water:** 4.8 sq. mi.

Beekmantown   Town
ZIP: 12901   **Lat:** 44-46-15 N **Long:** 73-30-00 W
Pop: 5,108 (1990); 4,275 (1980)   **Pop Density:** 84.4
Land: 60.5 sq. mi.; **Water:** 9.1 sq. mi.

Black Brook   Town
                        Lat: 44-30-15 N **Long:** 73-47-46 W
Pop: 1,556 (1990); 1,505 (1980)   **Pop Density:** 12.0
Land: 130.2 sq. mi.; **Water:** 4.1 sq. mi.

Champlain   Town
ZIP: 12919   **Lat:** 44-57-56 N **Long:** 73-26-12 W
Pop: 5,796 (1990); 5,889 (1980)   **Pop Density:** 113.2
Land: 51.2 sq. mi.; **Water:** 7.6 sq. mi.

*Champlain   Village
ZIP: 12919   **Lat:** 44-59-14 N **Long:** 73-26-40 W
Pop: 1,273 (1990); 1,410 (1980)   **Pop Density:** 1060.8
Land: 1.2 sq. mi.; **Water:** 0.0 sq. mi.   **Elev:** 152 ft.
Not coextensive with the town of the same name.
Name origin: For the early French explorer.

Chazy   Town
                        Lat: 44-51-28 N **Long:** 73-27-48 W
Pop: 3,890 (1990); 3,766 (1980)   **Pop Density:** 71.8
Land: 54.2 sq. mi.; **Water:** 7.1 sq. mi.
In northeastern NY near Lake Champlain.
Name origin: For Lt. de Chezy, who was killed here in 1666.

Clinton
Town
Lat: 44-57-19 N Long: 73-55-36 W
Pop: 663 (1990); 685 (1980)   Pop Density: 9.9
Land: 67.1 sq. mi.; Water: 0.0 sq. mi.

Cumberland Head
CDP
Lat: 44-42-58 N Long: 73-24-10 W
Pop: 1,698 (1990)   Pop Density: 458.9
Land: 3.7 sq. mi.; Water: 0.0 sq. mi.

Dannemora
Town
ZIP: 12929   Lat: 44-44-20 N Long: 73-49-59 W
Pop: 5,232 (1990); 4,717 (1980)   Pop Density: 88.4
Land: 59.2 sq. mi.; Water: 6.6 sq. mi.

*Dannemora
Village
ZIP: 12929   Lat: 44-43-15 N Long: 73-43-09 W
Pop: 4,005 (1990); 3,327 (1980)   Pop Density: 3337.5
Land: 1.2 sq. mi.; Water: 0.0 sq. mi.   Elev: 1439 ft.
Not coextensive with the town of the same name.

Name origin: For Dannemora, Sweden, which was known for its iron mines.

Ellenburg
Town
Lat: 44-50-24 N Long: 73-53-22 W
Pop: 1,847 (1990); 1,751 (1980)   Pop Density: 17.3
Land: 106.8 sq. mi.; Water: 0.6 sq. mi.

Keeseville
Village
ZIP: 12944   Lat: 44-30-19 N Long: 73-29-06 W
Pop: 972 (1990); 1,055 (1980)   Pop Density: 1388.6
Land: 0.7 sq. mi.; Water: 0.0 sq. mi.   Elev: 503 ft.

In northeastern NY, near the western shore of Lake Champlain. Part of the town is in Essex County.

Name origin: For John Keese, a Quaker settler who arrived in 1806.

Mooers
Town
ZIP: 12958   Lat: 44-57-46 N Long: 73-39-35 W
Pop: 2,995 (1990); 2,927 (1980)   Pop Density: 34.2
Land: 87.7 sq. mi.; Water: 0.3 sq. mi.

*Mooers
Village
ZIP: 12958   Lat: 44-57-54 N Long: 73-35-09 W
Pop: 467 (1990); 549 (1980)   Pop Density: 518.9
Land: 0.9 sq. mi.; Water: 0.0 sq. mi.
Not coextensive with the town of the same name.

Morrisonville
CDP
ZIP: 12962   Lat: 44-41-26 N Long: 73-33-04 W
Pop: 1,742 (1990); 1,043 (1980)   Pop Density: 670.0
Land: 2.6 sq. mi.; Water: 0.1 sq. mi.

Peru
Town
ZIP: 12972   Lat: 44-34-49 N Long 73-33-25 W
Pop: 6,254 (1990); 5,352 (1980)   Pop Density: 78.8
Land: 79.4 sq. mi.; Water: 13.1 sq. mi.

In northeastern NY on the western shore of Lake Champlain.

Name origin: Named by some stretch of the imagination for the South American country because of its proximity to the mountains.

Plattsburgh
City
ZIP: 12901   Lat: 44-41-43 N Long 73-27-24 W
Pop: 21,255 (1990); 21,057 (1980)   Pop Density: 4251.0
Land: 5.0 sq. mi.; Water: 1.5 sq. mi.   Elev: 135 ft.

In northeastern NY on the west shore of Lake Champlain, 20 mi. south of the Canadian border.

Name origin: For Zephaniah Platt, landowner, fur trader, and "a man of uncompromising integrity."

*Plattsburgh
Town
ZIP: 12918   Lat: 44-41-52 N Long: 73-29-09 W
Pop: 17,231 (1990); 16,384 (1980)   Pop Density: 374.6
Land: 46.0 sq. mi.; Water: 22.1 sq. mi.

Plattsburgh Air Force Base
Military facility
ZIP: 12903   Lat: 44-39-48 N Long: 73-27-12 W
Pop: 5,483 (1990); 5,905 (1980)   Pop Density: 4569.2
Land: 1.2 sq. mi.; Water: 0.0 sq. mi.

Plattsburgh West
CDP
Lat: 44-40-57 N Long: 73-30-11 W
Pop: 1,274 (1990); 1,210 (1980)   Pop Density: 707.8
Land: 1.8 sq. mi.; Water: 0.1 sq. mi.

Rouses Point
Village
ZIP: 12979   Lat: 44-59-31 N Long: 73-21-57 W
Pop: 2,377 (1990); 2,266 (1980)   Pop Density: 1320.6
Land: 1.8 sq. mi.; Water: 0.4 sq. mi.   Elev: 116 ft.

In northeastern NY at the upper end of Lake Champlain on the border of the Canadian province of Quebec.

Name origin: For an early settler.

Saranac
Town
ZIP: 12981   Lat: 44-39-13 N Long: 73-48-35 W
Pop: 3,710 (1990); 3,389 (1980)   Pop Density: 32.4
Land: 114.5 sq. mi.; Water: 0.6 sq. mi.

Name origin: From an Indian term of uncertain meaning.

Schuyler Falls
Town
ZIP: 12985   Lat: 44-39-34 N Long: 73-35-04 W
Pop: 4,787 (1990); 4,184 (1980)   Pop Density: 128.0
Land: 37.4 sq. mi.; Water: 0.3 sq. mi.

Name origin: For Gen. Phillip Schuyler (1733–1804).

Columbia County
County Seat: Hudson (ZIP: 12534)

Pop: 62,982 (1990); 59,487 (1980) **Pop Density:** 99.1
Land: 635.8 sq. mi.; **Water:** 12.5 sq. mi. **Area Code:** 518

On central eastern border of NY, southeast of Albany; organized Apr 4, 1786 (prior to statehood) from Albany County.

Name origin: Feminine form of Columbus, a poetic and honorific reference to Christopher Columbus (1451–1506) and America.

Ancram
Town
ZIP: 12502 **Lat:** 42-01-51 N **Long:** 73-34-30 W
Pop: 1,510 (1990); 1,332 (1980) **Pop Density:** 35.4
Land: 42.6 sq. mi.; **Water:** 0.2 sq. mi.

Austerlitz
Town
Lat: 42-18-23 N **Long:** 73-30-25 W
Pop: 1,456 (1990); 1,314 (1980) **Pop Density:** 29.9
Land: 48.7 sq. mi.; **Water:** 0.1 sq. mi.
On the eastern border of NY.
Name origin: Named by Martin Van Buren (1782–1862), an ardent admirer of Napoleon (1769–1821), for the site of Napoleon's 1805 victory.

Canaan
Town
ZIP: 12029 **Lat:** 42-23-33 N **Long:** 73-27-22 W
Pop: 1,773 (1990); 1,654 (1980) **Pop Density:** 48.3
Land: 36.7 sq. mi.; **Water:** 0.2 sq. mi.
Name origin: For the biblical city.

Chatham
Town
ZIP: 12037 **Lat:** 42-25-04 N **Long:** 73-34-37 W
Pop: 4,413 (1990); 4,294 (1980) **Pop Density:** 82.8
Land: 53.3 sq. mi.; **Water:** 0.3 sq. mi.

*Chatham
Village
ZIP: 12037 **Lat:** 42-21-40 N **Long:** 73-35-52 W
Pop: 1,920 (1990); 889 (1980) **Pop Density:** 1600.0
Land: 1.2 sq. mi.; **Water:** 0.0 sq. mi. **Elev:** 473 ft.
Not coextensive with the town of the same name.
Name origin: For William Pitt, Lord Chatham.

Claverack
Town
ZIP: 12513 **Lat:** 42-13-00 N **Long:** 73-40-49 W
Pop: 6,414 (1990); 6,061 (1980) **Pop Density:** 134.5
Land: 47.7 sq. mi.; **Water:** 0.3 sq. mi.
Name origin: From Dutch meaning 'clover stretch.'

Clermont
Town
ZIP: 12526 **Lat:** 42-05-09 N **Long:** 73-51-17 W
Pop: 1,443 (1990); 1,269 (1980) **Pop Density:** 80.2
Land: 18.0 sq. mi.; **Water:** 1.2 sq. mi.

Copake
Town
ZIP: 12516 **Lat:** 42-07-44 N **Long:** 73-32-55 W
Pop: 3,118 (1990); 2,854 (1980) **Pop Density:** 76.0
Land: 41.0 sq. mi.; **Water:** 1.2 sq. mi.
Name origin: From an Indian term possibly meaning 'snake pond.'

Gallatin
Town
Lat: 42-02-59 N **Long:** 73-42-48 W
Pop: 1,658 (1990); 1,292 (1980) **Pop Density:** 42.2
Land: 39.3 sq. mi.; **Water:** 0.4 sq. mi.

Germantown
Town
ZIP: 12526 **Lat:** 42-08-02 N **Long:** 73-52-18 W
Pop: 2,010 (1990); 1,922 (1980) **Pop Density:** 164.8
Land: 12.2 sq. mi.; **Water:** 1.8 sq. mi.
Name origin: For the 1,200 settlers from the German Palatinates brought over in 1710.

Ghent
Town
ZIP: 12075 **Lat:** 42-18-33 N **Long:** 73-39-06 W
Pop: 4,812 (1990); 4,636 (1980) **Pop Density:** 106.5
Land: 45.2 sq. mi.; **Water:** 0.2 sq. mi.
Name origin: For the Belgian city.

Greenport
Town
Lat: 42-13-49 N **Long:** 73-47-44 W
Pop: 4,101 (1990); 4,029 (1980) **Pop Density:** 218.1
Land: 18.8 sq. mi.; **Water:** 1.7 sq. mi.

Hillsdale
Town
ZIP: 12529 **Lat:** 42-13-36 N **Long:** 73-32-14 W
Pop: 1,793 (1990); 1,648 (1980) **Pop Density:** 37.7
Land: 47.6 sq. mi.; **Water:** 0.1 sq. mi.

Hudson
City
ZIP: 12534 **Lat:** 42-15-04 N **Long:** 73-47-11 W
Pop: 8,034 (1990); 7,986 (1980) **Pop Density:** 3651.8
Land: 2.2 sq. mi.; **Water:** 0.2 sq. mi.
In southeastern NY on the east bank of the Hudson River, 28 mi. south of Albany.
Name origin: For the Hudson River.

Kinderhook
Town
ZIP: 12106 **Lat:** 42-24-46 N **Long:** 73-40-54 W
Pop: 8,112 (1990); 7,674 (1980) **Pop Density:** 255.1
Land: 31.8 sq. mi.; **Water:** 0.6 sq. mi.

*Kinderhook
Village
ZIP: 12106 **Lat:** 42-23-40 N **Long:** 73-42-14 W
Pop: 1,293 (1990); 1,377 (1980) **Pop Density:** 680.5
Land: 1.9 sq. mi.; **Water:** 0.0 sq. mi. **Elev:** 256 ft.
In southeastern NY, on the east bank of the Hudson River, southeast of Albany. Not coextensive with the town of the same name.
Name origin: Dutch 'children's corner,' so named by Henry Hudson (d.1611) because of the many Indian children assembled on the bluffs of the Hudson River to see his boat, *Half Moon.*

Livingston
Town
Lat: 42-08-23 N **Long:** 73-47-15 W
Pop: 3,582 (1990); 3,087 (1980) **Pop Density:** 93.8
Land: 38.2 sq. mi.; **Water:** 0.7 sq. mi.
Name origin: For Robert R. Livingston (1746–1813), a signer of the Declaration of Independence.

Lorenz Park
CDP
Lat: 42-15-49 N Long: 73-46-07 W
Pop: 1,811 (1990); 1,720 (1980)   **Pop Density:** 1006.1
Land: 1.8 sq. mi.; **Water:** 0.1 sq. mi.

New Lebanon
Town
ZIP: 12125   Lat: 42-27-59 N Long: 73-26-37 W
Pop: 2,379 (1990); 2,271 (1980)   **Pop Density:** 66.3
Land: 35.9 sq. mi.; **Water:** 0.1 sq. mi.

Niverville
CDP
ZIP: 12130   Lat: 42-26-43 N Long: 73-38-55 W
Pop: 1,809 (1990); 328 (1980)   **Pop Density:** 623.8
Land: 2.9 sq. mi.; **Water:** 0.5 sq. mi.

Philmont
Village
ZIP: 12565   Lat: 42-14-54 N Long: 73-38-47 W
Pop: 1,623 (1990); 1,539 (1980)   **Pop Density:** 1352.5
Land: 1.2 sq. mi.; **Water:** 0.0 sq. mi.

Stockport
Town
Lat: 42-19-04 N Long: 73-45-18 W
Pop: 3,085 (1990); 2,847 (1980)   **Pop Density:** 265.9
Land: 11.6 sq. mi.; **Water:** 1.5 sq. mi.

Stottville
CDP
Lat: 42-17-21 N Long: 73-45-08 W
Pop: 1,369 (1990); 225 (1980)   **Pop Density:** 311.1
Land: 4.4 sq. mi.; **Water:** 0.0 sq. mi.

Stuyvesant
Town
ZIP: 12173   Lat: 42-24-31 N Long: 73-45-20 W
Pop: 2,178 (1990); 2,216 (1980)   **Pop Density:** 86.8
Land: 25.1 sq. mi.; **Water:** 1.7 sq. mi.
Name origin: For Peter Stuyvesant (c.1610–72), Dutch governor of Nieuw Amsterdam, later named New York.

Taghkanic
Town
ZIP: 12502   Lat: 42-08-04 N Long: 73-40-05 W
Pop: 1,111 (1990); 1,101 (1980)   **Pop Density:** 27.8
Land: 40.0 sq. mi.; **Water:** 0.1 sq. mi.

Valatie
Village
ZIP: 12184   Lat: 42-24-53 N Long: 73-40-35 W
Pop: 1,487 (1990); 1,492 (1980)   **Pop Density:** 1062.1
Land: 1.4 sq. mi.; **Water:** 0.0 sq. mi.
Name origin: From Dutch meaning 'little valley.'

Cortland County
County Seat: Cortland (ZIP: 13045)

Pop: 48,963 (1990); 48,820 (1980)   **Pop Density:** 98.0
Land: 499.7 sq. mi.; **Water:** 1.9 sq. mi.   **Area Code:** 607

In south-central NY, south of Syracuse; organized Apr 8, 1808 from Onondaga County.

Name origin: For Pierre Van Cortland, Jr. (1762–1848), NY legislator, U.S. representative (1811–13), and banker.

Cincinnatus
Town
ZIP: 13040   Lat: 42-31-20 N Long: 75-55-28 W
Pop: 1,122 (1990); 1,151 (1980)   **Pop Density:** 44.2
Land: 25.4 sq. mi.; **Water:** 0.1 sq. mi.
Name origin: For the ancient Roman hero (6th century B.C.).

Cortland
City
ZIP: 13045   Lat: 42-36-03 N Long: 76-10-45 W
Pop: 19,801 (1990); 20,138 (1980)   **Pop Density:** 5077.2
Land: 3.9 sq. mi.; **Water:** 0.0 sq. mi.
In central NY, 30 mi. south of Syracuse. Settled 1792.
Name origin: For the prominent Van Cortlandt family, with a spelling alteration.

Cortlandville
Town
ZIP: 13045   Lat: 42-35-31 N Long: 76-09-25 W
Pop: 8,054 (1990); 8,299 (1980)   **Pop Density:** 161.7
Land: 49.8 sq. mi.; **Water:** 0.1 sq. mi.

Cortland West
CDP
Lat: 42-35-20 N Long: 76-13-40 W
Pop: 1,270 (1990); 1,149 (1980)   **Pop Density:** 239.6
Land: 5.3 sq. mi.; **Water:** 0.0 sq. mi.

Cuyler
Town
ZIP: 13050   Lat: 42-43-28 N Long: 75-56-20 W
Pop: 850 (1990); 846 (1980)   **Pop Density:** 19.5
Land: 43.5 sq. mi.; **Water:** 0.0 sq. mi.

Freetown
Town
ZIP: 13803   Lat: 42-31-15 N Long: 76-01-27 W
Pop: 688 (1990); 572 (1980)   **Pop Density:** 27.0
Land: 25.5 sq. mi.; **Water:** 0.1 sq. mi.

Harford
Town
ZIP: 13784   Lat: 42-26-34 N Long: 76-12-24 W
Pop: 886 (1990); 855 (1980)   **Pop Density:** 36.6
Land: 24.2 sq. mi.; **Water:** 0.0 sq. mi.

Homer
Town
ZIP: 13077   Lat: 42-39-56 N Long: 76-10-07 W
Pop: 6,508 (1990); 6,599 (1980)   **Pop Density:** 129.1
Land: 50.4 sq. mi.; **Water:** 0.3 sq. mi.

*Homer
Village
ZIP: 13077   Lat: 42-38-16 N Long: 76-11-00 W
Pop: 3,476 (1990); 21 (1980)   **Pop Density:** 2172.5
Land: 1.6 sq. mi.; **Water:** 0.0 sq. mi.   **Elev:** 1133 ft.
In central NY, 28 mi. south of Syracuse. Settled 1791. Not coextensive with the town of the same name.
Name origin: For the ancient Greek poet (9th–8th? century B.C.).

Lapeer
Town
ZIP: 13803   Lat: 42-26-47 N Long: 76-06-41 W
Pop: 613 (1990); 592 (1980)   **Pop Density:** 24.4
Land: 25.1 sq. mi.; **Water:** 0.1 sq. mi.   **Elev:** 1326 ft.

McGraw Village
ZIP: 13101 Lat: 42-35-31 N Long: 76-05-53 W
Pop: 1,074 (1990); 1,188 (1980) Pop Density: 1074.0
Land: 1.0 sq. mi.; Water: 0.0 sq. mi.

Marathon Town
ZIP: 13803 Lat: 42-27-08 N Long: 76-00-44 W
Pop: 2,019 (1990); 1,804 (1980) Pop Density: 80.8
Land: 25.0 sq. mi.; Water: 0.1 sq. mi.

*Marathon Village
ZIP: 13803 Lat: 42-26-34 N Long: 76-02-06 W
Pop: 1,107 (1990); 1,046 (1980) Pop Density: 1107.0
Land: 1.0 sq. mi.; Water: 0.0 sq. mi. Elev: 1020 ft.
Not coextensive with the town of the same name.

Munsons Corners CDP
ZIP: 13045 Lat: 42-34-48 N Long: 76-12-18 W
Pop: 2,436 (1990); 2,478 (1980) Pop Density: 1059.1
Land: 2.3 sq. mi.; Water: 0.0 sq. mi.

Preble Town
ZIP: 13141 Lat: 42-44-35 N Long: 76-07-55 W
Pop: 1,577 (1990); 1,637 (1980) Pop Density: 58.4
Land: 27.0 sq. mi.; Water: 0.6 sq. mi.

Scott Town
ZIP: 13077 Lat: 42-43-46 N Long: 76-13-54 W
Pop: 1,167 (1990); 1,193 (1980) Pop Density: 52.3
Land: 22.3 sq. mi.; Water: 0.1 sq. mi.

Solon Town
Lat: 42-36-07 N Long: 76-01-03 W
Pop: 1,008 (1990); 865 (1980) Pop Density: 33.9
Land: 29.7 sq. mi.; Water: 0.0 sq. mi.

Taylor Town
ZIP: 13040 Lat: 42-36-01 N Long: 75-55-47 W
Pop: 542 (1990); 481 (1980) Pop Density: 18.1
Land: 30.0 sq. mi.; Water: 0.1 sq. mi.

Truxton Town
ZIP: 13158 Lat: 42-42-36 N Long: 76-01-32 W
Pop: 1,064 (1990); 988 (1980) Pop Density: 23.8
Land: 44.7 sq. mi.; Water: 0.0 sq. mi.

Virgil Town
ZIP: 13045 Lat: 42-30-56 N Long: 76-09-55 W
Pop: 2,172 (1990); 2,053 (1980) Pop Density: 45.9
Land: 47.3 sq. mi.; Water: 0.0 sq. mi.
Name origin: For the Roman poet (70–19 B.C.).

Willet Town
ZIP: 13863 Lat: 42-26-51 N Long: 75-55-05 W
Pop: 892 (1990); 747 (1980) Pop Density: 34.6
Land: 25.8 sq. mi.; Water: 0.2 sq. mi.

Delaware County
County Seat: Delhi (ZIP: 13753)

Pop: 47,225 (1990); 46,824 (1980) Pop Density: 32.6
Land: 1446.4 sq. mi.; Water: 21.7 sq. mi. Area Code: 607

In south-central NY, east of Binghamton; organized Mar 10, 1797 from Ulster and Otsego counties.

Name origin: For the Delaware River, whose two main branches flow through the county.

Andes Town
ZIP: 13731 Lat: 42-07-45 N Long: 74-47-19 W
Pop: 1,291 (1990); 1,312 (1980) Pop Density: 11.8
Land: 109.1 sq. mi.; Water: 3.5 sq. mi.

*Andes Village
ZIP: 13731 Lat: 42-11-24 N Long: 74-47-03 W
Pop: 292 (1990); 372 (1980) Pop Density: 265.5
Land: 1.1 sq. mi.; Water: 0.0 sq. mi.
Not coextensive with the town of the same name.

Bovina Town
ZIP: 13740 Lat: 42-15-51 N Long: 74-45-30 W
Pop: 550 (1990); 562 (1980) Pop Density: 12.4
Land: 44.4 sq. mi.; Water: 0.2 sq. mi.

Colchester Town
ZIP: 13755 Lat: 42-02-25 N Long: 74-57-18 W
Pop: 1,928 (1990); 1,848 (1980) Pop Density: 14.0
Land: 137.4 sq. mi.; Water: 4.8 sq. mi.

Davenport Town
ZIP: 13750 Lat: 42-27-05 N Long: 74-54-31 W
Pop: 2,438 (1990); 1,971 (1980) Pop Density: 46.6
Land: 52.3 sq. mi.; Water: 0.1 sq. mi.

Delhi Town
ZIP: 13753 Lat: 42-16-37 N Long: 74-54-36 W
Pop: 5,015 (1990); 5,295 (1980) Pop Density: 77.6
Land: 64.6 sq. mi.; Water: 0.0 sq. mi.

*Delhi Village
ZIP: 13753 Lat: 42-16-47 N Long: 74-54-52 W
Pop: 3,064 (1990); 3,374 (1980) Pop Density: 957.5
Land: 3.2 sq. mi.; Water: 0.0 sq. mi. Elev: 1370 ft.
In southern NY on the Delaware River. Not coextensive with the town of the same name.
Name origin: Named by the local citizens for Delhi, India.

Deposit Town
Lat: 42-05-33 N Long: 75-22-21 W
Pop: 1,824 (1990); 1,810 (1980) Pop Density: 42.4
Land: 43.0 sq. mi.; Water: 3.1 sq. mi.

*Deposit Village
ZIP: 13754 Lat: 42-03-50 N Long: 75-24-55 W
Pop: 999 (1990); 880 (1980) Pop Density: 1665.0
Land: 0.6 sq. mi.; Water: 0.1 sq. mi. Elev: 991 ft.
Part of the town is in Broome County. Not coextensive with the town of the same name.

Fleischmanns
Village
ZIP: 12430 **Lat:** 42-09-20 N **Long:** 74-32-00 W
Pop: 351 (1990); 346 (1980) **Pop Density:** 501.4
Land: 0.7 sq. mi.; **Water:** 0.0 sq. mi.
Name origin: For a prominent citizen.

Franklin
Town
Lat: 42-20-02 N **Long:** 75-06-42 W
Pop: 2,471 (1990); 2,431 (1980) **Pop Density:** 30.3
Land: 81.5 sq. mi.; **Water:** 0.1 sq. mi.

*Franklin
Village
ZIP: 13775 **Lat:** 42-20-33 N **Long:** 75-09-59 W
Pop: 409 (1990); 440 (1980) **Pop Density:** 1363.3
Land: 0.3 sq. mi.; **Water:** 0.0 sq. mi.
Not coextensive with the town of the same name.

Hamden
Town
ZIP: 13782 **Lat:** 42-12-11 N **Long:** 74-58-51 W
Pop: 1,144 (1990); 1,276 (1980) **Pop Density:** 19.1
Land: 59.8 sq. mi.; **Water:** 0.0 sq. mi.

Hancock
Town
ZIP: 13783 **Lat:** 41-57-29 N **Long:** 75-09-44 W
Pop: 3,384 (1990); 3,497 (1980) **Pop Density:** 21.2
Land: 159.3 sq. mi.; **Water:** 2.5 sq. mi.

*Hancock
Village
ZIP: 13783 **Lat:** 41-57-12 N **Long:** 75-17-00 W
Pop: 1,330 (1990); 1,526 (1980) **Pop Density:** 831.3
Land: 1.6 sq. mi.; **Water:** 0.1 sq. mi.
Not coextensive with the town of the same name.
Name origin: For the prominent Hancock family.

Harpersfield
Town
ZIP: 13786 **Lat:** 42-26-42 N **Long:** 74-42-08 W
Pop: 1,450 (1990); 1,495 (1980) **Pop Density:** 34.4
Land: 42.1 sq. mi.; **Water:** 0.2 sq. mi.
In central NY, southwest of Albany. Settled 1771.
Name origin: For Col. John Harper.

Hobart
Village
ZIP: 13788 **Lat:** 42-22-16 N **Long:** 74-40-07 W
Pop: 385 (1990); 473 (1980) **Pop Density:** 770.0
Land: 0.5 sq. mi.; **Water:** 0.0 sq. mi.

Kortright
Town
ZIP: 13739 **Lat:** 42-23-45 N **Long:** 74-47-30 W
Pop: 1,410 (1990); 1,250 (1980) **Pop Density:** 22.5
Land: 62.6 sq. mi.; **Water:** 0.1 sq. mi.

Margaretville
Village
ZIP: 12455 **Lat:** 42-08-39 N **Long:** 74-39-07 W
Pop: 639 (1990); 755 (1980) **Pop Density:** 912.9
Land: 0.7 sq. mi.; **Water:** 0.0 sq. mi.

Masonville
Town
ZIP: 13804 **Lat:** 42-14-09 N **Long:** 75-20-47 W
Pop: 1,352 (1990); 1,156 (1980) **Pop Density:** 25.4
Land: 53.3 sq. mi.; **Water:** 0.1 sq. mi.

Meredith
Town
Lat: 42-21-53 N **Long:** 74-56-34 W
Pop: 1,513 (1990); 1,374 (1980) **Pop Density:** 26.0
Land: 58.2 sq. mi.; **Water:** 0.1 sq. mi.

Middletown
Town
Lat: 42-09-33 N **Long:** 74-37-30 W
Pop: 3,406 (1990); 3,555 (1980) **Pop Density:** 35.3
Land: 96.4 sq. mi.; **Water:** 0.9 sq. mi.

Roxbury
Town
ZIP: 12474 **Lat:** 42-18-01 N **Long:** 74-33-12 W
Pop: 2,388 (1990); 2,291 (1980) **Pop Density:** 27.4
Land: 87.2 sq. mi.; **Water:** 0.5 sq. mi.
In southern NY, 18 mi. east of Delhi.
Name origin: From an English term meaning 'rocky.'

Sidney
Town
ZIP: 13838 **Lat:** 42-18-24 N **Long:** 75-16-32 W
Pop: 6,667 (1990); 6,856 (1980) **Pop Density:** 130.2
Land: 51.2 sq. mi.; **Water:** 0.4 sq. mi.

*Sidney
Village
ZIP: 13838 **Lat:** 42-18-21 N **Long:** 75-23-51 W
Pop: 4,720 (1990); 4,861 (1980) **Pop Density:** 1966.7
Land: 2.4 sq. mi.; **Water:** 0.0 sq. mi. **Elev:** 992 ft.
Not coextensive with the town of the same name.

Stamford
Town
ZIP: 12167 **Lat:** 42-21-40 N **Long:** 74-39-44 W
Pop: 2,047 (1990); 2,038 (1980) **Pop Density:** 42.2
Land: 48.5 sq. mi.; **Water:** 0.0 sq. mi.

*Stamford
Village
ZIP: 12167 **Lat:** 42-24-31 N **Long:** 74-37-03 W
Pop: 1,211 (1990); 499 (1980) **Pop Density:** 931.5
Land: 1.3 sq. mi.; **Water:** 0.0 sq. mi. **Elev:** 1827 ft.
Not coextensive with the town of the same name.
Name origin: For a town in England.

Tompkins
Town
Lat: 42-06-40 N **Long:** 75-15-43 W
Pop: 994 (1990); 968 (1980) **Pop Density:** 10.1
Land: 98.2 sq. mi.; **Water:** 4.7 sq. mi.

Walton
Town
ZIP: 13856 **Lat:** 42-10-35 N **Long:** 75-07-32 W
Pop: 5,953 (1990); 5,839 (1980) **Pop Density:** 61.2
Land: 97.2 sq. mi.; **Water:** 0.4 sq. mi.

*Walton
Village
ZIP: 13856 **Lat:** 42-10-10 N **Long:** 75-07-50 W
Pop: 3,326 (1990); 3,329 (1980) **Pop Density:** 2217.3
Land: 1.5 sq. mi.; **Water:** 0.0 sq. mi. **Elev:** 1226 ft.
Not coextensive with the town of the same name.
Name origin: For an early settler.

Dutchess County
County Seat: Poughkeepsie (ZIP: 12601)

Pop: 259,462 (1990); 245,055 (1980)　　　　**Pop Density:** 323.7
Land: 801.7 sq. mi.; **Water:** 23.8 sq. mi.　　　　**Area Code:** 914
In southeastern NY, north of NYC; original county, organized Nov 1, 1683.
Name origin: For Mary (1658–1718), Duchess of York, wife of James, Duke of York and Albany, later James II, king of England; spelling is 17th–century variant of *duchess*.

Amenia　　　　　　　　　　　　　　　Town
ZIP: 12501　　　　**Lat:** 41-49-22 N **Long:** 73-33-32 W
Pop: 5,195 (1990); 6,299 (1980)　　**Pop Density:** 120.0
Land: 43.3 sq. mi.; **Water:** 0.2 sq. mi.

Arlington　　　　　　　　　　　　　　CDP
ZIP: 12603　　　　**Lat:** 41-41-44 N **Long:** 73-53-05 W
Pop: 11,948 (1990); 11,305 (1980)　　**Pop Density:** 2438.4
Land: 4.9 sq. mi.; **Water:** 0.0 sq. mi.

Beacon　　　　　　　　　　　　　　　City
ZIP: 12508　　　　**Lat:** 41-30-14 N **Long:** 73-57-57 W
Pop: 13,243 (1990); 12,937 (1980)　　**Pop Density:** 2817.7
Land: 4.7 sq. mi.; **Water:** 0.1 sq. mi.

In southeastern NY on the Hudson River across from Newburgh.
Name origin: For nearby Mt. Beacon.

Beekman　　　　　　　　　　　　　　Town
ZIP: 12570　　　　**Lat:** 41-35-58 N **Long:** 73-41-44 W
Pop: 10,447 (1990); 7,139 (1980)　　**Pop Density:** 348.2
Land: 30.0 sq. mi.; **Water:** 0.3 sq. mi.

Brinckerhoff　　　　　　　　　　　　CDP
　　　　　　　　　　Lat: 41-33-01 N **Long:** 73-52-11 W
Pop: 2,756 (1990); 3,030 (1980)　　**Pop Density:** 2505.5
Land: 1.1 sq. mi.; **Water:** 0.0 sq. mi.

Clinton　　　　　　　　　　　　　　Town
　　　　　　　　　　Lat: 41-52-02 N **Long:** 73-49-22 W
Pop: 3,760 (1990); 3,394 (1980)　　**Pop Density:** 97.7
Land: 38.5 sq. mi.; **Water:** 0.4 sq. mi.

Crown Heights　　　　　　　　　　　CDP
　　　　　　　　　　Lat: 41-38-13 N **Long:** 73-56-18 W
Pop: 3,200 (1990); 3,225 (1980)　　**Pop Density:** 1523.8
Land: 2.1 sq. mi.; **Water:** 0.6 sq. mi.

Dover　　　　　　　　　　　　　　　Town
ZIP: 12522　　　　**Lat:** 41-40-40 N **Long:** 73-34-10 W
Pop: 7,778 (1990); 7,261 (1980)　　**Pop Density:** 139.6
Land: 55.7 sq. mi.; **Water:** 0.6 sq. mi.

Dover Plains　　　　　　　　　　　　CDP
ZIP: 12522　　　　**Lat:** 41-44-42 N **Long:** 73-34-48 W
Pop: 1,847 (1990); 511 (1980)　　**Pop Density:** 1539.2
Land: 1.2 sq. mi.; **Water:** 0.0 sq. mi.

East Fishkill　　　　　　　　　　　　Town
ZIP: 12533　　　　**Lat:** 41-33-25 N **Long:** 73-46-50 W
Pop: 22,101 (1990); 18,091 (1980)　　**Pop Density:** 388.4
Land: 56.9 sq. mi.; **Water:** 0.4 sq. mi.

Fairview　　　　　　　　　　　　　　CDP
　　　　　　　　　　Lat: 41-43-54 N **Long:** 73-54-48 W
Pop: 4,811 (1990); 1,930 (1980)　　**Pop Density:** 1374.6
Land: 3.5 sq. mi.; **Water:** 0.1 sq. mi.

Fishkill　　　　　　　　　　　　　　Town
ZIP: 12524　　　　**Lat:** 41-30-32 N **Long:** 73-55-45 W
Pop: 17,655 (1990); 15,506 (1980)　　**Pop Density:** 642.0
Land: 27.5 sq. mi.; **Water:** 4.6 sq. mi.

*Fishkill　　　　　　　　　　　　　Village
ZIP: 12524　　　　**Lat:** 41-32-04 N **Long:** 73-53-38 W
Pop: 1,957 (1990); 1,555 (1980)　　**Pop Density:** 2174.4
Land: 0.9 sq. mi.; **Water:** 0.0 sq. mi.

In southeastern NY on the east bank of the Hudson River. Not coextensive with the town of the same name.
Name origin: For the stream that runs through it; from an anglicized version of a Dutch term meaning 'fish stream.'

Haviland　　　　　　　　　　　　　　CDP
　　　　　　　　　　Lat: 41-45-59 N **Long:** 73-54-06 W
Pop: 3,605 (1990); 3,578 (1980)　　**Pop Density:** 924.4
Land: 3.9 sq. mi.; **Water:** 0.0 sq. mi.

Hillside Lake　　　　　　　　　　　　CDP
　　　　　　　　　　Lat: 41-36-53 N **Long:** 73-47-55 W
Pop: 1,692 (1990); 1,382 (1980)　　**Pop Density:** 1128.0
Land: 1.5 sq. mi.; **Water:** 0.0 sq. mi.

Hopewell Junction　　　　　　　　　CDP
ZIP: 12533　　　　**Lat:** 41-35-08 N **Long:** 73-48-04 W
Pop: 1,786 (1990); 1,754 (1980)　　**Pop Density:** 637.9
Land: 2.8 sq. mi.; **Water:** 0.0 sq. mi.

Hyde Park　　　　　　　　　　　　　Town
ZIP: 12538　　　　**Lat:** 41-48-10 N **Long:** 73-54-37 W
Pop: 21,230 (1990); 20,768 (1980)　　**Pop Density:** 573.8
Land: 37.0 sq. mi.; **Water:** 2.9 sq. mi.

In southeastern NY on the east bank of the Hudson River, 6 mi. north of Poughkeepsie. Birthplace of Pres. Franklin D. Roosevelt (1882–1945).
Name origin: Previously called Stoutenburgh for first settler Jacobus Stoutenburgh.

La Grange　　　　　　　　　　　　　Town
ZIP: 12540　　　　**Lat:** 41-40-21 N **Long:** 73-48-10 W
Pop: 13,274 (1990); 12,375 (1980)　　**Pop Density:** 334.4
Land: 39.7 sq. mi.; **Water:** 0.2 sq. mi.

Milan　　　　　　　　　　　　　　　Town
　　　　　　　　　　Lat: 41-58-39 N **Long:** 73-46-51 W
Pop: 1,895 (1990); 1,668 (1980)　　**Pop Density:** 52.5
Land: 36.1 sq. mi.; **Water:** 0.2 sq. mi.
Name origin: For the Italian city.

Millbrook　　　　　　　　　　　　　Village
ZIP: 12545　　　　**Lat:** 41-47-03 N **Long:** 73-41-41 W
Pop: 1,339 (1990); 1,343 (1980)　　**Pop Density:** 704.7
Land: 1.9 sq. mi.; **Water:** 0.0 sq. mi.　　**Elev:** 569 ft.

Millerton Village
ZIP: 12546 Lat: 41-57-13 N Long: 73-30-40 W
Pop: 884 (1990); 1,013 (1980) Pop Density: 1473.3
Land: 0.6 sq. mi.; Water: 0.0 sq. mi. Elev: 701 ft.

Myers Corner CDP
ZIP: 12590 Lat: 41-35-49 N Long: 73-51-57 W
Pop: 5,599 (1990); 5,180 (1980) Pop Density: 1302.1
Land: 4.3 sq. mi.; Water: 0.0 sq. mi.

North East Town
ZIP: 12546 Lat: 41-56-53 N Long: 73-32-48 W
Pop: 2,918 (1990); 2,877 (1980) Pop Density: 67.2
Land: 43.4 sq. mi.; Water: 0.3 sq. mi.

Pawling Town
ZIP: 12564 Lat: 41-33-58 N Long: 73-35-50 W
Pop: 5,947 (1990); 5,795 (1980) Pop Density: 134.5
Land: 44.2 sq. mi.; Water: 0.8 sq. mi.

*Pawling Village
ZIP: 12564 Lat: 41-33-48 N Long: 73-35-59 W
Pop: 1,974 (1990); 1,996 (1980) Pop Density: 987.0
Land: 2.0 sq. mi.; Water: 0.0 sq. mi. Elev: 465 ft.

In southeastern NY, 20 mi. southeast of Poughkeepsie. Settled c. 1740 by English Quakers. Not coextensive with the town of the same name.

Pine Plains Town
ZIP: 12567 Lat: 41-58-17 N Long: 73-38-53 W
Pop: 2,287 (1990); 2,199 (1980) Pop Density: 74.0
Land: 30.9 sq. mi.; Water: 0.5 sq. mi.

Pleasant Valley Town
ZIP: 12569 Lat: 41-46-12 N Long: 73-48-17 W
Pop: 8,063 (1990); 6,892 (1980) Pop Density: 245.1
Land: 32.9 sq. mi.; Water: 0.3 sq. mi.

Poughkeepsie Town
ZIP: 12602 Lat: 41-40-15 N Long: 73-54-26 W
Pop: 40,143 (1990); 39,549 (1980) Pop Density: 1393.9
Land: 28.8 sq. mi.; Water: 2.4 sq. mi.

*Poughkeepsie City
ZIP: 12601 Lat: 41-41-44 N Long: 73-55-20 W
Pop: 28,844 (1990); 29,757 (1980) Pop Density: 5655.7
Land: 5.1 sq. mi.; Water: 0.6 sq. mi. Elev: 209 ft.

In southeastern NY on the east bank of the Hudson River, 65 mi. north of New York City. Not coextensive with the town of the same name.

Name origin: From an Algonquian Indian term whose meaning is unclear, but definitely referring to water. Possibly 'waterfall,' or perhaps 'pool at the base of the fall'; an early definition was given as 'safe harbor.'

Red Hook Town
ZIP: 12571 Lat: 42-00-56 N Long: 73-52-35 W
Pop: 9,565 (1990); 8,351 (1980) Pop Density: 260.6
Land: 36.7 sq. mi.; Water: 3.4 sq. mi.

*Red Hook Village
ZIP: 12571 Lat: 41-59-44 N Long: 73-52-35 W
Pop: 1,794 (1990); 1,692 (1980) Pop Density: 1630.9
Land: 1.1 sq. mi.; Water: 0.0 sq. mi. Elev: 218 ft.

In southeastern NY, northeast of Kingston on the east bank of the Hudson River. Not coextensive with the town of the same name.

Name origin: Origin of the name is in doubt. Previously

called Roode Hoeck by early Dutch navigators, possibly because of the profusion of red berries they saw growing on the hillsides, or perhaps for the Red Brick Tavern.

Red Oaks Mill CDP
Lat: 41-39-20 N Long: 73-52-24 W
Pop: 4,906 (1990); 2,287 (1980) Pop Density: 1401.7
Land: 3.5 sq. mi.; Water: 0.1 sq. mi.

Rhinebeck Town
ZIP: 12572 Lat: 41-55-38 N Long 73-53-56 W
Pop: 7,558 (1990); 7,062 (1980) Pop Density: 208.2
Land: 36.3 sq. mi.; Water: 3.6 sq. mi.

*Rhinebeck Village
ZIP: 12572 Lat: 41-55-43 N Long 73-54-27 W
Pop: 2,725 (1990); 2,542 (1980) Pop Density: 1703.1
Land: 1.6 sq. mi.; Water: 0.0 sq. mi. Elev: 200 ft.

Near the east bank of the Hudson River, 16 mi. north of Poughkeepsie. Not coextensive with the town of the same name.

Name origin: For the Hudson River's resemblance to the Rhine River in Germany.

Spackenkill CDP
Lat: 41-39-21 N Long: 73-54-50 W
Pop: 4,660 (1990); 4,848 (1980) Pop Density: 1606.9
Land: 2.9 sq. mi.; Water: 0.0 sq. mi.

Stanford Town
Lat: 41-53-20 N Long: 73-41-52 W
Pop: 3,495 (1990); 3,319 (1980) Pop Density: 69.9
Land: 50.0 sq. mi.; Water: 0.3 sq. mi.

Tivoli Village
ZIP: 12583 Lat: 42-03-33 N Long: 73-54-39 W
Pop: 1,035 (1990); 711 (1980) Pop Density: 575.0
Land: 1.8 sq. mi.; Water: 0.0 sq. mi.

In southeastern NY on the east bank of the Hudson River, northeast of Kingston.

Name origin: For the Chateau de Tivoli, the first unit of a projected model community built by Peter de Labigarre, who came to America after the French Revolution.

Union Vale Town
Lat: 41-40-40 N Long: 73-40-39 W
Pop: 3,577 (1990); 2,658 (1980) Pop Density: 94.9
Land: 37.7 sq. mi.; Water: 0.1 sq. mi.

Wappinger Town
ZIP: 12590 Lat: 41-35-24 N Long: 73-53-33 W
Pop: 26,008 (1990); 26,776 (1980) Pop Density: 952.7
Land: 27.3 sq. mi.; Water: 1.3 sq. mi.

Wappingers Falls Village
ZIP: 12590 Lat: 41-35-56 N Long: 73-55-06 W
Pop: 4,605 (1990); 955 (1980) Pop Density: 4186.4
Land: 1.1 sq. mi.; Water: 0.1 sq. mi.

In southeastern NY, 8 mi. south of Poughkeepsie near the Hudson River.

Name origin: For the 75-foot cascade in Wappinger Creek that has provided water power since the place was settled.

Washington Town
Lat: 41-47-28 N Long: 73-40-41 W
Pop: 4,479 (1990); 4,382 (1980) Pop Density: 75.8
Land: 59.1 sq. mi.; Water: 0.3 sq. mi.

Erie County
County Seat: Buffalo (ZIP: 14202)

Pop: 968,532 (1990); 1,015,470 (1980)　　　　**Pop Density:** 927.1
Land: 1044.7 sq. mi.; **Water:** 182.3 sq. mi.　　　**Area Code:** 716

On central western border of NY on Lake Erie, south of Niagara Falls; organized Apr 2, 1821 from Niagara County.

Name origin: For the Erie Indian tribe of Iroquoian linguistic stock, who lived along the southern shore of Lake Erie.

Akron
Village
ZIP: 14001　　　**Lat:** 43-01-09 N **Long:** 78-29-44 W
Pop: 2,906 (1990); 2,971 (1980)　　**Pop Density:** 1529.5
Land: 1.9 sq. mi.; **Water:** 0.0 sq. mi.

In northwestern NY on State 93, 15 mi. east of Buffalo.

Name origin: From the Greek term meaning 'summit.'

Alden
Town
ZIP: 14004　　　**Lat:** 42-54-10 N **Long:** 78-31-00 W
Pop: 10,372 (1990); 10,093 (1980)　　**Pop Density:** 300.6
Land: 34.5 sq. mi.; **Water:** 0.0 sq. mi.

*Alden
Village
ZIP: 14004　　　**Lat:** 42-53-54 N **Long:** 78-29-40 W
Pop: 2,457 (1990); 2,488 (1980)　　**Pop Density:** 910.0
Land: 2.7 sq. mi.; **Water:** 0.0 sq. mi.　　**Elev:** 866 ft.

In northwestern NY, 20 mi. northeast of Buffalo. Not coextensive with the town of the same name.

Name origin: For the English town.

Amherst
Town
ZIP: 14051　　　**Lat:** 43-00-35 N **Long:** 78-45-21 W
Pop: 111,711 (1990); 108,706 (1980)　　**Pop Density:** 2095.9
Land: 53.3 sq. mi.; **Water:** 0.3 sq. mi.

A major suburb of Buffalo, 10 mi. northeast of the city center.

Name origin: For British commander Lord Jeffrey Amherst (1717–97), hero of the French and Indian War.

Angola
Village
ZIP: 14006　　　**Lat:** 42-38-15 N **Long:** 79-01-47 W
Pop: 2,231 (1990); 2,292 (1980)　　**Pop Density:** 1593.6
Land: 1.4 sq. mi.; **Water:** 0.0 sq. mi.　　**Elev:** 689 ft.

Name origin: For the country in Africa.

Angola on the Lake
CDP
Lat: 42-39-17 N **Long:** 79-02-56 W
Pop: 1,719 (1990); 1,907 (1980)　　**Pop Density:** 687.6
Land: 2.5 sq. mi.; **Water:** 0.0 sq. mi.

Aurora
Town
ZIP: 14052　　　**Lat:** 42-44-27 N **Long:** 78-37-52 W
Pop: 13,433 (1990); 13,872 (1980)　　**Pop Density:** 369.0
Land: 36.4 sq. mi.; **Water:** 0.0 sq. mi.

In central NY on east shore of Cayuga Lake, 40 mi. southwest of Syracuse.

Billington Heights
CDP
Lat: 42-47-03 N **Long:** 78-37-35 W
Pop: 1,729 (1990); 740 (1980)　　**Pop Density:** 557.7
Land: 3.1 sq. mi.; **Water:** 0.0 sq. mi.

Blasdell
Village
ZIP: 14219　　　**Lat:** 42-47-46 N **Long:** 78-50-00 W
Pop: 2,900 (1990); 3,288 (1980)　　**Pop Density:** 2636.4
Land: 1.1 sq. mi.; **Water:** 0.0 sq. mi.

Boston
Town
ZIP: 14025　　　**Lat:** 42-39-18 N **Long:** 78-45-15 W
Pop: 7,445 (1990); 7,687 (1980)　　**Pop Density:** 208.0
Land: 35.8 sq. mi.; **Water:** 0.0 sq. mi.

Name origin: For Boston, MA.

Brant
Town
Lat: 42-35-20 N **Long:** 79-00-59 W
Pop: 2,119 (1990); 2,437 (1980)　　**Pop Density:** 87.2
Land: 24.3 sq. mi.; **Water:** 0.4 sq. mi.

Buffalo
City
ZIP: 14201　　　**Lat:** 42-53-23 N **Long:** 78-51-34 W
Pop: 328,123 (1990); 357,870 (1980)　　**Pop Density:** 8081.8
Land: 40.6 sq. mi.; **Water:** 11.9 sq. mi.

In northwestern NY at the northeast point of Lake Erie and on the Niagara River, 16 mi. southeast of Niagara Falls. A major industrial and transportation center of the U.S., nation's largest producer of flour, and one of the biggest grain-handling ports.

Name origin: For a creek that flows into Lake Erie. Origin of name is in dispute because no buffalo inhabited the area. Indians called it Beaver Creek and the place *te-osah-way* 'basswood,' for the trees. Bones of large animals may have led to the name *Buffalo*, although they were probably from elk or moose. Another theory is that the name derives from French *beau fleuve* 'beautiful river.'

Cattaraugus Reservation
Pop. Place
Lat: 42-32-17 N **Long:** 79-00-36 W
Pop: 1,789 (1990); 1,628 (1980)　　**Pop Density:** 70.7
Land: 25.3 sq. mi.; **Water:** 0.4 sq. mi.

Cheektowaga
Town
ZIP: 14225　　　**Lat:** 42-54-32 N **Long:** 78-45-00 W
Pop: 99,314 (1990); 109,442 (1980)　　**Pop Density:** 3366.6
Land: 29.5 sq. mi.; **Water:** 0.0 sq. mi.　　**Elev:** 659 ft.

In western NY, east of Buffalo.

Name origin: From the Iroquoian term probably meaning 'crab apple place.'

Clarence
Town
ZIP: 14031　　　**Lat:** 43-01-11 N **Long:** 78-38-06 W
Pop: 20,041 (1990); 18,146 (1980)　　**Pop Density:** 375.3
Land: 53.4 sq. mi.; **Water:** 0.0 sq. mi.

Colden
Town
ZIP: 14033　　　**Lat:** 42-39-09 N **Long:** 78-38-21 W
Pop: 2,899 (1990); 3,128 (1980)　　**Pop Density:** 81.2
Land: 35.7 sq. mi.; **Water:** 0.1 sq. mi.

Name origin: For historian Cadwallader Colden (1688–1776).

Collins
Town
ZIP: 14034　　　**Lat:** 42-29-34 N **Long:** 78-51-42 W
Pop: 6,020 (1990); 5,037 (1980)　　**Pop Density:** 125.2
Land: 48.1 sq. mi.; **Water:** 0.0 sq. mi.

Concord
Town
ZIP: 14141   **Lat:** 42-32-26 N **Long:** 78-42-30 W
Pop: 8,387 (1990); 8,171 (1980)   **Pop Density:** 119.6
Land: 70.1 sq. mi.; **Water:** 0.1 sq. mi.

Depew
Village
ZIP: 14043   **Lat:** 42-54-43 N **Long:** 78-42-16 W
Pop: 17,673 (1990); 12,768 (1980)   **Pop Density:** 3465.3
Land: 5.1 sq. mi.; **Water:** 0.0 sq. mi.

In western NY, 9 mi. east of Buffalo.
Name origin: For Chauncey M. Depew (1834–1928), railroad executive, Republican Party leader, and NY senator.

East Aurora
Village
ZIP: 14052   **Lat:** 42-46-00 N **Long:** 78-37-02 W
Pop: 6,647 (1990); 6,803 (1980)   **Pop Density:** 2658.8
Land: 2.5 sq. mi.; **Water:** 0.0 sq. mi.   **Elev:** 917 ft.

In western NY, 15 mi. east-southeast of Buffalo.

Eden
Town
ZIP: 14057   **Lat:** 42-39-06 N **Long:** 78-52-35 W
Pop: 7,416 (1990); 7,327 (1980)   **Pop Density:** 186.3
Land: 39.8 sq. mi.; **Water:** 0.0 sq. mi.

Name origin: For the biblical garden.

Elma
Town
ZIP: 14059   **Lat:** 42-49-17 N **Long:** 78-38-14 W
Pop: 10,355 (1990); 10,574 (1980)   **Pop Density:** 300.1
Land: 34.5 sq. mi.; **Water:** 0.0 sq. mi.

Name origin: For the many elm trees once abundant in the area.

Evans
Town
ZIP: 14006   **Lat:** 42-39-12 N **Long:** 79-00-34 W
Pop: 17,478 (1990); 17,961 (1980)   **Pop Density:** 418.1
Land: 41.8 sq. mi.; **Water:** 0.0 sq. mi.

Farnham
Village
ZIP: 14061   **Lat:** 42-35-48 N **Long:** 79-04-43 W
Pop: 427 (1990); 404 (1980)   **Pop Density:** 355.8
Land: 1.2 sq. mi.; **Water:** 0.0 sq. mi.   **Elev:** 631 ft.

Gowanda
Village
ZIP: 14070   **Lat:** 42-28-08 N **Long:** 78-56-14 W
Pop: 885 (1990); 849 (1980)   **Pop Density:** 1475.0
Land: 0.6 sq. mi.; **Water:** 0.0 sq. mi.

Name origin: Part of the town is also in Cattaraugus County. From an Indian term probably meaning 'surrounded by a hill.'

Grand Island
Town
ZIP: 14072   **Lat:** 43-01-19 N **Long:** 78-57-51 W
Pop: 17,561 (1990); 16,770 (1980)   **Pop Density:** 614.0
Land: 28.6 sq. mi.; **Water:** 4.5 sq. mi.

In western NY, an island in the upper Niagara River, northwest of Buffalo.
Name origin: For its descriptive connotations.

Hamburg
Town
ZIP: 14075   **Lat:** 42-44-29 N **Long:** 78-51-28 W
Pop: 53,735 (1990); 53,270 (1980)   **Pop Density:** 1301.1
Land: 41.3 sq. mi.; **Water:** 0.0 sq. mi.

*Hamburg
Village
ZIP: 14075   **Lat:** 42-43-26 N **Long:** 78-50-05 W
Pop: 10,442 (1990); 10,582 (1980)   **Pop Density:** 4176.8
Land: 2.5 sq. mi.; **Water:** 0.0 sq. mi.   **Elev:** 825 ft.

In western NY, 10 mi. south of Buffalo. Settled c. 1805 by German immigrants. Not coextensive with the town of the same name.
Name origin: For the German city.

Harris Hill
CDP
     Lat: 42-58-35 N **Long:** 78-40-57 W
Pop: 4,577 (1990); 5,087 (1980)   **Pop Density:** 1144.3
Land: 4.0 sq. mi.; **Water:** 0.0 sq. mi.

Holland
Town
ZIP: 14080   **Lat:** 42-38-51 N **Long:** 78-30-50 W
Pop: 3,572 (1990); 3,446 (1980)   **Pop Density:** 100.1
Land: 35.7 sq. mi.; **Water:** 0.0 sq. mi.
Name origin: For the Netherlands.

Kenmore
Village
ZIP: 14217   **Lat:** 42-57-53 N **Long:** 78-52-18 W
Pop: 17,180 (1990); 18,474 (1980)   **Pop Density:** 12271.4
Land: 1.4 sq. mi.; **Water:** 0.0 sq. mi.

In western NY on the Niagara River, 5 mi. north of Buffalo.
Name origin: For a prominent citizen.

Lackawanna
City
ZIP: 14218   **Lat:** 42-49-00 N **Long:** 78-49-45 W
Pop: 20,585 (1990); 22,701 (1980)   **Pop Density:** 3374.6
Land: 6.1 sq. mi.; **Water:** 0.0 sq. mi.

In western NY on Lake Erie, 5 mi. south of Buffalo.
Name origin: For the steel company that moved from Scranton, PA, and erected its plant here in 1899.

Lake Erie Beach
CDP
     Lat: 42-37-25 N **Long:** 79-04-39 W
Pop: 4,509 (1990); 4,625 (1980)   **Pop Density:** 1156.2
Land: 3.9 sq. mi.; **Water:** 0.0 sq. mi.

Lancaster
Town
ZIP: 14086   **Lat:** 42-54-25 N **Long:** 78-38-05 W
Pop: 32,181 (1990); 30,144 (1980)   **Pop Density:** 849.1
Land: 37.9 sq. mi.; **Water:** 0.0 sq. mi.

*Lancaster
Village
ZIP: 14086   **Lat:** 42-54-05 N **Long:** 78-40-11 W
Pop: 11,940 (1990); 13,056 (1980)   **Pop Density:** 4422.2
Land: 2.7 sq. mi.; **Water:** 0.0 sq. mi.

In western NY, 11 mi. east of Buffalo. Not coextensive with the town of the same name.
Name origin: For the English county.

Marilla
Town
ZIP: 14102   **Lat:** 42-49-36 N **Long:** 78-32-15 W
Pop: 5,250 (1990); 4,861 (1980)   **Pop Density:** 190.2
Land: 27.6 sq. mi.; **Water:** 0.0 sq. mi.

Newstead
Town
ZIP: 14001   **Lat:** 43-01-01 N **Long:** 78-31-31 W
Pop: 7,440 (1990); 7,231 (1980)   **Pop Density:** 145.6
Land: 51.1 sq. mi.; **Water:** 0.0 sq. mi.

North Boston
CDP
     Lat: 42-40-19 N **Long:** 78-47-02 W
Pop: 2,581 (1990); 2,743 (1980)   **Pop Density:** 629.5
Land: 4.1 sq. mi.; **Water:** 0.0 sq. mi.

North Collins
Town
ZIP: 14111   **Lat:** 42-34-06 N **Long:** 78-51-33 W
Pop: 3,502 (1990); 3,791 (1980)   **Pop Density:** 81.6
Land: 42.9 sq. mi.; **Water:** 0.2 sq. mi.

*North Collins — Village
ZIP: 14111 Lat: 42-35-40 N Long: 78-56-12 W
Pop: 1,335 (1990); 1,496 (1980) Pop Density: 1668.8
Land: 0.8 sq. mi.; Water: 0.0 sq. mi. Elev: 847 ft.

Settled c. 1809 by Quakers, who in 1813 built the first meetinghouse. Not coextensive with the town of the same name.

Orchard Park — Town
ZIP: 14127 Lat: 42-45-03 N Long: 78-44-51 W
Pop: 24,632 (1990); 24,359 (1980) Pop Density: 639.8
Land: 38.5 sq. mi.; Water: 0.1 sq. mi.

*Orchard Park — Village
ZIP: 14127 Lat: 42-45-48 N Long: 78-44-44 W
Pop: 3,280 (1990); 3,671 (1980) Pop Density: 2523.1
Land: 1.3 sq. mi.; Water: 0.0 sq. mi.

In western NY, 10 mi. southeast of Buffalo. Not coextensive with the town of the same name.

Name origin: For its descriptive connotations.

Sardinia — Town
ZIP: 14134 Lat: 42-33-06 N Long: 78-32-59 W
Pop: 2,667 (1990); 2,792 (1980) Pop Density: 53.0
Land: 50.3 sq. mi.; Water: 0.2 sq. mi.

Name origin: For the island in the Mediterranean.

Sloan — Village
ZIP: 14225 Lat: 42-53-31 N Long: 78-47-29 W
Pop: 3,830 (1990); 4,529 (1980) Pop Density: 4787.5
Land: 0.8 sq. mi.; Water: 0.0 sq. mi.

In western NY, an eastern suburb of Buffalo.

Springville — Village
ZIP: 14141 Lat: 42-30-33 N Long: 78-40-12 W
Pop: 4,310 (1990); 4,285 (1980) Pop Density: 1231.4
Land: 3.5 sq. mi.; Water: 0.0 sq. mi. Elev: 1341 ft.

In western NY, 27 mi. southeast of Buffalo.

Tonawanda — Town
ZIP: 14150 Lat: 42-58-56 N Long: 78-52-31 W
Pop: 82,464 (1990); 91,269 (1980) Pop Density: 4386.4
Land: 18.8 sq. mi.; Water: 1.7 sq. mi.

*Tonawanda — City
ZIP: 14150 Lat: 43-00-38 N Long: 78-52-54 W
Pop: 17,284 (1990); 18,693 (1980) Pop Density: 4548.4
Land: 3.8 sq. mi.; Water: 0.3 sq. mi.

In western NY, 9 mi. north of Buffalo. Not coextensive with the town of the same name.

Name origin: From an Iroquoian term probably meaning 'swift water.'

Tonawanda Reservation — Pop. Place
Lat: 43-04-24 N Long: 78-28-53 W
Pop: 10 (1990); 12 (1980) Pop Density: 5.6
Land: 1.8 sq. mi.; Water: 0.0 sq. mi.

Town Line — CDP
Lat: 42-53-05 N Long: 78-33-31 W
Pop: 2,721 (1990); 2,720 (1980) Pop Density: 591.5
Land: 4.6 sq. mi.; Water: 0.0 sq. mi.

Wales — Town
Lat: 42-43-45 N Long: 78-31-12 W
Pop: 2,917 (1990); 2,844 (1980) Pop Density: 81.9
Land: 35.6 sq. mi.; Water: 0.0 sq. mi.

Name origin: For the country.

West Seneca — Town
ZIP: 14224 Lat: 42-50-15 N Long: 78-45-05 W
Pop: 47,830 (1990); 51,210 (1980) Pop Density: 2235.0
Land: 21.4 sq. mi.; Water: 0.0 sq. mi.

In western NY, a southeastern suburb of Buffalo.

Williamsville — Village
ZIP: 14221 Lat: 42-57-46 N Long: 78-44-27 W
Pop: 5,583 (1990); 6,017 (1980) Pop Density: 4294.6
Land: 1.3 sq. mi.; Water: 0.0 sq. mi. Elev: 672 ft.

Essex County
County Seat: Elizabethtown (ZIP: 12932)

Pop: 37,152 (1990); 36,176 (1980) Pop Density: 20.7
Land: 1797.0 sq. mi.; Water: 119.7 sq. mi. Area Code: 518

On northeastern border of NY, southwest of Burlington, VT; organized Mar 1, 1799 from Clinton County.

Name origin: For the county of Essex, England.

Chesterfield — Town
Lat: 44-27-32 N Long: 73-29-06 W
Pop: 2,267 (1990); 2,398 (1980) Pop Density: 28.4
Land: 79.7 sq. mi.; Water: 26.4 sq. mi.

Crown Point — Town
ZIP: 12928 Lat: 43-57-48 N Long: 73-31-30 W
Pop: 1,963 (1990); 1,837 (1980) Pop Density: 26.1
Land: 75.3 sq. mi.; Water: 5.6 sq. mi.

Elizabethtown — Town
ZIP: 12932 Lat: 44-10-27 N Long: 73-37-01 W
Pop: 1,314 (1990); 1,267 (1980) Pop Density: 16.3
Land: 80.8 sq. mi.; Water: 1.4 sq. mi.

Essex — Town
ZIP: 12936 Lat: 44-16-59 N Long: 73-23-49 W
Pop: 687 (1990); 880 (1980) Pop Density: 21.9
Land: 31.3 sq. mi.; Water: 5.9 sq. mi.

Name origin: For the English county.

Jay — Town
ZIP: 12941 Lat: 44-22-35 N Long: 73-41-44 W
Pop: 2,244 (1990); 2,221 (1980) Pop Density: 32.5
Land: 69.0 sq. mi.; Water: 0.5 sq. mi.

Name origin: For John Jay (1745–1829), first U.S. Chief Justice.

Keene
Town

ZIP: 12942   **Lat:** 44-11-11 N   **Long:** 73-48-26 W
Pop: 908 (1990); 919 (1980)   **Pop Density:** 5.7
Land: 159.3 sq. mi.; **Water:** 0.6 sq. mi.

Keeseville
Village

ZIP: 12944   **Lat:** 44-30-06 N   **Long:** 73-28-48 W
Pop: 882 (1990); 970 (1980)   **Pop Density:** 1764.0
Land: 0.5 sq. mi.; **Water:** 0.0 sq. mi.   **Elev:** 503 ft.

In northeastern NY, near the western shore of Lake Champlain. Part of the town is in Clinton County.
Name origin: For John Keese, a Quaker settler who arrived in 1806.

Lake Placid
Village

ZIP: 12946   **Lat:** 44-17-00 N   **Long:** 73-59-06 W
Pop: 2,485 (1990); 2,490 (1980)   **Pop Density:** 1775.0
Land: 1.4 sq. mi.; **Water:** 0.1 sq. mi.

In northeastern NY in the Adirondack Mts.
Name origin: For the nearby lake resort.

Lewis
Town

ZIP: 12950   **Lat:** 44-17-52 N   **Long:** 73-33-58 W
Pop: 1,057 (1990); 922 (1980)   **Pop Density:** 12.6
Land: 83.9 sq. mi.; **Water:** 0.2 sq. mi.

Minerva
Town

ZIP: 12851   **Lat:** 43-51-10 N   **Long:** 74-03-12 W
Pop: 758 (1990); 781 (1980)   **Pop Density:** 4.9
Land: 155.3 sq. mi.; **Water:** 3.5 sq. mi.

Mineville-Witherbee
CDP

     Lat: 44-05-20 N   **Long:** 73-31-39 W
Pop: 1,740 (1990); 1,925 (1980)   **Pop Density:** 414.3
Land: 4.2 sq. mi.; **Water:** 0.0 sq. mi.

Moriah
Town

ZIP: 12960   **Lat:** 44-03-16 N   **Long:** 73-31-40 W
Pop: 4,884 (1990); 5,139 (1980)   **Pop Density:** 73.4
Land: 66.5 sq. mi.; **Water:** 6.6 sq. mi.

Name origin: For the biblical mountain.

Newcomb
Town

ZIP: 12852   **Lat:** 44-01-14 N   **Long:** 74-08-06 W
Pop: 544 (1990); 681 (1980)   **Pop Density:** 2.5
Land: 218.7 sq. mi.; **Water:** 6.5 sq. mi.

North Elba
Town

ZIP: 12946   **Lat:** 44-15-39 N   **Long:** 74-00-27 W
Pop: 7,870 (1990); 6,597 (1980)   **Pop Density:** 51.8
Land: 151.9 sq. mi.; **Water:** 4.6 sq. mi.

North Hudson
Town

ZIP: 12855   **Lat:** 43-59-02 N   **Long:** 73-47-35 W
Pop: 266 (1990); 179 (1980)   **Pop Density:** 1.4
Land: 186.9 sq. mi.; **Water:** 3.1 sq. mi.

Port Henry
Village

ZIP: 12974   **Lat:** 44-02-49 N   **Long** 73-27-38 W
Pop: 1,263 (1990); 1,450 (1980)   **Pop Density:** 1052.5
Land: 1.2 sq. mi.; **Water:** 0.3 sq. mi.   **Elev:** 108 ft.

St. Armand
Town

     Lat: 44-22-20 N   **Long:** 74-03-41 W
Pop: 1,318 (1990); 1,064 (1980)   **Pop Density:** 23.3
Land: 56.6 sq. mi.; **Water:** 0.9 sq. mi.

Saranac Lake
Village

ZIP: 12983   **Lat:** 44-19-26 N   **Long:** 74-07-19 W
Pop: 1,365 (1990); 1,288 (1980)   **Pop Density:** 1365.0
Land: 1.0 sq. mi.; **Water:** 0.1 sq. mi.   **Elev:** 1547 ft.

Part of the town is also in Franklin County.

Schroon
Town

     Lat: 43-50-42 N   **Long:** 73-46-05 W
Pop: 1,721 (1990); 1,606 (1980)   **Pop Density:** 12.8
Land: 134.4 sq. mi.; **Water:** 8.1 sq. mi.

Ticonderoga
Town

ZIP: 12883   **Lat:** 43-49-35 N   **Long:** 73-29-35 W
Pop: 5,149 (1990); 5,436 (1980)   **Pop Density:** 62.9
Land: 81.9 sq. mi.; **Water:** 6.5 sq. mi.

*Ticonderoga
Village

ZIP: 12883   **Lat:** 43-50-49 N   **Long:** 73-25-32 W
Pop: 2,770 (1990); 2,938 (1980)   **Pop Density:** 1978.6
Land: 1.4 sq. mi.; **Water:** 0.0 sq. mi.   **Elev:** 154 ft.

In northeastern NY on the neck of land between Lake George and Lake Champlain. Not coextensive with the town of the same name.
Name origin: From Iroquoian Indian *cheonderoga*, probably 'between two waters' or 'where the waters meet.'

Westport
Town

ZIP: 12993   **Lat:** 44-11-10 N   **Long:** 73-26-55 W
Pop: 1,446 (1990); 1,439 (1980)   **Pop Density:** 24.8
Land: 58.4 sq. mi.; **Water:** 8.5 sq. mi.

*Westport
Village

ZIP: 12993   **Lat:** 44-10-43 N   **Long:** 73-26-09 W
Pop: 539 (1990); 613 (1980)   **Pop Density:** 539.0
Land: 1.0 sq. mi.; **Water:** 0.0 sq. mi.

Not coextensive with the town of the same name.

Willsboro
Town

ZIP: 12996   **Lat:** 44-23-41 N   **Long:** 73-23-24 W
Pop: 1,736 (1990); 1,759 (1980)   **Pop Density:** 41.4
Land: 41.9 sq. mi.; **Water:** 30.7 sq. mi.

In northeastern NY, 25 mi. south of Plattsburg.

Wilmington
Town

ZIP: 12997   **Lat:** 44-21-56 N   **Long:** 73-50-29 W
Pop: 1,020 (1990); 1,051 (1980)   **Pop Density:** 15.6
Land: 65.2 sq. mi.; **Water:** 0.3 sq. mi.

Franklin County
County Seat: Malone (ZIP: 12953)

Pop: 46,540 (1990); 44,929 (1980)   **Pop Density:** 28.5
Land: 1631.6 sq. mi.; **Water:** 65.9 sq. mi.   **Area Code:** 518

On northeastern border of NY, south of Montreal, prov. of Quebec, Canada; organized Mar 11, 1808 from Clinton County.

Name origin: For Benjamin Franklin (1706–90), U.S. patriot, diplomat, and statesman.

Altamont   Town
ZIP: 12986   **Lat:** 44-14-26 N **Long:** 74-28-31 W
Pop: 6,199 (1990); 6,318 (1980)   **Pop Density:** 52.7
Land: 117.6 sq. mi.; **Water:** 12.5 sq. mi.

Bangor   Town
                       Lat: 44-50-26 N **Long:** 74-25-52 W
Pop: 2,080 (1990); 1,960 (1980)   **Pop Density:** 48.3
Land: 43.1 sq. mi.; **Water:** 0.0 sq. mi.
Name origin: For the town in Wales.

Bellmont   Town
                       Lat: 44-45-21 N **Long:** 74-06-22 W
Pop: 1,246 (1990); 1,045 (1980)   **Pop Density:** 7.6
Land: 164.4 sq. mi.; **Water:** 2.8 sq. mi.

Bombay   Town
ZIP: 12914   **Lat:** 44-55-22 N **Long:** 74-35-06 W
Pop: 1,158 (1990); 1,247 (1980)   **Pop Density:** 32.3
Land: 35.8 sq. mi.; **Water:** 0.1 sq. mi.
Name origin: For Bombay, India.

Brandon   Town
                       Lat: 44-44-48 N **Long:** 74-25-08 W
Pop: 394 (1990); 499 (1980)   **Pop Density:** 9.5
Land: 41.3 sq. mi.; **Water:** 0.0 sq. mi.

Brighton   Town
                       Lat: 44-28-44 N **Long:** 74-14-51 W
Pop: 1,511 (1990); 1,625 (1980)   **Pop Density:** 19.4
Land: 78.0 sq. mi.; **Water:** 5.0 sq. mi.

Brushton   Village
ZIP: 12916   **Lat:** 44-49-51 N **Long:** 74-30-46 W
Pop: 522 (1990); 577 (1980)   **Pop Density:** 1740.0
Land: 0.3 sq. mi.; **Water:** 0.0 sq. mi.

Burke   Town
ZIP: 12917   **Lat:** 44-55-35 N **Long:** 74-11-13 W
Pop: 1,231 (1990); 1,237 (1980)   **Pop Density:** 27.7
Land: 44.4 sq. mi.; **Water:** 0.0 sq. mi.

*Burke   Village
ZIP: 12917   **Lat:** 44-54-12 N **Long:** 74-10-15 W
Pop: 209 (1990); 226 (1980)   **Pop Density:** 696.7
Land: 0.3 sq. mi.; **Water:** 0.0 sq. mi.
Not coextensive with the town of the same name.

Chateaugay   Town
ZIP: 12920   **Lat:** 44-55-49 N **Long:** 74-04-20 W
Pop: 1,659 (1990); 1,863 (1980)   **Pop Density:** 33.4
Land: 49.7 sq. mi.; **Water:** 0.0 sq. mi.

*Chateaugay   Village
ZIP: 12920   **Lat:** 44-55-38 N **Long:** 74-04-50 W
Pop: 845 (1990); 869 (1980)   **Pop Density:** 845.0
Land: 1.0 sq. mi.; **Water:** 0.0 sq. mi.   **Elev:** 972 ft.
Not coextensive with the town of the same name.
Name origin: For the adjoining Canadian land grant owned by Charles Lemoyne, founder of an eminent Canadian family.

Constable   Town
ZIP: 12926   **Lat:** 44-56-26 N **Long:** 74-17-26 W
Pop: 1,203 (1990); 1,218 (1980)   **Pop Density:** 36.7
Land: 32.8 sq. mi.; **Water:** 0.0 sq. mi.

Dickinson   Town
                       Lat: 44-43-42 N **Long:** 74-32-55 W
Pop: 751 (1990); 786 (1980)   **Pop Density:** 17.0
Land: 44.3 sq. mi.; **Water:** 0.0 sq. mi.

Duane   Town
ZIP: 12953   **Lat:** 44-36-59 N **Long:** 74-15-55 W
Pop: 152 (1990); 184 (1980)   **Pop Density:** 2.0
Land: 75.1 sq. mi.; **Water:** 2.9 sq. mi.

Fort Covington   Town
ZIP: 12937   **Lat:** 44-56-54 N **Long:** 74-29-30 W
Pop: 1,676 (1990); 1,804 (1980)   **Pop Density:** 45.5
Land: 36.8 sq. mi.; **Water:** 0.0 sq. mi.
On the northern border of NY with Quebec, Canada.
Name origin: In 1812 Gen. Wade Hampton (1751?–1835) built a blockhouse here and named it for Gen. Leonard Covington, who became a hero of the War of 1812.

Franklin   Town
ZIP: 12983   **Lat:** 44-31-45 N **Long:** 74-02-31 W
Pop: 1,016 (1990); 926 (1980)   **Pop Density:** 6.0
Land: 170.2 sq. mi.; **Water:** 5.0 sq. mi.

Harrietstown   Town
ZIP: 12983   **Lat:** 44-15-07 N **Long:** 74-14-51 W
Pop: 5,621 (1990); 5,604 (1980)   **Pop Density:** 28.6
Land: 196.8 sq. mi.; **Water:** 16.8 sq. mi.

Malone   Town
ZIP: 12953   **Lat:** 44-47-19 N **Long:** 74-17-12 W
Pop: 12,982 (1990); 11,276 (1980)   **Pop Density:** 127.4
Land: 101.9 sq. mi.; **Water:** 0.9 sq. mi.

*Malone   Village
ZIP: 12953   **Lat:** 44-50-53 N **Long:** 74-17-29 W
Pop: 6,777 (1990); 7,668 (1980)   **Pop Density:** 2259.0
Land: 3.0 sq. mi.; **Water:** 0.0 sq. mi.   **Elev:** 722 ft.
In northeastern NY, 45 mi. west-northwest of Plattsburg. Settled 1802. Not coextensive with the town of the same name.
Name origin: For Edmund Malone (1741–1812), Shakespearean scholar.

Moira
Town
ZIP: 12957   Lat: 44-49-26 N Long: 74-33-42 W
Pop: 2,684 (1990); 2,624 (1980)   Pop Density: 59.4
Land: 45.2 sq. mi.; Water: 0.0 sq. mi.
Name origin: From a personal name.

St. Regis Reservation
Pop. Place
Lat: 44-58-54 N Long: 74-38-58 W
Pop: 1,978 (1990); 1,802 (1980)   Pop Density: 104.1
Land: 19.0 sq. mi.; Water: 2.0 sq. mi.

Santa Clara
Town
ZIP: 12980   Lat: 44-27-46 N Long: 74-23-30 W
Pop: 311 (1990); 310 (1980)   Pop Density: 1.8
Land: 175.0 sq. mi.; Water: 16.7 sq. mi.

Saranac Lake
Village
ZIP: 12983   Lat: 44-19-29 N Long: 74-08-13 W
Pop: 4,012 (1990); 4,116 (1980)   Pop Density: 2228.9
Land: 1.8 sq. mi.; Water: 0.1 sq. mi.   Elev: 1547 ft.
Part of the town is also in Essex County.

Tupper Lake
Village
ZIP: 12986   Lat: 44-14-03 N Long: 74-28-08 W
Pop: 4,087 (1990); 4,478 (1980)   Pop Density: 2270.6
Land: 1.8 sq. mi.; Water: 0.0 sq. mi.   Elev: 560 ft.

Waverly
Town
Lat: 44-32-23 N Long: 74-31-26 W
Pop: 1,068 (1990); 1,110 (1980)   Pop Density: 8.5
Land: 125.2 sq. mi.; Water: 1.2 sq. mi.

Westville
Town
Lat: 44-56-35 N Long: 74-23-05 W
Pop: 1,620 (1990); 1,491 (1980)   Pop Density: 46.6
Land: 34.8 sq. mi.; Water: 0.0 sq. mi.

Fulton County
County Seat: Johnstown (ZIP: 12095)

Pop: 54,191 (1990); 55,153 (1980)   Pop Density: 109.2
Land: 496.2 sq. mi.; Water: 36.8 sq. mi.   Area Code: 518

In east-central NY, east of Utica; organized Apr 18, 1838 from Montgomery County.

Name origin: For Robert Fulton (1765–1815), developer of the *Clermont*, the first commercially successful steamboat.

Bleecker
Town
ZIP: 12078   Lat: 43-11-12 N Long: 74-22-48 W
Pop: 515 (1990); 463 (1980)   Pop Density: 9.0
Land: 57.2 sq. mi.; Water: 2.3 sq. mi.

Broadalbin
Town
ZIP: 12025   Lat: 43-04-36 N Long: 74-09-13 W
Pop: 4,397 (1990); 4,074 (1980)   Pop Density: 138.7
Land: 31.7 sq. mi.; Water: 8.0 sq. mi.

*Broadalbin
Village
ZIP: 12025   Lat: 43-03-34 N Long: 74-11-51 W
Pop: 1,397 (1990); 1,363 (1980)   Pop Density: 1397.0
Land: 1.0 sq. mi.; Water: 0.0 sq. mi.
Settled 1770. Not coextensive with the town of the same name.
Name origin: Adapted from Breadalbane, a district of Scotland; named by Scottish-born settlers when the post office was established in 1804.

Caroga
Town
ZIP: 12032   Lat: 43-10-07 N Long: 74-30-25 W
Pop: 1,337 (1990); 1,177 (1980)   Pop Density: 26.3
Land: 50.9 sq. mi.; Water: 3.4 sq. mi.

Dolgeville
Village
ZIP: 13329   Lat: 43-06-00 N Long: 74-45-56 W
Pop: 108 (1990); 162 (1980)   Pop Density: 360.0
Land: 0.3 sq. mi.; Water: 0.0 sq. mi.   Elev: 802 ft.
Part of the county is in Herkimer County.
Name origin: Named in 1881 for businessman Alfred Dolge, who transformed the village of Brockett's Bridge into a factory town of several thousand workers.

Ephratah
Town
Lat: 43-02-27 N Long: 74-32-57 W
Pop: 1,556 (1990); 1,564 (1980)   Pop Density: 39.7
Land: 39.2 sq. mi.; Water: 0.2 sq. mi.

Gloversville
City
ZIP: 12078   Lat: 43-03-00 N Long: 74-20-49 W
Pop: 16,656 (1990); 17,836 (1980)   Pop Density: 3331.2
Land: 5.0 sq. mi.; Water: 0.0 sq. mi.
In eastern NY, northwest of Schenectady.
Name origin: For its major industry.

Johnstown
City
ZIP: 12095   Lat: 43-00-30 N Long: 74-22-27 W
Pop: 9,058 (1990); 9,360 (1980)   Pop Density: 1927.2
Land: 4.7 sq. mi.; Water: 0.0 sq. mi.
In eastern NY on the Cayadutta Plateau, northwest of Schenectady.
Name origin: For Sir William Johnson (1715–74), who settled here in 1762 at the height of his picturesque life as a frontier statesman and empire builder.

*Johnstown
Town
ZIP: 12095   Lat: 43-02-59 N Long: 74-24-01 W
Pop: 6,418 (1990); 6,719 (1980)   Pop Density: 91.0
Land: 70.5 sq. mi.; Water: 1.2 sq. mi.

Mayfield
Town
ZIP: 12117   Lat: 43-07-29 N Long: 74-15-45 W
Pop: 5,738 (1990); 5,439 (1980)   Pop Density: 98.3
Land: 58.4 sq. mi.; Water: 6.3 sq. mi.

*Mayfield
Village
ZIP: 12117 **Lat:** 43-06-07 N **Long:** 74-15-59 W
Pop: 817 (1990); 944 (1980) **Pop Density:** 907.8
Land: 0.9 sq. mi.; **Water:** 0.2 sq. mi.

Not coextensive with the town of the same name.

Northampton
Town
ZIP: 12134 **Lat:** 43-11-26 N **Long:** 74-10-32 W
Pop: 2,705 (1990); 2,829 (1980) **Pop Density:** 128.2
Land: 21.1 sq. mi.; **Water:** 13.7 sq. mi.

Northville
Village
ZIP: 12134 **Lat:** 43-13-19 N **Long:** 74-10-15 W
Pop: 1,180 (1990); 1,304 (1980) **Pop Density:** 1072.7
Land: 1.1 sq. mi.; **Water:** 0.4 sq. mi.

Oppenheim
Town
ZIP: 13329 **Lat:** 43-05-02 N **Long:** 74-41-08 W
Pop: 1,848 (1990); 1,806 (1980) **Pop Density:** 32.8
Land: 56.3 sq. mi.; **Water:** 0.2 sq. mi.

Perth
Town
Lat: 43-00-21 N **Long:** 74-12-19 W
Pop: 3,377 (1990); 3,261 (1980) **Pop Density:** 129.4
Land: 26.1 sq. mi.; **Water:** 0.0 sq. mi.

Stratford
Town
ZIP: 13470 **Lat:** 43-10-41 N **Long:** 74-37-55 W
Pop: 586 (1990); 625 (1980) **Pop Density:** 7.8
Land: 75.2 sq. mi.; **Water:** 1.5 sq. mi.

Genesee County
County Seat: Batavia (ZIP: 14020)

Pop: 60,060 (1990); 59,400 (1980) **Pop Density:** 121.5
Land: 494.1 sq. mi.; **Water:** 1.2 sq. mi. **Area Code:** 716

In northwestern NY, southeast of Rochester; organized Mar 30, 1802 from Ontario County.

Name origin: From the Iroquoian word probably meaning 'beautiful valley.'

Alabama
Town
Lat: 43-05-23 N **Long:** 78-22-59 W
Pop: 1,998 (1990); 1,926 (1980) **Pop Density:** 46.9
Land: 42.6 sq. mi.; **Water:** 0.2 sq. mi.

In northwestern NY, 35 mi. west of Buffalo on State Highway 63.

Name origin: For the state.

Alexander
Town
ZIP: 14005 **Lat:** 42-54-21 N **Long:** 78-15-09 W
Pop: 2,233 (1990); 2,367 (1980) **Pop Density:** 62.9
Land: 35.5 sq. mi.; **Water:** 0.0 sq. mi.

*Alexander
Village
ZIP: 14005 **Lat:** 42-54-06 N **Long:** 78-15-38 W
Pop: 445 (1990); 483 (1980) **Pop Density:** 1112.5
Land: 0.4 sq. mi.; **Water:** 0.0 sq. mi. **Elev:** 940 ft.

In northwestern NY, 30 mi. east of Buffalo. Not coextensive with the town of the same name.

Name origin: For Alexander Rea, first settler and state senator.

Attica
Village
ZIP: 14011 **Lat:** 42-52-36 N **Long:** 78-16-39 W
Pop: 8 (1990); 16 (1980) **Pop Density:** 40.0
Land: 0.2 sq. mi.; **Water:** 0.0 sq. mi.

In northwestern NY. Site of the Attica Correctional Facility. Most of the village is in Wyoming County.

Name origin: For the district in ancient Greece.

Batavia
City
ZIP: 14020 **Lat:** 42-59-55 N **Long:** 78-10-52 W
Pop: 16,310 (1990); 16,703 (1980) **Pop Density:** 3136.5
Land: 5.2 sq. mi.; **Water:** 0.1 sq. mi. **Elev:** 895 ft.

In northwestern NY, 33 mi. west-southwest of Rochester. Not coextensive with the town of the same name.

Name origin: For the area between the North Sea and the Rhine River (in present-day Netherlands) to which the proprietors belonged.

*Batavia
Town
ZIP: 14020 **Lat:** 43-00-20 N **Long:** 78-13-41 W
Pop: 6,055 (1990); 5,565 (1980) **Pop Density:** 125.1
Land: 48.4 sq. mi.; **Water:** 0.0 sq. mi.

Bergen
Town
ZIP: 14416 **Lat:** 43-05-24 N **Long:** 77-58-40 W
Pop: 2,794 (1990); 2,568 (1980) **Pop Density:** 101.2
Land: 27.6 sq. mi.; **Water:** 0.0 sq. mi.

*Bergen
Village
ZIP: 14416 **Lat:** 43-04-59 N **Long:** 77-56-31 W
Pop: 1,103 (1990); 976 (1980) **Pop Density:** 1838.3
Land: 0.6 sq. mi.; **Water:** 0.0 sq. mi. **Elev:** 606 ft.

Not coextensive with the town of the same name.

Bethany
Town
Lat: 42-54-31 N **Long:** 78-08-04 W
Pop: 1,808 (1990); 1,876 (1980) **Pop Density:** 50.1
Land: 36.1 sq. mi.; **Water:** 0.0 sq. mi.

Byron
Town
ZIP: 14422 **Lat:** 43-05-04 N **Long:** 78-04-02 W
Pop: 2,345 (1990); 2,242 (1980) **Pop Density:** 72.8
Land: 32.2 sq. mi.; **Water:** 0.1 sq. mi.

Name origin: For the English poet George Gordon, Lord Byron (1788–1824).

Corfu
Village
ZIP: 14036 **Lat:** 42-57-37 N **Long:** 78-24-01 W
Pop: 755 (1990); 689 (1980) **Pop Density:** 755.0
Land: 1.0 sq. mi.; **Water:** 0.0 sq. mi. **Elev:** 861 ft.

Name origin: For the Greek island.

Darien
Town
Lat: 42-54-48 N **Long:** 78-23-21 W
Pop: 2,979 (1990); 2,950 (1980) **Pop Density:** 62.7
Land: 47.5 sq. mi.; **Water:** 0.1 sq. mi.

Elba   Town
ZIP: 14058   **Lat:** 43-05-31 N **Long:** 78-10-11 W
Pop: 2,407 (1990); 2,487 (1980)   **Pop Density:** 67.4
Land: 35.7 sq. mi.; **Water:** 0.0 sq. mi.

*Elba   Village
ZIP: 14058   **Lat:** 43-04-30 N **Long:** 78-11-19 W
Pop: 703 (1990); 750 (1980)   **Pop Density:** 703.0
Land: 1.0 sq. mi.; **Water:** 0.0 sq. mi.   **Elev:** 761 ft.
Not coextensive with the town of the same name.

Le Roy   Town
ZIP: 14482   **Lat:** 42-59-29 N **Long:** 77-58-04 W
Pop: 8,176 (1990); 8,019 (1980)   **Pop Density:** 193.7
Land: 42.2 sq. mi.; **Water:** 0.0 sq. mi.

*Le Roy   Village
ZIP: 14482   **Lat:** 42-58-40 N **Long:** 77-59-27 W
Pop: 4,974 (1990); 4,900 (1980)   **Pop Density:** 1842.2
Land: 2.7 sq. mi.; **Water:** 0.0 sq. mi.   **Elev:** 869 ft.
In western NY, 24 mi. southwest of Rochester. Not coextensive with the town of the same name.
Name origin: For a prominent citizen.

Oakfield   Town
ZIP: 14125   **Lat:** 43-05-03 N **Long:** 78-16-27 W
Pop: 3,312 (1990); 3,213 (1980)   **Pop Density:** 140.9
Land: 23.5 sq. mi.; **Water:** 0.5 sq. mi.

*Oakfield   Village
ZIP: 14125   **Lat:** 43-03-51 N **Long:** 78-16-14 W
Pop: 1,818 (1990); 1,791 (1980)   **Pop Density:** 2597.1
Land: 0.7 sq. mi.; **Water:** 0.0 sq. mi.   **Elev:** 753 ft.
Not coextensive with the town of the same name.

Pavilion   Town
ZIP: 14525   **Lat:** 42-54-09 N **Long:** 78-00-29 W
Pop: 2,327 (1990); 2,375 (1980)   **Pop Density:** 65.4
Land: 35.6 sq. mi.; **Water:** 0.1 sq. mi.

Pembroke   Town
ZIP: 14036   **Lat:** 43-00-05 N **Long:** 78-23-08 W
Pop: 4,232 (1990); 4,146 (1980)   **Pop Density:** 101.5
Land: 41.7 sq. mi.; **Water:** 0.0 sq. mi.

Stafford   Town
ZIP: 14143   **Lat:** 42-59-40 N **Long:** 78-05-06 W
Pop: 2,593 (1990); 2,508 (1980)   **Pop Density:** 83.4
Land: 31.1 sq. mi.; **Water:** 0.1 sq. mi.
Name origin: For the town in England.

Tonawanda Reservation   Pop. Place
                        Lat: 43-03-58 N **Long:** 78-26-11 W
Pop: 491 (1990); 455 (1980)   **Pop Density:** 53.4
Land: 9.2 sq. mi.; **Water:** 0.1 sq. mi.

Greene County
County Seat: Catskill (ZIP: 12414)

Pop: 44,739 (1990); 40,861 (1980)   **Pop Density:** 69.1
Land: 647.8 sq. mi.; **Water:** 10.3 sq. mi.   **Area Code:** 518
In southeastern NY, southwest of Albany; organized Mar 25, 1800 from Albany and Ulster counties.
Name origin: For Gen. Nathanael Greene (1742–86), hero of the Revolutionary War; quartermaster general (1778–80).

Ashland   Town
ZIP: 12407   **Lat:** 42-19-08 N **Long:** 74-20-19 W
Pop: 803 (1990); 744 (1980)   **Pop Density:** 30.9
Land: 26.0 sq. mi.; **Water:** 0.0 sq. mi.

Athens   Town
ZIP: 12015   **Lat:** 42-16-46 N **Long:** 73-51-43 W
Pop: 3,561 (1990); 3,462 (1980)   **Pop Density:** 135.9
Land: 26.2 sq. mi.; **Water:** 2.7 sq. mi.

*Athens   Village
ZIP: 12015   **Lat:** 42-16-01 N **Long:** 73-48-46 W
Pop: 1,708 (1990); 1,738 (1980)   **Pop Density:** 502.4
Land: 3.4 sq. mi.; **Water:** 1.2 sq. mi.
Not coextensive with the town of the same name.
Name origin: For the Greek city.

Cairo   Town
ZIP: 12413   **Lat:** 42-17-58 N **Long:** 74-00-59 W
Pop: 5,418 (1990); 4,729 (1980)   **Pop Density:** 90.3
Land: 60.0 sq. mi.; **Water:** 0.2 sq. mi.
Name origin: For the great Egyptian city.

Catskill   Town
ZIP: 12414   **Lat:** 42-12-37 N **Long:** 73-56-18 W
Pop: 11,965 (1990); 11,453 (1980)   **Pop Density:** 197.8
Land: 60.5 sq. mi.; **Water:** 3.6 sq. mi.

*Catskill   Village
ZIP: 12414   **Lat:** 42-12-53 N **Long:** 73-51-55 W
Pop: 4,690 (1990); 4,718 (1980)   **Pop Density:** 2131.8
Land: 2.2 sq. mi.; **Water:** 0.6 sq. mi.   **Elev:** 47 ft.
In southeastern NY, 30 mi. south of Albany on the Hudson River. Not coextensive with the town of the same name.
Name origin: Named from the Dutch for 'cat's stream,' in reference to the wildcats that came down from the hills.

Coxsackie   Town
ZIP: 12051   **Lat:** 42-20-44 N **Long:** 73-51-53 W
Pop: 7,633 (1990); 6,018 (1980)   **Pop Density:** 206.9
Land: 36.9 sq. mi.; **Water:** 1.5 sq. mi.

*Coxsackie   Village
ZIP: 12051   **Lat:** 42-21-29 N **Long:** 73-48-33 W
Pop: 2,789 (1990); 2,786 (1980)   **Pop Density:** 1267.7
Land: 2.2 sq. mi.; **Water:** 0.4 sq. mi.
In southeastern NY on the Hudson River, south of Albany. Not coextensive with the town of the same name.
Name origin: From an Indian term possibly meaning 'stream outlet.'

Durham
Town
Lat: 42-22-43 N Long: 74-08-58 W
Pop: 2,324 (1990); 2,283 (1980)   Pop Density: 47.1
Land: 49.3 sq. mi.; Water: 0.0 sq. mi.

Greenville
Town
ZIP: 12083   Lat: 42-23-17 N Long: 74-00-37 W
Pop: 3,135 (1990); 2,849 (1980)   Pop Density: 80.6
Land: 38.9 sq. mi.; Water: 0.2 sq. mi.

Halcott
Town
Lat: 42-13-08 N Long: 74-28-17 W
Pop: 189 (1990); 150 (1980)   Pop Density: 8.2
Land: 23.0 sq. mi.; Water: 0.0 sq. mi.

Hunter
Town
ZIP: 12442   Lat: 42-09-30 N Long: 74-08-55 W
Pop: 2,116 (1990); 2,252 (1980)   Pop Density: 23.4
Land: 90.5 sq. mi.; Water: 0.2 sq. mi.

*Hunter
Village
ZIP: 12442   Lat: 42-12-40 N Long: 74-12-56 W
Pop: 429 (1990); 511 (1980)   Pop Density: 268.1
Land: 1.6 sq. mi.; Water: 0.0 sq. mi.
Not coextensive with the town of the same name.

Jefferson Heights
CDP
Lat: 42-14-11 N Long: 73-52-21 W
Pop: 1,512 (1990); 1,610 (1980)   Pop Density: 521.4
Land: 2.9 sq. mi.; Water: 0.2 sq. mi.

Jewett
Town
ZIP: 12444   Lat: 42-14-59 N Long: 74-13-39 W
Pop: 933 (1990); 723 (1980)   Pop Density: 18.6
Land: 50.1 sq. mi.; Water: 0.2 sq. mi.

Lexington
Town
Lat: 42-11-51 N Long: 74-21-39 W
Pop: 835 (1990); 819 (1980)   Pop Density: 10.5
Land: 79.9 sq. mi.; Water: 0.0 sq. mi.
Name origin: For Lexington, MA.

New Baltimore
Town
Lat: 42-24-57 N Long: 73-51-32 W
Pop: 3,371 (1990); 3,050 (1980)   Pop Density: 81.0
Land: 41.6 sq. mi.; Water: 1.5 sq. mi.
Name origin: For Lord Baltimore of the Calvert family, proprietors of the colony of MD.

Prattsville
Town
ZIP: 12468   Lat: 42-19-42 N Long: 74-25-17 W
Pop: 774 (1990); 666 (1980)   Pop Density: 39.5
Land: 19.6 sq. mi.; Water: 0.1 sq. mi.

Tannersville
Village
ZIP: 12424   Lat: 42-11-37 N Long: 74-08-05 W
Pop: 465 (1990); 685 (1980)   Pop Density: 422.7
Land: 1.1 sq. mi.; Water: 0.0 sq. mi.

Windham
Town
ZIP: 12496   Lat: 42-19-02 N Long: 74-12-13 W
Pop: 1,682 (1990); 1,663 (1980)   Pop Density: 37.1
Land: 45.3 sq. mi.; Water: 0.1 sq. mi.
Name origin: For the English town.

Hamilton County
County Seat: Lake Pleasant (ZIP: 12108)

Pop: 5,279 (1990); 5,034 (1980)   Pop Density: 3.1
Land: 1720.7 sq. mi.; Water: 87.2 sq. mi.   Area Code: 518
In north-central NY, northeast of Utica; organized Apr 12, 1816 from Montgomery County.
Name origin: For Alexander Hamilton (1757–1804), first U.S. secretary of the treasury (1789–95).

Arietta
Town
ZIP: 12139   Lat: 43-32-42 N Long: 74-33-49 W
Pop: 300 (1990); 314 (1980)   Pop Density: 0.9
Land: 317.8 sq. mi.; Water: 11.6 sq. mi.

Benson
Town
Lat: 43-17-25 N Long: 74-21-39 W
Pop: 168 (1990); 156 (1980)   Pop Density: 2.0
Land: 82.7 sq. mi.; Water: 0.5 sq. mi.

Hope
Town
Lat: 43-17-57 N Long: 74-13-08 W
Pop: 358 (1990); 311 (1980)   Pop Density: 8.8
Land: 40.7 sq. mi.; Water: 0.9 sq. mi.

Indian Lake
Town
ZIP: 12842   Lat: 43-47-14 N Long: 74-18-46 W
Pop: 1,481 (1990); 1,410 (1980)   Pop Density: 5.9
Land: 252.5 sq. mi.; Water: 13.4 sq. mi.

Inlet
Town
ZIP: 13360   Lat: 43-44-15 N Long: 74-44-34 W
Pop: 343 (1990); 320 (1980)   Pop Density: 5.5
Land: 62.3 sq. mi.; Water: 4.1 sq. mi.

Lake Pleasant
Town
ZIP: 12108   Lat: 43-34-26 N Long: 74-25-46 W
Pop: 887 (1990); 859 (1980)   Pop Density: 4.7
Land: 188.1 sq. mi.; Water: 9.9 sq. mi.

Long Lake
Town
ZIP: 12847   Lat: 43-57-52 N Long: 74-35-52 W
Pop: 930 (1990); 935 (1980)   Pop Density: 2.3
Land: 407.9 sq. mi.; Water: 42.0 sq. mi.

Morehouse
Town
Lat: 43-28-27 N Long: 74-42-33 W
Pop: 106 (1990); 102 (1980)   Pop Density: 0.6
Land: 191.1 sq. mi.; Water: 3.6 sq. mi.

Speculator Village
ZIP: 12164   **Lat:** 43-34-50 N   **Long:** 74-22-50 W
Pop: 400 (1990); 408 (1980)   **Pop Density:** 9.0
Land: 44.6 sq. mi.; **Water:** 2.6 sq. mi.   **Elev:** 1739 ft.

Wells Town
ZIP: 12190   **Lat:** 43-27-51 N   **Long:** 74-16-51 W
Pop: 706 (1990); 627 (1980)   **Pop Density:** 4.0
Land: 177.5 sq. mi.; **Water:** 1.2 sq. mi.

Herkimer County
County Seat: Herkimer (ZIP: 13350)

Pop: 65,797 (1990); 66,714 (1980)   **Pop Density:** 46.6
Land: 1411.8 sq. mi.; **Water:** 46.6 sq. mi.   **Area Code:** 315

In north-central NY, east of Utica; organized Feb 16, 1791 from Montgomery County.

Name origin: For Gen. Nicholas Herkimer (1728–77), Revolutionary War officer and patriot, fatally wounded at the Battle of Oriskany. An earlier name was German Flats, for German settlers.

Cold Brook Village
ZIP: 13324   **Lat:** 43-14-27 N   **Long:** 75-02-15 W
Pop: 310 (1990); 402 (1980)   **Pop Density:** 775.0
Land: 0.4 sq. mi.; **Water:** 0.0 sq. mi.

Columbia Town
ZIP: 13357   **Lat:** 42-55-31 N   **Long:** 75-02-26 W
Pop: 1,587 (1990); 1,537 (1980)   **Pop Density:** 45.3
Land: 35.0 sq. mi.; **Water:** 0.0 sq. mi.

Danube Town
Lat: 42-59-14 N   **Long:** 74-47-52 W
Pop: 1,077 (1990); 1,081 (1980)   **Pop Density:** 37.4
Land: 28.8 sq. mi.; **Water:** 0.3 sq. mi.

Dolgeville Village
ZIP: 13329   **Lat:** 43-06-06 N   **Long:** 74-46-38 W
Pop: 2,344 (1990); 2,440 (1980)   **Pop Density:** 1562.7
Land: 1.5 sq. mi.; **Water:** 0.0 sq. mi.   **Elev:** 802 ft.
Part of the town is in Fulton County.
Name origin: Named in 1881 for businessman Alfred Dolge, who transformed the village of Brockett's Bridge into a factory town of several thousand workers.

Fairfield Town
Lat: 43-07-02 N   **Long:** 74-55-14 W
Pop: 1,442 (1990); 1,455 (1980)   **Pop Density:** 35.1
Land: 41.1 sq. mi.; **Water:** 0.2 sq. mi.

Frankfort Town
ZIP: 13340   **Lat:** 43-02-17 N   **Long:** 75-08-09 W
Pop: 7,494 (1990); 7,686 (1980)   **Pop Density:** 201.5
Land: 37.2 sq. mi.; **Water:** 0.1 sq. mi.

*Frankfort Village
ZIP: 13340   **Lat:** 43-02-17 N   **Long:** 75-04-18 W
Pop: 2,693 (1990); 2,995 (1980)   **Pop Density:** 2693.0
Land: 1.0 sq. mi.; **Water:** 0.0 sq. mi.
Not coextensive with the town of the same name.
Name origin: For Frankfort, Germany.

German Flatts Town
ZIP: 13407   **Lat:** 42-59-17 N   **Long:** 74-59-07 W
Pop: 14,345 (1990); 14,981 (1980)   **Pop Density:** 425.7
Land: 33.7 sq. mi.; **Water:** 0.5 sq. mi.

Herkimer Town
ZIP: 13350   **Lat:** 43-03-28 N   **Long:** 74-59-21 W
Pop: 10,401 (1990); 11,027 (1980)   **Pop Density:** 329.1
Land: 31.6 sq. mi.; **Water:** 0.6 sq. mi.

*Herkimer Village
ZIP: 13350   **Lat:** 43-01-43 N   **Long:** 74-59-33 W
Pop: 7,945 (1990); 8,383 (1980)   **Pop Density:** 3310.4
Land: 2.4 sq. mi.; **Water:** 0.1 sq. mi.   **Elev:** 407 ft.
In northeast-central NY on the Mohawk River, 14 mi. southeast of Utica. Not coextensive with the town of the same name.
Name origin: For Gen. Nicholas Herkimer (1728–77), killed in the Battle of Oriskany in 1777.

Ilion Village
ZIP: 13357   **Lat:** 43-00-40 N   **Long:** 75-02-26 W
Pop: 8,888 (1990); 9,450 (1980)   **Pop Density:** 3555.2
Land: 2.5 sq. mi.; **Water:** 0.0 sq. mi.   **Elev:** 410 ft.
In northeast-central NY on the Mohawk River, 11 mi. east-southeast of Utica.
Name origin: From the Greek term for Troy.

Litchfield Town
Lat: 42-58-38 N   **Long:** 75-09-04 W
Pop: 1,414 (1990); 1,187 (1980)   **Pop Density:** 47.8
Land: 29.6 sq. mi.; **Water:** 0.1 sq. mi.

Little Falls City
ZIP: 13365   **Lat:** 43-02-43 N   **Long:** 74-51-21 W
Pop: 5,829 (1990); 6,156 (1980)   **Pop Density:** 1533.9
Land: 3.8 sq. mi.; **Water:** 0.2 sq. mi.
In northeast-central NY, 20 mi. east of Utica.
Name origin: For a local geographic feature.

*Little Falls Town
ZIP: 13365   **Lat:** 43-01-01 N   **Long:** 74-53-27 W
Pop: 1,635 (1990); 1,434 (1980)   **Pop Density:** 74.0
Land: 22.1 sq. mi.; **Water:** 0.2 sq. mi.

Manheim Town
Lat: 43-04-07 N   **Long:** 74-48-21 W
Pop: 3,527 (1990); 3,634 (1980)   **Pop Density:** 121.6
Land: 29.0 sq. mi.; **Water:** 0.6 sq. mi.

Middleville Village
ZIP: 13406   **Lat:** 43-08-17 N   **Long:** 74-58-15 W
Pop: 624 (1990); 454 (1980)   **Pop Density:** 891.4
Land: 0.7 sq. mi.; **Water:** 0.0 sq. mi.

Mohawk　　　　　　　　　　　　　　Village
ZIP: 13407　　　　**Lat:** 43-00-33 N **Long:** 75-00-25 W
Pop: 2,986 (1990); 2,956 (1980)　　**Pop Density:** 3317.8
Land: 0.9 sq. mi.; **Water:** 0.0 sq. mi.　　　**Elev:** 407 ft.
In north-central NY east of Syracuse on the Mohawk River.
Name origin: For the river, itself named for the Indian tribe.

Newport　　　　　　　　　　　　　　Town
ZIP: 13416　　　　**Lat:** 43-10-52 N **Long:** 75-02-29 W
Pop: 2,148 (1990); 2,206 (1980)　　**Pop Density:** 67.1
Land: 32.0 sq. mi.; **Water:** 0.5 sq. mi.

*Newport　　　　　　　　　　　　　Village
ZIP: 13416　　　　**Lat:** 43-11-14 N **Long:** 75-00-53 W
Pop: 676 (1990); 746 (1980)　　**Pop Density:** 1352.0
Land: 0.5 sq. mi.; **Water:** 0.1 sq. mi.
Not coextensive with the town of the same name.

Norway　　　　　　　　　　　　　　Town
　　　　　　　　Lat: 43-13-06 N **Long:** 74-56-54 W
Pop: 663 (1990); 662 (1980)　　**Pop Density:** 18.6
Land: 35.6 sq. mi.; **Water:** 0.3 sq. mi.
Name origin: For the country.

Ohio　　　　　　　　　　　　　　　Town
ZIP: 13324　　　　**Lat:** 43-27-40 N **Long:** 74-54-06 W
Pop: 880 (1990); 788 (1980)　　**Pop Density:** 2.9
Land: 302.6 sq. mi.; **Water:** 6.4 sq. mi.

Poland　　　　　　　　　　　　　　Village
ZIP: 13431　　　　**Lat:** 43-13-34 N **Long:** 75-03-41 W
Pop: 444 (1990); 449 (1980)　　**Pop Density:** 740.0
Land: 0.6 sq. mi.; **Water:** 0.0 sq. mi.

Russia　　　　　　　　　　　　　　Town
ZIP: 13431　　　　**Lat:** 43-18-05 N **Long:** 75-04-03 W
Pop: 2,294 (1990); 2,405 (1980)　　**Pop Density:** 40.3
Land: 56.9 sq. mi.; **Water:** 3.5 sq. mi.
Name origin: For the country.

Salisbury　　　　　　　　　　　　　Town
ZIP: 13365　　　　**Lat:** 43-13-19 N **Long:** 74-48-09 W
Pop: 1,934 (1990); 1,946 (1980)　　**Pop Density:** 18.0
Land: 107.4 sq. mi.; **Water:** 0.8 sq. mi.

Schuyler　　　　　　　　　　　　　Town
ZIP: 13340　　　　**Lat:** 43-05-55 N **Long:** 75-05-29 W
Pop: 3,508 (1990); 2,886 (1980)　　**Pop Density:** 88.1
Land: 39.8 sq. mi.; **Water:** 0.5 sq. mi.

Stark　　　　　　　　　　　　　　Town
　　　　　　　　Lat: 42-54-54 N **Long:** 74-48-57 W
Pop: 759 (1990); 824 (1980)　　**Pop Density:** 23.4
Land: 32.4 sq. mi.; **Water:** 0.0 sq. mi.

Warren　　　　　　　　　　　　　　Town
　　　　　　　　Lat: 42-53-20 N **Long:** 74-55-50 W
Pop: 1,077 (1990); 1,065 (1980)　　**Pop Density:** 28.2
Land: 38.2 sq. mi.; **Water:** 0.3 sq. mi.

Webb　　　　　　　　　　　　　　Town
　　　　　　　　Lat: 43-51-00 N **Long:** 74-59-53 W
Pop: 1,637 (1990); 1,701 (1980)　　**Pop Density:** 3.6
Land: 451.2 sq. mi.; **Water:** 31.8 sq. mi.

West Winfield　　　　　　　　　　　Village
ZIP: 13491　　　　**Lat:** 42-53-01 N **Long:** 75-11-30 W
Pop: 871 (1990); 979 (1980)　　**Pop Density:** 967.8
Land: 0.9 sq. mi.; **Water:** 0.0 sq. mi.　　**Elev:** 1220 ft.

Winfield　　　　　　　　　　　　　Town
ZIP: 13491　　　　**Lat:** 42-53-49 N **Long:** 75-10-00 W
Pop: 2,146 (1990); 2,053 (1980)　　**Pop Density:** 90.9
Land: 23.6 sq. mi.; **Water:** 0.0 sq. mi.

Jefferson County
County Seat: Watertown (ZIP: 13601)

Pop: 110,943 (1990); 88,151 (1980)　　**Pop Density:** 87.2
Land: 1272.3 sq. mi.; **Water:** 585.0 sq. mi.　　**Area Code:** 315
On central western border of NY on Lake Ontario; organized Mar 28, 1805 from Oneida County.
Name origin: For Thomas Jefferson (1743–1826), U.S. patriot and statesman; third U.S. president.

Adams　　　　　　　　　　　　　　Town
ZIP: 13605　　　　**Lat:** 43-51-19 N **Long:** 76-02-16 W
Pop: 4,977 (1990); 4,390 (1980)　　**Pop Density:** 117.4
Land: 42.4 sq. mi.; **Water:** 0.0 sq. mi.

*Adams　　　　　　　　　　　　　　Village
ZIP: 13605　　　　**Lat:** 43-48-35 N **Long:** 76-01-21 W
Pop: 1,753 (1990); 1,701 (1980)　　**Pop Density:** 1252.1
Land: 1.4 sq. mi.; **Water:** 0.0 sq. mi.
In northern NY, 15 mi. south of Watertown. Not coextensive with the town of the same name.
Name origin: For John Adams (1735–1826), second U.S. president.

Alexandria　　　　　　　　　　　　Town
ZIP: 13607　　　　**Lat:** 44-19-08 N **Long:** 75-52-37 W
Pop: 3,949 (1990); 3,587 (1980)　　**Pop Density:** 54.1
Land: 73.0 sq. mi.; **Water:** 11.6 sq. mi.

Alexandria Bay　　　　　　　　　　Village
ZIP: 13607　　　　**Lat:** 44-20-14 N **Long:** 75-55-03 W
Pop: 1,194 (1990); 1,265 (1980)　　**Pop Density:** 1705.7
Land: 0.7 sq. mi.; **Water:** 0.8 sq. mi.　　**Elev:** 284 ft.

Antwerp　　　　　　　　　　　　　Town
　　　　　　　　Lat: 44-12-51 N **Long:** 75-36-19 W
Pop: 1,856 (1990); 1,859 (1980)　　**Pop Density:** 17.4
Land: 106.9 sq. mi.; **Water:** 1.5 sq. mi.

*Antwerp
Village
ZIP: 13608   Lat: 44-11-59 N Long: 75-36-32 W
Pop: 739 (1990); 749 (1980)   Pop Density: 739.0
Land: 1.0 sq. mi.; Water: 0.0 sq. mi.   Elev: 545 ft.
Not coextensive with the town of the same name.
Name origin: For the city in Belgium.

Black River
Village
ZIP: 13612   Lat: 44-00-34 N Long: 75-47-48 W
Pop: 1,349 (1990); 824 (1980)   Pop Density: 749.4
Land: 1.8 sq. mi.; Water: 0.0 sq. mi.

Brownville
Town
ZIP: 13615   Lat: 44-01-55 N Long: 76-03-35 W
Pop: 5,604 (1990); 5,113 (1980)   Pop Density: 94.5
Land: 59.3 sq. mi.; Water: 7.3 sq. mi.

*Brownville
Village
Lat: 44-00-19 N Long: 75-59-00 W
Pop: 1,138 (1990); 1,099 (1980)   Pop Density: 1896.7
Land: 0.6 sq. mi.; Water: 0.0 sq. mi.

Calcium
CDP
ZIP: 13616   Lat: 44-02-04 N Long: 75-50-52 W
Pop: 2,465 (1990)   Pop Density: 440.2
Land: 5.6 sq. mi.; Water: 0.0 sq. mi.

Cape Vincent
Town
ZIP: 13618   Lat: 44-07-39 N Long: 76-16-57 W
Pop: 2,768 (1990); 1,823 (1980)   Pop Density: 49.0
Land: 56.5 sq. mi.; Water: 33.4 sq. mi.

*Cape Vincent
Village
ZIP: 13618   Lat: 44-07-34 N Long: 76-19-51 W
Pop: 683 (1990); 785 (1980)   Pop Density: 975.7
Land: 0.7 sq. mi.; Water: 0.0 sq. mi.   Elev: 253 ft.
Not coextensive with the town of the same name.

Carthage
Village
ZIP: 13619   Lat: 43-59-05 N Long: 75-36-16 W
Pop: 4,344 (1990); 3,643 (1980)   Pop Density: 1737.6
Land: 2.5 sq. mi.; Water: 0.2 sq. mi.   Elev: 743 ft.

Champion
Town
Lat: 43-57-56 N Long: 75-41-32 W
Pop: 4,574 (1990); 4,056 (1980)   Pop Density: 103.3
Land: 44.3 sq. mi.; Water: 0.8 sq. mi.

Chaumont
Village
ZIP: 13622   Lat: 44-03-55 N Long: 76-08-00 W
Pop: 593 (1990); 620 (1980)   Pop Density: 847.1
Land: 0.7 sq. mi.; Water: 0.1 sq. mi.   Elev: 293 ft.

Clayton
Town
ZIP: 13624   Lat: 44-11-50 N Long: 76-04-52 W
Pop: 4,629 (1990); 4,028 (1980)   Pop Density: 56.0
Land: 82.6 sq. mi.; Water: 21.5 sq. mi.

*Clayton
Village
ZIP: 13624   Lat: 44-14-08 N Long: 76-05-12 W
Pop: 2,160 (1990); 1,816 (1980)   Pop Density: 1350.0
Land: 1.6 sq. mi.; Water: 0.9 sq. mi.
Not coextensive with the town of the same name.

Deferiet
Village
ZIP: 13628   Lat: 44-02-04 N Long: 75-40-47 W
Pop: 293 (1990); 326 (1980)   Pop Density: 418.6
Land: 0.7 sq. mi.; Water: 0.0 sq. mi.
In north-central NY, northeast of Watertown.
Name origin: For Baroness Jenika de Ferriet, who built (c.

1830) a beautiful mansion, called the Hermitage, on the bank of the Black River. The spelling of the name has been altered.

Dexter
Village
ZIP: 13634   Lat: 44-00-29 N Long: 76-02-44 W
Pop: 1,030 (1990); 1,053 (1980)   Pop Density: 2575.0
Land: 0.4 sq. mi.; Water: 0.1 sq. mi.   Elev: 325 ft.

Ellisburg
Town
ZIP: 13636   Lat: 43-44-31 N Long: 76-07-16 W
Pop: 3,386 (1990); 3,312 (1980)   Pop Density: 39.7
Land: 85.3 sq. mi.; Water: 1.3 sq. mi.

*Ellisburg
Village
ZIP: 13636   Lat: 43-44-09 N Long 76-08-01 W
Pop: 246 (1990); 307 (1980)   Pop Density: 246.0
Land: 1.0 sq. mi.; Water: 0.0 sq. mi.
Not coextensive with the town of the same name.

Evans Mills
Village
ZIP: 13637   Lat: 44-05-16 N Long 75-48-29 W
Pop: 661 (1990); 651 (1980)   Pop Density: 826.3
Land: 0.8 sq. mi.; Water: 0.0 sq. mi.   Elev: 430 ft.
Name origin: For Ethni Evans, a millwright from NH who settled here in 1803.

Fort Drum
Military facility
ZIP: 13612   Lat: 44-03-12 N Long 75-46-25 W
Pop: 11,578 (1990)   Pop Density: 737.5
Land: 15.7 sq. mi.; Water: 0.0 sq. mi.

Glen Park
Village
ZIP: 13601   Lat: 44-00-02 N Long 75-57-18 W
Pop: 527 (1990); 470 (1980)   Pop Density: 752.9
Land: 0.7 sq. mi.; Water: 0.0 sq. mi.   Elev: 347 ft.

Henderson
Town
ZIP: 13650   Lat: 43-51-23 N Long 76-10-49 W
Pop: 1,268 (1990); 1,330 (1980)   Pop Density: 30.7
Land: 41.3 sq. mi.; Water: 11.7 sq. mi.

Herrings
Village
ZIP: 13653   Lat: 44-01-24 N Long 75-39-27 W
Pop: 140 (1990); 170 (1980)   Pop Density: 466.7
Land: 0.3 sq. mi.; Water: 0.0 sq. mi.

Hounsfield
Town
ZIP: 13685   Lat: 43-54-43 N Long 76-10-36 W
Pop: 3,089 (1990); 2,645 (1980)   Pop Density: 62.7
Land: 49.3 sq. mi.; Water: 71.2 sq. mi.

Le Ray
Town
ZIP: 13637   Lat: 44-04-46 N Long 75-47-46 W
Pop: 17,973 (1990); 5,039 (1980)   Pop Density: 243.9
Land: 73.7 sq. mi.; Water: 0.3 sq. mi.

Lorraine
Town
ZIP: 13659   Lat: 43-45-02 N Long 75-57-59 W
Pop: 766 (1990); 720 (1980)   Pop Density: 19.6
Land: 39.0 sq. mi.; Water: 0.0 sq. mi.

Lyme
Town
Lat: 44-01-49 N Long 76-12-48 W
Pop: 1,701 (1990); 1,695 (1980)   Pop Density: 30.3
Land: 56.1 sq. mi.; Water: 50.8 sq. mi.

Mannsville
Village
ZIP: 13661   Lat: 43-42-54 N Long 76-03-59 W
Pop: 444 (1990); 431 (1980)   Pop Density: 493.3
Land: 0.9 sq. mi.; Water: 0.0 sq. mi.

Orleans
Town
Lat: 44-12-00 N　Long: 75-58-00 W
Pop: 2,248 (1990); 2,007 (1980)　　Pop Density: 31.6
Land: 71.1 sq. mi.; Water: 6.7 sq. mi.

Pamelia
Town
ZIP: 13637　　　Lat: 44-03-08 N　Long: 75-54-37 W
Pop: 2,811 (1990); 2,417 (1980)　　Pop Density: 82.2
Land: 34.2 sq. mi.; Water: 1.6 sq. mi.

Philadelphia
Town
ZIP: 13673　　　Lat: 44-08-48 N　Long: 75-42-23 W
Pop: 2,136 (1990); 1,417 (1980)　　Pop Density: 56.8
Land: 37.6 sq. mi.; Water: 0.0 sq. mi.

*Philadelphia
Village
ZIP: 13673　　　Lat: 44-09-17 N　Long: 75-42-33 W
Pop: 1,478 (1990); 855 (1980)　　Pop Density: 1642.2
Land: 0.9 sq. mi.; Water: 0.0 sq. mi.　　Elev: 490 ft.
Not coextensive with the town of the same name.

Rodman
Town
Lat: 43-50-33 N　Long: 75-54-13 W
Pop: 1,016 (1990); 836 (1980)　　Pop Density: 24.1
Land: 42.2 sq. mi.; Water: 0.0 sq. mi.

Rutland
Town
ZIP: 13638　　　Lat: 43-57-03 N　Long: 75-47-47 W
Pop: 3,023 (1990); 2,685 (1980)　　Pop Density: 66.9
Land: 45.2 sq. mi.; Water: 0.2 sq. mi.

Sackets Harbor
Village
ZIP: 13685　　　Lat: 43-56-29 N　Long: 76-07-19 W
Pop: 1,313 (1990); 1,017 (1980)　　Pop Density: 570.9
Land: 2.3 sq. mi.; Water: 0.0 sq. mi.　　Elev: 278 ft.
In northern NY on Lake Ontario, 11 mi. west-southwest of Watertown.

Theresa
Town
ZIP: 13691　　　Lat: 44-14-35 N　Long: 75-46-32 W
Pop: 2,281 (1990); 1,853 (1980)　　Pop Density: 34.9
Land: 65.4 sq. mi.; Water: 4.3 sq. mi.

*Theresa
Village
ZIP: 13691　　　Lat: 44-12-53 N　Long: 75-47-49 W
Pop: 889 (1990); 827 (1980)　　Pop Density: 683.8
Land: 1.3 sq. mi.; Water: 0.1 sq. mi.　　Elev: 391 ft.
Not coextensive with the town of the same name.

Watertown
City
ZIP: 13601　　　Lat: 43-58-24 N　Long: 75-54-36 W
Pop: 29,429 (1990); 27,861 (1980)　　Pop Density: 3382.6
Land: 8.7 sq. mi.; Water: 0.2 sq. mi.　　Elev: 478 ft.
In northern NY, 10 mi. east of Lake Ontario.
Name origin: Named in 1800 by five New Englanders who hacked their way up from the Mohawk Valley and stopped at the rocky Black River Falls.

*Watertown
Town
Lat: 43-56-05 N　Long: 75-55-06 W
Pop: 4,341 (1990); 3,098 (1980)　　Pop Density: 120.6
Land: 36.0 sq. mi.; Water: 0.1 sq. mi.

West Carthage
Village
ZIP: 13619　　　Lat: 43-58-24 N　Long: 75-37-18 W
Pop: 2,166 (1990); 1,824 (1980)　　Pop Density: 1969.1
Land: 1.1 sq. mi.; Water: 0.1 sq. mi.

Wilna
Town
ZIP: 13619　　　Lat: 44-03-04 N　Long: 75-35-15 W
Pop: 6,899 (1990); 6,227 (1980)　　Pop Density: 87.4
Land: 78.9 sq. mi.; Water: 0.6 sq. mi.

Worth
Town
ZIP: 13659　　　Lat: 43-44-35 N　Long: 75-50-38 W
Pop: 219 (1990); 153 (1980)　　Pop Density: 5.1
Land: 43.2 sq. mi.; Water: 0.1 sq. mi.

Kings County (Brooklyn)
County Seat: Brooklyn (ZIP: 11201)

Pop: 2,300,664 (1990); 2,231,028 (1980)　　Pop Density: 32633.5
Land: 70.5 sq. mi.; Water: 26.3 sq. mi.　　Area Code: 718

On the southwestern end of Long Island, east of Manhattan Island; original county, organized Nov 1, 1683. The county is coterminous with the borough of Brooklyn, part of New York City.
Name origin: For Charles II (1630–85), king of England.

Brooklyn
Borough
The borough of Brooklyn is on the western end of Long Island, across the East River from Manhattan. First settled 1636. Incorporated as a village in 1816, as a city in 1834. Became a borough of New York City on January 1, 1898. Includes many residential districts, such as Bay Ridge, Bedford-Stuyvesant, Bensonhurst, Brighton Beach, Brooklyn Heights, Brownsville, Bushwick, Canarsie, Carroll Gardens, Coney Island, Crown Heights, Ditmas Park, Dyker Heights, East New York, Flatbush, Gravesend, Greenpoint, Park Slope, Sunset Park, and Williamsburg.
Name origin: From Dutch *Breuckelyn,* a village in Holland, with Anglicized spelling.

Lewis County
County Seat: Lowville (ZIP: 13367)

Pop: 26,796 (1990); 25,035 (1980)
Land: 1275.6 sq. mi.; **Water:** 14.4 sq. mi.

Pop Density: 21.0
Area Code: 315

In north-central NY, east of Syracuse; organized Mar 28, 1805 from Oneida County.
Name origin: For Morgan Lewis (1754–1844), officer in the Revolutionary War and the War of 1812, NY legislator, and governor (1804–07).

Castorland
Village
ZIP: 13620   **Lat:** 43-53-03 N   **Long:** 75-31-03 W
Pop: 292 (1990); 277 (1980)   **Pop Density:** 973.3
Land: 0.3 sq. mi.; **Water:** 0.0 sq. mi.   **Elev:** 739 ft.

Constableville
Village
ZIP: 13325   **Lat:** 43-33-51 N   **Long:** 75-25-42 W
Pop: 307 (1990); 330 (1980)   **Pop Density:** 279.1
Land: 1.1 sq. mi.; **Water:** 0.0 sq. mi.

Copenhagen
Village
ZIP: 13626   **Lat:** 43-53-37 N   **Long:** 75-40-26 W
Pop: 876 (1990); 656 (1980)   **Pop Density:** 730.0
Land: 1.2 sq. mi.; **Water:** 0.0 sq. mi.   **Elev:** 1174 ft.
Name origin: For the capital of Denmark.

Croghan
Town
ZIP: 13327   **Lat:** 43-58-13 N   **Long:** 75-21-24 W
Pop: 3,071 (1990); 2,824 (1980)   **Pop Density:** 17.1
Land: 179.4 sq. mi.; **Water:** 2.6 sq. mi.

*Croghan
Village
ZIP: 13327   **Lat:** 43-53-42 N   **Long:** 75-23-28 W
Pop: 664 (1990); 383 (1980)   **Pop Density:** 1660.0
Land: 0.4 sq. mi.; **Water:** 0.0 sq. mi.

Not coextensive with the town of the same name.

Denmark
Town
Lat: 43-53-45 N   **Long:** 75-36-57 W
Pop: 2,718 (1990); 2,448 (1980)   **Pop Density:** 53.7
Land: 50.6 sq. mi.; **Water:** 0.4 sq. mi.

In north-central NY, southeast of Watertown.
Name origin: For the country in Europe.

Diana
Town
ZIP: 13648   **Lat:** 44-06-42 N   **Long:** 75-22-23 W
Pop: 1,743 (1990); 1,709 (1980)   **Pop Density:** 12.7
Land: 137.4 sq. mi.; **Water:** 3.5 sq. mi.

Greig
Town
ZIP: 13345   **Lat:** 43-41-42 N   **Long:** 75-15-56 W
Pop: 1,323 (1990); 1,115 (1980)   **Pop Density:** 14.2
Land: 92.9 sq. mi.; **Water:** 1.4 sq. mi.

Harrisburg
Town
ZIP: 13367   **Lat:** 43-49-29 N   **Long:** 75-39-47 W
Pop: 425 (1990); 418 (1980)   **Pop Density:** 10.7
Land: 39.9 sq. mi.; **Water:** 0.0 sq. mi.   **Elev:** 1365 ft.

Harrisville
Village
ZIP: 13648   **Lat:** 44-09-12 N   **Long:** 75-19-17 W
Pop: 703 (1990); 937 (1980)   **Pop Density:** 878.8
Land: 0.8 sq. mi.; **Water:** 0.0 sq. mi.   **Elev:** 777 ft.

Lewis
Town
ZIP: 13489   **Lat:** 43-29-08 N   **Long:** 75-33-53 W
Pop: 858 (1990); 720 (1980)   **Pop Density:** 13.3
Land: 64.7 sq. mi.; **Water:** 0.5 sq. mi.

Leyden
Town
ZIP: 13433   **Lat:** 43-32-12 N   **Long:** 75-22-39 W
Pop: 1,796 (1990); 1,660 (1980)   **Pop Density:** 53.9
Land: 33.3 sq. mi.; **Water:** 0.2 sq. mi.

Lowville
Town
ZIP: 13367   **Lat:** 43-49-15 N   **Long:** 75-31-33 W
Pop: 4,849 (1990); 4,575 (1980)   **Pop Density:** 128.3
Land: 37.8 sq. mi.; **Water:** 0.3 sq. mi.

*Lowville
Village
ZIP: 13367   **Lat:** 43-47-08 N   **Long:** 75-29-23 W
Pop: 3,632 (1990); 3,364 (1980)   **Pop Density:** 1816.0
Land: 2.0 sq. mi.; **Water:** 0.0 sq. mi.

In north-central NY, 26 mi. southeast of Watertown. Not coextensive with the town of the same name.

Lyonsdale
Town
ZIP: 13368   **Lat:** 43-36-27 N   **Long:** 75-14-47 W
Pop: 1,281 (1990); 1,135 (1980)   **Pop Density:** 18.6
Land: 68.8 sq. mi.; **Water:** 1.3 sq. mi.

Lyons Falls
Village
ZIP: 13368   **Lat:** 43-37-00 N   **Long:** 75-21-43 W
Pop: 698 (1990); 84 (1980)   **Pop Density:** 698.0
Land: 1.0 sq. mi.; **Water:** 0.1 sq. mi.

Martinsburg
Town
Lat: 43-43-02 N   **Long:** 75-31-36 W
Pop: 1,358 (1990); 1,494 (1980)   **Pop Density:** 17.9
Land: 75.8 sq. mi.; **Water:** 0.3 sq. mi.

Montague
Town
ZIP: 13367   **Lat:** 43-42-43 N   **Long:** 75-42-57 W
Pop: 47 (1990); 32 (1980)   **Pop Density:** 0.7
Land: 65.1 sq. mi.; **Water:** 0.2 sq. mi.

New Bremen
Town
Lat: 43-51-10 N   **Long:** 75-22-20 W
Pop: 2,526 (1990); 2,316 (1980)   **Pop Density:** 45.5
Land: 55.5 sq. mi.; **Water:** 0.2 sq. mi.
Name origin: For the city in Germany, former home of early settlers.

Osceola
Town
Lat: 43-34-01 N   **Long:** 75-41-23 W
Pop: 239 (1990); 321 (1980)   **Pop Density:** 2.7
Land: 87.0 sq. mi.; **Water:** 0.0 sq. mi.
Name origin: For the Seminole Indian chief (c.1804–38).

Pinckney
Town
Lat: 43-50-23 N   **Long:** 75-46-56 W
Pop: 323 (1990); 305 (1980)   **Pop Density:** 7.9
Land: 41.1 sq. mi.; **Water:** 0.0 sq. mi.

Port Leyden
Village
ZIP: 13433   **Lat:** 43-35-02 N   **Long:** 75-20-27 W
Pop: 723 (1990); 539 (1980)   **Pop Density:** 1205.0
Land: 0.6 sq. mi.; **Water:** 0.1 sq. mi.   **Elev:** 897 ft.

Turin Town
ZIP: 13473 Lat: 43-40-03 N Long: 75-25-56 W
Pop: 873 (1990); 824 (1980) Pop Density: 28.0
Land: 31.2 sq. mi.; **Water:** 0.2 sq. mi.

*Turin Village
ZIP: 13473 Lat: 43-37-43 N Long: 75-24-35 W
Pop: 295 (1990); 284 (1980) Pop Density: 295.0
Land: 1.0 sq. mi.; **Water:** 0.0 sq. mi. Elev: 1264 ft.
Not coextensive with the town of the same name.
Name origin: For the city in Italy.

Watson Town
ZIP: 13367 Lat: 43-49-09 N Long: 75-15-09 W
Pop: 1,613 (1990); 1,272 (1980) Pop Density: 14.3
Land: 112.7 sq. mi.; **Water:** 3.0 sq. mi.

West Turin Town
ZIP: 13325 Lat: 43-35-47 N Long: 75-30-18 W
Pop: 1,753 (1990); 1,867 (1980) Pop Density: 17.2
Land: 102.2 sq. mi.; **Water:** 0.2 sq. mi.

Livingston County
County Seat: Geneseo (ZIP: 14454)

Pop: 62,372 (1990); 57,006 (1980) Pop Density: 98.7
Land: 632.2 sq. mi.; **Water:** 8.3 sq. mi. Area Code: 716

In western NY, south of Rochester; organized Feb 23, 1821 from Genesee and Ontario counties.
Name origin: For Robert R. Livingston (1746–1813), NY patriot, statesman, and a drafter of the Declaration of Independence.

Avon Town
ZIP: 14414 Lat: 42-53-57 N Long: 77-44-04 W
Pop: 6,283 (1990); 6,185 (1980) Pop Density: 152.5
Land: 41.2 sq. mi.; **Water:** 0.1 sq. mi.

*Avon Village
ZIP: 14414 Lat: 42-54-44 N Long: 77-44-46 W
Pop: 2,995 (1990); 3,006 (1980) Pop Density: 998.3
Land: 3.0 sq. mi.; **Water:** 0.0 sq. mi. Elev: 651 ft.
In western NY on the Genesee River. Not coextensive with the town of the same name.
Name origin: For the famous English river.

Caledonia Town
ZIP: 14423 Lat: 42-57-02 N Long: 77-49-39 W
Pop: 4,441 (1990); 4,034 (1980) Pop Density: 100.7
Land: 44.1 sq. mi.; **Water:** 0.2 sq. mi.

*Caledonia Village
ZIP: 14423 Lat: 42-58-32 N Long: 77-51-26 W
Pop: 2,262 (1990); 2,188 (1980) Pop Density: 1077.1
Land: 2.1 sq. mi.; **Water:** 0.0 sq. mi. Elev: 666 ft.
Not coextensive with the town of the same name.
Name origin: From the ancient name for Scotland.

Conesus Town
ZIP: 14435 Lat: 42-43-13 N Long: 77-39-39 W
Pop: 2,196 (1990); 1,970 (1980) Pop Density: 66.7
Land: 32.9 sq. mi.; **Water:** 2.9 sq. mi.
Name origin: From an Indian term possibly meaning 'berry place.'

Dansville Village
ZIP: 14437 Lat: 42-33-39 N Long: 77-41-43 W
Pop: 5,002 (1990); 4,979 (1980) Pop Density: 2174.8
Land: 2.3 sq. mi.; **Water:** 0.0 sq. mi.

Geneseo Town
ZIP: 14454 Lat: 42-48-20 N Long: 77-46-45 W
Pop: 9,178 (1990); 8,673 (1980) Pop Density: 208.6
Land: 44.0 sq. mi.; **Water:** 1.2 sq. mi.

*Geneseo Village
ZIP: 14454 Lat: 42-47-53 N Long: 77-48-38 W
Pop: 7,187 (1990); 6,746 (1980) Pop Density: 2764.2
Land: 2.6 sq. mi.; **Water:** 0.0 sq. mi.
In west-central NY in the Genesee Valley, southwest of Rochester. Not coextensive with the town of the same name.
Name origin: From an Indian term possibly meaning 'beautiful valley.'

Groveland Town
ZIP: 14462 Lat: 42-42-14 N Long: 77-46-24 W
Pop: 3,190 (1990); 2,140 (1980) Pop Density: 81.4
Land: 39.2 sq. mi.; **Water:** 0.7 sq. mi.

Leicester Town
ZIP: 14481 Lat: 42-45-58 N Long: 77-54-29 W
Pop: 2,223 (1990); 1,888 (1980) Pop Density: 66.4
Land: 33.5 sq. mi.; **Water:** 0.0 sq. mi.

*Leicester Village
ZIP: 14481 Lat: 42-46-17 N Long: 77-53-52 W
Pop: 405 (1990); 462 (1980) Pop Density: 1350.0
Land: 0.3 sq. mi.; **Water:** 0.0 sq. mi.
Not coextensive with the town of the same name.

Lima Town
ZIP: 14485 Lat: 42-53-46 N Long: 77-36-30 W
Pop: 4,187 (1990); 3,859 (1980) Pop Density: 131.3
Land: 31.9 sq. mi.; **Water:** 0.0 sq. mi.

*Lima Village
ZIP: 14485 Lat: 42-54-23 N Long: 77-36-47 W
Pop: 2,165 (1990); 2,025 (1980) Pop Density: 1546.4
Land: 1.4 sq. mi.; **Water:** 0.0 sq. mi.
Not coextensive with the town of the same name.

Livonia Town
ZIP: 14487 Lat: 42-48-35 N Long: 77-39-11 W
Pop: 6,804 (1990); 5,742 (1980) Pop Density: 177.7
Land: 38.3 sq. mi.; **Water:** 2.7 sq. mi.

*Livonia Village
ZIP: 14487 Lat: 42-49-15 N Long: 77-40-07 W
Pop: 1,434 (1990); 1,238 (1980) Pop Density: 1434.0
Land: 1.0 sq. mi.; Water: 0.0 sq. mi. Elev: 1047 ft.
Not coextensive with the town of the same name.

Mount Morris Town
ZIP: 14510 Lat: 42-39-45 N Long: 77-53-55 W
Pop: 4,633 (1990); 4,478 (1980) Pop Density: 91.4
Land: 50.7 sq. mi.; Water: 0.1 sq. mi.

*Mount Morris Village
ZIP: 14510 Lat: 42-43-25 N Long: 77-52-29 W
Pop: 3,102 (1990); 3,039 (1980) Pop Density: 1551.0
Land: 2.0 sq. mi.; Water: 0.0 sq. mi. Elev: 626 ft.
Not coextensive with the town of the same name.

North Dansville Town
ZIP: 14437 Lat: 42-33-28 N Long: 77-41-32 W
Pop: 5,783 (1990); 5,994 (1980) Pop Density: 590.1
Land: 9.8 sq. mi.; Water: 0.0 sq. mi.

Nunda Town
ZIP: 14517 Lat: 42-33-37 N Long: 77-54-11 W
Pop: 2,931 (1990); 2,692 (1980) Pop Density: 79.0
Land: 37.1 sq. mi.; Water: 0.0 sq. mi.

*Nunda Village
ZIP: 14517 Lat: 42-34-50 N Long: 77-56-19 W
Pop: 1,347 (1990); 1,169 (1980) Pop Density: 1496.7
Land: 0.9 sq. mi.; Water: 0.0 sq. mi. Elev: 944 ft.
Not coextensive with the town of the same name.
Name origin: From an Indian term possibly meaning 'hilly.'

Ossian Town
Lat: 42-31-30 N Long: 77-46-55 W
Pop: 797 (1990); 667 (1980) Pop Density: 20.1
Land: 39.6 sq. mi.; Water: 0.0 sq. mi.

Portage Town
Lat: 42-33-31 N Long: 77-59-41 W
Pop: 893 (1990); 771 (1980) Pop Density: 33.8
Land: 26.4 sq. mi.; Water: 0.3 sq. mi.

Sparta Town
Lat: 42-37-40 N Long: 77-41-50 W
Pop: 1,578 (1990); 1,458 (1980) Pop Density: 57.0
Land: 27.7 sq. mi.; Water: 0.0 sq. mi.
Name origin: For the city in ancient Greece.

Springwater Town
ZIP: 14560 Lat: 42-37-35 N Long: 77-34-25 W
Pop: 2,407 (1990); 2,143 (1980) Pop Density: 45.2
Land: 53.3 sq. mi.; Water: 0.0 sq. mi.
In west-central NY, 40 mi. south of Rochester.

West Sparta Town
Lat: 42-36-53 N Long: 77-47-23 W
Pop: 1,335 (1990); 1,100 (1980) Pop Density: 40.0
Land: 33.4 sq. mi.; Water: 0.0 sq. mi.

York Town
Lat: 42-52-13 N Long: 77-53-02 W
Pop: 3,513 (1990); 3,212 (1980) Pop Density: 71.5
Land: 49.1 sq. mi.; Water: 0.0 sq. mi.
Name origin: For the county in England.

Madison County
County Seat: Wampsville (ZIP: 13163)

Pop: 69,120 (1990); 65,150 (1980) Pop Density: 105.4
Land: 655.9 sq. mi.; Water: 5.7 sq. mi. Area Code: 315
In central NY, east of Syracuse; organized Mar 21, 1806 from Chenango County.
Name origin: For James Madison (1751–1836), U.S. secretary of state at the time of the county's creation, later fourth U.S. president.

Bridgeport CDP
Lat: 43-09-29 N Long: 75-57-47 W
Pop: 456 (1990) Pop Density: 414.5
Land: 1.1 sq. mi.; Water: 0.0 sq. mi.
Part of the town is also in Onondaga County.

Brookfield Town
ZIP: 13314 Lat: 42-48-27 N Long: 75-20-37 W
Pop: 2,225 (1990); 2,037 (1980) Pop Density: 28.5
Land: 78.0 sq. mi.; Water: 0.1 sq. mi.

Canastota Village
ZIP: 13032 Lat: 43-05-03 N Long: 75-45-20 W
Pop: 4,673 (1990); 4,773 (1980) Pop Density: 1416.1
Land: 3.3 sq. mi.; Water: 0.0 sq. mi.
Name origin: From an Iroquoian term probably meaning 'lone pine grove.'

Cazenovia Town
ZIP: 13035 Lat: 42-54-34 N Long: 75-51-44 W
Pop: 6,514 (1990); 5,880 (1980) Pop Density: 130.5
Land: 49.9 sq. mi.; Water: 1.8 sq. mi.

*Cazenovia Village
ZIP: 13035 Lat: 42-55-45 N Long: 75-51-07 W
Pop: 3,007 (1990); 2,599 (1980) Pop Density: 1879.4
Land: 1.6 sq. mi.; Water: 0.0 sq. mi.
Not coextensive with the town of the same name.

Chittenango Village
ZIP: 13037 Lat: 43-02-44 N Long: 75-52-24 W
Pop: 4,734 (1990); 4,290 (1980) Pop Density: 1972.5
Land: 2.4 sq. mi.; Water: 0.0 sq. mi.
In central NY, 16 mi. east of Syracuse.

De Ruyter Town
ZIP: 13052 Lat: 42-46-16 N Long: 75-50-33 W
Pop: 1,458 (1990); 1,349 (1980) Pop Density: 47.8
Land: 30.5 sq. mi.; Water: 0.8 sq. mi.

*De Ruyter Village
ZIP: 13052 Lat: 42-45-32 N Long: 75-53-14 W
Pop: 568 (1990); 542 (1980) Pop Density: 1893.3
Land: 0.3 sq. mi.; Water: 0.0 sq. mi.
Not coextensive with the town of the same name.

Earlville   Village
ZIP: 13332   **Lat:** 42-44-30 N **Long:** 75-32-40 W
Pop: 542 (1990); 622 (1980)   **Pop Density:** 1084.0
Land: 0.5 sq. mi.; **Water:** 0.0 sq. mi.   **Elev:** 1100 ft.
Part of the town is in Chenango County.

Eaton   Town
ZIP: 13334   **Lat:** 42-52-54 N **Long:** 75-37-37 W
Pop: 5,362 (1990); 5,182 (1980)   **Pop Density:** 120.0
Land: 44.7 sq. mi.; **Water:** 0.8 sq. mi.

Fenner   Town
ZIP: 13035   **Lat:** 42-58-17 N **Long:** 75-46-33 W
Pop: 1,694 (1990); 1,580 (1980)   **Pop Density:** 54.5
Land: 31.1 sq. mi.; **Water:** 0.0 sq. mi.

Georgetown   Town
                       Lat: 42-46-34 N **Long:** 75-44-53 W
Pop: 932 (1990); 779 (1980)   **Pop Density:** 23.2
Land: 40.1 sq. mi.; **Water:** 0.1 sq. mi.

Hamilton   Town
ZIP: 13346   **Lat:** 42-47-24 N **Long:** 75-29-37 W
Pop: 6,221 (1990); 6,027 (1980)   **Pop Density:** 150.3
Land: 41.4 sq. mi.; **Water:** 0.1 sq. mi.

*Hamilton   Village
ZIP: 13346   **Lat:** 42-49-28 N **Long:** 75-32-50 W
Pop: 3,790 (1990); 3,725 (1980)   **Pop Density:** 1994.7
Land: 1.9 sq. mi.; **Water:** 0.0 sq. mi.   **Elev:** 1126 ft.
In central NY southwest of Utica. Settled 1792. Not coextensive with the town of the same name.
Name origin: For Alexander Hamilton (1757–1804), first U.S. secretary of the treasury.

Lebanon   Town
ZIP: 13085   **Lat:** 42-47-07 N **Long:** 75-37-24 W
Pop: 1,265 (1990); 1,117 (1980)   **Pop Density:** 29.1
Land: 43.4 sq. mi.; **Water:** 0.2 sq. mi.
Name origin: For the biblical reference to the country.

Lenox   Town
ZIP: 13032   **Lat:** 43-06-39 N **Long:** 75-45-30 W
Pop: 8,621 (1990); 8,539 (1980)   **Pop Density:** 236.8
Land: 36.4 sq. mi.; **Water:** 0.0 sq. mi.

Lincoln   Town
                       Lat: 43-01-46 N **Long:** 75-43-52 W
Pop: 1,669 (1990); 1,722 (1980)   **Pop Density:** 66.8
Land: 25.0 sq. mi.; **Water:** 0.0 sq. mi.

Madison   Town
ZIP: 13402   **Lat:** 42-52-50 N **Long:** 75-30-02 W
Pop: 2,774 (1990); 2,314 (1980)   **Pop Density:** 67.8
Land: 40.9 sq. mi.; **Water:** 0.5 sq. mi.

*Madison   Village
ZIP: 13402   **Lat:** 42-53-52 N **Long:** 75-30-39 W
Pop: 316 (1990); 396 (1980)   **Pop Density:** 632.0
Land: 0.5 sq. mi.; **Water:** 0.0 sq. mi.
Not coextensive with the town of the same name.

Morrisville   Village
ZIP: 13408   **Lat:** 42-53-52 N **Long:** 75-38-41 W
Pop: 2,732 (1990); 2,707 (1980)   **Pop Density:** 2276.7
Land: 1.2 sq. mi.; **Water:** 0.0 sq. mi.

Munnsville   Village
ZIP: 13409   **Lat:** 42-58-37 N **Long:** 75-35-15 W
Pop: 438 (1990); 499 (1980)   **Pop Density:** 486.7
Land: 0.9 sq. mi.; **Water:** 0.0 sq. mi.

Nelson   Town
ZIP: 13035   **Lat:** 42-52-32 N **Long:** 75-45-31 W
Pop: 1,892 (1990); 1,495 (1980)   **Pop Density:** 43.9
Land: 43.1 sq. mi.; **Water:** 0.9 sq. mi.

Oneida   City
ZIP: 13421   **Lat:** 43-04-32 N **Long:** 75-39-49 W
Pop: 10,850 (1990); 10,810 (1980)   **Pop Density:** 493.2
Land: 22.0 sq. mi.; **Water:** 0.0 sq. mi.
In central NY, 5 mi. southeast of Oneida Lake.
Name origin: For the lake, itself named for the Indian tribe.

Smithfield   Town
                       Lat: 42-58-16 N **Long:** 75-40-37 W
Pop: 1,053 (1990); 1,001 (1980)   **Pop Density:** 43.3
Land: 24.3 sq. mi.; **Water:** 0.0 sq. mi.

Stockbridge   Town
ZIP: 13409   **Lat:** 42-59-07 N **Long:** 75-35-25 W
Pop: 1,968 (1990); 1,947 (1980)   **Pop Density:** 62.1
Land: 31.7 sq. mi.; **Water:** 0.0 sq. mi.

Sullivan   Town
ZIP: 13037   **Lat:** 43-05-41 N **Long:** 75-52-50 W
Pop: 14,622 (1990); 13,371 (1980)   **Pop Density:** 199.2
Land: 73.4 sq. mi.; **Water:** 0.2 sq. mi.

Wampsville   Village
ZIP: 13163   **Lat:** 43-04-39 N **Long:** 75-42-34 W
Pop: 501 (1990); 569 (1980)   **Pop Density:** 501.0
Land: 1.0 sq. mi.; **Water:** 0.0 sq. mi.

Monroe County
County Seat: Rochester (ZIP: 14614)

Pop: 713,968 (1990); 702,238 (1980)   **Pop Density:** 1082.9
Land: 659.3 sq. mi.; **Water:** 706.7 sq. mi.   **Area Code:** 716

On northwestern border of NY on Lake Ontario; organized Feb 23, 1821 from Genesee and Ontario counties.

Name origin: For James Monroe (1758–1831), fifth U.S. president, in office at the time of the county's creation.

Brighton   Town
ZIP: 14610   **Lat:** 43-07-06 N **Long:** 77-35-03 W
Pop: 34,455 (1990); 35,776 (1980)   **Pop Density:** 2222.9
Land: 15.5 sq. mi.; **Water:** 0.2 sq. mi.

Brockport   Village
ZIP: 14420   **Lat:** 43-12-48 N **Long:** 77-56-27 W
Pop: 8,749 (1990)   **Pop Density:** 3976.8
Land: 2.2 sq. mi.; **Water:** 0.0 sq. mi.
Name origin: For Hiel Brockway (1775–1842), a local landowner, and the fact that the village is on the Erie Canal.

Chili   Town
ZIP: 14428   **Lat:** 43-05-16 N **Long:** 77-45-32 W
Pop: 25,178 (1990); 23,676 (1980)   **Pop Density:** 634.2
Land: 39.7 sq. mi.; **Water:** 0.2 sq. mi.

Churchville   Village
ZIP: 14428   **Lat:** 43-06-05 N **Long:** 77-53-02 W
Pop: 1,731 (1990); 1,399 (1980)   **Pop Density:** 1442.5
Land: 1.2 sq. mi.; **Water:** 0.0 sq. mi.

Clarkson   Town
                    Lat: 43-15-24 N **Long:** 77-55-12 W
Pop: 4,517 (1990); 4,016 (1980)   **Pop Density:** 136.1
Land: 33.2 sq. mi.; **Water:** 0.0 sq. mi.

East Rochester   Village
ZIP: 14445   **Lat:** 43-06-41 N **Long:** 77-29-14 W
Pop: 6,932 (1990); 3,473 (1980)   **Pop Density:** 4951.4
Land: 1.4 sq. mi.; **Water:** 0.0 sq. mi.
Coterminous with the town of the same name.

Fairport   Village
ZIP: 14450   **Lat:** 43-06-00 N **Long:** 77-26-35 W
Pop: 5,943 (1990); 5,970 (1980)   **Pop Density:** 3714.4
Land: 1.6 sq. mi.; **Water:** 0.0 sq. mi.
In western NY, 10 mi. east of Rochester.
Name origin: For its descriptive connotations.

Gates   Town
ZIP: 14624   **Lat:** 43-09-07 N **Long:** 77-42-45 W
Pop: 28,583 (1990)   **Pop Density:** 1880.5
Land: 15.2 sq. mi.; **Water:** 0.1 sq. mi.

Greece   Town
ZIP: 14616   **Lat:** 43-14-48 N **Long:** 77-42-02 W
Pop: 90,106 (1990)   **Pop Density:** 1901.0
Land: 47.4 sq. mi.; **Water:** 4.0 sq. mi.
Name origin: For the country.

Hamlin   Town
ZIP: 14464   **Lat:** 43-19-20 N **Long:** 77-55-10 W
Pop: 9,203 (1990)   **Pop Density:** 212.1
Land: 43.4 sq. mi.; **Water:** 1.1 sq. mi.
Name origin: For Hamlin, Germany.

Henrietta   Town
ZIP: 14467   **Lat:** 43-03-18 N **Long:** 77-38-34 W
Pop: 36,376 (1990)   **Pop Density:** 1027.6
Land: 35.4 sq. mi.; **Water:** 0.2 sq. mi.

Hilton   Village
ZIP: 14468   **Lat:** 43-17-23 N **Long:** 77-47-34 W
Pop: 5,216 (1990); 4,151 (1980)   **Pop Density:** 3260.0
Land: 1.6 sq. mi.; **Water:** 0.0 sq. mi.

Honeoye Falls   Village
ZIP: 14472   **Lat:** 42-57-15 N **Long:** 77-35-30 W
Pop: 2,340 (1990); 2,410 (1980)   **Pop Density:** 900.0
Land: 2.6 sq. mi.; **Water:** 0.0 sq. mi.   **Elev:** 668 ft.

Irondequoit   Town
ZIP: 14617   **Lat:** 43-12-36 N **Long:** 77-34-19 W
Pop: 52,377 (1990)   **Pop Density:** 3423.3
Land: 15.3 sq. mi.; **Water:** 1.6 sq. mi.
In northern NY east of Rochester on Irondequoit Bay, an inlet of Lake Ontario.
Name origin: From an Iroquoian term probably meaning 'bay.'

Mendon   Town
ZIP: 14506   **Lat:** 42-58-36 N **Long:** 77-32-30 W
Pop: 6,845 (1990)   **Pop Density:** 172.0
Land: 39.8 sq. mi.; **Water:** 0.1 sq. mi.

Ogden   Town
ZIP: 14559   **Lat:** 43-09-26 N **Long:** 77-48-56 W
Pop: 16,912 (1990)   **Pop Density:** 462.1
Land: 36.6 sq. mi.; **Water:** 0.2 sq. mi.

Parma   Town
ZIP: 14468   **Lat:** 43-15-39 N **Long:** 77-47-48 W
Pop: 13,873 (1990)   **Pop Density:** 331.1
Land: 41.9 sq. mi.; **Water:** 1.0 sq. mi.
Name origin: For the city in Italy.

Penfield   Town
ZIP: 14526   **Lat:** 43-09-30 N **Long:** 77-26-55 W
Pop: 30,219 (1990)   **Pop Density:** 805.8
Land: 37.5 sq. mi.; **Water:** 0.4 sq. mi.
In western NY, 7 mi. southeast of Rochester.

Perinton   Town
ZIP: 14450   **Lat:** 43-04-32 N **Long:** 77-25-31 W
Pop: 43,015 (1990)   **Pop Density:** 1261.4
Land: 34.1 sq. mi.; **Water:** 0.3 sq. mi.
Name origin: For first settler Glover Perin.

Pittsford   Town
ZIP: 14534   **Lat:** 43-04-32 N **Long:** 77-31-33 W
Pop: 24,497 (1990)   **Pop Density:** 1055.9
Land: 23.2 sq. mi.; **Water:** 0.2 sq. mi.

*Pittsford   Village
ZIP: 14534   **Lat:** 43-05-25 N **Long:** 77-31-01 W
Pop: 1,488 (1990); 1,568 (1980)   **Pop Density:** 2125.7
Land: 0.7 sq. mi.; **Water:** 0.0 sq. mi.

In western NY, 7 mi. southeast of Rochester. Not coextensive with the town of the same name.

Riga   Town
ZIP: 14428   **Lat:** 43-04-44 N **Long:** 77-52-24 W
Pop: 5,114 (1990)   **Pop Density:** 145.7
Land: 35.1 sq. mi.; **Water:** 0.1 sq. mi.

Rochester   City
ZIP: 14601   **Lat:** 43-10-07 N **Long:** 77-36-57 W
Pop: 231,636 (1990); 241,741 (1980)   **Pop Density:** 6470.3
Land: 35.8 sq. mi.; **Water:** 1.3 sq. mi.

On the northern border of NY, on Lake Ontario, 80 mi. northwest of Syracuse. Incorporated 1817. Major producer of cameras, dental and optical equipment, nonelectrical machinery, and electronic equipment. Site of Univ. of Rochester and Eastman School of Music.

Name origin: For Col. Nathaniel Rochester (1752–1831), who, along with Col. William Fitzhugh and Maj. Charles Carroll, purchased the site in 1803; in 1811 he offered lots for sale.

Rush   Town
ZIP: 14543   **Lat:** 42-58-59 N **Long:** 77-40-14 W
Pop: 3,217 (1990)   **Pop Density:** 105.5
Land: 30.5 sq. mi.; **Water:** 0.2 sq. mi.

Name origin: For the rush reeds growing in the area.

Scottsville   Village
ZIP: 14546   **Lat:** 43-01-18 N **Long:** 77-45-13 W
Pop: 1,912 (1990); 1,789 (1980)   **Pop Density:** 1738.2
Land: 1.1 sq. mi.; **Water:** 0.0 sq. mi.

Spencerport   Village
ZIP: 14559   **Lat:** 43-11-16 N **Long:** 77-48-31 W
Pop: 3,606 (1990); 3,424 (1980)   **Pop Density:** 2575.7
Land: 1.4 sq. mi.; **Water:** 0.0 sq. mi.

In western NY, 10 mi. northwest of Rochester.

Name origin: From a personal name and for being a port on the Erie Canal.

Sweden   Town
ZIP: 14420   **Lat:** 43-10-10 N **Long:** 77-57-09 W
Pop: 14,181 (1990)   **Pop Density:** 422.1
Land: 33.6 sq. mi.; **Water:** 0.2 sq. mi.
Name origin: For the country.

Webster   Town
ZIP: 14580   **Lat:** 43-13-50 N **Long:** 77-26-36 W
Pop: 31,639 (1990)   **Pop Density:** 930.6
Land: 34.0 sq. mi.; **Water:** 1.5 sq. mi.

*Webster   Village
ZIP: 14580   **Lat:** 43-12-50 N **Long:** 77-25-20 W
Pop: 5,464 (1990); 5,499 (1980)   **Pop Density:** 2483.6
Land: 2.2 sq. mi.; **Water:** 0.0 sq. mi.

In western NY, 10 mi. northeast of Rochester. Not coextensive with the town of the same name.

Name origin: For an early settler.

Wheatland   Town
ZIP: 14546   **Lat:** 43-00-43 N **Long:** 77-48-45 W
Pop: 5,093 (1990)   **Pop Density:** 166.4
Land: 30.6 sq. mi.; **Water:** 0.1 sq. mi.

Montgomery County
County Seat: Fonda (ZIP: 12068)

Pop: 51,981 (1990); 53,439 (1980)   **Pop Density:** 128.4
Land: 404.8 sq. mi.; **Water:** 5.5 sq. mi.   **Area Code:** 518

In south-central NY, northwest of Albany; organized as Tryon County Mar 12, 1772 (prior to statehood) from Albany County; name changed Apr 2, 1784.

Name origin: For Gen. Richard Montgomery (1736–75), Revolutionary War officer.

Ames   Village
ZIP: 13317   **Lat:** 42-50-08 N **Long:** 74-36-10 W
Pop: 166 (1990); 224 (1980)   **Pop Density:** 1660.0
Land: 0.1 sq. mi.; **Water:** 0.0 sq. mi.   **Elev:** 713 ft.

Amsterdam   City
ZIP: 12010   **Lat:** 42-56-30 N **Long:** 74-11-27 W
Pop: 20,714 (1990); 21,872 (1980)   **Pop Density:** 3452.3
Land: 6.0 sq. mi.; **Water:** 0.3 sq. mi.

In northern NY on the NY State Barge Canal and Mohawk River, 28 mi. northwest of Albany. Not coextensive with the town of the same name.

Name origin: Named in 1804 for the Dutch city. Previously called Veedersburg.

*Amsterdam   Town
ZIP: 12010   **Lat:** 42-57-21 N **Long:** 74-10-00 W
Pop: 5,962 (1990)   **Pop Density:** 201.4
Land: 29.6 sq. mi.; **Water:** 0.7 sq. mi.

Canajoharie   Town
ZIP: 13317   **Lat:** 42-51-40 N **Long:** 74-36-30 W
Pop: 3,909 (1990)   **Pop Density:** 91.1
Land: 42.9 sq. mi.; **Water:** 0.2 sq. mi.

*Canajoharie   Village
ZIP: 13317   **Lat:** 42-54-10 N **Long:** 74-34-17 W
Pop: 2,278 (1990); 2,412 (1980)   **Pop Density:** 2278.0
Land: 1.0 sq. mi.; **Water:** 0.0 sq. mi.   **Elev:** 311 ft.

In northeastern NY on the Mohawk River; a western suburb of Schenectady. Not coextensive with the town of the same name.

Name origin: From the Indian term possibly meaning 'the pot that washes itself,' referring to a large pothole at the entrance to Canajoharie Gorge.

Charleston
Town
Lat: 42-49-24 N **Long:** 74-20-36 W
Pop: 1,107 (1990)   **Pop Density:** 26.0
Land: 42.6 sq. mi.; **Water:** 0.2 sq. mi.

Florida
Town
Lat: 42-53-12 N **Long:** 74-12-59 W
Pop: 2,637 (1990)   **Pop Density:** 52.3
Land: 50.4 sq. mi.; **Water:** 1.1 sq. mi.
Name origin: For the state.

Fonda
Village
ZIP: 12068   **Lat:** 42-57-11 N **Long:** 74-22-23 W
Pop: 1,007 (1990); 1,006 (1980)   **Pop Density:** 2014.0
Land: 0.5 sq. mi.; **Water:** 0.1 sq. mi.   **Elev:** 294 ft.
In eastern NY on the Mohawk River, 12 mi. west of Amsterdam. Settled in the early 1700s by the Dutch.
Name origin: Originally known as Caughnawaa.

Fort Johnson
Village
ZIP: 12070   **Lat:** 42-57-26 N **Long:** 74-14-21 W
Pop: 615 (1990); 646 (1980)   **Pop Density:** 878.6
Land: 0.7 sq. mi.; **Water:** 0.1 sq. mi.
During the French and Indian War a palisade was built around the settlement.
Name origin: For Sir William Johnson.

Fort Plain
Village
ZIP: 13339   **Lat:** 42-55-54 N **Long:** 74-37-41 W
Pop: 2,416 (1990); 7 (1980)   **Pop Density:** 1725.7
Land: 1.4 sq. mi.; **Water:** 0.1 sq. mi.   **Elev:** 317 ft.
In eastern NY at the confluence of Otsuquago Creek and the Mohawk River, 23 mi. west of Amsterdam.
Name origin: For its level topography.

Fultonville
Village
ZIP: 12072   **Lat:** 42-56-42 N **Long:** 74-22-13 W
Pop: 748 (1990); 777 (1980)   **Pop Density:** 1496.0
Land: 0.5 sq. mi.; **Water:** 0.0 sq. mi.

Glen
Town
Lat: 42-53-58 N **Long:** 74-21-07 W
Pop: 1,950 (1990)   **Pop Density:** 50.4
Land: 38.7 sq. mi.; **Water:** 0.6 sq. mi.

Hagaman
Village
ZIP: 12086   **Lat:** 42-58-29 N **Long:** 74-09-13 W
Pop: 1,377 (1990); 1,331 (1980)   **Pop Density:** 918.0
Land: 1.5 sq. mi.; **Water:** 0.0 sq. mi.

Minden
Town
ZIP: 13339   **Lat:** 42-55-22 N **Long:** 74-41-38 W
Pop: 4,474 (1990)   **Pop Density:** 87.7
Land: 51.0 sq. mi.; **Water:** 0.4 sq. mi.

Mohawk
Town
ZIP: 12068   **Lat:** 42-57-30 N **Long:** 74-23-40 W
Pop: 3,976 (1990)   **Pop Density:** 114.6
Land: 34.7 sq. mi.; **Water:** 0.7 sq. mi.

Nelliston
Village
Lat: 42-55-55 N **Long** 74-36-29 W
Pop: 569 (1990); 691 (1980)   **Pop Density:** 517.3
Land: 1.1 sq. mi.; **Water:** 0.1 sq. mi.

Palatine
Town
ZIP: 13428   **Lat:** 42-56-29 N **Long** 74-33-27 W
Pop: 2,787 (1990)   **Pop Density:** 67.6
Land: 41.2 sq. mi.; **Water:** 0.5 sq. mi.
Name origin: For the Rhenish Palatine, Germany, former home of many early settlers.

Palatine Bridge
Village
ZIP: 13428   **Lat:** 42-54-38 N **Long:** 74-34-30 W
Pop: 520 (1990); 604 (1980)   **Pop Density:** 866.7
Land: 0.6 sq. mi.; **Water:** 0.1 sq. mi.   **Elev:** 337 ft.

Root
Town
ZIP: 12166   **Lat:** 42-50-07 N **Long:** 74-28-59 W
Pop: 1,692 (1990)   **Pop Density:** 33.3
Land: 50.8 sq. mi.; **Water:** 0.2 sq. mi.

St. Johnsville
Town
Lat: 43-00-20 N **Long:** 74-40-43 W
Pop: 2,773 (1990)   **Pop Density:** 165.1
Land: 16.8 sq. mi.; **Water:** 0.5 sq. mi.

*St. Johnsville
Village
Lat: 43-00-01 N **Long:** 74-40-36 W
Pop: 1,825 (1990); 1,974 (1980)   **Pop Density:** 2281.3
Land: 0.8 sq. mi.; **Water:** 0.0 sq. mi.
Not coextensive with the town of the same name.

Tribes Hill
CDP
Lat: 42-56-51 N **Long:** 74-18-06 W
Pop: 1,060 (1990); 197 (1980)   **Pop Density:** 460.9
Land: 2.3 sq. mi.; **Water:** 0.1 sq. mi.

Nassau County
County Seat: Mineola (ZIP: 11501)

Pop: 1,287,350 (1990); 1,321,580 (1980)   **Pop Density:** 4489.1
Land: 286.8 sq. mi.; **Water:** 166.6 sq. mi.   **Area Code:** 516
On the western end of Long Island, east of Manhattan Island; organized Apr 27, 1898 from Queens County.
Name origin: For the duchy in Germany associated with the House of Orange, hence with William, Prince of Orange (1650–1702), later William III, King of England.

Albertson
CDP
ZIP: 11507   **Lat:** 40-46-16 N **Long:** 73-38-57 W
Pop: 5,166 (1990); 5,561 (1980)   **Pop Density:** 7380.0
Land: 0.7 sq. mi.; **Water:** 0.0 sq. mi.

Atlantic Beach
Village
ZIP: 11509   **Lat:** 40-35-16 N **Long:** 73-43-46 W
Pop: 1,933 (1990); 1,775 (1980)   **Pop Density:** 3866.0
Land: 0.5 sq. mi.; **Water:** 0.5 sq. mi.

In southeastern NY at the western point of Long Beach on western Long Island.
Name origin: For its location.

Baldwin   CDP
ZIP: 11510   **Lat:** 40-39-46 N **Long:** 73-36-40 W
Pop: 22,719 (1990); 31,630 (1980)   **Pop Density:** 7834.1
Land: 2.9 sq. mi.; **Water:** 0.0 sq. mi.

Baldwin Harbor   CDP
ZIP: 11510   **Lat:** 40-37-47 N **Long:** 73-36-08 W
Pop: 7,899 (1990)   **Pop Density:** 6582.5
Land: 1.2 sq. mi.; **Water:** 0.5 sq. mi.

Barnum Island   CDP
ZIP: 11558   **Lat:** 40-36-16 N **Long:** 73-38-39 W
Pop: 2,624 (1990)   **Pop Density:** 2915.6
Land: 0.9 sq. mi.; **Water:** 0.4 sq. mi.

Baxter Estates   Village
ZIP: 11050   **Lat:** 40-50-02 N **Long:** 73-41-46 W
Pop: 961 (1990); 911 (1980)   **Pop Density:** 4805.0
Land: 0.2 sq. mi.; **Water:** 0.0 sq. mi.

Bayville   Village
ZIP: 11709   **Lat:** 40-54-25 N **Long:** 73-33-47 W
Pop: 7,193 (1990); 7,034 (1980)   **Pop Density:** 5137.9
Land: 1.4 sq. mi.; **Water:** 0.1 sq. mi.   **Elev:** 40 ft.
On the northwestern end of Long Island.
Name origin: For its location on Oyster Bay.

Bellerose   Village
ZIP: 11426   **Lat:** 40-43-27 N **Long:** 73-43-00 W
Pop: 1,101 (1990); 1,187 (1980)   **Pop Density:** 11010.0
Land: 0.1 sq. mi.; **Water:** 0.0 sq. mi.

Bellmore   CDP
ZIP: 11710   **Lat:** 40-39-25 N **Long:** 73-31-45 W
Pop: 16,438 (1990); 18,106 (1980)   **Pop Density:** 6575.2
Land: 2.5 sq. mi.; **Water:** 0.5 sq. mi.

Bethpage   CDP
ZIP: 11714   **Lat:** 40-44-58 N **Long:** 73-29-08 W
Pop: 15,761 (1990); 16,840 (1980)   **Pop Density:** 4378.1
Land: 3.6 sq. mi.; **Water:** 0.0 sq. mi.

Brookville   Village
ZIP: 11545   **Lat:** 40-48-27 N **Long:** 73-34-12 W
Pop: 3,716 (1990); 3,290 (1980)   **Pop Density:** 929.0
Land: 4.0 sq. mi.; **Water:** 0.0 sq. mi.

Carle Place   CDP
ZIP: 11514   **Lat:** 40-45-03 N **Long:** 73-36-41 W
Pop: 5,107 (1990); 5,470 (1980)   **Pop Density:** 5674.4
Land: 0.9 sq. mi.; **Water:** 0.0 sq. mi.

Cedarhurst   Village
ZIP: 11516   **Lat:** 40-37-31 N **Long:** 73-43-40 W
Pop: 5,716 (1990); 6,162 (1980)   **Pop Density:** 8165.7
Land: 0.7 sq. mi.; **Water:** 0.0 sq. mi.
On southwestern Long Island near the Queens County border.
Name origin: For the numerous cedar trees.

Centre Island   Village
ZIP: 11771   **Lat:** 40-54-00 N **Long:** 73-31-19 W
Pop: 439 (1990); 378 (1980)   **Pop Density:** 399.1
Land: 1.1 sq. mi.; **Water:** 0.0 sq. mi.   **Elev:** 35 ft.

Cove Neck   Village
ZIP: 11771   **Lat:** 40-53-03 N **Long:** 73-29-47 W
Pop: 332 (1990); 331 (1980)   **Pop Density:** 255.4
Land: 1.3 sq. mi.; **Water:** 0.3 sq. mi.   **Elev:** 22 ft.

East Hills   Village
ZIP: 11548   **Lat:** 40-47-47 N **Long:** 73-37-44 W
Pop: 6,746 (1990); 7,146 (1980)   **Pop Density:** 2933.0
Land: 2.3 sq. mi.; **Water:** 0.0 sq. mi.

East Massapequa   CDP
ZIP: 11758   **Lat:** 40-40-24 N **Long:** 73-26-12 W
Pop: 19,550 (1990); 13,987 (1980)   **Pop Density:** 5585.7
Land: 3.5 sq. mi.; **Water:** 0.1 sq. mi.

East Meadow   CDP
ZIP: 11554   **Lat:** 40-43-11 N **Long:** 73-33-33 W
Pop: 36,909 (1990); 39,317 (1980)   **Pop Density:** 5858.6
Land: 6.3 sq. mi.; **Water:** 0.0 sq. mi.

East Norwich   CDP
ZIP: 11732   **Lat:** 40-50-49 N **Long:** 73-31-45 W
Pop: 2,698 (1990)   **Pop Density:** 2698.0
Land: 1.0 sq. mi.; **Water:** 0.0 sq. mi.

East Rockaway   Village
ZIP: 11518   **Lat:** 40-38-37 N **Long:** 73-40-02 W
Pop: 10,152 (1990); 10,917 (1980)   **Pop Density:** 10152.0
Land: 1.0 sq. mi.; **Water:** 0.0 sq. mi.
In southeastern NY on southwestern Long Island, 20 mi. east of New York City.

East Williston   Village
ZIP: 11596   **Lat:** 40-45-38 N **Long:** 73-38-01 W
Pop: 2,515 (1990); 2,708 (1980)   **Pop Density:** 4191.7
Land: 0.6 sq. mi.; **Water:** 0.0 sq. mi.   **Elev:** 119 ft.

Elmont   CDP
ZIP: 11003   **Lat:** 40-42-14 N **Long:** 73-42-27 W
Pop: 28,612 (1990); 27,592 (1980)   **Pop Density:** 8415.3
Land: 3.4 sq. mi.; **Water:** 0.0 sq. mi.

Farmingdale   Village
ZIP: 11735   **Lat:** 40-43-59 N **Long:** 73-26-51 W
Pop: 8,022 (1990); 7,946 (1980)   **Pop Density:** 7292.7
Land: 1.1 sq. mi.; **Water:** 0.0 sq. mi.
In southeastern NY, 30 mi. east of New York City on Long Island.

Floral Park   Village
ZIP: 11001   **Lat:** 40-43-20 N **Long:** 73-42-13 W
Pop: 15,947 (1990); 14,478 (1980)   **Pop Density:** 11390.7
Land: 1.4 sq. mi.; **Water:** 0.0 sq. mi.
In southeastern NY on Long Island, 15 mi. east of New York City.
Name origin: For its descriptive connotations.

Flower Hill   Village
ZIP: 11050   **Lat:** 40-48-30 N **Long:** 73-40-33 W
Pop: 4,490 (1990); 4,558 (1980)   **Pop Density:** 2806.3
Land: 1.6 sq. mi.; **Water:** 0.0 sq. mi.

Franklin Square   CDP
ZIP: 11010   **Lat:** 40-41-59 N **Long:** 73-40-37 W
Pop: 28,205 (1990); 29,051 (1980)   **Pop Density:** 9725.9
Land: 2.9 sq. mi.; **Water:** 0.0 sq. mi.

Freeport
Village
ZIP: 11520   **Lat:** 40-39-02 N **Long:** 73-35-05 W
Pop: 39,894 (1990); 38,272 (1980)   **Pop Density:** 8672.6
Land: 4.6 sq. mi.; **Water:** 0.2 sq. mi.

In southeastern NY on the south shore of Long Island, 25 mi. southeast of New York City.
Name origin: The port was used in colonial days by cargo ships to avoid British taxes.

Garden City
Village
ZIP: 11530   **Lat:** 40-43-33 N **Long:** 73-38-40 W
Pop: 21,686 (1990); 22,927 (1980)   **Pop Density:** 4091.7
Land: 5.3 sq. mi.; **Water:** 0.0 sq. mi.

In southeastern NY on Long Island, 18 mi. east of New York City.
Name origin: Named by its developers.

Garden City Park
CDP
ZIP: 11040   **Lat:** 40-44-39 N **Long:** 73-39-48 W
Pop: 7,437 (1990); 7,712 (1980)   **Pop Density:** 7437.0
Land: 1.0 sq. mi.; **Water:** 0.0 sq. mi.

Garden City South
CDP
     Lat: 40-42-40 N **Long:** 73-39-38 W
Pop: 4,073 (1990)   **Pop Density:** 10182.5
Land: 0.4 sq. mi.; **Water:** 0.0 sq. mi.

Glen Cove
City
ZIP: 11542   **Lat:** 40-53-29 N **Long:** 73-38-19 W
Pop: 24,149 (1990); 24,618 (1980)   **Pop Density:** 3658.9
Land: 6.6 sq. mi.; **Water:** 12.6 sq. mi.

In southeastern NY on Long Island's north shore, 22 mi. northeast of New York City.

Glen Head
CDP
ZIP: 11545   **Lat:** 40-50-35 N **Long:** 73-37-09 W
Pop: 4,488 (1990)   **Pop Density:** 2805.0
Land: 1.6 sq. mi.; **Water:** 0.0 sq. mi.

Glenwood Landing
CDP
     Lat: 40-49-47 N **Long:** 73-38-15 W
Pop: 3,407 (1990)   **Pop Density:** 3407.0
Land: 1.0 sq. mi.; **Water:** 0.0 sq. mi.

Great Neck
Village
ZIP: 11020   **Lat:** 40-48-08 N **Long:** 73-44-00 W
Pop: 8,745 (1990); 9,168 (1980)   **Pop Density:** 6726.9
Land: 1.3 sq. mi.; **Water:** 0.0 sq. mi.

In southeastern NY, on the north shore of Long Island, near the Queens County border.

Great Neck Estates
Village
ZIP: 11021   **Lat:** 40-47-05 N **Long:** 73-44-20 W
Pop: 2,790 (1990); 2,936 (1980)   **Pop Density:** 3487.5
Land: 0.8 sq. mi.; **Water:** 0.0 sq. mi.

Great Neck Plaza
Village
ZIP: 11020   **Lat:** 40-47-12 N **Long:** 73-43-35 W
Pop: 5,897 (1990); 5,604 (1980)   **Pop Density:** 19656.7
Land: 0.3 sq. mi.; **Water:** 0.0 sq. mi.

Hempstead
Town
ZIP: 11550   **Lat:** 40-39-33 N **Long:** 73-36-32 W
Pop: 725,639 (1990)   **Pop Density:** 6036.9
Land: 120.2 sq. mi.; **Water:** 23.9 sq. mi.

*Hempstead
Village
ZIP: 11550   **Lat:** 40-42-12 N **Long:** 73-37-08 W
Pop: 49,453 (1990); 40,404 (1980)   **Pop Density:** 13365.7
Land: 3.7 sq. mi.; **Water:** 0.0 sq. mi.

In southeastern NY, 20 mi. east of New York City on Long Island. Not coextensive with the town of the same name.
Name origin: For the town in the Netherlands.

Herricks
CDP
     Lat: 40-45-24 N **Long:** 73-39-51 W
Pop: 4,097 (1990); 8,123 (1980)   **Pop Density:** 6828.3
Land: 0.6 sq. mi.; **Water:** 0.0 sq. mi.

Hewlett
CDP
ZIP: 11557   **Lat:** 40-38-30 N **Long:** 73-41-40 W
Pop: 6,620 (1990); 6,986 (1980)   **Pop Density:** 7355.6
Land: 0.9 sq. mi.; **Water:** 0.0 sq. mi.

Hewlett Bay Park
Village
ZIP: 11557   **Lat:** 40-38-05 N **Long:** 73-41-46 W
Pop: 440 (1990); 489 (1980)   **Pop Density:** 1100.0
Land: 0.4 sq. mi.; **Water:** 0.0 sq. mi.

Hewlett Harbor
Village
ZIP: 11557   **Lat:** 40-37-55 N **Long:** 73-41-04 W
Pop: 1,193 (1990); 1,331 (1980)   **Pop Density:** 1704.3
Land: 0.7 sq. mi.; **Water:** 0.1 sq. mi.

Hewlett Neck
Village
ZIP: 11598   **Lat:** 40-37-28 N **Long:** 73-41-50 W
Pop: 547 (1990); 472 (1980)   **Pop Density:** 2735.0
Land: 0.2 sq. mi.; **Water:** 0.0 sq. mi.

Hicksville
CDP
ZIP: 11801   **Lat:** 40-45-49 N **Long:** 73-31-30 W
Pop: 40,174 (1990); 43,245 (1980)   **Pop Density:** 5907.9
Land: 6.8 sq. mi.; **Water:** 0.0 sq. mi.

Inwood
CDP
ZIP: 11696   **Lat:** 40-37-22 N **Long:** 73-45-00 W
Pop: 7,767 (1990); 8,228 (1980)   **Pop Density:** 4854.4
Land: 1.6 sq. mi.; **Water:** 0.5 sq. mi.

Island Park
Village
ZIP: 11558   **Lat:** 40-36-12 N **Long:** 73-39-19 W
Pop: 4,860 (1990); 4,847 (1980)   **Pop Density:** 12150.0
Land: 0.4 sq. mi.; **Water:** 0.0 sq. mi.

In southeastern NY on the southern shore of Long Island, 29 mi. east-southeast of New York City.

Jericho
CDP
ZIP: 11753   **Lat:** 40-47-18 N **Long:** 73-32-30 W
Pop: 13,141 (1990); 12,739 (1980)   **Pop Density:** 3285.3
Land: 4.0 sq. mi.; **Water:** 0.0 sq. mi.

Kensington
Village
ZIP: 11021   **Lat:** 40-47-39 N **Long:** 73-43-24 W
Pop: 1,104 (1990); 1,132 (1980)   **Pop Density:** 3680.0
Land: 0.3 sq. mi.; **Water:** 0.0 sq. mi.

Kings Point
Village
ZIP: 11024   **Lat:** 40-49-01 N **Long:** 73-44-38 W
Pop: 4,843 (1990); 5,234 (1980)   **Pop Density:** 1467.6
Land: 3.3 sq. mi.; **Water:** 0.6 sq. mi.   **Elev:** 26 ft.

In southeastern NY, on the north shore of Long Island, near Great Neck. Site of the U.S. Merchant Marine Academy.

Lake Success
Village
ZIP: 11040   **Lat:** 40-46-07 N **Long:** 73-42-36 W
Pop: 2,484 (1990); 2,396 (1980)   **Pop Density:** 1380.0
Land: 1.8 sq. mi.; **Water:** 0.0 sq. mi.

Lakeview   CDP
ZIP: 11552   **Lat:** 40-40-30 N **Long:** 73-39-05 W
Pop: 5,476 (1990); 5,276 (1980)   **Pop Density:** 5476.0
Land: 1.0 sq. mi.; **Water:** 0.2 sq. mi.

Lattingtown   Village
ZIP: 11560   **Lat:** 40-53-41 N **Long:** 73-35-41 W
Pop: 1,859 (1990); 1,749 (1980)   **Pop Density:** 489.2
Land: 3.8 sq. mi.; **Water:** 0.0 sq. mi.   **Elev:** 65 ft.

Laurel Hollow   Village
ZIP: 11791   **Lat:** 40-51-26 N **Long:** 73-28-40 W
Pop: 1,748 (1990); 1,527 (1980)   **Pop Density:** 602.8
Land: 2.9 sq. mi.; **Water:** 0.1 sq. mi.   **Elev:** 91 ft.

Lawrence   Village
ZIP: 11559   **Lat:** 40-36-15 N **Long:** 73-42-46 W
Pop: 6,513 (1990); 6,175 (1980)   **Pop Density:** 1713.9
Land: 3.8 sq. mi.; **Water:** 0.9 sq. mi.

In southeastern NY on the south shore of Long Island, 16 mi.
east-southeast of New York.

Name origin: For naval hero James Lawrence (1781–1813).

Levittown   CDP
ZIP: 11756   **Lat:** 40-43-25 N **Long:** 73-30-47 W
Pop: 53,286 (1990); 57,045 (1980)   **Pop Density:** 7722.6
Land: 6.9 sq. mi.; **Water:** 0.0 sq. mi.

Lido Beach   CDP
ZIP: 11561   **Lat:** 40-35-31 N **Long:** 73-36-27 W
Pop: 2,786 (1990)   **Pop Density:** 1638.8
Land: 1.7 sq. mi.; **Water:** 0.0 sq. mi.

Locust Valley   CDP
ZIP: 11560   **Lat:** 40-52-50 N **Long:** 73-35-15 W
Pop: 3,963 (1990)   **Pop Density:** 3963.0
Land: 1.0 sq. mi.; **Water:** 0.0 sq. mi.

Long Beach   City
ZIP: 11561   **Lat:** 40-35-06 N **Long:** 73-39-56 W
Pop: 33,510 (1990); 34,073 (1980)   **Pop Density:** 15957.1
Land: 2.1 sq. mi.; **Water:** 1.8 sq. mi.

In southeastern NY on the west end of the Outer Barrier
beach between the south shore of Long Island and the Atlantic Ocean, 21 mi. southeast of New York City.

Lynbrook   Village
ZIP: 11563   **Lat:** 40-39-31 N **Long:** 73-40-27 W
Pop: 19,208 (1990); 20,424 (1980)   **Pop Density:** 9604.0
Land: 2.0 sq. mi.; **Water:** 0.0 sq. mi.   **Elev:** 21 ft.

In southeastern NY on the south shore of Long Island, 18 mi.
east of New York City.

Malverne   Village
ZIP: 11565   **Lat:** 40-40-28 N **Long:** 73-40-21 W
Pop: 9,054 (1990); 9,262 (1980)   **Pop Density:** 8230.9
Land: 1.1 sq. mi.; **Water:** 0.0 sq. mi.

In southeastern NY on Long Island, 17 mi. east of New York.

Manhasset   CDP
ZIP: 11030   **Lat:** 40-47-29 N **Long:** 73-41-34 W
Pop: 7,718 (1990); 8,485 (1980)   **Pop Density:** 3215.8
Land: 2.4 sq. mi.; **Water:** 0.0 sq. mi.

Manhasset Hills   CDP
                       Lat: 40-45-32 N **Long:** 73-40-48 W
Pop: 3,722 (1990)   **Pop Density:** 6203.3
Land: 0.6 sq. mi.; **Water:** 0.0 sq. mi.

Manorhaven   Village
ZIP: 11050   **Lat:** 40-50-30 N **Long:** 73-42-51 W
Pop: 5,672 (1990); 5,384 (1980)   **Pop Density:** 11344.0
Land: 0.5 sq. mi.; **Water:** 0.2 sq. mi.

Massapequa   CDP
ZIP: 11758   **Lat:** 40-40-05 N **Long:** 73-28-18 W
Pop: 22,018 (1990); 24,454 (1980)   **Pop Density:** 6116.1
Land: 3.6 sq. mi.; **Water:** 0.4 sq. mi.

Massapequa Park   Village
ZIP: 11762   **Lat:** 40-40-50 N **Long:** 73-26-59 W
Pop: 18,044 (1990); 19,779 (1980)   **Pop Density:** 8201.8
Land: 2.2 sq. mi.; **Water:** 0.0 sq. mi.   **Elev:** 24 ft.

In southeastern NY on Long Island.

Matinecock   Village
ZIP: 11560   **Lat:** 40-51-51 N **Long:** 73-35-02 W
Pop: 872 (1990); 985 (1980)   **Pop Density:** 335.4
Land: 2.6 sq. mi.; **Water:** 0.0 sq. mi.

Merrick   CDP
ZIP: 11566   **Lat:** 40-39-02 N **Long:** 73-33-16 W
Pop: 23,042 (1990); 24,478 (1980)   **Pop Density:** 5486.2
Land: 4.2 sq. mi.; **Water:** 1.0 sq. mi.

Mill Neck   Village
ZIP: 11765   **Lat:** 40-52-48 N **Long:** 73-33-22 W
Pop: 977 (1990); 959 (1980)   **Pop Density:** 375.8
Land: 2.6 sq. mi.; **Water:** 0.3 sq. mi.

Mineola   Village
ZIP: 11501   **Lat:** 40-44-49 N **Long:** 73-38-19 W
Pop: 18,994 (1990); 52 (1980)   **Pop Density:** 9996.8
Land: 1.9 sq. mi.; **Water:** 0.0 sq. mi.

In southeastern NY on Long Island, 20 mi. east of New York
City.

Name origin: From an Indian term possibly meaning 'much
water.'

Munsey Park   Village
ZIP: 11030   **Lat:** 40-47-57 N **Long:** 73-40-48 W
Pop: 2,692 (1990); 2,806 (1980)   **Pop Density:** 5384.0
Land: 0.5 sq. mi.; **Water:** 0.0 sq. mi.

Muttontown   Village
ZIP: 11545   **Lat:** 40-49-14 N **Long:** 73-32-28 W
Pop: 3,024 (1990); 2,725 (1980)   **Pop Density:** 495.7
Land: 6.1 sq. mi.; **Water:** 0.0 sq. mi.

New Cassel   CDP
ZIP: 11590   **Lat:** 40-45-32 N **Long:** 73-33-56 W
Pop: 10,257 (1990); 9,635 (1980)   **Pop Density:** 6838.0
Land: 1.5 sq. mi.; **Water:** 0.0 sq. mi.

New Hyde Park   Village
ZIP: 11040   **Lat:** 40-43-55 N **Long:** 73-41-09 W
Pop: 9,728 (1990); 4,047 (1980)   **Pop Density:** 12160.0
Land: 0.8 sq. mi.; **Water:** 0.0 sq. mi.

In southeastern NY on Long Island.

North Bellmore   CDP
ZIP: 11710   **Lat:** 40-41-23 N **Long:** 73-32-18 W
Pop: 19,707 (1990); 20,630 (1980)   **Pop Density:** 7579.6
Land: 2.6 sq. mi.; **Water:** 0.0 sq. mi.

North Hempstead   Town
ZIP: 11040   **Lat:** 40-48-11 N **Long:** 73-40-43 W
Pop: 211,393 (1990)   **Pop Density:** 3951.3
Land: 53.5 sq. mi.; **Water:** 15.5 sq. mi.

North Hills
Village

ZIP: 11040   **Lat:** 40-46-35 N **Long:** 73-40-51 W
Pop: 3,453 (1990); 1,587 (1980)   **Pop Density:** 1233.2
Land: 2.8 sq. mi.; **Water:** 0.0 sq. mi.

North Massapequa
CDP

ZIP: 11758   **Lat:** 40-42-10 N **Long:** 73-27-59 W
Pop: 19,365 (1990); 21,385 (1980)   **Pop Density:** 6455.0
Land: 3.0 sq. mi.; **Water:** 0.0 sq. mi.

North Merrick
CDP

ZIP: 11566   **Lat:** 40-41-13 N **Long:** 73-33-38 W
Pop: 12,113 (1990); 12,848 (1980)   **Pop Density:** 6729.4
Land: 1.8 sq. mi.; **Water:** 0.0 sq. mi.

North New Hyde Park
CDP

ZIP: 11040   **Lat:** 40-44-44 N **Long:** 73-41-16 W
Pop: 14,359 (1990); 15,114 (1980)   **Pop Density:** 7179.5
Land: 2.0 sq. mi.; **Water:** 0.0 sq. mi.

North Valley Stream
CDP

ZIP: 11580   **Lat:** 40-41-03 N **Long:** 73-42-27 W
Pop: 14,574 (1990); 14,530 (1980)   **Pop Density:** 7670.5
Land: 1.9 sq. mi.; **Water:** 0.0 sq. mi.

North Wantagh
CDP

ZIP: 11793   **Lat:** 40-41-56 N **Long:** 73-30-31 W
Pop: 12,276 (1990); 12,677 (1980)   **Pop Density:** 6461.1
Land: 1.9 sq. mi.; **Water:** 0.0 sq. mi.

Oceanside
CDP

ZIP: 11572   **Lat:** 40-37-56 N **Long:** 73-38-08 W
Pop: 32,423 (1990); 33,639 (1980)   **Pop Density:** 6484.6
Land: 5.0 sq. mi.; **Water:** 0.4 sq. mi.

Old Bethpage
CDP

ZIP: 11804   **Lat:** 40-45-15 N **Long:** 73-27-19 W
Pop: 5,610 (1990); 6,215 (1980)   **Pop Density:** 1368.3
Land: 4.1 sq. mi.; **Water:** 0.0 sq. mi.

Old Brookville
Village

ZIP: 11545   **Lat:** 40-49-39 N **Long:** 73-36-17 W
Pop: 1,823 (1990); 1,574 (1980)   **Pop Density:** 455.8
Land: 4.0 sq. mi.; **Water:** 0.0 sq. mi.   **Elev:** 92 ft.

Old Westbury
Village

ZIP: 11568   **Lat:** 40-47-10 N **Long:** 73-35-46 W
Pop: 3,897 (1990); 2,175 (1980)   **Pop Density:** 458.5
Land: 8.5 sq. mi.; **Water:** 0.0 sq. mi.

In southeastern NY in west-central Long Island, southeast of Roslyn.

Oyster Bay
Town

ZIP: 11771   **Lat:** 40-47-17 N **Long:** 73-30-50 W
Pop: 292,657 (1990)   **Pop Density:** 2805.9
Land: 104.3 sq. mi.; **Water:** 16.7 sq. mi.

In southeastern NY on the north shore of Long Island on inlet of Oyster Bay Harbor.

Name origin: For its descriptive connotations.

Oyster Bay Cove
Village

ZIP: 11771   **Lat:** 40-51-33 N **Long:** 73-30-15 W
Pop: 2,109 (1990); 1,799 (1980)   **Pop Density:** 502.1
Land: 4.2 sq. mi.; **Water:** 0.1 sq. mi.

Plainedge
CDP

ZIP: 11756   **Lat:** 40-43-27 N **Long:** 73-28-40 W
Pop: 8,739 (1990); 9,629 (1980)   **Pop Density:** 6242.1
Land: 1.4 sq. mi.; **Water:** 0.0 sq. mi.

Plainview
CDP

ZIP: 11803   **Lat:** 40-46-59 N **Long:** 73-28-21 W
Pop: 26,207 (1990); 28,037 (1980)   **Pop Density:** 4597.7
Land: 5.7 sq. mi.; **Water:** 0.0 sq. mi.

Plandome
Village

ZIP: 11030   **Lat:** 40-48-27 N **Long:** 73-42-01 W
Pop: 1,347 (1990); 1,503 (1980)   **Pop Density:** 2694.0
Land: 0.5 sq. mi.; **Water:** 0.0 sq. mi.

Plandome Heights
Village

ZIP: 11030   **Lat:** 40-48-04 N **Long:** 73-42-18 W
Pop: 852 (1990); 963 (1980)   **Pop Density:** 4260.0
Land: 0.2 sq. mi.; **Water:** 0.0 sq. mi.   **Elev:** 90 ft.

Plandome Manor
Village

ZIP: 11030   **Lat:** 40-48-48 N **Long:** 73-41-51 W
Pop: 790 (1990); 883 (1980)   **Pop Density:** 1580.0
Land: 0.5 sq. mi.; **Water:** 0.1 sq. mi.

Port Washington
CDP

ZIP: 11050   **Lat:** 40-49-38 N **Long:** 73-40-49 W
Pop: 15,387 (1990); 14,521 (1980)   **Pop Density:** 3663.6
Land: 4.2 sq. mi.; **Water:** 1.4 sq. mi.

Port Washington North
Village

ZIP: 11050   **Lat:** 40-50-35 N **Long** 73-42-09 W
Pop: 2,736 (1990); 3,147 (1980)   **Pop Density:** 5472.0
Land: 0.5 sq. mi.; **Water:** 0.0 sq. mi.

Rockville Centre
Village

ZIP: 11570   **Lat:** 40-39-49 N **Long** 73-38-17 W
Pop: 24,727 (1990); 25,412 (1980)   **Pop Density:** 7493.0
Land: 3.3 sq. mi.; **Water:** 0.1 sq. mi.   **Elev:** 31 ft.

In southeastern NY on southeastern Long Island, 19 mi. southeast of New York City.

Name origin: For the Reverend Mordecai "Rock" Smith.

Roosevelt
CDP

ZIP: 11575   **Lat:** 40-40-46 N **Long** 73-35-02 W
Pop: 15,030 (1990); 14,109 (1980)   **Pop Density:** 8350.0
Land: 1.8 sq. mi.; **Water:** 0.0 sq. mi.

Roslyn
Village

ZIP: 11576   **Lat:** 40-47-58 N **Long** 73-38-55 W
Pop: 1,965 (1990); 2,134 (1980)   **Pop Density:** 3275.0
Land: 0.6 sq. mi.; **Water:** 0.0 sq. mi.

In southeastern NY on the north shore of Long Island, about 4 mi. north of Mineola.

Name origin: For the wife of an early settler.

Roslyn Estates
Village

ZIP: 11576   **Lat:** 40-47-38 N **Long** 73-39-44 W
Pop: 1,184 (1990); 1,292 (1980)   **Pop Density:** 2960.0
Land: 0.4 sq. mi.; **Water:** 0.0 sq. mi.

Roslyn Harbor
Village

ZIP: 11545   **Lat:** 40-49-06 N **Long** 73-38-26 W
Pop: 1,114 (1990); 785 (1980)   **Pop Density:** 928.3
Land: 1.2 sq. mi.; **Water:** 0.0 sq. mi.

Russell Gardens
Village

ZIP: 11021   **Lat:** 40-46-52 N **Long** 73-43-31 W
Pop: 1,027 (1990); 1,263 (1980)   **Pop Density:** 5135.0
Land: 0.2 sq. mi.; **Water:** 0.0 sq. mi.

Saddle Rock
Village

ZIP: 11023   **Lat:** 40-47-39 N **Long** 73-44-57 W
Pop: 832 (1990); 921 (1980)   **Pop Density:** 4160.0
Land: 0.2 sq. mi.; **Water:** 0.0 sq. mi.

Salisbury
CDP
Lat: 40-44-44 N **Long:** 73-33-38 W
Pop: 12,226 (1990)   **Pop Density:** 7191.8
Land: 1.7 sq. mi.; **Water:** 0.0 sq. mi.

Sands Point
Village
ZIP: 11050   **Lat:** 40-51-10 N **Long:** 73-42-10 W
Pop: 2,477 (1990); 2,742 (1980)   **Pop Density:** 589.8
Land: 4.2 sq. mi.; **Water:** 1.4 sq. mi.

Sea Cliff
Village
ZIP: 11579   **Lat:** 40-50-54 N **Long:** 73-39-04 W
Pop: 5,054 (1990); 5,364 (1980)   **Pop Density:** 4594.5
Land: 1.1 sq. mi.; **Water:** 0.9 sq. mi.

In southeastern NY on the north shore of western Long Island.

Name origin: For its descriptive connotations.

Seaford
CDP
ZIP: 11783   **Lat:** 40-40-04 N **Long:** 73-29-34 W
Pop: 15,597 (1990); 16,117 (1980)   **Pop Density:** 5998.8
Land: 2.6 sq. mi.; **Water:** 0.0 sq. mi.

Searingtown
CDP
ZIP: 11507   **Lat:** 40-46-12 N **Long:** 73-39-36 W
Pop: 5,020 (1990)   **Pop Density:** 5577.8
Land: 0.9 sq. mi.; **Water:** 0.0 sq. mi.

South Farmingdale
CDP
ZIP: 11735   **Lat:** 40-43-04 N **Long:** 73-26-54 W
Pop: 15,377 (1990); 16,439 (1980)   **Pop Density:** 6989.5
Land: 2.2 sq. mi.; **Water:** 0.0 sq. mi.

South Floral Park
Village
Lat: 40-42-46 N **Long:** 73-42-03 W
Pop: 1,478 (1990); 1,490 (1980)   **Pop Density:** 14780.0
Land: 0.1 sq. mi.; **Water:** 0.0 sq. mi.

South Hempstead
CDP
Lat: 40-40-57 N **Long:** 73-37-25 W
Pop: 3,014 (1990)   **Pop Density:** 5023.3
Land: 0.6 sq. mi.; **Water:** 0.0 sq. mi.

South Valley Stream
CDP
ZIP: 11581   **Lat:** 40-39-21 N **Long:** 73-43-05 W
Pop: 5,328 (1990); 5,462 (1980)   **Pop Density:** 5920.0
Land: 0.9 sq. mi.; **Water:** 0.0 sq. mi.

Stewart Manor
Village
ZIP: 11530   **Lat:** 40-43-13 N **Long:** 73-41-08 W
Pop: 2,002 (1990); 2,373 (1980)   **Pop Density:** 10010.0
Land: 0.2 sq. mi.; **Water:** 0.0 sq. mi.

Syosset
CDP
ZIP: 11791   **Lat:** 40-48-55 N **Long:** 73-30-10 W
Pop: 18,967 (1990); 9,818 (1980)   **Pop Density:** 3793.4
Land: 5.0 sq. mi.; **Water:** 0.0 sq. mi.

Thomaston
Village
ZIP: 11021   **Lat:** 40-47-16 N **Long:** 73-42-52 W
Pop: 2,612 (1990); 2,684 (1980)   **Pop Density:** 6530.0
Land: 0.4 sq. mi.; **Water:** 0.0 sq. mi.

Uniondale
CDP
ZIP: 11553   **Lat:** 40-42-08 N **Long:** 73-35-29 W
Pop: 20,328 (1990); 20,016 (1980)   **Pop Density:** 7528.9
Land: 2.7 sq. mi.; **Water:** 0.0 sq. mi.

University Gardens
CDP
Lat: 40-46-29 N **Long:** 73-43-40 W
Pop: 4,419 (1990)   **Pop Density:** 7365.0
Land: 0.6 sq. mi.; **Water:** 0.0 sq. mi.

Upper Brookville
Village
ZIP: 11545   **Lat:** 40-50-38 N **Long:** 73-33-53 W
Pop: 1,453 (1990); 1,245 (1980)   **Pop Density:** 337.9
Land: 4.3 sq. mi.; **Water:** 0.0 sq. mi.   **Elev:** 156 ft.

Valley Stream
Village
ZIP: 11580   **Lat:** 40-39-52 N **Long:** 73-42-18 W
Pop: 33,946 (1990); 35,769 (1980)   **Pop Density:** 9984.1
Land: 3.4 sq. mi.; **Water:** 0.0 sq. mi.

In southeastern NY on Long Island, 18 mi. from the Manhattan Bridge.

Wantagh
CDP
ZIP: 11793   **Lat:** 40-40-03 N **Long:** 73-30-38 W
Pop: 18,567 (1990); 19,817 (1980)   **Pop Density:** 4886.1
Land: 3.8 sq. mi.; **Water:** 0.3 sq. mi.

Westbury
Village
ZIP: 11590   **Lat:** 40-45-34 N **Long:** 73-35-20 W
Pop: 13,060 (1990); 13,871 (1980)   **Pop Density:** 5441.7
Land: 2.4 sq. mi.; **Water:** 0.0 sq. mi.   **Elev:** 107 ft.

In southeastern NY, in central-western Long Island, 23 mi. east of New York City.

Name origin: For one of two Westburys in England.

West Hempstead
CDP
ZIP: 11552   **Lat:** 40-41-43 N **Long:** 73-39-03 W
Pop: 17,689 (1990); 18,536 (1980)   **Pop Density:** 6551.5
Land: 2.7 sq. mi.; **Water:** 0.1 sq. mi.

Williston Park
Village
ZIP: 11596   **Lat:** 40-45-31 N **Long:** 73-38-48 W
Pop: 7,516 (1990); 8,216 (1980)   **Pop Density:** 12526.7
Land: 0.6 sq. mi.; **Water:** 0.0 sq. mi.   **Elev:** 127 ft.

In southeastern NY on Long Island, 18 mi. east of New York City.

Woodbury
CDP
ZIP: 11797   **Lat:** 40-48-53 N **Long:** 73-28-13 W
Pop: 8,008 (1990); 7,043 (1980)   **Pop Density:** 1570.2
Land: 5.1 sq. mi.; **Water:** 0.0 sq. mi.

Woodmere
CDP
ZIP: 11598   **Lat:** 40-38-16 N **Long:** 73-43-18 W
Pop: 15,578 (1990); 17,205 (1980)   **Pop Density:** 5991.5
Land: 2.6 sq. mi.; **Water:** 0.1 sq. mi.

Woodsburgh
Village
ZIP: 11598   **Lat:** 40-37-15 N **Long:** 73-42-23 W
Pop: 1,190 (1990); 847 (1980)   **Pop Density:** 2975.0
Land: 0.4 sq. mi.; **Water:** 0.0 sq. mi.   **Elev:** 8 ft.

New York City

ZIP: 10001
Pop: 7,322,564 (1990); 7,071,639 (1980)
Land: 308.9 sq. mi.; **Water:** 159.0 sq. mi.

Lat: 40-42-51 N **Long:** 74-00-23 W
Pop Density: 23705.3
Area Code: 212; 718; 917

In southeastern NY at the mouth of the Hudson River. First incorporated as the city of New Amsterdam by Dutch colonists in 1653. The English took possession in 1664, and the city (then encompassing Manhattan only) became known as New York City. Greater New York was formed in 1898 from five boroughs: Manhattan, Brooklyn, the Bronx, Queens, and Richmond (Staten Island). Most populous city and center of the most populous metropolitan area in the United States. One of the world's most important centers of business (corporate headquarters, advertising), finance (stock exchanges, commodities markets), culture (publishing, theater, dance, music, museums, colleges and universities), and trade; also a major port. Site of the United Nations headquarters, Statue of Liberty, Empire State Building, World Trade Center Towers. Nicknamed *The Big Apple.* Each of the five boroughs is coextensive with a county: Manhattan/New York County; Bronx/Bronx County; Brooklyn/Kings County; Queens/Queens County; Staten Island/Richmond County.

Name origin: Named in 1664 when Col. Richard Nicolls seized the Dutch territories for King Charles II of England, who granted them to his brother, James (1633–1701), Duke of York and Albany, later James II, King of England. Lands east of the Hudson River were called Yorkshire, later New York. Called Nieuw Amsterdam by the Dutch.

New York County (Manhattan)
County Seat: New York (ZIP: 10007)

Pop: 1,487,536 (1990); 1,428,285 (1980)
Land: 28.4 sq. mi.; **Water:** 5.3 sq. mi.

Pop Density: 52378.0
Area Code: 212; 917

Primarily on Manhattan Island at the southeastern tip of NY, west of Long Island; original county, organized Nov 1, 1683. The county is coterminous with the borough of Manhattan, part of New York City.

Name origin: See New York City.

Manhattan
Borough
Lat: 40-46-27 N **Long:** 73-58-19 W

Includes Manhattan Island, a small portion (Marble Hill) on the mainland, and several islands in the East River. The borough of Manhattan is one part of New York City, but is generally what is meant when referring to "New York City." The area was known as New York City until the formation of Greater New York in 1898, which joined Manhattan with four other boroughs. Includes the following neighborhoods: Greenwich Village, Harlem.

Name origin: For the Manhattan tribe of Indians, from whom Dutch colonist Peter Minuit (1580–1638) purchased the island in 1626.

Niagara County
County Seat: Lockport (ZIP: 14094)

Pop: 220,756 (1990); 227,354 (1980)
Land: 523.0 sq. mi.; **Water:** 616.9 sq. mi.

Pop Density: 422.1
Area Code: 716

In northwestern corner of NY on Lake Ontario; organized Mar 11, 1808 from Genesee County.

Name origin: For the Niagara River, which forms its western border.

Barker
Village
ZIP: 14012
Pop: 569 (1990); 535 (1980)
Land: 0.4 sq. mi.; **Water:** 0.0 sq. mi.
Lat: 43-19-38 N **Long:** 78-33-13 W
Pop Density: 1422.5
Elev: 331 ft.

Cambria
Town
Pop: 4,779 (1990)
Land: 39.9 sq. mi.; **Water:** 0.0 sq. mi.
Lat: 43-10-14 N **Long:** 78-49-48 W
Pop Density: 119.8

Gasport
CDP
ZIP: 14067   **Lat:** 43-11-43 N **Long:** 78-34-37 W
Pop: 1,336 (1990); 1,339 (1980)   **Pop Density:** 460.7
Land: 2.9 sq. mi.; **Water:** 0.1 sq. mi.

Hartland
Town
Lat: 43-15-48 N **Long:** 78-33-11 W
Pop: 3,911 (1990)   **Pop Density:** 74.6
Land: 52.4 sq. mi.; **Water:** 0.0 sq. mi.

Lewiston
Town
ZIP: 14092   **Lat:** 43-10-44 N **Long:** 78-58-42 W
Pop: 15,453 (1990)   **Pop Density:** 415.4
Land: 37.2 sq. mi.; **Water:** 3.8 sq. mi.

*Lewiston
Village
ZIP: 14092   **Lat:** 43-10-17 N **Long:** 79-02-26 W
Pop: 3,048 (1990); 3,326 (1980)   **Pop Density:** 2770.9
Land: 1.1 sq. mi.; **Water:** 0.1 sq. mi.

In western NY along the Niagara River, 7 mi. north of Niagara Falls. Not coextensive with the town of the same name.

Lockport
City
ZIP: 14094   **Lat:** 43-10-10 N **Long:** 78-41-46 W
Pop: 24,426 (1990); 24,844 (1980)   **Pop Density:** 2873.6
Land: 8.5 sq. mi.; **Water:** 0.1 sq. mi.

In western NY, 20 mi. northeast of Niagara Falls. Not coextensive with the town of the same name.

Name origin: For the series of locks built to carry the Erie Canal through the Lockport gorge.

*Lockport
Town
ZIP: 14094   **Lat:** 43-09-11 N **Long:** 78-40-34 W
Pop: 16,596 (1990)   **Pop Density:** 372.1
Land: 44.6 sq. mi.; **Water:** 0.1 sq. mi.

Middleport
Village
ZIP: 14105   **Lat:** 43-12-42 N **Long:** 78-28-33 W
Pop: 1,876 (1990); 163 (1980)   **Pop Density:** 2084.4
Land: 0.9 sq. mi.; **Water:** 0.0 sq. mi.

In western NY, 30 mi. east-northeast of Niagara Falls. Settled upon completion of the Erie Canal in 1825.

Name origin: For its location midway between Lockport and Albion.

Newfane
Town
ZIP: 14108   **Lat:** 43-17-13 N **Long:** 78-41-57 W
Pop: 8,996 (1990)   **Pop Density:** 173.7
Land: 51.8 sq. mi.; **Water:** 1.6 sq. mi.

In northern NY on Lake Ontario, northwest of Niagara Falls.

Name origin: For settler John Fane.

Niagara
Town
ZIP: 14302   **Lat:** 43-07-05 N **Long:** 78-58-47 W
Pop: 9,880 (1990)   **Pop Density:** 1051.1
Land: 9.4 sq. mi.; **Water:** 0.0 sq. mi.

Niagara Falls
City
ZIP: 14301   **Lat:** 43-05-28 N **Long:** 79-00-58 W
Pop: 61,840 (1990); 71,384 (1980)   **Pop Density:** 4385.8
Land: 14.1 sq. mi.; **Water:** 2.7 sq. mi.   **Elev:** 618 ft.

In northwestern NY on the Niagara River at the Falls; 20 mi. north of Buffalo.

North Tonawanda
City
ZIP: 14120   **Lat:** 43-02-37 N **Long:** 78-51-57 W
Pop: 34,989 (1990); 35,760 (1980)   **Pop Density:** 3464.3
Land: 10.1 sq. mi.; **Water:** 0.8 sq. mi.   **Elev:** 575 ft.

In western NY, 10 mi. east of Niagara Falls.

Olcott
CDP
Lat: 43-20-07 N **Long:** 78-42-44 W
Pop: 1,432 (1990); 1,571 (1980)   **Pop Density:** 311.3
Land: 4.6 sq. mi.; **Water:** 0.7 sq. mi.

Pendleton
Town
ZIP: 14094   **Lat:** 43-06-13 N **Long:** 78-45-53 W
Pop: 5,010 (1990)   **Pop Density:** 184.2
Land: 27.2 sq. mi.; **Water:** 0.3 sq. mi.

Porter
Town
ZIP: 14131   **Lat:** 43-15-23 N **Long:** 78-58-17 W
Pop: 7,110 (1990)   **Pop Density:** 214.2
Land: 33.2 sq. mi.; **Water:** 4.5 sq. mi.

Ransomville
CDP
ZIP: 14131   **Lat:** 43-14-16 N **Long:** 78-54-32 W
Pop: 1,542 (1990); 1,103 (1980)   **Pop Density:** 248.7
Land: 6.2 sq. mi.; **Water:** 0.0 sq. mi.

Rapids
CDP
Lat: 43-06-04 N **Long:** 78-38-28 W
Pop: 1,152 (1990)   **Pop Density:** 311.4
Land: 3.7 sq. mi.; **Water:** 0.0 sq. mi.

Royalton
Town
ZIP: 14067   **Lat:** 43-08-43 N **Long:** 78-33-01 W
Pop: 7,453 (1990)   **Pop Density:** 106.8
Land: 69.8 sq. mi.; **Water:** 0.3 sq. mi.

Somerset
Town
Lat: 43-20-11 N **Long:** 78-32-46 W
Pop: 2,655 (1990)   **Pop Density:** 71.4
Land: 37.2 sq. mi.; **Water:** 0.1 sq. mi.

South Lockport
CDP
ZIP: 14094   **Lat:** 43-08-02 N **Long:** 78-41-10 W
Pop: 7,112 (1990); 3,366 (1980)   **Pop Density:** 1247.7
Land: 5.7 sq. mi.; **Water:** 0.0 sq. mi.

Tonawanda Reservation
Pop. Place
Lat: 43-05-19 N **Long:** 78-28-41 W
Pop: 0 (1990)
Land: 0.8 sq. mi.; **Water:** 0.0 sq. mi.

Tuscarora Reservation
Pop. Place
Lat: 43-09-59 N **Long:** 78-57-27 W
Pop: 772 (1990)   **Pop Density:** 83.0
Land: 9.3 sq. mi.; **Water:** 0.0 sq. mi.

Wheatfield
Town
ZIP: 14120   **Lat:** 43-05-44 N **Long:** 78-53-08 W
Pop: 11,125 (1990)   **Pop Density:** 398.7
Land: 27.9 sq. mi.; **Water:** 0.7 sq. mi.

Wilson
Town
ZIP: 14172   **Lat:** 43-16-21 N **Long:** 78-48-47 W
Pop: 5,761 (1990)   **Pop Density:** 116.4
Land: 49.5 sq. mi.; **Water:** 1.9 sq. mi.

*Wilson
Village
ZIP: 14172   **Lat:** 43-18-38 N **Long:** 78-49-37 W
Pop: 1,307 (1990); 1,259 (1980)   **Pop Density:** 1633.8
Land: 0.8 sq. mi.; **Water:** 0.2 sq. mi.   **Elev:** 290 ft.

Not coextensive with the town of the same name.

Youngstown
Village
ZIP: 14174   **Lat:** 43-14-55 N **Long:** 79-02-33 W
Pop: 2,075 (1990); 2,191 (1980)   **Pop Density:** 1729.2
Land: 1.2 sq. mi.; **Water:** 0.2 sq. mi.   **Elev:** 301 ft.

In western NY, 35 mi. north of Buffalo.

Oneida County
County Seat: Utica (ZIP: 13501)

Pop: 250,836 (1990); 253,466 (1980)   **Pop Density:** 206.8
Land: 1212.8 sq. mi.; **Water:** 44.4 sq. mi.   **Area Code:** 315

In central NY, northeast of Syracuse; organized May 15, 1798 from Herkimer County.

Name origin: For the Oneida Indian tribe of Iroquoian linguistic stock; one of the Five Nations of the Iroquois. The name probably means 'stone people,' perhaps in praise of their bravery.

Annsville   Town
ZIP: 13471   **Lat:** 43-20-51 N **Long:** 75-37-09 W
Pop: 2,786 (1990)   **Pop Density:** 46.3
Land: 60.2 sq. mi.; **Water:** 0.3 sq. mi.

Augusta   Town
ZIP: 13425   **Lat:** 42-58-46 N **Long:** 75-30-07 W
Pop: 2,070 (1990)   **Pop Density:** 74.7
Land: 27.7 sq. mi.; **Water:** 0.0 sq. mi.

Ava   Town
ZIP: 13303   **Lat:** 43-24-58 N **Long:** 75-27-44 W
Pop: 792 (1990)   **Pop Density:** 21.0
Land: 37.7 sq. mi.; **Water:** 0.0 sq. mi.

Barneveld   Village
ZIP: 13304   **Lat:** 43-16-26 N **Long:** 75-11-20 W
Pop: 272 (1990); 396 (1980)   **Pop Density:** 1360.0
Land: 0.2 sq. mi.; **Water:** 0.0 sq. mi.

Boonville   Town
ZIP: 13309   **Lat:** 43-27-59 N **Long:** 75-17-55 W
Pop: 4,246 (1990)   **Pop Density:** 59.0
Land: 72.0 sq. mi.; **Water:** 0.7 sq. mi.

*Boonville   Village
ZIP: 13309   **Lat:** 43-28-51 N **Long:** 75-19-48 W
Pop: 2,220 (1990); 2,344 (1980)   **Pop Density:** 1233.3
Land: 1.8 sq. mi.; **Water:** 0.0 sq. mi.   **Elev:** 1146 ft.
Not coextensive with the town of the same name.

Bridgewater   Town
          Lat: 42-54-26 N **Long:** 75-15-21 W
Pop: 1,591 (1990)   **Pop Density:** 66.6
Land: 23.9 sq. mi.; **Water:** 0.0 sq. mi.

*Bridgewater   Village
ZIP: 13313   **Lat:** 42-52-39 N **Long:** 75-15-00 W
Pop: 537 (1990); 578 (1980)   **Pop Density:** 895.0
Land: 0.6 sq. mi.; **Water:** 0.0 sq. mi.
Not coextensive with the town of the same name.

Camden   Town
ZIP: 13316   **Lat:** 43-20-34 N **Long:** 75-47-04 W
Pop: 5,134 (1990)   **Pop Density:** 95.1
Land: 54.0 sq. mi.; **Water:** 0.1 sq. mi.

*Camden   Village
ZIP: 13316   **Lat:** 43-20-10 N **Long:** 75-44-51 W
Pop: 2,552 (1990); 2,667 (1980)   **Pop Density:** 1109.6
Land: 2.3 sq. mi.; **Water:** 0.0 sq. mi.
Not coextensive with the town of the same name.
Name origin: For Lord Camden, who supported the American cause before the Revolution.

Clark Mills   CDP
          Lat: 43-05-03 N **Long:** 75-22-35 W
Pop: 1,303 (1990); 1,412 (1980)   **Pop Density:** 1447.8
Land: 0.9 sq. mi.; **Water:** 0.0 sq. mi.

Clayville   Village
ZIP: 13322   **Lat:** 42-58-27 N **Long:** 75-14-59 W
Pop: 463 (1990); 478 (1980)   **Pop Density:** 926.0
Land: 0.5 sq. mi.; **Water:** 0.0 sq. mi.

Clinton   Village
ZIP: 13323   **Lat:** 43-02-56 N **Long:** 75-22-43 W
Pop: 2,238 (1990); 2,107 (1980)   **Pop Density:** 3730.0
Land: 0.6 sq. mi.; **Water:** 0.0 sq. mi.

Deerfield   Town
          Lat: 43-10-53 N **Long:** 75-08-53 W
Pop: 3,942 (1990)   **Pop Density:** 119.8
Land: 32.9 sq. mi.; **Water:** 0.1 sq. mi.

Florence   Town
ZIP: 13316   **Lat:** 43-25-11 N **Long:** 75-44-16 W
Pop: 852 (1990)   **Pop Density:** 15.5
Land: 55.0 sq. mi.; **Water:** 0.1 sq. mi.

Floyd   Town
          Lat: 43-14-59 N **Long:** 75-19-46 W
Pop: 3,856 (1990)   **Pop Density:** 111.4
Land: 34.6 sq. mi.; **Water:** 0.2 sq. mi.

Forestport   Town
ZIP: 13338   **Lat:** 43-29-31 N **Long:** 75-09-37 W
Pop: 1,556 (1990)   **Pop Density:** 20.2
Land: 77.2 sq. mi.; **Water:** 1.8 sq. mi.

Holland Patent   Village
ZIP: 13354   **Lat:** 43-14-30 N **Long:** 75-15-26 W
Pop: 411 (1990); 534 (1980)   **Pop Density:** 822.0
Land: 0.5 sq. mi.; **Water:** 0.0 sq. mi.

Kirkland   Town
ZIP: 13323   **Lat:** 43-02-10 N **Long:** 75-23-15 W
Pop: 10,153 (1990)   **Pop Density:** 300.4
Land: 33.8 sq. mi.; **Water:** 0.1 sq. mi.

Lee   Town
ZIP: 13440   **Lat:** 43-19-31 N **Long:** 75-31-07 W
Pop: 7,115 (1990)   **Pop Density:** 157.4
Land: 45.2 sq. mi.; **Water:** 0.4 sq. mi.

Marcy   Town
ZIP: 13403   **Lat:** 43-10-20 N **Long:** 75-15-53 W
Pop: 8,685 (1990)   **Pop Density:** 263.2
Land: 33.0 sq. mi.; **Water:** 0.4 sq. mi.

Marshall   Town
          Lat: 42-57-49 N **Long:** 75-23-37 W
Pop: 2,125 (1990)   **Pop Density:** 64.8
Land: 32.8 sq. mi.; **Water:** 0.0 sq. mi.

New Hartford   Town
ZIP: 13413   Lat: 43-03-32 N **Long:** 75-16-49 W
Pop: 21,640 (1990)   **Pop Density:** 852.0
Land: 25.4 sq. mi.; **Water:** 0.1 sq. mi.

*New Hartford   Village
ZIP: 13413   Lat: 43-04-15 N **Long:** 75-17-22 W
Pop: 2,111 (1990); 2,313 (1980)   **Pop Density:** 3518.3
Land: 0.6 sq. mi.; **Water:** 0.0 sq. mi.

In central NY, a southern suburb of Utica. Not coextensive with the town of the same name.
Name origin: For the city in England.

New York Mills   Village
ZIP: 13417   Lat: 43-06-01 N **Long:** 75-17-35 W
Pop: 3,534 (1990); 1,930 (1980)   **Pop Density:** 3212.7
Land: 1.1 sq. mi.; **Water:** 0.0 sq. mi.

Oneida Castle   Village
ZIP: 13421   Lat: 43-05-01 N **Long:** 75-37-56 W
Pop: 671 (1990); 751 (1980)   **Pop Density:** 1342.0
Land: 0.5 sq. mi.; **Water:** 0.0 sq. mi.

Oriskany   Village
ZIP: 13424   Lat: 43-09-21 N **Long:** 75-19-58 W
Pop: 1,450 (1990); 1,680 (1980)   **Pop Density:** 1812.5
Land: 0.8 sq. mi.; **Water:** 0.0 sq. mi.

In central NY on the Mohawk River, 7 mi. west-northwest of Utica.
Name origin: Located on the site of the former Indian village of Oriska, which means 'nettles.'

Oriskany Falls   Village
ZIP: 13425   Lat: 42-56-16 N **Long:** 75-27-47 W
Pop: 795 (1990); 802 (1980)   **Pop Density:** 1590.0
Land: 0.5 sq. mi.; **Water:** 0.0 sq. mi.

Paris   Town
Lat: 42-58-59 N **Long:** 75-16-05 W
Pop: 4,414 (1990)   **Pop Density:** 140.6
Land: 31.4 sq. mi.; **Water:** 0.0 sq. mi.

In central NY, a southeastern suburb of Rome.
Name origin: For early settler Isaac Paris, Jr.

Prospect   Village
ZIP: 13435   Lat: 43-18-15 N **Long:** 75-09-10 W
Pop: 312 (1990); 368 (1980)   **Pop Density:** 1560.0
Land: 0.2 sq. mi.; **Water:** 0.0 sq. mi.

Remsen   Town
ZIP: 13438   Lat: 43-21-56 N **Long:** 75-08-46 W
Pop: 1,739 (1990)   **Pop Density:** 49.3
Land: 35.3 sq. mi.; **Water:** 1.5 sq. mi.

*Remsen   Village
ZIP: 13438   Lat: 43-19-39 N **Long:** 75-11-13 W
Pop: 518 (1990); 587 (1980)   **Pop Density:** 1295.0
Land: 0.4 sq. mi.; **Water:** 0.0 sq. mi.   **Elev:** 1171 ft.

Not coextensive with the town of the same name.

Rome   City
ZIP: 13440   Lat: 43-13-31 N **Long:** 75-29-21 W
Pop: 44,350 (1990); 43,826 (1980)   **Pop Density:** 592.1
Land: 74.9 sq. mi.; **Water:** 0.7 sq. mi.

In central NY on the Mohawk River, 15 mi. northwest of Utica. Incorporated 1819.
Name origin: For the capital of Italy. Previously called Lynchville.

Sangerfield   Town
Lat: 42-54-03 N **Long:** 75-22-18 W
Pop: 2,460 (1990)   **Pop Density:** 79.9
Land: 30.8 sq. mi.; **Water:** 0.2 sq. mi.
Name origin: For a local citizen.

Sherrill   City
ZIP: 13461   Lat: 43-04-11 N **Long:** 75-36-00 W
Pop: 2,864 (1990); 2,830 (1980)   **Pop Density:** 1432.0
Land: 2.0 sq. mi.; **Water:** 0.0 sq. mi.

Steuben   Town
ZIP: 13354   Lat: 43-20-57 N **Long:** 75-15-58 W
Pop: 1,006 (1990)   **Pop Density:** 23.6
Land: 42.7 sq. mi.; **Water:** 0.0 sq. mi.

Sylvan Beach   Village
ZIP: 13157   Lat: 43-12-23 N **Long:** 75-43-31 W
Pop: 1,119 (1990)   **Pop Density:** 1598.6
Land: 0.7 sq. mi.; **Water:** 0.0 sq. mi.

Trenton   Town
Lat: 43-15-15 N **Long:** 75-12-05 W
Pop: 4,682 (1990); 4,930 (1980)   **Pop Density:** 108.1
Land: 43.3 sq. mi.; **Water:** 0.4 sq. mi.

Utica   City
ZIP: 13501   Lat: 43-05-48 N **Long:** 75-13-42 W
Pop: 68,637 (1990); 75,632 (1980)   **Pop Density:** 4210.9
Land: 16.3 sq. mi.; **Water:** 0.3 sq. mi.

In central NY on the Mohawk River, 90 mi. west of Albany.
Name origin: For the ancient city on the Mediterranean coast of Tunisia. Previously called Yahnundadasis.

Vernon   Town
ZIP: 13476   Lat: 43-04-01 N **Long:** 75-31-48 W
Pop: 5,338 (1990)   **Pop Density:** 139.7
Land: 38.2 sq. mi.; **Water:** 0.0 sq. mi.

*Vernon   Village
ZIP: 13476   Lat: 43-04-49 N **Long:** 75-32-18 W
Pop: 1,274 (1990); 1,373 (1980)   **Pop Density:** 1415.6
Land: 0.9 sq. mi.; **Water:** 0.0 sq. mi.

Not coextensive with the town of the same name.
Name origin: For Edward Vernon (1684–1757), British admiral.

Verona   Town
ZIP: 13478   Lat: 43-09-12 N **Long:** 75-36-59 W
Pop: 6,460 (1990)   **Pop Density:** 93.2
Land: 69.3 sq. mi.; **Water:** 0.4 sq. mi.
Name origin: For Verona, Italy.

Vienna   Town
ZIP: 13308   Lat: 43-13-47 N **Long:** 75-46-40 W
Pop: 5,564 (1990)   **Pop Density:** 90.5
Land: 61.5 sq. mi.; **Water:** 33.3 sq. mi.
Name origin: For the capital of Austria.

Waterville   Village
ZIP: 13480   Lat: 42-55-51 N **Long:** 75-22-52 W
Pop: 1,664 (1990); 306 (1980)   **Pop Density:** 1280.0
Land: 1.3 sq. mi.; **Water:** 0.0 sq. mi.   **Elev:** 1237 ft.

Western   Town
Lat: 43-20-43 N **Long:** 75-23-35 W
Pop: 2,057 (1990)   **Pop Density:** 40.0
Land: 51.4 sq. mi.; **Water:** 3.3 sq. mi.

Westmoreland
Town
ZIP: 13490   **Lat:** 43-07-22 N **Long:** 75-26-51 W
Pop: 5,737 (1990)   **Pop Density:** 133.1
Land: 43.1 sq. mi.; **Water:** 0.0 sq. mi.

Name origin: For the county in England.

Whitesboro
Village
ZIP: 13492   **Lat:** 43-07-25 N **Long:** 75-17-49 W
Pop: 4,195 (1990); 4,460 (1980)   **Pop Density:** 3813.6
Land: 1.1 sq. mi.; **Water:** 0.0 sq. mi.

In central NY on the Mohawk River, 5 mi. northwest of Utica.

Name origin: For Judge Hugh White (1733–1812), originally from Middletown, CT.

Whitestown
Town
ZIP: 13492   **Lat:** 43-08-15 N **Long:** 75-20-37 W
Pop: 18,985 (1990)   **Pop Density:** 698.0
Land: 27.2 sq. mi.; **Water:** 0.0 sq. mi.

Yorkville
Village
ZIP: 13495   **Lat:** 43-06-42 N **Long:** 75-16-26 W
Pop: 2,972 (1990); 3,115 (1980)   **Pop Density:** 4245.7
Land: 0.7 sq. mi.; **Water:** 0.0 sq. mi.

Onondaga County
County Seat: Syracuse (ZIP: 13202)

Pop: 468,973 (1990); 463,920 (1980)   **Pop Density:** 601.0
Land: 780.3 sq. mi.; **Water:** 25.4 sq. mi.   **Area Code:** 315

In north-central NY, southwest of Rome; organized Mar 5, 1794.

Name origin: For the lake, named for the Onondaga Indian tribe, one of the Five Nations of the Iroquois; name probably means 'hill people.'

Baldwinsville
Village
ZIP: 13027   **Lat:** 43-09-23 N **Long:** 76-20-01 W
Pop: 6,591 (1990); 3,932 (1980)   **Pop Density:** 2126.1
Land: 3.1 sq. mi.; **Water:** 0.2 sq. mi.

In northern NY on the Seneca River, a northwestern suburb of Syracuse.

Brewerton
CDP
ZIP: 13029   **Lat:** 43-13-46 N **Long:** 76-08-35 W
Pop: 2,127 (1990); 1,586 (1980)   **Pop Density:** 1012.9
Land: 2.1 sq. mi.; **Water:** 0.0 sq. mi.

Part of the town is also in Oswego County.

Bridgeport
CDP
ZIP: 13030   **Lat:** 43-09-09 N **Long:** 75-58-51 W
Pop: 1,651 (1990)   **Pop Density:** 1834.4
Land: 0.9 sq. mi.; **Water:** 0.0 sq. mi.

Part of the town is also in Madison County.

Camillus
Town
ZIP: 13031   **Lat:** 43-03-02 N **Long:** 76-18-09 W
Pop: 23,625 (1990)   **Pop Density:** 684.8
Land: 34.5 sq. mi.; **Water:** 0.0 sq. mi.

*Camillus
Village
ZIP: 13031   **Lat:** 43-02-21 N **Long:** 76-18-29 W
Pop: 1,150 (1990); 1,298 (1980)   **Pop Density:** 2875.0
Land: 0.4 sq. mi.; **Water:** 0.0 sq. mi.

In central NY, 9 mi. west of Syracuse. Not coextensive with the town of the same name.

Cicero
Town
ZIP: 13039   **Lat:** 43-09-46 N **Long:** 76-03-42 W
Pop: 25,560 (1990)   **Pop Density:** 527.0
Land: 48.5 sq. mi.; **Water:** 0.0 sq. mi.

Name origin: For the famous Roman writer (106–43 B.C.).

Clay
Town
ZIP: 13041   **Lat:** 43-10-40 N **Long:** 76-11-34 W
Pop: 59,749 (1990)   **Pop Density:** 1244.8
Land: 48.0 sq. mi.; **Water:** 0.8 sq. mi.

Name origin: For the local soil type.

De Witt
Town
ZIP: 13214   **Lat:** 43-02-59 N **Long** 76-04-14 W
Pop: 25,148 (1990)   **Pop Density:** 741.8
Land: 33.9 sq. mi.; **Water:** 0.1 sq. mi.

Name origin: For Major Moses DeWitt, a local mayor, surveyor, and judge.

East Syracuse
Village
ZIP: 13057   **Lat:** 43-03-49 N **Long** 76-04-11 W
Pop: 3,343 (1990); 3,412 (1980)   **Pop Density:** 2089.4
Land: 1.6 sq. mi.; **Water:** 0.0 sq. mi.

Elbridge
Town
ZIP: 13060   **Lat:** 43-03-18 N **Long** 76-26-08 W
Pop: 6,192 (1990)   **Pop Density:** 164.7
Land: 37.6 sq. mi.; **Water:** 0.7 sq. mi.

*Elbridge
Village
ZIP: 13060   **Lat:** 43-02-03 N **Long** 76-26-37 W
Pop: 1,219 (1990); 1,099 (1980)   **Pop Density:** 1219.0
Land: 1.0 sq. mi.; **Water:** 0.0 sq. mi.

Not coextensive with the town of the same name.

Fabius
Town
ZIP: 13063   **Lat:** 42-49-26 N **Long** 75-59-36 W
Pop: 1,760 (1990)   **Pop Density:** 37.8
Land: 46.6 sq. mi.; **Water:** 0.2 sq. mi.

*Fabius
Village
ZIP: 13063   **Lat:** 42-50-07 N **Long** 75-59-07 W
Pop: 310 (1990); 367 (1980)   **Pop Density:** 775.0
Land: 0.4 sq. mi.; **Water:** 0.0 sq. mi.

Not coextensive with the town of the same name.

Name origin: For the Roman hero.

Fairmount   CDP
ZIP: 13031   **Lat:** 43-02-25 N **Long:** 76-14-50 W
Pop: 12,266 (1990); 11,852 (1980)   **Pop Density:** 3315.1
Land: 3.7 sq. mi.; **Water:** 0.0 sq. mi.

Fayetteville   Village
ZIP: 13066   **Lat:** 43-01-48 N **Long:** 75-59-52 W
Pop: 4,248 (1990); 4,709 (1980)   **Pop Density:** 2498.8
Land: 1.7 sq. mi.; **Water:** 0.0 sq. mi.   **Elev:** 531 ft.

Geddes   Town
ZIP: 13209   **Lat:** 43-04-42 N **Long:** 76-13-35 W
Pop: 17,677 (1990)   **Pop Density:** 1921.4
Land: 9.2 sq. mi.; **Water:** 3.0 sq. mi.

Jordan   Village
ZIP: 13080   **Lat:** 43-03-56 N **Long:** 76-28-23 W
Pop: 1,325 (1990); 1,371 (1980)   **Pop Density:** 1325.0
Land: 1.0 sq. mi.; **Water:** 0.0 sq. mi.

LaFayette   Town
ZIP: 13084   **Lat:** 42-54-44 N **Long:** 76-06-23 W
Pop: 5,105 (1990)   **Pop Density:** 130.2
Land: 39.2 sq. mi.; **Water:** 0.3 sq. mi.

Name origin: For the Marquis de Lafayette (1757–1834), French statesman and soldier who fought with the Americans during the Revolutionary War.

Liverpool   Village
ZIP: 13088-99   **Lat:** 43-06-21 N **Long:** 76-12-35 W
Pop: 2,624 (1990); 2,849 (1980)   **Pop Density:** 3280.0
Land: 0.8 sq. mi.; **Water:** 0.0 sq. mi.

In central NY, 5 mi. north of Syracuse.

Name origin: For the English city.

Lyncourt   CDP
          Lat: 43-04-52 N **Long:** 76-07-34 W
Pop: 4,516 (1990); 492 (1980)   **Pop Density:** 3763.3
Land: 1.2 sq. mi.; **Water:** 0.0 sq. mi.

Lyndon   CDP
          Lat: 43-01-40 N **Long:** 76-02-26 W
Pop: 4,593 (1990)   **Pop Density:** 1020.7
Land: 4.5 sq. mi.; **Water:** 0.0 sq. mi.

Lysander   Town
ZIP: 13027   **Lat:** 43-10-42 N **Long:** 76-22-34 W
Pop: 16,346 (1990)   **Pop Density:** 264.1
Land: 61.9 sq. mi.; **Water:** 2.7 sq. mi.

Name origin: For the ancient Spartan general (d. 395 B.C.).

Manlius   Town
ZIP: 13104   **Lat:** 43-02-52 N **Long:** 75-58-58 W
Pop: 30,656 (1990)   **Pop Density:** 618.1
Land: 49.6 sq. mi.; **Water:** 0.3 sq. mi.

*Manlius   Village
ZIP: 13104   **Lat:** 43-00-03 N **Long:** 75-58-56 W
Pop: 4,764 (1990); 5,241 (1980)   **Pop Density:** 2802.4
Land: 1.7 sq. mi.; **Water:** 0.0 sq. mi.

In central NY, 10 mi. east of Syracuse. Not coextensive with the town of the same name.

Marcellus   Town
ZIP: 13108   **Lat:** 42-57-20 N **Long:** 76-19-30 W
Pop: 6,465 (1990)   **Pop Density:** 198.3
Land: 32.6 sq. mi.; **Water:** 0.1 sq. mi.

*Marcellus   Village
ZIP: 13108   **Lat:** 42-59-02 N **Long:** 76-20-23 W
Pop: 1,840 (1990); 1,870 (1980)   **Pop Density:** 3066.7
Land: 0.6 sq. mi.; **Water:** 0.0 sq. mi.

Not coextensive with the town of the same name.

Mattydale   CDP
ZIP: 13211   **Lat:** 43-05-57 N **Long:** 76-08-45 W
Pop: 6,418 (1990); 7,511 (1980)   **Pop Density:** 4936.9
Land: 1.3 sq. mi.; **Water:** 0.0 sq. mi.

Minoa   Village
ZIP: 13116   **Lat:** 43-04-31 N **Long:** 76-00-37 W
Pop: 3,745 (1990); 3,640 (1980)   **Pop Density:** 3120.8
Land: 1.2 sq. mi.; **Water:** 0.0 sq. mi.

North Syracuse   Village
ZIP: 13212   **Lat:** 43-07-56 N **Long:** 76-07-48 W
Pop: 7,363 (1990); 2,095 (1980)   **Pop Density:** 3681.5
Land: 2.0 sq. mi.; **Water:** 0.0 sq. mi.

In central NY, 8 mi. north-northeast of Syracuse.

Onondaga   Town
ZIP: 13215   **Lat:** 42-57-42 N **Long:** 76-12-42 W
Pop: 18,396 (1990)   **Pop Density:** 318.8
Land: 57.7 sq. mi.; **Water:** 0.1 sq. mi.

In central NY, a southern suburb of Syracuse.

Name origin: For one of the Five Nations of the Iroquois, settled mainly in this county; the name probably means 'hill people.'

Onondaga Reservation   Pop. Place
          Lat: 42-56-35 N **Long:** 76-09-38 W
Pop: 771 (1990)   **Pop Density:** 83.8
Land: 9.2 sq. mi.; **Water:** 0.1 sq. mi.

Otisco   Town
ZIP: 13159   **Lat:** 42-51-43 N **Long:** 76-13-41 W
Pop: 2,255 (1990)   **Pop Density:** 76.2
Land: 29.6 sq. mi.; **Water:** 1.5 sq. mi.

Pompey   Town
ZIP: 13138   **Lat:** 42-55-17 N **Long:** 75-59-13 W
Pop: 5,317 (1990)   **Pop Density:** 80.1
Land: 66.4 sq. mi.; **Water:** 0.1 sq. mi.

Name origin: For the Roman general.

Salina   Town
ZIP: 13088   **Lat:** 43-06-14 N **Long:** 76-10-30 W
Pop: 35,145 (1990)   **Pop Density:** 2546.7
Land: 13.8 sq. mi.; **Water:** 1.3 sq. mi.

Name origin: From Spanish meaning 'salt mine' or 'salt pit.'

Skaneateles   Town
ZIP: 13152   **Lat:** 42-55-52 N **Long:** 76-24-37 W
Pop: 7,526 (1990)   **Pop Density:** 176.3
Land: 42.7 sq. mi.; **Water:** 6.1 sq. mi.

*Skaneateles   Village
ZIP: 13152   **Lat:** 42-56-41 N **Long:** 76-25-31 W
Pop: 2,724 (1990); 2,789 (1980)   **Pop Density:** 2095.4
Land: 1.3 sq. mi.; **Water:** 0.3 sq. mi.

In central NY at the northern end of Skaneateles Lake, 8 mi. east of Auburn. Not coextensive with the town of the same name.

Name origin: From an Indian term possibly meaning 'long lake.'

Solvay
Village
ZIP: 13209   **Lat:** 43-03-29 N **Long:** 76-12-43 W
Pop: 6,717 (1990); 7,140 (1980)   **Pop Density:** 4198.1
Land: 1.6 sq. mi.; **Water:** 0.0 sq. mi.   **Elev:** 503 ft.
In central NY, 5 mi. west of Syracuse.

Spafford
Town
Lat: 42-50-16 N **Long:** 76-18-05 W
Pop: 1,675 (1990)   **Pop Density:** 51.1
Land: 32.8 sq. mi.; **Water:** 6.4 sq. mi.

Syracuse
City
ZIP: 13201   **Lat:** 43-02-27 N **Long:** 76-08-38 W
Pop: 163,860 (1990); 170,105 (1980)   **Pop Density:** 6528.3
Land: 25.1 sq. mi.; **Water:** 0.6 sq. mi.
In north-central NY, 12 mi. south of the west end of Oneida
Lake, and southeast of Rochester. Manufacturing of chemi-
cals, chinaware, drugs, and transportation equipment; a con-
vention center. Site of Syracuse University.
Name origin: Named by Abraham Walton for the ancient
Greek city in Sicily, supposedly because the terrains were
similar.

Tully
Town
ZIP: 13159   **Lat:** 42-49-07 N **Long:** 76-08-24 W
Pop: 2,378 (1990)   **Pop Density:** 91.8
Land: 25.9 sq. mi.; **Water:** 0.4 sq. mi.

*Tully
Village
ZIP: 13159   **Lat:** 42-47-52 N **Long:** 76-06-28 W
Pop: 911 (1990); 1,049 (1980)   **Pop Density:** 1518.3
Land: 0.6 sq. mi.; **Water:** 0.0 sq. mi.   **Elev:** 1252 ft.
Not coextensive with the town of the same name.
Name origin: For the nickname of Marcus Tullius Cicero
(106–43 B.C.), the Roman orator, statesman, and writer.

Van Buren
Town
ZIP: 13027   **Lat:** 43-07-11 N **Long:** 76-21-17 W
Pop: 13,367 (1990)   **Pop Density:** 375.5
Land: 35.6 sq. mi.; **Water:** 0.6 sq. mi.

Village Green
CDP
Lat: 43-07-59 N **Long:** 76-18-48 W
Pop: 4,198 (1990)   **Pop Density:** 3498.3
Land: 1.2 sq. mi.; **Water:** 0.0 sq. mi.

Westvale
CDP
ZIP: 13219   **Lat:** 43-02-30 N **Long:** 76-12-44 W
Pop: 5,952 (1990); 6,169 (1980)   **Pop Density:** 3720.0
Land: 1.6 sq. mi.; **Water:** 0.0 sq. mi.

Ontario County
County Seat: Canandaigua (ZIP: 14424)

Pop: 95,101 (1990); 88,909 (1980)   **Pop Density:** 147.6
Land: 644.4 sq. mi.; **Water:** 18.0 sq. mi.   **Area Code:** 716
In west-central NY, southeast of Rochester; organized Jan 27, 1789 from Montgom-
ery County.
Name origin: For Lake Ontario.

Bristol
Town
Lat: 42-48-30 N **Long:** 77-25-32 W
Pop: 2,071 (1990)   **Pop Density:** 56.4
Land: 36.7 sq. mi.; **Water:** 0.0 sq. mi.

Canadice
Town
Lat: 42-42-57 N **Long:** 77-33-05 W
Pop: 1,857 (1990)   **Pop Density:** 61.9
Land: 30.0 sq. mi.; **Water:** 2.4 sq. mi.

Canandaigua
City
ZIP: 14424   **Lat:** 42-53-20 N **Long:** 77-16-50 W
Pop: 10,725 (1990); 10,419 (1980)   **Pop Density:** 2331.5
Land: 4.6 sq. mi.; **Water:** 0.2 sq. mi.   **Elev:** 767 ft.
In western NY at the north end of Canandaigua Lake, 26 mi.
southeast of Rochester.
Name origin: An Iroquoian term probably meaning 'town
site.'

*Canandaigua
Town
ZIP: 14424   **Lat:** 42-51-38 N **Long:** 77-18-55 W
Pop: 7,160 (1990)   **Pop Density:** 125.8
Land: 56.9 sq. mi.; **Water:** 5.7 sq. mi.

Clifton Springs
Village
ZIP: 14432   **Lat:** 42-57-35 N **Long:** 77-08-00 W
Pop: 2,175 (1990); 1,533 (1980)   **Pop Density:** 1553.6
Land: 1.4 sq. mi.; **Water:** 0.0 sq. mi.

East Bloomfield
Town
Lat: 42-53-47 N **Long:** 77-25-19 W
Pop: 3,258 (1990)   **Pop Density:** 98.1
Land: 33.2 sq. mi.; **Water:** 0.1 sq. mi.

*East Bloomfield
Village
ZIP: 14443   **Lat:** 42-53-49 N **Long:** 77-26-01 W
Pop: 541 (1990); 587 (1980)   **Pop Density:** 1082.0
Land: 0.5 sq. mi.; **Water:** 0.0 sq. mi.
Not coextensive with the town of the same name.

Farmington
Town
ZIP: 14425   **Lat:** 42-59-32 N **Long:** 77-18-44 W
Pop: 10,381 (1990)   **Pop Density:** 262.8
Land: 39.5 sq. mi.; **Water:** 0.0 sq. mi.

Geneva
City
ZIP: 14456   **Lat:** 42-52-00 N **Long:** 76-59-13 W
Pop: 14,143 (1990); 15,133 (1980)   **Pop Density:** 3367.4
Land: 4.2 sq. mi.; **Water:** 0.0 sq. mi.   **Elev:** 494 ft.
In western NY at the north end of Seneca Lake. Part of the
town is in Seneca County.
Name origin: For the Swiss city. Not coextensive with the
town of the same name.

*Geneva   Town
ZIP: 14456   **Lat:** 42-49-47 N **Long:** 76-59-59 W
Pop: 2,967 (1990)   **Pop Density:** 155.3
Land: 19.1 sq. mi.; **Water:** 0.0 sq. mi.

Gorham   Town
Lat: 42-48-08 N **Long:** 77-12-33 W
Pop: 3,497 (1990)   **Pop Density:** 71.5
Land: 48.9 sq. mi.; **Water:** 4.3 sq. mi.

Holcomb   Village
ZIP: 14469   **Lat:** 42-54-00 N **Long:** 77-25-05 W
Pop: 790 (1990); 952 (1980)   **Pop Density:** 877.8
Land: 0.9 sq. mi.; **Water:** 0.0 sq. mi.

Hopewell   Town
Lat: 42-53-36 N **Long:** 77-11-46 W
Pop: 3,016 (1990)   **Pop Density:** 84.7
Land: 35.6 sq. mi.; **Water:** 0.0 sq. mi.

Manchester   Town
ZIP: 14504   **Lat:** 42-59-14 N **Long:** 77-11-40 W
Pop: 9,351 (1990)   **Pop Density:** 247.4
Land: 37.8 sq. mi.; **Water:** 0.0 sq. mi.

*Manchester   Village
ZIP: 14504   **Lat:** 42-58-07 N **Long:** 77-13-53 W
Pop: 1,598 (1990); 1,698 (1980) **Pop Density:** 1331.7
Land: 1.2 sq. mi.; **Water:** 0.0 sq. mi.

In western NY in the Finger Lakes resort area, 24 mi. southeast of Rochester. Not coextensive with the town of the same name.
Name origin: Named by early residents for Manchester, England.

Naples   Town
ZIP: 14512   **Lat:** 42-37-07 N **Long:** 77-25-40 W
Pop: 2,559 (1990)   **Pop Density:** 64.8
Land: 39.5 sq. mi.; **Water:** 0.0 sq. mi.

*Naples   Village
ZIP: 14512   **Lat:** 42-37-00 N **Long:** 77-24-06 W
Pop: 1,237 (1990); 1,225 (1980) **Pop Density:** 1237.0
Land: 1.0 sq. mi.; **Water:** 0.0 sq. mi.

Not coextensive with the town of the same name.
Name origin: For the city in Italy.

Phelps   Town
ZIP: 14532   **Lat:** 42-57-25 N **Long:** 77-02-54 W
Pop: 6,749 (1990)   **Pop Density:** 103.8
Land: 65.0 sq. mi.; **Water:** 0.3 sq. mi.

*Phelps   Village
ZIP: 14532   **Lat:** 42-57-29 N **Long:** 77-03-45 W
Pop: 1,978 (1990); 2,004 (1980) **Pop Density:** 1648.3
Land: 1.2 sq. mi.; **Water:** 0.0 sq. mi.

Not coextensive with the town of the same name.

Richmond   Town
Lat: 42-47-20 N **Long:** 77-31-26 W
Pop: 3,230 (1990)   **Pop Density:** 76.2
Land: 42.4 sq. mi.; **Water:** 1.9 sq. mi.

Rushville   Village
ZIP: 14544   **Lat:** 42-45-48 N **Long:** 77-13-39 W
Pop: 201 (1990); 148 (1980)   **Pop Density:** 670.0
Land: 0.3 sq. mi.; **Water:** 0.0 sq. mi.

Part of the town is also in Yates County.

Seneca   Town
Lat: 42-50-12 N **Long:** 77-04-32 W
Pop: 2,747 (1990)   **Pop Density:** 54.5
Land: 50.4 sq. mi.; **Water:** 0.0 sq. mi.

Shortsville   Village
ZIP: 14548   **Lat:** 42-57-21 N **Long:** 77-13-20 W
Pop: 1,485 (1990); 1,669 (1980) **Pop Density:** 2475.0
Land: 0.6 sq. mi.; **Water:** 0.0 sq. mi.

In west-central NY, 7 mi. north of Canadaigua.

South Bristol   Town
Lat: 42-43-24 N **Long:** 77-24-29 W
Pop: 1,663 (1990)   **Pop Density:** 42.5
Land: 39.1 sq. mi.; **Water:** 3.0 sq. mi.

Victor   Town
ZIP: 14564   **Lat:** 42-59-16 N **Long:** 77-25-54 W
Pop: 7,191 (1990)   **Pop Density:** 200.3
Land: 35.9 sq. mi.; **Water:** 0.0 sq. mi.

*Victor   Village
ZIP: 14564   **Lat:** 42-58-57 N **Long:** 77-24-42 W
Pop: 2,308 (1990); 2,370 (1980) **Pop Density:** 1648.6
Land: 1.4 sq. mi.; **Water:** 0.0 sq. mi.   **Elev:** 586 ft.

Not coextensive with the town of the same name.

West Bloomfield   Town
Lat: 42-54-10 N **Long:** 77-30-53 W
Pop: 2,536 (1990)   **Pop Density:** 99.5
Land: 25.5 sq. mi.; **Water:** 0.0 sq. mi.

Orange County
County Seat: Goshen (ZIP: 10924)

Pop: 307,647 (1990); 259,603 (1980)   **Pop Density:** 376.8
Land: 816.4 sq. mi.; **Water:** 22.2 sq. mi.   **Area Code:** 914

In southeastern NY, southwest of Poughkeepsie; original county, organized Nov 1, 1683.

Name origin: For William of Orange (1650–1702), later William III, king of England.

Balmville   CDP
Lat: 41-31-36 N   Long: 74-01-24 W
Pop: 2,963 (1990); 2,919 (1980)   **Pop Density:** 1411.0
Land: 2.1 sq. mi.; **Water:** 0.0 sq. mi.

Beaverdam Lake-Salisbury Mills   CDP
Lat: 41-26-40 N   Long: 74-07-04 W
Pop: 2,354 (1990); 13 (1980)   **Pop Density:** 980.8
Land: 2.4 sq. mi.; **Water:** 0.3 sq. mi.

Blooming Grove   Town
ZIP: 10914   Lat: 41-23-40 N   Long: 74-10-56 W
Pop: 16,673 (1990)   **Pop Density:** 477.7
Land: 34.9 sq. mi.; **Water:** 0.5 sq. mi.

Central Valley   CDP
ZIP: 10917   Lat: 41-19-44 N   Long: 74-07-38 W
Pop: 1,929 (1990); 1,705 (1980)   **Pop Density:** 714.4
Land: 2.7 sq. mi.; **Water:** 0.0 sq. mi.

Chester   Town
ZIP: 10918   Lat: 41-20-02 N   Long: 74-16-11 W
Pop: 9,138 (1990)   **Pop Density:** 362.6
Land: 25.2 sq. mi.; **Water:** 0.1 sq. mi.

*Chester   Village
ZIP: 10918   Lat: 41-21-25 N   Long: 74-16-34 W
Pop: 3,270 (1990); 1,910 (1980)   **Pop Density:** 1557.1
Land: 2.1 sq. mi.; **Water:** 0.0 sq. mi.

Not coextensive with the town of the same name.
Name origin: For the city in England.

Cornwall   Town
ZIP: 12518   Lat: 41-25-13 N   Long: 74-03-33 W
Pop: 11,270 (1990)   **Pop Density:** 420.5
Land: 26.8 sq. mi.; **Water:** 1.3 sq. mi.

In southeastern NY on the Hudson River, south of Newburgh.
Name origin: For the county in England.

Cornwall on Hudson   Village
ZIP: 12520   Lat: 41-26-19 N   Long: 74-01-02 W
Pop: 3,093 (1990); 3,164 (1980)   **Pop Density:** 1546.5
Land: 2.0 sq. mi.; **Water:** 0.1 sq. mi.

Crawford   Town
ZIP: 12566   Lat: 41-34-21 N   Long: 74-18-48 W
Pop: 6,394 (1990)   **Pop Density:** 159.5
Land: 40.1 sq. mi.; **Water:** 0.0 sq. mi.

Deerpark   Town
ZIP: 12729   Lat: 41-26-47 N   Long: 74-40-24 W
Pop: 7,832 (1990)   **Pop Density:** 118.0
Land: 66.4 sq. mi.; **Water:** 1.4 sq. mi.

East Middletown   CDP
Lat: 41-26-51 N   Long: 74-23-36 W
Pop: 4,974 (1990); 4,330 (1980)   **Pop Density:** 1507.3
Land: 3.3 sq. mi.; **Water:** 0.1 sq. mi.

Firthcliffe   CDP
Lat: 41-26-23 N   Long: 74-02-03 W
Pop: 4,427 (1990); 4,250 (1980)   **Pop Density:** 1475.7
Land: 3.0 sq. mi.; **Water:** 0.0 sq. mi.

Florida   Village
ZIP: 10921   Lat: 41-19-48 N   Long: 74-21-15 W
Pop: 2,497 (1990)   **Pop Density:** 1314.2
Land: 1.9 sq. mi.; **Water:** 0.0 sq. mi.
Name origin: For the state.

Fort Montgomery   CDP
Lat: 41-20-15 N   Long: 73-59-15 W
Pop: 1,450 (1990); 1,396 (1980)   **Pop Density:** 1318.2
Land: 1.1 sq. mi.; **Water:** 0.0 sq. mi.

Gardnertown   CDP
Lat: 41-32-02 N   Long: 74-03-35 W
Pop: 4,209 (1990); 4,238 (1980)   **Pop Density:** 859.0
Land: 4.9 sq. mi.; **Water:** 0.0 sq. mi.

Goshen   Town
ZIP: 10924   Lat: 41-22-52 N   Long: 74-21-05 W
Pop: 11,500 (1990)   **Pop Density:** 261.4
Land: 44.0 sq. mi.; **Water:** 0.1 sq. mi.

*Goshen   Village
ZIP: 10924   Lat: 41-24-04 N   Long: 74-19-39 W
Pop: 5,255 (1990); 4,874 (1980)   **Pop Density:** 1642.2
Land: 3.2 sq. mi.; **Water:** 0.0 sq. mi.

In southern NY, 18 mi. southwest of Newburgh. Not coextensive with the town of the same name.
Name origin: Named by settlers who arrived in the early eighteenth century and believed that the fertility of the soil would rival that of the biblical land of Goshen.

Greenville   Town
Lat: 41-22-03 N   Long: 74-35-40 W
Pop: 3,120 (1990)   **Pop Density:** 103.3
Land: 30.2 sq. mi.; **Water:** 0.3 sq. mi.

Greenwood Lake   Village
ZIP: 10925   Lat: 41-13-19 N   Long: 74-17-20 W
Pop: 3,208 (1990); 2,809 (1980)   **Pop Density:** 1527.6
Land: 2.1 sq. mi.; **Water:** 0.4 sq. mi.   **Elev:** 624 ft.

Hamptonburgh   Town
Lat: 41-27-01 N   Long: 74-15-10 W
Pop: 3,910 (1990)   **Pop Density:** 147.0
Land: 26.6 sq. mi.; **Water:** 0.2 sq. mi.

Harriman
Village
ZIP: 10926   **Lat:** 41-18-32 N **Long:** 74-08-41 W
Pop: 2,288 (1990); 781 (1980)   **Pop Density:** 2288.0
Land: 1.0 sq. mi.; **Water:** 0.0 sq. mi.   **Elev:** 542 ft.

Highland Falls
Village
ZIP: 10928   **Lat:** 41-21-45 N **Long:** 73-58-09 W
Pop: 3,937 (1990); 4,187 (1980)   **Pop Density:** 3579.1
Land: 1.1 sq. mi.; **Water:** 0.0 sq. mi.

In southeastern NY on the west bank of the Hudson River, 5 mi. south-southwest of Newburgh.
Name origin: For a local geographic feature.

Highland Mills
CDP
ZIP: 10930   **Lat:** 41-21-06 N **Long:** 74-07-36 W
Pop: 2,576 (1990); 2,034 (1980)   **Pop Density:** 1515.3
Land: 1.7 sq. mi.; **Water:** 0.0 sq. mi.

Highlands
Town
ZIP: 10928   **Lat:** 41-21-35 N **Long:** 74-01-02 W
Pop: 13,667 (1990)   **Pop Density:** 442.3
Land: 30.9 sq. mi.; **Water:** 2.6 sq. mi.

Kiryas Joel
Village
ZIP: 10950   **Lat:** 41-20-23 N **Long:** 74-10-03 W
Pop: 7,437 (1990); 2,088 (1980)   **Pop Density:** 6760.9
Land: 1.1 sq. mi.; **Water:** 0.0 sq. mi.

Maybrook
Village
ZIP: 12543   **Lat:** 41-29-08 N **Long:** 74-12-51 W
Pop: 2,802 (1990); 13 (1980)   **Pop Density:** 2155.4
Land: 1.3 sq. mi.; **Water:** 0.0 sq. mi.

Middletown
City
ZIP: 10940   **Lat:** 41-26-44 N **Long:** 74-25-20 W
Pop: 24,160 (1990); 21,454 (1980)   **Pop Density:** 4832.0
Land: 5.0 sq. mi.; **Water:** 0.0 sq. mi.

In southeastern NY, 23 mi. west of Newburgh.

Minisink
Town
ZIP: 10998   **Lat:** 41-19-59 N **Long:** 74-32-13 W
Pop: 2,981 (1990)   **Pop Density:** 129.0
Land: 23.1 sq. mi.; **Water:** 0.1 sq. mi.

Monroe
Town
ZIP: 10950   **Lat:** 41-18-30 N **Long:** 74-11-34 W
Pop: 23,035 (1990)   **Pop Density:** 1146.0
Land: 20.1 sq. mi.; **Water:** 1.2 sq. mi.

*Monroe
Village
ZIP: 10950   **Lat:** 41-19-14 N **Long:** 74-11-10 W
Pop: 6,672 (1990); 5,996 (1980)   **Pop Density:** 1962.4
Land: 3.4 sq. mi.; **Water:** 0.0 sq. mi.   **Elev:** 679 ft.

In southeastern NY, 15 mi. southwest of Newburgh. Not coextensive with the town of the same name.
Name origin: For James Monroe (1758–1831), fifth U.S. president.

Montgomery
Town
ZIP: 12549   **Lat:** 41-32-22 N **Long:** 74-12-29 W
Pop: 18,501 (1990)   **Pop Density:** 367.1
Land: 50.4 sq. mi.; **Water:** 0.6 sq. mi.

*Montgomery
Village
ZIP: 12549   **Lat:** 41-31-19 N **Long:** 74-14-17 W
Pop: 2,696 (1990); 2,316 (1980)   **Pop Density:** 1925.7
Land: 1.4 sq. mi.; **Water:** 0.1 sq. mi.   **Elev:** 354 ft.

In southeastern NY, northwest of Newburgh. Not coextensive with the town of the same name.
Name origin: For Revolutionary War hero Gen. Richard Montgomery (1736–75).

Mount Hope
Town
ZIP: 10940   **Lat:** 41-27-38 N **Long:** 74-31-36 W
Pop: 5,971 (1990)   **Pop Density:** 236.9
Land: 25.2 sq. mi.; **Water:** 0.3 sq. mi.

Newburgh
City
ZIP: 12550   **Lat:** 41-30-11 N **Long:** 74-01-12 W
Pop: 26,454 (1990); 23,438 (1980)   **Pop Density:** 6961.6
Land: 3.8 sq. mi.; **Water:** 1.0 sq. mi.   **Elev:** 139 ft.

On the west bank of the Hudson River; above the broad expanse of Newburgh Bay, 15 mi. south of Poughkeepsie. Not coextensive with the town of the same name.
Name origin: Named in 1762 for the town in Scotland on the River Tay.

*Newburgh
Town
ZIP: 12550   **Lat:** 41-33-06 N **Long:** 74-03-49 W
Pop: 24,058 (1990)   **Pop Density:** 550.5
Land: 43.7 sq. mi.; **Water:** 3.3 sq. mi.

New Windsor
Town
ZIP: 12553   **Lat:** 41-28-24 N **Long:** 74-06-55 W
Pop: 22,937 (1990)   **Pop Density:** 659.1
Land: 34.8 sq. mi.; **Water:** 2.2 sq. mi.

Orange Lake
CDP
ZIP: 12550   **Lat:** 41-31-54 N **Long:** 74-05-38 W
Pop: 5,196 (1990); 5,120 (1980)   **Pop Density:** 962.2
Land: 5.4 sq. mi.; **Water:** 0.6 sq. mi.

Otisville
Village
ZIP: 10963   **Lat:** 41-28-14 N **Long:** 74-32-23 W
Pop: 1,078 (1990); 953 (1980)   **Pop Density:** 1540.0
Land: 0.7 sq. mi.; **Water:** 0.0 sq. mi.   **Elev:** 852 ft.

Pine Bush
CDP
ZIP: 12566   **Lat:** 41-36-32 N **Long:** 74-17-50 W
Pop: 1,445 (1990); 1,255 (1980)   **Pop Density:** 688.1
Land: 2.1 sq. mi.; **Water:** 0.0 sq. mi.

Port Jervis
City
ZIP: 12771   **Lat:** 41-22-40 N **Long:** 74-41-28 W
Pop: 9,060 (1990); 8,699 (1980)   **Pop Density:** 3624.0
Land: 2.5 sq. mi.; **Water:** 0.2 sq. mi.   **Elev:** 442 ft.

In southeastern NY on the Delaware River, 38 mi. west of Newburgh.
Name origin: For John P. Jervis, general superintendent in the construction of the Delaware and Hudson Canal.

Scotchtown
CDP
ZIP: 10940   **Lat:** 41-28-34 N **Long:** 74-22-07 W
Pop: 8,765 (1990); 7,352 (1980)   **Pop Density:** 2086.9
Land: 4.2 sq. mi.; **Water:** 0.0 sq. mi.

Tuxedo
Town
ZIP: 10987   **Lat:** 41-13-44 N **Long:** 74-11-06 W
Pop: 3,023 (1990)   **Pop Density:** 63.6
Land: 47.5 sq. mi.; **Water:** 1.9 sq. mi.

Tuxedo Park
Village
ZIP: 10987   **Lat:** 41-12-14 N   **Long:** 74-12-25 W
Pop: 706 (1990); 809 (1980)   **Pop Density:** 261.5
Land: 2.7 sq. mi.; **Water:** 0.6 sq. mi.   **Elev:** 420 ft.

Unionville
Village
ZIP: 10988   **Lat:** 41-18-07 N   **Long:** 74-33-45 W
Pop: 548 (1990); 574 (1980)   **Pop Density:** 1826.7
Land: 0.3 sq. mi.; **Water:** 0.0 sq. mi.   **Elev:** 1518 ft.

Vails Gate
CDP
    Lat: 41-27-28 N   **Long:** 74-03-14 W
Pop: 3,014 (1990); 3,156 (1980)   **Pop Density:** 3014.0
Land: 1.0 sq. mi.; **Water:** 0.0 sq. mi.

Walden
Village
ZIP: 12586   **Lat:** 41-33-35 N   **Long:** 74-11-19 W
Pop: 5,836 (1990); 5,659 (1980)   **Pop Density:** 2918.0
Land: 2.0 sq. mi.; **Water:** 0.1 sq. mi.

In southeastern NY, northwest of Newburgh.

Wallkill
Town
ZIP: 10919   **Lat:** 41-28-59 N   **Long:** 74-23-31 W
Pop: 23,016 (1990)   **Pop Density:** 370.0
Land: 62.2 sq. mi.; **Water:** 0.6 sq. mi.

Warwick
Town
ZIP: 10990   **Lat:** 41-15-30 N   **Long:** 74-21-41 W
Pop: 27,193 (1990)   **Pop Density:** 267.6
Land: 101.6 sq. mi.; **Water:** 3.2 sq. mi.

*Warwick
Village
ZIP: 10990   **Lat:** 41-15-22 N   **Long:** 74-21-19 W
Pop: 5,984 (1990); 4,320 (1980)   **Pop Density:** 2720.0
Land: 2.2 sq. mi.; **Water:** 0.0 sq. mi.   **Elev:** 538 ft.

In southern NY, 40 mi. northwest of New York City. Settled 1746. Not coextensive with the town of the same name.

Name origin: Named by English immigrants for Warwickshire, England.

Washington Heights
CDP
    Lat: 41-28-10 N   **Long:** 74-25-03 W
Pop: 1,159 (1990); 1,233 (1980)   **Pop Density:** 772.7
Land: 1.5 sq. mi.; **Water:** 0.0 sq. mi.

Washingtonville
Village
ZIP: 10992   **Lat:** 41-25-46 N   **Long:** 74-09-27 W
Pop: 4,906 (1990); 2,380 (1980)   **Pop Density:** 1886.9
Land: 2.6 sq. mi.; **Water:** 0.0 sq. mi.

Name origin: For George Washington (1732–99), first U.S. president.

Wawayanda
Town
ZIP: 10973   **Lat:** 41-23-02 N   **Long:** 74-27-24 W
Pop: 5,518 (1990)   **Pop Density:** 156.8
Land: 35.2 sq. mi.; **Water:** 0.1 sq. mi.

West Point
Military facility
ZIP: 10996   **Lat:** 41-21-44 N   **Long:** 74-01-38 W
Pop: 8,024 (1990); 8,105 (1980)   **Pop Density:** 330.2
Land: 24.3 sq. mi.; **Water:** 0.7 sq. mi.

Woodbury
Town
ZIP: 10930   **Lat:** 41-19-50 N   **Long:** 74-06-06 W
Pop: 8,236 (1990)   **Pop Density:** 227.5
Land: 36.2 sq. mi.; **Water:** 1.0 sq. mi.

Orleans County
County Seat: Albion (ZIP: 14411)

Pop: 41,846 (1990); 38,496 (1980)   **Pop Density:** 106.9
Land: 391.4 sq. mi.; **Water:** 426.1 sq. mi.   **Area Code:** 716

On northwestern border of NY, on Lake Ontario, west of Rochester; organized Nov 12, 1824 from Genesee County.

Name origin: For the French city of Orleans.

Albion
Town
ZIP: 14411   **Lat:** 43-13-35 N   **Long:** 78-12-33 W
Pop: 8,178 (1990)   **Pop Density:** 324.5
Land: 25.2 sq. mi.; **Water:** 0.1 sq. mi.

*Albion
Village
ZIP: 14411   **Lat:** 43-14-45 N   **Long:** 78-11-21 W
Pop: 5,863 (1990); 4,198 (1980)   **Pop Density:** 2021.7
Land: 2.9 sq. mi.; **Water:** 0.0 sq. mi.

Not coextensive with the town of the same name.

Name origin: From the ancient name for England.

Barre
Town
    Lat: 43-10-06 N   **Long:** 78-13-02 W
Pop: 2,093 (1990)   **Pop Density:** 38.0
Land: 55.1 sq. mi.; **Water:** 0.0 sq. mi.

Carlton
Town
    Lat: 43-20-23 N   **Long:** 78-12-59 W
Pop: 2,808 (1990)   **Pop Density:** 64.3
Land: 43.7 sq. mi.; **Water:** 0.8 sq. mi.

Clarendon
Town
    Lat: 43-10-27 N   **Long:** 78-03-15 W
Pop: 2,705 (1990)   **Pop Density:** 76.8
Land: 35.2 sq. mi.; **Water:** 0.0 sq. mi.

Name origin: For the Earl of Clarendon.

Gaines
Town
    Lat: 43-17-06 N   **Long:** 78-12-15 W
Pop: 3,025 (1990)   **Pop Density:** 87.9
Land: 34.4 sq. mi.; **Water:** 0.0 sq. mi.

Holley
Village
ZIP: 14470   **Lat:** 43-13-27 N   **Long:** 78-01-41 W
Pop: 1,890 (1990); 1,882 (1980)   **Pop Density:** 1453.8
Land: 1.3 sq. mi.; **Water:** 0.0 sq. mi.

Kendall
Town
ZIP: 14476   **Lat:** 43-19-56 N   **Long:** 78-03-14 W
Pop: 2,769 (1990)   **Pop Density:** 84.2
Land: 32.9 sq. mi.; **Water:** 0.1 sq. mi.

Name origin: For an early settler.

Lyndonville
Village
ZIP: 14098   **Lat:** 43-19-18 N **Long:** 78-23-13 W
Pop: 953 (1990); 916 (1980)   **Pop Density:** 953.0
Land: 1.0 sq. mi.; **Water:** 0.0 sq. mi.   **Elev:** 324 ft.

Medina
Village
ZIP: 14103   **Lat:** 43-13-11 N **Long:** 78-23-16 W
Pop: 6,686 (1990); 3,766 (1980)   **Pop Density:** 2089.4
Land: 3.2 sq. mi.; **Water:** 0.1 sq. mi.   **Elev:** 542 ft.
Name origin: For the city in Arabia.

Murray
Town
Lat: 43-14-58 N **Long:** 78-03-30 W
Pop: 4,921 (1990)   **Pop Density:** 158.7
Land: 31.0 sq. mi.; **Water:** 0.1 sq. mi.

Ridgeway
Town
ZIP: 14103   **Lat:** 43-15-42 N **Long:** 78-22-38 W
Pop: 7,341 (1990)   **Pop Density:** 146.8
Land: 50.0 sq. mi.; **Water:** 0.2 sq. mi.

Shelby
Town
ZIP: 14103   **Lat:** 43-10-17 N **Long:** 78-23-13 W
Pop: 5,509 (1990)   **Pop Density:** 119.0
Land: 46.3 sq. mi.; **Water:** 0.4 sq. mi.

Yates
Town
Lat: 43-20-12 N **Long:** 78-23-15 W
Pop: 2,497 (1990)   **Pop Density:** 66.6
Land: 37.5 sq. mi.; **Water:** 0.0 sq. mi.

Oswego County
County Seat: Oswego (ZIP: 13126)

Pop: 121,771 (1990); 113,901 (1980)   **Pop Density:** 127.7
Land: 953.3 sq. mi.; **Water:** 358.9 sq. mi.   **Area Code:** 315

In northwestern NY on Lake Ontario, north of Syracuse; organized Mar 1, 1816 from Oneida and Onondaga counties.

Name origin: For the Oswego River, which runs through its western part; from Iroquoian *osh-we-go*, probably 'outpouring,' in reference to the mouth of the Oswego River where it empties into Lake Ontario; also translated 'the place where the valley widens.'

Albion
Town
Lat: 43-29-52 N **Long:** 76-01-53 W
Pop: 2,043 (1990)   **Pop Density:** 43.2
Land: 47.3 sq. mi.; **Water:** 0.6 sq. mi.

Altmar
Village
ZIP: 13302   **Lat:** 43-30-38 N **Long:** 76-00-17 W
Pop: 336 (1990); 347 (1980)   **Pop Density:** 152.7
Land: 2.2 sq. mi.; **Water:** 0.0 sq. mi.   **Elev:** 577 ft.

Amboy
Town
ZIP: 13493   **Lat:** 43-22-37 N **Long:** 75-56-12 W
Pop: 1,010 (1990)   **Pop Density:** 27.2
Land: 37.1 sq. mi.; **Water:** 0.6 sq. mi.

Boylston
Town
ZIP: 13083   **Lat:** 43-39-16 N **Long:** 75-57-51 W
Pop: 443 (1990)   **Pop Density:** 11.3
Land: 39.1 sq. mi.; **Water:** 0.0 sq. mi.

Brewerton
CDP
Lat: 43-14-39 N **Long:** 76-08-12 W
Pop: 827 (1990); 384 (1980)   **Pop Density:** 751.8
Land: 1.1 sq. mi.; **Water:** 0.1 sq. mi.
Part of the town is also in Onondaga County.

Central Square
Village
ZIP: 13036   **Lat:** 43-17-12 N **Long:** 76-08-26 W
Pop: 1,671 (1990); 1,418 (1980)   **Pop Density:** 879.5
Land: 1.9 sq. mi.; **Water:** 0.0 sq. mi.

Cleveland
Village
ZIP: 13042   **Lat:** 43-14-21 N **Long:** 75-53-06 W
Pop: 784 (1990); 855 (1980)   **Pop Density:** 712.7
Land: 1.1 sq. mi.; **Water:** 0.1 sq. mi.

Constantia
Town
ZIP: 13044   **Lat:** 43-15-03 N **Long:** 75-57-41 W
Pop: 4,868 (1990)   **Pop Density:** 85.6
Land: 56.9 sq. mi.; **Water:** 42.8 sq. mi.

Fulton
City
ZIP: 13069   **Lat:** 43-19-00 N **Long:** 76-24-56 W
Pop: 12,929 (1990); 13,312 (1980)   **Pop Density:** 3402.4
Land: 3.8 sq. mi.; **Water:** 0.9 sq. mi.   **Elev:** 364 ft.
In central NY, 24 mi. northwest of Syracuse.
Name origin: For inventor Robert Fulton (1765–1815).

Granby
Town
ZIP: 13069   **Lat:** 43-17-31 N **Long:** 76-26-24 W
Pop: 7,013 (1990)   **Pop Density:** 156.2
Land: 44.9 sq. mi.; **Water:** 1.6 sq. mi.

Hannibal
Town
ZIP: 13074   **Lat:** 43-18-36 N **Long:** 76-33-01 W
Pop: 4,616 (1990)   **Pop Density:** 103.0
Land: 44.8 sq. mi.; **Water:** 0.0 sq. mi.

*Hannibal
Village
ZIP: 13074   **Lat:** 43-19-03 N **Long:** 76-34-39 W
Pop: 613 (1990); 680 (1980)   **Pop Density:** 557.3
Land: 1.1 sq. mi.; **Water:** 0.0 sq. mi.   **Elev:** 327 ft.
Not coextensive with the town of the same name.
Name origin: For the Carthaginian general (247–183 B.C.).

Hastings
Town
ZIP: 13076   **Lat:** 43-19-19 N **Long:** 76-09-33 W
Pop: 8,113 (1990)   **Pop Density:** 177.1
Land: 45.8 sq. mi.; **Water:** 0.3 sq. mi.

Lacona
Village
ZIP: 13083   **Lat:** 43-38-37 N **Long:** 76-04-08 W
Pop: 593 (1990); 582 (1980)   **Pop Density:** 593.0
Land: 1.0 sq. mi.; **Water:** 0.0 sq. mi.

Mexico
Village
ZIP: 13114   Lat: 43-27-17 N   Long: 76-12-17 W
Pop: 5,050 (1990)   Pop Density: 109.1
Land: 46.3 sq. mi.; Water: 0.6 sq. mi.
Name origin: For the country.

*Mexico
Village
ZIP: 13114   Lat: 43-27-50 N   Long: 76-14-05 W
Pop: 1,555 (1990); 1,621 (1980)   Pop Density: 740.5
Land: 2.1 sq. mi.; Water: 0.0 sq. mi.

Minetto
Town
Lat: 43-23-56 N   Long: 76-28-53 W
Pop: 1,822 (1990)   Pop Density: 314.1
Land: 5.8 sq. mi.; Water: 0.3 sq. mi.

New Haven
Town
Lat: 43-28-36 N   Long: 76-18-43 W
Pop: 2,778 (1990)   Pop Density: 89.0
Land: 31.2 sq. mi.; Water: 2.3 sq. mi.

Orwell
Town
Lat: 43-33-17 N   Long: 75-56-58 W
Pop: 1,171 (1990)   Pop Density: 29.4
Land: 39.8 sq. mi.; Water: 1.6 sq. mi.

Oswego
City
ZIP: 13126   Lat: 43-27-30 N   Long: 76-30-10 W
Pop: 19,195 (1990); 19,793 (1980)   Pop Density: 2492.9
Land: 7.7 sq. mi.; Water: 3.6 sq. mi.   Elev: 298 ft.
In central NY on Lake Ontario at the mouth of the Oswego River, 33 mi. northwest of Syracuse. Not coextensive with the town of the same name.
Name origin: Iroquoian Indian *osh-we-go,* perhaps 'pouring out of waters' in reference to the mouth of the Oswego River; or possibly 'the place where the valley widens.'

*Oswego
Town
ZIP: 13126   Lat: 43-24-13 N   Long: 76-33-39 W
Pop: 8,027 (1990)   Pop Density: 293.0
Land: 27.4 sq. mi.; Water: 1.9 sq. mi.

Palermo
Town
ZIP: 13069   Lat: 43-22-04 N   Long: 76-15-45 W
Pop: 3,582 (1990)   Pop Density: 88.2
Land: 40.6 sq. mi.; Water: 0.2 sq. mi.
Name origin: For the city in Italy.

Parish
Town
ZIP: 13131   Lat: 43-24-13 N   Long: 76-04-03 W
Pop: 2,425 (1990)   Pop Density: 58.0
Land: 41.8 sq. mi.; Water: 0.2 sq. mi.

*Parish
Village
ZIP: 13131   Lat: 43-24-15 N   Long: 76-07-44 W
Pop: 473 (1990); 535 (1980)   Pop Density: 337.9
Land: 1.4 sq. mi.; Water: 0.0 sq. mi.
Not coextensive with the town of the same name.

Phoenix
Village
ZIP: 13135   Lat: 43-13-54 N   Long: 76-17-50 W
Pop: 2,435 (1990); 2,357 (1980)   Pop Density: 2213.6
Land: 1.1 sq. mi.; Water: 0.1 sq. mi.
In central NY, 14 mi. north-northwest of Syracuse.
Name origin: For Daniel Phoenix, owner of the townsite.

Pulaski
Village
ZIP: 13142   Lat: 43-33-55 N   Long: 76-07-41 W
Pop: 2,525 (1990); 2,415 (1980)   Pop Density: 765.2
Land: 3.3 sq. mi.; Water: 0.1 sq. mi.
In central NY near Lake Ontario, 30 mi. south-southwest of Watertown.
Name origin: For Count Casimir Pulaski (1747–79), a Polish soldier who aided the Americans during the Revolutionary War.

Redfield
Town
ZIP: 13437   Lat: 43-35-13 N   Long: 75-49-58 W
Pop: 564 (1990)   Pop Density: 6.3
Land: 90.1 sq. mi.; Water: 3.4 sq. mi.

Richland
Town
ZIP: 13144   Lat: 43-32-52 N   Long: 76-08-08 W
Pop: 5,917 (1990)   Pop Density: 103.4
Land: 57.2 sq. mi.; Water: 2.9 sq. mi.

Sand Ridge
CDP
Lat: 43-15-21 N   Long: 76-13-49 W
Pop: 1,312 (1990); 1,293 (1980)   Pop Density: 546.7
Land: 2.4 sq. mi.; Water: 0.0 sq. mi.

Sandy Creek
Town
ZIP: 13145   Lat: 43-38-18 N   Long: 76-06-29 W
Pop: 3,454 (1990)   Pop Density: 81.7
Land: 42.3 sq. mi.; Water: 4.3 sq. mi.

*Sandy Creek
Village
ZIP: 13145   Lat: 43-38-34 N   Long 76-05-09 W
Pop: 793 (1990); 765 (1980)   Pop Density: 566.4
Land: 1.4 sq. mi.; Water: 0.0 sq. mi.   Elev: 498 ft.
Not coextensive with the town of the same name.

Schroeppel
Town
ZIP: 13135   Lat: 43-15-44 N   Long 76-16-46 W
Pop: 8,931 (1990)   Pop Density: 211.1
Land: 42.3 sq. mi.; Water: 0.9 sq. mi.

Scriba
Town
ZIP: 13126   Lat: 43-27-58 N   Long 76-24-56 W
Pop: 6,472 (1990)   Pop Density: 159.4
Land: 40.6 sq. mi.; Water: 3.3 sq. mi.

Volney
Town
ZIP: 13069   Lat: 43-21-33 N   Long 76-22-07 W
Pop: 5,676 (1990)   Pop Density: 117.5
Land: 48.3 sq. mi.; Water: 0.9 sq. mi.

West Monroe
Town
ZIP: 13167   Lat: 43-17-47 N   Long 76-04-10 W
Pop: 4,393 (1990)   Pop Density: 130.4
Land: 33.7 sq. mi.; Water: 4.8 sq. mi.

Williamstown
Town
ZIP: 13493   Lat: 43-27-10 N   Long 75-54-00 W
Pop: 1,279 (1990)   Pop Density: 33.0
Land: 38.7 sq. mi.; Water: 0.5 sq. mi.

Otsego County
County Seat: Cooperstown (ZIP: 13326)

Pop: 60,517 (1990); 59,075 (1980)   **Pop Density:** 60.3
Land: 1002.9 sq. mi.; **Water:** 12.3 sq. mi.   **Area Code:** 607

In south-central NY, south of Utica; organized Feb 16, 1791 from Montgomery County.

Name origin: Iroquoian 'rock site' or 'place of the rock.'

Burlington   Town
ZIP: 13315   **Lat:** 42-42-59 N **Long:** 75-08-45 W
Pop: 1,036 (1990)   **Pop Density:** 23.0
Land: 45.0 sq. mi.; **Water:** 0.1 sq. mi.

Butternuts   Town
ZIP: 13776   **Lat:** 42-28-09 N **Long:** 75-19-16 W
Pop: 1,626 (1990)   **Pop Density:** 30.1
Land: 54.1 sq. mi.; **Water:** 0.0 sq. mi.

Cherry Valley   Town
ZIP: 13320   **Lat:** 42-48-32 N **Long:** 74-44-14 W
Pop: 1,210 (1990)   **Pop Density:** 30.2
Land: 40.1 sq. mi.; **Water:** 0.0 sq. mi.

*Cherry Valley   Village
ZIP: 13320   **Lat:** 42-47-52 N **Long:** 74-45-09 W
Pop: 617 (1990); 684 (1980)   **Pop Density:** 1028.3
Land: 0.6 sq. mi.; **Water:** 0.0 sq. mi.   **Elev:** 1326 ft.
Not coextensive with the town of the same name.

Cooperstown   Village
ZIP: 13326   **Lat:** 42-41-59 N **Long:** 74-55-50 W
Pop: 2,180 (1990); 238 (1980)   **Pop Density:** 1453.3
Land: 1.5 sq. mi.; **Water:** 0.0 sq. mi.   **Elev:** 1264 ft.
Name origin: For founder William Cooper who bought land here in 1785.

Decatur   Town
ZIP: 12197   **Lat:** 42-39-24 N **Long:** 74-42-23 W
Pop: 356 (1990)   **Pop Density:** 17.3
Land: 20.6 sq. mi.; **Water:** 0.2 sq. mi.

Edmeston   Town
ZIP: 13335   **Lat:** 42-42-43 N **Long:** 75-14-49 W
Pop: 1,717 (1990)   **Pop Density:** 38.5
Land: 44.6 sq. mi.; **Water:** 0.0 sq. mi.

Exeter   Town
ZIP: 13315   **Lat:** 42-47-29 N **Long:** 75-05-04 W
Pop: 967 (1990)   **Pop Density:** 30.1
Land: 32.1 sq. mi.; **Water:** 0.6 sq. mi.

Gilbertsville   Village
ZIP: 13776   **Lat:** 42-28-09 N **Long:** 75-19-16 W
Pop: 388 (1990); 455 (1980)   **Pop Density:** 388.0
Land: 1.0 sq. mi.; **Water:** 0.0 sq. mi.   **Elev:** 1108 ft.

Hartwick   Town
ZIP: 13348   **Lat:** 42-38-32 N **Long:** 75-00-56 W
Pop: 2,045 (1990)   **Pop Density:** 50.9
Land: 40.2 sq. mi.; **Water:** 0.2 sq. mi.

Laurens   Town
ZIP: 13796   **Lat:** 42-32-10 N **Long:** 75-07-11 W
Pop: 2,349 (1990)   **Pop Density:** 55.1
Land: 42.6 sq. mi.; **Water:** 0.1 sq. mi.

*Laurens   Village
ZIP: 13796   **Lat:** 42-31-52 N **Long:** 75-05-18 W
Pop: 293 (1990); 276 (1980)   **Pop Density:** 2930.0
Land: 0.1 sq. mi.; **Water:** 0.0 sq. mi.   **Elev:** 1116 ft.
Not coextensive with the town of the same name.

Maryland   Town
ZIP: 12116   **Lat:** 42-32-27 N **Long:** 74-51-24 W
Pop: 1,716 (1990)   **Pop Density:** 33.1
Land: 51.8 sq. mi.; **Water:** 0.1 sq. mi.
Name origin: For the state.

Middlefield   Town
                       Lat: 42-42-18 N **Long:** 74-52-17 W
Pop: 2,231 (1990)   **Pop Density:** 34.6
Land: 64.4 sq. mi.; **Water:** 1.5 sq. mi.

Milford   Town
ZIP: 13807   **Lat:** 42-32-46 N **Long:** 74-58-38 W
Pop: 2,845 (1990)   **Pop Density:** 61.7
Land: 46.1 sq. mi.; **Water:** 1.1 sq. mi.

*Milford   Village
ZIP: 13807   **Lat:** 42-35-24 N **Long:** 74-56-50 W
Pop: 462 (1990); 514 (1980)   **Pop Density:** 924.0
Land: 0.5 sq. mi.; **Water:** 0.0 sq. mi.
Not coextensive with the town of the same name.

Morris   Town
ZIP: 13808   **Lat:** 42-32-33 N **Long:** 75-15-50 W
Pop: 1,787 (1990)   **Pop Density:** 45.8
Land: 39.0 sq. mi.; **Water:** 0.1 sq. mi.

*Morris   Village
ZIP: 13808   **Lat:** 42-32-52 N **Long:** 75-14-43 W
Pop: 642 (1990); 681 (1980)   **Pop Density:** 917.1
Land: 0.7 sq. mi.; **Water:** 0.0 sq. mi.
Not coextensive with the town of the same name.

New Lisbon   Town
ZIP: 13415   **Lat:** 42-37-24 N **Long:** 75-08-41 W
Pop: 996 (1990)   **Pop Density:** 22.4
Land: 44.5 sq. mi.; **Water:** 0.1 sq. mi.

Oneonta   City
ZIP: 13820   **Lat:** 42-27-16 N **Long:** 75-04-02 W
Pop: 13,954 (1990); 14,933 (1980)   **Pop Density:** 3171.4
Land: 4.4 sq. mi.; **Water:** 0.0 sq. mi.   **Elev:** 1085 ft.
In central NY on the Susquehanna River, 45 mi. south of Utica. Not coextensive with the town of the same name.
Name origin: Iroquoian Indian 'stony place' or 'hills.'

*Oneonta   Town
ZIP: 13820   **Lat:** 42-28-09 N **Long:** 75-04-03 W
Pop: 4,963 (1990)   **Pop Density:** 147.7
Land: 33.6 sq. mi.; **Water:** 0.1 sq. mi.

Otego Town
ZIP: 13825 Lat: 42-25-02 N Long: 75-11-11 W
Pop: 3,128 (1990) Pop Density: 69.7
Land: 44.9 sq. mi.; Water: 0.0 sq. mi.

*Otego Village
ZIP: 13825 Lat: 42-23-29 N Long: 75-10-42 W
Pop: 1,068 (1990); 1,089 (1980) Pop Density: 970.9
Land: 1.1 sq. mi.; Water: 0.0 sq. mi.
Not coextensive with the town of the same name.
Name origin: From an Iroquois term probably meaning 'to have fire there.'

Otsego Town
ZIP: 13337 Lat: 42-44-34 N Long: 74-58-38 W
Pop: 3,932 (1990) Pop Density: 72.5
Land: 54.2 sq. mi.; Water: 3.6 sq. mi.

Pittsfield Town
Lat: 42-36-50 N Long: 75-16-19 W
Pop: 1,116 (1990) Pop Density: 29.6
Land: 37.7 sq. mi.; Water: 0.1 sq. mi.

Plainfield Town
Lat: 42-50-08 N Long: 75-11-39 W
Pop: 850 (1990) Pop Density: 28.8
Land: 29.5 sq. mi.; Water: 0.0 sq. mi.

Richfield Town
ZIP: 13439 Lat: 42-51-07 N Long: 75-02-53 W
Pop: 2,711 (1990) Pop Density: 87.7
Land: 30.9 sq. mi.; Water: 1.5 sq. mi.

Richfield Springs Village
ZIP: 13439 Lat: 42-51-15 N Long: 74-59-10 W
Pop: 1,565 (1990); 1,561 (1980) Pop Density: 1565.0
Land: 1.0 sq. mi.; Water: 0.0 sq. mi. Elev: 1315 ft.
In central NY, 20 mi. southeast of Utica.

Roseboom Town
ZIP: 13450 Lat: 42-42-40 N Long: 74-43-37 W
Pop: 668 (1990) Pop Density: 20.2
Land: 33.0 sq. mi.; Water: 0.1 sq. mi.

Schenevus Village
ZIP: 12155 Lat: 42-32-50 N Long: 74-49-28 W
Pop: 513 (1990); 625 (1980) Pop Density: 1026.0
Land: 0.5 sq. mi.; Water: 0.0 sq. mi. Elev: 1266 ft.

Springfield Town
ZIP: 13468 Lat: 42-49-54 N Long: 74-51-38 W
Pop: 1,267 (1990) Pop Density: 29.5
Land: 43.0 sq. mi.; Water: 2.5 sq. mi.

Unadilla Town
ZIP: 13849 Lat: 42-21-57 N Long: 75-19-41 W
Pop: 4,343 (1990) Pop Density: 93.6
Land: 46.4 sq. mi.; Water: 0.2 sq. mi.

*Unadilla Village
ZIP: 13849 Lat: 42-19-37 N Long: 75-18-59 W
Pop: 1,265 (1990); 1,367 (1980) Pop Density: 1150.0
Land: 1.1 sq. mi.; Water: 0.0 sq. mi. Elev: 1024 ft.
In southern NY on the Susquehanna River, northeast of Binghamton. Not coextensive with the town of the same name.
Name origin: For the Unadilla River, which forms the western border of the borough, itself named from an Iroquoian term probably meaning 'meeting.'

West End CDP
ZIP: 13820 Lat: 42-28-06 N Long: 75-05-38 W
Pop: 1,825 (1990); 1,715 (1980) Pop Density: 480.3
Land: 3.8 sq. mi.; Water: 0.0 sq. mi.

Westford Town
ZIP: 13488 Lat: 42-38-21 N Long: 74-48-51 W
Pop: 634 (1990) Pop Density: 18.8
Land: 33.8 sq. mi.; Water: 0.0 sq. mi.

Worcester Town
ZIP: 12197 Lat: 42-35-37 N Long: 74-43-02 W
Pop: 2,070 (1990) Pop Density: 44.3
Land: 46.7 sq. mi.; Water: 0.1 sq. mi.

Putnam County
County Seat: Carmel (ZIP: 10512)

Pop: 83,941 (1990); 77,193 (1980) Pop Density: 362.5
Land: 231.5 sq. mi.; Water: 14.7 sq. mi. Area Code: 914
In southeastern NY, southeast of Poughkeepsie; organized Jun 12, 1812 from Dutchess County.
Name origin: For Israel Putnam (1718–90), MA general and American commander at the Battle of Bunker Hill.

Brewster Village
ZIP: 10509 Lat: 41-23-48 N Long: 73-36-54 W
Pop: 1,566 (1990); 1,650 (1980) Pop Density: 3132.0
Land: 0.5 sq. mi.; Water: 0.0 sq. mi. Elev: 395 ft.

Brewster Hill CDP
Lat: 41-25-25 N Long: 73-36-17 W
Pop: 2,226 (1990); 2,371 (1980) Pop Density: 2473.3
Land: 0.9 sq. mi.; Water: 0.1 sq. mi.

Carmel Town
ZIP: 10512 Lat: 41-23-31 N Long: 73-43-30 W
Pop: 28,816 (1990) Pop Density: 798.2
Land: 36.1 sq. mi.; Water: 4.6 sq. mi.
In southeastern NY, 20 mi. east-southeast of Newburgh.
Name origin: For the biblical mountain.

Carmel Hamlet CDP
Lat: 41-24-52 N Long: 73-41-01 W
Pop: 4,800 (1990) Pop Density: 564.7
Land: 8.5 sq. mi.; Water: 2.0 sq. mi.

Cold Spring
Village
ZIP: 10516　　　　**Lat:** 41-25-07 N　**Long:** 73-57-17 W
Pop: 1,998 (1990); 2,161 (1980)　　**Pop Density:** 3330.0
Land: 0.6 sq. mi.; **Water:** 0.0 sq. mi.　　**Elev:** 108 ft.
On the Hudson River.

Kent
Town
ZIP: 10512　　　　**Lat:** 41-28-30 N　**Long:** 73-43-45 W
Pop: 13,183 (1990)　　　**Pop Density:** 323.9
Land: 40.7 sq. mi.; **Water:** 2.5 sq. mi.

Lake Carmel
CDP
ZIP: 10512　　　　**Lat:** 41-27-40 N　**Long:** 73-40-12 W
Pop: 8,489 (1990); 7,210 (1980)　　**Pop Density:** 1632.5
Land: 5.2 sq. mi.; **Water:** 0.3 sq. mi.

Mahopac
CDP
ZIP: 10541　　　　**Lat:** 41-22-10 N　**Long:** 73-44-29 W
Pop: 7,755 (1990); 7,681 (1980)　　**Pop Density:** 1463.2
Land: 5.3 sq. mi.; **Water:** 1.1 sq. mi.

Nelsonville
Village
ZIP: 10516　　　　**Lat:** 41-25-46 N　**Long:** 73-56-54 W
Pop: 585 (1990); 567 (1980)　　**Pop Density:** 585.0
Land: 1.0 sq. mi.; **Water:** 0.0 sq. mi.　　**Elev:** 198 ft.

Patterson
Town
ZIP: 12563　　　　**Lat:** 41-29-23 N　**Long:** 73-35-38 W
Pop: 8,679 (1990)　　　**Pop Density:** 268.7
Land: 32.3 sq. mi.; **Water:** 0.6 sq. mi.
In southeastern NY on the CT border.
Name origin: Named in 1808 for early settler Matthew Patterson.

Peach Lake
CDP
Lat: 41-22-06 N　**Long:** 73-34-45 W
Pop: 960 (1990); 998 (1980)　　**Pop Density:** 480.0
Land: 2.0 sq. mi.; **Water:** 0.2 sq. mi.
Part of the town is also in Westchester County.

Philipstown
Town
ZIP: 10516　　　　**Lat:** 41-25-06 N　**Long:** 73-54-49 W
Pop: 9,242 (1990)　　　**Pop Density:** 189.0
Land: 48.9 sq. mi.; **Water:** 2.7 sq. mi.

Putnam Lake
CDP
ZIP: 10509　　　　**Lat:** 41-28-39 N　**Long:** 73-32-59 W
Pop: 3,459 (1990)　　　**Pop Density:** 886.9
Land: 3.9 sq. mi.; **Water:** 0.4 sq. mi.

Putnam Valley
Town
ZIP: 10579　　　　**Lat:** 41-23-56 N　**Long:** 73-50-23 W
Pop: 9,094 (1990)　　　**Pop Density:** 219.1
Land: 41.5 sq. mi.; **Water:** 1.5 sq. mi.

Southeast
Town
ZIP: 10509　　　　**Lat:** 41-24-19 N　**Long:** 73-36-01 W
Pop: 14,927 (1990)　　　**Pop Density:** 465.0
Land: 32.1 sq. mi.; **Water:** 2.9 sq. mi.

Queens County and Borough
County Seat: Jamaica (ZIP: 11435)

Pop: 1,951,598 (1990); 1,891,325 (1980)　　**Pop Density:** 17839.1
Land: 109.4 sq. mi.; **Water:** 68.0 sq. mi.　　**Area Code:** 718

In western end of Long Island, east of Brooklyn; original county, organized Nov 1, 1683. The county is coterminous with the borough of Queens, part of New York City. Includes the following areas: Astoria, Bay Ridge, Flushing, Forest Hills, Howard Beach, Jackson Heights, and Ozone Park.

Name origin: For Queen Catharine of Braganza (1638–1705), wife of King Charles II of England.

Rensselaer County
County Seat: Troy (ZIP: 12180)

Pop: 154,429 (1990); 151,966 (1980)　　**Pop Density:** 236.1
Land: 654.0 sq. mi.; **Water:** 11.4 sq. mi.　　**Area Code:** 518

On central eastern border of NY, east of Albany; organized Feb 7, 1791 from Albany County.

Name origin: For Kiliaen Van Rensselaer (1595–1644), one of the early patrons of the Dutch New Netherlands territories and a founder of the Dutch West India Company. Much of the territory of the county had been granted him by patent in 1630.

Averill Park
CDP
ZIP: 12018　　　　**Lat:** 42-38-06 N　**Long:** 73-33-12 W
Pop: 1,656 (1990); 1,337 (1980)　　**Pop Density:** 552.0
Land: 3.0 sq. mi.; **Water:** 0.1 sq. mi.

Berlin
Town
ZIP: 12022　　　　**Lat:** 42-40-03 N　**Long:** 73-22-17 W
Pop: 1,929 (1990)　　　**Pop Density:** 31.8
Land: 60.7 sq. mi.; **Water:** 0.3 sq. mi.

Brunswick
Town
ZIP: 12180   **Lat:** 42-44-57 N   **Long:** 73-35-25 W
Pop: 11,093 (1990)   **Pop Density:** 249.3
Land: 44.5 sq. mi.; **Water:** 0.1 sq. mi.

Castleton-on-Hudson
Village
ZIP: 12033   **Lat:** 42-31-56 N   **Long:** 73-45-02 W
Pop: 1,491 (1990); 1,627 (1980)   **Pop Density:** 1863.8
Land: 0.8 sq. mi.; **Water:** 0.0 sq. mi.

East Greenbush
Town
ZIP: 12061   **Lat:** 42-36-43 N   **Long:** 73-42-00 W
Pop: 14,076 (1990)   **Pop Density:** 584.1
Land: 24.1 sq. mi.; **Water:** 0.3 sq. mi.

Grafton
Town
     Lat: 42-46-02 N   **Long:** 73-27-12 W
Pop: 1,917 (1990)   **Pop Density:** 42.7
Land: 44.9 sq. mi.; **Water:** 1.1 sq. mi.
Name origin: For the English town.

Hampton Manor
CDP
     Lat: 42-37-14 N   **Long:** 73-43-44 W
Pop: 2,600 (1990)   **Pop Density:** 4333.3
Land: 0.6 sq. mi.; **Water:** 0.0 sq. mi.

Hoosick
Town
ZIP: 12089   **Lat:** 42-53-19 N   **Long:** 73-21-21 W
Pop: 6,696 (1990)   **Pop Density:** 106.3
Land: 63.0 sq. mi.; **Water:** 0.1 sq. mi.
In northeastern NY on the Hoosick River, northeast of Albany.
Name origin: From an Indian term possibly meaning 'stony place.'

Hoosick Falls
Village
ZIP: 12090   **Lat:** 42-54-01 N   **Long:** 73-21-01 W
Pop: 3,490 (1990); 3,609 (1980)   **Pop Density:** 2052.9
Land: 1.7 sq. mi.; **Water:** 0.0 sq. mi.   **Elev:** 460 ft.

Nassau
Town
ZIP: 12123   **Lat:** 42-32-48 N   **Long:** 73-32-35 W
Pop: 4,989 (1990)   **Pop Density:** 112.1
Land: 44.5 sq. mi.; **Water:** 0.7 sq. mi.

*Nassau
Village
ZIP: 12123   **Lat:** 42-30-49 N   **Long:** 73-36-41 W
Pop: 1,254 (1990); 1,206 (1980)   **Pop Density:** 1791.4
Land: 0.7 sq. mi.; **Water:** 0.0 sq. mi.
Not coextensive with the town of the same name.
Name origin: Named by Dutch settlers for the duchy in Germany associated with the House of Orange.

North Greenbush
Town
ZIP: 12198   **Lat:** 42-40-22 N   **Long:** 73-39-33 W
Pop: 10,891 (1990)   **Pop Density:** 573.2
Land: 19.0 sq. mi.; **Water:** 0.3 sq. mi.

Petersburg
Town
ZIP: 12138   **Lat:** 42-47-01 N   **Long:** 73-20-11 W
Pop: 1,461 (1990)   **Pop Density:** 36.1
Land: 40.5 sq. mi.; **Water:** 0.0 sq. mi.
In eastern NY, 20 mi. east of Troy.

Pittstown
Town
ZIP: 12094   **Lat:** 42-51-37 N   **Long:** 73-30-10 W
Pop: 5,468 (1990)   **Pop Density:** 88.6
Land: 61.7 sq. mi.; **Water:** 3.1 sq. mi.

Poestenkill
Town
ZIP: 12140   **Lat:** 42-41-15 N   **Long:** 73-31-19 W
Pop: 3,809 (1990)   **Pop Density:** 117.2
In eastern NY, near Troy.

Rensselaer
City
ZIP: 12144   **Lat:** 42-38-39 N   **Long:** 73-44-07 W
Pop: 8,255 (1990); 9,047 (1980)   **Pop Density:** 2948.2
Land: 2.8 sq. mi.; **Water:** 0.3 sq. mi.
In eastern NY on the east bank of the Hudson River across from Albany. Formed in 1897 by the union of the villages of East Albany, Greenbush, and Bath-on-the-Hudson.
Name origin: Located on part of Rensselaerswyck, most successful of the patronships.

Sand Lake
Town
ZIP: 12153   **Lat:** 42-37-46 N   **Long:** 73-33-05 W
Pop: 7,642 (1990)   **Pop Density:** 217.1
Land: 35.2 sq. mi.; **Water:** 0.9 sq. mi.
Name origin: For its descriptive connotations.

Schaghticoke
Town
ZIP: 12154   **Lat:** 42-52-50 N   **Long:** 73-36-36 W
Pop: 7,574 (1990)   **Pop Density:** 151.8
Land: 49.9 sq. mi.; **Water:** 2.0 sq. mi.

*Schaghticoke
Village
ZIP: 12154   **Lat:** 42-53-58 N   **Long:** 73-35-11 W
Pop: 794 (1990); 677 (1980)   **Pop Density:** 1134.3
Land: 0.7 sq. mi.; **Water:** 0.2 sq. mi.
Not coextensive with the town of the same name.
Name origin: From an Indian term possibly meaning 'branching stream.'

Schodack
Town
ZIP: 12033   **Lat:** 42-31-31 N   **Long:** 73-41-07 W
Pop: 11,839 (1990)   **Pop Density:** 190.3
Land: 62.2 sq. mi.; **Water:** 1.4 sq. mi.

Stephentown
Town
     Lat: 42-33-14 N   **Long:** 73-24-19 W
Pop: 2,521 (1990)   **Pop Density:** 43.5
Land: 58.0 sq. mi.; **Water:** 0.1 sq. mi.

Troy
City
ZIP: 12180   **Lat:** 42-44-03 N   **Long:** 73-40-31 W
Pop: 54,269 (1990); 56,638 (1980)   **Pop Density:** 5218.2
Land: 10.4 sq. mi.; **Water:** 0.1 sq. mi.
In eastern NY on the east bank of the Hudson River at the mouth of the Mohawk River, 8 mi. northeast of Albany.
Name origin: Named at a public meeting in Ashley's Tavern on January 5, 1789, for the ancient city in Asia Minor.

Valley Falls
Village
ZIP: 12185   **Lat:** 42-54-02 N   **Long:** 73-33-46 W
Pop: 527 (1990); 453 (1980)   **Pop Density:** 1317.5
Land: 0.4 sq. mi.; **Water:** 0.0 sq. mi.   **Elev:** 330 ft.

West Sand Lake
CDP
ZIP: 12196   **Lat:** 42-38-19 N   **Long:** 73-36-23 W
Pop: 2,251 (1990); 2,153 (1980)   **Pop Density:** 478.9
Land: 4.7 sq. mi.; **Water:** 0.0 sq. mi.

Wyantskill
CDP
     Lat: 42-41-20 N   **Long:** 73-38-57 W
Pop: 3,329 (1990)   **Pop Density:** 1387.1
Land: 2.4 sq. mi.; **Water:** 0.0 sq. mi.

Richmond County (Staten Island)
County Seat: Staten Island (ZIP: 10301)

Pop: 378,977 (1990); 352,029 (1980)   **Pop Density:** 6466.5
Land: 58.6 sq. mi.; **Water:** 44.0 sq. mi.   **Area Code:** 718

Coterminous with Staten Island in New York Bay between Long Island and New Jersey; original county, organized Nov 1, 1683. The county is coterminous with the borough of Staten Island, part of New York City.

Name origin: For Charles Lennox (1672–1723), first Duke of Richmond, son of King Charles II of England (1630–85).

Rockland County
County Seat: New City (ZIP: 10956)

Pop: 265,475 (1990); 259,530 (1980)   **Pop Density:** 1523.8
Land: 174.2 sq. mi.; **Water:** 25.1 sq. mi.   **Area Code:** 914

In southeastern NY, northwest of NYC; organized Feb 23, 1798 from Orange County.

Name origin: For the rugged land and the Palisades on the Hudson River, which form its eastern border.

Airmont CDP
ZIP: 10901   **Lat:** 41-05-56 N **Long:** 74-06-01 W
Pop: 7,835 (1990)   **Pop Density:** 1667.0
Land: 4.7 sq. mi.; **Water:** 0.0 sq. mi.

Bardonia CDP
Lat: 41-06-40 N **Long:** 73-58-52 W
Pop: 4,487 (1990)   **Pop Density:** 1725.8
Land: 2.6 sq. mi.; **Water:** 0.3 sq. mi.

Blauvelt CDP
ZIP: 10913   **Lat:** 41-04-04 N **Long:** 73-57-18 W
Pop: 4,838 (1990)   **Pop Density:** 1075.1
Land: 4.5 sq. mi.; **Water:** 0.1 sq. mi.

Chestnut Ridge Village
ZIP: 10977   **Lat:** 41-04-54 N **Long:** 74-03-06 W
Pop: 7,517 (1990)   **Pop Density:** 1534.1
Land: 4.9 sq. mi.; **Water:** 0.0 sq. mi.

Clarkstown Town
ZIP: 10956   **Lat:** 41-07-56 N **Long:** 73-58-15 W
Pop: 79,346 (1990)   **Pop Density:** 2060.9
Land: 38.5 sq. mi.; **Water:** 8.4 sq. mi.

Congers CDP
ZIP: 10920   **Lat:** 41-08-52 N **Long:** 73-56-48 W
Pop: 8,003 (1990); 7,123 (1980)   **Pop Density:** 2500.9
Land: 3.2 sq. mi.; **Water:** 0.7 sq. mi.

Grand View-on-Hudson Village
Lat: 41-03-30 N **Long:** 73-54-26 W
Pop: 271 (1990); 312 (1980)   **Pop Density:** 1355.0
Land: 0.2 sq. mi.; **Water:** 2.3 sq. mi.

Haverstraw Town
ZIP: 10927   **Lat:** 41-12-03 N **Long:** 74-02-17 W
Pop: 32,712 (1990)   **Pop Density:** 1460.4
Land: 22.4 sq. mi.; **Water:** 5.1 sq. mi.

*Haverstraw Village
ZIP: 10927   **Lat:** 41-11-07 N **Long:** 73-57-18 W
Pop: 9,438 (1990); 8,800 (1980)   **Pop Density:** 4719.0
Land: 2.0 sq. mi.; **Water:** 3.1 sq. mi.

In southeastern NY on the west bank of the Hudson River, 32 mi. north of New York City. Not coextensive with the town of the same name.

Hillburn Village
ZIP: 10931   **Lat:** 41-07-38 N **Long:** 74-10-13 W
Pop: 892 (1990); 926 (1980)   **Pop Density:** 405.5
Land: 2.2 sq. mi.; **Water:** 0.0 sq. mi.

Hillcrest CDP
ZIP: 10977   **Lat:** 41-07-46 N **Long:** 74-02-09 W
Pop: 6,447 (1990); 5,733 (1980)   **Pop Density:** 4959.2
Land: 1.3 sq. mi.; **Water:** 0.0 sq. mi.

Monsey CDP
ZIP: 10952   **Lat:** 41-07-05 N **Long:** 74-04-03 W
Pop: 13,986 (1990); 12,380 (1980)   **Pop Density:** 5827.5
Land: 2.4 sq. mi.; **Water:** 0.0 sq. mi.

Montebello Village
ZIP: 10901   **Lat:** 41-07-43 N **Long:** 74-07-05 W
Pop: 2,950 (1990)   **Pop Density:** 670.5
Land: 4.4 sq. mi.; **Water:** 0.0 sq. mi.

Mount Ivy CDP
ZIP: 10970   **Lat:** 41-11-34 N **Long:** 74-01-43 W
Pop: 6,013 (1990)   **Pop Density:** 4008.7
Land: 1.5 sq. mi.; **Water:** 0.0 sq. mi.

Nanuet CDP
ZIP: 10954   **Lat:** 41-05-42 N **Long:** 74-00-57 W
Pop: 14,065 (1990); 12,578 (1980)   **Pop Density:** 2604.6
Land: 5.4 sq. mi.; **Water:** 0.0 sq. mi.

New City CDP
ZIP: 10956   **Lat:** 41-09-13 N **Long:** 73-59-30 W
Pop: 33,673 (1990); 35,859 (1980)   **Pop Density:** 2158.5
Land: 15.6 sq. mi.; **Water:** 0.7 sq. mi.

New Hempstead Village
ZIP: 10977 Lat: 41-08-58 N Long: 74-02-58 W
Pop: 4,200 (1990) Pop Density: 1448.3
Land: 2.9 sq. mi.; Water: 0.0 sq. mi.

New Square Village
ZIP: 10977 Lat: 41-08-22 N Long: 74-01-43 W
Pop: 2,605 (1990); 1,750 (1980) Pop Density: 6512.5
Land: 0.4 sq. mi.; Water: 0.0 sq. mi. Elev: 540 ft.

Nyack Village
ZIP: 10960 Lat: 41-05-24 N Long: 73-54-54 W
Pop: 6,558 (1990); 696 (1980) Pop Density: 8197.5
Land: 0.8 sq. mi.; Water: 0.8 sq. mi.
In southeastern NY on the west bank of the Hudson River,
25 mi. north of New York City.
Name origin: From an Indian term possibly meaning 'point
of land.'

Orangeburg CDP
ZIP: 10962 Lat: 41-03-00 N Long: 73-56-44 W
Pop: 3,583 (1990) Pop Density: 1155.8
Land: 3.1 sq. mi.; Water: 0.0 sq. mi.

Orangetown Town
ZIP: 10960 Lat: 41-03-09 N Long: 73-56-53 W
Pop: 46,742 (1990) Pop Density: 1931.5
Land: 24.2 sq. mi.; Water: 7.2 sq. mi.

Pearl River CDP
ZIP: 10965 Lat: 41-03-37 N Long: 74-00-11 W
Pop: 15,314 (1990); 15,893 (1980) Pop Density: 2252.1
Land: 6.8 sq. mi.; Water: 0.4 sq. mi.

Piermont Village
ZIP: 10968 Lat: 41-02-22 N Long: 73-54-55 W
Pop: 2,163 (1990); 2,269 (1980) Pop Density: 3090.0
Land: 0.7 sq. mi.; Water: 0.5 sq. mi.
In southeastern NY on the west bank of the Hudson River,
22 mi. north of New York City.
Name origin: From the mile-long pier of the Erie Railroad.

Pomona Village
ZIP: 10970 Lat: 41-11-23 N Long: 74-03-13 W
Pop: 2,611 (1990); 1,170 (1980) Pop Density: 1087.9
Land: 2.4 sq. mi.; Water: 0.0 sq. mi.
Name origin: For the Roman goddess of fruit.

Ramapo Town
ZIP: 10931 Lat: 41-08-15 N Long: 74-06-27 W
Pop: 93,861 (1990) Pop Density: 1533.7
Land: 61.2 sq. mi.; Water: 0.7 sq. mi.

Sloatsburg Village
ZIP: 10974 Lat: 41-09-38 N Long: 74-11-28 W
Pop: 3,035 (1990); 3,154 (1980) Pop Density: 1214.0
Land: 2.5 sq. mi.; Water: 0.0 sq. mi. Elev: 343 ft.
In southeastern NY near the NJ border.
Name origin: For Jacob Sloat, an early settler.

South Nyack Village
ZIP: 10960 Lat: 41-04-39 N Long: 73-55-01 W
Pop: 3,352 (1990); 3,602 (1980) Pop Density: 5586.7
Land: 0.6 sq. mi.; Water: 1.1 sq. mi.

Spring Valley Village
ZIP: 10977 Lat: 41-06-51 N Long: 74-02-57 W
Pop: 21,802 (1990); 1,970 (1980) Pop Density: 10381.9
Land: 2.1 sq. mi.; Water: 0.0 sq. mi.
In southeastern NY near the NJ border.

Stony Point Town
ZIP: 10980 Lat: 41-15-35 N Long: 74-00-47 W
Pop: 12,814 (1990) Pop Density: 460.9
Land: 27.8 sq. mi.; Water: 3.7 sq. mi.
Name origin: For a rocky bluff that projects into the Hudson.

Suffern Village
ZIP: 10901 Lat: 41-06-48 N Long: 74-08-38 W
Pop: 11,055 (1990); 10,794 (1980) Pop Density: 5264.3
Land: 2.1 sq. mi.; Water: 0.0 sq. mi. Elev: 313 ft.
In southeastern NY, 30 mi. northwest of New York City.
Name origin: For an early pioneer family.

Tappan CDP
ZIP: 10983 Lat: 41-01-32 N Long: 73-57-05 W
Pop: 6,867 (1990); 8,267 (1980) Pop Density: 2452.5
Land: 2.8 sq. mi.; Water: 0.0 sq. mi.

Thiells CDP
ZIP: 10984 Lat: 41-12-27 N Long: 74-00-37 W
Pop: 5,204 (1990) Pop Density: 2738.9
Land: 1.9 sq. mi.; Water: 0.0 sq. mi.

Upper Nyack Village
ZIP: 10960 Lat: 41-06-52 N Long: 73-54-52 W
Pop: 2,084 (1990); 1,906 (1980) Pop Density: 1603.1
Land: 1.3 sq. mi.; Water: 2.9 sq. mi.

Valley Cottage CDP
ZIP: 10989 Lat: 41-06-55 N Long: 73-56-37 W
Pop: 9,007 (1990); 8,214 (1980) Pop Density: 2094.7
Land: 4.3 sq. mi.; Water: 0.0 sq. mi.

Viola CDP
Lat: 41-07-45 N Long: 74-04-56 W
Pop: 4,504 (1990); 5,340 (1980) Pop Density: 1668.1
Land: 2.7 sq. mi.; Water: 0.0 sq. mi.

Wesley Hills Village
ZIP: 10977 Lat: 41-09-27 N Long: 74-04-45 W
Pop: 4,305 (1990) Pop Density: 1266.2
Land: 3.4 sq. mi.; Water: 0.0 sq. mi.

West Haverstraw Village
ZIP: 10993 Lat: 41-12-23 N Long: 73-59-15 W
Pop: 9,183 (1990); 9,181 (1980) Pop Density: 6122.0
Land: 1.5 sq. mi.; Water: 0.0 sq. mi.

West Nyack CDP
ZIP: 10994 Lat: 41-05-27 N Long: 73-58-09 W
Pop: 3,437 (1990); 8,553 (1980) Pop Density: 1185.2
Land: 2.9 sq. mi.; Water: 0.0 sq. mi.

St. Lawrence County
County Seat: Canton (ZIP: 13617)

Pop: 111,974 (1990); 114,347 (1980)   **Pop Density:** 41.7
Land: 2685.7 sq. mi.; **Water:** 135.9 sq. mi.   **Area Code:** 315

On northwestern border of NY, north of Watertown; organized Mar 3, 1802 from Clinton, Montgomery, and Herkimer counties.
Name origin: For the Saint Lawrence River, which forms its western boundary.

Brasher   Town
Lat: 44-53-12 N **Long:** 74-43-28 W
Pop: 2,124 (1990)   **Pop Density:** 23.3
Land: 91.2 sq. mi.; **Water:** 0.9 sq. mi.

Brasher Falls-Winthrop   CDP
Lat: 44-48-17 N **Long:** 74-47-37 W
Pop: 1,271 (1990); 817 (1980)   **Pop Density:** 282.4
Land: 4.5 sq. mi.; **Water:** 0.1 sq. mi.

Canton   Town
ZIP: 13617   **Lat:** 44-34-47 N **Long:** 75-11-36 W
Pop: 11,120 (1990)   **Pop Density:** 106.1
Land: 104.8 sq. mi.; **Water:** 1.1 sq. mi.

*Canton   Village
ZIP: 13617   **Lat:** 44-35-47 N **Long:** 75-10-21 W
Pop: 6,379 (1990); 7,055 (1980)   **Pop Density:** 2899.5
Land: 2.2 sq. mi.; **Water:** 0.1 sq. mi.   **Elev:** 409 ft.
In northern NY, 18 mi. east-southeast of Ogdensburg. Not coextensive with the town of the same name.
Name origin: For the Chinese city.

Clare   Town
ZIP: 13684   **Lat:** 44-21-15 N **Long:** 74-59-32 W
Pop: 78 (1990)   **Pop Density:** 0.8
Land: 96.6 sq. mi.; **Water:** 0.7 sq. mi.

Clifton   Town
Lat: 44-12-03 N **Long:** 74-53-12 W
Pop: 917 (1990)   **Pop Density:** 6.8
Land: 135.1 sq. mi.; **Water:** 15.2 sq. mi.

Colton   Town
ZIP: 13625   **Lat:** 44-19-12 N **Long:** 74-47-39 W
Pop: 1,274 (1990)   **Pop Density:** 5.3
Land: 242.1 sq. mi.; **Water:** 12.8 sq. mi.

De Kalb   Town
ZIP: 13630   **Lat:** 44-29-16 N **Long:** 75-21-12 W
Pop: 2,153 (1990)   **Pop Density:** 26.1
Land: 82.5 sq. mi.; **Water:** 0.7 sq. mi.

De Peyster   Town
ZIP: 13633   **Lat:** 44-32-31 N **Long:** 75-27-40 W
Pop: 913 (1990)   **Pop Density:** 21.2
Land: 43.1 sq. mi.; **Water:** 2.0 sq. mi.
Name origin: For a wealthy NY merchant.

Edwards   Town
ZIP: 13635   **Lat:** 44-17-24 N **Long:** 75-15-53 W
Pop: 1,083 (1990)   **Pop Density:** 21.4
Land: 50.7 sq. mi.; **Water:** 0.6 sq. mi.

*Edwards   Village
ZIP: 13635   **Lat:** 44-19-24 N **Long:** 75-15-11 W
Pop: 487 (1990); 561 (1980)   **Pop Density:** 487.0
Land: 1.0 sq. mi.; **Water:** 0.0 sq. mi.
Not coextensive with the town of the same name.

Fine   Town
ZIP: 13639   **Lat:** 44-08-59 N **Long:** 75-04-11 W
Pop: 1,813 (1990)   **Pop Density:** 10.8
Land: 167.1 sq. mi.; **Water:** 2.3 sq. mi.

Fowler   Town
ZIP: 13642   **Lat:** 44-16-39 N **Long:** 75-24-54 W
Pop: 1,885 (1990)   **Pop Density:** 31.7
Land: 59.5 sq. mi.; **Water:** 1.2 sq. mi.

Gouverneur   Town
ZIP: 13642   **Lat:** 44-21-57 N **Long:** 75-29-48 W
Pop: 6,985 (1990)   **Pop Density:** 97.7
Land: 71.5 sq. mi.; **Water:** 0.9 sq. mi.

*Gouverneur   Village
ZIP: 13642   **Lat:** 44-20-11 N **Long:** 75-27-58 W
Pop: 4,604 (1990); 4,285 (1980)   **Pop Density:** 2192.4
Land: 2.1 sq. mi.; **Water:** 0.1 sq. mi.   **Elev:** 447 ft.
In northern NY on both banks of the Oswegatchie River. Settled 1805. Not coextensive with the town of the same name.
Name origin: For Gouverneur Morris who purchased land here in 1798.

Hammond   Town
ZIP: 13646   **Lat:** 44-26-28 N **Long:** 75-44-38 W
Pop: 1,168 (1990)   **Pop Density:** 18.8
Land: 62.2 sq. mi.; **Water:** 15.7 sq. mi.

*Hammond   Village
ZIP: 13646   **Lat:** 44-26-49 N **Long:** 75-41-39 W
Pop: 270 (1990); 271 (1980)   **Pop Density:** 450.0
Land: 0.6 sq. mi.; **Water:** 0.0 sq. mi.   **Elev:** 360 ft.
Not coextensive with the town of the same name.

Hermon   Town
ZIP: 13652   **Lat:** 44-24-03 N **Long:** 75-17-20 W
Pop: 1,041 (1990)   **Pop Density:** 19.5
Land: 53.4 sq. mi.; **Water:** 0.8 sq. mi.

*Hermon   Village
ZIP: 13652   **Lat:** 44-28-06 N **Long:** 75-13-57 W
Pop: 407 (1990); 490 (1980)   **Pop Density:** 1017.5
Land: 0.4 sq. mi.; **Water:** 0.0 sq. mi.
Not coextensive with the town of the same name.

Heuvelton   Village
ZIP: 13654   **Lat:** 44-37-01 N **Long:** 75-24-15 W
Pop: 771 (1990); 777 (1980)   **Pop Density:** 963.8
Land: 0.8 sq. mi.; **Water:** 0.1 sq. mi.   **Elev:** 315 ft.

Hopkinton   Town
Lat: 44-32-24 N **Long:** 74-39-51 W
Pop: 957 (1990)   **Pop Density:** 5.2
Land: 185.4 sq. mi.; **Water:** 1.6 sq. mi.

Lawrence
Town
Lat: 44-45-13 N Long: 74-40-19 W
Pop: 1,516 (1990)   Pop Density: 31.8
Land: 47.7 sq. mi.; Water: 0.0 sq. mi.

Lisbon
Town
ZIP: 13658   Lat: 44-42-09 N Long: 75-19-33 W
Pop: 3,746 (1990)   Pop Density: 34.6
Land: 108.2 sq. mi.; Water: 5.4 sq. mi.
Name origin: For the capital of Portugal.

Louisville
Town
Lat: 44-54-26 N Long: 75-00-56 W
Pop: 3,040 (1990)   Pop Density: 63.1
Land: 48.2 sq. mi.; Water: 15.7 sq. mi.

Macomb
Town
ZIP: 13642   Lat: 44-26-28 N Long: 75-34-03 W
Pop: 790 (1990)   Pop Density: 12.9
Land: 61.2 sq. mi.; Water: 1.9 sq. mi.

Madrid
Town
ZIP: 13660   Lat: 44-46-06 N Long: 75-07-49 W
Pop: 1,568 (1990)   Pop Density: 29.6
Land: 52.9 sq. mi.; Water: 0.7 sq. mi.
Name origin: For the capital of Spain.

Massena
Town
ZIP: 13662   Lat: 44-57-30 N Long: 74-50-03 W
Pop: 13,826 (1990)   Pop Density: 294.2
Land: 47.0 sq. mi.; Water: 11.5 sq. mi.

*Massena
Village
ZIP: 13662   Lat: 44-55-42 N Long: 74-53-36 W
Pop: 11,719 (1990); 217 (1980)   Pop Density: 2663.4
Land: 4.4 sq. mi.; Water: 0.2 sq. mi.
In northern NY near the St. Lawrence River, 31 mi. west of
Malone. Not coextensive with the town of the same name.
Name origin: For French Gen. André Masséna (1758–1817).

Morristown
Town
ZIP: 13664   Lat: 44-31-58 N Long: 75-38-03 W
Pop: 2,019 (1990)   Pop Density: 44.0
Land: 45.9 sq. mi.; Water: 13.6 sq. mi.

*Morristown
Village
ZIP: 13664   Lat: 44-34-59 N Long: 75-38-42 W
Pop: 490 (1990); 461 (1980)   Pop Density: 490.0
Land: 1.0 sq. mi.; Water: 0.0 sq. mi.
Not coextensive with the town of the same name.

Norfolk
Town
ZIP: 13667   Lat: 44-49-20 N Long: 74-56-50 W
Pop: 4,258 (1990)   Pop Density: 78.0
Land: 54.6 sq. mi.; Water: 0.8 sq. mi.
Name origin: For the English county.

Norwood
Village
ZIP: 13668   Lat: 44-44-54 N Long: 74-59-51 W
Pop: 1,841 (1990); 70 (1980)   Pop Density: 876.7
Land: 2.1 sq. mi.; Water: 0.2 sq. mi.

Ogdensburg
City
ZIP: 13669   Lat: 44-42-25 N Long: 75-28-13 W
Pop: 13,521 (1990); 12,375 (1980)   Pop Density: 2651.2
Land: 5.1 sq. mi.; Water: 3.1 sq. mi.
In northern NY on the St. Lawrence River, 55 mi. northeast
of Watertown.
Name origin: For Col. Samuel Ogden, who purchased the site

in 1792 and promoted its resettlement after the British evac-
uation.

Oswegatchie
Town
ZIP: 13654   Lat: 44-37-54 N Long: 75-29-07 W
Pop: 4,036 (1990)   Pop Density: 61.3
Land: 65.8 sq. mi.; Water: 5.5 sq. mi.
Name origin: From an Iroquoian term possibly meaning
'black water.'

Parishville
Town
ZIP: 13672   Lat: 44-34-30 N Long: 74-49-49 W
Pop: 1,901 (1990)   Pop Density: 19.4
Land: 98.2 sq. mi.; Water: 3.2 sq. mi.

Piercefield
Town
ZIP: 12973   Lat: 44-13-24 N Long: 74-36-16 W
Pop: 285 (1990)   Pop Density: 2.7
Land: 104.3 sq. mi.; Water: 6.8 sq. mi.

Pierrepont
Town
ZIP: 13617   Lat: 44-31-33 N Long: 75-00-45 W
Pop: 2,375 (1990)   Pop Density: 39.3
Land: 60.4 sq. mi.; Water: 0.3 sq. mi.

Pitcairn
Town
Lat: 44-11-18 N Long: 75-17-15 W
Pop: 751 (1990)   Pop Density: 12.7
Land: 59.0 sq. mi.; Water: 0.5 sq. mi.

Potsdam
Town
ZIP: 13676   Lat: 44-40-15 N Long: 75-02-42 W
Pop: 16,822 (1990)   Pop Density: 165.7
Land: 101.5 sq. mi.; Water: 2.0 sq. mi.

*Potsdam
Village
ZIP: 13676   Lat: 44-40-05 N Long: 74-59-08 W
Pop: 10,251 (1990); 10,635 (1980)   Pop Density: 2329.8
Land: 4.4 sq. mi.; Water: 0.5 sq. mi.
In northern NY, 27 mi. east of Ogdensburg. Not coextensive
with the town of the same name.
Name origin: For the city in Germany.

Rensselaer Falls
Village
ZIP: 13680   Lat: 44-35-26 N Long: 75-19-12 W
Pop: 316 (1990); 360 (1980)   Pop Density: 1053.3
Land: 0.3 sq. mi.; Water: 0.0 sq. mi.   Elev: 328 ft.

Richville
Village
ZIP: 13681   Lat: 44-24-55 N Long: 75-23-27 W
Pop: 311 (1990); 336 (1980)   Pop Density: 444.3
Land: 0.7 sq. mi.; Water: 0.0 sq. mi.

Rossie
Town
ZIP: 13646   Lat: 44-20-01 N Long: 75-38-13 W
Pop: 770 (1990)   Pop Density: 20.2
Land: 38.1 sq. mi.; Water: 1.0 sq. mi.

Russell
Town
ZIP: 13684   Lat: 44-24-10 N Long: 75-08-29 W
Pop: 1,716 (1990)   Pop Density: 17.7
Land: 96.8 sq. mi.; Water: 0.5 sq. mi.
Name origin: For a prominent citizen.

Star Lake
CDP
ZIP: 13690   Lat: 44-09-36 N Long: 75-02-15 W
Pop: 1,092 (1990); 275 (1980)   Pop Density: 248.2
Land: 4.4 sq. mi.; Water: 0.4 sq. mi.

Stockholm Town
Lat: 44-44-16 N **Long:** 74-51-08 W
Pop: 3,533 (1990)   **Pop Density:** 37.6
Land: 93.9 sq. mi.; **Water:** 0.3 sq. mi.

Waddington Town
ZIP: 13694   Lat: 44-49-35 N **Long:** 75-11-44 W
Pop: 1,990 (1990)   **Pop Density:** 38.6
Land: 51.5 sq. mi.; **Water:** 6.4 sq. mi.

*Waddington Village
ZIP: 13694   Lat: 44-51-31 N **Long:** 75-11-47 W
Pop: 944 (1990); 980 (1980)   **Pop Density:** 429.1
Land: 2.2 sq. mi.; **Water:** 0.2 sq. mi.

Not coextensive with the town of the same name.

Saratoga County
County Seat: Ballston Spa (ZIP: 12020)

Pop: 181,276 (1990); 153,759 (1980)   **Pop Density:** 223.3
Land: 811.9 sq. mi.; **Water:** 31.9 sq. mi.   **Area Code:** 518

In east-central NY, north of Albany; organized Feb 7, 1791 from Albany County.

Name origin: Of Indian origin; possibly from Mohawk word meaning 'springs from the hillside'; or from Iroquois for 'beaver place.'

Ballston Town
ZIP: 12019   Lat: 42-57-16 N **Long:** 73-52-46 W
Pop: 8,078 (1990)   **Pop Density:** 272.9
Land: 29.6 sq. mi.; **Water:** 0.4 sq. mi.

Name origin: For a prominent settler.

Ballston Spa Village
ZIP: 12020   Lat: 43-00-21 N **Long:** 73-51-05 W
Pop: 4,937 (1990); 995 (1980)   **Pop Density:** 3085.6
Land: 1.6 sq. mi.; **Water:** 0.0 sq. mi.   **Elev:** 288 ft.

Name origin: For Eliphalet Ball, a relative of George Washington (1732–99), and its mineral springs, a once-popular resort.

Charlton Town
Lat: 42-57-47 N **Long:** 73-59-35 W
Pop: 3,984 (1990)   **Pop Density:** 121.5
Land: 32.8 sq. mi.; **Water:** 0.0 sq. mi.

Clifton Park Town
ZIP: 12065   Lat: 42-51-30 N **Long:** 73-49-20 W
Pop: 30,117 (1990)   **Pop Density:** 619.7
Land: 48.6 sq. mi.; **Water:** 1.7 sq. mi.

Corinth Town
ZIP: 12822   Lat: 43-14-11 N **Long:** 73-53-37 W
Pop: 5,935 (1990)   **Pop Density:** 104.5
Land: 56.8 sq. mi.; **Water:** 1.3 sq. mi.

*Corinth Village
ZIP: 12822   Lat: 43-14-43 N **Long:** 73-49-50 W
Pop: 2,760 (1990); 2,702 (1980)   **Pop Density:** 2509.1
Land: 1.1 sq. mi.; **Water:** 0.0 sq. mi.

Not coextensive with the town of the same name.

Name origin: For the ancient Greek city.

Country Knolls CDP
Lat: 42-54-53 N **Long:** 73-48-20 W
Pop: 2,287 (1990); 2,497 (1980)   **Pop Density:** 1429.4
Land: 1.6 sq. mi.; **Water:** 0.0 sq. mi.

Day Town
ZIP: 12835   Lat: 43-19-18 N **Long:** 74-00-54 W
Pop: 746 (1990)   **Pop Density:** 11.6
Land: 64.3 sq. mi.; **Water:** 5.2 sq. mi.

Edinburg Town
ZIP: 12835   Lat: 43-12-49 N **Long:** 74-03-57 W
Pop: 1,041 (1990)   **Pop Density:** 17.3
Land: 60.1 sq. mi.; **Water:** 7.0 sq. mi.

Galway Town
ZIP: 12074   Lat: 43-01-53 N **Long:** 74-01-54 W
Pop: 3,266 (1990)   **Pop Density:** 74.2
Land: 44.0 sq. mi.; **Water:** 1.0 sq. mi.

*Galway Village
ZIP: 12074   Lat: 43-01-07 N **Long:** 74-01-54 W
Pop: 151 (1990); 245 (1980)   **Pop Density:** 503.3
Land: 0.3 sq. mi.; **Water:** 0.0 sq. mi.

Not coextensive with the town of the same name.

Greenfield Town
ZIP: 12833   Lat: 43-08-14 N **Long:** 73-52-27 W
Pop: 6,338 (1990)   **Pop Density:** 94.0
Land: 67.4 sq. mi.; **Water:** 0.3 sq. mi.

Hadley Town
ZIP: 12835   Lat: 43-20-16 N **Long:** 73-54-20 W
Pop: 1,628 (1990)   **Pop Density:** 40.9
Land: 39.8 sq. mi.; **Water:** 1.3 sq. mi.

Name origin: For Hadley, England.

Halfmoon Town
ZIP: 12065   Lat: 42-52-00 N **Long:** 73-43-38 W
Pop: 13,879 (1990)   **Pop Density:** 425.7
Land: 32.6 sq. mi.; **Water:** 1.0 sq. mi.

Lake Luzerne-Hadley CDP
Lat: 43-18-46 N **Long:** 73-50-42 W
Pop: 877 (1990); 825 (1980)   **Pop Density:** 730.8
Land: 1.2 sq. mi.; **Water:** 0.2 sq. mi.

Part of the town is also in Warren County.

Malta Town
ZIP: 12020   Lat: 42-59-16 N **Long:** 73-47-10 W
Pop: 11,709 (1990)   **Pop Density:** 418.2
Land: 28.0 sq. mi.; **Water:** 3.4 sq. mi.

Name origin: For the Mediterranean island.

Mechanicville
City
ZIP: 12118   Lat: 42-54-14 N Long: 73-41-24 W
Pop: 5,249 (1990); 5,500 (1980)   Pop Density: 6561.3
Land: 0.8 sq. mi.; Water: 0.1 sq. mi.   Elev: 104 ft.
In eastern NY on the west bank of the Hudson River, 17 mi. north of Albany.
Name origin: For early local industry.

Milton
Town
ZIP: 12020   Lat: 43-02-21 N Long: 73-53-48 W
Pop: 14,658 (1990)   Pop Density: 411.7
Land: 35.6 sq. mi.; Water: 0.0 sq. mi.

Moreau
Town
ZIP: 12801   Lat: 43-14-49 N Long: 73-39-59 W
Pop: 13,022 (1990)   Pop Density: 308.6
Land: 42.2 sq. mi.; Water: 1.4 sq. mi.

North Ballston Spa
CDP
Lat: 43-01-09 N Long: 73-51-10 W
Pop: 1,362 (1990); 1,350 (1980)   Pop Density: 1513.3
Land: 0.9 sq. mi.; Water: 0.0 sq. mi.

Northumberland
Town
Lat: 43-09-39 N Long: 73-38-00 W
Pop: 3,645 (1990)   Pop Density: 112.5
Land: 32.4 sq. mi.; Water: 0.5 sq. mi.

Providence
Town
ZIP: 12850   Lat: 43-07-04 N Long: 74-02-48 W
Pop: 1,360 (1990)   Pop Density: 30.9
Land: 44.0 sq. mi.; Water: 1.1 sq. mi.

Round Lake
Village
ZIP: 12151   Lat: 42-56-13 N Long: 73-47-45 W
Pop: 765 (1990); 791 (1980)   Pop Density: 695.5
Land: 1.1 sq. mi.; Water: 0.1 sq. mi.   Elev: 159 ft.

Saratoga
Town
ZIP: 12871   Lat: 43-03-54 N Long: 73-39-00 W
Pop: 5,069 (1990)   Pop Density: 124.5
Land: 40.7 sq. mi.; Water: 2.2 sq. mi.

Saratoga Springs
City
ZIP: 12866   Lat: 43-04-03 N Long: 73-46-43 W
Pop: 25,001 (1990); 23,906 (1980)   Pop Density: 880.3
Land: 28.4 sq. mi.; Water: 0.6 sq. mi.
In eastern NY, 33 mi. north of Albany. Famous health resort noted for its mineral springs. Large numbers of wild animals, attracted by the saline properties of the water, made this section a favorite hunting ground for the Indians.
Name origin: Meaning of the name is in dispute: possibly a Mohawk name 'springs from the hillside,' or Iroquois 'beaver place.'

Schuylerville
Village
ZIP: 12871   Lat: 43-06-07 N Long: 73-34-49 W
Pop: 1,364 (1990); 1,256 (1980)   Pop Density: 2728.0
Land: 0.5 sq. mi.; Water: 0.1 sq. mi.
In eastern NY on the west bank of the Hudson River, 32 mi. north of Albany.

South Glens Falls
Village
ZIP: 12801   Lat: 43-17-36 N Long: 73-38-06 W
Pop: 3,506 (1990); 3,714 (1980)   Pop Density: 2696.9
Land: 1.3 sq. mi.; Water: 0.1 sq. mi.   Elev: 345 ft.
In eastern NY, 17 mi. northeast of Sarasota Springs.
Name origin: For its location relative to Glens Falls across the Hudson River to the north.

Stillwater
Town
ZIP: 12170   Lat: 42-58-06 N Long: 73-41-14 W
Pop: 7,233 (1990)   Pop Density: 174.7
Land: 41.4 sq. mi.; Water: 2.2 sq. mi.

*Stillwater
Village
ZIP: 12170   Lat: 42-57-00 N Long 73-38-41 W
Pop: 1,531 (1990); 1,572 (1980)   Pop Density: 1275.8
Land: 1.2 sq. mi.; Water: 0.2 sq. mi.
In northern NY on the Hudson River, about 20 mi. north of Albany. Not coextensive with the town of the same name.

Victory
Village
ZIP: 12884   Lat: 43-05-36 N Long: 73-35-32 W
Pop: 581 (1990); 571 (1980)   Pop Density: 1162.0
Land: 0.5 sq. mi.; Water: 0.0 sq. mi.

Waterford
Town
ZIP: 12188   Lat: 42-48-24 N Long: 73-41-23 W
Pop: 8,695 (1990)   Pop Density: 1317.4
Land: 6.6 sq. mi.; Water: 0.9 sq. mi.

*Waterford
Village
ZIP: 12188   Lat: 42-47-30 N Long: 73-40-45 W
Pop: 2,370 (1990); 2,405 (1980)   Pop Density: 7900.0
Land: 0.3 sq. mi.; Water: 0.1 sq. mi.
In eastern NY, 10 mi. north of Albany on the Hudson River. Not coextensive with the town of the same name.

Wilton
Town
ZIP: 12866   Lat: 43-09-19 N Long: 73-43-28 W
Pop: 10,623 (1990)   Pop Density: 295.9
Land: 35.9 sq. mi.; Water: 0.1 sq. mi.
Name origin: For a prominent citizen.

Schenectady County
County Seat: Schenectady (ZIP: 12305)

Pop: 149,285 (1990); 149,946 (1980)   **Pop Density:** 724.2
Land: 206.1 sq. mi.; **Water:** 3.5 sq. mi.   **Area Code:** 518
In east-central NY, northwest of Albany; organized Mar 7, 1809 from Albany County.
Name origin: For the city, its county seat.

Delanson   Village
ZIP: 12053   **Lat:** 42-44-51 N **Long:** 74-11-05 W
Pop: 361 (1990); 448 (1980)   **Pop Density:** 601.7
Land: 0.6 sq. mi.; **Water:** 0.0 sq. mi.

Duanesburg   Town
ZIP: 12056   **Lat:** 42-46-59 N **Long:** 74-10-37 W
Pop: 5,474 (1990)   **Pop Density:** 76.9
Land: 71.2 sq. mi.; **Water:** 0.9 sq. mi.
Name origin: For James Duane (1733–97), jurist, land speculator, and mayor of Manhattan (1748–49).

East Glenville   CDP
ZIP: 12302   **Lat:** 42-51-36 N **Long:** 73-54-57 W
Pop: 6,518 (1990); 6,537 (1980)   **Pop Density:** 892.9
Land: 7.3 sq. mi.; **Water:** 0.2 sq. mi.

Glenville   Town
ZIP: 12302   **Lat:** 42-53-17 N **Long:** 73-59-20 W
Pop: 28,771 (1990)   **Pop Density:** 576.6
Land: 49.9 sq. mi.; **Water:** 1.0 sq. mi.

Niskayuna   Town
ZIP: 12309   **Lat:** 42-48-08 N **Long:** 73-52-25 W
Pop: 19,048 (1990)   **Pop Density:** 1350.9
Land: 14.1 sq. mi.; **Water:** 0.9 sq. mi.
Name origin: From an Indian term probably meaning 'big cornfields.'

*Niskayuna   CDP
   Lat: 42-49-01 N **Long:** 73-53-52 W
Pop: 4,942 (1990); 5,223 (1980)   **Pop Density:** 4942.0
Land: 1.0 sq. mi.; **Water:** 0.0 sq. mi.

Princetown   Town
ZIP: 12056   **Lat:** 42-48-41 N **Long:** 74-04-31 W
Pop: 2,031 (1990)   **Pop Density:** 84.3
Land: 24.1 sq. mi.; **Water:** 0.0 sq. mi.

Rotterdam   Town
ZIP: 12303   **Lat:** 42-48-41 N **Long:** 74-00-48 W
Pop: 28,395 (1990)   **Pop Density:** 788.8
Land: 36.0 sq. mi.; **Water:** 0.5 sq. mi.
In eastern NY, northwest of Schenectady.
Name origin: For the Dutch city.

*Rotterdam   CDP
ZIP: 12303   **Lat:** 42-46-42 N **Long:** 73-57-16 W
Pop: 21,228 (1990); 22,933 (1980)   **Pop Density:** 3076.5
Land: 6.9 sq. mi.; **Water:** 0.0 sq. mi.

Schenectady   City
ZIP: 12301   **Lat:** 42-48-06 N **Long:** 73-55-41 W
Pop: 65,566 (1990); 67,972 (1980)   **Pop Density:** 6015.2
Land: 10.9 sq. mi.; **Water:** 0.1 sq. mi.
In eastern NY on the Mohawk River, 13 mi. northwest of Albany.
Name origin: From an Indian term probably meaning 'on the other side of the pinelands' or 'the other side of the plains,' referring to the sites of both Albany and Schenectady as the termini of the aboriginal portage between the Hudson and Mohawk rivers. Previously called Schonowe.

Scotia   Village
ZIP: 12302   **Lat:** 42-49-55 N **Long:** 73-57-39 W
Pop: 7,359 (1990); 7,280 (1980)   **Pop Density:** 4328.8
Land: 1.7 sq. mi.; **Water:** 0.1 sq. mi.
In eastern NY, 25 mi. northwest of Albany.

Schoharie County
County Seat: Schoharie (ZIP: 12157)

Pop: 31,859 (1990); 29,710 (1980)   **Pop Density:** 51.2
Land: 621.8 sq. mi.; **Water:** 4.3 sq. mi.   **Area Code:** 518
In south-central NY, west of Albany; organized Apr 6, 1795 from Albany and Otsego counties.
Name origin: For the Schoharie Creek, which runs through it; from Iroquoian for 'driftwood.' Variants include: *skoharle, towasschoher, shoary, skohary,* and *schughhorre.*

Blenheim   Town
ZIP: 12131   **Lat:** 42-28-47 N **Long:** 74-29-15 W
Pop: 332 (1990)   **Pop Density:** 9.8
Land: 33.9 sq. mi.; **Water:** 0.4 sq. mi.

Broome   Town
   Lat: 42-30-08 N **Long:** 74-17-36 W
Pop: 926 (1990)   **Pop Density:** 19.5
Land: 47.5 sq. mi.; **Water:** 0.3 sq. mi.

Carlisle
Town
ZIP: 12031   **Lat:** 42-45-21 N   **Long:** 74-26-23 W
Pop: 1,672 (1990)   **Pop Density:** 48.9
Land: 34.2 sq. mi.; **Water:** 0.1 sq. mi.

Cobleskill
Town
ZIP: 12043   **Lat:** 42-40-56 N   **Long:** 74-26-57 W
Pop: 7,270 (1990)   **Pop Density:** 237.6
Land: 30.6 sq. mi.; **Water:** 0.2 sq. mi.

*Cobleskill
Village
ZIP: 12043   **Lat:** 42-40-44 N   **Long:** 74-29-09 W
Pop: 5,268 (1990); 5,272 (1980)   **Pop Density:** 1699.4
Land: 3.1 sq. mi.; **Water:** 0.0 sq. mi.   **Elev:** 932 ft.
In eastern NY, southwest of Amsterdam. Not coextensive with the town of the same name.
Name origin: From Dutch 'Coble's stream,' for Jacob Kobell, an early Dutch settler; with a spelling alteration.

Conesville
Town
     Lat: 42-23-19 N   **Long:** 74-20-11 W
Pop: 684 (1990)   **Pop Density:** 17.3
Land: 39.5 sq. mi.; **Water:** 0.4 sq. mi.

Esperance
Town
     Lat: 42-45-16 N   **Long:** 74-18-53 W
Pop: 2,101 (1990)   **Pop Density:** 107.2
Land: 19.6 sq. mi.; **Water:** 0.5 sq. mi.

*Esperance
Village
ZIP: 12066   **Lat:** 42-45-51 N   **Long:** 74-15-27 W
Pop: 324 (1990); 374 (1980)   **Pop Density:** 648.0
Land: 0.5 sq. mi.; **Water:** 0.0 sq. mi.
Not coextensive with the town of the same name.

Fulton
Town
     Lat: 42-33-30 N   **Long:** 74-26-35 W
Pop: 1,514 (1990)   **Pop Density:** 23.3
Land: 65.0 sq. mi.; **Water:** 0.0 sq. mi.

Gilboa
Town
ZIP: 12076   **Lat:** 42-25-47 N   **Long:** 74-27-20 W
Pop: 1,207 (1990)   **Pop Density:** 20.9
Land: 57.8 sq. mi.; **Water:** 1.6 sq. mi.
Name origin: For the biblical hill.

Jefferson
Town
ZIP: 12093   **Lat:** 42-29-33 N   **Long:** 74-37-04 W
Pop: 1,190 (1990)   **Pop Density:** 27.5
Land: 43.3 sq. mi.; **Water:** 0.1 sq. mi.
Name origin: For Thomas Jefferson (1743–1826), third U.S. president.

Middleburgh
Town
ZIP: 12122   **Lat:** 42-36-32 N   **Long:** 74-19-34 W
Pop: 3,296 (1990)   **Pop Density:** 66.9
Land: 49.3 sq. mi.; **Water:** 0.1 sq. mi.

*Middleburgh
Village
ZIP: 12122   **Lat:** 42-35-56 N   **Long:** 74-19-47 W
Pop: 1,436 (1990); 1,358 (1980)   **Pop Density:** 1196.7
Land: 1.2 sq. mi.; **Water:** 0.0 sq. mi.
Founded in 1712 by John Conrad Weiser and the first group of German Palatine pioneers.

Richmondville
Town
ZIP: 12149   **Lat:** 42-38-16 N   **Long:** 74-32-51 W
Pop: 2,397 (1990)   **Pop Density:** 79.4
Land: 30.2 sq. mi.; **Water:** 0.0 sq. mi.

*Richmondville
Village
ZIP: 12149   **Lat:** 42-37-59 N   **Long:** 74-33-52 W
Pop: 843 (1990); 792 (1980)   **Pop Density:** 468.3
Land: 1.8 sq. mi.; **Water:** 0.0 sq. mi.   **Elev:** 1148 ft.
Not coextensive with the town of the same name.

Schoharie
Town
ZIP: 12157   **Lat:** 42-40-43 N   **Long:** 74-18-46 W
Pop: 3,369 (1990)   **Pop Density:** 113.1
Land: 29.8 sq. mi.; **Water:** 0.2 sq. mi.

*Schoharie
Village
ZIP: 12157   **Lat:** 42-40-00 N   **Long:** 74-18-46 W
Pop: 1,045 (1990); 1,016 (1980)   **Pop Density:** 614.7
Land: 1.7 sq. mi.; **Water:** 0.0 sq. mi.   **Elev:** 611 ft.
Not coextensive with the town of the same name.

Seward
Town
ZIP: 12043   **Lat:** 42-42-08 N   **Long:** 74-34-43 W
Pop: 1,651 (1990)   **Pop Density:** 45.4
Land: 36.4 sq. mi.; **Water:** 0.1 sq. mi.

Sharon
Town
     Lat: 42-46-47 N   **Long:** 74-35-35 W
Pop: 1,892 (1990)   **Pop Density:** 48.4
Land: 39.1 sq. mi.; **Water:** 0.1 sq. mi.

Sharon Springs
Village
ZIP: 13459   **Lat:** 42-47-41 N   **Long:** 74-37-03 W
Pop: 543 (1990); 514 (1980)   **Pop Density:** 417.7
Land: 1.3 sq. mi.; **Water:** 0.0 sq. mi.   **Elev:** 1137 ft.

Summit
Town
ZIP: 12175   **Lat:** 42-34-02 N   **Long:** 74-36-46 W
Pop: 973 (1990)   **Pop Density:** 26.2
Land: 37.1 sq. mi.; **Water:** 0.3 sq. mi.

Wright
Town
     Lat: 42-39-44 N   **Long:** 74-13-12 W
Pop: 1,385 (1990)   **Pop Density:** 48.4
Land: 28.6 sq. mi.; **Water:** 0.1 sq. mi.

Schuyler County
County Seat: Watkins Glen (ZIP: 14891)

Pop: 18,662 (1990); 17,686 (1980)   **Pop Density:** 56.8
Land: 328.7 sq. mi.; **Water:** 17.4 sq. mi.   **Area Code:** 607

In north-central NY, southeast of Rochester; organized Apr 17, 1854 from Tompkins, Steuben, and Chemung counties.

Name origin: For Gen. Philip John Schuyler (1733–1804), an officer in the Revolutionary War, NY legislator, and U.S. senator (1789–91; 1797–98).

Burdett   Village
ZIP: 14818   **Lat:** 42-25-01 N **Long:** 76-50-50 W
Pop: 372 (1990); 410 (1980)   **Pop Density:** 372.0
Land: 1.0 sq. mi.; **Water:** 0.0 sq. mi.

Catharine   Town
              Lat: 42-20-37 N **Long:** 76-44-24 W
Pop: 1,991 (1990)   **Pop Density:** 60.7
Land: 32.8 sq. mi.; **Water:** 0.6 sq. mi.

Cayuta   Town
ZIP: 14824   **Lat:** 42-15-52 N **Long:** 76-40-52 W
Pop: 599 (1990)   **Pop Density:** 30.1
Land: 19.9 sq. mi.; **Water:** 0.0 sq. mi.

Dix   Town
              Lat: 42-19-39 N **Long:** 76-54-26 W
Pop: 4,130 (1990)   **Pop Density:** 114.1
Land: 36.2 sq. mi.; **Water:** 0.5 sq. mi.

Hector   Town
ZIP: 14841   **Lat:** 42-28-22 N **Long:** 76-47-38 W
Pop: 4,423 (1990)   **Pop Density:** 43.2
Land: 102.5 sq. mi.; **Water:** 13.9 sq. mi.

Name origin: For the mythological Trojan hero.

Montour   Town
              Lat: 42-20-18 N **Long:** 76-49-32 W
Pop: 2,528 (1990)   **Pop Density:** 135.9
Land: 18.6 sq. mi.; **Water:** 0.0 sq. mi.

Montour Falls   Village
ZIP: 14865   **Lat:** 42-21-00 N **Long:** 76-50-57 W
Pop: 1,845 (1990); 94 (1980)   **Pop Density:** 615.0
Land: 3.0 sq. mi.; **Water:** 0.0 sq. mi.

In southwest-central NY near the northern point of Seneca Lake.

Odessa   Village
ZIP: 14869   **Lat:** 42-18-39 N **Long:** 76-49-02 W
Pop: 986 (1990); 529 (1980)   **Pop Density:** 133.2
Land: 7.4 sq. mi.; **Water:** 0.0 sq. mi.   **Elev:** 1050 ft.

Name origin: For the city in Ukraine.

Orange   Town
              Lat: 42-19-58 N **Long:** 77-02-08 W
Pop: 1,561 (1990)   **Pop Density:** 28.9
Land: 54.1 sq. mi.; **Water:** 0.3 sq. mi.

Reading   Town
              Lat: 42-25-11 N **Long:** 76-56-17 W
Pop: 1,810 (1990)   **Pop Density:** 66.5
Land: 27.2 sq. mi.; **Water:** 0.0 sq. mi.

Tyrone   Town
              Lat: 42-26-28 N **Long:** 77-02-39 W
Pop: 1,620 (1990)   **Pop Density:** 43.2
Land: 37.5 sq. mi.; **Water:** 2.1 sq. mi.

Name origin: For the county in Ireland.

Watkins Glen   Village
ZIP: 14891   **Lat:** 42-22-49 N **Long:** 76-52-04 W
Pop: 2,207 (1990); 2,008 (1980)   **Pop Density:** 1471.3
Land: 1.5 sq. mi.; **Water:** 0.4 sq. mi.

In southwest-central NY, 18 mi. north of Elmira.

Seneca County
County Seat: Waterloo (ZIP: 13165)

Pop: 33,683 (1990); 33,733 (1980)   **Pop Density:** 103.7
Land: 324.9 sq. mi.; **Water:** 65.6 sq. mi.   **Area Code:** 315

In north-central NY, southeast of Rochester; organized Mar 24, 1804 from Cayuga County.

Name origin: For the Seneca Indians, one of the Five Nations of the Iroquois.

Covert   Town
              Lat: 42-35-05 N **Long:** 76-41-42 W
Pop: 2,246 (1990)   **Pop Density:** 71.3
Land: 31.5 sq. mi.; **Water:** 6.1 sq. mi.

Fayette   Town
              Lat: 42-50-42 N **Long:** 76-50-56 W
Pop: 3,636 (1990)   **Pop Density:** 65.9
Land: 55.2 sq. mi.; **Water:** 11.3 sq. mi.

Geneva   City
ZIP: 14456   **Lat:** 42-52-08 N **Long:** 07-65-84 W
Pop: 0 (1990); 15,620 (1980)

              Elev: 494 ft.

In western NY at the north end of Seneca Lake. Part of the town is in Ontario County.

Name origin: For the Swiss city.

Interlaken Village
ZIP: 14847 Lat: 42-37-07 N Long: 76-43-29 W
Pop: 680 (1990); 685 (1980) Pop Density: 2266.7
Land: 0.3 sq. mi.; Water: 0.0 sq. mi.
Name origin: For its location between Cayuga and Seneca
lakes; from German 'between lakes.'

Junius Town
ZIP: 13165 Lat: 42-58-15 N Long: 76-54-35 W
Pop: 1,354 (1990) Pop Density: 50.7
Land: 26.7 sq. mi.; Water: 0.1 sq. mi.

Lodi Town
ZIP: 14860 Lat: 42-35-32 N Long: 76-49-55 W
Pop: 1,429 (1990) Pop Density: 41.7
Land: 34.3 sq. mi.; Water: 5.5 sq. mi.

*Lodi Village
ZIP: 14860 Lat: 42-36-47 N Long: 76-49-20 W
Pop: 364 (1990); 334 (1980) Pop Density: 606.7
Land: 0.6 sq. mi.; Water: 0.0 sq. mi.
Not coextensive with the town of the same name.

Ovid Town
ZIP: 14521 Lat: 42-39-27 N Long: 76-47-34 W
Pop: 2,306 (1990) Pop Density: 74.4
Land: 31.0 sq. mi.; Water: 7.8 sq. mi.

*Ovid Village
ZIP: 14521 Lat: 42-40-31 N Long: 76-49-17 W
Pop: 660 (1990); 642 (1980) Pop Density: 1650.0
Land: 0.4 sq. mi.; Water: 0.0 sq. mi.
In west-central NY between Seneca and Cayuga lakes. Not
coextensive with the town of the same name.
Name origin: For the Roman poet (48 B.C.–17 A.D.).

Romulus Town
ZIP: 14541 Lat: 42-43-10 N Long: 76-49-46 W
Pop: 2,532 (1990) Pop Density: 67.0
Land: 37.8 sq. mi.; Water: 13.5 sq. mi.
Name origin: For one of the mythological founders, along
with his brother Remus, of Rome.

Seneca Falls Town
ZIP: 13148 Lat: 42-54-43 N Long: 76-47-25 W
Pop: 9,384 (1990) Pop Density: 387.8
Land: 24.2 sq. mi.; Water: 3.2 sq. mi.

*Seneca Falls Village
ZIP: 13148 Lat: 42-54-33 N Long: 76-47-44 W
Pop: 7,370 (1990); 7,466 (1980) Pop Density: 1675.0
Land: 4.4 sq. mi.; Water: 0.2 sq. mi.
In west-central NY where the Seneca River cascades into
Cayuga Lake. Not coextensive with the town of the same
name.
Name origin: For the river, itself named for the Seneca In-
dians.

Tyre Town
ZIP: 13148 Lat: 42-59-00 N Long: 76-47-39 W
Pop: 870 (1990) Pop Density: 28.8
Land: 30.2 sq. mi.; Water: 3.0 sq. mi.

Varick Town
Lat: 42-46-42 N Long: 76-51-18 W
Pop: 2,161 (1990) Pop Density: 66.9
Land: 32.3 sq. mi.; Water: 13.3 sq. mi.

Waterloo Town
ZIP: 13165 Lat: 42-54-32 N Long: 76-54-44 W
Pop: 7,765 (1990) Pop Density: 357.8
Land: 21.7 sq. mi.; Water: 0.2 sq. mi.

*Waterloo Village
ZIP: 13165 Lat: 42-54-16 N Long: 76-51-33 W
Pop: 5,116 (1990); 732 (1980) Pop Density: 2558.0
Land: 2.0 sq. mi.; Water: 0.1 sq. mi. Elev: 455 ft.
Not coextensive with the town of the same name.
Name origin: For the great European battle at which Napo-
leon (1769–1821) was decisively defeated.

Steuben County
County Seat: Bath (ZIP: 14810)

Pop: 99,088 (1990); 99,217 (1980) Pop Density: 71.1
Land: 1392.7 sq. mi.; Water: 11.4 sq. mi. Area Code: 607
On central southern border of NY, south of Rochester; organized Mar 17, 1796 from
Ontario County.
Name origin: For Baron Friedrich Wilhelm von Steuben (1730–94), Prussian soldier
and inspector general of the Continental Army during the American Revolution.

Addison Town
ZIP: 14801 Lat: 42-08-13 N Long: 77-14-23 W
Pop: 2,645 (1990) Pop Density: 103.3
Land: 25.6 sq. mi.; Water: 0.0 sq. mi.

*Addison Village
ZIP: 14801 Lat: 42-06-20 N Long: 77-14-00 W
Pop: 1,842 (1990); 2,028 (1980) Pop Density: 969.5
Land: 1.9 sq. mi.; Water: 0.0 sq. mi.
Not coextensive with the town of the same name.

Almond Village
ZIP: 14804 Lat: 42-19-13 N Long: 77-44-05 W
Pop: 16 (1990); 39 (1980) Pop Density: 160.0
Land: 0.1 sq. mi.; Water: 0.0 sq. mi.
Most of the village is in Allegany County.

Arkport Village
ZIP: 14807 Lat: 42-23-30 N Long: 77-41-47 W
Pop: 770 (1990); 811 (1980) Pop Density: 1100.0
Land: 0.7 sq. mi.; Water: 0.0 sq. mi. Elev: 1194 ft.

Avoca　　　　　　　　　　　　　　　Town
ZIP: 14809　　　Lat: 42-25-02 N　**Long:** 77-26-25 W
Pop: 2,269 (1990)　　　　　　**Pop Density:** 62.5
Land: 36.3 sq. mi.; **Water:** 0.0 sq. mi.

*Avoca　　　　　　　　　　　　　Village
ZIP: 14809　　　Lat: 42-24-30 N　**Long:** 77-25-23 W
Pop: 1,033 (1990); 1,144 (1980)　**Pop Density:** 860.8
Land: 1.2 sq. mi.; **Water:** 0.0 sq. mi.　**Elev:** 1192 ft.
Not coextensive with the town of the same name.

Bath　　　　　　　　　　　　　　　Town
ZIP: 14810　　　Lat: 42-19-29 N　**Long:** 77-18-20 W
Pop: 12,724 (1990)　　　　　　**Pop Density:** 132.5
Land: 96.0 sq. mi.; **Water:** 0.3 sq. mi.

*Bath　　　　　　　　　　　　　Village
ZIP: 14810　　　Lat: 42-20-13 N　**Long:** 77-19-06 W
Pop: 5,801 (1990); 6,042 (1980)　**Pop Density:** 2000.3
Land: 2.9 sq. mi.; **Water:** 0.0 sq. mi.　**Elev:** 1106 ft.
In southern NY, 19 mi. east of Hornell. Not coextensive with
the town of the same name.
Name origin: For the English city.

Bradford　　　　　　　　　　　　　Town
ZIP: 14815　　　Lat: 42-19-50 N　**Long:** 77-08-01 W
Pop: 699 (1990)　　　　　　　**Pop Density:** 28.2
Land: 24.8 sq. mi.; **Water:** 0.0 sq. mi.

Cameron　　　　　　　　　　　　　Town
ZIP: 14819　　　Lat: 42-12-52 N　**Long:** 77-23-50 W
Pop: 916 (1990)　　　　　　　**Pop Density:** 19.6
Land: 46.7 sq. mi.; **Water:** 0.0 sq. mi.

Campbell　　　　　　　　　　　　Town
ZIP: 14821　　　Lat: 42-14-04 N　**Long:** 77-10-08 W
Pop: 3,658 (1990)　　　　　　**Pop Density:** 89.7
Land: 40.8 sq. mi.; **Water:** 0.0 sq. mi.
Name origin: For the famous Scottish clan.

Canisteo　　　　　　　　　　　　Town
ZIP: 14823　　　Lat: 42-14-12 N　**Long:** 77-32-05 W
Pop: 3,636 (1990)　　　　　　**Pop Density:** 66.8
Land: 54.4 sq. mi.; **Water:** 0.0 sq. mi.

*Canisteo　　　　　　　　　　　Village
ZIP: 14823　　　Lat: 42-16-13 N　**Long:** 77-36-18 W
Pop: 2,421 (1990); 2,679 (1980)　**Pop Density:** 2690.0
Land: 0.9 sq. mi.; **Water:** 0.0 sq. mi.　**Elev:** 1132 ft.
In southwestern NY on the Canisteo River, northwest of
Elmira. Not coextensive with the town of the same name.
Name origin: An Indian term possibly referring to the pick-
erel fish.

Caton　　　　　　　　　　　　　　Town
　　　　　　　　Lat: 42-02-58 N　**Long:** 77-01-44 W
Pop: 1,888 (1990)　　　　　　**Pop Density:** 49.9
Land: 37.8 sq. mi.; **Water:** 0.2 sq. mi.

Cohocton　　　　　　　　　　　　Town
ZIP: 14826　　　Lat: 42-30-56 N　**Long:** 77-28-56 W
Pop: 2,520 (1990)　　　　　　**Pop Density:** 44.9
Land: 56.1 sq. mi.; **Water:** 0.0 sq. mi.

*Cohocton　　　　　　　　　　　Village
ZIP: 14826　　　Lat: 42-30-00 N　**Long:** 77-29-57 W
Pop: 859 (1990); 902 (1980)　**Pop Density:** 572.7
Land: 1.5 sq. mi.; **Water:** 0.0 sq. mi.
Not coextensive with the town of the same name.
Name origin: From Iroquois probably meaning 'log-in-the-
water.'

Corning　　　　　　　　　　　　　City
ZIP: 14830　　　Lat: 42-08-50 N　**Long:** 77-03-24 W
Pop: 11,938 (1990); 12,953 (1980)　**Pop Density:** 3851.0
Land: 3.1 sq. mi.; **Water:** 0.2 sq. mi.　**Elev:** 937 ft.
In southern NY on the Chemung River, 14 mi. west of
Elmira. Not coextensive with the town of the same name.
Name origin: For founder Erastus Corning.

*Corning　　　　　　　　　　　　Town
ZIP: 14830　　　Lat: 42-08-14 N　**Long:** 77-00-57 W
Pop: 6,367 (1990)　　　　　　**Pop Density:** 172.5
Land: 36.9 sq. mi.; **Water:** 0.4 sq. mi.

Dansville　　　　　　　　　　　　Town
　　　　　　　　Lat: 42-28-28 N　**Long:** 77-39-55 W
Pop: 1,811 (1990)　　　　　　**Pop Density:** 37.7
Land: 48.0 sq. mi.; **Water:** 0.1 sq. mi.

Erwin　　　　　　　　　　　　　Town
ZIP: 14870　　　Lat: 42-08-28 N　**Long:** 77-08-28 W
Pop: 6,763 (1990)　　　　　　**Pop Density:** 174.8
Land: 38.7 sq. mi.; **Water:** 0.5 sq. mi.

Fremont　　　　　　　　　　　　Town
　　　　　　　　Lat: 42-24-18 N　**Long:** 77-36-23 W
Pop: 912 (1990)　　　　　　　**Pop Density:** 28.3
Land: 32.2 sq. mi.; **Water:** 0.1 sq. mi.

Gang Mills　　　　　　　　　　　CDP
　　　　　　　　Lat: 42-09-12 N　**Long:** 77-08-04 W
Pop: 2,738 (1990); 2,300 (1980)　**Pop Density:** 414.8
Land: 6.6 sq. mi.; **Water:** 0.0 sq. mi.

Greenwood　　　　　　　　　　　Town
ZIP: 14839　　　Lat: 42-08-50 N　**Long:** 77-41-09 W
Pop: 898 (1990)　　　　　　　**Pop Density:** 21.7
Land: 41.3 sq. mi.; **Water:** 0.0 sq. mi.

Hammondsport　　　　　　　　　Village
ZIP: 14840　　　Lat: 42-24-31 N　**Long:** 77-13-23 W
Pop: 929 (1990); 1,065 (1980)　**Pop Density:** 2322.5
Land: 0.4 sq. mi.; **Water:** 0.0 sq. mi.　**Elev:** 743 ft.

Hartsville　　　　　　　　　　　Town
　　　　　　　　Lat: 42-14-28 N　**Long:** 77-40-04 W
Pop: 546 (1990)　　　　　　　**Pop Density:** 15.1
Land: 36.2 sq. mi.; **Water:** 0.0 sq. mi.

Hornby　　　　　　　　　　　　　Town
　　　　　　　　Lat: 42-13-37 N　**Long:** 77-01-36 W
Pop: 1,655 (1990)　　　　　　**Pop Density:** 40.5
Land: 40.9 sq. mi.; **Water:** 0.0 sq. mi.

Hornell　　　　　　　　　　　　　City
ZIP: 14843　　　Lat: 42-19-27 N　**Long:** 77-39-37 W
Pop: 9,877 (1990); 10,234 (1980)　**Pop Density:** 3798.8
Land: 2.6 sq. mi.; **Water:** 0.0 sq. mi.　**Elev:** 1164 ft.
In southwestern NY, 56 mi. south of Rochester.
Name origin: For George Hornell, an Indian trader who
purchased the site in 1793, built the first gristmill and tavern,
and became the leading citizen of the upper Canisteo Valley.

Hornellsville
Town
Lat: 42-20-04 N **Long:** 77-40-39 W
Pop: 4,149 (1990) **Pop Density:** 95.2
Land: 43.6 sq. mi.; **Water:** 0.2 sq. mi.

Howard
Town
Lat: 42-20-29 N **Long:** 77-31-04 W
Pop: 1,331 (1990) **Pop Density:** 22.0
Land: 60.6 sq. mi.; **Water:** 0.1 sq. mi.

Jasper
Town
ZIP: 14855 **Lat:** 42-08-37 N **Long:** 77-32-02 W
Pop: 1,232 (1990) **Pop Density:** 23.4
Land: 52.7 sq. mi.; **Water:** 0.0 sq. mi.

Lindley
Town
ZIP: 14858 **Lat:** 42-02-46 N **Long:** 77-08-42 W
Pop: 1,862 (1990) **Pop Density:** 49.7
Land: 37.5 sq. mi.; **Water:** 0.3 sq. mi.

North Hornell
Village
ZIP: 14843 **Lat:** 42-20-44 N **Long:** 77-39-45 W
Pop: 822 (1990); 813 (1980) **Pop Density:** 1174.3
Land: 0.7 sq. mi.; **Water:** 0.0 sq. mi.

Painted Post
Village
ZIP: 14870 **Lat:** 42-09-46 N **Long:** 77-05-30 W
Pop: 1,950 (1990); 2,196 (1980) **Pop Density:** 1500.0
Land: 1.3 sq. mi.; **Water:** 0.1 sq. mi.

Name origin: For a red-painted oaken post that was once here, probably erected as a memorial either to an Indian victory or to an Indian chief.

Prattsburg
Town
ZIP: 14873 **Lat:** 42-31-49 N **Long:** 77-18-53 W
Pop: 1,894 (1990) **Pop Density:** 36.6
Land: 51.7 sq. mi.; **Water:** 0.0 sq. mi.

In southern NY.

Pulteney
Town
ZIP: 14874 **Lat:** 42-31-11 N **Long:** 77-11-36 W
Pop: 1,417 (1990) **Pop Density:** 42.7
Land: 33.2 sq. mi.; **Water:** 3.2 sq. mi.

Name origin: For Sir William Pulteney, head of the London Associates.

Rathbone
Town
Lat: 42-08-08 N **Long:** 77-19-40 W
Pop: 892 (1990) **Pop Density:** 24.7
Land: 36.1 sq. mi.; **Water:** 0.0 sq. mi.

Riverside
Village
ZIP: 14830 **Lat:** 42-09-21 N **Long:** 77-04-51 W
Pop: 585 (1990); 684 (1980) **Pop Density:** 1950.0
Land: 0.3 sq. mi.; **Water:** 0.0 sq. mi.

Savona
Village
ZIP: 14879 **Lat:** 42-17-02 N **Long:** 77-13-23 W
Pop: 974 (1990); 932 (1980) **Pop Density:** 974.0
Land: 1.0 sq. mi.; **Water:** 0.0 sq. mi.

Name origin: For Savona, Italy.

South Corning
Village
ZIP: 14830 **Lat:** 42-07-26 N **Long:** 77-02-12 W
Pop: 1,025 (1990); 1,195 (1980) **Pop Density:** 1708.3
Land: 0.6 sq. mi.; **Water:** 0.0 sq. mi.

Thurston
Town
Lat: 42-13-31 N **Long:** 77-16-40 W
Pop: 1,054 (1990) **Pop Density:** 29.0
Land: 36.4 sq. mi.; **Water:** 0.1 sq. mi.

Troupsburg
Town
ZIP: 14885 **Lat:** 42-02-58 N **Long:** 77-32-54 W
Pop: 1,006 (1990) **Pop Density:** 16.4
Land: 61.2 sq. mi.; **Water:** 0.0 sq. mi.

Tuscarora
Town
Lat: 42-03-00 N **Long:** 77-15-27 W
Pop: 1,368 (1990) **Pop Density:** 36.2
Land: 37.8 sq. mi.; **Water:** 0.0 sq. mi.

Urbana
Town
Lat: 42-24-35 N **Long:** 77-13-38 W
Pop: 2,807 (1990) **Pop Density:** 68.3
Land: 41.1 sq. mi.; **Water:** 3.0 sq. mi.

Wayland
Town
ZIP: 14572 **Lat:** 42-31-50 N **Long:** 77-35-23 W
Pop: 4,311 (1990) **Pop Density:** 110.5
Land: 39.0 sq. mi.; **Water:** 0.5 sq. mi.

*Wayland
Village
ZIP: 14572 **Lat:** 42-34-05 N **Long:** 77-35-31 W
Pop: 1,976 (1990); 1,846 (1980) **Pop Density:** 1976.0
Land: 1.0 sq. mi.; **Water:** 0.0 sq. mi. **Elev:** 1372 ft.

Not coextensive with the town of the same name.

Wayne
Town
Lat: 42-26-47 N **Long:** 77-07-52 W
Pop: 1,029 (1990) **Pop Density:** 49.7
Land: 20.7 sq. mi.; **Water:** 1.9 sq. mi.

West Union
Town
Lat: 42-03-22 N **Long:** 77-41-07 W
Pop: 412 (1990) **Pop Density:** 10.0
Land: 41.0 sq. mi.; **Water:** 0.1 sq. mi.

Wheeler
Town
Lat: 42-26-35 N **Long:** 77-20-49 W
Pop: 1,084 (1990) **Pop Density:** 23.5
Land: 46.1 sq. mi.; **Water:** 0.0 sq. mi.

Woodhull
Town
ZIP: 14898 **Lat:** 42-03-43 N **Long:** 77-23-14 W
Pop: 1,518 (1990) **Pop Density:** 27.4
Land: 55.4 sq. mi.; **Water:** 0.0 sq. mi.

Suffolk County
County Seat: Riverhead (ZIP: 11901)

Pop: 1,321,860 (1990); 1,284,230 (1980)   **Pop Density:** 1450.6
Land: 911.2 sq. mi.; **Water:** 1462.2 sq. mi.   **Area Code:** 516
On eastern end of Long Island, NY; original county, organized Nov 1, 1683.
Name origin: For Suffolk County, England.

Amityville   Village
ZIP: 11701   **Lat:** 40-40-11 N **Long:** 73-24-58 W
Pop: 9,286 (1990); 9,076 (1980)   **Pop Density:** 4421.9
Land: 2.1 sq. mi.; **Water:** 0.4 sq. mi.   **Elev:** 25 ft.
In southeastern NY on Great South Bay, south shore of Long Island.
Name origin: For the amicable settling of an argument over the name of the village.

Aquebogue   CDP
    Lat: 40-56-17 N **Long:** 72-36-50 W
Pop: 2,060 (1990)   **Pop Density:** 542.1
Land: 3.8 sq. mi.; **Water:** 0.7 sq. mi.

Asharoken   Village
ZIP: 11768   **Lat:** 40-56-41 N **Long:** 73-23-28 W
Pop: 807 (1990); 635 (1980)   **Pop Density:** 576.4
Land: 1.4 sq. mi.; **Water:** 5.1 sq. mi.

Babylon   Town
ZIP: 11702   **Lat:** 40-38-49 N **Long:** 73-21-07 W
Pop: 202,889 (1990)   **Pop Density:** 3879.3
Land: 52.3 sq. mi.; **Water:** 61.9 sq. mi.

*Babylon   Village
ZIP: 11702   **Lat:** 40-41-45 N **Long:** 73-19-37 W
Pop: 12,249 (1990); 12,388 (1980)   **Pop Density:** 5103.8
Land: 2.4 sq. mi.; **Water:** 0.3 sq. mi.
On Great South Bay in Long Island, 37 mi. east of New York City. Not coextensive with the town of the same name.
Name origin: For the ancient city.

Bayport   CDP
ZIP: 11705   **Lat:** 40-44-51 N **Long:** 73-03-16 W
Pop: 7,702 (1990); 9,282 (1980)   **Pop Density:** 2081.6
Land: 3.7 sq. mi.; **Water:** 0.1 sq. mi.

Bay Shore   CDP
ZIP: 11706   **Lat:** 40-43-34 N **Long:** 73-15-01 W
Pop: 21,279 (1990); 10,784 (1980)   **Pop Density:** 4014.9
Land: 5.3 sq. mi.; **Water:** 0.8 sq. mi.

Baywood   CDP
    Lat: 40-45-04 N **Long:** 73-17-27 W
Pop: 7,351 (1990)   **Pop Density:** 3341.4
Land: 2.2 sq. mi.; **Water:** 0.0 sq. mi.

Belle Terre   Village
ZIP: 11777   **Lat:** 40-57-44 N **Long:** 73-04-01 W
Pop: 839 (1990); 826 (1980)   **Pop Density:** 932.2
Land: 0.9 sq. mi.; **Water:** 0.0 sq. mi.
Name origin: From the French for 'beautiful land.'

Bellport   Village
ZIP: 11713   **Lat:** 40-45-24 N **Long:** 72-56-31 W
Pop: 2,572 (1990); 2,809 (1980)   **Pop Density:** 1714.7
Land: 1.5 sq. mi.; **Water:** 0.1 sq. mi.   **Elev:** 26 ft.

Blue Point   CDP
ZIP: 11715   **Lat:** 40-45-00 N **Long:** 73-02-06 W
Pop: 4,230 (1990)   **Pop Density:** 2350.0
Land: 1.8 sq. mi.; **Water:** 0.0 sq. mi.

Bohemia   CDP
ZIP: 11716   **Lat:** 40-46-26 N **Long:** 73-07-16 W
Pop: 9,556 (1990); 9,308 (1980)   **Pop Density:** 1098.4
Land: 8.7 sq. mi.; **Water:** 0.0 sq. mi.

Brentwood   CDP
ZIP: 11717   **Lat:** 40-46-52 N **Long:** 73-14-54 W
Pop: 45,218 (1990); 44,321 (1980)   **Pop Density:** 4477.0
Land: 10.1 sq. mi.; **Water:** 0.0 sq. mi.

Bridgehampton   CDP
    Lat: 40-56-36 N **Long:** 72-17-56 W
Pop: 1,997 (1990); 1,941 (1980)   **Pop Density:** 217.1
Land: 9.2 sq. mi.; **Water:** 0.7 sq. mi.

Brightwaters   Village
ZIP: 11718   **Lat:** 40-43-04 N **Long:** 73-15-57 W
Pop: 3,265 (1990); 3,286 (1980)   **Pop Density:** 3265.0
Land: 1.0 sq. mi.; **Water:** 0.1 sq. mi.
On Great South Bay on the southern shore of Long Island.
Name origin: Descriptive of the lakes and marina of this shoreline community.

Brookhaven   Town
ZIP: 11719   **Lat:** 40-48-17 N **Long:** 72-56-55 W
Pop: 407,779 (1990)   **Pop Density:** 1572.6
Land: 259.3 sq. mi.; **Water:** 154.9 sq. mi.
In southeastern NY east of Patchogue, on Long Island.

Calverton   CDP
ZIP: 11933   **Lat:** 40-55-26 N **Long:** 72-45-42 W
Pop: 4,759 (1990); 4,952 (1980)   **Pop Density:** 170.0
Land: 28.0 sq. mi.; **Water:** 0.5 sq. mi.

Centereach   CDP
ZIP: 11720   **Lat:** 40-52-14 N **Long:** 73-04-59 W
Pop: 26,720 (1990); 30,136 (1980)   **Pop Density:** 3340.0
Land: 8.0 sq. mi.; **Water:** 0.0 sq. mi.

Center Moriches   CDP
ZIP: 11934   **Lat:** 40-47-56 N **Long:** 72-47-48 W
Pop: 5,987 (1990); 5,703 (1980)   **Pop Density:** 1197.4
Land: 5.0 sq. mi.; **Water:** 0.4 sq. mi.

Centerport   CDP
ZIP: 11721   **Lat:** 40-54-02 N **Long:** 73-22-19 W
Pop: 5,333 (1990); 6,576 (1980)   **Pop Density:** 2539.5
Land: 2.1 sq. mi.; **Water:** 1.4 sq. mi.

Central Islip   CDP
ZIP: 11722   **Lat:** 40-47-07 N **Long:** 73-11-48 W
Pop: 26,028 (1990); 19,734 (1980)   **Pop Density:** 4411.5
Land: 5.9 sq. mi.; **Water:** 0.0 sq. mi.

Cold Spring Harbor   CDP
ZIP: 11724   Lat: 40-51-46 N Long: 73-26-52 W
Pop: 4,789 (1990); 5,336 (1980)   Pop Density: 1294.3
Land: 3.7 sq. mi.; Water: 0.2 sq. mi.

Commack   CDP
ZIP: 11725   Lat: 40-50-41 N Long: 73-17-01 W
Pop: 36,124 (1990); 13,687 (1980)   Pop Density: 2985.5
Land: 12.1 sq. mi.; Water: 0.0 sq. mi.

Copiague   CDP
ZIP: 11726   Lat: 40-40-16 N Long: 73-23-31 W
Pop: 20,769 (1990); 20,132 (1980)   Pop Density: 6490.3
Land: 3.2 sq. mi.; Water: 0.5 sq. mi.

Coram   CDP
ZIP: 11727   Lat: 40-52-46 N Long: 73-00-16 W
Pop: 30,111 (1990); 24,752 (1980)   Pop Density: 2182.0
Land: 13.8 sq. mi.; Water: 0.0 sq. mi.

Cutchogue   CDP
ZIP: 11935   Lat: 41-00-46 N Long: 72-29-10 W
Pop: 2,627 (1990); 2,788 (1980)   Pop Density: 324.3
Land: 8.1 sq. mi.; Water: 0.4 sq. mi.

Deer Park   CDP
ZIP: 11729   Lat: 40-45-44 N Long: 73-19-21 W
Pop: 28,840 (1990); 30,394 (1980)   Pop Density: 4651.6
Land: 6.2 sq. mi.; Water: 0.0 sq. mi.

Dering Harbor   Village
ZIP: 11964   Lat: 41-05-25 N Long: 72-20-26 W
Pop: 28 (1990); 16 (1980)   Pop Density: 140.0
Land: 0.2 sq. mi.; Water: 0.0 sq. mi.

Dix Hills   CDP
ZIP: 11746   Lat: 40-48-17 N Long: 73-20-11 W
Pop: 25,849 (1990); 26,693 (1980)   Pop Density: 1625.7
Land: 15.9 sq. mi.; Water: 0.0 sq. mi.

East Farmingdale   CDP
                    Lat: 40-43-44 N Long: 73-25-02 W
Pop: 4,510 (1990); 5,522 (1980)   Pop Density: 835.2
Land: 5.4 sq. mi.; Water: 0.0 sq. mi.

East Hampton   Village
ZIP: 11937   Lat: 40-57-02 N Long: 72-11-48 W
Pop: 1,402 (1990); 1,886 (1980)   Pop Density: 292.1
Land: 4.8 sq. mi.; Water: 0.1 sq. mi.   Elev: 36 ft.

In southeastern NY on Long Island, on the Atlantic Ocean,
20 mi. west of Montauk Point. Settled 1648. Not coextensive
with the town of the same name.
Name origin: For the English county.

*East Hampton   Town
ZIP: 11937   Lat: 41-01-53 N Long: 72-02-06 W
Pop: 16,132 (1990)   Pop Density: 220.1
Land: 73.3 sq. mi.; Water: 286.6 sq. mi.

East Islip   CDP
ZIP: 11730   Lat: 40-43-30 N Long: 73-11-13 W
Pop: 14,325 (1990); 13,852 (1980)   Pop Density: 3410.7
Land: 4.2 sq. mi.; Water: 0.3 sq. mi.

East Moriches   CDP
ZIP: 11940   Lat: 40-48-36 N Long: 72-45-37 W
Pop: 4,021 (1990)   Pop Density: 744.6
Land: 5.4 sq. mi.; Water: 0.1 sq. mi.

East Northport   CDP
ZIP: 11731   Lat: 40-52-44 N Long: 73-19-28 W
Pop: 20,411 (1990); 20,187 (1980)   Pop Density: 4002.2
Land: 5.1 sq. mi.; Water: 0.0 sq. mi.

East Patchogue   CDP
ZIP: 11772   Lat: 40-46-11 N Long: 72-58-56 W
Pop: 20,195 (1990); 18,139 (1980)   Pop Density: 2433.1
Land: 8.3 sq. mi.; Water: 0.2 sq. mi.

East Quogue   CDP
ZIP: 11942   Lat: 40-51-11 N Long: 72-34-36 W
Pop: 4,372 (1990); 3,668 (1980)   Pop Density: 470.1
Land: 9.3 sq. mi.; Water: 1.7 sq. mi.

East Shoreham   CDP
ZIP: 11786   Lat: 40-56-40 N Long: 72-52-48 W
Pop: 5,461 (1990)   Pop Density: 1011.3
Land: 5.4 sq. mi.; Water: 0.0 sq. mi.

Eatons Neck   CDP
ZIP: 11768   Lat: 40-55-50 N Long: 73-24-06 W
Pop: 1,499 (1990); 1,574 (1980)   Pop Density: 1499.0
Land: 1.0 sq. mi.; Water: 3.0 sq. mi.

Elwood   CDP
ZIP: 11731   Lat: 40-50-46 N Long: 73-20-31 W
Pop: 10,916 (1990); 11,847 (1980)   Pop Density: 2274.2
Land: 4.8 sq. mi.; Water: 0.0 sq. mi.

Farmingville   CDP
ZIP: 11738   Lat: 40-50-33 N Long: 73-02-39 W
Pop: 14,842 (1990); 13,398 (1980)   Pop Density: 3298.2
Land: 4.5 sq. mi.; Water: 0.0 sq. mi.

Flanders   CDP
ZIP: 11901   Lat: 40-53-27 N Long: 72-36-17 W
Pop: 3,231 (1990)   Pop Density: 285.9
Land: 11.3 sq. mi.; Water: 2.4 sq. mi.

Fort Salonga   CDP
ZIP: 11768   Lat: 40-54-40 N Long: 73-17-39 W
Pop: 9,176 (1990); 5,760 (1980)   Pop Density: 986.7
Land: 9.3 sq. mi.; Water: 3.7 sq. mi.

Greenlawn   CDP
ZIP: 11740   Lat: 40-51-47 N Long: 73-21-59 W
Pop: 13,208 (1990); 13,869 (1980)   Pop Density: 3569.7
Land: 3.7 sq. mi.; Water: 0.0 sq. mi.

Greenport   Village
ZIP: 11944   Lat: 41-06-09 N Long: 72-22-03 W
Pop: 2,070 (1990); 2,273 (1980)   Pop Density: 2070.0
Land: 1.0 sq. mi.; Water: 0.3 sq. mi.

In southeastern NY on the north fork of Long Island between
Gardiners Bay and Long Island Sound.

Greenport West   CDP
                    Lat: 41-05-58 N Long: 72-22-29 W
Pop: 1,614 (1990); 1,571 (1980)   Pop Density: 489.1
Land: 3.3 sq. mi.; Water: 0.1 sq. mi.

Halesite   CDP
                    Lat: 40-53-13 N Long: 73-24-50 W
Pop: 2,687 (1990)   Pop Density: 2985.6
Land: 0.9 sq. mi.; Water: 0.1 sq. mi.

Hampton Bays   CDP
ZIP: 11946   Lat: 40-51-43 N Long: 72-31-27 W
Pop: 7,893 (1990); 7,256 (1980)   Pop Density: 686.3
Land: 11.5 sq. mi.; Water: 9.6 sq. mi.

Hauppauge   CDP
ZIP: 11788   **Lat:** 40-49-11 N **Long:** 73-12-45 W
Pop: 19,750 (1990); 10,196 (1980)   **Pop Density:** 1828.7
Land: 10.8 sq. mi.; **Water:** 0.1 sq. mi.

Head of the Harbor   Village
ZIP: 11780   **Lat:** 40-53-53 N **Long:** 73-09-45 W
Pop: 1,354 (1990); 1,023 (1980)   **Pop Density:** 483.6
Land: 2.8 sq. mi.; **Water:** 0.2 sq. mi.

Holbrook   CDP
ZIP: 11741   **Lat:** 40-47-33 N **Long:** 73-04-14 W
Pop: 25,273 (1990); 4,899 (1980)   **Pop Density:** 3716.6
Land: 6.8 sq. mi.; **Water:** 0.0 sq. mi.

Holtsville   CDP
ZIP: 11742   **Lat:** 40-48-47 N **Long:** 73-02-51 W
Pop: 14,972 (1990); 11,073 (1980)   **Pop Density:** 2138.9
Land: 7.0 sq. mi.; **Water:** 0.0 sq. mi.

Huntington   Town
ZIP: 11743   **Lat:** 40-53-08 N **Long:** 73-22-48 W
Pop: 191,474 (1990)   **Pop Density:** 2037.0
Land: 94.0 sq. mi.; **Water:** 43.2 sq. mi.
In southeastern NY on the north shore of Long Island, just east of the Suffolk County line.

Huntington Bay   Village
ZIP: 11743   **Lat:** 40-54-38 N **Long:** 73-24-58 W
Pop: 1,521 (1990); 1,783 (1980)   **Pop Density:** 1521.0
Land: 1.0 sq. mi.; **Water:** 1.5 sq. mi.

Huntington Station   CDP
ZIP: 11746   **Lat:** 40-50-41 N **Long:** 73-24-18 W
Pop: 28,247 (1990); 28,769 (1980)   **Pop Density:** 5230.9
Land: 5.4 sq. mi.; **Water:** 0.0 sq. mi.

Islandia   Village
ZIP: 11722   **Lat:** 40-48-24 N **Long:** 73-10-18 W
Pop: 2,769 (1990)   **Pop Density:** 1258.6
Land: 2.2 sq. mi.; **Water:** 0.0 sq. mi.

Islip   Town
ZIP: 11751   **Lat:** 40-43-03 N **Long:** 73-11-37 W
Pop: 299,587 (1990)   **Pop Density:** 2847.8
Land: 105.2 sq. mi.; **Water:** 57.9 sq. mi.
In southeastern NY on southern Long Island, 10 mi. west of Patchogue.
Name origin: For the English town.

Islip Terrace   CDP
ZIP: 11752   **Lat:** 40-44-55 N **Long:** 73-11-12 W
Pop: 5,530 (1990); 5,588 (1980)   **Pop Density:** 3950.0
Land: 1.4 sq. mi.; **Water:** 0.0 sq. mi.

Jamesport   CDP
    Lat: 40-56-43 N **Long:** 72-34-30 W
Pop: 1,532 (1990); 1,069 (1980)   **Pop Density:** 340.4
Land: 4.5 sq. mi.; **Water:** 3.3 sq. mi.

Kings Park   CDP
ZIP: 11754   **Lat:** 40-53-26 N **Long:** 73-14-43 W
Pop: 17,773 (1990); 16,131 (1980)   **Pop Density:** 2962.2
Land: 6.0 sq. mi.; **Water:** 0.4 sq. mi.

Lake Grove   Village
ZIP: 11755   **Lat:** 40-51-28 N **Long:** 73-07-00 W
Pop: 9,612 (1990); 9,692 (1980)   **Pop Density:** 3204.0
Land: 3.0 sq. mi.; **Water:** 0.0 sq. mi.   **Elev:** 119 ft.
In southeastern NY on Long Island, 7 mi. northeast of Islip.
Name origin: For the groves of trees once abundant in the area.

Lake Ronkonkoma   CDP
ZIP: 11779   **Lat:** 40-49-53 N **Long:** 73-06-39 W
Pop: 18,997 (1990); 14,305 (1980)   **Pop Density:** 3876.9
Land: 4.9 sq. mi.; **Water:** 0.0 sq. mi.

Laurel   CDP
ZIP: 11948   **Lat:** 40-58-31 N **Long:** 72-33-13 W
Pop: 1,094 (1990)   **Pop Density:** 321.8
Land: 3.4 sq. mi.; **Water:** 0.1 sq. mi.

Lindenhurst   Village
ZIP: 11757   **Lat:** 40-41-08 N **Long:** 73-22-18 W
Pop: 26,879 (1990); 26,919 (1980)   **Pop Density:** 7073.4
Land: 3.8 sq. mi.; **Water:** 0.1 sq. mi.   **Elev:** 27 ft.
In southeastern NY on Long Island on Great South Bay, 35 mi. east of New York City.

Lloyd Harbor   Village
ZIP: 11743   **Lat:** 40-55-03 N **Long:** 73-27-50 W
Pop: 3,343 (1990); 3,405 (1980)   **Pop Density:** 359.5
Land: 9.3 sq. mi.; **Water:** 1.3 sq. mi.

Manorville   CDP
ZIP: 11949   **Lat:** 40-51-30 N **Long:** 72-47-38 W
Pop: 6,198 (1990)   **Pop Density:** 242.1
Land: 25.6 sq. mi.; **Water:** 0.0 sq. mi.

Mastic   CDP
ZIP: 11950   **Lat:** 40-48-07 N **Long:** 72-50-39 W
Pop: 13,778 (1990); 10,413 (1980)   **Pop Density:** 3131.4
Land: 4.4 sq. mi.; **Water:** 0.3 sq. mi.

Mastic Beach   CDP
ZIP: 11951   **Lat:** 40-45-41 N **Long:** 72-50-24 W
Pop: 10,293 (1990); 8,318 (1980)   **Pop Density:** 2450.7
Land: 4.2 sq. mi.; **Water:** 1.1 sq. mi.

Mattituck   CDP
ZIP: 11952   **Lat:** 41-00-09 N **Long:** 72-32-47 W
Pop: 3,902 (1990); 3,923 (1980)   **Pop Density:** 453.7
Land: 8.6 sq. mi.; **Water:** 1.6 sq. mi.

Medford   CDP
ZIP: 11763   **Lat:** 40-49-20 N **Long:** 72-59-04 W
Pop: 21,274 (1990); 20,418 (1980)   **Pop Density:** 1969.8
Land: 10.8 sq. mi.; **Water:** 0.0 sq. mi.

Melville   CDP
ZIP: 11747   **Lat:** 40-46-55 N **Long:** 73-24-43 W
Pop: 12,586 (1990); 8,139 (1980)   **Pop Density:** 1113.8
Land: 11.3 sq. mi.; **Water:** 0.0 sq. mi.

Middle Island   CDP
ZIP: 11953   **Lat:** 40-53-05 N **Long:** 72-56-38 W
Pop: 7,848 (1990); 5,703 (1980)   **Pop Density:** 945.5
Land: 8.3 sq. mi.; **Water:** 0.1 sq. mi.

Miller Place   CDP
ZIP: 11764   **Lat:** 40-55-57 N **Long:** 72-59-14 W
Pop: 9,315 (1990); 7,877 (1980)   **Pop Density:** 1433.1
Land: 6.5 sq. mi.; **Water:** 0.0 sq. mi.

Montauk CDP
ZIP: 11954   **Lat:** 41-02-50 N **Long:** 71-56-42 W
Pop: 3,001 (1990); 2,828 (1980)   **Pop Density:** 172.5
Land: 17.4 sq. mi.; **Water:** 2.3 sq. mi.

Mount Sinai CDP
ZIP: 11766   **Lat:** 40-56-18 N **Long:** 73-01-08 W
Pop: 8,023 (1990); 6,591 (1980)   **Pop Density:** 1337.2
Land: 6.0 sq. mi.; **Water:** 0.4 sq. mi.

Nesconset CDP
ZIP: 11767   **Lat:** 40-50-48 N **Long:** 73-09-08 W
Pop: 10,712 (1990); 10,706 (1980)   **Pop Density:** 2818.9
Land: 3.8 sq. mi.; **Water:** 0.0 sq. mi.

Nissequogue Village
ZIP: 11780   **Lat:** 40-54-20 N **Long:** 73-11-18 W
Pop: 1,620 (1990); 1,462 (1980)   **Pop Density:** 395.1
Land: 4.1 sq. mi.; **Water:** 1.2 sq. mi.   **Elev:** 106 ft.

North Amityville CDP
ZIP: 11701   **Lat:** 40-42-00 N **Long:** 73-24-47 W
Pop: 13,849 (1990); 13,140 (1980)   **Pop Density:** 5770.4
Land: 2.4 sq. mi.; **Water:** 0.0 sq. mi.

North Babylon CDP
ZIP: 11703   **Lat:** 40-43-53 N **Long:** 73-19-31 W
Pop: 18,081 (1990); 19,019 (1980)   **Pop Density:** 5317.9
Land: 3.4 sq. mi.; **Water:** 0.1 sq. mi.

North Bay Shore CDP
ZIP: 11706   **Lat:** 40-45-32 N **Long:** 73-15-39 W
Pop: 12,799 (1990); 35,020 (1980)   **Pop Density:** 4266.3
Land: 3.0 sq. mi.; **Water:** 0.0 sq. mi.

North Bellport CDP
ZIP: 11713   **Lat:** 40-47-18 N **Long:** 72-56-46 W
Pop: 8,182 (1990); 7,432 (1980)   **Pop Density:** 1778.7
Land: 4.6 sq. mi.; **Water:** 0.0 sq. mi.

North Great River CDP
ZIP: 11722   **Lat:** 40-45-22 N **Long:** 73-10-12 W
Pop: 3,964 (1990); 11,416 (1980)   **Pop Density:** 1723.5
Land: 2.3 sq. mi.; **Water:** 0.0 sq. mi.

North Haven Village
ZIP: 11963   **Lat:** 41-01-25 N **Long:** 72-18-56 W
Pop: 713 (1990); 738 (1980)   **Pop Density:** 264.1
Land: 2.7 sq. mi.; **Water:** 0.0 sq. mi.

North Lindenhurst CDP
ZIP: 11757   **Lat:** 40-42-24 N **Long:** 73-23-07 W
Pop: 10,563 (1990); 11,511 (1980)   **Pop Density:** 5559.5
Land: 1.9 sq. mi.; **Water:** 0.0 sq. mi.

North Patchogue CDP
ZIP: 11772   **Lat:** 40-47-03 N **Long:** 73-01-28 W
Pop: 7,374 (1990); 7,126 (1980)   **Pop Density:** 3511.4
Land: 2.1 sq. mi.; **Water:** 0.0 sq. mi.

Northport Village
ZIP: 11768   **Lat:** 40-54-13 N **Long:** 73-20-43 W
Pop: 7,572 (1990); 7,651 (1980)   **Pop Density:** 3292.2
Land: 2.3 sq. mi.; **Water:** 0.2 sq. mi.

In southeastern NY on the north shore of Long Island on Northport Bay.

Name origin: For its location.

North Sea CDP
ZIP: 11963   **Lat:** 40-56-14 N **Long:** 72-24-21 W
Pop: 2,530 (1990); 1,171 (1980)   **Pop Density:** 275.0
Land: 9.2 sq. mi.; **Water:** 1.1 sq. mi.

Northwest Harbor CDP
    Lat: 41-00-34 N **Long:** 72-13-17 W
Pop: 2,167 (1990); 2,459 (1980)   **Pop Density:** 147.4
Land: 14.7 sq. mi.; **Water:** 2.2 sq. mi.

Noyack CDP
    Lat: 40-58-36 N **Long:** 72-19-59 W
Pop: 2,059 (1990); 2,657 (1980)   **Pop Density:** 248.1
Land: 8.3 sq. mi.; **Water:** 0.2 sq. mi.

Oakdale CDP
ZIP: 11769   **Lat:** 40-44-15 N **Long:** 73-08-03 W
Pop: 7,875 (1990); 8,090 (1980)   **Pop Density:** 2386.4
Land: 3.3 sq. mi.; **Water:** 0.4 sq. mi.

Ocean Beach Village
ZIP: 11770   **Lat:** 40-38-43 N **Long:** 73-09-23 W
Pop: 131 (1990); 155 (1980)   **Pop Density:** 655.0
Land: 0.2 sq. mi.; **Water:** 0.0 sq. mi.

Old Field Village
ZIP: 11733   **Lat:** 40-57-44 N **Long:** 73-07-50 W
Pop: 765 (1990); 829 (1980)   **Pop Density:** 364.3
Land: 2.1 sq. mi.; **Water:** 0.1 sq. mi.

Patchogue Village
ZIP: 11772   **Lat:** 40-45-40 N **Long:** 73-01-09 W
Pop: 11,060 (1990); 11,291 (1980)   **Pop Density:** 4808.7
Land: 2.3 sq. mi.; **Water:** 0.3 sq. mi.

In southeastern NY on the south shore of Long Island, on Great South Bay, 53 mi. east of New York City.

Name origin: For an Indian tribe, whose name may possibly derive from *Pachaug* 'turning place.'

Peconic CDP
ZIP: 11958   **Lat:** 41-02-20 N **Long:** 72-27-53 W
Pop: 1,100 (1990); 1,056 (1980)   **Pop Density:** 229.2
Land: 4.8 sq. mi.; **Water:** 0.1 sq. mi.

Pine Valley Village
    Lat: 40-54-16 N **Long:** 72-40-46 W
Pop: 1,486 (1990)   **Pop Density:** 479.4
Land: 3.1 sq. mi.; **Water:** 0.2 sq. mi.

Poospatuck Reservation Pop. Place
    Lat: 40-47-23 N **Long:** 72-50-00 W
Pop: 136 (1990)   **Pop Density:** 1360.0
Land: 0.1 sq. mi.; **Water:** 0.0 sq. mi.

Poquott Village
ZIP: 11733   **Lat:** 40-57-07 N **Long:** 73-05-21 W
Pop: 770 (1990); 588 (1980)   **Pop Density:** 1925.0
Land: 0.4 sq. mi.; **Water:** 0.2 sq. mi.

Port Jefferson Village
ZIP: 11777   **Lat:** 40-56-51 N **Long:** 73-03-32 W
Pop: 7,455 (1990); 6,731 (1980)   **Pop Density:** 2485.0
Land: 3.0 sq. mi.; **Water:** 0.0 sq. mi.   **Elev:** 12 ft.

In southeastern NY on the north shore of Long Island, on Long Island Sound.

Port Jefferson Station CDP
ZIP: 11776   **Lat:** 40-55-24 N **Long:** 73-04-03 W
Pop: 7,232 (1990); 17,009 (1980)   **Pop Density:** 2781.5
Land: 2.6 sq. mi.; **Water:** 0.0 sq. mi.

Quogue   Village
ZIP: 11959   **Lat:** 40-49-03 N **Long:** 72-35-50 W
Pop: 898 (1990); 966 (1980)   **Pop Density:** 213.8
Land: 4.2 sq. mi.; **Water:** 2.4 sq. mi.

In southeastern NY on the south shore of Long Island between Moriches and Shinnecock bays.
Name origin: From Indian term possibly meaning 'trembling river.'

Remsenburg-Speonk   CDP
                        Lat: 40-48-48 N **Long:** 72-42-20 W
Pop: 1,851 (1990); 1,868 (1980)   **Pop Density:** 617.0
Land: 3.0 sq. mi.; **Water:** 0.1 sq. mi.

Ridge   CDP
ZIP: 11961   **Lat:** 40-54-36 N **Long:** 72-52-55 W
Pop: 11,734 (1990); 8,977 (1980)   **Pop Density:** 888.9
Land: 13.2 sq. mi.; **Water:** 0.1 sq. mi.

Riverhead   Town
ZIP: 11901   **Lat:** 40-58-39 N **Long:** 72-43-38 W
Pop: 23,011 (1990)   **Pop Density:** 341.4
Land: 67.4 sq. mi.; **Water:** 134.1 sq. mi.

In southeastern NY on the Peconic River, at the eastern end of Long Island where the forks begin. Settled 1690.

Riverside   CDP
ZIP: 11901   **Lat:** 40-52-52 N **Long:** 72-40-41 W
Pop: 1,300 (1990); 5,400 (1980)   **Pop Density:** 117.1
Land: 11.1 sq. mi.; **Water:** 0.0 sq. mi.

Rocky Point   CDP
ZIP: 11778   **Lat:** 40-55-37 N **Long:** 72-55-24 W
Pop: 8,596 (1990); 7,012 (1980)   **Pop Density:** 834.6
Land: 10.3 sq. mi.; **Water:** 0.0 sq. mi.

Ronkonkoma   CDP
ZIP: 11779   **Lat:** 40-48-12 N **Long:** 73-07-29 W
Pop: 20,391 (1990)   **Pop Density:** 2486.7
Land: 8.2 sq. mi.; **Water:** 0.4 sq. mi.

Sag Harbor   Village
ZIP: 11963   **Lat:** 40-59-46 N **Long:** 72-17-24 W
Pop: 2,134 (1990); 895 (1980)   **Pop Density:** 1255.3
Land: 1.7 sq. mi.; **Water:** 0.7 sq. mi.

In southeastern NY, 25 mi. west of Montauk Point at the west end of the south fork of Long Island.
Name origin: From an Indian term possibly meaning 'outlet of the stream.'

St. James   CDP
ZIP: 11780   **Lat:** 40-52-35 N **Long:** 73-09-09 W
Pop: 12,703 (1990); 12,122 (1980) **Pop Density:** 2822.9
Land: 4.5 sq. mi.; **Water:** 0.0 sq. mi.

Saltaire   Village
ZIP: 11706   **Lat:** 40-38-16 N **Long:** 73-11-42 W
Pop: 38 (1990); 35 (1980)   **Pop Density:** 126.7
Land: 0.3 sq. mi.; **Water:** 0.1 sq. mi.

Sayville   CDP
ZIP: 11782   **Lat:** 40-44-48 N **Long:** 73-05-08 W
Pop: 16,550 (1990); 12,013 (1980) **Pop Density:** 3009.1
Land: 5.5 sq. mi.; **Water:** 0.1 sq. mi.

Selden   CDP
ZIP: 11784   **Lat:** 40-52-10 N **Long:** 73-02-52 W
Pop: 20,608 (1990); 17,259 (1980) **Pop Density:** 4384.7
Land: 4.7 sq. mi.; **Water:** 0.0 sq. mi.

Setauket-East Setauket   CDP
ZIP: 11733   **Lat:** 40-55-47 N **Long:** 73-06-09 W
Pop: 13,634 (1990); 10,176 (1980) **Pop Density:** 1604.0
Land: 8.5 sq. mi.; **Water:** 0.8 sq. mi.

Shelter Island   Town
                        Lat: 41-04-04 N **Long:** 72-18-58 W
Pop: 2,263 (1990)   **Pop Density:** 187.0
Land: 12.1 sq. mi.; **Water:** 15.0 sq. mi.

In southeastern NY, an island in Gardiners Bay between the forks at the eastern end of Long Island.
Name origin: As early as 1652 Quakers sought refuge on the island.

*Shelter Island   CDP
                        Lat: 41-03-35 N **Long:** 72-19-12 W
Pop: 1,193 (1990); 1,115 (1980)   **Pop Density:** 183.5
Land: 6.5 sq. mi.; **Water:** 0.1 sq. mi.

Shelter Island Heights   CDP
                        Lat: 41-04-32 N **Long:** 72-20-33 W
Pop: 1,042 (1990)   **Pop Density:** 193.0
Land: 5.4 sq. mi.; **Water:** 0.3 sq. mi.

Shinnecock Hills   CDP
ZIP: 11946   **Lat:** 40-53-43 N **Long:** 72-27-23 W
Pop: 2,847 (1990); 2,344 (1980)   **Pop Density:** 466.7
Land: 6.1 sq. mi.; **Water:** 0.7 sq. mi.

Shinnecock Reservation   Pop. Place
                        Lat: 40-52-31 N **Long:** 72-25-52 W
Pop: 375 (1990)   **Pop Density:** 288.5
Land: 1.3 sq. mi.; **Water:** 0.0 sq. mi.

Shirley   CDP
ZIP: 11967   **Lat:** 40-47-42 N **Long:** 72-52-26 W
Pop: 22,936 (1990); 18,072 (1980) **Pop Density:** 2104.2
Land: 10.9 sq. mi.; **Water:** 0.3 sq. mi.

Shoreham   Village
ZIP: 11786   **Lat:** 40-57-20 N **Long:** 72-54-23 W
Pop: 540 (1990); 555 (1980)   **Pop Density:** 1350.0
Land: 0.4 sq. mi.; **Water:** 0.0 sq. mi.

Smithtown   Town
ZIP: 11787   **Lat:** 40-52-12 N **Long:** 73-13-02 W
Pop: 113,406 (1990)   **Pop Density:** 2115.8
Land: 53.6 sq. mi.; **Water:** 7.3 sq. mi.

In southeastern NY on central Long Island.
Name origin: For a prominent resident.

*Smithtown   CDP
ZIP: 11787   **Lat:** 40-51-25 N **Long:** 73-12-53 W
Pop: 25,638 (1990); 30,906 (1980) **Pop Density:** 2172.7
Land: 11.8 sq. mi.; **Water:** 0.5 sq. mi.

Sound Beach   CDP
ZIP: 11789   **Lat:** 40-57-19 N **Long:** 72-58-00 W
Pop: 9,102 (1990); 8,071 (1980)   **Pop Density:** 3371.1
Land: 2.7 sq. mi.; **Water:** 0.0 sq. mi.

Southampton   Town
ZIP: 11968   **Lat:** 40-53-14 N **Long:** 72-28-35 W
Pop: 44,976 (1990)   **Pop Density:** 323.8
Land: 3.4 sq. mi.; **Water:** 107.2 sq. mi.

*Southampton   Village
ZIP: 11968   **Lat:** 40-52-49 N **Long:** 72-23-43 W
Pop: 3,980 (1990); 4,000 (1980)   **Pop Density:** 631.7
Land: 6.3 sq. mi.; **Water:** 0.4 sq. mi.

In southeastern NY on the south shore of Long Island, 33 mi.

west of Montauk Point. Not coextensive with the town of the same name.
Name origin: For the English city.

South Huntington
CDP
ZIP: 11746 **Lat:** 40-49-14 N **Long:** 73-23-31 W
Pop: 9,624 (1990); 14,854 (1980) **Pop Density:** 2830.6
Land: 3.4 sq. mi.; **Water:** 0.0 sq. mi.

Southold
Town
ZIP: 11971 **Lat:** 41-08-01 N **Long:** 72-15-39 W
Pop: 19,836 (1990) **Pop Density:** 369.4
Land: 53.7 sq. mi.; **Water:** 169.5 sq. mi.

In southeastern NY, 18 mi. northeast of Riverhead on the north fork of Long Island.

Springs
CDP
ZIP: 11937 **Lat:** 41-01-15 N **Long:** 72-09-25 W
Pop: 4,355 (1990); 3,197 (1980) **Pop Density:** 512.4
Land: 8.5 sq. mi.; **Water:** 0.8 sq. mi.

Stony Brook
CDP
ZIP: 11790 **Lat:** 40-54-28 N **Long:** 73-07-42 W
Pop: 13,726 (1990); 16,155 (1980) **Pop Density:** 2408.1
Land: 5.7 sq. mi.; **Water:** 0.4 sq. mi.

Terryville
CDP
ZIP: 11776 **Lat:** 40-54-30 N **Long:** 73-02-59 W
Pop: 10,275 (1990) **Pop Density:** 3210.9
Land: 3.2 sq. mi.; **Water:** 0.0 sq. mi.

Village of The Branch
Village
Lat: 40-51-04 N **Long:** 73-11-04 W
Pop: 1,669 (1990); 1,707 (1980) **Pop Density:** 1854.4
Land: 0.9 sq. mi.; **Water:** 0.0 sq. mi. **Elev:** 63 ft.

Wading River
CDP
ZIP: 11792 **Lat:** 40-56-49 N **Long:** 72-49-11 W
Pop: 5,317 (1990) **Pop Density:** 542.6
Land: 9.8 sq. mi.; **Water:** 0.0 sq. mi.

Watermill
CDP
Lat: 40-55-44 N **Long:** 72-20-53 W
Pop: 1,893 (1990) **Pop Density:** 128.8
Land: 14.7 sq. mi.; **Water:** 1.6 sq. mi.

West Babylon
CDP
ZIP: 11704 **Lat:** 40-42-36 N **Long:** 73-21-30 W
Pop: 42,410 (1990); 41,699 (1980) **Pop Density:** 5507.8
Land: 7.7 sq. mi.; **Water:** 0.3 sq. mi.

West Bay Shore
CDP
ZIP: 11706 **Lat:** 40-42-27 N **Long:** 73-16-16 W
Pop: 4,907 (1990); 5,118 (1980) **Pop Density:** 2044.6
Land: 2.4 sq. mi.; **Water:** 0.0 sq. mi.

Westhampton
CDP
ZIP: 11977 **Lat:** 40-50-19 N **Long:** 72-39-53 W
Pop: 2,129 (1990); 2,774 (1980) **Pop Density:** 143.9
Land: 14.8 sq. mi.; **Water:** 0.1 sq. mi.

Westhampton Beach
Village
ZIP: 11978 **Lat:** 40-48-32 N **Long:** 72-38-47 W
Pop: 1,571 (1990); 1,629 (1980) **Pop Density:** 541.7
Land: 2.9 sq. mi.; **Water:** 0.1 sq. mi.

In southeastern NY on the south shore of Long Island, south of Riverhead.

West Hills
CDP
ZIP: 11743 **Lat:** 40-49-09 N **Long:** 73-25-54 W
Pop: 5,849 (1990); 6,071 (1980) **Pop Density:** 1169.8
Land: 5.0 sq. mi.; **Water:** 0.0 sq. mi.

West Islip
CDP
ZIP: 11795 **Lat:** 40-42-31 N **Long:** 73-17-47 W
Pop: 28,419 (1990); 29,533 (1980) **Pop Density:** 4583.7
Land: 6.2 sq. mi.; **Water:** 0.4 sq. mi.

West Sayville
CDP
ZIP: 11796 **Lat:** 40-43-41 N **Long:** 73-06-20 W
Pop: 4,680 (1990); 8,185 (1980) **Pop Density:** 2463.2
Land: 1.9 sq. mi.; **Water:** 0.0 sq. mi.

Wheatley Heights
CDP
ZIP: 11798 **Lat:** 40-45-49 N **Long:** 73-22-13 W
Pop: 5,027 (1990) **Pop Density:** 3590.7
Land: 1.4 sq. mi.; **Water:** 0.0 sq. mi.

Wyandanch
CDP
ZIP: 11798 **Lat:** 40-44-47 N **Long:** 73-22-37 W
Pop: 8,950 (1990); 13,215 (1980) **Pop Density:** 2034.1
Land: 4.4 sq. mi.; **Water:** 0.0 sq. mi.

Yaphank
CDP
ZIP: 11980 **Lat:** 40-49-53 N **Long:** 72-55-32 W
Pop: 4,637 (1990) **Pop Density:** 338.5
Land: 13.7 sq. mi.; **Water:** 0.1 sq. mi.

Sullivan County
County Seat: Monticello (ZIP: 12701)

Pop: 69,277 (1990); 65,155 (1980) **Pop Density:** 71.4
Land: 969.8 sq. mi.; **Water:** 27.1 sq. mi. **Area Code:** 914

In south-central NY, west of Poughkeepsie; organized Mar 27, 1809 from Ulster County.

Name origin: For Gen. John Sullivan (1740–95), Revolutionary War officer, member of the Continental Congress (1780–81), and president of NH (1786, 1787, 1789).

Bethel
Town
ZIP: 12720 **Lat:** 41-41-19 N **Long:** 74-50-55 W
Pop: 3,693 (1990) **Pop Density:** 43.2
Land: 85.4 sq. mi.; **Water:** 4.6 sq. mi.

Bloomingburgh
Village
ZIP: 12721 **Lat:** 41-33-21 N **Long:** 74-26-29 W
Pop: 316 (1990); 338 (1980) **Pop Density:** 1053.3
Land: 0.3 sq. mi.; **Water:** 0.0 sq. mi.

Callicoon
Town
ZIP: 12723 Lat: 41-50-05 N Long: 74-55-30 W
Pop: 3,024 (1990) Pop Density: 62.1
Land: 48.7 sq. mi.; Water: 0.3 sq. mi.

Cochecton
Town
ZIP: 12726 Lat: 41-40-43 N Long: 74-59-39 W
Pop: 1,318 (1990) Pop Density: 35.9
Land: 36.7 sq. mi.; Water: 0.7 sq. mi.

Delaware
Town
Lat: 41-45-29 N Long: 75-00-12 W
Pop: 2,633 (1990) Pop Density: 75.9
Land: 34.7 sq. mi.; Water: 0.6 sq. mi.

Fallsburg
Town
ZIP: 12733 Lat: 41-44-09 N Long: 74-36-14 W
Pop: 11,445 (1990) Pop Density: 147.5
Land: 77.6 sq. mi.; Water: 1.4 sq. mi.
Name origin: For a local geographical feature.

Forestburgh
Town
Lat: 41-32-39 N Long: 74-42-00 W
Pop: 614 (1990) Pop Density: 11.2
Land: 54.9 sq. mi.; Water: 1.6 sq. mi.

Fremont
Town
ZIP: 12736 Lat: 41-51-28 N Long: 75-01-44 W
Pop: 1,332 (1990) Pop Density: 26.5
Land: 50.3 sq. mi.; Water: 0.9 sq. mi.

Highland
Town
Lat: 41-32-05 N Long: 74-53-41 W
Pop: 2,147 (1990) Pop Density: 42.9
Land: 50.0 sq. mi.; Water: 1.7 sq. mi.

Jeffersonville
Village
ZIP: 12748 Lat: 41-46-45 N Long: 74-55-57 W
Pop: 484 (1990); 554 (1980) Pop Density: 1210.0
Land: 0.4 sq. mi.; Water: 0.0 sq. mi. Elev: 1058 ft.

Liberty
Town
ZIP: 12754 Lat: 41-48-33 N Long: 74-46-30 W
Pop: 9,825 (1990) Pop Density: 123.4
Land: 79.6 sq. mi.; Water: 1.1 sq. mi.

*Liberty
Village
ZIP: 12754 Lat: 41-47-50 N Long: 74-44-46 W
Pop: 4,128 (1990); 4,293 (1980) Pop Density: 1794.8
Land: 2.3 sq. mi.; Water: 0.0 sq. mi. Elev: 1509 ft.
Not coextensive with the town of the same name.

Livingston Manor
CDP
ZIP: 12758 Lat: 41-53-42 N Long: 74-49-35 W
Pop: 1,482 (1990); 1,436 (1980) Pop Density: 478.1
Land: 3.1 sq. mi.; Water: 0.0 sq. mi.

Lumberland
Town
Lat: 41-29-31 N Long: 74-48-45 W
Pop: 1,425 (1990) Pop Density: 30.3
Land: 47.0 sq. mi.; Water: 2.6 sq. mi.

Mamakating
Town
ZIP: 12790 Lat: 41-34-58 N Long: 74-29-47 W
Pop: 9,792 (1990) Pop Density: 101.8
Land: 96.2 sq. mi.; Water: 2.3 sq. mi.

Monticello
Village
ZIP: 12701 Lat: 41-39-08 N Long: 74-41-16 W
Pop: 6,597 (1990); 6,306 (1980) Pop Density: 1736.1
Land: 3.8 sq. mi.; Water: 0.0 sq. mi.
In southeastern NY, 42 mi. west of Poughkeepsie.
Name origin: For the VA estate of Thomas Jefferson (1743–1826), but pronounced "mont-i-SELL-o."

Neversink
Town
ZIP: 12765 Lat: 41-52-46 N Long: 74-36-13 W
Pop: 2,951 (1990) Pop Density: 35.6
Land: 82.9 sq. mi.; Water: 3.4 sq. mi.
Name origin: A folk etymologized form of an Algonquian word, possibly *navesink* meaning 'at the point.'

Rockland
Town
Lat: 41-56-51 N Long: 74-47-58 W
Pop: 4,096 (1990) Pop Density: 43.4
Land: 94.3 sq. mi.; Water: 1.0 sq. mi.

South Fallsburg
CDP
ZIP: 12779 Lat: 41-43-13 N Long: 74-38-05 W
Pop: 2,115 (1990); 2,196 (1980) Pop Density: 352.5
Land: 6.0 sq. mi.; Water: 0.1 sq. mi.

Thompson
Town
ZIP: 12701 Lat: 41-38-48 N Long: 74-40-36 W
Pop: 13,711 (1990) Pop Density: 163.0
Land: 84.1 sq. mi.; Water: 3.3 sq. mi.

Tusten
Town
Lat: 41-35-09 N Long: 74-58-51 W
Pop: 1,271 (1990) Pop Density: 26.9
Land: 47.3 sq. mi.; Water: 1.5 sq. mi.

Woodridge
Village
ZIP: 12789 Lat: 41-42-40 N Long: 74-34-24 W
Pop: 783 (1990); 809 (1980) Pop Density: 489.4
Land: 1.6 sq. mi.; Water: 0.1 sq. mi.

Wurtsboro
Village
ZIP: 12790 Lat: 41-34-34 N Long: 74-29-07 W
Pop: 1,048 (1990); 1,128 (1980) Pop Density: 806.2
Land: 1.3 sq. mi.; Water: 0.0 sq. mi.

Tioga County
County Seat: Owego (ZIP: 13827)

Pop: 52,337 (1990); 49,812 (1980)
Land: 518.7 sq. mi.; **Water:** 4.2 sq. mi.

Pop Density: 100.9
Area Code: 607

On central southern border of NY, south of Ithaca; organized Feb 16, 1791 from Montgomery County.

Name origin: For the Iroquoian town on the Susquehanna River near Athens, PA, just south of the county line; from Iroquoian probably meaning 'place between two points' or 'at the forks.'

Apalachin   CDP
ZIP: 13732   **Lat:** 42-04-20 N **Long:** 76-09-57 W
Pop: 1,208 (1990); 1,227 (1980)   **Pop Density:** 805.3
Land: 1.5 sq. mi.; **Water:** 0.0 sq. mi.

Barton   Town
ZIP: 13734   **Lat:** 42-04-46 N **Long:** 76-29-57 W
Pop: 8,925 (1990)   **Pop Density:** 150.3
Land: 59.4 sq. mi.; **Water:** 0.4 sq. mi.
Name origin: From a personal name.

Berkshire   Town
ZIP: 13736   **Lat:** 42-18-03 N **Long:** 76-10-57 W
Pop: 1,303 (1990)   **Pop Density:** 43.1
Land: 30.2 sq. mi.; **Water:** 0.0 sq. mi.

Candor   Town
ZIP: 13743   **Lat:** 42-13-52 N **Long:** 76-19-58 W
Pop: 5,310 (1990)   **Pop Density:** 56.2
Land: 94.5 sq. mi.; **Water:** 0.1 sq. mi.

*Candor   Village
ZIP: 13743   **Lat:** 42-13-38 N **Long:** 76-20-15 W
Pop: 869 (1990); 917 (1980)   **Pop Density:** 2172.5
Land: 0.4 sq. mi.; **Water:** 0.0 sq. mi.
Not coextensive with the town of the same name.

Newark Valley   Town
ZIP: 13811   **Lat:** 42-13-46 N **Long:** 76-09-45 W
Pop: 4,189 (1990)   **Pop Density:** 83.3
Land: 50.3 sq. mi.; **Water:** 0.1 sq. mi.

*Newark Valley   Village
ZIP: 13811   **Lat:** 42-13-22 N **Long:** 76-11-09 W
Pop: 1,082 (1990); 1,190 (1980)   **Pop Density:** 1082.0
Land: 1.0 sq. mi.; **Water:** 0.0 sq. mi.
Not coextensive with the town of the same name.

Nichols   Town
ZIP: 13812   **Lat:** 42-02-07 N **Long:** 76-20-49 W
Pop: 2,525 (1990)   **Pop Density:** 74.9
Land: 33.7 sq. mi.; **Water:** 1.0 sq. mi.

*Nichols   Village
ZIP: 13812   **Lat:** 42-01-11 N **Long:** 76-22-07 W
Pop: 573 (1990); 613 (1980)   **Pop Density:** 1146.0
Land: 0.5 sq. mi.; **Water:** 0.0 sq. mi.
Not coextensive with the town of the same name.

Owego   Town
ZIP: 13827   **Lat:** 42-05-21 N **Long:** 76-11-12 W
Pop: 21,279 (1990)   **Pop Density:** 204.2
Land: 104.2 sq. mi.; **Water:** 1.6 sq. mi.

*Owego   Village
ZIP: 13827   **Lat:** 42-06-17 N **Long:** 76-15-45 W
Pop: 4,442 (1990); 4,364 (1980)   **Pop Density:** 1776.8
Land: 2.5 sq. mi.; **Water:** 0.2 sq. mi.   **Elev:** 817 ft.
In southern NY on the Susquehana River, 20 mi. west of Binghamton. Not coextensive with the town of the same name.
Name origin: Located on the site of Ah-wah-ga 'where the valley widens,' one of the Indian towns destroyed by the Sullivan-Clinton troops in 1779.

Richford   Town
ZIP: 13835   **Lat:** 42-21-52 N **Long:** 76-11-23 W
Pop: 1,153 (1990)   **Pop Density:** 30.2
Land: 38.2 sq. mi.; **Water:** 0.0 sq. mi.

Spencer   Town
ZIP: 14883   **Lat:** 42-12-57 N **Long:** 76-28-48 W
Pop: 2,881 (1990)   **Pop Density:** 58.1
Land: 49.6 sq. mi.; **Water:** 0.3 sq. mi.

*Spencer   Village
ZIP: 14883   **Lat:** 42-12-54 N **Long:** 76-29-41 W
Pop: 815 (1990); 863 (1980)   **Pop Density:** 815.0
Land: 1.0 sq. mi.; **Water:** 0.0 sq. mi.
Not coextensive with the town of the same name.

Tioga   Town
                     Lat: 42-06-10 N **Long:** 76-21-59 W
Pop: 4,772 (1990)   **Pop Density:** 81.3
Land: 58.7 sq. mi.; **Water:** 0.8 sq. mi.

Waverly   Village
ZIP: 14892   **Lat:** 42-00-43 N **Long:** 76-32-28 W
Pop: 4,787 (1990); 4,738 (1980)   **Pop Density:** 2081.3
Land: 2.3 sq. mi.; **Water:** 0.0 sq. mi.
In southeastern NY, 15 mi. southeast of Elmira.

Tompkins County
County Seat: Ithaca (ZIP: 14850)

Pop: 94,097 (1990); 87,085 (1980)   **Pop Density:** 197.7
Land: 476.1 sq. mi.; **Water:** 15.6 sq. mi.   **Area Code:** 607

In south-central NY, northeast of Elmira; organized Apr 7, 1817 from Cayuga and Seneca counties.

Name origin: For Daniel D. Tompkins (1774–1825), associate justice of the NY supreme court (1804–07), governor (1807–17) and U.S. vice president (1817–25).

Caroline
Town
Lat: 42-21-18 N **Long:** 76-19-48 W
Pop: 3,044 (1990)   **Pop Density:** 55.3
Land: 55.0 sq. mi.; **Water:** 0.1 sq. mi.

Cayuga Heights
Village
ZIP: 14850   **Lat:** 42-28-08 N **Long:** 76-29-12 W
Pop: 3,457 (1990); 3,170 (1980)   **Pop Density:** 1920.6
Land: 1.8 sq. mi.; **Water:** 0.0 sq. mi.

Danby
Town
Lat: 42-20-14 N **Long:** 76-28-23 W
Pop: 2,858 (1990)   **Pop Density:** 53.3
Land: 53.6 sq. mi.; **Water:** 0.2 sq. mi.

Dryden
Town
ZIP: 13053   **Lat:** 42-28-36 N **Long:** 76-21-18 W
Pop: 13,251 (1990)   **Pop Density:** 141.1
Land: 93.9 sq. mi.; **Water:** 0.3 sq. mi.

*Dryden
Village
ZIP: 13053   **Lat:** 42-29-24 N **Long:** 76-17-56 W
Pop: 1,908 (1990); 1,761 (1980)   **Pop Density:** 1122.4
Land: 1.7 sq. mi.; **Water:** 0.0 sq. mi.

Not coextensive with the town of the same name.

Name origin: For the English poet, John (1631–1700).

East Ithaca
CDP
Lat: 42-25-37 N **Long:** 76-27-56 W
Pop: 2,152 (1990)   **Pop Density:** 1265.9
Land: 1.7 sq. mi.; **Water:** 0.0 sq. mi.

Enfield
Town
Lat: 42-26-03 N **Long:** 76-37-54 W
Pop: 3,054 (1990)   **Pop Density:** 82.8
Land: 36.9 sq. mi.; **Water:** 0.0 sq. mi.

Forest Home
CDP
Lat: 42-27-11 N **Long:** 76-28-18 W
Pop: 1,125 (1990)   **Pop Density:** 3750.0
Land: 0.3 sq. mi.; **Water:** 0.0 sq. mi.

Freeville
Village
ZIP: 13068   **Lat:** 42-30-42 N **Long:** 76-20-45 W
Pop: 437 (1990); 449 (1980)   **Pop Density:** 397.3
Land: 1.1 sq. mi.; **Water:** 0.0 sq. mi.   **Elev:** 1048 ft.

Groton
Town
ZIP: 13073   **Lat:** 42-35-03 N **Long:** 76-21-34 W
Pop: 5,483 (1990)   **Pop Density:** 110.5
Land: 49.6 sq. mi.; **Water:** 0.0 sq. mi.

*Groton
Village
ZIP: 13073   **Lat:** 42-35-12 N **Long:** 76-21-54 W
Pop: 2,398 (1990); 2,313 (1980)   **Pop Density:** 1498.8
Land: 1.6 sq. mi.; **Water:** 0.0 sq. mi.

Not coextensive with the town of the same name.
Name origin: For the English town.

Ithaca
City
ZIP: 14850   **Lat:** 42-26-37 N **Long:** 76-30-12 W
Pop: 29,541 (1990); 28,732 (1980)   **Pop Density:** 5371.1
Land: 5.5 sq. mi.; **Water:** 0.6 sq. mi.

In south-central NY on the southern end of Cayuga Lake, 29 mi. northeast of Elmira. Site of Cornell Univ.

Name origin: Named by U.S. surveyor Gen. Simeon DeWitt for the legendary Greek home of Ulysses.

*Ithaca
Town
ZIP: 14850   **Lat:** 42-25-46 N **Long:** 76-31-15 W
Pop: 17,797 (1990)   **Pop Density:** 611.6
Land: 29.1 sq. mi.; **Water:** 1.2 sq. mi.

Lansing
Town
ZIP: 14882   **Lat:** 42-33-59 N **Long:** 76-31-55 W
Pop: 9,296 (1990)   **Pop Density:** 153.1
Land: 60.7 sq. mi.; **Water:** 9.2 sq. mi.

*Lansing
Village
ZIP: 14882   **Lat:** 42-29-26 N **Long:** 76-29-11 W
Pop: 3,281 (1990); 3,039 (1980)   **Pop Density:** 713.3
Land: 4.6 sq. mi.; **Water:** 0.0 sq. mi.

Name origin: For jurist John Lansing.

Newfield
Town
ZIP: 14867   **Lat:** 42-20-00 N **Long:** 76-36-34 W
Pop: 4,867 (1990)   **Pop Density:** 82.6
Land: 58.9 sq. mi.; **Water:** 0.1 sq. mi.

Newfield Hamlet
CDP
Lat: 42-21-28 N **Long:** 76-35-38 W
Pop: 692 (1990)   **Pop Density:** 576.7
Land: 1.2 sq. mi.; **Water:** 0.0 sq. mi.

Northeast Ithaca
CDP
Lat: 42-28-16 N **Long:** 76-28-04 W
Pop: 2,533 (1990)   **Pop Density:** 1948.5
Land: 1.3 sq. mi.; **Water:** 0.0 sq. mi.

Northwest Ithaca
CDP
Lat: 42-28-14 N **Long:** 76-32-35 W
Pop: 1,144 (1990)   **Pop Density:** 394.5
Land: 2.9 sq. mi.; **Water:** 0.6 sq. mi.

South Hill
CDP
ZIP: 14850   **Lat:** 42-24-41 N **Long:** 76-29-27 W
Pop: 5,423 (1990)   **Pop Density:** 919.2
Land: 5.9 sq. mi.; **Water:** 0.1 sq. mi.

Trumansburg
Village
ZIP: 14886   **Lat:** 42-32-25 N **Long:** 76-39-37 W
Pop: 1,611 (1990); 1,722 (1980)   **Pop Density:** 1342.5
Land: 1.2 sq. mi.; **Water:** 0.0 sq. mi.

Name origin: For Abner Treman, first settler and Revolutionary War veteran, who came here in 1792; with spelling variation.

Ulysses
Town
Lat: 42-30-45 N **Long:** 76-37-05 W
Pop: 4,906 (1990)   **Pop Density:** 148.7
Land: 33.0 sq. mi.; **Water:** 3.9 sq. mi.

Ulster County
County Seat: Kingston (ZIP: 12401)

Pop: 165,304 (1990); 158,158 (1980)   **Pop Density:** 146.7
Land: 1126.6 sq. mi.; **Water:** 34.2 sq. mi.   **Area Code:** 914
In southeastern NY, west of Poughkeepsie; original county, organized Nov 1, 1683.
Name origin: For Ulster, Ireland, the earldom of the Duke of York, specifically honoring James Stuart (1633–1701), later James II, king of England.

Clintondale
CDP
ZIP: 12515   **Lat:** 41-41-30 N **Long:** 74-02-50 W
Pop: 1,394 (1990); 279 (1980)   **Pop Density:** 248.9
Land: 5.6 sq. mi.; **Water:** 0.0 sq. mi.

Denning
Town
Lat: 41-56-44 N **Long:** 74-29-43 W
Pop: 524 (1990)   **Pop Density:** 5.0
Land: 105.2 sq. mi.; **Water:** 0.1 sq. mi.

Ellenville
Village
ZIP: 12428   **Lat:** 41-42-10 N **Long:** 74-21-50 W
Pop: 4,243 (1990); 4,405 (1980)   **Pop Density:** 471.4
Land: 9.0 sq. mi.; **Water:** 0.1 sq. mi.
Name origin: For the wife of an early settler.

Esopus
Town
ZIP: 12429   **Lat:** 41-50-50 N **Long:** 73-59-37 W
Pop: 8,860 (1990)   **Pop Density:** 238.2
Land: 37.2 sq. mi.; **Water:** 4.6 sq. mi.
In southeastern NY at the mouth of Roundout Creek in the Catskill Mts., a suburb of Kingston.
Name origin: Named in 1615 by Dutch traders for a trading post at the mouth of Roundout Creek. Probably from an Algonquian term meaning 'rivulet.'

Gardiner
Town
ZIP: 12525   **Lat:** 41-41-53 N **Long:** 74-11-33 W
Pop: 4,278 (1990)   **Pop Density:** 96.6
Land: 44.3 sq. mi.; **Water:** 0.5 sq. mi.

Glasco
CDP
Lat: 42-02-44 N **Long:** 73-57-02 W
Pop: 1,538 (1990); 1,179 (1980)   **Pop Density:** 854.4
Land: 1.8 sq. mi.; **Water:** 0.8 sq. mi.

Hardenburgh
Town
Lat: 42-03-29 N **Long:** 74-35-55 W
Pop: 204 (1990)   **Pop Density:** 2.5
Land: 81.3 sq. mi.; **Water:** 0.2 sq. mi.

Highland
CDP
ZIP: 12528   **Lat:** 41-43-02 N **Long:** 73-57-56 W
Pop: 4,492 (1990); 3,967 (1980)   **Pop Density:** 976.5
Land: 4.6 sq. mi.; **Water:** 0.4 sq. mi.

Hurley
Town
ZIP: 12443   **Lat:** 41-58-07 N **Long:** 74-07-04 W
Pop: 6,741 (1990)   **Pop Density:** 225.5
Land: 29.9 sq. mi.; **Water:** 6.0 sq. mi.
Name origin: Named in 1669 for Francis Loveace, Baron Hurley of Ireland. Previously called Neiuw Dorp, from Dutch meaning 'new village'.

Kerhonkson
CDP
ZIP: 12446   **Lat:** 41-46-44 N **Long:** 74-17-45 W
Pop: 1,629 (1990); 655 (1980)   **Pop Density:** 307.4
Land: 5.3 sq. mi.; **Water:** 0.0 sq. mi.

Kingston
City
ZIP: 12401   **Lat:** 41-55-48 N **Long:** 73-59-50 W
Pop: 23,095 (1990); 24,481 (1980)   **Pop Density:** 3120.9
Land: 7.4 sq. mi.; **Water:** 1.3 sq. mi.
In southeastern NY on the Hudson River, 15 mi. north of Poughkeepsie.

*Kingston
Town
ZIP: 12401   **Lat:** 41-59-08 N **Long:** 74-02-37 W
Pop: 864 (1990)   **Pop Density:** 110.8
Land: 7.8 sq. mi.; **Water:** 0.1 sq. mi.

Lake Katrine
CDP
ZIP: 12449   **Lat:** 41-58-59 N **Long:** 73-59-24 W
Pop: 1,998 (1990); 2,011 (1980)   **Pop Density:** 908.2
Land: 2.2 sq. mi.; **Water:** 0.0 sq. mi.

Lincoln Park
CDP
Lat: 41-57-27 N **Long:** 74-00-09 W
Pop: 2,457 (1990); 2,664 (1980)   **Pop Density:** 1890.0
Land: 1.3 sq. mi.; **Water:** 0.0 sq. mi.

Lloyd
Town
ZIP: 12528   **Lat:** 41-43-53 N **Long:** 73-59-56 W
Pop: 9,231 (1990)   **Pop Density:** 291.2
Land: 31.7 sq. mi.; **Water:** 1.6 sq. mi.

Marbletown
Town
ZIP: 12401   **Lat:** 41-52-39 N **Long:** 74-09-58 W
Pop: 5,285 (1990)   **Pop Density:** 96.8
Land: 54.6 sq. mi.; **Water:** 0.6 sq. mi.

Marlboro
CDP
ZIP: 12542   **Lat:** 41-36-11 N **Long:** 73-58-23 W
Pop: 2,200 (1990); 2,275 (1980)   **Pop Density:** 785.7
Land: 2.8 sq. mi.; **Water:** 0.6 sq. mi.

Marlborough
Town
ZIP: 12542   **Lat:** 41-38-25 N **Long:** 73-59-18 W
Pop: 7,430 (1990)   **Pop Density:** 298.4
Land: 24.9 sq. mi.; **Water:** 1.6 sq. mi.

Milton
CDP
ZIP: 12547   **Lat:** 41-39-27 N **Long:** 73-57-40 W
Pop: 1,140 (1990); 1,253 (1980)   **Pop Density:** 518.2
Land: 2.2 sq. mi.; **Water:** 0.0 sq. mi.

Napanoch　　　　　　　　　　　　CDP
ZIP: 12458　　　　　**Lat:** 41-45-03 N **Long:** 74-22-28 W
Pop: 1,068 (1990); 1,260 (1980)　　　**Pop Density:** 890.0
Land: 1.2 sq. mi.; **Water:** 0.0 sq. mi.

New Paltz　　　　　　　　　　　　Town
ZIP: 12561　　　　　**Lat:** 41-45-30 N **Long:** 74-05-13 W
Pop: 11,388 (1990)　　　　**Pop Density:** 334.9
Land: 34.0 sq. mi.; **Water:** 0.4 sq. mi.

*New Paltz　　　　　　　　　　　　Village
ZIP: 12561　　　　　**Lat:** 41-44-53 N **Long:** 74-04-54 W
Pop: 5,463 (1990); 4,938 (1980)　　**Pop Density:** 3213.5
Land: 1.7 sq. mi.; **Water:** 0.0 sq. mi.　　**Elev:** 236 ft.

In southeastern NY, 10 mi. west of Poughkeepsie. Established 1678. Not coextensive with the town of the same name.

Name origin: For the Rheinish Pfalz, former home of early settlers.

Olive　　　　　　　　　　　　Town
ZIP: 12461　　　　　**Lat:** 41-56-40 N **Long:** 74-15-26 W
Pop: 4,086 (1990)　　　　**Pop Density:** 69.6
Land: 58.7 sq. mi.; **Water:** 6.5 sq. mi.

Plattekill　　　　　　　　　　　　Town
ZIP: 12568　　　　　**Lat:** 41-38-34 N **Long:** 74-04-08 W
Pop: 8,891 (1990)　　　　**Pop Density:** 249.7
Land: 35.6 sq. mi.; **Water:** 0.1 sq. mi.

Name origin: From Dutch term meaning 'flat water.'

Port Ewen　　　　　　　　　　　　CDP
ZIP: 12466　　　　　**Lat:** 41-54-22 N **Long:** 73-58-44 W
Pop: 3,444 (1990); 2,813 (1980)　　**Pop Density:** 1722.0
Land: 2.0 sq. mi.; **Water:** 0.7 sq. mi.

Rochester　　　　　　　　　　　　Town
ZIP: 12404　　　　　**Lat:** 41-48-49 N **Long:** 74-16-51 W
Pop: 5,679 (1990)　　　　**Pop Density:** 64.2
Land: 88.4 sq. mi.; **Water:** 0.4 sq. mi.

Rosendale　　　　　　　　　　　　Town
ZIP: 12472　　　　　**Lat:** 41-50-50 N **Long:** 74-04-41 W
Pop: 6,220 (1990)　　　　**Pop Density:** 312.6
Land: 19.9 sq. mi.; **Water:** 0.8 sq. mi.

Rosendale Village　　　　　　　　　　　　CDP
ZIP: 12472　　　　　**Lat:** 41-50-57 N **Long:** 74-04-34 W
Pop: 1,284 (1990); 1,134 (1980)　　**Pop Density:** 713.3
Land: 1.8 sq. mi.; **Water:** 0.1 sq. mi.

Saugerties　　　　　　　　　　　　Town
ZIP: 12477　　　　　**Lat:** 42-04-59 N **Long:** 74-00-05 W
Pop: 18,467 (1990)　　　　**Pop Density:** 286.3
Land: 64.5 sq. mi.; **Water:** 3.5 sq. mi.

*Saugerties　　　　　　　　　　　　Village
ZIP: 12477　　　　　**Lat:** 42-04-29 N **Long:** 73-56-53 W
Pop: 3,915 (1990); 3,882 (1980)　　**Pop Density:** 2060.5
Land: 1.9 sq. mi.; **Water:** 0.5 sq. mi.　　**Elev:** 155 ft.

In southeastern NY on the west side of the Hudson River, 11 mi. north of Kingston. Not coextensive with the town of the same name.

Name origin: A folk etymologized form of the town name recorded in 1663 as *Zager's kiletie,* Dutch 'Zager's streamlet.' Zaget was the first Dutch settler on the stream.

Saugerties South　　　　　　　　　　　　CDP
　　　　　Lat: 42-03-31 N **Long:** 73-57-08 W
Pop: 2,346 (1990); 2,919 (1980)　　**Pop Density:** 2346.0
Land: 1.0 sq. mi.; **Water:** 0.2 sq. mi.

Shandaken　　　　　　　　　　　　Town
ZIP: 12480　　　　　**Lat:** 42-04-01 N **Long:** 74-21-52 W
Pop: 3,013 (1990)　　　　**Pop Density:** 25.2
Land: 119.8 sq. mi.; **Water:** 0.0 sq. mi.

In southeastern NY, northwest of Kingston.

Name origin: From an Indian term possibly meaning 'hemlock.'

Shawangunk　　　　　　　　　　　　Town
ZIP: 12589　　　　　**Lat:** 41-38-02 N **Long:** 74-15-34 W
Pop: 10,081 (1990)　　　　**Pop Density:** 178.7
Land: 56.4 sq. mi.; **Water:** 0.3 sq. mi.

Tillson　　　　　　　　　　　　CDP
ZIP: 12486　　　　　**Lat:** 41-49-53 N **Long:** 74-04-09 W
Pop: 1,688 (1990); 1,529 (1980)　　**Pop Density:** 703.3
Land: 2.4 sq. mi.; **Water:** 0.0 sq. mi.

Ulster　　　　　　　　　　　　Town
ZIP: 12401　　　　　**Lat:** 41-58-09 N **Long:** 74-00-22 W
Pop: 12,329 (1990)　　　　**Pop Density:** 460.0
Land: 26.8 sq. mi.; **Water:** 2.1 sq. mi.

Wallkill　　　　　　　　　　　　CDP
ZIP: 12589　　　　　**Lat:** 41-36-31 N **Long:** 74-09-53 W
Pop: 2,125 (1990); 2,064 (1980)　　**Pop Density:** 685.5
Land: 3.1 sq. mi.; **Water:** 0.0 sq. mi.

Wawarsing　　　　　　　　　　　　Town
ZIP: 12489　　　　　**Lat:** 41-44-51 N **Long:** 74-25-19 W
Pop: 12,348 (1990)　　　　**Pop Density:** 94.5
Land: 130.6 sq. mi.; **Water:** 3.1 sq. mi.

West Hurley　　　　　　　　　　　　CDP
ZIP: 12491　　　　　**Lat:** 42-00-23 N **Long:** 74-06-40 W
Pop: 2,252 (1990); 2,344 (1980)　　**Pop Density:** 549.3
Land: 4.1 sq. mi.; **Water:** 0.0 sq. mi.

Woodstock　　　　　　　　　　　　Town
ZIP: 12498　　　　　**Lat:** 42-03-27 N **Long:** 74-10-04 W
Pop: 6,290 (1990)　　　　**Pop Density:** 93.2
Land: 67.5 sq. mi.; **Water:** 0.4 sq. mi.

Zena　　　　　　　　　　　　CDP
　　　　　Lat: 42-01-19 N **Long:** 74-05-10 W
Pop: 1,177 (1990); 1,435 (1980)　　**Pop Density:** 435.9
Land: 2.7 sq. mi.; **Water:** 0.0 sq. mi.

Warren County
County Seat: Lake George (ZIP: 12845)

Pop: 59,209 (1990); 54,854 (1980)　　　　　　**Pop Density:** 68.1
Land: 869.7 sq. mi.; **Water:** 62.0 sq. mi.　　　**Area Code:** 518

In northeastern NY, north of Saratoga; organized Mar 12, 1813 from Washington County.

Name origin: For Joseph Warren (1741–75), Revolutionary War patriot and member of the Continental Congress who dispatched Paul Revere (1735–1818) on his famous ride.

Bolton
Town
Lat: 43-34-45 N **Long:** 73-39-26 W
Pop: 1,855 (1990)　　　　**Pop Density:** 29.3
Land: 63.4 sq. mi.; **Water:** 22.2 sq. mi.

Chester
Town
Lat: 43-41-17 N **Long:** 73-52-11 W
Pop: 3,465 (1990)　　　　**Pop Density:** 41.0
Land: 84.5 sq. mi.; **Water:** 2.6 sq. mi.

Glens Falls
City
ZIP: 12801　　　**Lat:** 43-18-39 N **Long:** 73-38-43 W
Pop: 15,023 (1990); 15,897 (1980)　　**Pop Density:** 3852.1
Land: 3.9 sq. mi.; **Water:** 0.1 sq. mi.　　**Elev:** 348 ft.

In eastern NY on the west bank of the Hudson River at Falls, north of Albany.
Name origin: For a geographic feature.

Glens Falls North
CDP
ZIP: 12801　　　**Lat:** 43-20-04 N **Long:** 73-41-03 W
Pop: 7,978 (1990); 6,956 (1980)　　**Pop Density:** 984.9
Land: 8.1 sq. mi.; **Water:** 0.1 sq. mi.

Hague
Town
ZIP: 12836　　　**Lat:** 43-42-50 N **Long:** 73-32-13 W
Pop: 699 (1990)　　　　**Pop Density:** 10.9
Land: 64.0 sq. mi.; **Water:** 15.6 sq. mi.

In eastern NY on Lake George.
Name origin: For the Dutch city.

Horicon
Town
ZIP: 12815　　　**Lat:** 43-42-12 N **Long:** 73-42-41 W
Pop: 1,269 (1990)　　　　**Pop Density:** 19.2
Land: 66.1 sq. mi.; **Water:** 5.7 sq. mi.

Johnsburg
Town
ZIP: 12843　　　**Lat:** 43-38-37 N **Long:** 74-03-06 W
Pop: 2,352 (1990)　　　　**Pop Density:** 11.5
Land: 204.6 sq. mi.; **Water:** 2.2 sq. mi.

Name origin: For an early settler.

Lake George
Town
ZIP: 12845　　　**Lat:** 43-26-20 N **Long:** 73-43-27 W
Pop: 3,211 (1990)　　　　**Pop Density:** 106.3
Land: 30.2 sq. mi.; **Water:** 3.7 sq. mi.

*Lake George
Village
ZIP: 12845　　　**Lat:** 43-25-32 N **Long:** 73-42-54 W
Pop: 933 (1990); 1,047 (1980)　　**Pop Density:** 1555.0
Land: 0.6 sq. mi.; **Water:** 0.0 sq. mi.　　**Elev:** 353 ft.

Not coextensive with the town of the same name.

Lake Luzerne
Town
ZIP: 12846　　　**Lat:** 43-19-33 N **Long:** 73-48-47 W
Pop: 2,816 (1990)　　　　**Pop Density:** 53.5
Land: 52.6 sq. mi.; **Water:** 1.4 sq. mi.

Name origin: For the famous Swiss lake.

Queensbury
Town
ZIP: 12804　　　**Lat:** 43-21-29 N **Long:** 73-40-23 W
Pop: 22,630 (1990)　　　　**Pop Density:** 359.2
Land: 63.0 sq. mi.; **Water:** 5.1 sq. mi.

Stony Creek
Town
ZIP: 12878　　　**Lat:** 43-25-02 N **Long:** 74-01-33 W
Pop: 670 (1990)　　　　**Pop Density:** 8.1
Land: 82.4 sq. mi.; **Water:** 0.8 sq. mi.

Thurman
Town
ZIP: 12885　　　**Lat:** 43-29-59 N **Long:** 73-59-09 W
Pop: 1,045 (1990)　　　　**Pop Density:** 11.4
Land: 91.4 sq. mi.; **Water:** 1.4 sq. mi.

Warrensburg
Town
ZIP: 12885　　　**Lat:** 43-30-10 N **Long:** 73-47-32 W
Pop: 4,174 (1990)　　　　**Pop Density:** 65.5
Land: 63.7 sq. mi.; **Water:** 1.1 sq. mi.

In east-central NY on the Schroon River at the southwestern end of Lake George.
Name origin: For James Warren, who settled here in 1804.

West Glens Falls
CDP
ZIP: 12801　　　**Lat:** 43-18-09 N **Long:** 73-41-16 W
Pop: 5,964 (1990); 5,331 (1980)　　**Pop Density:** 1296.5
Land: 4.6 sq. mi.; **Water:** 0.1 sq. mi.

Washington County
County Seat: Fort Edward (ZIP: 12828)

Pop: 59,330 (1990); 54,795 (1980)   **Pop Density:** 71.0
Land: 835.5 sq. mi.; **Water:** 10.4 sq. mi.   **Area Code:** 518

On central eastern border of NY, east of Glens Falls; organized as Charlotte County Mar 12, 1772 (prior to statehood) from Albany County.

Name origin: For George Washington (1732–99), American patriot and first U.S. president. Name changed Apr 2, 1784 from Charlotte, which had been given to honor the wife of King George III of England (1738–1820).

Argyle   Town
ZIP: 12809   **Lat:** 43-14-17 N **Long:** 73-27-59 W
Pop: 3,031 (1990)   **Pop Density:** 53.6
Land: 56.6 sq. mi.; **Water:** 1.1 sq. mi.

*Argyle   Village
ZIP: 12809   **Lat:** 43-14-13 N **Long:** 73-29-25 W
Pop: 295 (1990); 320 (1980)   **Pop Density:** 737.5
Land: 0.4 sq. mi.; **Water:** 0.0 sq. mi.
Not coextensive with the town of the same name.

Cambridge   Town
ZIP: 12816   **Lat:** 42-59-44 N **Long:** 73-26-51 W
Pop: 1,938 (1990)   **Pop Density:** 53.2
Land: 36.4 sq. mi.; **Water:** 0.1 sq. mi.

*Cambridge   Village
ZIP: 12816   **Lat:** 43-01-35 N **Long:** 73-22-51 W
Pop: 1,906 (1990); 550 (1980)   **Pop Density:** 1191.3
Land: 1.6 sq. mi.; **Water:** 0.0 sq. mi.   **Elev:** 496 ft.
Not coextensive with the town of the same name.
Name origin: For the English university town.

Dresden   Town
ZIP: 12887   **Lat:** 43-36-30 N **Long:** 73-28-46 W
Pop: 561 (1990)   **Pop Density:** 10.2
Land: 55.2 sq. mi.; **Water:** 1.7 sq. mi.

Easton   Town
ZIP: 12834   **Lat:** 43-01-48 N **Long:** 73-32-16 W
Pop: 2,203 (1990)   **Pop Density:** 35.4
Land: 62.3 sq. mi.; **Water:** 0.9 sq. mi.

Fort Ann   Town
ZIP: 12827   **Lat:** 43-28-29 N **Long:** 73-30-07 W
Pop: 6,368 (1990)   **Pop Density:** 59.1
Land: 107.7 sq. mi.; **Water:** 1.3 sq. mi.

*Fort Ann   Village
ZIP: 12827   **Lat:** 43-24-53 N **Long:** 73-29-26 W
Pop: 419 (1990); 509 (1980)   **Pop Density:** 1396.7
Land: 0.3 sq. mi.; **Water:** 0.0 sq. mi.   **Elev:** 138 ft.
Not coextensive with the town of the same name.

Fort Edward   Town
ZIP: 12828   **Lat:** 43-14-08 N **Long:** 73-33-53 W
Pop: 6,330 (1990)   **Pop Density:** 235.3
Land: 26.9 sq. mi.; **Water:** 0.6 sq. mi.

*Fort Edward   Village
ZIP: 12828   **Lat:** 43-16-08 N **Long:** 73-34-58 W
Pop: 3,561 (1990); 3,561 (1980)   **Pop Density:** 1978.3
Land: 1.8 sq. mi.; **Water:** 0.1 sq. mi.   **Elev:** 144 ft.
In eastern NY on the Hudson River, 38 mi. north of Troy. Not coextensive with the town of the same name.

Granville   Town
ZIP: 12832   **Lat:** 43-25-19 N **Long:** 73-18-21 W
Pop: 5,935 (1990)   **Pop Density:** 105.8
Land: 56.1 sq. mi.; **Water:** 0.0 sq. mi.

*Granville   Village
ZIP: 12832   **Lat:** 43-24-30 N **Long:** 73-15-39 W
Pop: 2,646 (1990); 2,696 (1980)   **Pop Density:** 1653.8
Land: 1.6 sq. mi.; **Water:** 0.0 sq. mi.   **Elev:** 407 ft.
Not coextensive with the town of the same name.
Name origin: Previously called Bishop's Corners.

Greenwich   Town
ZIP: 12834   **Lat:** 43-07-56 N **Long:** 73-28-38 W
Pop: 4,557 (1990)   **Pop Density:** 103.6
Land: 44.0 sq. mi.; **Water:** 0.4 sq. mi.

*Greenwich   Village
ZIP: 12834   **Lat:** 43-05-11 N **Long:** 73-29-48 W
Pop: 1,961 (1990); 282 (1980)   **Pop Density:** 1307.3
Land: 1.5 sq. mi.; **Water:** 0.0 sq. mi.
Not coextensive with the town of the same name.

Hampton   Town
ZIP: 12837   **Lat:** 43-32-51 N **Long:** 73-17-55 W
Pop: 756 (1990)   **Pop Density:** 33.5
Land: 22.6 sq. mi.; **Water:** 0.1 sq. mi.

Hartford   Town
ZIP: 12838   **Lat:** 43-21-38 N **Long:** 73-25-19 W
Pop: 1,989 (1990)   **Pop Density:** 45.8
Land: 43.4 sq. mi.; **Water:** 0.0 sq. mi.
Name origin: For Hartford, England.

Hebron   Town
ZIP: 12832   **Lat:** 43-16-27 N **Long:** 73-19-18 W
Pop: 1,540 (1990)   **Pop Density:** 27.4
Land: 56.3 sq. mi.; **Water:** 0.2 sq. mi.

Hudson Falls   Village
ZIP: 12839   **Lat:** 43-18-16 N **Long:** 73-34-55 W
Pop: 7,651 (1990); 7,419 (1980)   **Pop Density:** 4026.8
Land: 1.9 sq. mi.; **Water:** 0.0 sq. mi.   **Elev:** 294 ft.

Jackson   Town
Lat: 43-05-18 N **Long:** 73-22-36 W
Pop: 1,581 (1990)   **Pop Density:** 42.5
Land: 37.2 sq. mi.; **Water:** 0.3 sq. mi.

Kingsbury   Town
ZIP: 12839   **Lat:** 43-20-19 N **Long:** 73-32-53 W
Pop: 11,851 (1990)   **Pop Density:** 297.0
Land: 39.9 sq. mi.; **Water:** 0.1 sq. mi.

Putnam
Town
Lat: 43-44-42 N Long: 73-24-58 W
Pop: 477 (1990)   Pop Density: 14.4
Land: 33.2 sq. mi.; Water: 2.3 sq. mi.

Salem
Town
ZIP: 12865   Lat: 43-09-52 N Long: 73-19-28 W
Pop: 2,608 (1990)   Pop Density: 49.7
Land: 52.5 sq. mi.; Water: 0.0 sq. mi.

*Salem
Village
ZIP: 12865   Lat: 43-10-26 N Long: 73-19-41 W
Pop: 958 (1990); 959 (1980)   Pop Density: 330.3
Land: 2.9 sq. mi.; Water: 0.0 sq. mi.

Not coextensive with the town of the same name.

Name origin: An anglicization of the Hebrew term *shalom* meaning 'peace.'

White Creek
Town
Lat: 43-00-01 N Long: 73-20-40 W
Pop: 3,196 (1990)   Pop Density: 66.7
Land: 47.9 sq. mi.; Water: 0.1 sq. mi.

Whitehall
Town
ZIP: 12887   Lat: 43-32-28 N Long: 73-23-11 W
Pop: 4,409 (1990)   Pop Density: 76.5
Land: 57.6 sq. mi.; Water: 1.1 sq. mi.

*Whitehall
Village
ZIP: 12887   Lat: 43-33-36 N Long: 73-25-06 W
Pop: 3,071 (1990); 3,241 (1980)   Pop Density: 653.4
Land: 4.7 sq. mi.; Water: 0.1 sq. mi.   Elev: 125 ft.

Not coextensive with the town of the same name.

Wayne County
County Seat: Lyons (ZIP: 14489)

Pop: 89,123 (1990); 84,581 (1980)   Pop Density: 147.5
Land: 604.2 sq. mi.; Water: 780.0 sq. mi.   Area Code: 315

On central western border of NY on Lake Ontario, east of Rochester; organized Apr 11, 1823 from Ontario and Seneca counties.

Name origin: For Gen. Anthony Wayne (1745–1796), PA soldier and statesman, nicknamed "Mad Anthony" for his daring during the American Revolution.

Arcadia
Town
ZIP: 14513   Lat: 43-05-09 N Long: 77-05-13 W
Pop: 14,855 (1990)   Pop Density: 285.1
Land: 52.1 sq. mi.; Water: 0.1 sq. mi.

Name origin: For the district in ancient Greece.

Butler
Town
Lat: 43-10-12 N Long: 76-45-58 W
Pop: 2,152 (1990)   Pop Density: 58.0
Land: 37.1 sq. mi.; Water: 0.1 sq. mi.

Clyde
Village
ZIP: 14433   Lat: 43-05-00 N Long: 76-52-15 W
Pop: 2,409 (1990); 2,491 (1980)   Pop Density: 1095.0
Land: 2.2 sq. mi.; Water: 0.1 sq. mi.   Elev: 400 ft.

Name origin: For the river in Scotland.

Galen
Town
Lat: 43-04-02 N Long: 76-52-50 W
Pop: 4,413 (1990)   Pop Density: 74.3
Land: 59.4 sq. mi.; Water: 0.6 sq. mi.

Huron
Town
Lat: 43-14-47 N Long: 76-53-47 W
Pop: 2,025 (1990)   Pop Density: 51.3
Land: 39.5 sq. mi.; Water: 3.7 sq. mi.

Lyons
Town
ZIP: 14489   Lat: 43-05-23 N Long: 77-00-08 W
Pop: 6,315 (1990)   Pop Density: 168.9
Land: 37.4 sq. mi.; Water: 0.1 sq. mi.

*Lyons
Village
ZIP: 14489   Lat: 43-03-48 N Long: 76-59-37 W
Pop: 4,280 (1990); 4,160 (1980)   Pop Density: 1043.9
Land: 4.1 sq. mi.; Water: 0.1 sq. mi.   Elev: 438 ft.

Not coextensive with the town of the same name.

Macedon
Town
ZIP: 14502   Lat: 43-04-42 N Long: 77-18-41 W
Pop: 7,375 (1990)   Pop Density: 190.6
Land: 38.7 sq. mi.; Water: 0.2 sq. mi.

*Macedon
Village
ZIP: 14502   Lat: 43-04-07 N Long: 77-18-09 W
Pop: 1,400 (1990); 1,400 (1980)   Pop Density: 1166.7
Land: 1.2 sq. mi.; Water: 0.0 sq. mi.   Elev: 478 ft.

Not coextensive with the town of the same name.

Marion
Town
ZIP: 14505   Lat: 43-09-36 N Long: 77-12-01 W
Pop: 4,901 (1990)   Pop Density: 167.8
Land: 29.2 sq. mi.; Water: 0.1 sq. mi.

Name origin: For Gen. Francis Marion (1732?–95), Revolutionary War hero known as the "Swamp Fox."

Newark
Village
ZIP: 14513   Lat: 43-02-30 N Long: 77-05-39 W
Pop: 9,849 (1990); 10,017 (1980)   Pop Density: 1894.0
Land: 5.2 sq. mi.; Water: 0.0 sq. mi.   Elev: 457 ft.

Ontario
Town
ZIP: 14519   Lat: 43-14-42 N Long: 77-18-58 W
Pop: 8,560 (1990)   Pop Density: 265.8
Land: 32.2 sq. mi.; Water: 0.1 sq. mi.

In western NY, about 17 mi. northeast of Rochester.

Name origin: For the Indian tribe whose name origin is in dispute. Either from *ontare* 'lake' plus *io* 'beautiful'; or from *Entouhonorons*, a name Samuel de Champlain (c.1567–1635) used to designate the Lake of the Seneca or Iroquois.

Palmyra
Town
ZIP: 14522   Lat: 43-05-13 N Long: 77-11-34 W
Pop: 7,690 (1990)   Pop Density: 229.6
Land: 33.5 sq. mi.; Water: 0.2 sq. mi.

*Palmyra
Village
ZIP: 14522 Lat: 43-03-41 N Long: 77-13-50 W
Pop: 3,566 (1990); 3,729 (1980) Pop Density: 2743.1
Land: 1.3 sq. mi.; Water: 0.0 sq. mi.

Not coextensive with the town of the same name.

Name origin: For the ancient city in Syria.

Red Creek
Village
ZIP: 13143 Lat: 43-14-52 N Long: 76-43-23 W
Pop: 566 (1990); 645 (1980) Pop Density: 628.9
Land: 0.9 sq. mi.; Water: 0.0 sq. mi.

Rose
Town
Lat: 43-09-28 N Long: 76-53-58 W
Pop: 2,424 (1990) Pop Density: 71.5
Land: 33.9 sq. mi.; Water: 0.0 sq. mi.

Savannah
Town
ZIP: 13146 Lat: 43-04-29 N Long: 76-45-37 W
Pop: 1,768 (1990) Pop Density: 49.1
Land: 36.0 sq. mi.; Water: 0.2 sq. mi.

Name origin: From a Spanish form of a Carib Indian term possibly meaning 'meadow.'

Sodus
Town
ZIP: 14551 Lat: 43-12-59 N Long: 77-02-56 W
Pop: 8,877 (1990) Pop Density: 131.7
Land: 67.4 sq. mi.; Water: 1.9 sq. mi.

*Sodus
Village
ZIP: 14551 Lat: 43-14-12 N Long: 77-03-50 W
Pop: 1,904 (1990); 1,790 (1980) Pop Density: 2115.6
Land: 0.9 sq. mi.; Water: 0.0 sq. mi. Elev: 432 ft.

Not coextensive with the town of the same name.

Name origin: From an Indian term of uncertain meaning.

Sodus Point
Village
ZIP: 14555 Lat: 43-15-45 N Long: 76-59-39 W
Pop: 1,190 (1990); 1,334 (1980) Pop Density: 793.3
Land: 1.5 sq. mi.; Water: 0.0 sq. mi.

Walworth
Town
ZIP: 14568 Lat: 43-09-50 N Long: 77-19-07 W
Pop: 6,945 (1990) Pop Density: 205.5
Land: 33.8 sq. mi.; Water: 0.0 sq. mi.

Name origin: For a prominent citizen.

Williamson
Town
ZIP: 14589 Lat: 43-14-42 N Long: 77-11-39 W
Pop: 6,540 (1990) Pop Density: 189.0
Land: 34.6 sq. mi.; Water: 2.3 sq. mi.

In western NY, 25 mi. northeast of Rochester.

Name origin: For an early settler.

Wolcott
Town
ZIP: 14590 Lat: 43-16-27 N Long: 76-45-53 W
Pop: 4,283 (1990) Pop Density: 109.0
Land: 39.3 sq. mi.; Water: 0.9 sq. mi.

*Wolcott
Village
ZIP: 14590 Lat: 43-13-21 N Long: 76-48-45 W
Pop: 1,544 (1990); 246 (1980) Pop Density: 812.6
Land: 1.9 sq. mi.; Water: 0.0 sq. mi. Elev: 378 ft.

In north-central NY, 47 mi. east of Rochester. Not coextensive with the town of the same name.

Westchester County
County Seat: White Plains (ZIP: 10601)

Pop: 874,866 (1990); 866,599 (1980) Pop Density: 2021.0
Land: 432.9 sq. mi.; Water: 67.3 sq. mi. Area Code: 914

In southwestern NY, north of New York City; original county, organized Nov 1, 1683.

Name origin: For the town and county of Chester in England.

Ardsley
Village
ZIP: 10502 Lat: 41-00-52 N Long: 73-50-28 W
Pop: 4,272 (1990); 4,183 (1980) Pop Density: 3286.2
Land: 1.3 sq. mi.; Water: 0.0 sq. mi.

Armonk
CDP
ZIP: 10504 Lat: 41-07-56 N Long: 73-42-46 W
Pop: 2,745 (1990); 2,238 (1980) Pop Density: 450.0
Land: 6.1 sq. mi.; Water: 0.0 sq. mi.

Bedford
Town
ZIP: 10506 Lat: 41-13-32 N Long: 73-39-55 W
Pop: 16,906 (1990) Pop Density: 454.5
Land: 37.2 sq. mi.; Water: 2.1 sq. mi.

In southeastern NY just west of the CT border.

Name origin: For the town in England.

Briarcliff Manor
Village
ZIP: 10510 Lat: 41-08-19 N Long: 73-50-31 W
Pop: 7,070 (1990); 795 (1980) Pop Density: 1198.3
Land: 5.9 sq. mi.; Water: 0.7 sq. mi. Elev: 266 ft.

Bronxville
Village
ZIP: 10708 Lat: 40-56-19 N Long: 73-49-38 W
Pop: 6,028 (1990); 6,267 (1980) Pop Density: 6028.0
Land: 1.0 sq. mi.; Water: 0.0 sq. mi.

Incorporated 1898.

Name origin: Adopted on incorporation at the suggestion of James Swain, a local cutlery manufacturer. Previously called Underhill's Crossing, for John Underhill, who dammed the Bronx River in the early 1700s and built a bridge.

Buchanan
Village
ZIP: 10511 Lat: 41-15-47 N Long: 73-56-41 W
Pop: 1,970 (1990); 2,041 (1980) Pop Density: 1407.1
Land: 1.4 sq. mi.; Water: 0.3 sq. mi.

Cortlandt
Town
ZIP: 10520 Lat: 41-15-16 N Long: 73-54-02 W
Pop: 37,357 (1990) Pop Density: 941.0
Land: 39.7 sq. mi.; Water: 10.5 sq. mi.

Croton-on-Hudson — Village
ZIP: 10520 **Lat:** 41-12-11 N **Long:** 73-53-26 W
Pop: 7,018 (1990); 6,889 (1980) **Pop Density:** 1462.1
Land: 4.8 sq. mi.; **Water:** 6.1 sq. mi.

In southeastern NY on the east bank of the Hudson River, a northern suburb of New York City. Incorporated 1898.

Name origin: An adaptation of *Kenotin* or *Knoten*, the name of an Indian chief who lived near the mouth of the Croton River. Previously called Collabaugh Landing, Cortlandt Town, and Croton Landing.

Dobbs Ferry — Village
ZIP: 10522 **Lat:** 41-00-52 N **Long:** 73-52-11 W
Pop: 9,940 (1990); 10,053 (1980) **Pop Density:** 4141.7
Land: 2.4 sq. mi.; **Water:** 0.7 sq. mi. **Elev:** 210 ft.

Name origin: For Jan Dobbs, a Swedish immigrant who operated a ferry across the Hudson River until 1759.

Eastchester — Town
ZIP: 10709 **Lat:** 40-57-09 N **Long:** 73-48-50 W
Pop: 30,867 (1990) **Pop Density:** 6299.4
Land: 4.9 sq. mi.; **Water:** 0.1 sq. mi.

Name origin: For the English county of Chester (Cheshire).

*Eastchester — CDP
ZIP: 10709 **Lat:** 40-57-29 N **Long:** 73-48-28 W
Pop: 18,537 (1990); 20,305 (1980) **Pop Density:** 5617.3
Land: 3.3 sq. mi.; **Water:** 0.1 sq. mi.

Elmsford — Village
ZIP: 10523 **Lat:** 41-03-11 N **Long:** 73-48-52 W
Pop: 3,938 (1990); 3,361 (1980) **Pop Density:** 3938.0
Land: 1.0 sq. mi.; **Water:** 0.0 sq. mi.

In southeastern NY, 26 mi. north of New York City.

Name origin: For the many elm trees that used to be in the area.

Golden's Bridge — CDP
Lat: 41-17-09 N **Long:** 73-40-13 W
Pop: 1,589 (1990); 1,367 (1980) **Pop Density:** 467.4
Land: 3.4 sq. mi.; **Water:** 0.6 sq. mi.

Greenburgh — Town
ZIP: 10591 **Lat:** 41-01-58 N **Long:** 73-50-36 W
Pop: 83,816 (1990) **Pop Density:** 2748.1
Land: 30.5 sq. mi.; **Water:** 5.7 sq. mi.

Greenville — CDP
ZIP: 10583 **Lat:** 41-00-03 N **Long:** 73-49-07 W
Pop: 9,528 (1990); 8,706 (1980) **Pop Density:** 3073.5
Land: 3.1 sq. mi.; **Water:** 0.0 sq. mi.

Harrison — Town and Village
ZIP: 10528 **Lat:** 41-01-21 N **Long:** 73-43-12 W
Pop: 23,308 (1990); 23,046 (1980) **Pop Density:** 1387.4
Land: 16.8 sq. mi.; **Water:** 0.6 sq. mi.

The town and the village are coextensive.

Name origin: For John Harrison, a Quaker leader from Long Island.

Hartsdale — CDP
ZIP: 10530 **Lat:** 41-01-32 N **Long:** 73-48-18 W
Pop: 9,587 (1990); 10,216 (1980) **Pop Density:** 3195.7
Land: 3.0 sq. mi.; **Water:** 0.0 sq. mi.

Hastings-on-Hudson — Village
ZIP: 10706 **Lat:** 40-59-16 N **Long:** 73-52-46 W
Pop: 8,000 (1990); 8,573 (1980) **Pop Density:** 4000.0
Land: 2.0 sq. mi.; **Water:** 0.9 sq. mi. **Elev:** 199 ft.

In southeastern NY on the west bank of the Hudson River, 18 mi. north of New York City. Post office opened 1849; incorporated 1879.

Name origin: Because the residents thought the village resembled the town in England. Originally Hastings-upon-Hudson; changed to present form in 1935.

Hawthorne — CDP
ZIP: 10532 **Lat:** 41-06-15 N **Long:** 73-47-37 W
Pop: 4,764 (1990); 5,010 (1980) **Pop Density:** 2802.4
Land: 1.7 sq. mi.; **Water:** 0.0 sq. mi.

Irvington — Village
ZIP: 10533 **Lat:** 41-02-18 N **Long:** 73-52-02 W
Pop: 6,348 (1990); 5,774 (1980) **Pop Density:** 2267.1
Land: 2.8 sq. mi.; **Water:** 1.2 sq. mi.

In southeastern NY on the east bank of the Hudson River, 22 mi. north of New York City and 3 mi. south of Tarrytown.

Name origin: For Washington Irving (1783–1859).

Jefferson Valley-Yorktown — CDP
ZIP: 10535 **Lat:** 41-19-06 N **Long:** 73-48-06 W
Pop: 14,118 (1990); 13,380 (1980) **Pop Density:** 2046.1
Land: 6.9 sq. mi.; **Water:** 0.1 sq. mi.

Larchmont — Village
ZIP: 10538 **Lat:** 40-55-33 N **Long:** 73-45-12 W
Pop: 6,181 (1990); 6,308 (1980) **Pop Density:** 5619.1
Land: 1.1 sq. mi.; **Water:** 0.0 sq. mi.

In southeastern NY on Long Island Sound.

Name origin: For the estate of Peter Jay Munro, located on a hill and planted with larch trees.

Lewisboro — Town
ZIP: 10590 **Lat:** 41-16-27 N **Long:** 73-35-07 W
Pop: 11,313 (1990) **Pop Density:** 406.9
Land: 27.8 sq. mi.; **Water:** 1.3 sq. mi.

In southeastern NY, north of New York City on the west bank of the Hudson River.

Name origin: For John Lewis, who in 1840 gave the town the income from $10,000 for its schools, with the proviso that the town's name of South Salem be changed to Lewisborough. The present spelling was adopted in the 1890s.

Mamaroneck — Town
ZIP: 10543 **Lat:** 40-55-38 N **Long:** 73-44-29 W
Pop: 27,706 (1990) **Pop Density:** 4197.9
Land: 6.6 sq. mi.; **Water:** 7.4 sq. mi.

*Mamaroneck — Village
ZIP: 10543 **Lat:** 40-56-04 N **Long:** 73-43-38 W
Pop: 17,325 (1990); 10,281 (1980) **Pop Density:** 5414.1
Land: 3.2 sq. mi.; **Water:** 3.5 sq. mi.

In southeastern NY on Long Island Sound, 22 mi. northeast of New York. Not coextensive with the town of the same name.

Name origin: Origin of the name is unclear: an Indian chief of that name lived near the Croton River, which was called, in a 1661 deed, *Merrimack* 'sturgeon.'

Mount Kisco — Village
ZIP: 10549 **Lat:** 41-12-06 N **Long:** 73-43-49 W
Pop: 9,108 (1990); 8,025 (1980) **Pop Density:** 2938.1
Land: 3.1 sq. mi.; **Water:** 0.0 sq. mi. **Elev:** 289 ft.

Not coextensive with the town of the same name.

Name origin: Formerly called Kisco Plain, from Indian *Cisqua* 'muddy place.'

Mount Pleasant   Town
ZIP: 10591   Lat: 41-06-26 N Long: 73-48-30 W
Pop: 40,590 (1990)   Pop Density: 1465.3
Land: 27.7 sq. mi.; Water: 5.0 sq. mi.

Mount Vernon   City
ZIP: 10550   Lat: 40-54-46 N Long: 73-49-47 W
Pop: 67,153 (1990); 66,713 (1980)   Pop Density: 15262.0
Land: 4.4 sq. mi.; Water: 0.0 sq. mi.

In southeastern NY on the Bronx River, a northern suburb of
New York City. Incorporated as a village 1854; as a city
1892.

Name origin: For the VA estate of George Washington (1732–
99).

New Castle   Town
ZIP: 10514   Lat: 41-11-09 N Long: 73-46-30 W
Pop: 16,648 (1990)   Pop Density: 720.7
Land: 23.1 sq. mi.; Water: 0.3 sq. mi.

New Rochelle   City
ZIP: 10801   Lat: 40-55-23 N Long: 73-46-47 W
Pop: 67,265 (1990); 70,794 (1980)   Pop Density: 6530.6
Land: 10.3 sq. mi.; Water: 2.9 sq. mi.   Elev: 94 ft.

In southeastern NY on Long Island Sound, 16 mi. northeast
of New York City. Settled 1688 by a small group of Huguenot
refugees.

Name origin: For La Rochelle, France, former home of early
settlers.

North Castle   Town
ZIP: 10504   Lat: 41-08-03 N Long: 73-41-55 W
Pop: 10,061 (1990)   Pop Density: 417.5
Land: 24.1 sq. mi.; Water: 2.4 sq. mi.

North Salem   Town
ZIP: 10560   Lat: 41-19-57 N Long: 73-36-22 W
Pop: 4,725 (1990)   Pop Density: 220.8
Land: 21.4 sq. mi.; Water: 1.5 sq. mi.

North Tarrytown   Village
ZIP: 10591   Lat: 41-05-30 N Long: 73-52-16 W
Pop: 8,152 (1990); 7,994 (1980)   Pop Density: 3544.3
Land: 2.3 sq. mi.; Water: 2.6 sq. mi.

Ossining   Town
ZIP: 10562   Lat: 41-09-14 N Long: 73-51-31 W
Pop: 34,124 (1990)   Pop Density: 2916.6
Land: 11.7 sq. mi.; Water: 3.9 sq. mi.

*Ossining   Village
ZIP: 10562   Lat: 41-09-30 N Long: 73-52-17 W
Pop: 22,582 (1990); 20,196 (1980)   Pop Density: 7056.9
Land: 3.2 sq. mi.; Water: 3.1 sq. mi.

On the eastern bank of the Hudson River, north of White
Plains. Site of Sing Sing prison. Incorporated as city 1813.
Not coextensive with the town of the same name.

Name origin: From an Ojibway Indian term *ossinee* 'stones.'
Earlier names were Hunter's Landing and Sing Sing.

Peach Lake   CDP
                    Lat: 41-21-34 N Long: 73-34-24 W
Pop: 539 (1990); 466 (1980)   Pop Density: 770.0
Land: 0.7 sq. mi.; Water: 0.2 sq. mi.

Part of the town is also in Putnam County.

Peekskill   City
ZIP: 10566   Lat: 41-17-21 N Long: 73-55-25 W
Pop: 19,536 (1990); 18,236 (1980)   Pop Density: 4543.3
Land: 4.3 sq. mi.; Water: 1.2 sq. mi.

In southeastern NY on the east bank of the Hudson River, 39
mi. north of New York City.

Name origin: For Peeck's Kill, the creek along the city's
northern boundary, named for Jan Peeck, a Dutch trader
who settled on its bank.

Pelham   Town
ZIP: 10803   Lat: 40-53-57 N Long: 73-48-22 W
Pop: 11,903 (1990)   Pop Density: 5410.5
Land: 2.2 sq. mi.; Water: 0.1 sq. mi.

*Pelham   Village
ZIP: 10803   Lat: 40-54-39 N Long: 73-48-29 W
Pop: 6,413 (1990); 6,848 (1980)   Pop Density: 8016.3
Land: 0.8 sq. mi.; Water: 0.0 sq. mi.

In southeastern NY, 17 mi. northeast of New York City. Not
coextensive with the town of the same name.

Name origin: For Thomas Pell, who in 1664 purchased from
the Siwanoy Indians the land on which the townsite was
built.

Pelham Manor   Village
ZIP: 10803   Lat: 40-53-37 N Long: 73-48-18 W
Pop: 5,443 (1990); 6,130 (1980)   Pop Density: 4186.9
Land: 1.3 sq. mi.; Water: 0.1 sq. mi.

Pleasantville   Village
ZIP: 10570   Lat: 41-08-17 N Long: 73-47-04 W
Pop: 6,592 (1990); 6,749 (1980)   Pop Density: 3662.2
Land: 1.8 sq. mi.; Water: 0.0 sq. mi.   Elev: 304 ft.

In southeastern NY, 30 mi. north-northeast of New York
City.

Name origin: Descriptively named by its settlers.

Port Chester   Village
ZIP: 10573   Lat: 41-00-16 N Long: 73-40-03 W
Pop: 24,728 (1990); 23,565 (1980)   Pop Density: 10303.3
Land: 2.4 sq. mi.; Water: 0.1 sq. mi.

In southeastern NY on Long Island Sound, 25 mi. northeast
of New York City. Settled c. 1650.

Name origin: For being the port of West Chester. Originally
known as Saw Log Swamp and Sawpits.

Pound Ridge   Town
ZIP: 10576   Lat: 41-12-58 N Long: 73-34-35 W
Pop: 4,550 (1990)   Pop Density: 199.6
Land: 22.8 sq. mi.; Water: 0.7 sq. mi.

Rye   Town
ZIP: 10580   Lat: 41-00-21 N Long: 73-41-18 W
Pop: 39,524 (1990)   Pop Density: 5646.3
Land: 7.0 sq. mi.; Water: 0.5 sq. mi.

*Rye   City
ZIP: 10580   Lat: 40-57-10 N Long: 73-41-01 W
Pop: 14,936 (1990); 15,083 (1980)   Pop Density: 2575.2
Land: 5.8 sq. mi.; Water: 14.2 sq. mi.

In southeastern NY on Long Island Sound, 24 mi. northeast
of New York City. Settled 1660; incorporated 1942.

Name origin: For Rye, England, former home of John Budd,
delegate to the General Court in Hartford.

Rye Brook
Village

ZIP: 10573   **Lat:** 41-01-49 N   **Long:** 73-41-11 W
Pop: 7,765 (1990)   **Pop Density:** 2218.6
Land: 3.5 sq. mi.; **Water:** 0.0 sq. mi.

Scarsdale
Village & Town

ZIP: 10583   **Lat:** 40-59-18 N   **Long:** 73-46-35 W
Pop: 16,987 (1990); 17,650 (1980)   **Pop Density:** 2573.8
Land: 6.6 sq. mi.; **Water:** 0.0 sq. mi.

In southeastern NY, 20 mi. northeast of New York City. Town incorporated in 1701. Village incorporated in 1916. Village and town are coterminous and are administered by a single government.

Name origin: For the Manor of Scarsdale, established by Caleb Heathcote in 1701 and named for his birthplace of Scarsdale, Derbyshire, England.

Somers
Town

ZIP: 10589   **Lat:** 41-18-29 N   **Long:** 73-43-35 W
Pop: 16,216 (1990)   **Pop Density:** 540.5
Land: 30.0 sq. mi.; **Water:** 2.2 sq. mi.

In southeastern NY, about 5 mi. west of the CT border.

Name origin: For Capt. Richard Somers, a naval hero of the Tripolitan War. Pronounced "summers" to differentiate it from a town with the same name in Rensselaer County.

Tarrytown
Village

ZIP: 10591   **Lat:** 41-03-53 N   **Long:** 73-52-07 W
Pop: 10,739 (1990); 10,648 (1980)   **Pop Density:** 3579.7
Land: 3.0 sq. mi.; **Water:** 2.7 sq. mi.

In southeastern NY on the Hudson River, 24 mi. north of New York City. Settled in the 1680s; incorporated as a village in 1870.

Name origin: Origin of the name is debatable, but most likely it is from Dutch *Tarwe dorp* 'wheat town,' since much wheat was grown, milled, and exported from here.

Thornwood
CDP

ZIP: 10594   **Lat:** 41-06-49 N   **Long:** 73-45-53 W
Pop: 7,025 (1990); 7,197 (1980)   **Pop Density:** 1596.6
Land: 4.4 sq. mi.; **Water:** 0.8 sq. mi.

Tuckahoe
Village

ZIP: 10707   **Lat:** 40-57-09 N   **Long:** 73-49-23 W
Pop: 6,302 (1990); 6,076 (1980)   **Pop Density:** 10503.3
Land: 0.6 sq. mi.; **Water:** 0.0 sq. mi.

In southeastern NY, 18 mi. north-northeast of New York City. Incorporated as a village in 1903.

Name origin: From an Indian term probably meaning 'place

of the tuckah,' the root of the golden club, an aquatic plant roasted and ground into flour by the Indians.

White Plains
City

ZIP: 10601   **Lat:** 41-01-15 N   **Long:** 73-45-26 W
Pop: 48,718 (1990); 46,999 (1980)   **Pop Density:** 4971.2
Land: 9.8 sq. mi.; **Water:** 0.1 sq. mi.

In southeastern NY on the west bank of the Hudson River, 25 mi. northeast of New York City. Village created 1866; incorporated as a city 1916.

Name origin: A euphemistic translation of the Indian name for the area *Qua-ro-pas* 'white marshes.'

Yonkers
City

ZIP: 10701   **Lat:** 40-56-49 N   **Long:** 73-52-03 W
Pop: 188,082 (1990); 195,351 (1980)   **Pop Density:** 10391.3
Land: 18.1 sq. mi.; **Water:** 2.3 sq. mi.

In southeastern NY on the Hudson River, a northeastern suburb of New York City. Manufacturing city: chemicals, corn syrup and molasses, electronic parts for air- and space-craft.

Name origin: From Dutch *jonker* meaning 'his young lordship.' An Indian village, Nappeckamack, stood on the site of Yonkers, which was part of the Kekeskick Purchase (1639) made by the Dutch West India Company from the Indians. The city site was included in a grant of land made in 1646 by the company to Adriaen Cornelissen Van der Donck, the first lawyer and first historian of New Netherland. By reason of his wealth and social position Van der Donck enjoyed the courtesy title of *jonker*.

Yorktown
Town

ZIP: 10598   **Lat:** 41-16-10 N   **Long:** 73-48-24 W
Pop: 33,467 (1990)   **Pop Density:** 911.9
Land: 36.7 sq. mi.; **Water:** 2.6 sq. mi.

Yorktown Heights
CDP

ZIP: 10598   **Lat:** 41-16-16 N   **Long:** 73-46-57 W
Pop: 7,690 (1990); 7,696 (1980)   **Pop Density:** 1349.1
Land: 5.7 sq. mi.; **Water:** 0.0 sq. mi.

Wyoming County
County Seat: Warsaw (ZIP: 14569)

Pop: 42,507 (1990); 39,895 (1980)   **Pop Density: 71.7**
Land: 593.0 sq. mi.; **Water:** 3.5 sq. mi.   **Area Code: 716**

In northwestern NY, southeast of Buffalo; organized May 19, 1841 from Genesee County.

Name origin: From an Indian word *maughwauwame* 'large meadows,' originally applied to a valley in northeastern PA, but made famous in the popular poem "Gertrude of Wyoming," published in 1809 by British poet Thomas Campbell (1777–1844).

Arcade   Town
ZIP: 14009   Lat: 42-33-26 N Long: 78-23-19 W
Pop: 3,938 (1990)   Pop Density: 83.6
Land: 47.1 sq. mi.; **Water:** 0.1 sq. mi.

*Arcade   Village
ZIP: 14009   Lat: 42-32-00 N Long: 78-25-59 W
Pop: 2,081 (1990); 2,052 (1980)   Pop Density: 832.4
Land: 2.5 sq. mi.; **Water:** 0.0 sq. mi.
Not coextensive with the town of the same name.

Attica   Town
ZIP: 14011   Lat: 42-49-53 N Long: 78-14-59 W
Pop: 7,383 (1990)   Pop Density: 206.8
Land: 35.7 sq. mi.; **Water:** 0.3 sq. mi.

*Attica   Village
ZIP: 14011   Lat: 42-51-48 N Long: 78-16-56 W
Pop: 2,622 (1990); 2,643 (1980)   Pop Density: 1748.0
Land: 1.5 sq. mi.; **Water:** 0.0 sq. mi.
In northwestern NY. Site of the Attica Correctional Facility. Part of the village is in Genesee County. Not coextensive with the town of the same name.
Name origin: For the district in ancient Greece.

Bennington   Town
Lat: 42-49-51 N Long: 78-23-56 W
Pop: 3,046 (1990)   Pop Density: 55.3
Land: 55.1 sq. mi.; **Water:** 0.2 sq. mi.

Castile   Town
ZIP: 14427   Lat: 42-39-42 N Long: 78-01-22 W
Pop: 3,042 (1990)   Pop Density: 82.2
Land: 37.0 sq. mi.; **Water:** 1.4 sq. mi.

*Castile   Village
ZIP: 14427   Lat: 42-37-51 N Long: 78-03-09 W
Pop: 1,078 (1990); 1,135 (1980)   Pop Density: 770.0
Land: 1.4 sq. mi.; **Water:** 0.0 sq. mi.
Not coextensive with the town of the same name.

Covington   Town
Lat: 42-50-23 N Long: 78-00-41 W
Pop: 1,266 (1990)   Pop Density: 48.5
Land: 26.1 sq. mi.; **Water:** 0.0 sq. mi.

Eagle   Town
Lat: 42-34-15 N Long: 78-15-00 W
Pop: 1,155 (1990)   Pop Density: 31.7
Land: 36.4 sq. mi.; **Water:** 0.1 sq. mi.

Gainesville   Town
ZIP: 14066   Lat: 42-39-10 N Long: 78-08-06 W
Pop: 2,288 (1990)   Pop Density: 64.3
Land: 35.6 sq. mi.; **Water:** 0.1 sq. mi.

*Gainesville   Village
ZIP: 14066   Lat: 42-38-26 N Long: 78-08-06 W
Pop: 340 (1990); 334 (1980)   Pop Density: 377.8
Land: 0.9 sq. mi.; **Water:** 0.0 sq. mi.
Not coextensive with the town of the same name.

Genesee Falls   Town
Lat: 42-34-02 N Long: 78-03-35 W
Pop: 488 (1990)   Pop Density: 31.5
Land: 15.5 sq. mi.; **Water:** 0.2 sq. mi.

Java   Town
Lat: 42-38-58 N Long: 78-23-14 W
Pop: 2,197 (1990)   Pop Density: 46.6
Land: 47.1 sq. mi.; **Water:** 0.2 sq. mi.

Middlebury   Town
Lat: 42-49-28 N Long: 78-08-04 W
Pop: 1,532 (1990)   Pop Density: 42.9
Land: 35.7 sq. mi.; **Water:** 0.0 sq. mi.

Orangeville   Town
Lat: 42-44-31 N Long: 78-14-37 W
Pop: 1,115 (1990)   Pop Density: 31.3
Land: 35.6 sq. mi.; **Water:** 0.1 sq. mi.

Perry   Town
ZIP: 14530   Lat: 42-45-31 N Long: 78-00-53 W
Pop: 5,353 (1990)   Pop Density: 147.1
Land: 36.4 sq. mi.; **Water:** 0.2 sq. mi.

*Perry   Village
ZIP: 14530   Lat: 42-43-02 N Long: 78-00-24 W
Pop: 4,219 (1990); 317 (1980)   Pop Density: 1834.3
Land: 2.3 sq. mi.; **Water:** 0.1 sq. mi.   **Elev:** 1363 ft.
In western NY, 37 mi. southeast of Rochester. Not coextensive with the town of the same name.
Name origin: For naval hero Oliver Hazard Perry (1785–1819).

Pike   Town
Lat: 42-33-57 N Long: 78-08-14 W
Pop: 1,081 (1990)   Pop Density: 34.8
Land: 31.1 sq. mi.; **Water:** 0.1 sq. mi.

*Pike   Village
ZIP: 14130   Lat: 42-33-21 N Long: 78-09-15 W
Pop: 384 (1990); 367 (1980)   Pop Density: 384.0
Land: 1.0 sq. mi.; **Water:** 0.0 sq. mi.   **Elev:** 1551 ft.
Not coextensive with the town of the same name.

Sheldon   Town
ZIP: 14145   Lat: 42-44-38 N Long: 78-22-34 W
Pop: 2,487 (1990)   Pop Density: 52.6
Land: 47.3 sq. mi.; **Water:** 0.0 sq. mi.

Silver Springs
Village
ZIP: 14550   Lat: 42-39-36 N Long: 78-05-05 W
Pop: 852 (1990); 801 (1980)   Pop Density: 946.7
Land: 0.9 sq. mi.; Water: 0.0 sq. mi.

Warsaw
Town
ZIP: 14569   Lat: 42-44-22 N Long: 78-07-54 W
Pop: 5,342 (1990)   Pop Density: 150.9
Land: 35.4 sq. mi.; Water: 0.0 sq. mi.

*Warsaw
Village
ZIP: 14569   Lat: 42-44-29 N Long: 78-08-27 W
Pop: 3,830 (1990); 3,619 (1980)   Pop Density: 934.1
Land: 4.1 sq. mi.; Water: 0.0 sq. mi.

Not coextensive with the town of the same name.

Name origin: For the capital of Poland.

Wethersfield
Town
Lat: 42-39-14 N Long: 78-14-51 W
Pop: 794 (1990)   Pop Density: 22.2
Land: 35.8 sq. mi.; Water: 0.3 sq. mi.

Wyoming
Village
ZIP: 14591   Lat: 42-49-30 N Long: 78-05-07 W
Pop: 478 (1990); 507 (1980)   Pop Density: 682.9
Land: 0.7 sq. mi.; Water: 0.0 sq. mi.   Elev: 991 ft.

In northwestern NY, 30 mi. southwest of Batavia.

Name origin: From an Indian term possibly meaning 'large meadows.'

Yates County
County Seat: Penn Yan (ZIP: 14527)

Pop: 22,810 (1990); 21,459 (1980)   Pop Density: 67.4
Land: 338.2 sq. mi.; Water: 33.6 sq. mi.   Area Code: 315

In northwestern NY, southeast of Rochester; organized Feb 5, 1823 from Ontario County.

Name origin: For Joseph Christopher Yates (1768–1837), NY supreme court justice (1808–22) and governor (1823–24) at the time of the county's creation.

Barrington
Town
Lat: 42-31-14 N Long: 77-03-13 W
Pop: 1,195 (1990)   Pop Density: 33.5
Land: 35.7 sq. mi.; Water: 1.4 sq. mi.

Benton
Town
Lat: 42-43-19 N Long: 77-02-58 W
Pop: 2,380 (1990)   Pop Density: 57.3
Land: 41.5 sq. mi.; Water: 3.0 sq. mi.

Dresden
Village
ZIP: 14441   Lat: 42-40-59 N Long: 76-57-24 W
Pop: 339 (1990); 378 (1980)   Pop Density: 1130.0
Land: 0.3 sq. mi.; Water: 0.0 sq. mi.

Dundee
Village
ZIP: 14837   Lat: 42-31-24 N Long: 76-58-41 W
Pop: 1,588 (1990); 1,556 (1980)   Pop Density: 1443.6
Land: 1.1 sq. mi.; Water: 0.0 sq. mi.   Elev: 994 ft.

Italy
Town
Lat: 42-37-08 N Long: 77-18-38 W
Pop: 1,120 (1990)   Pop Density: 27.9
Land: 40.2 sq. mi.; Water: 0.1 sq. mi.

Name origin: For the European country.

Jerusalem
Town
Lat: 42-36-41 N Long: 77-09-30 W
Pop: 3,784 (1990)   Pop Density: 64.2
Land: 58.9 sq. mi.; Water: 6.5 sq. mi.

Name origin: For the biblical city.

Middlesex
Town
ZIP: 14507   Lat: 42-43-04 N Long: 77-17-22 W
Pop: 1,249 (1990)   Pop Density: 40.4
Land: 30.9 sq. mi.; Water: 3.2 sq. mi.

Name origin: For the English county.

Milo
Town
ZIP: 14527   Lat: 42-37-07 N Long: 77-00-06 W
Pop: 7,023 (1990)   Pop Density: 182.9
Land: 38.4 sq. mi.; Water: 5.9 sq. mi.

Penn Yan
Village
ZIP: 14527   Lat: 42-39-40 N Long: 77-03-17 W
Pop: 5,248 (1990); 410 (1980)   Pop Density: 2499.0
Land: 2.1 sq. mi.; Water: 0.1 sq. mi.   Elev: 737 ft.

In western NY at the outlet of Lake Keuka, 30 mi. southwest of Auburn.

Name origin: A controversy between the settlers from PA and those from New England over a name for the place was compromised by combining the first syllables of PA and Yankee.

Potter
Town
Lat: 42-42-47 N Long: 77-10-53 W
Pop: 1,617 (1990)   Pop Density: 43.5
Land: 37.2 sq. mi.; Water: 0.0 sq. mi.

Rushville
Village
ZIP: 14544   Lat: 42-45-30 N Long: 77-13-35 W
Pop: 408 (1990); 400 (1980)   Pop Density: 1360.0
Land: 0.3 sq. mi.; Water: 0.0 sq. mi.

Part of the town is also in Ontario County.

Starkey
Town
Lat: 42-31-25 N Long: 76-57-00 W
Pop: 3,173 (1990)   Pop Density: 96.7
Land: 32.8 sq. mi.; Water: 2.5 sq. mi.

Torrey
Town
Lat: 42-40-36 N Long: 76-57-16 W
Pop: 1,269 (1990)   Pop Density: 55.9
Land: 22.7 sq. mi.; Water: 11.0 sq. mi.

Index to Places and Counties in New York

Pennsylvania

PENNSYLVANIA

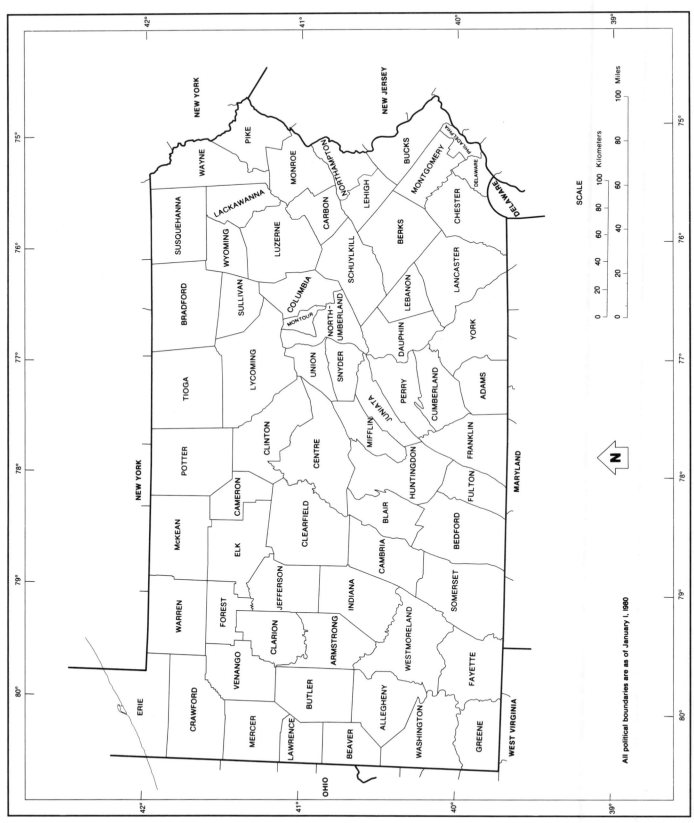

All political boundaries are as of January 1, 1980

SCALE

Kilometers

Miles

Pennsylvania

Population: 11,881,643 (1990); 11,863,895 (1980)
Population rank (1990): 5
Percent population change (1980-1990): 0.1
Population projection: 12,070,000 (1995);
12,073,000 (2000)

Area: total 46,058 sq. mi.; 44,820 sq. mi. land, 1,239 sq. mi. water
Area rank: 33
Highest elevation: 3,213 ft., Mount Davis (Markleton County)
Lowest point: sea level along the Delaware River (Delaware County)

State capital: Harrisburg (Dauphin County)
Largest city: Philadelphia (1,585,577)
Second largest city: Pittsburgh (369,879)
Largest county: Philadelphia (1,585,577)

Total housing units: 4,938,140
No. of occupied housing units: 4,495,966
Vacant housing units (%): 9.0
Distribution of population by race & Hispanic origin (%):
White: 88.5
Black: 9.2
Hispanic (any race): 2.0
Native American: 0.1
Asian/Pacific: 1.2
Other: 1.0

Admission date: December 12, 1787 (2nd state).

Location: In the northeastern United States, bordering Delaware, Maryland, West Virginia, Ohio, Lake Erie, New York, and New Jersey. One of the thirteen original English colonies.

Name Origin: Named in 1681 by Charles II of England for Admiral Sir William Penn (1621-70), father of William Penn (1644-1718), founder of Pennsylvania; a combination of Penn + sylvania from Latin *silva* 'forest, woodlands'; thus, 'Penn's woods.'

State animal: white-tailed deer *(Odocoileus virginianus)*
State beverage: milk
State bird: ruffed grouse *(Bonasa umbellus)*
State dog: Great Dane
State fish: brook trout *(Salvelinus fontinalis)*
State flagship: U.S. Brig Niagara
State flower: mountain laurel *(Kalmia latifolia)*
State fossil: Phacops rana
State insect: firefly *(Photuris pennsylvanica)*
State plant: Penngift crownvetch *(Coronilla varia)*
State tree: eastern hemlock *(Tsuga canadensis)*

State motto: Virtue, Liberty, and Independence
State nickname: Keystone State; Quaker State

Area codes: 215 (Philadelphia), 412 (Pittsburgh), 717 (Harrisburg), 814 (Altoona)
Time zone: Eastern
Abbreviations: PA (postal); Pa., Penn., Penna. (traditional)
Part of (region): Northeast; Middle Atlantic

Local Government

Counties

Pennsylvania has 67 counties. Philadelphia County is coterminous with the consolidated city of Philadelphia.

Municipalities

Other forms of local government include 52 cities, 968 boroughs, 1550 townships, and one incorporated town. In addition, there are 501 autonomous local school districts.

Settlement History and Early Development

Much of the area now officially called the Commonwealth of Pennsylvania was originally inhabited by the Erie, Monongahela, Susquehannock, and Delaware (also called Lenni Lenape) Indians. There is evidence of farming in the region some 3,000 years before the first Europeans arrived.

Beginning about 1608, the English, French, and Dutch explored from Delaware Bay north up the Delaware River to the Schuylkill River, and inland from the headwaters of the Susquehanna River to its mouth in Chesapeake Bay, establishing trading posts and forts. But Swedish settlers organized the first permanent European settlement in 1643 on Tinicum Island, across the Schuylkill River from the Dutch Fort Nassau, near the present-day site of Philadelphia. In 1651, Peter Stuyvesant, director of the Dutch colony of New Netherlands, built Fort Casimir south of the Swedish settlement at Wilmington, Delaware, and gained control of the Delaware River. In 1654, the Swedes accepted the surrender of the fort; later in the year they surrendered Fort Christina at Wilmington to the Dutch, and Stuyvesant became governor of Pennsylvania.

On March 22, 1664, King Charles II of England granted all lands from the west side of the Connecticut River to the east side of Delaware Bay (present-day New York and New Jersey), plus the lands to the west, to his brother, James, Duke of York and Albany. On August 18, 1664, the English under Col. Richard Nicolls accepted Stuyvesant's surrender of New Netherlands and Nicholls became the first English governor.

Fortunately, each change of power from one country to another was bloodless and the lives of the settlers were not affected. When the Susquehannock Indians lost their battle with the Iroquois Confederacy and were dispersed, European settlers were free to expand inland.

The Duke of York controlled the region until 1681 when King Charles II granted a large tract of land to William Penn, a Quaker. Penn arrived from England in 1682 with the colony's first constitution, the Frame of Government. He founded Philadelphia (Greek 'brotherly love') in the same year as a "greene countrie towne" and planned it to be a center of religious freedom. It became the capital of Pennsylvania Colony the following year and was incorporated as a city in 1701. He also voluntarily paid the Indians for most of the land in his grant. In 1701 he granted a new constitution, the Charter of Privileges, which gave greater control of the government to the people. He died in England in 1718, but his family governed the colony until 1775.

The colony was originally settled by English, Irish, and Welsh Quakers. Their settlements were generally north and west of Philadelphia on the Schuylkill River. German Pietists arrived in 1683, followed by a group of Mennonite Germans, and later German Quakers, most of whom settled in Germantown, northwest of Philadelphia. In 1710, German, Scotch-Irish, and French Huguenot immigrants began arriving, followed in 1719 by German "Dunkards" (German Baptists). The Pennsylvania Dutch (German-born settlers, so named owing to a misuse of *Deutsch* 'German'), who include such religious groups as the Amish, Mennonites, and Dunkards, settled primarily in Lancaster County. Moravians established the city of Bethlehem in 1741 and Nazareth in 1742. The colony and its port, Philadelphia, grew prosperous as the rich Piedmont soil of southeastern Pennsylvania was developed. Philadelphia became the center for shipment of goods and supplies, and the business activity that went along with such commerce.

Significance in United States History

On Sep 5, 1774, the First Continental Congress met in Philadelphia to discuss how to resist the growing taxes and trade restrictions levied on the colonies by Britain. They voted to cease trading with Britain. The Second Continental Congress met again in Philadelphia in May 1775, after the start of the Revolutionary War in April of that year in Massachusetts. They voted to become independent from Britain, and on July 4, 1776, the Declaration of Independence was adopted in the Pennsylvania State House (now Independence Hall) in Philadelphia.

After the Revolutionary War, the Constitutional Convention met in Philadelphia from May to September 1787 to draft the U.S. Constitution. Pennsylvania became the second state (after Delaware) to ratify it, on December 12, 1787.

In June-July 1863 the bloodiest battle of the Civil War was fought at Gettysburg in south-central Pennsylvania; it was a major defeat for the Confederacy. Abraham Lincoln's Gettysburg Address was delivered at the ceremony,

November 19, 1863, dedicating part of the battlefield to those who had died there.

Mining and Industry

Large coal deposits had been worked in Pennsylvania since the beginning of the eighteenth century, and steel had been manufactured since 1732. The anthracite of eastern Pennsylvania became an important heating fuel in the U.S. in the 1800s. Later, softer bituminous coal was found in vast supply in western Pennsylvania. Processed into coke to fuel iron and steel furnaces, this coal was the key to development of the region as a mining and iron and steel center, with Pittsburgh as its hub.

In 1859 Edwin Drake drilled the first commercially successful oil well in western Pennsylvania near Titusville. In the late nineteenth century Pennsylvania petroleum was an important source of kerosene (used as fuel for lamps), and of lubricants for machinery. Lumber from north Pennsylvania forests became a major source of building materials in the latter part of the nineteenth century.

Industrial growth continued into the early 1900s and expanded further during World War I. The adverse effects of the Great Depression were alleviated by World War II when the state's industries produced huge quantities of cement, clothing, coal, petroleum, ships, steel, and weapons. But during the 1950s foreign competition caused coal production to fall sharply, and textile mills were either automated or moved south, resulting in a large loss of jobs. Pittsburgh, once an important center of steel manufacturing, saw the decline of this industry to near non-existence. Recently, however, both Philadelphia and Pittsburgh have revitalized themselves, and as centers of industry are now the headquarters for many corporations. The state is shifting to educational, financial, and other service industries, while restoring historic sites and buildings to attract both new investment and tourism.

State Boundaries

William Penn's charter established Pennsylvania colony's eastern boundary as the Delaware River, from a point 12 miles upriver from New Castle, Delaware to "43 degrees north latitude, [actually the 42nd parallel] to extend westward five degrees in longitude," and the southern border to be decided by drawing the circumference of a circle in a 12-mile radius from New Castle (note present northern border of Delaware). The circle was to touch the 39th parallel, which it failed to do; it also extended into the claims of Lord Baltimore and the Duke of York. In 1701 Penn granted rights to the "Lower Counties" of New Castle, Sussex, and Kent (now Delaware) to function as a separate government. But boundary disputes continued until July 4, 1760 when the Pennsylvania-Maryland-Delaware border was established on a line 15 miles south of Philadelphia, and running west from the circumference of the 12-mile circle drawn from New Castle. A resurvey in 1892-93 refined the Pennsylvania-Delaware boundary, which was formally accepted by the latter on March 28, 1921.

The grant also included a large tract in the northeastern part of present-day Pennsylvania, known as the Wyoming Valley. Connecticut claimed this land under its charter of 1662 and in 1776 organized it as Westmoreland County.

After many years of dispute and a few battles, the Continental Congress awarded it to Pennsylvania in 1782.

In 1737, surveyors claimed all the land from Wrightstown in Bucks County, to almost the northeastern border of present-day Pike County. Further treaties with the Indians granted the colony land farther west to the forks of the Ohio River, almost to present-day Pittsburgh, and settlers kept pushing farther west into other land claimed by Connecticut (the east bank of the Susquehanna River in present-day Wyoming County and all of northern Pennsylvania above the 41st parallel).

The first surveys to divide U.S. public lands into ranges and townships began at the marker established in 1785 on the north bank of the Ohio River on the western boundary of Pennsylvania, known as "the point of beginning." The original marker disappeared and was replaced by a large granite monument in 1881.

The Mason-Dixon Line

In 1763, in order to settle their boundary dispute, Pennsylvania and Maryland hired two English astronomers, Charles Mason and Jeremiah Dixon, to survey the land. The survey, completed in 1767, established the Mason-Dixon line, the traditional border between Northern and Southern states. The Mason-Dixon survey also established the east-west border between what is now Delaware and Maryland, and the north-south boundary of Pennsylvania with present-day Maryland and West Virginia.

A meridian drawn from the western end of the Mason-Dixon line north to Lake Erie completed Pennsylvania's western border with Ohio and West Virginia in 1786. In 1789, the Pennsylvania Assembly ratified the 42nd parallel as the northern boundary of the state (ratified by New York's legislature in 1829). The Erie Triangle, ceded to the U.S. by New York, was bought by Pennsylvania in March 1792, giving the state direct access to Lake Erie.

Counties

Adams	Chester	Fulton	McKean	Snyder
Allegheny	Clarion	Greene	Mercer	Somerset
Armstrong	Clearfield	Huntingdon	Mifflin	Sullivan
Beaver	Clinton	Indiana	Monroe	Susquehanna
Bedford	Columbia	Jefferson	Montgomery	Tioga
Berks	Crawford	Juniata	Montour	Union
Blair	Cumberland	Lackawanna	Northampton	Venango
Bradford	Dauphin	Lancaster	Northumber-	Warren
Bucks	Delaware	Lawrence	land	Washington
Butler	Elk	Lebanon	Perry	Wayne
Cambria	Erie	Lehigh	Philadelphia	Westmoreland
Cameron	Fayette	Luzerne	Pike	Wyoming
Carbon	Forest	Lycoming	Potter	York
Centre	Franklin		Schuylkill	

Multi-County Places

The following places are in more than one county. Given here is the total population for each multi-county place, and the names of the counties it is in.

Adamstown, pop. 1,108; Lancaster (1,108), Berks (0)
Ardmore, pop. 12,646; Montgomery (7,325), Delaware (5,321)
Ashland, pop. 3,859; Schuylkill (3,856), Columbia (3)
Bethlehem, pop. 71,428; Northampton (52,561), Lehigh (18,867)
Ellwood City, pop. 8,894; Lawrence (8,044), Beaver (850)
Emlenton, pop. 834; Venango (824), Clarion (10)
Falls Creek, pop. 1,087; Jefferson (1,033), Clearfield (54)
Lynnwood-Pricedale, pop. 2,664; Westmoreland (1,598), Fayette (1,066)
McDonald, pop. 2,252; Washington (1,809), Allegheny (443)
Seven Springs, pop. 22; Somerset (22), Fayette (0)
Shippensburg, pop. 5,331; Cumberland (4,328), Franklin (1,003)
Telford, pop. 4,238; Montgomery (2,565), Bucks (1,673)
Trafford, pop. 3,345; Westmoreland (3,255), Allegheny (90)
Tunnelhill, pop. 365; Cambria (259), Blair (106)

Adams County
County Seat: Gettysburg (ZIP: 17325)

Pop: 78,274 (1990); 68,292 (1980) **Pop Density:** 150.5
Land: 520.1 sq. mi.; **Water:** 1.5 sq. mi. **Area Code:** 717

On central southern border of PA, southwest of Harrisburg; organized Jan 22, 1800 from York County.

Name origin: For John Adams (1735–1826), second U.S. president.

Abbottstown
Borough
ZIP: 17301 **Lat:** 39-53-04 N **Long:** 76-59-22 W
Pop: 539 (1990); 689 (1980) **Pop Density:** 898.3
Land: 0.6 sq. mi.; **Water:** 0.0 sq. mi. **Elev:** 549 ft.
In southern PA on Beaver Creek.

Arendtsville
Borough
ZIP: 17303 **Lat:** 39-55-29 N **Long:** 77-18-04 W
Pop: 693 (1990); 600 (1980) **Pop Density:** 990.0
Land: 0.7 sq. mi.; **Water:** 0.0 sq. mi. **Elev:** 711 ft.

Bendersville
Borough
ZIP: 17306 **Lat:** 39-58-56 N **Long:** 77-14-59 W
Pop: 560 (1990); 533 (1980) **Pop Density:** 1400.0
Land: 0.4 sq. mi.; **Water:** 0.0 sq. mi. **Elev:** 760 ft.
In southern PA.

Berwick
Township
Lat: 39-51-43 N **Long:** 76-59-03 W
Pop: 1,831 (1990); 1,492 (1980) **Pop Density:** 237.8
Land: 7.7 sq. mi.; **Water:** 0.0 sq. mi.

Biglerville
Borough
ZIP: 17307 **Lat:** 39-55-48 N **Long:** 77-14-50 W
Pop: 993 (1990); 991 (1980) **Pop Density:** 1655.0
Land: 0.6 sq. mi.; **Water:** 0.0 sq. mi. **Elev:** 636 ft.
In southern PA, 7 mi. north of Gettysburg. Surveyed 1817.

Bonneauville
Borough
ZIP: 17325 **Lat:** 39-48-41 N **Long:** 77-08-12 W
Pop: 1,282 (1990); 920 (1980) **Pop Density:** 1282.0
Land: 1.0 sq. mi.; **Water:** 0.0 sq. mi. **Elev:** 558 ft.

Butler
Township
Lat: 39-55-40 N **Long:** 77-13-51 W
Pop: 2,514 (1990); 2,166 (1980) **Pop Density:** 104.8
Land: 24.0 sq. mi.; **Water:** 0.0 sq. mi.

Carroll Valley
Borough
ZIP: 17320 **Lat:** 39-45-02 N **Long:** 77-22-51 W
Pop: 1,457 (1990); 817 (1980) **Pop Density:** 269.8
Land: 5.4 sq. mi.; **Water:** 0.1 sq. mi.

Conewago
Township
Lat: 39-47-48 N **Long:** 77-01-22 W
Pop: 4,532 (1990); 3,405 (1980) **Pop Density:** 431.6
Land: 10.5 sq. mi.; **Water:** 0.0 sq. mi.
For Conewago Creek, which runs through the county.
Name origin: An Indian term possibly meaning 'at the rapids.'

Cumberland
Township
ZIP: 17325 **Lat:** 39-48-05 N **Long:** 77-14-56 W
Pop: 5,431 (1990); 4,637 (1980) **Pop Density:** 162.6
Land: 33.4 sq. mi.; **Water:** 0.1 sq. mi.

East Berlin
Borough
ZIP: 17316 **Lat:** 39-56-12 N **Long:** 76-58-49 W
Pop: 1,175 (1990); 1,054 (1980) **Pop Density:** 1678.6
Land: 0.7 sq. mi.; **Water:** 0.0 sq. mi. **Elev:** 420 ft.
In southern PA along the Conewago Creek, west of York.
Name origin: Named by German settlers for the capital of Germany.

Fairfield
Borough
ZIP: 17320 **Lat:** 39-47-15 N **Long:** 77-22-09 W
Pop: 524 (1990); 591 (1980) **Pop Density:** 748.6
Land: 0.7 sq. mi.; **Water:** 0.0 sq. mi. **Elev:** 600 ft.
In southern PA in a hilly, densely forested area, 8 mi. southwest of Gettysburg.

Franklin
Township
Lat: 39-54-24 N **Long:** 77-22-41 W
Pop: 4,126 (1990); 3,692 (1980) **Pop Density:** 60.2
Land: 68.5 sq. mi.; **Water:** 0.4 sq. mi.

Freedom
Township
Lat: 39-45-04 N **Long:** 77-18-05 W
Pop: 692 (1990); 650 (1980) **Pop Density:** 49.8
Land: 13.9 sq. mi.; **Water:** 0.0 sq. mi.

Germany
Township
Lat: 39-43-58 N **Long:** 77-06-35 W
Pop: 1,949 (1990); 1,652 (1980) **Pop Density:** 178.8
Land: 10.9 sq. mi.; **Water:** 0.0 sq. mi.

Gettysburg
Borough
ZIP: 17325 **Lat:** 39-49-48 N **Long:** 77-14-04 W
Pop: 7,025 (1990); 7,194 (1980) **Pop Density:** 4390.6
Land: 1.6 sq. mi.; **Water:** 0.0 sq. mi. **Elev:** 520 ft.
In southern PA, about 5 mi. north of the MD border. Incorporated Mar 10, 1806.
Name origin: For James Gettys, who bought a tract of land and laid out a village. Previously called Gettys-town. Site of a decisive battle in the Civil War.

Hamilton
Township
Lat: 39-53-58 N **Long:** 77-01-17 W
Pop: 1,760 (1990); 1,692 (1980) **Pop Density:** 128.5
Land: 13.7 sq. mi.; **Water:** 0.0 sq. mi.

Hamiltonban
Township
Lat: 39-48-11 N **Long:** 77-24-52 W
Pop: 1,872 (1990); 1,835 (1980) **Pop Density:** 47.9
Land: 39.1 sq. mi.; **Water:** 0.1 sq. mi.

Highland
Township
Lat: 39-49-23 N **Long:** 77-19-46 W
Pop: 815 (1990); 717 (1980) **Pop Density:** 67.4
Land: 12.1 sq. mi.; **Water:** 0.0 sq. mi.

Huntington
Township
Lat: 40-00-01 N **Long:** 77-08-26 W
Pop: 1,989 (1990); 1,557 (1980)   **Pop Density:** 78.9
Land: 25.2 sq. mi.; **Water:** 0.0 sq. mi.

Latimore
Township
Lat: 40-01-25 N **Long:** 77-05-14 W
Pop: 2,209 (1990); 1,369 (1980)   **Pop Density:** 104.2
Land: 21.2 sq. mi.; **Water:** 0.2 sq. mi.

Liberty
Township
Lat: 39-44-47 N **Long:** 77-21-59 W
Pop: 938 (1990); 823 (1980)   **Pop Density:** 57.9
Land: 16.2 sq. mi.; **Water:** 0.0 sq. mi.

Littlestown
Borough
ZIP: 17340   **Lat:** 39-44-38 N **Long:** 77-05-19 W
Pop: 2,974 (1990); 2,870 (1980)   **Pop Density:** 1858.8
Land: 1.6 sq. mi.; **Water:** 0.0 sq. mi.   **Elev:** 635 ft.
In southern PA. Settled in 1765 by Adam Klein, a German immigrant.
Name origin: Originally referred to as Petersburg and Kleinestaedtel before being translated into present name.

McSherrystown
Borough
ZIP: 17344   **Lat:** 39-48-14 N **Long:** 77-01-10 W
Pop: 2,769 (1990); 2,764 (1980)   **Pop Density:** 5538.0
Land: 0.5 sq. mi.; **Water:** 0.0 sq. mi.   **Elev:** 571 ft.
Name origin: For a settler, Patrick McSherry, who came here in 1765.

Menallen
Township
Lat: 39-58-59 N **Long:** 77-18-40 W
Pop: 2,700 (1990); 2,354 (1980)   **Pop Density:** 63.1
Land: 42.8 sq. mi.; **Water:** 0.1 sq. mi.

Midway
CDP
Lat: 39-48-14 N **Long:** 77-00-18 W
Pop: 2,254 (1990); 1,599 (1980)   **Pop Density:** 3220.0
Land: 0.7 sq. mi.; **Water:** 0.0 sq. mi.

Mount Joy
Township
Lat: 39-45-44 N **Long:** 77-10-58 W
Pop: 2,848 (1990); 2,564 (1980)   **Pop Density:** 110.0
Land: 25.9 sq. mi.; **Water:** 0.2 sq. mi.

Mount Pleasant
Township
Lat: 39-49-27 N **Long:** 77-06-35 W
Pop: 4,076 (1990); 3,473 (1980)   **Pop Density:** 133.2
Land: 30.6 sq. mi.; **Water:** 0.1 sq. mi.

New Oxford
Borough
ZIP: 17350   **Lat:** 39-51-43 N **Long:** 77-03-20 W
Pop: 1,617 (1990); 1,921 (1980)   **Pop Density:** 2695.0
Land: 0.6 sq. mi.; **Water:** 0.0 sq. mi.   **Elev:** 561 ft.
Laid out in 1792.
Name origin: For the English university town.

Oxford
Township
Lat: 39-50-56 N **Long:** 77-02-45 W
Pop: 3,437 (1990); 2,302 (1980)   **Pop Density:** 354.3
Land: 9.7 sq. mi.; **Water:** 0.0 sq. mi.

Reading
Township
Lat: 39-57-02 N **Long:** 77-02-25 W
Pop: 3,828 (1990); 2,660 (1980)   **Pop Density:** 143.9
Land: 26.6 sq. mi.; **Water:** 0.2 sq. mi.

Straban
Township
Lat: 39-52-11 N **Long:** 77-10-14 W
Pop: 4,565 (1990); 4,240 (1980)   **Pop Density:** 132.7
Land: 34.4 sq. mi.; **Water:** 0.0 sq. mi.

Tyrone
Township
Lat: 39-57-28 N **Long:** 77-09-29 W
Pop: 1,829 (1990); 1,534 (1980)   **Pop Density:** 85.1
Land: 21.5 sq. mi.; **Water:** 0.0 sq. mi.

Union
Township
Lat: 39-45-18 N **Long:** 77-03-01 W
Pop: 2,178 (1990); 1,978 (1980)   **Pop Density:** 124.5
Land: 17.5 sq. mi.; **Water:** 0.0 sq. mi.

York Springs
Borough
ZIP: 17372   **Lat:** 40-00-31 N **Long:** 77-06-59 W
Pop: 547 (1990); 556 (1980)   **Pop Density:** 2735.0
Land: 0.2 sq. mi.; **Water:** 0.0 sq. mi.   **Elev:** 600 ft.

Allegheny County
County Seat: Pittsburgh (ZIP: 15219)

Pop: 1,336,450 (1990); 1,450,200 (1980)   **Pop Density:** 1830.2
Land: 730.2 sq. mi.; **Water:** 14.5 sq. mi.   **Area Code:** 412
In southwestern PA; organized Sep 24, 1788 from Westmoreland and Washington counties.
Name origin: For the Allegheny River.

Aleppo
Township
Lat: 40-31-58 N **Long:** 80-08-22 W
Pop: 1,246 (1990); 1,134 (1980)   **Pop Density:** 692.2
Land: 1.8 sq. mi.; **Water:** 0.0 sq. mi.

Aspinwall
Borough
ZIP: 15215   **Lat:** 40-29-32 N **Long:** 79-54-13 W
Pop: 2,880 (1990); 3,284 (1980)   **Pop Density:** 9600.0
Land: 0.3 sq. mi.; **Water:** 0.0 sq. mi.   **Elev:** 750 ft.
In southwestern PA on the Allegheny River. Founded 1796.
Name origin: For the Aspinwall family, early landowners.

Avalon
Borough
ZIP: 15202   **Lat:** 40-30-03 N **Long:** 80-04-07 W
Pop: 5,784 (1990); 6,240 (1980)   **Pop Density:** 9640.0
Land: 0.6 sq. mi.; **Water:** 0.1 sq. mi.   **Elev:** 900 ft.
In southwestern PA, a suburb of Pittsburgh. Settled in the late 1700s by an Irish trader, James Taylor. Incorporated in 1874 as West Bellevue.
Name origin: Railroad station called Birmingham, for Capt. John Birmingham who purchased land from Taylor; incorporated as West Bellevue; and post office named Myler. To

avoid confusion, it was given its present name in 1893. Avalon is the world of the dead in Arthurian legend.

Baldwin
Borough
ZIP: 15234   Lat: 40-21-47 N Long: 79-57-58 W
Pop: 21,923 (1990); 24,598 (1980)   Pop Density: 3779.8
Land: 5.8 sq. mi.; Water: 0.2 sq. mi.   Elev: 1200 ft.
In southwestern PA on the Monongahela River, a southern suburb of Pittsburgh.
Name origin: For Henry Baldwin, PA Supreme Court justice.

*Baldwin
Township
ZIP: 15234   Lat: 40-22-46 N Long: 80-00-57 W
Pop: 2,479 (1990); 2,680 (1980)   Pop Density: 4958.0
Land: 0.5 sq. mi.; Water: 0.0 sq. mi.

Bell Acres
Borough
ZIP: 15143   Lat: 40-35-31 N Long: 80-10-34 W
Pop: 1,436 (1990); 1,307 (1980)   Pop Density: 276.2
Land: 5.2 sq. mi.; Water: 0.0 sq. mi.   Elev: 1180 ft.

Bellevue
Borough
ZIP: 15202   Lat: 40-29-38 N Long: 80-03-21 W
Pop: 9,126 (1990); 10,128 (1980)   Pop Density: 9126.0
Land: 1.0 sq. mi.; Water: 0.1 sq. mi.   Elev: 970 ft.
In southwestern PA on the Ohio River; a suburb of Pittsburgh. Settled 1802; incorporated 1867.
Name origin: From French meaning 'beautiful view.'

Ben Avon
Borough
ZIP: 15202   Lat: 40-30-23 N Long: 80-04-56 W
Pop: 2,096 (1990); 2,314 (1980)   Pop Density: 5240.0
Land: 0.4 sq. mi.; Water: 0.1 sq. mi.   Elev: 800 ft.
In southwestern PA, a suburb to the northwest of Pittsburgh. Incorporated 1891.
Name origin: From a Scottish term meaning 'hill by the waters.'

Ben Avon Heights
Borough
ZIP: 15202   Lat: 40-30-41 N Long: 80-04-22 W
Pop: 373 (1990); 398 (1980)   Pop Density: 1865.0
Land: 0.2 sq. mi.; Water: 0.0 sq. mi.   Elev: 1100 ft.

Bethel Park
Borough
ZIP: 15102   Lat: 40-19-24 N Long: 80-02-09 W
Pop: 33,823 (1990); 34,755 (1980)   Pop Density: 2890.9
Land: 11.7 sq. mi.; Water: 0.0 sq. mi.   Elev: 1250 ft.
In southwestern PA, a suburb of Pittsburgh.

Blawnox
Borough
ZIP: 15238   Lat: 40-29-27 N Long: 79-51-44 W
Pop: 1,626 (1990); 1,653 (1980)   Pop Density: 5420.0
Land: 0.3 sq. mi.; Water: 0.1 sq. mi.   Elev: 740 ft.

Brackenridge
Borough
ZIP: 15014   Lat: 40-36-26 N Long: 79-44-31 W
Pop: 3,784 (1990); 4,297 (1980)   Pop Density: 7568.0
Land: 0.5 sq. mi.; Water: 0.0 sq. mi.   Elev: 916 ft.
In southwestern PA, a northern suburb of Pittsburgh. Incorporated 1901.
Name origin: For the Brackenridge family, prominent in the area during the 19th century.

Braddock
Borough
ZIP: 15104   Lat: 40-24-07 N Long: 79-52-09 W
Pop: 4,682 (1990); 5,634 (1980)   Pop Density: 7803.3
Land: 0.6 sq. mi.; Water: 0.1 sq. mi.   Elev: 825 ft.
In southwestern PA, 10 mi. east of Pittsburgh. Incorporated 1867.
Name origin: For Gen. Edward Braddock (1695–1755), a Revolutionary War officer who was fatally wounded nearby in a battle with the French and Indians in 1755.

Braddock Hills
Borough
ZIP: 15221   Lat: 40-25-00 N Long: 79-51-48 W
Pop: 2,026 (1990); 2,556 (1980)   Pop Density: 2026.0
Land: 1.0 sq. mi.; Water: 0.0 sq. mi.   Elev: 1232 ft.
Name origin: For its location 1 mi. north of Braddock.

Bradfordwoods
Borough
ZIP: 15015   Lat: 40-38-08 N Long: 80-04-49 W
Pop: 1,329 (1990); 1,264 (1980)   Pop Density: 1476.7
Land: 0.9 sq. mi.; Water: 0.0 sq. mi.

Brentwood
Borough
ZIP: 15227   Lat: 40-22-23 N Long: 79-58-33 W
Pop: 10,823 (1990); 11,907 (1980)   Pop Density: 7730.7
Land: 1.4 sq. mi.; Water: 0.0 sq. mi.   Elev: 1255 ft.
In southwestern PA, 5 mi. south of Pittsburgh. Incorporated 1915 when it merged with Whitehall and Point View.

Bridgeville
Borough
ZIP: 15017   Lat: 40-21-23 N Long: 80-06-21 W
Pop: 5,445 (1990); 6,154 (1980)   Pop Density: 4950.0
Land: 1.1 sq. mi.; Water: 0.0 sq. mi.   Elev: 900 ft.

Carnegie
Borough
ZIP: 15106   Lat: 40-24-27 N Long: 80-05-11 W
Pop: 9,278 (1990); 10,099 (1980)   Pop Density: 5457.6
Land: 1.7 sq. mi.; Water: 0.0 sq. mi.   Elev: 770 ft.
In southwestern PA, 6 mi. west of Pittsburgh.
Name origin: For Andrew Carnegie (1835–1919), steel manufacturer and philanthropist.

Carnot-Moon
CDP
ZIP: 15108   Lat: 40-31-06 N Long: 80-12-50 W
Pop: 10,187 (1990); 11,102 (1980)   Pop Density: 2079.0
Land: 4.9 sq. mi.; Water: 0.0 sq. mi.

Castle Shannon
Borough
ZIP: 15234   Lat: 40-21-58 N Long: 80-01-12 W
Pop: 9,135 (1990); 10,164 (1980)   Pop Density: 5709.4
Land: 1.6 sq. mi.; Water: 0.0 sq. mi.   Elev: 1160 ft.
In southwestern PA on Saw Mill Run, 8 mi. south of Pittsburgh.

Chalfant
Borough
ZIP: 15112   Lat: 40-24-35 N Long: 79-50-18 W
Pop: 959 (1990); 1,119 (1980)   Pop Density: 4795.0
Land: 0.2 sq. mi.; Water: 0.0 sq. mi.   Elev: 1100 ft.
In western PA, an eastern suburb of Pittsburgh.

Cheswick
Borough
ZIP: 15024   Lat: 40-32-34 N Long: 79-48-04 W
Pop: 1,971 (1990); 2,336 (1980)   Pop Density: 3942.0
Land: 0.5 sq. mi.; Water: 0.1 sq. mi.   Elev: 770 ft.
In southwestern PA on the Allegheny River, 12 mi. northeast of Pittsburgh.

Churchill
Borough
ZIP: 15221   **Lat:** 40-26-17 N **Long:** 79-50-26 W
Pop: 3,883 (1990); 4,285 (1980)   **Pop Density:** 1765.0
Land: 2.2 sq. mi.; **Water:** 0.0 sq. mi.   **Elev:** 1050 ft.

In southwestern PA, an eastern suburb of Pittsburgh.

Clairton
City
ZIP: 15025   **Lat:** 40-17-47 N **Long:** 79-53-07 W
Pop: 9,656 (1990); 12,188 (1980)   **Pop Density:** 3448.6
Land: 2.8 sq. mi.; **Water:** 0.2 sq. mi.   **Elev:** 900 ft.

In southwestern PA on the Monongahela River, 12 mi. southeast of Pittsburgh.

Name origin: For Samuel Sinclair, who once owned a tract of 215 acres of land on which part of the present city is built.

Collier
Township
Lat: 40-24-04 N **Long:** 80-07-59 W
Pop: 4,841 (1990); 5,063 (1980)   **Pop Density:** 340.9
Land: 14.2 sq. mi.; **Water:** 0.0 sq. mi.

Coraopolis
Borough
ZIP: 15108   **Lat:** 40-30-50 N **Long:** 80-09-43 W
Pop: 6,747 (1990); 7,308 (1980)   **Pop Density:** 5190.0
Land: 1.3 sq. mi.; **Water:** 0.1 sq. mi.   **Elev:** 800 ft.

In southwestern PA, 10 mi. northwest of Pittsburgh. Settled c. 1760.

Name origin: Named for Cora Watson, daughter of an influential citizen. From the Greek *kore* 'a girl' and -*opolis* 'a city.'

Crafton
Borough
ZIP: 15205   **Lat:** 40-25-59 N **Long:** 80-04-15 W
Pop: 7,188 (1990); 7,623 (1980)   **Pop Density:** 6534.5
Land: 1.1 sq. mi.; **Water:** 0.0 sq. mi.   **Elev:** 880 ft.

In southwestern PA on Chartiers Creek, a southeastern suburb of Pittsburgh. Laid out in 1870.

Name origin: For Pittsburgh lawyer James S. Craft, whose son, Charles C. Craft, laid out the town on land he had inherited from his father.

Crescent
Township
Lat: 40-33-25 N **Long:** 80-13-31 W
Pop: 2,490 (1990); 2,862 (1980)   **Pop Density:** 1185.7
Land: 2.1 sq. mi.; **Water:** 0.2 sq. mi.

Curtisville
CDP
Lat: 40-38-55 N **Long:** 79-50-58 W
Pop: 1,285 (1990); 1,404 (1980)   **Pop Density:** 917.9
Land: 1.4 sq. mi.; **Water:** 0.0 sq. mi.

Dormont
Borough
ZIP: 15216   **Lat:** 40-23-34 N **Long:** 80-02-15 W
Pop: 9,772 (1990); 11,275 (1980)   **Pop Density:** 13960.0
Land: 0.7 sq. mi.; **Water:** 0.0 sq. mi.   **Elev:** 1190 ft.

In southwestern PA, a southern suburb of Pittsburgh.

Name origin: Suggested by Gilbert M. Brown, the first burgess of Dormont, from the French term *d'or mont* 'mount of gold,' with reference to the beautiful hills on which the town is built and for the wonderful opportunities that they offered.

Dravosburg
Borough
ZIP: 15034   **Lat:** 40-21-07 N **Long:** 79-53-19 W
Pop: 2,377 (1990); 2,511 (1980)   **Pop Density:** 2377.0
Land: 1.0 sq. mi.; **Water:** 0.1 sq. mi.   **Elev:** 800 ft.

In southwestern PA on the Monongahela River, bordered by Allegheny County airport.

Name origin: For John F. Drava, pioneer coal operator.

Duquesne
City
ZIP: 15110   **Lat:** 40-22-23 N **Long:** 79-51-02 W
Pop: 8,525 (1990); 10,094 (1980)   **Pop Density:** 4736.1
Land: 1.8 sq. mi.; **Water:** 0.2 sq. mi.   **Elev:** 900 ft.

Incorporated 1891.

Name origin: For Fort Duquesne, which was built at the forks of the Ohio in 1754 and named in honor of the Marquis Duquesne de Menneville, then governor of New France.

East Deer
Township
Lat: 40-35-14 N **Long:** 79-46-39 W
Pop: 1,558 (1990); 1,658 (1980)   **Pop Density:** 677.4
Land: 2.3 sq. mi.; **Water:** 0.3 sq. mi.

East McKeesport
Borough
ZIP: 15035   **Lat:** 40-23-03 N **Long:** 79-48-24 W
Pop: 2,678 (1990); 2,940 (1980)   **Pop Density:** 6695.0
Land: 0.4 sq. mi.; **Water:** 0.0 sq. mi.   **Elev:** 900 ft.

East Pittsburgh
Borough
ZIP: 15112   **Lat:** 40-23-49 N **Long:** 79-50-12 W
Pop: 2,160 (1990); 2,493 (1980)   **Pop Density:** 5400.0
Land: 0.4 sq. mi.; **Water:** 0.0 sq. mi.   **Elev:** 1200 ft.

In southwestern PA near the Monongahela River, adjacent to Pittsburgh.

Edgewood
Borough
ZIP: 15218   **Lat:** 40-25-53 N **Long:** 79-53-01 W
Pop: 3,581 (1990); 4,382 (1980)   **Pop Density:** 5968.3
Land: 0.6 sq. mi.; **Water:** 0.0 sq. mi.   **Elev:** 980 ft.

In southwestern PA, an eastern suburb of Pittsburgh.

Edgeworth
Borough
ZIP: 15143   **Lat:** 40-33-15 N **Long:** 80-11-31 W
Pop: 1,670 (1990); 1,738 (1980)   **Pop Density:** 1113.3
Land: 1.5 sq. mi.; **Water:** 0.2 sq. mi.   **Elev:** 721 ft.

In southwestern PA on the Ohio River, northwest of Pittsburgh.

Elizabeth
Township
ZIP: 15037   **Lat:** 40-16-00 N **Long:** 79-49-31 W
Pop: 14,712 (1990); 16,269 (1980)   **Pop Density:** 656.8
Land: 22.4 sq. mi.; **Water:** 0.5 sq. mi.

*Elizabeth
Borough
ZIP: 15037   **Lat:** 40-16-17 N **Long:** 79-53-11 W
Pop: 1,610 (1990); 1,892 (1980)   **Pop Density:** 4025.0
Land: 0.4 sq. mi.; **Water:** 0.1 sq. mi.   **Elev:** 780 ft.

In southwestern PA, a southeastern suburb of Pittsburgh. Laid out in 1787 by Stephen Bayard.

Name origin: For Elizabeth Mackay Bayard, wife of Stephen Bayard and daughter of Col. Aeneas Mackay, a former commandant of Fort Pitt.

Emsworth
Borough
ZIP: 15202   **Lat:** 40-30-38 N **Long:** 80-05-47 W
Pop: 2,892 (1990); 3,074 (1980)   **Pop Density:** 4820.0
Land: 0.6 sq. mi.; **Water:** 0.1 sq. mi.   **Elev:** 800 ft.

Etna
Borough
ZIP: 15223   **Lat:** 40-29-54 N **Long:** 79-56-50 W
Pop: 4,200 (1990); 4,534 (1980)   **Pop Density:** 6000.0
Land: 0.7 sq. mi.; **Water:** 0.0 sq. mi.   **Elev:** 743 ft.

In southwestern PA, a suburb of Pittsburgh. An ironmaking establishment was set up here in 1832. Established as borough 1868.

Name origin: For Sicily's famed volcano, Mt. Etna, because it was a town of flaming furnaces, iron works, and steel mills.

Fawn Township
Lat: 40-38-29 N Long: 79-46-10 W
Pop: 2,712 (1990); 2,899 (1980) Pop Density: 210.2
Land: 12.9 sq. mi.; Water: 0.0 sq. mi.

Findlay Township
Lat: 40-28-33 N Long: 80-16-59 W
Pop: 4,500 (1990); 4,573 (1980) Pop Density: 138.0
Land: 32.6 sq. mi.; Water: 0.0 sq. mi.

Forest Hills Borough
ZIP: 15221 Lat: 40-25-29 N Long: 79-51-09 W
Pop: 7,335 (1990); 8,198 (1980) Pop Density: 4584.4
Land: 1.6 sq. mi.; Water: 0.0 sq. mi. Elev: 966 ft.
In southwestern PA, an eastern suburb of Pittsburgh.

Forward Township
Lat: 40-13-34 N Long: 79-54-22 W
Pop: 3,877 (1990); 4,335 (1980) Pop Density: 205.1
Land: 18.9 sq. mi.; Water: 1.0 sq. mi.

Fox Chapel Borough
ZIP: 15238 Lat: 40-31-31 N Long: 79-53-22 W
Pop: 5,319 (1990); 5,049 (1980) Pop Density: 673.3
Land: 7.9 sq. mi.; Water: 0.0 sq. mi. Elev: 980 ft.
In southwestern PA, a northeastern suburb of Pittsburgh.

Franklin Park Borough
ZIP: 15143 Lat: 40-35-30 N Long: 80-05-55 W
Pop: 10,109 (1990); 6,135 (1980) Pop Density: 743.3
Land: 13.6 sq. mi.; Water: 0.0 sq. mi. Elev: 1246 ft.

Frazer Township
Lat: 40-36-11 N Long: 79-47-37 W
Pop: 1,388 (1990); 1,509 (1980) Pop Density: 147.7
Land: 9.4 sq. mi.; Water: 0.0 sq. mi.

Glassport Borough
ZIP: 15045 Lat: 40-19-31 N Long: 79-53-11 W
Pop: 5,582 (1990); 6,242 (1980) Pop Density: 3283.5
Land: 1.7 sq. mi.; Water: 0.2 sq. mi. Elev: 760 ft.
In southwestern PA on the east bank of the Monongahela River, a southern suburb of Pittsburgh. Incorporated 1902.
Name origin: Named in 1888 when the United States Glass Company established a plant here.

Glenfield Borough
ZIP: 15143 Lat: 40-31-18 N Long: 80-07-55 W
Pop: 201 (1990); 246 (1980) Pop Density: 251.3
Land: 0.8 sq. mi.; Water: 0.2 sq. mi.

Green Tree Borough
ZIP: 15242 Lat: 40-25-06 N Long: 80-03-18 W
Pop: 4,905 (1990); 5,722 (1980) Pop Density: 2335.7
Land: 2.1 sq. mi.; Water: 0.0 sq. mi.
In southwestern PA, a southern suburb of Pittsburgh.

Hampton Township
ZIP: 15101 Lat: 40-35-09 N Long: 79-57-17 W
Pop: 15,568 (1990); 14,260 (1980) Pop Density: 973.0
Land: 16.0 sq. mi.; Water: 0.0 sq. mi.

Harmar Township
Lat: 40-32-36 N Long: 79-50-17 W
Pop: 3,144 (1990); 3,461 (1980) Pop Density: 524.0
Land: 6.0 sq. mi.; Water: 0.5 sq. mi.

Harrison Township
ZIP: 15065 Lat: 40-38-11 N Long: 79-43-00 W
Pop: 11,763 (1990); 13,252 (1980) Pop Density: 1611.4
Land: 7.3 sq. mi.; Water: 0.5 sq. mi.
In southwestern PA, a northeastern suburb of Pittsburgh.

Haysville Borough
ZIP: 15143 Lat: 40-31-33 N Long: 80-09-15 W
Pop: 100 (1990); 117 (1980) Pop Density: 500.0
Land: 0.2 sq. mi.; Water: 0.1 sq. mi. Elev: 724 ft.

Heidelberg Borough
ZIP: 15106 Lat: 40-23-29 N Long: 80-05-31 W
Pop: 1,238 (1990); 1,606 (1980) Pop Density: 4126.7
Land: 0.3 sq. mi.; Water: 0.0 sq. mi. Elev: 820 ft.
Name origin: Named by German founders for the medieval city in their native land.

Homestead Borough
ZIP: 15120 Lat: 40-24-24 N Long: 79-54-35 W
Pop: 4,179 (1990); 5,092 (1980) Pop Density: 6965.0
Land: 0.6 sq. mi.; Water: 0.1 sq. mi. Elev: 780 ft.
In southwestern PA adjoining Pittsburgh. Laid out in 1871 by a Pittsburgh corporation; incorporated 1880.
Name origin: For either the Homestead Bank and Life Insurance Company, or for the fact that one of the farms the company bought belonged to Abdiel McClure, whose fine old farmhouse was locally known as "the McClure homestead."

Imperial-Enlow CDP
Lat: 40-27-12 N Long: 80-14-54 W
Pop: 3,449 (1990); 1,587 (1980) Pop Density: 841.2
Land: 4.1 sq. mi.; Water: 0.0 sq. mi.

Indiana Township
ZIP: 15051 Lat: 40-34-27 N Long: 79-52-26 W
Pop: 6,024 (1990); 6,080 (1980) Pop Density: 340.3
Land: 17.7 sq. mi.; Water: 0.0 sq. mi.

Ingram Borough
ZIP: 15205 Lat: 40-26-44 N Long: 80-04-06 W
Pop: 3,901 (1990); 4,346 (1980) Pop Density: 9752.5
Land: 0.4 sq. mi.; Water: 0.0 sq. mi. Elev: 930 ft.
In southwestern PA, a southern suburb of Pittsburgh.

Jefferson Borough
ZIP: 15025 Lat: 40-17-37 N Long 79-55-55 W
Pop: 9,533 (1990); 8,643 (1980) Pop Density: 574.3
Land: 16.6 sq. mi.; Water: 0.0 sq. mi.
In southwestern PA, a southeastern suburb of Pittsburgh. Incorporated 1950.
Name origin: For Thomas Jefferson (1743–1825), third U.S. president.

Kennedy Township
ZIP: 15108 Lat: 40-28-34 N Long 80-06-06 W
Pop: 7,265 (1990); 7,159 (1980) Pop Density: 1345.4
Land: 5.4 sq. mi.; Water: 0.1 sq. mi.

Kilbuck Township
Lat: 40-31-01 N Long 80-05-56 W
Pop: 890 (1990); 1,219 (1980) Pop Density: 356.0
Land: 2.5 sq. mi.; Water: 0.0 sq. mi.

Leet Township
Lat: 40-34-16 N Long 80-12-19 W
Pop: 1,731 (1990); 1,854 (1980) Pop Density: 1081.9
Land: 1.6 sq. mi.; Water: 0.0 sq. mi.

Leetsdale
Borough
ZIP: 15056 **Lat:** 40-34-05 N **Long:** 80-12-53 W
Pop: 1,387 (1990); 1,604 (1980) **Pop Density:** 1387.0
Land: 1.0 sq. mi.; **Water:** 0.2 sq. mi. **Elev:** 700 ft.

In southeastern PA, a suburb of Pittsburgh. Settled in 1796 by William Leet.

Name origin: For William Leet.

Liberty
Borough
ZIP: 15133 **Lat:** 40-19-25 N **Long:** 79-51-28 W
Pop: 2,744 (1990); 3,112 (1980) **Pop Density:** 1960.0
Land: 1.4 sq. mi.; **Water:** 0.1 sq. mi. **Elev:** 880 ft.

Lincoln
Borough
ZIP: 15037 **Lat:** 40-17-35 N **Long:** 79-51-08 W
Pop: 1,187 (1990); 1,428 (1980) **Pop Density:** 237.4
Land: 5.0 sq. mi.; **Water:** 0.2 sq. mi. **Elev:** 1120 ft.

In southwestern PA, a suburb of Pittsburgh.

Name origin: For Abraham Lincoln (1809–65), sixteenth U.S. president.

Marshall
Township
Lat: 40-38-45 N **Long:** 80-06-29 W
Pop: 4,010 (1990); 2,594 (1980) **Pop Density:** 257.1
Land: 15.6 sq. mi.; **Water:** 0.0 sq. mi.

McCandless
Township
ZIP: 15237 **Lat:** 40-35-00 N **Long:** 80-01-47 W
Pop: 28,781 (1990); 26,250 (1980) **Pop Density:** 1744.3
Land: 16.5 sq. mi.; **Water:** 0.1 sq. mi.

McDonald
Borough
Lat: 40-22-17 N **Long:** 80-13-40 W
Pop: 443 (1990); 539 (1980) **Pop Density:** 2215.0
Land: 0.2 sq. mi.; **Water:** 0.0 sq. mi.

Laid out in 1781. Part of the town is also in Washington County.

Name origin: For old Fort McDonald, which was built during the Revolutionary War on the land of John McDonald, who settled here in 1775.

McKeesport
City
ZIP: 15130 **Lat:** 40-20-29 N **Long:** 79-50-39 W
Pop: 26,016 (1990); 31,012 (1980) **Pop Density:** 5203.2
Land: 5.0 sq. mi.; **Water:** 0.4 sq. mi. **Elev:** 1020 ft.

In southwestern PA at the junction of the Youghiogheny and Monongahela rivers, 10 mi. southeast of Pittsburgh. Laid out in 1795.

Name origin: For David McKee and his family. He was a north-country Irishman who settled here in 1755, acquired title to 844 acres, and in 1755 obtained ferry privileges from colonial authorities. His son, John, laid out the town and named it for his father..After 1830 coal mining and shipping developed the town into a large industrial city.

McKees Rocks
Borough
ZIP: 15136 **Lat:** 40-28-09 N **Long:** 80-03-43 W
Pop: 7,691 (1990); 8,742 (1980) **Pop Density:** 7691.0
Land: 1.0 sq. mi.; **Water:** 0.1 sq. mi. **Elev:** 750 ft.

In southwestern PA, west of Pittsburgh.

Name origin: For Alexander McKee, an early settler, and for the rock formations along the Ohio River.

Millvale
Borough
ZIP: 15209 **Lat:** 40-28-55 N **Long:** 79-58-28 W
Pop: 4,341 (1990); 4,772 (1980) **Pop Density:** 6201.4
Land: 0.7 sq. mi.; **Water:** 0.1 sq. mi. **Elev:** 800 ft.

Monroeville
Borough
ZIP: 15146 **Lat:** 40-25-33 N **Long:** 79-45-39 W
Pop: 29,169 (1990); 29,510 (1980) **Pop Density:** 1473.2
Land: 19.8 sq. mi.; **Water:** 0.0 sq. mi. **Elev:** 1200 ft.

In southwestern PA, 13 mi. east of Pittsburgh.

Name origin: For James Monroe (1758–1831), fifth U.S. president.

Moon
Township
ZIP: 15108 **Lat:** 40-30-27 N **Long:** 80-12-27 W
Pop: 19,631 (1990); 20,935 (1980) **Pop Density:** 828.3
Land: 23.7 sq. mi.; **Water:** 0.3 sq. mi.

Mount Lebanon
Township
ZIP: 15228 **Lat:** 40-22-26 N **Long:** 80-02-55 W
Pop: 33,362 (1990); 34,414 (1980) **Pop Density:** 5560.3
Land: 6.0 sq. mi.; **Water:** 0.0 sq. mi.

Mount Oliver
Borough
ZIP: 15210 **Lat:** 40-24-39 N **Long:** 79-59-11 W
Pop: 4,160 (1990); 4,576 (1980) **Pop Density:** 13866.7
Land: 0.3 sq. mi.; **Water:** 0.0 sq. mi. **Elev:** 1130 ft.

Name origin: For Oliver Ormsby, who owned several hundred acres of land here.

Munhall
Borough
ZIP: 15120 **Lat:** 40-23-36 N **Long:** 79-54-04 W
Pop: 13,158 (1990); 14,532 (1980) **Pop Density:** 5720.9
Land: 2.3 sq. mi.; **Water:** 0.1 sq. mi. **Elev:** 860 ft.

In southwestern PA on the Monongahela River, 7 mi. east of Pittsburgh.

Name origin: For Capt. John Munhall, who gave the Pittsburgh, Virginia & Charleston Railroad the right of way through his land on the condition that he choose the location for the station.

Neville
Township
Lat: 40-30-16 N **Long:** 80-06-46 W
Pop: 1,273 (1990); 1,416 (1980) **Pop Density:** 979.2
Land: 1.3 sq. mi.; **Water:** 0.9 sq. mi.

North Braddock
Borough
ZIP: 15104 **Lat:** 40-24-03 N **Long:** 79-51-07 W
Pop: 7,036 (1990); 8,711 (1980) **Pop Density:** 4690.7
Land: 1.5 sq. mi.; **Water:** 0.1 sq. mi. **Elev:** 1200 ft.

In southwestern PA, 10 mi. east of Pittsburgh. Incorporated in 1897.

Name origin: For its geographic relationship to its southern neighbor, Braddock.

North Fayette
Township
Lat: 40-24-46 N **Long:** 80-13-33 W
Pop: 9,537 (1990); 7,351 (1980) **Pop Density:** 380.0
Land: 25.1 sq. mi.; **Water:** 0.0 sq. mi.

North Versailles
Township
ZIP: 15137 **Lat:** 40-22-47 N **Long:** 79-48-34 W
Pop: 12,302 (1990); 13,294 (1980) **Pop Density:** 1518.8
Land: 8.1 sq. mi.; **Water:** 0.2 sq. mi.

In southwestern PA, southeast of Pittsburgh.

Oakdale
Borough
ZIP: 15071 **Lat:** 40-23-58 N **Long:** 80-11-15 W
Pop: 1,752 (1990); 1,955 (1980) **Pop Density:** 3504.0
Land: 0.5 sq. mi.; **Water:** 0.0 sq. mi. **Elev:** 902 ft.

In southwestern PA, a western suburb of Pittsburgh.

Oakmont
Borough
ZIP: 15139 **Lat:** 40-31-09 N **Long:** 79-50-11 W
Pop: 6,961 (1990); 7,039 (1980) **Pop Density:** 4350.6
Land: 1.6 sq. mi.; **Water:** 0.2 sq. mi. **Elev:** 760 ft.
In southwestern PA, 11 mi. northeast of Pittsburgh.

O'Hara
Township
ZIP: 15238 **Lat:** 40-29-57 N **Long:** 79-54-06 W
Pop: 9,096 (1990); 9,233 (1980) **Pop Density:** 1299.4
Land: 7.0 sq. mi.; **Water:** 0.3 sq. mi.

Ohio
Township
Lat: 40-32-37 N **Long:** 80-05-20 W
Pop: 2,459 (1990); 2,072 (1980) **Pop Density:** 356.4
Land: 6.9 sq. mi.; **Water:** 0.0 sq. mi.

Osborne
Borough
ZIP: 15143 **Lat:** 40-31-50 N **Long:** 80-10-10 W
Pop: 565 (1990); 529 (1980) **Pop Density:** 1412.5
Land: 0.4 sq. mi.; **Water:** 0.1 sq. mi. **Elev:** 1000 ft.

Penn Hills
Township
ZIP: 15235 **Lat:** 40-28-33 N **Long:** 79-49-37 W
Pop: 51,479 (1990); 57,632 (1980) **Pop Density:** 2709.4
Land: 19.0 sq. mi.; **Water:** 0.3 sq. mi.
In southwestern PA, an eastern suburb of Pittsburgh.

Pennsbury Village
Borough
ZIP: 15205 **Lat:** 40-25-39 N **Long:** 80-06-03 W
Pop: 774 (1990); 798 (1980) **Pop Density:** 7740.0
Land: 0.1 sq. mi.; **Water:** 0.0 sq. mi.

Pine
Township
Lat: 40-38-39 N **Long:** 80-01-47 W
Pop: 4,048 (1990); 3,908 (1980) **Pop Density:** 241.0
Land: 16.8 sq. mi.; **Water:** 0.0 sq. mi.

Pitcairn
Borough
ZIP: 15140 **Lat:** 40-24-27 N **Long:** 79-46-33 W
Pop: 4,087 (1990); 4,175 (1980) **Pop Density:** 8174.0
Land: 0.5 sq. mi.; **Water:** 0.0 sq. mi. **Elev:** 900 ft.
In southwestern PA, 13 mi. east of Pittsburgh.
Name origin: For Robert Pitcairn, then superintendent of the Pittsburgh division of the Pennsylvania Railroad.

Pittsburgh
City
ZIP: 15122 **Lat:** 40-26-21 N **Long:** 79-58-36 W
Pop: 369,879 (1990); 423,938 (1980) **Pop Density:** 6652.5
Land: 55.6 sq. mi.; **Water:** 2.7 sq. mi. **Elev:** 770 ft.
In southwestern PA where the Monongahela and Allegheny rivers unite to form the Ohio River; incorporated as borough Apr 22, 1794, as city Mar 18, 1816. Second city of importance in the state, port, and one of the greatest steel centers of the world. Originated in a cluster of log cabins built near Fort Pitt after 1758. Manufacturing city: steel, pig iron, coke; also computer services and health care.
Name origin: For William Pitt, the Elder (1708–78), English statesman who defended the American colonies before the Revolutionary War.

Pleasant Hills
Borough
ZIP: 15236 **Lat:** 40-19-43 N **Long:** 79-57-39 W
Pop: 8,884 (1990); 9,676 (1980) **Pop Density:** 3290.4
Land: 2.7 sq. mi.; **Water:** 0.0 sq. mi. **Elev:** 1200 ft.

Plum
Borough
ZIP: 15239 **Lat:** 40-30-08 N **Long:** 79-45-14 W
Pop: 25,609 (1990); 25,390 (1980) **Pop Density:** 895.4
Land: 28.6 sq. mi.; **Water:** 0.4 sq. mi. **Elev:** 1040 ft.
In southwestern PA, an eastern suburb of Pittsburgh.
Name origin: For the abundant wild plum trees in the area.

Port Vue
Borough
ZIP: 15133 **Lat:** 40-20-12 N **Long:** 79-52-13 W
Pop: 4,641 (1990); 5,316 (1980) **Pop Density:** 4219.1
Land: 1.1 sq. mi.; **Water:** 0.0 sq. mi. **Elev:** 1185 ft.

Rankin
Borough
ZIP: 15104 **Lat:** 40-24-40 N **Long:** 79-52-55 W
Pop: 2,503 (1990); 2,892 (1980) **Pop Density:** 6257.5
Land: 0.4 sq. mi.; **Water:** 0.1 sq. mi. **Elev:** 870 ft.
In southwestern PA on the Monongahela River, 5 mi. east of Pittsburgh.
Name origin: For Thomas Rankin, whose house in 1870 was the only one in sight and was made a stop by the Baltimore & Ohio Railroad.

Reserve
Township
Lat: 40-28-57 N **Long:** 79-59-13 W
Pop: 3,866 (1990); 4,306 (1980) **Pop Density:** 1933.0
Land: 2.0 sq. mi.; **Water:** 0.0 sq. mi.

Richland
Township
ZIP: 15044 **Lat:** 40-38-38 N **Long:** 79-57-31 W
Pop: 8,600 (1990); 7,749 (1980) **Pop Density:** 589.0
Land: 14.6 sq. mi.; **Water:** 0.0 sq. mi.

Robinson
Township
ZIP: 15136 **Lat:** 40-27-43 N **Long:** 80-07-36 W
Pop: 10,830 (1990); 9,416 (1980) **Pop Density:** 736.7
Land: 14.7 sq. mi.; **Water:** 0.2 sq. mi.

Ross
Township
ZIP: 15237 **Lat:** 40-31-35 N **Long:** 80-01-29 W
Pop: 33,482 (1990); 35,102 (1980) **Pop Density:** 2325.1
Land: 14.4 sq. mi.; **Water:** 0.0 sq. mi.
In southwestern PA, north of Pittsburgh.

Rosslyn Farms
Borough
Lat: 40-25-17 N **Long:** 80-05-23 W
Pop: 483 (1990); 521 (1980) **Pop Density:** 805.0
Land: 0.6 sq. mi.; **Water:** 0.0 sq. mi. **Elev:** 1120 ft.

Scott
Township
ZIP: 15106 **Lat:** 40-23-10 N **Long:** 80-04-38 W
Pop: 17,118 (1990); 20,413 (1980) **Pop Density:** 4279.5
Land: 4.0 sq. mi.; **Water:** 0.0 sq. mi.
In southwestern PA, southwest of Pittsburgh.

Sewickley
Borough
ZIP: 15143 **Lat:** 40-32-22 N **Long:** 80-10-49 W
Pop: 4,134 (1990); 4,778 (1980) **Pop Density:** 4134.0
Land: 1.0 sq. mi.; **Water:** 0.1 sq. mi. **Elev:** 840 ft.
In southwestern PA on the Ohio River, 10 mi. northwest of Pittsburgh.
Name origin: For an Indian tribe; meaning of the name unknown.

Sewickley Heights
Borough
ZIP: 15143 **Lat:** 40-33-39 N **Long:** 80-09-20 W
Pop: 984 (1990); 899 (1980) **Pop Density:** 134.8
Land: 7.3 sq. mi.; **Water:** 0.0 sq. mi. **Elev:** 1000 ft.

Sewickley Hills
Borough
ZIP: 15143   **Lat:** 40-33-36 N   **Long:** 80-07-12 W
Pop: 622 (1990); 419 (1980)   **Pop Density:** 248.8
Land: 2.5 sq. mi.; **Water:** 0.0 sq. mi.   **Elev:** 1140 ft.

Shaler
Township
ZIP: 15116   **Lat:** 40-31-15 N   **Long:** 79-57-50 W
Pop: 30,533 (1990); 33,694 (1980)   **Pop Density:** 2750.7
Land: 11.1 sq. mi.; **Water:** 0.2 sq. mi.

In southwestern PA, north of Pittsburgh.

Sharpsburg
Borough
ZIP: 15215   **Lat:** 40-29-35 N   **Long:** 79-55-35 W
Pop: 3,781 (1990); 4,351 (1980)   **Pop Density:** 7562.0
Land: 0.5 sq. mi.; **Water:** 0.2 sq. mi.   **Elev:** 770 ft.

In southwestern PA on the Allegheny River, 5 mi. northeast of Pittsburgh. Founded in 1826; incorporated 1841. Eight-year-old Howard J. Heinz began his billion dollar business here by selling produce from his mother's garden patch.
Name origin: For founder James Sharp, who kept a temperance hotel here until his death in 1861.

South Fayette
Township
ZIP: 15064   **Lat:** 40-20-58 N   **Long:** 80-09-42 W
Pop: 10,329 (1990); 9,707 (1980)   **Pop Density:** 508.8
Land: 20.3 sq. mi.; **Water:** 0.0 sq. mi.

South Park
Township
ZIP: 15129   **Lat:** 40-17-49 N   **Long:** 79-59-37 W
Pop: 14,292 (1990); 13,535 (1980)   **Pop Density:** 1553.5
Land: 9.2 sq. mi.; **Water:** 0.0 sq. mi.

South Versailles
Township
Lat: 40-18-05 N   **Long:** 79-47-50 W
Pop: 515 (1990); 425 (1980)   **Pop Density:** 572.2
Land: 0.9 sq. mi.; **Water:** 0.1 sq. mi.

Springdale
Borough
ZIP: 15144   **Lat:** 40-32-22 N   **Long:** 79-46-55 W
Pop: 3,992 (1990); 4,418 (1980)   **Pop Density:** 4435.6
Land: 0.9 sq. mi.; **Water:** 0.2 sq. mi.   **Elev:** 805 ft.

In southwestern PA on the Allegheny River, 15 mi. northeast of Pittsburgh. Settled in 1795.
Name origin: For springs in a nearby hollow.

*Springdale
Township
ZIP: 15144   **Lat:** 40-33-01 N   **Long:** 79-47-00 W
Pop: 1,777 (1990); 1,918 (1980)   **Pop Density:** 807.7
Land: 2.2 sq. mi.; **Water:** 0.2 sq. mi.

Stowe
Township
ZIP: 15136   **Lat:** 40-28-59 N   **Long:** 80-04-23 W
Pop: 7,681 (1990); 9,202 (1980)   **Pop Density:** 3840.5
Land: 2.0 sq. mi.; **Water:** 0.4 sq. mi.

Swissvale
Borough
ZIP: 15218   **Lat:** 40-25-13 N   **Long:** 79-53-11 W
Pop: 10,637 (1990); 11,345 (1980)   **Pop Density:** 8864.2
Land: 1.2 sq. mi.; **Water:** 0.1 sq. mi.   **Elev:** 1020 ft.

In southwestern PA, 5 mi. east of Pittsburgh.
Name origin: Name said to have been invented by Jane Gray Swisshelm, wife of James, on whose farm the town was built.

Tarentum
Borough
ZIP: 15084   **Lat:** 40-36-18 N   **Long:** 79-45-36 W
Pop: 5,674 (1990); 6,419 (1980)   **Pop Density:** 4728.3
Land: 1.2 sq. mi.; **Water:** 0.2 sq. mi.   **Elev:** 768 ft.

In southwestern PA, a northeastern suburb of Pittsburgh.

Settled in the 1790s when a gristmill was erected on Bull Creek. Laid out in 1829.
Name origin: Named by Judge Henry Marie Brackenridge, an ancient history and classical languages student and scholar, for the ancient city in southern Italy called Tarentum by the Romans and Taras by the Greeks.

Thornburg
Borough
ZIP: 15205   **Lat:** 40-26-00 N   **Long:** 80-05-00 W
Pop: 461 (1990); 526 (1980)   **Pop Density:** 1152.5
Land: 0.4 sq. mi.; **Water:** 0.0 sq. mi.   **Elev:** 850 ft.

Turtle Creek
Borough
ZIP: 15145   **Lat:** 40-24-28 N   **Long:** 79-49-15 W
Pop: 6,556 (1990); 6,959 (1980)   **Pop Density:** 6556.0
Land: 1.0 sq. mi.; **Water:** 0.0 sq. mi.   **Elev:** 900 ft.

Settled in 1765; incorporated 1892.
Name origin: Transliteration of *Tulpewi-sysu*, the Indian name for the place.

Upper St. Clair
Township
ZIP: 15241   **Lat:** 40-20-08 N   **Long:** 80-05-01 W
Pop: 19,692 (1990); 19,023 (1980)   **Pop Density:** 2009.4
Land: 9.8 sq. mi.; **Water:** 0.0 sq. mi.

Verona
Borough
ZIP: 15147   **Lat:** 40-30-18 N   **Long:** 79-50-28 W
Pop: 3,260 (1990); 3,179 (1980)   **Pop Density:** 6520.0
Land: 0.5 sq. mi.; **Water:** 0.1 sq. mi.   **Elev:** 760 ft.
Name origin: For Verona, Italy.

Versailles
Borough
ZIP: 15132   **Lat:** 40-19-01 N   **Long:** 79-49-49 W
Pop: 1,821 (1990); 2,150 (1980)   **Pop Density:** 3642.0
Land: 0.5 sq. mi.; **Water:** 0.0 sq. mi.   **Elev:** 840 ft.

In southwestern PA on the Youghiogheny River, 15 mi. southeast of Pittsburgh.
Name origin: From old Versailles Township, itself named for the palace of the French kings in commemoration of the valiant but vain French effort to possess western PA.

Wall
Borough
ZIP: 15148   **Lat:** 40-23-35 N   **Long:** 79-47-06 W
Pop: 853 (1990); 989 (1980)   **Pop Density:** 2132.5
Land: 0.4 sq. mi.; **Water:** 0.0 sq. mi.   **Elev:** 800 ft.

West Deer
Township
ZIP: 15076   **Lat:** 40-38-03 N   **Long:** 79-52-23 W
Pop: 11,371 (1990); 10,897 (1980)   **Pop Density:** 392.1
Land: 29.0 sq. mi.; **Water:** 0.0 sq. mi.

West Elizabeth
Borough
ZIP: 15088   **Lat:** 40-16-23 N   **Long:** 79-53-38 W
Pop: 634 (1990); 808 (1980)   **Pop Density:** 3170.0
Land: 0.2 sq. mi.; **Water:** 0.1 sq. mi.   **Elev:** 760 ft.

West Homestead
Borough
ZIP: 15120   **Lat:** 40-23-56 N   **Long:** 79-55-13 W
Pop: 2,495 (1990); 3,128 (1980)   **Pop Density:** 2772.2
Land: 0.9 sq. mi.; **Water:** 0.1 sq. mi.   **Elev:** 930 ft.

In southwestern PA adjacent to Homestead on the Monongahela River, a southeastern suburb of Pittsburgh.

West Mifflin
Borough
ZIP: 15122   **Lat:** 40-21-25 N   **Long:** 79-54-28 W
Pop: 23,644 (1990); 26,279 (1980)   **Pop Density:** 1665.1
Land: 14.2 sq. mi.; **Water:** 0.3 sq. mi.   **Elev:** 1100 ft.

In southwestern PA, a southeastern suburb of Pittsburgh.

West View
Borough
ZIP: 15229   **Lat:** 40-31-05 N   **Long:** 80-02-01 W
Pop: 7,734 (1990); 7,648 (1980)   **Pop Density:** 7734.0
Land: 1.0 sq. mi.; **Water:** 0.0 sq. mi.   **Elev:** 1100 ft.

Whitaker
Borough
ZIP: 15120   **Lat:** 40-23-58 N   **Long:** 79-53-14 W
Pop: 1,416 (1990); 1,615 (1980)   **Pop Density:** 4720.0
Land: 0.3 sq. mi.; **Water:** 0.0 sq. mi.   **Elev:** 990 ft.

Whitehall
Borough
ZIP: 15210   **Lat:** 40-21-32 N   **Long:** 79-59-30 W
Pop: 14,451 (1990); 15,206 (1980)   **Pop Density:** 4379.1
Land: 3.3 sq. mi.; **Water:** 0.0 sq. mi.   **Elev:** 1257 ft.
In southwestern PA, a southern suburb of Pittsburgh.
Name origin: For the site of Whitehall Palace, site of the principal government offices in London, England.

White Oak
Borough
ZIP: 15131   **Lat:** 40-20-21 N   **Long:** 79-48-15 W
Pop: 8,761 (1990); 9,480 (1980)   **Pop Density:** 1307.6
Land: 6.7 sq. mi.; **Water:** 0.0 sq. mi.   **Elev:** 818 ft.

Wilkins
Township
ZIP: 15145   **Lat:** 40-25-34 N   **Long:** 79-49-27 W
Pop: 7,585 (1990); 8,472 (1980)   **Pop Density:** 2917.3
Land: 2.6 sq. mi.; **Water:** 0.0 sq. mi.

Wilkinsburg
Borough
ZIP: 15221   **Lat:** 40-26-41 N   **Long:** 79-52-23 W
Pop: 21,080 (1990); 23,669 (1980)   **Pop Density:** 9165.2
Land: 2.3 sq. mi.; **Water:** 0.0 sq. mi.
In southwestern PA, 10 mi. east of Pittsburgh. Settled in 1780; incorporated 1887.
Name origin: For Judge William Wilkins, minister to Russia and Pres. Tyler's secretary of war. Formerly called McNairsville and Rippeysville.

Wilmerding
Borough
ZIP: 15148   **Lat:** 40-23-36 N   **Long:** 79-48-39 W
Pop: 2,222 (1990); 2,421 (1980)   **Pop Density:** 4444.0
Land: 0.5 sq. mi.; **Water:** 0.0 sq. mi.   **Elev:** 800 ft.
In southwestern PA, 10 mi. east of Pittsburgh. Originally a railroad station, built about 1885, on land owned by Maj. William B. Negley.
Name origin: Named by Robert Pitcairn, then superintendent of the Pittsburgh division of the Pennsylvania Railroad, for his wife, Joanna Wilmerding Negley.

Armstrong County
County Seat: Kittanning (ZIP: 16201)

Pop: 73,478 (1990); 77,768 (1980)   **Pop Density:** 112.4
Land: 654.0 sq. mi.; **Water:** 10.5 sq. mi.   **Area Code:** 412
In central portion of western PA, northeast of Pittsburgh; organized Mar 12, 1800 from Allegheny, Lycoming, and Westmoreland counties.
Name origin: For John Armstrong (1758–1843), officer in the Revolutionary War and the War of 1812, U.S. senator from NY (1800–02; 1803–04), and U.S. secretary of war (1813–14).

Apollo
Borough
ZIP: 15613   **Lat:** 40-35-04 N   **Long:** 79-33-52 W
Pop: 1,895 (1990); 2,212 (1980)   **Pop Density:** 6316.7
Land: 0.3 sq. mi.; **Water:** 0.0 sq. mi.   **Elev:** 900 ft.
In western PA, northeast of Pittsburgh. Laid out in 1815.
Name origin: Named in 1848 for the Greek god by Dr. Robert McKisson, physician, poet, and student of the classics. Originally called Warren for an Indian trader who often stopped here.

Applewold
Borough
ZIP: 16201   **Lat:** 40-48-26 N   **Long:** 79-31-20 W
Pop: 388 (1990); 395 (1980)   **Pop Density:** 7760.0
Land: 0.05 sq. mi.; **Water:** 0.0 sq. mi.   **Elev:** 800 ft.

Atwood
Borough
ZIP: 16249   **Lat:** 40-44-52 N   **Long:** 79-15-42 W
Pop: 128 (1990); 107 (1980)   **Pop Density:** 61.0
Land: 2.1 sq. mi.; **Water:** 0.0 sq. mi.   **Elev:** 1230 ft.

Bethel
Township
Lat: 40-42-24 N   **Long:** 79-32-52 W
Pop: 1,261 (1990); 1,349 (1980)   **Pop Density:** 82.4
Land: 15.3 sq. mi.; **Water:** 0.6 sq. mi.

Boggs
Township
Lat: 40-53-18 N   **Long:** 79-25-01 W
Pop: 981 (1990); 953 (1980)   **Pop Density:** 40.7
Land: 24.1 sq. mi.; **Water:** 0.3 sq. mi.

Bradys Bend
Township
Lat: 40-59-12 N   **Long:** 79-38-48 W
Pop: 963 (1990); 1,124 (1980)   **Pop Density:** 75.8
Land: 12.7 sq. mi.; **Water:** 0.0 sq. mi.

Burrell
Township
Lat: 40-40-12 N   **Long:** 79-28-01 W
Pop: 728 (1990); 766 (1980)   **Pop Density:** 34.2
Land: 21.3 sq. mi.; **Water:** 0.5 sq. mi.
Name origin: For Jeremiah Murray Burrell, presiding judge of the judicial district.

Cadogan
Township
Lat: 40-45-12 N   **Long:** 79-35-02 W
Pop: 427 (1990); 459 (1980)   **Pop Density:** 474.4
Land: 0.9 sq. mi.; **Water:** 0.2 sq. mi.

Cowanshannock
Township
Lat: 40-47-51 N   **Long:** 79-17-46 W
Pop: 2,813 (1990); 3,178 (1980)   **Pop Density:** 61.7
Land: 45.6 sq. mi.; **Water:** 0.7 sq. mi.

Dayton   Borough
ZIP: 16222   **Lat:** 40-52-51 N **Long:** 79-14-30 W
Pop: 572 (1990); 648 (1980)   **Pop Density:** 1144.0
Land: 0.5 sq. mi.; **Water:** 0.0 sq. mi.   **Elev:** 1357 ft.

East Franklin   Township
                        Lat: 40-51-03 N **Long:** 79-33-05 W
Pop: 3,923 (1990); 3,716 (1980)   **Pop Density:** 127.0
Land: 30.9 sq. mi.; **Water:** 0.7 sq. mi.

Elderton   Borough
ZIP: 15736   **Lat:** 40-41-38 N **Long:** 79-20-30 W
Pop: 371 (1990); 420 (1980)   **Pop Density:** 1236.7
Land: 0.3 sq. mi.; **Water:** 0.0 sq. mi.   **Elev:** 1264 ft.

Ford City   Borough
ZIP: 16226   **Lat:** 40-46-05 N **Long:** 79-32-04 W
Pop: 3,413 (1990); 3,923 (1980)   **Pop Density:** 4875.7
Land: 0.7 sq. mi.; **Water:** 0.1 sq. mi.   **Elev:** 794 ft.

In western PA on the Allegheny River, northeast of Pittsburgh.

Name origin: For Capt. John B. Ford, "father of the plate glass industry in America," who built a factory here in 1887.

Ford Cliff   Borough
                        Lat: 40-45-35 N **Long:** 79-32-11 W
Pop: 450 (1990); 516 (1980)   **Pop Density:** 4500.0
Land: 0.1 sq. mi.; **Water:** 0.0 sq. mi.   **Elev:** 965 ft.

Freeport   Borough
ZIP: 16229   **Lat:** 40-40-57 N **Long:** 79-40-58 W
Pop: 1,983 (1990); 2,381 (1980)   **Pop Density:** 1652.5
Land: 1.2 sq. mi.; **Water:** 0.0 sq. mi.   **Elev:** 780 ft.

In western PA at the confluence of the Allegheny and Kiskiminetas rivers and Buffalo Creek. Laid out in 1796 by William and David Todd.

Name origin: For being a free port for river craft.

Gilpin   Township
                        Lat: 40-40-10 N **Long:** 79-36-17 W
Pop: 2,804 (1990); 2,967 (1980)   **Pop Density:** 169.9
Land: 16.5 sq. mi.; **Water:** 0.7 sq. mi.

Hovey   Township
                        Lat: 41-08-04 N **Long:** 79-41-07 W
Pop: 99 (1990); 103 (1980)   **Pop Density:** 47.1
Land: 2.1 sq. mi.; **Water:** 0.0 sq. mi.

Kiskiminetas   Township
ZIP: 15613   **Lat:** 40-35-10 N **Long:** 79-29-18 W
Pop: 5,456 (1990); 5,875 (1980)   **Pop Density:** 134.1
Land: 40.7 sq. mi.; **Water:** 0.3 sq. mi.

Kittanning   Borough
ZIP: 16201   **Lat:** 40-49-37 N **Long:** 79-31-24 W
Pop: 5,120 (1990); 5,432 (1980)   **Pop Density:** 5120.0
Land: 1.0 sq. mi.; **Water:** 0.0 sq. mi.

In western PA, 43 mi. northeast of Pittsburgh. Laid out in 1803 by Judge George Rose; incorporated Apr 2, 1821.

Name origin: For being the starting point of an Indian trail, the Kittanning Path, which led across the mountains to Standing Stone, now Huntingdon. A corruption of an Indian term *Kit-hannink* 'the town on the great river,' a reference to the Allegheny.

*Kittanning   Township
ZIP: 16201   **Lat:** 40-45-27 N **Long:** 79-26-35 W
Pop: 2,310 (1990); 2,160 (1980)   **Pop Density:** 75.2
Land: 30.7 sq. mi.; **Water:** 0.1 sq. mi.

Leechburg   Borough
ZIP: 15656   **Lat:** 40-37-49 N **Long:** 79-36-10 W
Pop: 2,504 (1990); 2,682 (1980)   **Pop Density:** 6260.0
Land: 0.4 sq. mi.; **Water:** 0.0 sq. mi.   **Elev:** 800 ft.

In southwestern PA, northeast of Pittsburgh on the Kiskiminetas River. Laid out in 1828.

Name origin: For David Leech, a native of Mercer County.

Lenape Heights   CDP
                        Lat: 40-45-51 N **Long:** 79-31-14 W
Pop: 1,355 (1990); 1,548 (1980)   **Pop Density:** 1355.0
Land: 1.0 sq. mi.; **Water:** 0.0 sq. mi.

Madison   Township
                        Lat: 40-57-13 N **Long:** 79-27-28 W
Pop: 941 (1990); 1,030 (1980)   **Pop Density:** 31.1
Land: 30.3 sq. mi.; **Water:** 0.9 sq. mi.

Mahoning   Township
                        Lat: 40-57-43 N **Long:** 79-20-38 W
Pop: 1,504 (1990); 1,649 (1980)   **Pop Density:** 60.6
Land: 24.8 sq. mi.; **Water:** 0.5 sq. mi.

Manor   Township
                        Lat: 40-45-53 N **Long:** 79-30-35 W
Pop: 4,482 (1990); 4,819 (1980)   **Pop Density:** 270.0
Land: 16.6 sq. mi.; **Water:** 0.6 sq. mi.

Name origin: For Kittanning or Appleby Manor, one of the twenty manors in PA owned by the Penns.

Manorville   Borough
ZIP: 16238   **Lat:** 40-47-15 N **Long:** 79-31-15 W
Pop: 418 (1990); 409 (1980)   **Pop Density:** 4180.0
Land: 0.1 sq. mi.; **Water:** 0.0 sq. mi.   **Elev:** 1000 ft.

Name origin: For Kittanning or Appleby Manor, one of twenty manors in PA owned by the Penn family.

North Apollo   Borough
ZIP: 15673   **Lat:** 40-35-35 N **Long:** 79-33-25 W
Pop: 1,391 (1990); 1,487 (1980)   **Pop Density:** 2782.0
Land: 0.5 sq. mi.; **Water:** 0.0 sq. mi.   **Elev:** 900 ft.

North Buffalo   Township
                        Lat: 40-47-02 N **Long:** 79-36-18 W
Pop: 2,897 (1990); 2,827 (1980)   **Pop Density:** 117.3
Land: 24.7 sq. mi.; **Water:** 0.5 sq. mi.

Parker   City
ZIP: 16049   **Lat:** 41-05-31 N **Long:** 79-41-03 W
Pop: 853 (1990); 808 (1980)   **Pop Density:** 775.5
Land: 1.1 sq. mi.; **Water:** 0.0 sq. mi.   **Elev:** 1100 ft.

Parks   Township
                        Lat: 40-38-16 N **Long:** 79-32-23 W
Pop: 2,739 (1990); 3,123 (1980)   **Pop Density:** 194.3
Land: 14.1 sq. mi.; **Water:** 0.1 sq. mi.

Perry   Township
                        Lat: 41-02-01 N **Long:** 79-39-36 W
Pop: 322 (1990); 396 (1980)   **Pop Density:** 21.5
Land: 15.0 sq. mi.; **Water:** 0.0 sq. mi.

Pine   Township
                        Lat: 40-55-14 N **Long:** 79-25-39 W
Pop: 534 (1990); 656 (1980)   **Pop Density:** 109.0
Land: 4.9 sq. mi.; **Water:** 0.2 sq. mi.

Plumcreek   Township
                        Lat: 40-43-08 N **Long:** 79-20-30 W
Pop: 2,400 (1990); 2,303 (1980)   **Pop Density:** 56.6
Land: 42.4 sq. mi.; **Water:** 0.7 sq. mi.

Rayburn
Township
Lat: 40-50-17 N **Long:** 79-29-04 W
Pop: 1,823 (1990); 1,971 (1980) **Pop Density:** 153.2
Land: 11.9 sq. mi.; **Water:** 0.5 sq. mi.

Redbank
Township
Lat: 40-58-41 N **Long:** 79-14-54 W
Pop: 1,058 (1990); 1,161 (1980) **Pop Density:** 32.7
Land: 32.4 sq. mi.; **Water:** 0.3 sq. mi.

Rural Valley
Borough
ZIP: 16249 **Lat:** 40-47-56 N **Long:** 79-18-52 W
Pop: 957 (1990); 1,033 (1980) **Pop Density:** 455.7
Land: 2.1 sq. mi.; **Water:** 0.0 sq. mi. **Elev:** 1130 ft.

South Bend
Township
Lat: 40-37-57 N **Long:** 79-23-56 W
Pop: 1,304 (1990); 1,237 (1980) **Pop Density:** 57.4
Land: 22.7 sq. mi.; **Water:** 0.1 sq. mi.

South Bethlehem
Borough
ZIP: 16242 **Lat:** 40-59-58 N **Long:** 79-20-22 W
Pop: 479 (1990); 476 (1980) **Pop Density:** 2395.0
Land: 0.2 sq. mi.; **Water:** 0.0 sq. mi. **Elev:** 1100 ft.

South Buffalo
Township
Lat: 40-43-33 N **Long:** 79-38-24 W
Pop: 2,687 (1990); 2,636 (1980) **Pop Density:** 99.2
Land: 27.1 sq. mi.; **Water:** 0.9 sq. mi.

Sugarcreek
Township
Lat: 40-55-41 N **Long:** 79-38-17 W
Pop: 1,496 (1990); 1,511 (1980) **Pop Density:** 55.2
Land: 27.1 sq. mi.; **Water:** 0.0 sq. mi.

Valley
Township
Lat: 40-49-14 N **Long:** 79-24-24 W
Pop: 709 (1990); 628 (1980) **Pop Density:** 48.2
Land: 14.7 sq. mi.; **Water:** 0.0 sq. mi.

Washington
Township
Lat: 40-55-26 N **Long:** 79-32-04 W
Pop: 984 (1990); 1,008 (1980) **Pop Density:** 44.7
Land: 22.0 sq. mi.; **Water:** 1.0 sq. mi.
Name origin: For George Washington (1732-99), first U.S. president.

Wayne
Township
Lat: 40-53-16 N **Long:** 79-17-10 W
Pop: 937 (1990); 1,020 (1980) **Pop Density:** 21.0
Land: 44.7 sq. mi.; **Water:** 0.2 sq. mi.

West Franklin
Township
Lat: 40-51-03 N **Long:** 79-38-59 W
Pop: 2,008 (1990); 1,863 (1980) **Pop Density:** 76.3
Land: 26.3 sq. mi.; **Water:** 0.0 sq. mi.

West Kittanning
Borough
ZIP: 16201 **Lat:** 40-48-42 N **Long:** 79-31-54 W
Pop: 1,253 (1990); 1,591 (1980) **Pop Density:** 3132.5
Land: 0.4 sq. mi.; **Water:** 0.0 sq. mi. **Elev:** 980 ft.

Worthington
Borough
ZIP: 16262 **Lat:** 40-50-16 N **Long:** 79-38-03 W
Pop: 713 (1990); 760 (1980) **Pop Density:** 1188.3
Land: 0.6 sq. mi.; **Water:** 0.0 sq. mi. **Elev:** 1140 ft.

Beaver County
County Seat: Beaver (ZIP: 15009)

Pop: 186,093 (1990); 204,441 (1980) **Pop Density:** 427.5
Land: 435.3 sq. mi.; **Water:** 8.7 sq. mi. **Area Code:** 412
On central western border of PA, northwest of Pittsburgh; organized Mar 12, 1800 from Allegheny and Washington counties.
Name origin: For the Beaver River, which traverses it.

Aliquippa
Borough
ZIP: 15001 **Lat:** 40-37-02 N **Long:** 80-15-18 W
Pop: 13,374 (1990); 17,094 (1980) **Pop Density:** 3262.0
Land: 4.1 sq. mi.; **Water:** 0.4 sq. mi. **Elev:** 700 ft.
In western PA on the Ohio River, 19 mi. west-northwest of Pittsburgh.
Name origin: For the Iroquois queen, Aliquippa, who is said to have lived on the site of McKeesport in the 1750s and whose name is probably from an Iroquois term meaning 'hat.'

Ambridge
Borough
ZIP: 15003 **Lat:** 40-35-35 N **Long:** 80-13-31 W
Pop: 8,133 (1990); 9,575 (1980) **Pop Density:** 5422.0
Land: 1.5 sq. mi.; **Water:** 0.0 sq. mi. **Elev:** 800 ft.
Name origin: For the American Bridge Company, which bought the community called Harmony Society here in 1901.

Baden
Borough
ZIP: 15005 **Lat:** 40-38-18 N **Long:** 80-13-18 W
Pop: 5,074 (1990); 5,318 (1980) **Pop Density:** 2206.1
Land: 2.3 sq. mi.; **Water:** 0.2 sq. mi. **Elev:** 900 ft.
In western PA just north of Ambridge. Incorporated 1868.

Beaver
Borough
ZIP: 15009 **Lat:** 40-41-34 N **Long:** 80-18-27 W
Pop: 5,028 (1990); 5,441 (1980) **Pop Density:** 5586.7
Land: 0.9 sq. mi.; **Water:** 0.2 sq. mi. **Elev:** 780 ft.
In western PA, 25 mi. northwest of Pittsburgh; incorporated Mar 29, 1802.
Name origin: For the county, located at the mouth of the Beaver River.

Beaver Falls
City
ZIP: 15010 **Lat:** 40-45-39 N **Long:** 80-19-20 W
Pop: 10,687 (1990); 12,525 (1980) **Pop Density:** 5089.0
Land: 2.1 sq. mi.; **Water:** 0.2 sq. mi. **Elev:** 780 ft.
In western PA on the west bank of the Beaver River where it forms falls, 30 mi. northwest of Pittsburgh. Laid out in 1806.
Name origin: Named in 1866 by members of the Harmony

Society. Previously called Brighton by the Constable brothers of Brighton, England.

Big Beaver   Borough
ZIP: 15010   **Lat:** 40-49-06 N **Long:** 80-21-48 W
Pop: 2,298 (1990); 2,815 (1980)   **Pop Density:** 129.1
Land: 17.8 sq. mi.; **Water:** 0.2 sq. mi.

Bridgewater   Borough
                        Lat: 40-42-32 N **Long:** 80-18-01 W
Pop: 751 (1990); 879 (1980)   **Pop Density:** 1072.9
Land: 0.7 sq. mi.; **Water:** 0.1 sq. mi.

Brighton   Township
ZIP: 15009   **Lat:** 40-42-05 N **Long:** 80-22-00 W
Pop: 7,489 (1990); 7,858 (1980)   **Pop Density:** 386.0
Land: 19.4 sq. mi.; **Water:** 0.0 sq. mi.

In central-western PA, a northwestern suburb of Pittsburgh.
Name origin: For the English seaside resort.

Center   Township
ZIP: 15001   **Lat:** 40-38-50 N **Long:** 80-18-00 W
Pop: 10,742 (1990); 10,733 (1980)   **Pop Density:** 697.5
Land: 15.4 sq. mi.; **Water:** 0.3 sq. mi.

Chippewa   Township
ZIP: 15010   **Lat:** 40-45-32 N **Long:** 80-23-05 W
Pop: 6,988 (1990); 7,245 (1980)   **Pop Density:** 426.1
Land: 16.4 sq. mi.; **Water:** 0.0 sq. mi.

Conway   Borough
ZIP: 15207   **Lat:** 40-39-52 N **Long:** 80-14-27 W
Pop: 2,424 (1990); 2,747 (1980)   **Pop Density:** 1864.6
Land: 1.3 sq. mi.; **Water:** 0.2 sq. mi.   **Elev:** 760 ft.

In western PA on the east bank of the Ohio River, 19 mi. northwest of Pittsburgh.

Darlington   Township
ZIP: 16115   **Lat:** 40-49-21 N **Long:** 80-28-09 W
Pop: 2,040 (1990); 2,090 (1980)   **Pop Density:** 92.7
Land: 22.0 sq. mi.; **Water:** 0.1 sq. mi.

*Darlington   Borough
ZIP: 16115   **Lat:** 40-48-36 N **Long:** 80-25-26 W
Pop: 311 (1990); 377 (1980)   **Pop Density:** 3110.0
Land: 0.1 sq. mi.; **Water:** 0.0 sq. mi.   **Elev:** 912 ft.

Daugherty   Township
                        Lat: 40-44-52 N **Long:** 80-16-29 W
Pop: 3,433 (1990); 3,605 (1980)   **Pop Density:** 343.3
Land: 10.0 sq. mi.; **Water:** 0.0 sq. mi.

East Rochester   Borough
ZIP: 15074   **Lat:** 40-41-53 N **Long:** 80-16-05 W
Pop: 672 (1990); 789 (1980)   **Pop Density:** 1680.0
Land: 0.4 sq. mi.; **Water:** 0.1 sq. mi.   **Elev:** 800 ft.

Eastvale   Borough
ZIP: 15010   **Lat:** 40-46-03 N **Long:** 80-18-55 W
Pop: 328 (1990); 379 (1980)   **Pop Density:** 3280.0
Land: 0.1 sq. mi.; **Water:** 0.0 sq. mi.   **Elev:** 800 ft.

Economy   Borough
ZIP: 15005   **Lat:** 40-38-18 N **Long:** 80-11-06 W
Pop: 9,519 (1990); 9,538 (1980)   **Pop Density:** 537.8
Land: 17.7 sq. mi.; **Water:** 0.1 sq. mi.   **Elev:** 1000 ft.

Founded 1825 by the Harmony Society, a religious organization noted for its thrift and efficiency, that bought c. 3,000 acres of land here. Through the group's economy and business administration the members became immensely

wealthy, especially after oil was discovered on their lands. Incorporated 1958.

Ellwood City   Borough
ZIP: 16117   **Lat:** 40-51-05 N **Long:** 80-17-05 W
Pop: 850 (1990); 795 (1980)   **Pop Density:** 2125.0
Land: 0.4 sq. mi.; **Water:** 0.0 sq. mi.   **Elev:** 1210 ft.

In western PA on the Shenango River, 10 mi. north of Beaver Falls. Laid out in 1890 by the Pittsburgh Company. Part of the town is also in Lawrence County.
Name origin: For Col. I. L. Ellwood of IN, who pioneered the manufacturing of wire fencing.

Fallston   Borough
ZIP: 15066   **Lat:** 40-43-17 N **Long:** 80-18-52 W
Pop: 392 (1990); 312 (1980)   **Pop Density:** 784.0
Land: 0.5 sq. mi.; **Water:** 0.0 sq. mi.   **Elev:** 720 ft.

Frankfort Springs   Borough
ZIP: 15050   **Lat:** 40-28-52 N **Long:** 80-26-44 W
Pop: 134 (1990); 187 (1980)   **Pop Density:** 670.0
Land: 0.2 sq. mi.; **Water:** 0.0 sq. mi.   **Elev:** 1186 ft.

Franklin   Township
                        Lat: 40-49-59 N **Long:** 80-12-21 W
Pop: 3,821 (1990); 3,772 (1980)   **Pop Density:** 215.9
Land: 17.7 sq. mi.; **Water:** 0.1 sq. mi.

Freedom   Borough
ZIP: 15042   **Lat:** 40-41-04 N **Long:** 80-15-12 W
Pop: 1,897 (1990); 2,272 (1980)   **Pop Density:** 3161.7
Land: 0.6 sq. mi.; **Water:** 0.1 sq. mi.   **Elev:** 900 ft.

In western PA on a bend of the Ohio River; a northwestern suburb of Pittsburgh.

Georgetown   Borough
ZIP: 15043   **Lat:** 40-38-30 N **Long:** 80-29-59 W
Pop: 194 (1990); 231 (1980)   **Pop Density:** 970.0
Land: 0.2 sq. mi.; **Water:** 0.1 sq. mi.   **Elev:** 838 ft.

Glasgow   Borough
ZIP: 15059   **Lat:** 40-38-40 N **Long:** 80-30-30 W
Pop: 74 (1990); 106 (1980)   **Pop Density:** 740.0
Land: 0.1 sq. mi.; **Water:** 0.1 sq. mi.   **Elev:** 700 ft.

Greene   Township
                        Lat: 40-35-45 N **Long:** 80-28-22 W
Pop: 2,573 (1990); 2,422 (1980)   **Pop Density:** 99.7
Land: 25.8 sq. mi.; **Water:** 0.4 sq. mi.

Hanover   Township
                        Lat: 40-31-02 N **Long:** 80-26-31 W
Pop: 3,470 (1990); 3,443 (1980)   **Pop Density:** 77.3
Land: 44.9 sq. mi.; **Water:** 0.2 sq. mi.

Harmony   Township
                        Lat: 40-36-25 N **Long:** 80-13-13 W
Pop: 3,694 (1990); 3,977 (1980)   **Pop Density:** 1273.8
Land: 2.9 sq. mi.; **Water:** 0.4 sq. mi.

Homewood   Borough
ZIP: 15010   **Lat:** 40-48-48 N **Long:** 80-19-45 W
Pop: 162 (1990); 188 (1980)   **Pop Density:** 810.0
Land: 0.2 sq. mi.; **Water:** 0.0 sq. mi.   **Elev:** 1100 ft.

Hookstown   Borough
ZIP: 15050   **Lat:** 40-35-55 N **Long:** 80-28-27 W
Pop: 169 (1990); 228 (1980)   **Pop Density:** 1690.0
Land: 0.1 sq. mi.; **Water:** 0.0 sq. mi.   **Elev:** 1010 ft.

Hopewell
Township
ZIP: 15001   **Lat:** 40-35-29 N **Long:** 80-16-26 W
Pop: 13,274 (1990); 14,662 (1980)   **Pop Density:** 785.4
Land: 16.9 sq. mi.; **Water:** 0.2 sq. mi.

Independence
Township
Lat: 40-32-23 N **Long:** 80-19-57 W
Pop: 2,563 (1990); 2,534 (1980)   **Pop Density:** 111.9
Land: 22.9 sq. mi.; **Water:** 0.4 sq. mi.

Industry
Borough
ZIP: 15052   **Lat:** 40-39-21 N **Long:** 80-24-35 W
Pop: 2,124 (1990); 2,417 (1980)   **Pop Density:** 223.6
Land: 9.5 sq. mi.; **Water:** 0.7 sq. mi.   **Elev:** 696 ft.

Koppel
Borough
ZIP: 16136   **Lat:** 40-50-05 N **Long:** 80-19-20 W
Pop: 1,024 (1990); 1,146 (1980)   **Pop Density:** 2048.0
Land: 0.5 sq. mi.; **Water:** 0.0 sq. mi.   **Elev:** 960 ft.
Name origin: For Arthur Koppel of Germany, who established a freight car factory here a few years before World War I.

Marion
Township
Lat: 40-47-12 N **Long:** 80-12-46 W
Pop: 909 (1990); 941 (1980)   **Pop Density:** 88.3
Land: 10.3 sq. mi.; **Water:** 0.3 sq. mi.

Midland
Borough
ZIP: 15059   **Lat:** 40-38-23 N **Long:** 80-27-28 W
Pop: 3,321 (1990); 4,310 (1980)   **Pop Density:** 1581.4
Land: 2.1 sq. mi.; **Water:** 0.2 sq. mi.   **Elev:** 781 ft.
In western PA on the north bank of the Ohio River, 7 mi. east of Liverpool.
Name origin: For the Midland Steel Company.

Monaca
Borough
ZIP: 15061   **Lat:** 40-41-00 N **Long:** 80-16-23 W
Pop: 6,739 (1990); 7,661 (1980)   **Pop Density:** 3209.0
Land: 2.1 sq. mi.; **Water:** 0.4 sq. mi.   **Elev:** 900 ft.
In western PA, 2 mi. south of Beaver.

New Brighton
Borough
ZIP: 15066   **Lat:** 40-44-08 N **Long:** 80-18-31 W
Pop: 6,854 (1990); 7,364 (1980)   **Pop Density:** 6854.0
Land: 1.0 sq. mi.; **Water:** 0.1 sq. mi.   **Elev:** 760 ft.
In western PA, just south of Beaver Falls.
Name origin: For the English seaside resort.

New Galilee
Borough
ZIP: 16141   **Lat:** 40-49-59 N **Long:** 80-24-03 W
Pop: 500 (1990); 596 (1980)   **Pop Density:** 1666.7
Land: 0.3 sq. mi.; **Water:** 0.0 sq. mi.   **Elev:** 955 ft.
In southwestern PA, a suburb of Pittsburgh.
Name origin: Named by religious settlers for Jesus's homeland.

New Sewickley
Township
ZIP: 15074   **Lat:** 40-43-03 N **Long:** 80-12-00 W
Pop: 6,861 (1990); 7,340 (1980)   **Pop Density:** 209.8
Land: 32.7 sq. mi.; **Water:** 0.0 sq. mi.

North Sewickley
Township
ZIP: 15010   **Lat:** 40-47-53 N **Long:** 80-17-00 W
Pop: 6,178 (1990); 6,758 (1980)   **Pop Density:** 298.5
Land: 20.7 sq. mi.; **Water:** 0.4 sq. mi.

Ohioville
Borough
ZIP: 15059   **Lat:** 40-40-58 N **Long:** 80-28-38 W
Pop: 3,865 (1990); 4,217 (1980)   **Pop Density:** 165.9
Land: 23.3 sq. mi.; **Water:** 0.3 sq. mi.   **Elev:** 1137 ft.
Incorporated in the early 1960s.

Patterson
Township
Lat: 40-44-35 N **Long:** 80-19-56 W
Pop: 3,074 (1990); 3,288 (1980)   **Pop Density:** 1808.2
Land: 1.7 sq. mi.; **Water:** 0.0 sq. mi.

Patterson Heights
Borough
ZIP: 15010   **Lat:** 40-44-20 N **Long:** 80-19-37 W
Pop: 576 (1990); 797 (1980)   **Pop Density:** 2880.0
Land: 0.2 sq. mi.; **Water:** 0.0 sq. mi.   **Elev:** 1040 ft.

Potter
Township
Lat: 40-39-13 N **Long:** 80-21-09 W
Pop: 546 (1990); 605 (1980)   **Pop Density:** 89.5
Land: 6.1 sq. mi.; **Water:** 0.6 sq. mi.

Pulaski
Township
Lat: 40-43-54 N **Long** 80-17-45 W
Pop: 1,697 (1990); 1,998 (1980)   **Pop Density:** 2121.3
Land: 0.8 sq. mi.; **Water:** 0.0 sq. mi.   **Elev:** 1060 ft.

Raccoon
Township
Lat: 40-36-03 N **Long:** 80-22-40 W
Pop: 3,426 (1990); 3,133 (1980)   **Pop Density:** 185.2
Land: 18.5 sq. mi.; **Water:** 0.7 sq. mi.

Rochester
Borough
ZIP: 15074   **Lat:** 40-42-07 N **Long** 80-16-59 W
Pop: 4,156 (1990); 4,759 (1980)   **Pop Density:** 6926.7
Land: 0.6 sq. mi.; **Water:** 0.1 sq. mi.   **Elev:** 860 ft.
In western PA at the confluence of the Beaver and Ohio rivers, where the latter turns southwestward.
Name origin: Named in 1838 by Ovid Pinney for his native Rochester, NY.

*Rochester
Township
ZIP: 15074   **Lat:** 40-42-29 N **Long:** 80-16-24 W
Pop: 3,247 (1990); 3,427 (1980)   **Pop Density:** 854.5
Land: 3.8 sq. mi.; **Water:** 0.1 sq. mi.

Shippingport
Borough
ZIP: 15077   **Lat:** 40-37-31 N **Long:** 80-25-27 W
Pop: 227 (1990); 255 (1980)   **Pop Density:** 68.8
Land: 3.3 sq. mi.; **Water:** 0.4 sq. mi.   **Elev:** 781 ft.
In western PA on the Ohio River, a northwestern suburb of Pittsburgh.
Name origin: For being a coal shipment point.

South Beaver
Township
Lat: 40-45-24 N **Long:** 80-27-31 W
Pop: 2,942 (1990); 2,932 (1980)   **Pop Density:** 99.4
Land: 29.6 sq. mi.; **Water:** 0.1 sq. mi.

South Heights
Borough
ZIP: 15081   **Lat:** 40-34-28 N **Long:** 80-14-10 W
Pop: 647 (1990); 765 (1980)   **Pop Density:** 2156.7
Land: 0.3 sq. mi.; **Water:** 0.1 sq. mi.   **Elev:** 760 ft.

Vanport
Township
Lat: 40-41-03 N **Long:** 80-19-48 W
Pop: 1,700 (1990); 2,013 (1980)   **Pop Density:** 1888.9
Land: 0.9 sq. mi.; **Water:** 0.3 sq. mi.
In western PA, a suburb of Beaver Falls.
Name origin: Named for Martin Van Buren (1782–1862) during his 1836 presidential campaign.

West Mayfield　　　　　　　　　　　Borough
ZIP: 15010　　**Lat:** 40-46-44 N **Long:** 80-20-17 W
Pop: 1,312 (1990); 1,712 (1980)　　**Pop Density:** 1640.0
Land: 0.8 sq. mi.; **Water:** 0.0 sq. mi.　　**Elev:** 1000 ft.

White　　　　　　　　　　　Township
ZIP: 15010　　**Lat:** 40-46-00 N **Long:** 80-20-05 W
Pop: 1,610 (1990); 1,870 (1980)　　**Pop Density:** 2300.0
Land: 0.7 sq. mi.; **Water:** 0.0 sq. mi.

Bedford County
County Seat: Bedford (ZIP: 15522)

Pop: 47,919 (1990); 46,784 (1980)　　**Pop Density:** 47.2
Land: 1014.6 sq. mi.; **Water:** 2.9 sq. mi.　　**Area Code:** 814

On southern border with MD, southeast of Johnstown; organized Mar 9, 1771 (prior to statehood) from Cumberland County.

Name origin: For Fort Bedford, which became the site of the county seat of Bedford. The fort was named in 1759 to honor England's Duke of Bedford.

Bedford　　　　　　　　　　　Township
ZIP: 15522　　**Lat:** 40-02-52 N **Long:** 78-29-23 W
Pop: 4,945 (1990); 4,692 (1980)　　**Pop Density:** 72.1
Land: 68.6 sq. mi.; **Water:** 0.0 sq. mi.

*Bedford　　　　　　　　　　　Borough
ZIP: 15522　　**Lat:** 40-00-53 N **Long:** 78-30-15 W
Pop: 3,137 (1990); 3,326 (1980)　　**Pop Density:** 2851.8
Land: 1.1 sq. mi.; **Water:** 0.0 sq. mi.　　**Elev:** 1106 ft.

In southern PA, southwest of Altoona. Settled c. 1750; incorporated Mar 13, 1795.

Name origin: For Fort Bedford, an important outpost during the colonial period. Originally called Raystown for a Scottish trader, John Wray, who had a post here.

Bloomfield　　　　　　　　　　　Township
Lat: 40-14-51 N **Long:** 78-25-21 W
Pop: 766 (1990); 631 (1980)　　**Pop Density:** 39.3
Land: 19.5 sq. mi.; **Water:** 0.0 sq. mi.

Broad Top　　　　　　　　　　　Township
Lat: 40-08-28 N **Long:** 78-13-18 W
Pop: 1,918 (1990); 1,837 (1980)　　**Pop Density:** 39.8
Land: 48.2 sq. mi.; **Water:** 0.3 sq. mi.

Coaldale　　　　　　　　　　　Borough
Lat: 40-10-04 N **Long:** 78-13-01 W
Pop: 143 (1990); 233 (1980)　　**Pop Density:** 2860.0
Land: 0.05 sq. mi.; **Water:** 0.0 sq. mi.　　**Elev:** 1130 ft.

Colerain　　　　　　　　　　　Township
Lat: 39-55-55 N **Long:** 78-29-56 W
Pop: 1,058 (1990); 1,015 (1980)　　**Pop Density:** 25.2
Land: 42.0 sq. mi.; **Water:** 0.0 sq. mi.

Cumberland Valley　　　　　　　　　　　Township
Lat: 39-48-57 N **Long:** 78-38-15 W
Pop: 1,473 (1990); 1,494 (1980)　　**Pop Density:** 24.8
Land: 59.4 sq. mi.; **Water:** 0.6 sq. mi.

East Providence　　　　　　　　　　　Township
Lat: 39-59-58 N **Long:** 78-15-48 W
Pop: 1,785 (1990); 1,808 (1980)　　**Pop Density:** 35.3
Land: 50.5 sq. mi.; **Water:** 0.2 sq. mi.

East St. Clair　　　　　　　　　　　Township
Lat: 40-07-35 N **Long:** 78-33-07 W
Pop: 2,765 (1990); 2,492 (1980)　　**Pop Density:** 81.6
Land: 33.9 sq. mi.; **Water:** 0.0 sq. mi.

Everett　　　　　　　　　　　Borough
ZIP: 15537　　**Lat:** 40-00-45 N **Long:** 78-21-58 W
Pop: 1,777 (1990); 1,828 (1980)　　**Pop Density:** 1615.5
Land: 1.1 sq. mi.; **Water:** 0.0 sq. mi.　　**Elev:** 1017 ft.

In southern PA in the Tussey Mountains, 42 mi. south of Altoona.

Harrison　　　　　　　　　　　Township
Lat: 39-57-27 N **Long:** 78-38-03 W
Pop: 967 (1990); 951 (1980)　　**Pop Density:** 25.6
Land: 37.7 sq. mi.; **Water:** 0.0 sq. mi.

Hopewell　　　　　　　　　　　Township
ZIP: 16650　　**Lat:** 40-07-19 N **Long:** 78-19-15 W
Pop: 1,928 (1990); 1,926 (1980)　　**Pop Density:** 56.4
Land: 34.2 sq. mi.; **Water:** 0.2 sq. mi.

*Hopewell　　　　　　　　　　　Borough
ZIP: 16650　　**Lat:** 40-08-04 N **Long:** 78-16-00 W
Pop: 194 (1990); 256 (1980)　　**Pop Density:** 1940.0
Land: 0.1 sq. mi.; **Water:** 0.0 sq. mi.　　**Elev:** 901 ft.

Hyndman　　　　　　　　　　　Borough
ZIP: 15545　　**Lat:** 39-49-15 N **Long:** 78-43-16 W
Pop: 1,019 (1990); 1,106 (1980)　　**Pop Density:** 2547.5
Land: 0.4 sq. mi.; **Water:** 0.0 sq. mi.　　**Elev:** 948 ft.

In southern PA on Wills Creek, 50 mi. southwest of Altoona. Incorporated 1877.

Name origin: For E. K. Hyndman, president of the Pittsburgh & Western Railroad. Originally called Bridgeport.

Juniata　　　　　　　　　　　Township
Lat: 39-59-13 N **Long:** 78-43-20 W
Pop: 865 (1990); 799 (1980)　　**Pop Density:** 18.2
Land: 47.4 sq. mi.; **Water:** 0.0 sq. mi.

Kimmel　　　　　　　　　　　Township
Lat: 40-14-42 N **Long:** 78-30-03 W
Pop: 1,605 (1990); 1,492 (1980)　　**Pop Density:** 78.7
Land: 20.4 sq. mi.; **Water:** 0.0 sq. mi.

King　　　　　　　　　　　Township
Lat: 40-11-46 N **Long:** 78-30-50 W
Pop: 1,226 (1990); 1,154 (1980)　　**Pop Density:** 79.6
Land: 15.4 sq. mi.; **Water:** 0.0 sq. mi.

Liberty　　　　　　　　　　　Township
Lat: 40-12-30 N **Long:** 78-16-42 W
Pop: 1,478 (1990); 1,534 (1980)　　**Pop Density:** 56.2
Land: 26.3 sq. mi.; **Water:** 0.3 sq. mi.

Lincoln
Township
Lat: 40-13-34 N **Long:** 78-36-36 W
Pop: 394 (1990); 349 (1980) **Pop Density:** 24.3
Land: 16.2 sq. mi.; **Water:** 0.0 sq. mi.
Name origin: For Abraham Lincoln (1809–65), sixteenth U.S. president.

Londonderry
Township
Lat: 39-50-11 N **Long:** 78-43-21 W
Pop: 1,893 (1990); 1,899 (1980) **Pop Density:** 34.5
Land: 54.8 sq. mi.; **Water:** 0.0 sq. mi.

Mann
Township
ZIP: 17211 **Lat:** 39-45-42 N **Long:** 78-24-06 W
Pop: 481 (1990); 455 (1980) **Pop Density:** 13.4
Land: 35.9 sq. mi.; **Water:** 0.0 sq. mi.

Manns Choice
Borough
ZIP: 15550 **Lat:** 40-00-09 N **Long:** 78-35-30 W
Pop: 249 (1990); 286 (1980) **Pop Density:** 498.0
Land: 0.5 sq. mi.; **Water:** 0.0 sq. mi. **Elev:** 1200 ft.

Monroe
Township
Lat: 39-52-40 N **Long:** 78-22-48 W
Pop: 1,305 (1990); 1,202 (1980) **Pop Density:** 14.8
Land: 88.0 sq. mi.; **Water:** 0.0 sq. mi.

Napier
Township
Lat: 40-04-46 N **Long:** 78-38-37 W
Pop: 2,054 (1990); 1,977 (1980) **Pop Density:** 35.5
Land: 57.9 sq. mi.; **Water:** 0.7 sq. mi.

New Paris
Borough
ZIP: 15554 **Lat:** 40-06-27 N **Long:** 78-38-35 W
Pop: 223 (1990); 199 (1980) **Pop Density:** 2230.0
Land: 0.1 sq. mi.; **Water:** 0.0 sq. mi. **Elev:** 1258 ft.

Pleasantville
Borough
ZIP: 15521 **Lat:** 40-10-49 N **Long:** 78-36-47 W
Pop: 215 (1990); 275 (1980) **Pop Density:** 2150.0
Land: 0.1 sq. mi.; **Water:** 0.0 sq. mi.
In southern PA on the Juniata River.

Rainsburg
Borough
ZIP: 15522 **Lat:** 39-53-42 N **Long:** 78-30-58 W
Pop: 175 (1990); 201 (1980) **Pop Density:** 875.0
Land: 0.2 sq. mi.; **Water:** 0.0 sq. mi. **Elev:** 1398 ft.

St. Clairsville
Borough
Lat: 40-09-21 N **Long:** 78-30-38 W
Pop: 88 (1990); 90 (1980)
Land: 0.0 sq. mi.; **Water:** 0.0 sq. mi. **Elev:** 1220 ft.

Saxton
Borough
ZIP: 16678 **Lat:** 40-12-46 N **Long:** 78-14-50 W
Pop: 838 (1990); 814 (1980) **Pop Density:** 2095.0
Land: 0.4 sq. mi.; **Water:** 0.0 sq. mi. **Elev:** 918 ft.

Schellsburg
Borough
ZIP: 15559 **Lat:** 40-02-54 N **Long:** 78-38-34 W
Pop: 245 (1990); 325 (1980) **Pop Density:** 612.5
Land: 0.4 sq. mi.; **Water:** 0.0 sq. mi. **Elev:** 1258 ft.

Snake Spring
Township
Lat: 40-02-11 N **Long:** 78-25-05 W
Pop: 1,511 (1990); 1,498 (1980) **Pop Density:** 58.6
Land: 25.8 sq. mi.; **Water:** 0.0 sq. mi.

Southampton
Township
Lat: 39-47-24 N **Long:** 78-31-07 W
Pop: 920 (1990); 825 (1980) **Pop Density:** 11.5
Land: 79.9 sq. mi.; **Water:** 0.0 sq. mi.

South Woodbury
Township
Lat: 40-09-33 N **Long:** 78-25-05 W
Pop: 1,839 (1990); 1,755 (1980) **Pop Density:** 53.9
Land: 34.1 sq. mi.; **Water:** 0.0 sq. mi.

Union
Township
Lat: 40-16-23 N **Long:** 78-35-34 W
Pop: 296 (1990); 215 (1980) **Pop Density:** 13.5
Land: 22.0 sq. mi.; **Water:** 0.0 sq. mi.

West Providence
Township
Lat: 39-59-42 N **Long:** 78-21-11 W
Pop: 3,233 (1990); 3,361 (1980) **Pop Density:** 84.0
Land: 38.5 sq. mi.; **Water:** 0.4 sq. mi.

West St. Clair
Township
Lat: 40-10-18 N **Long:** 78-38-06 W
Pop: 1,543 (1990); 1,251 (1980) **Pop Density:** 51.4
Land: 30.0 sq. mi.; **Water:** 0.0 sq. mi.

Woodbury
Township
ZIP: 16695 **Lat:** 40-13-48 N **Long:** 78-21-05 W
Pop: 1,129 (1990); 966 (1980) **Pop Density:** 47.6
Land: 23.7 sq. mi.; **Water:** 0.0 sq. mi.

*Woodbury
Borough
ZIP: 16695 **Lat:** 40-13-32 N **Long:** 78-22-00 W
Pop: 239 (1990); 267 (1980) **Pop Density:** 2390.0
Land: 0.1 sq. mi.; **Water:** 0.0 sq. mi. **Elev:** 1225 ft.

Berks County
County Seat: Reading (ZIP: 19601)

Pop: 336,523 (1990); 312,509 (1980) **Pop Density:** 391.7
Land: 859.2 sq. mi.; **Water:** 6.5 sq. mi. **Area Code:** 215

In southeastern PA, southwest of Allentown; established Mar 11, 1752 from Chester, Lancaster, and Philadelphia counties.

Name origin: The shortened form for Berkshire, England, which also has a Reading as its county seat; site of large land holdings of the Penn family.

Adamstown
Borough
ZIP: 19501 **Lat:** 40-14-54 N **Long:** 76-02-45 W
Pop: 0 (1990); 12 (1980)
Water: 0.0 sq. mi. **Elev:** 980 ft.

In southern PA, south of Reading. Part of the borough is also in Lancaster County.

Name origin: For the Adams Mill, included in a patent for 356 acres obtained by William Bird in 1739.

Albany
Township
ZIP: 19529 **Lat:** 40-37-28 N **Long:** 75-53-54 W
Pop: 1,547 (1990); 1,381 (1980) **Pop Density:** 38.5
Land: 40.2 sq. mi.; **Water:** 0.0 sq. mi.

In east-central PA, west of Allentown.

Name origin: For the Duke of Albany, the Scottish title of King James II of England.

Alsace
Township
Lat: 40-22-55 N **Long:** 75-51-56 W
Pop: 3,459 (1990); 3,456 (1980) **Pop Density:** 283.5
Land: 12.2 sq. mi.; **Water:** 0.0 sq. mi.

Amity
Township
ZIP: 19518 **Lat:** 40-17-28 N **Long:** 75-44-45 W
Pop: 6,434 (1990); 5,883 (1980) **Pop Density:** 351.6
Land: 18.3 sq. mi.; **Water:** 0.1 sq. mi.

In southeastern PA, southeast of Reading. Formed 1719.

Name origin: For the friendly relations existing between the Indians and the Swedes, whom William Penn (1644–1718) convinced to settle here.

Amity Gardens
CDP
Lat: 40-16-26 N **Long:** 75-44-08 W
Pop: 2,714 (1990) **Pop Density:** 2714.0
Land: 1.0 sq. mi.; **Water:** 0.0 sq. mi.

Bally
Borough
ZIP: 19503 **Lat:** 40-24-03 N **Long:** 75-35-19 W
Pop: 973 (1990); 1,051 (1980) **Pop Density:** 1946.0
Land: 0.5 sq. mi.; **Water:** 0.0 sq. mi. **Elev:** 468 ft.

In southeastern PA, northeast of Reading. Laid out in 1742 on ground owned by the Society of Jesus.

Name origin: For the Rev. Augustin Bally, S.J.

Bechtelsville
Borough
ZIP: 19505 **Lat:** 40-22-15 N **Long:** 75-37-50 W
Pop: 884 (1990); 832 (1980) **Pop Density:** 1768.0
Land: 0.5 sq. mi.; **Water:** 0.0 sq. mi. **Elev:** 420 ft.

Bern
Township
ZIP: 19605 **Lat:** 40-23-50 N **Long:** 75-59-47 W
Pop: 6,303 (1990); 5,097 (1980) **Pop Density:** 328.3
Land: 19.2 sq. mi.; **Water:** 0.8 sq. mi.
Settled early 1700s.

Name origin: Named by settlers from the Berne region in Switzerland; with spelling alteration.

Bernville
Borough
ZIP: 19506 **Lat:** 40-26-02 N **Long:** 76-06-38 W
Pop: 789 (1990); 798 (1980) **Pop Density:** 1972.5
Land: 0.4 sq. mi.; **Water:** 0.0 sq. mi.

Bethel
Village & Township
ZIP: 19507 **Lat:** 40-29-16 N **Long:** 76-18-42 W
Pop: 3,676 (1990); 3,312 (1980) **Pop Density:** 87.1
Land: 42.2 sq. mi.; **Water:** 0.0 sq. mi.

In southeastern PA, 40 mi. east of Harrisburg.

Birdsboro
Borough
ZIP: 19508 **Lat:** 40-15-38 N **Long:** 75-48-37 W
Pop: 4,222 (1990); 3,481 (1980) **Pop Density:** 3015.7
Land: 1.4 sq. mi.; **Water:** 0.0 sq. mi. **Elev:** 163 ft.

In southeastern PA on the Schuylkill River, 11 mi. west of Pottstown. Founded 1740.

Name origin: For ironmaster William Bird, who obtained a patent for 356 acres here in 1739.

Boyertown
Borough
ZIP: 19512 **Lat:** 40-19-54 N **Long:** 75-38-16 W
Pop: 3,759 (1990); 3,979 (1980) **Pop Density:** 4698.8
Land: 0.8 sq. mi.; **Water:** 0.0 sq. mi. **Elev:** 415 ft.

In southeast-central PA, 25 mi. south of Allentown. Settled 1720; founded 1834.

Name origin: For Henry Boyer, an early settler.

Brecknock
Township
Lat: 40-13-46 N **Long:** 75-58-41 W
Pop: 3,770 (1990); 2,641 (1980) **Pop Density:** 211.8
Land: 17.8 sq. mi.; **Water:** 0.0 sq. mi.

Caernarvon
Township
Lat: 40-10-12 N **Long:** 75-52-53 W
Pop: 1,951 (1990); 1,710 (1980) **Pop Density:** 154.8
Land: 12.6 sq. mi.; **Water:** 0.0 sq. mi.

Centerport
Borough
ZIP: 19516 **Lat:** 40-29-11 N **Long:** 76-00-22 W
Pop: 284 (1990); 246 (1980) **Pop Density:** 1420.0
Land: 0.2 sq. mi.; **Water:** 0.0 sq. mi. **Elev:** 340 ft.

In southeastern PA on Irish Creek, northwest of Reading.

Centre
Township
ZIP: 19541 **Lat:** 40-28-33 N **Long:** 76-01-04 W
Pop: 3,154 (1990); 2,329 (1980) **Pop Density:** 147.4
Land: 21.4 sq. mi.; **Water:** 0.2 sq. mi.

Colebrookdale
Township
ZIP: 19512 **Lat:** 40-20-40 N **Long:** 75-38-32 W
Pop: 5,469 (1990); 4,748 (1980) **Pop Density:** 651.1
Land: 8.4 sq. mi.; **Water:** 0.0 sq. mi.

Cumru
Township
ZIP: 19540 **Lat:** 40-17-00 N **Long:** 75-57-32 W
Pop: 13,142 (1990); 11,474 (1980) **Pop Density:** 638.0
Land: 20.6 sq. mi.; **Water:** 0.2 sq. mi.

District
Township
ZIP: 19512 **Lat:** 40-26-04 N **Long:** 75-39-05 W
Pop: 1,211 (1990); 1,094 (1980) **Pop Density:** 104.4
Land: 11.6 sq. mi.; **Water:** 0.0 sq. mi.

Douglass
Township
Lat: 40-17-21 N **Long:** 75-40-57 W
Pop: 3,570 (1990); 3,128 (1980) **Pop Density:** 278.9
Land: 12.8 sq. mi.; **Water:** 0.0 sq. mi.

Earl
Township
ZIP: 19512 **Lat:** 40-20-56 N **Long:** 75-42-36 W
Pop: 3,016 (1990); 2,607 (1980) **Pop Density:** 218.6
Land: 13.8 sq. mi.; **Water:** 0.0 sq. mi.

Exeter
Township
ZIP: 19606 **Lat:** 40-18-24 N **Long:** 75-50-11 W
Pop: 17,260 (1990); 14,419 (1980) **Pop Density:** 707.4
Land: 24.4 sq. mi.; **Water:** 0.2 sq. mi.

In eastern PA on the Susquehanna River, 9 mi. west of Scranton.
Name origin: For Exeter, RI, former home of many early settlers.

Fleetwood
Borough
ZIP: 19522 **Lat:** 40-27-20 N **Long:** 75-49-17 W
Pop: 3,478 (1990); 3,422 (1980) **Pop Density:** 3478.0
Land: 1.0 sq. mi.; **Water:** 0.0 sq. mi. **Elev:** 440 ft.

In southeastern PA, 15 mi. northeast of Reading.
Name origin: Named in 1859 for an English capitalist, who encouraged the construction of the railroad.

Flying Hills
CDP
Lat: 40-16-36 N **Long:** 75-54-52 W
Pop: 1,526 (1990) **Pop Density:** 5086.7
Land: 0.3 sq. mi.; **Water:** 0.0 sq. mi.

Greenwich
Township
ZIP: 19530 **Lat:** 40-33-47 N **Long:** 75-49-46 W
Pop: 2,977 (1990); 2,432 (1980) **Pop Density:** 95.1
Land: 31.3 sq. mi.; **Water:** 0.0 sq. mi.

Hamburg
Borough
ZIP: 19526 **Lat:** 40-33-22 N **Long:** 75-58-58 W
Pop: 3,987 (1990); 4,011 (1980) **Pop Density:** 2098.4
Land: 1.9 sq. mi.; **Water:** 0.1 sq. mi. **Elev:** 373 ft.

In southeastern PA on the east bank of the Schuykill River, 17 mi. north of Reading.

Heidelberg
Township
Lat: 40-21-25 N **Long:** 76-08-48 W
Pop: 1,513 (1990); 1,561 (1980) **Pop Density:** 105.8
Land: 14.3 sq. mi.; **Water:** 0.0 sq. mi.

Hereford
Township
ZIP: 18056 **Lat:** 40-26-29 N **Long:** 75-35-07 W
Pop: 3,026 (1990); 2,837 (1980) **Pop Density:** 196.5
Land: 15.4 sq. mi.; **Water:** 0.0 sq. mi.

Jefferson
Township
ZIP: 19506 **Lat:** 40-26-41 N **Long:** 76-09-39 W
Pop: 1,410 (1990); 1,310 (1980) **Pop Density:** 86.5
Land: 16.3 sq. mi.; **Water:** 0.0 sq. mi.

Kenhorst
Borough
ZIP: 19607 **Lat:** 40-18-24 N **Long:** 75-56-38 W
Pop: 2,918 (1990); 3,187 (1980) **Pop Density:** 4863.3
Land: 0.6 sq. mi.; **Water:** 0.0 sq. mi. **Elev:** 320 ft.

In southeastern PA, a suburb of Reading.

Kutztown
Borough
ZIP: 19530 **Lat:** 40-31-15 N **Long:** 75-46-41 W
Pop: 4,704 (1990); 4,040 (1980) **Pop Density:** 2940.0
Land: 1.6 sq. mi.; **Water:** 0.0 sq. mi. **Elev:** 417 ft.

In southeastern PA, 18 mi. north of Reading. Founded 1771.
Name origin: For George Kutz, who laid out the town.

Laureldale
Borough
ZIP: 19605 **Lat:** 40-23-21 N **Long:** 75-54-52 W
Pop: 3,726 (1990); 4,047 (1980) **Pop Density:** 4657.5
Land: 0.8 sq. mi.; **Water:** 0.0 sq. mi. **Elev:** 370 ft.

In southeastern PA, a northern suburb of Reading.

Leesport
Borough
ZIP: 19533 **Lat:** 40-26-41 N **Long:** 75-58-11 W
Pop: 1,270 (1990); 1,258 (1980) **Pop Density:** 1814.3
Land: 0.7 sq. mi.; **Water:** 0.0 sq. mi. **Elev:** 300 ft.

Name origin: Named in 1958. Previously called West Leesport.

Lenhartsville
Borough
ZIP: 19534 **Lat:** 40-34-21 N **Long:** 75-53-28 W
Pop: 195 (1990); 200 (1980) **Pop Density:** 1950.0
Land: 0.1 sq. mi.; **Water:** 0.0 sq. mi. **Elev:** 370 ft.

Longswamp
Township
ZIP: 19539 **Lat:** 40-29-20 N **Long:** 75-39-37 W
Pop: 5,387 (1990); 4,627 (1980) **Pop Density:** 236.3
Land: 22.8 sq. mi.; **Water:** 0.0 sq. mi.

Lorane
CDP
Lat: 40-17-37 N **Long:** 75-50-46 W
Pop: 2,580 (1990) **Pop Density:** 1612.5
Land: 1.6 sq. mi.; **Water:** 0.0 sq. mi.

Lower Alsace
Township
Lat: 40-20-53 N **Long:** 75-53-08 W
Pop: 4,627 (1990); 4,906 (1980) **Pop Density:** 984.5
Land: 4.7 sq. mi.; **Water:** 0.0 sq. mi.

Lower Heidelberg
Township
Lat: 40-21-28 N **Long:** 76-03-29 W
Pop: 2,209 (1990); 1,819 (1980) **Pop Density:** 148.3
Land: 14.9 sq. mi.; **Water:** 0.5 sq. mi.

Lyons
Borough
ZIP: 19536 **Lat:** 40-28-51 N **Long:** 75-45-36 W
Pop: 499 (1990); 579 (1980) **Pop Density:** 1247.5
Land: 0.4 sq. mi.; **Water:** 0.0 sq. mi. **Elev:** 465 ft.

Maidencreek
Township
Lat: 40-27-38 N **Long:** 75-53-43 W
Pop: 3,397 (1990); 2,377 (1980) **Pop Density:** 257.3
Land: 13.2 sq. mi.; **Water:** 1.1 sq. mi.

Marion
Township
ZIP: 19567 **Lat:** 40-23-30 N **Long:** 76-13-50 W
Pop: 1,415 (1990); 1,341 (1980) **Pop Density:** 92.5
Land: 15.3 sq. mi.; **Water:** 0.0 sq. mi.

Maxatawny
Township
ZIP: 19538 **Lat:** 40-31-31 N **Long:** 75-44-50 W
Pop: 5,724 (1990); 5,269 (1980) **Pop Density:** 218.5
Land: 26.2 sq. mi.; **Water:** 0.0 sq. mi.

Mohnton
Borough
ZIP: 19540 **Lat:** 40-17-11 N **Long:** 75-59-15 W
Pop: 2,484 (1990); 2,156 (1980) **Pop Density:** 2760.0
Land: 0.9 sq. mi.; **Water:** 0.0 sq. mi. **Elev:** 401 ft.

Mount Penn
Borough
ZIP: 19606   **Lat:** 40-19-42 N **Long:** 75-53-21 W
Pop: 2,883 (1990); 3,025 (1980)   **Pop Density:** 7207.5
Land: 0.4 sq. mi.; **Water:** 0.0 sq. mi.   **Elev:** 500 ft.

Muhlenberg
Township
ZIP: 19560   **Lat:** 40-23-42 N **Long:** 75-55-30 W
Pop: 12,636 (1990); 13,031 (1980)   **Pop Density:** 1089.3
Land: 11.6 sq. mi.; **Water:** 0.2 sq. mi.

Name origin: For Gen. John Peter Gabriel Muhlenberg (1746–1807), Revolutionary War officer, legislator, and U.S. representative.

North Heidelberg
Township
ZIP: 19506   **Lat:** 40-23-42 N **Long:** 76-07-15 W
Pop: 1,288 (1990); 953 (1980)   **Pop Density:** 95.4
Land: 13.5 sq. mi.; **Water:** 0.4 sq. mi.

Oley
Township
ZIP: 19547   **Lat:** 40-22-33 N **Long:** 75-46-27 W
Pop: 3,362 (1990); 3,024 (1980)   **Pop Density:** 138.9
Land: 24.2 sq. mi.; **Water:** 0.0 sq. mi.

Ontelaunee
Township
Lat: 40-26-45 N **Long:** 75-56-17 W
Pop: 1,359 (1990); 1,408 (1980)   **Pop Density:** 158.0
Land: 8.6 sq. mi.; **Water:** 0.6 sq. mi.

Penn
Township
ZIP: 19506   **Lat:** 40-26-18 N **Long:** 76-04-12 W
Pop: 1,831 (1990); 1,254 (1980)   **Pop Density:** 98.4
Land: 18.6 sq. mi.; **Water:** 0.5 sq. mi.

Perry
Township
ZIP: 19526   **Lat:** 40-30-39 N **Long:** 75-56-19 W
Pop: 2,516 (1990); 2,420 (1980)   **Pop Density:** 137.5
Land: 18.3 sq. mi.; **Water:** 0.1 sq. mi.

Pike
Township
ZIP: 19547   **Lat:** 40-24-24 N **Long:** 75-41-39 W
Pop: 1,359 (1990); 1,056 (1980)   **Pop Density:** 97.8
Land: 13.9 sq. mi.; **Water:** 0.0 sq. mi.

Reading
City
ZIP: 19601   **Lat:** 40-20-20 N **Long:** 75-55-35 W
Pop: 78,380 (1990); 78,686 (1980)   **Pop Density:** 7998.0
Land: 9.8 sq. mi.; **Water:** 0.3 sq. mi.   **Elev:** 266 ft.

In southeastern PA on the Schuylkill River, 70 mi. northwest of Philadelphia; incorporated as borough Sep 12, 1783, as city Mar 16, 1847.

Name origin: For the seat of Berkshire, England, which was derived from the Saxon term *rhedin* meaning 'a fern' and *-ing* meaning 'a meadow.'

Richmond
Township
ZIP: 19530   **Lat:** 40-29-15 N **Long:** 75-49-33 W
Pop: 3,439 (1990); 3,204 (1980)   **Pop Density:** 145.7
Land: 23.6 sq. mi.; **Water:** 0.0 sq. mi.

Robeson
Township
ZIP: 19508   **Lat:** 40-13-41 N **Long:** 75-52-08 W
Pop: 5,972 (1990); 4,729 (1980)   **Pop Density:** 166.4
Land: 35.9 sq. mi.; **Water:** 0.2 sq. mi.

Robesonia
Borough
ZIP: 19551   **Lat:** 40-20-54 N **Long:** 76-08-28 W
Pop: 1,944 (1990); 1,748 (1980)   **Pop Density:** 2160.0
Land: 0.9 sq. mi.; **Water:** 0.0 sq. mi.   **Elev:** 444 ft.
Founded in 1855.

Name origin: For Andrew Robeson, an early settler from Sweden.

Rockland
Township
ZIP: 19522   **Lat:** 40-27-13 N **Long:** 75-44-43 W
Pop: 2,675 (1990); 1,911 (1980)   **Pop Density:** 156.4
Land: 17.1 sq. mi.; **Water:** 0.0 sq. mi.

Ruscombmanor
Township
Lat: 40-25-25 N **Long:** 75-49-40 W
Pop: 3,129 (1990); 2,546 (1980)   **Pop Density:** 225.1
Land: 13.9 sq. mi.; **Water:** 0.0 sq. mi.

St. Lawrence
Borough
Lat: 40-19-33 N **Long:** 75-51-53 W
Pop: 1,542 (1990); 1,376 (1980)   **Pop Density:** 1713.3
Land: 0.9 sq. mi.; **Water:** 0.0 sq. mi.   **Elev:** 340 ft.

Shillington
Borough
ZIP: 19607   **Lat:** 40-18-09 N **Long:** 75-58-01 W
Pop: 5,062 (1990); 5,601 (1980)   **Pop Density:** 5062.0
Land: 1.0 sq. mi.; **Water:** 0.0 sq. mi.   **Elev:** 330 ft.

In southeastern PA, 5 mi. southwest of Reading. Laid out in 1860.

Name origin: For Samuel Shilling, who located his 130-acre farm here.

Shoemakersville
Borough
ZIP: 19555   **Lat:** 40-29-59 N **Long:** 75-58-09 W
Pop: 1,443 (1990); 1,391 (1980)   **Pop Density:** 2886.0
Land: 0.5 sq. mi.; **Water:** 0.0 sq. mi.   **Elev:** 360 ft.

Sinking Spring
Borough
ZIP: 19608   **Lat:** 40-19-28 N **Long:** 76-01-21 W
Pop: 2,467 (1990); 2,617 (1980)   **Pop Density:** 1897.7
Land: 1.3 sq. mi.; **Water:** 0.0 sq. mi.   **Elev:** 347 ft.

In southeastern PA, 5 mi. west of Reading. Founded in 1793.

Name origin: For the sinking spring, which fills up each February when water begins to ooze from the frost-packed ground but dries up before summer.

South Heidelberg
Township
Lat: 40-18-38 N **Long:** 76-05-54 W
Pop: 4,382 (1990); 3,355 (1980)   **Pop Density:** 317.5
Land: 13.8 sq. mi.; **Water:** 0.0 sq. mi.

Spring
Township
ZIP: 19609   **Lat:** 40-18-04 N **Long:** 76-01-30 W
Pop: 18,899 (1990); 17,193 (1980)   **Pop Density:** 1038.4
Land: 18.2 sq. mi.; **Water:** 0.0 sq. mi.

Strausstown
Borough
ZIP: 19559   **Lat:** 40-29-31 N **Long:** 76-11-03 W
Pop: 353 (1990); 377 (1980)   **Pop Density:** 1765.0
Land: 0.2 sq. mi.; **Water:** 0.0 sq. mi.   **Elev:** 581 ft.

Temple
Borough
ZIP: 19560   **Lat:** 40-24-29 N **Long:** 75-55-15 W
Pop: 1,491 (1990); 1,486 (1980)   **Pop Density:** 3727.5
Land: 0.4 sq. mi.; **Water:** 0.0 sq. mi.   **Elev:** 386 ft.

In southeastern PA, near Reading.

Name origin: For an old hotel sign that bore the invitation, "Stop at Solomon's Temple." Originally called Solomon's Temple.

Tilden
Township
ZIP: 19526   **Lat:** 40-32-41 N **Long:** 76-01-52 W
Pop: 2,622 (1990); 2,247 (1980)   **Pop Density:** 138.7
Land: 18.9 sq. mi.; **Water:** 0.1 sq. mi.

Topton
Borough
ZIP: 19562   **Lat:** 40-30-12 N **Long:** 75-42-09 W
Pop: 1,987 (1990); 1,818 (1980)   **Pop Density:** 2838.6
Land: 0.7 sq. mi.; **Water:** 0.0 sq. mi.   **Elev:** 485 ft.

Tulpehocken
Township
Lat: 40-26-13 N **Long:** 76-15-01 W
Pop: 2,843 (1990); 2,569 (1980)   **Pop Density:** 122.0
Land: 23.3 sq. mi.; **Water:** 0.0 sq. mi.

Union
Township
ZIP: 19508   **Lat:** 40-14-04 N **Long:** 75-46-52 W
Pop: 3,440 (1990); 2,815 (1980)   **Pop Density:** 148.3
Land: 23.2 sq. mi.; **Water:** 0.2 sq. mi.

Upper Bern
Township
ZIP: 19506   **Lat:** 40-31-12 N **Long:** 76-05-44 W
Pop: 1,458 (1990); 1,159 (1980)   **Pop Density:** 79.7
Land: 18.3 sq. mi.; **Water:** 0.0 sq. mi.

Upper Tulpehocken
Township
Lat: 40-30-13 N **Long:** 76-09-46 W
Pop: 1,289 (1990); 1,154 (1980)   **Pop Density:** 56.8
Land: 22.7 sq. mi.; **Water:** 0.0 sq. mi.

Washington
Township
ZIP: 19512   **Lat:** 40-23-44 N **Long:** 75-36-34 W
Pop: 2,799 (1990); 2,568 (1980)   **Pop Density:** 199.9
Land: 14.0 sq. mi.; **Water:** 0.0 sq. mi.

Name origin: For George Washington (1732–99), first U.S. president.

Wernersville
Borough
ZIP: 19565   **Lat:** 40-19-49 N **Long:** 76-04-59 W
Pop: 1,934 (1990); 1,811 (1980)   **Pop Density:** 2417.5
Land: 0.8 sq. mi.; **Water:** 0.0 sq. mi.   **Elev:** 388 ft.

West Lawn
Borough
ZIP: 19609   **Lat:** 40-19-42 N **Long:** 75-59-36 W
Pop: 1,606 (1990); 1,686 (1980)   **Pop Density:** 8030.0
Land: 0.2 sq. mi.; **Water:** 0.0 sq. mi.   **Elev:** 343 ft.

West Reading
Borough
ZIP: 19611   **Lat:** 40-20-00 N **Long:** 75-56-48 W
Pop: 4,142 (1990); 4,507 (1980)   **Pop Density:** 6903.3
Land: 0.6 sq. mi.; **Water:** 0.0 sq. mi.   **Elev:** 300 ft.

In southeastern PA on the Schuylkill River, across from Reading. Laid out in 1873; incorporated 1907

Windsor
Township
ZIP: 19526   **Lat:** 40-34-11 N **Long** 75-56-56 W
Pop: 2,101 (1990); 2,199 (1980)   **Pop Density:** 93.4
Land: 22.5 sq. mi.; **Water:** 0.1 sq. mi.

Womelsdorf
Borough
ZIP: 19567   **Lat:** 40-21-56 N **Long** 76-11-12 W
Pop: 2,270 (1990); 1,827 (1980)   **Pop Density:** 2522.2
Land: 0.9 sq. mi.; **Water:** 0.0 sq. mi.   **Elev:** 440 ft.

Founded in 1723 by Germans.

Name origin: Named in 1762 for John Womelsdorf, leader of emigrants from the German Palatinate. Originally called Middletown.

Wyomissing
Borough
ZIP: 19610   **Lat:** 40-19-49 N **Long** 75-58-03 W
Pop: 7,332 (1990); 6,551 (1980)   **Pop Density:** 1929.5
Land: 3.8 sq. mi.; **Water:** 0.0 sq. mi.   **Elev:** 320 ft.

In southeastern PA, 45 mi. west of Reading.

Name origin: From an Indian term probably meaning 'place of flats.'

Wyomissing Hills
Borough
ZIP: 19609   **Lat:** 40-20-05 N **Long** 75-58-55 W
Pop: 2,469 (1990); 2,150 (1980)   **Pop Density:** 3527.1
Land: 0.7 sq. mi.; **Water:** 0.0 sq. mi.   **Elev:** 350 ft.

Blair County
County Seat: Holidaysburg (ZIP: 16648)

Pop: 130,542 (1990); 136,621 (1980)   **Pop Density:** 248.2
Land: 525.9 sq. mi.; **Water:** 1.3 sq. mi.   **Area Code:** 814

In western PA, east of Johnstown; organized Feb 26, 1846 from Huntingdon and Bedford counties.

Name origin: For John Blair, PA legislator and prominent citizen. The only county in PA named for a local citizen.

Allegheny   Township
ZIP: 16635   **Lat:** 40-27-27 N **Long:** 78-28-33 W
Pop: 7,023 (1990); 7,463 (1980)   **Pop Density:** 239.7
Land: 29.3 sq. mi.; **Water:** 0.0 sq. mi.

Name origin: For the river.

Altoona   City
ZIP: 16601   **Lat:** 40-30-28 N **Long:** 78-24-04 W
Pop: 51,881 (1990); 57,078 (1980)   **Pop Density:** 5294.0
Land: 9.8 sq. mi.; **Water:** 0.0 sq. mi.   **Elev:** 1170 ft.

In south-central PA near the source of the Juniata River in a bituminous coal region, 90 mi. east of Pittsburgh.

Name origin: Origin uncertain. Its nickname is "Mountain City," so the name may come from Latin *altus* 'elevated; lofty,' or possibly from either Altona, Germany, or the Cherokee name *Allatoona*.

Antis   Township
ZIP: 16617   **Lat:** 40-36-45 N **Long:** 78-21-11 W
Pop: 6,176 (1990); 6,524 (1980)   **Pop Density:** 101.6
Land: 60.8 sq. mi.; **Water:** 0.2 sq. mi.

Bellwood   Borough
ZIP: 16617   **Lat:** 40-36-04 N **Long:** 78-20-03 W
Pop: 1,976 (1990); 2,114 (1980)   **Pop Density:** 3952.0
Land: 0.5 sq. mi.; **Water:** 0.0 sq. mi.   **Elev:** 1020 ft.

Laid out in 1877 by Dr. A. K. Bell.

Name origin: Originally called Bell's Mills for a prominent pioneer family named Bell; the latter part of the name was changed later.

Blair   Township
                         Lat: 40-23-57 N **Long:** 78-24-12 W
Pop: 3,994 (1990); 3,937 (1980)   **Pop Density:** 293.7
Land: 13.6 sq. mi.; **Water:** 0.1 sq. mi.

In central PA, south of Altoona.

Name origin: For the Hon. John Blair, who was among the first promoters of the turnpike and canal-portage system.

Catharine   Township
                         Lat: 40-31-32 N **Long:** 78-12-03 W
Pop: 738 (1990); 691 (1980)   **Pop Density:** 23.9
Land: 30.9 sq. mi.; **Water:** 0.0 sq. mi.

Claysburg   CDP
ZIP: 16625   **Lat:** 40-17-31 N **Long:** 78-26-58 W
Pop: 1,399 (1990); 1,346 (1980)   **Pop Density:** 582.9
Land: 2.4 sq. mi.; **Water:** 0.0 sq. mi.

Duncansville   Borough
ZIP: 16635   **Lat:** 40-25-34 N **Long:** 78-25-46 W
Pop: 1,309 (1990); 1,355 (1980)   **Pop Density:** 2618.0
Land: 0.5 sq. mi.; **Water:** 0.0 sq. mi.   **Elev:** 1015 ft.

Name origin: For founder Samuel Duncan after he and Jacob Walter, who owned a site to the east called Walterstown, met on a bridge spanning Blair Creek and tossed a penny to decide what the common name should be.

Frankstown   Township
ZIP: 16648   **Lat:** 40-26-30 N **Long:** 78-19-04 W
Pop: 7,243 (1990); 6,363 (1980)   **Pop Density:** 148.7
Land: 48.7 sq. mi.; **Water:** 0.5 sq. mi.

Freedom   Township
                         Lat: 40-21-17 N **Long:** 78-28-01 W
Pop: 2,959 (1990); 3,060 (1980)   **Pop Density:** 170.1
Land: 17.4 sq. mi.; **Water:** 0.0 sq. mi.

Greenfield   Township
                         Lat: 40-18-52 N **Long:** 78-30-39 W
Pop: 3,802 (1990); 3,758 (1980)   **Pop Density:** 105.9
Land: 35.9 sq. mi.; **Water:** 0.0 sq. mi.

Hollidaysburg   Borough
ZIP: 16648   **Lat:** 40-25-48 N **Long:** 78-23-35 W
Pop: 5,624 (1990); 5,892 (1980)   **Pop Density:** 2343.3
Land: 2.4 sq. mi.; **Water:** 0.0 sq. mi.   **Elev:** 958 ft.

In west-central PA, 5 mi. south of Altoona. Founded in 1768; incorporated Aug 10, 1836.

Name origin: For the borough's founders, Adam and William Holliday, Irish immigrants.

Huston   Township
                         Lat: 40-21-50 N **Long:** 78-16-39 W
Pop: 1,189 (1990); 1,049 (1980)   **Pop Density:** 33.9
Land: 35.1 sq. mi.; **Water:** 0.0 sq. mi.

Juniata   Township
                         Lat: 40-23-48 N **Long:** 78-31-32 W
Pop: 1,116 (1990); 1,129 (1980)   **Pop Density:** 42.0
Land: 26.6 sq. mi.; **Water:** 0.1 sq. mi.

Logan   Township
ZIP: 16602   **Lat:** 40-31-27 N **Long:** 78-25-22 W
Pop: 12,381 (1990); 12,183 (1980)   **Pop Density:** 265.7
Land: 46.6 sq. mi.; **Water:** 0.3 sq. mi.

Martinsburg   Borough
ZIP: 16662   **Lat:** 40-18-36 N **Long:** 78-19-28 W
Pop: 2,119 (1990); 2,231 (1980)   **Pop Density:** 3531.7
Land: 0.6 sq. mi.; **Water:** 0.0 sq. mi.   **Elev:** 1407 ft.

Newry   Borough
ZIP: 16665   **Lat:** 40-23-35 N **Long:** 78-26-07 W
Pop: 288 (1990); 353 (1980)   **Pop Density:** 2880.0
Land: 0.1 sq. mi.; **Water:** 0.0 sq. mi.   **Elev:** 1055 ft.

North Woodbury   Township
                         Lat: 40-17-25 N **Long:** 78-18-57 W
Pop: 2,219 (1990); 1,851 (1980)   **Pop Density:** 106.7
Land: 20.8 sq. mi.; **Water:** 0.0 sq. mi.

Roaring Spring
Borough
ZIP: 16673   Lat: 40-20-01 N Long: 78-23-48 W
Pop: 2,615 (1990); 2,962 (1980)   Pop Density: 3268.8
Land: 0.8 sq. mi.; Water: 0.0 sq. mi.   Elev: 1300 ft.

Snyder
Township
Lat: 40-42-11 N Long: 78-15-02 W
Pop: 3,163 (1990); 3,454 (1980)   Pop Density: 70.0
Land: 45.2 sq. mi.; Water: 0.0 sq. mi.

Taylor
Township
Lat: 40-19-50 N Long: 78-23-15 W
Pop: 2,327 (1990); 2,108 (1980)   Pop Density: 100.7
Land: 23.1 sq. mi.; Water: 0.0 sq. mi.

Tyrone
Borough
ZIP: 16686   Lat: 40-40-36 N Long: 78-14-46 W
Pop: 5,743 (1990); 6,346 (1980)   Pop Density: 2871.5
Land: 2.0 sq. mi.; Water: 0.0 sq. mi.   Elev: 896 ft.

In south-central PA, 15 mi. northeast of Altoona. Settled in 1850.

Name origin: For Tyrone, in Northern Ireland, the native county of early settlers.

*Tyrone
Township
ZIP: 16686   Lat: 40-34-46 N Long: 78-15-45 W
Pop: 1,677 (1990); 1,647 (1980)   Pop Density: 40.1
Land: 41.8 sq. mi.; Water: 0.1 sq. mi.

Williamsburg
Borough
ZIP: 16693   Lat: 40-27-49 N Long: 78-12-20 W
Pop: 1,456 (1990); 1,400 (1980)   Pop Density: 3640.0
Land: 0.4 sq. mi.; Water: 0.0 sq. mi.   Elev: 884 ft.

Woodbury
Township
Lat: 40-27-09 N Long: 78-12-43 W
Pop: 1,418 (1990); 1,519 (1980)   Pop Density: 43.6
Land: 32.5 sq. mi.; Water: 0.0 sq. mi.

Bradford County
County Seat: Towanda (ZIP: 18848)

Pop: 60,967 (1990); 62,919 (1980)   Pop Density: 53.0
Land: 1150.7 sq. mi.; Water: 10.3 sq. mi.   Area Code: 717

On northern border of PA, northwest of Scranton; organized as Ontario County Feb 10, 1810 from Luzerne and Lycoming counties.

Name origin: For William Bradford (1755–95), associate justice of the PA supreme court (1791) and U.S. attorney general (1794–95). Name changed Mar 24, 1812 from Ontario (named for the lake).

Alba
Borough
ZIP: 16910   Lat: 41-42-15 N Long: 76-49-40 W
Pop: 170 (1990); 222 (1980)   Pop Density: 242.9
Land: 0.7 sq. mi.; Water: 0.0 sq. mi.   Elev: 1360 ft.

Albany
Township
Lat: 41-35-51 N Long: 76-25-32 W
Pop: 927 (1990); 853 (1980)   Pop Density: 28.8
Land: 32.2 sq. mi.; Water: 0.1 sq. mi.

Armenia
Township
Lat: 41-44-24 N Long: 76-51-55 W
Pop: 134 (1990); 191 (1980)   Pop Density: 7.4
Land: 18.1 sq. mi.; Water: 0.1 sq. mi.

Asylum
Township
Lat: 41-42-51 N Long: 76-22-31 W
Pop: 981 (1990); 1,027 (1980)   Pop Density: 38.3
Land: 25.6 sq. mi.; Water: 1.0 sq. mi.

In northern PA, northwest of Scranton in the Towanda area. Established 1794.

Name origin: Promoted by Robert Morris and John Nicholson as an asylum for refugees of the French Revolution.

Athens
Township
ZIP: 18810   Lat: 41-57-17 N Long: 76-33-37 W
Pop: 4,755 (1990); 4,994 (1980)   Pop Density: 108.6
Land: 43.8 sq. mi.; Water: 1.3 sq. mi.

*Athens
Borough
ZIP: 18810   Lat: 41-57-01 N Long: 76-31-01 W
Pop: 3,468 (1990); 3,622 (1980)   Pop Density: 1926.7
Land: 1.8 sq. mi.; Water: 0.1 sq. mi.   Elev: 740 ft.

In northern PA on the border with NY. Founded 1786; borough incorporated 1831.

Name origin: For the capital of Greece, possibly because the ring of hills surrounding the city resembles the Greek metropolis. Previously called Tioga Point.

Burlington
Township
Lat: 41-45-33 N Long: 76-34-24 W
Pop: 705 (1990); 765 (1980)   Pop Density: 28.1
Land: 25.1 sq. mi.; Water: 0.1 sq. mi.

*Burlington
Borough
ZIP: 18814   Lat: 41-46-58 N Long: 76-36-31 W
Pop: 479 (1990); 162 (1980)   Pop Density: 798.3
Land: 0.6 sq. mi.; Water: 0.0 sq. mi.   Elev: 894 ft.

Canton
Township
Lat: 41-38-59 N Long: 76-49-24 W
Pop: 2,099 (1990); 1,898 (1980)   Pop Density: 56.9
Land: 36.9 sq. mi.; Water: 0.1 sq. mi.

*Canton   Borough
ZIP: 17724   **Lat:** 41-39-25 N **Long:** 76-51-10 W
Pop: 1,966 (1990); 1,959 (1980)   **Pop Density:** 1638.3
Land: 1.2 sq. mi.; **Water:** 0.0 sq. mi.   **Elev:** 1248 ft.
In northern PA, 30 mi. northeast of Williamsport. Founded 1800.
Name origin: Named by early settlers for Canton, CT.

Columbia   Township
           Lat: 41-50-43 N **Long:** 76-50-37 W
Pop: 1,077 (1990); 1,119 (1980)   **Pop Density:** 26.0
Land: 41.5 sq. mi.; **Water:** 0.0 sq. mi.

Franklin   Township
           Lat: 41-40-01 N **Long:** 76-35-21 W
Pop: 557 (1990); 559 (1980)   **Pop Density:** 16.6
Land: 33.6 sq. mi.; **Water:** 0.1 sq. mi.

Granville   Township
ZIP: 16926   **Lat:** 41-42-51 N **Long:** 76-42-49 W
Pop: 837 (1990); 903 (1980)   **Pop Density:** 33.9
Land: 24.7 sq. mi.; **Water:** 0.0 sq. mi.

Herrick   Township
           Lat: 41-47-04 N **Long:** 76-15-00 W
Pop: 647 (1990); 601 (1980)   **Pop Density:** 28.8
Land: 22.5 sq. mi.; **Water:** 0.1 sq. mi.

Le Raysville   Borough
ZIP: 18829   **Lat:** 41-50-15 N **Long:** 76-10-50 W
Pop: 336 (1990); 356 (1980)   **Pop Density:** 420.0
Land: 0.8 sq. mi.; **Water:** 0.0 sq. mi.

Leroy   Township
           Lat: 41-38-57 N **Long:** 76-43-31 W
Pop: 610 (1990); 639 (1980)   **Pop Density:** 13.6
Land: 44.8 sq. mi.; **Water:** 0.2 sq. mi.

Litchfield   Township
           Lat: 41-57-13 N **Long:** 76-25-50 W
Pop: 1,296 (1990); 1,203 (1980)   **Pop Density:** 43.1
Land: 30.1 sq. mi.; **Water:** 0.2 sq. mi.

Monroe   Township
           Lat: 41-40-40 N **Long:** 76-27-39 W
Pop: 1,235 (1990); 1,214 (1980)   **Pop Density:** 33.8
Land: 36.5 sq. mi.; **Water:** 0.0 sq. mi.

*Monroe   Borough
ZIP: 18832   **Lat:** 41-42-48 N **Long:** 76-28-32 W
Pop: 540 (1990); 627 (1980)   **Pop Density:** 771.4
Land: 0.7 sq. mi.; **Water:** 0.0 sq. mi.   **Elev:** 751 ft.

New Albany   Borough
ZIP: 18833   **Lat:** 41-36-02 N **Long:** 76-26-35 W
Pop: 306 (1990); 336 (1980)   **Pop Density:** 612.0
Land: 0.5 sq. mi.; **Water:** 0.0 sq. mi.   **Elev:** 1220 ft.

North Towanda   Township
           Lat: 41-47-28 N **Long:** 76-29-12 W
Pop: 909 (1990); 1,003 (1980)   **Pop Density:** 102.1
Land: 8.9 sq. mi.; **Water:** 0.2 sq. mi.

Orwell   Township
           Lat: 41-52-27 N **Long:** 76-16-21 W
Pop: 1,107 (1990); 1,020 (1980)   **Pop Density:** 34.7
Land: 31.9 sq. mi.; **Water:** 0.2 sq. mi.

Overton   Township
           Lat: 41-35-31 N **Long:** 76-34-45 W
Pop: 157 (1990); 239 (1980)   **Pop Density:** 3.3
Land: 47.0 sq. mi.; **Water:** 0.2 sq. mi.

Pike   Township
           Lat: 41-51-01 N **Long:** 76-10-25 W
Pop: 684 (1990); 598 (1980)   **Pop Density:** 23.8
Land: 28.7 sq. mi.; **Water:** 0.2 sq. mi.

Ridgebury   Township
           Lat: 41-56-58 N **Long:** 76-41-33 W
Pop: 2,026 (1990); 2,102 (1980)   **Pop Density:** 52.9
Land: 38.3 sq. mi.; **Water:** 0.1 sq. mi.

Rome   Township
ZIP: 18837   **Lat:** 41-52-29 N **Long:** 76-21-34 W
Pop: 1,043 (1990); 938 (1980)   **Pop Density:** 34.9
Land: 29.9 sq. mi.; **Water:** 0.1 sq. mi.

*Rome   Borough
ZIP: 18837   **Lat:** 41-51-28 N **Long:** 76-20-29 W
Pop: 475 (1990); 426 (1980)   **Pop Density:** 791.7
Land: 0.6 sq. mi.; **Water:** 0.0 sq. mi.   **Elev:** 835 ft.
Name origin: Named by the first settlers for Rome, NY.

Sayre   Borough
ZIP: 18840   **Lat:** 41-59-09 N **Long:** 76-31-15 W
Pop: 5,791 (1990); 6,951 (1980)   **Pop Density:** 2895.5
Land: 2.0 sq. mi.; **Water:** 0.0 sq. mi.   **Elev:** 780 ft.
In northern PA, 20 mi. southeast of Elmira, NY.
Name origin: Named in 1871 for Robert H. Sayre, superintendent of the railroad.

Sheshequin   Township
           Lat: 41-51-44 N **Long:** 76-27-30 W
Pop: 1,211 (1990); 1,141 (1980)   **Pop Density:** 34.3
Land: 35.3 sq. mi.; **Water:** 0.8 sq. mi.

Smithfield   Township
           Lat: 41-51-43 N **Long:** 76-36-33 W
Pop: 1,520 (1990); 1,536 (1980)   **Pop Density:** 36.5
Land: 41.6 sq. mi.; **Water:** 0.1 sq. mi.

South Creek   Township
ZIP: 16925   **Lat:** 41-57-27 N **Long:** 76-47-26 W
Pop: 1,229 (1990); 1,345 (1980)   **Pop Density:** 43.9
Land: 28.0 sq. mi.; **Water:** 0.0 sq. mi.

South Waverly   Borough
ZIP: 14892   **Lat:** 41-59-44 N **Long:** 76-32-39 W
Pop: 1,049 (1990); 1,176 (1980)   **Pop Density:** 1165.6
Land: 0.9 sq. mi.; **Water:** 0.0 sq. mi.   **Elev:** 820 ft.

Springfield   Township
ZIP: 16914   **Lat:** 41-51-17 N **Long:** 76-43-31 W
Pop: 1,118 (1990); 1,121 (1980)   **Pop Density:** 26.7
Land: 41.9 sq. mi.; **Water:** 0.1 sq. mi.

Standing Stone   Township
           Lat: 41-46-02 N **Long:** 76-19-19 W
Pop: 436 (1990); 419 (1980)   **Pop Density:** 27.6
Land: 15.8 sq. mi.; **Water:** 0.4 sq. mi.

Stevens   Township
           Lat: 41-46-20 N **Long:** 76-10-11 W
Pop: 401 (1990); 412 (1980)   **Pop Density:** 26.0
Land: 15.4 sq. mi.; **Water:** 0.1 sq. mi.

Sylvania   Borough
ZIP: 16945   **Lat:** 41-48-18 N **Long:** 76-51-27 W
Pop: 203 (1990); 236 (1980)   **Pop Density:** 338.3
Land: 0.6 sq. mi.; **Water:** 0.0 sq. mi.   **Elev:** 1280 ft.

Terry Township
Lat: 41-38-33 N Long: 76-19-49 W
Pop: 871 (1990); 823 (1980) **Pop Density:** 26.6
Land: 32.7 sq. mi.; **Water:** 0.7 sq. mi.

Towanda Borough
ZIP: 18848 Lat: 41-46-15 N Long: 76-26-49 W
Pop: 3,242 (1990); 3,526 (1980) **Pop Density:** 2947.3
Land: 1.1 sq. mi.; **Water:** 0.0 sq. mi. **Elev:** 737 ft.
In northern PA on the west shore of the Susquehanna River at the convergence of three valleys, 50 mi. northwest of Wilkes-Barre; incorporated Mar 5, 1828.
Name origin: From an Indian term possibly meaning 'where we bury the dead.'

*Towanda Township
ZIP: 18848 Lat: 41-44-52 N Long: 76-28-32 W
Pop: 1,133 (1990); 1,269 (1980) **Pop Density:** 74.5
Land: 15.2 sq. mi.; **Water:** 0.2 sq. mi.

Troy Township
ZIP: 16947 Lat: 41-46-08 N Long: 76-46-43 W
Pop: 1,797 (1990); 1,666 (1980) **Pop Density:** 49.1
Land: 36.6 sq. mi.; **Water:** 0.0 sq. mi.

*Troy Borough
ZIP: 16947 Lat: 41-47-04 N Long: 76-47-22 W
Pop: 1,262 (1990); 1,381 (1980) **Pop Density:** 1577.5
Land: 0.8 sq. mi.; **Water:** 0.0 sq. mi. **Elev:** 1095 ft.

Tuscarora Township
Lat: 41-41-40 N Long: 76-09-27 W
Pop: 996 (1990); 930 (1980) **Pop Density:** 34.0
Land: 29.3 sq. mi.; **Water:** 0.3 sq. mi.

Ulster Township
ZIP: 18850 Lat: 41-50-48 N Long: 76-31-39 W
Pop: 1,295 (1990); 1,321 (1980) **Pop Density:** 68.2
Land: 19.0 sq. mi.; **Water:** 0.5 sq. mi.
Name origin: Named by Irish immigrants for their homeland.

Warren Township
Lat: 41-56-12 N Long: 76-11-47 W
Pop: 927 (1990); 874 (1980) **Pop Density:** 22.1
Land: 42.0 sq. mi.; **Water:** 0.2 sq. mi.

Wells Township
ZIP: 16925 Lat: 41-56-53 N Long: 76-52-40 W
Pop: 1,018 (1990); 1,080 (1980) **Pop Density:** 30.0
Land: 33.9 sq. mi.; **Water:** 0.0 sq. mi.

West Burlington Township
Lat: 41-46-04 N Long: 76-39-03 W
Pop: 417 (1990); 637 (1980) **Pop Density:** 17.3
Land: 24.1 sq. mi.; **Water:** 0.1 sq. mi.

Wilmot Township
Lat: 41-35-56 N Long: 76-15-56 W
Pop: 1,057 (1990); 995 (1980) **Pop Density:** 24.0
Land: 44.0 sq. mi.; **Water:** 0.9 sq. mi.

Windham Township
Lat: 41-57-37 N Long: 76-19-17 W
Pop: 862 (1990); 800 (1980) **Pop Density:** 26.6
Land: 32.4 sq. mi.; **Water:** 0.2 sq. mi.

Wyalusing Township
ZIP: 18853 Lat: 41-42-20 N Long: 76-15-22 W
Pop: 1,235 (1990); 1,192 (1980) **Pop Density:** 44.0
Land: 28.1 sq. mi.; **Water:** 0.7 sq. mi.

*Wyalusing Borough
ZIP: 18853 Lat: 41-40-08 N Long: 76-15-45 W
Pop: 686 (1990); 716 (1980) **Pop Density:** 857.5
Land: 0.8 sq. mi.; **Water:** 0.0 sq. mi. **Elev:** 686 ft.

Wysox Township
ZIP: 18854 Lat: 41-47-46 N Long: 76-22-55 W
Pop: 1,685 (1990); 1,796 (1980) **Pop Density:** 74.9
Land: 22.5 sq. mi.; **Water:** 0.7 sq. mi.
Name origin: An Indian term possibly meaning 'place of grapes.'

Bucks County
County Seat: Doylestown (ZIP: 18901)

Pop: 541,174 (1990); 479,180 (1980) **Pop Density:** 890.6
Land: 607.6 sq. mi.; **Water:** 14.5 sq. mi. **Area Code:** 215
On southeastern border of PA, north of Philadelphia; original county, organized as Buckingham County Mar 10, 1682.
Name origin: Shortened from the original name, Buckingham, for the English county of Buckinghamshire (also called Bucks), home of the Penn family and of many original settlers.

Bedminster Village & Township
Lat: 40-25-12 N Long: 75-11-41 W
Pop: 4,602 (1990); 3,611 (1980) **Pop Density:** 152.4
Land: 30.2 sq. mi.; **Water:** 1.0 sq. mi.
In southeastern PA, c. 35 mi. north of Philadelphia.

Bensalem Township
ZIP: 19020 Lat: 40-06-38 N Long: 74-56-26 W
Pop: 56,788 (1990); 52,399 (1980) **Pop Density:** 2839.4
Land: 20.0 sq. mi.; **Water:** 1.0 sq. mi.

Bridgeton Township
Lat: 40-33-16 N Long: 75-07-06 W
Pop: 1,378 (1990); 1,242 (1980) **Pop Density:** 212.0
Land: 6.5 sq. mi.; **Water:** 0.2 sq. mi.

Bristol Township
ZIP: 19007 Lat: 40-07-13 N Long: 74-51-59 W
Pop: 57,129 (1990); 58,733 (1980) **Pop Density:** 3570.6
Land: 16.0 sq. mi.; **Water:** 1.1 sq. mi.

*Bristol
Borough
ZIP: 19007   **Lat:** 40-06-05 N **Long:** 74-51-11 W
Pop: 10,405 (1990); 10,867 (1980)   **Pop Density:** 6120.6
Land: 1.7 sq. mi.; **Water:** 0.2 sq. mi.   **Elev:** 20 ft.

In southeastern PA on the Delaware River, 20 mi. northeast of Philadelphia. Settled 1697. County seat 1705.

Name origin: For Bristol, England, the seaport where some of the ancestors of William Penn (1644–1718) lived.

Brittany Farms-Highlands
CDP
Lat: 40-16-07 N **Long:** 75-12-52 W
Pop: 2,747 (1990)   **Pop Density:** 2289.2
Land: 1.2 sq. mi.; **Water:** 0.0 sq. mi.

Buckingham
Township
ZIP: 18912   **Lat:** 40-19-12 N **Long:** 75-03-36 W
Pop: 9,364 (1990); 8,839 (1980)   **Pop Density:** 282.9
Land: 33.1 sq. mi.; **Water:** 0.0 sq. mi.

Chalfont
Borough
ZIP: 18914   **Lat:** 40-17-20 N **Long:** 75-12-34 W
Pop: 3,069 (1990); 2,802 (1980)   **Pop Density:** 1805.3
Land: 1.7 sq. mi.; **Water:** 0.0 sq. mi.   **Elev:** 260 ft.

In southeastern PA, north of Philadelphia.

Name origin: For the station on the Doylestown branch of the Philadelphia and Reading Railroad. Probably named by a Quaker railway official for Chalfont St. Giles, the English parish where William Penn (1644–1718) is buried. Originally called Butlers Mill.

Churchville
CDP
Lat: 40-12-02 N **Long:** 74-59-50 W
Pop: 4,255 (1990)   **Pop Density:** 2127.5
Land: 2.0 sq. mi.; **Water:** 0.0 sq. mi.

Cornwells Heights-Eddington
CDP
Lat: 40-04-54 N **Long:** 74-56-49 W
Pop: 3,621 (1990)   **Pop Density:** 3621.0
Land: 1.0 sq. mi.; **Water:** 0.0 sq. mi.

Croydon
CDP
Lat: 40-05-24 N **Long:** 74-53-43 W
Pop: 9,967 (1990)   **Pop Density:** 4152.9
Land: 2.4 sq. mi.; **Water:** 0.0 sq. mi.

Doylestown
Township
ZIP: 18901   **Lat:** 40-17-43 N **Long:** 75-08-18 W
Pop: 14,510 (1990); 11,824 (1980)   **Pop Density:** 936.1
Land: 15.5 sq. mi.; **Water:** 0.0 sq. mi.

*Doylestown
Borough
ZIP: 18901   **Lat:** 40-18-50 N **Long:** 75-07-40 W
Pop: 8,575 (1990); 8,717 (1980)   **Pop Density:** 3897.7
Land: 2.2 sq. mi.; **Water:** 0.0 sq. mi.   **Elev:** 400 ft.

In southeastern PA, 25 mi. north of Philadelphia. Settled 1735; incorporated Apr 16, 1838. Once an overnight stop for stage travelers between Easton and Philadelphia.

Name origin: For settler William Doyle.

Dublin
Borough
ZIP: 18917   **Lat:** 40-22-14 N **Long:** 75-12-16 W
Pop: 1,985 (1990); 1,565 (1980)   **Pop Density:** 3970.0
Land: 0.5 sq. mi.; **Water:** 0.0 sq. mi.   **Elev:** 580 ft.

Durham
Township
Lat: 40-34-25 N **Long:** 75-13-07 W
Pop: 1,209 (1990); 915 (1980)   **Pop Density:** 131.4
Land: 9.2 sq. mi.; **Water:** 0.2 sq. mi.

East Rockhill
Township
Lat: 40-24-26 N **Long:** 75-16-54 W
Pop: 3,753 (1990); 2,971 (1980)   **Pop Density:** 290.9
Land: 12.9 sq. mi.; **Water:** 0.1 sq. mi.

Fairless Hills
CDP
ZIP: 19030   **Lat:** 40-10-43 N **Long:** 74-51-12 W
Pop: 9,026 (1990)   **Pop Density:** 4750.5
Land: 1.9 sq. mi.; **Water:** 0.0 sq. mi.

Falls
Township
ZIP: 19054   **Lat:** 40-10-12 N **Long:** 74-47-23 W
Pop: 34,997 (1990); 36,083 (1980)   **Pop Density:** 1569.4
Land: 22.3 sq. mi.; **Water:** 4.3 sq. mi.

Feasterville-Trevose
CDP
Lat: 40-09-09 N **Long:** 74-59-11 W
Pop: 6,696 (1990)   **Pop Density:** 5150.8
Land: 1.3 sq. mi.; **Water:** 0.0 sq. mi.

Haycock
Township
Lat: 40-28-59 N **Long:** 75-15-00 W
Pop: 2,165 (1990); 1,750 (1980)   **Pop Density:** 107.7
Land: 20.1 sq. mi.; **Water:** 1.2 sq. mi.

Hilltown
Township
ZIP: 18927   **Lat:** 40-20-34 N **Long:** 75-15-02 W
Pop: 10,582 (1990); 9,326 (1980)   **Pop Density:** 393.4
Land: 26.9 sq. mi.; **Water:** 0.0 sq. mi.

Hulmeville
Borough
ZIP: 19047   **Lat:** 40-08-35 N **Long:** 74-54-27 W
Pop: 916 (1990); 1,014 (1980)   **Pop Density:** 2290.0
Land: 0.4 sq. mi.; **Water:** 0.0 sq. mi.   **Elev:** 40 ft.

In southeastern PA, a northeastern suburb of Philadelphia.

Ivyland
Borough
ZIP: 18974   **Lat:** 40-12-29 N **Long:** 75-04-22 W
Pop: 490 (1990); 581 (1980)   **Pop Density:** 1225.0
Land: 0.4 sq. mi.; **Water:** 0.0 sq. mi.   **Elev:** 289 ft.

Langhorne
Borough
ZIP: 19047   **Lat:** 40-10-38 N **Long:** 74-55-09 W
Pop: 1,361 (1990); 1,697 (1980)   **Pop Density:** 2722.0
Land: 0.5 sq. mi.; **Water:** 0.0 sq. mi.   **Elev:** 220 ft.

In southeastern PA, a suburb of Philadelphia.

Name origin: For early settler Jeremiah Langhorne, chief justice of the province in 1739–43.

Langhorne Manor
Borough
ZIP: 19047   **Lat:** 40-09-56 N **Long:** 74-55-05 W
Pop: 807 (1990); 1,103 (1980)   **Pop Density:** 1345.0
Land: 0.6 sq. mi.; **Water:** 0.0 sq. mi.   **Elev:** 220 ft.

Levittown
CDP
ZIP: 19053   **Lat:** 40-09-12 N **Long:** 74-51-11 W
Pop: 55,362 (1990)   **Pop Density:** 5427.6
Land: 10.2 sq. mi.; **Water:** 0.1 sq. mi.

Lower Makefield
Township
ZIP: 19067   **Lat:** 40-13-47 N **Long:** 74-51-19 W
Pop: 25,083 (1990); 17,351 (1980)   **Pop Density:** 1401.3
Land: 17.9 sq. mi.; **Water:** 0.4 sq. mi.

Lower Southampton
Township
ZIP: 19047   **Lat:** 40-09-15 N **Long:** 74-59-27 W
Pop: 19,860 (1990); 18,305 (1980)   **Pop Density:** 2964.2
Land: 6.7 sq. mi.; **Water:** 0.0 sq. mi.

In southeastern PA, northeast of Philadelphia.

Middletown
Township
ZIP: 19056   **Lat:** 40-10-42 N   **Long:** 74-54-27 W
Pop: 43,063 (1990); 34,246 (1980)   **Pop Density:** 2219.7
Land: 19.4 sq. mi.; **Water:** 0.0 sq. mi.

Milford
Township
ZIP: 18968   **Lat:** 40-25-59 N   **Long:** 75-25-01 W
Pop: 7,360 (1990); 6,053 (1980)   **Pop Density:** 261.9
Land: 28.1 sq. mi.; **Water:** 0.0 sq. mi.

Morrisville
Borough
ZIP: 19067   **Lat:** 40-12-26 N   **Long:** 74-46-49 W
Pop: 9,765 (1990); 9,845 (1980)   **Pop Density:** 5425.0
Land: 1.8 sq. mi.; **Water:** 0.2 sq. mi.   **Elev:** 60 ft.
In southeastern PA on the Delaware River, across from Trenton, NJ.
Name origin: For Robert Morris (1734–1806), a signer of the Declaration of Independence.

New Britain
Township
ZIP: 18914   **Lat:** 40-18-24 N   **Long:** 75-12-22 W
Pop: 9,099 (1990); 7,415 (1980)   **Pop Density:** 619.0
Land: 14.7 sq. mi.; **Water:** 0.6 sq. mi.

*New Britain
Borough
ZIP: 18901   **Lat:** 40-17-56 N   **Long:** 75-10-42 W
Pop: 2,174 (1990); 2,519 (1980)   **Pop Density:** 1672.3
Land: 1.3 sq. mi.; **Water:** 0.0 sq. mi.   **Elev:** 289 ft.
In southeastern PA, a northern suburb of Philadelphia.
Name origin: Named by westward-moving pioneers for the industrial city in CT.

New Hope
Borough
ZIP: 18938   **Lat:** 40-21-41 N   **Long:** 74-57-33 W
Pop: 1,400 (1990); 1,473 (1980)   **Pop Density:** 1076.9
Land: 1.3 sq. mi.; **Water:** 0.2 sq. mi.   **Elev:** 76 ft.

Newtown
Township
ZIP: 18940   **Lat:** 40-14-34 N   **Long:** 74-56-24 W
Pop: 13,685 (1990); 4,527 (1980)   **Pop Density:** 1140.4
Land: 12.0 sq. mi.; **Water:** 0.0 sq. mi.

*Newtown
Borough
ZIP: 18940   **Lat:** 40-13-41 N   **Long:** 74-55-57 W
Pop: 2,565 (1990); 2,519 (1980)   **Pop Density:** 5130.0
Land: 0.5 sq. mi.; **Water:** 0.0 sq. mi.   **Elev:** 62 ft.
In southeastern PA, 22 mi. northeast of Philadelphia.

Nockamixon
Township
         Lat: 40-31-12 N   **Long:** 75-10-31 W
Pop: 3,329 (1990); 2,787 (1980)   **Pop Density:** 150.0
Land: 22.2 sq. mi.; **Water:** 0.4 sq. mi.

Northampton
Township
ZIP: 18954   **Lat:** 40-12-35 N   **Long:** 75-00-02 W
Pop: 35,406 (1990); 27,392 (1980)   **Pop Density:** 1372.3
Land: 25.8 sq. mi.; **Water:** 0.3 sq. mi.
Name origin: For the neighboring county.

Penndel
Borough
ZIP: 19047   **Lat:** 40-09-17 N   **Long:** 74-54-49 W
Pop: 2,703 (1990); 2,703 (1980)   **Pop Density:** 6757.5
Land: 0.4 sq. mi.; **Water:** 0.0 sq. mi.   **Elev:** 100 ft.
In southeastern PA, a suburb of Philadelphia.
Name origin: For William Penn (1644–1718), founder of Philadelphia.

Perkasie
Borough
ZIP: 18944   **Lat:** 40-22-15 N   **Long:** 75-17-32 W
Pop: 7,878 (1990); 5,241 (1980)   **Pop Density:** 3030.0
Land: 2.6 sq. mi.; **Water:** 0.0 sq. mi.   **Elev:** 340 ft.
In southeastern PA, 20 mi. southeast of Allentown.

Plumstead
Township
ZIP: 18923   **Lat:** 40-23-14 N   **Long:** 75-07-12 W
Pop: 6,289 (1990); 5,153 (1980)   **Pop Density:** 231.2
Land: 27.2 sq. mi.; **Water:** 0.0 sq. mi.

Quakertown
Borough
ZIP: 18951   **Lat:** 40-26-22 N   **Long:** 75-20-45 W
Pop: 8,982 (1990); 8,867 (1980)   **Pop Density:** 4491.0
Land: 2.0 sq. mi.; **Water:** 0.0 sq. mi.   **Elev:** 505 ft.
In southeastern PA, 15 mi. southeast of Allentown. Founded in 1715.
Name origin: For the founders, who were Quakers from Gwynedd, Wales.

Richland
Township
ZIP: 18951   **Lat:** 40-26-59 N   **Long:** 75-19-58 W
Pop: 8,560 (1990); 6,286 (1980)   **Pop Density:** 417.6
Land: 20.5 sq. mi.; **Water:** 0.0 sq. mi.

Richlandtown
Borough
ZIP: 18955   **Lat:** 40-28-20 N   **Long:** 75-19-16 W
Pop: 1,195 (1990); 1,180 (1980)   **Pop Density:** 3983.3
Land: 0.3 sq. mi.; **Water:** 0.0 sq. mi.   **Elev:** 530 ft.

Riegelsville
Borough
ZIP: 18077   **Lat:** 40-35-48 N   **Long:** 75-11-52 W
Pop: 912 (1990); 993 (1980)   **Pop Density:** 912.0
Land: 1.0 sq. mi.; **Water:** 0.1 sq. mi.   **Elev:** 179 ft.

Sellersville
Borough
ZIP: 18960   **Lat:** 40-21-37 N   **Long:** 75-18-29 W
Pop: 4,479 (1990); 3,143 (1980)   **Pop Density:** 3732.5
Land: 1.2 sq. mi.; **Water:** 0.0 sq. mi.   **Elev:** 310 ft.
In southeastern PA, 20 mi. southeast of Allentown. Founded in 1738.
Name origin: For Samuel Sellers, who operated Old Sellers Tavern, a three-story stuccoed stone building that served as an early stage stop along the road to Allentown.

Silverdale
Borough
ZIP: 18962   **Lat:** 40-20-46 N   **Long:** 75-16-16 W
Pop: 881 (1990); 499 (1980)   **Pop Density:** 1762.0
Land: 0.5 sq. mi.; **Water:** 0.0 sq. mi.   **Elev:** 430 ft.

Solebury
Township
ZIP: 18963   **Lat:** 40-22-00 N   **Long:** 75-00-28 W
Pop: 5,998 (1990); 4,827 (1980)   **Pop Density:** 225.5
Land: 26.6 sq. mi.; **Water:** 0.6 sq. mi.

Springfield
Township
ZIP: 18951   **Lat:** 40-31-20 N   **Long:** 75-17-56 W
Pop: 5,177 (1990); 4,817 (1980)   **Pop Density:** 168.1
Land: 30.8 sq. mi.; **Water:** 0.0 sq. mi.

Tinicum
Township
         Lat: 40-28-34 N   **Long:** 75-06-35 W
Pop: 4,167 (1990); 3,533 (1980)   **Pop Density:** 138.0
Land: 30.2 sq. mi.; **Water:** 1.0 sq. mi.

Trumbauersville
Borough
ZIP: 18970   **Lat:** 40-24-50 N   **Long:** 75-22-45 W
Pop: 894 (1990); 781 (1980)   **Pop Density:** 2235.0
Land: 0.4 sq. mi.; **Water:** 0.0 sq. mi.   **Elev:** 460 ft.

Tullytown
Borough
ZIP: 19007 **Lat:** 40-08-21 N **Long:** 74-48-46 W
Pop: 2,339 (1990); 2,277 (1980) **Pop Density:** 1461.9
Land: 1.6 sq. mi.; **Water:** 0.5 sq. mi. **Elev:** 25 ft.

In southeast PA, an eastern suburb of Philadelphia.

Upper Makefield
Township
ZIP: 18940 **Lat:** 40-17-46 N **Long:** 74-55-24 W
Pop: 5,949 (1990); 4,577 (1980) **Pop Density:** 284.6
Land: 20.9 sq. mi.; **Water:** 0.6 sq. mi.

Upper Southampton
Township
ZIP: 18966 **Lat:** 40-10-17 N **Long:** 75-02-10 W
Pop: 16,076 (1990); 15,806 (1980) **Pop Density:** 2435.8
Land: 6.6 sq. mi.; **Water:** 0.0 sq. mi.

Warminster
Village
ZIP: 18974 **Lat:** 40-12-23 N **Long:** 75-05-27 W
Pop: 32,832 (1990); 35,543 (1980) **Pop Density:** 3218.8
Land: 10.2 sq. mi.; **Water:** 0.0 sq. mi.

In southeastern PA, 20 mi. northeast of Philadelphia. Home of Burpee Seed Company and the Society for Individual Liberty.

Warrington
Township
ZIP: 18976 **Lat:** 40-15-00 N **Long:** 75-09-32 W
Pop: 12,169 (1990); 10,704 (1980) **Pop Density:** 881.8
Land: 13.8 sq. mi.; **Water:** 0.0 sq. mi.

Warwick
Township
ZIP: 18929 **Lat:** 40-15-03 N **Long:** 75-04-55 W
Pop: 5,915 (1990); 2,307 (1980) **Pop Density:** 532.9
Land: 11.1 sq. mi.; **Water:** 0.0 sq. mi.

West Rockhill
Township
Lat: 40-21-48 N **Long:** 75-21-08 W
Pop: 4,518 (1990); 3,776 (1980) **Pop Density:** 277.2
Land: 16.3 sq. mi.; **Water:** 0.1 sq. mi.

Wrightstown
Township
ZIP: 18940 **Lat:** 40-15-55 N **Long:** 74-59-49 W
Pop: 2,426 (1990); 2,207 (1980) **Pop Density:** 245.1
Land: 9.9 sq. mi.; **Water:** 0.0 sq. mi.

Yardley
Borough
ZIP: 19067 **Lat:** 40-14-23 N **Long:** 74-50-18 W
Pop: 2,288 (1990); 2,533 (1980) **Pop Density:** 2542.2
Land: 0.9 sq. mi.; **Water:** 0.1 sq. mi. **Elev:** 80 ft.

Butler County
County Seat: Butler (ZIP: 16001)

Pop: 152,013 (1990); 147,912 (1980) **Pop Density:** 192.8
Land: 788.6 sq. mi.; **Water:** 6.3 sq. mi. **Area Code:** 412

In central portion of western PA, north of Pittsburgh; organized Mar 12, 1800 from Allegheny County.

Name origin: For Maj. Gen. Richard Butler (1743–91), officer and Indian commissioner after the American Revolution.

Adams
Township
Lat: 40-42-36 N **Long:** 80-00-44 W
Pop: 3,911 (1990); 3,816 (1980) **Pop Density:** 173.1
Land: 22.6 sq. mi.; **Water:** 0.0 sq. mi.

Allegheny
Township
Lat: 41-08-36 N **Long:** 79-44-02 W
Pop: 504 (1990); 565 (1980) **Pop Density:** 20.8
Land: 24.2 sq. mi.; **Water:** 0.0 sq. mi.

Name origin: For the river.

Brady
Township
Lat: 40-59-26 N **Long:** 80-01-12 W
Pop: 834 (1990); 684 (1980) **Pop Density:** 49.3
Land: 16.9 sq. mi.; **Water:** 0.3 sq. mi.

Bruin
Borough
ZIP: 16022 **Lat:** 41-03-18 N **Long:** 79-43-38 W
Pop: 646 (1990); 722 (1980) **Pop Density:** 380.0
Land: 1.7 sq. mi.; **Water:** 0.0 sq. mi. **Elev:** 1100 ft.

Name origin: For Bear Creek, which runs through the village.

Buffalo
Township
ZIP: 16055 **Lat:** 40-42-24 N **Long:** 79-44-13 W
Pop: 6,317 (1990); 6,371 (1980) **Pop Density:** 261.0
Land: 24.2 sq. mi.; **Water:** 0.1 sq. mi.

Butler
Township
ZIP: 16045 **Lat:** 40-51-01 N **Long:** 79-55-40 W
Pop: 17,625 (1990); 18,651 (1980) **Pop Density:** 816.0
Land: 21.6 sq. mi.; **Water:** 0.1 sq. mi.

*Butler
City
ZIP: 16001 **Lat:** 40-51-42 N **Long:** 79-53-48 W
Pop: 15,714 (1990); 17,026 (1980) **Pop Density:** 5820.0
Land: 2.7 sq. mi.; **Water:** 0.0 sq. mi. **Elev:** 1040 ft.

In western PA, bisected by Conoquenessing Creek, 33 mi. north of Pittsburgh. Laid out in 1803; incorporated as borough Feb 26, 1817, as city Jan 7, 1918. Originally owned by Robert Morris (1734–1806) of Philadelphia, financier of the Revolutionary War.

Name origin: For Richard Butler of York County, a lieutenant colonel with Morgan's Rifles in 1777, an Indian agent in OH in 1787, and a major general in the St. Clair expedition of 1791, in which he was killed.

Callery
Borough
ZIP: 16024 **Lat:** 40-44-22 N **Long:** 80-02-15 W
Pop: 420 (1990); 415 (1980) **Pop Density:** 840.0
Land: 0.5 sq. mi.; **Water:** 0.0 sq. mi. **Elev:** 974 ft.

Center
Township
ZIP: 16001 **Lat:** 40-55-24 N **Long:** 79-55-48 W
Pop: 6,239 (1990); 6,224 (1980) **Pop Density:** 255.7
Land: 24.4 sq. mi.; **Water:** 0.0 sq. mi.

Cherry
Township
Lat: 41-03-40 N **Long:** 79-56-10 W
Pop: 814 (1990); 778 (1980) **Pop Density:** 31.4
Land: 25.9 sq. mi.; **Water:** 0.3 sq. mi.

Cherry Valley
Borough
ZIP: 16373   Lat: 41-09-42 N   Long: 79-47-56 W
Pop: 96 (1990); 91 (1980)   Pop Density: 33.1
Land: 2.9 sq. mi.; Water: 0.0 sq. mi.   Elev: 1322 ft.

Chicora
Borough
Lat: 40-56-56 N   Long: 79-44-30 W
Pop: 1,058 (1990); 1,192 (1980)   Pop Density: 1763.3
Land: 0.6 sq. mi.; Water: 0.0 sq. mi.   Elev: 1200 ft.

In western PA on the B & O Railroad line, 10 mi. northeast of Butler.
Name origin: Named in 1956. Previously called Millerstown.

Clay
Township
Lat: 40-59-33 N   Long: 79-55-46 W
Pop: 2,360 (1990); 2,102 (1980)   Pop Density: 93.7
Land: 25.2 sq. mi.; Water: 0.0 sq. mi.

Clearfield
Township
Lat: 40-51-02 N   Long: 79-44-11 W
Pop: 2,635 (1990); 2,308 (1980)   Pop Density: 112.6
Land: 23.4 sq. mi.; Water: 0.0 sq. mi.

Clinton
Township
Lat: 40-42-25 N   Long: 79-49-44 W
Pop: 2,556 (1990); 2,432 (1980)   Pop Density: 107.4
Land: 23.8 sq. mi.; Water: 0.0 sq. mi.   Elev: 1240 ft.

Concord
Township
Lat: 40-59-29 N   Long: 79-49-54 W
Pop: 1,336 (1990); 1,367 (1980)   Pop Density: 53.7
Land: 24.9 sq. mi.; Water: 0.0 sq. mi.

Connoquenessing
Township
Lat: 40-51-06 N   Long: 80-01-01 W
Pop: 3,093 (1990); 2,840 (1980)   Pop Density: 137.5
Land: 22.5 sq. mi.; Water: 0.0 sq. mi.

In central-western PA, a northern suburb of Pittsburgh.
Name origin: For Connoquenessing Creek, from an Indian term probably meaning ' [it runs] for a long time straight.'

*Connoquenessing
Borough
ZIP: 16027   Lat: 40-49-04 N   Long: 80-00-50 W
Pop: 507 (1990); 539 (1980)   Pop Density: 362.1
Land: 1.4 sq. mi.; Water: 0.0 sq. mi.   Elev: 1280 ft.

Cranberry
Township
ZIP: 16046   Lat: 40-42-35 N   Long: 80-06-21 W
Pop: 14,816 (1990); 11,066 (1980)   Pop Density: 649.8
Land: 22.8 sq. mi.; Water: 0.0 sq. mi.

Donegal
Township
Lat: 40-55-09 N   Long: 79-44-02 W
Pop: 1,563 (1990); 1,540 (1980)   Pop Density: 68.0
Land: 23.0 sq. mi.; Water: 0.0 sq. mi.

East Butler
Borough
ZIP: 16029   Lat: 40-52-42 N   Long: 79-50-51 W
Pop: 725 (1990); 799 (1980)   Pop Density: 725.0
Land: 1.0 sq. mi.; Water: 0.0 sq. mi.   Elev: 1040 ft.

Eau Claire
Borough
ZIP: 16030   Lat: 41-08-12 N   Long: 79-47-53 W
Pop: 371 (1990); 420 (1980)   Pop Density: 265.0
Land: 1.4 sq. mi.; Water: 0.0 sq. mi.   Elev: 1500 ft.

Evans City
Borough
ZIP: 16033   Lat: 40-46-06 N   Long: 80-03-31 W
Pop: 2,054 (1990); 2,299 (1980)   Pop Density: 2567.5
Land: 0.8 sq. mi.; Water: 0.0 sq. mi.   Elev: 939 ft.

In southwestern PA, a northern suburb of Pittsburgh. Settled 1796 by Robert Boggs, who exchanged a mare for a 400-acre tract on which he built a cabin and a mill.
Name origin: For Thomas B. Evans, who laid out the village after buying half of Boggs's land.

Fairview
Township
Lat: 40-59-36 N   Long: 79-44-12 W
Pop: 2,009 (1990); 1,934 (1980)   Pop Density: 83.4
Land: 24.1 sq. mi.; Water: 0.0 sq. mi.

*Fairview
Borough
ZIP: 16050   Lat: 41-00-54 N   Long: 79-44-36 W
Pop: 224 (1990); 226 (1980)   Pop Density: 2240.0
Land: 0.1 sq. mi.; Water: 0.0 sq. mi.   Elev: 1400 ft.

Fernway
CDP
ZIP: 16063   Lat: 40-41-40 N   Long: 80-07-51 W
Pop: 9,072 (1990); 3,843 (1980)   Pop Density: 1711.7
Land: 5.3 sq. mi.; Water: 0.0 sq. mi.

Forward
Township
Lat: 40-47-02 N   Long: 80-01-00 W
Pop: 2,339 (1990); 2,146 (1980)   Pop Density: 100.4
Land: 23.3 sq. mi.; Water: 0.1 sq. mi.

Fox Run
CDP
Lat: 40-42-08 N   Long: 80-04-58 W
Pop: 2,384 (1990)   Pop Density: 1036.5
Land: 2.3 sq. mi.; Water: 0.0 sq. mi.

Franklin
Township
Lat: 40-55-38 N   Long: 80-00-51 W
Pop: 2,156 (1990); 2,254 (1980)   Pop Density: 103.7
Land: 20.8 sq. mi.; Water: 1.6 sq. mi.

Harmony
Borough
ZIP: 16037   Lat: 40-48-04 N   Long: 80-07-30 W
Pop: 1,054 (1990); 1,334 (1980)   Pop Density: 2635.0
Land: 0.4 sq. mi.; Water: 0.0 sq. mi.   Elev: 925 ft.

In western PA, a northern suburb of Pittsburgh.
Name origin: For the Harmony Society, organized in 1805 by George Rapp (1757–1847), the group's religious and industrial leader.

Harrisville
Borough
ZIP: 16038   Lat: 41-08-09 N   Long: 80-00-39 W
Pop: 862 (1990); 1,033 (1980)   Pop Density: 1077.5
Land: 0.8 sq. mi.; Water: 0.0 sq. mi.   Elev: 1313 ft.

Homeacre—Lyndora
CDP
ZIP: 16001   Lat: 40-52-15 N   Long: 79-55-22 W
Pop: 7,511 (1990); 8,333 (1980)   Pop Density: 1121.0
Land: 6.7 sq. mi.; Water: 0.0 sq. mi.

Jackson
Township
Lat: 40-46-55 N   Long: 80-06-34 W
Pop: 3,078 (1990); 2,441 (1980)   Pop Density: 145.2
Land: 21.2 sq. mi.; Water: 0.0 sq. mi.

Name origin: For Andrew Jackson (1767–1845), seventh U.S. president.

Jefferson
Township
Lat: 40-46-38 N   Long: 79-49-58 W
Pop: 4,812 (1990); 3,777 (1980)   Pop Density: 205.6
Land: 23.4 sq. mi.; Water: 0.0 sq. mi.

Karns City
Borough
ZIP: 16041   Lat: 40-59-49 N   Long: 79-43-33 W
Pop: 226 (1990); 354 (1980)   Pop Density: 565.0
Land: 0.4 sq. mi.; Water: 0.0 sq. mi.   Elev: 1200 ft.

Lancaster
Township
Lat: 40-50-31 N **Long:** 80-06-52 W
Pop: 2,268 (1990); 2,300 (1980) **Pop Density:** 96.9
Land: 23.4 sq. mi.; **Water:** 0.0 sq. mi.

Marion
Township
Lat: 41-08-17 N **Long:** 79-55-53 W
Pop: 1,113 (1990); 1,204 (1980) **Pop Density:** 43.6
Land: 25.5 sq. mi.; **Water:** 0.0 sq. mi.

Mars
Borough
ZIP: 16046 **Lat:** 40-41-47 N **Long:** 80-00-50 W
Pop: 1,713 (1990); 1,803 (1980) **Pop Density:** 4282.5
Land: 0.4 sq. mi.; **Water:** 0.0 sq. mi. **Elev:** 1031 ft.

Meadowood
CDP
Lat: 40-50-31 N **Long:** 79-53-38 W
Pop: 3,011 (1990); 3,320 (1980) **Pop Density:** 2007.3
Land: 1.5 sq. mi.; **Water:** 0.0 sq. mi.

Mercer
Township
Lat: 41-07-35 N **Long:** 80-00-24 W
Pop: 1,110 (1990); 1,103 (1980) **Pop Density:** 87.4
Land: 12.7 sq. mi.; **Water:** 0.0 sq. mi.

Meridian
CDP
Lat: 40-51-15 N **Long:** 79-57-23 W
Pop: 3,473 (1990); 2,513 (1980) **Pop Density:** 1240.4
Land: 2.8 sq. mi.; **Water:** 0.0 sq. mi.

Middlesex
Township
ZIP: 16059 **Lat:** 40-42-47 N **Long:** 79-55-10 W
Pop: 5,578 (1990); 5,480 (1980) **Pop Density:** 242.5
Land: 23.0 sq. mi.; **Water:** 0.1 sq. mi.

Muddy Creek
Township
Lat: 40-55-42 N **Long:** 80-07-12 W
Pop: 2,139 (1990); 1,832 (1980) **Pop Density:** 98.1
Land: 21.8 sq. mi.; **Water:** 2.0 sq. mi. **Elev:** 1210 ft.

Oakland
Township
Lat: 40-55-21 N **Long:** 79-49-54 W
Pop: 2,820 (1990); 2,767 (1980) **Pop Density:** 123.1
Land: 22.9 sq. mi.; **Water:** 0.3 sq. mi.

Parker
Township
Lat: 41-03-50 N **Long:** 79-44-21 W
Pop: 601 (1990); 614 (1980) **Pop Density:** 25.5
Land: 23.6 sq. mi.; **Water:** 0.0 sq. mi.

Penn
Township
ZIP: 16001 **Lat:** 40-46-44 N **Long:** 79-55-18 W
Pop: 5,080 (1990); 5,219 (1980) **Pop Density:** 209.9
Land: 24.2 sq. mi.; **Water:** 0.0 sq. mi.
Name origin: For William Penn (1644–1718), founder of Pennsylvania.

Petrolia
Borough
ZIP: 16050 **Lat:** 41-01-18 N **Long:** 79-43-01 W
Pop: 292 (1990); 472 (1980) **Pop Density:** 730.0
Land: 0.4 sq. mi.; **Water:** 0.0 sq. mi. **Elev:** 1180 ft.

Portersville
Borough
ZIP: 16051 **Lat:** 40-55-30 N **Long:** 80-08-40 W
Pop: 307 (1990); 320 (1980) **Pop Density:** 383.8
Land: 0.8 sq. mi.; **Water:** 0.0 sq. mi. **Elev:** 1364 ft.

Prospect
Borough
ZIP: 16052 **Lat:** 40-54-02 N **Long:** 80-02-58 W
Pop: 1,122 (1990); 1,016 (1980) **Pop Density:** 233.7
Land: 4.8 sq. mi.; **Water:** 0.0 sq. mi. **Elev:** 1369 ft.
In western PA, a suburb of Butler. Settled in 1796.

Saxonburg
Borough
ZIP: 16056 **Lat:** 40-45-07 N **Long:** 79-48-55 W
Pop: 1,345 (1990); 1,336 (1980) **Pop Density:** 1494.4
Land: 0.9 sq. mi.; **Water:** 0.0 sq. mi. **Elev:** 1288 ft.
In western PA, a northeastern suburb of Pittsburgh. Founded by John A. Roebling, who later became a civil engineer and builder of suspension bridges.
Name origin: For Old Saxony, Germany, former home of many German settlers.

Seven Fields
Borough
ZIP: 16046 **Lat:** 40-41-18 N **Long:** 80-03-43 W
Pop: 556 (1990) **Pop Density:** 695.0
Land: 0.8 sq. mi.; **Water:** 0.0 sq. mi. **Elev:** 1090 ft.

Slippery Rock
Township
ZIP: 16057 **Lat:** 41-03-44 N **Long:** 80-01-52 W
Pop: 4,638 (1990) **Pop Density:** 179.8
Land: 25.8 sq. mi.; **Water:** 0.0 sq. mi.

*Slippery Rock
Borough
ZIP: 16057 **Lat:** 41-04-12 N **Long:** 80-03-37 W
Pop: 3,008 (1990); 3,047 (1980) **Pop Density:** 1769.4
Land: 1.7 sq. mi.; **Water:** 0.0 sq. mi. **Elev:** 1302 ft.
In western PA, a northern suburb of Pittsburgh.
Name origin: For Slippery Rock Creek, which Capt. Samuel Brady is said to have crossed in a single 23-ft. leap to escape an Indian. Previously called Ginger Hill for the free ginger given by the local tavern keeper with the whiskey he sold.

Summit
Township
Lat: 40-51-01 N **Long:** 79-49-33 W
Pop: 4,284 (1990) **Pop Density:** 192.1
Land: 22.3 sq. mi.; **Water:** 0.0 sq. mi.

Valencia
Borough
ZIP: 16059 **Lat:** 40-40-32 N **Long:** 79-59-17 W
Pop: 364 (1990); 340 (1980) **Pop Density:** 910.0
Land: 0.4 sq. mi.; **Water:** 0.0 sq. mi. **Elev:** 1083 ft.

Venango
Township
Lat: 41-08-10 N **Long:** 79-50-23 W
Pop: 707 (1990) **Pop Density:** 34.0
Land: 20.8 sq. mi.; **Water:** 0.0 sq. mi.
Name origin: For the Venango River, now called French Creek, which flows through the western part of the county and joins the Allegheny River at Franklin.

Washington
Township
Lat: 41-03-51 N **Long:** 79-49-49 W
Pop: 1,280 (1990) **Pop Density:** 51.2
Land: 25.0 sq. mi.; **Water:** 0.0 sq. mi.
Name origin: For George Washington (1732–99), first U.S. president.

West Liberty
Borough
ZIP: 16057 **Lat:** 41-00-26 N **Long:** 80-03-18 W
Pop: 282 (1990); 301 (1980) **Pop Density:** 72.3
Land: 3.9 sq. mi.; **Water:** 0.0 sq. mi. **Elev:** 1193 ft.

West Sunbury
Borough
ZIP: 16061 **Lat:** 41-00-21 N **Long:** 79-53-46 W
Pop: 177 (1990); 203 (1980) **Pop Density:** 1770.0
Land: 0.1 sq. mi.; **Water:** 0.0 sq. mi. **Elev:** 1400 ft.

Winfield
Township
Lat: 40-47-11 N **Long:** 79-44-15 W
Pop: 3,162 (1990) **Pop Density:** 129.6
Land: 24.4 sq. mi.; **Water:** 0.0 sq. mi.

Worth
Township
Lat: 41-00-11 N **Long:** 80-06-50 W
Pop: 955 (1990) **Pop Density:** 39.3
Land: 24.3 sq. mi.; **Water:** 1.0 sq. mi.

Zelienople
Borough
ZIP: 16063 **Lat:** 40-47-21 N **Long:** 80-08-36 W
Pop: 4,158 (1990); 3,502 (1980) **Pop Density:** 1980.0
Land: 2.1 sq. mi.; **Water:** 0.0 sq. mi. **Elev:** 911 ft.

In western PA on Connoquenessing Creek, 30 mi. northwest of Pittsburgh.

Name origin: Named in 1802 by founder Baron Dettmar Basse, for his daughter, who was nicknamed Zelie, plus -*ople* 'city.'

Cambria County
County Seat: Ebensburg (ZIP: 15931)

Pop: 163,029 (1990); 183,263 (1980) **Pop Density:** 236.9
Land: 688.1 sq. mi.; **Water:** 5.4 sq. mi. **Area Code:** 814

In western PA, west of Altoona; organized Mar 26, 1804 from Somerset, Bedford, and Huntingdon counties.

Name origin: For Cambria township in Somerset County. Cambria is an ancient, poetic name for Wales, from Welsh *cymy* or *cumbri* 'brotherhood' or 'fraternity.'

Adams
Township
ZIP: 15955 **Lat:** 40-17-29 N **Long:** 78-44-53 W
Pop: 6,869 (1990) **Pop Density:** 146.1
Land: 47.0 sq. mi.; **Water:** 0.1 sq. mi.

Allegheny
Township
Lat: 40-31-42 N **Long:** 78-37-28 W
Pop: 2,075 (1990) **Pop Density:** 70.3
Land: 29.5 sq. mi.; **Water:** 0.1 sq. mi.
Name origin: For the river.

Ashville
Borough
ZIP: 16613 **Lat:** 40-33-32 N **Long:** 78-32-50 W
Pop: 306 (1990); 383 (1980) **Pop Density:** 1530.0
Land: 0.2 sq. mi.; **Water:** 0.0 sq. mi. **Elev:** 1626 ft.

Barnesboro
Borough
ZIP: 15714 **Lat:** 40-39-58 N **Long:** 78-47-05 W
Pop: 2,530 (1990); 2,741 (1980) **Pop Density:** 1581.3
Land: 1.6 sq. mi.; **Water:** 0.0 sq. mi. **Elev:** 1500 ft.

Name origin: For coal miner operator Thomas Barnes, who laid out the town in 1891 after coal was discovered.

Barr
Township
Lat: 40-36-26 N **Long:** 78-49-05 W
Pop: 2,260 (1990) **Pop Density:** 71.7
Land: 31.5 sq. mi.; **Water:** 0.1 sq. mi.

Beaverdale-Lloydell
CDP
Lat: 40-19-22 N **Long:** 78-41-55 W
Pop: 1,278 (1990); 1,187 (1980) **Pop Density:** 983.1
Land: 1.3 sq. mi.; **Water:** 0.0 sq. mi.

Belmont
CDP
Lat: 40-16-56 N **Long:** 78-53-30 W
Pop: 3,184 (1990); 2,296 (1980) **Pop Density:** 1768.9
Land: 1.8 sq. mi.; **Water:** 0.0 sq. mi.

Blacklick
Township
Lat: 40-31-25 N **Long:** 78-51-28 W
Pop: 2,206 (1990) **Pop Density:** 70.9
Land: 31.1 sq. mi.; **Water:** 0.1 sq. mi.

Brownstown
Village
ZIP: 15906 **Lat:** 40-19-58 N **Long:** 78-56-13 W
Pop: 937 (1990); 1,077 (1980) **Pop Density:** 3123.3
Land: 0.3 sq. mi.; **Water:** 0.0 sq. mi. **Elev:** 1443 ft.

In southern PA, a northeast suburb of Lancaster.

Cambria
Township
ZIP: 15931 **Lat:** 40-29-29 N **Long:** 78-44-43 W
Pop: 6,357 (1990) **Pop Density:** 128.9
Land: 49.3 sq. mi.; **Water:** 0.3 sq. mi.

Created 1798.

Name origin: The poetic name for Wales, former home of most of the early settlers.

Carrolltown
Borough
ZIP: 15722 **Lat:** 40-36-15 N **Long:** 78-42-25 W
Pop: 1,286 (1990); 1,395 (1980) **Pop Density:** 1837.1
Land: 0.7 sq. mi.; **Water:** 0.0 sq. mi. **Elev:** 2060 ft.

Laid out in 1840.

Name origin: Named by Prince Demetrius Gallitzin (1770–1840) for John Carroll (1735–1815) who, in 1788, became the first Roman Catholic bishop in the United States and 20 years later the archbishop of Baltimore. His cousin, Charles Carroll (1737–1832), signed the Declaration of Independence and later resided here.

Cassandra
Borough
ZIP: 15925 **Lat:** 40-24-29 N **Long:** 78-38-29 W
Pop: 192 (1990); 238 (1980) **Pop Density:** 1920.0
Land: 0.1 sq. mi.; **Water:** 0.0 sq. mi.

Chest
Township
Lat: 40-40-37 N **Long:** 78-37-12 W
Pop: 312 (1990) **Pop Density:** 10.6
Land: 29.3 sq. mi.; **Water:** 0.0 sq. mi.

Chest Springs
Borough
ZIP: 16624 **Lat:** 40-34-43 N **Long:** 78-36-36 W
Pop: 166 (1990); 198 (1980) **Pop Density:** 830.0
Land: 0.2 sq. mi.; **Water:** 0.0 sq. mi. **Elev:** 1960 ft.

Clearfield
Township
Lat: 40-36-45 N Long: 78-34-41 W
Pop: 1,749 (1990) Pop Density: 56.2
Land: 31.1 sq. mi.; Water: 0.0 sq. mi.

Colver
CDP
ZIP: 15927 Lat: 40-32-34 N Long: 78-47-15 W
Pop: 1,024 (1990); 1,165 (1980) Pop Density: 930.9
Land: 1.1 sq. mi.; Water: 0.0 sq. mi.

Conemaugh
Township
Lat: 40-20-28 N Long: 78-50-55 W
Pop: 2,399 (1990) Pop Density: 212.3
Land: 11.3 sq. mi.; Water: 0.1 sq. mi. Elev: 1200 ft.
In southwestern PA, south of Johnstown. Established 1801.
Name origin: For the Conemaugh River, which forms part of its eastern border; from the Indian term possibly meaning 'otter creek.'

Cresson
Township
ZIP: 16630 Lat: 40-26-46 N Long: 78-35-03 W
Pop: 3,284 (1990) Pop Density: 278.3
Land: 11.8 sq. mi.; Water: 0.0 sq. mi.

*Cresson
City
ZIP: 16630 Lat: 40-27-45 N Long: 78-35-11 W
Pop: 1,784 (1990); 2,184 (1980) Pop Density: 3568.0
Land: 0.5 sq. mi.; Water: 0.0 sq. mi. Elev: 2030 ft.

Croyle
Township
Lat: 40-22-16 N Long: 78-45-36 W
Pop: 2,451 (1990) Pop Density: 133.9
Land: 18.3 sq. mi.; Water: 0.1 sq. mi.

Daisytown
Borough
ZIP: 15902 Lat: 40-19-13 N Long: 78-54-12 W
Pop: 367 (1990); 421 (1980) Pop Density: 1223.3
Land: 0.3 sq. mi.; Water: 0.0 sq. mi. Elev: 1800 ft.

Dale
Borough
ZIP: 15902 Lat: 40-18-42 N Long: 78-54-14 W
Pop: 1,642 (1990); 1,906 (1980) Pop Density: 8210.0
Land: 0.2 sq. mi.; Water: 0.0 sq. mi.
In southwest-central PA, a suburb of Johnstown.
Name origin: For its location in a hilly area.

Dean
Township
Lat: 40-36-06 N Long: 78-28-48 W
Pop: 398 (1990) Pop Density: 19.2
Land: 20.7 sq. mi.; Water: 0.0 sq. mi.

East Carroll
Township
Lat: 40-34-55 N Long: 78-41-33 W
Pop: 1,951 (1990) Pop Density: 77.1
Land: 25.3 sq. mi.; Water: 0.0 sq. mi.

East Conemaugh
Borough
ZIP: 15909 Lat: 40-20-50 N Long: 78-53-09 W
Pop: 1,470 (1990); 2,128 (1980) Pop Density: 4900.0
Land: 0.3 sq. mi.; Water: 0.0 sq. mi.
In southwest-central PA, 1 mi. north of Johnstown.
Name origin: For the Conemaugh River, famous at the time of the 1889 Johnstown flood; from the Indian term *connemach* possibly meaning 'otter creek.'

East Taylor
Township
Lat: 40-22-16 N Long: 78-51-29 W
Pop: 3,073 (1990) Pop Density: 341.4
Land: 9.0 sq. mi.; Water: 0.3 sq. mi.

Ebensburg
Borough
ZIP: 15931 Lat: 40-29-19 N Long: 78-43-37 W
Pop: 3,872 (1990); 4,096 (1980) Pop Density: 2277.6
Land: 1.7 sq. mi.; Water: 0.0 sq. mi. Elev: 2140 ft.
In southwest-central PA on the north branch of Conemaugh Creek, 18 mi. northeast of Johnstown. Founded in the early 1800s by the Rev. Rees Lloyd, a religious dissenter and leader of Welsh immigrants; incorporated Jan 15, 1825.
Name origin: For Eben, the Rev. Lloyd's eldest son, who died in childhood.

Ehrenfeld
Borough
ZIP: 15956 Lat: 40-22-21 N Long: 78-46-34 W
Pop: 307 (1990); 360 (1980) Pop Density: 767.5
Land: 0.4 sq. mi.; Water: 0.0 sq. mi. Elev: 1560 ft.

Elder
Township
Lat: 40-40-45 N Long: 78-41-16 W
Pop: 1,185 (1990) Pop Density: 91.2
Land: 13.0 sq. mi.; Water: 0.0 sq. mi.

Elim
CDP
Lat: 40-17-52 N Long: 78-56-34 W
Pop: 3,861 (1990); 4,669 (1980) Pop Density: 1930.5
Land: 2.0 sq. mi.; Water: 0.0 sq. mi.

Ferndale
Borough
ZIP: 15905 Lat: 40-17-18 N Long: 78-55-01 W
Pop: 2,020 (1990); 2,204 (1980) Pop Density: 5050.0
Land: 0.4 sq. mi.; Water: 0.0 sq. mi. Elev: 1208 ft.
In southwest-central PA, a southern suburb of Johnstown.

Franklin
City
ZIP: 15909 Lat: 40-20-31 N Long: 78-53-00 W
Pop: 565 (1990); 559 (1980) Pop Density: 941.7
Land: 0.6 sq. mi.; Water: 0.0 sq. mi. Elev: 1280 ft.

Gallitzin
Borough
ZIP: 16641 Lat: 40-28-55 N Long: 78-33-21 W
Pop: 2,003 (1990); 2,315 (1980) Pop Density: 2861.4
Land: 0.7 sq. mi.; Water: 0.0 sq. mi. Elev: 2167 ft.
In southwest-central PA, 10 mi. west of Altoona.
Name origin: For Prince Demetrius Augustine Gallitzin (1770–1840), priest, son of a Russian diplomat, and the scion of an ancient and noble family, one of the pioneers of Cambria County, who moved to Baltimore during his *wanderjahr* in 1792 at the age of 22.

*Gallitzin
Township
ZIP: 16641 Lat: 40-31-29 N Long: 78-32-50 W
Pop: 1,289 (1990) Pop Density: 75.8
Land: 17.0 sq. mi.; Water: 0.0 sq. mi.

Geistown
Borough
ZIP: 15904 Lat: 40-17-37 N Long: 78-52-18 W
Pop: 2,749 (1990); 3,304 (1980) Pop Density: 2499.1
Land: 1.1 sq. mi.; Water: 0.0 sq. mi. Elev: 2052 ft.
In southwest-central PA, 6 mi. southeast of Johnstown.

Hastings
Borough
ZIP: 16646 Lat: 40-39-53 N Long: 78-42-32 W
Pop: 1,431 (1990); 1,574 (1980) Pop Density: 2385.0
Land: 0.6 sq. mi.; Water: 0.0 sq. mi. Elev: 1758 ft.

Jackson
Township
ZIP: 15909 Lat: 40-25-56 N Long: 78-51-53 W
Pop: 5,213 (1990) Pop Density: 107.9
Land: 48.3 sq. mi.; Water: 0.1 sq. mi.
Name origin: For Andrew Jackson (1767–1845), seventh U.S. president.

Johnstown — City
ZIP: 15901   Lat: 40-19-31 N Long: 78-55-10 W
Pop: 28,134 (1990); 35,496 (1980)   Pop Density: 4850.7
Land: 5.8 sq. mi.; Water: 0.2 sq. mi.

In southwest-central PA between narrow valley walls, 75 mi. east of Pittsburgh.

Name origin: For Joseph Johns, Jahns, or Yahns (as the name was variously spelled), a native of Switzerland, who came to America in 1769, at the age of 19. Previously called Conemaugh. Site of a flood in May 1889 that destroyed the town and killed more than 2,000 inhabitants.

Lilly — Borough
ZIP: 15938   Lat: 40-25-26 N Long: 78-37-11 W
Pop: 1,162 (1990); 1,462 (1980)   Pop Density: 2324.0
Land: 0.5 sq. mi.; Water: 0.0 sq. mi.   Elev: 1920 ft.

In southwest-central PA, 20 mi. southwest of Altoona.

Lorain — Borough
ZIP: 15902   Lat: 40-17-44 N Long: 78-53-42 W
Pop: 824 (1990); 989 (1980)   Pop Density: 2746.7
Land: 0.3 sq. mi.; Water: 0.0 sq. mi.   Elev: 1280 ft.

Loretto — Borough
ZIP: 15940   Lat: 40-30-31 N Long: 78-38-10 W
Pop: 1,072 (1990); 1,395 (1980)   Pop Density: 1072.0
Land: 1.0 sq. mi.; Water: 0.0 sq. mi.   Elev: 1944 ft.

In southwest-central PA, southwest of Altoona.

Name origin: Named by Fr. Demetrius Gallatzin (1770–1840) for the celebrated religious shrine in Italy near the Adriatic Sea.

Lower Yoder — Township
Lat: 40-19-54 N Long: 78-59-06 W
Pop: 3,342 (1990)   Pop Density: 251.3
Land: 13.3 sq. mi.; Water: 0.1 sq. mi.

Middle Taylor — Township
Lat: 40-22-08 N Long: 78-54-17 W
Pop: 802 (1990)   Pop Density: 167.1
Land: 4.8 sq. mi.; Water: 0.1 sq. mi.

Munster — Township
Lat: 40-28-05 N Long: 78-39-41 W
Pop: 688 (1990)   Pop Density: 48.8
Land: 14.1 sq. mi.; Water: 0.1 sq. mi.

Nanty-Glo — Borough
ZIP: 15943   Lat: 40-28-13 N Long: 78-50-05 W
Pop: 3,190 (1990); 3,936 (1980)   Pop Density: 1772.2
Land: 1.8 sq. mi.; Water: 0.0 sq. mi.   Elev: 1711 ft.
Name origin: From a Welsh phrase meaning 'the coal brook.'

Patton — Borough
ZIP: 16668   Lat: 40-37-57 N Long: 78-38-57 W
Pop: 2,206 (1990); 2,441 (1980)   Pop Density: 2451.1
Land: 0.9 sq. mi.; Water: 0.0 sq. mi.   Elev: 1820 ft.

In southwest-central PA, 20 mi. northwest of Altoona.

Name origin: For Col. John Patton of Curwensville.

Portage — Township
ZIP: 15946   Lat: 40-22-49 N Long: 78-38-12 W
Pop: 4,089 (1990)   Pop Density: 168.3
Land: 24.3 sq. mi.; Water: 0.1 sq. mi.

*Portage — Borough
ZIP: 15946   Lat: 40-23-12 N Long: 78-40-31 W
Pop: 3,105 (1990); 3,510 (1980)   Pop Density: 4435.7
Land: 0.7 sq. mi.; Water: 0.0 sq. mi.   Elev: 1677 ft.

In southwest-central PA, 20 mi. northeast of Johnstown.

Name origin: For the old Portage Railroad, which once extended from Hollidaysburg to Johnstown.

Reade — Township
Lat: 40-41-15 N Long: 78-26-41 W
Pop: 1,716 (1990)   Pop Density: 44.0
Land: 39.0 sq. mi.; Water: 0.0 sq. mi.

Richland — Township
ZIP: 15904   Lat: 40-17-02 N Long: 78-50-50 W
Pop: 12,777 (1990)   Pop Density: 655.2
Land: 19.5 sq. mi.; Water: 0.0 sq. mi.

Sankertown — Borough
ZIP: 16630   Lat: 40-28-14 N Long: 78-35-34 W
Pop: 770 (1990); 804 (1980)   Pop Density: 2566.7
Land: 0.3 sq. mi.; Water: 0.0 sq. mi.   Elev: 2060 ft.

Scalp Level — Borough
ZIP: 15963   Lat: 40-14-57 N Long: 78-50-38 W
Pop: 1,158 (1990); 1,186 (1980)   Pop Density: 1930.0
Land: 0.6 sq. mi.; Water: 0.0 sq. mi.   Elev: 1860 ft.

Name origin: From Jacob Eash, Jr.'s exhortation to those helping him clear the land around his mill, "Scalp 'em level."

South Fork — Borough
ZIP: 15956   Lat: 40-21-49 N Long: 78-47-29 W
Pop: 1,197 (1990); 1,401 (1980)   Pop Density: 2394.0
Land: 0.5 sq. mi.; Water: 0.0 sq. mi.   Elev: 1496 ft.

Southmont — Borough
ZIP: 15905   Lat: 40-18-37 N Long: 78-55-51 W
Pop: 2,415 (1990); 2,683 (1980)   Pop Density: 2195.5
Land: 1.1 sq. mi.; Water: 0.0 sq. mi.   Elev: 1640 ft.

Spangler — Borough
ZIP: 15775   Lat: 40-38-42 N Long: 78-46-23 W
Pop: 2,068 (1990); 2,399 (1980)   Pop Density: 1477.1
Land: 1.4 sq. mi.; Water: 0.0 sq. mi.   Elev: 1500 ft.

In southwestern PA, 20 mi. northwest of Altoona. Incorporated in 1893.

Name origin: For Col. J. L. Spangler of Bellefonte.

Stonycreek — Township
Lat: 40-17-54 N Long: 78-53-24 W
Pop: 3,562 (1990)   Pop Density: 1047.6
Land: 3.4 sq. mi.; Water: 0.0 sq. mi.

Summerhill — Township
ZIP: 15958   Lat: 40-21-01 N Long: 78-41-25 W
Pop: 2,798 (1990)   Pop Density: 97.2
Land: 28.8 sq. mi.; Water: 0.7 sq. mi.

*Summerhill — Borough
ZIP: 15958   Lat: 40-22-32 N Long: 78-45-40 W
Pop: 614 (1990); 725 (1980)   Pop Density: 2046.7
Land: 0.3 sq. mi.; Water: 0.0 sq. mi.   Elev: 1640 ft.

Name origin: For old Summerhill Township. Originally called Somerhill for Joseph and David Somer, two landowners in the area.

Susquehanna — Township
Lat: 40-41-18 N Long: 78-45-28 W
Pop: 2,299 (1990)   Pop Density: 83.0
Land: 27.7 sq. mi.; Water: 0.0 sq. mi.

Tunnelhill
Borough
ZIP: 16641   Lat: 40-28-36 N Long: 78-32-42 W
Pop: 259 (1990); 359 (1980)   Pop Density: 1295.0
Land: 0.2 sq. mi.; Water: 0.0 sq. mi.   Elev: 2300 ft.
Part of the town is also in Blair County.

Upper Yoder
Township
ZIP: 15905   Lat: 40-17-55 N Long: 78-59-23 W
Pop: 5,435 (1990)   Pop Density: 464.5
Land: 11.7 sq. mi.; Water: 0.0 sq. mi.

Vintondale
Borough
ZIP: 15961   Lat: 40-28-42 N Long: 78-54-45 W
Pop: 582 (1990); 697 (1980)   Pop Density: 1164.0
Land: 0.5 sq. mi.; Water: 0.0 sq. mi.   Elev: 1500 ft.

Washington
Township
Lat: 40-24-32 N Long: 78-36-13 W
Pop: 929 (1990)   Pop Density: 72.0
Land: 12.9 sq. mi.; Water: 0.0 sq. mi.

West Carroll
Township
Lat: 40-36-28 N Long: 78-44-21 W
Pop: 1,524 (1990)   Pop Density: 142.4
Land: 10.7 sq. mi.; Water: 0.0 sq. mi.

Westmont
Borough
ZIP: 15905   Lat: 40-19-08 N Long: 78-57-08 W
Pop: 5,789 (1990); 6,113 (1980)   Pop Density: 2412.1
Land: 2.4 sq. mi.; Water: 0.0 sq. mi.   Elev: 1794 ft.
In southwest-central PA in a highlands area, near Altoona.

West Taylor
Township
Lat: 40-23-06 N Long: 78-56-23 W
Pop: 995 (1990)   Pop Density: 168.6
Land: 5.9 sq. mi.; Water: 0.1 sq. mi.

White
Township
Lat: 40-40-44 N Long: 78-32-17 W
Pop: 553 (1990)   Pop Density: 27.4
Land: 20.2 sq. mi.; Water: 2.4 sq. mi.

Wilmore
Borough
ZIP: 15962   Lat: 40-23-10 N Long: 78-43-00 W
Pop: 277 (1990); 299 (1980)   Pop Density: 923.3
Land: 0.3 sq. mi.; Water: 0.0 sq. mi.   Elev: 1700 ft.

Cameron County
County Seat: Emporium (ZIP: 15834)

Pop: 5,913 (1990); 6,674 (1980)   Pop Density: 14.9
Land: 397.2 sq. mi.; Water: 1.4 sq. mi.   Area Code: 814

In north-west central PA, west of Williamsport; organized Mar 29, 1860 from Clinton, Elk, McKean, and Potter counties.

Name origin: For Simon Cameron (1799–1889), U.S. senator from PA (1845–49; 1857–61; 1867–77), U.S. secretary of war (1861–62), and U.S. Minister to Russia (1862).

Driftwood
Borough
ZIP: 15832   Lat: 41-20-35 N Long: 78-08-07 W
Pop: 116 (1990); 163 (1980)   Pop Density: 64.4
Land: 1.8 sq. mi.; Water: 0.1 sq. mi.   Elev: 860 ft.

Emporium
Borough
ZIP: 15834   Lat: 41-30-39 N Long: 78-14-13 W
Pop: 2,513 (1990); 2,837 (1980)   Pop Density: 3590.0
Land: 0.7 sq. mi.; Water: 0.0 sq. mi.   Elev: 1075 ft.
In north-central PA on Bucktail Trail, near the NY state line; incorporated Oct 13, 1864.

Name origin: A Latinized form of the Greek word meaning 'market,' or 'center of trade.'

Gibson
Township
Lat: 41-19-40 N Long: 78-10-37 W
Pop: 215 (1990)   Pop Density: 2.3
Land: 94.5 sq. mi.; Water: 0.8 sq. mi.

Grove
Township
Lat: 41-22-33 N Long: 78-03-27 W
Pop: 168 (1990)   Pop Density: 2.3
Land: 73.5 sq. mi.; Water: 0.5 sq. mi.

Lumber
Township
Lat: 41-27-35 N Long: 78-09-55 W
Pop: 195 (1990)   Pop Density: 3.8
Land: 51.4 sq. mi.; Water: 0.1 sq. mi.

Portage
Township
Lat: 41-32-59 N Long: 78-10-21 W
Pop: 211 (1990)   Pop Density: 11.7
Land: 18.1 sq. mi.; Water: 0.0 sq. mi.

Shippen
Township
Lat: 41-31-00 N Long: 78-19-18 W
Pop: 2,495 (1990)   Pop Density: 15.9
Land: 157.2 sq. mi.; Water: 0.0 sq. mi.

Carbon County
County Seat: Jim Thorpe (ZIP: 18229)

Pop: 56,846 (1990); 53,285 (1980) **Pop Density:** 148.6
Land: 382.6 sq. mi.; **Water:** 6.2 sq. mi. **Area Code:** 717

In eastern PA, south of Scranton; organized Mar 13, 1843 from Northampton and Monroe counties.

Name origin: For its rich deposits of anthracite coal.

Banks
Township
Lat: 40-55-56 N Long: 75-56-13 W
Pop: 1,485 (1990) **Pop Density:** 135.0
Land: 11.0 sq. mi.; **Water:** 0.0 sq. mi.

Beaver Meadows
Borough
Lat: 40-55-46 N Long: 75-54-45 W
Pop: 985 (1990); 1,078 (1980) **Pop Density:** 3283.3
Land: 0.3 sq. mi.; **Water:** 0.0 sq. mi. **Elev:** 1559 ft.
In eastern PA, near Hazelton.
Name origin: For nearby Beaver Creek.

Bowmanstown
Borough
ZIP: 18030 Lat: 40-48-05 N Long: 75-39-41 W
Pop: 888 (1990); 1,078 (1980) **Pop Density:** 1110.0
Land: 0.8 sq. mi.; **Water:** 0.0 sq. mi. **Elev:** 495 ft.
Founded 1796.

East Penn
Township
Lat: 40-46-41 N Long: 75-43-23 W
Pop: 2,091 (1990) **Pop Density:** 92.9
Land: 22.5 sq. mi.; **Water:** 0.1 sq. mi.

East Side
Borough
ZIP: 18661 Lat: 41-03-45 N Long: 75-45-43 W
Pop: 330 (1990); 302 (1980) **Pop Density:** 275.0
Land: 1.2 sq. mi.; **Water:** 0.0 sq. mi. **Elev:** 1112 ft.

Franklin
Township
Lat: 40-51-06 N Long: 75-39-25 W
Pop: 3,706 (1990) **Pop Density:** 253.8
Land: 14.6 sq. mi.; **Water:** 0.5 sq. mi.

Jim Thorpe
Borough
ZIP: 18229 Lat: 40-52-16 N Long: 75-44-23 W
Pop: 5,048 (1990); 5,263 (1980) **Pop Density:** 348.1
Land: 14.5 sq. mi.; **Water:** 0.3 sq. mi. **Elev:** 1000 ft.
Incorporated as Mauch Chunk Jan 26, 1850; name changed 1954.
Name origin: For the famous Olympic athlete (1886–1953), buried here. Mauch Chunk was an Indian place name meaning 'bear mountain.'

Kidder
Township
Lat: 41-03-24 N Long: 75-40-28 W
Pop: 1,319 (1990) **Pop Density:** 19.1
Land: 69.0 sq. mi.; **Water:** 0.8 sq. mi.

Lansford
Borough
ZIP: 18232 Lat: 40-49-55 N Long: 75-53-09 W
Pop: 4,583 (1990); 4,466 (1980) **Pop Density:** 2864.4
Land: 1.6 sq. mi.; **Water:** 0.0 sq. mi. **Elev:** 1134 ft.
In eastern PA. Founded 1846.
Name origin: For Asa Lansford Foster, mining engineer, coal operator, and early champion of the public school system.

Lausanne
Township
Lat: 40-58-44 N Long: 75-49-12 W
Pop: 237 (1990) **Pop Density:** 40.9
Land: 5.8 sq. mi.; **Water:** 0.0 sq. mi.

Lehigh
Township
Lat: 40-56-41 N Long: 75-45-44 W
Pop: 500 (1990) **Pop Density:** 19.0
Land: 26.3 sq. mi.; **Water:** 0.3 sq. mi.

Lehighton
Borough
ZIP: 18235 Lat: 40-49-52 N Long: 75-42-59 W
Pop: 5,914 (1990); 5,826 (1980) **Pop Density:** 3478.8
Land: 1.7 sq. mi.; **Water:** 0.0 sq. mi. **Elev:** 570 ft.
In eastern PA on a plateau overlooking the Lehigh River and valley, 26 mi. northwest of Allentown. Laid out in 1794 by Col. Jacob Weiss and William Henry.
Name origin: For the Lehigh River, on which the borough is situated.

Lower Towamensing
Township
Lat: 40-49-02 N Long: 75-33-27 W
Pop: 2,948 (1990) **Pop Density:** 139.7
Land: 21.1 sq. mi.; **Water:** 0.0 sq. mi.

Mahoning
Township
Lat: 40-48-54 N Long: 75-46-28 W
Pop: 4,198 (1990) **Pop Density:** 177.9
Land: 23.6 sq. mi.; **Water:** 0.1 sq. mi.

Nesquehoning
Borough
ZIP: 18240 Lat: 40-51-43 N Long: 75-49-46 W
Pop: 3,364 (1990); 3,346 (1980) **Pop Density:** 158.7
Land: 21.2 sq. mi.; **Water:** 0.4 sq. mi. **Elev:** 820 ft.
In eastern PA, 28 mi. south of Wilkes-Barre.
Name origin: From an Indian term possibly meaning 'at the black lick,' probably a reference to coal.

Packer
Township
Lat: 40-54-27 N Long: 75-52-50 W
Pop: 918 (1990) **Pop Density:** 31.9
Land: 28.8 sq. mi.; **Water:** 0.0 sq. mi.

Palmerton
Borough
ZIP: 18071 Lat: 40-48-04 N Long: 75-37-01 W
Pop: 5,394 (1990); 5,455 (1980) **Pop Density:** 2157.6
Land: 2.5 sq. mi.; **Water:** 0.0 sq. mi. **Elev:** 400 ft.
In eastern PA, 15 mi. northwest of Allentown. Laid out in 1898 by the New Jersey Zinc Company; incorporated 1913.
Name origin: For Stephen J. Palmer, president of the New Jersey Zinc Company.

Parryville
Borough
ZIP: 18244 Lat: 40-49-27 N Long: 75-40-10 W
Pop: 488 (1990); 481 (1980) **Pop Density:** 305.0
Land: 1.6 sq. mi.; **Water:** 0.0 sq. mi. **Elev:** 470 ft.

Penn Forest
Township
Lat: 40-57-35 N **Long:** 75-37-31 W
Pop: 2,895 (1990)   **Pop Density:** 38.3
Land: 75.5 sq. mi.; **Water:** 1.2 sq. mi.

Summit Hill
Borough
ZIP: 18250   **Lat:** 40-49-29 N **Long:** 75-50-47 W
Pop: 3,332 (1990); 3,418 (1980)   **Pop Density:** 374.4
Land: 8.9 sq. mi.; **Water:** 0.5 sq. mi.   **Elev:** 1411 ft.
Name origin: For its location at the summit of Sharp Mountain.

Towamensing
Township
Lat: 40-52-26 N **Long:** 75-34-30 W
Pop: 3,111 (1990)   **Pop Density:** 114.4
Land: 27.2 sq. mi.; **Water:** 1.7 sq. mi.

Weatherly
Borough
ZIP: 18255   **Lat:** 40-56-34 N **Long:** 75-49-18 W
Pop: 2,640 (1990); 2,891 (1980)   **Pop Density:** 880.0
Land: 3.0 sq. mi.; **Water:** 0.0 sq. mi.   **Elev:** 1094 ft.
In eastern PA, 10 mi. east of Hazleton. Settled in 1840.
Name origin: For a clockmaker, David Weatherly.

Weissport
Borough
ZIP: 18235   **Lat:** 40-49-44 N **Long:** 75-42-04 W
Pop: 472 (1990); 486 (1980)   **Pop Density:** 4720.0
Land: 0.1 sq. mi.; **Water:** 0.0 sq. mi.   **Elev:** 500 ft.

Centre County
County Seat: Bellefonte (ZIP: 16823)

Pop: 123,786 (1990); 112,760 (1980)   **Pop Density:** 111.8
Land: 1107.6 sq. mi.; **Water:** 4.3 sq. mi.   **Area Code:** 814
In central PA, southwest of Williamsport; organized Feb 13, 1800 from Lycoming, Mifflin, Northumberland, and Huntingdon counties.
Name origin: For its location in the geographic center of the state, with the British spelling of the time.

Bellefonte
Borough
ZIP: 16823   **Lat:** 40-54-49 N **Long:** 77-46-06 W
Pop: 6,358 (1990); 6,300 (1980)   **Pop Density:** 3532.2
Land: 1.8 sq. mi.; **Water:** 0.0 sq. mi.   **Elev:** 809 ft.
In central PA; occupies 7 hills at the southeastern base of Bald Eagle Mountain. Surveyed 1769; settled shortly afterward; incorporated Mar 28, 1806.
Name origin: From French meaning 'beautiful fountain.' The name is traditionally attributed to Charles-Maurice Talleyrand-Périgord (1754–1838), who made the remark upon seeing the big spring here during his exile from France in 1794–95.

Benner
Township
ZIP: 16823   **Lat:** 40-51-51 N **Long:** 77-49-07 W
Pop: 5,085 (1990)   **Pop Density:** 178.4
Land: 28.5 sq. mi.; **Water:** 0.0 sq. mi.
In central PA, northeast of Altoona.
Name origin: Named in 1853 for Gen. Philip Benner, a prominent politician and founder of a local newspaper.

Boalsburg
CDP
ZIP: 16827   **Lat:** 40-46-24 N **Long:** 77-47-29 W
Pop: 2,206 (1990); 2,295 (1980)   **Pop Density:** 848.5
Land: 2.6 sq. mi.; **Water:** 0.0 sq. mi.

Boggs
Township
Lat: 40-59-30 N **Long:** 77-47-57 W
Pop: 2,686 (1990)   **Pop Density:** 48.3
Land: 55.6 sq. mi.; **Water:** 0.1 sq. mi.

Burnside
Township
Lat: 41-07-30 N **Long:** 77-58-47 W
Pop: 390 (1990)   **Pop Density:** 4.6
Land: 85.2 sq. mi.; **Water:** 0.9 sq. mi.

Centre Hall
Borough
ZIP: 16828   **Lat:** 40-50-39 N **Long:** 77-41-04 W
Pop: 1,203 (1990); 1,233 (1980)   **Pop Density:** 2005.0
Land: 0.6 sq. mi.; **Water:** 0.0 sq. mi.   **Elev:** 1343 ft.
In central PA, northeast of State College.
Name origin: For its central position in Penn's Valley, one of the state's finest hunting and fishing areas; origin of *Hall* unknown.

College
Township
ZIP: 16801   **Lat:** 40-48-50 N **Long:** 77-48-58 W
Pop: 6,709 (1990)   **Pop Density:** 364.6
Land: 18.4 sq. mi.; **Water:** 0.0 sq. mi.
In central PA, a suburb of State College.
Name origin: For Pennsylvania State College (now Pennsylvania State University).

Curtin
Township
Lat: 41-06-02 N **Long:** 77-45-26 W
Pop: 516 (1990)   **Pop Density:** 11.7
Land: 44.2 sq. mi.; **Water:** 0.0 sq. mi.

Ferguson
Township
ZIP: 16801   **Lat:** 40-44-35 N **Long:** 77-56-49 W
Pop: 9,368 (1990)   **Pop Density:** 194.8
Land: 48.1 sq. mi.; **Water:** 0.0 sq. mi.

Gregg
Township
Lat: 40-51-25 N **Long:** 77-34-28 W
Pop: 1,805 (1990)   **Pop Density:** 39.7
Land: 45.5 sq. mi.; **Water:** 0.0 sq. mi.

Haines
Township
Lat: 40-54-04 N **Long:** 77-21-36 W
Pop: 1,315 (1990)   **Pop Density:** 22.8
Land: 57.8 sq. mi.; **Water:** 0.0 sq. mi.

Halfmoon
Township
Lat: 40-46-31 N **Long:** 78-01-15 W
Pop: 1,469 (1990) **Pop Density:** 65.0
Land: 22.6 sq. mi.; **Water:** 0.0 sq. mi.

Harris
Township
Lat: 40-45-53 N **Long:** 77-45-55 W
Pop: 4,167 (1990) **Pop Density:** 130.6
Land: 31.9 sq. mi.; **Water:** 0.0 sq. mi.

Howard
Township
ZIP: 16841 **Lat:** 41-00-18 N **Long:** 77-41-11 W
Pop: 1,004 (1990) **Pop Density:** 55.8
Land: 18.0 sq. mi.; **Water:** 1.6 sq. mi.

*Howard
Borough
ZIP: 16841 **Lat:** 41-00-43 N **Long:** 77-39-25 W
Pop: 749 (1990); 838 (1980) **Pop Density:** 2496.7
Land: 0.3 sq. mi.; **Water:** 0.0 sq. mi. **Elev:** 664 ft.

Huston
Township
Lat: 40-52-06 N **Long:** 77-58-06 W
Pop: 1,282 (1990) **Pop Density:** 49.3
Land: 26.0 sq. mi.; **Water:** 0.0 sq. mi.

Liberty
Township
Lat: 41-04-20 N **Long:** 77-38-00 W
Pop: 1,747 (1990) **Pop Density:** 80.1
Land: 21.8 sq. mi.; **Water:** 1.1 sq. mi.

Marion
Township
Lat: 40-59-12 N **Long:** 77-38-35 W
Pop: 730 (1990) **Pop Density:** 33.3
Land: 21.9 sq. mi.; **Water:** 0.0 sq. mi.

Miles
Township
Lat: 40-57-44 N **Long:** 77-22-09 W
Pop: 1,494 (1990) **Pop Density:** 23.8
Land: 62.7 sq. mi.; **Water:** 0.0 sq. mi.

Milesburg
Borough
ZIP: 16853 **Lat:** 40-56-33 N **Long:** 77-47-30 W
Pop: 1,144 (1990); 1,309 (1980) **Pop Density:** 2860.0
Land: 0.4 sq. mi.; **Water:** 0.0 sq. mi. **Elev:** 700 ft.
In central PA, north of State College. Founded 1793.
Name origin: For Gen. Samuel Miles, Indian fighter, patriot, landowner, iron manufacturer, and one-time mayor of Philadelphia (1790).

Millheim
Borough
ZIP: 16854 **Lat:** 40-53-33 N **Long:** 77-28-34 W
Pop: 847 (1990); 800 (1980) **Pop Density:** 651.5
Land: 1.3 sq. mi.; **Water:** 0.0 sq. mi. **Elev:** 1093 ft.

Patton
Township
ZIP: 16801 **Lat:** 40-49-38 N **Long:** 77-55-10 W
Pop: 9,971 (1990) **Pop Density:** 402.1
Land: 24.8 sq. mi.; **Water:** 0.0 sq. mi.

Penn
Township
Lat: 40-51-29 N **Long:** 77-29-30 W
Pop: 935 (1990) **Pop Density:** 33.2
Land: 28.2 sq. mi.; **Water:** 0.0 sq. mi.

Philipsburg
Borough
ZIP: 16866 **Lat:** 40-53-33 N **Long:** 78-12-42 W
Pop: 3,048 (1990); 3,533 (1980) **Pop Density:** 2770.9
Land: 1.1 sq. mi.; **Water:** 0.0 sq. mi. **Elev:** 1435 ft.
In central PA, 28 mi. northeast of Altoona. Founded 1797.
Name origin: For founders Henry and James Phillips, two Englishmen.

Port Matilda
Borough
ZIP: 16870 **Lat:** 40-47-56 N **Long:** 78-03-09 W
Pop: 669 (1990); 647 (1980) **Pop Density:** 1338.0
Land: 0.5 sq. mi.; **Water:** 0.0 sq. mi. **Elev:** 1014 ft.

Potter
Township
Lat: 40-47-56 N **Long:** 77-39-09 W
Pop: 3,020 (1990) **Pop Density:** 52.0
Land: 58.1 sq. mi.; **Water:** 0.1 sq. mi.

Rush
Township
Lat: 40-51-50 N **Long:** 78-10-05 W
Pop: 3,411 (1990) **Pop Density:** 23.0
Land: 148.4 sq. mi.; **Water:** 0.4 sq. mi.

Snow Shoe
Township
ZIP: 16874 **Lat:** 41-02-43 N **Long:** 77-56-01 W
Pop: 1,756 (1990) **Pop Density:** 21.1
Land: 83.1 sq. mi.; **Water:** 0.0 sq. mi.

*Snow Shoe
Borough
ZIP: 16874 **Lat:** 41-01-37 N **Long:** 77-57-01 W
Pop: 800 (1990); 852 (1980) **Pop Density:** 1333.3
Land: 0.6 sq. mi.; **Water:** 0.0 sq. mi. **Elev:** 1703 ft.
In central PA, north of State College.
Name origin: For Snow Shoe Camp Survey, because the surveyor found a snowshoe at a deserted Indian camp here in 1773.

South Philipsburg
Borough
ZIP: 16866 **Lat:** 40-53-13 N **Long:** 78-13-06 W
Pop: 438 (1990); 523 (1980) **Pop Density:** 1460.0
Land: 0.3 sq. mi.; **Water:** 0.0 sq. mi. **Elev:** 1458 ft.

Spring
Township
ZIP: 16823 **Lat:** 40-53-33 N **Long:** 77-43-42 W
Pop: 5,344 (1990) **Pop Density:** 206.3
Land: 25.9 sq. mi.; **Water:** 0.0 sq. mi.

State College
Borough
ZIP: 16801 **Lat:** 40-47-25 N **Long:** 77-51-28 W
Pop: 38,923 (1990); 36,130 (1980) **Pop Density:** 8649.6
Land: 4.5 sq. mi.; **Water:** 0.0 sq. mi. **Elev:** 1154 ft.
In central PA, in the Nittany Valley between the Bald Eagle Ridge (northwest) and the Seven Mountains (southeast), 50 mi. northeast of Altoona.
Name origin: The site of the Pennsylvania State University.

Taylor
Township
Lat: 40-46-36 N **Long:** 78-08-40 W
Pop: 714 (1990) **Pop Density:** 23.5
Land: 30.4 sq. mi.; **Water:** 0.0 sq. mi.

Union
Township
Lat: 40-55-54 N **Long:** 77-54-39 W
Pop: 895 (1990) **Pop Density:** 19.2
Land: 46.5 sq. mi.; **Water:** 0.0 sq. mi.

Unionville
Borough
ZIP: 16835 **Lat:** 40-54-21 N **Long:** 77-52-35 W
Pop: 284 (1990); 361 (1980) **Pop Density:** 946.7
Land: 0.3 sq. mi.; **Water:** 0.0 sq. mi.

Walker
Township
Lat: 40-56-53 N **Long:** 77-37-32 W
Pop: 2,801 (1990) **Pop Density:** 69.2
Land: 40.5 sq. mi.; **Water:** 0.0 sq. mi.

Worth   Township
Lat: 40-49-10 N **Long:** 78-03-48 W
Pop: 709 (1990)   **Pop Density:** 32.7
Land: 21.7 sq. mi.; **Water:** 0.0 sq. mi.

Chester County
County Seat: West Chester (ZIP: 19380)

Pop: 376,396 (1990); 316,660 (1980)   **Pop Density:** 497.9
Land: 756.0 sq. mi.; **Water:** 3.8 sq. mi.   **Area Code:** 215

On southeastern border of PA, west of Philadelphia; original county, organized as Upland County Mar 10, 1682; name changed soon after.

Name origin: For Chester, Cheshire, England, home of many settlers brought to America by William Penn (1644–1718).

Atglen   Borough
ZIP: 19310   **Lat:** 39-56-49 N **Long:** 75-58-30 W
Pop: 825 (1990); 669 (1980)   **Pop Density:** 916.7
Land: 0.9 sq. mi.; **Water:** 0.0 sq. mi.   **Elev:** 504 ft.

Avondale   Borough
ZIP: 19311   **Lat:** 39-49-26 N **Long:** 75-46-56 W
Pop: 954 (1990); 891 (1980)   **Pop Density:** 1908.0
Land: 0.5 sq. mi.; **Water:** 0.0 sq. mi.   **Elev:** 272 ft.

In southeastern PA on White Clay Creek, in a mushroom-producing agricultural area.

Birmingham   Township
Lat: 39-53-49 N **Long:** 75-36-05 W
Pop: 2,636 (1990)   **Pop Density:** 411.9
Land: 6.4 sq. mi.; **Water:** 0.1 sq. mi.

Caln   Township
ZIP: 19320   **Lat:** 39-59-58 N **Long:** 75-45-49 W
Pop: 11,997 (1990)   **Pop Density:** 1363.3
Land: 8.8 sq. mi.; **Water:** 0.0 sq. mi.

Charlestown   Township
Lat: 40-05-05 N **Long:** 75-33-16 W
Pop: 2,754 (1990)   **Pop Density:** 220.3
Land: 12.5 sq. mi.; **Water:** 0.0 sq. mi.

In southeastern PA, a suburb of Pittsburgh on Pickering Creek, which flows through the town.

Name origin: The creek and township are both named for Charles Pickering, an early settler.

Chesterbrook   CDP
Lat: 40-04-32 N **Long:** 75-27-33 W
Pop: 4,561 (1990)   **Pop Density:** 2850.6
Land: 1.6 sq. mi.; **Water:** 0.0 sq. mi.

Coatesville   City
ZIP: 19320   **Lat:** 39-59-05 N **Long:** 75-49-09 W
Pop: 11,038 (1990); 10,698 (1980)   **Pop Density:** 5809.5
Land: 1.9 sq. mi.; **Water:** 0.0 sq. mi.   **Elev:** 320 ft.

In southeastern PA, 28 mi. east of Lancaster. Post office established 1812.

Name origin: For first postmaster Moses Coates, who owned a large tract of land upon which the town was built.

Devon-Berwyn   CDP
ZIP: 19312   **Lat:** 40-02-36 N **Long:** 75-26-19 W
Pop: 5,019 (1990); 5,246 (1980)   **Pop Density:** 2007.6
Land: 2.5 sq. mi.; **Water:** 0.0 sq. mi.

Downingtown   Borough
ZIP: 19335   **Lat:** 40-00-25 N **Long:** 75-42-08 W
Pop: 7,749 (1990); 7,650 (1980)   **Pop Density:** 3522.3
Land: 2.2 sq. mi.; **Water:** 0.0 sq. mi.   **Elev:** 250 ft.

In southeastern PA on the east branch of Brandywine Creek, 32 mi. west of Philadelphia. Incorporated 1859; settled by immigrants from Birmingham, England.

Name origin: For Thomas Downing, who purchased a mill here in 1739. Originally called Milltown.

East Bradford   Township
ZIP: 19380   **Lat:** 39-57-35 N **Long:** 75-38-52 W
Pop: 6,440 (1990)   **Pop Density:** 429.3
Land: 15.0 sq. mi.; **Water:** 0.0 sq. mi.

East Brandywine   Township
ZIP: 19335   **Lat:** 40-02-15 N **Long:** 75-45-18 W
Pop: 5,179 (1990)   **Pop Density:** 454.3
Land: 11.4 sq. mi.; **Water:** 0.0 sq. mi.

East Caln   Township
Lat: 40-00-52 N **Long:** 75-40-59 W
Pop: 2,619 (1990)   **Pop Density:** 727.5
Land: 3.6 sq. mi.; **Water:** 0.1 sq. mi.

East Coventry   Township
Lat: 40-11-56 N **Long:** 75-36-45 W
Pop: 4,450 (1990)   **Pop Density:** 412.0
Land: 10.8 sq. mi.; **Water:** 0.2 sq. mi.

East Fallowfield   Township
Lat: 39-57-13 N **Long:** 75-49-03 W
Pop: 4,433 (1990)   **Pop Density:** 282.4
Land: 15.7 sq. mi.; **Water:** 0.0 sq. mi.

East Goshen   Township
ZIP: 19380   **Lat:** 39-59-29 N **Long:** 75-32-45 W
Pop: 15,138 (1990)   **Pop Density:** 1498.8
Land: 10.1 sq. mi.; **Water:** 0.0 sq. mi.

East Marlborough   Township
Lat: 39-52-34 N **Long:** 75-43-30 W
Pop: 4,781 (1990)   **Pop Density:** 306.5
Land: 15.6 sq. mi.; **Water:** 0.0 sq. mi.

East Nantmeal   Township
Lat: 40-08-15 N **Long:** 75-44-36 W
Pop: 1,448 (1990)   **Pop Density:** 88.3
Land: 16.4 sq. mi.; **Water:** 0.0 sq. mi.   **Elev:** 735 ft.

East Nottingham
Township
Lat: 39-45-31 N Long: 75-58-03 W
Pop: 3,841 (1990) **Pop Density:** 192.1
Land: 20.0 sq. mi.; **Water:** 0.0 sq. mi.

East Pikeland
Township
ZIP: 19460 Lat: 40-07-52 N Long: 75-33-44 W
Pop: 5,825 (1990) **Pop Density:** 661.9
Land: 8.8 sq. mi.; **Water:** 0.1 sq. mi.

Easttown
Township
ZIP: 19312 Lat: 40-01-43 N Long: 75-26-21 W
Pop: 9,570 (1990) **Pop Density:** 1167.1
Land: 8.2 sq. mi.; **Water:** 0.0 sq. mi.

East Vincent
Township
Lat: 40-10-17 N Long: 75-36-01 W
Pop: 4,161 (1990) **Pop Density:** 308.2
Land: 13.5 sq. mi.; **Water:** 0.2 sq. mi.

East Whiteland
Township
ZIP: 19355 Lat: 40-02-49 N Long: 75-33-13 W
Pop: 8,398 (1990) **Pop Density:** 763.5
Land: 11.0 sq. mi.; **Water:** 0.0 sq. mi.

Elk
Township
Lat: 39-44-13 N Long: 75-54-29 W
Pop: 1,129 (1990) **Pop Density:** 110.7
Land: 10.2 sq. mi.; **Water:** 0.0 sq. mi.

Elverson
Borough
ZIP: 19520 Lat: 40-09-28 N Long: 75-49-53 W
Pop: 470 (1990); 530 (1980) **Pop Density:** 470.0
Land: 1.0 sq. mi.; **Water:** 0.0 sq. mi. **Elev:** 680 ft.

Exton
CDP
ZIP: 19341 Lat: 40-01-53 N Long: 75-37-48 W
Pop: 2,550 (1990); 1,853 (1980) **Pop Density:** 796.9
Land: 3.2 sq. mi.; **Water:** 0.0 sq. mi.

Franklin
Township
Lat: 39-46-01 N Long: 75-49-45 W
Pop: 2,779 (1990) **Pop Density:** 210.5
Land: 13.2 sq. mi.; **Water:** 0.0 sq. mi.

Highland
Township
Lat: 39-55-33 N Long: 75-53-42 W
Pop: 1,199 (1990) **Pop Density:** 69.7
Land: 17.2 sq. mi.; **Water:** 0.0 sq. mi.

Honey Brook
Township
ZIP: 19344 Lat: 40-05-29 N Long: 75-53-28 W
Pop: 5,449 (1990) **Pop Density:** 217.1
Land: 25.1 sq. mi.; **Water:** 0.3 sq. mi.

*Honey Brook
Borough
ZIP: 19344 Lat: 40-05-36 N Long: 75-54-39 W
Pop: 1,184 (1990); 1,164 (1980) **Pop Density:** 2368.0
Land: 0.5 sq. mi.; **Water:** 0.0 sq. mi. **Elev:** 750 ft.
Name origin: The area was formerly named Nantmel. Nantmel Township was divided into East and West Nantmeal and Honey Brook townships. Nantmel was named for the former home of Welsh settlers; the name means 'sweet water.'

Kenilworth
CDP
Lat: 40-13-31 N Long: 75-38-33 W
Pop: 1,890 (1990); 1,686 (1980) **Pop Density:** 994.7
Land: 1.9 sq. mi.; **Water:** 0.0 sq. mi.

Kennett
Township
Lat: 39-49-58 N Long: 75-40-50 W
Pop: 4,624 (1990) **Pop Density:** 296.4
Land: 15.6 sq. mi.; **Water:** 0.0 sq. mi.

Kennett Square
Borough
ZIP: 19348 Lat: 39-50-37 N Long: 75-42-42 W
Pop: 5,218 (1990); 4,715 (1980) **Pop Density:** 4743.6
Land: 1.1 sq. mi.; **Water:** 0.0 sq. mi. **Elev:** 310 ft.
In southeastern PA, 12 mi. northwest of Wilmington, DE. Settled 1686.
Name origin: Named by Francis Smith, who had come from Kennett, Wiltshire, England.

Lionville-Marchwood
CDP
Lat: 40-03-09 N Long: 75-38-44 W
Pop: 6,468 (1990) **Pop Density:** 2587.2
Land: 2.5 sq. mi.; **Water:** 0.0 sq. mi.

London Britain
Township
Lat: 39-44-47 N Long: 75-47-05 W
Pop: 2,671 (1990) **Pop Density:** 269.8
Land: 9.9 sq. mi.; **Water:** 0.0 sq. mi.
Name origin: For the London Company, which once had large holdings in the county.

Londonderry
Township
Lat: 39-52-45 N Long: 75-52-39 W
Pop: 1,243 (1990) **Pop Density:** 110.0
Land: 11.3 sq. mi.; **Water:** 0.0 sq. mi.

London Grove
Township
Lat: 39-49-55 N Long: 75-48-55 W
Pop: 3,922 (1990) **Pop Density:** 228.0
Land: 17.2 sq. mi.; **Water:** 0.0 sq. mi.

Lower Oxford
Township
Lat: 39-48-13 N Long: 75-59-15 W
Pop: 3,264 (1990) **Pop Density:** 180.3
Land: 18.1 sq. mi.; **Water:** 0.3 sq. mi.

Malvern
Borough
ZIP: 19355 Lat: 40-02-00 N Long: 75-30-50 W
Pop: 2,944 (1990); 2,999 (1980) **Pop Density:** 2264.6
Land: 1.3 sq. mi.; **Water:** 0.0 sq. mi. **Elev:** 590 ft.
In southeastern PA, a suburb of Philadelphia, near Paoli.

Modena
Borough
ZIP: 19358 Lat: 39-57-43 N Long: 75-48-08 W
Pop: 563 (1990); 672 (1980) **Pop Density:** 1876.7
Land: 0.3 sq. mi.; **Water:** 0.0 sq. mi. **Elev:** 290 ft.

New Garden
Township
ZIP: 19350 Lat: 39-48-39 N Long: 75-44-59 W
Pop: 5,430 (1990) **Pop Density:** 337.3
Land: 16.1 sq. mi.; **Water:** 0.1 sq. mi.

Newlin
Township
Lat: 39-55-26 N Long: 75-44-12 W
Pop: 1,092 (1990) **Pop Density:** 91.0
Land: 12.0 sq. mi.; **Water:** 0.0 sq. mi.

New London
Township
Lat: 39-46-18 N Long: 75-52-34 W
Pop: 2,721 (1990) **Pop Density:** 228.7
Land: 11.9 sq. mi.; **Water:** 0.0 sq. mi.

North Coventry
Township
ZIP: 19464 Lat: 40-13-15 N Long: 75-40-45 W
Pop: 7,506 (1990) **Pop Density:** 560.1
Land: 13.4 sq. mi.; **Water:** 0.2 sq. mi.

Oxford
Borough
ZIP: 19363   **Lat:** 39-47-08 N   **Long:** 75-58-49 W
Pop: 3,769 (1990); 3,633 (1980)   **Pop Density:** 1983.7
Land: 1.9 sq. mi.; **Water:** 0.0 sq. mi.   **Elev:** 567 ft.
In southeastern PA. Founded in 1801.
Name origin: For the English university town.

Parkesburg
Borough
ZIP: 19365   **Lat:** 39-57-31 N   **Long:** 75-55-00 W
Pop: 2,981 (1990); 2,578 (1980)   **Pop Density:** 2484.2
Land: 1.2 sq. mi.; **Water:** 0.0 sq. mi.   **Elev:** 543 ft.
Name origin: For the influential Parkes family.

Penn
Township
     Lat: 39-49-19 N   **Long:** 75-52-35 W
Pop: 2,257 (1990)   **Pop Density:** 235.1
Land: 9.6 sq. mi.; **Water:** 0.0 sq. mi.

Pennsbury
Township
     Lat: 39-51-52 N   **Long:** 75-37-19 W
Pop: 3,326 (1990)   **Pop Density:** 336.0
Land: 9.9 sq. mi.; **Water:** 0.1 sq. mi.

Phoenixville
Borough
ZIP: 19460   **Lat:** 40-08-09 N   **Long:** 75-31-09 W
Pop: 15,066 (1990); 14,165 (1980)   **Pop Density:** 4185.0
Land: 3.6 sq. mi.; **Water:** 0.2 sq. mi.   **Elev:** 140 ft.
In southeastern PA on the Schuylkill River, 10 mi. west of Norristown.
Name origin: For the Phoenix Iron Works.

Pocopson
Township
     Lat: 39-54-26 N   **Long:** 75-39-45 W
Pop: 3,266 (1990)   **Pop Density:** 393.5
Land: 8.3 sq. mi.; **Water:** 0.1 sq. mi.

Sadsbury
Township
     Lat: 39-58-38 N   **Long:** 75-54-21 W
Pop: 2,510 (1990)   **Pop Density:** 404.8
Land: 6.2 sq. mi.; **Water:** 0.0 sq. mi.

Schuylkill
Township
ZIP: 19460   **Lat:** 40-06-29 N   **Long:** 75-29-46 W
Pop: 5,538 (1990)   **Pop Density:** 644.0
Land: 8.6 sq. mi.; **Water:** 0.3 sq. mi.

South Coatesville
Borough
ZIP: 19320   **Lat:** 39-58-05 N   **Long:** 75-48-55 W
Pop: 1,026 (1990); 1,359 (1980)   **Pop Density:** 603.5
Land: 1.7 sq. mi.; **Water:** 0.0 sq. mi.   **Elev:** 370 ft.

South Coventry
Township
     Lat: 40-10-36 N   **Long:** 75-40-38 W
Pop: 1,682 (1990)   **Pop Density:** 224.3
Land: 7.5 sq. mi.; **Water:** 0.0 sq. mi.

Spring City
Borough
ZIP: 19475   **Lat:** 40-10-36 N   **Long:** 75-32-48 W
Pop: 3,433 (1990); 3,389 (1980)   **Pop Density:** 4291.3
Land: 0.8 sq. mi.; **Water:** 0.1 sq. mi.   **Elev:** 200 ft.
In southwestern PA on the Schuylkill River, 30 mi. northwest of Philadelphia. Incorporated c. 1872.
Name origin: Previously called Springville for a large spring situated at the corner of Yost and Main Streets.

Thornbury
Township
     Lat: 39-54-56 N   **Long:** 75-33-05 W
Pop: 1,131 (1990)   **Pop Density:** 290.0
Land: 3.9 sq. mi.; **Water:** 0.0 sq. mi.

Tredyffrin
Township
ZIP: 19312   **Lat:** 40-03-59 N   **Long:** 75-27-16 W
Pop: 28,028 (1990)   **Pop Density:** 1415.6
Land: 19.8 sq. mi.; **Water:** 0.0 sq. mi.

Upper Oxford
Township
     Lat: 39-50-27 N   **Long:** 75-56-48 W
Pop: 1,615 (1990)   **Pop Density:** 96.1
Land: 16.8 sq. mi.; **Water:** 0.0 sq. mi.

Upper Uwchlan
Township
ZIP: 19353   **Lat:** 40-04-53 N   **Long:** 75-42-26 W
Pop: 4,396 (1990)   **Pop Density:** 407.0
Land: 10.8 sq. mi.; **Water:** 0.9 sq. mi.

Uwchlan
Township
ZIP: 19353   **Lat:** 40-02-46 N   **Long:** 75-40-19 W
Pop: 12,999 (1990)   **Pop Density:** 1249.9
Land: 10.4 sq. mi.; **Water:** 0.0 sq. mi.
Name origin: Welsh 'upland' or 'above the valley.'

Valley
Township
     Lat: 39-59-07 N   **Long:** 75-50-59 W
Pop: 4,007 (1990)   **Pop Density:** 667.8
Land: 6.0 sq. mi.; **Water:** 0.0 sq. mi.

Wallace
Township
     Lat: 40-05-14 N   **Long:** 75-46-14 W
Pop: 2,541 (1990)   **Pop Density:** 211.8
Land: 12.0 sq. mi.; **Water:** 0.1 sq. mi.

Warwick
Township
     Lat: 40-11-07 N   **Long:** 75-45-18 W
Pop: 2,575 (1990)   **Pop Density:** 134.1
Land: 19.2 sq. mi.; **Water:** 0.0 sq. mi.

West Bradford
Township
ZIP: 19335   **Lat:** 39-57-56 N   **Long:** 75-42-50 W
Pop: 10,406 (1990)   **Pop Density:** 559.5
Land: 18.6 sq. mi.; **Water:** 0.1 sq. mi.

West Brandywine
Township
ZIP: 19320   **Lat:** 40-02-27 N   **Long:** 75-48-24 W
Pop: 5,984 (1990)   **Pop Density:** 446.6
Land: 13.4 sq. mi.; **Water:** 0.0 sq. mi.

West Caln
Township
ZIP: 19376   **Lat:** 40-01-21 N   **Long:** 75-53-10 W
Pop: 6,143 (1990)   **Pop Density:** 281.8
Land: 21.8 sq. mi.; **Water:** 0.1 sq. mi.

West Chester
Borough
ZIP: 19380   **Lat:** 39-57-35 N   **Long:** 75-36-21 W
Pop: 18,041 (1990); 17,435 (1980)   **Pop Density:** 10022.8
Land: 1.8 sq. mi.; **Water:** 0.0 sq. mi.   **Elev:** 459 ft.
In southeastern PA near Brandywine, Paoli, Valley Forge, and other hallowed places of the Revolutionary War, 25 mi. west of Philadelphia; incorporated Mar 28, 1799. County seat.
Name origin: For its location 16 mi. northwest of old Chester.

West Fallowfield
Township
     Lat: 39-54-05 N   **Long:** 75-57-12 W
Pop: 2,342 (1990)   **Pop Density:** 129.4
Land: 18.1 sq. mi.; **Water:** 0.0 sq. mi.

West Goshen
Township
ZIP: 19380   **Lat:** 39-58-34 N   **Long:** 75-35-35 W
Pop: 18,082 (1990)   **Pop Density:** 1519.5
Land: 11.9 sq. mi.; **Water:** 0.1 sq. mi.

West Grove Borough
ZIP: 19390 Lat: 39-49-17 N Long: 75-49-44 W
Pop: 2,128 (1990); 1,820 (1980) Pop Density: 3546.7
Land: 0.6 sq. mi.; Water: 0.0 sq. mi. Elev: 440 ft.
In southeastern PA, a residential suburb of Philadelphia.

West Marlborough Township
Lat: 39-53-18 N Long: 75-48-27 W
Pop: 874 (1990) Pop Density: 51.1
Land: 17.1 sq. mi.; Water: 0.0 sq. mi.

West Nantmeal Township
Lat: 40-07-21 N Long: 75-49-47 W
Pop: 1,958 (1990) Pop Density: 146.1
Land: 13.4 sq. mi.; Water: 0.1 sq. mi.

West Nottingham Township
Lat: 39-44-28 N Long: 76-03-19 W
Pop: 2,183 (1990) Pop Density: 155.9
Land: 14.0 sq. mi.; Water: 0.0 sq. mi.

West Pikeland Township
Lat: 40-05-15 N Long: 75-37-15 W
Pop: 2,323 (1990) Pop Density: 232.3
Land: 10.0 sq. mi.; Water: 0.0 sq. mi. Elev: 360 ft.

West Sadsbury Township
Lat: 39-58-20 N Long: 75-57-20 W
Pop: 2,160 (1990) Pop Density: 201.9
Land: 10.7 sq. mi.; Water: 0.0 sq. mi.

Westtown Township
ZIP: 19395 Lat: 39-56-38 N Long: 75-33-29 W
Pop: 9,937 (1990) Pop Density: 1142.2
Land: 8.7 sq. mi.; Water: 0.0 sq. mi.

West Vincent Township
Lat: 40-07-31 N Long: 75-38-55 W
Pop: 2,262 (1990) Pop Density: 127.8
Land: 17.7 sq. mi.; Water: 0.0 sq. mi.

West Whiteland Township
ZIP: 19341 Lat: 40-01-18 N Long: 75-37-25 W
Pop: 12,403 (1990) Pop Density: 954.1
Land: 13.0 sq. mi.; Water: 0.0 sq. mi.

Willistown Township
ZIP: 19355 Lat: 40-00-11 N Long: 75-29-23 W
Pop: 9,380 (1990) Pop Density: 515.4
Land: 18.2 sq. mi.; Water: 0.0 sq. mi.

Clarion County
County Seat: Clarion (ZIP: 16214)

Pop: 41,699 (1990); 43,362 (1980) Pop Density: 69.2
Land: 602.5 sq. mi.; Water: 6.5 sq. mi. Area Code: 814
In central portion of western PA, northeast of Pittsburgh; organized Mar 11, 1839 from Venango and Armstrong counties.
Name origin: For the Clarion River, which flows through it. The rippling waters of the river sounded "like the notes of a distant clarion" to Daniel Stanard, one of the state surveyors.

Ashland Township
Lat: 41-17-06 N Long: 79-33-52 W
Pop: 1,019 (1990) Pop Density: 45.1
Land: 22.6 sq. mi.; Water: 0.0 sq. mi.

Beaver Township
Lat: 41-11-58 N Long: 79-31-58 W
Pop: 1,840 (1990) Pop Density: 54.6
Land: 33.7 sq. mi.; Water: 0.2 sq. mi.

Brady Township
Lat: 40-58-48 N Long: 79-35-51 W
Pop: 78 (1990) Pop Density: 45.9
Land: 1.7 sq. mi.; Water: 0.5 sq. mi.

Callensburg Borough
ZIP: 16213 Lat: 41-07-32 N Long: 79-33-30 W
Pop: 205 (1990); 248 (1980) Pop Density: 1025.0
Land: 0.2 sq. mi.; Water: 0.0 sq. mi. Elev: 1094 ft.

Clarion Borough
ZIP: 16214 Lat: 41-12-36 N Long: 79-22-49 W
Pop: 6,457 (1990); 6,664 (1980) Pop Density: 4304.7
Land: 1.5 sq. mi.; Water: 0.0 sq. mi. Elev: 1491 ft.
In western PA, 28 mi. southeast of Oil City; incorporated Apr 6, 1841.
Name origin: For the Clarion River, itself named because the clear sound of the ripples reflected by a then dense grove of

giant trees sounded to a surveyor "like the notes of a distant clarion."

*Clarion Township
ZIP: 16214 Lat: 41-11-50 N Long: 79-18-14 W
Pop: 3,306 (1990) Pop Density: 105.0
Land: 31.5 sq. mi.; Water: 0.2 sq. mi.

East Brady Borough
ZIP: 16028 Lat: 40-59-05 N Long: 79-36-50 W
Pop: 1,047 (1990); 1,153 (1980) Pop Density: 1308.8
Land: 0.8 sq. mi.; Water: 0.3 sq. mi. Elev: 900 ft.
In western PA on Brady's Bend of the Allegheny River, southeast of Oil City. Laid out in 1866.
Name origin: For Capt. Brady, who led expeditions against Indians in retaliation for the deaths during the Revolutionary War of his father and brother.

Elk Township
Lat: 41-16-24 N Long: 79-28-45 W
Pop: 1,526 (1990) Pop Density: 48.8
Land: 31.3 sq. mi.; Water: 0.0 sq. mi.

Emlenton Borough
ZIP: 16373 Lat: 41-10-52 N Long: 79-41-51 W
Pop: 10 (1990); 13 (1980) Pop Density: 100.0
Land: 0.1 sq. mi.; Water: 0.0 sq. mi. Elev: 902 ft.
Part of the town is also in Venango County.

Farmington　　　　　　　　　　　　　Township
　　　　　　　　Lat: 41-22-53 N **Long:** 79-16-54 W
Pop: 1,927 (1990)　　　　　　　　**Pop Density:** 31.1
Land: 62.0 sq. mi.; **Water:** 0.2 sq. mi.

Foxburg　　　　　　　　　　　　　　Borough
ZIP: 16036　　　　　　**Lat:** 41-08-41 N **Long:** 79-40-50 W
Pop: 262 (1990); 289 (1980)　　**Pop Density:** 873.3
Land: 0.3 sq. mi.; **Water:** 0.1 sq. mi.　　**Elev:** 1100 ft.

Hawthorn　　　　　　　　　　　　　Borough
ZIP: 16230　　　　　　**Lat:** 41-01-14 N **Long:** 79-16-34 W
Pop: 528 (1990); 547 (1980)　　**Pop Density:** 480.0
Land: 1.1 sq. mi.; **Water:** 0.0 sq. mi.
In western PA on Red Bank Creek.

Highland　　　　　　　　　　　　　Township
　　　　　　　　Lat: 41-15-44 N **Long:** 79-19-58 W
Pop: 573 (1990)　　　　　　　　**Pop Density:** 30.0
Land: 19.1 sq. mi.; **Water:** 0.4 sq. mi.

Knox　　　　　　　　　　　　　　　Township
ZIP: 16232　　　　　　**Lat:** 41-18-37 N **Long:** 79-22-51 W
Pop: 1,281 (1990)　　　　　　　**Pop Density:** 73.2
Land: 17.5 sq. mi.; **Water:** 0.0 sq. mi.

*Knox　　　　　　　　　　　　　　Borough
　　　　　　　　Lat: 41-14-05 N **Long:** 79-32-08 W
Pop: 1,182 (1990); 1,364 (1980)　**Pop Density:** 1970.0
Land: 0.6 sq. mi.; **Water:** 0.0 sq. mi.　　**Elev:** 1380 ft.
In western PA, 20 mi. southeast of Oil City.

Licking　　　　　　　　　　　　　Township
　　　　　　　　Lat: 41-07-52 N **Long:** 79-33-29 W
Pop: 483 (1990)　　　　　　　　**Pop Density:** 27.8
Land: 17.4 sq. mi.; **Water:** 0.4 sq. mi.

Limestone　　　　　　　　　　　　Township
　　　　　　　　Lat: 41-07-54 N **Long:** 79-17-13 W
Pop: 1,686 (1990)　　　　　　　**Pop Density:** 44.7
Land: 37.7 sq. mi.; **Water:** 0.0 sq. mi.

Madison　　　　　　　　　　　　　Township
　　　　　　　　Lat: 41-00-40 N **Long:** 79-31-20 W
Pop: 1,423 (1990)　　　　　　　**Pop Density:** 52.5
Land: 27.1 sq. mi.; **Water:** 0.8 sq. mi.

Millcreek　　　　　　　　　　　　Township
　　　　　　　　Lat: 41-15-40 N **Long:** 79-14-54 W
Pop: 407 (1990)　　　　　　　　**Pop Density:** 14.1
Land: 28.9 sq. mi.; **Water:** 0.3 sq. mi.

Monroe　　　　　　　　　　　　　Township
　　　　　　　　Lat: 41-08-06 N **Long:** 79-24-20 W
Pop: 1,314 (1990)　　　　　　　**Pop Density:** 44.5
Land: 29.5 sq. mi.; **Water:** 0.3 sq. mi.

New Bethlehem　　　　　　　　　　Borough
ZIP: 16242　　　　　　**Lat:** 41-00-10 N **Long:** 79-19-43 W
Pop: 1,151 (1990); 1,441 (1980)　**Pop Density:** 2302.0
Land: 0.5 sq. mi.; **Water:** 0.0 sq. mi.　　**Elev:** 1072 ft.
In western PA, 36 mi. southeast of Oil City.

Paint　　　　　　　　　　　　　　Township
　　　　　　　　Lat: 41-15-08 N **Long:** 79-24-30 W
Pop: 1,730 (1990)　　　　　　　**Pop Density:** 84.4
Land: 20.5 sq. mi.; **Water:** 0.3 sq. mi.

Perry　　　　　　　　　　　　　　Township
　　　　　　　　Lat: 41-05-47 N **Long:** 79-37-17 W
Pop: 1,076 (1990)　　　　　　　**Pop Density:** 37.1
Land: 29.0 sq. mi.; **Water:** 1.3 sq. mi.

Piney　　　　　　　　　　　　　　Township
　　　　　　　　Lat: 41-08-07 N **Long:** 79-28-37 W
Pop: 515 (1990)　　　　　　　　**Pop Density:** 28.9
Land: 17.8 sq. mi.; **Water:** 0.1 sq. mi.

Porter　　　　　　　　　　　　　　Township
　　　　　　　　Lat: 41-02-22 N **Long:** 79-23-11 W
Pop: 1,564 (1990)　　　　　　　**Pop Density:** 35.1
Land: 44.5 sq. mi.; **Water:** 0.0 sq. mi.

Redbank　　　　　　　　　　　　　Township
　　　　　　　　Lat: 41-04-04 N **Long:** 79-16-25 W
Pop: 1,576 (1990)　　　　　　　**Pop Density:** 52.4
Land: 30.1 sq. mi.; **Water:** 0.0 sq. mi.

Richland　　　　　　　　　　　　　Township
　　　　　　　　Lat: 41-09-55 N **Long:** 79-38-39 W
Pop: 490 (1990)　　　　　　　　**Pop Density:** 32.5
Land: 15.1 sq. mi.; **Water:** 0.6 sq. mi.

Rimersburg　　　　　　　　　　　Borough
ZIP: 16248　　　　　　**Lat:** 41-02-28 N **Long:** 79-30-07 W
Pop: 1,053 (1990); 1,096 (1980)　**Pop Density:** 2632.5
Land: 0.4 sq. mi.; **Water:** 0.0 sq. mi.　　**Elev:** 1480 ft.
Name origin: For John Rimer, who settled here in 1829 and
later opened a tavern.

St. Petersburg　　　　　　　　　　Borough
　　　　　　　　Lat: 41-09-39 N **Long:** 79-39-15 W
Pop: 349 (1990); 452 (1980)　　**Pop Density:** 1163.3
Land: 0.3 sq. mi.; **Water:** 0.0 sq. mi.　　**Elev:** 1360 ft.
Name origin: Previously called Petersburg.

Salem　　　　　　　　　　　　　　Township
　　　　　　　　Lat: 41-13-05 N **Long:** 79-36-48 W
Pop: 893 (1990)　　　　　　　　**Pop Density:** 55.5
Land: 16.1 sq. mi.; **Water:** 0.2 sq. mi.

Shippenville　　　　　　　　　　　Borough
ZIP: 16254　　　　　　**Lat:** 41-15-03 N **Long:** 79-27-46 W
Pop: 474 (1990); 558 (1980)　　**Pop Density:** 1185.0
Land: 0.4 sq. mi.; **Water:** 0.0 sq. mi.　　**Elev:** 1388 ft.
Name origin: For Judge Henry Shippen, who laid out the
town.

Sligo　　　　　　　　　　　　　　Borough
ZIP: 16255　　　　　　**Lat:** 41-06-31 N **Long:** 79-29-45 W
Pop: 706 (1990); 798 (1980)　　**Pop Density:** 504.3
Land: 1.4 sq. mi.; **Water:** 0.0 sq. mi.　　**Elev:** 1250 ft.
In western PA, bisected by Big Licking and Little Licking
creeks, southeast of Oil City.
Name origin: Named in 1845 by four men from Sligo, Ire-
land, who built Sligo Furnace, which was shut down after the
panic of 1873.

Strattanville　　　　　　　　　　　Borough
ZIP: 16258　　　　　　**Lat:** 41-12-10 N **Long:** 79-19-39 W
Pop: 490 (1990); 555 (1980)　　**Pop Density:** 980.0
Land: 0.5 sq. mi.; **Water:** 0.0 sq. mi.　　**Elev:** 1531 ft.

Toby　　　　　　　　　　　　　　Township
　　　　　　　　Lat: 41-03-58 N **Long:** 79-31-34 W
Pop: 1,153 (1990)　　　　　　　**Pop Density:** 39.9
Land: 28.9 sq. mi.; **Water:** 0.2 sq. mi.

Washington　　　　　　　　　　　Township
　　　　　　　　Lat: 41-22-01 N **Long:** 79-25-08 W
Pop: 1,925 (1990)　　　　　　　**Pop Density:** 59.2
Land: 32.5 sq. mi.; **Water:** 0.0 sq. mi.
Name origin: For George Washington (1732–99), first U.S.
president.

Clearfield County
County Seat: Clearfield (ZIP: 16830)

Pop: 78,097 (1990); 83,578 (1980)
Land: 1147.4 sq. mi.; **Water:** 6.5 sq. mi.
Pop Density: 68.1
Area Code: 814

In west-central PA, north of Altoona; organized Mar 26, 1804 from Lycoming and Huntingdon counties. Functioned as part of Centre County in early years; first county commissioners elected 1812, courts established 1822.

Name origin: For Clearfield Creek, which runs through a part of the county where buffalo had cleared the undergrowth.

Beccaria Township
ZIP: 16616 Lat: 40-45-43 N Long: 78-30-40 W
Pop: 1,917 (1990) Pop Density: 52.7
Land: 36.4 sq. mi.; Water: 0.0 sq. mi.
In central PA, northwest of Altoona.
Name origin: For an Italian publicist and philosopher, Cesare, Marquis of Beccaria (1735–94).

Bell Township
Lat: 40-55-05 N Long: 78-45-02 W
Pop: 925 (1990) Pop Density: 16.1
Land: 57.3 sq. mi.; Water: 0.2 sq. mi.

Bigler Township
Lat: 40-49-39 N Long: 78-26-20 W
Pop: 1,391 (1990) Pop Density: 56.1
Land: 24.8 sq. mi.; Water: 0.0 sq. mi.
In central PA, northwest of Altoona.
Name origin: For William Bigler, PA governor (1852–55).

Bloom Township
Lat: 41-01-22 N Long: 78-38-28 W
Pop: 454 (1990) Pop Density: 23.8
Land: 19.1 sq. mi.; Water: 0.0 sq. mi.

Boggs Township
Lat: 40-57-04 N Long: 78-21-26 W
Pop: 1,907 (1990) Pop Density: 52.5
Land: 36.3 sq. mi.; Water: 0.1 sq. mi.

Bradford Township
Lat: 41-01-08 N Long: 78-19-34 W
Pop: 2,504 (1990) Pop Density: 65.4
Land: 38.3 sq. mi.; Water: 0.5 sq. mi.

Brady Township
ZIP: 15801 Lat: 41-02-14 N Long: 78-44-11 W
Pop: 2,023 (1990) Pop Density: 54.1
Land: 37.4 sq. mi.; Water: 0.0 sq. mi.

Brisbin Borough
ZIP: 16620 Lat: 40-50-21 N Long: 78-21-07 W
Pop: 369 (1990); 387 (1980) Pop Density: 615.0
Land: 0.6 sq. mi.; Water: 0.0 sq. mi. Elev: 1521 ft.

Burnside Township
Lat: 40-46-27 N Long: 78-45-13 W
Pop: 1,137 (1990) Pop Density: 25.7
Land: 44.3 sq. mi.; Water: 0.0 sq. mi.

*Burnside Borough
ZIP: 15721 Lat: 40-48-46 N Long: 78-47-23 W
Pop: 350 (1990); 347 (1980) Pop Density: 205.9
Land: 1.7 sq. mi.; Water: 0.0 sq. mi. Elev: 1340 ft.

Chest Township
Lat: 40-46-16 N Long: 78-38-29 W
Pop: 565 (1990) Pop Density: 15.8
Land: 35.8 sq. mi.; Water: 0.0 sq. mi.

Chester Hill Borough
Lat: 40-53-23 N Long: 78-13-45 W
Pop: 945 (1990); 1,054 (1980) Pop Density: 1890.0
Land: 0.5 sq. mi.; Water: 0.0 sq. mi. Elev: 1500 ft.
In western PA on the Moshannon Creek near Phillipsburg.

Clearfield Borough
ZIP: 16830 Lat: 41-01-16 N Long: 78-26-21 W
Pop: 6,633 (1990); 7,580 (1980) Pop Density: 3685.0
Land: 1.8 sq. mi.; Water: 0.1 sq. mi. Elev: 1114 ft.
In central PA, 50 mi. north of Altoona; incorporated Apr 21, 1840.
Name origin: For nearby Clearfield Creek, so called because buffalo are believed to have cleared the undergrowth from large tracts along the creek, giving them the appearance of cleared fields.

Coalport Borough
ZIP: 16627 Lat: 40-44-54 N Long: 78-31-55 W
Pop: 578 (1990); 739 (1980) Pop Density: 1445.0
Land: 0.4 sq. mi.; Water: 0.0 sq. mi. Elev: 1382 ft.

Cooper Township
Lat: 41-00-42 N Long: 78-07-29 W
Pop: 2,590 (1990) Pop Density: 63.8
Land: 40.6 sq. mi.; Water: 0.2 sq. mi.

Covington Township
Lat: 41-09-14 N Long: 78-11-36 W
Pop: 648 (1990) Pop Density: 12.4
Land: 52.4 sq. mi.; Water: 0.2 sq. mi.

Curwensville Borough
ZIP: 16833 Lat: 40-58-21 N Long: 78-31-04 W
Pop: 2,924 (1990); 3,116 (1980) Pop Density: 1329.1
Land: 2.2 sq. mi.; Water: 0.1 sq. mi. Elev: 1161 ft.
Settled 1812.
Name origin: For John Curwen, who obtained title to the tract but never resided there.

Decatur Township
Lat: 40-52-55 N Long: 78-18-16 W
Pop: 3,004 (1990) Pop Density: 78.6
Land: 38.2 sq. mi.; Water: 0.0 sq. mi.

DuBois City
ZIP: 15801 Lat: 41-07-20 N Long: 78-45-20 W
Pop: 8,286 (1990); 9,290 (1980) Pop Density: 2437.1
Land: 3.4 sq. mi.; Water: 0.0 sq. mi. Elev: 1410 ft.
In west-central PA, bisected by Sandy Lick Creek in a narrow

basin at the lowest pass in the Allegheny Mountains. Incorporated 1880.

Name origin: For John DuBois, an important citizen.

Falls Creek   Borough
ZIP: 15840   **Lat:** 41-08-35 N **Long:** 78-47-49 W
Pop: 54 (1990); 50 (1980)   **Pop Density:** 5400.0
Land: 0.01 sq. mi.; **Water:** 0.0 sq. mi.   **Elev:** 1460 ft.

Part of the town is also in Jefferson County.

Ferguson   Township
                     Lat: 40-52-30 N **Long:** 78-36-43 W
Pop: 437 (1990)   **Pop Density:** 18.7
Land: 23.4 sq. mi.; **Water:** 0.2 sq. mi.

Girard   Township
                     Lat: 41-09-16 N **Long:** 78-17-05 W
Pop: 630 (1990)   **Pop Density:** 9.9
Land: 63.4 sq. mi.; **Water:** 0.3 sq. mi.

Glen Hope   Borough
ZIP: 16645   **Lat:** 40-47-56 N **Long:** 78-29-53 W
Pop: 187 (1990); 206 (1980)   **Pop Density:** 89.0
Land: 2.1 sq. mi.; **Water:** 0.0 sq. mi.   **Elev:** 1360 ft.

Goshen   Township
                     Lat: 41-09-32 N **Long:** 78-22-38 W
Pop: 346 (1990)   **Pop Density:** 7.1
Land: 48.8 sq. mi.; **Water:** 0.2 sq. mi.

Graham   Township
                     Lat: 41-00-49 N **Long:** 78-13-15 W
Pop: 1,231 (1990)   **Pop Density:** 40.6
Land: 30.3 sq. mi.; **Water:** 0.2 sq. mi.

Grampian   Borough
ZIP: 16838   **Lat:** 40-57-50 N **Long:** 78-36-39 W
Pop: 395 (1990); 464 (1980)   **Pop Density:** 1316.7
Land: 0.3 sq. mi.; **Water:** 0.0 sq. mi.   **Elev:** 1560 ft.

Greenwood   Township
                     Lat: 40-54-33 N **Long:** 78-39-49 W
Pop: 415 (1990)   **Pop Density:** 21.3
Land: 19.5 sq. mi.; **Water:** 0.2 sq. mi.

Gulich   Township
                     Lat: 40-45-47 N **Long:** 78-24-00 W
Pop: 1,192 (1990)   **Pop Density:** 59.3
Land: 20.1 sq. mi.; **Water:** 0.0 sq. mi.

Houtzdale   Borough
ZIP: 16651   **Lat:** 40-49-29 N **Long:** 78-21-03 W
Pop: 1,204 (1990); 1,222 (1980)   **Pop Density:** 2006.7
Land: 0.6 sq. mi.; **Water:** 0.0 sq. mi.   **Elev:** 1518 ft.

In west-central PA, 30 mi. northeast of Altoona.

Name origin: For Dr. Daniel Houtz, who owned the land upon which the town was built in 1870.

Huston   Township
                     Lat: 41-11-22 N **Long:** 78-34-32 W
Pop: 1,352 (1990)   **Pop Density:** 21.3
Land: 63.6 sq. mi.; **Water:** 0.0 sq. mi.

Hyde   CDP
                     Lat: 41-00-26 N **Long:** 78-28-05 W
Pop: 1,643 (1990); 1,791 (1980)   **Pop Density:** 966.5
Land: 1.7 sq. mi.; **Water:** 0.0 sq. mi.

Irvona   Borough
ZIP: 16656   **Lat:** 40-46-24 N **Long:** 78-33-10 W
Pop: 666 (1990); 644 (1980)   **Pop Density:** 1332.0
Land: 0.5 sq. mi.; **Water:** 0.0 sq. mi.   **Elev:** 1379 ft.

Jordan   Township
                     Lat: 40-50-17 N **Long:** 78-33-49 W
Pop: 533 (1990)   **Pop Density:** 22.0
Land: 24.2 sq. mi.; **Water:** 0.0 sq. mi.

Karthaus   Township
ZIP: 16845   **Lat:** 41-09-21 N **Long:** 78-06-50 W
Pop: 547 (1990)   **Pop Density:** 15.4
Land: 35.6 sq. mi.; **Water:** 0.6 sq. mi.

Knox   Township
                     Lat: 40-53-05 N **Long:** 78-29-13 W
Pop: 704 (1990)   **Pop Density:** 27.8
Land: 25.3 sq. mi.; **Water:** 0.0 sq. mi.

Lawrence   Township
ZIP: 16830   **Lat:** 41-05-29 N **Long:** 78-26-42 W
Pop: 8,000 (1990)   **Pop Density:** 95.8
Land: 83.5 sq. mi.; **Water:** 0.6 sq. mi.

Lumber City   Borough
                     Lat: 40-55-43 N **Long:** 78-34-19 W
Pop: 83 (1990); 117 (1980)   **Pop Density:** 30.7
Land: 2.7 sq. mi.; **Water:** 0.0 sq. mi.   **Elev:** 1183 ft.

Mahaffey   Borough
ZIP: 15757   **Lat:** 40-52-30 N **Long:** 78-43-41 W
Pop: 341 (1990); 513 (1980)   **Pop Density:** 852.5
Land: 0.4 sq. mi.; **Water:** 0.0 sq. mi.   **Elev:** 1323 ft.

In west-central PA on the west branch of the Susquehanna River.

Morris   Township
                     Lat: 40-56-50 N **Long:** 78-12-55 W
Pop: 2,680 (1990)   **Pop Density:** 137.4
Land: 19.5 sq. mi.; **Water:** 0.0 sq. mi.

Newburg   Borough
ZIP: 15753   **Lat:** 40-50-20 N **Long:** 78-41-13 W
Pop: 117 (1990); 132 (1980)   **Pop Density:** 68.8
Land: 1.7 sq. mi.; **Water:** 0.0 sq. mi.   **Elev:** 1296 ft.

New Washington   Borough
ZIP: 15757   **Lat:** 40-49-21 N **Long:** 78-42-05 W
Pop: 78 (1990); 103 (1980)   **Pop Density:** 35.5
Land: 2.2 sq. mi.; **Water:** 0.0 sq. mi.   **Elev:** 1669 ft.

Osceola Mills   Borough
ZIP: 16666   **Lat:** 40-51-09 N **Long:** 78-16-11 W
Pop: 1,310 (1990); 1,466 (1980)   **Pop Density:** 4366.7
Land: 0.3 sq. mi.; **Water:** 0.0 sq. mi.   **Elev:** 1458 ft.

Penn   Township
                     Lat: 40-57-50 N **Long:** 78-38-36 W
Pop: 1,372 (1990)   **Pop Density:** 54.0
Land: 25.4 sq. mi.; **Water:** 0.0 sq. mi.

Pike   Township
                     Lat: 40-58-58 N **Long:** 78-32-08 W
Pop: 2,044 (1990)   **Pop Density:** 50.6
Land: 40.4 sq. mi.; **Water:** 1.4 sq. mi.

Pine   Township
                     Lat: 41-06-07 N **Long:** 78-32-06 W
Pop: 43 (1990)   **Pop Density:** 1.3
Land: 32.0 sq. mi.; **Water:** 0.0 sq. mi.

Ramey   Borough
ZIP: 16671   **Lat:** 40-48-02 N **Long:** 78-23-55 W
Pop: 536 (1990); 568 (1980)   **Pop Density:** 595.6
Land: 0.9 sq. mi.; **Water:** 0.0 sq. mi.   **Elev:** 1613 ft.

Sandy Township
ZIP: 15801   **Lat:** 41-08-36 N   **Long:** 78-43-38 W
Pop: 9,005 (1990)   **Pop Density:** 173.8
Land: 51.8 sq. mi.; **Water:** 1.0 sq. mi.

Troutville Borough
ZIP: 15866   **Lat:** 41-01-29 N   **Long:** 78-47-07 W
Pop: 226 (1990); 204 (1980)   **Pop Density:** 282.5
Land: 0.8 sq. mi.; **Water:** 0.0 sq. mi.   **Elev:** 1569 ft.

Union Township
Lat: 41-05-30 N   **Long:** 78-38-10 W
Pop: 833 (1990)   **Pop Density:** 26.8
Land: 31.1 sq. mi.; **Water:** 0.3 sq. mi.

Wallaceton Borough
ZIP: 16876   **Lat:** 40-57-55 N   **Long:** 78-17-32 W
Pop: 319 (1990); 393 (1980)   **Pop Density:** 455.7
Land: 0.7 sq. mi.; **Water:** 0.0 sq. mi.   **Elev:** 1721 ft.

Westover Borough
ZIP: 16692   **Lat:** 40-44-58 N   **Long:** 78-40-54 W
Pop: 446 (1990); 517 (1980)   **Pop Density:** 165.2
Land: 2.7 sq. mi.; **Water:** 0.0 sq. mi.   **Elev:** 1360 ft.

Woodward Township
Lat: 40-51-02 N   **Long:** 78-22-30 W
Pop: 1,621 (1990)   **Pop Density:** 73.7
Land: 22.0 sq. mi.; **Water:** 0.0 sq. mi.

Clinton County
County Seat: Lock Haven (ZIP: 17745)

Pop: 37,182 (1990); 38,971 (1980)   **Pop Density:** 41.7
Land: 890.9 sq. mi.; **Water:** 7.2 sq. mi.   **Area Code:** 717

In north-central PA, west of Williamsport; organized Jun 21, 1839 from Lycoming and Centre counties.

Name origin: Most likely for DeWitt Clinton (1769–1828), governor of NY, and supporter of the Erie Canal. The name may have been a substitute to the originally proposed name, Eagle, to thwart political opponents of county formation.

Allison Township
Lat: 41-09-06 N   **Long:** 77-28-39 W
Pop: 191 (1990)   **Pop Density:** 100.5
Land: 1.9 sq. mi.; **Water:** 0.2 sq. mi.

Avis Borough
ZIP: 17721   **Lat:** 41-11-10 N   **Long:** 77-18-59 W
Pop: 1,506 (1990); 1,718 (1980)   **Pop Density:** 3012.0
Land: 0.5 sq. mi.; **Water:** 0.0 sq. mi.   **Elev:** 613 ft.
Name origin: For Avis Cochran, daughter of one of the chief promoters of the town in the early 20th century.

Bald Eagle Township
Lat: 41-08-52 N   **Long:** 77-33-02 W
Pop: 1,809 (1990)   **Pop Density:** 43.9
Land: 41.2 sq. mi.; **Water:** 0.4 sq. mi.
Name origin: For an Indian chief who once lived here.

Beech Creek Township
ZIP: 16822   **Lat:** 41-09-56 N   **Long:** 77-43-15 W
Pop: 1,007 (1990)   **Pop Density:** 10.5
Land: 96.2 sq. mi.; **Water:** 0.0 sq. mi.

***Beech Creek** Borough
ZIP: 16822   **Lat:** 41-04-28 N   **Long:** 77-35-09 W
Pop: 716 (1990)   **Pop Density:** 1193.3
Land: 0.6 sq. mi.; **Water:** 0.0 sq. mi.   **Elev:** 600 ft.
In central PA on the east bank of Beech Creek, near Lock Haven.

Castanea Township
ZIP: 17745   **Lat:** 41-07-37 N   **Long:** 77-24-58 W
Pop: 1,188 (1990)   **Pop Density:** 212.1
Land: 5.6 sq. mi.; **Water:** 0.3 sq. mi.

Chapman Township
Lat: 41-24-15 N   **Long:** 77-41-08 W
Pop: 978 (1990)   **Pop Density:** 9.8
Land: 100.0 sq. mi.; **Water:** 0.8 sq. mi.

Colebrook Township
ZIP: 17734   **Lat:** 41-13-09 N   **Long:** 77-31-55 W
Pop: 180 (1990)   **Pop Density:** 9.9
Land: 18.2 sq. mi.; **Water:** 0.5 sq. mi.

Crawford Township
Lat: 41-06-20 N   **Long:** 77-15-23 W
Pop: 665 (1990)   **Pop Density:** 30.1
Land: 22.1 sq. mi.; **Water:** 0.0 sq. mi.

Dunnstable Township
Lat: 41-10-23 N   **Long:** 77-23-35 W
Pop: 846 (1990)   **Pop Density:** 91.0
Land: 9.3 sq. mi.; **Water:** 0.2 sq. mi.

Dunnstown CDP
ZIP: 17745   **Lat:** 41-08-48 N   **Long:** 77-25-16 W
Pop: 1,486 (1990); 1,486 (1980)   **Pop Density:** 1857.5
Land: 0.8 sq. mi.; **Water:** 0.0 sq. mi.

East Keating Township
ZIP: 17778   **Lat:** 41-18-37 N   **Long:** 77-58-16 W
Pop: 22 (1990)   **Pop Density:** 0.4
Land: 50.8 sq. mi.; **Water:** 0.6 sq. mi.

Flemington Borough
ZIP: 17745   **Lat:** 41-07-37 N   **Long:** 77-28-13 W
Pop: 1,321 (1990); 1,416 (1980)   **Pop Density:** 3302.5
Land: 0.4 sq. mi.; **Water:** 0.0 sq. mi.   **Elev:** 639 ft.
Name origin: For John Fleming, an associate justice in Lycoming County (1798), who once owned this site.

Gallagher Township
Lat: 41-16-25 N   **Long:** 77-29-19 W
Pop: 213 (1990)   **Pop Density:** 4.0
Land: 53.6 sq. mi.; **Water:** 0.0 sq. mi.   **Elev:** 1620 ft.

Greene Township
ZIP: 17747   **Lat:** 41-02-58 N   **Long:** 77-15-44 W
Pop: 1,153 (1990)   **Pop Density:** 24.7
Land: 46.7 sq. mi.; **Water:** 0.2 sq. mi.

Grugan
Township
Lat: 41-16-36 N Long: 77-36-14 W
Pop: 52 (1990)   Pop Density: 0.8
Land: 68.3 sq. mi.; Water: 1.0 sq. mi.

Lamar
Township
Lat: 41-04-26 N Long: 77-24-46 W
Pop: 2,345 (1990)   Pop Density: 57.2
Land: 41.0 sq. mi.; Water: 0.0 sq. mi.

Leidy
Township
ZIP: 17764   Lat: 41-25-13 N Long: 77-52-52 W
Pop: 214 (1990)   Pop Density: 2.2
Land: 97.0 sq. mi.; Water: 0.2 sq. mi.

Lock Haven
City
ZIP: 17745   Lat: 41-08-09 N Long: 77-27-11 W
Pop: 9,230 (1990); 9,617 (1980)   Pop Density: 3692.0
Land: 2.5 sq. mi.; Water: 0.0 sq. mi.   Elev: 564 ft.
In central PA on the Susquehanna River in the Bald Eagle Mountains. Incorporated as borough May 25, 1840, as city Mar 28, 1870.
Name origin: For the lock on the canal, and because the river furnished an excellent harbor, or haven, for rafts.

Logan
Township
ZIP: 17747   Lat: 40-59-53 N Long: 77-24-48 W
Pop: 730 (1990)   Pop Density: 30.4
Land: 24.0 sq. mi.; Water: 0.0 sq. mi.

Loganton
Borough
ZIP: 17747   Lat: 41-02-01 N Long: 77-18-08 W
Pop: 443 (1990); 474 (1980)   Pop Density: 402.7
Land: 1.1 sq. mi.; Water: 0.0 sq. mi.   Elev: 1297 ft.

Mill Hall
Borough
ZIP: 17751   Lat: 41-06-15 N Long: 77-29-25 W
Pop: 1,702 (1990); 1,744 (1980)   Pop Density: 1702.0
Land: 1.0 sq. mi.; Water: 0.0 sq. mi.   Elev: 580 ft.

Noyes
Township
ZIP: 17764   Lat: 41-17-40 N Long: 77-47-20 W
Pop: 463 (1990)   Pop Density: 5.2
Land: 89.1 sq. mi.; Water: 1.0 sq. mi.

Pine Creek
Township
Lat: 41-11-10 N Long: 77-20-10 W
Pop: 3,188 (1990)   Pop Density: 221.4
Land: 14.4 sq. mi.; Water: 0.5 sq. mi.

Porter
Township
Lat: 41-01-51 N Long: 77-31-04 W
Pop: 1,437 (1990)   Pop Density: 55.9
Land: 25.7 sq. mi.; Water: 0.0 sq. mi.

Renovo
Borough
ZIP: 17764   Lat: 41-19-44 N Long: 77-44-52 W
Pop: 1,526 (1990); 1,812 (1980)   Pop Density: 1271.7
Land: 1.2 sq. mi.; Water: 0.0 sq. mi.   Elev: 668 ft.
In central PA on the Susquehanna River, 60 mi. northwest of Williamsport.
Name origin: From the Latin meaning 'I renew.'

South Renovo
Borough
ZIP: 17764   Lat: 41-19-27 N Long: 77-44-33 W
Pop: 579 (1990); 663 (1980)   Pop Density: 2895.0
Land: 0.2 sq. mi.; Water: 0.0 sq. mi.   Elev: 680 ft.

Wayne
Township
Lat: 41-08-40 N Long: 77-19-52 W
Pop: 782 (1990)   Pop Density: 35.1
Land: 22.3 sq. mi.; Water: 0.5 sq. mi.

West Keating
Township
Lat: 41-12-33 N Long: 78-00-56 W
Pop: 34 (1990)   Pop Density: 0.9
Land: 38.2 sq. mi.; Water: 0.3 sq. mi.

Woodward
Township
Lat: 41-10-42 N Long: 77-27-25 W
Pop: 2,662 (1990)   Pop Density: 148.7
Land: 17.9 sq. mi.; Water: 0.3 sq. mi.

Columbia County
County Seat: Bloomsburg (ZIP: 17815)

Pop: 63,202 (1990); 61,967 (1980) **Pop Density:** 130.2
Land: 485.6 sq. mi.; **Water:** 4.2 sq. mi. **Area Code:** 717

In east-central PA, southwest of Scranton; organized Mar 22, 1813 from Northumberland County.

Name origin: Feminine form of Columbus, a poetic and honorific reference to Christopher Columbus (1451–1506) and America.

Almedia
CDP
Lat: 41-00-51 N **Long:** 76-23-16 W
Pop: 1,116 (1990); 711 (1980) **Pop Density:** 1860.0
Land: 0.6 sq. mi.; **Water:** 0.2 sq. mi.

Ashland
Borough
ZIP: 17921 **Lat:** 40-46-56 N **Long:** 76-21-46 W
Pop: 3 (1990); 9 (1980) **Pop Density:** 300.0
Land: 0.01 sq. mi.; **Water:** 0.0 sq. mi. **Elev:** 1700 ft.
Laid out in 1847. Part of the town is also in Schuylkill County.

Name origin: Named in 1847 by Samuel Lewis for the estate of Henry Clay (1777–1852) in Lexington, KY.

Beaver
Township
Lat: 40-57-03 N **Long:** 76-17-03 W
Pop: 928 (1990) **Pop Density:** 26.0
Land: 35.7 sq. mi.; **Water:** 0.1 sq. mi.

Benton
Township
ZIP: 17814 **Lat:** 41-12-17 N **Long:** 76-21-40 W
Pop: 1,094 (1990) **Pop Density:** 54.4
Land: 20.1 sq. mi.; **Water:** 0.0 sq. mi.

*Benton
Borough
ZIP: 17814 **Lat:** 41-11-41 N **Long:** 76-23-06 W
Pop: 958 (1990); 981 (1980) **Pop Density:** 1596.7
Land: 0.6 sq. mi.; **Water:** 0.0 sq. mi. **Elev:** 800 ft.
In east-central PA, 15 mi. north of Bloomsburg. Incorporated 1850.

Name origin: For Thomas Hart Benton (1782–1858), popular U.S. senator from MO.

Berwick
Borough
ZIP: 18603 **Lat:** 41-03-20 N **Long:** 76-14-56 W
Pop: 10,976 (1990); 11,850 (1980) **Pop Density:** 3540.6
Land: 3.1 sq. mi.; **Water:** 0.1 sq. mi. **Elev:** 569 ft.
In east-central PA on the Susquehanna River, 23 mi. southwest of Wilkes-Barre. Laid out in 1786.

Name origin: Named by Evan Owen, town founder, for his former home in England, Berwick-upon-Tweed.

Bloomsburg
Town
ZIP: 17815 **Lat:** 41-00-08 N **Long:** 76-27-24 W
Pop: 12,439 (1990); 11,717 (1980) **Pop Density:** 2827.0
Land: 4.4 sq. mi.; **Water:** 0.2 sq. mi. **Elev:** 530 ft.
In east-central PA at the foot of Spectator Bluff and on Fishing Creek, 26 mi. north-northwest of Pottsville. Laid out 1802 by Ludwig Eyer. Incorporated Mar 4, 1870; the only incorporated town in PA.

Name origin: For Samuel Bloom, who was a county commissioner when the old Bloom Township was organized in 1797.

Briar Creek
Township
Lat: 41-05-36 N **Long:** 76-16-20 W
Pop: 3,010 (1990) **Pop Density:** 142.7
Land: 21.1 sq. mi.; **Water:** 0.1 sq. mi.

*Briar Creek
Borough
ZIP: 18603 **Lat:** 41-02-49 N **Long:** 76-17-12 W
Pop: 616 (1990); 637 (1980) **Pop Density:** 385.0
Land: 1.6 sq. mi.; **Water:** 0.0 sq. mi. **Elev:** 502 ft.

Catawissa
Borough
ZIP: 17820 **Lat:** 40-57-10 N **Long:** 76-27-37 W
Pop: 1,683 (1990); 1,568 (1980) **Pop Density:** 3366.0
Land: 0.5 sq. mi.; **Water:** 0.0 sq. mi. **Elev:** 477 ft.
In east-central PA on the Susquehanna River. Laid out in 1787 by William Hughes.

Name origin: For the creek, its name a corruption of the Indian term *gattawisi* probably meaning 'growing fat,' possibly referring to a deer killed at the creek in the season when deer fatten.

*Catawissa
Township
ZIP: 17820 **Lat:** 40-57-17 N **Long:** 76-25-58 W
Pop: 1,037 (1990) **Pop Density:** 83.0
Land: 12.5 sq. mi.; **Water:** 0.4 sq. mi.

Centralia
Borough
ZIP: 17927 **Lat:** 40-48-15 N **Long:** 76-20-39 W
Pop: 63 (1990); 1,017 (1980) **Pop Density:** 315.0
Land: 0.2 sq. mi.; **Water:** 0.0 sq. mi. **Elev:** 1500 ft.
Founded 1826.

Name origin: For its strategic commercial location at the time.

Cleveland
Township
ZIP: 17820 **Lat:** 40-52-03 N **Long:** 76-27-17 W
Pop: 997 (1990) **Pop Density:** 42.8
Land: 23.3 sq. mi.; **Water:** 0.1 sq. mi.

Name origin: For Grover Cleveland (1837–1908), twenty-second U.S. president.

Conyngham
Township
Lat: 40-49-11 N **Long:** 76-21-15 W
Pop: 1,038 (1990) **Pop Density:** 51.4
Land: 20.2 sq. mi.; **Water:** 0.2 sq. mi.

Espy
CDP
Lat: 41-00-17 N **Long:** 76-25-03 W
Pop: 1,430 (1990); 1,571 (1980) **Pop Density:** 1588.9
Land: 0.9 sq. mi.; **Water:** 0.2 sq. mi.

Fishing Creek
Township
ZIP: 17859 **Lat:** 41-08-20 N **Long:** 76-21-01 W
Pop: 1,378 (1990) **Pop Density:** 48.7
Land: 28.3 sq. mi.; **Water:** 0.0 sq. mi.

Franklin Township
ZIP: 17820   Lat: 40-54-46 N Long: 76-29-26 W
Pop: 624 (1990)   Pop Density: 47.3
Land: 13.2 sq. mi.; Water: 0.3 sq. mi.

Greenwood Township
ZIP: 17846   Lat: 41-08-29 N Long: 76-28-03 W
Pop: 1,972 (1990)   Pop Density: 70.7
Land: 27.9 sq. mi.; Water: 0.0 sq. mi.

Hemlock Township
Lat: 41-01-18 N Long: 76-31-04 W
Pop: 1,546 (1990)   Pop Density: 87.8
Land: 17.6 sq. mi.; Water: 0.0 sq. mi.

Jackson Township
ZIP: 17814   Lat: 41-14-04 N Long: 76-26-00 W
Pop: 508 (1990)   Pop Density: 27.3
Land: 18.6 sq. mi.; Water: 0.0 sq. mi.

Lime Ridge CDP
Lat: 41-01-25 N Long: 76-21-18 W
Pop: 1,051 (1990)   Pop Density: 808.5
Land: 1.3 sq. mi.; Water: 0.3 sq. mi.

Locust Township
ZIP: 17820   Lat: 40-52-57 N Long: 76-23-08 W
Pop: 1,308 (1990)   Pop Density: 72.7
Land: 18.0 sq. mi.; Water: 0.0 sq. mi.

Madison Township
ZIP: 17846   Lat: 41-05-39 N Long: 76-34-18 W
Pop: 1,565 (1990)   Pop Density: 44.3
Land: 35.3 sq. mi.; Water: 0.0 sq. mi.

Main Township
Lat: 40-58-47 N Long: 76-22-59 W
Pop: 1,241 (1990)   Pop Density: 76.6
Land: 16.2 sq. mi.; Water: 0.5 sq. mi.

Mifflin Township
Lat: 41-00-43 N Long: 76-17-28 W
Pop: 2,305 (1990)   Pop Density: 120.1
Land: 19.2 sq. mi.; Water: 0.8 sq. mi.

Mifflinville CDP
Lat: 41-01-45 N Long: 76-18-02 W
Pop: 1,329 (1990); 1,341 (1980)   Pop Density: 949.3
Land: 1.4 sq. mi.; Water: 0.0 sq. mi.

Millville Borough
ZIP: 17846   Lat: 41-07-16 N Long: 76-31-38 W
Pop: 969 (1990); 975 (1980)   Pop Density: 969.0
Land: 1.0 sq. mi.; Water: 0.0 sq. mi.   Elev: 640 ft.

Montour Township
Lat: 40-58-35 N Long: 76-30-05 W
Pop: 1,419 (1990)   Pop Density: 154.2
Land: 9.2 sq. mi.; Water: 0.4 sq. mi.

Mount Pleasant Township
Lat: 41-04-06 N Long: 76-27-51 W
Pop: 1,383 (1990)   Pop Density: 79.0
Land: 17.5 sq. mi.; Water: 0.0 sq. mi.

North Centre Township
Lat: 41-03-46 N Long: 76-21-10 W
Pop: 1,860 (1990)   Pop Density: 120.8
Land: 15.4 sq. mi.; Water: 0.0 sq. mi.

Orange Township
ZIP: 17859   Lat: 41-05-11 N Long: 76-24-59 W
Pop: 1,043 (1990)   Pop Density: 79.6
Land: 13.1 sq. mi.; Water: 0.0 sq. mi.

Orangeville Borough
ZIP: 17859   Lat: 41-04-35 N Long: 76-24-47 W
Pop: 504 (1990); 507 (1980)   Pop Density: 1260.0
Land: 0.4 sq. mi.; Water: 0.0 sq. mi.   Elev: 580 ft.
Name origin: Named by early settlers for Orange County, NY.

Pine Township
ZIP: 17846   Lat: 41-11-24 N Long: 76-30-56 W
Pop: 990 (1990)   Pop Density: 37.2
Land: 26.6 sq. mi.; Water: 0.0 sq. mi.

Roaring Creek Township
ZIP: 17820   Lat: 40-53-52 N Long: 76-20-01 W
Pop: 478 (1990)   Pop Density: 20.3
Land: 23.5 sq. mi.; Water: 0.0 sq. mi.

Scott Township
Lat: 41-01-08 N Long: 76-25-02 W
Pop: 4,423 (1990)   Pop Density: 614.3
Land: 7.2 sq. mi.; Water: 0.3 sq. mi.

South Centre Township
Lat: 41-01-45 N Long: 76-21-03 W
Pop: 1,891 (1990)   Pop Density: 356.8
Land: 5.3 sq. mi.; Water: 0.5 sq. mi.

Stillwater Borough
ZIP: 17878   Lat: 41-09-00 N Long: 76-22-01 W
Pop: 223 (1990); 201 (1980)   Pop Density: 71.9
Land: 3.1 sq. mi.; Water: 0.0 sq. mi.   Elev: 710 ft.

Sugarloaf Township
Lat: 41-15-59 N Long: 76-21-50 W
Pop: 730 (1990)   Pop Density: 28.2
Land: 25.9 sq. mi.; Water: 0.0 sq. mi.

Crawford County
County Seat: Meadville (ZIP: 16335)

Pop: 86,169 (1990); 88,869 (1980)   **Pop Density:** 85.1
Land: 1012.9 sq. mi.; **Water:** 24.9 sq. mi.   **Area Code:** 814

On northwest border of PA, south of Erie; organized Mar 12, 1800 from Allegheny County.

Name origin: For Col. William Crawford (1732–82), surveyor, army officer, and Indian fighter.

Athens
Township
Lat: 41-44-55 N **Long:** 79-50-15 W
Pop: 699 (1990)   **Pop Density:** 24.7
Land: 28.3 sq. mi.; **Water:** 0.0 sq. mi.

Beaver
Township
Lat: 41-48-10 N **Long:** 80-27-59 W
Pop: 831 (1990)   **Pop Density:** 22.6
Land: 36.7 sq. mi.; **Water:** 0.0 sq. mi.

Bloomfield
Township
Lat: 41-48-53 N **Long:** 79-50-32 W
Pop: 1,839 (1990)   **Pop Density:** 48.4
Land: 38.0 sq. mi.; **Water:** 0.3 sq. mi.
Formed 1811.

Name origin: For Thomas Bloomfield, one of the earliest permanent settlers.

Blooming Valley
Borough
ZIP: 16335   **Lat:** 41-40-48 N **Long:** 80-02-29 W
Pop: 391 (1990); 374 (1980)   **Pop Density:** 205.8
Land: 1.9 sq. mi.; **Water:** 0.0 sq. mi.   **Elev:** 1280 ft.

Cambridge
Township
ZIP: 16403   **Lat:** 41-47-45 N **Long:** 80-03-15 W
Pop: 1,496 (1990)   **Pop Density:** 69.6
Land: 21.5 sq. mi.; **Water:** 0.1 sq. mi.

Cambridge Springs
Borough
ZIP: 16403   **Lat:** 41-48-06 N **Long:** 80-03-36 W
Pop: 1,837 (1990); 2,102 (1980)   **Pop Density:** 2041.1
Land: 0.9 sq. mi.; **Water:** 0.0 sq. mi.   **Elev:** 1160 ft.
In northwestern PA on French Creek.

Name origin: For a mineral spring found here in 1884 by Dr. John H. Gray while he was prospecting for oil.

Centerville
Borough
ZIP: 16404   **Lat:** 41-44-10 N **Long:** 79-45-40 W
Pop: 249 (1990); 245 (1980)   **Pop Density:** 138.3
Land: 1.8 sq. mi.; **Water:** 0.0 sq. mi.   **Elev:** 1308 ft.
In northwestern PA, north of Oil City. Laid out 1821.

Name origin: For its position between Uniontown (Venango Co.) and Washington (Erie Co.).

Cochranton
Borough
ZIP: 16314   **Lat:** 41-31-06 N **Long:** 80-02-48 W
Pop: 1,174 (1990); 1,240 (1980)   **Pop Density:** 978.3
Land: 1.2 sq. mi.; **Water:** 0.0 sq. mi.   **Elev:** 1069 ft.
In northwestern PA on French Creek, 10 mi. southeast of Meadville.

Conneaut
Township
Lat: 41-42-42 N **Long:** 80-27-31 W
Pop: 1,399 (1990)   **Pop Density:** 34.2
Land: 40.9 sq. mi.; **Water:** 0.7 sq. mi.
Name origin: For Conneaut Lake, from an Indian term possi-

bly meaning 'snow place,' so called because the snow on the lake lasted long after that on the land had melted.

Conneaut Lake
Borough
ZIP: 16316   **Lat:** 41-36-08 N **Long:** 80-18-33 W
Pop: 699 (1990); 767 (1980)   **Pop Density:** 1747.5
Land: 0.4 sq. mi.; **Water:** 0.0 sq. mi.   **Elev:** 1080 ft.

Conneaut Lakeshore
CDP
Lat: 41-37-26 N **Long:** 80-18-25 W
Pop: 1,852 (1990)   **Pop Density:** 394.0
Land: 4.7 sq. mi.; **Water:** 1.4 sq. mi.

Conneautville
Borough
ZIP: 16406   **Lat:** 41-45-27 N **Long:** 80-22-05 W
Pop: 822 (1990); 971 (1980)   **Pop Density:** 747.3
Land: 1.1 sq. mi.; **Water:** 0.0 sq. mi.   **Elev:** 949 ft.

Cussewago
Township
Lat: 41-48-07 N **Long:** 80-12-42 W
Pop: 1,409 (1990)   **Pop Density:** 34.4
Land: 41.0 sq. mi.; **Water:** 0.1 sq. mi.

East Fairfield
Township
Lat: 41-33-39 N **Long:** 80-04-44 W
Pop: 890 (1990)   **Pop Density:** 69.5
Land: 12.8 sq. mi.; **Water:** 0.0 sq. mi.

East Fallowfield
Township
Lat: 41-31-52 N **Long:** 80-19-15 W
Pop: 1,280 (1990)   **Pop Density:** 45.7
Land: 28.0 sq. mi.; **Water:** 0.0 sq. mi.

East Mead
Township
Lat: 41-37-33 N **Long:** 80-03-42 W
Pop: 1,441 (1990)   **Pop Density:** 62.9
Land: 22.9 sq. mi.; **Water:** 0.6 sq. mi.

Fairfield
Township
Lat: 41-30-27 N **Long:** 80-06-40 W
Pop: 997 (1990)   **Pop Density:** 51.4
Land: 19.4 sq. mi.; **Water:** 0.0 sq. mi.

Fredericksburg
CDP
Lat: 41-38-51 N **Long:** 80-10-46 W
Pop: 1,269 (1990); 1,202 (1980)   **Pop Density:** 325.4
Land: 3.9 sq. mi.; **Water:** 0.0 sq. mi.

Greenwood
Township
Lat: 41-31-36 N **Long:** 80-13-12 W
Pop: 1,361 (1990)   **Pop Density:** 37.6
Land: 36.2 sq. mi.; **Water:** 0.2 sq. mi.

Hayfield
Township
Lat: 41-42-35 N **Long:** 80-12-14 W
Pop: 2,937 (1990)   **Pop Density:** 75.5
Land: 38.9 sq. mi.; **Water:** 0.1 sq. mi.

Hydetown
Borough
ZIP: 16328   **Lat:** 41-39-05 N   **Long:** 79-43-27 W
Pop: 681 (1990); 760 (1980)   **Pop Density:** 309.5
Land: 2.2 sq. mi.; **Water:** 0.0 sq. mi.   **Elev:** 1245 ft.

Linesville
Borough
ZIP: 16424   **Lat:** 41-39-24 N   **Long:** 80-25-18 W
Pop: 1,166 (1990); 1,198 (1980)   **Pop Density:** 1457.5
Land: 0.8 sq. mi.; **Water:** 0.0 sq. mi.   **Elev:** 1050 ft.
Laid out in 1825.
Name origin: For Amos Line, who was employed as a surveyor by the Pennsylvania Population Company.

Meadville
City
ZIP: 16335   **Lat:** 41-38-46 N   **Long:** 80-08-47 W
Pop: 14,318 (1990); 15,544 (1980)   **Pop Density:** 3254.1
Land: 4.4 sq. mi.; **Water:** 0.0 sq. mi.   **Elev:** 1140 ft.
In northwestern PA on French Creek in the western foothills of the Allegheny Mountains, 33 mi. south of Erie. Settled in 1778; incorporated as borough Mar 29, 1823, as city Feb 15, 1866.
Name origin: For David Mead, who, along with his brothers and other pioneers from Sunburgh, established the first European settlement in northwestern PA.

North Shenango
Township
     Lat: 41-36-55 N   **Long:** 80-28-22 W
Pop: 902 (1990)   **Pop Density:** 48.0
Land: 18.8 sq. mi.; **Water:** 7.4 sq. mi.

Oil Creek
Township
     Lat: 41-39-42 N   **Long:** 79-41-15 W
Pop: 2,069 (1990)   **Pop Density:** 64.1
Land: 32.3 sq. mi.; **Water:** 0.0 sq. mi.

Pine
Township
     Lat: 41-38-48 N   **Long:** 80-26-18 W
Pop: 455 (1990)   **Pop Density:** 68.9
Land: 6.6 sq. mi.; **Water:** 6.0 sq. mi.

Randolph
Township
     Lat: 41-37-45 N   **Long:** 79-57-12 W
Pop: 1,661 (1990)   **Pop Density:** 38.4
Land: 43.3 sq. mi.; **Water:** 0.3 sq. mi.

Richmond
Township
     Lat: 41-43-04 N   **Long:** 79-58-05 W
Pop: 1,370 (1990)   **Pop Density:** 37.6
Land: 36.4 sq. mi.; **Water:** 0.1 sq. mi.

Rockdale
Township
     Lat: 41-48-22 N   **Long:** 79-58-05 W
Pop: 1,045 (1990)   **Pop Density:** 29.0
Land: 36.0 sq. mi.; **Water:** 0.2 sq. mi.

Rome
Township
     Lat: 41-43-51 N   **Long:** 79-41-09 W
Pop: 1,491 (1990)   **Pop Density:** 36.2
Land: 41.2 sq. mi.; **Water:** 0.0 sq. mi.

Sadsbury
Township
     Lat: 41-36-15 N   **Long:** 80-20-03 W
Pop: 2,575 (1990)   **Pop Density:** 108.6
Land: 23.7 sq. mi.; **Water:** 1.4 sq. mi.

Saegertown
Borough
ZIP: 16433   **Lat:** 41-42-47 N   **Long:** 80-08-18 W
Pop: 1,066 (1990); 942 (1980)   **Pop Density:** 761.4
Land: 1.4 sq. mi.; **Water:** 0.0 sq. mi.   **Elev:** 1128 ft.

South Shenango
Township
     Lat: 41-32-18 N   **Long:** 80-26-53 W
Pop: 1,560 (1990)   **Pop Density:** 58.6
Land: 26.6 sq. mi.; **Water:** 3.4 sq. mi.

Sparta
Township
     Lat: 41-48-55 N   **Long:** 79-41-40 W
Pop: 1,554 (1990)   **Pop Density:** 37.0
Land: 42.0 sq. mi.; **Water:** 0.2 sq. mi.

Spartansburg
Borough
ZIP: 16434   **Lat:** 41-49-25 N   **Long:** 79-40-56 W
Pop: 403 (1990); 403 (1980)   **Pop Density:** 575.7
Land: 0.7 sq. mi.; **Water:** 0.0 sq. mi.   **Elev:** 1445 ft.
Name origin: For the spartan character of the town's early settlers.

Spring
Township
     Lat: 41-48-21 N   **Long:** 80-20-15 W
Pop: 1,561 (1990)   **Pop Density:** 34.2
Land: 45.6 sq. mi.; **Water:** 0.0 sq. mi.   **Elev:** 1225 ft.

Springboro
Borough
ZIP: 16435   **Lat:** 41-48-00 N   **Long:** 80-22-16 W
Pop: 471 (1990); 557 (1980)   **Pop Density:** 523.3
Land: 0.9 sq. mi.; **Water:** 0.0 sq. mi.   **Elev:** 940 ft.

Steuben
Township
     Lat: 41-41-56 N   **Long:** 79-49-17 W
Pop: 820 (1990)   **Pop Density:** 33.5
Land: 24.5 sq. mi.; **Water:** 0.0 sq. mi.

Summerhill
Township
     Lat: 41-43-28 N   **Long:** 80-19-51 W
Pop: 1,264 (1990)   **Pop Density:** 49.8
Land: 25.4 sq. mi.; **Water:** 0.0 sq. mi.

Summit
Township
     Lat: 41-40-02 N   **Long:** 80-19-54 W
Pop: 1,890 (1990)   **Pop Density:** 73.3
Land: 25.8 sq. mi.; **Water:** 0.2 sq. mi.

Titusville
Borough
ZIP: 16354   **Lat:** 41-37-36 N   **Long:** 79-40-15 W
Pop: 6,434 (1990)   **Pop Density:** 2218.6
Land: 2.9 sq. mi.; **Water:** 0.0 sq. mi.   **Elev:** 1199 ft.
In northwestern PA on Oil Creek, 15 mi. north of Oil City.
Name origin: For Jonathan Titus, a pioneer surveyor. A vast oil field was discovered here in 1859.

Townville
Borough
ZIP: 16360   **Lat:** 41-40-46 N   **Long:** 79-52-55 W
Pop: 358 (1990); 364 (1980)   **Pop Density:** 596.7
Land: 0.6 sq. mi.; **Water:** 0.0 sq. mi.   **Elev:** 1411 ft.

Troy
Township
     Lat: 41-38-25 N   **Long:** 79-49-29 W
Pop: 1,235 (1990)   **Pop Density:** 39.1
Land: 31.6 sq. mi.; **Water:** 0.0 sq. mi.

Union
Township
     Lat: 41-34-05 N   **Long:** 80-09-37 W
Pop: 895 (1990)   **Pop Density:** 56.6
Land: 15.8 sq. mi.; **Water:** 0.1 sq. mi.

Venango
Township
ZIP: 16440   **Lat:** 41-48-34 N   **Long:** 80-07-12 W
Pop: 729 (1990)   **Pop Density:** 43.1
Land: 16.9 sq. mi.; **Water:** 0.0 sq. mi.

*Venango   Borough
ZIP: 16440   **Lat:** 41-46-21 N **Long:** 80-06-43 W
Pop: 289 (1990); 298 (1980)   **Pop Density:** 963.3
Land: 0.3 sq. mi.; **Water:** 0.0 sq. mi.   **Elev:** 1140 ft.

In northwestern PA, northwest of Oil City. Originally an Indian village.

Name origin: From an Indian term of uncertain meaning, possibly 'tract of level, fertile ground,' 'a mink,' or 'bull thistles.'

Vernon   Township
ZIP: 16335   **Lat:** 41-37-36 N **Long:** 80-12-49 W
Pop: 5,605 (1990)   **Pop Density:** 189.4
Land: 29.6 sq. mi.; **Water:** 0.0 sq. mi.

Wayne   Township
                        Lat: 41-32-45 N **Long:** 79-58-43 W
Pop: 1,401 (1990)   **Pop Density:** 40.0
Land: 35.0 sq. mi.; **Water:** 0.3 sq. mi.

West Fallowfield   Township
                        Lat: 41-31-45 N **Long:** 80-23-07 W
Pop: 693 (1990)   **Pop Density:** 60.3
Land: 11.5 sq. mi.; **Water:** 0.1 sq. mi.

West Mead   Township
ZIP: 16335   **Lat:** 41-37-29 N **Long:** 80-07-29 W
Pop: 5,401 (1990)   **Pop Density:** 296.8
Land: 18.2 sq. mi.; **Water:** 0.3 sq. mi.

West Shenango   Township
                        Lat: 41-30-37 N **Long:** 80-29-33 W
Pop: 496 (1990)   **Pop Density:** 72.9
Land: 6.8 sq. mi.; **Water:** 2.1 sq. mi.

Woodcock   Township
                        Lat: 41-42-50 N **Long** 80-04-55 W
Pop: 2,412 (1990)   **Pop Density:** 74.0
Land: 32.6 sq. mi.; **Water:** 0.5 sq. mi.

*Woodcock   Borough
ZIP: 16433   **Lat:** 41-45-12 N **Long** 80-05-03 W
Pop: 148 (1990); 126 (1980)   **Pop Density:** 246.7
Land: 0.6 sq. mi.; **Water:** 0.0 sq. mi.   **Elev:** 1200 ft.

Cumberland County
County Seat: Carlisle (ZIP: 17013)

Pop: 195,257 (1990); 179,625 (1980)   **Pop Density:** 354.9
Land: 550.2 sq. mi.; **Water:** 1.0 sq. mi.   **Area Code:** 717

In south-central PA, west of Harrisburg; organized Jan 27, 1750 from Lancaster County.

Name origin: For William Augustus, Duke of Cumberland (1721–65), British general and second son of George II (1683–1760).

Boiling Springs   CDP
ZIP: 17007   **Lat:** 40-09-27 N **Long:** 77-08-14 W
Pop: 1,978 (1990); 2,323 (1980)   **Pop Density:** 1978.0
Land: 1.0 sq. mi.; **Water:** 0.0 sq. mi.

Camp Hill   Borough
ZIP: 17011   **Lat:** 40-14-33 N **Long:** 76-55-36 W
Pop: 7,831 (1990); 8,422 (1980)   **Pop Density:** 3729.0
Land: 2.1 sq. mi.; **Water:** 0.0 sq. mi.   **Elev:** 410 ft.

Carlisle   Borough
ZIP: 17013   **Lat:** 40-12-03 N **Long:** 77-12-15 W
Pop: 18,419 (1990); 18,314 (1980)   **Pop Density:** 3410.9
Land: 5.4 sq. mi.; **Water:** 0.0 sq. mi.   **Elev:** 480 ft.

In southern PA, 15 mi. west of Harrisburg; incorporated Apr 13, 1782. Molly Pitcher (1754–1832), the famous Revolutionary War fighter and nurse, died and was buried here. The Carlisle Barracks from the Civil War have been preserved nearby.

Name origin: For the city in England.

Cooke   Township
ZIP: 17013   **Lat:** 40-02-18 N **Long:** 77-18-54 W
Pop: 90 (1990)   **Pop Density:** 4.5
Land: 19.9 sq. mi.; **Water:** 0.0 sq. mi.

Dickinson   Township
                        Lat: 40-06-00 N **Long:** 77-14-27 W
Pop: 3,870 (1990)   **Pop Density:** 84.9
Land: 45.6 sq. mi.; **Water:** 0.0 sq. mi.

East Pennsboro   Township
ZIP: 17025   **Lat:** 40-17-21 N **Long:** 76-56-20 W
Pop: 15,185 (1990)   **Pop Density:** 1432.5
Land: 10.6 sq. mi.; **Water:** 0.0 sq. mi.

Enola   CDP
ZIP: 17025   **Lat:** 40-17-18 N **Long:** 76-56-09 W
Pop: 5,961 (1990)   **Pop Density:** 3137.4
Land: 1.9 sq. mi.; **Water:** 0.0 sq. mi.

Hampden   Township
ZIP: 17055   **Lat:** 40-15-35 N **Long:** 76-58-51 W
Pop: 20,384 (1990)   **Pop Density:** 1145.2
Land: 17.8 sq. mi.; **Water:** 0.2 sq. mi.

Hopewell   Township
ZIP: 17240   **Lat:** 40-09-11 N **Long:** 77-33-12 W
Pop: 1,913 (1990)   **Pop Density:** 68.3
Land: 28.0 sq. mi.; **Water:** 0.0 sq. mi.

Lemoyne   Borough
ZIP: 17043   **Lat:** 40-14-40 N **Long:** 76-53-57 W
Pop: 3,959 (1990); 4,178 (1980)   **Pop Density:** 2474.4
Land: 1.6 sq. mi.; **Water:** 0.0 sq. mi.   **Elev:** 400 ft.

Lower Allen   Township
ZIP: 17011   **Lat:** 40-12-29 N **Long:** 76-55-41 W
Pop: 15,254 (1990)   **Pop Density:** 1481.0
Land: 10.3 sq. mi.; **Water:** 0.0 sq. mi.

Lower Frankford
Township
ZIP: 17013   **Lat:** 40-14-28 N **Long:** 77-17-31 W
Pop: 1,491 (1990)   **Pop Density:** 99.4
Land: 15.0 sq. mi.; **Water:** 0.1 sq. mi.

Lower Mifflin
Township
ZIP: 17241   **Lat:** 40-14-19 N **Long:** 77-25-40 W
Pop: 1,700 (1990)   **Pop Density:** 70.8
Land: 24.0 sq. mi.; **Water:** 0.0 sq. mi.

Mechanicsburg
Borough
ZIP: 17055   **Lat:** 40-12-36 N **Long:** 77-00-19 W
Pop: 9,452 (1990); 9,487 (1980)   **Pop Density:** 3635.4
Land: 2.6 sq. mi.; **Water:** 0.0 sq. mi.   **Elev:** 456 ft.

In southern PA, 9 mi. southwest of Harrisburg.

Name origin: For the large number of inhabitants who were mechanics in the foundries and machine shops here.

Middlesex
Township
ZIP: 17013   **Lat:** 40-15-07 N **Long:** 77-07-44 W
Pop: 5,780 (1990)   **Pop Density:** 222.3
Land: 26.0 sq. mi.; **Water:** 0.1 sq. mi.

Monroe
Township
ZIP: 17055   **Lat:** 40-09-29 N **Long:** 77-04-22 W
Pop: 5,468 (1990)   **Pop Density:** 209.5
Land: 26.1 sq. mi.; **Water:** 0.0 sq. mi.

Mount Holly Springs
Borough
ZIP: 17065   **Lat:** 40-06-45 N **Long:** 77-11-05 W
Pop: 1,925 (1990); 2,068 (1980)   **Pop Density:** 1283.3
Land: 1.5 sq. mi.; **Water:** 0.1 sq. mi.   **Elev:** 572 ft.

Newburg
Borough
ZIP: 17240   **Lat:** 40-08-15 N **Long:** 77-33-16 W
Pop: 312 (1990); 303 (1980)   **Pop Density:** 1040.0
Land: 0.3 sq. mi.; **Water:** 0.0 sq. mi.   **Elev:** 595 ft.

New Cumberland
Borough
ZIP: 17070   **Lat:** 40-13-49 N **Long:** 76-52-30 W
Pop: 7,665 (1990); 8,051 (1980)   **Pop Density:** 4508.8
Land: 1.7 sq. mi.; **Water:** 0.0 sq. mi.   **Elev:** 383 ft.

In southern PA on the Susquehanna River, a suburb of Harrisburg.

Name origin: For the county, from a Welsh term meaning 'land of compatriots.'

Newville
Borough
ZIP: 17241   **Lat:** 40-10-15 N **Long:** 77-24-06 W
Pop: 1,349 (1990); 1,370 (1980)   **Pop Density:** 3372.5
Land: 0.4 sq. mi.; **Water:** 0.0 sq. mi.   **Elev:** 530 ft.

North Middleton
Township
ZIP: 17013   **Lat:** 40-14-42 N **Long:** 77-13-12 W
Pop: 9,833 (1990)   **Pop Density:** 420.2
Land: 23.4 sq. mi.; **Water:** 0.0 sq. mi.

North Newton
Township
ZIP: 17241   **Lat:** 40-08-31 N **Long:** 77-26-42 W
Pop: 1,779 (1990)   **Pop Density:** 79.1
Land: 22.5 sq. mi.; **Water:** 0.0 sq. mi.

Penn
Township
ZIP: 17013   **Lat:** 40-06-06 N **Long:** 77-20-37 W
Pop: 2,425 (1990)   **Pop Density:** 82.8
Land: 29.3 sq. mi.; **Water:** 0.0 sq. mi.

Shippensburg
Township
ZIP: 17257   **Lat:** 40-03-33 N **Long:** 77-30-29 W
Pop: 4,606 (1990)   **Pop Density:** 1842.4
Land: 2.5 sq. mi.; **Water:** 0.0 sq. mi.

*Shippensburg
Borough
ZIP: 17257   **Lat:** 40-03-01 N **Long:** 77-30-53 W
Pop: 4,328 (1990); 4,376 (1980)   **Pop Density:** 3329.2
Land: 1.3 sq. mi.; **Water:** 0.0 sq. mi.   **Elev:** 660 ft.

In southern PA, 10 mi. north of Chambersburg. Founded in 1730. Second oldest town in PA. Part of the town is also in Franklin County.

Name origin: For Edward Shippen, elected mayor of Philadelphia in 1744.

Shiremanstown
Borough
ZIP: 17011   **Lat:** 40-13-20 N **Long:** 76-57-22 W
Pop: 1,567 (1990); 1,719 (1980)   **Pop Density:** 5223.3
Land: 0.3 sq. mi.; **Water:** 0.0 sq. mi.   **Elev:** 421 ft.

Silver Spring
Township
ZIP: 17055   **Lat:** 40-15-02 N **Long:** 77-03-13 W
Pop: 8,369 (1990)   **Pop Density:** 257.5
Land: 32.5 sq. mi.; **Water:** 0.4 sq. mi.

Southampton
Township
Lat: 40-02-27 N **Long:** 77-27-30 W
Pop: 3,552 (1990)   **Pop Density:** 67.7
Land: 52.5 sq. mi.; **Water:** 0.0 sq. mi.

South Middleton
Township
ZIP: 17007   **Lat:** 40-08-16 N **Long:** 77-09-56 W
Pop: 10,340 (1990)   **Pop Density:** 208.9
Land: 49.5 sq. mi.; **Water:** 0.1 sq. mi.

South Newton
Township
ZIP: 17266   **Lat:** 40-04-48 N **Long:** 77-24-20 W
Pop: 1,153 (1990)   **Pop Density:** 104.8
Land: 11.0 sq. mi.; **Water:** 0.0 sq. mi.

Upper Allen
Township
ZIP: 17055   **Lat:** 40-10-44 N **Long:** 76-58-45 W
Pop: 13,347 (1990)   **Pop Density:** 1011.1
Land: 13.2 sq. mi.; **Water:** 0.0 sq. mi.

Upper Frankford
Township
ZIP: 17241   **Lat:** 40-14-05 N **Long:** 77-22-30 W
Pop: 1,703 (1990)   **Pop Density:** 87.3
Land: 19.5 sq. mi.; **Water:** 0.0 sq. mi.

Upper Mifflin
Township
ZIP: 17241   **Lat:** 40-11-50 N **Long:** 77-30-12 W
Pop: 1,013 (1990)   **Pop Density:** 46.3
Land: 21.9 sq. mi.; **Water:** 0.0 sq. mi.

West Fairview
Borough
ZIP: 17025   **Lat:** 40-16-38 N **Long:** 76-55-07 W
Pop: 1,403 (1990); 1,426 (1980)   **Pop Density:** 4676.7
Land: 0.3 sq. mi.; **Water:** 0.0 sq. mi.   **Elev:** 340 ft.

West Pennsboro
Township
ZIP: 17241   **Lat:** 40-10-40 N **Long:** 77-19-49 W
Pop: 4,945 (1990)   **Pop Density:** 162.1
Land: 30.5 sq. mi.; **Water:** 0.0 sq. mi.

Wormleysburg
Borough
ZIP: 17043   **Lat:** 40-15-42 N **Long:** 76-54-29 W
Pop: 2,847 (1990); 2,772 (1980)   **Pop Density:** 3163.3
Land: 0.9 sq. mi.; **Water:** 0.0 sq. mi.   **Elev:** 440 ft.

In southern PA, a suburb of Harrisburg.

Dauphin County
County Seat: Harrisburg (ZIP: 17108)

Pop: 237,813 (1990); 232,317 (1980)   **Pop Density:** 452.7
Land: 525.3 sq. mi.; **Water:** 32.2 sq. mi.   **Area Code:** 717

In south-central PA, northwest of Lancaster; organized Mar 4, 1785 from Lancaster County.

Name origin: To honor France, ally of the American states in the Revolutionary War, by use of the hereditary title of the eldest son of the king of France, *dauphin*. Louis Joseph (1781–89), son of Louis XVI (1754–93) and Marie Antoinette (1755–93), was dauphin at the time the county was established.

Berrysburg
Borough
ZIP: 17005   **Lat:** 40-36-10 N **Long:** 76-48-32 W
Pop: 376 (1990); 447 (1980)   **Pop Density:** 537.1
Land: 0.7 sq. mi.; **Water:** 0.0 sq. mi.

Bressler-Enhaut-Oberlin
CDP
Lat: 40-13-57 N **Long:** 76-49-10 W
Pop: 2,660 (1990)   **Pop Density:** 4433.3
Land: 0.6 sq. mi.; **Water:** 0.0 sq. mi.

Colonial Park
CDP
ZIP: 17109   **Lat:** 40-17-59 N **Long:** 76-48-23 W
Pop: 13,777 (1990)   **Pop Density:** 2870.2
Land: 4.8 sq. mi.; **Water:** 0.0 sq. mi.

Conewago
Township
Lat: 40-12-51 N **Long:** 76-36-57 W
Pop: 2,832 (1990)   **Pop Density:** 169.6
Land: 16.7 sq. mi.; **Water:** 0.0 sq. mi.

In southern PA on the Susquehanna River; a southeastern suburb of Harrisburg.

Name origin: An Indian term possibly meaning 'at the rapids.'

Dauphin
Borough
ZIP: 17018   **Lat:** 40-22-07 N **Long:** 76-55-49 W
Pop: 845 (1990); 901 (1980)   **Pop Density:** 2112.5
Land: 0.4 sq. mi.; **Water:** 0.0 sq. mi.   **Elev:** 375 ft.

Derry
Township
ZIP: 17033   **Lat:** 40-16-18 N **Long:** 76-39-28 W
Pop: 18,408 (1990)   **Pop Density:** 676.8
Land: 27.2 sq. mi.; **Water:** 0.2 sq. mi.

East Hanover
Township
Lat: 40-23-26 N **Long:** 76-40-59 W
Pop: 4,569 (1990)   **Pop Density:** 114.5
Land: 39.9 sq. mi.; **Water:** 0.0 sq. mi.

Elizabethville
Borough
ZIP: 17023   **Lat:** 40-32-50 N **Long:** 76-48-57 W
Pop: 1,467 (1990); 1,531 (1980)   **Pop Density:** 2934.0
Land: 0.5 sq. mi.; **Water:** 0.0 sq. mi.   **Elev:** 700 ft.

Gratz
Borough
ZIP: 17030   **Lat:** 40-36-20 N **Long:** 76-43-02 W
Pop: 696 (1990); 678 (1980)   **Pop Density:** 232.0
Land: 3.0 sq. mi.; **Water:** 0.0 sq. mi.   **Elev:** 820 ft.

Halifax
Township
ZIP: 17032   **Lat:** 40-28-13 N **Long:** 76-55-44 W
Pop: 3,449 (1990)   **Pop Density:** 123.6
Land: 27.9 sq. mi.; **Water:** 4.2 sq. mi.

*Halifax
Borough
ZIP: 17032   **Lat:** 40-27-53 N **Long:** 76-56-00 W
Pop: 911 (1990); 909 (1980)   **Pop Density:** 3036.7
Land: 0.3 sq. mi.; **Water:** 0.0 sq. mi.   **Elev:** 400 ft.

Harrisburg
City
ZIP: 17101   **Lat:** 40-16-33 N **Long:** 76-53-04 W
Pop: 52,376 (1990); 53,264 (1980)   **Pop Density:** 6466.2
Land: 8.1 sq. mi.; **Water:** 3.3 sq. mi.   **Elev:** 320 ft.

In south-central PA on the Susquehanna River. 100 mi. west of Philadelphia. State capital; incorporated as borough Apr 13, 1791, chartered as city Mar 19, 1860.

Name origin: For Yorkshireman John Harris, licensed in 1705 as an Indian trader, who settled at Paxtang c. 1712 and established a trading post. His son, John, Jr., established a ferry and the place was then called Harris's Ferry. In 1785 he laid out the town and gave it its present name.

Hershey
CDP
ZIP: 17033   **Lat:** 40-16-48 N **Long:** 76-38-51 W
Pop: 11,860 (1990); 13,249 (1980)   **Pop Density:** 812.3
Land: 14.6 sq. mi.; **Water:** 0.0 sq. mi.

Highspire
Borough
ZIP: 17034   **Lat:** 40-12-30 N **Long:** 76-47-09 W
Pop: 2,668 (1990); 2,959 (1980)   **Pop Density:** 3811.4
Land: 0.7 sq. mi.; **Water:** 0.0 sq. mi.   **Elev:** 320 ft.

In southeast-central PA, 5 mi. southeast of Harrisburg.

Name origin: For the old church spire here that served as a landmark for Susquehanna River boatmen.

Hummelstown
Borough
ZIP: 17036   **Lat:** 40-15-59 N **Long:** 76-42-46 W
Pop: 3,981 (1990); 4,267 (1980)   **Pop Density:** 3062.3
Land: 1.3 sq. mi.; **Water:** 0.0 sq. mi.   **Elev:** 400 ft.

In southeast-central PA. Founded c. 1740. An important depot of arms and munitions for garrisons and forts situated to the west and the north during the Revolutionary War.

Name origin: Named in 1780 for founder Frederick Hummel. Originally called Frederickstown.

Jackson
Township
ZIP: 17032   **Lat:** 40-30-46 N **Long:** 76-46-32 W
Pop: 1,797 (1990)   **Pop Density:** 46.2
Land: 38.9 sq. mi.; **Water:** 0.0 sq. mi.

Jefferson
Township
ZIP: 17032   **Lat:** 40-30-44 N **Long:** 76-41-45 W
Pop: 385 (1990)   **Pop Density:** 15.9
Land: 24.2 sq. mi.; **Water:** 0.0 sq. mi.

Lawnton
CDP
Lat: 40-15-56 N **Long:** 76-47-56 W
Pop: 3,221 (1990)   **Pop Density:** 2684.2
Land: 1.2 sq. mi.; **Water:** 0.0 sq. mi.

Linglestown   CDP
ZIP: 17112   **Lat:** 40-20-35 N **Long:** 76-47-38 W
Pop: 5,862 (1990)   **Pop Density:** 1584.3
Land: 3.7 sq. mi.; **Water:** 0.0 sq. mi.

Londonderry   Township
ZIP: 17057   **Lat:** 40-10-15 N **Long:** 76-41-36 W
Pop: 4,926 (1990)   **Pop Density:** 216.1
Land: 22.8 sq. mi.; **Water:** 4.1 sq. mi.

Lower Paxton   Township
ZIP: 17109   **Lat:** 40-19-07 N **Long:** 76-47-57 W
Pop: 39,162 (1990)   **Pop Density:** 1393.7
Land: 28.1 sq. mi.; **Water:** 0.0 sq. mi.

Lower Swatara   Township
ZIP: 17057   **Lat:** 40-13-01 N **Long:** 76-45-46 W
Pop: 7,072 (1990)   **Pop Density:** 584.5
Land: 12.1 sq. mi.; **Water:** 2.7 sq. mi.

Lykens   Borough
ZIP: 17048   **Lat:** 40-33-47 N **Long:** 76-41-52 W
Pop: 1,986 (1990); 2,181 (1980)   **Pop Density:** 1527.7
Land: 1.3 sq. mi.; **Water:** 0.0 sq. mi.   **Elev:** 690 ft.

Founded 1826, 1 year after the discovery of anthracite at the lower end of Short Mountain.

Name origin: For Andrew Lycan, or Lykens, who settled here in 1732.

*Lykens   Township
ZIP: 17048   **Lat:** 40-37-19 N **Long:** 76-43-56 W
Pop: 1,238 (1990)   **Pop Density:** 46.9
Land: 26.4 sq. mi.; **Water:** 0.0 sq. mi.

Middle Paxton   Township
ZIP: 17018   **Lat:** 40-23-31 N **Long:** 76-52-12 W
Pop: 5,129 (1990)   **Pop Density:** 93.9
Land: 54.6 sq. mi.; **Water:** 4.6 sq. mi.

Middletown   Borough
ZIP: 17057   **Lat:** 40-12-03 N **Long:** 76-43-45 W
Pop: 9,254 (1990); 10,122 (1980)   **Pop Density:** 4627.0
Land: 2.0 sq. mi.; **Water:** 0.1 sq. mi.   **Elev:** 343 ft.

In southeast-central PA on the Susquehanna River, 8 mi. southeast of Harrisburg. Founded 1755.

Name origin: For its location halfway between Lancaster and Carlisle.

Mifflin   Township
ZIP: 17061   **Lat:** 40-36-03 N **Long:** 76-50-30 W
Pop: 676 (1990)   **Pop Density:** 43.9
Land: 15.4 sq. mi.; **Water:** 0.0 sq. mi.

Millersburg   Borough
ZIP: 17061   **Lat:** 40-32-32 N **Long:** 76-57-21 W
Pop: 2,729 (1990); 2,770 (1980)   **Pop Density:** 3411.3
Land: 0.8 sq. mi.; **Water:** 0.0 sq. mi.   **Elev:** 440 ft.

In southeast-central PA on the Susquehanna River, 28 mi. north of Harrisburg. Settled 1790.

Name origin: For brothers Daniel and John Miller, who owned 400 acres here.

Paxtang   Borough
ZIP: 17111   **Lat:** 40-15-42 N **Long:** 76-50-03 W
Pop: 1,599 (1990); 1,649 (1980)   **Pop Density:** 3997.5
Land: 0.4 sq. mi.; **Water:** 0.0 sq. mi.   **Elev:** 380 ft.

Penbrook   Borough
ZIP: 17103   **Lat:** 40-16-41 N **Long:** 76-50-55 W
Pop: 2,791 (1990); 3,006 (1980)   **Pop Density:** 5582.0
Land: 0.5 sq. mi.; **Water:** 0.0 sq. mi.   **Elev:** 480 ft.

In southeast-central PA, 5 mi. northeast of Harrisburg.

Pillow   Borough
ZIP: 17080   **Lat:** 40-38-28 N **Long:** 76-48-08 W
Pop: 341 (1990); 359 (1980)   **Pop Density:** 682.0
Land: 0.5 sq. mi.; **Water:** 0.0 sq. mi.   **Elev:** 588 ft.

Reed   Township
ZIP: 17032   **Lat:** 40-24-47 N **Long:** 76-59-17 W
Pop: 259 (1990)   **Pop Density:** 43.9
Land: 5.9 sq. mi.; **Water:** 2.5 sq. mi.

Royalton   Borough
ZIP: 17057   **Lat:** 40-11-13 N **Long:** 76-43-34 W
Pop: 1,120 (1990); 981 (1980)   **Pop Density:** 3733.3
Land: 0.3 sq. mi.; **Water:** 0.0 sq. mi.   **Elev:** 320 ft.

In southeast-central PA, a suburb of Harrisburg.

Rush   Township
Lat: 40-30-45 N **Long:** 76-38-06 W
Pop: 201 (1990)   **Pop Density:** 8.6
Land: 23.4 sq. mi.; **Water:** 1.0 sq. mi.

South Hanover   Township
ZIP: 17036   **Lat:** 40-17-50 N **Long:** 76-42-27 W
Pop: 4,626 (1990)   **Pop Density:** 405.8
Land: 11.4 sq. mi.; **Water:** 0.1 sq. mi.

Steelton   Borough
ZIP: 17113   **Lat:** 40-13-34 N **Long:** 76-49-33 W
Pop: 5,152 (1990); 6,484 (1980)   **Pop Density:** 2862.2
Land: 1.8 sq. mi.; **Water:** 0.0 sq. mi.   **Elev:** 315 ft.

In southeast-central PA.

Name origin: Named in 1880 by steel works superintendent Luther Bent. Previously called Baldwin for Matthew Baldwin, a large stockholder in the steel company; post office named Steel Works.

Susquehanna   Township
ZIP: 17109   **Lat:** 40-18-44 N **Long:** 76-52-19 W
Pop: 18,636 (1990)   **Pop Density:** 1390.7
Land: 13.4 sq. mi.; **Water:** 1.8 sq. mi.

In south-central PA, a northern suburb of Harrisburg.

Name origin: For the Susquehanna River, which forms the western boundary of the county.

Swatara   Township
ZIP: 17111   **Lat:** 40-14-34 N **Long:** 76-48-12 W
Pop: 19,661 (1990)   **Pop Density:** 1489.5
Land: 13.2 sq. mi.; **Water:** 2.5 sq. mi.

Upper Paxton   Township
ZIP: 17061   **Lat:** 40-34-13 N **Long:** 76-55-44 W
Pop: 3,680 (1990)   **Pop Density:** 141.5
Land: 26.0 sq. mi.; **Water:** 5.1 sq. mi.

Washington   Township
ZIP: 17061   **Lat:** 40-33-30 N **Long:** 76-48-22 W
Pop: 1,816 (1990)   **Pop Density:** 97.6
Land: 18.6 sq. mi.; **Water:** 0.0 sq. mi.

Name origin: For George Washington (1732–99), first U.S. president.

Wayne　　　　　　　　　　　　Township
ZIP: 17032　　　Lat: 40-27-41 N　Long: 76-49-59 W
Pop: 847 (1990)　　　　　　Pop Density: 60.9
Land: 13.9 sq. mi.; Water: 0.0 sq. mi.

West Hanover　　　　　　　　Township
ZIP: 17112　　　Lat: 40-21-54 N　Long: 76-45-04 W
Pop: 6,125 (1990)　　　　　Pop Density: 264.0
Land: 23.2 sq. mi.; Water: 0.0 sq. mi.

Wiconisco　　　　　　　　　Township
　　　　　　　Lat: 40-34-15 N　Long: 76-42-25 W
Pop: 1,372 (1990)　　　　　Pop Density: 135.8
Land: 10.1 sq. mi.; Water: 0.0 sq. mi.

Williams　　　　　　　　　　Township
ZIP: 17098　　　Lat: 40-35-24 N　Long: 76-37-29 W
Pop: 1,146 (1990)　　　　　Pop Density: 130.2
Land: 8.8 sq. mi.; Water: 0.0 sq. mi.

Williamstown　　　　　　　　Borough
ZIP: 17098　　　Lat: 40-34-50 N　Long: 76-37-04 W
Pop: 1,509 (1990); 1,664 (1980)　Pop Density: 5030.0
Land: 0.3 sq. mi.; Water: 0.0 sq. mi.　Elev: 736 ft.

Delaware County
County Seat: Media (ZIP: 19063)

Pop: 547,651 (1990); 555,029 (1980)　　Pop Density: 2972.7
Land: 184.2 sq. mi.; Water: 6.5 sq. mi.　　Area Code: 215

On southeastern border of PA, west of Philadelphia; organized Sep 6, 1789 from Chester County.

Name origin: For the Delaware River, which forms its southeastern border.

Aldan　　　　　　　　　　　Borough
ZIP: 19018　　　Lat: 39-55-22 N　Long: 75-17-19 W
Pop: 4,549 (1990); 4,671 (1980)　Pop Density: 7581.7
Land: 0.6 sq. mi.; Water: 0.0 sq. mi.　Elev: 126 ft.
In southeastern PA, a suburb of Chester.

Ardmore　　　　　　　　　　CDP
ZIP: 19003　　　Lat: 39-59-50 N　Long: 75-18-19 W
Pop: 5,321 (1990)　　　　　Pop Density: 6651.3
Land: 0.8 sq. mi.; Water: 0.0 sq. mi.
Part of the town is also in Montgomery County.

Aston　　　　　　　　　　　Township
ZIP: 19014　　　Lat: 39-52-22 N　Long: 75-25-59 W
Pop: 15,080 (1990)　　　　Pop Density: 2645.6
Land: 5.7 sq. mi.; Water: 0.0 sq. mi.
In southeastern PA near the Delaware River; a suburb of Philadelphia.

Bethel　　　　　　　　　　　Township
ZIP: 19061　　　Lat: 39-50-41 N　Long: 75-29-03 W
Pop: 3,330 (1990)　　　　　Pop Density: 584.2
Land: 5.7 sq. mi.; Water: 0.0 sq. mi.

Birmingham　　　　　　　　Township
　　　　　　　Lat: 39-51-58 N　Long: 75-34-21 W
Pop: 3,118 (1990)　　　　　Pop Density: 358.4
Land: 8.7 sq. mi.; Water: 0.1 sq. mi.

Boothwyn　　　　　　　　　CDP
ZIP: 19061　　　Lat: 39-50-07 N　Long: 75-26-42 W
Pop: 5,069 (1990)　　　　　Pop Density: 4224.2
Land: 1.2 sq. mi.; Water: 0.0 sq. mi.

Brookhaven　　　　　　　　Borough
ZIP: 19015　　　Lat: 39-52-13 N　Long: 75-23-28 W
Pop: 8,567 (1990); 7,912 (1980)　Pop Density: 5039.4
Land: 1.7 sq. mi.; Water: 0.0 sq. mi.　Elev: 119 ft.

Broomall　　　　　　　　　CDP
ZIP: 19008　　　Lat: 39-58-11 N　Long: 75-21-10 W
Pop: 10,930 (1990)　　　　Pop Density: 3769.0
Land: 2.9 sq. mi.; Water: 0.0 sq. mi.

Chester　　　　　　　　　　City
ZIP: 19013　　　Lat: 39-50-43 N　Long: 75-22-19 W
Pop: 41,856 (1990); 45,794 (1980)　Pop Density: 8720.0
Land: 4.8 sq. mi.; Water: 1.2 sq. mi.　Elev: 20 ft.
In southeastern PA on the Delaware River, 15 mi. southwest of Philadelphia. Second oldest settlement in PA.

Name origin: Named by William Penn (1644–1718), allegedly for Chester (Cheshire), England, former home of many early settlers. Previously called Upland.

*Chester　　　　　　　　　Township
ZIP: 19013　　　Lat: 39-51-00 N　Long 75-23-50 W
Pop: 5,399 (1990); 5,687 (1980)　Pop Density: 3856.4
Land: 1.4 sq. mi.; Water: 0.0 sq. mi.

Chester Heights　　　　　　Borough
ZIP: 19017　　　Lat: 39-53-39 N　Long 75-28-03 W
Pop: 2,273 (1990); 1,302 (1980)　Pop Density: 1082.4
Land: 2.1 sq. mi.; Water: 0.0 sq. mi.　Elev: 336 ft.
In southeastern PA, southwest of Philadelphia

Clifton Heights　　　　　　Borough
　　　　　　　Lat: 39-55-44 N　Long 75-17-46 W
Pop: 7,111 (1990); 7,320 (1980)　Pop Density: 11851.7
Land: 0.6 sq. mi.; Water: 0.0 sq. mi.　Elev: 191 ft.
In southeastern PA, southwest of Philadelphia. Settled late 18th century; incorporated 1885.

Collingdale　　　　　　　　Borough
ZIP: 19023　　　Lat: 39-54-52 N　Long 75-16-38 W
Pop: 9,175 (1990); 9,539 (1980)　Pop Density: 10194.4
Land: 0.9 sq. mi.; Water: 0.0 sq. mi.　Elev: 83 ft.

Colwyn　　　　　　　　　　Borough
ZIP: 19023　　　Lat: 39-54-41 N　Long 75-15-11 W
Pop: 2,613 (1990); 2,851 (1980)　Pop Density: 8710.0
Land: 0.3 sq. mi.; Water: 0.0 sq. mi.　Elev: 44 ft.
In southeastern PA on Cobbs Creek, 10 mi. southwest of downtown Philadelphia.

Concord
Township
ZIP: 19331   **Lat:** 39-52-19 N **Long:** 75-31-01 W
Pop: 6,933 (1990)   **Pop Density:** 506.1
Land: 13.7 sq. mi.; **Water:** 0.0 sq. mi.

In southeastern PA, southwest of Philadelphia.

Name origin: For "the harmonious feelings which in early times prevailed among the settlers there."

Darby
Borough
ZIP: 19023   **Lat:** 39-55-13 N **Long:** 75-15-39 W
Pop: 11,140 (1990); 11,513 (1980)   **Pop Density:** 13925.0
Land: 0.8 sq. mi.; **Water:** 0.0 sq. mi.   **Elev:** 50 ft.

In southeastern PA in a residential area along Darby Creek, southwest of downtown Philadelphia.

Name origin: For Derby, England. Spelled Derbytown in 1698; spelling altered to reflect pronunciation.

*Darby
Township
ZIP: 19023   **Lat:** 39-53-58 N **Long:** 75-16-23 W
Pop: 10,955 (1990); 12,264 (1980)   **Pop Density:** 7825.0
Land: 1.4 sq. mi.; **Water:** 0.0 sq. mi.

Drexel Hill
CDP
ZIP: 19026   **Lat:** 39-56-57 N **Long:** 75-18-13 W
Pop: 29,744 (1990)   **Pop Density:** 9295.0
Land: 3.2 sq. mi.; **Water:** 0.0 sq. mi.

East Lansdowne
Borough
ZIP: 19050   **Lat:** 39-56-37 N **Long:** 75-15-42 W
Pop: 2,691 (1990); 2,806 (1980)   **Pop Density:** 13455.0
Land: 0.2 sq. mi.; **Water:** 0.0 sq. mi.   **Elev:** 120 ft.

In southeastern PA along Cobbs Creek, 5 mi. west of Philadelphia.

Eddystone
Borough
ZIP: 19013   **Lat:** 39-51-21 N **Long:** 75-19-58 W
Pop: 2,446 (1990); 2,555 (1980)   **Pop Density:** 2446.0
Land: 1.0 sq. mi.; **Water:** 0.5 sq. mi.   **Elev:** 20 ft.

In southwestern PA on the Delaware River, 15 mi. southwest of Philadelphia.

Edgmont
Township
Lat: 39-56-59 N **Long:** 75-27-56 W
Pop: 2,735 (1990)   **Pop Density:** 279.1
Land: 9.8 sq. mi.; **Water:** 0.0 sq. mi.

Folcroft
Borough
ZIP: 19032   **Lat:** 39-53-18 N **Long:** 75-16-35 W
Pop: 7,506 (1990); 8,231 (1980)   **Pop Density:** 5361.4
Land: 1.4 sq. mi.; **Water:** 0.1 sq. mi.   **Elev:** 80 ft.

In southeastern PA, a southwestern suburb of Philadelphia.

Folsom
CDP
ZIP: 19033   **Lat:** 39-53-28 N **Long:** 75-19-44 W
Pop: 8,173 (1990)   **Pop Density:** 6810.8
Land: 1.2 sq. mi.; **Water:** 0.0 sq. mi.

Glenolden
Borough
ZIP: 19036   **Lat:** 39-53-55 N **Long:** 75-17-34 W
Pop: 7,260 (1990); 7,633 (1980)   **Pop Density:** 7260.0
Land: 1.0 sq. mi.; **Water:** 0.0 sq. mi.   **Elev:** 100 ft.

In southeastern PA, 5 mi. southwest of central Philadelphia.

Haverford
Township
ZIP: 19041   **Lat:** 39-59-12 N **Long:** 75-19-01 W
Pop: 49,848 (1990)   **Pop Density:** 4984.8
Land: 10.0 sq. mi.; **Water:** 0.0 sq. mi.

Lansdowne
Borough
ZIP: 19050   **Lat:** 39-56-25 N **Long:** 75-16-30 W
Pop: 11,712 (1990); 11,891 (1980)   **Pop Density:** 9760.0
Land: 1.2 sq. mi.; **Water:** 0.0 sq. mi.   **Elev:** 140 ft.

In southeastern PA, 5 mi. west of Philadelphia.

Name origin: Probably named for Lord Lansdowne.

Lima
CDP
Lat: 39-55-00 N **Long:** 75-26-32 W
Pop: 2,670 (1990)   **Pop Density:** 1780.0
Land: 1.5 sq. mi.; **Water:** 0.0 sq. mi.

Linwood
CDP
Lat: 39-49-24 N **Long:** 75-25-28 W
Pop: 3,425 (1990)   **Pop Density:** 6850.0
Land: 0.5 sq. mi.; **Water:** 0.0 sq. mi.

Lower Chichester
Township
ZIP: 19061   **Lat:** 39-49-22 N **Long:** 75-25-48 W
Pop: 3,660 (1990)   **Pop Density:** 3327.3
Land: 1.1 sq. mi.; **Water:** 0.0 sq. mi.

Marcus Hook
Borough
ZIP: 19061   **Lat:** 39-48-45 N **Long:** 75-24-58 W
Pop: 2,546 (1990); 2,638 (1980)   **Pop Density:** 2314.5
Land: 1.1 sq. mi.; **Water:** 0.5 sq. mi.   **Elev:** 33 ft.

Marple
Township
ZIP: 19008   **Lat:** 39-57-54 N **Long:** 75-21-53 W
Pop: 23,123 (1990)   **Pop Density:** 2267.0
Land: 10.2 sq. mi.; **Water:** 0.3 sq. mi.

In southeastern PA, a western suburb of Chester.

Media
Borough
ZIP: 19063   **Lat:** 39-55-10 N **Long:** 75-23-19 W
Pop: 5,957 (1990); 6,119 (1980)   **Pop Density:** 7446.3
Land: 0.8 sq. mi.; **Water:** 0.0 sq. mi.   **Elev:** 330 ft.

Incorporated Mar 11, 1850.

Middletown
Township
ZIP: 19037   **Lat:** 39-54-30 N **Long:** 75-25-55 W
Pop: 14,130 (1990)   **Pop Density:** 1046.7
Land: 13.5 sq. mi.; **Water:** 0.0 sq. mi.

Millbourne
Borough
ZIP: 19082   **Lat:** 39-57-47 N **Long:** 75-15-09 W
Pop: 831 (1990); 652 (1980)   **Pop Density:** 8310.0
Land: 0.1 sq. mi.; **Water:** 0.0 sq. mi.   **Elev:** 80 ft.

Morton
Borough
ZIP: 19070   **Lat:** 39-54-39 N **Long:** 75-19-37 W
Pop: 2,851 (1990); 2,412 (1980)   **Pop Density:** 7127.5
Land: 0.4 sq. mi.; **Water:** 0.0 sq. mi.   **Elev:** 138 ft.

In southeastern PA, a southwestern suburb of Philadelphia.

Name origin: For John Morton (1724?–77), who may have cast the deciding vote from PA in favor of the Declaration of Independence, and who signed the historic document.

Nether Providence
Township
ZIP: 19086   **Lat:** 39-53-52 N **Long:** 75-22-05 W
Pop: 13,229 (1990); 12,730 (1980)   **Pop Density:** 2814.7
Land: 4.7 sq. mi.; **Water:** 0.0 sq. mi.

Newtown
Township
ZIP: 19073   **Lat:** 39-59-17 N **Long:** 75-24-32 W
Pop: 11,366 (1990)   **Pop Density:** 1136.6
Land: 10.0 sq. mi.; **Water:** 0.1 sq. mi.

Norwood
Borough
ZIP: 19074   **Lat:** 39-53-09 N **Long:** 75-17-45 W
Pop: 6,162 (1990); 6,647 (1980)   **Pop Density:** 7702.5
Land: 0.8 sq. mi.; **Water:** 0.0 sq. mi.   **Elev:** 79 ft.
In southeastern PA, 9 mi. southwest of Philadelphia.

Parkside
Borough
ZIP: 19013   **Lat:** 39-51-59 N **Long:** 75-22-43 W
Pop: 2,369 (1990); 2,464 (1980)   **Pop Density:** 11845.0
Land: 0.2 sq. mi.; **Water:** 0.0 sq. mi.   **Elev:** 100 ft.
In southeastern PA, a southwestern suburb of Philadelphia.

Prospect Park
Borough
ZIP: 19076   **Lat:** 39-53-08 N **Long:** 75-18-27 W
Pop: 6,764 (1990); 6,593 (1980)   **Pop Density:** 9662.9
Land: 0.7 sq. mi.; **Water:** 0.0 sq. mi.   **Elev:** 97 ft.

Radnor
Township
ZIP: 19087   **Lat:** 40-01-42 N **Long:** 75-22-05 W
Pop: 28,703 (1990)   **Pop Density:** 2079.9
Land: 13.8 sq. mi.; **Water:** 0.0 sq. mi.
In southeastern PA, a residential suburb west of Philadelphia. Settled in 1683.
Name origin: Named by Quakers for their homeland, Radnorshire, Wales.

Ridley
Township
ZIP: 19033   **Lat:** 39-53-11 N **Long:** 75-19-38 W
Pop: 31,169 (1990)   **Pop Density:** 6111.6
Land: 5.1 sq. mi.; **Water:** 0.2 sq. mi.

Ridley Park
Borough
ZIP: 19078   **Lat:** 39-52-39 N **Long:** 75-19-32 W
Pop: 7,592 (1990); 7,889 (1980)   **Pop Density:** 6901.8
Land: 1.1 sq. mi.; **Water:** 0.0 sq. mi.   **Elev:** 79 ft.

Rose Valley
Borough
ZIP: 19063   **Lat:** 39-53-41 N **Long:** 75-23-10 W
Pop: 982 (1990); 1,038 (1980)   **Pop Density:** 1402.9
Land: 0.7 sq. mi.; **Water:** 0.0 sq. mi.   **Elev:** 200 ft.

Rutledge
Borough
ZIP: 19070   **Lat:** 39-54-02 N **Long:** 75-19-39 W
Pop: 843 (1990); 934 (1980)   **Pop Density:** 8430.0
Land: 0.1 sq. mi.; **Water:** 0.0 sq. mi.   **Elev:** 120 ft.
In southeastern PA, a southwestern suburb of Philadelphia.

Sharon Hill
Borough
ZIP: 19079   **Lat:** 39-54-27 N **Long:** 75-16-09 W
Pop: 5,771 (1990); 6,221 (1980)   **Pop Density:** 7213.8
Land: 0.8 sq. mi.; **Water:** 0.0 sq. mi.   **Elev:** 40 ft.

Springfield
Township
ZIP: 19064   **Lat:** 39-55-39 N **Long:** 75-20-15 W
Pop: 24,160 (1990)   **Pop Density:** 3775.0
Land: 6.4 sq. mi.; **Water:** 0.0 sq. mi.
In southeastern PA, 15 mi. west of Philadelphia.
Name origin: For Springfield, MA.

Swarthmore
Borough
ZIP: 19081   **Lat:** 39-54-07 N **Long:** 75-20-53 W
Pop: 6,157 (1990); 5,950 (1980)   **Pop Density:** 4397.9
Land: 1.4 sq. mi.; **Water:** 0.0 sq. mi.   **Elev:** 120 ft.
In southeastern PA, 10 mi. southwest of Philadelphia.
Name origin: For Swarthmore College, around which the town has grown. The college was named for Swarthmore Hall, home of George Fox (1624–91), founder of the Society of Friends (Quakers).

Thornbury
Township
ZIP: 19373   **Lat:** 39-55-05 N **Long:** 75-30-48 W
Pop: 5,056 (1990)   **Pop Density:** 549.6
Land: 9.2 sq. mi.; **Water:** 0.0 sq. mi.

Tinicum
Township
ZIP: 19029   **Lat:** 39-51-53 N **Long:** 75-16-30 W
Pop: 4,440 (1990)   **Pop Density:** 778.9
Land: 5.7 sq. mi.; **Water:** 3.0 sq. mi.

Trainer
Borough
ZIP: 19013   **Lat:** 39-49-24 N **Long:** 75-24-18 W
Pop: 2,271 (1990); 2,056 (1980)   **Pop Density:** 2064.5
Land: 1.1 sq. mi.; **Water:** 0.3 sq. mi.   **Elev:** 60 ft.
In southeastern PA, a southwestern suburb of Philadelphia.
Name origin: For David Trainer.

Upland
Borough
ZIP: 19015   **Lat:** 39-51-23 N **Long:** 75-22-47 W
Pop: 3,334 (1990); 3,458 (1980)   **Pop Density:** 4762.9
Land: 0.7 sq. mi.; **Water:** 0.0 sq. mi.   **Elev:** 50 ft.
In southeastern PA near Chester, a southwestern suburb of Philadelphia.

Upper Chichester
Township
ZIP: 19061   **Lat:** 39-50-30 N **Long:** 75-26-26 W
Pop: 15,004 (1990)   **Pop Density:** 2239.4
Land: 6.7 sq. mi.; **Water:** 0.0 sq. mi.

Upper Darby
Township
ZIP: 19082   **Lat:** 39-56-53 N **Long:** 75-17-23 W
Pop: 81,177 (1990)   **Pop Density:** 10275.6
Land: 7.9 sq. mi.; **Water:** 0.0 sq. mi.

Upper Providence
Township
ZIP: 19063   **Lat:** 39-56-15 N **Long:** 75-23-47 W
Pop: 9,727 (1990)   **Pop Density:** 1737.0
Land: 5.6 sq. mi.; **Water:** 0.3 sq. mi.   **Elev:** 325 ft.

Yeadon
Borough
ZIP: 19050   **Lat:** 39-55-57 N **Long:** 75-15-06 W
Pop: 11,980 (1990); 11,727 (1980)   **Pop Density:** 7487.5
Land: 1.6 sq. mi.; **Water:** 0.0 sq. mi.   **Elev:** 103 ft.
In southeastern PA, 5 mi. southwest of Philadelphia.

Elk County
County Seat: Ridgway (ZIP: 15853)

Pop: 34,878 (1990); 38,338 (1980)   **Pop Density:** 42.1
Land: 828.7 sq. mi.; **Water:** 3.6 sq. mi.   **Area Code:** 814

In west-central PA, west of Williamsport; organized Apr 18, 1843 from Jefferson, Clearfield, and McKean counties.

Name origin: For the North American elk, once common in the county.

Benezette
                                                          Township
                           Lat: 41-18-26 N **Long:** 78-19-51 W
Pop: 243 (1990)   **Pop Density:** 2.3
Land: 106.8 sq. mi.; **Water:** 0.4 sq. mi.   **Elev:** 1140 ft.
In north-central PA on the Trout Run and Bennett branch of the Sinnemahoning River.

Benzinger
ZIP: 15857   **Lat:** 41-27-35 N **Long:** 78-32-07 W
Pop: 8,509 (1990)   **Pop Density:** 87.2
Land: 97.6 sq. mi.; **Water:** 0.2 sq. mi.
Name origin: For Col. Mathias Benzinger, who bought about 60,000 acres for German Catholic settlers from Baltimore.

Fox
                                                          Township
                           Lat: 41-19-10 N **Long:** 78-37-08 W
Pop: 3,392 (1990)   **Pop Density:** 50.4
Land: 67.3 sq. mi.; **Water:** 0.0 sq. mi.

Grandview Park
                                                          CDP
                           Lat: 41-25-01 N **Long:** 78-32-32 W
Pop: 2,170 (1990); 2,471 (1980)   **Pop Density:** 1033.3
Land: 2.1 sq. mi.; **Water:** 0.0 sq. mi.

Highland
                                                          Township
                           Lat: 41-32-41 N **Long:** 78-52-35 W
Pop: 551 (1990)   **Pop Density:** 6.3
Land: 86.9 sq. mi.; **Water:** 0.1 sq. mi.

Horton
                                                          Township
                           Lat: 41-17-49 N **Long:** 78-43-54 W
Pop: 1,655 (1990)   **Pop Density:** 29.0
Land: 57.0 sq. mi.; **Water:** 0.1 sq. mi.

Jay
                                                          Township
                           Lat: 41-19-20 N **Long:** 78-29-21 W
Pop: 2,087 (1990)   **Pop Density:** 30.8
Land: 67.8 sq. mi.; **Water:** 0.0 sq. mi.

Johnsonburg
ZIP: 15845   **Lat:** 41-29-30 N **Long:** 78-40-43 W
Pop: 3,350 (1990); 3,938 (1980)   **Pop Density:** 1116.7
Land: 3.0 sq. mi.; **Water:** 0.0 sq. mi.   **Elev:** 1465 ft.
In northwest-central PA at the forks of the Clarion River, 100 mi. northeast of Pittsburgh. Laid out in 1888.
Name origin: For John Johnson, pioneer settler in that region, who about 50 years before the town was laid out occupied a small cabin at the junction of the east and west branches of the Clarion River, near the center of the present town.

Jones
                                                          Township
                           Lat: 41-34-08 N **Long:** 78-37-34 W
Pop: 1,870 (1990)   **Pop Density:** 12.9
Land: 145.4 sq. mi.; **Water:** 1.7 sq. mi.

Millstone
                                                          Township
                           Lat: 41-23-37 N **Long:** 79-01-46 W
Pop: 85 (1990)   **Pop Density:** 2.0
Land: 41.6 sq. mi.; **Water:** 0.1 sq. mi.

Ridgway
                                                          Borough
ZIP: 15853   **Lat:** 41-25-32 N **Long:** 78-43-43 W
Pop: 4,793 (1990); 5,604 (1980)   **Pop Density:** 1775.2
Land: 2.7 sq. mi.; **Water:** 0.0 sq. mi.   **Elev:** 1400 ft.
In northwest-central PA in a crook of the Clarion River at the mouth of Elk Creek, east of Oil City. Laid out in 1833, incorporated Feb 15, 1881.
Name origin: For Jacob Ridgway, a Philadephia Quaker merchant who in 1817 purchased an 80,000-acre tract, part of which the town occupies.

*Ridgway
                                                          Township
ZIP: 15853   **Lat:** 41-26-19 N **Long:** 78-43-58 W
Pop: 2,617 (1990)   **Pop Density:** 30.0
Land: 87.3 sq. mi.; **Water:** 0.5 sq. mi.
In southeastern PA, southwest of Philadelphia.

St. Marys
                                                          Borough
ZIP: 15857   **Lat:** 41-25-42 N **Long:** 78-33-27 W
Pop: 5,511 (1990); 6,417 (1980)   **Pop Density:** 3241.8
Land: 1.7 sq. mi.; **Water:** 0.0 sq. mi.   **Elev:** 1667 ft.
In northwest-central PA, near the NY state line.

Spring Creek
                                                          Township
                           Lat: 41-23-26 N **Long:** 78-52-54 W
Pop: 215 (1990)   **Pop Density:** 3.4
Land: 63.6 sq. mi.; **Water:** 0.6 sq. mi.

Erie County
County Seat: Erie (ZIP: 16501)

Pop: 275,572 (1990); 279,780 (1980)
Land: 802.0 sq. mi.; **Water:** 756.5 sq. mi.

Pop Density: 343.6
Area Code: 814

At northwestern corner of PA, along southern shore of Lake Erie; organized Mar 12, 1800 from Allegheny County.

Name origin: For Lake Erie, which forms its northern border.

Albion — Borough
ZIP: 16401   **Lat:** 41-53-22 N   **Long:** 80-21-49 W
Pop: 1,575 (1990); 1,818 (1980)   **Pop Density:** 1431.8
Land: 1.1 sq. mi.; **Water:** 0.0 sq. mi.   **Elev:** 900 ft.
Settled 1815.
Name origin: Originally called Jackson Cross Roads.

Amity — Township
Lat: 41-57-57 N   **Long:** 79-49-37 W
Pop: 1,034 (1990)   **Pop Density:** 36.5
Land: 28.3 sq. mi.; **Water:** 0.0 sq. mi.

Avonia — CDP
Lat: 42-02-38 N   **Long:** 80-16-24 W
Pop: 1,336 (1990); 1,365 (1980)   **Pop Density:** 513.8
Land: 2.6 sq. mi.; **Water:** 0.0 sq. mi.

Concord — Township
Lat: 41-53-04 N   **Long:** 79-41-34 W
Pop: 1,384 (1990)   **Pop Density:** 41.9
Land: 33.0 sq. mi.; **Water:** 0.0 sq. mi.

Conneaut — Township
Lat: 41-53-17 N   **Long:** 80-25-22 W
Pop: 1,938 (1990)   **Pop Density:** 44.7
Land: 43.4 sq. mi.; **Water:** 0.0 sq. mi.
In northwestern PA, southwest of Erie.
Name origin: From an Indian term possibly meaning 'snow place,' so called because the snow on the water lasted long after that on the land had melted. Probably a reference to Lake Erie.

Corry — City
ZIP: 16407   **Lat:** 41-55-33 N   **Long:** 79-38-14 W
Pop: 7,216 (1990); 7,149 (1980)   **Pop Density:** 1183.0
Land: 6.1 sq. mi.; **Water:** 0.0 sq. mi.   **Elev:** 1428 ft.
In northwestern PA on the south branch of French Creek, 28 mi. southeast of Erie. Established 1861.
Name origin: For its location at the rights of way of two railroads that intersected on Hiram Corry's farm; grew due to the oil discovered by Drake at Titusville, some 25 miles to the south.

Cranesville — Borough
ZIP: 16410   **Lat:** 41-54-13 N   **Long:** 80-20-41 W
Pop: 598 (1990); 703 (1980)   **Pop Density:** 664.4
Land: 0.9 sq. mi.; **Water:** 0.0 sq. mi.   **Elev:** 950 ft.

Edinboro — Borough
ZIP: 16412   **Lat:** 41-52-28 N   **Long:** 80-07-28 W
Pop: 7,736 (1990); 6,324 (1980)   **Pop Density:** 3363.5
Land: 2.3 sq. mi.; **Water:** 0.1 sq. mi.   **Elev:** 1220 ft.
In northwestern PA, 20 mi. south of Lake Erie Shore.
Name origin: For Edinburgh, Scotland; spelling altered to reflect pronunciation.

Elgin — Borough
ZIP: 16413   **Lat:** 41-54-38 N   **Long:** 79-44-36 W
Pop: 229 (1990); 235 (1980)   **Pop Density:** 143.1
Land: 1.6 sq. mi.; **Water:** 0.0 sq. mi.   **Elev:** 1388 ft.

Elk Creek — Township
Lat: 41-53-09 N   **Long:** 80-17-40 W
Pop: 1,738 (1990)   **Pop Density:** 50.2
Land: 34.6 sq. mi.; **Water:** 0.0 sq. mi.

Erie — City
ZIP: 16501   **Lat:** 42-07-33 N   **Long:** 80-05-11 W
Pop: 108,718 (1990); 119,123 (1980)   **Pop Density:** 4941.7
Land: 22.0 sq. mi.; **Water:** 6.0 sq. mi.   **Elev:** 650 ft.
In northwestern PA on Lake Erie, 90 mi. west of Buffalo, NY. Incorporated as borough Mar 29, 1805, as city Apr 14, 1851. The Erie Indians were exterminated by the Seneca about 1654, and for decades thereafter the region remained under control of the Iroquois Confederacy.
Name origin: For Lake Erie.

Fairview — Township
ZIP: 16415   **Lat:** 42-01-35 N   **Long:** 80-14-10 W
Pop: 7,839 (1990)   **Pop Density:** 282.0
Land: 27.8 sq. mi.; **Water:** 0.0 sq. mi.

*Fairview — Borough
ZIP: 16415   **Lat:** 42-01-45 N   **Long:** 80-15-19 W
Pop: 1,988 (1990); 1,855 (1980)   **Pop Density:** 1420.0
Land: 1.4 sq. mi.; **Water:** 0.0 sq. mi.   **Elev:** 670 ft.

Franklin — Township
Lat: 41-55-38 N   **Long:** 80-12-54 W
Pop: 1,429 (1990)   **Pop Density:** 49.6
Land: 28.8 sq. mi.; **Water:** 0.0 sq. mi.

Girard — Township
ZIP: 16417   **Lat:** 41-59-00 N   **Long:** 80-19-32 W
Pop: 4,722 (1990)   **Pop Density:** 149.0
Land: 31.7 sq. mi.; **Water:** 0.0 sq. mi.

*Girard — Borough
ZIP: 16417   **Lat:** 42-00-14 N   **Long:** 80-19-09 W
Pop: 2,879 (1990); 2,615 (1980)   **Pop Density:** 1199.6
Land: 2.4 sq. mi.; **Water:** 0.0 sq. mi.   **Elev:** 777 ft.
In northwestern PA on Elk Creek, 10 mi. southwest of Erie. Settled 1800. Incorporated 1846.
Name origin: For Philadelphia merchant Stephen Girard, who owned land in the vicinity.

Greene — Township
Lat: 42-03-20 N   **Long:** 79-57-38 W
Pop: 4,959 (1990)   **Pop Density:** 132.2
Land: 37.5 sq. mi.; **Water:** 0.1 sq. mi.

Greenfield — Township
Lat: 42-07-50 N   **Long:** 79-49-58 W
Pop: 1,770 (1990)   **Pop Density:** 52.4
Land: 33.8 sq. mi.; **Water:** 0.3 sq. mi.

Harborcreek
Township
ZIP: 16421   **Lat:** 42-09-09 N   **Long:** 79-56-35 W
Pop: 15,108 (1990)   **Pop Density:** 441.8
Land: 34.2 sq. mi.; **Water:** 0.0 sq. mi.

Lake City
Borough
ZIP: 16423   **Lat:** 42-01-02 N   **Long:** 80-20-48 W
Pop: 2,519 (1990); 2,384 (1980)   **Pop Density:** 1399.4
Land: 1.8 sq. mi.; **Water:** 0.0 sq. mi.   **Elev:** 725 ft.
In northwestern PA on Lake Erie, 15 mi. south of Erie.
Name origin: Named in 1954. Previously called North Girard.

Lawrence Park
Township
Lat: 42-09-06 N   **Long:** 80-01-18 W
Pop: 4,310 (1990); 4,584 (1980)   **Pop Density:** 2268.4
Land: 1.9 sq. mi.; **Water:** 0.0 sq. mi.

Le Boeuf
Township
Lat: 41-53-05 N   **Long:** 79-57-45 W
Pop: 1,521 (1990)   **Pop Density:** 45.1
Land: 33.7 sq. mi.; **Water:** 0.0 sq. mi.

McKean
Township
Lat: 41-59-28 N   **Long:** 80-07-37 W
Pop: 4,503 (1990)   **Pop Density:** 123.0
Land: 36.6 sq. mi.; **Water:** 0.1 sq. mi.

*McKean
Borough
ZIP: 16426   **Lat:** 41-59-56 N   **Long:** 80-08-17 W
Pop: 418 (1990); 465 (1980)   **Pop Density:** 696.7
Land: 0.6 sq. mi.; **Water:** 0.0 sq. mi.

Millcreek
Township
ZIP: 16505   **Lat:** 42-04-42 N   **Long:** 80-07-08 W
Pop: 46,820 (1990)   **Pop Density:** 1587.1
Land: 29.5 sq. mi.; **Water:** 0.0 sq. mi.

Mill Village
Borough
ZIP: 16427   **Lat:** 41-52-39 N   **Long:** 79-58-21 W
Pop: 429 (1990); 427 (1980)   **Pop Density:** 476.7
Land: 0.9 sq. mi.; **Water:** 0.0 sq. mi.   **Elev:** 1206 ft.

North East
Township
ZIP: 16428   **Lat:** 42-11-44 N   **Long:** 79-49-27 W
Pop: 6,283 (1990)   **Pop Density:** 148.2
Land: 42.4 sq. mi.; **Water:** 0.1 sq. mi.

*North East
Borough
ZIP: 16428   **Lat:** 42-12-47 N   **Long:** 79-50-02 W
Pop: 4,617 (1990); 4,568 (1980)   **Pop Density:** 3551.5
Land: 1.3 sq. mi.; **Water:** 0.0 sq. mi.   **Elev:** 801 ft.
In northwestern PA on Lake Erie, 15 mi. northeast of Erie.
Name origin: For North East Township, which occupies the northeast corner of the Erie Triangle, a wedge-shaped slice of land once claimed by NY, MA, and CT.

Platea
Borough
ZIP: 16417   **Lat:** 41-57-05 N   **Long:** 80-19-49 W
Pop: 467 (1990); 492 (1980)   **Pop Density:** 141.5
Land: 3.3 sq. mi.; **Water:** 0.0 sq. mi.   **Elev:** 876 ft.

Springfield
Township
Lat: 41-57-37 N   **Long:** 80-27-05 W
Pop: 3,218 (1990)   **Pop Density:** 85.4
Land: 37.7 sq. mi.; **Water:** 0.1 sq. mi.

Summit
Township
ZIP: 16509   **Lat:** 42-02-34 N   **Long:** 80-02-57 W
Pop: 5,284 (1990)   **Pop Density:** 221.1
Land: 23.9 sq. mi.; **Water:** 0.0 sq. mi.

Union
Township
Lat: 41-53-36 N   **Long:** 79-49-33 W
Pop: 1,735 (1990)   **Pop Density:** 47.5
Land: 36.5 sq. mi.; **Water:** 0.1 sq. mi.

Union City
Borough
ZIP: 16438   **Lat:** 41-53-45 N   **Long:** 79-50-40 W
Pop: 3,537 (1990); 3,623 (1980)   **Pop Density:** 1861.6
Land: 1.9 sq. mi.; **Water:** 0.0 sq. mi.   **Elev:** 1261 ft.
In northwestern PA, 20 mi. southeast of Erie.

Venango
Township
Lat: 42-02-23 N   **Long:** 79-49-59 W
Pop: 2,235 (1990)   **Pop Density:** 51.3
Land: 43.6 sq. mi.; **Water:** 0.1 sq. mi.
Name origin: From an Indian term of uncertain meaning, possibly 'tract of level, fertile ground,' 'a mink,' or 'bull thistles.'

Washington
Township
Lat: 41-53-28 N   **Long:** 80-07-08 W
Pop: 4,102 (1990)   **Pop Density:** 91.0
Land: 45.1 sq. mi.; **Water:** 0.3 sq. mi.
Name origin: For George Washington (1732–99), first U.S. president.

Waterford
Township
ZIP: 16441   **Lat:** 41-57-14 N   **Long:** 79-58-21 W
Pop: 3,402 (1990)   **Pop Density:** 67.9
Land: 50.1 sq. mi.; **Water:** 0.3 sq. mi.

*Waterford
Borough
ZIP: 16441   **Lat:** 41-56-43 N   **Long:** 79-59-07 W
Pop: 1,492 (1990); 1,568 (1980)   **Pop Density:** 1243.3
Land: 1.2 sq. mi.; **Water:** 0.0 sq. mi.   **Elev:** 1207 ft.

Wattsburg
Borough
ZIP: 16442   **Lat:** 42-00-10 N   **Long:** 79-48-25 W
Pop: 486 (1990); 513 (1980)   **Pop Density:** 1620.0
Land: 0.3 sq. mi.; **Water:** 0.0 sq. mi.   **Elev:** 1290 ft.

Wayne
Township
Lat: 41-57-47 N   **Long:** 79-41-21 W
Pop: 1,679 (1990)   **Pop Density:** 43.8
Land: 38.3 sq. mi.; **Water:** 0.0 sq. mi.

Wesleyville
Borough
ZIP: 16510   **Lat:** 42-08-13 N   **Long:** 80-00-45 W
Pop: 3,655 (1990); 3,998 (1980)   **Pop Density:** 7310.0
Land: 0.5 sq. mi.; **Water:** 0.0 sq. mi.   **Elev:** 740 ft.
In northwestern PA. Laid out by John Shadduck in 1828.
Name origin: For John Wesley (1703–91), founder of Methodism.

Fayette County
County Seat: Uniontown (ZIP: 15401)

Pop: 145,351 (1990); 159,417 (1980)   **Pop Density:** 184.0
Land: 790.1 sq. mi.; **Water:** 7.9 sq. mi.   **Area Code:** 412

On southern border of western PA, southeast of Pittsburgh; organized Sep 26, 1783 from Westmoreland County.

Name origin: For the Marquis de Lafayette or La Fayette (1757–1834), French statesman and soldier who fought with the Americans during the Revolutionary War.

Belle Vernon   Borough
ZIP: 15012   **Lat:** 40-07-28 N **Long:** 79-51-56 W
Pop: 1,213 (1990); 1,489 (1980)   **Pop Density:** 4043.3
Land: 0.3 sq. mi.; **Water:** 0.1 sq. mi.   **Elev:** 1000 ft.
In southwestern PA on the Monongahela River.

Brownsville   Borough
ZIP: 15417   **Lat:** 40-01-08 N **Long:** 79-53-29 W
Pop: 3,164 (1990); 4,043 (1980)   **Pop Density:** 3164.0
Land: 1.0 sq. mi.; **Water:** 0.1 sq. mi.   **Elev:** 900 ft.
In southwestern PA, a southern suburb of Pittsburgh. Laid out in 1785. Combined with South Brownsville borough since 1933.
Name origin: For Thomas Brown who, according to his tombstone, "was once the owner of this town."

*Brownsville   Township
ZIP: 15417   **Lat:** 40-01-06 N **Long:** 79-52-30 W
Pop: 847 (1990)   **Pop Density:** 529.4
Land: 1.6 sq. mi.; **Water:** 0.0 sq. mi.

Bullskin   Township
ZIP: 15666   **Lat:** 40-04-56 N **Long:** 79-30-42 W
Pop: 7,323 (1990)   **Pop Density:** 168.7
Land: 43.4 sq. mi.; **Water:** 0.1 sq. mi.

Connellsville   City
ZIP: 15425   **Lat:** 40-00-58 N **Long:** 79-35-20 W
Pop: 9,229 (1990); 10,319 (1980)   **Pop Density:** 4012.6
Land: 2.3 sq. mi.; **Water:** 0.1 sq. mi.   **Elev:** 920 ft.

*Connellsville   Township
ZIP: 15425   **Lat:** 40-00-29 N **Long:** 79-34-05 W
Pop: 2,553 (1990)   **Pop Density:** 238.6
Land: 10.7 sq. mi.; **Water:** 0.1 sq. mi.
In southwestern PA, 47 mi. southeast of Pittsburgh. Laid out about 1793.
Name origin: For Zachariah Connell who, along with several other pioneers, came here in 1770, about the time coal was discovered.

Dawson   Borough
ZIP: 15428   **Lat:** 40-02-52 N **Long:** 79-39-32 W
Pop: 535 (1990); 661 (1980)   **Pop Density:** 2675.0
Land: 0.2 sq. mi.; **Water:** 0.0 sq. mi.   **Elev:** 849 ft.

Dunbar   Township
ZIP: 15431   **Lat:** 39-57-53 N **Long:** 79-36-04 W
Pop: 7,460 (1990)   **Pop Density:** 126.2
Land: 59.1 sq. mi.; **Water:** 0.4 sq. mi.

*Dunbar   Borough
ZIP: 15431   **Lat:** 39-58-46 N **Long:** 79-36-50 W
Pop: 1,213 (1990); 1,369 (1980)   **Pop Density:** 2021.7
Land: 0.6 sq. mi.; **Water:** 0.0 sq. mi.   **Elev:** 1000 ft.
In southwestern PA, 7 mi. northeast of Uniontown.
Name origin: For Col. Thomas Dunbar, who was defeated by a French and Indian army here in 1755.

East Uniontown   CDP
          Lat: 39-53-58 N **Long:** 79-41-53 W
Pop: 2,822 (1990); 2,492 (1980)   **Pop Density:** 1411.0
Land: 2.0 sq. mi.; **Water:** 0.0 sq. mi.

Everson   Borough
ZIP: 15631   **Lat:** 40-05-25 N **Long:** 79-35-14 W
Pop: 939 (1990); 1,032 (1980)   **Pop Density:** 4695.0
Land: 0.2 sq. mi.; **Water:** 0.0 sq. mi.   **Elev:** 1060 ft.

Fairchance   Borough
ZIP: 15436   **Lat:** 39-49-33 N **Long:** 79-45-16 W
Pop: 1,918 (1990); 2,106 (1980)   **Pop Density:** 1598.3
Land: 1.2 sq. mi.; **Water:** 0.0 sq. mi.   **Elev:** 1100 ft.
In southwestern PA, 6 mi. south of Uniontown.

Fayette City   Borough
ZIP: 15438   **Lat:** 40-06-00 N **Long:** 79-50-20 W
Pop: 713 (1990); 788 (1980)   **Pop Density:** 2376.7
Land: 0.3 sq. mi.; **Water:** 0.0 sq. mi.   **Elev:** 900 ft.

Franklin   Township
          Lat: 40-00-17 N **Long:** 79-44-29 W
Pop: 2,640 (1990)   **Pop Density:** 89.2
Land: 29.6 sq. mi.; **Water:** 0.2 sq. mi.

Georges   Township
ZIP: 15401   **Lat:** 39-48-43 N **Long:** 79-45-47 W
Pop: 6,525 (1990)   **Pop Density:** 136.2
Land: 47.9 sq. mi.; **Water:** 0.0 sq. mi.

German   Township
ZIP: 15458   **Lat:** 39-53-10 N **Long:** 79-52-05 W
Pop: 5,596 (1990)   **Pop Density:** 168.0
Land: 33.3 sq. mi.; **Water:** 0.4 sq. mi.

Grindstone-Rowes Run   CDP
          Lat: 40-00-54 N **Long:** 79-48-54 W
Pop: 1,041 (1990)   **Pop Density:** 743.6
Land: 1.4 sq. mi.; **Water:** 0.0 sq. mi.

Henry Clay   Township
          Lat: 39-46-56 N **Long:** 79-26-08 W
Pop: 1,860 (1990)   **Pop Density:** 36.3
Land: 51.3 sq. mi.; **Water:** 1.7 sq. mi.
Name origin: For Henry Clay (1777–1852) U.S. senator from KY known as the "Great Pacificator."

Hiller
CDP
ZIP: 15444   **Lat:** 40-00-26 N **Long:** 79-54-13 W
Pop: 1,401 (1990); 1,577 (1980)   **Pop Density:** 934.0
Land: 1.5 sq. mi.; **Water:** 0.0 sq. mi.

Hopwood
CDP
ZIP: 15445   **Lat:** 39-52-38 N **Long:** 79-42-06 W
Pop: 2,021 (1990); 897 (1980)   **Pop Density:** 1063.7
Land: 1.9 sq. mi.; **Water:** 0.0 sq. mi.

Jefferson
Township
Lat: 40-03-21 N **Long:** 79-50-00 W
Pop: 2,047 (1990)   **Pop Density:** 101.3
Land: 20.2 sq. mi.; **Water:** 0.3 sq. mi.

Leith-Hatfield
CDP
Lat: 39-52-47 N **Long:** 79-44-04 W
Pop: 2,437 (1990); 2,297 (1980)   **Pop Density:** 1353.9
Land: 1.8 sq. mi.; **Water:** 0.0 sq. mi.

Lower Tyrone
Township
Lat: 40-04-26 N **Long:** 79-39-52 W
Pop: 1,138 (1990)   **Pop Density:** 72.0
Land: 15.8 sq. mi.; **Water:** 0.3 sq. mi.

Luzerne
Township
Lat: 39-58-26 N **Long:** 79-56-08 W
Pop: 4,904 (1990)   **Pop Density:** 165.7
Land: 29.6 sq. mi.; **Water:** 1.2 sq. mi.

Lynnwood-Pricedale
CDP
Lat: 40-07-28 N **Long:** 79-51-08 W
Pop: 1,066 (1990); 1,178 (1980)   **Pop Density:** 2132.0
Land: 0.5 sq. mi.; **Water:** 0.0 sq. mi.
Part of the town is also in Westmoreland County.

Markleysburg
Borough
ZIP: 15459   **Lat:** 39-44-13 N **Long:** 79-27-10 W
Pop: 320 (1990); 356 (1980)   **Pop Density:** 1066.7
Land: 0.3 sq. mi.; **Water:** 0.0 sq. mi.   **Elev:** 1985 ft.

Masontown
Borough
ZIP: 15461   **Lat:** 39-50-53 N **Long:** 79-54-31 W
Pop: 3,759 (1990); 4,909 (1980)   **Pop Density:** 2506.0
Land: 1.5 sq. mi.; **Water:** 0.0 sq. mi.   **Elev:** 1020 ft.

Menallen
Township
Lat: 39-56-29 N **Long:** 79-47-48 W
Pop: 4,739 (1990)   **Pop Density:** 222.5
Land: 21.3 sq. mi.; **Water:** 0.0 sq. mi.

Newell
Borough
ZIP: 15466   **Lat:** 40-04-24 N **Long:** 79-53-19 W
Pop: 518 (1990); 629 (1980)   **Pop Density:** 863.3
Land: 0.6 sq. mi.; **Water:** 0.1 sq. mi.   **Elev:** 760 ft.
Incorporated 1952 from Jefferson Township.

Nicholson
Township
Lat: 39-48-35 N **Long:** 79-52-14 W
Pop: 1,995 (1990)   **Pop Density:** 91.1
Land: 21.9 sq. mi.; **Water:** 0.2 sq. mi.

North Union
Township
ZIP: 15401   **Lat:** 39-54-33 N **Long:** 79-40-23 W
Pop: 13,910 (1990)   **Pop Density:** 359.4
Land: 38.7 sq. mi.; **Water:** 0.0 sq. mi.

Ohiopyle
Borough
ZIP: 15470   **Lat:** 39-52-03 N **Long:** 79-29-39 W
Pop: 81 (1990); 124 (1980)   **Pop Density:** 202.5
Land: 0.4 sq. mi.; **Water:** 0.1 sq. mi.
Name origin: A corruption of an Indian term probably mean-

ing 'water whitened by froth,' a reference to rapids in the Youghiogheny River.

Perry
Township
Lat: 40-04-51 N **Long:** 79-44-23 W
Pop: 2,817 (1990)   **Pop Density:** 143.0
Land: 19.7 sq. mi.; **Water:** 0.5 sq. mi.

Perryopolis
Borough
ZIP: 15473   **Lat:** 40-05-11 N **Long:** 79-45-11 W
Pop: 1,833 (1990); 2,139 (1980)   **Pop Density:** 1018.3
Land: 1.8 sq. mi.; **Water:** 0.0 sq. mi.   **Elev:** 900 ft.
In southwestern PA. Laid out in 1814.
Name origin: For Oliver Hazard Perry (1785–1819), American naval hero.

Point Marion
Borough
ZIP: 15474   **Lat:** 39-44-04 N **Long:** 79-54-02 W
Pop: 1,344 (1990); 1,642 (1980)   **Pop Density:** 3360.0
Land: 0.4 sq. mi.; **Water:** 0.0 sq. mi.   **Elev:** 817 ft.
In southwestern PA at the confluence of the Cheat and Monongahela rivers, 20 mi. southwest of Uniontown. Laid out in 1842.
Name origin: For Gen. Francis Marion (1732?–95), the "Swamp Fox," hero of the Revolutionary War.

Redstone
Township
ZIP: 15442   **Lat:** 39-58-40 N **Long:** 79-50-45 W
Pop: 6,459 (1990)   **Pop Density:** 285.8
Land: 22.6 sq. mi.; **Water:** 0.1 sq. mi.   **Elev:** 899 ft.

Saltlick
Township
Lat: 40-02-55 N **Long:** 79-23-38 W
Pop: 3,253 (1990)   **Pop Density:** 86.3
Land: 37.7 sq. mi.; **Water:** 0.0 sq. mi.

Smithfield
Borough
ZIP: 15478   **Lat:** 39-48-07 N **Long:** 79-48-34 W
Pop: 1,000 (1990); 1,084 (1980)   **Pop Density:** 1428.6
Land: 0.7 sq. mi.; **Water:** 0.0 sq. mi.   **Elev:** 1089 ft.
Laid out in 1799; incorporated 1916.

South Connellsville
Borough
ZIP: 15425   **Lat:** 39-59-33 N **Long:** 79-34-56 W
Pop: 2,204 (1990); 2,296 (1980)   **Pop Density:** 1296.5
Land: 1.7 sq. mi.; **Water:** 0.1 sq. mi.   **Elev:** 1034 ft.

South Union
Township
ZIP: 15401   **Lat:** 39-52-11 N **Long:** 79-43-30 W
Pop: 10,223 (1990)   **Pop Density:** 612.2
Land: 16.7 sq. mi.; **Water:** 0.0 sq. mi.

Springfield
Township
Lat: 39-58-26 N **Long:** 79-26-38 W
Pop: 2,968 (1990)   **Pop Density:** 49.6
Land: 59.8 sq. mi.; **Water:** 0.2 sq. mi.

Springhill
Township
Lat: 39-45-13 N **Long:** 79-50-26 W
Pop: 2,800 (1990)   **Pop Density:** 83.6
Land: 33.5 sq. mi.; **Water:** 0.6 sq. mi.

Stewart
Township
Lat: 39-52-33 N **Long:** 79-28-52 W
Pop: 734 (1990)   **Pop Density:** 14.5
Land: 50.6 sq. mi.; **Water:** 0.5 sq. mi.

Uniontown
City
ZIP: 15401   **Lat:** 39-53-56 N **Long:** 79-43-28 W
Pop: 12,034 (1990)   **Pop Density:** 6017.0
Land: 2.0 sq. mi.; **Water:** 0.0 sq. mi.   **Elev:** 1150 ft.
In southwestern PA, 45 mi. southeast of Pittsburgh. Laid out in 1776, incorporated as borough Apr 4, 1796, as city Dec 19, 1913.

Upper Tyrone
Township
Lat: 40-04-42 N **Long:** 79-35-40 W
Pop: 1,995 (1990)   **Pop Density:** 259.1
Land: 7.7 sq. mi.; **Water:** 0.0 sq. mi.

Vanderbilt
Borough
ZIP: 15486   **Lat:** 40-01-59 N **Long:** 79-39-46 W
Pop: 545 (1990); 689 (1980)   **Pop Density:** 2725.0
Land: 0.2 sq. mi.; **Water:** 0.0 sq. mi.   **Elev:** 840 ft.

Washington
Township
Lat: 40-06-21 N **Long:** 79-49-04 W
Pop: 4,613 (1990)   **Pop Density:** 480.5
Land: 9.6 sq. mi.; **Water:** 0.2 sq. mi.
Name origin: For George Washington (1732–99), first U.S. president.

Wharton
Township
Lat: 39-47-29 N **Long:** 79-36-30 W
Pop: 3,390 (1990)   **Pop Density:** 36.9
Land: 91.9 sq. mi.; **Water:** 0.2 sq. mi.

Forest County
County Seat: Tionesta (ZIP: 16353)

Pop: 4,802 (1990); 5,072 (1980)   **Pop Density:** 11.2
Land: 428.1 sq. mi.; **Water:** 3.3 sq. mi.   **Area Code:** 814
In north-western PA, east of Oil City; organized Apr 11, 1848 from Jefferson County.
Name origin: Named by Cyrus Blood (1795– ?), pioneer settler, because the county was virgin forestland.

Barnett
Township
Lat: 41-22-57 N **Long:** 79-09-11 W
Pop: 400 (1990)   **Pop Density:** 11.7
Land: 34.3 sq. mi.; **Water:** 0.0 sq. mi.

Green
Township
Lat: 41-28-35 N **Long:** 79-19-33 W
Pop: 335 (1990)   **Pop Density:** 7.9
Land: 42.2 sq. mi.; **Water:** 0.3 sq. mi.

Harmony
Township
Lat: 41-34-32 N **Long:** 79-27-43 W
Pop: 499 (1990)   **Pop Density:** 14.6
Land: 34.1 sq. mi.; **Water:** 0.5 sq. mi.

Hickory
Township
Lat: 41-35-11 N **Long:** 79-20-59 W
Pop: 513 (1990)   **Pop Density:** 13.7
Land: 37.5 sq. mi.; **Water:** 0.4 sq. mi.

Howe
Township
Lat: 41-34-47 N **Long:** 79-04-38 W
Pop: 300 (1990)   **Pop Density:** 3.4
Land: 87.8 sq. mi.; **Water:** 0.0 sq. mi.

Jenks
Township
Lat: 41-28-13 N **Long:** 79-06-04 W
Pop: 1,321 (1990)   **Pop Density:** 15.6
Land: 84.5 sq. mi.; **Water:** 0.2 sq. mi.

Kingsley
Township
Lat: 41-32-16 N **Long:** 79-16-14 W
Pop: 218 (1990)   **Pop Density:** 3.6
Land: 61.4 sq. mi.; **Water:** 0.5 sq. mi.

Tionesta
Borough
ZIP: 16353   **Lat:** 41-29-45 N **Long:** 79-26-48 W
Pop: 634 (1990); 659 (1980)   **Pop Density:** 487.7
Land: 1.3 sq. mi.; **Water:** 0.0 sq. mi.   **Elev:** 1084 ft.
Incorporated Feb 28, 1856.

*Tionesta
Township
ZIP: 16353   **Lat:** 41-27-29 N **Long:** 79-27-06 W
Pop: 582 (1990)   **Pop Density:** 13.0
Land: 44.9 sq. mi.; **Water:** 1.5 sq. mi.

Franklin County
County Seat: Chambersburg (ZIP: 17201)

Pop: 121,082 (1990); 113,629 (1980)   **Pop Density:** 156.8
Land: 772.0 sq. mi.; **Water:** 0.7 sq. mi.   **Area Code:** 717
On central southern border of PA, southwest of Harrisburg; organized Sep 9, 1784 from Cumberland County.
Name origin: For Benjamin Franklin (1706–90), U.S. patriot, diplomat, and statesman.

Antrim
Township
ZIP: 17225   **Lat:** 39-46-53 N **Long:** 77-43-03 W
Pop: 10,107 (1990)   **Pop Density:** 144.2
Land: 70.1 sq. mi.; **Water:** 0.1 sq. mi.

Chambersburg
Borough
ZIP: 17201   **Lat:** 39-55-56 N **Long:** 77-39-23 W
Pop: 16,647 (1990); 16,174 (1980)   **Pop Density:** 2412.6
Land: 6.9 sq. mi.; **Water:** 0.0 sq. mi.   **Elev:** 621 ft.
In southern PA, 50 mi. southwest of Harrisburg. Laid out 1764; incorporated Mar 21, 1803.
Name origin: For Benjamin Chambers, miller, sawyer, trader, physician, militia colonel, judge, and arbitrator, who settled this tract.

Fannett
Township
ZIP: 17219   **Lat:** 40-11-46 N **Long:** 77-42-27 W
Pop: 2,309 (1990)   **Pop Density:** 33.8
Land: 68.4 sq. mi.; **Water:** 0.0 sq. mi.

Fayetteville
CDP
ZIP: 17222   **Lat:** 39-54-44 N **Long:** 77-33-56 W
Pop: 3,033 (1990); 1,565 (1980)   **Pop Density:** 919.1
Land: 3.3 sq. mi.; **Water:** 0.0 sq. mi.

Greencastle
Borough
ZIP: 17225   **Lat:** 39-47-25 N **Long:** 77-43-36 W
Pop: 3,600 (1990); 3,679 (1980)   **Pop Density:** 2250.0
Land: 1.6 sq. mi.; **Water:** 0.0 sq. mi.   **Elev:** 595 ft.
In southern PA, south of Chambersburg. Laid out in 1782.
Name origin: Named by Col. John Allison for his native town, a tiny seaport in County Donegal, Ireland.

Greene
Township
ZIP: 17201   **Lat:** 39-57-09 N **Long:** 77-33-51 W
Pop: 11,930 (1990)   **Pop Density:** 210.4
Land: 56.7 sq. mi.; **Water:** 0.0 sq. mi.

Guilford
Township
ZIP: 17201   **Lat:** 39-53-05 N **Long:** 77-35-50 W
Pop: 11,893 (1990)   **Pop Density:** 226.5
Land: 52.5 sq. mi.; **Water:** 0.0 sq. mi.

Hamilton
Township
ZIP: 17201   **Lat:** 39-56-38 N **Long:** 77-43-48 W
Pop: 7,745 (1990)   **Pop Density:** 216.3
Land: 35.8 sq. mi.; **Water:** 0.0 sq. mi.
Name origin: Named in 1752 for James Hamilton, then colonial governor of PA.

Letterkenny
Township
ZIP: 17246   **Lat:** 40-02-33 N **Long:** 77-43-27 W
Pop: 2,251 (1990)   **Pop Density:** 32.0
Land: 70.3 sq. mi.; **Water:** 0.1 sq. mi.

Lurgan
Township
ZIP: 17232   **Lat:** 40-06-54 N **Long:** 77-37-52 W
Pop: 2,026 (1990)   **Pop Density:** 61.8
Land: 32.8 sq. mi.; **Water:** 0.1 sq. mi.

Mercersburg
Borough
ZIP: 17236   **Lat:** 39-49-52 N **Long:** 77-54-06 W
Pop: 1,640 (1990); 1,617 (1980)   **Pop Density:** 1640.0
Land: 1.0 sq. mi.; **Water:** 0.0 sq. mi.   **Elev:** 540 ft.

Metal
Township
ZIP: 17224   **Lat:** 40-02-37 N **Long:** 77-50-52 W
Pop: 1,612 (1990)   **Pop Density:** 36.2
Land: 44.5 sq. mi.; **Water:** 0.1 sq. mi.

Mont Alto
Borough
ZIP: 17237   **Lat:** 39-50-22 N **Long:** 77-33-16 W
Pop: 1,395 (1990); 1,592 (1980)   **Pop Density:** 2325.0
Land: 0.6 sq. mi.; **Water:** 0.0 sq. mi.   **Elev:** 848 ft.

Montgomery
Township
ZIP: 17236   **Lat:** 39-46-15 N **Long:** 77-53-39 W
Pop: 4,558 (1990)   **Pop Density:** 67.9
Land: 67.1 sq. mi.; **Water:** 0.0 sq. mi.

Orrstown
Borough
ZIP: 17244   **Lat:** 40-03-29 N **Long:** 77-36-34 W
Pop: 220 (1990); 247 (1980)   **Pop Density:** 2200.0
Land: 0.1 sq. mi.; **Water:** 0.0 sq. mi.   **Elev:** 685 ft.

Peters
Township
ZIP: 17236   **Lat:** 39-52-38 N **Long:** 77-53-17 W
Pop: 4,090 (1990)   **Pop Density:** 73.2
Land: 55.9 sq. mi.; **Water:** 0.1 sq. mi.

Quincy
Township
ZIP: 17247   **Lat:** 39-48-42 N **Long:** 77-33-21 W
Pop: 5,704 (1990)   **Pop Density:** 127.6
Land: 44.7 sq. mi.; **Water:** 0.0 sq. mi.

St. Thomas
Township
ZIP: 17201   **Lat:** 39-55-17 N **Long:** 77-48-18 W
Pop: 5,861 (1990)   **Pop Density:** 113.4
Land: 51.7 sq. mi.; **Water:** 0.0 sq. mi.

Shippensburg
Borough
ZIP: 17257   **Lat:** 40-02-39 N **Long:** 77-32-20 W
Pop: 1,003 (1990); 885 (1980)   **Pop Density:** 1432.9
Land: 0.7 sq. mi.; **Water:** 0.0 sq. mi.   **Elev:** 660 ft.
In southern PA, 10 mi. north of Chambersburg. Founded in 1730. Second oldest town in PA. Part of the town is also in Cumberland County.
Name origin: For Edward Shippen, elected mayor of Philadelphia in 1744.

Southampton
Township
ZIP: 17244   **Lat:** 40-01-47 N **Long:** 77-33-04 W
Pop: 5,484 (1990)   **Pop Density:** 144.3
Land: 38.0 sq. mi.; **Water:** 0.0 sq. mi.

Warren
Township
Lat: 39-45-12 N Long: 78-01-30 W
Pop: 310 (1990)   **Pop Density:** 10.2
Land: 30.5 sq. mi.; **Water:** 0.0 sq. mi.

Washington
Township
ZIP: 17268   Lat: 39-45-00 N Long: 77-33-30 W
Pop: 11,119 (1990)   **Pop Density:** 285.8
Land: 38.9 sq. mi.; **Water:** 0.0 sq. mi.
Name origin: For George Washington (1732–99), first U.S. president.

Waynesboro
Borough
ZIP: 17268   Lat: 39-45-07 N Long: 77-34-56 W
Pop: 9,578 (1990); 9,726 (1980)   **Pop Density:** 2817.1
Land: 3.4 sq. mi.; **Water:** 0.0 sq. mi.   **Elev:** 713 ft.

In southern PA set in a natural hollow, 10 mi northeast of Hagerstown, MD. Laid out in 1797; incorporated as town of Waynesborough in 1818.
Name origin: Named by James Wallace, Jr., town founder, who had served under Gen. "Mad" Anthony Wayne (1745–96). Originally called Wallacetown. Spelling altered to reflect pronunciation.

Fulton County
County Seat: McConnellsburg (ZIP: 17233)

Pop: 13,837 (1990); 12,842 (1980)   **Pop Density:** 31.6
Land: 437.6 sq. mi.; **Water:** 0.5 sq. mi.   **Area Code:** 717

On central southern border of PA, southeast of Altoona; organized Apr 19, 1851 from Bedford County.
Name origin: For Robert Fulton (1765–1815), developer of the *Clermont*, the first commercially successful steamboat.

Ayr
Township
ZIP: 17212   Lat: 39-51-57 N Long: 78-01-45 W
Pop: 2,167 (1990)   **Pop Density:** 46.9
Land: 46.2 sq. mi.; **Water:** 0.3 sq. mi.

Belfast
Township
ZIP: 17238   Lat: 39-52-53 N Long: 78-08-26 W
Pop: 1,208 (1990)   **Pop Density:** 24.1
Land: 50.2 sq. mi.; **Water:** 0.0 sq. mi.

Bethel
Township
ZIP: 17267   Lat: 39-46-35 N Long: 78-13-02 W
Pop: 1,317 (1990)   **Pop Density:** 35.5
Land: 37.1 sq. mi.; **Water:** 0.0 sq. mi.

Brush Creek
Township
Lat: 39-55-50 N Long: 78-13-06 W
Pop: 643 (1990)   **Pop Density:** 11.8
Land: 54.3 sq. mi.; **Water:** 0.0 sq. mi.

Dublin
Township
ZIP: 17223   Lat: 40-03-40 N Long: 77-57-21 W
Pop: 1,146 (1990)   **Pop Density:** 31.1
Land: 36.9 sq. mi.; **Water:** 0.0 sq. mi.

Licking Creek
Township
ZIP: 17228   Lat: 39-58-31 N Long: 78-05-15 W
Pop: 1,410 (1990)   **Pop Density:** 31.5
Land: 44.7 sq. mi.; **Water:** 0.0 sq. mi.

McConnellsburg
Borough
ZIP: 17233   Lat: 39-55-53 N Long: 77-59-43 W
Pop: 1,106 (1990); 1,178 (1980)   **Pop Density:** 2765.0
Land: 0.4 sq. mi.; **Water:** 0.0 sq. mi.   **Elev:** 890 ft.
Laid out in 1786; incorporated Mar 26, 1814.

Taylor
Township
Lat: 40-04-43 N Long: 78-03-14 W
Pop: 1,172 (1990)   **Pop Density:** 36.0
Land: 32.6 sq. mi.; **Water:** 0.0 sq. mi.

Thompson
Township
Lat: 39-46-01 N Long: 78-06-24 W
Pop: 1,048 (1990)   **Pop Density:** 27.7
Land: 37.9 sq. mi.; **Water:** 0.0 sq. mi.

Todd
Township
Lat: 39-58-42 N Long: 77-58-16 W
Pop: 1,434 (1990)   **Pop Density:** 49.6
Land: 28.9 sq. mi.; **Water:** 0.1 sq. mi.

Union
Township
Lat: 39-46-04 N Long: 78-17-41 W
Pop: 623 (1990)   **Pop Density:** 20.4
Land: 30.5 sq. mi.; **Water:** 0.0 sq. mi.

Valley-Hi
Borough
ZIP: 15533   Lat: 40-01-37 N Long: 78-11-26 W
Pop: 19 (1990)   **Pop Density:** 38.0
Land: 0.5 sq. mi.; **Water:** 0.1 sq. mi.   **Elev:** 1340 ft.

Wells
Township
Lat: 40-05-10 N Long: 78-08-09 W
Pop: 544 (1990)   **Pop Density:** 14.5
Land: 37.4 sq. mi.; **Water:** 0.0 sq. mi.

Greene County
County Seat: Waynesburg (ZIP: 15370)

Pop: 39,550 (1990); 40,476 (1980)   **Pop Density:** 68.7
Land: 575.9 sq. mi.; **Water:** 2.1 sq. mi.   **Area Code:** 412

At southwestern corner of PA, south of Pittsburgh; organized Feb 9, 1796 from Washington County.

Name origin: For Gen. Nathanael Greene (1742–86), hero of the Revolutionary War; quartermaster general (1778–80).

Aleppo
Township
ZIP: 15310   **Lat:** 39-49-35 N **Long:** 80-27-25 W
Pop: 656 (1990)   **Pop Density:** 24.0
Land: 27.3 sq. mi.; **Water:** 0.0 sq. mi.

Carmichaels
Borough
ZIP: 15320   **Lat:** 39-53-51 N **Long:** 79-58-30 W
Pop: 532 (1990); 630 (1980)   **Pop Density:** 2660.0
Land: 0.2 sq. mi.; **Water:** 0.0 sq. mi.   **Elev:** 1000 ft.

Center
Township
Lat: 39-52-50 N **Long:** 80-17-36 W
Pop: 1,460 (1990)   **Pop Density:** 30.0
Land: 48.6 sq. mi.; **Water:** 0.0 sq. mi.

Clarksville
Borough
ZIP: 15322   **Lat:** 39-58-28 N **Long:** 80-02-39 W
Pop: 211 (1990); 251 (1980)   **Pop Density:** 2110.0
Land: 0.1 sq. mi.; **Water:** 0.0 sq. mi.   **Elev:** 800 ft.

Cumberland
Township
ZIP: 15320   **Lat:** 39-53-39 N **Long:** 79-59-27 W
Pop: 6,742 (1990)   **Pop Density:** 176.0
Land: 38.3 sq. mi.; **Water:** 0.7 sq. mi.

Dunkard
Township
Lat: 39-45-29 N **Long:** 79-59-43 W
Pop: 2,386 (1990)   **Pop Density:** 75.3
Land: 31.7 sq. mi.; **Water:** 0.3 sq. mi.

Name origin: For a large colony of Dunkards, German Baptists.

Fairdale
CDP
ZIP: 15320   **Lat:** 39-53-18 N **Long:** 79-58-08 W
Pop: 2,049 (1990); 2,046 (1980)   **Pop Density:** 1463.6
Land: 1.4 sq. mi.; **Water:** 0.0 sq. mi.

Franklin
Township
ZIP: 15370   **Lat:** 39-53-03 N **Long:** 80-10-35 W
Pop: 5,562 (1990)   **Pop Density:** 136.0
Land: 40.9 sq. mi.; **Water:** 0.0 sq. mi.

Freeport
Township
Lat: 39-44-55 N **Long:** 80-25-07 W
Pop: 327 (1990)   **Pop Density:** 37.6
Land: 8.7 sq. mi.; **Water:** 0.0 sq. mi.

Gilmore
Township
Lat: 39-44-34 N **Long:** 80-20-37 W
Pop: 365 (1990)   **Pop Density:** 16.8
Land: 21.7 sq. mi.; **Water:** 0.0 sq. mi.

Gray
Township
Lat: 39-55-47 N **Long:** 80-23-04 W
Pop: 220 (1990)   **Pop Density:** 66.7
Land: 3.3 sq. mi.; **Water:** 0.0 sq. mi.

Greene
Township
Lat: 39-49-21 N **Long:** 80-01-34 W
Pop: 494 (1990)   **Pop Density:** 26.6
Land: 18.6 sq. mi.; **Water:** 0.0 sq. mi.

Name origin: For Gen. Nathanael Greene (1742–86), hero of the American Revolution.

Greensboro
Borough
ZIP: 15338   **Lat:** 39-47-31 N **Long:** 79-54-46 W
Pop: 307 (1990); 377 (1980)   **Pop Density:** 3070.0
Land: 0.1 sq. mi.; **Water:** 0.0 sq. mi.   **Elev:** 860 ft.

Name origin: For Gen. Nathanael Greene (1742–86), hero of the American Revolution.

Jackson
Township
Lat: 39-49-24 N **Long:** 80-21-21 W
Pop: 546 (1990)   **Pop Density:** 18.6
Land: 29.4 sq. mi.; **Water:** 0.0 sq. mi.

Jefferson
Township
ZIP: 15344   **Lat:** 39-55-40 N **Long:** 80-03-09 W
Pop: 2,536 (1990)   **Pop Density:** 117.4
Land: 21.6 sq. mi.; **Water:** 0.1 sq. mi.

*Jefferson
Borough
ZIP: 15344   **Lat:** 39-55-48 N **Long:** 80-03-28 W
Pop: 355 (1990); 413 (1980)   **Pop Density:** 1775.0
Land: 0.2 sq. mi.; **Water:** 0.0 sq. mi.   **Elev:** 960 ft.

In southwestern PA, a southeastern suburb of Pittsburgh. Incorporated 1950.

Name origin: For Thomas Jefferson (1743–1826), third U.S. president.

Monongahela
Township
Lat: 39-48-56 N **Long:** 79-57-09 W
Pop: 1,858 (1990)   **Pop Density:** 107.4
Land: 17.3 sq. mi.; **Water:** 0.6 sq. mi.

Morgan
Township
Lat: 39-57-42 N **Long:** 80-05-21 W
Pop: 2,887 (1990)   **Pop Density:** 117.8
Land: 24.5 sq. mi.; **Water:** 0.0 sq. mi.

Morris
Township
Lat: 39-58-00 N **Long:** 80-18-14 W
Pop: 898 (1990)   **Pop Density:** 25.1
Land: 35.8 sq. mi.; **Water:** 0.0 sq. mi.

Morrisville
CDP
Lat: 39-54-06 N **Long:** 80-10-00 W
Pop: 1,365 (1990); 1,518 (1980)   **Pop Density:** 910.0
Land: 1.5 sq. mi.; **Water:** 0.0 sq. mi.

Nemacolin
CDP
Lat: 39-52-39 N **Long:** 79-55-26 W
Pop: 1,097 (1990); 1,235 (1980)   **Pop Density:** 997.3
Land: 1.1 sq. mi.; **Water:** 0.1 sq. mi.

Perry
Township
Lat: 39-45-02 N **Long:** 80-06-45 W
Pop: 1,719 (1990) **Pop Density:** 56.7
Land: 30.3 sq. mi.; **Water:** 0.0 sq. mi.

Rices Landing
Borough
ZIP: 15357 **Lat:** 39-56-45 N **Long:** 79-59-41 W
Pop: 457 (1990); 516 (1980) **Pop Density:** 571.3
Land: 0.8 sq. mi.; **Water:** 0.1 sq. mi. **Elev:** 971 ft.

Richhill
Township
Lat: 39-54-34 N **Long:** 80-26-33 W
Pop: 1,102 (1990) **Pop Density:** 19.7
Land: 56.0 sq. mi.; **Water:** 0.1 sq. mi.

Springhill
Township
Lat: 39-45-21 N **Long:** 80-28-24 W
Pop: 506 (1990) **Pop Density:** 22.9
Land: 22.1 sq. mi.; **Water:** 0.0 sq. mi.

Washington
Township
Lat: 39-58-01 N **Long:** 80-11-48 W
Pop: 1,071 (1990) **Pop Density:** 39.7
Land: 27.0 sq. mi.; **Water:** 0.0 sq. mi.

Wayne
Township
Lat: 39-45-51 N **Long:** 80-14-28 W
Pop: 1,317 (1990) **Pop Density:** 33.3
Land: 39.5 sq. mi.; **Water:** 0.0 sq. mi.

Waynesburg
Borough
ZIP: 15370 **Lat:** 39-53-55 N **Long:** 80-11-08 W
Pop: 4,270 (1990); 4,482 (1980) **Pop Density:** 5337.5
Land: 0.8 sq. mi.; **Water:** 0.0 sq. mi. **Elev:** 1034 ft.
In southwestern PA, 50 mi. south of Pittsburgh. Laid out in 1796; incorporated Jan 29, 1816.
Name origin: For Gen. Anthony Wayne (1745–96), whose victory over the Indians at Fallen Timbers allowed for extensive settlement of western PA in the early 1800s.

Whiteley
Township
Lat: 39-49-06 N **Long:** 80-08-03 W
Pop: 766 (1990) **Pop Density:** 24.6
Land: 31.2 sq. mi.; **Water:** 0.0 sq. mi.

Huntingdon County
County Seat: Huntingdon (ZIP: 16652)

Pop: 44,164 (1990); 42,253 (1980) **Pop Density:** 50.5
Land: 875.4 sq. mi.; **Water:** 14.9 sq. mi. **Area Code:** 814
In south-central PA, east of Altoona; organized Sep 20, 1787 from Bedford County.
Name origin: For the county seat.

Alexandria
Borough
ZIP: 16611 **Lat:** 40-33-31 N **Long:** 78-06-00 W
Pop: 411 (1990); 435 (1980) **Pop Density:** 4110.0
Land: 0.1 sq. mi.; **Water:** 0.0 sq. mi. **Elev:** 720 ft.
In south-central PA on the Frankstown branch of the Juniata River in the Appalachian Mountains, near Huntington.

Barree
Township
Lat: 40-38-58 N **Long:** 77-55-17 W
Pop: 450 (1990) **Pop Density:** 18.8
Land: 23.9 sq. mi.; **Water:** 0.1 sq. mi.

Birmingham
Borough
ZIP: 16686 **Lat:** 40-38-49 N **Long:** 78-11-43 W
Pop: 109 (1990); 121 (1980) **Pop Density:** 1090.0
Land: 0.1 sq. mi.; **Water:** 0.0 sq. mi. **Elev:** 950 ft.
Laid out 1797 by John Cadwallader.
Name origin: For Birmingham, England, in the hopes that it would become as successful an industrial center as that city.

Brady
Township
Lat: 40-27-45 N **Long:** 77-53-13 W
Pop: 1,053 (1990) **Pop Density:** 32.3
Land: 32.6 sq. mi.; **Water:** 0.1 sq. mi.

Broad Top City
Borough
ZIP: 16621 **Lat:** 40-12-05 N **Long:** 78-08-26 W
Pop: 331 (1990); 340 (1980) **Pop Density:** 551.7
Land: 0.6 sq. mi.; **Water:** 0.0 sq. mi. **Elev:** 1989 ft.

Carbon
Township
Lat: 40-13-17 N **Long:** 78-09-59 W
Pop: 438 (1990) **Pop Density:** 23.5
Land: 18.6 sq. mi.; **Water:** 0.0 sq. mi.

Cass
Township
Lat: 40-17-19 N **Long:** 78-01-37 W
Pop: 998 (1990) **Pop Density:** 30.5
Land: 32.7 sq. mi.; **Water:** 0.0 sq. mi.
Name origin: Named in 1843 for Lewis Cass (1782–1866), U.S. minister to France.

Cassville
Borough
ZIP: 16623 **Lat:** 40-17-37 N **Long:** 78-01-39 W
Pop: 183 (1990); 183 (1980) **Pop Density:** 457.5
Land: 0.4 sq. mi.; **Water:** 0.0 sq. mi. **Elev:** 1241 ft.
Name origin: Named in 1843 for Cass Township, which was named for statesman Lewis Cass (1782–1866), U.S. minister to France.

Clay
Township
Lat: 40-10-53 N **Long:** 78-01-17 W
Pop: 921 (1990) **Pop Density:** 32.3
Land: 28.5 sq. mi.; **Water:** 0.0 sq. mi.

Coalmont
Borough
ZIP: 16678 **Lat:** 40-12-39 N **Long:** 78-12-02 W
Pop: 109 (1990); 128 (1980) **Pop Density:** 1090.0
Land: 0.1 sq. mi.; **Water:** 0.0 sq. mi.

Cromwell
Township
Lat: 40-14-35 N **Long:** 77-55-00 W
Pop: 1,500 (1990) **Pop Density:** 29.5
Land: 50.9 sq. mi.; **Water:** 0.0 sq. mi.

Dublin
Township
ZIP: 17239 **Lat:** 40-08-14 N **Long:** 77-51-30 W
Pop: 1,119 (1990) **Pop Density:** 30.5
Land: 36.7 sq. mi.; **Water:** 0.0 sq. mi.

Dudley
Borough
ZIP: 16634   **Lat:** 40-12-05 N **Long:** 78-10-35 W
Pop: 232 (1990); 282 (1980)   **Pop Density:** 580.0
Land: 0.4 sq. mi.; **Water:** 0.0 sq. mi.   **Elev:** 1540 ft.

Franklin
Township
Lat: 40-40-29 N **Long:** 78-03-02 W
Pop: 466 (1990)   **Pop Density:** 14.7
Land: 31.7 sq. mi.; **Water:** 0.0 sq. mi.

Henderson
Township
Lat: 40-29-44 N **Long:** 77-56-06 W
Pop: 933 (1990)   **Pop Density:** 36.0
Land: 25.9 sq. mi.; **Water:** 0.1 sq. mi.

Hopewell
Township
Lat: 40-16-53 N **Long:** 78-13-07 W
Pop: 540 (1990)   **Pop Density:** 35.8
Land: 15.1 sq. mi.; **Water:** 1.4 sq. mi.

Huntingdon
Borough
ZIP: 16652   **Lat:** 40-29-47 N **Long:** 78-00-37 W
Pop: 6,843 (1990); 7,042 (1980)   **Pop Density:** 1955.1
Land: 3.5 sq. mi.; **Water:** 0.1 sq. mi.   **Elev:** 643 ft.
In south-central PA, 35 mi. east of Altoona. Laid out in 1767 by Dr. William Smith; incorporated Mar 29, 1796.

Name origin: Named in 1767 by Dr. William Smith (1727–1803), provost of the University of PA, for Selina Hastings, Countess of Huntingdon (1707–91), famed for her religious zeal and a leader of a Calvinist sect within the Methodist Church, who had responded liberally to Smith's appeal for funds to aid the university. Dr. Smith owned the land where the town was laid out. Previously called Standing Stone.

Jackson
Township
Lat: 40-40-11 N **Long:** 77-48-00 W
Pop: 816 (1990)   **Pop Density:** 11.3
Land: 72.5 sq. mi.; **Water:** 0.0 sq. mi.

Juniata
Township
Lat: 40-25-34 N **Long:** 78-01-52 W
Pop: 429 (1990)   **Pop Density:** 26.0
Land: 16.5 sq. mi.; **Water:** 3.6 sq. mi.

Lincoln
Township
Lat: 40-20-03 N **Long:** 78-11-12 W
Pop: 320 (1990)   **Pop Density:** 16.9
Land: 18.9 sq. mi.; **Water:** 2.2 sq. mi.

Name origin: For Abraham Lincoln (1809–65), sixteenth U.S. president.

Logan
Township
Lat: 40-35-15 N **Long:** 78-02-22 W
Pop: 684 (1990)   **Pop Density:** 30.1
Land: 22.7 sq. mi.; **Water:** 0.1 sq. mi.

Mapleton
Borough
Lat: 40-23-34 N **Long:** 77-56-22 W
Pop: 529 (1990); 591 (1980)   **Pop Density:** 2645.0
Land: 0.2 sq. mi.; **Water:** 0.0 sq. mi.   **Elev:** 600 ft.

Marklesburg
Borough
ZIP: 16657   **Lat:** 40-23-02 N **Long:** 78-10-09 W
Pop: 165 (1990); 188 (1980)   **Pop Density:** 183.3
Land: 0.9 sq. mi.; **Water:** 0.0 sq. mi.   **Elev:** 888 ft.

Mill Creek
Borough
ZIP: 17060   **Lat:** 40-26-14 N **Long:** 77-55-45 W
Pop: 392 (1990); 367 (1980)   **Pop Density:** 980.0
Land: 0.4 sq. mi.; **Water:** 0.0 sq. mi.   **Elev:** 627 ft.

Miller
Township
Lat: 40-34-10 N **Long:** 77-52-18 W
Pop: 474 (1990)   **Pop Density:** 21.2
Land: 22.4 sq. mi.; **Water:** 0.0 sq. mi.

Morris
Township
Lat: 40-34-08 N **Long:** 78-10-03 W
Pop: 415 (1990)   **Pop Density:** 34.3
Land: 12.1 sq. mi.; **Water:** 0.0 sq. mi.

Mount Union
Borough
ZIP: 17066   **Lat:** 40-23-05 N **Long:** 77-52-55 W
Pop: 2,878 (1990); 3,101 (1980)   **Pop Density:** 2616.4
Land: 1.1 sq. mi.; **Water:** 0.0 sq. mi.   **Elev:** 626 ft.

Oneida
Township
Lat: 40-32-33 N **Long:** 77-58-09 W
Pop: 1,085 (1990)   **Pop Density:** 61.6
Land: 17.6 sq. mi.; **Water:** 0.0 sq. mi.

Orbisonia
Borough
ZIP: 17243   **Lat:** 40-14-35 N **Long:** 77-53-37 W
Pop: 447 (1990); 506 (1980)   **Pop Density:** 4470.0
Land: 0.1 sq. mi.; **Water:** 0.0 sq. mi.   **Elev:** 880 ft.
Founded in 1760.

Name origin: For an early landowner, Thomas E. Orbison.

Penn
Township
Lat: 40-23-52 N **Long:** 78-06-16 W
Pop: 956 (1990)   **Pop Density:** 33.9
Land: 28.2 sq. mi.; **Water:** 6.0 sq. mi.

Petersburg
Borough
ZIP: 16669   **Lat:** 40-34-24 N **Long:** 78-02-58 W
Pop: 469 (1990); 543 (1980)   **Pop Density:** 1172.5
Land: 0.4 sq. mi.; **Water:** 0.0 sq. mi.   **Elev:** 680 ft.

Porter
Township
Lat: 40-32-11 N **Long:** 78-05-28 W
Pop: 1,942 (1990)   **Pop Density:** 54.9
Land: 35.4 sq. mi.; **Water:** 0.2 sq. mi.

Rockhill Furnace
Borough
ZIP: 17249   **Lat:** 40-14-31 N **Long:** 77-54-02 W
Pop: 421 (1990); 472 (1980)   **Pop Density:** 1403.3
Land: 0.3 sq. mi.; **Water:** 0.0 sq. mi.   **Elev:** 629 ft.

Saltillo
Borough
ZIP: 17253   **Lat:** 40-12-42 N **Long:** 78-00-28 W
Pop: 347 (1990); 373 (1980)   **Pop Density:** 1156.7
Land: 0.3 sq. mi.; **Water:** 0.0 sq. mi.   **Elev:** 786 ft.

Name origin: For Saltillo in northeastern Mexico.

Shade Gap
Borough
ZIP: 17255   **Lat:** 40-10-48 N **Long:** 77-51-56 W
Pop: 113 (1990); 141 (1980)
Land: 0.0 sq. mi.; **Water:** 0.0 sq. mi.   **Elev:** 990 ft.

Shirley
Township
ZIP: 17066   **Lat:** 40-20-04 N **Long:** 77-51-27 W
Pop: 2,494 (1990)   **Pop Density:** 42.9
Land: 58.2 sq. mi.; **Water:** 0.4 sq. mi.

Shirleysburg
Borough
ZIP: 17260   **Lat:** 40-17-48 N **Long:** 77-52-38 W
Pop: 140 (1990); 147 (1980)   **Pop Density:** 700.0
Land: 0.2 sq. mi.; **Water:** 0.0 sq. mi.   **Elev:** 606 ft.
In south-central PA on Aughwick Creek, southeast of Altoona.

Name origin: For Fort Shirley, where, in 1754, Conrad Weiser, Indian interpreter and provincial agent, conferred with the Iroquoian representative, Tanacharison, and chiefs of the Shawnee and Delaware tribes.

Smithfield
Township
Lat: 40-28-51 N **Long:** 78-01-25 W
Pop: 4,181 (1990) **Pop Density:** 746.6
Land: 5.6 sq. mi.; **Water:** 0.1 sq. mi.

Springfield
Township
Lat: 40-09-15 N **Long:** 77-56-40 W
Pop: 507 (1990) **Pop Density:** 18.2
Land: 27.9 sq. mi.; **Water:** 0.0 sq. mi.

Spruce Creek
Township
ZIP: 16683 **Lat:** 40-36-44 N **Long:** 78-08-23 W
Pop: 281 (1990) **Pop Density:** 34.3
Land: 8.2 sq. mi.; **Water:** 0.1 sq. mi.

In south-central PA at the confluence of Spruce Creek and the Little Juniata River, northeast of Altoona. Settled prior to 1763.

Tell
Township
ZIP: 17213 **Lat:** 40-15-44 N **Long:** 77-46-03 W
Pop: 551 (1990) **Pop Density:** 12.9
Land: 42.6 sq. mi.; **Water:** 0.0 sq. mi.

Todd
Township
ZIP: 16685 **Lat:** 40-16-04 N **Long:** 78-06-19 W
Pop: 889 (1990) **Pop Density:** 19.8
Land: 44.8 sq. mi.; **Water:** 0.0 sq. mi.

Union
Township
Lat: 40-22-19 N **Long:** 77-59-37 W
Pop: 992 (1990) **Pop Density:** 25.3
Land: 39.2 sq. mi.; **Water:** 0.1 sq. mi.

Walker
Township
Lat: 40-27-47 N **Long:** 78-05-22 W
Pop: 1,515 (1990) **Pop Density:** 80.6
Land: 18.8 sq. mi.; **Water:** 0.0 sq. mi.

Warriors Mark
Township
ZIP: 16877 **Lat:** 40-41-42 N **Long:** 78-08-27 W
Pop: 1,375 (1990) **Pop Density:** 46.6
Land: 29.5 sq. mi.; **Water:** 0.0 sq. mi.

West
Township
Lat: 40-38-08 N **Long:** 77-59-31 W
Pop: 572 (1990) **Pop Density:** 18.5
Land: 31.0 sq. mi.; **Water:** 0.0 sq. mi.

Wood
Township
Lat: 40-10-53 N **Long:** 78-05-33 W
Pop: 727 (1990) **Pop Density:** 44.3
Land: 16.4 sq. mi.; **Water:** 0.0 sq. mi.

Indiana County
County Seat: Indiana (ZIP: 15701)

Pop: 89,994 (1990); 92,281 (1980) **Pop Density:** 108.5
Land: 829.5 sq. mi.; **Water:** 4.8 sq. mi. **Area Code:** 412

In central portion of western PA, northeast of Pittsburgh; organized Mar 30, 1803 from Westmoreland and Lycoming counties.

Name origin: For the Indiana Territory, which had been formed as part of the Northwest Territory in 1800.

Armagh
Borough
ZIP: 15920 **Lat:** 40-27-11 N **Long:** 79-01-59 W
Pop: 104 (1990); 133 (1980) **Pop Density:** 1040.0
Land: 0.1 sq. mi.; **Water:** 0.0 sq. mi. **Elev:** 1531 ft.

Armstrong
Township
Lat: 40-38-01 N **Long:** 79-16-46 W
Pop: 3,048 (1990) **Pop Density:** 80.8
Land: 37.7 sq. mi.; **Water:** 0.0 sq. mi.

Banks
Township
Lat: 40-51-51 N **Long:** 78-51-34 W
Pop: 995 (1990) **Pop Density:** 31.3
Land: 31.8 sq. mi.; **Water:** 0.0 sq. mi.

Black Lick
Township
Lat: 40-29-47 N **Long:** 79-15-20 W
Pop: 1,225 (1990) **Pop Density:** 45.0
Land: 27.2 sq. mi.; **Water:** 0.5 sq. mi.

In west-central PA on the Conemaugh River Reservoir, near Blainsville. Settled 1807; laid out 1860.

Name origin: For a nearby creek whose waters appeared coal-black; the creek once contained a salt lick.

Blairsville
Borough
ZIP: 15717 **Lat:** 40-25-53 N **Long:** 79-15-36 W
Pop: 3,595 (1990); 4,166 (1980) **Pop Density:** 2567.9
Land: 1.4 sq. mi.; **Water:** 0.0 sq. mi. **Elev:** 1015 ft.

In west-central PA on the Conemaugh River. Settled 1792.

Name origin: For the Hon. John Blair, who was among the first promoters of the turnpike and canal-portage system.

Brush Valley
Township
Lat: 40-32-04 N **Long:** 79-03-43 W
Pop: 1,811 (1990) **Pop Density:** 43.6
Land: 41.5 sq. mi.; **Water:** 1.0 sq. mi.

Buffington
Township
Lat: 40-30-40 N **Long:** 78-57-27 W
Pop: 1,217 (1990) **Pop Density:** 39.9
Land: 30.5 sq. mi.; **Water:** 0.2 sq. mi.

Burrell
Township
Lat: 40-27-08 N **Long:** 79-12-32 W
Pop: 3,669 (1990) **Pop Density:** 154.8
Land: 23.7 sq. mi.; **Water:** 0.8 sq. mi.

Name origin: For Jeremiah Murray Burrell, presiding judge of the judicial district.

Canoe
Township
Lat: 40-52-00 N **Long:** 78-56-48 W
Pop: 1,915 (1990)   **Pop Density:** 70.7
Land: 27.1 sq. mi.; **Water:** 0.0 sq. mi.

Center
Township
ZIP: 15748   **Lat:** 40-32-37 N **Long:** 79-11-20 W
Pop: 5,257 (1990)   **Pop Density:** 130.1
Land: 40.4 sq. mi.; **Water:** 0.1 sq. mi.

Cherryhill
Township
Lat: 40-37-57 N **Long:** 79-00-26 W
Pop: 2,764 (1990)   **Pop Density:** 56.6
Land: 48.8 sq. mi.; **Water:** 0.7 sq. mi.

Cherry Tree
Borough
ZIP: 15724   **Lat:** 40-43-32 N **Long:** 78-48-28 W
Pop: 431 (1990); 520 (1980)   **Pop Density:** 862.0
Land: 0.5 sq. mi.; **Water:** 0.0 sq. mi.   **Elev:** 1380 ft.
In west-central PA, northeast of Pittsburgh.
Name origin: For the cherry tree that was used to determine one of the boundaries of the territory conveyed to the PA proprietors by the Fort Stanwix Treaty of 1768. Originally called Canoe Place.

Chevy Chase Heights
CDP
Lat: 40-38-20 N **Long:** 79-08-37 W
Pop: 1,535 (1990); 1,824 (1980)   **Pop Density:** 1180.8
Land: 1.3 sq. mi.; **Water:** 0.0 sq. mi.

Clymer
Borough
ZIP: 15728   **Lat:** 40-40-05 N **Long:** 79-00-50 W
Pop: 1,499 (1990); 1,761 (1980)   **Pop Density:** 2498.3
Land: 0.6 sq. mi.; **Water:** 0.0 sq. mi.   **Elev:** 1218 ft.
In west-central PA on Two Lick Creek, north of Johnstown. Laid out 1905 by the Dixon Run Land Company.
Name origin: For George Clymer (1739–1813), a PA signer of the Declaration of Independence and one of the framers of the Constitution of the United States.

Conemaugh
Township
Lat: 40-29-55 N **Long:** 79-22-58 W
Pop: 2,448 (1990)   **Pop Density:** 72.0
Land: 34.0 sq. mi.; **Water:** 0.4 sq. mi.
In southwestern PA, east of Pittsburgh.
Name origin: For the Conemaugh River, which forms its southern boundary; from an Indian term probably meaning 'otter creek.'

Creekside
Borough
ZIP: 15732   **Lat:** 40-40-47 N **Long:** 79-11-36 W
Pop: 337 (1990); 383 (1980)   **Pop Density:** 1685.0
Land: 0.2 sq. mi.; **Water:** 0.0 sq. mi.   **Elev:** 1060 ft.

East Mahoning
Township
Lat: 40-47-31 N **Long:** 79-02-49 W
Pop: 1,140 (1990)   **Pop Density:** 36.3
Land: 31.4 sq. mi.; **Water:** 0.0 sq. mi.

East Wheatfield
Township
Lat: 40-26-29 N **Long:** 79-00-26 W
Pop: 2,735 (1990)   **Pop Density:** 101.7
Land: 26.9 sq. mi.; **Water:** 0.4 sq. mi.

Ernest
Borough
ZIP: 15739   **Lat:** 40-40-42 N **Long:** 79-09-54 W
Pop: 492 (1990); 584 (1980)   **Pop Density:** 2460.0
Land: 0.2 sq. mi.; **Water:** 0.0 sq. mi.   **Elev:** 1180 ft.

Glen Campbell
Borough
ZIP: 15742   **Lat:** 40-49-05 N **Long:** 78-49-49 W
Pop: 313 (1990); 352 (1980)   **Pop Density:** 347.8
Land: 0.9 sq. mi.; **Water:** 0.0 sq. mi.   **Elev:** 1500 ft.

Grant
Township
Lat: 40-46-48 N **Long:** 78-56-52 W
Pop: 729 (1990)   **Pop Density:** 27.0
Land: 27.0 sq. mi.; **Water:** 0.0 sq. mi.

Green
Township
Lat: 40-41-58 N **Long:** 78-54-35 W
Pop: 4,095 (1990)   **Pop Density:** 77.6
Land: 52.8 sq. mi.; **Water:** 0.0 sq. mi.

Homer City
Borough
ZIP: 15748   **Lat:** 40-32-22 N **Long:** 79-09-34 W
Pop: 1,809 (1990); 2,248 (1980)   **Pop Density:** 3015.0
Land: 0.6 sq. mi.; **Water:** 0.0 sq. mi.   **Elev:** 1080 ft.
In west-central PA, 7 mi. south of the town of Indiana. Founded 1854.

Indiana
Borough
ZIP: 15701   **Lat:** 40-37-18 N **Long:** 79-09-20 W
Pop: 15,174 (1990); 16,051 (1980)   **Pop Density:** 8430.0
Land: 1.8 sq. mi.; **Water:** 0.0 sq. mi.   **Elev:** 1301 ft.
In west-central PA, 46 mi. northeast of Pittsburgh. Founded 1805 when George Clymer (1739–1813) of Philadelphia, one of the signers of the Declaration of Independence, donated 250 acres for county buildings; incorporated Mar 11, 1816.
Name origin: For the newly formed Territory of IN, which Congress established from the Northwest Territory in 1800.

Jacksonville
Borough
ZIP: 15752   **Lat:** 40-32-29 N **Long:** 79-17-00 W
Pop: 89 (1990); 121 (1980)   **Pop Density:** 890.0
Land: 0.1 sq. mi.; **Water:** 0.0 sq. mi.   **Elev:** 1063 ft.

Lucerne Mines
CDP
Lat: 40-33-15 N **Long:** 79-09-20 W
Pop: 1,074 (1990); 1,195 (1980)   **Pop Density:** 1193.3
Land: 0.9 sq. mi.; **Water:** 0.0 sq. mi.

Marion Center
Borough
ZIP: 15759   **Lat:** 40-46-12 N **Long:** 79-02-52 W
Pop: 476 (1990); 494 (1980)   **Pop Density:** 680.0
Land: 0.7 sq. mi.; **Water:** 0.0 sq. mi.   **Elev:** 1283 ft.

Montgomery
Township
Lat: 40-46-36 N **Long:** 78-51-05 W
Pop: 1,729 (1990)   **Pop Density:** 60.2
Land: 28.7 sq. mi.; **Water:** 0.0 sq. mi.

North Mahoning
Township
Lat: 40-52-28 N **Long:** 79-02-34 W
Pop: 1,254 (1990)   **Pop Density:** 44.3
Land: 28.3 sq. mi.; **Water:** 0.0 sq. mi.

Pine
Township
Lat: 40-35-40 N **Long:** 78-54-50 W
Pop: 2,172 (1990)   **Pop Density:** 70.1
Land: 31.0 sq. mi.; **Water:** 0.0 sq. mi.

Plumville
Borough
ZIP: 16246   **Lat:** 40-47-37 N **Long:** 79-10-49 W
Pop: 390 (1990); 431 (1980)   **Pop Density:** 780.0
Land: 0.5 sq. mi.; **Water:** 0.0 sq. mi.   **Elev:** 1173 ft.

Rayne
Township
Lat: 40-42-49 N **Long:** 79-05-34 W
Pop: 3,339 (1990)   **Pop Density:** 70.7
Land: 47.2 sq. mi.; **Water:** 0.0 sq. mi.

Saltsburg
ZIP: 15681   Lat: 40-29-06 N Long: 79-26-47 W
Pop: 990 (1990)   Pop Density: 3300.0
Land: 0.3 sq. mi.; Water: 0.0 sq. mi.

In west-central PA, 30 mi. northeast of Pittsburgh.

Name origin: For salt deposits discovered by a Mrs. Deemer when she found the food she cooked in water that trickled from rocks along the Conemaugh River had a salty taste.

Shelocta
ZIP: 15774   Lat: 40-39-23 N Long: 79-18-08 W
Pop: 108 (1990); 139 (1980)   Pop Density: 1080.0
Land: 0.1 sq. mi.; Water: 0.0 sq. mi.   Elev: 992 ft.

Smicksburg
ZIP: 16256   Lat: 40-52-11 N Long: 79-10-18 W
Pop: 76 (1990); 82 (1980)   Pop Density: 760.0
Land: 0.1 sq. mi.; Water: 0.0 sq. mi.   Elev: 1165 ft.

South Mahoning   Township
Lat: 40-48-30 N Long: 79-09-07 W
Pop: 1,713 (1990)   Pop Density: 59.9
Land: 28.6 sq. mi.; Water: 0.0 sq. mi.

Washington   Township
Lat: 40-43-17 N Long: 79-12-44 W
Pop: 1,861 (1990)   Pop Density: 48.6
Land: 38.3 sq. mi.; Water: 0.0 sq. mi.

Name origin: For George Washington (1732–99), first U.S. president.

West Mahoning   Township
Lat: 40-51-58 N Long: 79-09-58 W
Pop: 1,032 (1990)   Pop Density: 35.1
Land: 29.4 sq. mi.; Water: 0.0 sq. mi.

West Wheatfield   Township
Lat: 40-25-41 N Long: 79-06-31 W
Pop: 2,370 (1990)   Pop Density: 75.0
Land: 31.6 sq. mi.; Water: 0.4 sq. mi.

White   Township
ZIP: 15701   Lat: 40-36-51 N Long: 79-08-57 W
Pop: 13,788 (1990)   Pop Density: 323.7
Land: 42.6 sq. mi.; Water: 0.3 sq. mi.

Young   Township
Lat: 40-33-52 N Long: 79-20-43 W
Pop: 1,805 (1990)   Pop Density: 51.6
Land: 35.0 sq. mi.; Water: 0.0 sq. mi.

Jefferson County
County Seat: Brookville (ZIP: 15825)

Pop: 46,083 (1990); 48,303 (1980)   Pop Density: 70.3
Land: 655.5 sq. mi.; Water: 1.4 sq. mi.   Area Code: 814

In central portion of western PA, northeast of Pittsburgh; organized Mar 26, 1804 from Lycoming County.

Name origin: For Thomas Jefferson (1743–1826), U.S. patriot and statesman; third U.S. president.

Barnett   Township
Lat: 41-18-31 N Long: 79-08-50 W
Pop: 269 (1990)   Pop Density: 18.6
Land: 14.5 sq. mi.; Water: 0.6 sq. mi.

Name origin: For Joseph Barnett, the first white settler, who arrived in 1800.

Beaver   Township
Lat: 41-03-38 N Long: 79-10-11 W
Pop: 551 (1990)   Pop Density: 25.5
Land: 21.6 sq. mi.; Water: 0.0 sq. mi.

Bell   Township
Lat: 40-57-10 N Long: 78-55-39 W
Pop: 2,055 (1990)   Pop Density: 109.9
Land: 18.7 sq. mi.; Water: 0.0 sq. mi.

Big Run   Borough
ZIP: 15715   Lat: 40-58-11 N Long: 78-52-41 W
Pop: 699 (1990); 822 (1980)   Pop Density: 998.6
Land: 0.7 sq. mi.; Water: 0.0 sq. mi.   Elev: 1283 ft.

In west-central PA, 7 mi. north of Punxsutawney. Founded 1822.

Name origin: For the Big Run stream that flows into Stump Creek here.

Brockway   Borough
ZIP: 15824   Lat: 41-14-49 N Long: 78-47-35 W
Pop: 2,207 (1990); 2,376 (1980) Pop Density: 2006.4
Land: 1.1 sq. mi.; Water: 0.0 sq. mi.   Elev: 1441 ft.
Laid out 1836.

Name origin: For Alonzo and Chauncey Brockway, who settled here in 1822 and laid out the town fourteen years later.

Brookville   Borough
ZIP: 15825   Lat: 41-09-41 N Long: 79-04-58 W
Pop: 4,184 (1990); 4,568 (1980) Pop Density: 1307.5
Land: 3.2 sq. mi.; Water: 0.0 sq. mi.   Elev: 1269 ft.

In west-central PA on Red Bank Creek and 3 of its tributaries, 80 mi. northwest of Pittsburgh. Settled 1801; laid out 1830; incorporated Apr 9, 1834. County seat.

Name origin: For the various brooks flowing in and around town.

Clover   Township
Lat: 41-07-42 N Long: 79-10-25 W
Pop: 523 (1990)   Pop Density: 32.3
Land: 16.2 sq. mi.; Water: 0.0 sq. mi.
Formed 1841.

Name origin: For Levi G. Clover, former county clerk.

Corsica
Borough
ZIP: 15829   **Lat:** 41-10-54 N **Long:** 79-12-10 W
Pop: 337 (1990); 381 (1980)   **Pop Density:** 674.0
Land: 0.5 sq. mi.; **Water:** 0.0 sq. mi.   **Elev:** 1613 ft.

Eldred
Township
          Lat: 41-15-31 N **Long:** 79-07-38 W
Pop: 1,197 (1990)   **Pop Density:** 25.7
Land: 46.6 sq. mi.; **Water:** 0.0 sq. mi.

Falls Creek
Borough
ZIP: 15840   **Lat:** 41-08-31 N **Long:** 78-48-26 W
Pop: 1,033 (1990); 1,158 (1980)   **Pop Density:** 1147.8
Land: 0.9 sq. mi.; **Water:** 0.0 sq. mi.   **Elev:** 1460 ft.
Part of the town is also in Clearfield County.

Gaskill
Township
          Lat: 40-56-01 N **Long:** 78-50-58 W
Pop: 675 (1990)   **Pop Density:** 31.4
Land: 21.5 sq. mi.; **Water:** 0.0 sq. mi.

Heath
Township
ZIP: 15842   **Lat:** 41-20-02 N **Long:** 79-00-54 W
Pop: 109 (1990)   **Pop Density:** 3.8
Land: 28.6 sq. mi.; **Water:** 0.4 sq. mi.

Henderson
Township
          Lat: 41-00-13 N **Long:** 78-50-51 W
Pop: 1,376 (1990)   **Pop Density:** 62.8
Land: 21.9 sq. mi.; **Water:** 0.0 sq. mi.

Knox
Township
          Lat: 41-05-25 N **Long:** 79-01-57 W
Pop: 1,014 (1990)   **Pop Density:** 32.5
Land: 31.2 sq. mi.; **Water:** 0.0 sq. mi.

McCalmont
Township
          Lat: 41-01-17 N **Long:** 78-57-19 W
Pop: 1,006 (1990)   **Pop Density:** 38.3
Land: 26.3 sq. mi.; **Water:** 0.0 sq. mi.

Oliver
Township
          Lat: 41-01-20 N **Long:** 79-04-27 W
Pop: 1,119 (1990)   **Pop Density:** 36.8
Land: 30.4 sq. mi.; **Water:** 0.0 sq. mi.

Perry
Township
          Lat: 40-56-54 N **Long:** 79-04-06 W
Pop: 1,293 (1990)   **Pop Density:** 45.1
Land: 28.7 sq. mi.; **Water:** 0.0 sq. mi.

Pine Creek
Township
          Lat: 41-08-58 N **Long:** 79-00-07 W
Pop: 1,413 (1990)   **Pop Density:** 49.6
Land: 28.5 sq. mi.; **Water:** 0.0 sq. mi.

Polk
Township
          Lat: 41-17-44 N **Long:** 78-56-15 W
Pop: 305 (1990)   **Pop Density:** 9.9
Land: 30.7 sq. mi.; **Water:** 0.0 sq. mi.

Porter
Township
          Lat: 40-56-06 N **Long:** 79-09-58 W
Pop: 310 (1990)   **Pop Density:** 17.5
Land: 17.7 sq. mi.; **Water:** 0.0 sq. mi.

Punxsutawney
Borough
ZIP: 15767   **Lat:** 40-56-38 N **Long:** 78-58-39 W
Pop: 6,782 (1990); 7,479 (1980)   **Pop Density:** 1994.7
Land: 3.4 sq. mi.; **Water:** 0.0 sq. mi.   **Elev:** 1238 ft.
In west-central PA on Mahoning Creek, 80 mi. northeast of
Pittsburgh. Site of the annual watch on Ground Hog Day,
Feb. 2, for "Punxsutawney Phil," the ground hog whose
emergence from his hole is awaited at Gobbler's Knob. If
Phil sees his shadow, the forecast is for six more weeks of
winter.
Name origin: Algonquian Indian *ponsetunik* 'land of the
ponkies,' referring to the swarms of gnats (living dust or
ashes, to the Indians), that plagued early settlers and their
livestock.

Reynoldsville
Borough
ZIP: 15851   **Lat:** 41-05-39 N **Long:** 78-53-16 W
Pop: 2,818 (1990); 3,016 (1980)   **Pop Density:** 2012.9
Land: 1.4 sq. mi.; **Water:** 0.0 sq. mi.

Ringgold
Township
ZIP: 15770   **Lat:** 40-59-56 N **Long:** 79-10-05 W
Pop: 705 (1990)   **Pop Density:** 36.7
Land: 19.2 sq. mi.; **Water:** 0.0 sq. mi.

Rose
Township
          Lat: 41-08-14 N **Long:** 79-06-22 W
Pop: 1,198 (1990)   **Pop Density:** 62.7
Land: 19.1 sq. mi.; **Water:** 0.0 sq. mi.

Snyder
Township
          Lat: 41-15-39 N **Long:** 78-48-49 W
Pop: 2,535 (1990)   **Pop Density:** 60.6
Land: 41.8 sq. mi.; **Water:** 0.0 sq. mi.

Summerville
Borough
ZIP: 15864   **Lat:** 41-06-58 N **Long:** 79-11-19 W
Pop: 675 (1990); 830 (1980)   **Pop Density:** 1125.0
Land: 0.6 sq. mi.; **Water:** 0.0 sq. mi.   **Elev:** 1163 ft.

Sykesville
Borough
ZIP: 15865   **Lat:** 41-02-57 N **Long:** 78-49-08 W
Pop: 1,387 (1990); 1,537 (1980)   **Pop Density:** 866.9
Land: 1.6 sq. mi.; **Water:** 0.0 sq. mi.   **Elev:** 1360 ft.
Settled in 1861.
Name origin: For Jacob Sykes, a sawmill owner of the 1880s.

Timblin
Borough
ZIP: 15778   **Lat:** 40-57-58 N **Long:** 79-11-57 W
Pop: 165 (1990); 197 (1980)   **Pop Density:** 183.3
Land: 0.9 sq. mi.; **Water:** 0.0 sq. mi.   **Elev:** 1269 ft.

Union
Township
          Lat: 41-11-34 N **Long:** 79-10-26 W
Pop: 733 (1990)   **Pop Density:** 41.2
Land: 17.8 sq. mi.; **Water:** 0.0 sq. mi.

Warsaw
Township
          Lat: 41-13-55 N **Long:** 78-59-45 W
Pop: 1,213 (1990)   **Pop Density:** 23.6
Land: 51.3 sq. mi.; **Water:** 0.0 sq. mi.

Washington
Township
          Lat: 41-10-56 N **Long:** 78-51-32 W
Pop: 1,939 (1990)   **Pop Density:** 40.8
Land: 47.5 sq. mi.; **Water:** 0.2 sq. mi.
Name origin: For George Washington (1732–99), first U.S.
president.

Winslow
Township
          Lat: 41-05-28 N **Long:** 78-52-29 W
Pop: 2,526 (1990)   **Pop Density:** 55.5
Land: 45.5 sq. mi.; **Water:** 0.0 sq. mi.

Worthville Borough
ZIP: 15784 Lat: 41-01-27 N Long: 79-08-27 W
Pop: 65 (1990); 87 (1980) Pop Density: 325.0
Land: 0.2 sq. mi.; Water: 0.0 sq. mi. Elev: 1199 ft.

Young Township
Lat: 40-57-28 N Long: 78-59-20 W
Pop: 1,667 (1990) Pop Density: 107.5
Land: 15.5 sq. mi.; Water: 0.0 sq. mi.

Juniata County
County Seat: Miffintown (ZIP: 17059)

Pop: 20,625 (1990); 19,188 (1980) Pop Density: 52.7
Land: 391.6 sq. mi.; Water: 2.0 sq. mi. Area Code: 717
In central PA, northwest of Harrisburg; organized Mar 2, 1831 from Mifflin County.
Name origin: For the Juniata River, which flows through it; it is named for an Indian word of uncertain origin.

Beale Township
ZIP: 17082 Lat: 40-30-12 N Long: 77-30-47 W
Pop: 629 (1990) Pop Density: 28.9
Land: 21.8 sq. mi.; Water: 0.0 sq. mi.

Delaware Township
ZIP: 17059 Lat: 40-35-07 N Long: 77-13-30 W
Pop: 1,440 (1990) Pop Density: 49.0
Land: 29.4 sq. mi.; Water: 0.5 sq. mi.

Fayette Township
ZIP: 17049 Lat: 40-39-09 N Long: 77-16-29 W
Pop: 3,002 (1990) Pop Density: 75.6
Land: 39.7 sq. mi.; Water: 0.0 sq. mi.

Fermanagh Township
ZIP: 17059 Lat: 40-37-06 N Long: 77-23-28 W
Pop: 2,249 (1990) Pop Density: 70.1
Land: 32.1 sq. mi.; Water: 0.4 sq. mi.

Greenwood Township
ZIP: 17094 Lat: 40-36-48 N Long: 77-07-08 W
Pop: 493 (1990) Pop Density: 25.0
Land: 19.7 sq. mi.; Water: 0.0 sq. mi.

Lack Township
Lat: 40-22-10 N Long: 77-39-59 W
Pop: 714 (1990) Pop Density: 12.5
Land: 56.9 sq. mi.; Water: 0.0 sq. mi.

Mifflin Borough
ZIP: 17058 Lat: 40-34-04 N Long: 77-24-17 W
Pop: 660 (1990); 648 (1980) Pop Density: 3300.0
Land: 0.2 sq. mi.; Water: 0.0 sq. mi. Elev: 440 ft.

Mifflintown Borough
ZIP: 17059 Lat: 40-34-15 N Long: 77-23-42 W
Pop: 866 (1990); 783 (1980) Pop Density: 8660.0
Land: 0.1 sq. mi.; Water: 0.0 sq. mi. Elev: 465 ft.
Laid out in 1791; incorporated Mar 6, 1833.

Milford Township
ZIP: 17059 Lat: 40-32-53 N Long: 77-29-15 W
Pop: 1,429 (1990) Pop Density: 35.7
Land: 40.0 sq. mi.; Water: 0.4 sq. mi.

Monroe Township
ZIP: 17014 Lat: 40-39-34 N Long: 77-07-26 W
Pop: 1,800 (1990) Pop Density: 91.8
Land: 19.6 sq. mi.; Water: 0.0 sq. mi.

Port Royal Borough
ZIP: 17082 Lat: 40-32-01 N Long: 77-23-27 W
Pop: 836 (1990); 835 (1980) Pop Density: 1194.3
Land: 0.7 sq. mi.; Water: 0.0 sq. mi. Elev: 444 ft.

Spruce Hill Township
ZIP: 17082 Lat: 40-27-47 N Long: 77-28-01 W
Pop: 694 (1990) Pop Density: 32.0
Land: 21.7 sq. mi.; Water: 0.0 sq. mi.

Susquehanna Township
Lat: 40-37-52 N Long: 77-01-12 W
Pop: 1,022 (1990) Pop Density: 61.9
Land: 16.5 sq. mi.; Water: 0.0 sq. mi.
In central PA, northwest of Harrisburg.
Name origin: For the Susquehanna River, which forms part of its eastern border.

Thompsontown Borough
ZIP: 17094 Lat: 40-33-58 N Long: 77-14-07 W
Pop: 582 (1990); 593 (1980) Pop Density: 1940.0
Land: 0.3 sq. mi.; Water: 0.0 sq. mi. Elev: 447 ft.

Turbett Township
ZIP: 17082 Lat: 40-30-30 N Long: 77-22-36 W
Pop: 779 (1990) Pop Density: 47.5
Land: 16.4 sq. mi.; Water: 0.1 sq. mi.

Tuscarora Township
ZIP: 17035 Lat: 40-25-49 N Long: 77-35-04 W
Pop: 1,099 (1990) Pop Density: 23.2
Land: 47.4 sq. mi.; Water: 0.0 sq. mi.

Walker Township
ZIP: 17059 Lat: 40-33-33 N Long: 77-19-08 W
Pop: 2,331 (1990) Pop Density: 80.4
Land: 29.0 sq. mi.; Water: 0.5 sq. mi.

Lackawanna County
County Seat: Scranton (ZIP: 18503)

Pop: 219,039 (1990); 227,908 (1980)   **Pop Density:** 477.4
Land: 458.8 sq. mi.; **Water:** 5.8 sq. mi.   **Area Code:** 717

In northeastern PA, northeast of Wilkes-Barre. Organized Aug 13, 1878 from Luzerne County; the last PA county to be created.

Name origin: For the Lackawanna River, which runs through it. From a Delaware Indian word probably meaning 'the stream that forks.'

Abington
Township
Lat: 41-31-27 N **Long:** 75-41-57 W
Pop: 1,533 (1990)   **Pop Density:** 333.3
Land: 4.6 sq. mi.; **Water:** 0.0 sq. mi.

Archbald
Borough
ZIP: 18403   **Lat:** 41-30-25 N **Long:** 75-32-31 W
Pop: 6,291 (1990); 6,295 (1980)   **Pop Density:** 374.5
Land: 16.8 sq. mi.; **Water:** 0.0 sq. mi.   **Elev:** 1000 ft.

In northeastern PA, northeast of Scranton.

Name origin: Named in 1846 for James Archbald, a company engineer, by the Delaware and Hudson Canal Company, who began exploiting the area's coal deposits. Previously called White Oak Run.

Benton
Township
Lat: 41-36-26 N **Long:** 75-42-12 W
Pop: 1,837 (1990)   **Pop Density:** 74.7
Land: 24.6 sq. mi.; **Water:** 0.5 sq. mi.

Blakely
Borough
ZIP: 18447   **Lat:** 41-29-16 N **Long:** 75-35-52 W
Pop: 7,222 (1990); 7,438 (1980)   **Pop Density:** 1851.8
Land: 3.9 sq. mi.; **Water:** 0.0 sq. mi.   **Elev:** 802 ft.

In northeastern PA on the Lackawanna River; a suburb of Scranton.

Name origin: For Capt. Johnston Blakely, naval commander during the War of 1812.

Carbondale
City
ZIP: 18407   **Lat:** 41-34-15 N **Long:** 75-30-19 W
Pop: 10,664 (1990); 11,255 (1980)   **Pop Density:** 3332.5
Land: 3.2 sq. mi.; **Water:** 0.0 sq. mi.   **Elev:** 1100 ft.

In northeastern PA on the Lackawanna River, 17 mi. northeast of Scranton.

Name origin: For its being an anthracite center since 1814, when William Wurts, a Philadelphia merchant who owned large tracts in the vicinity, and David Nobles, a hunter who knew the region, opened veins and obtained coal for exhibition and appraisal in New York and Philadelphia.

*Carbondale
Township
ZIP: 18407   **Lat:** 41-33-10 N **Long:** 75-30-27 W
Pop: 907 (1990)   **Pop Density:** 66.2
Land: 13.7 sq. mi.; **Water:** 0.2 sq. mi.

Clarks Green
Borough
ZIP: 18411   **Lat:** 41-29-58 N **Long:** 75-41-44 W
Pop: 1,603 (1990); 1,862 (1980)   **Pop Density:** 2671.7
Land: 0.6 sq. mi.; **Water:** 0.0 sq. mi.   **Elev:** 1302 ft.

Clarks Summit
Borough
ZIP: 18411   **Lat:** 41-29-24 N **Long:** 75-42-26 W
Pop: 5,433 (1990); 5,272 (1980)   **Pop Density:** 3395.6
Land: 1.6 sq. mi.; **Water:** 0.0 sq. mi.   **Elev:** 1460 ft.

In northeastern PA, 5 mi. northwest of Scranton.

Name origin: For Deacon William Clark, who in 1799 cleared the triangular green, and for the summit of a grade on the Legett's Gap Railroad, the northern division of the Lackawanna & Western Railroad.

Clifton
Township
Lat: 41-14-58 N **Long:** 75-31-58 W
Pop: 1,041 (1990)   **Pop Density:** 53.9
Land: 19.3 sq. mi.; **Water:** 0.4 sq. mi.

Covington
Township
Lat: 41-17-28 N **Long:** 75-29-59 W
Pop: 2,055 (1990)   **Pop Density:** 87.4
Land: 23.5 sq. mi.; **Water:** 0.1 sq. mi.

Dalton
Borough
ZIP: 18414   **Lat:** 41-32-16 N **Long:** 75-44-19 W
Pop: 1,369 (1990); 1,383 (1980)   **Pop Density:** 441.6
Land: 3.1 sq. mi.; **Water:** 0.1 sq. mi.   **Elev:** 992 ft.

Dickson City
Borough
ZIP: 18519   **Lat:** 41-28-07 N **Long:** 75-38-05 W
Pop: 6,276 (1990); 6,699 (1980)   **Pop Density:** 1335.3
Land: 4.7 sq. mi.; **Water:** 0.0 sq. mi.   **Elev:** 783 ft.

In northeastern PA, a northern suburb of Scranton. William H. Richmond of Scranton opened coal drifts here in 1859 and the following year the first breaker was erected.

Name origin: For Thomas Dickson, president of the Delaware & Hudson Canal Company (1869–84).

Dunmore
Borough
ZIP: 18512   **Lat:** 41-24-56 N **Long:** 75-36-25 W
Pop: 15,403 (1990); 16,781 (1980)   **Pop Density:** 1770.5
Land: 8.7 sq. mi.; **Water:** 0.1 sq. mi.   **Elev:** 900 ft.

Settled 1783 by shoemaker William Allsworth.

Name origin: Named in 1840 for the second son of the 5th Earl of Dunmore, a frequent hunter and fisher in the area, in the (futile) hope that he would invest in a railroad connecting the region with the Morris Canal in NJ. Formerly called Buckstown for the abundance of deer.

Elmhurst
Township
Lat: 41-22-26 N **Long:** 75-32-55 W
Pop: 834 (1990)   **Pop Density:** 463.3
Land: 1.8 sq. mi.; **Water:** 0.1 sq. mi.

Fell
Township
Lat: 41-36-31 N **Long:** 75-31-12 W
Pop: 2,426 (1990)   **Pop Density:** 158.6
Land: 15.3 sq. mi.; **Water:** 0.1 sq. mi.

Glenburn
Township
Lat: 41-30-33 N   Long: 75-44-06 W
Pop: 1,242 (1990)   **Pop Density:** 264.3
Land: 4.7 sq. mi.; **Water:** 0.2 sq. mi.

Greenfield
Township
Lat: 41-36-59 N   Long: 75-35-27 W
Pop: 1,743 (1990)   **Pop Density:** 83.8
Land: 20.8 sq. mi.; **Water:** 0.6 sq. mi.

Jefferson
Township
Lat: 41-26-58 N   Long: 75-28-34 W
Pop: 3,438 (1990)   **Pop Density:** 103.2
Land: 33.3 sq. mi.; **Water:** 0.5 sq. mi.

Jermyn
Borough
ZIP: 18433   Lat: 41-31-36 N   Long: 75-32-47 W
Pop: 2,263 (1990); 2,411 (1980)   **Pop Density:** 2828.8
Land: 0.8 sq. mi.; **Water:** 0.0 sq. mi.   **Elev:** 960 ft.
In northeastern PA, a northeastern suburb of Scranton. With Mayfield, forms the "twin boroughs."
Name origin: Named by the Delaware and Hudson Canal Company for a wealthy English merchant, John Jermyn.

Jessup
Borough
ZIP: 18434   Lat: 41-27-29 N   Long: 75-32-51 W
Pop: 4,605 (1990); 4,974 (1980)   **Pop Density:** 687.3
Land: 6.7 sq. mi.; **Water:** 0.0 sq. mi.   **Elev:** 957 ft.
Settled 1849.

La Plume
Township
Lat: 41-33-26 N   Long: 75-45-21 W
Pop: 647 (1990)   **Pop Density:** 269.6
Land: 2.4 sq. mi.; **Water:** 0.0 sq. mi.

Lehigh
Township
Lat: 41-12-45 N   Long: 75-36-48 W
Pop: 486 (1990)   **Pop Density:** 21.1
Land: 23.0 sq. mi.; **Water:** 0.2 sq. mi.

Madison
Township
Lat: 41-20-41 N   Long: 75-29-17 W
Pop: 2,207 (1990)   **Pop Density:** 129.8
Land: 17.0 sq. mi.; **Water:** 0.1 sq. mi.
Name origin: For James Madison (1751–1836), fourth U.S. president.

Mayfield
Borough
ZIP: 18433   Lat: 41-32-13 N   Long: 75-32-01 W
Pop: 1,890 (1990); 1,812 (1980)   **Pop Density:** 787.5
Land: 2.4 sq. mi.; **Water:** 0.0 sq. mi.   **Elev:** 960 ft.
Established before 1840 by John Gibson, who sold out in 1874 to the Delaware and Hudson Canal Company.

Moosic
Borough
ZIP: 18507   Lat: 41-21-25 N   Long: 75-42-08 W
Pop: 5,339 (1990); 6,068 (1980)   **Pop Density:** 821.4
Land: 6.5 sq. mi.; **Water:** 0.1 sq. mi.   **Elev:** 647 ft.
In northeastern PA, a suburb of Scranton.
Name origin: For the great herds of moose that once roamed the Lackawanna River Valley.

Moscow
Borough
ZIP: 18444   Lat: 41-20-25 N   Long: 75-31-44 W
Pop: 1,527 (1990); 1,536 (1980)   **Pop Density:** 545.4
Land: 2.8 sq. mi.; **Water:** 0.0 sq. mi.   **Elev:** 1559 ft.
In northeastern PA, 12 mi. southeast of Scranton.

Mount Cobb
CDP
Lat: 41-25-42 N   Long 75-29-50 W
Pop: 2,043 (1990)   **Pop Density:** 125.3
Land: 16.3 sq. mi.; **Water:** 0.2 sq. mi.

Newton
Township
Lat: 41-27-23 N   Long 75-45-59 W
Pop: 2,843 (1990)   **Pop Density:** 126.9
Land: 22.4 sq. mi.; **Water:** 0.3 sq. mi.

North Abington
Township
Lat: 41-33-19 N   Long 75-41-06 W
Pop: 691 (1990)   **Pop Density:** 72.7
Land: 9.5 sq. mi.; **Water:** 0.0 sq. mi.

Old Forge
Borough
ZIP: 18518   Lat: 41-22-08 N   Long: 75-44-32 W
Pop: 8,834 (1990); 9,304 (1980)   **Pop Density:** 2598.2
Land: 3.4 sq. mi.; **Water:** 0.0 sq. mi.   **Elev:** 740 ft.
In northeastern PA, 6 mi. southwest of Scranton. Founded 1789.
Name origin: For a forge that was built by Dr. William Hooker Smith, the pioneer physician of this region.

Olyphant
Borough
ZIP: 18447   Lat: 41-26-57 N   Long: 75-34-48 W
Pop: 5,222 (1990); 5,204 (1980)   **Pop Density:** 967.0
Land: 5.4 sq. mi.; **Water:** 0.1 sq. mi.   **Elev:** 960 ft.
In northeastern PA, 5 mi. northeast of Scranton.
Name origin: For George Talbot Olyphant of NY, who became president of the Delaware and Hudson Canal Company in 1858.

Ransom
Township
Lat: 41-24-25 N   Long: 75-45-56 W
Pop: 1,608 (1990)   **Pop Density:** 91.4
Land: 17.6 sq. mi.; **Water:** 0.3 sq. mi.

Roaring Brook
Township
Lat: 41-22-35 N   Long: 75-34-40 W
Pop: 1,966 (1990)   **Pop Density:** 89.8
Land: 21.9 sq. mi.; **Water:** 0.5 sq. mi.

Scott
Township
ZIP: 18447   Lat: 41-32-18 N   Long: 75-37-01 W
Pop: 5,350 (1990)   **Pop Density:** 196.0
Land: 27.3 sq. mi.; **Water:** 0.3 sq. mi.

Scranton
City
ZIP: 18501   Lat: 41-24-14 N   Long: 75-39-57 W
Pop: 81,805 (1990)   **Pop Density:** 3246.2
Land: 25.2 sq. mi.; **Water:** 0.2 sq. mi.   **Elev:** 754 ft.
In northeastern PA, northeast of Wilkes-Barre. Laid out in 1841; incorporated as borough 1856, as city Apr 23, 1866. Manufacturing city: appliances, books, cigars, machinery, textiles.
Name origin: For two brothers, George Whitfield (1811–61) and Selden T., and their cousin, Joseph H. Scranton (1813–72), who were attracted by the abundance of iron ore and anthracite nearby. With their partners William Henry, Sanford Grant, and Philip Mattes, they organized the firm of Scranton, Grant, and Company, which became the nucleus of the Lackawanna Iron and Steel Company. They succeeded in manufacturing iron using anthracite as a fuel. Earlier names were Lackawanna, Harrison, and Scrantonia.

South Abington
Township
ZIP: 18410   Lat: 41-29-16 N   Long: 75-41-18 W
Pop: 6,377 (1990)   **Pop Density:** 716.5
Land: 8.9 sq. mi.; **Water:** 0.1 sq. mi.

Spring Brook
                           Township
Lat: 41-18-04 N **Long:** 75-37-27 W
Pop: 2,097 (1990) **Pop Density:** 61.5
Land: 34.1 sq. mi.; **Water:** 0.6 sq. mi.

Taylor
                           Borough
ZIP: 18517 **Lat:** 41-23-55 N **Long:** 75-42-49 W
Pop: 6,941 (1990); 7,246 (1980) **Pop Density:** 1334.8
Land: 5.2 sq. mi.; **Water:** 0.0 sq. mi. **Elev:** 760 ft.

In northeastern PA, 5 mi. southwest of Scranton.

Name origin: For Moses Taylor, a prominent NY merchant and capitalist, who had extensive business interests in the area.

Throop
                           Borough
ZIP: 18512 **Lat:** 41-26-18 N **Long:** 75-35-45 W
Pop: 4,070 (1990); 4,166 (1980) **Pop Density:** 814.0
Land: 5.0 sq. mi.; **Water:** 0.0 sq. mi. **Elev:** 880 ft.

In northeastern PA, 5 mi. northeast of Scranton.

Name origin: For Dr. Benjamin Henry Throop, the pioneer physician of Scranton.

Vandling
                           Borough
ZIP: 18421 **Lat:** 41-37-52 N **Long:** 75-28-14 W
Pop: 660 (1990); 557 (1980) **Pop Density:** 507.7
Land: 1.3 sq. mi.; **Water:** 0.0 sq. mi. **Elev:** 1600 ft.

In northeastern PA, near Forest City.

West Abington
                           Township
Lat: 41-31-50 N **Long:** 75-46-09 W
Pop: 294 (1990) **Pop Density:** 53.5
Land: 5.5 sq. mi.; **Water:** 0.0 sq. mi.

Lancaster County
County Seat: Lancaster (ZIP: 17602)

Pop: 422,822 (1990); 362,346 (1980) **Pop Density:** 445.5
Land: 949.1 sq. mi.; **Water:** 34.8 sq. mi. **Area Code:** 717

In southeastern PA, southeast of Harrisburg; organized May 10, 1729 from Chester County.

Name origin: For Lancaster, Lancashire, England, former home of John Wright, a prime figure in the formation of the county.

Adamstown
                           Borough
ZIP: 19501 **Lat:** 40-14-27 N **Long:** 76-03-45 W
Pop: 1,108 (1990); 1,107 (1980) **Pop Density:** 791.4
Land: 1.4 sq. mi.; **Water:** 0.0 sq. mi. **Elev:** 980 ft.

In southern PA, south of Reading. Part of the borough is also in Berks County.

Name origin: For the Adams Mill, included in a patent for 356 acres obtained by William Bird in 1739.

Akron
                           Borough
ZIP: 17501 **Lat:** 40-09-27 N **Long:** 76-12-13 W
Pop: 3,869 (1990); 3,471 (1980) **Pop Density:** 2976.2
Land: 1.3 sq. mi.; **Water:** 0.0 sq. mi. **Elev:** 460 ft.

Settled in the 1800s by Germans; incorporated 1884.

Bart
                           Township
Lat: 39-55-28 N **Long:** 76-04-20 W
Pop: 2,774 (1990) **Pop Density:** 172.3
Land: 16.1 sq. mi.; **Water:** 0.0 sq. mi.

In southeastern PA, 15 mi. southeast of Lancaster.

Name origin: For the abbreviation of the title Baronet, for Sir William Keith, Bart., provincial governor of PA (1717–26).

Brecknock
                           Township
ZIP: 17517 **Lat:** 40-11-51 N **Long:** 76-01-45 W
Pop: 5,197 (1990) **Pop Density:** 208.7
Land: 24.9 sq. mi.; **Water:** 0.0 sq. mi.

Brickerville
                           CDP
ZIP: 17543 **Lat:** 40-13-36 N **Long:** 76-17-11 W
Pop: 1,268 (1990) **Pop Density:** 576.4
Land: 2.2 sq. mi.; **Water:** 0.0 sq. mi.

Caernarvon
                           Township
Lat: 40-08-27 N **Long:** 75-56-57 W
Pop: 3,946 (1990) **Pop Density:** 171.6
Land: 23.0 sq. mi.; **Water:** 0.0 sq. mi.

Christiana
                           Borough
ZIP: 17509 **Lat:** 39-57-14 N **Long:** 75-59-51 W
Pop: 1,045 (1990); 1,183 (1980) **Pop Density:** 2090.0
Land: 0.5 sq. mi.; **Water:** 0.0 sq. mi. **Elev:** 494 ft.

Clay
                           Township
ZIP: 17578 **Lat:** 40-14-11 N **Long:** 76-14-21 W
Pop: 5,050 (1990) **Pop Density:** 227.5
Land: 22.2 sq. mi.; **Water:** 0.5 sq. mi.

Colerain
                           Township
ZIP: 17536 **Lat:** 39-51-36 N **Long:** 76-03-45 W
Pop: 2,867 (1990) **Pop Density:** 99.5
Land: 28.8 sq. mi.; **Water:** 0.6 sq. mi.

Columbia
                           Borough
ZIP: 17512 **Lat:** 40-02-00 N **Long:** 76-29-42 W
Pop: 10,701 (1990); 10,466 (1980) **Pop Density:** 4458.8
Land: 2.4 sq. mi.; **Water:** 0.2 sq. mi. **Elev:** 300 ft.

In southeastern PA on the Susquehanna River, 12 mi. west of Lancaster. Laid out in 1788.

Name origin: Possibly in the hope of becoming the site of the national capital. Originally called Wright's Ferry for John Wright, an early settler.

Conestoga
                           Township
ZIP: 17516 **Lat:** 39-55-33 N **Long:** 76-21-23 W
Pop: 3,470 (1990) **Pop Density:** 237.7
Land: 14.6 sq. mi.; **Water:** 1.8 sq. mi.

Name origin: From the creek on which the township is located, from Susquehanna Indian term *Kanastoge*, possibly meaning 'at the place of the immersed pole.' The first Conestoga wagon was made here.

Conoy Township
ZIP: 17502 **Lat:** 40-06-12 N **Long:** 76-40-13 W
Pop: 2,687 (1990) **Pop Density:** 181.6
Land: 14.8 sq. mi.; **Water:** 3.7 sq. mi.
Name origin: For an Indian tribe called the Conoys or Gawanese; name probably means 'cornshellers.'

Denver Borough
ZIP: 17517 **Lat:** 40-13-57 N **Long:** 76-08-19 W
Pop: 2,861 (1990); 2,018 (1980) **Pop Density:** 2200.8
Land: 1.3 sq. mi.; **Water:** 0.0 sq. mi. **Elev:** 380 ft.

Drumore Township
ZIP: 17518 **Lat:** 39-49-07 N **Long:** 76-14-46 W
Pop: 2,114 (1990) **Pop Density:** 88.5
Land: 23.9 sq. mi.; **Water:** 5.0 sq. mi.

Earl Township
ZIP: 17557 **Lat:** 40-07-03 N **Long:** 76-05-43 W
Pop: 5,515 (1990) **Pop Density:** 251.8
Land: 21.9 sq. mi.; **Water:** 0.0 sq. mi.

East Cocalico Township
ZIP: 17517 **Lat:** 40-13-30 N **Long:** 76-06-30 W
Pop: 7,809 (1990) **Pop Density:** 379.1
Land: 20.6 sq. mi.; **Water:** 0.0 sq. mi.
Name origin: From an Indian term possibly meaning 'where snakes gather in holes.'

East Donegal Township
Lat: 40-05-05 N **Long:** 76-34-04 W
Pop: 4,484 (1990) **Pop Density:** 207.6
Land: 21.6 sq. mi.; **Water:** 2.3 sq. mi.

East Drumore Township
Lat: 39-51-07 N **Long:** 76-10-41 W
Pop: 3,225 (1990) **Pop Density:** 139.0
Land: 23.2 sq. mi.; **Water:** 0.0 sq. mi.

East Earl Township
ZIP: 17519 **Lat:** 40-07-37 N **Long:** 76-01-57 W
Pop: 5,491 (1990) **Pop Density:** 223.2
Land: 24.6 sq. mi.; **Water:** 0.1 sq. mi.

East Hempfield Township
ZIP: 17603 **Lat:** 40-04-56 N **Long:** 76-23-05 W
Pop: 18,597 (1990) **Pop Density:** 881.4
Land: 21.1 sq. mi.; **Water:** 0.0 sq. mi.

East Lampeter Township
ZIP: 17602 **Lat:** 40-02-14 N **Long:** 76-12-48 W
Pop: 11,999 (1990) **Pop Density:** 603.0
Land: 19.9 sq. mi.; **Water:** 0.1 sq. mi.

East Petersburg Borough
ZIP: 17520 **Lat:** 40-06-02 N **Long:** 76-21-12 W
Pop: 4,197 (1990); 3,600 (1980) **Pop Density:** 3228.5
Land: 1.3 sq. mi.; **Water:** 0.0 sq. mi. **Elev:** 357 ft.
In southeastern PA, 5 mi. north of Lancaster.

Eden Township
ZIP: 17566 **Lat:** 39-54-32 N **Long:** 76-08-01 W
Pop: 1,857 (1990) **Pop Density:** 149.8
Land: 12.4 sq. mi.; **Water:** 0.0 sq. mi.

Elizabeth Township
ZIP: 17543 **Lat:** 40-13-30 N **Long:** 76-18-22 W
Pop: 3,691 (1990) **Pop Density:** 209.7
Land: 17.6 sq. mi.; **Water:** 0.2 sq. mi.

Elizabethtown Borough
ZIP: 17022 **Lat:** 40-09-12 N **Long:** 76-35-55 W
Pop: 9,952 (1990); 8,233 (1980) **Pop Density:** 3827.7
Land: 2.6 sq. mi.; **Water:** 0.0 sq. mi. **Elev:** 456 ft.
In southeastern PA, 15 mi. southeast of Harrisburg.
Name origin: For the wife of Capt. Barnabas Hughes, who purchased the tavern and the original Harris tract in 1750.

Ephrata Borough
ZIP: 17522 **Lat:** 40-10-50 N **Long:** 76-10-57 W
Pop: 12,133 (1990); 11,095 (1980) **Pop Density:** 3370.3
Land: 3.6 sq. mi.; **Water:** 0.0 sq. mi. **Elev:** 400 ft.
In southeastern PA, 12 mi. northeast of Lancaster. Site of historic Ephrata Cloister along a scenic route. The German Seventh-Day Adventists established a monastic community here 1735.
Name origin: For the biblical city.

*Ephrata Township
ZIP: 17522 **Lat:** 40-10-14 N **Long:** 76-10-45 W
Pop: 7,116 (1990) **Pop Density:** 442.0
Land: 16.1 sq. mi.; **Water:** 0.0 sq. mi.

Fulton Township
ZIP: 17563 **Lat:** 39-45-39 N **Long:** 76-11-35 W
Pop: 2,688 (1990) **Pop Density:** 103.8
Land: 25.9 sq. mi.; **Water:** 3.4 sq. mi.

Gap CDP
ZIP: 17527 **Lat:** 39-59-20 N **Long:** 76-01-27 W
Pop: 1,226 (1990) **Pop Density:** 533.0
Land: 2.3 sq. mi.; **Water:** 0.0 sq. mi.

Lancaster City
ZIP: 17601 **Lat:** 40-02-30 N **Long:** 76-18-04 W
Pop: 55,551 (1990); 54,725 (1980) **Pop Density:** 7506.9
Land: 7.4 sq. mi.; **Water:** 0.0 sq. mi. **Elev:** 368 ft.
In southeastern PA near the Susquehanna River, 64 mi. west of Philadelphia. Laid out in 1730; chartered as borough May 1, 1742, as city Mar 10, 1818.
Name origin: Named by John Wright, chief magistrate, for his home shire of Lancaster, England.

*Lancaster Township
ZIP: 17603 **Lat:** 40-01-25 N **Long:** 76-19-22 W
Pop: 13,187 (1990) **Pop Density:** 2197.8
Land: 6.0 sq. mi.; **Water:** 0.0 sq. mi.

Leacock Township
ZIP: 17540 **Lat:** 40-02-24 N **Long:** 76-06-36 W
Pop: 4,668 (1990) **Pop Density:** 226.6
Land: 20.6 sq. mi.; **Water:** 0.0 sq. mi.

Lititz Borough
ZIP: 17543 **Lat:** 40-09-13 N **Long:** 76-18-19 W
Pop: 8,280 (1990); 7,590 (1980) **Pop Density:** 3600.0
Land: 2.3 sq. mi.; **Water:** 0.0 sq. mi. **Elev:** 387 ft.
In southeastern PA. Laid out in 1757 by Moravian missionaries from Bethlehem.
Name origin: For a barony in Moravia.

Little Britain Township
ZIP: 17566 **Lat:** 39-47-14 N **Long:** 76-06-21 W
Pop: 2,701 (1990) **Pop Density:** 98.6
Land: 27.4 sq. mi.; **Water:** 0.2 sq. mi.

Manheim
Township
ZIP: 17545   Lat: 40-05-42 N Long: 76-17-39 W
Pop: 28,880 (1990)   Pop Density: 1203.3
Land: 24.0 sq. mi.; Water: 0.1 sq. mi.

In southeastern PA, 10 mi. northeast of Lancaster.
Name origin: For Manheim, Germany.

*Manheim
Borough
ZIP: 17545   Lat: 40-09-47 N Long: 76-23-47 W
Pop: 5,011 (1990); 5,015 (1980)   Pop Density: 3579.3
Land: 1.4 sq. mi.; Water: 0.0 sq. mi.   Elev: 402 ft.

Manor
Township
ZIP: 17582   Lat: 39-58-56 N Long: 76-25-20 W
Pop: 14,130 (1990)   Pop Density: 367.0
Land: 38.5 sq. mi.; Water: 10.1 sq. mi.

Name origin: For Conestoga Manor, one of the twenty manors in PA belonging to the Penns.

Marietta
Borough
ZIP: 17547   Lat: 40-03-25 N Long: 76-33-10 W
Pop: 2,778 (1990); 2,740 (1980)   Pop Density: 3472.5
Land: 0.8 sq. mi.; Water: 0.0 sq. mi.   Elev: 280 ft.

In southeastern PA on the Susquehanna River, 22 mi. southeast of Harrisburg. Originally two distinct settlements: New Haven, laid out by David Cook in 1803, and Waterford, laid out at Anderson's Ferry by James Anderson in 1804. Incorporated under present name in 1812.
Name origin: Believed to be for Mary Cook and Etta Anderson.

Martic
Township
ZIP: 17565   Lat: 39-52-12 N Long: 76-18-46 W
Pop: 4,362 (1990)   Pop Density: 150.4
Land: 29.0 sq. mi.; Water: 3.7 sq. mi.

Maytown
CDP
Lat: 40-04-37 N Long: 76-34-49 W
Pop: 1,720 (1990); 1,479 (1980)   Pop Density: 464.9
Land: 3.7 sq. mi.; Water: 0.0 sq. mi.

Millersville
Borough
ZIP: 17551   Lat: 40-00-12 N Long: 76-21-13 W
Pop: 8,099 (1990); 7,668 (1980)   Pop Density: 4049.5
Land: 2.0 sq. mi.; Water: 0.0 sq. mi.   Elev: 312 ft.

In southeastern PA, a suburb of Lancaster.

Mount Joy
Borough
ZIP: 17552   Lat: 40-06-37 N Long: 76-30-28 W
Pop: 6,398 (1990); 5,680 (1980)   Pop Density: 2781.7
Land: 2.3 sq. mi.; Water: 0.0 sq. mi.   Elev: 362 ft.

*Mount Joy
Township
ZIP: 17022   Lat: 40-10-07 N Long: 76-33-04 W
Pop: 6,227 (1990)   Pop Density: 222.4
Land: 28.0 sq. mi.; Water: 0.0 sq. mi.

Mountville
Borough
ZIP: 17554   Lat: 40-02-26 N Long: 76-26-03 W
Pop: 1,977 (1990); 1,505 (1980)   Pop Density: 2196.7
Land: 0.9 sq. mi.; Water: 0.0 sq. mi.   Elev: 440 ft.

New Holland
Borough
ZIP: 17557   Lat: 40-06-03 N Long: 76-05-25 W
Pop: 4,484 (1990); 4,147 (1980)   Pop Density: 2135.2
Land: 2.1 sq. mi.; Water: 0.0 sq. mi.   Elev: 494 ft.

In southeastern PA, 13 mi. northeast of Lancaster.

Paradise
Township
ZIP: 17562   Lat: 39-59-19 N Long: 76-06-25 W
Pop: 4,430 (1990)   Pop Density: 236.9
Land: 18.7 sq. mi.; Water: 0.0 sq. mi.

Penn
Township
ZIP: 17545   Lat: 40-11-24 N Long: 76-22-24 W
Pop: 6,760 (1990)   Pop Density: 228.4
Land: 29.6 sq. mi.; Water: 0.0 sq. mi.

Name origin: For William Penn (1644–1718), founder of Pennsylvania.

Pequea
Township
ZIP: 17565   Lat: 39-58-08 N Long: 76-18-17 W
Pop: 4,512 (1990)   Pop Density: 331.8
Land: 13.6 sq. mi.; Water: 0.0 sq. mi.

Providence
Township
ZIP: 17560   Lat: 39-54-19 N Long: 76-13-52 W
Pop: 6,071 (1990)   Pop Density: 302.0
Land: 20.1 sq. mi.; Water: 0.0 sq. mi.

Quarryville
Borough
ZIP: 17566   Lat: 39-53-44 N Long: 76-09-40 W
Pop: 1,642 (1990); 1,558 (1980)   Pop Density: 1263.1
Land: 1.3 sq. mi.; Water: 0.0 sq. mi.   Elev: 503 ft.

Rapho
Township
ZIP: 17545   Lat: 40-09-21 N Long: 76-27-21 W
Pop: 8,211 (1990)   Pop Density: 172.9
Land: 47.5 sq. mi.; Water: 0.0 sq. mi.

Sadsbury
Township
Lat: 39-56-21 N Long: 76-01-03 W
Pop: 2,712 (1990)   Pop Density: 137.0
Land: 19.8 sq. mi.; Water: 0.0 sq. mi.

Salisbury
Township
ZIP: 17535   Lat: 40-02-19 N Long: 75-59-32 W
Pop: 8,527 (1990)   Pop Density: 203.5
Land: 41.9 sq. mi.; Water: 0.0 sq. mi.

Strasburg
Township
ZIP: 17579   Lat: 39-57-31 N Long: 76-11-00 W
Pop: 3,688 (1990)   Pop Density: 184.4
Land: 20.0 sq. mi.; Water: 0.0 sq. mi.

*Strasburg
Borough
ZIP: 17579   Lat: 39-59-00 N Long: 76-11-08 W
Pop: 2,568 (1990); 1,999 (1980)   Pop Density: 2568.0
Land: 1.0 sq. mi.; Water: 0.0 sq. mi.   Elev: 470 ft.

In southeastern PA, 10 mi. southeast of Lancaster. Settled in 1733 by the LeFevres, Ferrees, and other French immigrants.
Name origin: For Strasbourg in Alsace, former home of original settlers; with a spelling alteration.

Terre Hill
Borough
ZIP: 17581   Lat: 40-09-26 N Long: 76-03-02 W
Pop: 1,282 (1990); 1,217 (1980)   Pop Density: 2564.0
Land: 0.5 sq. mi.; Water: 0.0 sq. mi.   Elev: 540 ft.

Upper Leacock
Township
ZIP: 17540   Lat: 40-04-59 N Long: 76-11-13 W
Pop: 7,254 (1990)   Pop Density: 400.8
Land: 18.1 sq. mi.; Water: 0.1 sq. mi.

Warwick
Township
ZIP: 17543   Lat: 40-09-15 N Long: 76-17-02 W
Pop: 11,622 (1990)   Pop Density: 581.1
Land: 20.0 sq. mi.; Water: 0.1 sq. mi.   Elev: 400 ft.

West Cocalico
Township
ZIP: 17578   Lat: 40-15-50 N Long: 76-09-55 W
Pop: 5,521 (1990)   Pop Density: 199.3
Land: 27.7 sq. mi.; Water: 0.1 sq. mi.

West Donegal
Township
ZIP: 17022   Lat: 40-07-34 N Long: 76-37-13 W
Pop: 5,605 (1990)   Pop Density: 357.0
Land: 15.7 sq. mi.; Water: 0.0 sq. mi.

West Earl
Township
ZIP: 17508   Lat: 40-07-42 N Long: 76-10-47 W
Pop: 6,434 (1990)   Pop Density: 365.6
Land: 17.6 sq. mi.; Water: 0.4 sq. mi.

West Hempfield
Township
ZIP: 17601   Lat: 40-03-21 N Long: 76-27-49 W
Pop: 12,942 (1990)   Pop Density: 684.8
Land: 18.9 sq. mi.; Water: 2.1 sq. mi.

West Lampeter
Township
ZIP: 17537   Lat: 39-59-43 N Long: 76-15-24 W
Pop: 9,865 (1990)   Pop Density: 601.5
Land: 16.4 sq. mi.; Water: 0.0 sq. mi.   Elev: 300 ft.

Lawrence County
County Seat: New Castle (ZIP: 16101)

Pop: 96,246 (1990); 107,150 (1980)   Pop Density: 267.0
Land: 360.5 sq. mi.; Water: 2.3 sq. mi.   Area Code: 412
On central-western border of PA, northwest of Pittsburgh; organized Mar 20, 1849 from Beaver and Mercer counties.

Name origin: For the *Lawrence*, the flagship of American commander Oliver Hazard Perry (1785–1819) in the Battle of Lake Erie (1813).

Bessemer
Borough
ZIP: 16112   Lat: 40-58-36 N Long: 80-29-14 W
Pop: 1,196 (1990); 1,293 (1980)   Pop Density: 703.5
Land: 1.7 sq. mi.; Water: 0.1 sq. mi.   Elev: 1086 ft.

In western PA, 10 mi. west of New Castle.

Name origin: For Sir Henry Bessemer (1813–98), inventor of an economical process to make steel that revolutionized the industry.

Ellport
Borough
ZIP: 16117   Lat: 40-51-40 N Long: 80-15-44 W
Pop: 1,243 (1990); 1,290 (1980)   Pop Density: 3107.5
Land: 0.4 sq. mi.; Water: 0.0 sq. mi.   Elev: 900 ft.

Ellwood City
Borough
ZIP: 16117   Lat: 40-51-51 N Long: 80-16-58 W
Pop: 8,044 (1990); 9,203 (1980)   Pop Density: 4022.0
Land: 2.0 sq. mi.; Water: 0.0 sq. mi.

In western PA on the Shenango River, 10 mi. north of Beaver Falls. Laid out in 1890 by the Pittsburgh Company. Part of the town is also in Beaver County.

Name origin: For Col. I. L. Ellwood of IN, who pioneered the manufacturing of wire fencing.

Enon Valley
Borough
ZIP: 16120   Lat: 40-51-20 N Long: 80-27-26 W
Pop: 355 (1990); 408 (1980)   Pop Density: 710.0
Land: 0.5 sq. mi.; Water: 0.0 sq. mi.   Elev: 995 ft.

Hickory
Township
Lat: 41-02-15 N Long: 80-17-08 W
Pop: 2,317 (1990)   Pop Density: 143.9
Land: 16.1 sq. mi.; Water: 0.0 sq. mi.

Little Beaver
Township
Lat: 40-52-33 N Long: 80-28-07 W
Pop: 1,251 (1990)   Pop Density: 61.3
Land: 20.4 sq. mi.; Water: 0.1 sq. mi.

Mahoning
Township
Lat: 41-01-34 N Long: 80-28-05 W
Pop: 3,560 (1990)   Pop Density: 144.7
Land: 24.6 sq. mi.; Water: 0.4 sq. mi.

Neshannock
Township
ZIP: 16105   Lat: 41-03-06 N Long: 80-21-05 W
Pop: 8,373 (1990)   Pop Density: 484.0
Land: 17.3 sq. mi.; Water: 0.1 sq. mi.

New Beaver
Borough
ZIP: 16141   Lat: 40-52-56 N Long: 80-21-52 W
Pop: 1,736 (1990); 1,885 (1980)   Pop Density: 119.7
Land: 14.5 sq. mi.; Water: 0.0 sq. mi.

In western PA, a suburb of Beaver Falls. Incorporated 1960.
Name origin: For Big Beaver Township.

New Castle
City
ZIP: 16101   Lat: 40-59-44 N Long: 80-20-46 W
Pop: 28,334 (1990); 33,621 (1980)   Pop Density: 3333.4
Land: 8.5 sq. mi.; Water: 0.0 sq. mi.   Elev: 807 ft.

In western PA on the Shenango River, 44 mi northwest of Pittsburgh. Laid out in 1802; incorporated as borough Mar 25, 1825, as city Feb 25, 1869.

Name origin: For Newcastle-upon-Tyne, the English industrial city.

New Wilmington
Borough
ZIP: 16142   Lat: 41-07-03 N Long: 80-19-55 W
Pop: 2,706 (1990); 2,774 (1980)   Pop Density: 2460.0
Land: 1.1 sq. mi.; Water: 0.0 sq. mi.   Elev: 999 ft.

In western PA on Little Neshannock Creek, 9 mi. north of New Castle. Incorporated in 1863 from Wilmington Township.

North Beaver
Township
Lat: 40-56-56 N Long: 80-26-29 W
Pop: 3,982 (1990)   Pop Density: 92.4
Land: 43.1 sq. mi.; Water: 0.2 sq. mi.

Perry
Township
Lat: 40-53-25 N Long: 80-11-39 W
Pop: 1,841 (1990) Pop Density: 100.1
Land: 18.4 sq. mi.; Water: 0.1 sq. mi.

Plain Grove
Township
Lat: 41-04-04 N Long: 80-09-14 W
Pop: 791 (1990) Pop Density: 44.2
Land: 17.9 sq. mi.; Water: 0.1 sq. mi.

Pulaski
Township
ZIP: 16143 Lat: 41-05-52 N Long: 80-26-55 W
Pop: 3,469 (1990) Pop Density: 113.7
Land: 30.5 sq. mi.; Water: 0.1 sq. mi.

Scott
Township
Lat: 41-01-23 N Long: 80-12-33 W
Pop: 2,200 (1990) Pop Density: 111.7
Land: 19.7 sq. mi.; Water: 0.0 sq. mi.

Shenango
Township
ZIP: 16101 Lat: 40-56-49 N Long: 80-18-19 W
Pop: 7,187 (1990) Pop Density: 294.5
Land: 24.4 sq. mi.; Water: 0.0 sq. mi.

Slippery Rock
Township
Lat: 40-57-15 N Long: 80-13-07 W
Pop: 3,196 (1990) Pop Density: 105.8
Land: 30.2 sq. mi.; Water: 0.1 sq. mi.

S.N.P.J.
Borough
ZIP: 16120 Lat: 40-55-43 N Long: 80-29-56 W
Pop: 12 (1990); 16 (1980) Pop Density: 17.1
Land: 0.7 sq. mi.; Water: 0.0 sq. mi.

South New Castle
Borough
ZIP: 16101 Lat: 40-58-27 N Long: 80-20-45 W
Pop: 805 (1990); 879 (1980) Pop Density: 2683.3
Land: 0.3 sq. mi.; Water: 0.0 sq. mi. Elev: 1000 ft.

Taylor
Township
Lat: 40-56-25 N Long: 80-21-40 W
Pop: 1,326 (1990) Pop Density: 260.0
Land: 5.1 sq. mi.; Water: 0.2 sq. mi.

Union
Township
Lat: 41-00-44 N Long: 80-23-38 W
Pop: 5,581 (1990) Pop Density: 581.4
Land: 9.6 sq. mi.; Water: 0.0 sq. mi.

Volant
Borough
ZIP: 16156 Lat: 41-06-49 N Long: 80-15-32 W
Pop: 152 (1990); 203 (1980) Pop Density: 1520.0
Land: 0.1 sq. mi.; Water: 0.0 sq. mi.

Wampum
Borough
ZIP: 16157 Lat: 40-53-11 N Long: 80-20-19 W
Pop: 666 (1990); 851 (1980) Pop Density: 740.0
Land: 0.9 sq. mi.; Water: 0.0 sq. mi. Elev: 800 ft.

In western PA on the Beaver River, south of New Castle.
Settled in 1796; incorporated 1876.
Name origin: From a contraction of an Indian term
wampumpeak probably meaning 'a string of shell beads.'

Washington
Township
Lat: 41-04-59 N Long: 80-13-28 W
Pop: 671 (1990) Pop Density: 40.9
Land: 16.4 sq. mi.; Water: 0.2 sq. mi.

Wayne
Township
Lat: 40-53-24 N Long: 80-16-53 W
Pop: 2,785 (1990) Pop Density: 173.0
Land: 16.1 sq. mi.; Water: 0.3 sq. mi.

Wilmington
Township
Lat: 41-06-14 N Long: 80-19-21 W
Pop: 2,467 (1990) Pop Density: 123.3
Land: 20.0 sq. mi.; Water: 0.0 sq. mi.

Lebanon County
County Seat: Lebanon (ZIP: 17042)

Pop: 113,744 (1990); 108,582 (1980) Pop Density: 314.4
Land: 361.8 sq. mi.; Water: 0.8 sq. mi. Area Code: 717
In east-central PA, east of Harrisburg; organized Feb 16, 1815 from Dauphin and
Lancaster counties.
Name origin: For Lebanon Township, from which the county was formed.

Annville
Township
ZIP: 17003 Lat: 40-19-57 N Long: 76-30-23 W
Pop: 4,294 (1990) Pop Density: 2862.7
Land: 1.5 sq. mi.; Water: 0.0 sq. mi.

In south-central PA, northeast of Harrisburg, on Quitapahilla
Creek.
Name origin: For the wife of Abraham Miller, who laid out
the town in 1762. Originally called Millersville for Miller
himself.

Avon Heights
CDP
ZIP: 17042 Lat: 40-20-44 N Long: 76-23-13 W
Pop: 2,714 (1990) Pop Density: 2261.7
Land: 1.2 sq. mi.; Water: 0.0 sq. mi.

Bethel
Township
Lat: 40-26-49 N Long: 76-25-20 W
Pop: 4,343 (1990) Pop Density: 125.2
Land: 34.7 sq. mi.; Water: 0.0 sq. mi.

Campbelltown
CDP
Lat: 40-16-34 N Long: 76-35-04 W
Pop: 1,609 (1990); 1,250 (1980) Pop Density: 536.3
Land: 3.0 sq. mi.; Water: 0.0 sq. mi.

Cleona
Borough
ZIP: 17042 Lat: 40-20-19 N Long: 76-28-38 W
Pop: 2,322 (1990); 2,003 (1980) Pop Density: 2580.0
Land: 0.9 sq. mi.; Water: 0.0 sq. mi. Elev: 560 ft.

In southeast-central PA, just west of Lebanon.

Cold Spring
Township
Lat: 40-30-19 N Long: 76-35-55 W
Pop: 3 (1990) **Pop Density:** 0.2
Land: 19.7 sq. mi.; **Water:** 0.0 sq. mi.

Cornwall
Borough
ZIP: 17016 **Lat:** 40-16-10 N **Long:** 76-24-29 W
Pop: 3,231 (1990); 2,653 (1980) **Pop Density:** 333.1
Land: 9.7 sq. mi.; **Water:** 0.2 sq. mi. **Elev:** 640 ft.
In southeast-central PA, served by major rail lines heading to and from Lebanon. Site of an old Cornwall Blast furnace.
Name origin: For a region in England.

East Hanover
Township
ZIP: 17003 **Lat:** 40-24-11 N **Long:** 76-36-02 W
Pop: 3,058 (1990) **Pop Density:** 93.2
Land: 32.8 sq. mi.; **Water:** 0.2 sq. mi.

Fredericksburg
CDP
ZIP: 17026 **Lat:** 40-27-22 N **Long:** 76-25-32 W
Pop: 2,338 (1990) **Pop Density:** 152.8
Land: 15.3 sq. mi.; **Water:** 0.0 sq. mi.

Heidelberg
Township
Lat: 40-17-44 N Long: 76-17-35 W
Pop: 3,797 (1990) **Pop Density:** 156.9
Land: 24.2 sq. mi.; **Water:** 0.0 sq. mi.

Jackson
Township
ZIP: 17042 **Lat:** 40-22-37 N **Long:** 76-18-45 W
Pop: 5,732 (1990) **Pop Density:** 240.8
Land: 23.8 sq. mi.; **Water:** 0.1 sq. mi.
Name origin: For Andrew Jackson (1767–1845), seventh U.S. president.

Jonestown
Borough
ZIP: 17038 **Lat:** 40-24-47 N **Long:** 76-28-50 W
Pop: 931 (1990); 814 (1980) **Pop Density:** 1551.7
Land: 0.6 sq. mi.; **Water:** 0.0 sq. mi. **Elev:** 475 ft.

Lebanon
City
ZIP: 17042 **Lat:** 40-20-28 N **Long:** 76-25-23 W
Pop: 24,800 (1990); 25,711 (1980) **Pop Density:** 5904.8
Land: 4.2 sq. mi.; **Water:** 0.0 sq. mi. **Elev:** 480 ft.
In southeast-central PA on a branch of Quitapahilla Creek between the South and Blue mountains, 80 mi. northwest of Philadelphia. Laid out in 1750 by George Steitz. First incorporated as borough Mar 28, 1799, but citizens did not accept incorporation; finally chartered as borough Feb 20, 1821, as city 1885.
Name origin: For cedar trees growing in the vicinity that may have reminded the Moravian settlers of the biblical "cedars of Lebanon."

Millcreek
Township
ZIP: 17073 **Lat:** 40-19-39 N **Long:** 76-13-20 W
Pop: 2,687 (1990) **Pop Density:** 131.7
Land: 20.4 sq. mi.; **Water:** 0.0 sq. mi.

Mount Gretna
Borough
ZIP: 17064 **Lat:** 40-14-43 N **Long:** 76-28-17 W
Pop: 303 (1990); 280 (1980) **Pop Density:** 1515.0
Land: 0.2 sq. mi.; **Water:** 0.0 sq. mi. **Elev:** 620 ft.

Myerstown
Borough
ZIP: 17067 **Lat:** 40-22-17 N **Long:** 76-18-19 W
Pop: 3,236 (1990); 3,131 (1980) **Pop Density:** 3595.6
Land: 0.9 sq. mi.; **Water:** 0.0 sq. mi. **Elev:** 481 ft.
In southeast-central PA, 8 mi. east of Lebanon.

North Annville
Township
Lat: 40-21-35 N Long: 76-32-28 W
Pop: 2,441 (1990) **Pop Density:** 139.5
Land: 17.5 sq. mi.; **Water:** 0.0 sq. mi.

North Cornwall
Township
ZIP: 17042 **Lat:** 40-18-56 N **Long:** 76-27-24 W
Pop: 4,886 (1990) **Pop Density:** 514.3
Land: 9.5 sq. mi.; **Water:** 0.0 sq. mi.

North Lebanon
Township
ZIP: 17042 **Lat:** 40-21-58 N **Long:** 76-25-18 W
Pop: 9,741 (1990) **Pop Density:** 576.4
Land: 16.9 sq. mi.; **Water:** 0.1 sq. mi.

North Londonderry
Township
ZIP: 17078 **Lat:** 40-19-20 N **Long** 76-34-52 W
Pop: 5,630 (1990) **Pop Density:** 531.1
Land: 10.6 sq. mi.; **Water:** 0.0 sq. mi.

Palmyra
Borough
ZIP: 17078 **Lat:** 40-18-34 N **Long:** 76-35-42 W
Pop: 6,910 (1990); 7,228 (1980) **Pop Density:** 3636.8
Land: 1.9 sq. mi.; **Water:** 0.0 sq. mi.
In southeast-central PA, 15 mi. east of Harrisburg. Settled in 1749 by John Palm, who came to America from Germany.
Name origin: For the ancient Syrian city. Previously called Palmstown.

Richland
Borough
ZIP: 17087 **Lat:** 40-21-25 N **Long:** 76-15-27 W
Pop: 1,457 (1990); 1,470 (1980) **Pop Density:** 910.6
Land: 1.6 sq. mi.; **Water:** 0.0 sq. mi. **Elev:** 489 ft.

South Annville
Township
Lat: 40-17-46 N Long: 76-30-41 W
Pop: 3,008 (1990) **Pop Density:** 152.7
Land: 19.7 sq. mi.; **Water:** 0.0 sq. mi.

South Lebanon
Township
ZIP: 17042 **Lat:** 40-18-14 N **Long:** 76-22-06 W
Pop: 7,491 (1990) **Pop Density:** 343.6
Land: 21.8 sq. mi.; **Water:** 0.1 sq. mi. **Elev:** 618 ft.

South Londonderry
Township
Lat: 40-14-46 N Long: 76-32-32 W
Pop: 4,502 (1990) **Pop Density:** 186.0
Land: 24.2 sq. mi.; **Water:** 0.0 sq. mi.

Swatara
Township
Lat: 40-25-57 N Long: 76-28-25 W
Pop: 3,318 (1990) **Pop Density:** 156.5
Land: 21.2 sq. mi.; **Water:** 0.0 sq. mi.

Union
Township
Lat: 40-27-29 N Long: 76-32-40 W
Pop: 2,755 (1990) **Pop Density:** 80.3
Land: 34.3 sq. mi.; **Water:** 0.0 sq. mi.

West Cornwall
Township
Lat: 40-16-07 N Long: 76-27-05 W
Pop: 1,996 (1990) **Pop Density:** 229.4
Land: 8.7 sq. mi.; **Water:** 0.0 sq. mi.

West Lebanon
Township
Lat: 40-20-35 N Long: 76-26-47 W
Pop: 872 (1990) **Pop Density:** 2180.0
Land: 0.4 sq. mi.; **Water:** 0.0 sq. mi.

Lehigh County
County Seat: Allentown (ZIP: 18105)

Pop: 291,130 (1990); 272,349 (1980)   **Pop Density:** 839.8
Land: 346.7 sq. mi.; **Water:** 1.7 sq. mi.   **Area Code:** 215

In mideastern PA, northeast of Reading; organized Mar 6, 1812 from Northampton County.

Name origin: For the Lehigh River, which forms most of its eastern border. From Algonquian *lechauwekink* 'where there are forks'; shortened by Germans to *Lecha*, then anglicized.

Alburtis   Borough
ZIP: 18011   **Lat:** 40-30-34 N **Long:** 75-36-02 W
Pop: 1,415 (1990); 1,428 (1980)   **Pop Density:** 2021.4
Land: 0.7 sq. mi.; **Water:** 0.0 sq. mi.   **Elev:** 560 ft.
In eastern PA near Allentown.

Allentown   City
ZIP: 18101   **Lat:** 40-35-46 N **Long:** 75-28-39 W
Pop: 105,090 (1990); 103,758 (1980)   **Pop Density:** 5937.3
Land: 17.7 sq. mi.; **Water:** 0.2 sq. mi.

In eastern PA on the Lehigh River near Bethlehem and Easton, 48 mi. north of Philadelphia. Settled by German immigrants in the 1720s. Laid out in 1762; incorporated as borough Mar 18, 1811; as city Mar 12, 1867. Diverse manufacturing city: electrical appliances, electronic equipment; leading center of truck manufacturing.

Name origin: For William Allen, founder and jurist. Earlier called Northampton Town. Nicknamed "Truck Capital of the World." ·

Ancient Oaks   CDP
Lat: 40-31-57 N **Long:** 75-35-08 W
Pop: 2,663 (1990)   **Pop Density:** 1210.5
Land: 2.2 sq. mi.; **Water:** 0.0 sq. mi.

Bethlehem   City
ZIP: 18015   **Lat:** 40-37-54 N **Long:** 75-24-29 W
Pop: 18,867 (1990); 19,865 (1980)   **Pop Density:** 4288.0
Land: 4.4 sq. mi.; **Water:** 0.1 sq. mi.   **Elev:** 360 ft.

In eastern PA on the Lehigh River, 5 mi. east of Allentown. Founded in 1741 by the Moravian Brethren. Site of Lehigh Univ. Part of the city is also in Northampton County.

Name origin: Named on Christmas Eve 1741 for the birthplace of Jesus, when the congregation and their leader, Count Nicholas Ludwig, sang an old German hymn with the words "Bethlehem gave us that which makes life rich."

Catasauqua   Borough
ZIP: 18032   **Lat:** 40-39-07 N **Long:** 75-27-52 W
Pop: 6,662 (1990); 6,711 (1980)   **Pop Density:** 5124.6
Land: 1.3 sq. mi.; **Water:** 0.0 sq. mi.   **Elev:** 358 ft.

In eastern PA on the Lehigh River, north of Allentown. Incorporated 1853.

Name origin: For the creek flowing nearby, a name corrupted from the Delaware Indian term *gotto-shacki* possibly meaning 'burnt ground,' 'parched land,' or 'the earth thirsts.'

Coopersburg   Borough
ZIP: 18036   **Lat:** 40-30-37 N **Long:** 75-23-28 W
Pop: 2,599 (1990); 2,595 (1980)   **Pop Density:** 2887.8
Land: 0.9 sq. mi.; **Water:** 0.0 sq. mi.   **Elev:** 500 ft.
In eastern PA, 10 mi. south of Allentown. Founded 1780.

Coplay   Borough
ZIP: 18037   **Lat:** 40-40-15 N **Long:** 75-29-47 W
Pop: 3,267 (1990); 3,130 (1980)   **Pop Density:** 5445.0
Land: 0.6 sq. mi.; **Water:** 0.0 sq. mi.   **Elev:** 400 ft.

In eastern PA on the Lehigh River, north of Allentown.

Name origin: From an Indian term possibly meaning 'smooth running stream.'

Emmaus   Borough
ZIP: 18049   **Lat:** 40-32-09 N **Long:** 75-29-52 W
Pop: 11,157 (1990); 11,001 (1980)   **Pop Density:** 3847.2
Land: 2.9 sq. mi.; **Water:** 0.0 sq. mi.   **Elev:** 448 ft.

In eastern PA, 5 mi. south of Allentown. Founded in 1740 by the Moravians.

Name origin: Named in 1761 when Bishop August Spangenberg (1704–92), founder of the Moravian Church in America, conducted a feast here and named it for the biblical town of Emmaus; in succeeding years one "m" was dropped from the name, but in 1939 the earlier spelling was officially restored. Previously called Maguntchi, from an Indian term possibly meaning 'place of the bears.'

Fountain Hill   Borough
ZIP: 18015   **Lat:** 40-36-09 N **Long:** 75-23-47 W
Pop: 4,637 (1990); 4,805 (1980)   **Pop Density:** 6624.3
Land: 0.7 sq. mi.; **Water:** 0.0 sq. mi.   **Elev:** 366 ft.
In eastern PA, 1 mi. west of Bethlehem.

Fullerton   CDP
ZIP: 18052   **Lat:** 40-37-55 N **Long:** 75-29-09 W
Pop: 13,127 (1990); 8,055 (1980)   **Pop Density:** 3547.8
Land: 3.7 sq. mi.; **Water:** 0.0 sq. mi.

Hanover   Township
Lat: 40-38-45 N **Long:** 75-26-39 W
Pop: 2,243 (1990)   **Pop Density:** 534.0
Land: 4.2 sq. mi.; **Water:** 0.0 sq. mi.

Heidelberg   Township
Lat: 40-42-39 N **Long:** 75-41-54 W
Pop: 3,250 (1990)   **Pop Density:** 131.6
Land: 24.7 sq. mi.; **Water:** 0.0 sq. mi.

Hokendauqua   CDP
Lat: 40-39-31 N **Long:** 75-29-44 W
Pop: 3,413 (1990)   **Pop Density:** 3102.7
Land: 1.1 sq. mi.; **Water:** 0.0 sq. mi.

Lower Macungie   Township
ZIP: 18062   **Lat:** 40-31-50 N **Long:** 75-34-03 W
Pop: 16,871 (1990)   **Pop Density:** 746.5
Land: 22.6 sq. mi.; **Water:** 0.0 sq. mi.

Lower Milford
Township
Lat: 40-28-05 N **Long:** 75-28-30 W
Pop: 3,269 (1990) **Pop Density:** 165.9
Land: 19.7 sq. mi.; **Water:** 0.0 sq. mi.

Lowhill
Township
Lat: 40-38-28 N **Long:** 75-39-29 W
Pop: 1,602 (1990) **Pop Density:** 114.4
Land: 14.0 sq. mi.; **Water:** 0.0 sq. mi.

Lynn
Township
Lat: 40-40-13 N **Long:** 75-47-29 W
Pop: 3,220 (1990) **Pop Density:** 77.8
Land: 41.4 sq. mi.; **Water:** 0.2 sq. mi.

Macungie
Borough
ZIP: 18062 **Lat:** 40-30-56 N **Long:** 75-33-15 W
Pop: 2,597 (1990); 1,899 (1980) **Pop Density:** 2597.0
Land: 1.0 sq. mi.; **Water:** 0.0 sq. mi. **Elev:** 374 ft.
In eastern PA on Swope Creek, a southern suburb of Allentown.
Name origin: From an Indian term possibly meaning 'feeding place of the bears.'

North Whitehall
Township
ZIP: 18037 **Lat:** 40-40-44 N **Long:** 75-34-41 W
Pop: 10,827 (1990) **Pop Density:** 377.2
Land: 28.7 sq. mi.; **Water:** 0.4 sq. mi.

Salisbury
Township
ZIP: 18103 **Lat:** 40-34-54 N **Long:** 75-26-53 W
Pop: 13,401 (1990) **Pop Density:** 1218.3
Land: 11.0 sq. mi.; **Water:** 0.1 sq. mi.

Slatington
Borough
ZIP: 18080 **Lat:** 40-45-15 N **Long:** 75-36-44 W
Pop: 4,678 (1990); 4,277 (1980) **Pop Density:** 3598.5
Land: 1.3 sq. mi.; **Water:** 0.1 sq. mi. **Elev:** 500 ft.
In eastern PA, 15 mi. northwest of Allentown.
Name origin: For being a slate center where quarrying began in 1845.

South Whitehall
Township
ZIP: 18104 **Lat:** 40-36-45 N **Long:** 75-32-56 W
Pop: 18,261 (1990) **Pop Density:** 1061.7
Land: 17.2 sq. mi.; **Water:** 0.1 sq. mi.

Upper Macungie
Township
ZIP: 18087 **Lat:** 40-34-08 N **Long:** 75-37-34 W
Pop: 8,757 (1990) **Pop Density:** 334.2
Land: 26.2 sq. mi.; **Water:** 0.1 sq. mi.

Upper Milford
Township
ZIP: 18092 **Lat:** 40-29-25 N **Long:** 75-31-05 W
Pop: 6,304 (1990) **Pop Density:** 352.2
Land: 17.9 sq. mi.; **Water:** 0.0 sq. mi.

Upper Saucon
Township
ZIP: 18034 **Lat:** 40-32-15 N **Long:** 75-24-23 W
Pop: 9,775 (1990) **Pop Density:** 395.7
Land: 24.7 sq. mi.; **Water:** 0.0 sq. mi.

Washington
Township
ZIP: 18080 **Lat:** 40-44-18 N **Long:** 75-38-21 W
Pop: 6,356 (1990) **Pop Density:** 269.3
Land: 23.6 sq. mi.; **Water:** 0.1 sq. mi.
Name origin: For George Washington (1732–99), first U.S. president.

Weisenberg
Township
Lat: 40-36-16 N **Long:** 75-42-39 W
Pop: 3,246 (1990) **Pop Density:** 121.1
Land: 26.8 sq. mi.; **Water:** 0.0 sq. mi.

Whitehall
Township
ZIP: 18052 **Lat:** 40-39-29 N **Long:** 75-30-18 W
Pop: 22,779 (1990) **Pop Density:** 1822.3
Land: 12.5 sq. mi.; **Water:** 0.2 sq. mi.

Luzerne County
County Seat: Wilkes-Barre (ZIP: 18702)

Pop: 328,149 (1990); 343,079 (1980) **Pop Density:** 368.3
Land: 891.0 sq. mi.; **Water:** 16.2 sq. mi. **Area Code:** 717
In north-central PA, southwest of Scranton; organized Sep 25, 1786 from Northumberland County.
Name origin: For Anne Cesar, Chevalier de la Luzerne (1741–91), French diplomat who helped negotiate the termination of the American Revolution.

Ashley
Borough
ZIP: 18706 **Lat:** 41-12-49 N **Long:** 75-53-56 W
Pop: 3,291 (1990); 3,512 (1980) **Pop Density:** 3656.7
Land: 0.9 sq. mi.; **Water:** 0.0 sq. mi. **Elev:** 660 ft.
In northeastern PA, south of Wilkes-Barre. Settled 1810; incorporated 1870.
Name origin: Named in 1870 for a prominent family of coal operators, including Herbert Henry Ashley of Wilkes-Barre. Formerly called Scrabbletown, Coalville, Skunktown, Peestone, Hightown, Newton, Hendricksburg, Nanticoke Junction, and Alberts.

Avoca
Borough
ZIP: 18641 **Lat:** 41-20-15 N **Long:** 75-44-35 W
Pop: 2,897 (1990); 3,536 (1980) **Pop Density:** 2897.0
Land: 1.0 sq. mi.; **Water:** 0.0 sq. mi. **Elev:** 840 ft.
In eastern PA at the junction of the Lackawanna and Wyoming valleys.
Name origin: Originally called Pleasant Valley.

Bear Creek
Township
Lat: 41-11-09 N **Long:** 75-44-56 W
Pop: 2,721 (1990)   **Pop Density:** 39.6
Land: 68.7 sq. mi.; **Water:** 1.8 sq. mi.

In northeastern PA on the west bank of Bear Creek, near Wilkes-Barre.

Name origin: For the creek, itself named for the numerous bears in the region.

Black Creek
Township
Lat: 40-58-58 N **Long:** 76-09-50 W
Pop: 1,937 (1990)   **Pop Density:** 79.4
Land: 24.4 sq. mi.; **Water:** 0.1 sq. mi.

In east-central PA, south of Wilkes-Barre.

Name origin: For the creek that runs through the township.

Buck
Township
Lat: 41-09-52 N **Long:** 75-38-23 W
Pop: 375 (1990)   **Pop Density:** 22.6
Land: 16.6 sq. mi.; **Water:** 0.1 sq. mi.

Name origin: For George Buck, an early settler and the first tavern owner.

Butler
Township
ZIP: 18222   **Lat:** 41-01-51 N **Long:** 75-59-04 W
Pop: 6,020 (1990)   **Pop Density:** 181.3
Land: 33.2 sq. mi.; **Water:** 0.3 sq. mi.

Conyngham
Borough
ZIP: 18219   **Lat:** 40-59-29 N **Long:** 76-03-36 W
Pop: 2,060 (1990); 2,242 (1980)   **Pop Density:** 1872.7
Land: 1.1 sq. mi.; **Water:** 0.0 sq. mi.   **Elev:** 948 ft.

In eastern PA, 5 mi. northwest of Hazleton in an old mining area.

*Conyngham
Township
Lat: 41-07-27 N **Long:** 76-06-53 W
Pop: 1,509 (1990)   **Pop Density:** 89.8
Land: 16.8 sq. mi.; **Water:** 0.9 sq. mi.

Courtdale
Borough
ZIP: 18704   **Lat:** 41-17-07 N **Long:** 75-54-54 W
Pop: 784 (1990); 844 (1980)   **Pop Density:** 784.0
Land: 1.0 sq. mi.; **Water:** 0.0 sq. mi.   **Elev:** 740 ft.

Dallas
Township
ZIP: 18612   **Lat:** 41-21-31 N **Long:** 75-58-03 W
Pop: 7,625 (1990)   **Pop Density:** 412.2
Land: 18.5 sq. mi.; **Water:** 0.2 sq. mi.

*Dallas
Borough
ZIP: 18612   **Lat:** 41-19-54 N **Long:** 75-58-20 W
Pop: 2,567 (1990); 2,679 (1980)   **Pop Density:** 1116.1
Land: 2.3 sq. mi.; **Water:** 0.1 sq. mi.   **Elev:** 1128 ft.

Name origin: For Alexander James Dallas (1759–1817), Philadelphia author, lawyer, statesman, and financier who won fame by his efficient administration as secretary of the treasury (1814–17).

Dennison
Township
Lat: 41-05-51 N **Long:** 75-50-02 W
Pop: 809 (1990)   **Pop Density:** 23.5
Land: 34.4 sq. mi.; **Water:** 0.2 sq. mi.

Dorrance
Township
Lat: 41-05-40 N **Long:** 76-00-07 W
Pop: 1,778 (1990)   **Pop Density:** 73.8
Land: 24.1 sq. mi.; **Water:** 0.2 sq. mi.

Dupont
Borough
ZIP: 18641   **Lat:** 41-19-26 N **Long:** 75-44-32 W
Pop: 2,984 (1990); 3,460 (1980)   **Pop Density:** 1989.3
Land: 1.5 sq. mi.; **Water:** 0.0 sq. mi.   **Elev:** 735 ft.

In eastern PA, a northeastern suburb of Wilkes-Barre. Founded 1917.

Name origin: For the duPont family, operators of a nearby powder plant.

Duryea
Borough
ZIP: 18642   **Lat:** 41-21-06 N **Long:** 75-46-34 W
Pop: 4,869 (1990); 5,415 (1980)   **Pop Density:** 885.3
Land: 5.5 sq. mi.; **Water:** 0.2 sq. mi.   **Elev:** 820 ft.

In eastern PA.

Name origin: For Abram Duryea, 5th NY Infantry Civil War colonel, who opened coal mines here in 1845. Previously called Babylon because of the babel of languages occasioned by the influx of immigrant miners.

East Berwick
CDP
Lat: 41-03-52 N **Long:** 76-13-14 W
Pop: 2,128 (1990); 2,324 (1980)   **Pop Density:** 2364.4
Land: 0.9 sq. mi.; **Water:** 0.1 sq. mi.

Edwardsville
Borough
ZIP: 18704   **Lat:** 41-15-37 N **Long:** 75-54-25 W
Pop: 5,399 (1990); 5,729 (1980)   **Pop Density:** 4499.2
Land: 1.2 sq. mi.; **Water:** 0.0 sq. mi.   **Elev:** 700 ft.

In eastern PA, 3 mi. northwest of Wilkes-Barre. Incorporated 1884.

Name origin: For Daniel Edwards, superintendent of the Kingston Coal Company, whose mining operations opened here soon after the borough was incorporated.

Exeter
Borough
ZIP: 18643   **Lat:** 41-19-48 N **Long:** 75-49-20 W
Pop: 5,691 (1990); 5,493 (1980)   **Pop Density:** 1210.9
Land: 4.7 sq. mi.; **Water:** 0.3 sq. mi.   **Elev:** 580 ft.

Name origin: For Exeter Township.

*Exeter
Township
Lat: 41-23-01 N **Long:** 75-50-18 W
Pop: 2,457 (1990)   **Pop Density:** 190.5
Land: 12.9 sq. mi.; **Water:** 0.5 sq. mi.

Fairmount
Township
Lat: 41-16-49 N **Long:** 76-16-21 W
Pop: 1,211 (1990)   **Pop Density:** 26.6
Land: 45.6 sq. mi.; **Water:** 0.7 sq. mi.

Fairview
Township
Lat: 41-09-47 N **Long:** 75-51-48 W
Pop: 3,014 (1990)   **Pop Density:** 310.7
Land: 9.7 sq. mi.; **Water:** 0.0 sq. mi.   **Elev:** 1600 ft.

Forty Fort
Borough
ZIP: 18704   **Lat:** 41-17-20 N **Long:** 75-52-13 W
Pop: 5,049 (1990); 5,590 (1980)   **Pop Density:** 3883.8
Land: 1.3 sq. mi.; **Water:** 0.2 sq. mi.   **Elev:** 555 ft.

Name origin: For the fort, named for the first 40 settlers from CT who came to the valley.

Foster
Township
Lat: 41-01-04 N **Long:** 75-49-48 W
Pop: 3,372 (1990)   **Pop Density:** 75.9
Land: 44.4 sq. mi.; **Water:** 0.3 sq. mi.

Franklin
Township
Lat: 41-23-05 N Long: 75-53-55 W
Pop: 1,414 (1990) **Pop Density:** 109.6
Land: 12.9 sq. mi.; **Water:** 0.3 sq. mi.

Freeland
Borough
ZIP: 18224 Lat: 41-01-14 N Long: 75-53-46 W
Pop: 3,909 (1990); 4,285 (1980) **Pop Density:** 5584.3
Land: 0.7 sq. mi.; **Water:** 0.0 sq. mi. **Elev:** 1900 ft.
In eastern PA, 10 mi. northeast of Hazelton.
Name origin: Named in 1874 by townspeople for the free land that could be purchased as compared to the coal company's land that could not be purchased. Originally known as Freehold.

Glen Lyon
CDP
ZIP: 18617 Lat: 41-11-02 N Long: 76-04-17 W
Pop: 2,082 (1990); 2,352 (1980) **Pop Density:** 594.9
Land: 3.5 sq. mi.; **Water:** 0.2 sq. mi.

Hanover
Township
ZIP: 18702 Lat: 41-12-16 N Long: 75-55-51 W
Pop: 12,050 (1990) **Pop Density:** 641.0
Land: 18.8 sq. mi.; **Water:** 0.3 sq. mi.

Harveys Lake
Borough
ZIP: 18618 Lat: 41-21-43 N Long: 76-01-55 W
Pop: 2,746 (1990); 2,318 (1980) **Pop Density:** 518.1
Land: 5.3 sq. mi.; **Water:** 1.0 sq. mi. **Elev:** 1330 ft.
In eastern PA, north of Wilkes-Barre.

Hazle
Township
ZIP: 18201 Lat: 40-57-15 N Long: 76-00-03 W
Pop: 9,323 (1990) **Pop Density:** 207.6
Land: 44.9 sq. mi.; **Water:** 0.2 sq. mi.

Hazleton
City
ZIP: 18201 Lat: 40-57-00 N Long: 75-58-20 W
Pop: 24,730 (1990); 27,318 (1980) **Pop Density:** 4121.7
Land: 6.0 sq. mi.; **Water:** 0.0 sq. mi. **Elev:** 1620 ft.
In eastern PA, 20 mi. south of Wilkes-Barre.
Name origin: For Hazel Creek.

Hollenback
Township
Lat: 41-03-47 N Long: 76-04-45 W
Pop: 1,198 (1990) **Pop Density:** 81.5
Land: 14.7 sq. mi.; **Water:** 0.0 sq. mi.

Hughestown
Borough
ZIP: 18640 Lat: 41-19-48 N Long: 75-46-18 W
Pop: 1,734 (1990); 1,783 (1980) **Pop Density:** 1926.7
Land: 0.9 sq. mi.; **Water:** 0.0 sq. mi. **Elev:** 727 ft.
In eastern PA northeast of Pittston, a southern suburb of Scranton.

Hunlock
Township
Lat: 41-13-42 N Long: 76-05-49 W
Pop: 2,496 (1990) **Pop Density:** 118.9
Land: 21.0 sq. mi.; **Water:** 0.3 sq. mi. **Elev:** 684 ft.

Huntington
Township
Lat: 41-10-54 N Long: 76-14-35 W
Pop: 1,905 (1990) **Pop Density:** 67.1
Land: 28.4 sq. mi.; **Water:** 0.2 sq. mi.

Jackson
Township
ZIP: 18708 Lat: 41-16-46 N Long: 75-59-06 W
Pop: 5,336 (1990) **Pop Density:** 401.2
Land: 13.3 sq. mi.; **Water:** 0.0 sq. mi.
Name origin: For Andrew Jackson (1767–1845), seventh U.S. president.

Jeddo
Borough
ZIP: 18224 Lat: 40-59-32 N Long: 75-53-51 W
Pop: 124 (1990); 128 (1980) **Pop Density:** 413.3
Land: 0.3 sq. mi.; **Water:** 0.0 sq. mi. **Elev:** 1661 ft.

Jenkins
Township
Lat: 41-17-10 N Long: 75-44-54 W
Pop: 4,740 (1990) **Pop Density:** 343.5
Land: 13.8 sq. mi.; **Water:** 0.3 sq. mi.

Kingston
Borough
ZIP: 18704 Lat: 41-15-50 N Long: 75-53-14 W
Pop: 14,507 (1990); 15,681 (1980) **Pop Density:** 6908.1
Land: 2.1 sq. mi.; **Water:** 0.1 sq. mi.
In eastern PA, 3 mi. north of Wilkes-Barre.
Name origin: For Kingston, RI, from which some of the "first 40" of the early settlers had migrated.

*Kingston
Township
ZIP: 18708 Lat: 41-19-40 N Long: 75-54-20 W
Pop: 6,763 (1990) **Pop Density:** 497.3
Land: 13.6 sq. mi.; **Water:** 0.3 sq. mi. **Elev:** 544 ft.

Laflin
Borough
ZIP: 18702 Lat: 41-17-22 N Long: 75-47-46 W
Pop: 1,498 (1990); 1,650 (1980) **Pop Density:** 1070.0
Land: 1.4 sq. mi.; **Water:** 0.0 sq. mi. **Elev:** 727 ft.
In eastern PA on Gardner's Creek, 4 mi. north of Wilkes-Barre.

Lake
Township
Lat: 41-20-55 N Long: 76-06-22 W
Pop: 1,924 (1990) **Pop Density:** 71.5
Land: 26.9 sq. mi.; **Water:** 0.0 sq. mi. **Elev:** 1270 ft.

Larksville
Borough
ZIP: 18704 Lat: 41-15-33 N Long: 75-55-56 W
Pop: 4,700 (1990); 4,410 (1980) **Pop Density:** 979.2
Land: 4.8 sq. mi.; **Water:** 0.2 sq. mi. **Elev:** 581 ft.
In eastern PA, an eastern suburb of Wilkes-Barre.
Name origin: Named in 1895 for Peggy Lark, who had owned the village site and died here at the reputed age of 106. Previously called Blindtown.

Laurel Run
Borough
ZIP: 18702 Lat: 41-13-09 N Long: 75-50-51 W
Pop: 708 (1990); 725 (1980) **Pop Density:** 138.8
Land: 5.1 sq. mi.; **Water:** 0.0 sq. mi. **Elev:** 979 ft.
In eastern PA, a suburb of Wilkes-Barre.

Lehman
Township
Lat: 41-18-13 N Long: 76-02-47 W
Pop: 3,076 (1990) **Pop Density:** 141.8
Land: 21.7 sq. mi.; **Water:** 1.3 sq. mi.

Luzerne
Borough
ZIP: 18709 Lat: 41-17-09 N Long: 75-53-50 W
Pop: 3,206 (1990); 3,703 (1980) **Pop Density:** 4580.0
Land: 0.7 sq. mi.; **Water:** 0.0 sq. mi. **Elev:** 630 ft.
In eastern PA, a suburb of Wilkes-Barre.

Nanticoke　　　　　　　　　　　　City
ZIP: 18634　　　　**Lat:** 41-12-00 N **Long:** 76-00-00 W
Pop: 12,267 (1990); 13,044 (1980)　**Pop Density:** 3504.9
Land: 3.5 sq. mi.; **Water:** 0.1 sq. mi.　　**Elev:** 540 ft.

In northeastern PA on the Susquehanna River, a suburb of Wilkes-Barre.

Name origin: For the Indian tribe; the meaning of the name is possibly 'seashore settlers' or 'tidewater people.'

Nescopeck　　　　　　　　　　Borough
ZIP: 18635　　　　**Lat:** 41-03-09 N **Long:** 76-12-45 W
Pop: 1,651 (1990); 1,768 (1980)　**Pop Density:** 1651.0
Land: 1.0 sq. mi.; **Water:** 0.0 sq. mi.　　**Elev:** 520 ft.

*Nescopeck　　　　　　　　　Township
ZIP: 18635　　　　**Lat:** 41-02-19 N **Long:** 76-10-28 W
Pop: 1,072 (1990)　　　　**Pop Density:** 59.2
Land: 18.1 sq. mi.; **Water:** 0.7 sq. mi.

New Columbus　　　　　　　Borough
ZIP: 17878　　　　**Lat:** 41-10-07 N **Long:** 76-17-11 W
Pop: 228 (1990); 214 (1980)　**Pop Density:** 71.3
Land: 3.2 sq. mi.; **Water:** 0.0 sq. mi.　　**Elev:** 994 ft.

Newport　　　　　　　　　　Township
　　　　　　　Lat: 41-10-42 N **Long:** 76-02-55 W
Pop: 4,593 (1990)　　　　**Pop Density:** 276.7
Land: 16.6 sq. mi.; **Water:** 0.4 sq. mi.

Nuangola　　　　　　　　　　Borough
ZIP: 18637　　　　**Lat:** 41-09-29 N **Long:** 75-58-40 W
Pop: 701 (1990); 726 (1980)　**Pop Density:** 637.3
Land: 1.1 sq. mi.; **Water:** 0.2 sq. mi.　　**Elev:** 1245 ft.

Penn Lake Park　　　　　　　Borough
ZIP: 18661　　　　**Lat:** 41-06-53 N **Long:** 75-46-28 W
Pop: 242 (1990); 217 (1980)　**Pop Density:** 127.4
Land: 1.9 sq. mi.; **Water:** 0.1 sq. mi.

Pittston　　　　　　　　　　　　City
ZIP: 18640　　　　**Lat:** 41-19-34 N **Long:** 75-47-16 W
Pop: 9,389 (1990)　　　　**Pop Density:** 5868.1
Land: 1.6 sq. mi.; **Water:** 0.1 sq. mi.　　**Elev:** 650 ft.

In eastern PA on the Susquehanna River, 10 mi. northeast of Wilkes-Barre.

Name origin: For the elder William Pitt (1708–78), British statesman.

*Pittston　　　　　　　　　　Township
　　　　　　　Lat: 41-18-50 N **Long:** 75-43-00 W
Pop: 2,725 (1990)　　　　**Pop Density:** 191.9
Land: 14.2 sq. mi.; **Water:** 0.0 sq. mi.

Plains　　　　　　　　　　　Township
ZIP: 18705　　　　**Lat:** 41-15-49 N **Long:** 75-48-52 W
Pop: 10,988 (1990)　　　　**Pop Density:** 845.2
Land: 13.0 sq. mi.; **Water:** 0.3 sq. mi.

Plymouth　　　　　　　　　　Borough
ZIP: 18651　　　　**Lat:** 41-14-27 N **Long:** 75-57-00 W
Pop: 7,134 (1990); 7,605 (1980)　**Pop Density:** 6485.5
Land: 1.1 sq. mi.; **Water:** 0.1 sq. mi.　　**Elev:** 540 ft.

In eastern PA on the Susquehanna River, a western suburb of Wilkes-Barre. Incorporated Dec 28, 1768, from Plymouth Township.

Name origin: For Plymouth in Litchfield County, CT, which was named for Plymouth, MA, the oldest settlement in New England.

*Plymouth　　　　　　　　　Township
ZIP: 18651　　　　**Lat:** 41-14-43 N **Long:** 75-59-56 W
Pop: 1,773 (1990)　　　　**Pop Density:** 114.4
Land: 15.5 sq. mi.; **Water:** 0.5 sq. mi.

Pringle　　　　　　　　　　　Borough
ZIP: 18704　　　　**Lat:** 41-16-35 N **Long:** 75-54-11 W
Pop: 1,161 (1990); 1,221 (1980)　**Pop Density:** 2322.0
Land: 0.5 sq. mi.; **Water:** 0.0 sq. mi.　　**Elev:** 650 ft.

In eastern PA near Wilkes-Barre.

Rice　　　　　　　　　　　　Township
　　　　　　　Lat: 41-09-18 N **Long:** 75-56-43 W
Pop: 1,907 (1990)　　　　**Pop Density:** 171.8
Land: 11.1 sq. mi.; **Water:** 0.2 sq. mi.

Ross　　　　　　　　　　　　Township
　　　　　　　Lat: 41-18-02 N **Long:** 76-10-50 W
Pop: 2,634 (1990)　　　　**Pop Density:** 61.0
Land: 43.2 sq. mi.; **Water:** 0.5 sq. mi.

Salem　　　　　　　　　　　Township
　　　　　　　Lat: 41-06-25 N **Long:** 76-11-10 W
Pop: 4,503 (1990)　　　　**Pop Density:** 155.3
Land: 29.0 sq. mi.; **Water:** 1.0 sq. mi.

Shickshinny　　　　　　　　　Borough
ZIP: 18655　　　　**Lat:** 41-09-11 N **Long:** 76-09-05 W
Pop: 1,108 (1990); 1,192 (1980)　**Pop Density:** 2770.0
Land: 0.4 sq. mi.; **Water:** 0.0 sq. mi.　　**Elev:** 518 ft.

In eastern PA, southwest of Wilkes Barre.

Name origin: Choctaw Indian term probably meaning 'five mountains,' referring to Newport, Lee's, Rocky, Knob, and River mountains surrounding the area.

Slocum　　　　　　　　　　　Township
　　　　　　　Lat: 41-08-09 N **Long:** 76-02-25 W
Pop: 1,159 (1990)　　　　**Pop Density:** 117.1
Land: 9.9 sq. mi.; **Water:** 0.4 sq. mi.

Sugarloaf　　　　　　　　　　Township
ZIP: 18249　　　　**Lat:** 41-00-06 N **Long:** 76-04-53 W
Pop: 3,534 (1990)　　　　**Pop Density:** 159.9
Land: 22.1 sq. mi.; **Water:** 0.0 sq. mi.

Sugar Notch　　　　　　　　　Borough
ZIP: 18706　　　　**Lat:** 41-11-32 N **Long:** 75-55-55 W
Pop: 1,044 (1990); 1,191 (1980)　**Pop Density:** 1044.0
Land: 1.0 sq. mi.; **Water:** 0.0 sq. mi.　　**Elev:** 1100 ft.

Name origin: For the mountain gap nearby, which is covered with sugar maple trees.

Swoyersville　　　　　　　　　Borough
ZIP: 18704　　　　**Lat:** 41-17-54 N **Long:** 75-52-44 W
Pop: 5,630 (1990); 5,795 (1980)　**Pop Density:** 2559.1
Land: 2.2 sq. mi.; **Water:** 0.0 sq. mi.　　**Elev:** 560 ft.

In eastern PA, 5 mi. north of Wilkes-Barre.

Name origin: For an early coal operator, Henry Swoyer.

Union　　　　　　　　　　　Township
　　　　　　　Lat: 41-11-55 N **Long:** 76-09-10 W
Pop: 2,028 (1990)　　　　**Pop Density:** 100.4
Land: 20.2 sq. mi.; **Water:** 0.5 sq. mi.

Warrior Run　　　　　　　　　Borough
ZIP: 18706　　　　**Lat:** 41-11-14 N **Long:** 75-57-10 W
Pop: 656 (1990); 784 (1980)　**Pop Density:** 820.0
Land: 0.8 sq. mi.; **Water:** 0.0 sq. mi.

West Hazleton
Borough
ZIP: 18201   **Lat:** 40-58-14 N   **Long:** 76-00-47 W
Pop: 4,136 (1990); 4,871 (1980)   **Pop Density:** 2585.0
Land: 1.6 sq. mi.; **Water:** 0.0 sq. mi.   **Elev:** 1700 ft.

In eastern PA, adjacent to Hazleton.

West Pittston
Borough
ZIP: 18643   **Lat:** 41-19-45 N   **Long:** 75-48-00 W
Pop: 5,590 (1990); 5,980 (1980)   **Pop Density:** 6987.5
Land: 0.8 sq. mi.; **Water:** 0.1 sq. mi.   **Elev:** 562 ft.

West Wyoming
Borough
ZIP: 18644   **Lat:** 41-19-09 N   **Long:** 75-51-08 W
Pop: 3,117 (1990); 3,288 (1980)   **Pop Density:** 865.8
Land: 3.6 sq. mi.; **Water:** 0.0 sq. mi.   **Elev:** 599 ft.

White Haven
Borough
ZIP: 18661   **Lat:** 41-03-18 N   **Long:** 75-46-38 W
Pop: 1,132 (1990); 1,921 (1980)   **Pop Density:** 943.3
Land: 1.2 sq. mi.; **Water:** 0.0 sq. mi.   **Elev:** 1221 ft.

Wilkes-Barre
City
ZIP: 18701   **Lat:** 41-14-47 N   **Long:** 75-52-32 W
Pop: 47,523 (1990)   **Pop Density:** 6988.7
Land: 6.8 sq. mi.; **Water:** 0.3 sq. mi.   **Elev:** 550 ft.

In northeastern PA on the Susquehanna River, 20 mi. southwest of Scranton. Laid out in 1772; incorporated as borough Mar 17, 1806, as city May 4, 1871.

Name origin: Named in 1769 by Maj. John Durkee, who brought about one hundred settlers with him from Norwich, CT. Origin of the name is uncertain: possibly for John Wilkes and Isaac Barré, liberal leaders in Parliament and champions of the American colonies; or else for the sons of John Durkee and his cousin, Andrew, each named for one of the Englishmen.

*Wilkes-Barre
Township
ZIP: 18702   **Lat:** 41-14-14 N   **Long:** 75-51-46 W
Pop: 3,572 (1990)   **Pop Density:** 1190.7
Land: 3.0 sq. mi.; **Water:** 0.0 sq. mi.

Wright
Township
    Lat: 41-07-17 N   **Long:** 75-54-01 W
Pop: 4,685 (1990)   **Pop Density:** 347.0
Land: 13.5 sq. mi.; **Water:** 0.0 sq. mi.

Wyoming
Borough
ZIP: 18644   **Lat:** 41-18-20 N   **Long:** 75-50-30 W
Pop: 3,255 (1990); 3,655 (1980)   **Pop Density:** 2325.0
Land: 1.4 sq. mi.; **Water:** 0.1 sq. mi.   **Elev:** 599 ft.

In eastern PA on the Susquehanna River, 5 mi. northeast of Wilkes-Barre. Site of the Battle of Wyoming, where valley settlers fought an invading party of Tories, known as Butler's Rangers, and a band of Iroquois on July 3, 1778.

Name origin: For the Wyoming Valley, from the Indian name *M'chwewormink,* probably 'extensive plains or meadows.'

Yatesville
Borough
ZIP: 18640   **Lat:** 41-18-10 N   **Long:** 75-46-55 W
Pop: 506 (1990); 555 (1980)   **Pop Density:** 843.3
Land: 0.6 sq. mi.; **Water:** 0.0 sq. mi.   **Elev:** 750 ft.

Lycoming County
County Seat: Williamsport (ZIP: 17701)

Pop: 118,710 (1990); 118,416 (1980)   **Pop Density:** 96.1
Land: 1234.9 sq. mi.; **Water:** 8.9 sq. mi.   **Area Code:** 717

In north-central PA, west of Wilkes-Barre; organized Apr 13, 1795 from Northumberland County.

Name origin: For Lycoming Creek, which runs through it and had for many years been the dividing line between settled and disputed Indian lands. From Delaware Indian word probably meaning 'sandy or gravel-bed creek.'

Anthony
Township
    Lat: 41-17-52 N   **Long:** 77-10-14 W
Pop: 727 (1990)   **Pop Density:** 45.7
Land: 15.9 sq. mi.; **Water:** 0.0 sq. mi.

Armstrong
Township
    Lat: 41-12-41 N   **Long:** 77-00-38 W
Pop: 676 (1990)   **Pop Density:** 27.0
Land: 25.0 sq. mi.; **Water:** 0.5 sq. mi.

Bastress
Township
    Lat: 41-11-36 N   **Long:** 77-07-48 W
Pop: 513 (1990)   **Pop Density:** 59.0
Land: 8.7 sq. mi.; **Water:** 0.0 sq. mi.

Brady
Township
ZIP: 17752   **Lat:** 41-10-25 N   **Long:** 76-56-39 W
Pop: 822 (1990)
Land: 8.6 sq. mi.; **Water:** 0.0 sq. mi.

Brown
Township
    Lat: 41-30-25 N   **Long:** 77-29-27 W
Pop: 102 (1990)   **Pop Density:** 1.4
Land: 73.3 sq. mi.; **Water:** 0.4 sq. mi.

Cascade
Township
ZIP: 17771   **Lat:** 41-27-23 N   **Long:** 76-53-25 W
Pop: 382 (1990)   **Pop Density:** 9.3
Land: 40.9 sq. mi.; **Water:** 0.0 sq. mi.

Clinton
Township
ZIP: 17752   **Lat:** 41-12-43 N   **Long:** 76-52-53 W
Pop: 3,086 (1990)   **Pop Density:** 110.2
Land: 28.0 sq. mi.; **Water:** 0.8 sq. mi.

Cogan House
Township
ZIP: 17771   **Lat:** 41-25-00 N   **Long:** 77-09-55 W
Pop: 807 (1990)   **Pop Density:** 11.5
Land: 69.9 sq. mi.; **Water:** 0.0 sq. mi.

Settled c. 1825; township formed 1843.

Name origin: For David Cogan, the first settler, whose house fell into decay and was referred to by hunters as Cogan's House.

Cummings
Township
ZIP: 17776   Lat: 41-20-09 N Long: 77-20-40 W
Pop: 334 (1990)   Pop Density: 4.8
Land: 68.9 sq. mi.; Water: 0.5 sq. mi.

Duboistown
Borough
ZIP: 17702   Lat: 41-13-22 N Long: 77-02-17 W
Pop: 1,201 (1990); 1,218 (1980)   Pop Density: 2001.7
Land: 0.6 sq. mi.; Water: 0.1 sq. mi.   Elev: 536 ft.

Eldred
Township
ZIP: 17754   Lat: 41-19-33 N Long: 76-57-13 W
Pop: 2,055 (1990)   Pop Density: 143.7
Land: 14.3 sq. mi.; Water: 0.0 sq. mi.

Fairfield
Township
ZIP: 17754   Lat: 41-15-25 N Long: 76-52-21 W
Pop: 2,580 (1990)   Pop Density: 222.4
Land: 11.6 sq. mi.; Water: 0.1 sq. mi.

Franklin
Township
Lat: 41-13-59 N Long: 76-34-38 W
Pop: 914 (1990)   Pop Density: 37.3
Land: 24.5 sq. mi.; Water: 0.0 sq. mi.

Gamble
Township
ZIP: 17771   Lat: 41-23-30 N Long: 76-56-54 W
Pop: 744 (1990)   Pop Density: 16.4
Land: 45.5 sq. mi.; Water: 0.6 sq. mi.

Garden View
CDP
Lat: 41-15-23 N Long: 77-02-55 W
Pop: 2,687 (1990); 2,777 (1980)   Pop Density: 2687.0
Land: 1.0 sq. mi.; Water: 0.0 sq. mi.

Hepburn
Township
ZIP: 17728   Lat: 41-19-56 N Long: 77-02-01 W
Pop: 2,834 (1990)   Pop Density: 170.7
Land: 16.6 sq. mi.; Water: 0.0 sq. mi.

Hughesville
Borough
ZIP: 17737   Lat: 41-14-18 N Long: 76-43-34 W
Pop: 2,049 (1990); 2,174 (1980)   Pop Density: 3415.0
Land: 0.6 sq. mi.; Water: 0.0 sq. mi.   Elev: 580 ft.
In north-central PA, 15 mi. east of Williamsport. Laid out in 1816.
Name origin: Named in 1827 for Jeptha Hughes. Previously called Hughesburg.

Jackson
Township
Lat: 41-31-04 N Long: 77-06-50 W
Pop: 421 (1990)   Pop Density: 11.8
Land: 35.6 sq. mi.; Water: 0.0 sq. mi.

Jersey Shore
Borough
ZIP: 17740   Lat: 41-12-02 N Long: 77-16-01 W
Pop: 4,353 (1990); 4,631 (1980)   Pop Density: 3627.5
Land: 1.2 sq. mi.; Water: 0.0 sq. mi.   Elev: 600 ft.
In north-central PA, 16 mi. west of Williamsport. Settled 1785.
Name origin: A nickname given by Irish settlers to the area where settlers from NJ lived, on the opposite shore of the Susquehanna River. Formerly called Waynesburg.

Jordan
Township
ZIP: 17774   Lat: 41-14-51 N Long: 76-31-06 W
Pop: 871 (1990)   Pop Density: 42.1
Land: 20.7 sq. mi.; Water: 0.0 sq. mi.

Lewis
Township
ZIP: 17771   Lat: 41-24-46 N Long: 77-02-36 W
Pop: 1,194 (1990)   Pop Density: 31.6
Land: 37.8 sq. mi.; Water: 0.0 sq. mi.

Limestone
Township
Lat: 41-08-42 N Long: 77-09-15 W
Pop: 1,893 (1990)   Pop Density: 55.5
Land: 34.1 sq. mi.; Water: 0.1 sq. mi.

Loyalsock
Township
ZIP: 17701   Lat: 41-16-08 N Long: 76-59-03 W
Pop: 10,644 (1990)   Pop Density: 506.9
Land: 21.0 sq. mi.; Water: 0.2 sq. mi.   Elev: 518 ft.
Name origin: Indian name for the creek running through the township, possibly meaning 'middle creek.'

Lycoming
Township
ZIP: 17728   Lat: 41-18-47 N Long: 77-06-21 W
Pop: 1,748 (1990)   Pop Density: 115.0
Land: 15.2 sq. mi.; Water: 0.1 sq. mi.

McHenry
Township
ZIP: 17739   Lat: 41-24-17 N Long: 77-27-34 W
Pop: 246 (1990)   Pop Density: 3.2
Land: 76.0 sq. mi.; Water: 0.5 sq. mi.

McIntyre
Township
Lat: 41-30-55 N Long: 76-57-59 W
Pop: 588 (1990)   Pop Density: 12.5
Land: 47.2 sq. mi.; Water: 0.1 sq. mi.

McNett
Township
Lat: 41-33-11 N Long: 76-50-56 W
Pop: 200 (1990)   Pop Density: 5.9
Land: 33.8 sq. mi.; Water: 0.0 sq. mi.

Mifflin
Township
Lat: 41-17-28 N Long: 77-13-54 W
Pop: 1,110 (1990)   Pop Density: 39.8
Land: 27.9 sq. mi.; Water: 0.0 sq. mi.

Mill Creek
Township
ZIP: 17756   Lat: 41-18-29 N Long: 76-47-16 W
Pop: 477 (1990)   Pop Density: 41.8
Land: 11.4 sq. mi.; Water: 0.0 sq. mi.

Montgomery
Borough
ZIP: 17752   Lat: 41-10-15 N Long: 76-52-30 W
Pop: 1,631 (1990); 1,653 (1980)   Pop Density: 3262.0
Land: 0.5 sq. mi.; Water: 0.0 sq. mi.   Elev: 497 ft.

Montoursville
Borough
ZIP: 17754   Lat: 41-14-49 N Long: 76-55-11 W
Pop: 4,983 (1990); 5,403 (1980)   Pop Density: 1245.8
Land: 4.0 sq. mi.; Water: 0.1 sq. mi.   Elev: 535 ft.
In north-central PA on the Susquehanna River, near Williamsport.
Name origin: Named in 1768 for Andrew Montour, a half-breed Indian interpreter who was given the site once occupied by the Indian village of Otzinachson for his loyalty to the provincial government.

Moreland
Township
ZIP: 17756   Lat: 41-11-46 N Long: 76-39-23 W
Pop: 984 (1990)   Pop Density: 41.2
Land: 23.9 sq. mi.; Water: 0.0 sq. mi.

Muncy
Borough
ZIP: 17756   **Lat:** 41-12-06 N   **Long:** 76-47-09 W
Pop: 2,702 (1990); 2,700 (1980)   **Pop Density:** 3377.5
Land: 0.8 sq. mi.; **Water:** 0.0 sq. mi.   **Elev:** 519 ft.

In north-central PA on the Susquehanna River, 12 mi. east of Williamsport. Laid out in 1797.

Name origin: For the Munsee Indians.

*Muncy
Township
ZIP: 17756   **Lat:** 41-15-13 N   **Long:** 76-47-57 W
Pop: 1,036 (1990)   **Pop Density:** 66.0
Land: 15.7 sq. mi.; **Water:** 0.2 sq. mi.

Muncy Creek
Township
ZIP: 17756   **Lat:** 41-11-36 N   **Long:** 76-45-44 W
Pop: 3,401 (1990)   **Pop Density:** 169.2
Land: 20.1 sq. mi.; **Water:** 0.6 sq. mi.

Nippenose
Township
Lat: 41-11-13 N   **Long:** 77-13-31 W
Pop: 742 (1990)   **Pop Density:** 69.3
Land: 10.7 sq. mi.; **Water:** 0.5 sq. mi.

Old Lycoming
Township
ZIP: 17701   **Lat:** 41-15-54 N   **Long:** 77-04-35 W
Pop: 5,526 (1990)   **Pop Density:** 581.7
Land: 9.5 sq. mi.; **Water:** 0.1 sq. mi.

Penn
Township
ZIP: 17737   **Lat:** 41-16-47 N   **Long:** 76-38-37 W
Pop: 788 (1990)   **Pop Density:** 29.6
Land: 26.6 sq. mi.; **Water:** 0.1 sq. mi.

Piatt
Township
Lat: 41-13-08 N   **Long:** 77-12-56 W
Pop: 1,097 (1990)   **Pop Density:** 110.8
Land: 9.9 sq. mi.; **Water:** 0.3 sq. mi.

Picture Rocks
Borough
ZIP: 17762   **Lat:** 41-16-48 N   **Long:** 76-42-33 W
Pop: 660 (1990); 615 (1980)   **Pop Density:** 733.3
Land: 0.9 sq. mi.; **Water:** 0.0 sq. mi.   **Elev:** 659 ft.

Pine
Township
Lat: 41-29-00 N   **Long:** 77-16-39 W
Pop: 290 (1990)   **Pop Density:** 3.8
Land: 75.8 sq. mi.; **Water:** 0.0 sq. mi.

Plunketts Creek
Township
Lat: 41-23-15 N   **Long:** 76-48-07 W
Pop: 905 (1990)   **Pop Density:** 16.4
Land: 55.2 sq. mi.; **Water:** 0.0 sq. mi.

Porter
Township
Lat: 41-12-19 N   **Long:** 77-16-33 W
Pop: 1,441 (1990)   **Pop Density:** 189.6
Land: 7.6 sq. mi.; **Water:** 0.3 sq. mi.

Salladasburg
Borough
ZIP: 17740   **Lat:** 41-16-35 N   **Long:** 77-13-39 W
Pop: 301 (1990); 273 (1980)   **Pop Density:** 376.3
Land: 0.8 sq. mi.; **Water:** 0.0 sq. mi.   **Elev:** 652 ft.

Name origin: For founder Jacob P. Sallada.

Shrewsbury
Township
ZIP: 17737   **Lat:** 41-19-50 N   **Long:** 76-41-00 W
Pop: 402 (1990)   **Pop Density:** 23.0
Land: 17.5 sq. mi.; **Water:** 0.0 sq. mi.

South Williamsport
Borough
ZIP: 17701   **Lat:** 41-13-47 N   **Long:** 77-00-04 W
Pop: 6,496 (1990); 6,581 (1980)   **Pop Density:** 3418.9
Land: 1.9 sq. mi.; **Water:** 0.2 sq. mi.   **Elev:** 520 ft.

Susquehanna
Township
Lat: 41-12-17 N   **Long:** 77-08-06 W
Pop: 1,046 (1990)   **Pop Density:** 147.3
Land: 7.1 sq. mi.; **Water:** 0.7 sq. mi.

In north-central PA, southwest of Williamsport.

Name origin: For the Susquehanna River, which flows through it.

Upper Fairfield
Township
ZIP: 17754   **Lat:** 41-18-11 N   **Long:** 76-51-44 W
Pop: 1,774 (1990)   **Pop Density:** 98.0
Land: 18.1 sq. mi.; **Water:** 0.1 sq. mi.

Washington
Township
Lat: 41-07-08 N   **Long:** 77-02-37 W
Pop: 1,552 (1990)   **Pop Density:** 31.9
Land: 48.6 sq. mi.; **Water:** 0.0 sq. mi.

Name origin: For George Washington (1732–99), first U.S. president.

Watson
Township
Lat: 41-15-18 N   **Long:** 77-19-46 W
Pop: 565 (1990)   **Pop Density:** 24.4
Land: 23.2 sq. mi.; **Water:** 0.4 sq. mi.

Williamsport
City
ZIP: 17701   **Lat:** 41-14-20 N   **Long:** 77-02-15 W
Pop: 31,933 (1990)   **Pop Density:** 3588.0
Land: 8.9 sq. mi.; **Water:** 0.7 sq. mi.   **Elev:** 528 ft.

In north-central PA on the west branch of the Susquehanna River, 70 mi. north of Harrisburg. Laid out in 1795; incorporated as borough Mar 1, 1806, as city Jan 15, 1866.

Name origin: Origin uncertain: possibly for Sen. William Hepburn; or William, son of Michael Ross who laid out the town; or for William Russell, a boatman who discovered a port or landing place long before the town was laid out, near the site of the Philadelphia and Reading Railroad station.

Wolf
Township
ZIP: 17737   **Lat:** 41-16-04 N   **Long:** 76-43-53 W
Pop: 2,617 (1990)   **Pop Density:** 134.2
Land: 19.5 sq. mi.; **Water:** 0.0 sq. mi.

Woodward
Township
ZIP: 17744   **Lat:** 41-14-02 N   **Long:** 77-09-00 W
Pop: 2,267 (1990)   **Pop Density:** 171.7
Land: 13.2 sq. mi.; **Water:** 0.5 sq. mi.

McKean County
County Seat: Smethport (ZIP: 16749)

Pop: 47,131 (1990); 50,635 (1980)   **Pop Density:** 48.0
Land: 981.6 sq. mi.; **Water:** 2.6 sq. mi.   **Area Code:** 814

On northern border of western PA. Organized Mar 26, 1804 from Lycoming County, but administered through Centre County until 1814, then Potter and Lycoming counties; fully organized in 1826.

Name origin: For Thomas McKean (1734–1817), signer of the Declaration of Independence, chief justice of PA (1777–79), and governor (1799–1808).

Annin   Township
Lat: 41-53-24 N **Long:** 78-17-24 W
Pop: 805 (1990)   **Pop Density:** 24.0
Land: 33.6 sq. mi.; **Water:** 0.0 sq. mi.

Bradford   City
ZIP: 16701   Lat: 41-57-37 N **Long:** 78-38-24 W
Pop: 9,625 (1990); 11,211 (1980)   **Pop Density:** 2830.9
Land: 3.4 sq. mi.; **Water:** 0.0 sq. mi.   **Elev:** 1442 ft.
In northern PA, 4 mi. south of the NY state line.
Name origin: Named for William Bradford by Daniel Kingsbury. Originally called Littleton for the first landowner, Col. L. C. Little of Boston.

*Bradford   Township
ZIP: 16701   Lat: 41-54-56 N **Long:** 78-41-16 W
Pop: 5,065 (1990)   **Pop Density:** 91.1
Land: 55.6 sq. mi.; **Water:** 0.3 sq. mi.

Ceres   Township
Lat: 41-57-11 N **Long:** 78-16-41 W
Pop: 981 (1990)   **Pop Density:** 24.1
Land: 40.7 sq. mi.; **Water:** 0.0 sq. mi.
Name origin: For the Ceres Land Company, which was intimately connected with the settlement, development, and early history of the area.

Corydon   Township
Lat: 41-55-04 N **Long:** 78-50-46 W
Pop: 319 (1990)   **Pop Density:** 4.4
Land: 73.2 sq. mi.; **Water:** 0.4 sq. mi.

Eldred   Township
ZIP: 16731   Lat: 41-56-29 N **Long:** 78-23-35 W
Pop: 1,768 (1990)   **Pop Density:** 44.9
Land: 39.4 sq. mi.; **Water:** 0.0 sq. mi.

*Eldred   Borough
ZIP: 16731   Lat: 41-57-24 N **Long:** 78-22-51 W
Pop: 869 (1990); 965 (1980)   **Pop Density:** 965.6
Land: 0.9 sq. mi.; **Water:** 0.0 sq. mi.   **Elev:** 1500 ft.

Foster   Township
Lat: 41-57-51 N **Long:** 78-37-06 W
Pop: 4,691 (1990)   **Pop Density:** 101.1
Land: 46.4 sq. mi.; **Water:** 0.0 sq. mi.

Hamilton   Township
Lat: 41-46-21 N **Long:** 78-52-26 W
Pop: 612 (1990)   **Pop Density:** 8.5
Land: 72.0 sq. mi.; **Water:** 1.8 sq. mi.

Hamlin   Township
Lat: 41-43-59 N **Long:** 78-38-44 W
Pop: 822 (1990)   **Pop Density:** 12.7
Land: 64.6 sq. mi.; **Water:** 0.0 sq. mi.

Kane   Borough
ZIP: 16735   Lat: 41-39-46 N **Long:** 78-48-33 W
Pop: 4,590 (1990); 4,916 (1980)   **Pop Density:** 2868.8
Land: 1.6 sq. mi.; **Water:** 0.0 sq. mi.   **Elev:** 2020 ft.
In northern PA on the eastern border of the Allegheny National Forest.

Keating   Township
Lat: 41-48-49 N **Long:** 78-29-04 W
Pop: 3,070 (1990)   **Pop Density:** 31.3
Land: 98.1 sq. mi.; **Water:** 0.0 sq. mi.

Lafayette   Township
Lat: 41-49-07 N **Long:** 78-41-19 W
Pop: 2,106 (1990)   **Pop Density:** 29.6
Land: 71.2 sq. mi.; **Water:** 0.0 sq. mi.

Lewis Run   Borough
ZIP: 16738   Lat: 41-52-14 N **Long:** 78-39-38 W
Pop: 578 (1990); 677 (1980)   **Pop Density:** 304.2
Land: 1.9 sq. mi.; **Water:** 0.0 sq. mi.   **Elev:** 1560 ft.
In northern PA on a plain at the southern edge of the Bradford oil field.
Name origin: For the stream, which bisects the town.

Liberty   Township
Lat: 41-46-22 N **Long:** 78-16-15 W
Pop: 1,764 (1990)   **Pop Density:** 21.1
Land: 83.5 sq. mi.; **Water:** 0.0 sq. mi.

Mount Jewett   Borough
ZIP: 16740   Lat: 41-43-29 N **Long:** 78-38-38 W
Pop: 1,029 (1990); 1,053 (1980)   **Pop Density:** 428.7
Land: 2.4 sq. mi.; **Water:** 0.0 sq. mi.   **Elev:** 2240 ft.

Norwich   Township
Lat: 41-40-37 N **Long:** 78-21-18 W
Pop: 593 (1990)   **Pop Density:** 6.2
Land: 95.6 sq. mi.; **Water:** 0.0 sq. mi.   **Elev:** 1584 ft.

Otto   Township
Lat: 41-56-51 N **Long:** 78-29-28 W
Pop: 1,820 (1990)   **Pop Density:** 52.3
Land: 34.8 sq. mi.; **Water:** 0.0 sq. mi.

Port Allegany   Borough
ZIP: 16743   Lat: 41-48-48 N **Long:** 78-16-39 W
Pop: 2,391 (1990); 2,593 (1980)   **Pop Density:** 1328.3
Land: 1.8 sq. mi.; **Water:** 0.0 sq. mi.   **Elev:** 1481 ft.
In northern PA on the Allegheny River, 20 mi. southeast of Olean, NY.
Name origin: For being the center of lumbering operations along the Allegheny River that reached their peak between 1830 and 1840.

Sergeant
Township
Lat: 41-40-32 N **Long:** 78-33-15 W
Pop: 154 (1990) **Pop Density:** 1.9
Land: 80.3 sq. mi.; **Water:** 0.0 sq. mi.

Smethport
Borough
ZIP: 16749 **Lat:** 41-48-26 N **Long:** 78-26-39 W
Pop: 1,734 (1990); 1,797 (1980) **Pop Density:** 1020.0
Land: 1.7 sq. mi.; **Water:** 0.0 sq. mi. **Elev:** 1560 ft.
In northern PA, 20 mi. south of Bradford. Laid out in 1870; incorporated Feb 11, 1853.
Name origin: For Raymond and Theodore de Smeth, Dutch

bankers and business agents for the exiled French nobility in their dealings with the Ceres Land Company.

Wetmore
Township
Lat: 41-40-37 N **Long:** 78-49-40 W
Pop: 1,745 (1990) **Pop Density:** 22.1
Land: 79.0 sq. mi.; **Water:** 0.0 sq. mi.

Mercer County
County Seat: Mercer (ZIP: 16137)

Pop: 121,003 (1990); 128,299 (1980) **Pop Density:** 180.1
Land: 671.9 sq. mi.; **Water:** 10.8 sq. mi. **Area Code:** 412
On central-western border of PA, north of New Castle; organized Mar 12, 1800 from Allegheny County.
Name origin: For Gen. Hugh Mercer (1721–77), Revolutionary War officer and physician.

Clark
Borough
ZIP: 16113 **Lat:** 41-17-07 N **Long:** 80-24-14 W
Pop: 610 (1990); 667 (1980) **Pop Density:** 203.3
Land: 3.0 sq. mi.; **Water:** 0.7 sq. mi. **Elev:** 920 ft.

Coolspring
Township
Lat: 41-15-59 N **Long:** 80-12-54 W
Pop: 2,140 (1990) **Pop Density:** 111.5
Land: 19.2 sq. mi.; **Water:** 0.4 sq. mi.

Deer Creek
Township
Lat: 41-27-04 N **Long:** 80-08-18 W
Pop: 513 (1990) **Pop Density:** 35.4
Land: 14.5 sq. mi.; **Water:** 0.3 sq. mi.

Delaware
Township
Lat: 41-19-46 N **Long:** 80-19-25 W
Pop: 2,064 (1990) **Pop Density:** 63.5
Land: 32.5 sq. mi.; **Water:** 0.3 sq. mi.

East Lackawannock
Township
Lat: 41-12-00 N **Long:** 80-16-37 W
Pop: 1,606 (1990) **Pop Density:** 75.8
Land: 21.2 sq. mi.; **Water:** 0.0 sq. mi.

Fairview
Township
Lat: 41-20-02 N **Long:** 80-13-02 W
Pop: 910 (1990) **Pop Density:** 48.7
Land: 18.7 sq. mi.; **Water:** 0.0 sq. mi.

Farrell
City
ZIP: 16121 **Lat:** 41-12-34 N **Long:** 80-29-50 W
Pop: 6,841 (1990); 8,645 (1980) **Pop Density:** 2974.3
Land: 2.3 sq. mi.; **Water:** 0.0 sq. mi. **Elev:** 1050 ft.
Incorporated 1901.
Name origin: For James A. Farrell, president of the United States Steel Corp. Originally called South Sharon.

Findley
Township
Lat: 41-12-11 N **Long:** 80-10-24 W
Pop: 2,284 (1990) **Pop Density:** 108.2
Land: 21.1 sq. mi.; **Water:** 0.1 sq. mi.

Fredonia
Borough
ZIP: 16124 **Lat:** 41-19-19 N **Long:** 80-15-31 W
Pop: 683 (1990); 712 (1980) **Pop Density:** 1707.5
Land: 0.4 sq. mi.; **Water:** 0.0 sq. mi. **Elev:** 1175 ft.

French Creek
Township
Lat: 41-27-31 N **Long:** 80-03-15 W
Pop: 789 (1990) **Pop Density:** 38.1
Land: 20.7 sq. mi.; **Water:** 0.1 sq. mi.

Greene
Township
Lat: 41-27-51 N **Long:** 80-27-00 W
Pop: 1,247 (1990) **Pop Density:** 56.9
Land: 21.9 sq. mi.; **Water:** 0.0 sq. mi.

Greenville
Borough
ZIP: 16125 **Lat:** 41-24-21 N **Long:** 80-23-03 W
Pop: 6,734 (1990); 7,730 (1980) **Pop Density:** 3544.2
Land: 1.9 sq. mi.; **Water:** 0.0 sq. mi. **Elev:** 965 ft.
In western PA, 70 mi. north of Pittsburgh.
Name origin: For Gen. Nathanael Greene (1742–86), hero of the American Revolution. Previously called West Greenville.

Grove City
Borough
ZIP: 16127 **Lat:** 41-09-24 N **Long:** 80-05-19 W
Pop: 8,240 (1990); 8,162 (1980) **Pop Density:** 3051.9
Land: 2.7 sq. mi.; **Water:** 0.0 sq. mi. **Elev:** 1256 ft.
In western PA, 55 mi. north of Pittsburgh.

Hempfield
Township
Lat: 41-23-27 N **Long:** 80-21-15 W
Pop: 3,826 (1990) **Pop Density:** 271.3
Land: 14.1 sq. mi.; **Water:** 0.0 sq. mi.

Hermitage
City
ZIP: 16148 **Lat:** 41-13-47 N **Long:** 80-26-34 W
Pop: 15,300 (1990) **Pop Density:** 515.2
Land: 29.7 sq. mi.; **Water:** 0.1 sq. mi. **Elev:** 1090 ft.

Jackson
Township
Lat: 41-16-14 N **Long:** 80-08-49 W
Pop: 1,089 (1990) **Pop Density:** 63.7
Land: 17.1 sq. mi.; **Water:** 0.2 sq. mi.

Jackson Center Borough
ZIP: 16133 Lat: 41-16-23 N Long: 80-08-19 W
Pop: 244 (1990); 265 (1980) Pop Density: 221.8
Land: 1.1 sq. mi.; Water: 0.0 sq. mi. Elev: 1318 ft.

Jamestown Borough
ZIP: 16134 Lat: 41-29-05 N Long: 80-26-13 W
Pop: 761 (1990); 854 (1980) Pop Density: 951.3
Land: 0.8 sq. mi.; Water: 0.0 sq. mi. Elev: 982 ft.

Jefferson Township
Lat: 41-15-48 N Long: 80-19-38 W
Pop: 1,998 (1990) Pop Density: 81.6
Land: 24.5 sq. mi.; Water: 0.8 sq. mi.

Lackawannock Township
Lat: 41-11-42 N Long: 80-21-12 W
Pop: 2,677 (1990) Pop Density: 130.0
Land: 20.6 sq. mi.; Water: 0.0 sq. mi.

Lake Township
Lat: 41-20-00 N Long: 80-08-46 W
Pop: 651 (1990) Pop Density: 41.2
Land: 15.8 sq. mi.; Water: 0.2 sq. mi.

Liberty Township
Lat: 41-06-42 N Long: 80-06-19 W
Pop: 1,223 (1990) Pop Density: 83.8
Land: 14.6 sq. mi.; Water: 0.1 sq. mi.

Mercer Borough
ZIP: 16137 Lat: 41-13-34 N Long: 80-14-11 W
Pop: 2,444 (1990); 2,532 (1980) Pop Density: 1880.0
Land: 1.3 sq. mi.; Water: 0.0 sq. mi. Elev: 1259 ft.
Laid out in 1803; incorporated Mar 28, 1814.

Mill Creek Township
Lat: 41-24-11 N Long: 80-02-34 W
Pop: 604 (1990) Pop Density: 32.0
Land: 18.9 sq. mi.; Water: 0.4 sq. mi.

New Lebanon Borough
ZIP: 16145 Lat: 41-25-00 N Long: 80-04-33 W
Pop: 209 (1990); 197 (1980) Pop Density: 160.8
Land: 1.3 sq. mi.; Water: 0.0 sq. mi. Elev: 1400 ft.

New Vernon Township
Lat: 41-24-28 N Long: 80-08-19 W
Pop: 493 (1990) Pop Density: 32.6
Land: 15.1 sq. mi.; Water: 1.4 sq. mi.

Otter Creek Township
Lat: 41-23-54 N Long: 80-17-48 W
Pop: 583 (1990) Pop Density: 49.4
Land: 11.8 sq. mi.; Water: 0.0 sq. mi.

Perry Township
Lat: 41-23-55 N Long: 80-13-00 W
Pop: 1,468 (1990) Pop Density: 81.6
Land: 18.0 sq. mi.; Water: 0.0 sq. mi.

Pine Township
Lat: 41-10-15 N Long: 80-04-07 W
Pop: 4,193 (1990) Pop Density: 163.2
Land: 25.7 sq. mi.; Water: 0.3 sq. mi.

Pymatuning Township
Lat: 41-19-33 N Long: 80-25-17 W
Pop: 3,736 (1990) Pop Density: 226.4
Land: 16.5 sq. mi.; Water: 1.6 sq. mi.

Salem Township
Lat: 41-26-48 N Long: 80-17-48 W
Pop: 678 (1990) Pop Density: 51.0
Land: 13.3 sq. mi.; Water: 0.0 sq. mi.

Sandy Creek Township
Lat: 41-27-36 N Long: 80-13-34 W
Pop: 806 (1990) Pop Density: 50.7
Land: 15.9 sq. mi.; Water: 0.3 sq. mi.

Sandy Lake Township
ZIP: 16145 Lat: 41-20-13 N Long: 80-03-01 W
Pop: 1,161 (1990) Pop Density: 47.8
Land: 24.3 sq. mi.; Water: 0.3 sq. mi.

*Sandy Lake Borough
ZIP: 16145 Lat: 41-20-51 N Long: 80-05-04 W
Pop: 722 (1990); 779 (1980) Pop Density: 722.0
Land: 1.0 sq. mi.; Water: 0.0 sq. mi. Elev: 1160 ft.

Sharon City
ZIP: 16146 Lat: 41-14-03 N Long: 80-29-59 W
Pop: 17,493 (1990) Pop Density: 4727.8
Land: 3.7 sq. mi.; Water: 0.0 sq. mi. Elev: 998 ft.
In western PA on the Ohio River, 18 mi. northwest of New Castle.

Name origin: Probably for the biblical plain of Sharon in Palestine for the similarity of the local flat topography.

Sharpsville Borough
ZIP: 16150 Lat: 41-15-32 N Long: 80-28-55 W
Pop: 4,729 (1990); 5,375 (1980) Pop Density: 3377.9
Land: 1.4 sq. mi.; Water: 0.0 sq. mi. Elev: 1000 ft.
In western PA, 20 mi. northwest of New Castle.

Name origin: For James Sharp, one of the original owners of the town site.

Sheakleyville Borough
ZIP: 16151 Lat: 41-26-40 N Long: 80-12-25 W
Pop: 145 (1990); 155 (1980) Pop Density: 725.0
Land: 0.2 sq. mi.; Water: 0.0 sq. mi. Elev: 1282 ft.

Shenango Township
Lat: 41-09-51 N Long: 80-26-52 W
Pop: 4,339 (1990) Pop Density: 145.1
Land: 29.9 sq. mi.; Water: 0.0 sq. mi.

South Pymatuning Township
Lat: 41-18-49 N Long: 80-29-13 W
Pop: 2,775 (1990) Pop Density: 143.8
Land: 19.3 sq. mi.; Water: 2.1 sq. mi.

Springfield Township
Lat: 41-08-24 N Long: 80-11-49 W
Pop: 1,892 (1990) Pop Density: 69.6
Land: 27.2 sq. mi.; Water: 0.2 sq. mi.

Stoneboro Borough
ZIP: 16153 Lat: 41-20-11 N Long: 80-06-35 W
Pop: 1,091 (1990); 1,177 (1980) Pop Density: 389.6
Land: 2.8 sq. mi.; Water: 0.1 sq. mi. Elev: 1184 ft.

Sugar Grove Township
Lat: 41-26-58 N Long: 80-20-54 W
Pop: 987 (1990) Pop Density: 80.2
Land: 12.3 sq. mi.; Water: 0.0 sq. mi.

West Middlesex Borough
ZIP: 16159 Lat: 41-10-26 N Long: 80-27-22 W
Pop: 982 (1990); 1,064 (1980) Pop Density: 1091.1
Land: 0.9 sq. mi.; Water: 0.0 sq. mi. Elev: 865 ft.

West Salem
Township
Lat: 41-24-06 N **Long:** 80-27-18 W
Pop: 3,547 (1990) **Pop Density:** 95.9
Land: 37.0 sq. mi.; **Water:** 0.0 sq. mi.

Wheatland
Borough
ZIP: 16161 **Lat:** 41-11-48 N **Long:** 80-29-45 W
Pop: 760 (1990); 1,132 (1980) **Pop Density:** 950.0
Land: 0.8 sq. mi.; **Water:** 0.0 sq. mi. **Elev:** 900 ft.

In western PA, northwest of New Castle on the OH border.
Laid out c. 1865 by Philadelphia Democrat James Wood.
Name origin: For the Lancaster County estate of Pres. James
Buchanan (1791–1868).

Wilmington
Township
Lat: 41-08-25 N **Long:** 80-19-23 W
Pop: 1,177 (1990) **Pop Density:** 89.8
Land: 13.1 sq. mi.; **Water:** 0.0 sq. mi.

Wolf Creek
Township
Lat: 41-13-33 N **Long:** 80-03-40 W
Pop: 653 (1990) **Pop Density:** 39.3
Land: 16.6 sq. mi.; **Water:** 0.2 sq. mi.

Worth
Township
Lat: 41-16-22 N **Long:** 80-03-00 W
Pop: 906 (1990) **Pop Density:** 36.5
Land: 24.8 sq. mi.; **Water:** 0.2 sq. mi.

Mifflin County
County Seat: Lewistown (ZIP: 17044)

Pop: 46,197 (1990); 46,908 (1980) **Pop Density:** 112.5
Land: 410.7 sq. mi.; **Water:** 2.7 sq. mi. **Area Code:** 717

In central PA, east of Altoona; organized Sep 19, 1789 from Cumberland and
Northumberland counties.
Name origin: For Gen. Thomas Mifflin (1744–1800), member of the Continental
Congress (1774–76; 1782–84), PA legislator, and longest-serving governor of PA
(1788–99).

Armagh
Township
ZIP: 17063 **Lat:** 40-45-08 N **Long:** 77-29-33 W
Pop: 3,627 (1990) **Pop Density:** 39.1
Land: 92.8 sq. mi.; **Water:** 0.1 sq. mi.

Belleville
CDP
ZIP: 17004 **Lat:** 40-36-10 N **Long:** 77-43-32 W
Pop: 1,589 (1990); 1,689 (1980) **Pop Density:** 722.3
Land: 2.2 sq. mi.; **Water:** 0.0 sq. mi.

Bratton
Township
ZIP: 17044 **Lat:** 40-28-54 N **Long:** 77-41-39 W
Pop: 1,427 (1990) **Pop Density:** 43.5
Land: 32.8 sq. mi.; **Water:** 0.5 sq. mi.

Brown
Township
ZIP: 17084 **Lat:** 40-40-51 N **Long:** 77-38-41 W
Pop: 3,320 (1990) **Pop Density:** 100.0
Land: 33.2 sq. mi.; **Water:** 0.0 sq. mi.

Burnham
Borough
ZIP: 17009 **Lat:** 40-38-11 N **Long:** 77-33-47 W
Pop: 2,197 (1990); 2,457 (1980) **Pop Density:** 1997.3
Land: 1.1 sq. mi.; **Water:** 0.0 sq. mi. **Elev:** 560 ft.
In central PA, northwest of Harrisburg.
Name origin: For William Burnham, official of a local steel
plant. Formerly called Freedom Forge and Logan.

Decatur
Township
Lat: 40-41-15 N **Long:** 77-24-41 W
Pop: 2,735 (1990) **Pop Density:** 60.5
Land: 45.2 sq. mi.; **Water:** 0.0 sq. mi.

Derry
Township
ZIP: 17099 **Lat:** 40-37-36 N **Long:** 77-32-02 W
Pop: 7,650 (1990) **Pop Density:** 246.0
Land: 31.1 sq. mi.; **Water:** 0.1 sq. mi.

Granville
Township
ZIP: 17029 **Lat:** 40-34-12 N **Long:** 77-37-03 W
Pop: 5,090 (1990) **Pop Density:** 126.9
Land: 40.1 sq. mi.; **Water:** 0.7 sq. mi.

Highland Park
CDP
ZIP: 17044 **Lat:** 40-37-18 N **Long:** 77-34-14 W
Pop: 1,583 (1990); 1,879 (1980) **Pop Density:** 2261.4
Land: 0.7 sq. mi.; **Water:** 0.0 sq. mi.

Juniata Terrace
Borough
ZIP: 17044 **Lat:** 40-35-03 N **Long:** 77-34-28 W
Pop: 556 (1990); 631 (1980) **Pop Density:** 5560.0
Land: 0.1 sq. mi.; **Water:** 0.0 sq. mi. **Elev:** 550 ft.

Kistler
Borough
ZIP: 17066 **Lat:** 40-22-38 N **Long:** 77-52-04 W
Pop: 314 (1990); 364 (1980) **Pop Density:** 1046.7
Land: 0.3 sq. mi.; **Water:** 0.0 sq. mi. **Elev:** 660 ft.

Lewistown
Borough
ZIP: 17044 **Lat:** 40-35-50 N **Long:** 77-34-24 W
Pop: 9,341 (1990); 9,830 (1980) **Pop Density:** 4670.5
Land: 2.0 sq. mi.; **Water:** 0.0 sq. mi. **Elev:** 504 ft.
In south-central PA, near the western end of Lewistown Nar-
rows. Laid out in 1790; incorporated as borough Apr 11,
1795; reincorporated Feb 6, 1811.
Name origin: For William Lewis, an ironmaster, who then
owned and operated Hope Furnace, which was situated in
old Derry Township, a few miles west of the new town.

McVeytown
Borough
ZIP: 17051 **Lat:** 40-29-53 N **Long:** 77-44-28 W
Pop: 408 (1990); 447 (1980) **Pop Density:** 4080.0
Land: 0.1 sq. mi.; **Water:** 0.0 sq. mi. **Elev:** 506 ft.

Menno
Township
ZIP: 17004 **Lat:** 40-33-32 N **Long:** 77-47-18 W
Pop: 1,637 (1990) **Pop Density:** 68.8
Land: 23.8 sq. mi.; **Water:** 0.0 sq. mi.

Milroy   CDP
ZIP: 17063   **Lat:** 40-42-53 N **Long:** 77-35-12 W
Pop: 1,456 (1990); 1,594 (1980)   **Pop Density:** 2080.0
Land: 0.7 sq. mi.; **Water:** 0.0 sq. mi.

Newton Hamilton   Borough
ZIP: 17075   **Lat:** 40-23-33 N **Long:** 77-50-07 W
Pop: 287 (1990); 317 (1980)   **Pop Density:** 1435.0
Land: 0.2 sq. mi.; **Water:** 0.0 sq. mi.   **Elev:** 600 ft.

Oliver   Township
ZIP: 17044   **Lat:** 40-31-02 N **Long:** 77-44-47 W
Pop: 1,822 (1990)   **Pop Density:** 52.7
Land: 34.6 sq. mi.; **Water:** 0.4 sq. mi.

Union   Township
ZIP: 17004   **Lat:** 40-36-45 N **Long:** 77-42-53 W
Pop: 3,265 (1990)   **Pop Density:** 128.0
Land: 25.5 sq. mi.; **Water:** 0.0 sq. mi.

Wayne   Township
                        Lat: 40-25-16 N **Long:** 77-48-55 W
Pop: 2,521 (1990)   **Pop Density:** 52.6
Land: 47.9 sq. mi.; **Water:** 0.8 sq. mi.

Monroe County
County Seat: Stroudsburg (ZIP: 18360)

Pop: 95,709 (1990); 69,409 (1980)   **Pop Density:** 157.6
Land: 607.3 sq. mi.; **Water:** 8.7 sq. mi.   **Area Code:** 717
On central eastern border of PA, southeast of Scranton; organized Apr 1, 1836 from Northampton and Pike counties.
Name origin: For James Monroe (1758–1831), fifth U.S. president.

Arlington Heights   CDP
                        Lat: 41-00-15 N **Long:** 75-12-47 W
Pop: 4,768 (1990); 1,198 (1980)   **Pop Density:** 899.6
Land: 5.3 sq. mi.; **Water:** 0.0 sq. mi.

Barrett   Township
                        Lat: 41-12-20 N **Long:** 75-14-37 W
Pop: 3,216 (1990)   **Pop Density:** 61.1
Land: 52.6 sq. mi.; **Water:** 0.7 sq. mi.
Formed in 1859.
Name origin: For George R. Barrett, then presiding judge of the county courts.

Brodheadsville   CDP
ZIP: 18322   **Lat:** 40-55-26 N **Long:** 75-24-11 W
Pop: 1,389 (1990)   **Pop Density:** 323.0
Land: 4.3 sq. mi.; **Water:** 0.0 sq. mi.

Chestnuthill   Township
ZIP: 18331   **Lat:** 40-57-26 N **Long:** 75-25-05 W
Pop: 8,798 (1990)   **Pop Density:** 235.9
Land: 37.3 sq. mi.; **Water:** 0.1 sq. mi.

Coolbaugh   Township
ZIP: 18466   **Lat:** 41-11-20 N **Long:** 75-26-17 W
Pop: 6,756 (1990)   **Pop Density:** 78.8
Land: 85.7 sq. mi.; **Water:** 1.9 sq. mi.

Delaware Water Gap   Borough
ZIP: 18327   **Lat:** 40-58-42 N **Long:** 75-08-15 W
Pop: 733 (1990); 597 (1980)   **Pop Density:** 431.2
Land: 1.7 sq. mi.; **Water:** 0.0 sq. mi.   **Elev:** 520 ft.
Name origin: For the gap in the Blue Ridge Mountains between Mount Minsi and Mount Tammany, through which the Delaware River flows.

East Stroudsburg   Borough
ZIP: 18301   **Lat:** 41-00-05 N **Long:** 75-10-42 W
Pop: 8,781 (1990); 8,039 (1980)   **Pop Density:** 3027.9
Land: 2.9 sq. mi.; **Water:** 0.0 sq. mi.   **Elev:** 422 ft.
In eastern PA, north of Allentown. Originally an extension of Stroudsburg.

Eldred   Township
                        Lat: 40-51-29 N **Long:** 75-26-51 W
Pop: 2,202 (1990)   **Pop Density:** 90.6
Land: 24.3 sq. mi.; **Water:** 0.0 sq. mi.

Hamilton   Township
ZIP: 18354   **Lat:** 40-56-11 N **Long:** 75-16-59 W
Pop: 6,681 (1990)   **Pop Density:** 174.4
Land: 38.3 sq. mi.; **Water:** 0.2 sq. mi.

Jackson   Township
                        Lat: 41-00-22 N **Long:** 75-21-20 W
Pop: 3,757 (1990)   **Pop Density:** 127.8
Land: 29.4 sq. mi.; **Water:** 0.4 sq. mi.   **Elev:** 710 ft.
Name origin: For Andrew Jackson (1767–1845), seventh U.S. president.

Middle Smithfield   Township
ZIP: 18301   **Lat:** 41-05-34 N **Long:** 75-06-10 W
Pop: 6,382 (1990)   **Pop Density:** 120.2
Land: 53.1 sq. mi.; **Water:** 1.0 sq. mi.

Mountainhome   CDP
                        Lat: 41-10-35 N **Long:** 75-15-47 W
Pop: 1,042 (1990)   **Pop Density:** 578.9
Land: 1.8 sq. mi.; **Water:** 0.0 sq. mi.

Mount Pocono   Borough
ZIP: 18344   **Lat:** 41-07-20 N **Long:** 75-21-28 W
Pop: 1,795 (1990); 1,237 (1980)   **Pop Density:** 512.9
Land: 3.5 sq. mi.; **Water:** 0.0 sq. mi.   **Elev:** 1860 ft.

Paradise   Township
                        Lat: 41-06-58 N **Long:** 75-17-10 W
Pop: 2,251 (1990)   **Pop Density:** 104.2
Land: 21.6 sq. mi.; **Water:** 0.1 sq. mi.

Pocono   Township
ZIP: 18372   **Lat:** 41-03-38 N **Long:** 75-18-38 W
Pop: 7,529 (1990)   **Pop Density:** 221.4
Land: 34.0 sq. mi.; **Water:** 0.2 sq. mi.

Polk
Township
Lat: 40-55-43 N Long: 75-30-16 W
Pop: 4,517 (1990) **Pop Density:** 151.6
Land: 29.8 sq. mi.; **Water:** 0.4 sq. mi.

Price
Township
Lat: 41-08-21 N Long: 75-12-00 W
Pop: 1,633 (1990) **Pop Density:** 64.8
Land: 25.2 sq. mi.; **Water:** 0.2 sq. mi.

Ross
Township
Lat: 40-52-37 N Long: 75-21-46 W
Pop: 3,696 (1990) **Pop Density:** 163.5
Land: 22.6 sq. mi.; **Water:** 0.0 sq. mi.

Smithfield
Township
Lat: 41-01-20 N Long: 75-07-56 W
Pop: 4,692 (1990) **Pop Density:** 202.2
Land: 23.2 sq. mi.; **Water:** 0.7 sq. mi.

Stroud
Township
ZIP: 18360 Lat: 40-59-59 N Long: 75-13-15 W
Pop: 10,600 (1990) **Pop Density:** 339.7
Land: 31.2 sq. mi.; **Water:** 0.2 sq. mi.

Stroudsburg
Borough
ZIP: 18360 **Lat:** 40-59-01 N **Long:** 75-11-51 W
Pop: 5,312 (1990); 5,148 (1980) **Pop Density:** 2951.1
Land: 1.8 sq. mi.; **Water:** 0.0 sq. mi. **Elev:** 430 ft.

In eastern PA in the Pocono foothills at the confluence of McMichaels, Pocono, and Brodhead creeks, 30 mi. north of Easton; incorporated Feb 6, 1815.

Name origin: For Col. Jacob Stroud, a veteran of the French and Indian War, who erected a stockaded house here and called it Fort Penn.

Tobyhanna
Township
ZIP: 18466 **Lat:** 41-06-49 N **Long:** 75-31-30 W
Pop: 4,318 (1990) **Pop Density:** 85.5
Land: 50.5 sq. mi.; **Water:** 2.3 sq. mi.

Name origin: From an Indian term possibly meaning 'alder stream.'

Tunkhannock
Township
Lat: 41-02-56 N **Long:** 75-28-39 W
Pop: 2,060 (1990) **Pop Density:** 53.2
Land: 38.7 sq. mi.; **Water:** 0.3 sq. mi.

Montgomery County
County Seat: Norristown (ZIP: 19404)

Pop: 678,111 (1990); 643,371 (1980) **Pop Density:** 1403.5
Land: 483.1 sq. mi.; **Water:** 4.3 sq. mi. **Area Code:** 215

In southeastern PA, northwest of Philadelphia; organized Sep 10, 1784 from old Philadelphia County.

Name origin: For Gen. Richard Montgomery (1736–1775), Revolutionary War officer and hero.

Abington
Township
ZIP: 19001 Lat: 40-06-38 N Long: 75-06-46 W
Pop: 56,322 (1990) **Pop Density:** 3633.7
Land: 15.5 sq. mi.; **Water:** 0.0 sq. mi.

In southeastern PA, north of Philadelphia. Founded 1714 when the Abington Presbyterian Church was built.

Name origin: For Great and Little Abington, Cambridgeshire, England.

Ambler
Borough
ZIP: 19002 Lat: 40-09-21 N Long: 75-13-19 W
Pop: 6,609 (1990); 6,628 (1980) **Pop Density:** 8261.3
Land: 0.8 sq. mi.; **Water:** 0.0 sq. mi. **Elev:** 250 ft.

Name origin: For a prominent family of early settlers, one of whom, Joseph Amber, settled here in 1723.

Ardmore
CDP
ZIP: 19003 Lat: 40-00-25 N Long: 75-17-13 W
Pop: 7,325 (1990) **Pop Density:** 6659.1
Land: 1.1 sq. mi.; **Water:** 0.0 sq. mi.

Part of the town is also in Delaware County.

Audubon
CDP
ZIP: 19407 Lat: 40-07-47 N Long: 75-25-42 W
Pop: 6,328 (1990) **Pop Density:** 1406.2
Land: 4.5 sq. mi.; **Water:** 0.0 sq. mi.

Blue Bell
CDP
ZIP: 19422 Lat: 40-08-44 N Long: 75-16-03 W
Pop: 6,091 (1990) **Pop Density:** 1128.0
Land: 5.4 sq. mi.; **Water:** 0.0 sq. mi.

Bridgeport
Borough
ZIP: 19405 **Lat:** 40-06-14 N **Long:** 75-20-36 W
Pop: 4,292 (1990); 4,843 (1980) **Pop Density:** 6131.4
Land: 0.7 sq. mi.; **Water:** 0.1 sq. mi. **Elev:** 108 ft.

Bryn Athyn
Borough
ZIP: 19009 **Lat:** 40-08-18 N **Long:** 75-03-57 W
Pop: 1,081 (1990); 947 (1980) **Pop Density:** 568.9
Land: 1.9 sq. mi.; **Water:** 0.0 sq. mi. **Elev:** 287 ft.

Bryn Mawr
CDP
Lat: 40-01-18 N **Long:** 75-18-57 W
Pop: 3,271 (1990) **Pop Density:** 5451.7
Land: 0.6 sq. mi.; **Water:** 0.0 sq. mi.

Cheltenham
Village & Township
ZIP: 19012 **Lat:** 40-04-39 N **Long:** 75-08-19 W
Pop: 34,923 (1990) **Pop Density:** 3880.3
Land: 9.0 sq. mi.; **Water:** 0.0 sq. mi.

In southeastern PA, a northern suburb of Philadelphia.

Collegeville
Borough
ZIP: 19426 **Lat:** 40-11-13 N **Long:** 75-27-26 W
Pop: 4,227 (1990); 3,406 (1980) **Pop Density:** 2641.9
Land: 1.6 sq. mi.; **Water:** 0.1 sq. mi. **Elev:** 150 ft.

In southeastern PA, 20 mi. northwest of Philadelphia.

Name origin: Formerly called Perkiomen Bridge and Freeland. Changed to present name in 1869 when the Reformed Church established Ursinus College.

Conshohocken
Borough
ZIP: 19428　　　**Lat:** 40-04-39 N **Long:** 75-18-11 W
Pop: 8,064 (1990); 8,475 (1980)　　**Pop Density:** 8064.0
Land: 1.0 sq. mi.; **Water:** 0.0 sq. mi.　　**Elev:** 95 ft.

In southeastern PA on the Schuylkill River, 11 mi. northwest of Philadelphia.
Name origin: From an Indian term possibly meaning 'pleasant valley.'

Douglass
Township
ZIP: 19525　　　**Lat:** 40-20-51 N **Long:** 75-35-27 W
Pop: 7,048 (1990)　　　**Pop Density:** 460.7
Land: 15.3 sq. mi.; **Water:** 0.0 sq. mi.

Eagleville
CDP
　　　　　　　Lat: 40-09-28 N **Long:** 75-24-27 W
Pop: 3,637 (1990)　　　**Pop Density:** 2273.1
Land: 1.6 sq. mi.; **Water:** 0.0 sq. mi.

East Greenville
Borough
ZIP: 18041　　　**Lat:** 40-24-21 N **Long:** 75-30-23 W
Pop: 3,117 (1990); 2,456 (1980)　　**Pop Density:** 6234.0
Land: 0.5 sq. mi.; **Water:** 0.0 sq. mi.　　**Elev:** 400 ft.

In southeastern PA near Perkiomen Creek, 20 mi. south of Allentown on the main line between that city and Philadelphia.

East Norriton
Township
ZIP: 19401　　　**Lat:** 40-09-06 N **Long:** 75-20-12 W
Pop: 13,324 (1990); 12,711 (1980)　　**Pop Density:** 2184.3
Land: 6.1 sq. mi.; **Water:** 0.0 sq. mi.

In southeastern PA near Norristown.

Evansburg
CDP
　　　　　　　Lat: 40-11-24 N **Long:** 75-26-09 W
Pop: 1,047 (1990); 605 (1980)　　**Pop Density:** 698.0
Land: 1.5 sq. mi.; **Water:** 0.0 sq. mi.

Flourtown
CDP
ZIP: 19031　　　**Lat:** 40-06-10 N **Long:** 75-12-31 W
Pop: 4,754 (1990)　　　**Pop Density:** 3395.7
Land: 1.4 sq. mi.; **Water:** 0.0 sq. mi.

Fort Washington
CDP
ZIP: 19025　　　**Lat:** 40-08-18 N **Long:** 75-11-30 W
Pop: 3,699 (1990)　　　**Pop Density:** 1370.0
Land: 2.7 sq. mi.; **Water:** 0.0 sq. mi.

Franconia
Township
ZIP: 18924　　　**Lat:** 40-18-14 N **Long:** 75-21-32 W
Pop: 7,224 (1990)　　　**Pop Density:** 523.5
Land: 13.8 sq. mi.; **Water:** 0.0 sq. mi.

Gilbertsville
CDP
ZIP: 19525　　　**Lat:** 40-19-22 N **Long:** 75-36-32 W
Pop: 3,994 (1990); 3,160 (1980)　　**Pop Density:** 1174.7
Land: 3.4 sq. mi.; **Water:** 0.0 sq. mi.

Glenside
CDP
ZIP: 19038　　　**Lat:** 40-06-10 N **Long:** 75-09-09 W
Pop: 8,704 (1990)　　　**Pop Density:** 6695.4
Land: 1.3 sq. mi.; **Water:** 0.0 sq. mi.

Green Lane
Borough
ZIP: 18054　　　**Lat:** 40-20-08 N **Long:** 75-28-14 W
Pop: 442 (1990); 542 (1980)　　**Pop Density:** 1473.3
Land: 0.3 sq. mi.; **Water:** 0.0 sq. mi.　　**Elev:** 220 ft.

Halfway House
CDP
　　　　　　　Lat: 40-16-54 N **Long:** 75-38-37 W
Pop: 1,415 (1990); 1,415 (1980)　　**Pop Density:** 707.5
Land: 2.0 sq. mi.; **Water:** 0.0 sq. mi.

Harleysville
CDP
ZIP: 19438　　　**Lat:** 40-16-42 N **Long:** 75-23-16 W
Pop: 7,405 (1990); 510 (1980)　　**Pop Density:** 1763.1
Land: 4.2 sq. mi.; **Water:** 0.0 sq. mi.

Hatboro
Borough
ZIP: 19040　　　**Lat:** 40-10-39 N **Long:** 75-06-17 W
Pop: 7,382 (1990); 7,579 (1980)　　**Pop Density:** 5272.9
Land: 1.4 sq. mi.; **Water:** 0.0 sq. mi.　　**Elev:** 250 ft.

Hatfield
Township
ZIP: 19440　　　**Lat:** 40-16-36 N **Long:** 75-17-15 W
Pop: 15,357 (1990)　　　**Pop Density:** 1535.7
Land: 10.0 sq. mi.; **Water:** 0.0 sq. mi.

*Hatfield
Borough
ZIP: 19440　　　**Lat:** 40-16-40 N **Long:** 75-17-57 W
Pop: 2,650 (1990); 2,533 (1980)　　**Pop Density:** 4416.7
Land: 0.6 sq. mi.; **Water:** 0.0 sq. mi.　　**Elev:** 332 ft.

In southeastern PA, a northern suburb of Philadelphia, 10 mi. west of Doylestown.

Horsham
Township
ZIP: 19044　　　**Lat:** 40-11-57 N **Long:** 75-09-58 W
Pop: 21,896 (1990)　　　**Pop Density:** 1265.7
Land: 17.3 sq. mi.; **Water:** 0.0 sq. mi.

Jenkintown
Borough
ZIP: 19046　　　**Lat:** 40-05-45 N **Long:** 75-07-47 W
Pop: 4,574 (1990); 4,942 (1980)　　**Pop Density:** 7623.3
Land: 0.6 sq. mi.; **Water:** 0.0 sq. mi.　　**Elev:** 300 ft.

In southeastern PA, a northern suburb of Philadelphia.
Name origin: For Welsh pioneer William Jenkins, who settled here before 1697. Previously called Jenkins'-town.

King of Prussia
CDP
ZIP: 19406　　　**Lat:** 40-05-43 N **Long:** 75-23-00 W
Pop: 18,406 (1990)　　　**Pop Density:** 2191.2
Land: 8.4 sq. mi.; **Water:** 0.1 sq. mi.

Kulpsville
CDP
ZIP: 19443　　　**Lat:** 40-14-37 N **Long:** 75-20-27 W
Pop: 5,183 (1990)　　　**Pop Density:** 1671.9
Land: 3.1 sq. mi.; **Water:** 0.0 sq. mi.

Lansdale
Borough
ZIP: 19446　　　**Lat:** 40-14-30 N **Long:** 75-16-55 W
Pop: 16,362 (1990); 16,526 (1980)　　**Pop Density:** 5278.1
Land: 3.1 sq. mi.; **Water:** 0.0 sq. mi.　　**Elev:** 360 ft.

In southeastern PA, a suburb 24 mi. northwest of Philadelphia.
Name origin: For a railroad surveyor, Philip Lansdale Fox.

Limerick
Township
ZIP: 19468　　　**Lat:** 40-13-57 N **Long:** 75-32-03 W
Pop: 6,691 (1990)　　　**Pop Density:** 296.1
Land: 22.6 sq. mi.; **Water:** 0.2 sq. mi.

Lower Frederick
Township
　　　　　　　Lat: 40-16-42 N **Long:** 75-28-43 W
Pop: 3,396 (1990)　　　**Pop Density:** 424.5
Land: 8.0 sq. mi.; **Water:** 0.1 sq. mi.

Lower Gwynedd
Township
ZIP: 19437   Lat: 40-11-09 N **Long:** 75-14-11 W
Pop: 9,958 (1990)   **Pop Density:** 1070.8
Land: 9.3 sq. mi.; **Water:** 0.0 sq. mi.

Lower Merion
Township
ZIP: 19003   Lat: 40-01-41 N **Long:** 75-16-45 W
Pop: 58,003 (1990)   **Pop Density:** 2447.4
Land: 23.7 sq. mi.; **Water:** 0.2 sq. mi.

In southeastern PA, northwest of Philadelphia.

Lower Moreland
Township
ZIP: 19006   Lat: 40-08-05 N **Long:** 75-02-54 W
Pop: 11,768 (1990)   **Pop Density:** 1612.1
Land: 7.3 sq. mi.; **Water:** 0.0 sq. mi.

Lower Pottsgrove
Township
ZIP: 19464   Lat: 40-15-04 N **Long:** 75-35-53 W
Pop: 8,808 (1990)   **Pop Density:** 1114.9
Land: 7.9 sq. mi.; **Water:** 0.1 sq. mi.

Lower Providence
Township
ZIP: 19401   Lat: 40-08-35 N **Long:** 75-25-24 W
Pop: 19,351 (1990)   **Pop Density:** 1264.8
Land: 15.3 sq. mi.; **Water:** 0.2 sq. mi.

Lower Salford
Township
ZIP: 19438   Lat: 40-15-56 N **Long:** 75-23-30 W
Pop: 10,735 (1990)   **Pop Density:** 745.5
Land: 14.4 sq. mi.; **Water:** 0.1 sq. mi.

Maple Glen
CDP
ZIP: 19002   Lat: 40-10-30 N **Long:** 75-10-49 W
Pop: 5,881 (1990)   **Pop Density:** 1897.1
Land: 3.1 sq. mi.; **Water:** 0.0 sq. mi.

Marlborough
Township
Lat: 40-21-28 N **Long:** 75-27-02 W
Pop: 3,116 (1990)   **Pop Density:** 249.3
Land: 12.5 sq. mi.; **Water:** 0.2 sq. mi.

Montgomery
Township
ZIP: 18936   Lat: 40-14-32 N **Long:** 75-13-59 W
Pop: 12,179 (1990)   **Pop Density:** 1138.2
Land: 10.7 sq. mi.; **Water:** 0.0 sq. mi.

Montgomeryville
CDP
ZIP: 18936   Lat: 40-14-52 N **Long:** 75-14-30 W
Pop: 9,114 (1990)   **Pop Density:** 1898.7
Land: 4.8 sq. mi.; **Water:** 0.0 sq. mi.

Narberth
Borough
ZIP: 19072   Lat: 40-00-28 N **Long:** 75-15-49 W
Pop: 4,278 (1990); 4,496 (1980)   **Pop Density:** 8556.0
Land: 0.5 sq. mi.; **Water:** 0.0 sq. mi.   **Elev:** 319 ft.

In southeastern PA, a northwestern suburb of Philadelphia.

New Hanover
Township
ZIP: 19525   Lat: 40-18-52 N **Long:** 75-33-41 W
Pop: 5,956 (1990)   **Pop Density:** 275.7
Land: 21.6 sq. mi.; **Water:** 0.0 sq. mi.

Norristown
Borough
ZIP: 19401   Lat: 40-07-19 N **Long:** 75-20-23 W
Pop: 30,749 (1990); 34,684 (1980)   **Pop Density:** 8785.4
Land: 3.5 sq. mi.; **Water:** 0.0 sq. mi.   **Elev:** 179 ft.

In southeastern PA on the Schuylkill River, 15 mi. northwest of Philadelphia in a fertile rolling section of the Schuylkill Valley. Laid out in 1784; incorporated Mar 31, 1812.

Name origin: For Isaac Norris, who, with William Trent on Oct 7, 1704, purchased the land now occupied by the borough for 50 cents an acre.

North Wales
Borough
ZIP: 19454   Lat: 40-12-38 N **Long:** 75-16-31 W
Pop: 3,802 (1990); 3,391 (1980)   **Pop Density:** 6336.7
Land: 0.6 sq. mi.; **Water:** 0.0 sq. mi.   **Elev:** 377 ft.

In southeastern PA, 20 mi. north of Philadelphia.

Pennsburg
Borough
ZIP: 18073   Lat: 40-23-36 N **Long:** 75-29-45 W
Pop: 2,460 (1990); 2,339 (1980)   **Pop Density:** 3075.0
Land: 0.8 sq. mi.; **Water:** 0.0 sq. mi.

In southeastern PA, 40 mi. north of Philadelphia.

Perkiomen
Township
Lat: 40-13-58 N **Long:** 75-27-56 W
Pop: 3,200 (1990)   **Pop Density:** 653.1
Land: 4.9 sq. mi.; **Water:** 0.1 sq. mi.   **Elev:** 120 ft.

Plymouth
Township
ZIP: 19401   Lat: 40-06-46 N **Long:** 75-17-51 W
Pop: 15,958 (1990)   **Pop Density:** 1899.8
Land: 8.4 sq. mi.; **Water:** 0.1 sq. mi.

Pottstown
Borough
ZIP: 19464   Lat: 40-15-00 N **Long:** 75-38-38 W
Pop: 21,831 (1990); 22,729 (1980)   **Pop Density:** 4548.1
Land: 4.8 sq. mi.; **Water:** 0.1 sq. mi.   **Elev:** 150 ft.

In southeastern PA at the junction of Manatawny Creek and the Schuylkill River. Laid out in 1754; incorporated 1815.

Name origin: For a prominent ironmaster, John Potts.

Red Hill
Borough
ZIP: 18076   Lat: 40-22-36 N **Long:** 75-29-01 W
Pop: 1,794 (1990); 1,727 (1980)   **Pop Density:** 2562.9
Land: 0.7 sq. mi.; **Water:** 0.0 sq. mi.   **Elev:** 380 ft.

Rockledge
Borough
ZIP: 19111   Lat: 40-04-55 N **Long:** 75-05-23 W
Pop: 2,679 (1990); 2,538 (1980)   **Pop Density:** 8930.0
Land: 0.3 sq. mi.; **Water:** 0.0 sq. mi.   **Elev:** 200 ft.

In southeastern PA, 10 mi. northeast of Philadelphia.

Royersford
Borough
ZIP: 19468   Lat: 40-11-06 N **Long:** 75-32-16 W
Pop: 4,458 (1990); 4,243 (1980)   **Pop Density:** 5572.5
Land: 0.8 sq. mi.; **Water:** 0.0 sq. mi.   **Elev:** 200 ft.

In southeastern PA, 5 mi. north of Phoenixville.

Salford
Township
Lat: 40-20-15 N **Long:** 75-24-00 W
Pop: 2,216 (1990)   **Pop Density:** 233.3
Land: 9.5 sq. mi.; **Water:** 0.0 sq. mi.

Schwenksville
Borough
ZIP: 19473   Lat: 40-15-28 N **Long:** 75-27-59 W
Pop: 1,326 (1990); 1,041 (1980)   **Pop Density:** 3315.0
Land: 0.4 sq. mi.; **Water:** 0.0 sq. mi.   **Elev:** 148 ft.

Skippack
Township
ZIP: 19474   Lat: 40-13-05 N **Long:** 75-25-14 W
Pop: 8,790 (1990)   **Pop Density:** 637.0
Land: 13.8 sq. mi.; **Water:** 0.2 sq. mi.

Souderton
Borough
ZIP: 18964   Lat: 40-18-36 N **Long:** 75-19-19 W
Pop: 5,957 (1990); 6,657 (1980)   **Pop Density:** 5415.5
Land: 1.1 sq. mi.; **Water:** 0.0 sq. mi.   **Elev:** 449 ft.

In southeastern PA, a northern suburb of Philadelphia. Founded in 1876.

Springfield
Township
ZIP: 19118   **Lat:** 40-05-49 N **Long:** 75-12-09 W
Pop: 19,612 (1990)   **Pop Density:** 2884.1
Land: 6.8 sq. mi.; **Water:** 0.0 sq. mi.

Telford
Borough
ZIP: 18969   **Lat:** 40-19-21 N **Long:** 75-19-49 W
Pop: 2,565 (1990); 2,520 (1980)   **Pop Density:** 5130.0
Land: 0.5 sq. mi.; **Water:** 0.0 sq. mi.   **Elev:** 449 ft.
In southeastern PA, 25 mi. east of Reading. Part of the town
is also in Bucks County.

Towamencin
Township
ZIP: 19443   **Lat:** 40-14-30 N **Long:** 75-20-19 W
Pop: 14,167 (1990)   **Pop Density:** 1460.5
Land: 9.7 sq. mi.; **Water:** 0.0 sq. mi.

Trappe
Borough
ZIP: 19426   **Lat:** 40-11-38 N **Long:** 75-28-38 W
Pop: 2,115 (1990); 1,800 (1980)   **Pop Density:** 1007.1
Land: 2.1 sq. mi.; **Water:** 0.0 sq. mi.   **Elev:** 290 ft.
Name origin: Either because an early tavern's high stoop
often became a "trap" for the unsteady feet of its patrons, or
an anglicization of *treppe* 'steps,' which the German settlers
called the high stoop.

Upper Dublin
Township
ZIP: 19034   **Lat:** 40-08-58 N **Long:** 75-10-59 W
Pop: 24,028 (1990)   **Pop Density:** 1820.3
Land: 13.2 sq. mi.; **Water:** 0.0 sq. mi.

Upper Frederick
Township
Lat: 40-18-39 N **Long:** 75-30-24 W
Pop: 2,165 (1990)   **Pop Density:** 218.7
Land: 9.9 sq. mi.; **Water:** 0.2 sq. mi.

Upper Gwynedd
Township
ZIP: 19454   **Lat:** 40-12-58 N **Long:** 75-17-29 W
Pop: 12,197 (1990)   **Pop Density:** 1505.8
Land: 8.1 sq. mi.; **Water:** 0.0 sq. mi.

Upper Hanover
Township
Lat: 40-23-47 N **Long:** 75-30-47 W
Pop: 4,604 (1990)   **Pop Density:** 227.9
Land: 20.2 sq. mi.; **Water:** 1.0 sq. mi.

Upper Merion
Township
ZIP: 19406   **Lat:** 40-05-24 N **Long:** 75-22-45 W
Pop: 25,722 (1990)   **Pop Density:** 1531.1
Land: 16.8 sq. mi.; **Water:** 0.4 sq. mi.

Upper Moreland
Township
ZIP: 19090   **Lat:** 40-09-22 N **Long:** 75-06-13 W
Pop: 25,313 (1990)   **Pop Density:** 3164.1
Land: 8.0 sq. mi.; **Water:** 0.0 sq. mi.
In southeastern PA, north of Philadelphia.

Upper Pottsgrove
Township
Lat: 40-17-00 N **Long:** 75-38-04 W
Pop: 3,315 (1990)   **Pop Density:** 663.0
Land: 5.0 sq. mi.; **Water:** 0.0 sq. mi.

Upper Providence
Township
ZIP: 19456   **Lat:** 40-09-54 N **Long:** 75-29-25 W
Pop: 9,682 (1990)   **Pop Density:** 543.9
Land: 17.8 sq. mi.; **Water:** 0.4 sq. mi.

Upper Salford
Township
Lat: 40-17-24 N **Long:** 75-26-38 W
Pop: 2,719 (1990)   **Pop Density:** 302.1
Land: 9.0 sq. mi.; **Water:** 0.1 sq. mi.

West Conshohocken
Borough
ZIP: 19428   **Lat:** 40-04-11 N **Long:** 75-19-08 W
Pop: 1,294 (1990); 1,516 (1980)   **Pop Density:** 1617.5
Land: 0.8 sq. mi.; **Water:** 0.0 sq. mi.   **Elev:** 130 ft.

West Norriton
Township
ZIP: 19401   **Lat:** 40-07-45 N **Long:** 75-22-44 W
Pop: 15,209 (1990)   **Pop Density:** 2577.8
Land: 5.9 sq. mi.; **Water:** 0.3 sq. mi.
In southeastern PA, west of Philadelphia.

West Pottsgrove
Township
Lat: 40-15-26 N **Long:** 75-40-19 W
Pop: 3,829 (1990)   **Pop Density:** 1595.4
Land: 2.4 sq. mi.; **Water:** 0.0 sq. mi.   **Elev:** 260 ft.

Whitemarsh
Township & Village
ZIP: 19428   **Lat:** 40-05-59 N **Long:** 75-15-08 W
Pop: 14,863 (1990)   **Pop Density:** 1018.0
Land: 14.6 sq. mi.; **Water:** 0.1 sq. mi.
In southeastern PA on Wissahickon Creek, 15 mi. north of
Philadelphia.

Whitpain
Township
ZIP: 19422   **Lat:** 40-09-26 N **Long:** 75-16-42 W
Pop: 15,673 (1990)   **Pop Density:** 1215.0
Land: 12.9 sq. mi.; **Water:** 0.0 sq. mi.

Worcester
Township
Lat: 40-11-29 N **Long:** 75-20-59 W
Pop: 4,686 (1990)   **Pop Density:** 289.3
Land: 16.2 sq. mi.; **Water:** 0.0 sq. mi.

Montour County
County Seat: Danville (ZIP: 17821)

Pop: 17,735 (1990); 16,675 (1980)   **Pop Density:** 135.6
Land: 130.8 sq. mi.; **Water:** 1.5 sq. mi.   **Area Code:** 717

In central PA, southeast of Williamsport; organized May 3, 1850 from Columbia County.

Name origin: For Madame Montour (c. 1682–1752), an early PA settler. Of French-Canadian and Indian stock, she was captured and adopted at age ten by an Iroquois tribe. She later used her background as an Indian interpreter and greatly influenced Indian affairs in PA and NY.

Anthony
Township
Lat: 41-07-08 N **Long:** 76-41-11 W
Pop: 1,287 (1990)   **Pop Density:** 49.7
Land: 25.9 sq. mi.; **Water:** 0.3 sq. mi.

Cooper
Township
Lat: 40-57-50 N **Long:** 76-32-36 W
Pop: 934 (1990)   **Pop Density:** 135.4
Land: 6.9 sq. mi.; **Water:** 0.3 sq. mi.

Danville
Borough
ZIP: 17821   **Lat:** 40-57-41 N **Long:** 76-36-44 W
Pop: 5,165 (1990); 5,239 (1980)   **Pop Density:** 3228.1
Land: 1.6 sq. mi.; **Water:** 0.0 sq. mi.   **Elev:** 500 ft.
Laid out in 1792; incorporated Feb 27, 1849.

Derry
Township
Lat: 41-03-28 N **Long:** 76-38-53 W
Pop: 1,272 (1990)   **Pop Density:** 79.0
Land: 16.1 sq. mi.; **Water:** 0.2 sq. mi.

Liberty
Township
Lat: 40-59-23 N **Long:** 76-43-45 W
Pop: 1,309 (1990)   **Pop Density:** 48.3
Land: 27.1 sq. mi.; **Water:** 0.0 sq. mi.

Limestone
Township
Lat: 41-03-40 N **Long:** 76-43-28 W
Pop: 787 (1990)   **Pop Density:** 58.7
Land: 13.4 sq. mi.; **Water:** 0.0 sq. mi.

Mahoning
Township
Lat: 40-57-53 N **Long:** 76-36-11 W
Pop: 4,134 (1990)   **Pop Density:** 480.7
Land: 8.6 sq. mi.; **Water:** 0.6 sq. mi.

Mayberry
Township
Lat: 40-54-30 N **Long:** 76-32-49 W
Pop: 207 (1990)   **Pop Density:** 29.2
Land: 7.1 sq. mi.; **Water:** 0.1 sq. mi.

Mechanicsville
CDP
Lat: 40-57-59 N **Long:** 76-35-07 W
Pop: 2,803 (1990); 2,613 (1980)   **Pop Density:** 1401.5
Land: 2.0 sq. mi.; **Water:** 0.0 sq. mi.

Valley
Township
Lat: 41-00-01 N **Long:** 76-37-52 W
Pop: 2,010 (1990)   **Pop Density:** 124.1
Land: 16.2 sq. mi.; **Water:** 0.0 sq. mi.

Washingtonville
Borough
ZIP: 17884   **Lat:** 41-03-06 N **Long:** 76-40-30 W
Pop: 228 (1990); 218 (1980)   **Pop Density:** 2280.0
Land: 0.1 sq. mi.; **Water:** 0.0 sq. mi.   **Elev:** 566 ft.
Name origin: For George Washington (1732–99), first U.S. president.

West Hemlock
Township
Lat: 41-01-30 N **Long:** 76-34-49 W
Pop: 402 (1990)   **Pop Density:** 52.2
Land: 7.7 sq. mi.; **Water:** 0.0 sq. mi.

Northampton County
County Seat: Easton (ZIP: 18042)

Pop: 247,105 (1990); 225,418 (1980)   **Pop Density:** 661.0
Land: 373.9 sq. mi.; **Water:** 3.6 sq. mi.   **Area Code:** 215

On central eastern border of PA, east of Allentown; organized Mar 11, 1752 from Bucks County.

Name origin: For Northamptonshire, England, home of Thomas Penn's father-in-law, Thomas Fermor, the Earl of Pomfret.

Allen
Township
Lat: 40-42-37 N **Long:** 75-29-13 W
Pop: 2,626 (1990)   **Pop Density:** 236.6
Land: 11.1 sq. mi.; **Water:** 0.1 sq. mi.

In central-eastern PA, north of Allentown.

Name origin: For William Allen, who was chief justice of PA (1750–74) and received 3,000 acres here in 1748.

Bangor
Borough
ZIP: 18013   **Lat:** 40-52-06 N **Long:** 75-12-29 W
Pop: 5,383 (1990); 5,006 (1980)   **Pop Density:** 3588.7
Land: 1.5 sq. mi.; **Water:** 0.0 sq. mi.   **Elev:** 600 ft.

Founded 1773; incorporated c. 1875. Center of PA's slate-quarrying area.

Name origin: For the slate-producing city of Bangor, Wales, former home of many early settlers.

Bath
Borough
ZIP: 18014   **Lat:** 40-43-39 N **Long:** 75-23-30 W
Pop: 2,358 (1990); 1,953 (1980)   **Pop Density:** 2620.0
Land: 0.9 sq. mi.; **Water:** 0.0 sq. mi.   **Elev:** 432 ft.

Belfast
CDP
Lat: 40-46-57 N **Long:** 75-16-23 W
Pop: 1,102 (1990)   **Pop Density:** 1001.8
Land: 1.1 sq. mi.; **Water:** 0.0 sq. mi.

Bethlehem
City
ZIP: 18015   **Lat:** 40-37-30 N **Long:** 75-21-28 W
Pop: 52,561 (1990); 50,554 (1980)   **Pop Density:** 3527.6
Land: 14.9 sq. mi.; **Water:** 0.1 sq. mi.   **Elev:** 360 ft.

In eastern PA on the Lehigh River, 5 mi. east of Allentown. Founded in 1741 by the Moravian Brethren. Site of Lehigh Univ. Part of the city is also in Lehigh County.

Name origin: Named on Christmas Eve 1741 for birthplace of Jesus, when the congregation and their leader, Count Nicholas Ludwig, sang an old German hymn with the words, "Bethlehem gave us that which makes life rich."

*Bethlehem
Township
ZIP: 18017   **Lat:** 40-39-51 N **Long:** 75-18-49 W
Pop: 16,425 (1990)   **Pop Density:** 1125.0
Land: 14.6 sq. mi.; **Water:** 0.1 sq. mi.

Bushkill
Township
ZIP: 18064   **Lat:** 40-47-52 N **Long:** 75-19-46 W
Pop: 5,512 (1990)   **Pop Density:** 217.9
Land: 25.3 sq. mi.; **Water:** 0.1 sq. mi.

Chapman
Borough
Lat: 40-45-33 N **Long:** 75-24-05 W
Pop: 254 (1990); 255 (1980)   **Pop Density:** 635.0
Land: 0.4 sq. mi.; **Water:** 0.0 sq. mi.   **Elev:** 581 ft.

East Allen
Township
Lat: 40-42-24 N **Long:** 75-25-24 W
Pop: 4,572 (1990)   **Pop Density:** 317.5
Land: 14.4 sq. mi.; **Water:** 0.0 sq. mi.

East Bangor
Borough
ZIP: 18013   **Lat:** 40-52-50 N **Long:** 75-11-11 W
Pop: 1,006 (1990); 955 (1980)   **Pop Density:** 1676.7
Land: 0.6 sq. mi.; **Water:** 0.0 sq. mi.   **Elev:** 700 ft.

Eastlawn Gardens
CDP
Lat: 40-45-02 N **Long:** 75-17-46 W
Pop: 1,794 (1990); 1,771 (1980)   **Pop Density:** 1630.9
Land: 1.1 sq. mi.; **Water:** 0.0 sq. mi.

Easton
City
ZIP: 18042   **Lat:** 40-41-10 N **Long:** 75-13-14 W
Pop: 26,276 (1990); 26,027 (1980)   **Pop Density:** 6110.7
Land: 4.3 sq. mi.; **Water:** 0.4 sq. mi.   **Elev:** 300 ft.

In eastern PA on the Lehigh and Delaware rivers, 15 mi. northeast of Allentown near Phillipsburg, NJ. Incorporated as borough Sep 23, 1789, as city Nov 2, 1886; home rule charter adopted Apr 1976.

Name origin: For the Northamptonshire estate (Easton-Weston) of Lord Pomfret, Thomas Penn's father-in-law.

Forks
Township
ZIP: 18042   **Lat:** 40-44-05 N **Long:** 75-13-29 W
Pop: 5,923 (1990)   **Pop Density:** 489.5
Land: 12.1 sq. mi.; **Water:** 0.2 sq. mi.

Freemansburg
Borough
ZIP: 18017   **Lat:** 40-37-38 N **Long:** 75-20-24 W
Pop: 1,946 (1990); 1,879 (1980)   **Pop Density:** 2780.0
Land: 0.7 sq. mi.; **Water:** 0.0 sq. mi.   **Elev:** 310 ft.

Glendon
Borough
ZIP: 18042   **Lat:** 40-39-40 N **Long:** 75-14-08 W
Pop: 391 (1990); 354 (1980)   **Pop Density:** 651.7
Land: 0.6 sq. mi.; **Water:** 0.0 sq. mi.   **Elev:** 300 ft.

Hanover
Township
ZIP: 18017   **Lat:** 40-40-13 N **Long:** 75-23-56 W
Pop: 7,176 (1990)   **Pop Density:** 1071.0
Land: 6.7 sq. mi.; **Water:** 0.0 sq. mi.

Hellertown
Borough
ZIP: 18055   **Lat:** 40-34-52 N **Long:** 75-20-17 W
Pop: 5,662 (1990); 6,025 (1980)   **Pop Density:** 4044.3
Land: 1.4 sq. mi.; **Water:** 0.0 sq. mi.

Lehigh
Township
ZIP: 18088   **Lat:** 40-46-15 N **Long:** 75-32-12 W
Pop: 9,296 (1990)   **Pop Density:** 313.0
Land: 29.7 sq. mi.; **Water:** 0.3 sq. mi.

Name origin: For the Lehigh River, which forms the township's western border.

Lower Mount Bethel
Township
Lat: 40-48-12 N Long: 75-09-14 W
Pop: 3,187 (1990)   Pop Density: 131.7
Land: 24.2 sq. mi.; Water: 0.5 sq. mi.

Lower Nazareth
Township
Lat: 40-42-16 N Long: 75-19-53 W
Pop: 4,483 (1990)   Pop Density: 334.6
Land: 13.4 sq. mi.; Water: 0.0 sq. mi.

Lower Saucon
Township
ZIP: 18015   Lat: 40-35-07 N Long: 75-19-35 W
Pop: 8,448 (1990)   Pop Density: 349.1
Land: 24.2 sq. mi.; Water: 0.2 sq. mi.   Elev: 345 ft.

Middletown
CDP
ZIP: 18017   Lat: 40-38-37 N Long: 75-19-32 W
Pop: 6,866 (1990); 5,801 (1980)   Pop Density: 2746.4
Land: 2.5 sq. mi.; Water: 0.0 sq. mi.

Moore
Township
ZIP: 18014   Lat: 40-46-50 N Long: 75-25-19 W
Pop: 8,418 (1990)   Pop Density: 225.1
Land: 37.4 sq. mi.; Water: 0.0 sq. mi.

Nazareth
Borough
ZIP: 18064   Lat: 40-44-23 N Long: 75-18-46 W
Pop: 5,713 (1990); 5,443 (1980)   Pop Density: 3360.6
Land: 1.7 sq. mi.; Water: 0.0 sq. mi.   Elev: 500 ft.
In eastern PA, 13 mi. northeast of Allentown. The second Moravian settlement in PA.
Name origin: For the biblical town where Jesus lived.

Northampton
Borough
ZIP: 18067   Lat: 40-41-16 N Long: 75-29-19 W
Pop: 8,717 (1990); 8,240 (1980)   Pop Density: 3352.7
Land: 2.6 sq. mi.; Water: 0.1 sq. mi.   Elev: 380 ft.
In eastern PA on the Lehigh River, 5 mi. north of Allentown.
Name origin: For the county.

North Catasauqua
Borough
ZIP: 18032   Lat: 40-39-51 N Long: 75-28-27 W
Pop: 2,867 (1990); 2,554 (1980)   Pop Density: 4095.7
Land: 0.7 sq. mi.; Water: 0.0 sq. mi.   Elev: 350 ft.

Palmer
Township
ZIP: 18042   Lat: 40-42-07 N Long: 75-15-57 W
Pop: 14,965 (1990)   Pop Density: 1398.6
Land: 10.7 sq. mi.; Water: 0.0 sq. mi.

Pen Argyl
Borough
ZIP: 18072   Lat: 40-52-04 N Long: 75-15-15 W
Pop: 3,492 (1990); 3,388 (1980)   Pop Density: 2494.3
Land: 1.4 sq. mi.; Water: 0.0 sq. mi.   Elev: 847 ft.
In eastern PA, 20 mi. northeast of Allentown.

Plainfield
Township
ZIP: 18064   Lat: 40-49-11 N Long: 75-15-40 W
Pop: 5,444 (1990)   Pop Density: 220.4
Land: 24.7 sq. mi.; Water: 0.0 sq. mi.

Portland
Borough
ZIP: 18351   Lat: 40-55-13 N Long: 75-05-53 W
Pop: 516 (1990); 540 (1980)   Pop Density: 1032.0
Land: 0.5 sq. mi.; Water: 0.0 sq. mi.   Elev: 299 ft.
Founded 1845 by Capt. James Ginn.
Name origin: For Portland, ME.

Roseto
Borough
ZIP: 18013   Lat: 40-52-41 N Long: 75-13-14 W
Pop: 1,555 (1990); 1,484 (1980)   Pop Density: 2591.7
Land: 0.6 sq. mi.; Water: 0.0 sq. mi.   Elev: 860 ft.
In eastern PA, north of Easton.

Stockertown
Borough
ZIP: 18083   Lat: 40-45-19 N Long: 75-15-49 W
Pop: 641 (1990); 661 (1980)   Pop Density: 641.0
Land: 1.0 sq. mi.; Water: 0.0 sq. mi.   Elev: 400 ft.
Laid out in 1774.
Name origin: For Andrew Stocker.

Tatamy
Borough
ZIP: 18085   Lat: 40-44-28 N Long: 75-15-18 W
Pop: 873 (1990); 910 (1980)   Pop Density: 1746.0
Land: 0.5 sq. mi.; Water: 0.0 sq. mi.   Elev: 328 ft.

Upper Mount Bethel
Township
ZIP: 18013   Lat: 40-53-47 N Long: 75-08-17 W
Pop: 5,476 (1990)   Pop Density: 125.9
Land: 43.5 sq. mi.; Water: 0.9 sq. mi.

Upper Nazareth
Township
Lat: 40-44-11 N Long: 75-20-04 W
Pop: 3,413 (1990)   Pop Density: 467.5
Land: 7.3 sq. mi.; Water: 0.1 sq. mi.

Walnutport
Borough
ZIP: 18088   Lat: 40-45-05 N Long: 75-35-44 W
Pop: 2,055 (1990); 2,007 (1980)   Pop Density: 2935.7
Land: 0.7 sq. mi.; Water: 0.0 sq. mi.   Elev: 380 ft.
In eastern PA.

Washington
Township
Lat: 40-50-45 N Long: 75-11-40 W
Pop: 3,759 (1990)   Pop Density: 207.7
Land: 18.1 sq. mi.; Water: 0.0 sq. mi.
Name origin: For George Washington (1732–99), first U.S. president.

West Easton
Borough
ZIP: 18042   Lat: 40-40-41 N Long: 75-14-11 W
Pop: 1,163 (1990); 1,033 (1980)   Pop Density: 3876.7
Land: 0.3 sq. mi.; Water: 0.0 sq. mi.   Elev: 300 ft.

Williams
Township
Lat: 40-37-41 N Long: 75-13-35 W
Pop: 3,982 (1990)   Pop Density: 216.4
Land: 18.4 sq. mi.; Water: 0.3 sq. mi.

Wilson
Borough
ZIP: 18042   Lat: 40-41-06 N Long: 75-14-24 W
Pop: 7,830 (1990); 7,564 (1980)   Pop Density: 6525.0
Land: 1.2 sq. mi.; Water: 0.0 sq. mi.   Elev: 400 ft.
In eastern PA, northeast of Allentown.

Wind Gap
Borough
ZIP: 18091   Lat: 40-50-51 N Long: 75-17-30 W
Pop: 2,741 (1990); 2,651 (1980)   Pop Density: 1957.9
Land: 1.4 sq. mi.; Water: 0.0 sq. mi.   Elev: 752 ft.
Incorporated 1893.
Name origin: For the "wind gap" in the Blue Mountains, the first notch to the south of the Delaware Water Gap.

Northumberland County
County Seat: Sunbury (ZIP: 17801)

Pop: 96,771 (1990); 100,381 (1980)　　　**Pop Density:** 210.4
Land: 459.9 sq. mi.; **Water:** 17.5 sq. mi.　　**Area Code:** 717

In central PA, southeast of Williamsport; organized Mar 21, 1772 from Lancaster, Bedford, Berks, Northampton, and Cumberland counties.
Name origin: For the county of Northumberland in England.

Coal　　　　　　　　　　　　　　Township
ZIP: 17872　　　**Lat:** 40-47-13 N **Long:** 76-32-49 W
Pop: 9,922 (1990)　　　**Pop Density:** 374.4
Land: 26.5 sq. mi.; **Water:** 0.0 sq. mi.

Delaware　　　　　　　　　　　　Township
ZIP: 17777　　　**Lat:** 41-07-20 N **Long:** 76-50-31 W
Pop: 4,018 (1990)　　　**Pop Density:** 132.2
Land: 30.4 sq. mi.; **Water:** 1.0 sq. mi.

East Cameron　　　　　　　　　　Township
　　　　　　　Lat: 40-44-56 N **Long:** 76-31-02 W
Pop: 646 (1990)　　　**Pop Density:** 54.3
Land: 11.9 sq. mi.; **Water:** 0.0 sq. mi.

East Chillisquaque　　　　　　　Township
ZIP: 17847　　　**Lat:** 40-58-56 N **Long:** 76-47-58 W
Pop: 679 (1990)　　　**Pop Density:** 83.8
Land: 8.1 sq. mi.; **Water:** 0.0 sq. mi.
Name origin: An Indian term possibly meaning 'resort of snow birds.'

Edgewood　　　　　　　　　　　　CDP
ZIP: 17872　　　**Lat:** 40-47-16 N **Long:** 76-34-43 W
Pop: 2,719 (1990); 3,115 (1980)　　　**Pop Density:** 5438.0
Land: 0.5 sq. mi.; **Water:** 0.0 sq. mi.

Elysburg　　　　　　　　　　　　CDP
ZIP: 17824　　　**Lat:** 40-52-05 N **Long:** 76-32-57 W
Pop: 1,890 (1990); 1,447 (1980)　　　**Pop Density:** 651.7
Land: 2.9 sq. mi.; **Water:** 0.0 sq. mi.

Fairview-Ferndale　　　　　　　　CDP
　　　　　　　Lat: 40-46-47 N **Long:** 76-34-32 W
Pop: 2,895 (1990); 3,167 (1980)　　　**Pop Density:** 3216.7
Land: 0.9 sq. mi.; **Water:** 0.0 sq. mi.

Herndon　　　　　　　　　　　　Borough
ZIP: 17830　　　**Lat:** 40-42-37 N **Long:** 76-51-16 W
Pop: 422 (1990); 483 (1980)　　　**Pop Density:** 527.5
Land: 0.8 sq. mi.; **Water:** 1.0 sq. mi.　　**Elev:** 460 ft.

Jackson　　　　　　　　　　　　Township
ZIP: 17830　　　**Lat:** 40-42-29 N **Long:** 76-49-02 W
Pop: 845 (1990)　　　**Pop Density:** 66.5
Land: 12.7 sq. mi.; **Water:** 1.5 sq. mi.

Jordan　　　　　　　　　　　　Township
ZIP: 17830　　　**Lat:** 40-40-08 N **Long:** 76-45-55 W
Pop: 847 (1990)　　　**Pop Density:** 49.0
Land: 17.3 sq. mi.; **Water:** 0.0 sq. mi.

Kulpmont　　　　　　　　　　　Borough
ZIP: 17834　　　**Lat:** 40-47-43 N **Long:** 76-28-19 W
Pop: 3,233 (1990); 3,675 (1980)　　　**Pop Density:** 3592.2
Land: 0.9 sq. mi.; **Water:** 0.0 sq. mi.　　**Elev:** 1100 ft.
Founded 1875; incorporated 1914.

Lewis　　　　　　　　　　　　Township
ZIP: 17772　　　**Lat:** 41-06-43 N **Long:** 76-46-10 W
Pop: 1,881 (1990)　　　**Pop Density:** 71.3
Land: 26.4 sq. mi.; **Water:** 0.0 sq. mi.

Little Mahanoy　　　　　　　　Township
ZIP: 17823　　　**Lat:** 40-45-23 N **Long:** 76-45-51 W
Pop: 432 (1990)　　　**Pop Density:** 41.1
Land: 10.5 sq. mi.; **Water:** 0.0 sq. mi.

Lower Augusta　　　　　　　　Township
　　　　　　　Lat: 40-46-54 N **Long:** 76-48-40 W
Pop: 1,024 (1990)　　　**Pop Density:** 56.0
Land: 18.3 sq. mi.; **Water:** 2.2 sq. mi.

Lower Mahanoy　　　　　　　　Township
　　　　　　　Lat: 40-39-12 N **Long:** 76-52-27 W
Pop: 1,669 (1990)　　　**Pop Density:** 76.2
Land: 21.9 sq. mi.; **Water:** 3.5 sq. mi.

Marion Heights　　　　　　　　Borough
ZIP: 17832　　　**Lat:** 40-48-11 N **Long:** 76-27-54 W
Pop: 837 (1990); 921 (1980)　　　**Pop Density:** 4185.0
Land: 0.2 sq. mi.; **Water:** 0.0 sq. mi.　　**Elev:** 1323 ft.

Marshallton　　　　　　　　　　CDP
ZIP: 17872　　　**Lat:** 40-47-07 N **Long:** 76-32-04 W
Pop: 1,482 (1990); 1,692 (1980)　　　**Pop Density:** 1646.7
Land: 0.9 sq. mi.; **Water:** 0.0 sq. mi.

McEwensville　　　　　　　　　Borough
ZIP: 17749　　　**Lat:** 41-04-19 N **Long:** 76-49-08 W
Pop: 273 (1990); 247 (1980)　　　**Pop Density:** 2730.0
Land: 0.1 sq. mi.; **Water:** 0.0 sq. mi.　　**Elev:** 511 ft.

Milton　　　　　　　　　　　　Borough
ZIP: 17847　　　**Lat:** 41-00-28 N **Long:** 76-51-02 W
Pop: 6,746 (1990); 6,730 (1980)　　　**Pop Density:** 1984.1
Land: 3.4 sq. mi.; **Water:** 0.3 sq. mi.　　**Elev:** 480 ft.
In east-central PA on the Susquehanna River, 23 mi. southeast of Williamsport.

Mount Carmel　　　　　　　　　Borough
ZIP: 17851　　　**Lat:** 40-47-43 N **Long:** 76-24-44 W
Pop: 7,196 (1990); 8,190 (1980)　　　**Pop Density:** 10280.0
Land: 0.7 sq. mi.; **Water:** 0.0 sq. mi.　　**Elev:** 1100 ft.

*Mount Carmel　　　　　　　　Township
ZIP: 17851　　　**Lat:** 40-47-46 N **Long:** 76-26-30 W
Pop: 2,679 (1990)　　　**Pop Density:** 122.9
Land: 21.8 sq. mi.; **Water:** 0.2 sq. mi.

Northumberland　　　　　　　　Borough
ZIP: 17857　　　**Lat:** 40-53-49 N **Long:** 76-47-37 W
Pop: 3,860 (1990); 3,636 (1980)　　　**Pop Density:** 2412.5
Land: 1.6 sq. mi.; **Water:** 0.0 sq. mi.　　**Elev:** 586 ft.
In east-central PA on the Susquehanna River, 28 mi. southeast of Williamsport. Laid out in 1772 on a wedge of land

formed by the junction of the two branches of the Susquehanna River.

Name origin: For the newly-formed county.

Point
Township
ZIP: 17857 **Lat:** 40-55-50 N **Long:** 76-45-42 W
Pop: 3,466 (1990) **Pop Density:** 137.5
Land: 25.2 sq. mi.; **Water:** 2.2 sq. mi.

Ralpho
Township
ZIP: 17872 **Lat:** 40-51-14 N **Long:** 76-32-49 W
Pop: 3,625 (1990) **Pop Density:** 195.9
Land: 18.5 sq. mi.; **Water:** 0.0 sq. mi.

Riverside
Borough
ZIP: 17868 **Lat:** 40-56-33 N **Long:** 76-38-44 W
Pop: 1,991 (1990); 2,266 (1980) **Pop Density:** 414.8
Land: 4.8 sq. mi.; **Water:** 0.5 sq. mi. **Elev:** 598 ft.

In east-central PA, annexed to Gearheaert Township in 1950.

Rockefeller
Township
Lat: 40-49-28 N **Long:** 76-44-02 W
Pop: 2,029 (1990) **Pop Density:** 98.5
Land: 20.6 sq. mi.; **Water:** 0.0 sq. mi.

Rush
Township
Lat: 40-54-20 N **Long:** 76-37-29 W
Pop: 1,097 (1990) **Pop Density:** 40.9
Land: 26.8 sq. mi.; **Water:** 0.6 sq. mi.

Shamokin
City
ZIP: 17866 **Lat:** 40-47-17 N **Long:** 76-33-17 W
Pop: 9,184 (1990) **Pop Density:** 11480.0
Land: 0.8 sq. mi.; **Water:** 0.0 sq. mi. **Elev:** 720 ft.

In east-central PA, southwest of Wilkes-Barre. Laid out in 1835.

Name origin: For the old Indian village, *Schachamekhan,* probably meaning 'eel stream,' that once stood on the present site of Sunbury.

*Shamokin
Township
ZIP: 17866 **Lat:** 40-49-42 N **Long:** 76-38-22 W
Pop: 1,697 (1990) **Pop Density:** 54.7
Land: 31.0 sq. mi.; **Water:** 0.1 sq. mi.

Snydertown
Borough
Lat: 40-52-20 N **Long:** 76-40-28 W
Pop: 416 (1990); 358 (1980) **Pop Density:** 118.9
Land: 3.5 sq. mi.; **Water:** 0.0 sq. mi. **Elev:** 502 ft.

Sunbury
City
ZIP: 17801 **Lat:** 40-51-43 N **Long:** 76-47-17 W
Pop: 11,591 (1990) **Pop Density:** 5519.5
Land: 2.1 sq. mi.; **Water:** 0.0 sq. mi. **Elev:** 450 ft.

In east-central PA, bounded roughly by the Shamokin Creek and the Susquehanna River, 50 mi. north of Harrisburg. Laid out in 1772; incorporated as borough Mar 24, 1797, as city 1921.

Name origin: For Sunbury village, about 15 mi. southwest of London, England.

Turbot
Township
Lat: 41-02-22 N **Long:** 76-48-11 W
Pop: 1,846 (1990) **Pop Density:** 132.8
Land: 13.9 sq. mi.; **Water:** 0.2 sq. mi.

Turbotville
Borough
ZIP: 17772 **Lat:** 41-06-03 N **Long:** 76-46-09 W
Pop: 675 (1990); 675 (1980) **Pop Density:** 1687.5
Land: 0.4 sq. mi.; **Water:** 0.0 sq. mi. **Elev:** 591 ft.

Upper Augusta
Township
Lat: 40-52-20 N **Long:** 76-45-33 W
Pop: 2,681 (1990) **Pop Density:** 132.1
Land: 20.3 sq. mi.; **Water:** 3.0 sq. mi.

Upper Mahanoy
Township
ZIP: 17836 **Lat:** 40-42-31 N **Long:** 76-37-46 W
Pop: 621 (1990) **Pop Density:** 26.5
Land: 23.4 sq. mi.; **Water:** 0.0 sq. mi.

Washington
Township
ZIP: 17867 **Lat:** 40-43-11 N **Long:** 76-44-00 W
Pop: 620 (1990) **Pop Density:** 34.3
Land: 18.1 sq. mi.; **Water:** 0.0 sq. mi.

Watsontown
Borough
ZIP: 17777 **Lat:** 41-05-04 N **Long:** 76-51-52 W
Pop: 2,310 (1990); 2,366 (1980) **Pop Density:** 3300.0
Land: 0.7 sq. mi.; **Water:** 0.2 sq. mi. **Elev:** 481 ft.

Name origin: For John Watson, who bought 610 acres here in 1792, and two years later laid out the town.

West Cameron
Township
ZIP: 17872 **Lat:** 40-45-01 N **Long:** 76-38-42 W
Pop: 527 (1990) **Pop Density:** 44.7
Land: 11.8 sq. mi.; **Water:** 0.0 sq. mi.

West Chillisquaque
Township
Lat: 40-58-01 N **Long:** 76-50-50 W
Pop: 3,119 (1990) **Pop Density:** 241.8
Land: 12.9 sq. mi.; **Water:** 0.9 sq. mi.

Zerbe
Township
Lat: 40-46-28 N **Long:** 76-39-47 W
Pop: 2,067 (1990) **Pop Density:** 178.2
Land: 11.6 sq. mi.; **Water:** 0.0 sq. mi.

Perry County
County Seat: New Bloomfield (ZIP: 17068)

Pop: 41,172 (1990); 35,718 (1980)   **Pop Density:** 74.4
Land: 553.6 sq. mi.; **Water:** 2.2 sq. mi.   **Area Code:** 717

In south-central PA, northwest of Harrisburg; organized Mar 22, 1820 from Cumberland County.

Name origin: For Oliver Hazard Perry (1785–1819), U.S. naval officer during the War of 1812, famous for the message, "We have met the enemy and they are ours."

Blain
Borough
ZIP: 17006   **Lat:** 40-20-13 N   **Long:** 77-30-44 W
Pop: 266 (1990); 274 (1980)   **Pop Density:** 665.0
Land: 0.4 sq. mi.; **Water:** 0.0 sq. mi.   **Elev:** 700 ft.

In south-central PA on Sherman Creek, 40 mi. west of Harrisburg.

Bloomfield
Borough
ZIP: 17068   **Lat:** 40-25-10 N   **Long:** 77-11-19 W
Pop: 1,092 (1990); 1,109 (1980)   **Pop Density:** 992.7
Land: 1.1 sq. mi.; **Water:** 0.0 sq. mi.   **Elev:** 680 ft.

In south-central PA; northwest of Harrisburg. Laid out in Jun 1822; incorporated Mar 14, 1831.

Name origin: For the name of Thomas Barnett's tract of land, on which the town was built. The post office name is New Bloomfield.

Buffalo
Township
ZIP: 17045   **Lat:** 40-30-33 N   **Long:** 77-01-28 W
Pop: 1,080 (1990)   **Pop Density:** 53.5
Land: 20.2 sq. mi.; **Water:** 0.0 sq. mi.

Carroll
Township
ZIP: 17090   **Lat:** 40-20-22 N   **Long:** 77-10-22 W
Pop: 4,597 (1990)   **Pop Density:** 133.6
Land: 34.4 sq. mi.; **Water:** 0.0 sq. mi.

Centre
Township
ZIP: 17068   **Lat:** 40-25-25 N   **Long:** 77-11-48 W
Pop: 1,974 (1990)   **Pop Density:** 66.7
Land: 29.6 sq. mi.; **Water:** 0.1 sq. mi.

Duncannon
Borough
ZIP: 17020   **Lat:** 40-23-44 N   **Long:** 77-01-37 W
Pop: 1,450 (1990); 1,645 (1980)   **Pop Density:** 3625.0
Land: 0.4 sq. mi.; **Water:** 0.0 sq. mi.   **Elev:** 360 ft.

In south-central PA on the Susquehanna River, north of Harrisburg.

Greenwood
Township
Lat: 40-33-17 N   **Long:** 77-06-31 W
Pop: 943 (1990)   **Pop Density:** 37.4
Land: 25.2 sq. mi.; **Water:** 0.2 sq. mi.

Howe
Township
ZIP: 17074   **Lat:** 40-29-51 N   **Long:** 77-05-26 W
Pop: 459 (1990)   **Pop Density:** 56.0
Land: 8.2 sq. mi.; **Water:** 0.4 sq. mi.

Jackson
Township
ZIP: 17006   **Lat:** 40-19-00 N   **Long:** 77-30-32 W
Pop: 489 (1990)   **Pop Density:** 13.1
Land: 37.3 sq. mi.; **Water:** 0.0 sq. mi.

Juniata
Township
ZIP: 17074   **Lat:** 40-28-31 N   **Long:** 77-12-48 W
Pop: 1,278 (1990)   **Pop Density:** 60.9
Land: 21.0 sq. mi.; **Water:** 0.1 sq. mi.

Landisburg
Borough
ZIP: 17040   **Lat:** 40-20-35 N   **Long:** 77-18-21 W
Pop: 178 (1990); 227 (1980)   **Pop Density:** 1780.0
Land: 0.1 sq. mi.; **Water:** 0.0 sq. mi.   **Elev:** 580 ft.

Liverpool
Borough
ZIP: 17045   **Lat:** 40-34-20 N   **Long:** 76-59-33 W
Pop: 934 (1990); 809 (1980)   **Pop Density:** 934.0
Land: 1.0 sq. mi.; **Water:** 0.0 sq. mi.   **Elev:** 394 ft.

*Liverpool
Township
ZIP: 17045   **Lat:** 40-34-54 N   **Long:** 77-00-56 W
Pop: 915 (1990)   **Pop Density:** 43.6
Land: 21.0 sq. mi.; **Water:** 0.0 sq. mi.

Marysville
Borough
ZIP: 17053   **Lat:** 40-20-15 N   **Long:** 76-55-57 W
Pop: 2,425 (1990); 2,452 (1980)   **Pop Density:** 1010.4
Land: 2.4 sq. mi.; **Water:** 0.0 sq. mi.

In south-central PA on the Susquehanna River, north of Harrisburg.

Miller
Township
Lat: 40-28-12 N   **Long:** 77-04-30 W
Pop: 894 (1990)   **Pop Density:** 71.5
Land: 12.5 sq. mi.; **Water:** 0.3 sq. mi.

Millerstown
Borough
ZIP: 17062   **Lat:** 40-33-10 N   **Long:** 77-09-10 W
Pop: 646 (1990); 550 (1980)   **Pop Density:** 717.8
Land: 0.9 sq. mi.; **Water:** 0.1 sq. mi.   **Elev:** 340 ft.

New Bloomfield *See* Bloomfield

New Buffalo
Borough
ZIP: 17069   **Lat:** 40-27-15 N   **Long:** 76-58-15 W
Pop: 145 (1990); 156 (1980)   **Pop Density:** 1450.0
Land: 0.1 sq. mi.; **Water:** 0.0 sq. mi.   **Elev:** 380 ft.

Newport
Borough
ZIP: 17074   **Lat:** 40-28-41 N   **Long:** 77-08-02 W
Pop: 1,568 (1990); 1,600 (1980)   **Pop Density:** 5226.7
Land: 0.3 sq. mi.; **Water:** 0.0 sq. mi.   **Elev:** 395 ft.

Northeast Madison
Township
ZIP: 17047   **Lat:** 40-23-29 N   **Long:** 77-27-53 W
Pop: 674 (1990)   **Pop Density:** 26.1
Land: 25.8 sq. mi.; **Water:** 0.0 sq. mi.

Oliver
Township
ZIP: 17074   **Lat:** 40-29-16 N   **Long:** 77-08-41 W
Pop: 2,039 (1990)   **Pop Density:** 245.7
Land: 8.3 sq. mi.; **Water:** 0.3 sq. mi.

Penn
Township
ZIP: 17020   **Lat:** 40-21-54 N   **Long:** 77-01-55 W
Pop: 3,283 (1990)   **Pop Density:** 153.4
Land: 21.4 sq. mi.; **Water:** 0.2 sq. mi.

Rye
Township
Lat: 40-19-27 N   Long: 77-02-18 W
Pop: 2,136 (1990)   **Pop Density:** 83.4
Land: 25.6 sq. mi.; **Water:** 0.0 sq. mi.

Saville
Township
ZIP: 17074   Lat: 40-26-08 N   Long: 77-20-53 W
Pop: 1,818 (1990)   **Pop Density:** 39.5
Land: 46.0 sq. mi.; **Water:** 0.0 sq. mi.

Southwest Madison
Township
ZIP: 17047   Lat: 40-20-27 N   Long: 77-26-08 W
Pop: 745 (1990)   **Pop Density:** 27.0
Land: 27.6 sq. mi.; **Water:** 0.0 sq. mi.

Spring
Township
ZIP: 17040   Lat: 40-20-39 N   Long: 77-15-28 W
Pop: 1,665 (1990)   **Pop Density:** 57.8
Land: 28.8 sq. mi.; **Water:** 0.0 sq. mi.

Toboyne
Township
Lat: 40-16-10 N   Long: 77-35-02 W
Pop: 455 (1990)   **Pop Density:** 8.1
Land: 56.3 sq. mi.; **Water:** 0.0 sq. mi.

Tuscarora
Township
ZIP: 17074   Lat: 40-30-20 N   Long: 77-14-29 W
Pop: 1,034 (1990)   **Pop Density:** 35.2
Land: 29.4 sq. mi.; **Water:** 0.1 sq. mi.

Tyrone
Township
ZIP: 17040   Lat: 40-20-04 N   Long: 77-19-36 W
Pop: 1,741 (1990)   **Pop Density:** 48.8
Land: 35.7 sq. mi.; **Water:** 0.0 sq. mi.

Watts
Township
ZIP: 17020   Lat: 40-28-05 N   Long: 76-59-35 W
Pop: 1,152 (1990)   **Pop Density:** 98.5
Land: 11.7 sq. mi.; **Water:** 0.3 sq. mi.

Wheatfield
Township
ZIP: 17020   Lat: 40-24-12 N   Long: 77-05-47 W
Pop: 3,097 (1990)   **Pop Density:** 148.2
Land: 20.9 sq. mi.; **Water:** 0.2 sq. mi.

Philadelphia County
County Seat: Philadelphia (ZIP: 19107)

Pop: 1,585,580 (1990); 1,688,210 (1980)   **Pop Density:** 11733.7
Land: 135.1 sq. mi.; **Water:** 7.5 sq. mi.   **Area Code:** 215

On southeastern border of PA, southwest of Trenton, NJ; original county, organized Mar 10, 1682. The county is coterminous with the city.

Name origin: Named by William Penn (1644–1718) for either Philadelphia, an ancient biblical city of Lydia, in western Asia Minor, seat of one of the seven early Christian churches, or the abstract Greek noun *philadelphia* 'brotherly love.'

Philadelphia
City
ZIP: 19101   Lat: 40-00-24 N   Long: 75-08-04 W
Pop: 1,585,577 (1990)   **Pop Density:** 11736.3
Land: 135.1 sq. mi.; **Water:** 7.5 sq. mi.   **Elev:** 40 ft.

On the southeastern border of PA, southwest of Trenton, NJ, at the confluence of the Delaware and Schuylkill rivers. City coextensive with the county. Laid out in 1682; chartered Oct 25, 1701, rechartered Mar 11, 1789. Nicknamed *Quaker City* because founder William Penn (1644–1718) and many of the first settlers were Quakers. Capital of the American Colonies during most of the American Revolution; birthplace of the U.S.: the Declaration of Independence and the Constitution of the U.S. both adopted here in Independence Hall. Site of many historic attractions. Service industry city: finance, trade, health care.

Pike County
County Seat: Milford (ZIP: 18337)

Pop: 27,966 (1990); 18,271 (1980)   **Pop Density:** 51.1
Land: 547.1 sq. mi.; **Water:** 19.6 sq. mi.   **Area Code:** 717

On northeastern border of PA, east of Scranton; organized Mar 26, 1814 from Wayne County.

Name origin: For Gen. Zebulon Montgomery Pike (1779–1813), U.S. army officer and discoverer of Pikes Peak, CO.

Blooming Grove
Township
Lat: 41-21-20 N   Long: 75-06-03 W
Pop: 2,022 (1990)   **Pop Density:** 26.9
Land: 75.3 sq. mi.; **Water:** 1.8 sq. mi.

Delaware
Township
Lat: 41-14-29 N   Long: 74-55-22 W
Pop: 3,527 (1990)   **Pop Density:** 79.8
Land: 44.2 sq. mi.; **Water:** 1.5 sq. mi.   **Elev:** 370 ft.

Dingman   Township
Lat: 41-19-17 N   **Long:** 74-55-32 W
Pop: 4,591 (1990)   **Pop Density:** 78.9
Land: 58.2 sq. mi.; **Water:** 1.7 sq. mi.

Greene   Township
Lat: 41-17-12 N   **Long:** 75-15-10 W
Pop: 2,097 (1990)   **Pop Density:** 34.8
Land: 60.2 sq. mi.; **Water:** 1.7 sq. mi.

Lackawaxen   Township
ZIP: 18435   Lat: 41-29-07 N   **Long:** 75-03-34 W
Pop: 2,832 (1990)   **Pop Density:** 36.0
Land: 78.6 sq. mi.; **Water:** 2.5 sq. mi.
Founded 1770.
Name origin: From an Indian term possibly meaning 'where the way forks,' a reference to the confluence of the Lackawaxen Stream with the Delaware River.

Lehman   Township
Lat: 41-09-04 N   **Long:** 74-59-28 W
Pop: 3,055 (1990)   **Pop Density:** 62.5
Land: 48.9 sq. mi.; **Water:** 1.2 sq. mi.

Matamoras   Borough
ZIP: 18336   Lat: 41-21-59 N   **Long:** 74-42-00 W
Pop: 1,934 (1990); 2,111 (1980)   **Pop Density:** 2762.9
Land: 0.7 sq. mi.; **Water:** 0.1 sq. mi.   **Elev:** 444 ft.
In northeastern PA on the Delaware River, near the NY and NJ state lines.

Milford   Borough
ZIP: 18337   **Lat:** 41-19-26 N   **Long:** 74-48-06 W
Pop: 1,064 (1990); 1,143 (1980)   **Pop Density:** 2128.0
Land: 0.5 sq. mi.; **Water:** 0.0 sq. mi.   **Elev:** 503 ft.
Incorporated Dec 25, 1874.

*Milford   Township
ZIP: 18337   **Lat:** 41-20-50 N   **Long:** 74-50-09 W
Pop: 1,013 (1990)   **Pop Density:** 81.0
Land: 12.5 sq. mi.; **Water:** 0.1 sq. mi.

Palmyra   Township
Lat: 41-23-07 N   **Long:** 75-12-25 W
Pop: 1,976 (1990)   **Pop Density:** 57.4
Land: 34.4 sq. mi.; **Water:** 5.3 sq. mi.

Porter   Township
Lat: 41-12-38 N   **Long:** 75-05-00 W
Pop: 163 (1990)   **Pop Density:** 2.8
Land: 58.6 sq. mi.; **Water:** 1.8 sq. mi.

Shohola   Township
ZIP: 18458   **Lat:** 41-25-20 N   **Long:** 74-54-32 W
Pop: 1,586 (1990)   **Pop Density:** 35.5
Land: 44.7 sq. mi.; **Water:** 1.2 sq. mi.

Westfall   Township
Lat: 41-22-52 N   **Long:** 74-45-27 W
Pop: 2,106 (1990)   **Pop Density:** 69.3
Land: 30.4 sq. mi.; **Water:** 0.6 sq. mi.

Potter County
County Seat: Coudersport (ZIP: 16915)

Pop: 16,717 (1990); 17,726 (1980)   **Pop Density:** 15.5
Land: 1081.2 sq. mi.; **Water:** 0.2 sq. mi.   **Area Code:** 814
On central northern border of PA; organized Mar 26, 1804 from Lycoming County.
Name origin: For Gen. James Potter (1729–89), hero of the Revolutionary War.

Abbott   Township
ZIP: 16922   **Lat:** 41-36-36 N   **Long:** 77-42-23 W
Pop: 173 (1990)   **Pop Density:** 2.5
Land: 69.9 sq. mi.; **Water:** 0.0 sq. mi.

Allegany   Township
Lat: 41-52-00 N   **Long:** 77-54-09 W
Pop: 413 (1990)   **Pop Density:** 10.2
Land: 40.3 sq. mi.; **Water:** 0.0 sq. mi.
Name origin: For the river.

Austin   Borough
ZIP: 16720   **Lat:** 41-38-09 N   **Long:** 78-05-20 W
Pop: 569 (1990); 740 (1980)   **Pop Density:** 142.3
Land: 4.0 sq. mi.; **Water:** 0.0 sq. mi.   **Elev:** 1352 ft.

Bingham   Township
ZIP: 16948   **Lat:** 41-56-56 N   **Long:** 77-47-28 W
Pop: 557 (1990)   **Pop Density:** 15.6
Land: 35.8 sq. mi.; **Water:** 0.1 sq. mi.

Clara   Township
Lat: 41-52-29 N   **Long:** 78-06-49 W
Pop: 133 (1990)   **Pop Density:** 6.7
Land: 19.8 sq. mi.; **Water:** 0.0 sq. mi.

Coudersport   Borough
ZIP: 16915   **Lat:** 41-46-27 N   **Long:** 78-00-51 W
Pop: 2,854 (1990); 2,791 (1980)   **Pop Density:** 500.7
Land: 5.7 sq. mi.; **Water:** 0.0 sq. mi.   **Elev:** 1655 ft.
In northern PA near the NY state line. Laid out 1807; incorporated Feb 7, 1848.
Name origin: For its location on the Allegheny River, and for Jean Samuel Couderc, of the Amsterdam banking firm that had managed the interests of the exiled Frenchmen of Asylum who had invested in the Ceres Land Company. The final letter in Couderc's name was dropped for the sake of euphony.

Eulalia   Township
ZIP: 16915   **Lat:** 41-45-31 N   **Long:** 78-01-27 W
Pop: 686 (1990)   **Pop Density:** 22.1
Land: 31.1 sq. mi.; **Water:** 0.0 sq. mi.

Galeton   Borough
ZIP: 16922   **Lat:** 41-43-59 N   **Long:** 77-38-38 W
Pop: 1,370 (1990); 1,462 (1980)   **Pop Density:** 1957.1
Land: 0.7 sq. mi.; **Water:** 0.0 sq. mi.   **Elev:** 1344 ft.
In northern PA at the forks of Pine Creek, near Lyman Run State Park.

Genesee
Township
Lat: 41-57-54 N **Long:** 77-54-42 W
Pop: 803 (1990) **Pop Density:** 22.3
Land: 36.0 sq. mi.; **Water:** 0.0 sq. mi.

Harrison
Township
ZIP: 16927 **Lat:** 41-57-38 N **Long:** 77-40-13 W
Pop: 1,129 (1990) **Pop Density:** 31.4
Land: 36.0 sq. mi.; **Water:** 0.0 sq. mi. **Elev:** 2280 ft.

Hebron
Township
ZIP: 16915 **Lat:** 41-51-21 N **Long:** 78-01-05 W
Pop: 525 (1990) **Pop Density:** 12.1
Land: 43.3 sq. mi.; **Water:** 0.0 sq. mi.

Hector
Township
ZIP: 16948 **Lat:** 41-51-41 N **Long:** 77-40-10 W
Pop: 336 (1990) **Pop Density:** 8.1
Land: 41.4 sq. mi.; **Water:** 0.0 sq. mi.

Homer
Township
ZIP: 16915 **Lat:** 41-42-26 N **Long:** 78-01-34 W
Pop: 216 (1990) **Pop Density:** 6.8
Land: 31.9 sq. mi.; **Water:** 0.0 sq. mi.

Keating
Township
Lat: 41-41-24 N **Long:** 78-08-00 W
Pop: 304 (1990) **Pop Density:** 7.3
Land: 41.4 sq. mi.; **Water:** 0.0 sq. mi.

Oswayo
Township
Lat: 41-57-38 N **Long:** 78-01-39 W
Pop: 214 (1990) **Pop Density:** 5.7
Land: 37.8 sq. mi.; **Water:** 0.0 sq. mi.

*Oswayo
Borough
ZIP: 16915 **Lat:** 41-55-12 N **Long:** 78-01-13 W
Pop: 156 (1990); 183 (1980) **Pop Density:** 141.8
Land: 1.1 sq. mi.; **Water:** 0.0 sq. mi. **Elev:** 1704 ft.

Pike
Township
ZIP: 16922 **Lat:** 41-46-22 N **Long:** 77-40-02 W
Pop: 252 (1990) **Pop Density:** 6.8
Land: 37.1 sq. mi.; **Water:** 0.0 sq. mi.

Pleasant Valley
Township
Lat: 41-51-20 N **Long:** 78-11-11 W
Pop: 78 (1990) **Pop Density:** 4.0
Land: 19.6 sq. mi.; **Water:** 0.0 sq. mi.

Portage
Township
Lat: 41-36-27 N **Long:** 78-08-00 W
Pop: 176 (1990) **Pop Density:** 4.7
Land: 37.7 sq. mi.; **Water:** 0.0 sq. mi.

Roulette
Township
Lat: 41-46-36 N **Long:** 78-09-09 W
Pop: 1,266 (1990) **Pop Density:** 38.7
Land: 32.7 sq. mi.; **Water:** 0.0 sq. mi.
Name origin: For Jean Roulette, a businessman

Sharon
Township
Lat: 41-56-55 N **Long:** 78-08-33 W
Pop: 841 (1990) **Pop Density:** 24.7
Land: 34.0 sq. mi.; **Water:** 0.0 sq. mi.

Shinglehouse
Borough
ZIP: 16748 **Lat:** 41-57-55 N **Long:** 78-11-29 W
Pop: 1,243 (1990); 1,310 (1980) **Pop Density:** 591.9
Land: 2.1 sq. mi.; **Water:** 0.0 sq. mi. **Elev:** 1492 ft.
Name origin: For an old pioneer shingled house built by a French immigrant named Jaudrie in 1806.

Stewardson
Township
Lat: 41-31-47 N **Long:** 77-42-50 W
Pop: 66 (1990) **Pop Density:** 0.9
Land: 74.3 sq. mi.; **Water:** 0.0 sq. mi.

Summit
Township
ZIP: 16915 **Lat:** 41-40-15 N **Long** 77-54-46 W
Pop: 115 (1990) **Pop Density:** 2.3
Land: 49.4 sq. mi.; **Water:** 0.0 sq. mi.

Sweden
Township
ZIP: 16915 **Lat:** 41-46-44 N **Long** 77-54-05 W
Pop: 581 (1990) **Pop Density:** 17.2
Land: 33.7 sq. mi.; **Water:** 0.0 sq. mi.

Sylvania
Township
Lat: 41-37-42 N **Long** 78-00-37 W
Pop: 80 (1990) **Pop Density:** 2.7
Land: 29.9 sq. mi.; **Water:** 0.0 sq. mi.

Ulysses
Borough
ZIP: 16948 **Lat:** 41-54-14 N **Long** 77-45-18 W
Pop: 653 (1990); 654 (1980) **Pop Density:** 163.3
Land: 4.0 sq. mi.; **Water:** 0.0 sq. mi. **Elev:** 2110 ft.

*Ulysses
Township
ZIP: 16948 **Lat:** 41-48-49 N **Long** 77-47-21 W
Pop: 557 (1990) **Pop Density:** 7.4
Land: 75.1 sq. mi.; **Water:** 0.0 sq. mi.

West Branch
Township
ZIP: 16922 **Lat:** 41-42-03 N **Long** 77-43-44 W
Pop: 286 (1990) **Pop Density:** 4.6
Land: 62.6 sq. mi.; **Water:** 0.1 sq. mi.

Wharton
Township
Lat: 41-31-58 N **Long** 77-59-58 W
Pop: 70 (1990) **Pop Density:** 1.1
Land: 61.8 sq. mi.; **Water:** 0.0 sq. mi.

Schuylkill County
County Seat: Pottsville (ZIP: 17901)

Pop: 152,585 (1990); 160,630 (1980)   **Pop Density:** 196.0
Land: 778.6 sq. mi.; **Water:** 4.0 sq. mi.   **Area Code:** 717

In east-central PA, west of Allentown; organized Mar 1, 1811 from Berks and Northampton counties.

Name origin: For the Schuylkill River, which traverses it; from Dutch *schuy* 'hidden,' and *kill* 'stream.'

Ashland
Borough
ZIP: 17921   **Lat:** 40-46-51 N **Long:** 76-20-44 W
Pop: 3,856 (1990); 4,226 (1980)   **Pop Density:** 2410.0
Land: 1.6 sq. mi.; **Water:** 0.0 sq. mi.   **Elev:** 1700 ft.
Laid out in 1847. Part of the town is also in Columbia County.
Name origin: Named in 1847 by Samuel Lewis for the estate of Henry Clay (1777–1852) in Lexington, KY.

Auburn
Borough
ZIP: 17922   **Lat:** 40-35-46 N **Long:** 76-05-46 W
Pop: 913 (1990); 999 (1980)   **Pop Density:** 537.1
Land: 1.7 sq. mi.; **Water:** 0.0 sq. mi.   **Elev:** 500 ft.

Barry
Township
ZIP: 17938   **Lat:** 40-42-35 N **Long:** 76-24-55 W
Pop: 845 (1990)   **Pop Density:** 50.6
Land: 16.7 sq. mi.; **Water:** 0.0 sq. mi.

Blythe
Township
Lat: 40-43-53 N **Long:** 76-07-41 W
Pop: 1,023 (1990)   **Pop Density:** 37.2
Land: 27.5 sq. mi.; **Water:** 0.2 sq. mi.

Branch
Township
Lat: 40-39-36 N **Long:** 76-16-23 W
Pop: 2,051 (1990)   **Pop Density:** 175.3
Land: 11.7 sq. mi.; **Water:** 0.1 sq. mi.

Butler
Township
Lat: 40-45-55 N **Long:** 76-19-27 W
Pop: 4,099 (1990)   **Pop Density:** 152.4
Land: 26.9 sq. mi.; **Water:** 0.0 sq. mi.

Cass
Township
Lat: 40-43-05 N **Long:** 76-17-02 W
Pop: 2,088 (1990)   **Pop Density:** 157.0
Land: 13.3 sq. mi.; **Water:** 0.0 sq. mi.

Coaldale
Borough
ZIP: 18218   **Lat:** 40-49-14 N **Long:** 75-54-58 W
Pop: 2,531 (1990); 2,762 (1980)   **Pop Density:** 1150.5
Land: 2.2 sq. mi.; **Water:** 0.0 sq. mi.   **Elev:** 1040 ft.
Incorporated 1906.
Name origin: For a dale containing rich deposits of anthracite coal.

Cressona
Borough
ZIP: 17929   **Lat:** 40-37-49 N **Long:** 76-11-41 W
Pop: 1,694 (1990); 1,810 (1980)   **Pop Density:** 1694.0
Land: 1.0 sq. mi.; **Water:** 0.0 sq. mi.   **Elev:** 562 ft.
Name origin: For John Chapman Cresson, who laid out the town. He was a civil engineer in Philadelphia, manager of the Schuylkill Navigation Company, president of the Mine Hill & Schuylkill Haven Railroad Company, and chief engineer of Fairmount Park in Philadelphia.

Deer Lake
Borough
ZIP: 17961   **Lat:** 40-37-14 N **Long:** 76-03-23 W
Pop: 550 (1990); 515 (1980)   **Pop Density:** 1375.0
Land: 0.4 sq. mi.; **Water:** 0.0 sq. mi.   **Elev:** 500 ft.

Delano
Township
Lat: 40-50-44 N **Long:** 76-04-01 W
Pop: 573 (1990)   **Pop Density:** 69.9
Land: 8.2 sq. mi.; **Water:** 0.0 sq. mi.

East Brunswick
Township
ZIP: 17960   **Lat:** 40-40-48 N **Long:** 75-59-13 W
Pop: 1,506 (1990)   **Pop Density:** 49.4
Land: 30.5 sq. mi.; **Water:** 0.0 sq. mi.

East Norwegian
Township
Lat: 40-42-25 N **Long:** 76-09-51 W
Pop: 991 (1990)   **Pop Density:** 241.7
Land: 4.1 sq. mi.; **Water:** 0.0 sq. mi.

East Union
Township
Lat: 40-53-44 N **Long:** 76-07-11 W
Pop: 1,374 (1990)   **Pop Density:** 52.8
Land: 26.0 sq. mi.; **Water:** 0.0 sq. mi.

Eldred
Township
ZIP: 17964   **Lat:** 40-42-32 N **Long:** 76-29-59 W
Pop: 736 (1990)   **Pop Density:** 33.2
Land: 22.2 sq. mi.; **Water:** 0.0 sq. mi.

Foster
Township
Lat: 40-41-12 N **Long:** 76-21-10 W
Pop: 298 (1990)   **Pop Density:** 22.6
Land: 13.2 sq. mi.; **Water:** 0.0 sq. mi.

Frackville
Borough
ZIP: 17931   **Lat:** 40-47-01 N **Long:** 76-14-00 W
Pop: 4,700 (1990); 5,308 (1980)   **Pop Density:** 7833.3
Land: 0.6 sq. mi.; **Water:** 0.0 sq. mi.   **Elev:** 1476 ft.
In east-central PA, northwest of Allentown.

Frailey
Township
ZIP: 17981   **Lat:** 40-38-10 N **Long:** 76-24-41 W
Pop: 518 (1990)   **Pop Density:** 56.9
Land: 9.1 sq. mi.; **Water:** 0.0 sq. mi.

Gilberton
Borough
ZIP: 17934   **Lat:** 40-47-47 N **Long:** 76-13-23 W
Pop: 953 (1990); 1,096 (1980)   **Pop Density:** 680.7
Land: 1.4 sq. mi.; **Water:** 0.0 sq. mi.   **Elev:** 1140 ft.

Girardville
Borough
ZIP: 17935   **Lat:** 40-47-32 N **Long:** 76-17-03 W
Pop: 1,889 (1990); 2,268 (1980)   **Pop Density:** 3778.0
Land: 0.5 sq. mi.; **Water:** 0.0 sq. mi.   **Elev:** 1000 ft.

Gordon
Borough
ZIP: 17936   **Lat:** 40-45-01 N   **Long:** 76-20-26 W
Pop: 768 (1990); 892 (1980)   **Pop Density:** 1280.0
Land: 0.6 sq. mi.; **Water:** 0.0 sq. mi.   **Elev:** 900 ft.

Hegins
Township
ZIP: 17938   **Lat:** 40-38-50 N   **Long:** 76-30-27 W
Pop: 3,561 (1990)   **Pop Density:** 111.3
Land: 32.0 sq. mi.; **Water:** 0.0 sq. mi.

Hometown
CDP
Lat: 40-49-19 N   **Long:** 75-59-09 W
Pop: 1,545 (1990); 1,346 (1980)   **Pop Density:** 772.5
Land: 2.0 sq. mi.; **Water:** 0.0 sq. mi.

Hubley
Township
ZIP: 17983   **Lat:** 40-38-37 N   **Long:** 76-37-02 W
Pop: 928 (1990)   **Pop Density:** 70.8
Land: 13.1 sq. mi.; **Water:** 0.0 sq. mi.

Kline
Township
Lat: 40-52-52 N   **Long:** 76-01-03 W
Pop: 1,722 (1990)   **Pop Density:** 141.1
Land: 12.2 sq. mi.; **Water:** 0.1 sq. mi.

Lake Wynonah
CDP
Lat: 40-35-13 N   **Long:** 76-10-48 W
Pop: 1,055 (1990)   **Pop Density:** 363.8
Land: 2.9 sq. mi.; **Water:** 0.3 sq. mi.

Landingville
Borough
ZIP: 17942   **Lat:** 40-37-31 N   **Long:** 76-07-23 W
Pop: 192 (1990); 170 (1980)   **Pop Density:** 240.0
Land: 0.8 sq. mi.; **Water:** 0.0 sq. mi.   **Elev:** 502 ft.

Mahanoy
Township
ZIP: 17976   **Lat:** 40-49-23 N   **Long:** 76-08-27 W
Pop: 1,273 (1990)   **Pop Density:** 61.2
Land: 20.8 sq. mi.; **Water:** 0.3 sq. mi.

Mahanoy City
Borough
ZIP: 17948   **Lat:** 40-48-45 N   **Long:** 76-08-18 W
Pop: 5,209 (1990); 6,167 (1980)   **Pop Density:** 10418.0
Land: 0.5 sq. mi.; **Water:** 0.0 sq. mi.   **Elev:** 1256 ft.
Name origin: From the Delaware word *mahoni* probably meaning 'lick,' denoting a saline deposit where deer congregate.

McAdoo
Borough
ZIP: 18237   **Lat:** 40-54-03 N   **Long:** 75-59-32 W
Pop: 2,459 (1990); 2,940 (1980)   **Pop Density:** 8196.7
Land: 0.3 sq. mi.; **Water:** 0.0 sq. mi.   **Elev:** 1800 ft.
Name origin: Named by postal authorities for William Gibbs McAdoo.

Mechanicsville
Borough
ZIP: 17901   **Lat:** 40-41-22 N   **Long:** 76-10-53 W
Pop: 540 (1990); 519 (1980)   **Pop Density:** 1800.0
Land: 0.3 sq. mi.; **Water:** 0.0 sq. mi.   **Elev:** 630 ft.

Middleport
Borough
ZIP: 17953   **Lat:** 40-43-38 N   **Long:** 76-05-13 W
Pop: 520 (1990); 577 (1980)   **Pop Density:** 1300.0
Land: 0.4 sq. mi.; **Water:** 0.0 sq. mi.   **Elev:** 726 ft.

Minersville
Borough
ZIP: 17954   **Lat:** 40-41-26 N   **Long:** 76-15-33 W
Pop: 4,877 (1990); 5,635 (1980)   **Pop Density:** 6967.1
Land: 0.7 sq. mi.; **Water:** 0.0 sq. mi.   **Elev:** 740 ft.
In east-central PA, northwest of Allentown.
Name origin: Named for the large number of townspeople who have been coal miners.

Mount Carbon
Borough
ZIP: 17901   **Lat:** 40-40-26 N   **Long:** 76-11-16 W
Pop: 132 (1990); 157 (1980)   **Pop Density:** 1320.0
Land: 0.1 sq. mi.; **Water:** 0.0 sq. mi.   **Elev:** 800 ft.

New Castle
Township
ZIP: 17970   **Lat:** 40-44-28 N   **Long:** 76-13-02 W
Pop: 567 (1990)   **Pop Density:** 46.5
Land: 12.2 sq. mi.; **Water:** 0.2 sq. mi.

New Philadelphia
Borough
ZIP: 17959   **Lat:** 40-43-03 N   **Long:** 76-07-04 W
Pop: 1,283 (1990); 1,341 (1980)   **Pop Density:** 855.3
Land: 1.5 sq. mi.; **Water:** 0.0 sq. mi.   **Elev:** 693 ft.

New Ringgold
Borough
ZIP: 17960   **Lat:** 40-41-18 N   **Long:** 75-59-37 W
Pop: 315 (1990); 301 (1980)   **Pop Density:** 350.0
Land: 0.9 sq. mi.; **Water:** 0.0 sq. mi.   **Elev:** 560 ft.

North Manheim
Township
Lat: 40-39-13 N   **Long:** 76-09-50 W
Pop: 3,404 (1990)   **Pop Density:** 166.0
Land: 20.5 sq. mi.; **Water:** 0.1 sq. mi.

North Union
Township
ZIP: 17985   **Lat:** 40-54-34 N   **Long:** 76-12-19 W
Pop: 1,143 (1990)   **Pop Density:** 57.2
Land: 20.0 sq. mi.; **Water:** 0.0 sq. mi.

Norwegian
Township
Lat: 40-41-54 N   **Long:** 76-13-28 W
Pop: 1,938 (1990)   **Pop Density:** 334.1
Land: 5.8 sq. mi.; **Water:** 0.1 sq. mi.

Orwigsburg
Borough
ZIP: 17961   **Lat:** 40-39-13 N   **Long:** 76-06-13 W
Pop: 2,780 (1990); 2,700 (1980)   **Pop Density:** 1263.6
Land: 2.2 sq. mi.; **Water:** 0.0 sq. mi.   **Elev:** 620 ft.
In east-central PA, 5 mi. southeast of Pottsville. Laid out in 1796. County seat (1811–51).
Name origin: Named by Peter Orwig in 1796.

Palo Alto
Borough
ZIP: 17901   **Lat:** 40-40-58 N   **Long:** 76-10-36 W
Pop: 1,192 (1990); 1,321 (1980)   **Pop Density:** 1083.6
Land: 1.1 sq. mi.; **Water:** 0.0 sq. mi.   **Elev:** 700 ft.

Pine Grove
Township
ZIP: 17963   **Lat:** 40-32-01 N   **Long:** 76-25-10 W
Pop: 3,699 (1990)   **Pop Density:** 96.8
Land: 38.2 sq. mi.; **Water:** 0.1 sq. mi.

*Pine Grove
Borough
ZIP: 17963   **Lat:** 40-33-12 N   **Long:** 76-23-13 W
Pop: 2,118 (1990); 2,244 (1980)   **Pop Density:** 1925.5
Land: 1.1 sq. mi.; **Water:** 0.0 sq. mi.   **Elev:** 515 ft.
In east-central PA.

Port Carbon
Borough
ZIP: 17965   **Lat:** 40-41-49 N   **Long:** 76-10-01 W
Pop: 2,134 (1990); 2,576 (1980)   **Pop Density:** 2667.5
Land: 0.8 sq. mi.; **Water:** 0.0 sq. mi.   **Elev:** 700 ft.

Port Clinton
Borough
ZIP: 19549   Lat: 40-34-56 N Long: 76-01-36 W
Pop: 328 (1990); 337 (1980)   Pop Density: 656.0
Land: 0.5 sq. mi.; Water: 0.0 sq. mi.   Elev: 406 ft.

Porter
Township
ZIP: 17980   Lat: 40-35-53 N Long: 76-31-29 W
Pop: 2,560 (1990)   Pop Density: 143.0
Land: 17.9 sq. mi.; Water: 0.0 sq. mi.

Pottsville
City
ZIP: 17901   Lat: 40-40-45 N Long: 76-12-35 W
Pop: 16,603 (1990)   Pop Density: 3953.1
Land: 4.2 sq. mi.; Water: 0.0 sq. mi.   Elev: 659 ft.

In east-central PA on the Schuylkill River, 28 mi. northwest of Reading. Incorporated as borough Feb 19, 1828, as city, 1910.

Name origin: For John Potts, iron founder and furnace owner, who was also proprietor of the White Horse Tavern.

Reilly
Township
Lat: 40-38-45 N Long: 76-19-46 W
Pop: 835 (1990)   Pop Density: 51.5
Land: 16.2 sq. mi.; Water: 0.0 sq. mi.

Ringtown
Borough
ZIP: 17967   Lat: 40-51-24 N Long: 76-14-07 W
Pop: 853 (1990); 837 (1980)   Pop Density: 2132.5
Land: 0.4 sq. mi.; Water: 0.0 sq. mi.   Elev: 1160 ft.

Rush
Township
ZIP: 17980   Lat: 40-50-16 N Long: 75-59-40 W
Pop: 3,472 (1990)   Pop Density: 152.3
Land: 22.8 sq. mi.; Water: 1.0 sq. mi.

Ryan
Township
Lat: 40-47-24 N Long: 76-06-09 W
Pop: 1,363 (1990)   Pop Density: 75.7
Land: 18.0 sq. mi.; Water: 0.2 sq. mi.

St. Clair
Borough
Lat: 40-43-13 N Long: 76-11-26 W
Pop: 3,524 (1990); 4,037 (1980)   Pop Density: 2936.7
Land: 1.2 sq. mi.; Water: 0.0 sq. mi.   Elev: 715 ft.

In east-central PA, northwest of Reading. Founded in 1831.
Name origin: For St. Clair Nichols, who owned the farm on which the town was built.

Schuylkill
Township
Lat: 40-46-19 N Long: 76-02-14 W
Pop: 1,230 (1990)   Pop Density: 125.5
Land: 9.8 sq. mi.; Water: 0.0 sq. mi.

Schuylkill Haven
Borough
ZIP: 17972   Lat: 40-37-41 N Long: 76-10-22 W
Pop: 5,610 (1990); 5,977 (1980)   Pop Density: 4007.1
Land: 1.4 sq. mi.; Water: 0.0 sq. mi.   Elev: 515 ft.

In east-central PA, 5 mi. south of Pottsville.
Name origin: For completion of the Schuylkill Canal between Philadelphia and a point just north of here.

Shenandoah
Borough
ZIP: 17976   Lat: 40-48-59 N Long: 76-12-03 W
Pop: 6,221 (1990); 7,589 (1980)   Pop Density: 4147.3
Land: 1.5 sq. mi.; Water: 0.1 sq. mi.   Elev: 1300 ft.

In east-central PA, 10 mi. north of Pottsville. Settled in 1835. Laid out in 1862 as a mining town.
Name origin: For the Shenandoah Creek, which flows through the town. An Iroquois name probably meaning 'great plains.'

South Manheim
Township
ZIP: 17922   Lat: 40-35-20 N Long: 76-08-12 W
Pop: 1,558 (1990)   Pop Density: 75.3
Land: 20.7 sq. mi.; Water: 0.4 sq. mi.

Tamaqua
Borough
ZIP: 18252   Lat: 40-48-18 N Long: 75-56-05 W
Pop: 7,943 (1990); 8,843 (1980)   Pop Density: 810.5
Land: 9.8 sq. mi.; Water: 0.1 sq. mi.   Elev: 824 ft.

In east-central PA, 15 mi. northeast of Pottsville. Laid out in 1829 by the Lehigh Coal and Navigation Company.
Name origin: For the creek flowing by, from a Delaware Indian term probably meaning 'beaver.'

Tower City
Borough
ZIP: 17980   Lat: 40-35-22 N Long: 76-33-13 W
Pop: 1,518 (1990); 1,667 (1980)   Pop Density: 3036.0
Land: 0.5 sq. mi.; Water: 0.0 sq. mi.   Elev: 800 ft.

In east-central PA; built on reclaimed marsh lands 25 mi. west of Pottsville.
Name origin: Named in 1868 for Charlemagne Tower, founder of the borough.

Tremont
Borough
ZIP: 17981   Lat: 40-37-47 N Long: 76-23-31 W
Pop: 1,814 (1990); 1,796 (1980)   Pop Density: 2267.5
Land: 0.8 sq. mi.; Water: 0.0 sq. mi.   Elev: 800 ft.

*Tremont
Township
ZIP: 17981   Lat: 40-35-30 N Long: 76-26-48 W
Pop: 297 (1990)   Pop Density: 12.7
Land: 23.3 sq. mi.; Water: 0.0 sq. mi.

Union
Township
ZIP: 17967   Lat: 40-51-08 N Long: 76-14-55 W
Pop: 1,458 (1990)   Pop Density: 66.0
Land: 22.1 sq. mi.; Water: 0.2 sq. mi.

Upper Mahantongo
Township
ZIP: 17941   Lat: 40-40-17 N Long: 76-37-09 W
Pop: 696 (1990)   Pop Density: 47.0
Land: 14.8 sq. mi.; Water: 0.0 sq. mi.

Walker
Township
Lat: 40-45-07 N Long: 76-00-26 W
Pop: 949 (1990)   Pop Density: 41.6
Land: 22.8 sq. mi.; Water: 0.0 sq. mi.

Washington
Township
Lat: 40-33-39 N Long: 76-18-43 W
Pop: 2,423 (1990)   Pop Density: 78.2
Land: 31.0 sq. mi.; Water: 0.1 sq. mi.

Name origin: For George Washington (1732–99), first U.S. president.

Wayne
Township
ZIP: 17963   Lat: 40-34-44 N Long: 76-13-47 W
Pop: 3,929 (1990)   Pop Density: 112.3
Land: 35.0 sq. mi.; Water: 0.1 sq. mi.

West Brunswick
Township
ZIP: 17961   Lat: 40-37-59 N Long: 76-03-54 W
Pop: 3,227 (1990)   Pop Density: 106.5
Land: 30.3 sq. mi.; Water: 0.2 sq. mi.

West Mahanoy
Township
Lat: 40-48-44 N Long: 76-13-12 W
Pop: 4,539 (1990)   Pop Density: 436.4
Land: 10.4 sq. mi.; Water: 0.1 sq. mi.

West Penn Township
ZIP: 17960 Lat: 40-44-34 N Long: 75-52-53 W
Pop: 3,693 (1990) Pop Density: 63.5
Land: 58.2 sq. mi.; Water: 0.0 sq. mi.

Snyder County
County Seat: Middleburg (ZIP: 17842)

Pop: 36,680 (1990); 33,584 (1980) Pop Density: 110.7
Land: 331.2 sq. mi.; Water: 1.0 sq. mi. Area Code: 717
In central PA, south of Williamsport; organized Mar 2, 1855 from Union County.
Name origin: For Simon Snyder (1759–1819), member of the PA assembly (1797–1807), speaker of the house (1802–07), and governor (1808–17).

Adams Township
Lat: 40-48-54 N Long: 77-10-34 W
Pop: 833 (1990) Pop Density: 40.6
Land: 20.5 sq. mi.; Water: 0.4 sq. mi.

Beaver Township
ZIP: 17813 Lat: 40-45-17 N Long: 77-09-10 W
Pop: 516 (1990) Pop Density: 27.4
Land: 18.8 sq. mi.; Water: 0.0 sq. mi.

Beavertown Borough
ZIP: 17813 Lat: 40-45-09 N Long: 77-10-11 W
Pop: 877 (1990); 853 (1980) Pop Density: 1096.3
Land: 0.8 sq. mi.; Water: 0.0 sq. mi. Elev: 651 ft.
In central PA, 8 mi. west of Middleburg.
Name origin: For the beaver colonies once numerous here.

Centre Township
ZIP: 17842 Lat: 40-50-37 N Long: 77-04-43 W
Pop: 1,986 (1990) Pop Density: 93.2
Land: 21.3 sq. mi.; Water: 0.0 sq. mi.

Chapman Township
ZIP: 17864 Lat: 40-40-39 N Long: 76-56-05 W
Pop: 1,442 (1990) Pop Density: 108.4
Land: 13.3 sq. mi.; Water: 0.0 sq. mi.

Franklin Township
Lat: 40-46-30 N Long: 77-04-05 W
Pop: 2,158 (1990) Pop Density: 75.7
Land: 28.5 sq. mi.; Water: 0.0 sq. mi.

Freeburg Borough
ZIP: 17827 Lat: 40-45-46 N Long: 76-56-28 W
Pop: 640 (1990); 643 (1980) Pop Density: 2133.3
Land: 0.3 sq. mi.; Water: 0.0 sq. mi. Elev: 530 ft.

Hummels Wharf CDP
Lat: 40-50-00 N Long: 76-50-22 W
Pop: 1,069 (1990); 1,474 (1980) Pop Density: 2138.0
Land: 0.5 sq. mi.; Water: 0.0 sq. mi.

Jackson Township
ZIP: 17870 Lat: 40-51-50 N Long: 76-57-08 W
Pop: 1,383 (1990) Pop Density: 91.6
Land: 15.1 sq. mi.; Water: 0.0 sq. mi.

McClure Borough
ZIP: 17841 Lat: 40-42-27 N Long: 77-18-40 W
Pop: 1,070 (1990); 1,024 (1980) Pop Density: 289.2
Land: 3.7 sq. mi.; Water: 0.0 sq. mi. Elev: 689 ft.
Founded 1867.
Name origin: For Alexander Kelley McClure (1828–1909),

journalist, politician, author, and one of the founders of the Republican Party. Previously called Stricktown for a noted Indian fighter.

Middleburg Borough
ZIP: 17842 Lat: 40-47-20 N Long: 77-02-45 W
Pop: 1,422 (1990); 1,357 (1980) Pop Density: 1580.0
Land: 0.9 sq. mi.; Water: 0.0 sq. mi. Elev: 540 ft.
Laid out in 1800; incorporated Sep 25, 1860.

Middlecreek Township
Lat: 40-49-10 N Long: 76-58-13 W
Pop: 1,791 (1990) Pop Density: 125.2
Land: 14.3 sq. mi.; Water: 0.0 sq. mi.

Monroe Township
Lat: 40-51-29 N Long: 76-51-11 W
Pop: 3,881 (1990) Pop Density: 248.8
Land: 15.6 sq. mi.; Water: 0.1 sq. mi.

Penn Township
Lat: 40-48-30 N Long: 76-53-59 W
Pop: 3,208 (1990) Pop Density: 179.2
Land: 17.9 sq. mi.; Water: 0.2 sq. mi.

Perry Township
Lat: 40-41-38 N Long: 77-00-23 W
Pop: 1,873 (1990) Pop Density: 71.8
Land: 26.1 sq. mi.; Water: 0.0 sq. mi.

Selinsgrove Borough
ZIP: 17870 Lat: 40-48-03 N Long: 76-51-55 W
Pop: 5,384 (1990); 5,227 (1980) Pop Density: 2833.7
Land: 1.9 sq. mi.; Water: 0.0 sq. mi. Elev: 444 ft.
In central PA on the west banks of the Susquehanna River, 5 mi. south of Sunbury. Laid out in 1790 by Anthony Selin.
Name origin: For Anthony Selin, a Swiss soldier of fortune who accompanied the Marquis de Lafayette (1757–1834) to America.

Shamokin Dam Borough
ZIP: 17876 Lat: 40-51-11 N Long: 76-49-20 W
Pop: 1,690 (1990); 1,622 (1980) Pop Density: 938.9
Land: 1.8 sq. mi.; Water: 0.1 sq. mi. Elev: 500 ft.

Spring Township
Lat: 40-45-56 N Long: 77-14-41 W
Pop: 1,575 (1990) Pop Density: 42.7
Land: 36.9 sq. mi.; Water: 0.1 sq. mi.

Union
ZIP: 17864   **Lat:** 40-43-38 N   **Long:** 76-53-26 W
Pop: 1,466 (1990)   **Pop Density:** 100.4
Land: 14.6 sq. mi.; **Water:** 0.1 sq. mi.
Township

Washington
ZIP: 17842   **Lat:** 40-45-28 N   **Long:** 76-57-14 W
Pop: 1,420 (1990)   **Pop Density:** 58.0
Land: 24.5 sq. mi.; **Water:** 0.1 sq. mi.
Township

Name origin: For George Washington (1732–99), first U.S. president.

West Beaver
ZIP: 17841   **Lat:** 40-44-45 N   **Long:** 77-18-52 W
Pop: 1,096 (1990)   **Pop Density:** 39.3
Land: 27.9 sq. mi.; **Water:** 0.0 sq. mi.
Township

West Perry
Lat: 40-41-04 N   **Long:** 77-09-16 W
Pop: 969 (1990)   **Pop Density:** 36.7
Land: 26.4 sq. mi.; **Water:** 0.0 sq. mi.
Township

Somerset County
County Seat: Somerset (ZIP: 15501)

Pop: 78,218 (1990); 81,243 (1980)   **Pop Density:** 72.8
Land: 1074.8 sq. mi.; **Water:** 6.5 sq. mi.   **Area Code:** 814
On the southern border of western PA, south of Johnstown; organized Apr 17, 1795 from Bedford County.
Name origin: For Somersetshire, England.

Addison
ZIP: 15411   **Lat:** 39-46-18 N   **Long:** 79-17-11 W
Pop: 946 (1990)   **Pop Density:** 15.3
Land: 61.7 sq. mi.; **Water:** 1.7 sq. mi.
Township

*Addison
ZIP: 15411   **Lat:** 39-44-36 N   **Long:** 79-20-06 W
Pop: 212 (1990); 259 (1980)   **Pop Density:** 353.3
Land: 0.6 sq. mi.; **Water:** 0.0 sq. mi.   **Elev:** 2026 ft.
Borough

In southern PA near the MD state line and Youghiogheny Reservoir.

Allegheny
Lat: 39-56-42 N   **Long:** 78-48-47 W
Pop: 695 (1990)   **Pop Density:** 13.4
Land: 51.7 sq. mi.; **Water:** 0.0 sq. mi.
Township

Name origin: For the river.

Benson
Lat: 40-12-09 N   **Long:** 78-55-45 W
Pop: 277 (1990); 308 (1980)   **Pop Density:** 923.3
Land: 0.3 sq. mi.; **Water:** 0.0 sq. mi.   **Elev:** 1540 ft.
Borough

Berlin
ZIP: 15530   **Lat:** 39-55-20 N   **Long:** 78-57-09 W
Pop: 2,064 (1990); 1,999 (1980)   **Pop Density:** 2293.3
Land: 0.9 sq. mi.; **Water:** 0.0 sq. mi.   **Elev:** 2323 ft.
Borough

In southern PA on a ridge in Brothers Valley, 40 mi. south of Johnstown.
Name origin: Named for the capital of Germany, former home of many early settlers.

Black
Lat: 39-53-48 N   **Long:** 79-08-21 W
Pop: 942 (1990)   **Pop Density:** 22.2
Land: 42.5 sq. mi.; **Water:** 0.0 sq. mi.
Township

In southern PA, south of Johnstown.
Name origin: For Jeremiah Sullivan Black (1810–83), chief justice of PA (1851) and U.S. attorney-general under Pres. Buchanan (1791–1868).

Boswell
ZIP: 15531   **Lat:** 40-09-38 N   **Long:** 79-01-37 W
Pop: 1,485 (1990); 1,480 (1980)   **Pop Density:** 2121.4
Land: 0.7 sq. mi.; **Water:** 0.0 sq. mi.   **Elev:** 1825 ft.
Borough

Brothersvalley
Lat: 39-54-55 N   **Long:** 78-58-45 W
Pop: 2,395 (1990)   **Pop Density:** 38.2
Land: 62.7 sq. mi.; **Water:** 0.0 sq. mi.
Township

Name origin: For the Dunkard Brethren, a German sect that settled the area about 1769. Also spelled Brothers' Valley.

Callimont
ZIP: 15552   **Lat:** 39-47-47 N   **Long:** 78-55-13 W
Pop: 55 (1990); 32 (1980)   **Pop Density:** 12.2
Land: 4.5 sq. mi.; **Water:** 0.0 sq. mi.   **Elev:** 2240 ft.
Borough

Casselman
ZIP: 15557   **Lat:** 39-53-07 N   **Long:** 79-12-39 W
Pop: 89 (1990); 114 (1980)   **Pop Density:** 445.0
Land: 0.2 sq. mi.; **Water:** 0.0 sq. mi.   **Elev:** 1737 ft.
Borough

Central City
ZIP: 15926   **Lat:** 40-06-35 N   **Long:** 78-48-19 W
Pop: 1,246 (1990); 1,496 (1980)   **Pop Density:** 2492.0
Land: 0.5 sq. mi.; **Water:** 0.0 sq. mi.   **Elev:** 2200 ft.
Borough

Conemaugh
ZIP: 15905   **Lat:** 40-14-33 N   **Long:** 78-58-09 W
Pop: 7,737 (1990)   **Pop Density:** 187.3
Land: 41.3 sq. mi.; **Water:** 0.6 sq. mi.
Township

Confluence
ZIP: 15424   **Lat:** 39-48-34 N   **Long:** 79-21-15 W
Pop: 873 (1990); 968 (1980)   **Pop Density:** 545.6
Land: 1.6 sq. mi.; **Water:** 0.1 sq. mi.   **Elev:** 1336 ft.
Borough

In southwestern PA, southeast of Pittsburgh.
Name origin: For the confluence of Laurel and Casselman creeks with the Youghiogheny River.

Davidsville
ZIP: 15928   **Lat:** 40-13-54 N   **Long:** 78-56-12 W
Pop: 1,167 (1990); 1,155 (1980)   **Pop Density:** 583.5
Land: 2.0 sq. mi.; **Water:** 0.0 sq. mi.
CDP

Elk Lick Township
Lat: 39-45-51 N Long: 79-08-08 W
Pop: 2,313 (1990) **Pop Density:** 40.7
Land: 56.9 sq. mi.; **Water:** 0.6 sq. mi.

Fairhope Township
ZIP: 15538 Lat: 39-50-58 N Long: 78-47-47 W
Pop: 137 (1990) **Pop Density:** 9.3
Land: 14.8 sq. mi.; **Water:** 0.0 sq. mi.

Friedens CDP
ZIP: 15541 Lat: 40-02-33 N Long: 79-00-18 W
Pop: 1,576 (1990); 1,065 (1980) **Pop Density:** 508.4
Land: 3.1 sq. mi.; **Water:** 0.0 sq. mi.

Garrett Borough
ZIP: 15542 Lat: 39-51-51 N Long: 79-03-41 W
Pop: 520 (1990); 563 (1980) **Pop Density:** 742.9
Land: 0.7 sq. mi.; **Water:** 0.0 sq. mi. **Elev:** 1930 ft.

Greenville Township
Lat: 39-45-03 N Long: 78-58-26 W
Pop: 664 (1990) **Pop Density:** 26.3
Land: 25.2 sq. mi.; **Water:** 0.0 sq. mi.

Hooversville Borough
ZIP: 15936 Lat: 40-09-01 N Long: 78-54-52 W
Pop: 731 (1990); 863 (1980) **Pop Density:** 1044.3
Land: 0.7 sq. mi.; **Water:** 0.0 sq. mi. **Elev:** 1730 ft.

Indian Lake Borough
ZIP: 15926 Lat: 40-02-51 N Long: 78-51-34 W
Pop: 388 (1990); 306 (1980) **Pop Density:** 104.9
Land: 3.7 sq. mi.; **Water:** 0.8 sq. mi. **Elev:** 2281 ft.

Jefferson Township
Lat: 40-03-13 N Long: 79-13-04 W
Pop: 1,462 (1990) **Pop Density:** 35.4
Land: 41.3 sq. mi.; **Water:** 0.2 sq. mi.

Jenner Township
Lat: 40-10-36 N Long: 79-03-40 W
Pop: 4,147 (1990) **Pop Density:** 64.2
Land: 64.6 sq. mi.; **Water:** 0.5 sq. mi.

Jennerstown Borough
ZIP: 15547 Lat: 40-09-51 N Long: 79-03-43 W
Pop: 635 (1990); 656 (1980) **Pop Density:** 334.2
Land: 1.9 sq. mi.; **Water:** 0.1 sq. mi. **Elev:** 950 ft.
Name origin: For English physician Edward Jenner (1749–1823), developer of the vaccine against smallpox.

Jerome CDP
Lat: 40-12-48 N Long: 78-59-02 W
Pop: 1,074 (1990); 1,196 (1980) **Pop Density:** 397.8
Land: 2.7 sq. mi.; **Water:** 0.0 sq. mi.

Larimer Township
Lat: 39-47-26 N Long: 78-55-24 W
Pop: 547 (1990) **Pop Density:** 32.8
Land: 16.7 sq. mi.; **Water:** 0.0 sq. mi.

Lincoln Township
Lat: 40-05-30 N Long: 79-06-39 W
Pop: 1,655 (1990) **Pop Density:** 64.4
Land: 25.7 sq. mi.; **Water:** 0.0 sq. mi.
Name origin: For Abraham Lincoln (1809–65), sixteenth U.S. president.

Lower Turkeyfoot Township
Lat: 39-52-16 N Long: 79-21-19 W
Pop: 670 (1990) **Pop Density:** 18.6
Land: 36.0 sq. mi.; **Water:** 0.3 sq. mi.

Meyersdale Borough
ZIP: 15552 Lat: 39-48-47 N Long: 79-01-36 W
Pop: 2,518 (1990); 2,581 (1980) **Pop Density:** 3147.5
Land: 0.8 sq. mi.; **Water:** 0.0 sq. mi. **Elev:** 1975 ft.
In southern PA, northwest of Cumberland, MD. Laid out in a valley 1844.
Name origin: For Peter Meyers, an early settler who converted his farm into building lots.

Middlecreek Township
Lat: 39-58-00 N Long: 79-16-19 W
Pop: 764 (1990) **Pop Density:** 22.8
Land: 33.5 sq. mi.; **Water:** 0.1 sq. mi.

Milford Township
Lat: 39-57-29 N Long: 79-10-15 W
Pop: 1,544 (1990) **Pop Density:** 52.7
Land: 29.3 sq. mi.; **Water:** 0.0 sq. mi. **Elev:** 1940 ft.

New Baltimore Borough
ZIP: 15553 Lat: 39-59-08 N Long: 78-46-19 W
Pop: 162 (1990); 221 (1980) **Pop Density:** 405.0
Land: 0.4 sq. mi.; **Water:** 0.0 sq. mi. **Elev:** 1474 ft.

New Centerville Borough
Lat: 39-56-27 N Long: 79-11-31 W
Pop: 211 (1990); 213 (1980) **Pop Density:** 703.3
Land: 0.3 sq. mi.; **Water:** 0.0 sq. mi. **Elev:** 2130 ft.

Northampton Township
Lat: 39-50-13 N Long: 78-52-42 W
Pop: 356 (1990) **Pop Density:** 10.2
Land: 35.0 sq. mi.; **Water:** 0.0 sq. mi.

Ogle Township
Lat: 40-12-16 N Long: 78-43-35 W
Pop: 597 (1990) **Pop Density:** 16.5
Land: 36.2 sq. mi.; **Water:** 0.0 sq. mi.

Paint Township
ZIP: 15963 Lat: 40-12-05 N Long: 78-51-06 W
Pop: 3,491 (1990) **Pop Density:** 109.1
Land: 32.0 sq. mi.; **Water:** 0.1 sq. mi.

*Paint Borough
ZIP: 15963 Lat: 40-14-34 N Long: 78-50-56 W
Pop: 1,091 (1990); 1,177 (1980) **Pop Density:** 3636.7
Land: 0.3 sq. mi.; **Water:** 0.0 sq. mi. **Elev:** 1678 ft.

Quemahoning Township
Lat: 40-07-23 N Long: 78-57-53 W
Pop: 2,301 (1990) **Pop Density:** 64.8
Land: 35.5 sq. mi.; **Water:** 0.6 sq. mi.

Rockwood Borough
Lat: 39-55-00 N Long: 79-09-25 W
Pop: 1,014 (1990); 1,058 (1980) **Pop Density:** 3380.0
Land: 0.3 sq. mi.; **Water:** 0.0 sq. mi. **Elev:** 1913 ft.

Salisbury Borough
ZIP: 15558 Lat: 39-45-15 N Long: 79-05-04 W
Pop: 716 (1990); 817 (1980) **Pop Density:** 1790.0
Land: 0.4 sq. mi.; **Water:** 0.0 sq. mi. **Elev:** 2133 ft.

Seven Springs
Borough
ZIP: 15622   **Lat:** 40-01-30 N   **Long:** 79-17-29 W
Pop: 22 (1990); 30 (1980)   **Pop Density:** 22.0
Land: 1.0 sq. mi.; **Water:** 0.0 sq. mi.   **Elev:** 2530 ft.

Incorporated in 1964. Part of the town is also in Fayette County.

Shade
Township
Lat: 40-06-49 N   **Long:** 78-49-02 W
Pop: 3,177 (1990)   **Pop Density:** 47.3
Land: 67.2 sq. mi.; **Water:** 0.1 sq. mi.

Shanksville
Borough
ZIP: 15560   **Lat:** 40-01-02 N   **Long:** 78-54-24 W
Pop: 235 (1990); 273 (1980)   **Pop Density:** 1175.0
Land: 0.2 sq. mi.; **Water:** 0.0 sq. mi.   **Elev:** 2230 ft.

Somerset
Township
ZIP: 15501   **Lat:** 40-01-17 N   **Long:** 79-03-36 W
Pop: 8,732 (1990)   **Pop Density:** 136.7
Land: 63.9 sq. mi.; **Water:** 0.4 sq. mi.

*Somerset
Borough
ZIP: 15501   **Lat:** 40-00-18 N   **Long:** 79-04-41 W
Pop: 6,454 (1990); 6,474 (1980)   **Pop Density:** 2390.4
Land: 2.7 sq. mi.; **Water:** 0.0 sq. mi.   **Elev:** 2190 ft.

In southern PA, 30 mi. south of Johnstown. Laid out in 1795; incorporated Mar 5, 1804.

Name origin: For the shire of Somerset, England. Originally called Brunerstown, after Ulrich Bruner, who arrived in 1787.

Southampton
Township
Lat: 39-45-37 N   **Long:** 78-49-14 W
Pop: 553 (1990)   **Pop Density:** 18.8
Land: 29.4 sq. mi.; **Water:** 0.0 sq. mi.

Stonycreek
Township
Lat: 40-00-47 N   **Long:** 78-53-52 W
Pop: 2,083 (1990)   **Pop Density:** 34.0
Land: 61.2 sq. mi.; **Water:** 0.3 sq. mi.

Stoystown
Borough
ZIP: 15563   **Lat:** 40-06-12 N   **Long:** 78-57-18 W
Pop: 389 (1990); 432 (1980)   **Pop Density:** 1945.0
Land: 0.2 sq. mi.; **Water:** 0.0 sq. mi.   **Elev:** 2000 ft.

Summit
Township
Lat: 39-50-19 N   **Long:** 79-03-55 W
Pop: 2,495 (1990)   **Pop Density:** 55.3
Land: 45.1 sq. mi.; **Water:** 0.0 sq. mi.

Upper Turkeyfoot
Township
Lat: 39-53-34 N   **Long:** 79-17-18 W
Pop: 1,132 (1990)   **Pop Density:** 29.3
Land: 38.7 sq. mi.; **Water:** 0.0 sq. mi.

Ursina
Borough
ZIP: 15485   **Lat:** 39-48-56 N   **Long:** 79-19-58 W
Pop: 327 (1990); 311 (1980)   **Pop Density:** 467.1
Land: 0.7 sq. mi.; **Water:** 0.0 sq. mi.   **Elev:** 1356 ft.

Wellersburg
Borough
ZIP: 15564   **Lat:** 39-43-40 N   **Long:** 78-50-59 W
Pop: 213 (1990); 265 (1980)   **Pop Density:** 266.3
Land: 0.8 sq. mi.; **Water:** 0.0 sq. mi.   **Elev:** 1343 ft.

Windber
Borough
ZIP: 15963   **Lat:** 40-14-01 N   **Long:** 78-49-33 W
Pop: 4,756 (1990); 5,585 (1980)   **Pop Density:** 2264.8
Land: 2.1 sq. mi.; **Water:** 0.0 sq. mi.   **Elev:** 1853 ft.

Site selected for its new station by the Pennsylvania Railroad Company in 1897.

Name origin: Named by E. J. Berwind, the chief stockholder in the Berwind-White Coal Company, by transposing the two syllables of his family name.

Sullivan County
County Seat: Laporte (ZIP: 18626)

Pop: 6,104 (1990); 6,349 (1980)   **Pop Density:** 13.6
Land: 450.0 sq. mi.; **Water:** 2.4 sq. mi.   **Area Code:** 717

In north-central PA, west of Scranton; organized Mar 15, 1847 from Lycoming County.

Name origin: For Gen. John Sullivan (1740–95), Revolutionary War officer, member of the Continental Congress (1774–75), and chief executive of NH (1786–88; 1789–90). He led the punitive expedition against the Iroquois Indians (1779) who had caused the Wyoming Massacre.

Cherry
Township
Lat: 41-30-24 N   **Long:** 76-24-11 W
Pop: 1,481 (1990)   **Pop Density:** 25.7
Land: 57.6 sq. mi.; **Water:** 0.2 sq. mi.

Colley
Township
Lat: 41-27-51 N   **Long:** 76-17-59 W
Pop: 600 (1990)   **Pop Density:** 10.3
Land: 58.0 sq. mi.; **Water:** 1.0 sq. mi.

Davidson
Township
Lat: 41-19-48 N   **Long:** 76-26-37 W
Pop: 597 (1990)   **Pop Density:** 7.6
Land: 78.3 sq. mi.; **Water:** 0.1 sq. mi.

Dushore
Borough
ZIP: 18614   **Lat:** 41-31-31 N   **Long:** 76-23-56 W
Pop: 738 (1990); 692 (1980)   **Pop Density:** 820.0
Land: 0.9 sq. mi.; **Water:** 0.0 sq. mi.   **Elev:** 1450 ft.

Eagles Mere
Borough
ZIP: 17731   **Lat:** 41-24-34 N   **Long:** 76-34-59 W
Pop: 123 (1990); 164 (1980)   **Pop Density:** 58.6
Land: 2.1 sq. mi.; **Water:** 0.2 sq. mi.   **Elev:** 2061 ft.

Elkland
Township
Lat: 41-31-42 N   **Long:** 76-39-00 W
Pop: 565 (1990)   **Pop Density:** 14.7
Land: 38.5 sq. mi.; **Water:** 0.2 sq. mi.

Forks
Township
Lat: 41-30-25 N Long: 76-33-25 W
Pop: 355 (1990) **Pop Density:** 8.1
Land: 43.9 sq. mi.; **Water:** 0.0 sq. mi.

Forksville
Borough
ZIP: 18616 Lat: 41-29-27 N Long: 76-36-13 W
Pop: 160 (1990); 137 (1980) **Pop Density:** 106.7
Land: 1.5 sq. mi.; **Water:** 0.0 sq. mi. **Elev:** 1040 ft.

Fox
Township
ZIP: 17768 Lat: 41-32-16 N Long: 76-44-43 W
Pop: 300 (1990) **Pop Density:** 7.8
Land: 38.5 sq. mi.; **Water:** 0.1 sq. mi.

Hillsgrove
Township
ZIP: 18619 Lat: 41-25-51 N Long: 76-42-39 W
Pop: 337 (1990) **Pop Density:** 11.9
Land: 28.4 sq. mi.; **Water:** 0.0 sq. mi.

Laporte
Borough
ZIP: 18626 Lat: 41-25-06 N Long: 76-29-30 W
Pop: 328 (1990); 230 (1980) **Pop Density:** 298.2
Land: 1.1 sq. mi.; **Water:** 0.2 sq. mi. **Elev:** 1966 ft.
In northeast-central PA, west of Scranton. Laid out in 1850; incorporated 1853.
Name origin: Named by Michael Meylert for his friend, John Laporte, who was speaker of the general assembly (1832), a member of Congress (1832–36), and the last surveyor-general of PA (1845–51).

*Laporte
Township
Lat: 41-25-41 N Long: 76-27-03 W
Pop: 213 (1990) **Pop Density:** 4.0
Land: 53.3 sq. mi.; **Water:** 0.2 sq. mi.

Shrewsbury
Township
Lat: 41-23-42 N Long: 76-37-06 W
Pop: 307 (1990) **Pop Density:** 6.4
Land: 47.8 sq. mi.; **Water:** 0.3 sq. mi.

Susquehanna County
County Seat: Montrose (ZIP: 16801)

Pop: 40,380 (1990); 37,876 (1980) **Pop Density:** 49.1
Land: 823.0 sq. mi.; **Water:** 9.4 sq. mi. **Area Code:** 717
On northern border of eastern PA, north of Scranton; organized Feb 21, 1810 from Luzerne County.
Name origin: For the Susquehanna River, which runs through it.

Apolacon
Township
Lat: 41-57-21 N Long: 76-05-55 W
Pop: 493 (1990) **Pop Density:** 21.3
Land: 23.1 sq. mi.; **Water:** 0.3 sq. mi.

Ararat
Township
Lat: 41-48-42 N Long: 75-30-59 W
Pop: 420 (1990) **Pop Density:** 22.3
Land: 18.8 sq. mi.; **Water:** 0.7 sq. mi.

Auburn
Township
Lat: 41-41-15 N Long: 76-02-48 W
Pop: 1,639 (1990) **Pop Density:** 32.4
Land: 50.6 sq. mi.; **Water:** 0.3 sq. mi.

Bridgewater
Township
Lat: 41-50-09 N Long: 75-51-48 W
Pop: 2,368 (1990) **Pop Density:** 58.5
Land: 40.5 sq. mi.; **Water:** 0.5 sq. mi.

Brooklyn
Township
Lat: 41-45-39 N Long: 75-47-54 W
Pop: 873 (1990) **Pop Density:** 35.9
Land: 24.3 sq. mi.; **Water:** 0.2 sq. mi.
Name origin: For Brooklyn, CT, former home of early settlers.

Choconut
Township
Lat: 41-57-35 N Long: 76-01-36 W
Pop: 799 (1990) **Pop Density:** 39.8
Land: 20.1 sq. mi.; **Water:** 0.2 sq. mi.

Clifford
Township
Lat: 41-40-30 N Long: 75-33-22 W
Pop: 2,147 (1990) **Pop Density:** 53.4
Land: 40.2 sq. mi.; **Water:** 0.6 sq. mi.
In northeastern PA, a crossroads town on the east branch of Tunkhannock Creek. Settled 1800 by Adam Miller.

Dimock
Township
Lat: 41-44-57 N Long: 75-54-25 W
Pop: 1,226 (1990) **Pop Density:** 41.7
Land: 29.4 sq. mi.; **Water:** 0.4 sq. mi.

Forest City
Borough
ZIP: 18421 Lat: 41-39-05 N Long: 75-28-10 W
Pop: 1,846 (1990); 1,924 (1980) **Pop Density:** 2051.1
Land: 0.9 sq. mi.; **Water:** 0.0 sq. mi. **Elev:** 1482 ft.
In northeastern PA, 20 mi. northeast of Scranton.

Forest Lake
Township
Lat: 41-52-26 N Long: 75-59-19 W
Pop: 1,229 (1990) **Pop Density:** 41.4
Land: 29.7 sq. mi.; **Water:** 0.1 sq. mi.

Franklin
Township
Lat: 41-53-58 N Long: 75-49-40 W
Pop: 913 (1990) **Pop Density:** 38.4
Land: 23.8 sq. mi.; **Water:** 0.1 sq. mi.

Friendsville
Borough
ZIP: 18818 Lat: 41-55-04 N Long: 76-02-50 W
Pop: 102 (1990); 72 (1980) **Pop Density:** 68.0
Land: 1.5 sq. mi.; **Water:** 0.0 sq. mi. **Elev:** 1543 ft.

Gibson
　　　　　　　　　　　　　　　　　Township
　　　　　　　Lat: 41-46-21 N　Long: 75-36-45 W
Pop: 1,015 (1990)　　　　　　　**Pop Density:** 32.0
Land: 31.7 sq. mi.; **Water:** 0.3 sq. mi.

Great Bend
　　　　　　　　　　　　　　　　　Township
ZIP: 18821　　　　　Lat: 41-56-56 N　**Long:** 75-42-25 W
Pop: 1,817 (1990)　　　　　　　**Pop Density:** 50.1
Land: 36.3 sq. mi.; **Water:** 0.7 sq. mi.

*Great Bend
　　　　　　　　　　　　　　　　　Borough
ZIP: 18821　　　　　Lat: 41-58-21 N　**Long:** 75-44-44 W
Pop: 704 (1990); 740 (1980)　　**Pop Density:** 2346.7
Land: 0.3 sq. mi.; **Water:** 0.0 sq. mi.　　**Elev:** 920 ft.

Hallstead
　　　　　　　　　　　　　　　　　Borough
ZIP: 18822　　　　　Lat: 41-57-42 N　**Long:** 75-44-50 W
Pop: 1,274 (1990); 1,280 (1980)　**Pop Density:** 3185.0
Land: 0.4 sq. mi.; **Water:** 0.0 sq. mi.　　**Elev:** 883 ft.

In northeastern PA on the north branch of the Susquehanna River.

Name origin: For William F. Hallstead, an official of the Lackawanna Railroad.

Harford
　　　　　　　　　　　　　　　　　Township
ZIP: 18823　　　　　Lat: 41-46-12 N　**Long:** 75-42-40 W
Pop: 1,100 (1990)　　　　　　　**Pop Density:** 33.4
Land: 32.9 sq. mi.; **Water:** 0.4 sq. mi.

Harmony
　　　　　　　　　　　　　　　　　Township
　　　　　　　Lat: 41-57-31 N　Long: 75-31-57 W
Pop: 544 (1990)　　　　　　　**Pop Density:** 17.3
Land: 31.4 sq. mi.; **Water:** 0.3 sq. mi.

Herrick
　　　　　　　　　　　　　　　　　Township
　　　　　　　Lat: 41-44-25 N　Long: 75-31-03 W
Pop: 563 (1990)　　　　　　　**Pop Density:** 22.8
Land: 24.7 sq. mi.; **Water:** 0.2 sq. mi.

Hop Bottom
　　　　　　　　　　　　　　　　　Borough
ZIP: 18824　　　　　Lat: 41-42-23 N　**Long:** 75-46-02 W
Pop: 345 (1990); 405 (1980)　　**Pop Density:** 575.0
Land: 0.6 sq. mi.; **Water:** 0.0 sq. mi.　　**Elev:** 820 ft.

Jackson
　　　　　　　　　　　　　　　　　Township
ZIP: 18825　　　　　Lat: 41-51-44 N　**Long:** 75-36-06 W
Pop: 757 (1990)　　　　　　　**Pop Density:** 29.0
Land: 26.1 sq. mi.; **Water:** 0.4 sq. mi.

Jessup
　　　　　　　　　　　　　　　　　Township
　　　　　　　Lat: 41-48-36 N　Long: 75-58-25 W
Pop: 483 (1990)　　　　　　　**Pop Density:** 22.6
Land: 21.4 sq. mi.; **Water:** 0.1 sq. mi.

Lanesboro
　　　　　　　　　　　　　　　　　Borough
ZIP: 18827　　　　　Lat: 41-57-44 N　**Long:** 75-34-56 W
Pop: 659 (1990); 465 (1980)　　**Pop Density:** 253.5
Land: 2.6 sq. mi.; **Water:** 0.1 sq. mi.　　**Elev:** 965 ft.

Lathrop
　　　　　　　　　　　　　　　　　Township
　　　　　　　Lat: 41-40-38 N　Long: 75-48-22 W
Pop: 794 (1990)　　　　　　　**Pop Density:** 38.5
Land: 20.6 sq. mi.; **Water:** 0.1 sq. mi.

Lenox
　　　　　　　　　　　　　　　　　Township
　　　　　　　Lat: 41-40-37 N　Long: 75-42-08 W
Pop: 1,581 (1990)　　　　　　　**Pop Density:** 39.2
Land: 40.3 sq. mi.; **Water:** 0.6 sq. mi.

Liberty
　　　　　　　　　　　　　　　　　Township
　　　　　　　Lat: 41-57-36 N　Long: 75-49-34 W
Pop: 1,353 (1990)　　　　　　　**Pop Density:** 45.6
Land: 29.7 sq. mi.; **Water:** 0.3 sq. mi.

Little Meadows
　　　　　　　　　　　　　　　　　Borough
ZIP: 18830　　　　　Lat: 41-59-35 N　**Long:** 76-07-51 W
Pop: 326 (1990); 375 (1980)　　**Pop Density:** 141.7
Land: 2.3 sq. mi.; **Water:** 0.0 sq. mi.　　**Elev:** 1044 ft.

Middletown
　　　　　　　　　　　　　　　　　Township
　　　　　　　Lat: 41-52-17 N　Long: 76-05-34 W
Pop: 339 (1990)　　　　　　　**Pop Density:** 11.8
Land: 28.7 sq. mi.; **Water:** 0.0 sq. mi.

Montrose
　　　　　　　　　　　　　　　　　Borough
ZIP: 18801　　　　　Lat: 41-50-02 N　**Long:** 75-52-36 W
Pop: 1,982 (1990); 1,980 (1980)　**Pop Density:** 1524.6
Land: 1.3 sq. mi.; **Water:** 0.0 sq. mi.　　**Elev:** 1619 ft.

Laid out in 1812; incorporated Mar 19, 1824.

New Milford
　　　　　　　　　　　　　　　　　Township
ZIP: 18834　　　　　Lat: 41-51-39 N　**Long:** 75-42-29 W
Pop: 1,731 (1990)　　　　　　　**Pop Density:** 38.9
Land: 44.5 sq. mi.; **Water:** 0.7 sq. mi.

*New Milford
　　　　　　　　　　　　　　　　　Borough
ZIP: 18834　　　　　Lat: 41-52-33 N　**Long:** 75-43-36 W
Pop: 953 (1990); 1,040 (1980)　　**Pop Density:** 866.4
Land: 1.1 sq. mi.; **Water:** 0.0 sq. mi.　　**Elev:** 1107 ft.

Oakland
　　　　　　　　　　　　　　　　　Borough
ZIP: 18847　　　　　Lat: 41-56-56 N　**Long:** 75-36-40 W
Pop: 641 (1990); 734 (1980)　　**Pop Density:** 1282.0
Land: 0.5 sq. mi.; **Water:** 0.0 sq. mi.　　**Elev:** 1000 ft.

*Oakland
　　　　　　　　　　　　　　　　　Township
　　　　　　　Lat: 41-56-55 N　Long: 75-37-32 W
Pop: 544 (1990)　　　　　　　**Pop Density:** 33.2
Land: 16.4 sq. mi.; **Water:** 0.4 sq. mi.

Rush
　　　　　　　　　　　　　　　　　Township
　　　　　　　Lat: 41-46-39 N　Long: 76-03-43 W
Pop: 1,126 (1990)　　　　　　　**Pop Density:** 29.8
Land: 37.8 sq. mi.; **Water:** 0.1 sq. mi.

Silver Lake
　　　　　　　　　　　　　　　　　Township
　　　　　　　Lat: 41-57-02 N　Long: 75-56-15 W
Pop: 1,542 (1990)　　　　　　　**Pop Density:** 47.2
Land: 32.7 sq. mi.; **Water:** 0.6 sq. mi.

Springville
　　　　　　　　　　　　　　　　　Township
ZIP: 18844　　　　　Lat: 41-40-34 N　**Long:** 75-54-38 W
Pop: 1,424 (1990)　　　　　　　**Pop Density:** 46.8
Land: 30.4 sq. mi.; **Water:** 0.2 sq. mi.

Susquehanna Depot
　　　　　　　　　　　　　　　　　Borough
ZIP: 18847　　　　　Lat: 41-56-40 N　**Long:** 75-36-15 W
Pop: 1,760 (1990); 1,994 (1980)　**Pop Density:** 2514.3
Land: 0.7 sq. mi.; **Water:** 0.0 sq. mi.　　**Elev:** 903 ft.

In northeastern PA, near the NY state line.

Name origin: For the county and for the river, which flows through it.

Thompson
　　　　　　　　　　　　　　　　　Township
ZIP: 18465　　　　　Lat: 41-52-20 N　**Long:** 75-31-10 W
Pop: 374 (1990)　　　　　　　**Pop Density:** 17.2
Land: 21.7 sq. mi.; **Water:** 0.3 sq. mi.

*Thompson   Borough
ZIP: 18465   **Lat:** 41-51-44 N **Long:** 75-30-50 W
Pop: 291 (1990); 303 (1980)   **Pop Density:** 727.5
Land: 0.4 sq. mi.; **Water:** 0.0 sq. mi.   **Elev:** 1660 ft.
Name origin: For an early settler.

Union Dale   Borough
ZIP: 18470   **Lat:** 41-42-51 N **Long:** 75-29-01 W
Pop: 303 (1990); 321 (1980)   **Pop Density:** 121.2
Land: 2.5 sq. mi.; **Water:** 0.1 sq. mi.   **Elev:** 1697 ft.

Tioga County
County Seat: Wellsboro (ZIP: 16901)

Pop: 41,126 (1990); 40,973 (1980)   **Pop Density:** 36.3
Land: 1133.8 sq. mi.; **Water:** 3.6 sq. mi.   **Area Code:** 717

On central northern border of PA, north of Williamsport; organized Mar 26, 1804 from Lycoming County.

Name origin: For the Tioga River, which flows through it; from Iroquoian for 'place between two points' or 'at the forks,' for the Indian town on the Susquehanna River near Athens, PA; the town was called *Diahoga* or *Tioga*.

Bloss   Township
                             Lat: 41-39-56 N **Long:** 77-08-33 W
Pop: 388 (1990)   **Pop Density:** 16.8
Land: 23.1 sq. mi.; **Water:** 0.1 sq. mi.

Blossburg   Borough
ZIP: 16912   **Lat:** 41-40-58 N **Long:** 77-03-59 W
Pop: 1,571 (1990); 1,757 (1980)   **Pop Density:** 334.3
Land: 4.7 sq. mi.; **Water:** 0.0 sq. mi.   **Elev:** 1332 ft.
In north-central PA, north of Williamsport.
Name origin: For Aaron Bloss, who opened a tavern here in 1802. Originally called Peters Camp.

Brookfield   Township
ZIP: 16950   **Lat:** 41-57-46 N **Long:** 77-32-36 W
Pop: 432 (1990)   **Pop Density:** 13.6
Land: 31.8 sq. mi.; **Water:** 0.0 sq. mi.

Charleston   Township
ZIP: 16901   **Lat:** 41-45-13 N **Long:** 77-13-48 W
Pop: 2,957 (1990)   **Pop Density:** 56.2
Land: 52.6 sq. mi.; **Water:** 0.3 sq. mi.

Chatham   Township
ZIP: 16935   **Lat:** 41-52-21 N **Long:** 77-24-25 W
Pop: 607 (1990)   **Pop Density:** 17.3
Land: 35.0 sq. mi.; **Water:** 0.1 sq. mi.

Clymer   Township
ZIP: 16943   **Lat:** 41-50-58 N **Long:** 77-32-42 W
Pop: 597 (1990)   **Pop Density:** 17.8
Land: 33.5 sq. mi.; **Water:** 0.2 sq. mi.

Covington   Township
ZIP: 16917   **Lat:** 41-43-46 N **Long:** 77-05-53 W
Pop: 918 (1990)   **Pop Density:** 25.3
Land: 36.3 sq. mi.; **Water:** 0.0 sq. mi.
Name origin: For Gen. Leonard Covington, a noted Indian fighter and comrade of Gen. "Mad" Anthony Wayne (1745–96).

Deerfield   Township
ZIP: 16928   **Lat:** 41-57-15 N **Long:** 77-25-29 W
Pop: 647 (1990)   **Pop Density:** 22.0
Land: 29.4 sq. mi.; **Water:** 0.0 sq. mi.

Delmar   Township
ZIP: 16901   **Lat:** 41-43-02 N **Long:** 77-21-06 W
Pop: 3,048 (1990)   **Pop Density:** 37.9
Land: 80.4 sq. mi.; **Water:** 0.2 sq. mi.

Duncan   Township
ZIP: 16901   **Lat:** 41-38-27 N **Long:** 77-15-49 W
Pop: 248 (1990)   **Pop Density:** 12.5
Land: 19.8 sq. mi.; **Water:** 0.0 sq. mi.

Elk   Township
ZIP: 16921   **Lat:** 41-37-21 N **Long:** 77-31-59 W
Pop: 42 (1990)   **Pop Density:** 0.6
Land: 73.9 sq. mi.; **Water:** 0.1 sq. mi.

Elkland   Borough
ZIP: 16920   **Lat:** 41-59-21 N **Long** 77-18-53 W
Pop: 1,849 (1990); 1,974 (1980)   **Pop Density:** 840.5
Land: 2.2 sq. mi.; **Water:** 0.0 sq. mi.   **Elev:** 1135 ft.
In northern PA, just south of the NY state line.

*Elkland   Township
ZIP: 16920   **Lat:** 41-58-11 N **Long** 77-18-03 W
Pop: 61 (1990)   **Pop Density:** 23.5
Land: 2.6 sq. mi.; **Water:** 0.0 sq. mi.

Farmington   Township
                             Lat: 41-55-47 N **Long** 77-16-22 W
Pop: 644 (1990)   **Pop Density:** 20.1
Land: 32.0 sq. mi.; **Water:** 0.0 sq. mi.

Gaines   Township
ZIP: 16921   **Lat:** 41-44-51 N **Long** 77-32-51 W
Pop: 601 (1990)   **Pop Density:** 12.3
Land: 48.7 sq. mi.; **Water:** 0.0 sq. mi.

Hamilton   Township
                             Lat: 41-39-54 N **Long** 77-02-26 W
Pop: 496 (1990)   **Pop Density:** 45.1
Land: 11.0 sq. mi.; **Water:** 0.0 sq. mi.

Jackson   Township
ZIP: 16929   **Lat:** 41-57-27 N **Long** 76-59-05 W
Pop: 2,072 (1990)   **Pop Density:** 51.0
Land: 40.6 sq. mi.; **Water:** 0.0 sq. mi.

Knoxville
Borough
ZIP: 16928　　**Lat:** 41-57-24 N　**Long:** 77-26-08 W
Pop: 589 (1990); 650 (1980)　　**Pop Density:** 1178.0
Land: 0.5 sq. mi.; **Water:** 0.0 sq. mi.　　**Elev:** 1241 ft.

In northern PA at the foot of 2,000–ft. Fork Hill, north of Williamsport.

Lawrence
Township
Lat: 41-58-22 N　**Long:** 77-08-15 W
Pop: 1,519 (1990)　　**Pop Density:** 44.0
Land: 34.5 sq. mi.; **Water:** 0.0 sq. mi.

Lawrenceville
Borough
ZIP: 16929　　**Lat:** 41-59-56 N　**Long:** 77-07-46 W
Pop: 481 (1990); 327 (1980)　　**Pop Density:** 962.0
Land: 0.5 sq. mi.; **Water:** 0.0 sq. mi.　　**Elev:** 996 ft.

Liberty
Township
ZIP: 16930　　**Lat:** 41-35-49 N　**Long:** 77-06-54 W
Pop: 930 (1990)　　**Pop Density:** 14.3
Land: 65.1 sq. mi.; **Water:** 0.0 sq. mi.

*Liberty
Borough
ZIP: 16930　　**Lat:** 41-33-35 N　**Long:** 77-06-18 W
Pop: 199 (1990); 220 (1980)　　**Pop Density:** 398.0
Land: 0.5 sq. mi.; **Water:** 0.0 sq. mi.　　**Elev:** 1546 ft.

In north-central PA, north of Williamsport. Site of the Liberty Blockhouse, erected as a provision station and refuge in 1792 on Williamson Road, between Northumberland and Canoe Camp.

Mansfield
Borough
ZIP: 16933　　**Lat:** 41-48-20 N　**Long:** 77-04-43 W
Pop: 3,538 (1990); 3,322 (1980)　　**Pop Density:** 1862.1
Land: 1.9 sq. mi.; **Water:** 0.0 sq. mi.　　**Elev:** 1147 ft.

In northern PA, southwest of Elmira, NY.

Name origin: Named in 1824 for Asa Mann, an early settler.

Middlebury
Township
ZIP: 16935　　**Lat:** 41-51-35 N　**Long:** 77-16-02 W
Pop: 1,244 (1990)　　**Pop Density:** 25.7
Land: 48.4 sq. mi.; **Water:** 0.4 sq. mi.

Morris
Township
ZIP: 16938　　**Lat:** 41-34-44 N　**Long:** 77-20-34 W
Pop: 675 (1990)　　**Pop Density:** 9.2
Land: 73.5 sq. mi.; **Water:** 0.0 sq. mi.

Nelson
Township
Lat: 41-59-00 N　**Long:** 77-15-06 W
Pop: 514 (1990)　　**Pop Density:** 57.1
Land: 9.0 sq. mi.; **Water:** 0.0 sq. mi.

Osceola
Township
ZIP: 16942　　**Lat:** 41-58-34 N　**Long:** 77-22-06 W
Pop: 772 (1990)　　**Pop Density:** 55.9
Land: 13.8 sq. mi.; **Water:** 0.0 sq. mi.

Putnam
Township
Lat: 41-44-45 N　**Long:** 77-04-44 W
Pop: 444 (1990)　　**Pop Density:** 740.0
Land: 0.6 sq. mi.; **Water:** 0.0 sq. mi.

Richmond
Township
ZIP: 16933　　**Lat:** 41-48-29 N　**Long:** 77-06-17 W
Pop: 2,305 (1990)　　**Pop Density:** 45.4
Land: 50.8 sq. mi.; **Water:** 0.1 sq. mi.

Roseville
Borough
Lat: 41-51-55 N　**Long:** 76-57-32 W
Pop: 230 (1990); 211 (1980)　　**Pop Density:** 460.0
Land: 0.5 sq. mi.; **Water:** 0.0 sq. mi.　　**Elev:** 1355 ft.

Rutland
Township
ZIP: 16933　　**Lat:** 41-52-30 N　**Long:** 76-58-35 W
Pop: 646 (1990)　　**Pop Density:** 18.2
Land: 35.4 sq. mi.; **Water:** 0.0 sq. mi.

Shippen
Township
ZIP: 16901　　**Lat:** 41-45-46 N　**Long:** 77-27-12 W
Pop: 508 (1990)　　**Pop Density:** 10.4
Land: 48.8 sq. mi.; **Water:** 0.0 sq. mi.

Sullivan
Township
ZIP: 16932　　**Lat:** 41-46-59 N　**Long:** 76-57-42 W
Pop: 1,140 (1990)　　**Pop Density:** 27.0
Land: 42.2 sq. mi.; **Water:** 0.1 sq. mi.

Tioga
Township
ZIP: 16946　　**Lat:** 41-54-13 N　**Long:** 77-07-09 W
Pop: 1,019 (1990)　　**Pop Density:** 26.3
Land: 38.7 sq. mi.; **Water:** 1.8 sq. mi.

Name origin: For the Tioga River, which runs through the county.

*Tioga
Borough
ZIP: 16946　　**Lat:** 41-54-17 N　**Long:** 77-08-07 W
Pop: 638 (1990); 613 (1980)　　**Pop Density:** 1595.0
Land: 0.4 sq. mi.; **Water:** 0.1 sq. mi.　　**Elev:** 1039 ft.

Union
Township
Lat: 41-36-57 N　**Long:** 76-57-30 W
Pop: 931 (1990)　　**Pop Density:** 19.7
Land: 47.3 sq. mi.; **Water:** 0.0 sq. mi.

Ward
Township
Lat: 41-41-44 N　**Long:** 76-57-00 W
Pop: 55 (1990)　　**Pop Density:** 1.6
Land: 34.2 sq. mi.; **Water:** 0.0 sq. mi.

Wellsboro
Borough
ZIP: 16901　　**Lat:** 41-44-46 N　**Long:** 77-18-10 W
Pop: 3,430 (1990); 3,805 (1980)　　**Pop Density:** 700.0
Land: 4.9 sq. mi.; **Water:** 0.0 sq. mi.　　**Elev:** 1311 ft.

In northern PA, 40 mi. southwest of Elmira, NY. Laid out in 1806 by Benjamin Morris, a land agent who arrived in 1799; incorporated Mar 6, 1830.

Name origin: For Morris's wife, Mary Wells Morris, who with her brothers promoted the town to be the seat of the new county of Tioga in 1806.

Westfield
Borough
ZIP: 16950　　**Lat:** 41-55-04 N　**Long:** 77-32-26 W
Pop: 1,119 (1990); 1,268 (1980)　　**Pop Density:** 1119.0
Land: 1.0 sq. mi.; **Water:** 0.0 sq. mi.　　**Elev:** 1374 ft.

In northern PA, 50 mi. southwest of Elmira, NY.

Name origin: Named by Henry Trowbridge for Westfield, MA, his former home.

*Westfield
Township
ZIP: 16950　　**Lat:** 41-54-18 N　**Long:** 77-32-02 W
Pop: 1,022 (1990)　　**Pop Density:** 43.1
Land: 23.7 sq. mi.; **Water:** 0.0 sq. mi.

Union County
County Seat: Lewisburg (ZIP: 17837)

Pop: 36,176 (1990); 32,870 (1980)
Land: 316.8 sq. mi.; Water: 0.4 sq. mi.

Pop Density: 114.2
Area Code: 717

In central PA, south of Williamsport; organized Mar 22, 1813 from Northumberland County.
Name origin: As an expression of belief in the federal union of the states.

Buffalo — Township
ZIP: 17837 — Lat: 40-57-53 N Long: 76-59-11 W
Pop: 2,877 (1990) — Pop Density: 94.0
Land: 30.6 sq. mi.; Water: 0.0 sq. mi.

East Buffalo — Township
ZIP: 17837 — Lat: 40-55-43 N Long: 76-54-43 W
Pop: 5,245 (1990) — Pop Density: 336.2
Land: 15.6 sq. mi.; Water: 0.0 sq. mi.

Gregg — Township
ZIP: 17810 — Lat: 41-06-54 N Long: 76-55-50 W
Pop: 1,114 (1990) — Pop Density: 73.8
Land: 15.1 sq. mi.; Water: 0.0 sq. mi.

Hartleton — Borough
ZIP: 17829 — Lat: 40-53-58 N Long: 77-09-24 W
Pop: 246 (1990); 220 (1980) — Pop Density: 273.3
Land: 0.9 sq. mi.; Water: 0.0 sq. mi. — Elev: 640 ft.

Hartley — Township
Lat: 40-53-40 N Long: 77-13-20 W
Pop: 1,896 (1990) — Pop Density: 23.8
Land: 79.6 sq. mi.; Water: 0.1 sq. mi.

Kelly — Township
ZIP: 17837 — Lat: 40-59-54 N Long: 76-55-13 W
Pop: 4,561 (1990) — Pop Density: 266.7
Land: 17.1 sq. mi.; Water: 0.0 sq. mi.

Lewis — Township
ZIP: 17880 — Lat: 40-57-34 N Long: 77-07-36 W
Pop: 1,222 (1990) — Pop Density: 31.6
Land: 38.7 sq. mi.; Water: 0.1 sq. mi.

Lewisburg — Borough
ZIP: 17837 — Lat: 40-57-50 N Long: 76-53-25 W
Pop: 5,785 (1990); 5,407 (1980) — Pop Density: 5785.0
Land: 1.0 sq. mi.; Water: 0.0 sq. mi. — Elev: 456 ft.

In central PA on the Susquehanna River, 10 mi. northwest of Sunbury. Laid out in 1785; incorporated Mar 21, 1822.
Name origin: For storekeeper and early settler Ludwig (Lewis) Doerr.

Limestone — Township
ZIP: 17844 — Lat: 40-53-22 N Long: 77-02-19 W
Pop: 1,346 (1990) — Pop Density: 65.7
Land: 20.5 sq. mi.; Water: 0.0 sq. mi.

Linntown — CDP
ZIP: 17837 — Lat: 40-57-24 N Long: 76-54-03 W
Pop: 1,640 (1990); 1,842 (1980) — Pop Density: 2342.9
Land: 0.7 sq. mi.; Water: 0.0 sq. mi.

Mifflinburg — Borough
ZIP: 17844 — Lat: 40-55-12 N Long 77-02-49 W
Pop: 3,480 (1990); 3,151 (1980) — Pop Density: 1933.3
Land: 1.8 sq. mi.; Water: 0.0 sq. mi. — Elev: 583 ft.

New Berlin — Borough
ZIP: 17855 — Lat: 40-52-49 N Long 76-59-07 W
Pop: 892 (1990); 783 (1980) — Pop Density: 2230.0
Land: 0.4 sq. mi.; Water: 0.0 sq. mi. — Elev: 607 ft.

Union — Township
ZIP: 17889 — Lat: 40-53-51 N Long: 76-53-25 W
Pop: 1,300 (1990) — Pop Density: 120.4
Land: 10.8 sq. mi.; Water: 0.0 sq. mi.

West Buffalo — Township
ZIP: 17844 — Lat: 40-59-31 N Long: 77-04-34 W
Pop: 2,254 (1990) — Pop Density: 59.3
Land: 38.0 sq. mi.; Water: 0.0 sq. mi.

White Deer — Township
Lat: 41-03-15 N Long: 76-56-57 W
Pop: 3,958 (1990) — Pop Density: 85.1
Land: 46.5 sq. mi.; Water: 0.1 sq. mi.

Venango County
County Seat: Franklin (ZIP: 16323)

Pop: 59,381 (1990); 64,444 (1980)   **Pop Density:** 88.0
Land: 675.1 sq. mi.; **Water:** 8.0 sq. mi.   **Area Code:** 814

In northwestern PA, southeast of Erie; organized Mar 12, 1800 from Allegheny and Lycoming counties.

Name origin: For the Venango River (now called French Creek), which flows through it; from an Indian term of uncertain origin, possibly from *innungah* 'a figure carved on a tree.'

Allegheny
Township
Lat: 41-34-11 N **Long:** 79-32-37 W
Pop: 281 (1990)   **Pop Density:** 11.2
Land: 25.0 sq. mi.; **Water:** 0.0 sq. mi.
Name origin: For the river.

Barkeyville
Borough
ZIP: 16038   **Lat:** 41-12-00 N **Long:** 79-58-59 W
Pop: 274 (1990); 266 (1980)   **Pop Density:** 78.3
Land: 3.5 sq. mi.; **Water:** 0.0 sq. mi.   **Elev:** 1479 ft.

Canal
Township
Lat: 41-28-34 N **Long:** 79-56-48 W
Pop: 1,067 (1990)   **Pop Density:** 43.6
Land: 24.5 sq. mi.; **Water:** 0.1 sq. mi.

Cherrytree
Township
Lat: 41-34-17 N **Long:** 79-42-36 W
Pop: 1,601 (1990)   **Pop Density:** 43.5
Land: 36.8 sq. mi.; **Water:** 0.0 sq. mi.

Clinton
Township
Lat: 41-13-33 N **Long:** 79-51-54 W
Pop: 733 (1990)   **Pop Density:** 25.7
Land: 28.5 sq. mi.; **Water:** 0.3 sq. mi.

Clintonville
Borough
ZIP: 16372   **Lat:** 41-12-06 N **Long:** 79-52-34 W
Pop: 520 (1990); 512 (1980)   **Pop Density:** 472.7
Land: 1.1 sq. mi.; **Water:** 0.0 sq. mi.   **Elev:** 1473 ft.

Cooperstown
Borough
ZIP: 16317   **Lat:** 41-29-58 N **Long:** 79-52-26 W
Pop: 506 (1990); 644 (1980)   **Pop Density:** 843.3
Land: 0.6 sq. mi.; **Water:** 0.0 sq. mi.   **Elev:** 1131 ft.

Cornplanter
Township
Lat: 41-29-21 N **Long:** 79-39-07 W
Pop: 2,968 (1990)   **Pop Density:** 79.6
Land: 37.3 sq. mi.; **Water:** 0.5 sq. mi.
In northwestern PA, a northeastern suburb of Oil City.
Name origin: For Garganwahgah, nicknamed "the Cornplanter," a distinguished Seneca Indian chief and noted warrior.

Cranberry
Township
ZIP: 16319   **Lat:** 41-21-45 N **Long:** 79-41-44 W
Pop: 7,256 (1990)   **Pop Density:** 103.1
Land: 70.4 sq. mi.; **Water:** 0.9 sq. mi.

Emlenton
Borough
Lat: 41-10-46 N **Long:** 79-42-32 W
Pop: 824 (1990); 794 (1980)   **Pop Density:** 1177.1
Land: 0.7 sq. mi.; **Water:** 0.1 sq. mi.
Part of the town is also in Clarion County.

Franklin
City
ZIP: 16323   **Lat:** 41-23-31 N **Long:** 79-50-19 W
Pop: 7,329 (1990); 8,146 (1980)   **Pop Density:** 1593.3
Land: 4.6 sq. mi.; **Water:** 0.1 sq. mi.   **Elev:** 1000 ft.
In northwestern PA, 70 mi. north of Pittsburgh. Laid out in 1795 on a tract of 1,000 acres belonging to the state.
Name origin: For Fort Franklin.

Frenchcreek
Township
Lat: 41-23-43 N **Long:** 79-56-38 W
Pop: 1,676 (1990)   **Pop Density:** 57.2
Land: 29.3 sq. mi.; **Water:** 0.2 sq. mi.

Hasson Heights
CDP
Lat: 41-26-55 N **Long:** 79-40-37 W
Pop: 1,610 (1990); 1,066 (1980)   **Pop Density:** 805.0
Land: 2.0 sq. mi.; **Water:** 0.0 sq. mi.

Irwin
Township
Lat: 41-13-50 N **Long:** 79-57-15 W
Pop: 1,182 (1990)   **Pop Density:** 39.1
Land: 30.2 sq. mi.; **Water:** 0.0 sq. mi.

Jackson
Township
Lat: 41-30-18 N **Long:** 79-52-52 W
Pop: 1,089 (1990)   **Pop Density:** 44.1
Land: 24.7 sq. mi.; **Water:** 0.0 sq. mi.

Mineral
Township
Lat: 41-19-26 N **Long:** 79-57-50 W
Pop: 514 (1990)   **Pop Density:** 22.8
Land: 22.5 sq. mi.; **Water:** 0.0 sq. mi.

Oakland
Township
Lat: 41-29-58 N **Long:** 79-46-27 W
Pop: 1,527 (1990)   **Pop Density:** 52.7
Land: 29.0 sq. mi.; **Water:** 0.2 sq. mi.

Oil City
City
ZIP: 16301   **Lat:** 41-25-35 N **Long:** 79-42-15 W
Pop: 11,949 (1990)   **Pop Density:** 2655.3
Land: 4.5 sq. mi.; **Water:** 0.2 sq. mi.   **Elev:** 1200 ft.
In northwestern PA on the Allegheny River at the mouth of Oil Creek, 90 mi. north of Pittsburgh. Important oil center in 1860.
Name origin: For the rise and growth of the petroleum business.

Oilcreek
Township
Lat: 41-34-46 N **Long:** 79-37-04 W
Pop: 915 (1990)   **Pop Density:** 39.8
Land: 23.0 sq. mi.; **Water:** 0.0 sq. mi.

Pinegrove
Township
Lat: 41-22-18 N **Long:** 79-32-36 W
Pop: 1,395 (1990)   **Pop Density:** 37.7
Land: 37.0 sq. mi.; **Water:** 0.0 sq. mi.

Pleasantville
Borough
ZIP: 16341 **Lat:** 41-35-36 N **Long:** 79-34-45 W
Pop: 991 (1990); 1,099 (1980) **Pop Density:** 991.0
Land: 1.0 sq. mi.; **Water:** 0.0 sq. mi. **Elev:** 1635 ft.

Plum
Township
Lat: 41-34-52 N **Long:** 79-49-05 W
Pop: 1,031 (1990) **Pop Density:** 38.8
Land: 26.6 sq. mi.; **Water:** 0.0 sq. mi.

Polk
Borough
ZIP: 16342 **Lat:** 41-22-09 N **Long:** 79-55-48 W
Pop: 1,267 (1990); 1,884 (1980) **Pop Density:** 666.8
Land: 1.9 sq. mi.; **Water:** 0.0 sq. mi. **Elev:** 1116 ft.
In northwestern PA, 15 mi. southwest of Oil City. Settled c. 1798; laid out in 1839.
Name origin: For James K. Polk (1795–1849), eleventh U.S. president.

President
Township
Lat: 41-27-02 N **Long:** 79-33-36 W
Pop: 501 (1990) **Pop Density:** 13.4
Land: 37.4 sq. mi.; **Water:** 1.1 sq. mi.

Richland
Township
Lat: 41-14-45 N **Long:** 79-40-39 W
Pop: 775 (1990) **Pop Density:** 34.9
Land: 22.2 sq. mi.; **Water:** 0.2 sq. mi.

Rockland
Township
Lat: 41-17-08 N **Long:** 79-44-48 W
Pop: 1,320 (1990) **Pop Density:** 26.6
Land: 49.7 sq. mi.; **Water:** 0.0 sq. mi.

Rouseville
Borough
ZIP: 16344 **Lat:** 41-28-15 N **Long:** 79-41-09 W
Pop: 583 (1990); 734 (1980) **Pop Density:** 647.8
Land: 0.9 sq. mi.; **Water:** 0.0 sq. mi. **Elev:** 1035 ft.

Sandycreek
Township
Lat: 41-21-14 N **Long:** 79-50-41 W
Pop: 2,495 (1990) **Pop Density:** 140.2
Land: 17.8 sq. mi.; **Water:** 1.2 sq. mi.

Scrubgrass
Township
Lat: 41-13-15 N **Long:** 79-47-16 W
Pop: 673 (1990) **Pop Density:** 26.2
Land: 25.7 sq. mi.; **Water:** 1.7 sq. mi.

Sugarcreek
Borough
ZIP: 16323 **Lat:** 41-26-22 N **Long:** 79-48-41 W
Pop: 5,532 (1990); 5,954 (1980) **Pop Density:** 147.9
Land: 37.4 sq. mi.; **Water:** 0.5 sq. mi. **Elev:** 1035 ft.
In northwestern PA, 10 mi. west of Oil Creek. Incorporated in 1968.

Utica
Borough
ZIP: 16362 **Lat:** 41-26-13 N **Long:** 79-57-27 W
Pop: 242 (1990); 255 (1980) **Pop Density:** 186.2
Land: 1.3 sq. mi.; **Water:** 0.0 sq. mi. **Elev:** 1150 ft.

Victory
Township
Lat: 41-18-08 N **Long:** 79-53-31 W
Pop: 365 (1990) **Pop Density:** 18.3
Land: 19.9 sq. mi.; **Water:** 0.7 sq. mi.

Warren County
County Seat: Warren (ZIP: 16365)

Pop: 45,050 (1990); 47,449 (1980) **Pop Density:** 51.0
Land: 883.5 sq. mi.; **Water:** 14.4 sq. mi. **Area Code:** 814
On northern border of western PA, southeast of Erie; organized Mar 12, 1800 from Allegheny and Lycoming counties.
Name origin: For Gen. Joseph Warren (1741–75), Revolutionary War patriot and member of the Continental Congress who dispatched Paul Revere (1735–1818) on his famous ride.

Bear Lake
Borough
ZIP: 16402 **Lat:** 41-59-34 N **Long:** 79-30-03 W
Pop: 193 (1990); 249 (1980) **Pop Density:** 275.7
Land: 0.7 sq. mi.; **Water:** 0.0 sq. mi. **Elev:** 1552 ft.

Brokenstraw
Township
Lat: 41-50-44 N **Long:** 79-19-09 W
Pop: 1,962 (1990) **Pop Density:** 50.8
Land: 38.6 sq. mi.; **Water:** 0.2 sq. mi.
Name origin: A transliteration of the Indian name for the area where a tall stiff prairie grass grew. In autumn, the grass became brittle, broke off, and fell over. Previously called Irvine Flats.

Cherry Grove
Township
Lat: 41-40-53 N **Long:** 79-08-26 W
Pop: 155 (1990) **Pop Density:** 3.3
Land: 46.9 sq. mi.; **Water:** 0.0 sq. mi.

Clarendon
Borough
ZIP: 16313 **Lat:** 41-46-50 N **Long:** 79-05-47 W
Pop: 650 (1990); 776 (1980) **Pop Density:** 1625.0
Land: 0.4 sq. mi.; **Water:** 0.0 sq. mi. **Elev:** 1395 ft.
Laid out c. 1872.
Name origin: For Thomas Clarendon, owner of a tannery and large saw-mill.

Columbus
Township
ZIP: 16405 **Lat:** 41-56-37 N **Long:** 79-33-31 W
Pop: 1,776 (1990) **Pop Density:** 43.7
Land: 40.6 sq. mi.; **Water:** 0.0 sq. mi.
Name origin: For Christopher Columbus (1451–1506).

Conewango
Township
Lat: 41-52-28 N **Long:** 79-12-01 W
Pop: 4,475 (1990) **Pop Density:** 149.2
Land: 30.0 sq. mi.; **Water:** 0.5 sq. mi.
In northwestern PA, southeast of Erie.
Name origin: For Conewango Creek, which forms its eastern

border; a variant of the Indian term probably meaning 'at the rapids.'

Deerfield
Township
Lat: 41-44-07 N Long: 79-22-15 W
Pop: 274 (1990) Pop Density: 6.4
Land: 42.9 sq. mi.; Water: 0.5 sq. mi.

Eldred
Township
Lat: 41-44-32 N Long: 79-32-56 W
Pop: 669 (1990) Pop Density: 18.5
Land: 36.1 sq. mi.; Water: 0.0 sq. mi.

Elk
Township
Lat: 41-56-19 N Long: 79-00-04 W
Pop: 541 (1990) Pop Density: 13.1
Land: 41.3 sq. mi.; Water: 2.6 sq. mi.

Farmington
Township
Lat: 41-57-40 N Long: 79-13-52 W
Pop: 1,287 (1990) Pop Density: 37.7
Land: 34.1 sq. mi.; Water: 0.0 sq. mi.

Freehold
Township
Lat: 41-57-05 N Long: 79-26-55 W
Pop: 1,318 (1990) Pop Density: 37.0
Land: 35.6 sq. mi.; Water: 0.0 sq. mi.

Glade
Township
Lat: 41-52-13 N Long: 79-03-41 W
Pop: 2,372 (1990) Pop Density: 67.0
Land: 35.4 sq. mi.; Water: 0.9 sq. mi.

Limestone
Township
Lat: 41-39-36 N Long: 79-20-46 W
Pop: 359 (1990) Pop Density: 11.5
Land: 31.1 sq. mi.; Water: 0.4 sq. mi.

Mead
Township
Lat: 41-48-46 N Long: 79-01-11 W
Pop: 1,579 (1990) Pop Density: 20.1
Land: 78.5 sq. mi.; Water: 7.3 sq. mi.

Pine Grove
Township
Lat: 41-57-21 N Long: 79-07-39 W
Pop: 2,756 (1990) Pop Density: 69.4
Land: 39.7 sq. mi.; Water: 0.3 sq. mi.

Pittsfield
Township
ZIP: 16340 Lat: 41-49-36 N Long: 79-25-21 W
Pop: 1,543 (1990) Pop Density: 27.8
Land: 55.6 sq. mi.; Water: 0.0 sq. mi.

Pleasant
Township
Lat: 41-47-41 N Long: 79-11-48 W
Pop: 2,663 (1990) Pop Density: 77.6
Land: 34.3 sq. mi.; Water: 0.7 sq. mi.

Sheffield
Township
ZIP: 16347 Lat: 41-41-13 N Long: 79-01-15 W
Pop: 2,382 (1990) Pop Density: 40.6
Land: 58.7 sq. mi.; Water: 0.0 sq. mi.
In northwestern PA, 10 mi. southeast of Warren.

Southwest
Township
Lat: 41-40-00 N Long: 79-33-14 W
Pop: 626 (1990) Pop Density: 18.4
Land: 34.1 sq. mi.; Water: 0.0 sq. mi.

Spring Creek
Township
ZIP: 16436 Lat: 41-50-43 N Long: 79-32-22 W
Pop: 843 (1990) Pop Density: 17.3
Land: 48.7 sq. mi.; Water: 0.1 sq. mi.

Sugar Grove
Township
Lat: 41-56-53 N Long: 79-20-04 W
Pop: 1,745 (1990) Pop Density: 49.2
Land: 35.5 sq. mi.; Water: 0.0 sq. mi. Elev: 1400 ft.

*Sugar Grove
Borough
ZIP: 16350 Lat: 41-59-00 N Long: 79-20-23 W
Pop: 604 (1990); 630 (1980) Pop Density: 549.1
Land: 1.1 sq. mi.; Water: 0.0 sq. mi.

Tidioute
Borough
ZIP: 16351 Lat: 41-41-00 N Long: 79-24-07 W
Pop: 791 (1990); 844 (1980) Pop Density: 719.1
Land: 1.1 sq. mi.; Water: 0.3 sq. mi. Elev: 1114 ft.

Triumph
Township
Lat: 41-40-31 N Long: 79-27-09 W
Pop: 314 (1990) Pop Density: 11.1
Land: 28.4 sq. mi.; Water: 0.2 sq. mi. Elev: 1680 ft.

Warren
Borough
ZIP: 16365 Lat: 41-50-37 N Long: 79-08-38 W
Pop: 11,122 (1990) Pop Density: 3835.2
Land: 2.9 sq. mi.; Water: 0.2 sq. mi. Elev: 1200 ft.
In northwestern PA on the Allegheny River near the mouth of Conewago Creek, 20 mi. south of Jamestown, NY. Laid out in 1795; incorporated Apr 3, 1832.
Name origin: For Gen. Joseph Warren (1741–75), hero of the American Revolution.

Watson
Township
Lat: 41-42-29 N Long: 79-15-59 W
Pop: 276 (1990) Pop Density: 5.6
Land: 49.6 sq. mi.; Water: 0.3 sq. mi.

Youngsville
Borough
ZIP: 16371 Lat: 41-51-06 N Long: 79-18-56 W
Pop: 1,775 (1990); 2,006 (1980) Pop Density: 1365.4
Land: 1.3 sq. mi.; Water: 0.0 sq. mi. Elev: 1200 ft.
In northwestern PA, 10 mi. west of Warren. Settled in 1795 by John McKinney.
Name origin: For Matthew Young, who taught school from his tent here beginning in 1796.

Washington County
County Seat: Washington (ZIP: 15301)

Pop: 204,584 (1990); 217,074 (1980)
Land: 857.1 sq. mi.; **Water:** 3.9 sq. mi.

Pop Density: 238.7
Area Code: 412

On western border of PA, southwest of Pittsburgh; organized Mar 28, 1781 from Westmoreland County.

Name origin: For George Washington (1732–99), commander-in-chief of the Revolutionary forces at the time the county was formed; later the first U.S. president.

Allenport
Borough
ZIP: 15412   **Lat:** 40-05-27 N **Long:** 79-51-24 W
Pop: 595 (1990); 735 (1980)   **Pop Density:** 283.3
Land: 2.1 sq. mi.; **Water:** 0.2 sq. mi.   **Elev:** 767 ft.

Amwell
Township
Lat: 40-04-52 N **Long:** 80-11-37 W
Pop: 4,176 (1990)   **Pop Density:** 93.2
Land: 44.8 sq. mi.; **Water:** 0.0 sq. mi.

Baidland
CDP
Lat: 40-11-20 N **Long:** 79-57-18 W
Pop: 1,620 (1990)   **Pop Density:** 810.0
Land: 2.0 sq. mi.; **Water:** 0.0 sq. mi.

Beallsville
Borough
ZIP: 15313   **Lat:** 40-03-30 N **Long:** 80-01-59 W
Pop: 530 (1990); 588 (1980)   **Pop Density:** 220.8
Land: 2.4 sq. mi.; **Water:** 0.0 sq. mi.   **Elev:** 1136 ft.

Bentleyville
Borough
ZIP: 15314   **Lat:** 40-07-04 N **Long:** 80-00-13 W
Pop: 2,673 (1990); 2,525 (1980)   **Pop Density:** 722.4
Land: 3.7 sq. mi.; **Water:** 0.0 sq. mi.   **Elev:** 1100 ft.

In southwestern PA, about 25 mi. south of Pittsburgh.
Name origin: For Sheshbazzar Bentley, Jr., who laid out the town in 1816.

Blaine
Township
Lat: 40-10-33 N **Long:** 80-23-57 W
Pop: 682 (1990)   **Pop Density:** 57.3
Land: 11.9 sq. mi.; **Water:** 0.0 sq. mi.

Buffalo
Township
Lat: 40-08-57 N **Long:** 80-20-37 W
Pop: 2,148 (1990)   **Pop Density:** 105.8
Land: 20.3 sq. mi.; **Water:** 0.0 sq. mi.

Burgettstown
Borough
ZIP: 15021   **Lat:** 40-22-52 N **Long:** 80-23-32 W
Pop: 1,634 (1990); 1,867 (1980)   **Pop Density:** 2723.3
Land: 0.6 sq. mi.; **Water:** 0.0 sq. mi.   **Elev:** 989 ft.

In southwestern PA, 20 mi. west of Pittsburgh. Laid out in 1795 by George Burgett.
Name origin: For Fort Burgett, which was erected here during the Revolutionary War by George Burgett's father, Sebastian Burgett, a native of Germany.

California
Borough
ZIP: 15419   **Lat:** 40-03-58 N **Long:** 79-54-38 W
Pop: 5,748 (1990); 5,703 (1980)   **Pop Density:** 522.5
Land: 11.0 sq. mi.; **Water:** 0.2 sq. mi.   **Elev:** 1000 ft.

In southwestern PA, 40 mi. south of Pittsburgh. Laid out in 1849; annexed to East Pike Run Township 1954.
Name origin: For the western state.

Canonsburg
Borough
ZIP: 15317   **Lat:** 40-15-49 N **Long:** 80-11-12 W
Pop: 9,200 (1990); 10,459 (1980)   **Pop Density:** 4000.0
Land: 2.3 sq. mi.; **Water:** 0.0 sq. mi.   **Elev:** 1000 ft.

In southwestern PA, 17 mi. southwest of Pittsburgh. Settled 1773; laid out 1787.
Name origin: For Col. John Canon, militia officer and member of the state assembly.

Canton
Township
ZIP: 15301   **Lat:** 40-11-55 N **Long:** 80-17-58 W
Pop: 9,256 (1990)   **Pop Density:** 621.2
Land: 14.9 sq. mi.; **Water:** 0.0 sq. mi.

Carroll
Township
ZIP: 15063   **Lat:** 40-10-43 N **Long:** 79-55-44 W
Pop: 6,210 (1990)   **Pop Density:** 460.0
Land: 13.5 sq. mi.; **Water:** 0.3 sq. mi.

Cecil
Township
ZIP: 15321   **Lat:** 40-18-59 N **Long:** 80-11-47 W
Pop: 8,948 (1990)   **Pop Density:** 340.2
Land: 26.3 sq. mi.; **Water:** 0.1 sq. mi.

Centerville
Borough
ZIP: 15417   **Lat:** 40-01-50 N **Long:** 79-57-33 W
Pop: 3,842 (1990); 4,207 (1980)   **Pop Density:** 291.1
Land: 13.2 sq. mi.; **Water:** 0.4 sq. mi.   **Elev:** 1200 ft.

Laid out in 1821.

Charleroi
Borough
ZIP: 15022   **Lat:** 40-08-20 N **Long:** 79-54-01 W
Pop: 5,014 (1990); 5,717 (1980)   **Pop Density:** 6267.5
Land: 0.8 sq. mi.; **Water:** 0.1 sq. mi.   **Elev:** 780 ft.

In southwestern PA, south of Pittsburgh. Laid out 1890. Glass manufacturing region.
Name origin: For Charleroi, an industrial town in Belgium.

Chartiers
Township
ZIP: 15342   **Lat:** 40-15-05 N **Long:** 80-15-00 W
Pop: 7,603 (1990)   **Pop Density:** 310.3
Land: 24.5 sq. mi.; **Water:** 0.0 sq. mi.

Claysville
Borough
ZIP: 15323   **Lat:** 40-07-14 N **Long:** 80-24-47 W
Pop: 962 (1990); 1,029 (1980)   **Pop Density:** 3206.7
Land: 0.3 sq. mi.; **Water:** 0.0 sq. mi.   **Elev:** 1149 ft.

Name origin: Named by John Purviance, town founder, for Henry Clay, probably because he championed both the National Highway and a protective tariff on coal, once the comunity's chief support.

Coal Center
Borough
ZIP: 15423   **Lat:** 40-04-11 N **Long:** 79-54-04 W
Pop: 184 (1990); 255 (1980)   **Pop Density:** 1840.0
Land: 0.1 sq. mi.; **Water:** 0.0 sq. mi.   **Elev:** 780 ft.

Cokeburg
Borough
ZIP: 15324 Lat: 40-05-54 N Long: 80-03-58 W
Pop: 724 (1990); 796 (1980) Pop Density: 1810.0
Land: 0.4 sq. mi.; Water: 0.0 sq. mi. Elev: 1100 ft.

Cross Creek
Township
Lat: 40-17-42 N Long: 80-24-47 W
Pop: 1,727 (1990) Pop Density: 62.6
Land: 27.6 sq. mi.; Water: 0.0 sq. mi.

Deemston
Borough
ZIP: 15333 Lat: 40-01-55 N Long: 80-01-36 W
Pop: 770 (1990); 829 (1980) Pop Density: 80.2
Land: 9.6 sq. mi.; Water: 0.0 sq. mi. Elev: 1143 ft.

Donegal
Township
Lat: 40-08-11 N Long: 80-28-18 W
Pop: 2,347 (1990) Pop Density: 56.7
Land: 41.4 sq. mi.; Water: 0.1 sq. mi.

Donora
Borough
ZIP: 15033 Lat: 40-10-41 N Long: 79-51-48 W
Pop: 5,928 (1990); 7,524 (1980) Pop Density: 3120.0
Land: 1.9 sq. mi.; Water: 0.1 sq. mi. Elev: 900 ft.
In southwestern PA on the west bank of the Monongahela River. Founded 1900.
Name origin: For William H. Donner, president of the town's developing company, and Nora Mellon, wife of Andrew W. Mellon (1855–1937).

Dunlevy
Borough
ZIP: 15432 Lat: 40-06-44 N Long: 79-51-31 W
Pop: 417 (1990); 463 (1980) Pop Density: 834.0
Land: 0.5 sq. mi.; Water: 0.1 sq. mi. Elev: 860 ft.

East Bethlehem
Township
Lat: 39-59-33 N Long: 80-01-23 W
Pop: 2,799 (1990) Pop Density: 548.8
Land: 5.1 sq. mi.; Water: 0.2 sq. mi.

East Finley
Township
Lat: 40-02-57 N Long: 80-23-26 W
Pop: 1,479 (1990) Pop Density: 42.1
Land: 35.1 sq. mi.; Water: 0.0 sq. mi.

East Washington
Borough
ZIP: 15301 Lat: 40-10-25 N Long: 80-13-58 W
Pop: 2,126 (1990); 2,241 (1980) Pop Density: 5315.0
Land: 0.4 sq. mi.; Water: 0.0 sq. mi. Elev: 1204 ft.
In southwestern PA, adjacent to the city of Washington.

Elco
Borough
Lat: 40-05-06 N Long: 79-52-59 W
Pop: 373 (1990); 417 (1980) Pop Density: 1243.3
Land: 0.3 sq. mi.; Water: 0.1 sq. mi. Elev: 760 ft.

Ellsworth
Borough
ZIP: 15331 Lat: 40-06-28 N Long: 80-01-19 W
Pop: 1,048 (1990); 1,228 (1980) Pop Density: 1497.1
Land: 0.7 sq. mi.; Water: 0.0 sq. mi. Elev: 1000 ft.
In southwestern PA in an old coal mining region, 30 mi. south of Pittsburgh.

Fallowfield
Township
Lat: 40-08-31 N Long: 79-57-09 W
Pop: 4,972 (1990) Pop Density: 233.4
Land: 21.3 sq. mi.; Water: 0.0 sq. mi.

Finleyville
Borough
ZIP: 15332 Lat: 40-15-10 N Long: 80-00-07 W
Pop: 446 (1990); 402 (1980) Pop Density: 2230.0
Land: 0.2 sq. mi.; Water: 0.0 sq. mi. Elev: 960 ft.

Fredericktown-Millsboro
CDP
Lat: 39-59-50 N Long: 80-00-18 W
Pop: 1,237 (1990); 1,052 (1980) Pop Density: 687.2
Land: 1.8 sq. mi.; Water: 0.0 sq. mi.

Gastonville
CDP
Lat: 40-15-51 N Long: 80-00-26 W
Pop: 3,090 (1990) Pop Density: 1144.4
Land: 2.7 sq. mi.; Water: 0.0 sq. mi.

Green Hills
Borough
ZIP: 15301 Lat: 40-06-56 N Long: 80-18-31 W
Pop: 21 (1990); 18 (1980) Pop Density: 23.3
Land: 0.9 sq. mi.; Water: 0.0 sq. mi.

Hanover
Township
Lat: 40-26-01 N Long: 80-27-18 W
Pop: 2,883 (1990) Pop Density: 60.6
Land: 47.6 sq. mi.; Water: 0.0 sq. mi.

Hopewell
Township
Lat: 40-14-02 N Long: 80-23-21 W
Pop: 942 (1990) Pop Density: 46.0
Land: 20.5 sq. mi.; Water: 0.0 sq. mi.

Houston
Borough
ZIP: 15342 Lat: 40-14-59 N Long: 80-12-42 W
Pop: 1,445 (1990); 1,568 (1980) Pop Density: 3612.5
Land: 0.4 sq. mi.; Water: 0.0 sq. mi. Elev: 1020 ft.
In southwestern PA, 18 mi. southwest of Pittsburgh.

Independence
Township
Lat: 40-14-08 N Long: 80-28-40 W
Pop: 1,868 (1990) Pop Density: 72.4
Land: 25.8 sq. mi.; Water: 0.0 sq. mi.

Jefferson
Township
Lat: 40-20-08 N Long: 80-28-57 W
Pop: 1,212 (1990) Pop Density: 53.6
Land: 22.6 sq. mi.; Water: 0.0 sq. mi.

Long Branch
Borough
ZIP: 15423 Lat: 40-06-09 N Long: 79-52-44 W
Pop: 482 (1990); 610 (1980) Pop Density: 150.6
Land: 3.2 sq. mi.; Water: 0.0 sq. mi. Elev: 1095 ft.

Marianna
Borough
ZIP: 15345 Lat: 40-00-40 N Long: 80-06-51 W
Pop: 616 (1990); 907 (1980) Pop Density: 308.0
Land: 2.0 sq. mi.; Water: 0.0 sq. mi. Elev: 1051 ft.

McDonald
Borough
ZIP: 15057 Lat: 40-22-07 N Long: 80-14-09 W
Pop: 1,809 (1990); 2,233 (1980) Pop Density: 6030.0
Land: 0.3 sq. mi.; Water: 0.0 sq. mi. Elev: 1000 ft.
Laid out in 1781. Part of the town is also in Allegheny County.
Name origin: For old Fort McDonald, which was built during the Revolutionary War on the land of John McDonald, who settled here in 1775.

McGovern
CDP
Lat: 40-14-25 N Long: 80-13-44 W
Pop: 2,504 (1990) Pop Density: 1391.1
Land: 1.8 sq. mi.; Water: 0.0 sq. mi.

McMurray
CDP
Lat: 40-16-50 N **Long:** 80-05-17 W
Pop: 4,082 (1990) **Pop Density:** 1316.8
Land: 3.1 sq. mi.; **Water:** 0.0 sq. mi.

Midway
Borough
ZIP: 15060 **Lat:** 40-22-06 N **Long:** 80-17-30 W
Pop: 1,043 (1990); 1,187 (1980) **Pop Density:** 2607.5
Land: 0.4 sq. mi.; **Water:** 0.0 sq. mi. **Elev:** 1063 ft.
In southwestern PA.
Name origin: For its location between Pittsburgh and Steubenville, OH.

Monongahela
City
ZIP: 15063 **Lat:** 40-11-54 N **Long:** 79-55-21 W
Pop: 4,928 (1990); 5,950 (1980) **Pop Density:** 2593.7
Land: 1.9 sq. mi.; **Water:** 0.2 sq. mi. **Elev:** 887 ft.
In southwestern PA on the Monongahela River, 18 mi. south of Pittsburgh.
Name origin: For the river, itself named from the Indian term *menaun-gehilla* possibly meaning 'river with the sliding banks.' Previously called Williamsport and Parkinson's Ferry.

Morris
Township
Lat: 40-02-13 N **Long:** 80-17-54 W
Pop: 1,145 (1990) **Pop Density:** 40.3
Land: 28.4 sq. mi.; **Water:** 0.0 sq. mi.

Mount Pleasant
Township
Lat: 40-18-11 N **Long:** 80-18-24 W
Pop: 3,555 (1990) **Pop Density:** 99.9
Land: 35.6 sq. mi.; **Water:** 0.1 sq. mi. **Elev:** 1340 ft.

New Eagle
Borough
ZIP: 15067 **Lat:** 40-12-22 N **Long:** 79-57-16 W
Pop: 2,172 (1990); 2,617 (1980) **Pop Density:** 2172.0
Land: 1.0 sq. mi.; **Water:** 0.1 sq. mi. **Elev:** 950 ft.
In southwestern PA on the Monongahela River, 16 mi. south of Pittsburgh.

North Bethlehem
Township
Lat: 40-06-03 N **Long:** 80-06-24 W
Pop: 1,864 (1990) **Pop Density:** 83.6
Land: 22.3 sq. mi.; **Water:** 0.0 sq. mi.

North Charleroi
Borough
ZIP: 15022 **Lat:** 40-09-01 N **Long:** 79-54-30 W
Pop: 1,562 (1990); 1,760 (1980) **Pop Density:** 5206.7
Land: 0.3 sq. mi.; **Water:** 0.0 sq. mi. **Elev:** 800 ft.

North Franklin
Township
Lat: 40-08-47 N **Long:** 80-15-51 W
Pop: 4,997 (1990) **Pop Density:** 684.5
Land: 7.3 sq. mi.; **Water:** 0.2 sq. mi.

North Strabane
Township
ZIP: 15317 **Lat:** 40-14-07 N **Long:** 80-09-01 W
Pop: 8,157 (1990) **Pop Density:** 298.8
Land: 27.3 sq. mi.; **Water:** 0.1 sq. mi.

Nottingham
Township
Lat: 40-12-34 N **Long:** 80-03-33 W
Pop: 2,303 (1990) **Pop Density:** 113.4
Land: 20.3 sq. mi.; **Water:** 0.0 sq. mi.

Peters
Township
Lat: 40-16-24 N **Long:** 80-04-50 W
Pop: 14,467 (1990) **Pop Density:** 738.1
Land: 19.6 sq. mi.; **Water:** 0.2 sq. mi.

Robinson
Township
Lat: 40-24-16 N **Long:** 80-18-26 W
Pop: 2,160 (1990) **Pop Density:** 101.9
Land: 21.2 sq. mi.; **Water:** 0.1 sq. mi.

Roscoe
Borough
ZIP: 15477 **Lat:** 40-04-39 N **Long:** 79-51-53 W
Pop: 872 (1990); 1,123 (1980) **Pop Density:** 4360.0
Land: 0.2 sq. mi.; **Water:** 0.0 sq. mi. **Elev:** 760 ft.

Smith
Township
Lat: 40-22-22 N **Long:** 80-22-37 W
Pop: 4,844 (1990) **Pop Density:** 140.8
Land: 34.4 sq. mi.; **Water:** 0.0 sq. mi.

Somerset
Township
Lat: 40-08-51 N **Long:** 80-03-34 W
Pop: 2,947 (1990) **Pop Density:** 91.8
Land: 32.1 sq. mi.; **Water:** 0.1 sq. mi.

South Franklin
Township
Lat: 40-06-02 N **Long:** 80-17-22 W
Pop: 3,665 (1990) **Pop Density:** 177.9
Land: 20.6 sq. mi.; **Water:** 0.1 sq. mi.

South Strabane
Township
ZIP: 15301 **Lat:** 40-10-49 N **Long:** 80-11-27 W
Pop: 7,676 (1990) **Pop Density:** 332.3
Land: 23.1 sq. mi.; **Water:** 0.0 sq. mi.

Speers
Borough
ZIP: 15012 **Lat:** 40-07-21 N **Long:** 79-52-48 W
Pop: 1,284 (1990); 1,425 (1980) **Pop Density:** 1284.0
Land: 1.0 sq. mi.; **Water:** 0.1 sq. mi. **Elev:** 1020 ft.
In southwestern PA on the west bank of the Monongahela River, west of Belle Vernon.
Name origin: For Apollos Speers, who is closely identified with the early development of the Monongahela Valley.

Stockdale
Borough
ZIP: 15483 **Lat:** 40-04-59 N **Long:** 79-51-02 W
Pop: 630 (1990); 641 (1980) **Pop Density:** 2100.0
Land: 0.3 sq. mi.; **Water:** 0.0 sq. mi. **Elev:** 765 ft.
Name origin: For the dairy cows that formerly grazed on the land.

Twilight
Borough
ZIP: 15022 **Lat:** 40-06-51 N **Long:** 79-53-25 W
Pop: 252 (1990); 298 (1980) **Pop Density:** 157.5
Land: 1.6 sq. mi.; **Water:** 0.0 sq. mi. **Elev:** 1000 ft.

Union
Township
ZIP: 15332 **Lat:** 40-14-46 N **Long:** 79-58-54 W
Pop: 6,322 (1990) **Pop Density:** 410.5
Land: 15.4 sq. mi.; **Water:** 0.4 sq. mi.

Washington
City
ZIP: 15301 **Lat:** 40-10-27 N **Long:** 80-14-50 W
Pop: 15,864 (1990) **Pop Density:** 5470.3
Land: 2.9 sq. mi.; **Water:** 0.0 sq. mi. **Elev:** 1100 ft.
In southwestern PA, 30 mi. southwest of Pittsburgh. Laid out in 1781; incorporated as borough Feb 12, 1810; chartered as city 1924. County seat.
Name origin: For George Washington (1732–99), first U.S. president. Originally called Catfish's Camp, a Delaware Indian village that was the headquarters of Chief Tingoocqua. Later called Bassett-town to honor a kinsman of David Hoge, the founder. Given its present name in 1781.

West Alexander
Borough
ZIP: 15376   **Lat:** 40-06-14 N **Long:** 80-30-28 W
Pop: 301 (1990); 286 (1980)   **Pop Density:** 1505.0
Land: 0.2 sq. mi.; **Water:** 0.0 sq. mi.   **Elev:** 1173 ft.

West Bethlehem
Township
Lat: 40-02-16 N **Long:** 80-06-48 W
Pop: 1,609 (1990)   **Pop Density:** 72.8
Land: 22.1 sq. mi.; **Water:** 0.0 sq. mi.

West Brownsville
Borough
ZIP: 15417   **Lat:** 40-01-52 N **Long:** 79-53-31 W
Pop: 1,170 (1990); 1,433 (1980)   **Pop Density:** 900.0
Land: 1.3 sq. mi.; **Water:** 0.1 sq. mi.   **Elev:** 1100 ft.

West Finley
Township
ZIP: 15377   **Lat:** 40-01-33 N **Long:** 80-28-02 W
Pop: 972 (1990)   **Pop Density:** 24.9
Land: 39.1 sq. mi.; **Water:** 0.0 sq. mi.

West Middletown
Borough
ZIP: 15379   **Lat:** 40-14-42 N **Long:** 80-25-31 W
Pop: 166 (1990); 215 (1980)   **Pop Density:** 415.0
Land: 0.4 sq. mi.; **Water:** 0.0 sq. mi.   **Elev:** 1333 ft.

West Pike Run
Township
Lat: 40-04-20 N **Long:** 79-58-57 W
Pop: 1,818 (1990)   **Pop Density:** 111.5
Land: 16.3 sq. mi.; **Water:** 0.0 sq. mi.

Wayne County
County Seat: Honesdale (ZIP: 18431)

Pop: 39,944 (1990); 35,237 (1980)   **Pop Density:** 54.8
Land: 729.4 sq. mi.; **Water:** 21.2 sq. mi.   **Area Code:** 717

At the northeastern corner of PA, east of Scranton; organized Mar 21, 1798 from Northampton County.

Name origin: For Gen. Anthony Wayne (1745–1796), PA soldier and statesman, nicknamed "Mad Anthony" for his daring during the Revolutionary War.

Berlin
Township
Lat: 41-34-46 N **Long:** 75-09-43 W
Pop: 1,777 (1990)   **Pop Density:** 46.0
Land: 38.6 sq. mi.; **Water:** 0.9 sq. mi.

Bethany
Borough
ZIP: 18431   **Lat:** 41-36-51 N **Long:** 75-17-20 W
Pop: 238 (1990); 282 (1980)   **Pop Density:** 476.0
Land: 0.5 sq. mi.; **Water:** 0.0 sq. mi.   **Elev:** 1447 ft.

In northeastern PA, near Honesdale. Founded in 1801 by a Quaker, Henry Drinker.

Name origin: For the village in Palestine.

Buckingham
Township
Lat: 41-52-38 N **Long:** 75-17-32 W
Pop: 648 (1990)   **Pop Density:** 14.6
Land: 44.4 sq. mi.; **Water:** 1.2 sq. mi.

Canaan
Township
Lat: 41-34-12 N **Long:** 75-23-33 W
Pop: 1,267 (1990)   **Pop Density:** 70.4
Land: 18.0 sq. mi.; **Water:** 0.8 sq. mi.

Cherry Ridge
Township
Lat: 41-31-38 N **Long:** 75-17-25 W
Pop: 1,600 (1990)   **Pop Density:** 74.4
Land: 21.5 sq. mi.; **Water:** 0.6 sq. mi.

Clinton
Township
Lat: 41-38-15 N **Long:** 75-24-18 W
Pop: 1,582 (1990)   **Pop Density:** 41.1
Land: 38.5 sq. mi.; **Water:** 1.1 sq. mi.

Damascus
Township
ZIP: 18415   **Lat:** 41-41-57 N **Long:** 75-07-47 W
Pop: 3,081 (1990)   **Pop Density:** 39.0
Land: 79.0 sq. mi.; **Water:** 1.4 sq. mi.

Dreher
Township
Lat: 41-17-29 N **Long:** 75-21-13 W
Pop: 1,022 (1990)   **Pop Density:** 68.6
Land: 14.9 sq. mi.; **Water:** 0.1 sq. mi.

Dyberry
Township
Lat: 41-37-55 N **Long:** 75-17-27 W
Pop: 1,223 (1990)   **Pop Density:** 55.1
Land: 22.2 sq. mi.; **Water:** 0.4 sq. mi.

Hawley
Borough
ZIP: 18428   **Lat:** 41-28-35 N **Long:** 75-10-40 W
Pop: 1,244 (1990); 1,181 (1980)   **Pop Density:** 2073.3
Land: 0.6 sq. mi.; **Water:** 0.0 sq. mi.   **Elev:** 896 ft.

In northeastern PA, 25 mi. east of Scranton.

Honesdale
Borough
ZIP: 18431   **Lat:** 41-34-37 N **Long:** 75-15-12 W
Pop: 4,972 (1990); 5,128 (1980)   **Pop Density:** 1274.9
Land: 3.9 sq. mi.; **Water:** 0.1 sq. mi.   **Elev:** 970 ft.

In northeastern PA, 24 mi. northeast of Scranton. Laid out in 1827; incorporated Jan 28, 1831.

Name origin: For Philip Hone, mayor of New York City and later president of the Delaware & Hudson Canal Company. He came to the settlement to push construction of a canal that would divert the flow of coal to his city.

Lake
Township
Lat: 41-27-18 N **Long:** 75-22-14 W
Pop: 3,287 (1990)   **Pop Density:** 116.1
Land: 28.3 sq. mi.; **Water:** 1.7 sq. mi.

Lebanon
Township
Lat: 41-43-30 N **Long:** 75-15-48 W
Pop: 479 (1990)   **Pop Density:** 12.8
Land: 37.3 sq. mi.; **Water:** 0.7 sq. mi.

Lehigh
Township
Lat: 41-15-25 N **Long:** 75-25-05 W
Pop: 1,178 (1990)   **Pop Density:** 99.8
Land: 11.8 sq. mi.; **Water:** 0.6 sq. mi.

Manchester
Township
Lat: 41-48-50 N **Long:** 75-11-05 W
Pop: 663 (1990)   **Pop Density:** 14.8
Land: 44.7 sq. mi.; **Water:** 0.8 sq. mi.

Mount Pleasant
Township
Lat: 41-44-17 N   Long: 75-23-16 W
Pop: 1,271 (1990)   Pop Density: 22.5
Land: 56.4 sq. mi.; Water: 0.9 sq. mi.

Oregon
Township
Lat: 41-38-44 N   Long: 75-13-34 W
Pop: 606 (1990)   Pop Density: 34.6
Land: 17.5 sq. mi.; Water: 0.2 sq. mi.

Palmyra
Township
Lat: 41-30-30 N   Long: 75-11-13 W
Pop: 905 (1990)   Pop Density: 57.6
Land: 15.7 sq. mi.; Water: 0.3 sq. mi.

Paupack
Township
Lat: 41-26-28 N   Long: 75-15-28 W
Pop: 1,696 (1990)   Pop Density: 60.4
Land: 28.1 sq. mi.; Water: 5.1 sq. mi.
Name origin: A short form from the Wallenpaupack Creek, which forms part of the county border. An Indian term possibly meaning 'deep, stagnant water.'

Preston
Township
Lat: 41-50-20 N   Long: 75-24-17 W
Pop: 1,044 (1990)   Pop Density: 20.6
Land: 50.7 sq. mi.; Water: 2.0 sq. mi.

Prompton
Borough
ZIP: 18456   Lat: 41-35-23 N   Long: 75-19-46 W
Pop: 238 (1990); 249 (1980)   Pop Density: 148.8
Land: 1.6 sq. mi.; Water: 0.1 sq. mi.   Elev: 1093 ft.

Salem
Township
Lat: 41-24-15 N   Long: 75-22-06 W
Pop: 2,933 (1990)   Pop Density: 96.2
Land: 30.5 sq. mi.; Water: 0.7 sq. mi.

Scott
Township
Lat: 41-57-29 N   Long: 75-24-20 W
Pop: 590 (1990)   Pop Density: 13.3
Land: 44.3 sq. mi.; Water: 0.7 sq. mi.

South Canaan
Township
Lat: 41-30-56 N   Long: 75-23-47 W
Pop: 1,320 (1990)   Pop Density: 47.7
Land: 27.7 sq. mi.; Water: 0.5 sq. mi.

Starrucca
Borough
ZIP: 18462   Lat: 41-54-09 N   Long: 75-27-15 W
Pop: 199 (1990); 216 (1980)   Pop Density: 26.5
Land: 7.5 sq. mi.; Water: 0.0 sq. mi.   Elev: 1309 ft.

Sterling
Township
ZIP: 18463   Lat: 41-19-36 N   Long 75-24-17 W
Pop: 974 (1990)   Pop Density: 35.5
Land: 27.4 sq. mi.; Water: 0.1 sq. mi.

Texas
Township
Lat: 41-33-14 N   Long 75-15-38 W
Pop: 2,570 (1990)   Pop Density: 177.2
Land: 14.5 sq. mi.; Water: 0.1 sq. mi.

Waymart
Borough
ZIP: 18472   Lat: 41-35-13 N   Long 75-24-33 W
Pop: 1,337 (1990); 1,248 (1980)   Pop Density: 431.3
Land: 3.1 sq. mi.; Water: 0.1 sq. mi.   Elev: 1400 ft.

Westmoreland County
County Seat: Greensburg (ZIP: 15601)

Pop: 370,321 (1990); 392,184 (1980)   Pop Density: 362.1
Land: 1022.6 sq. mi.; Water: 13.9 sq. mi.   Area Code: 412

In southwestern PA, east of Pittsburgh; organized Feb 26, 1773 (prior to statehood) from Bedford County.
Name origin: For the former county of Westmorland in northwest England, with spelling change.

Adamsburg
Borough
ZIP: 15611   Lat: 40-18-37 N   Long: 79-39-16 W
Pop: 257 (1990); 236 (1980)   Pop Density: 856.7
Land: 0.3 sq. mi.; Water: 0.0 sq. mi.   Elev: 1180 ft.
In southwestern PA near Jeannette.
Name origin: For John Adams (1735–1826), second U.S. president.

Allegheny
Township
ZIP: 15656   Lat: 40-37-06 N   Long: 79-38-35 W
Pop: 7,895 (1990)   Pop Density: 256.3
Land: 30.8 sq. mi.; Water: 0.7 sq. mi.
Name origin: For the river.

Arnold
City
ZIP: 15068   Lat: 40-34-44 N   Long: 79-45-53 W
Pop: 6,113 (1990); 6,853 (1980)   Pop Density: 8732.9
Land: 0.7 sq. mi.; Water: 0.0 sq. mi.   Elev: 877 ft.
In southwestern PA, northeast of Pittsburgh on the Allegheny River. Incorporated as a borough 1896.

Name origin: For Andrew Arnold, owner of the town site at the time of the first settlement.

Arona
Borough
ZIP: 15617   Lat: 40-16-05 N   Long: 79-39-26 W
Pop: 397 (1990); 446 (1980)   Pop Density: 794.0
Land: 0.5 sq. mi.; Water: 0.0 sq. mi.   Elev: 1020 ft.

Avonmore
Borough
ZIP: 15618   Lat: 40-31-36 N   Long: 79-28-11 W
Pop: 1,089 (1990); 1,234 (1980)   Pop Density: 726.0
Land: 1.5 sq. mi.; Water: 0.1 sq. mi.   Elev: 880 ft.

Bell
Township
Lat: 40-30-39 N   Long: 79-31-25 W
Pop: 2,353 (1990)   Pop Density: 111.0
Land: 21.2 sq. mi.; Water: 0.7 sq. mi.

Bolivar
Borough
ZIP: 15923   Lat: 40-23-41 N   Long: 79-09-07 W
Pop: 544 (1990); 706 (1980)   Pop Density: 2720.0
Land: 0.2 sq. mi.; Water: 0.0 sq. mi.   Elev: 1040 ft.

Calumet-Norvelt
CDP
Lat: 40-12-26 N **Long:** 79-29-35 W
Pop: 1,790 (1990); 2,541 (1980)   **Pop Density:** 1193.3
Land: 1.5 sq. mi.; **Water:** 0.0 sq. mi.

Cook
Township
Lat: 40-10-00 N **Long:** 79-17-19 W
Pop: 2,033 (1990)   **Pop Density:** 43.7
Land: 46.5 sq. mi.; **Water:** 0.0 sq. mi.

Delmont
Borough
ZIP: 15626   **Lat:** 40-24-50 N **Long:** 79-34-24 W
Pop: 2,041 (1990); 2,159 (1980)   **Pop Density:** 1855.5
Land: 1.1 sq. mi.; **Water:** 0.0 sq. mi.   **Elev:** 1315 ft.

Derry
Township
ZIP: 15627   **Lat:** 40-22-35 N **Long:** 79-19-13 W
Pop: 15,446 (1990)   **Pop Density:** 163.4
Land: 94.5 sq. mi.; **Water:** 2.8 sq. mi.

*Derry
Borough
ZIP: 15627   **Lat:** 40-19-59 N **Long:** 79-18-06 W
Pop: 2,950 (1990); 3,072 (1980)   **Pop Density:** 3687.5
Land: 0.8 sq. mi.; **Water:** 0.0 sq. mi.   **Elev:** 1175 ft.
In southwestern PA, 35 mi. east of Pittsburgh.
Name origin: For the northern Irish town that was known as Derry before the British took control and renamed it Londonderry.

Donegal
Township
ZIP: 15628   **Lat:** 40-06-37 N **Long:** 79-19-53 W
Pop: 2,419 (1990)   **Pop Density:** 48.9
Land: 49.5 sq. mi.; **Water:** 0.1 sq. mi.

*Donegal
Borough
ZIP: 15628   **Lat:** 40-06-46 N **Long:** 79-22-57 W
Pop: 212 (1990); 212 (1980)   **Pop Density:** 706.7
Land: 0.3 sq. mi.; **Water:** 0.0 sq. mi.   **Elev:** 1814 ft.

East Huntingdon
Township
ZIP: 15612   **Lat:** 40-08-28 N **Long:** 79-35-55 W
Pop: 7,708 (1990)   **Pop Density:** 235.0
Land: 32.8 sq. mi.; **Water:** 0.0 sq. mi.

East Vandergrift
Borough
ZIP: 15629   **Lat:** 40-35-50 N **Long:** 79-33-46 W
Pop: 787 (1990); 955 (1980)   **Pop Density:** 7870.0
Land: 0.1 sq. mi.; **Water:** 0.0 sq. mi.   **Elev:** 860 ft.

Export
Borough
ZIP: 15632   **Lat:** 40-25-07 N **Long:** 79-37-29 W
Pop: 981 (1990); 1,143 (1980)   **Pop Density:** 1962.0
Land: 0.5 sq. mi.; **Water:** 0.0 sq. mi.   **Elev:** 985 ft.

Fairfield
Township
Lat: 40-19-15 N **Long:** 79-08-31 W
Pop: 2,276 (1990)   **Pop Density:** 37.6
Land: 60.5 sq. mi.; **Water:** 0.3 sq. mi.

Greensburg
City
ZIP: 15601   **Lat:** 40-18-39 N **Long:** 79-32-39 W
Pop: 16,318 (1990); 17,558 (1980)   **Pop Density:** 3885.2
Land: 4.2 sq. mi.; **Water:** 0.0 sq. mi.   **Elev:** 1100 ft.
In southwestern PA, 30 mi. east of Pittsburgh. Laid out on the land of Christopher Truby; incorporated as borough Feb 9, 1799, as city 1928.
Name origin: For Gen. Nathanael Greene (1742–86), hero of the American Revolution, under whom many a soldier from Westmoreland County had fought.

Hempfield
Township
ZIP: 15601   **Lat:** 40-17-05 N **Long:** 79-34-57 W
Pop: 42,609 (1990)   **Pop Density:** 556.3
Land: 76.6 sq. mi.; **Water:** 0.2 sq. mi.
In southwestern PA, southeast of Pittsburgh.

Hunker
Borough
ZIP: 15639   **Lat:** 40-12-14 N **Long:** 79-36-55 W
Pop: 328 (1990); 359 (1980)   **Pop Density:** 820.0
Land: 0.4 sq. mi.; **Water:** 0.0 sq. mi.   **Elev:** 935 ft.

Hyde Park
Borough
ZIP: 15641   **Lat:** 40-37-55 N **Long:** 79-35-20 W
Pop: 542 (1990); 633 (1980)   **Pop Density:** 2710.0
Land: 0.2 sq. mi.; **Water:** 0.1 sq. mi.   **Elev:** 793 ft.

Irwin
Borough
ZIP: 15642   **Lat:** 40-19-33 N **Long:** 79-41-58 W
Pop: 4,604 (1990); 4,995 (1980)   **Pop Density:** 5115.6
Land: 0.9 sq. mi.; **Water:** 0.0 sq. mi.   **Elev:** 992 ft.
In southwestern PA, 20 mi. southeast of Pittsburgh.

Jeannette
City
ZIP: 15644   **Lat:** 40-19-38 N **Long:** 79-36-50 W
Pop: 11,221 (1990); 13,106 (1980)   **Pop Density:** 4675.4
Land: 2.4 sq. mi.; **Water:** 0.0 sq. mi.   **Elev:** 1040 ft.
In southwestern PA, 23 mi. southeast of Pittsburgh.
Name origin: For the wife of H. Sellers McKee. He helped to establish a glass works in 1889 that led to the transformation of a farm site into an industrial city.

Latrobe
Borough
ZIP: 15650   **Lat:** 40-18-43 N **Long:** 79-22-57 W
Pop: 9,265 (1990); 10,799 (1980)   **Pop Density:** 4211.4
Land: 2.2 sq. mi.; **Water:** 0.1 sq. mi.   **Elev:** 1020 ft.
In southwestern PA on Loyalhanna Creek, 41 mi. southeast of Pittsburgh.
Name origin: For Benjamin Henry Latrobe, Jr., son of the "father of U.S. architecture."

Laurel Mountain
Borough
ZIP: 15655   **Lat:** 40-12-40 N **Long:** 79-11-05 W
Pop: 195 (1990)   **Pop Density:** 1950.0
Land: 0.1 sq. mi.; **Water:** 0.0 sq. mi.

Lawson Heights
CDP
Lat: 40-17-31 N **Long:** 79-23-17 W
Pop: 2,464 (1990); 2,626 (1980)   **Pop Density:** 1642.7
Land: 1.5 sq. mi.; **Water:** 0.0 sq. mi.

Ligonier
Township
ZIP: 15658   **Lat:** 40-14-18 N **Long:** 79-12-44 W
Pop: 6,979 (1990)   **Pop Density:** 76.0
Land: 91.8 sq. mi.; **Water:** 0.3 sq. mi.

*Ligonier
Borough
ZIP: 15658   **Lat:** 40-14-40 N **Long:** 79-14-14 W
Pop: 1,638 (1990); 1,917 (1980)   **Pop Density:** 3276.0
Land: 0.5 sq. mi.; **Water:** 0.0 sq. mi.   **Elev:** 1195 ft.
Laid out in 1816.
Name origin: For Fort Ligonier, erected in 1758 by Col. Henry Bouquet and named for a noted English soldier of French extraction, Field Marshal Sir John Louis Ligonier.

Lower Burrell
City
ZIP: 15068   **Lat:** 40-34-56 N **Long:** 79-42-46 W
Pop: 12,251 (1990); 13,200 (1980)   **Pop Density:** 1056.1
Land: 11.6 sq. mi.; **Water:** 0.3 sq. mi.   **Elev:** 840 ft.
In southeastern PA, a northern suburb of Pittsburgh.

Loyalhanna
Township
ZIP: 15661　　**Lat:** 40-27-14 N　**Long:** 79-26-51 W
Pop: 2,171 (1990)　　**Pop Density:** 109.1
Land: 19.9 sq. mi.; **Water:** 2.0 sq. mi.
Name origin: Indian name for the stream running through the township, probably meaning 'middle river.'

Lynnwood-Pricedale
CDP
Lat: 40-08-04 N　**Long:** 79-51-08 W
Pop: 1,598 (1990); 1,741 (1980)　　**Pop Density:** 1997.5
Land: 0.8 sq. mi.; **Water:** 0.0 sq. mi.
Part of the town is also in Fayette County.

Madison
Borough
ZIP: 15663　　**Lat:** 40-14-47 N　**Long:** 79-40-22 W
Pop: 539 (1990); 531 (1980)　　**Pop Density:** 1078.0
Land: 0.5 sq. mi.; **Water:** 0.0 sq. mi.　　**Elev:** 1132 ft.

Manor
Borough
ZIP: 15665　　**Lat:** 40-20-47 N　**Long:** 79-40-14 W
Pop: 2,627 (1990); 2,235 (1980)　　**Pop Density:** 1313.5
Land: 2.0 sq. mi.; **Water:** 0.0 sq. mi.　　**Elev:** 920 ft.
Name origin: For one of the manors built here that was owned by the Penn family.

McChesneytown-Loyalhanna
CDP
Lat: 40-18-46 N　**Long:** 79-21-21 W
Pop: 3,708 (1990); 4,108 (1980)　　**Pop Density:** 1612.2
Land: 2.3 sq. mi.; **Water:** 0.0 sq. mi.

Monessen
City
ZIP: 15062　　**Lat:** 40-09-08 N　**Long:** 79-52-55 W
Pop: 9,901 (1990); 11,928 (1980)　　**Pop Density:** 3414.1
Land: 2.9 sq. mi.; **Water:** 0.2 sq. mi.　　**Elev:** 920 ft.
In southwestern PA on the Monongahela River, 22 mi. south of Pittsburgh.
Name origin: A combination of the first syllable of Monongahela with Essen, the name of an iron town in Germany that is the home of the Krupp works.

Mount Pleasant
Township
ZIP: 15666　　**Lat:** 40-10-51 N　**Long:** 79-28-36 W
Pop: 11,341 (1990)　　**Pop Density:** 203.6
Land: 55.7 sq. mi.; **Water:** 0.2 sq. mi.
In southwestern PA, 21 mi. northeast of Uniontown.

*Mount Pleasant
Borough
ZIP: 15666　　**Lat:** 40-09-01 N　**Long:** 79-32-38 W
Pop: 4,787 (1990); 5,354 (1980)　　**Pop Density:** 4351.8
Land: 1.1 sq. mi.; **Water:** 0.0 sq. mi.　　**Elev:** 1223 ft.

Murrysville
Borough
ZIP: 15668　　**Lat:** 40-26-29 N　**Long:** 79-39-21 W
Pop: 17,240 (1990); 16,036 (1980)　　**Pop Density:** 467.2
Land: 36.9 sq. mi.; **Water:** 0.0 sq. mi.　　**Elev:** 900 ft.

New Alexandria
Borough
ZIP: 15670　　**Lat:** 40-23-36 N　**Long:** 79-25-06 W
Pop: 571 (1990); 697 (1980)　　**Pop Density:** 815.7
Land: 0.7 sq. mi.; **Water:** 0.2 sq. mi.　　**Elev:** 996 ft.

New Florence
Borough
ZIP: 15944　　**Lat:** 40-22-44 N　**Long:** 79-04-29 W
Pop: 854 (1990); 855 (1980)　　**Pop Density:** 2846.7
Land: 0.3 sq. mi.; **Water:** 0.0 sq. mi.　　**Elev:** 1086 ft.

New Kensington
City
ZIP: 15068　　**Lat:** 40-34-11 N　**Long:** 79-45-02 W
Pop: 15,894 (1990); 17,660 (1980)　　**Pop Density:** 3973.5
Land: 4.0 sq. mi.; **Water:** 0.3 sq. mi.　　**Elev:** 960 ft.
In southwestern PA on the Allegheny River, 16 mi. northeast of Pittsburgh.
Name origin: For the London district of Kensington.

New Stanton
Borough
ZIP: 15672　　**Lat:** 40-13-17 N　**Long:** 79-36-32 W
Pop: 2,081 (1990); 2,600 (1980)　　**Pop Density:** 533.6
Land: 3.9 sq. mi.; **Water:** 0.0 sq. mi.　　**Elev:** 1034 ft.

North Belle Vernon
Borough
ZIP: 15012　　**Lat:** 40-07-55 N　**Long:** 79-51-54 W
Pop: 2,112 (1990); 2,425 (1980)　　**Pop Density:** 5280.0
Land: 0.4 sq. mi.; **Water:** 0.0 sq. mi.　　**Elev:** 940 ft.

North Huntingdon
Township
ZIP: 15642　　**Lat:** 40-19-43 N　**Long:** 79-44-01 W
Pop: 28,158 (1990)　　**Pop Density:** 1027.7
Land: 27.4 sq. mi.; **Water:** 0.0 sq. mi.

North Irwin
Borough
ZIP: 15642　　**Lat:** 40-20-19 N　**Long:** 79-42-40 W
Pop: 956 (1990); 1,016 (1980)　　**Pop Density:** 4780.0
Land: 0.2 sq. mi.; **Water:** 0.0 sq. mi.　　**Elev:** 907 ft.
In southern PA, an eastern suburb of Pittsburgh.

Oklahoma
Borough
ZIP: 15613　　**Lat:** 40-34-51 N　**Long:** 79-34-28 W
Pop: 977 (1990); 1,078 (1980)　　**Pop Density:** 1395.7
Land: 0.7 sq. mi.; **Water:** 0.0 sq. mi.　　**Elev:** 975 ft.

Penn
Township
ZIP: 15675　　**Lat:** 40-22-12 N　**Long:** 79-38-53 W
Pop: 15,945 (1990)　　**Pop Density:** 526.2
Land: 30.3 sq. mi.; **Water:** 0.0 sq. mi.
In southwestern PA, east of Pittsburgh.
Name origin: For William Penn (1644–1718), founder of Pennsylvania.

*Penn
Borough
ZIP: 15675　　**Lat:** 40-19-43 N　**Long:** 79-38-30 W
Pop: 511 (1990); 619 (1980)　　**Pop Density:** 2555.0
Land: 0.2 sq. mi.; **Water:** 0.0 sq. mi.　　**Elev:** 950 ft.
In southwestern PA, an eastern suburb of Pittsburgh.
Name origin: For William Penn (1644–1718), founder of Pennsylvania.

Rostraver
Township
ZIP: 15012　　**Lat:** 40-10-09 N　**Long:** 79-48-14 W
Pop: 11,224 (1990)　　**Pop Density:** 348.6
Land: 32.2 sq. mi.; **Water:** 0.7 sq. mi.

St. Clair
Township
Lat: 40-22-11 N　**Long:** 79-02-36 W
Pop: 1,603 (1990)　　**Pop Density:** 56.4
Land: 28.4 sq. mi.; **Water:** 0.4 sq. mi.

Salem
Township
ZIP: 15601　　**Lat:** 40-24-11 N　**Long:** 79-30-48 W
Pop: 7,282 (1990)　　**Pop Density:** 156.6
Land: 46.5 sq. mi.; **Water:** 1.5 sq. mi.

Scottdale
Borough
ZIP: 15683   **Lat:** 40-06-10 N **Long:** 79-35-23 W
Pop: 5,184 (1990); 5,833 (1980)   **Pop Density:** 4320.0
Land: 1.2 sq. mi.; **Water:** 0.0 sq. mi.   **Elev:** 1020 ft.

In southwestern PA on Jacobs Creek, a southeastern suburb of Pittsburgh.

Name origin: For Thomas A. Scott, president of the Pennsylvania Railroad, after a spur was extended to the town in 1873. Originally called Fountain Hills.

Seward
Borough
ZIP: 15954   **Lat:** 40-24-45 N **Long:** 79-01-18 W
Pop: 522 (1990); 675 (1980)   **Pop Density:** 2610.0
Land: 0.2 sq. mi.; **Water:** 0.0 sq. mi.   **Elev:** 1139 ft.

Sewickley
Township
ZIP: 15637   **Lat:** 40-15-15 N **Long:** 79-44-01 W
Pop: 6,642 (1990)   **Pop Density:** 249.7
Land: 26.6 sq. mi.; **Water:** 0.2 sq. mi.

Smithton
Borough
ZIP: 15479   **Lat:** 40-09-11 N **Long:** 79-44-29 W
Pop: 388 (1990); 559 (1980)   **Pop Density:** 3880.0
Land: 0.1 sq. mi.; **Water:** 0.0 sq. mi.   **Elev:** 795 ft.

South Greensburg
Borough
ZIP: 15601   **Lat:** 40-16-36 N **Long:** 79-32-52 W
Pop: 2,293 (1990); 2,605 (1980)   **Pop Density:** 3275.7
Land: 0.7 sq. mi.; **Water:** 0.0 sq. mi.   **Elev:** 985 ft.

South Huntingdon
Township
ZIP: 15089   **Lat:** 40-10-33 N **Long:** 79-42-00 W
Pop: 6,352 (1990)   **Pop Density:** 140.2
Land: 45.3 sq. mi.; **Water:** 0.4 sq. mi.

Southwest Greensburg
Borough
ZIP: 15601   **Lat:** 40-17-31 N **Long:** 79-32-51 W
Pop: 2,456 (1990); 2,898 (1980)   **Pop Density:** 6140.0
Land: 0.4 sq. mi.; **Water:** 0.0 sq. mi.   **Elev:** 995 ft.

Sutersville
Borough
ZIP: 15083   **Lat:** 40-14-08 N **Long:** 79-48-09 W
Pop: 755 (1990); 863 (1980)   **Pop Density:** 2516.7
Land: 0.3 sq. mi.; **Water:** 0.0 sq. mi.   **Elev:** 900 ft.

Trafford
Borough
ZIP: 15085   **Lat:** 40-23-06 N **Long:** 79-45-19 W
Pop: 3,255 (1990); 3,662 (1980)   **Pop Density:** 2503.8
Land: 1.3 sq. mi.; **Water:** 0.0 sq. mi.   **Elev:** 900 ft.

In southwestern PA, an eastern suburb of Pittsburgh. Part of the town is also in Allegheny County.

Unity
Township
ZIP: 15650   **Lat:** 40-16-53 N **Long:** 79-25-30 W
Pop: 20,109 (1990)   **Pop Density:** 300.1
Land: 67.0 sq. mi.; **Water:** 0.7 sq. mi.

Upper Burrell
Township
Lat: 40-32-53 N **Long:** 79-40-10 W
Pop: 2,258 (1990)   **Pop Density:** 148.6
Land: 15.2 sq. mi.; **Water:** 0.0 sq. mi.

Vandergrift
Borough
ZIP: 15690   **Lat:** 40-35-58 N **Long:** 79-34-27 W
Pop: 5,904 (1990); 6,823 (1980)   **Pop Density:** 4541.5
Land: 1.3 sq. mi.; **Water:** 0.1 sq. mi.   **Elev:** 900 ft.

In southwestern PA, 30 mi. northeast of Pittsburgh.

Washington
Township
ZIP: 15613   **Lat:** 40-30-30 N **Long:** 79-36-05 W
Pop: 7,725 (1990)   **Pop Density:** 243.7
Land: 31.7 sq. mi.; **Water:** 0.9 sq. mi.

Name origin: For George Washington (1732–99), first U.S. president.

West Leechburg
Borough
ZIP: 15656   **Lat:** 40-37-55 N **Long:** 79-37-02 W
Pop: 1,359 (1990); 1,395 (1980)   **Pop Density:** 1510.0
Land: 0.9 sq. mi.; **Water:** 0.0 sq. mi.   **Elev:** 1000 ft.

West Newton
Borough
ZIP: 15089   **Lat:** 40-12-30 N **Long:** 79-46-10 W
Pop: 3,152 (1990); 3,387 (1980)   **Pop Density:** 2865.5
Land: 1.1 sq. mi.; **Water:** 0.1 sq. mi.   **Elev:** 800 ft.

Youngstown
Borough
ZIP: 15696   **Lat:** 40-16-51 N **Long:** 79-21-56 W
Pop: 370 (1990); 470 (1980)   **Pop Density:** 3700.0
Land: 0.1 sq. mi.; **Water:** 0.0 sq. mi.   **Elev:** 1100 ft.

Youngwood
Borough
ZIP: 15697   **Lat:** 40-14-37 N **Long:** 79-34-51 W
Pop: 3,372 (1990); 3,749 (1980)   **Pop Density:** 1873.3
Land: 1.8 sq. mi.; **Water:** 0.0 sq. mi.   **Elev:** 989 ft.

In southwestern PA in an industrial area, 30 mi. east of Pittsburgh.

Wyoming County
County Seat: Tunkhannock (ZIP: 18657)

Pop: 28,076 (1990); 26,433 (1980)   **Pop Density:** 70.7
Land: 397.2 sq. mi.; **Water:** 7.6 sq. mi.   **Area Code:** 717
In northeastern PA, west of Scranton; organized Apr 4, 1842 from Luzerne County.
Name origin: For the Wyoming Valley, the northern extent of which is in the county.

Braintrim
Township
Lat: 41-38-13 N   Long: 76-08-46 W
Pop: 465 (1990)   **Pop Density:** 77.5
Land: 6.0 sq. mi.; **Water:** 0.3 sq. mi.

Clinton
Township
Lat: 41-34-10 N   Long: 75-49-05 W
Pop: 1,063 (1990)   **Pop Density:** 87.1
Land: 12.2 sq. mi.; **Water:** 0.0 sq. mi.

Eaton
Township
Lat: 41-29-57 N   Long: 75-59-15 W
Pop: 1,600 (1990)   **Pop Density:** 44.6
Land: 35.9 sq. mi.; **Water:** 1.1 sq. mi.

Exeter
Township
Lat: 41-26-13 N   Long: 75-51-41 W
Pop: 763 (1990)   **Pop Density:** 246.1
Land: 3.1 sq. mi.; **Water:** 0.3 sq. mi.

Factoryville
Borough
ZIP: 18419   Lat: 41-33-36 N   Long: 75-47-00 W
Pop: 1,310 (1990); 924 (1980)   **Pop Density:** 1871.4
Land: 0.7 sq. mi.; **Water:** 0.0 sq. mi.   **Elev:** 840 ft.

Falls
Township
ZIP: 18615   Lat: 41-28-27 N   Long: 75-50-32 W
Pop: 2,055 (1990)   **Pop Density:** 99.3
Land: 20.7 sq. mi.; **Water:** 0.6 sq. mi.

Forkston
Township
Lat: 41-27-14 N   Long: 76-09-39 W
Pop: 316 (1990)   **Pop Density:** 4.5
Land: 70.8 sq. mi.; **Water:** 0.2 sq. mi.

Grantley
CDP
Lat: 39-56-24 N   Long: 76-43-46 W
Pop: 3,069 (1990)   **Pop Density:** 1805.3
Land: 1.7 sq. mi.; **Water:** 0.0 sq. mi.

Laceyville
Borough
ZIP: 18623   Lat: 41-38-42 N   Long: 76-09-34 W
Pop: 436 (1990); 498 (1980)   **Pop Density:** 2180.0
Land: 0.2 sq. mi.; **Water:** 0.0 sq. mi.   **Elev:** 657 ft.

Lemon
Township
Lat: 41-36-59 N   Long: 75-54-28 W
Pop: 1,264 (1990)   **Pop Density:** 79.5
Land: 15.9 sq. mi.; **Water:** 0.6 sq. mi.

Mehoopany
Township
ZIP: 18629   Lat: 41-33-54 N   Long: 76-04-12 W
Pop: 888 (1990)   **Pop Density:** 51.6
Land: 17.2 sq. mi.; **Water:** 0.7 sq. mi.

Meshoppen
Township
ZIP: 18630   Lat: 41-37-44 N   Long: 76-03-29 W
Pop: 879 (1990)   **Pop Density:** 56.7
Land: 15.5 sq. mi.; **Water:** 0.4 sq. mi.

*Meshoppen
Borough
ZIP: 18630   Lat: 41-36-48 N   Long: 76-02-45 W
Pop: 439 (1990); 571 (1980)   **Pop Density:** 627.1
Land: 0.7 sq. mi.; **Water:** 0.0 sq. mi.   **Elev:** 640 ft.

Monroe
Township
Lat: 41-25-38 N   Long: 76-00-36 W
Pop: 1,802 (1990)   **Pop Density:** 87.1
Land: 20.7 sq. mi.; **Water:** 0.1 sq. mi.

Nicholson
Township
ZIP: 18446   Lat: 41-36-59 N   Long: 75-48-32 W
Pop: 1,287 (1990)   **Pop Density:** 56.4
Land: 22.8 sq. mi.; **Water:** 0.3 sq. mi.

*Nicholson
Borough
ZIP: 18446   Lat: 41-37-38 N   Long: 75-47-08 W
Pop: 857 (1990); 945 (1980)   **Pop Density:** 714.2
Land: 1.2 sq. mi.; **Water:** 0.0 sq. mi.   **Elev:** 780 ft.

North Branch
Township
Lat: 41-31-54 N   Long: 76-11-58 W
Pop: 168 (1990)   **Pop Density:** 7.5
Land: 22.3 sq. mi.; **Water:** 0.1 sq. mi.

Northmoreland
Township
Lat: 41-26-06 N   Long: 75-55-54 W
Pop: 1,462 (1990)   **Pop Density:** 73.8
Land: 19.8 sq. mi.; **Water:** 0.1 sq. mi.

Noxen
Township
ZIP: 18636   Lat: 41-25-03 N   Long: 76-05-28 W
Pop: 944 (1990)   **Pop Density:** 33.1
Land: 28.5 sq. mi.; **Water:** 0.0 sq. mi.

Overfield
Township
Lat: 41-31-05 N   Long: 75-49-44 W
Pop: 1,466 (1990)   **Pop Density:** 148.1
Land: 9.9 sq. mi.; **Water:** 0.3 sq. mi.

Tunkhannock
Township
ZIP: 18657   Lat: 41-32-56 N   Long: 75-54-34 W
Pop: 4,371 (1990)   **Pop Density:** 140.5
Land: 31.1 sq. mi.; **Water:** 0.9 sq. mi.

*Tunkhannock
Borough
ZIP: 18657   Lat: 41-32-27 N   Long: 75-56-57 W
Pop: 2,251 (1990); 2,144 (1980)   **Pop Density:** 2501.1
Land: 0.9 sq. mi.; **Water:** 0.0 sq. mi.   **Elev:** 640 ft.
In northeastern PA at the confluence of Tunkhannock Creek and the Susquehanna River, 20 mi. northwest of Scranton; incorporated Aug 8, 1841.
Name origin: For Tunkhannock Creek, the name of which is a corruption of *tank-hanne*, meaning 'a small stream.'

Washington
Township
Lat: 41-35-40 N   Long: 76-00-27 W
Pop: 1,212 (1990)   **Pop Density:** 64.8
Land: 18.7 sq. mi.; **Water:** 0.6 sq. mi.

Windham   Township
　　　　　　　Lat: 41-35-35 N **Long:** 76-09-16 W
Pop: 778 (1990)   **Pop Density:** 34.9
Land: 22.3 sq. mi.; **Water:** 0.9 sq. mi.

York County
County Seat: York (ZIP: 17401)

Pop: 339,574 (1990); 312,963 (1980)   **Pop Density:** 375.4
Land: 904.6 sq. mi.; **Water:** 5.7 sq. mi.   **Area Code:** 717

On southeastern border of PA, south of Harrisburg; organized Aug 19, 1749 from Lancaster County.

Name origin: For York and Yorkshire, England, and for James, Duke of York and Albany (1633–1701), later James II, king of England. Name perhaps suggested by its proximity to Lancaster County; the houses of York and Lancaster are linked in English history.

Carroll   Township
　　　　　　　Lat: 40-06-59 N **Long:** 77-01-12 W
Pop: 3,287 (1990)   **Pop Density:** 219.1
Land: 15.0 sq. mi.; **Water:** 0.0 sq. mi.

Chanceford   Township
ZIP: 17309   Lat: 39-52-57 N **Long:** 76-28-50 W
Pop: 5,026 (1990)   **Pop Density:** 103.6
Land: 48.5 sq. mi.; **Water:** 0.0 sq. mi.

Codorus   Township
　　　　　　　Lat: 39-46-48 N **Long:** 76-47-47 W
Pop: 3,653; (1990); 4,030 (1980)   **Pop Density:** 109.0
Land: 33.5 sq. mi.; **Water:** 0.0 sq. mi.

Name origin: For Codorus Creek, itself named from an Indian term probably meaning 'rapid water.'

Conewago   Township
　　　　　　　Lat: 40-03-48 N **Long:** 76-47-41 W
Pop: 4,997 (1990)   **Pop Density:** 204.8
Land: 24.4 sq. mi.; **Water:** 0.2 sq. mi.

In southern PA on Edgegrove Creek, south of Harrisburg.

Name origin: An Indian term probably meaning 'at the rapids.'

Cross Roads   Borough
ZIP: 17322   Lat: 39-49-13 N **Long:** 76-34-13 W
Pop: 322 (1990); 267 (1980)   **Pop Density:** 169.5
Land: 1.9 sq. mi.; **Water:** 0.0 sq. mi.   **Elev:** 812 ft.

Dallastown   Borough
ZIP: 17313   Lat: 39-53-59 N **Long:** 76-38-27 W
Pop: 3,974 (1990); 3,949 (1980)   **Pop Density:** 5677.1
Land: 0.7 sq. mi.; **Water:** 0.0 sq. mi.   **Elev:** 900 ft.

Name origin: For George Mifflin Dallas (1792–1864) of Philadelphia, son of Alexander J. Dallas (1759–1817). He served as U.S. senator from PA (1831), as vice president of the United States during Pres. Polk's administration, and as minister to Great Britain (1856–61).

Delta   Borough
ZIP: 17314   Lat: 39-43-33 N **Long:** 76-19-39 W
Pop: 761 (1990); 692 (1980)   **Pop Density:** 2536.7
Land: 0.3 sq. mi.; **Water:** 0.0 sq. mi.   **Elev:** 360 ft.

Dillsburg   Borough
ZIP: 17019   Lat: 40-06-36 N **Long:** 77-02-05 W
Pop: 1,925 (1990); 1,733 (1980)   **Pop Density:** 2406.3
Land: 0.8 sq. mi.; **Water:** 0.0 sq. mi.   **Elev:** 600 ft.

In southern PA, 15 mi. north of Harrisburg.

Dover   Township
ZIP: 17315   Lat: 39-59-58 N **Long:** 76-52-08 W
Pop: 15,668 (1990)   **Pop Density:** 373.9
Land: 41.9 sq. mi.; **Water:** 0.1 sq. mi.

*Dover   Borough
ZIP: 17315   Lat: 40-00-13 N **Long:** 76-50-58 W
Pop: 1,884 (1990); 1,910 (1980)   **Pop Density:** 3768.0
Land: 0.5 sq. mi.; **Water:** 0.0 sq. mi.   **Elev:** 440 ft.

In southern PA on Fox Run Creek at the foot of the Conewago Mountains.

Name origin: For Dover, England.

East Hopewell   Township
　　　　　　　Lat: 39-48-04 N **Long:** 76-31-53 W
Pop: 1,929 (1990)   **Pop Density:** 93.6
Land: 20.6 sq. mi.; **Water:** 0.0 sq. mi.

East Manchester   Township
　　　　　　　Lat: 40-02-54 N **Long:** 76-41-43 W
Pop: 3,714 (1990)   **Pop Density:** 223.7
Land: 16.6 sq. mi.; **Water:** 0.6 sq. mi.

East Prospect   Borough
ZIP: 17317   Lat: 39-58-17 N **Long:** 76-31-15 W
Pop: 558 (1990); 529 (1980)   **Pop Density:** 1860.0
Land: 0.3 sq. mi.; **Water:** 0.0 sq. mi.   **Elev:** 493 ft.

East York   CDP
ZIP: 17402   Lat: 39-58-07 N **Long:** 76-40-29 W
Pop: 8,487 (1990)   **Pop Density:** 2926.6
Land: 2.9 sq. mi.; **Water:** 0.0 sq. mi.

Emigsville   CDP
　　　　　　　Lat: 40-00-28 N **Long:** 76-43-48 W
Pop: 2,580 (1990); 2,413 (1980)   **Pop Density:** 2150.0
Land: 1.2 sq. mi.; **Water:** 0.0 sq. mi.

Fairview   Township
ZIP: 17070   Lat: 40-10-06 N **Long:** 76-51-34 W
Pop: 13,258 (1990)   **Pop Density:** 372.4
Land: 35.6 sq. mi.; **Water:** 0.1 sq. mi.

Fawn
Township
ZIP: 17321 **Lat:** 39-45-12 N **Long:** 76-27-58 W
Pop: 2,175 (1990) **Pop Density:** 80.3
Land: 27.1 sq. mi.; **Water:** 0.0 sq. mi.

Fawn Grove
Borough
ZIP: 17321 **Lat:** 39-43-47 N **Long:** 76-27-03 W
Pop: 489 (1990); 516 (1980) **Pop Density:** 305.6
Land: 1.6 sq. mi.; **Water:** 0.0 sq. mi. **Elev:** 732 ft.

Felton
Borough
ZIP: 17322 **Lat:** 39-51-22 N **Long:** 76-33-41 W
Pop: 438 (1990); 483 (1980) **Pop Density:** 625.7
Land: 0.7 sq. mi.; **Water:** 0.0 sq. mi. **Elev:** 540 ft.

Franklin
Township
Lat: 40-04-14 N **Long:** 77-04-15 W
Pop: 3,852 (1990) **Pop Density:** 201.7
Land: 19.1 sq. mi.; **Water:** 0.1 sq. mi.

Franklintown
Borough
ZIP: 17323 **Lat:** 40-04-30 N **Long:** 77-01-44 W
Pop: 373 (1990); 280 (1980) **Pop Density:** 1865.0
Land: 0.2 sq. mi.; **Water:** 0.0 sq. mi. **Elev:** 700 ft.

Glen Rock
Borough
ZIP: 17327 **Lat:** 39-47-36 N **Long:** 76-43-49 W
Pop: 1,688 (1990); 1,662 (1980) **Pop Density:** 2110.0
Land: 0.8 sq. mi.; **Water:** 0.0 sq. mi. **Elev:** 650 ft.
In southern PA, 15 mi. south of York in a farming region.

Goldsboro
Borough
ZIP: 17319 **Lat:** 40-09-16 N **Long:** 76-45-01 W
Pop: 458 (1990); 477 (1980) **Pop Density:** 1145.0
Land: 0.4 sq. mi.; **Water:** 0.0 sq. mi. **Elev:** 509 ft.

Hanover
Borough
ZIP: 17331 **Lat:** 39-48-43 N **Long:** 76-59-01 W
Pop: 14,399 (1990); 14,890 (1980) **Pop Density:** 3891.6
Land: 3.7 sq. mi.; **Water:** 0.0 sq. mi. **Elev:** 609 ft.
In southern PA, 18 mi. southwest of York and 8 mi. north of the MD state line.
Name origin: For Hanover, Germany, former home of German settlers.

Heidelberg
Township
Lat: 39-49-40 N **Long:** 76-55-14 W
Pop: 2,622 (1990) **Pop Density:** 180.8
Land: 14.5 sq. mi.; **Water:** 0.5 sq. mi.

Hellam
Township
ZIP: 17368 **Lat:** 40-01-24 N **Long:** 76-35-53 W
Pop: 5,123 (1990) **Pop Density:** 184.9
Land: 27.7 sq. mi.; **Water:** 0.0 sq. mi.

*Hellam
Borough
ZIP: 17406 **Lat:** 40-00-08 N **Long:** 76-36-16 W
Pop: 1,375 (1990); 1,428 (1980) **Pop Density:** 1964.3
Land: 0.7 sq. mi.; **Water:** 0.0 sq. mi. **Elev:** 380 ft.
In southern PA, 5 mi. northeast of York along a scenic route.
Name origin: Named by early settler Samuel Blunston for his native town of Upper Hallam in Yorkshire, England.

Hopewell
Township
Lat: 39-45-28 N **Long:** 76-35-26 W
Pop: 3,177 (1990) **Pop Density:** 118.1
Land: 26.9 sq. mi.; **Water:** 0.0 sq. mi.

Jackson
Township
ZIP: 17362 **Lat:** 39-54-22 N **Long:** 76-53-01 W
Pop: 6,244 (1990) **Pop Density:** 278.8
Land: 22.4 sq. mi.; **Water:** 0.2 sq. mi.
Name origin: For Andrew Jackson (1767–1845), seventh U.S. president.

Jacobus
Borough
ZIP: 17407 **Lat:** 39-52-56 N **Long:** 76-42-44 W
Pop: 1,370 (1990); 1,396 (1980) **Pop Density:** 1522.2
Land: 0.9 sq. mi.; **Water:** 0.0 sq. mi. **Elev:** 704 ft.
In southern PA, 10 mi. south of York.

Jefferson
Borough
ZIP: 17311 **Lat:** 39-48-57 N **Long:** 76-50-28 W
Pop: 675 (1990); 685 (1980) **Pop Density:** 1125.0
Land: 0.6 sq. mi.; **Water:** 0.0 sq. mi.

Lewisberry
Borough
ZIP: 17339 **Lat:** 40-08-06 N **Long:** 76-51-38 W
Pop: 314 (1990); 309 (1980) **Pop Density:** 3140.0
Land: 0.1 sq. mi.; **Water:** 0.0 sq. mi. **Elev:** 450 ft.

Loganville
Borough
ZIP: 17342 **Lat:** 39-51-18 N **Long:** 76-42-31 W
Pop: 954 (1990); 1,020 (1980) **Pop Density:** 954.0
Land: 1.0 sq. mi.; **Water:** 0.0 sq. mi. **Elev:** 783 ft.
Laid out in 1820.
Name origin: For Col. Henry Logan, York County representative in Congress.

Lower Chanceford
Township
Lat: 39-49-07 N **Long:** 76-23-19 W
Pop: 2,454 (1990) **Pop Density:** 59.0
Land: 41.6 sq. mi.; **Water:** 0.1 sq. mi.

Lower Windsor
Township
ZIP: 17368 **Lat:** 39-57-48 N **Long:** 76-32-07 W
Pop: 7,051 (1990) **Pop Density:** 280.9
Land: 25.1 sq. mi.; **Water:** 0.0 sq. mi.

Manchester
Township
ZIP: 17345 **Lat:** 40-00-35 N **Long:** 76-45-11 W
Pop: 7,517 (1990) **Pop Density:** 472.8
Land: 15.9 sq. mi.; **Water:** 0.0 sq. mi.

*Manchester
Borough
ZIP: 17345 **Lat:** 40-03-40 N **Long:** 76-43-13 W
Pop: 1,830 (1990); 2,027 (1980) **Pop Density:** 2287.5
Land: 0.8 sq. mi.; **Water:** 0.0 sq. mi. **Elev:** 492 ft.

Manheim
Township
Lat: 39-45-25 N **Long:** 76-51-24 W
Pop: 2,692 (1990) **Pop Density:** 125.2
Land: 21.5 sq. mi.; **Water:** 0.9 sq. mi.

Monaghan
Township
Lat: 40-08-13 N **Long:** 76-57-20 W
Pop: 2,009 (1990) **Pop Density:** 154.5
Land: 13.0 sq. mi.; **Water:** 0.0 sq. mi.

Mount Wolf
Borough
ZIP: 17347 **Lat:** 40-03-36 N **Long:** 76-42-19 W
Pop: 1,365 (1990); 1,517 (1980) **Pop Density:** 2730.0
Land: 0.5 sq. mi.; **Water:** 0.0 sq. mi. **Elev:** 594 ft.

Newberry
Township
ZIP: 17370 **Lat:** 40-07-50 N **Long:** 76-47-29 W
Pop: 12,003 (1990) **Pop Density:** 394.8
Land: 30.4 sq. mi.; **Water:** 0.3 sq. mi.

New Freedom Borough
ZIP: 17349 Lat: 39-44-10 N **Long:** 76-41-48 W
Pop: 2,920 (1990); 2,205 (1980) **Pop Density:** 1390.5
Land: 2.1 sq. mi.; **Water:** 0.0 sq. mi. **Elev:** 818 ft.

New Salem Borough
ZIP: 17371 Lat: 39-54-08 N **Long:** 76-47-36 W
Pop: 669 (1990); 832 (1980) **Pop Density:** 1338.0
Land: 0.5 sq. mi.; **Water:** 0.0 sq. mi.

North Codorus Township
ZIP: 17362 Lat: 39-52-00 N **Long:** 76-49-17 W
Pop: 7,565 (1990) **Pop Density:** 234.2
Land: 32.3 sq. mi.; **Water:** 0.1 sq. mi.

North Hopewell Township
Lat: 39-49-34 N **Long:** 76-37-21 W
Pop: 2,205 (1990) **Pop Density:** 118.5
Land: 18.6 sq. mi.; **Water:** 0.0 sq. mi.

North York Borough
ZIP: 17404 Lat: 39-58-39 N **Long:** 76-43-54 W
Pop: 1,689 (1990); 1,755 (1980) **Pop Density:** 5630.0
Land: 0.3 sq. mi.; **Water:** 0.0 sq. mi. **Elev:** 400 ft.
In southern PA, just north of the city of York.

Paradise Township
Lat: 39-54-51 N **Long:** 76-56-43 W
Pop: 3,180 (1990) **Pop Density:** 156.7
Land: 20.3 sq. mi.; **Water:** 0.0 sq. mi.

Peach Bottom Township
ZIP: 17314 Lat: 39-44-55 N **Long:** 76-19-56 W
Pop: 3,444 (1990) **Pop Density:** 117.5
Land: 29.3 sq. mi.; **Water:** 0.4 sq. mi.

Penn Township
ZIP: 17331 Lat: 39-48-01 N **Long:** 76-57-54 W
Pop: 11,658 (1990) **Pop Density:** 910.8
Land: 12.8 sq. mi.; **Water:** 0.2 sq. mi.
Name origin: For William Penn (1644–1718), founder of Pennsylvania.

Railroad Borough
ZIP: 17355 Lat: 39-45-36 N **Long:** 76-41-48 W
Pop: 317 (1990); 272 (1980) **Pop Density:** 528.3
Land: 0.6 sq. mi.; **Water:** 0.0 sq. mi. **Elev:** 741 ft.

Red Lion Borough
ZIP: 17356 Lat: 39-53-55 N **Long:** 76-36-27 W
Pop: 6,130 (1990); 5,824 (1980) **Pop Density:** 4715.4
Land: 1.3 sq. mi.; **Water:** 0.0 sq. mi. **Elev:** 911 ft.
In southern PA, 10 mi. southeast of York.
Name origin: For a tavern built here in colonial times, which had a painted red lion as its emblem.

Seven Valleys Borough
ZIP: 17360 Lat: 39-51-09 N **Long:** 76-45-59 W
Pop: 483 (1990); 500 (1980) **Pop Density:** 439.1
Land: 1.1 sq. mi.; **Water:** 0.0 sq. mi.

Shrewsbury Township
ZIP: 17361 Lat: 39-45-55 N **Long:** 76-41-52 W
Pop: 5,898 (1990) **Pop Density:** 202.0
Land: 29.2 sq. mi.; **Water:** 0.0 sq. mi.

*Shrewsbury Borough
Lat: 39-46-15 N **Long:** 76-40-49 W
Pop: 2,672 (1990); 2,688 (1980) **Pop Density:** 1484.4
Land: 1.8 sq. mi.; **Water:** 0.0 sq. mi. **Elev:** 983 ft.
Founded 1739.
Name origin: Named by immigrants for Shrewsbury, England.

Springettsbury Township
ZIP: 17402 Lat: 39-59-28 N **Long:** 76-40-41 W
Pop: 21,564 (1990) **Pop Density:** 1283.6
Land: 16.8 sq. mi.; **Water:** 0.0 sq. mi.
Name origin: For Springettsbury Manor, named for the eldest son of William Penn.

Springfield Township
Lat: 39-50-28 N **Long:** 76-42-44 W
Pop: 3,918 (1990) **Pop Density:** 149.5
Land: 26.2 sq. mi.; **Water:** 0.3 sq. mi.

Spring Garden Township
ZIP: 17403 Lat: 39-56-44 N **Long:** 76-43-22 W
Pop: 11,207 (1990) **Pop Density:** 1698.0
Land: 6.6 sq. mi.; **Water:** 0.0 sq. mi.
In southern PA, south of York.

Spring Grove Borough
ZIP: 17362 Lat: 39-52-52 N **Long:** 76-51-51 W
Pop: 1,863 (1990); 1,832 (1980) **Pop Density:** 2328.8
Land: 0.8 sq. mi.; **Water:** 0.0 sq. mi. **Elev:** 467 ft.

Stewartstown Borough
ZIP: 17363 Lat: 39-45-08 N **Long:** 76-35-34 W
Pop: 1,308 (1990); 1,072 (1980) **Pop Density:** 1635.0
Land: 0.8 sq. mi.; **Water:** 0.0 sq. mi. **Elev:** 870 ft.

Warrington Township
Lat: 40-04-44 N **Long:** 76-55-43 W
Pop: 4,275 (1990) **Pop Density:** 120.8
Land: 35.4 sq. mi.; **Water:** 0.6 sq. mi.

Washington Township
Lat: 40-00-41 N **Long:** 76-59-09 W
Pop: 2,291 (1990) **Pop Density:** 82.1
Land: 27.9 sq. mi.; **Water:** 0.0 sq. mi.
Name origin: For George Washington (1732–99), first U.S. president.

Wellsville Borough
ZIP: 17365 Lat: 40-03-00 N **Long:** 76-56-27 W
Pop: 304 (1990); 347 (1980) **Pop Density:** 3040.0
Land: 0.1 sq. mi.; **Water:** 0.0 sq. mi. **Elev:** 500 ft.

West Manchester Township
ZIP: 17404 Lat: 39-56-39 N **Long:** 76-47-40 W
Pop: 14,369 (1990) **Pop Density:** 714.9
Land: 20.1 sq. mi.; **Water:** 0.0 sq. mi.

West Manheim Township
Lat: 39-44-45 N **Long:** 76-56-27 W
Pop: 4,590 (1990) **Pop Density:** 234.2
Land: 19.6 sq. mi.; **Water:** 0.6 sq. mi.

West York Borough
ZIP: 17404 Lat: 39-57-10 N **Long:** 76-45-36 W
Pop: 4,283 (1990); 4,526 (1980) **Pop Density:** 8566.0
Land: 0.5 sq. mi.; **Water:** 0.0 sq. mi. **Elev:** 398 ft.
In southern PA, 5 mi. west of York.
Name origin: Originally called Eberton for farmer Henry Ebert.

American Places Dictionary

Windsor Township
ZIP: 17366   Lat: 39-55-11 N Long: 76-35-35 W
Pop: 9,424 (1990)   Pop Density: 346.5
Land: 27.2 sq. mi.; Water: 0.0 sq. mi.

*Windsor Borough
ZIP: 17366   Lat: 39-54-55 N Long: 76-34-59 W
Pop: 1,355 (1990); 1,205 (1980)   Pop Density: 2710.0
Land: 0.5 sq. mi.; Water: 0.0 sq. mi.   Elev: 650 ft.
Name origin: Named for Windsor, England, by Thomas Armor, justice of the township in the 1750s.

Winterstown Borough
ZIP: 17356   Lat: 39-50-27 N Long: 76-36-47 W
Pop: 581 (1990); 491 (1980)   Pop Density: 252.6
Land: 2.3 sq. mi.; Water: 0.0 sq. mi.   Elev: 860 ft.

Wrightsville Borough
ZIP: 17368   Lat: 40-01-27 N Long: 76-31-53 W
Pop: 2,396 (1990); 2,365 (1980)   Pop Density: 3993.3
Land: 0.6 sq. mi.; Water: 0.0 sq. mi.   Elev: 300 ft.

Yoe Borough
ZIP: 17313   Lat: 39-54-34 N Long: 76-38-11 W
Pop: 947 (1990); 990 (1980)   Pop Density: 4735.0
Land: 0.2 sq. mi.; Water: 0.0 sq. mi.   Elev: 800 ft.

York City
ZIP: 17401   Lat: 39-57-52 N Long: 76-43-54 W
Pop: 42,192 (1990)   Pop Density: 8113.8
Land: 5.2 sq. mi.; Water: 0.1 sq. mi.   Elev: 400 ft.
In southeastern PA, 10 mi. west-southwest of the Susquehanna River. Laid out in 1741; incorporated as borough Sep 24, 1787, as city Jan 11, 1887.
Name origin: Named by Richard Thomas and John Penn for either the Duke of York, their royal patron and family benefactor, or for York, England.

*York Township
ZIP: 17403   Lat: 39-54-38 N Long: 76-40-38 W
Pop: 19,231 (1990)   Pop Density: 754.2
Land: 25.5 sq. mi.; Water: 0.3 sq. mi.

Yorkana Borough
ZIP: 17402   Lat: 39-58-27 N Long: 76-35-04 W
Pop: 285 (1990); 296 (1980)   Pop Density: 1425.0
Land: 0.2 sq. mi.; Water: 0.0 sq. mi.   Elev: 630 ft.

York Haven Borough
ZIP: 17370   Lat: 40-06-36 N Long: 76-42-56 W
Pop: 758 (1990); 746 (1980)   Pop Density: 2526.7
Land: 0.3 sq. mi.; Water: 0.0 sq. mi.   Elev: 334 ft.

Index to Places and Counties in Pennsylvania

Rhode Island

RHODE ISLAND

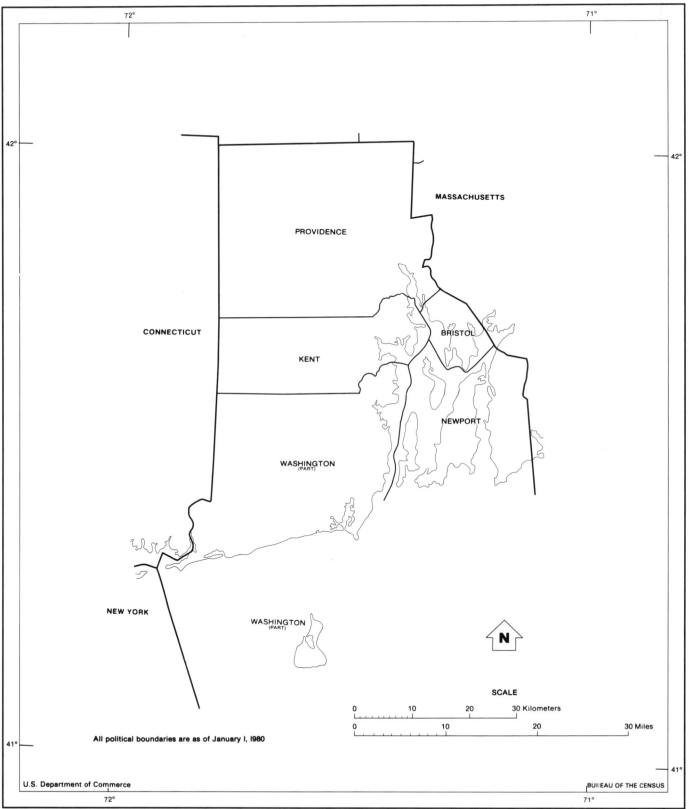

Rhode Island

Population: 1,003,464 (1990); 947,154 (1980)
Population rank (1990): 43
Percent population change (1980-1990): 5.9
Population projection: 1,027,000 (1995); 1,046,000 (2000)

Area: total 1,545 sq. mi.; 1,045 sq. mi. land, 500 sq. mi. water. Coastline 40 mi.
Area rank: 50
Highest elevation: 812 ft., Jerimoth Hill (Providence County)
Lowest point: sea level on Block Island and Rhode Island sounds

State capital: Providence (Providence County)
Largest city: Providence (160,728)
Second largest city: Warwick (85,427)
Largest county: Providence (596,270)

Total housing units: 414,572
No. of occupied housing units: 377,977
Vacant housing units (%): 8.8
Distribution of population by race and Hispanic origin (%):
White: 91.4
Black: 3.9
Hispanic (any race): 4.6
Native American: 0.4
Asian/Pacific: 1.8
Other: 2.5

Admission date: May 29, 1790 (13th state).

Location: In the northeastern United States, on the Atlantic coast, bordering Massachusetts and Connecticut. One of the thirteen original English colonies.

Name Origin: For Rhode Island in Narragansett Bay, which Italian explorer Giovanni da Verrazano, while navigating Narragansett Bay in 1524 in the service of France, is said to have named for its likeness to the Mediterranean isle of Rhodes off the coast of Turkey. It is the largest of several islands in the bay and was called Aquidneck by the Indians. In 1614 Dutch explorer Adriaen Block named an island in the bay *Roodt Eylandt* 'red island' because of the red clay along the shore. Early English settlers used the name Aquidneck, but in 1644 the name was officially established by royal charter as Rhode Island. Since the settlements on the mainland along Narragansett Bay were known as the Providence Plantations, the full, official name of the state became "Rhode Island and Providence Plantations."

State bird: Rhode Island Red chicken

State flower: violet
State mineral: bowenite
State rock: cumberlandite
State song: "Rhode Island"
State tree: red maple *(Acer rubrum)*

State motto: Hope
State nickname: The Ocean State; Little Rhody

Area code: 401
Time zone: Eastern
Abbreviations: RI (postal), R.I. (traditional)
Part of (region): New England

Local Government

Counties

Rhode Island, like Connecticut, has abolished county governments. Its five former counties merely provide judicial administration; city and town governments provide local-level administration.

Municipalities

The entire area of Rhode Island is within one of the eight cities or 31 towns. Towns may include rural areas and unincorporated villages, and are usually governed by town meetings.

Settlement History and Early Development

The Narragansett were the most numerous of the Indians who inhabited the area, now known as Rhode Island, before the arrival of the first Europeans. But four other Algonquian tribes also lived there: the Wampanoag, Niantic, Nipmuck, and Pequot.

Some historians believe Miguel de Cortereal, a Portuguese navigator, may have been the first to explore the coast in 1511, and Giovanni da Verrazano, sailing for France, is known to have explored the area in 1524. The first permanent settlement was not established until 1636 when Roger Williams, driven out of Massachusetts Bay Colony for demanding greater religious and political freedom, founded Providence. He was followed by others who settled Portsmouth in 1638, Newport in 1639, and Warwick in 1642. In 1644 Williams received a patent from the English Parliamentary Commission uniting these four towns into a colony they called the Providence Plantations. In 1663 King Charles II of England granted a royal charter to Rhode Island and Providence Plantations guaranteeing religious liberty, strengthening their territorial claims, and giving them the most local autonomy of any colony.

Despite the fact that Williams respected and maintained peace with the Indians, King Philip's war, which began in Massachusetts (see Massachusetts section), spilled over into Rhode Island in 1675, when troops from the Bay Colony defeated Indians near Kingston. The Indians retaliated by attacking Rhode Islanders. King Philip, king of the Wampanoag Indians, was killed near present-day Bristol in 1676.

The eighteenth century was a time of great prosperity in Rhode Island. Large plantations worked by slaves were established, similar to those in the Southern colonies. Cheese was a major product, and a fine breed of saddle horse, called the Narragansett Pacer, was developed. The merchants of Newport owned large fleets that exported plantation products to the other English colonies and to the West Indies, and they and the plantation owners invested in rum and the African slave trade. Despite this, Rhode Island in 1774 became the first colony to prohibit the importation of slaves.

The Revolutionary War and Statehood

Because Rhode Island had the greatest degree of self-rule of any of the colonies, it had the most to lose from the restrictive British laws and taxes and was among the first to fight back. In 1769 Rhode Islanders burned the British ship *Liberty* at Newport.

When the Revolutionary War began in Massachusetts in 1775, Rhode Islanders flocked to join the patriots. Stephen Hopkins and other Rhode Island men were the chief organizers of the Continental Navy, and Nathanael Greene became one of the leading generals of the Continental Army. On May 4, 1776, it was the first colony to formally declare its independence from Great Britain. British troops occupied Newport from December 1776 to October 1779 and they also raided other communities during the war, but no major battles took place in Rhode Island.

On July 9, 1778, Rhode Island ratified the Articles of Confederation, but because it resisted the centralizing tendencies of the federal constitution, it did not ratify the U.S. Constitution until May 29, 1790, when the Bill of Rights was ready to be added. It was the last of the thirteen original states to ratify the Constitution, and even then the ratification vote was 34-32.

Business and Industry

Textile manufacturing, the state's first important industry, began during the latter part of the eighteenth century. The first hand-operated cotton-spinning jenny in the U.S. was built in Providence in 1787, and the first water-powered spinning machines were manufactured in Pawtucket in 1790 by Samuel Slater. The early growth of the industry was spurred by power spinning, plus abundant water power, nearby markets in Boston and New York City, excellent transportation, and the Jefferson Embargo of 1807, which prohibited the importation of textiles. In 1794 Nehemiah Dodge of Providence and his brother, Seril, found a way to cover cheap metal with precious metals. This led to the establishment of jewelry and silverplate manufacturing, which has long been a major part of the Rhode Island economy. The Providence area is still one of the centers of the U.S. costume-jewelry

industry. Fishing was also an important industry, as was whaling (for whale oil and candle-making) in Newport, Providence, and Warren, leading U.S. whaling centers from 1775 to 1850. Both the population and industries expanded greatly during the late 1800s and early 1900s.

During World War I chemicals and munitions factories multiplied and the shipyards built both combat and cargo ships. World War II helped stimulate the state's recovery from the Great Depression, and by the 1960s industry had expanded to include plastics, electronics, chemicals, and machinery, although the production of jewelry, silverware, and other metal products remains a major segment of the manufacturing base. Improvement in roads increased the tourist industry, and today it is one of the state's major sources of income.

The Dorr Rebellion

Thousands of Canadian and European immigrants thronged to Rhode Island's textile mills in the early nineteenth century for work, but the state's royal charter of 1663, still in effect, made no provision for this change. The numerous rural towns were declining in economic significance, but still had disproportionate power in the legislature, and only landowners and their eldest sons could vote.

The general assembly had ignored those calling for moderate change, so a People's Convention was convened and Thomas Wilson Dorr, a Providence lawyer, began a movement to draft a "People's Constitution." It was ratified in a popular referendum in December 1841. The following April Dorr and his followers held an election in which he was elected governor. Since the assembly did not recognize his government, he formed an army and attempted a coup, but was soundly defeated and left the state. The assembly then bowed to popular pressure and drafted a new constitution almost as liberal as Dorr's, which took effect in 1843.

The Civil War and Late Nineteenth Century

No battles were fought in Rhode Island, but more than 24,000 of its men served in the Union army and navy. The most famous was Major General Ambrose E. Burnside, commander of the Army of the Potomac for a brief period, and for whom sideburn whiskers were named.

Newport became the home of the Newport Naval Station in 1883 (closed in the mid-1970s), and of the Naval War College in 1884. Many wealthy banking and railroad families built summer "cottages" in Newport, huge, rambling mansions with exquisite furnishings and fixtures, many of which are today on the National Register of Historic Places and are open to tourists. The city was long the home port for America's Cup races, the last of which was held off the Rhode Island coast in 1983.

State Boundaries

The Rhode Island-Connecticut border was established in 1703 along a line still known as the Dexter and Hopkins Line, but not finally accepted until 1888. See the Massachusetts section for the Rhode Island-Massachusetts border.

Rhode Island Counties

Bristol	Newport	Washington
Kent	Providence	

Bristol County
Former County Seat: Bristol (ZIP: 02809)

Pop: 48,859 (1990); 46,942 (1980)   **Pop Density:** 1979.6
Land: 24.7 sq. mi.; **Water:** 20.0 sq. mi.   **Area Code:** 401
Largely peninsular area in eastern RI, south of Providence; organized Feb 17, 1747 from Newport County.
Name origin: For Bristol, England.

Barrington   Town
ZIP: 02806   **Lat:** 41-44-06 N **Long:** 71-19-07 W
Pop: 15,849 (1990); 16,174 (1980)   **Pop Density:** 1886.8
Land: 8.4 sq. mi.; **Water:** 7.0 sq. mi.

In eastern RI, 7 mi. east-southeast of Providence. Incorporated by MA Nov 18, 1717, and by RI in Jun 1770.
Name origin: For English theologian Lord Barrington (1678–1734), an advocate of religious toleration.

Bristol   Town
ZIP: 02809   **Lat:** 41-40-39 N **Long:** 71-16-27 W
Pop: 21,625 (1990); 20,128 (1980)   **Pop Density:** 2141.1
Land: 10.1 sq. mi.; **Water:** 10.5 sq. mi.

In eastern RI on Narragansett Bay, 12 mi. east-southeast of Providence. County seat; settled 1669. Incorporated by

Plymouth Colony Oct 28, 1681; annexed to RI Feb 17, 1746. Includes Hog Island.
Name origin: For the seaport city of Bristol in England.

Warren   Town
ZIP: 02885   **Lat:** 41-43-08 N **Long:** 71-15-41 W
Pop: 11,385 (1990); 10,640 (1980)   **Pop Density:** 1836.3
Land: 6.2 sq. mi.; **Water:** 2.5 sq. mi.   **Elev:** 32 ft.

In eastern RI on Narragansett Bay, 9 mi. southeast of Providence. Settled 1632 as part of Swansea, MA; annexed by RI and incorporated Jan 27, 1747.
Name origin: For British navy admiral Sir Peter Warren (1703–52), who led a fleet in the capture of the French fortress at Louisburg in 1745.

Kent County
Former County Seat: East Greenwich (ZIP: 02818)

Pop: 161,135 (1990); 154,163 (1980)   **Pop Density:** 947.4
Land: 170.1 sq. mi.; **Water:** 17.9 sq. mi.   **Area Code:** 401
In central RI, south of Cranston; organized Jun 11, 1750 from Washington County.
Name origin: For the county in England.

Coventry   Town
ZIP: 02816   **Lat:** 41-41-20 N **Long:** 71-39-49 W
Pop: 31,083 (1990); 27,065 (1980)   **Pop Density:** 522.4
Land: 59.5 sq. mi.; **Water:** 2.8 sq. mi.

In central RI, 14 mi. southwest of Providence. Incorporated Aug 21, 1741.
Name origin: For Coventry, Warwickshire, England.

East Greenwich   Town
ZIP: 02818   **Lat:** 41-38-09 N **Long:** 71-30-16 W
Pop: 11,865 (1990); 10,211 (1980)   **Pop Density:** 719.1
Land: 16.5 sq. mi.; **Water:** 0.1 sq. mi.

In central RI, 11 mi. west-southwest of Providence. County seat; incorporated Oct 31, 1677.
Name origin: For the borough of Greenwich in London, England.

Warwick   City
ZIP: 02886   **Lat:** 41-42-07 N **Long:** 71-25-18 W
Pop: 85,427 (1990); 87,123 (1980)   **Pop Density:** 2406.4
Land: 35.5 sq. mi.; **Water:** 14.1 sq. mi.   **Elev:** 64 ft.
In central RI on Greenwich Bay, 9 mi. south of Providence.

Settled Oct 1642; received city charter 1931. A commercial center, produces textiles and metal products.
Name origin: For Robert Rich, Earl of Warwick (1587–1658), who granted a charter of self-government for the Colony of Rhode Island to Roger Williams, Mar 13, 1644. Indian name was Shawomet.

West Greenwich   Town
ZIP: 02817   **Lat:** 41-37-45 N **Long:** 71-39-38 W
Pop: 3,492 (1990); 2,738 (1980)   **Pop Density:** 69.0
Land: 50.6 sq. mi.; **Water:** 0.7 sq. mi.

Incorporated Apr 6, 1741.
Name origin: For a borough of London, England.

West Warwick   Town
ZIP: 02893   **Lat:** 41-41-51 N **Long:** 71-31-05 W
Pop: 29,268 (1990); 27,026 (1980)   **Pop Density:** 3704.8
Land: 7.9 sq. mi.; **Water:** 0.2 sq. mi.

In central RI, 10 mi. west-southwest of Providence. Incorporated Mar 14, 1913, after division from the town of Warwick.

Newport County
Former County Seat: Newport (ZIP: 02840)

Pop: 87,194 (1990); 81,383 (1980)   **Pop Density:** 838.0
Land: 104.1 sq. mi.; **Water:** 209.6 sq. mi.   **Area Code:** 401

In southeastern RI, comprising the islands in Narragansett Bay and mainland along the eastern border of RI, south of Fall River, MA. Original county, organized as Rhode Island County Jun 22, 1703; name changed Jun 16, 1729.

Name origin: Descriptive, or possibly recalling Newport, Monmouthshire, England.

Jamestown
Town
ZIP: 02835   **Lat:** 41-31-12 N **Long:** 71-22-14 W
Pop: 4,999 (1990); 4,040 (1980)   **Pop Density:** 515.4
Land: 9.7 sq. mi.; **Water:** 25.6 sq. mi.   **Elev:** 50 ft.
Incorporated Oct 30, 1678.

Name origin: For James (1633–1701), Duke of York and Albany, later King James II of England.

Little Compton
Town
ZIP: 02837   **Lat:** 41-30-32 N **Long:** 71-10-22 W
Pop: 3,339 (1990); 3,085 (1980)   **Pop Density:** 159.8
Land: 20.9 sq. mi.; **Water:** 8.0 sq. mi.
Incorporated Jan 27, 1746.

Melville
Military facility
ZIP: 02840   **Lat:** 41-33-49 N **Long:** 71-18-13 W
Pop: 4,426 (1990); 2,001 (1980)   **Pop Density:** 2011.8
Land: 2.2 sq. mi.; **Water:** 2.9 sq. mi.

Middletown
Town
ZIP: 02840   **Lat:** 41-31-11 N **Long:** 71-16-49 W
Pop: 19,460 (1990); 17,216 (1980)   **Pop Density:** 1496.9
Land: 13.0 sq. mi.; **Water:** 2.0 sq. mi.

On the island of Rhode Island, 4 mi. north of Newport. Incorporated Jun 16, 1743.

Name origin: For its central location on the island.

Newport
City
ZIP: 02840   **Lat:** 41-28-59 N **Long:** 71-19-12 W
Pop: 28,227 (1990); 29,259 (1980)   **Pop Density:** 3573.0
Land: 7.9 sq. mi.; **Water:** 3.5 sq. mi.   **Elev:** 96 ft.
In southeastern RI at the mouth of Narragansett Bay.

Founded Apr 29, 1639. Incorporated as a city Jun 1, 1784 (repealed Mar 27, 1787); reincorporated May 6, 1853. Summer resort, yachting and tourist center. Site of annual Newport Music Festival; Touro Synagogue, oldest Jewish house of worship in the U.S. (1763).

Name origin: For Newport, Monmouthshire, England.

Portsmouth
Town
ZIP: 02871   **Lat:** 41-35-56 N **Long:** 71-16-58 W
Pop: 16,857 (1990); 14,257 (1980)   **Pop Density:** 726.6
Land: 23.2 sq. mi.; **Water:** 36.1 sq. mi.

In southeastern RI on the Sakonnet River, 7 mi. northnortheast of Newport. Founded 1638.

Name origin: For Portsmouth, England. Indian name was Pocasset.

Tiverton
Town
ZIP: 02878   **Lat:** 41-36-53 N **Long:** 71-10-54 W
Pop: 14,312 (1990); 13,526 (1980)   **Pop Density:** 486.8
Land: 29.4 sq. mi.; **Water:** 7.0 sq. mi.

In southeastern RI on the Sakonnet River, just south of Fall River, MA. Incorporated as a MA town 1694; annexed to RI Jan 27, 1746.

Name origin: For Tiverton, Devonshire, England. Originally called Pocasset, for the Pocasset Indians from whom the land was purchased.

Providence County
Former County Seat: Providence (ZIP: 02903)

Pop: 596,270 (1990); 571,349 (1980)
Land: 413.3 sq. mi.; Water: 22.6 sq. mi.

Pop Density: 1442.7
Area Code: 401

In northern RI; original county, organized as the County of Providence Plantations Jun 22, 1703; name modified Jun 16, 1729.
Name origin: For the city, its county seat.

Burrillville   Town
ZIP: 02830   Lat: 41-58-10 N Long: 71-41-53 W
Pop: 16,230 (1990); 13,164 (1980)   Pop Density: 291.9
Land: 55.6 sq. mi.; Water: 1.6 sq. mi.

In northern RI, 23 mi. northwest of Providence. Incorporated Oct 29, 1806.
Name origin: For James Burrill, Jr. (1772–1820), RI attorney-general, chief justice, and U.S. senator.

Central Falls   City
ZIP: 02863   Lat: 41-53-21 N Long: 71-23-37 W
Pop: 17,637 (1990); 16,995 (1980)   Pop Density: 14697.5
Land: 1.2 sq. mi.; Water: 0.1 sq. mi.   Elev: 100 ft.

In northeastern RI on the Blackstone River, north of Pawtucket. Incorporated Feb 21, 1895.
Name origin: For its location between Valley Falls and Pawtucket Falls. Formerly called Chocolate Mill, for an early chocolate factory.

Cranston   City
ZIP: 02910   Lat: 41-45-59 N Long: 71-28-51 W
Pop: 76,060 (1990); 71,992 (1980)   Pop Density: 2659.4
Land: 28.6 sq. mi.; Water: 1.4 sq. mi.   Elev: 60 ft.

In northern RI on the Pawtuxet River, 4 mi. south of Providence. Settled 1636. Incorporated as town Jun 14, 1754; as city Mar 10, 1910.
Name origin: Probably for Samuel Cranston (1659–1727), governor of RI (1698–1727).

Cumberland   Town
ZIP: 02864   Lat: 41-57-52 N Long: 71-25-18 W
Pop: 29,038 (1990); 27,069 (1980)   Pop Density: 1083.5
Land: 26.8 sq. mi.; Water: 1.5 sq. mi.

In northeastern RI, 5 mi. southeast of Woonsocket. Incorporated Jan 27, 1747.
Name origin: For Prince William (1721–65), Duke of Cumberland. Formerly called Attleboro Gore.

Cumberland Hill   CDP
ZIP: 02864   Lat: 41-58-19 N Long: 71-27-36 W
Pop: 6,379 (1990); 5,421 (1980)   Pop Density: 1993.4
Land: 3.2 sq. mi.; Water: 0.1 sq. mi.

East Providence   City
ZIP: 02914   Lat: 41-48-00 N Long: 71-21-34 W
Pop: 50,380 (1990); 50,980 (1980)   Pop Density: 3759.7
Land: 13.4 sq. mi.; Water: 3.2 sq. mi.   Elev: 59 ft.

In northern RI, an eastern suburb of Providence. Once part of Seekonk, MA. Incorporated as town Mar 1, 1862; as city 1958.
Name origin: For its location east of Providence across the Providence River.

Foster   Town
ZIP: 02825   Lat: 41-47-20 N Long: 71-44-08 W
Pop: 4,316 (1990); 3,370 (1980)   Pop Density: 84.3
Land: 51.2 sq. mi.; Water: 0.7 sq. mi.

In west-central RI, about 4 mi. west of the CT border. Incorporated Aug 24, 1781.
Name origin: For U.S. Sen. Theodore Foster (1752–1828), who owned property in the town.

Glocester   Town
ZIP: 02814   Lat: 41-53-26 N Long: 71-41-27 W
Pop: 9,227 (1990); 7,550 (1980)   Pop Density: 168.4
Land: 54.8 sq. mi.; Water: 2.0 sq. mi.

In northwestern RI, near CT border. Incorporated Feb 20, 1730.
Name origin: For Gloucester, England, with spelling alteration.

Greenville   CDP
ZIP: 02828   Lat: 41-52-44 N Long: 71-33-23 W
Pop: 8,303 (1990); 7,576 (1980)   Pop Density: 1596.7
Land: 5.2 sq. mi.; Water: 0.5 sq. mi.

Harrisville   CDP
ZIP: 02830   Lat: 41-58-05 N Long: 71-40-38 W
Pop: 1,654 (1990); 1,224 (1980)   Pop Density: 2067.5
Land: 0.8 sq. mi.; Water: 0.0 sq. mi.

Johnston   Town
ZIP: 02919   Lat: 41-49-30 N Long: 71-31-29 W
Pop: 26,542 (1990); 24,907 (1980)   Pop Density: 1119.9
Land: 23.7 sq. mi.; Water: 0.7 sq. mi.

In northern RI, 4 mi. southwest of Providence. Settled 1650; originally part of Providence. Incorporated Mar 6, 1759.
Name origin: For Augustus Johnston (c. 1730–90), attorney-general of the colony from 1757–65.

Lincoln   Town
ZIP: 02838   Lat: 41-55-03 N Long: 71-27-06 W
Pop: 18,045 (1990); 16,949 (1980)   Pop Density: 991.5
Land: 18.2 sq. mi.; Water: 0.7 sq. mi.

In northeastern RI, 8 mi. southeast of Woonsocket. Incorporated Mar 8, 1871.
Name origin: For Abraham Lincoln (1809–65), sixteenth U.S. president.

North Providence   Town
ZIP: 02911   Lat: 41-51-40 N Long: 71-27-26 W
Pop: 32,090 (1990); 29,188 (1980)   Pop Density: 5629.8
Land: 5.7 sq. mi.; Water: 0.1 sq. mi.

In northeastern RI, a northwestern suburb of Providence. Incorporated Jun 13, 1765.

North Smithfield
Town
ZIP: 02876   **Lat:** 41-58-48 N   **Long:** 71-33-13 W
Pop: 10,497 (1990); 9,972 (1980)   **Pop Density:** 437.4
Land: 24.0 sq. mi.; **Water:** 0.7 sq. mi.

In north-central RI, near Woonsocket. Incorporated as Slater Mar 8, 1871; name changed Mar 24, 1871.

Pascoag
CDP
ZIP: 02859   **Lat:** 41-57-13 N   **Long:** 71-42-17 W
Pop: 5,011 (1990); 3,807 (1980)   **Pop Density:** 1022.7
Land: 4.9 sq. mi.; **Water:** 0.4 sq. mi.

Pawtucket
City
ZIP: 02860   **Lat:** 41-52-23 N   **Long:** 71-22-27 W
Pop: 72,644 (1990); 71,204 (1980)   **Pop Density:** 8349.9
Land: 8.7 sq. mi.; **Water:** 0.3 sq. mi.

In northeastern RI, 5 mi. northeast of Providence at Pawtucket Falls, on both sides of the Blackstone River. City on east bank belonged to Seekonk, MA; that on west bank was part of North Providence; villages joined to become the town of Pawtucket Mar 1, 1862. City charter granted Apr 1, 1885. Diverse manufacturing city: wire, cable, jewelry; textiles; machined products; home of Hasbro Toys.
Name origin: An Algonquian word probably meaning 'at the falls in the river.'

Providence
City
ZIP: 02901   **Lat:** 41-49-19 N   **Long:** 71-25-11 W
Pop: 160,728 (1990); 156,804 (1980)   **Pop Density:** 8688.0
Land: 18.5 sq. mi.; **Water:** 2.1 sq. mi.

In northeastern RI, at the head of the Providence River, an extension of Narragansett Bay. Founded in Jun 1636; incorporated as a city Nov 5, 1831. State capital, county seat, and largest city in RI; major New England seaport and depot for foreign cars. Manufacturing center: costume jewelry, elec-

tronic devices, silverware, textiles. Home of Brown University.
Name origin: Named by founder Roger Williams (1603?–83) for "God's merciful providence unto me in my distresse."

Scituate
Town
ZIP: 02825   **Lat:** 41-47-32 N   **Long:** 71-37-26 W
Pop: 9,796 (1990); 8,405 (1980)   **Pop Density:** 201.1
Land: 48.7 sq. mi.; **Water:** 6.1 sq. mi.

Incorporated Feb 20, 1730.
Name origin: For Scituate, MA, the former home of many early settlers.

Smithfield
Town
ZIP: 02828   **Lat:** 41-54-06 N   **Long:** 71-31-55 W
Pop: 19,163 (1990); 16,886 (1980)   **Pop Density:** 720.4
Land: 26.6 sq. mi.; **Water:** 1.2 sq. mi.   **Elev:** 266 ft.

In northern RI, 9 mi. northwest of Providence. Incorporated Feb 20, 1730.
Name origin: Possibly for a Mr. Smith who deeded the land on which the Quaker Meeting House was built.

Valley Falls
CDP
ZIP: 02864   **Lat:** 41-55-25 N   **Long:** 71-23-36 W
Pop: 11,175 (1990); 10,892 (1980)   **Pop Density:** 3104.2
Land: 3.6 sq. mi.; **Water:** 0.1 sq. mi.

Part of the town of Cumberland.

Woonsocket
City
ZIP: 02895   **Lat:** 41-59-59 N   **Long:** 71-30-01 W
Pop: 43,877 (1990); 45,914 (1980)   **Pop Density:** 5698.3
Land: 7.7 sq. mi.; **Water:** 0.2 sq. mi.   **Elev:** 162 ft.

In northern RI, 12 mi. northwest of Providence. Settled 1666. Town incorporated Jan 31, 1867; incorporated as a city Jun 13, 1888.
Name origin: From an Algonquian word meaning 'steep descent,' or possibly 'thunder mist,' for a nearby waterfall since replaced by a dam.

Washington County
Former County Seat: Wakefield (ZIP: 02879)

Pop: 110,006 (1990); 93,317 (1980)   **Pop Density:** 330.5
Land: 332.9 sq. mi.; **Water:** 230.0 sq. mi.   **Area Code:** 401

In southwestern RI; incorporated as King's County Jun 16, 1729 from Newport County.
Name origin: For George Washington (1732–99), American patriot and first U.S. president. Name changed from King's County on Oct 29, 1781. Originally called the Narragansett Country; changed to King's Province on Mar 20, 1654.

Ashaway
CDP
ZIP: 02804   **Lat:** 41-25-35 N   **Long:** 71-47-15 W
Pop: 1,584 (1990); 1,747 (1980)   **Pop Density:** 660.0
Land: 2.4 sq. mi.; **Water:** 0.0 sq. mi.

Bradford
CDP
ZIP: 02808   **Lat:** 41-23-37 N   **Long:** 71-45-01 W
Pop: 1,604 (1990); 1,354 (1980)   **Pop Density:** 572.9
Land: 2.8 sq. mi.; **Water:** 0.0 sq. mi.

Charlestown
Town
ZIP: 02812   **Lat:** 41-22-28 N   **Long:** 71-40-34 W
Pop: 6,478 (1990); 4,800 (1980)   **Pop Density:** 176.0
Land: 36.8 sq. mi.; **Water:** 22.5 sq. mi.

In south-central RI on Block Island Sound. Chartered 1663; incorporated Aug 22, 1738.
Name origin: For King Charles II (1630–85), king of England.

Exeter
Town
ZIP: 02822   **Lat:** 41-34-14 N   **Long:** 71-37-45 W
Pop: 5,461 (1990); 4,453 (1980)   **Pop Density:** 94.6
Land: 57.7 sq. mi.; **Water:** 0.7 sq. mi.

Incorporated Mar 8, 1742.

Name origin: For Exeter, England.

Hope Valley
CDP
ZIP: 02832   **Lat:** 41-30-53 N   **Long:** 71-43-20 W
Pop: 1,446 (1990); 1,414 (1980)   **Pop Density:** 466.5
Land: 3.1 sq. mi.; **Water:** 0.2 sq. mi.

Hopkinton
Town
ZIP: 02804   **Lat:** 41-28-34 N   **Long:** 71-45-10 W
Pop: 6,873 (1990); 6,406 (1980)   **Pop Density:** 159.8
Land: 43.0 sq. mi.; **Water:** 1.1 sq. mi.

Incorporated Mar 19, 1757.

Name origin: For Stephen Hopkins (1707–85), a signer of the Declaration of Independence and a justice of the Superior Court of RI.

Kingston
CDP
ZIP: 02881   **Lat:** 41-28-20 N   **Long:** 71-31-24 W
Pop: 6,504 (1990); 5,479 (1980)   **Pop Density:** 4065.0
Land: 1.6 sq. mi.; **Water:** 0.0 sq. mi.

Part of the town of South Kingstown. Site of the University of Rhode Island.

Name origin: Shortened from King's Towne, for Charles II (1630–85), king of England.

Narragansett
Town
ZIP: 02882   **Lat:** 41-23-39 N   **Long:** 71-29-12 W
Pop: 14,985 (1990); 12,088 (1980)   **Pop Density:** 1062.8
Land: 14.1 sq. mi.; **Water:** 23.6 sq. mi.

In southern RI at the entrance to Narragansett Bay, 8 mi. west-southwest of Newport. Settled 1675; incorporated as a separate town Mar 28, 1901.

Name origin: From the Algonquian term *nanhiggonsick* meaning either 'back and forth' or 'people of the point.'

Narragansett Pier
CDP
    Lat: 41-25-37 N   **Long:** 71-28-00 W
Pop: 3,721 (1990); 3,342 (1980)   **Pop Density:** 1033.6
Land: 3.6 sq. mi.; **Water:** 0.3 sq. mi.

New Shoreham
Town
ZIP: 02807   **Lat:** 41-07-43 N   **Long:** 71-34-46 W
Pop: 836 (1990); 620 (1980)   **Pop Density:** 86.2
Land: 9.7 sq. mi.; **Water:** 99.7 sq. mi.   **Elev:** 40 ft.

The only town on Block Island, off the southern coast of RI. Incorporated Nov 6, 1672.

North Kingstown
Town
ZIP: 02852   **Lat:** 41-34-14 N   **Long:** 71-27-01 W
Pop: 23,786 (1990); 21,938 (1980)   **Pop Density:** 544.3
Land: 43.7 sq. mi.; **Water:** 14.7 sq. mi.

In southern RI on Narragansett Bay. Incorporated as King's Towne Oct 28, 1674; divided into North and South Kingstown 1723.

Name origin: For Charles II (1630–85), king of England. Formerly called King's Towne and Rochester.

Richmond
Town
ZIP: 02812   **Lat:** 41-29-59 N   **Long:** 71-39-40 W
Pop: 5,351 (1990); 4,018 (1980)   **Pop Density:** 131.8
Land: 40.6 sq. mi.; **Water:** 0.2 sq. mi.

Incorporated Aug 18, 1747.

Name origin: For Edward Richmond, RI attorney-general (1677–80).

South Kingstown
Town
ZIP: 02874   **Lat:** 41-25-18 N   **Long:** 71-33-06 W
Pop: 24,631 (1990); 20,414 (1980)   **Pop Density:** 431.4
Land: 57.1 sq. mi.; **Water:** 22.7 sq. mi.

In southern RI on Narragansett Bay. Incorporated Feb 26, 1723, at separation from North Kingstown. Includes the village of Kingston.

Name origin: For Charles II (1630–85), king of England. Formerly called King's Towne and Rochester.

Wakefield-Peacedale
CDP
ZIP: 02883   **Lat:** 41-26-44 N   **Long:** 71-30-03 W
Pop: 7,134 (1990); 6,474 (1980)   **Pop Density:** 1455.9
Land: 4.9 sq. mi.; **Water:** 0.2 sq. mi.

Westerly
Town
ZIP: 02883   **Lat:** 41-19-38 N   **Long:** 71-47-55 W
Pop: 21,605 (1990); 18,580 (1980)   **Pop Density:** 717.8
Land: 30.1 sq. mi.; **Water:** 41.0 sq. mi.

In southwestern RI, separated from Pawcatuck, CT, by the Pawcatuck River. Incorporated May 14, 1669

Name origin: For its location in the most westerly part of the state. Indian name Misquamicut.

Index to Places and Counties in Rhode Island

Vermont

VERMONT

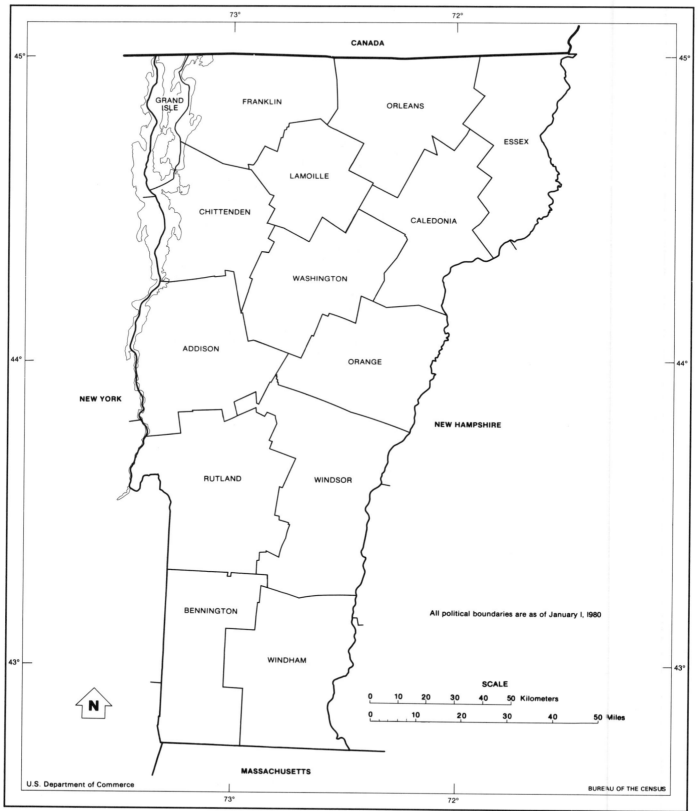

CANADA

GRAND ISLE

FRANKLIN

ORLEANS

ESSEX

LAMOILLE

CHITTENDEN

CALEDONIA

WASHINGTON

ADDISON

ORANGE

NEW YORK

NEW HAMPSHIRE

RUTLAND

WINDSOR

All political boundaries are as of January 1, 1980

BENNINGTON

WINDHAM

N

SCALE

0 10 20 30 40 50 Kilometers

0   10   20   30   40   50 Miles

U.S. Department of Commerce

BUREAU OF THE CENSUS

MASSACHUSETTS

Vermont

Population: 562,758 (1990); 511,456 (1980)
Population rank (1990): 48
Percent population change (1980-1990): 10.0
Population projection: 597,000 (1995);
  619,000 (2000)

Area: total 9,615 sq. mi.; 9,249 sq. mi. land, 366 sq. mi. water
Area rank: 45
Highest elevation: 4,393 ft., Mount Mansfield (Lamoille County)
Lowest point: 95 ft. at Lake Champlain (Franklin County)

State capital: Montpelier (Washington County)
Largest city: Burlington (39,127)
Second largest city: Rutland (18,230)
Largest county: Chittenden (131,761)

Total housing units: 271,214
No. of occupied housing units: 210,650
Vacant housing units (%): 22.3
Distribution of population by race and Hispanic origin (%):
  White: 98.6
  Black: 0.3
  Hispanic (any race): 0.7
  Native American: 0.3
  Asian/Pacific: 0.6
  Other: 0.1

Admission date: March 4, 1791 (14th state).

Location: In the northeastern United States, bordering Massachusetts, New York, the Canadian province of Quebec, and New Hampshire.

Name Origin: From French *vert* 'green' and *mont* 'mountain,' originally applied to the Green Mountains east of Lake Champlain by French explorer Samuel de Champlain on his map of 1612. Dr. Thomas Young, a framer of the Pennsylvania constitution and active in championing the cause of Vermont statehood, combined the words into Vermont in 1777. The region had previously been referred to as New Connecticut.

State animal: Morgan horse
State beverage: milk
State bird: hermit thrush *(Hylocichla guttata)*
State fish: cold water—brook trout *(Salvelinus fontinalis)*; **warm water**—walleye pike *(Stizostedion vitreum vitreum)*
State flower: red clover *(Trifolium pratense)*
State insect: honeybee *(Apis mellifera)*
State song: "Hail, Vermont!"

State tree: sugar maple *(Acer saccharum)*

State motto: Freedom and Unity
State nickname: The Green Mountain State

Area code: 802
Time zone: Eastern
Abbreviations: VT (postal); Vt. (traditional)
Part of (region): New England

Local Government

Counties

Vermont has 14 counties. A county seat is called a shire town, from the old English term for county.

Municipalities

There are nine cities, 237 organized towns, five unorganized towns, 45 incorporated villages, and three gores and one grant (nongoverned areas). The towns are similar to those in other parts of New England; there may be several communities within them, but they are all under a single town government. The first Tuesday in March of every year voters have a town meeting, debate the budget and other topics, and elect local officials for the coming year.

Settlement History and Early Development

Archaeological finds along the Otter River in the northwestern part of present-day Vermont show that the area has been inhabited since about 10,000 B.C. From about A.D. 1200 it was the hunting ground for the Abenaki, Mahican, and Penacook tribes of Algonquian Indians. Iroquois from the area of present-day New York State and elsewhere drove the Algonquians out for a time, but they returned in the early seventeenth century and, aided by the French, defeated the Iroquois.

Samuel de Champlain crossed the lake that now bears his name (in northwest Vermont) in 1609 and claimed the area for France. In 1666 the French built and briefly occupied Fort Ste. Anne on Isle La Motte in Lake Champlain. From 1650 to 1760 French, Iroquois from New York, Dutch, and English explorers passed through the state along trails connecting Montreal with Massachusetts and New York. In 1724 the first permanent white settlement was established at Fort Drummer near present-day Brattleboro by Massachusetts settlers to protect their western region from raids by the French and Indians.

The Lake Champlain region was the site of many major battles during the French and Indian War (1754–63). The Treaty of Paris (1763) granted control of Vermont and much of the rest of North America to England.

The royal governor of New Hampshire, Benning Wentworth, claiming his colony extended as far west as did Massachusetts and Connecticut, made 131 land grants by 1764. But New York claimed the same land and granted it to other settlers. That same year King George III of England declared that New York's northeastern boundary was the Connecticut River and recognized the grants New York had made. The crown ordered holders of the New Hampshire Grants to either surrender their land or pay New York for it. These settlers, under the leadership of Ethan Allen, organized the Green Mountain Boys in 1770 to defend their land and drive the New Yorkers from it.

The American Revolution and Statehood

The Revolutionary War broke out in Massachusetts in 1775 before the Vermont land disputes were settled. Vermonters united to aid the patriots and Ethan Allen, Benedict Arnold, and the Green Mountain Boys captured Fort Ticonderoga in May 1775 in what is generally considered the first offensive by the colonists in the Revolution. The Battle of Bennington, on August 16, 1777, was a major conflict that helped end British operations in the northern colonies. Often thought of as a Vermont battle, it was actually fought just to the west, in New York.

On January 15, 1777, Vermont declared itself an independent republic to be called New Connecticut. In July of that year Vermonters adopted their present name and their first constitution, which abolished slavery and gave all men the right to vote. Vermont was admitted as the fourteenth state on March 4, 1791, the first state that had not formerly been a colony.

The War of 1812 and the Civil War

Vermont volunteers fought the British during the War of 1812, but it was an unpopular war since the state's economy depended in large measure on trade with British-controlled Canada to the north. Northwestern Vermonters had smuggled to avoid the U.S. foreign trade embargo of 1808, and trade with Britain continued during the war.

About 34,000 Vermonters served with the Union forces during the Civil War. The only Civil War action that took place north of Pennsylvania occurred in St. Albans, Vermont on October 19, 1864, when about twenty-two Confederate soldiers robbed the banks there and fled to Canada with over $20,000.

Business and Industry

On July 31, 1790, the first patent issued by the U.S. government was granted to Samuel Hopkins for his method of making potash and pearl ash out of wood ash. During the nineteenth century, Vermont towns and villages grew, particularly along rivers that could provide water power. The Champlain-Hudson Canal opened in 1823, connecting Lake Champlain to the Hudson River in New York, and allowing local goods and produce to be shipped to New York City entirely by water. By 1840 rural-focused Vermont had six sheep for each person, and farmers in the Champlain Valley who raised Spanish Merino sheep for wool prospered. Many small water-powered mills were built to process the wool, but during the mid-1800s an abundant supply from western states and other countries caused the price of wool to drop. Vermont changed its emphasis from sheep-raising to dairy-farming.

After the Civil War agriculture declined and more and more farmers left either for work in the cities or moved to better farmland in the south and west. In the latter part of the nineteenth century the wood-processing and cheese-making industries grew. Burlington expanded as a port city, processing lumber from Canada and shipping it to other cities in the U.S. The granite industry in Barre boomed, but the formerly important textile industry declined, as many of the mills moved south where labor was cheaper. In the early 1900s Vermont became the first state to establish an official bureau to attract tourists.

After World War II, small manufacturing industries moved to Vermont. Electronics manufacturing, construction, and service industries all grew during the 1980s. Vermont's beauty has attracted tourists, winter-sports enthusiasts, and buyers of vacation homes, contributing to the state's economy but causing concern about the need to protect the environment and open spaces.

State Boundaries

The grants from King Henry of France in 1603 and from King James of England in 1606, as well as the charter of New England in 1620 included the territory of present-day Vermont. In 1772 a line was surveyed for Vermont's northern border with Canada at the supposed 45th parallel. It was later found to be up to 1.1 miles north of the parallel in some parts, but a convention between the U.S. and Great Britain in 1842 agreed upon the line as marked. The Vermont-Massachusetts border was set by the Crown on August 5, 1740. Vermont's border dispute with New York was settled in 1790 after Vermont paid New York $30,000. The Vermont-New Hampshire border, as decreed on May 29, 1933, by the U.S. Supreme Court, is formed by the Connecticut River, which is entirely within New Hampshire.

Vermont Counties

Addison	Chittenden	Grand Isle	Orleans	Windham
Bennington	Essex	Lamoille	Rutland	Windsor
Caledonia	Franklin	Orange	Washington	

Addison County
County Seat: Middlebury (ZIP: 05753)

Pop: 32,953 (1990); 29,406 (1980)   **Pop Density:** 42.8
Land: 770.0 sq. mi.; **Water:** 38.4 sq. mi.   **Area Code:** 802

On central western border of VT, west of Barre; organized Oct 18, 1785 (prior to statehood) from Rutland County.

Name origin: For the town of Addison.

Addison   Town
ZIP: 05491   **Lat:** 44-04-27 N **Long:** 73-20-48 W
Pop: 1,023 (1990); 889 (1980)   **Pop Density:** 24.5
Land: 41.8 sq. mi.; **Water:** 7.3 sq. mi.

Chartered Oct 14, 1761.

Name origin: For Joseph Addison (1672–1719), British author.

Bridport   Town
ZIP: 05734   **Lat:** 43-58-54 N **Long:** 73-19-59 W
Pop: 1,137 (1990); 997 (1980)   **Pop Density:** 25.9
Land: 43.9 sq. mi.; **Water:** 2.3 sq. mi.

Chartered Oct 9, 1761.

Name origin: For the English Channel port of Bridport.

Bristol   Town
ZIP: 05443   **Lat:** 44-07-45 N **Long:** 73-04-15 W
Pop: 3,762 (1990); 3,293 (1980)   **Pop Density:** 91.1
Land: 41.3 sq. mi.; **Water:** 0.4 sq. mi.

Chartered Jun 26, 1762; incorporated Mar 1903. Village and town are not coextensive.

Name origin: Named in 1789 for Bristol, RI. Previously named Pocock.

*Bristol   Village
ZIP: 05443   **Lat:** 44-08-11 N **Long:** 73-04-51 W
Pop: 1,801 (1990); 1,793 (1980)   **Pop Density:** 2001.1
Land: 0.9 sq. mi.; **Water:** 0.0 sq. mi.   **Elev:** 571 ft.

Cornwall   Town
          Lat: 43-57-44 N **Long:** 73-12-38 W
Pop: 1,101 (1990); 993 (1980)   **Pop Density:** 38.5
Land: 28.6 sq. mi.; **Water:** 0.0 sq. mi.

Chartered Nov 3, 1761.

Name origin: For Cornwall, England.

Ferrisburg   Town
ZIP: 05456   **Lat:** 44-12-08 N **Long:** 73-16-36 W
Pop: 2,317 (1990); 2,117 (1980)   **Pop Density:** 48.4
Land: 47.9 sq. mi.; **Water:** 13.3 sq. mi.

Chartered Jun 24, 1762.

Name origin: For founder Benjamin Ferris.

Goshen   Town
          Lat: 43-52-03 N **Long:** 73-00-28 W
Pop: 226 (1990); 163 (1980)   **Pop Density:** 10.4
Land: 21.7 sq. mi.; **Water:** 0.1 sq. mi.

Chartered Feb 2, 1792.

Name origin: For Goshen, CT.

Granville   Town
ZIP: 05747   **Lat:** 43-59-59 N **Long:** 72-50-22 W
Pop: 309 (1990); 288 (1980)   **Pop Density:** 6.0
Land: 51.9 sq. mi.; **Water:** 0.0 sq. mi.

Chartered Aug 2, 1781.

Name origin: For John Carteret (1690–1763), 1st Earl of Granville.

Hancock   Town
ZIP: 05748   **Lat:** 43-55-37 N **Long:** 72-55-00 W
Pop: 340 (1990); 334 (1980)   **Pop Density:** 8.7
Land: 38.9 sq. mi.; **Water:** 0.0 sq. mi.

Chartered Jul 31, 1781; organized Jun 18, 1792.

Name origin: For John Hancock (1737–93), noted signer of the Declaration of Independence and Revolutionary War patriot.

Leicester   Town
          Lat: 43-52-10 N **Long:** 73-05-57 W
Pop: 871 (1990); 803 (1980)   **Pop Density:** 41.7
Land: 20.9 sq. mi.; **Water:** 0.8 sq. mi.

Chartered Oct 20, 1761.

Name origin: Either for Leicester, MA, or the city in England.

Lincoln   Town
ZIP: 05443   **Lat:** 44-05-38 N **Long:** 72-58-19 W
Pop: 974 (1990); 870 (1980)   **Pop Density:** 22.2
Land: 43.9 sq. mi.; **Water:** 0.0 sq. mi.

Chartered Nov 9, 1780.

Name origin: For Revolutionary War general Benjamin Lincoln (1733–1810).

Middlebury   Town
ZIP: 05753   **Lat:** 44-00-29 N **Long:** 73-07-05 W
Pop: 8,034 (1990); 7,574 (1980)   **Pop Density:** 205.5
Land: 39.1 sq. mi.; **Water:** 0.1 sq. mi.

In west-central VT, northwest of Rutland. Chartered Nov 2, 1761. Site of Middlebury College (1800).

Name origin: For being the "middle" one of three towns in the area chartered at the same time.

Monkton   Town
          Lat: 44-13-12 N **Long:** 73-07-33 W
Pop: 1,482 (1990); 1,201 (1980)   **Pop Density:** 41.1
Land: 36.1 sq. mi.; **Water:** 0.2 sq. mi.

Chartered Jun 24, 1762.

Name origin: For Gen. Robert Monckton (1726–82), "just and moderate in his American dealings"; with spelling variation.

New Haven   Town
ZIP: 05472   **Lat:** 44-06-30 N **Long:** 73-10-17 W
Pop: 1,375 (1990); 1,217 (1980)   **Pop Density:** 33.1
Land: 41.5 sq. mi.; **Water:** 0.1 sq. mi.

Chartered Nov 2, 1761.

Name origin: For New Haven, CT.

Orwell
Town
ZIP: 05760   **Lat:** 43-48-30 N **Long:** 73-17-43 W
Pop: 1,114 (1990); 901 (1980)   **Pop Density:** 23.5
Land: 47.4 sq. mi.; **Water:** 2.3 sq. mi.
Chartered Aug 18, 1763.
Name origin: For Francis Vernon, the 1st Baron Orwell.

Panton
Town
ZIP: 05491   **Lat:** 44-08-24 N **Long:** 73-20-59 W
Pop: 606 (1990); 537 (1980)   **Pop Density:** 39.4
Land: 15.4 sq. mi.; **Water:** 6.5 sq. mi.
Chartered Nov 3, 1761.
Name origin: For Panton, Lincolnshire, England.

Ripton
Town
ZIP: 05766   **Lat:** 43-59-44 N **Long:** 72-58-57 W
Pop: 444 (1990); 327 (1980)   **Pop Density:** 8.9
Land: 49.7 sq. mi.; **Water:** 0.0 sq. mi.
Chartered Apr 13, 1781; organized 1828.
Name origin: For Ripton, Huntingdonshire, England.

Salisbury
Town
ZIP: 05769   **Lat:** 43-55-00 N **Long:** 73-06-46 W
Pop: 1,024 (1990); 881 (1980)   **Pop Density:** 35.2
Land: 29.1 sq. mi.; **Water:** 1.1 sq. mi.
Settled 1720; chartered Nov 3, 1761.
Name origin: For Salisbury, Wiltshire, England.

Shoreham
Town
ZIP: 05770   **Lat:** 43-53-30 N **Long:** 73-18-47 W
Pop: 1,115 (1990); 972 (1980)   **Pop Density:** 25.8
Land: 43.3 sq. mi.; **Water:** 2.9 sq. mi.
Chartered Oct 8, 1761; founded 1766.
Name origin: For Shoreham-by-the-Sea, England.

Starksboro
Town
ZIP: 05487   **Lat:** 44-13-36 N **Long:** 72-59-52 W
Pop: 1,511 (1990); 1,336 (1980)   **Pop Density:** 33.1
Land: 45.7 sq. mi.; **Water:** 0.0 sq. mi.
Chartered Nov 9, 1780.
Name origin: For Revolutionary War hero Gen. John Stark (1728–1822).

Vergennes
City
ZIP: 05491   **Lat:** 44-10-02 N **Long:** 73-15-20 W
Pop: 2,578 (1990); 2,273 (1980)   **Pop Density:** 1074.2
Land: 2.4 sq. mi.; **Water:** 0.1 sq. mi.   **Elev:** 205 ft.
Incorporated Oct 23, 1788.
Name origin: For French foreign affairs minister Charles Gravier, Comte de Vergennes, who assisted the colonies during the American Revolution.

Waltham
Town
ZIP: 05491   **Lat:** 44-07-25 N **Long:** 73-13-43 W
Pop: 454 (1990); 394 (1980)   **Pop Density:** 51.0
Land: 8.9 sq. mi.; **Water:** 0.1 sq. mi.
Organized Oct 31, 1796.
Name origin: Named by its founders for Waltham, MA.

Weybridge
Town
ZIP: 05753   **Lat:** 44-02-27 N **Long:** 73-13-48 W
Pop: 749 (1990); 667 (1980)   **Pop Density:** 44.1
Land: 17.0 sq. mi.; **Water:** 0.5 sq. mi.
Chartered Nov 3, 1761; organized 1789.
Name origin: Probably for Weybridge, Surrey, England.

Whiting
Town
ZIP: 05778   **Lat:** 43-51-52 N **Long:** 73-12-07 W
Pop: 407 (1990); 379 (1980)   **Pop Density:** 29.7
Land: 13.7 sq. mi.; **Water:** 0.0 sq. mi.
Chartered Aug 6, 1763.
Name origin: For five original settlers with the last name Whiting.

Bennington County
County Seat: Bennington (ZIP: 05201)

Pop: 35,845 (1990); 33,345 (1980)   **Pop Density:** 53.0
Land: 676.3 sq. mi.; **Water:** 1.4 sq. mi.   **Area Code:** 802
On the southwestern border of VT, south of Rutland. Oldest county, organized Feb 11, 1779 (prior to statehood).
Name origin: For the town, its county seat.

Arlington
Town
ZIP: 05250   **Lat:** 43-04-58 N **Long:** 73-11-22 W
Pop: 2,299 (1990); 2,184 (1980)   **Pop Density:** 54.2
Land: 42.4 sq. mi.; **Water:** 0.0 sq. mi.
Chartered Jul 28, 1761.
Name origin: For Augustus Henry Fitzroy (1735–1811), the 4th earl of Arlington, and a friend of the American colonies.

Bennington
Town
ZIP: 05201   **Lat:** 42-53-09 N **Long:** 73-12-47 W
Pop: 16,451 (1990); 15,815 (1980)   **Pop Density:** 388.0
Land: 42.4 sq. mi.; **Water:** 0.1 sq. mi.
In southwestern VT, 30 mi. west of Brattleboro. Knit-goods manufacturing. Chartered Jun 3, 1749.
Name origin: For Benning Wentworth (1696–1770), colonial

governor of NH and a founder of Dartmouth College. In 1750 he granted the land for the town, which was given his mother's maiden name.

Dorset
Town
ZIP: 05251   **Lat:** 43-16-08 N **Long:** 73-03-11 W
Pop: 1,918 (1990); 1,648 (1980)   **Pop Density:** 40.1
Land: 47.8 sq. mi.; **Water:** 0.0 sq. mi.
Chartered Aug 20, 1761.
Name origin: For Lionel Sackville, the 1st Duke of Dorset.

Glastenbury
Town
ZIP: 05262   **Lat:** 42-58-38 N **Long:** 73-04-29 W
Pop: 7 (1990); 3 (1980)   **Pop Density:** 0.2
Land: 44.5 sq. mi.; **Water:** 0.0 sq. mi.

Landgrove　　　　　　　　　　　　　　Town
ZIP: 05148　　　　**Lat:** 43-15-38 N　**Long:** 72-50-55 W
Pop: 134 (1990); 121 (1980)　　　**Pop Density:** 14.7
Land: 9.1 sq. mi.; **Water:** 0.0 sq. mi.

Chartered Nov 9, 1780.

Name origin: Named by its first settlers for the many trees covering the land.

Manchester　　　　　　　　　　　　　Town
ZIP: 05255　　　　**Lat:** 43-09-41 N　**Long:** 73-04-19 W
Pop: 3,622 (1990); 3,261 (1980)　　　**Pop Density:** 85.8
Land: 42.2 sq. mi.; **Water:** 0.1 sq. mi.

Chartered Aug 11, 1761. Village and town are not coextensive.

Name origin: For Manchester, England.

*Manchester　　　　　　　　　　　　Village
ZIP: 05255　　　　**Lat:** 43-09-43 N　**Long:** 73-04-19 W
Pop: 561 (1990); 563 (1980)　　　**Pop Density:** 155.8
Land: 3.6 sq. mi.; **Water:** 0.0 sq. mi.　　　**Elev:** 899 ft.

North Bennington　　　　　　　　　Village
ZIP: 05257　　　　**Lat:** 42-55-31 N　**Long:** 73-14-39 W
Pop: 1,520 (1990); 1,685 (1980)　　　**Pop Density:** 723.8
Land: 2.1 sq. mi.; **Water:** 0.0 sq. mi.

Name origin: For its location within the town of Bennington.

Old Bennington　　　　　　　　　　Village
ZIP: 05201　　　　**Lat:** 42-52-59 N　**Long:** 73-12-49 W
Pop: 279 (1990); 353 (1980)　　　**Pop Density:** 558.0
Land: 0.5 sq. mi.; **Water:** 0.0 sq. mi.

Name origin: Site of the earliest settlement in the town of Bennington.

Peru　　　　　　　　　　　　　　　Town
ZIP: 05152　　　　**Lat:** 43-15-43 N　**Long:** 72-54-11 W
Pop: 324 (1990); 312 (1980)　　　**Pop Density:** 8.7
Land: 37.3 sq. mi.; **Water:** 0.1 sq. mi.

Chartered Oct 13, 1761.

Name origin: For the South American country. Originally called Bromley.

Pownal　　　　　　　　　　　　　Town
ZIP: 05261　　　　**Lat:** 42-47-08 N　**Long:** 73-12-41 W
Pop: 3,485 (1990); 3,269 (1980)　　　**Pop Density:** 74.6
Land: 46.7 sq. mi.; **Water:** 0.1 sq. mi.

Chartered Jan 8, 1760.

Name origin: For John and Thomas Pownal, its original charterers.

Readsboro　　　　　　　　　　　　Town
　　　　　　　　　　Lat: 42-48-04 N　**Long:** 72-58-25 W
Pop: 762 (1990); 638 (1980)　　　**Pop Density:** 20.9
Land: 36.4 sq. mi.; **Water:** 0.1 sq. mi.

Chartered Jul 4, 1764. Village and town are not coextensive.
Name origin: For the first landowner, John Reade.

Rupert　　　　　　　　　　　　　Town
ZIP: 05768　　　　**Lat:** 43-15-59 N　**Long:** 73-12-03 W
Pop: 654 (1990); 605 (1980)　　　**Pop Density:** 14.7
Land: 44.6 sq. mi.; **Water:** 0.0 sq. mi.

Chartered Aug 20, 1761.

Name origin: Named by NH colonial Gov. Benning Went-

worth (1696–1770) for Prince Rupert (1619–82), Count Palatine of Rhine and Duke of Cumberland.

Sandgate　　　　　　　　　　　　Town
ZIP: 05250　　　　**Lat:** 43-09-12 N　**Long:** 73-11-22 W
Pop: 278 (1990); 234 (1980)　　　**Pop Density:** 6.6
Land: 42.2 sq. mi.; **Water:** 0.0 sq. mi.

Chartered Aug 11, 1761; settled late 1700s.
Name origin: For Sandgate, England.

Searsburg　　　　　　　　　　　　Town
ZIP: 05363　　　　**Lat:** 42-53-21 N　**Long:** 72-57-49 W
Pop: 85 (1990); 72 (1980)　　　**Pop Density:** 4.0
Land: 21.5 sq. mi.; **Water:** 0.0 sq. mi.

Chartered Feb 23, 1781.

Name origin: Probably for Revolutionary War patriot Isaac Sears (1730–86).

Shaftsbury　　　　　　　　　　　　Town
ZIP: 05262　　　　**Lat:** 42-58-45 N　**Long:** 73-12-22 W
Pop: 3,368 (1990); 3,001 (1980)　　　**Pop Density:** 78.1
Land: 43.1 sq. mi.; **Water:** 0.1 sq. mi.

Chartered Aug 20, 1761.

Name origin: Probably for Shaftesbury, England, with spelling variation.

Stamford　　　　　　　　　　　　Town
ZIP: 05352　　　　**Lat:** 42-46-43 N　**Long:** 73-04-41 W
Pop: 773 (1990); 773 (1980)　　　**Pop Density:** 19.6
Land: 39.5 sq. mi.; **Water:** 0.1 sq. mi.

Chartered Mar 6, 1753.

Name origin: Named by NH colonial Gov. Benning Wentworth (1696–1770), for Harry Grey, 4th Earl of Stamford.

Sunderland　　　　　　　　　　　Town
ZIP: 05250　　　　**Lat:** 43-03-56 N　**Long:** 73-04-43 W
Pop: 872 (1990); 768 (1980)　　　**Pop Density:** 19.2
Land: 45.4 sq. mi.; **Water:** 0.2 sq. mi.

Chartered Jul 29, 1796.

Name origin: For George Spencer, 6th Earl of Sunderland.

Winhall　　　　　　　　　　　　　Town
ZIP: 05340　　　　**Lat:** 43-10-09 N　**Long:** 72-55-21 W
Pop: 482 (1990); 327 (1980)　　　**Pop Density:** 11.0
Land: 43.7 sq. mi.; **Water:** 0.3 sq. mi.

Chartered Sep 15, 1761; settled after the Revolutionary War.
Name origin: Possibly for Winhall, England.

Woodford　　　　　　　　　　　　Town
ZIP: 05201　　　　**Lat:** 42-52-51 N　**Long:** 73-04-40 W
Pop: 331 (1990); 314 (1980)　　　**Pop Density:** 7.0
Land: 47.5 sq. mi.; **Water:** 0.1 sq. mi.

Chartered Mar 6, 1753; organized Feb 11, 1789.
Name origin: For Woodford, Essex, England.

Caledonia County
County Seat: Saint Johnsbury (ZIP: 05819)

Pop: 27,846 (1990); 25,808 (1980)
Land: 651.0 sq. mi.; **Water:** 6.8 sq. mi.

Pop Density: 42.8
Area Code: 802

In northeastern VT, east of Montpelier; organized Nov 5, 1792 from Chittenden and Orange counties.

Name origin: For the ancient name of Scotland; name given by the many Scots who had settled in this part of the state.

Barnet
Town
ZIP: 05821   **Lat:** 44-19-30 N **Long:** 72-04-38 W
Pop: 1,415 (1990); 1,338 (1980)   **Pop Density:** 33.4
Land: 42.4 sq. mi.; **Water:** 1.2 sq. mi.
Chartered Sep 16, 1763.
Name origin: For Barnet, Hertfordshire, England, former home of an early settler.

Burke
Town
ZIP: 05871   **Lat:** 44-36-53 N **Long:** 71-55-53 W
Pop: 1,406 (1990); 1,385 (1980)   **Pop Density:** 41.6
Land: 33.8 sq. mi.; **Water:** 0.0 sq. mi.
Chartered Feb 26, 1782.
Name origin: For Edmund Burke (1729–97), English statesman and supporter of the American colonies.

Danville
Town
ZIP: 05828   **Lat:** 44-25-26 N **Long:** 72-07-42 W
Pop: 1,917 (1990); 1,705 (1980)   **Pop Density:** 31.5
Land: 60.8 sq. mi.; **Water:** 0.3 sq. mi.
Chartered 1786; organized Oct 31, 1786.
Name origin: For Jean Baptiste Bourguignon d'Anville (1697–1782), royal cartographer of France.

Groton
Town
ZIP: 05046   **Lat:** 44-14-57 N **Long:** 72-15-30 W
Pop: 862 (1990); 667 (1980)   **Pop Density:** 16.0
Land: 53.9 sq. mi.; **Water:** 1.0 sq. mi.
Chartered Oct 20, 1789.
Name origin: For Groton, MA, which is named for Groton, Suffolk, England.

Hardwick
Town
ZIP: 05843   **Lat:** 44-31-45 N **Long:** 72-20-46 W
Pop: 2,964 (1990); 2,613 (1980)   **Pop Density:** 76.8
Land: 38.6 sq. mi.; **Water:** 0.4 sq. mi.
Chartered Aug 19, 1781. Village and town are not coextensive.
Name origin: For Philip Yorke, Earl of Hardwicke, with spelling variation.

Kirby
Town
ZIP: 05824   **Lat:** 44-30-10 N **Long:** 71-54-49 W
Pop: 347 (1990); 282 (1980)   **Pop Density:** 14.0
Land: 24.7 sq. mi.; **Water:** 0.0 sq. mi.
Chartered Oct 27, 1790; incorporated 1807.
Name origin: For Kirby, England.

Lyndon
Town
ZIP: 05849   **Lat:** 44-32-36 N **Long:** 72-00-26 W
Pop: 5,371 (1990); 4,924 (1980)   **Pop Density:** 136.3
Land: 39.4 sq. mi.; **Water:** 0.0 sq. mi.
Chartered Jun 27, 1781.
Name origin: For Josiah Lyndon Arnold, the son of a founder.

Lyndonville
Village
ZIP: 05851   **Lat:** 44-32-05 N **Long:** 72-00-10 W
Pop: 1,255 (1990); 1,401 (1980)   **Pop Density:** 1568.8
Land: 0.8 sq. mi.; **Water:** 0.0 sq. mi.   **Elev:** 714 ft.
Chartered to a group of Revolutionary War soldiers. Part of the town of Lyndon.

Newark
Town
ZIP: 05871   **Lat:** 44-42-22 N **Long:** 71-55-18 W
Pop: 354 (1990); 280 (1980)   **Pop Density:** 9.6
Land: 36.8 sq. mi.; **Water:** 0.4 sq. mi.
Chartered Aug 15, 1781.
Name origin: Named in the 1780s by its settlers, possibly referring to their town in the English sense as a 'new undertaking.'

Peacham
Town
ZIP: 05862   **Lat:** 44-19-42 N **Long:** 72-12-40 W
Pop: 627 (1990); 531 (1980)   **Pop Density:** 13.4
Land: 46.7 sq. mi.; **Water:** 1.0 sq. mi.
Chartered Dec 31, 1763.
Name origin: For the popular heroine in *The Beggar's Opera* by John Gay (1685–1732).

Ryegate
Town
ZIP: 05042   **Lat:** 44-13-31 N **Long:** 72-06-49 W
Pop: 1,058 (1990); 1,000 (1980)   **Pop Density:** 28.8
Land: 36.7 sq. mi.; **Water:** 0.2 sq. mi.
Chartered Sep 8, 1763.
Name origin: Named in 1760s by its settlers, for Reigate, England, with a spelling alteration.

St. Johnsbury
Town
ZIP: 05819   **Lat:** 44-27-18 N **Long:** 72-00-36 W
Pop: 7,608 (1990); 7,938 (1980)   **Pop Density:** 207.3
Land: 36.7 sq. mi.; **Water:** 0.1 sq. mi.
Chartered Nov 1, 1786.
Name origin: For author Michel Guillaume St. Jean Crèvecoeur (1735–1813), who wrote under the pen name of J. Hector St. John.

Sheffield
Town
ZIP: 05866   **Lat:** 44-38-25 N **Long:** 72-07-52 W
Pop: 541 (1990); 435 (1980)   **Pop Density:** 16.5
Land: 32.7 sq. mi.; **Water:** 0.1 sq. mi.
Chartered Oct 25, 1763.
Name origin: For Sheffield, MA.

Stannard
Town
ZIP: 05842   **Lat:** 44-32-38 N **Long:** 72-12-12 W
Pop: 148 (1990); 142 (1980)   **Pop Density:** 11.8
Land: 12.5 sq. mi.; **Water:** 0.0 sq. mi.
Organized Aug 18, 1867.
Name origin: Named in 1867 for VT's Civil War hero Gen. George Stannard. Originally called Goshen.

Sutton
Town
ZIP: 05867   **Lat:** 44-39-13 N   **Long:** 72-01-47 W
Pop: 854 (1990); 667 (1980)   **Pop Density:** 22.4
Land: 38.2 sq. mi.; **Water:** 0.1 sq. mi.

Chartered Feb 26, 1782.

Name origin: Named in the 1800s for Sutton, MA. Originally called Billymead.

Walden
Town
ZIP: 05873   **Lat:** 44-28-48 N   **Long:** 72-14-47 W
Pop: 703 (1990); 575 (1980)   **Pop Density:** 18.1
Land: 38.9 sq. mi.; **Water:** 0.3 sq. mi.

Chartered Aug 18, 1781.

Name origin: For Samuel Walden, the original grantee.

Waterford
Town
ZIP: 05848   **Lat:** 44-22-03 N   **Long:** 71-56-07 W
Pop: 1,190 (1990); 882 (1980)   **Pop Density:** 31.0
Land: 38.4 sq. mi.; **Water:** 1.4 sq. mi.

Chartered Nov 8, 1780.

Name origin: Either for Waterford, Ireland, or for being the site of a ford across the Connecticut River.

West Burke
Village
ZIP: 05871   **Lat:** 44-38-37 N   **Long:** 71-58-49 W
Pop: 353 (1990); 338 (1980)   **Pop Density:** 882.5
Land: 0.4 sq. mi.; **Water:** 0.0 sq. mi.

Name origin: For its location in relation to the town of Burke.

Wheelock
Town
ZIP: 05851   **Lat:** 44-34-44 N   **Long:** 72-08-25 W
Pop: 481 (1990); 444 (1980)   **Pop Density:** 12.1
Land: 39.8 sq. mi.; **Water:** 0.3 sq. mi.

Chartered Jun 14, 1785.

Name origin: For the Rev. Eleazar Wheelock (1711–79), the founder of Dartmouth College.

Chittenden County
County Seat: Burlington (ZIP: 05402)

Pop: 131,761 (1990); 115,534 (1980)   **Pop Density:** 244.5
Land: 539.0 sq. mi.; **Water:** 80.7 sq. mi.   **Area Code:** 802

In northwestern VT, west of Montpelier; organized Oct 22, 1787 (prior to statehood) from Addison County.

Name origin: For Thomas Chittenden (1730–97), first governor of the republic of VT (1778–89; 1790–91), and of the state (1791–97).

Bolton
Town
       Lat: 44-24-39 N   **Long:** 72-51-50 W
Pop: 971 (1990); 715 (1980)   **Pop Density:** 22.8
Land: 42.6 sq. mi.; **Water:** 0.3 sq. mi.

Granted Jun 7, 1763.

Name origin: Named by NH colonial Gov. Benning Wentworth (1696–1770), possibly for one of the Dukes of Bolton.

Buels Gore
Pop. Place
       Lat: 44-12-34 N   **Long:** 72-56-46 W
Pop: 2 (1990); 9 (1980)   **Pop Density:** 0.4
Land: 5.0 sq. mi.; **Water:** 0.0 sq. mi.

Burlington
City
ZIP: 05401   **Lat:** 44-29-17 N   **Long:** 73-13-34 W
Pop: 39,127 (1990); 37,712 (1980)   **Pop Density:** 3726.4
Land: 10.5 sq. mi.; **Water:** 4.9 sq. mi.   **Elev:** 113 ft.

In northwestern VT on Lake Champlain, 35 mi. northwest of Montpelier. State's largest city. Chartered Jun 7, 1763; settled 1773; organized 1797; incorporated 1864. Univ. of VT (1791), Trinity Coll. (1925). Revolutionary War hero Ethan Allen (1738–89) buried here.

Name origin: Named in the 18th century for one of the Earls of Burlington. Nicknamed the "Queen City."

Charlotte
Town
ZIP: 05445   **Lat:** 44-18-55 N   **Long:** 73-14-04 W
Pop: 3,148 (1990); 2,561 (1980)   **Pop Density:** 76.2
Land: 41.3 sq. mi.; **Water:** 9.0 sq. mi.

Chartered Jun 24, 1762.

Name origin: For Charlotte Sophia (1744–1818) of Mecklenburg-Strelitz, wife of George III (1738–1820), King of England.

Colchester
Town
ZIP: 05446   **Lat:** 44-33-34 N   **Long:** 73-12-39 W
Pop: 14,731 (1990); 12,629 (1980)   **Pop Density:** 398.1
Land: 37.0 sq. mi.; **Water:** 21.8 sq. mi.

In northwestern VT, 5 mi. northeast of Burlington. Chartered Jun 7, 1763.

Name origin: Named in 1763 either for British nobleman William Henry Nassau du Zurlostine, Baron of Colchester, or for Viscount Tunbridge, Baron of Enfield and Colchester, a political figure under George II (1683–1760), King of England.

Essex
Town
ZIP: 05451   **Lat:** 44-30-50 N   **Long:** 73-03-43 W
Pop: 16,498 (1990); 14,392 (1980)   **Pop Density:** 423.0
Land: 39.0 sq. mi.; **Water:** 0.3 sq. mi.

In northwest VT on the Winooski River, 4 mi. east of Burlington. Industrial village. Chartered Jun 7, 1763.

Name origin: For Essex, England.

Essex Junction
Village
ZIP: 05452   Lat: 44-29-25 N Long: 73-06-44 W
Pop: 8,396 (1990); 7,033 (1980)   Pop Density: 1679.2
Land: 5.0 sq. mi.; Water: 0.1 sq. mi.   Elev: 347 ft.
Granted 1763.
Name origin: For its location in the town of Essex; near its center is a railroad junction.

Hinesburg
Town
ZIP: 05461   Lat: 44-19-20 N Long: 73-05-01 W
Pop: 3,780 (1990); 2,690 (1980)   Pop Density: 94.7
Land: 39.9 sq. mi.; Water: 0.3 sq. mi.
Organized Jun 24, 1762; settled 1780s.
Name origin: For Abel Hine, the original town clerk.

Huntington
Town
ZIP: 05462   Lat: 44-18-02 N Long: 72-57-26 W
Pop: 1,609 (1990); 1,161 (1980)   Pop Density: 42.5
Land: 37.9 sq. mi.; Water: 0.0 sq. mi.
Chartered Jun 7, 1763.
Name origin: For the local Hunt family.

Jericho
Town
ZIP: 05465   Lat: 44-28-52 N Long: 72-57-53 W
Pop: 4,302 (1990); 3,575 (1980)   Pop Density: 122.2
Land: 35.2 sq. mi.; Water: 0.1 sq. mi.
Chartered Jun 8, 1763. Village and town are not coextensive.
Name origin: For the biblical city.

*Jericho
Village
ZIP: 05465   Lat: 44-30-06 N Long: 72-59-13 W
Pop: 1,405 (1990); 1,340 (1980)   Pop Density: 1003.6
Land: 1.4 sq. mi.; Water: 0.0 sq. mi.   Elev: 550 ft.

Milton
Town
ZIP: 05468   Lat: 44-38-27 N Long: 73-09-15 W
Pop: 8,404 (1990); 6,829 (1980)   Pop Density: 162.6
Land: 51.7 sq. mi.; Water: 9.5 sq. mi.
Chartered Jun 8, 1763. Village and town are not coextensive.
Name origin: For William Fitzwilliam (1720–56), Viscount Milton, a relative of NH colonial Gov. Benning Wentworth (1696–1770).

*Milton
Village
ZIP: 05468   Lat: 44-38-18 N Long: 73-06-44 W
Pop: 1,578 (1990); 1,411 (1980)   Pop Density: 1052.0
Land: 1.5 sq. mi.; Water: 0.2 sq. mi.

Richmond
Town
ZIP: 05477   Lat: 44-23-52 N Long: 72-59-37 W
Pop: 3,729 (1990); 3,159 (1980)   Pop Density: 116.5
Land: 32.0 sq. mi.; Water: 0.5 sq. mi.
Chartered Oct 27, 1792; incorporated 1794. Village and town are not coextensive.
Name origin: For Charles Lennox (1735–1806), the 3rd Duke of Richmond.

St. George
Town
Lat: 44-22-39 N Long: 73-07-32 W
Pop: 705 (1990); 677 (1980)   Pop Density: 195.8
Land: 3.6 sq. mi.; Water: 0.0 sq. mi.
Chartered Aug 16, 1763.
Name origin: For King George III (1738–1820), whom NH colonial Gov. Benning Wentworth (1696–1770) hoped to placate. The only other "saint" town in VT is St. Albans.

Shelburne
Town
ZIP: 05482   Lat: 44-23-03 N Long: 73-14-54 W
Pop: 5,871 (1990); 5,000 (1980)   Pop Density: 240.6
Land: 24.4 sq. mi.; Water: 20.5 sq. mi.
Granted by NH colonial Gov. Benning Wentworth (1696–1770). Chartered Aug 18, 1763; new charter May 16, 1967.
Name origin: For the Earl of Shelburne.

South Burlington
City
ZIP: 05401   Lat: 44-26-44 N Long: 73-12-58 W
Pop: 12,809 (1990); 10,679 (1980)   Pop Density: 771.6
Land: 16.6 sq. mi.; Water: 13.0 sq. mi.
In northwestern VT, 3 mi. south of Burlington. Incorporated 1864; organized 1865.
Name origin: Once part of the town of Burlington.

Underhill
Town
ZIP: 05489   Lat: 44-31-48 N Long: 72-52-57 W
Pop: 2,799 (1990); 2,172 (1980)   Pop Density: 54.7
Land: 51.2 sq. mi.; Water: 0.0 sq. mi.
Chartered Jun 8, 1763; settled late 1700s.
Name origin: For the local Underhill family.

Westford
Town
ZIP: 05494   Lat: 44-36-24 N Long: 73-00-15 W
Pop: 1,740 (1990); 1,413 (1980)   Pop Density: 44.6
Land: 39.0 sq. mi.; Water: 0.0 sq. mi.
Chartered Jun 8, 1763; organized 1793.
Name origin: For its being the most westerly of the towns granted at that time, and being at the ford on Browns River.

Williston
Town
ZIP: 05495   Lat: 44-26-07 N Long: 73-04-49 W
Pop: 4,887 (1990); 3,843 (1980)   Pop Density: 160.8
Land: 30.4 sq. mi.; Water: 0.4 sq. mi.
Chartered Jun 7, 1763.
Name origin: For Samuel Willis, a wealthy Quaker from Long Island.

Winooski
City
ZIP: 05404   Lat: 44-29-43 N Long: 73-11-06 W
Pop: 6,649 (1990); 6,318 (1980)   Pop Density: 4432.7
Land: 1.5 sq. mi.; Water: 0.1 sq. mi.
Organized Mar 7, 1922. Site of St. Michael's College (1904).
Name origin: For the adjacent Winooski River. The river's name derives from Abnaki, said to mean 'onion land.'

Essex County
County Seat: Guildhall (ZIP: 05905)

Pop: 6,405 (1990); 6,313 (1980)   **Pop Density:** 9.6
Land: 665.3 sq. mi.; **Water:** 8.5 sq. mi.   **Area Code:** 802

At the northeastern corner of VT; organized Nov 5, 1792 from Chittenden and Orange counties.

Name origin: For the county of Essex, England; many early residents had ancestors originally from there.

Averill
Town
Lat: 44-56-22 N **Long:** 71-39-59 W
Pop: 7 (1990); 15 (1980)   **Pop Density:** 0.2
Land: 36.1 sq. mi.; **Water:** 1.9 sq. mi.

Bloomfield
Town
Lat: 44-49-00 N **Long:** 71-37-47 W
Pop: 253 (1990); 188 (1980)   **Pop Density:** 6.3
Land: 40.4 sq. mi.; **Water:** 0.0 sq. mi.

Chartered Jun 29, 1762, as Minehead, former home of many early settlers.

Name origin: Renamed in 1830 either for its descriptive connotations, or possibly for Joseph Bloomfield (1753–1823), an officer in the American Revolution and the War of 1812.

Brighton
Town
ZIP: 05846   **Lat:** 44-47-57 N **Long:** 71-52-22 W
Pop: 1,562 (1990); 1,557 (1980)   **Pop Density:** 30.9
Land: 50.5 sq. mi.; **Water:** 1.2 sq. mi.

Chartered Aug 13, 1781; organized Mar 31, 1832.

Name origin: For Brighton, England.

Brunswick
Town
Lat: 44-43-43 N **Long:** 71-39-41 W
Pop: 92 (1990); 82 (1980)   **Pop Density:** 3.7
Land: 25.2 sq. mi.; **Water:** 0.3 sq. mi.

Chartered Oct 13, 1761.

Name origin: For George III (1738–1820), Duke of Brunswick-Luneburg and later king of England.

Canaan
Town
Lat: 44-58-09 N **Long:** 71-34-38 W
Pop: 1,121 (1990); 1,196 (1980)   **Pop Density:** 33.8
Land: 33.2 sq. mi.; **Water:** 0.2 sq. mi.

Chartered Feb 25, 1782.

Name origin: For the biblical "promised land."

Concord
Town
ZIP: 05824   **Lat:** 44-26-21 N **Long:** 71-50-22 W
Pop: 1,093 (1990); 1,125 (1980)   **Pop Density:** 21.2
Land: 51.6 sq. mi.; **Water:** 2.0 sq. mi.

Founded 1780; chartered Sep 15, 1781.

Name origin: For Concord, MA.

East Haven
Town
ZIP: 05837   **Lat:** 44-39-41 N **Long:** 71-49-34 W
Pop: 269 (1990); 280 (1980)   **Pop Density:** 7.2
Land: 37.5 sq. mi.; **Water:** 0.0 sq. mi.

Chartered Oct 22, 1790.

Name origin: For East Haven, CT.

Ferdinand
Town
ZIP: 05905   **Lat:** 44-43-01 N **Long:** 71-46-35 W
Pop: 23 (1990); 12 (1980)   **Pop Density:** 0.4
Land: 52.9 sq. mi.; **Water:** 0.1 sq. mi.

Granby
Town
Lat: 44-36-24 N **Long:** 71-43-56 W
Pop: 85 (1990); 70 (1980)   **Pop Density:** 2.2
Land: 38.9 sq. mi.; **Water:** 0.1 sq. mi.

Chartered Oct 10, 1761.

Name origin: For John Manners (1721–70), the Marquis of Granby, who helped defeat the French in 1759 at the Battle of Minden.

Guildhall
Town
ZIP: 05905   **Lat:** 44-32-30 N **Long:** 71-38-28 W
Pop: 270 (1990); 202 (1980)   **Pop Density:** 8.2
Land: 32.9 sq. mi.; **Water:** 0.0 sq. mi.

Chartered Oct 10, 1761.

Name origin: For London's famous Guildhall.

Island Pond
CDP
ZIP: 05846   **Lat:** 44-48-46 N **Long:** 71-53-07 W
Pop: 1,222 (1990); 1,216 (1980)   **Pop Density:** 291.0
Land: 4.2 sq. mi.; **Water:** 0.3 sq. mi.

Lemington
Town
Lat: 44-52-35 N **Long:** 71-36-44 W
Pop: 102 (1990); 108 (1980)   **Pop Density:** 2.9
Land: 35.2 sq. mi.; **Water:** 0.0 sq. mi.

Chartered Jun 29, 1762; settled late 1700s.

Name origin: For Leamington, England, with spelling alteration.

Lunenburg
Town
ZIP: 05906   **Lat:** 44-28-59 N **Long:** 71-42-17 W
Pop: 1,176 (1990); 1,138 (1980)   **Pop Density:** 26.2
Land: 44.9 sq. mi.; **Water:** 0.3 sq. mi.

Chartered Jul 5, 1763.

Name origin: For Prince Ferdinand of Brunswick-Luneburg, a relative of England's King George III (1738–1820); with spelling variation.

Maidstone
Town
ZIP: 05905   **Lat:** 44-38-23 N **Long:** 71-36-29 W
Pop: 131 (1990); 100 (1980)   **Pop Density:** 4.2
Land: 30.9 sq. mi.; **Water:** 1.3 sq. mi.

Chartered Oct 12, 1761.

Name origin: For Maidstone, England.

Norton
Town
Lat: 44-59-05 N **Long:** 71-48-53 W
Pop: 169 (1990); 184 (1980)   **Pop Density:** 4.4
Land: 38.8 sq. mi.; **Water:** 0.3 sq. mi.

Chartered Oct 26, 1769; incorporated 1779.

Name origin: For the Norton family, who were large landowners.

Victory
Town
ZIP: 05858 **Lat:** 44-32-47 N **Long:** 71-49-44 W
Pop: 50 (1990); 56 (1980) **Pop Density:** 1.2
Land: 42.9 sq. mi.; **Water:** 0.0 sq. mi.
Chartered Sep 6, 1781; organized May 3, 1841.
Name origin: For the anticipated victory over the British in the American Revolution.

Warren's Gore
Pop. Place
Lat: 44-54-08 N **Long:** 71-52-57 W
Pop: 2 (1990) **Pop Density:** 0.2
Land: 11.1 sq. mi.; **Water:** 0.7 sq. mi.

Franklin County
County Seat: Saint Albans (ZIP: 05478)

Pop: 39,980 (1990); 34,788 (1980) **Pop Density:** 62.8
Land: 637.1 sq. mi.; **Water:** 55.6 sq. mi. **Area Code:** 802
At the northwestern corner of VT, north of Burlington; organized Nov 5, 1792 from Chittenden County.
Name origin: For Benjamin Franklin (1706–90), U.S. patriot, diplomat, and statesman.

Bakersfield
Town
ZIP: 05441 **Lat:** 44-47-54 N **Long:** 72-47-31 W
Pop: 977 (1990); 852 (1980) **Pop Density:** 21.8
Land: 44.8 sq. mi.; **Water:** 0.0 sq. mi.
Chartered Jan 25, 1791.
Name origin: Named in 1788 by and for settler Joseph Baker.

Berkshire
Town
ZIP: 05447 **Lat:** 44-58-04 N **Long:** 72-46-06 W
Pop: 1,190 (1990); 1,116 (1980) **Pop Density:** 28.3
Land: 42.1 sq. mi.; **Water:** 0.0 sq. mi.
Settled 1780; chartered Jun 22, 1781.
Name origin: For Berkshire County, MA.

Enosburg
Town
ZIP: 05450 **Lat:** 44-52-10 N **Long:** 72-44-46 W
Pop: 2,535 (1990); 2,070 (1980) **Pop Density:** 52.2
Land: 48.6 sq. mi.; **Water:** 0.2 sq. mi.
Chartered May 15, 1780; organized 1798.
Name origin: For its first grantee, Gen. Roger Enos.

Enosburg Falls
Village
ZIP: 05450 **Lat:** 44-54-29 N **Long:** 72-48-15 W
Pop: 1,350 (1990); 1,207 (1980) **Pop Density:** 375.0
Land: 3.6 sq. mi.; **Water:** 0.1 sq. mi. **Elev:** 422 ft.
Part of the town of Enosburg.

Fairfax
Town
ZIP: 05454 **Lat:** 44-41-39 N **Long:** 73-00-37 W
Pop: 2,486 (1990); 1,805 (1980) **Pop Density:** 62.0
Land: 40.1 sq. mi.; **Water:** 0.3 sq. mi.
Chartered Aug 18, 1763; organized Mar 20, 1787.
Name origin: For Thomas Fairfax (1692–1780), 6th Baron Fairfax, who emigrated to VA in 1747.

Fairfield
Town
ZIP: 05455 **Lat:** 44-48-32 N **Long:** 72-56-17 W
Pop: 1,680 (1990); 1,493 (1980) **Pop Density:** 24.9
Land: 67.6 sq. mi.; **Water:** 0.7 sq. mi.
Chartered Aug 18, 1763.
Name origin: For Fairfield, CT.

Fletcher
Town
Lat: 44-42-17 N **Long:** 72-54-07 W
Pop: 941 (1990); 626 (1980) **Pop Density:** 24.8
Land: 38.0 sq. mi.; **Water:** 0.2 sq. mi.
Chartered Aug 20, 1781.
Name origin: For Gen. Samuel Fletcher, Revolutionary War hero.

Franklin
Town
ZIP: 05457 **Lat:** 44-58-44 N **Long:** 72-54-05 W
Pop: 1,068 (1990); 1,006 (1980) **Pop Density:** 27.5
Land: 38.9 sq. mi.; **Water:** 2.2 sq. mi.
Chartered Mar 19, 1789.
Name origin: For Benjamin Franklin (1706–90), U.S. patriot, diplomat, and statesman. Originally called Huntsburg.

Georgia
Town
ZIP: 05454 **Lat:** 44-43-42 N **Long:** 73-07-46 W
Pop: 3,753 (1990); 2,818 (1980) **Pop Density:** 95.3
Land: 39.4 sq. mi.; **Water:** 5.9 sq. mi.
Chartered Aug 17, 1763.
Name origin: For King George III of England (1738–1820).

Highgate
Town
ZIP: 05459 **Lat:** 44-57-31 N **Long:** 73-02-43 W
Pop: 3,020 (1990); 2,493 (1980) **Pop Density:** 59.0
Land: 51.2 sq. mi.; **Water:** 8.8 sq. mi.
Chartered Aug 17, 1763.
Name origin: Named by NH colonial Gov. Benning Wentworth (1696–1770) for Highgate, a well-known London suburb.

Montgomery
Town
Lat: 44-51-35 N **Long:** 72-36-37 W
Pop: 823 (1990); 681 (1980) **Pop Density:** 14.4
Land: 57.0 sq. mi.; **Water:** 0.0 sq. mi.
Chartered Mar 13, 1780.
Name origin: For Gen. Richard Montgomery (1736–75), Revolutionary War hero.

Richford   Town
ZIP: 05476   Lat: 44-58-02 N Long: 72-38-17 W
Pop: 2,178 (1990); 2,206 (1980)   Pop Density: 50.4
Land: 43.2 sq. mi.; Water: 0.0 sq. mi.

Organized Mar 30, 1799. Granted 1780 by VT, which was
raising money to pay its soldiers in the Continental Army.
Village and town are not coextensive.

Name origin: For its fertile soil, and its location at a ford in
the Missisquoi River.

*Richford   Village
ZIP: 05476   Lat: 44-59-44 N Long: 72-40-24 W
Pop: 1,425 (1990); 1,471 (1980)   Pop Density: 1187.5
Land: 1.2 sq. mi.; Water: 0.0 sq. mi.   Elev: 1477 ft.

St. Albans   City
ZIP: 05478   Lat: 44-48-40 N Long: 73-05-05 W
Pop: 7,339 (1990); 7,308 (1980)   Pop Density: 3669.5
Land: 2.0 sq. mi.; Water: 0.0 sq. mi.   Elev: 429 ft.

Incorporated as a village Nov 18, 1859; as a city on Mar 3,
1902.

*St. Albans   Town
ZIP: 05481   Lat: 44-48-37 N Long: 73-09-08 W
Pop: 4,606 (1990); 3,555 (1980)   Pop Density: 123.2
Land: 37.4 sq. mi.; Water: 23.2 sq. mi.

Chartered Aug 17, 1763; organized 1788. The only Civil War
action that took place north of Pennsylvania occurred in
Saint Albans on October 19, 1864, when about twenty-two
Confederate soldiers robbed the banks there and fled to
Canada with over $20,000.

Name origin: Named by NH colonial Gov. Benning Wentworth (1696–1770) on the day after St. Alban's Day, but
possibly for St. Albans, Hertfordshire, England. One of only
two towns with a "saint" name; the other is St. George.

Sheldon   Town
ZIP: 05483   Lat: 44-53-46 N Long: 72-55-24 W
Pop: 1,748 (1990); 1,618 (1980)   Pop Density: 45.4
Land: 38.5 sq. mi.; Water: 0.7 sq. mi.

Chartered Aug 18, 1763.

Name origin: Named in 1792 for Revolutionary War veteran
Col. Elisha Sheldon. Originally called Hungerford.

Swanton   Town
ZIP: 05488   Lat: 44-54-34 N Long: 73-07-13 W
Pop: 5,636 (1990); 5,141 (1980)   Pop Density: 116.4
Land: 48.4 sq. mi.; Water: 13.4 sq. mi.

Chartered Aug 17, 1763. Village and town are not coextensive.

Name origin: For British naval officer William Swanton, who
contributed to the victory over the French at Louisbourg in
1758.

*Swanton   Village
ZIP: 05488   Lat: 44-55-17 N Long: 73-07-15 W
Pop: 2,360 (1990); 2,520 (1980)   Pop Density: 2950.0
Land: 0.8 sq. mi.; Water: 0.0 sq. mi.   Elev: 157 ft.

Grand Isle County
County Seat: North Hero (ZIP: 05474)

Pop: 5,318 (1990); 4,613 (1980)   Pop Density: 64.4
Land: 82.6 sq. mi.; Water: 112.0 sq. mi.   Area Code: 802

Islands and peninsula in Lake Champlain, in northwestern VT; organized Nov 9,
1802 from Franklin and Chittenden counties.

Name origin: For the largest of the islands comprising the county. Often referred to
as "The Islands."

Alburg   Town
ZIP: 05440   Lat: 44-57-28 N Long: 73-17-32 W
Pop: 1,362 (1990); 1,352 (1980)   Pop Density: 46.2
Land: 29.5 sq. mi.; Water: 19.5 sq. mi.

Chartered Feb 23, 1781. Village and town are not coextensive.

Name origin: For founder Ira Allen, from a contraction of
Allenburg.

*Alburg   Village
ZIP: 05440   Lat: 44-58-38 N Long: 73-18-04 W
Pop: 436 (1990); 496 (1980)   Pop Density: 726.7
Land: 0.6 sq. mi.; Water: 0.0 sq. mi.   Elev: 124 ft.

Grand Isle   Town
ZIP: 05458   Lat: 44-43-22 N Long: 73-17-33 W
Pop: 1,642 (1990); 1,238 (1980)   Pop Density: 99.5
Land: 16.5 sq. mi.; Water: 18.7 sq. mi.

Chartered Oct 27, 1779, as part of the town of Two Heroes.
Separated from North Hero and South Hero Nov 7, 1798.

Name origin: French for 'big island'; it is on the largest island
in Lake Champlain.

Isle La Motte   Town
ZIP: 05463   Lat: 44-51-59 N Long: 73-19-53 W
Pop: 408 (1990); 393 (1980)   Pop Density: 51.6
Land: 7.9 sq. mi.; Water: 9.1 sq. mi.

Settled by a French army unit in 1666. Chartered Oct 27,
1770.

Name origin: For Pierre de St. Paul, Sieur de la Motte, commander of the original settlers.

North Hero   Town
ZIP: 05474   Lat: 44-50-30 N Long: 73-16-04 W
Pop: 502 (1990); 442 (1980)   Pop Density: 36.6
Land: 13.7 sq. mi.; Water: 32.2 sq. mi.

On an island in Lake Champlain. Originally granted as part
of the town of Two Heroes to Revolutionary War heroes
Ethan Allen (1738–89) and Samuel Herrick, Oct 27, 1779.

Name origin: Original name Two Heroes was for the grantees. Separated from Grand Isle and South Hero Nov 7, 1798.

South Hero
Town
ZIP: 05486   **Lat:** 44-37-45 N   **Long:** 73-18-52 W
Pop: 1,404 (1990); 1,188 (1980)   **Pop Density:** 93.6
Land: 15.0 sq. mi.; **Water:** 32.5 sq. mi.
On Grand Isle in Lake Champlain. Originally granted as part

of the town of Two Heroes to Revolutionary War heroes Ethan Allen (1738–89) and Samuel Herrick, Oct 27, 1779.
Name origin: Original name Two Heroes was for the grantees. Separated from Grand Isle and North Hero Nov 7, 1798.

Lamoille County
County Seat: Hyde Park (ZIP: 05655)

Pop: 19,735 (1990); 16,767 (1980)   **Pop Density:** 42.8
Land: 460.6 sq. mi.; **Water:** 2.9 sq. mi.   **Area Code:** 802
In north-central VT, north of Montpelier; organized Oct 26, 1835 from Orleans, Franklin, Washington, and Chittenden counties.
Name origin: For the Lamoille River, which runs through it; a corruption of French *la mouette* 'the seagull,' the name given to the river by Champlain. The 1744 Charlevois map of discoveries in America showed the river as *La Mouelle* owing to an engraver's neglecting to cross the *tt*s; with spelling variation.

Belvidere
Town
     Lat: 44-45-20 N   **Long:** 72-40-44 W
Pop: 228 (1990); 218 (1980)   **Pop Density:** 7.1
Land: 32.1 sq. mi.; **Water:** 0.0 sq. mi.
Chartered Nov 4, 1791.
Name origin: Named by landowner John Kelly for Lake Belvedere in Ireland, with spelling variation.

Cambridge
Town
ZIP: 05444   **Lat:** 44-37-36 N   **Long:** 72-48-56 W
Pop: 2,667 (1990); 2,019 (1980)   **Pop Density:** 41.9
Land: 63.6 sq. mi.; **Water:** 0.0 sq. mi.
Chartered Aug 30, 1781. Village and town are not coextensive.
Name origin: For Cambridge, MA, former home of many early settlers.

*Cambridge
Village
ZIP: 05444   **Lat:** 44-38-07 N   **Long:** 72-52-56 W
Pop: 292 (1990); 217 (1980)   **Pop Density:** 224.6
Land: 1.3 sq. mi.; **Water:** 0.0 sq. mi.   **Elev:** 455 ft.

Eden
Town
ZIP: 05652   **Lat:** 44-42-40 N   **Long:** 72-32-26 W
Pop: 840 (1990); 612 (1980)   **Pop Density:** 13.2
Land: 63.8 sq. mi.; **Water:** 0.7 sq. mi.
Settled after the American Revolution.
Name origin: For the biblical paradise.

Elmore
Town
     Lat: 44-30-10 N   **Long:** 72-30-40 W
Pop: 573 (1990); 421 (1980)   **Pop Density:** 14.8
Land: 38.6 sq. mi.; **Water:** 0.4 sq. mi.
Granted to a group of Revolutionary War veterans. Chartered Nov 7, 1780.
Name origin: For Col. Samuel Elmore.

Hyde Park
Town
ZIP: 05655   **Lat:** 44-37-09 N   **Long:** 72-33-41 W
Pop: 2,344 (1990); 2,021 (1980)   **Pop Density:** 62.0
Land: 37.8 sq. mi.; **Water:** 1.2 sq. mi.
Chartered Aug 27, 1781. Village and town are not coextensive.
Name origin: For Capt. Jedediah Hyde, its original grantee.

*Hyde Park
Village
ZIP: 05655   **Lat:** 44-35-39 N   **Long:** 72-36-46 W
Pop: 457 (1990); 475 (1980)   **Pop Density:** 380.8
Land: 1.2 sq. mi.; **Water:** 0.0 sq. mi.

Jeffersonville
Village
ZIP: 05464   **Lat:** 44-38-39 N   **Long:** 72-49-41 W
Pop: 462 (1990); 491 (1980)   **Pop Density:** 577.5
Land: 0.8 sq. mi.; **Water:** 0.0 sq. mi.   **Elev:** 459 ft.
Name origin: For Thomas Jefferson (1743–1826), third U.S. president.

Johnson
Town
ZIP: 05656   **Lat:** 44-38-37 N   **Long:** 72-40-54 W
Pop: 3,156 (1990); 2,581 (1980)   **Pop Density:** 68.3
Land: 46.2 sq. mi.; **Water:** 0.0 sq. mi.
Chartered Jan 2, 1792. Town and village are not coextensive.
Name origin: For William Samuel Johnson, its second grantee.

*Johnson
Village
ZIP: 05656   **Lat:** 44-38-14 N   **Long:** 72-40-40 W
Pop: 1,470 (1990); 1,393 (1980)   **Pop Density:** 1225.0
Land: 1.2 sq. mi.; **Water:** 0.0 sq. mi.   **Elev:** 516 ft.

Morristown
Town
ZIP: 05661   **Lat:** 44-33-14 N   **Long:** 72-38-22 W
Pop: 4,733 (1990); 4,448 (1980)   **Pop Density:** 94.1
Land: 50.3 sq. mi.; **Water:** 0.2 sq. mi.
Chartered Nov 6, 1780.
Name origin: For the prominent Morris family from NY.

Morrisville
Village
ZIP: 05661   **Lat:** 44-33-30 N   **Long:** 72-35-46 W
Pop: 1,984 (1990); 2,074 (1980)   **Pop Density:** 1102.2
Land: 1.8 sq. mi.; **Water:** 0.0 sq. mi.   **Elev:** 682 ft.
Settled just after the Revolutionary War; part of the Town of Morristown.

Stowe
Town
ZIP: 05672   **Lat:** 44-29-15 N   **Long:** 72-43-22 W
Pop: 3,433 (1990); 2,991 (1980)   **Pop Density:** 47.2
Land: 72.7 sq. mi.; **Water:** 0.1 sq. mi.
Chartered Jun 8, 1763. Village and town are not coextensive.
Name origin: For Stowe, MA.

*Stowe   Village
ZIP: 05672   **Lat:** 44-27-57 N **Long:** 72-41-08 W
Pop: 450 (1990); 531 (1980)   **Pop Density:** 642.9
Land: 0.7 sq. mi.; **Water:** 0.0 sq. mi.   **Elev:** 723 ft.

Waterville   Town
ZIP: 05492   **Lat:** 44-42-49 N **Long:** 72-44-51 W
Pop: 532 (1990); 470 (1980)   **Pop Density:** 32.4
Land: 16.4 sq. mi.; **Water:** 0.0 sq. mi.
Chartered Nov 15, 1824.

Name origin: For the town's central feature, the North
Branch of the Lamoille River.

Wolcott   Town
ZIP: 05680   **Lat:** 44-34-33 N **Long:** 72-26-27 W
Pop: 1,229 (1990); 986 (1980)   **Pop Density:** 31.4
Land: 39.1 sq. mi.; **Water:** 0.2 sq. mi.
Chartered Aug 22, 1781.

Name origin: For Revolutionary War statesman and soldier
Gen. Oliver Wolcott (1726–97).

Orange County
County Seat: Chelsea (ZIP: 05038)

Pop: 26,149 (1990); 22,739 (1980)   **Pop Density:** 38.0
Land: 688.7 sq. mi.; **Water:** 3.2 sq. mi.   **Area Code:** 802

On the central eastern border of VT, south of Montpelier; organized Feb 22, 1781
(prior to statehood) from the former Cumberland County.

Name origin: For William of Orange (1650–1702), later William III, king of England
(1689–1702).

Bradford   Town
ZIP: 05033   **Lat:** 44-00-43 N **Long:** 72-09-15 W
Pop: 2,522 (1990); 2,191 (1980)   **Pop Density:** 84.6
Land: 29.8 sq. mi.; **Water:** 0.1 sq. mi.
Chartered May 3, 1770. Settled during the late 1760s before
there was any grant, charter, or patent. Town and village are
not coextensive.

Name origin: Named after the Revolutionary War for MA
governor William Bradford. Previously named Mooretown
for a royal governor of NY, and Waits River Town or Waits-
town for its location on the river.

*Bradford   Village
ZIP: 05033   **Lat:** 43-59-38 N **Long:** 72-07-41 W
Pop: 672 (1990); 831 (1980)   **Pop Density:** 1344.0
Land: 0.5 sq. mi.; **Water:** 0.0 sq. mi.

Braintree   Town
ZIP: 05060   **Lat:** 43-58-02 N **Long:** 72-43-30 W
Pop: 1,174 (1990); 1,065 (1980)   **Pop Density:** 30.7
Land: 38.3 sq. mi.; **Water:** 0.0 sq. mi.
Chartered Aug 1, 1781; organized Apr 7, 1788.

Name origin: For Braintree, MA, which was named for
Braintree, Essex, England.

Brookfield   Town
ZIP: 05036   **Lat:** 44-01-50 N **Long:** 72-35-25 W
Pop: 1,089 (1990); 959 (1980)   **Pop Density:** 26.5
Land: 41.1 sq. mi.; **Water:** 0.3 sq. mi.
Chartered Aug 5, 1781.

Name origin: For Brookfield, MA.

Chelsea   Town
ZIP: 05038   **Lat:** 43-59-22 N **Long:** 72-27-47 W
Pop: 1,166 (1990); 1,091 (1980)   **Pop Density:** 29.2
Land: 39.9 sq. mi.; **Water:** 0.0 sq. mi.
Chartered Aug 4, 1781; organized Sep 1788.

Name origin: Named in 1794 for Chelsea, a section of Norwich, CT, home of early settlers. Previously called Turners-
burgh for Bela Turner, first grantee.

Corinth   Town
ZIP: 05039   **Lat:** 44-01-58 N **Long:** 72-17-39 W
Pop: 1,244 (1990); 904 (1980)   **Pop Density:** 25.6
Land: 48.6 sq. mi.; **Water:** 0.0 sq. mi.
Granted 1764 by NH colonial Gov. Benning Wentworth
(1696–1770); chartered Feb 4, 1764.

Name origin: For Corinth, Greece.

Fairlee   Town
ZIP: 05045   **Lat:** 43-56-14 N **Long:** 72-10-05 W
Pop: 883 (1990); 770 (1980)   **Pop Density:** 43.5
Land: 20.3 sq. mi.; **Water:** 1.0 sq. mi.
Chartered Sep 9, 1761; settled 1780s.

Name origin: For a town on the Isle of Wight.

Newbury   Town
ZIP: 05051   **Lat:** 44-06-13 N **Long:** 72-07-19 W
Pop: 1,985 (1990); 1,699 (1980)   **Pop Density:** 31.0
Land: 64.1 sq. mi.; **Water:** 0.3 sq. mi.
Chartered May 18, 1763. Town and village are not coexten-
sive.

Name origin: For Newbury, MA.

*Newbury   Village
ZIP: 05051   **Lat:** 44-04-49 N **Long:** 72-03-37 W
Pop: 412 (1990); 425 (1980)   **Pop Density:** 82.4
Land: 5.0 sq. mi.; **Water:** 0.0 sq. mi.

Orange   Town
                        Lat: 44-09-31 N **Long:** 72-23-20 W
Pop: 915 (1990); 752 (1980)   **Pop Density:** 23.6
Land: 38.8 sq. mi.; **Water:** 0.2 sq. mi.
Chartered Aug 11, 1781.

Name origin: For Orange, CT.

Randolph   Town
ZIP: 05060   **Lat:** 43-56-19 N **Long:** 72-36-23 W
Pop: 4,764 (1990); 4,689 (1980)   **Pop Density:** 99.0
Land: 48.1 sq. mi.; **Water:** 0.0 sq. mi.
Chartered Jun 29, 1781.

Name origin: For Edmund Randolph, VA statesman.

Strafford
Town
ZIP: 05072 **Lat:** 43-51-47 N **Long:** 72-21-34 W
Pop: 902 (1990); 731 (1980) **Pop Density:** 20.4
Land: 44.3 sq. mi.; **Water:** 0.1 sq. mi.
Chartered Aug 12, 1761.
Name origin: Named by NH colonial Gov. Benning Wentworth (1696–1770) for his family in England, who held the Earldom of Strafford.

Thetford
Town
Lat: 43-50-00 N **Long:** 72-15-02 W
Pop: 2,438 (1990); 2,188 (1980) **Pop Density:** 55.8
Land: 43.7 sq. mi.; **Water:** 0.6 sq. mi.
Chartered Aug 12, 1761; organized 1768.
Name origin: For Augustus Henry Fitzroy, Viscount Thetford.

Topsham
Town
Lat: 44-07-40 N **Long:** 72-15-19 W
Pop: 944 (1990); 767 (1980) **Pop Density:** 19.3
Land: 49.0 sq. mi.; **Water:** 0.1 sq. mi.
Chartered Aug 17, 1763; organized Mar 15, 1790.
Name origin: For Topsham, ME.

Tunbridge
Town
ZIP: 05077 **Lat:** 43-54-00 N **Long:** 72-29-09 W
Pop: 1,154 (1990); 925 (1980) **Pop Density:** 25.8
Land: 44.7 sq. mi.; **Water:** 0.0 sq. mi.
Chartered Sep 3, 1761; organized 1786; settled late 1700s.
Name origin: For William Henry Nassau du Zuylestein, Viscount Tunbridge.

Vershire
Town
ZIP: 05079 **Lat:** 43-57-33 N **Long:** 72-19-31 W
Pop: 560 (1990); 442 (1980) **Pop Density:** 15.3
Land: 36.5 sq. mi.; **Water:** 0.0 sq. mi.
Chartered Aug 3, 1781; organized 1783.
Name origin: A combination of Vermont and New Hampshire, indicative of its border location.

Washington
Town
ZIP: 05675 **Lat:** 44-04-47 N **Long:** 72-25-23 W
Pop: 937 (1990); 855 (1980) **Pop Density:** 24.1
Land: 38.8 sq. mi.; **Water:** 0.0 sq. mi.
Chartered Aug 8, 1781; organized Mar 7, 1793.
Name origin: For George Washington (1732–99), American patriot and first U.S. president.

Wells River
Village
ZIP: 05081 **Lat:** 44-09-04 N **Long:** 72-03-57 W
Pop: 424 (1990); 396 (1980) **Pop Density:** 212.0
Land: 2.0 sq. mi.; **Water:** 0.0 sq. mi.
Name origin: For its location on the river.

West Fairlee
Town
ZIP: 05083 **Lat:** 43-56-34 N **Long:** 72-13-35 W
Pop: 633 (1990); 427 (1980) **Pop Density:** 28.3
Land: 22.4 sq. mi.; **Water:** 0.2 sq. mi.
Chartered Feb 15, 1797.
Name origin: For its relation to Fairlee, from which it was created.

Williamstown
Town
ZIP: 05679 **Lat:** 44-06-24 N **Long:** 72-32-27 W
Pop: 2,839 (1990); 2,284 (1980) **Pop Density:** 70.4
Land: 40.3 sq. mi.; **Water:** 0.2 sq. mi.
Chartered Nov 6, 1780.
Name origin: For Williamstown, MA.

Orleans County
County Seat: Newport (ZIP: 05855)

Pop: 24,053 (1990); 23,440 (1980) **Pop Density:** 34.5
Land: 696.9 sq. mi.; **Water:** 23.5 sq. mi. **Area Code:** 802
On the central northern border of VT; organized Nov 5, 1792 from Chittenden and Orange counties.
Name origin: Probably for Louis Philippe Joseph (1747–93), Duke of Orleans, a friend of Marquis de Lafayette (1757–1834) and supporter of the American Revolution.

Albany
Town
ZIP: 05820 **Lat:** 44-43-50 N **Long:** 72-20-27 W
Pop: 782 (1990); 705 (1980) **Pop Density:** 20.3
Land: 38.5 sq. mi.; **Water:** 0.2 sq. mi.
Chartered Jun 26, 1782; organized Mar 27, 1782. Town and village are not coextensive.
Name origin: Probably for Albany County, NY. Originally called Lutterloh or Lutterlock for the original grantee, Col. Henry Emannuel Lutterloh (Lutterloth).

*Albany
Village
ZIP: 05820 **Lat:** 44-43-49 N **Long:** 72-22-55 W
Pop: 180 (1990); 174 (1980) **Pop Density:** 138.5
Land: 1.3 sq. mi.; **Water:** 0.0 sq. mi. **Elev:** 956 ft.

Barton
Town
ZIP: 05822 **Lat:** 44-45-08 N **Long:** 72-10-15 W
Pop: 2,967 (1990); 2,990 (1980) **Pop Density:** 67.9
Land: 43.7 sq. mi.; **Water:** 1.2 sq. mi.
Chartered Oct 20, 1789. Town and village are not coextensive. Settled after the Revolutionary War.
Name origin: For Col. William Barton (1747–1831). Originally called Providence, the former RI home of many early settlers.

*Barton
Village
ZIP: 05822 **Lat:** 44-44-58 N **Long:** 72-10-38 W
Pop: 908 (1990); 1,062 (1980) **Pop Density:** 648.6
Land: 1.4 sq. mi.; **Water:** 0.2 sq. mi. **Elev:** 952 ft.

Brownington
Town
ZIP: 05860   **Lat:** 44-49-52 N **Long:** 72-07-22 W
Pop: 705 (1990); 708 (1980)   **Pop Density:** 24.9
Land: 28.3 sq. mi.; **Water:** 0.1 sq. mi.
Chartered Feb 16, 1782.
Name origin: For grantees Daniel and Timothy Brown.

Charleston
Town
ZIP: 05872   **Lat:** 44-50-30 N **Long:** 72-00-48 W
Pop: 844 (1990); 851 (1980)   **Pop Density:** 22.2
Land: 38.1 sq. mi.; **Water:** 1.1 sq. mi.
Chartered Nov 10, 1780, as Navy by Commodore Abraham
Whipple (1733–1819), in honor of the American Navy.
Name origin: Present name adopted in 1825, but origin is
unclear. Probably for Charleston, SC, defended by Commo-
dore Whipple during the American Revolution.

Coventry
Town
          Lat: 44-52-31 N **Long:** 72-14-03 W
Pop: 806 (1990); 674 (1980)   **Pop Density:** 29.3
Land: 27.5 sq. mi.; **Water:** 0.2 sq. mi.
Chartered Nov 4, 1780.
Name origin: For Coventry, CT.

Craftsbury
Town
ZIP: 05826   **Lat:** 44-38-59 N **Long:** 72-24-07 W
Pop: 994 (1990); 844 (1980)   **Pop Density:** 25.4
Land: 39.1 sq. mi.; **Water:** 0.5 sq. mi.
Chartered Aug 23, 1781.
Name origin: For Col. Ebenezer Crafts (1740–1810), an origi-
nal charter grantee.

Derby
Town
ZIP: 05829   **Lat:** 44-57-03 N **Long:** 72-08-03 W
Pop: 4,479 (1990); 4,222 (1980)   **Pop Density:** 91.0
Land: 49.2 sq. mi.; **Water:** 8.3 sq. mi.   **Elev:** 1110 ft.
Chartered Oct 29, 1779.
Name origin: For Derby, CT.

Derby Center
Village
          Lat: 44-57-20 N **Long:** 72-07-56 W
Pop: 684 (1990); 598 (1980)   **Pop Density:** 488.6
Land: 1.4 sq. mi.; **Water:** 0.0 sq. mi.   **Elev:** 1110 ft.
Derby Center (also called Derby) is not coextensive with
town of Derby.

Derby Line
Village
ZIP: 05830   **Lat:** 45-00-08 N **Long:** 72-06-14 W
Pop: 855 (1990); 874 (1980)   **Pop Density:** 1068.8
Land: 0.8 sq. mi.; **Water:** 0.0 sq. mi.   **Elev:** 1029 ft.
Part of the town of Derby.
Name origin: For its location in the town of Derby, on the
border with the Canadian Province of Quebec.

Glover
Town
          Lat: 44-41-38 N **Long:** 72-13-17 W
Pop: 820 (1990); 843 (1980)   **Pop Density:** 21.8
Land: 37.6 sq. mi.; **Water:** 0.7 sq. mi.
Granted to Revolutionary War veterans. Chartered Nov 20,
1783.
Name origin: For Gen. John Glover (1732–97).

Greensboro
Town
ZIP: 05841   **Lat:** 44-36-17 N **Long:** 72-17-26 W
Pop: 717 (1990); 677 (1980)   **Pop Density:** 19.1
Land: 37.6 sq. mi.; **Water:** 1.6 sq. mi.
Chartered Aug 20, 1781.
Name origin: For printer Timothy Green.

Holland
Town
ZIP: 05830   **Lat:** 44-57-44 N **Long:** 71-59-45 W
Pop: 423 (1990); 473 (1980)   **Pop Density:** 11.2
Land: 37.8 sq. mi.; **Water:** 0.6 sq. mi.
Chartered Oct 26, 1779.
Name origin: For Samuel Holland, the king's surveyor gen-
eral of all colonies north of VA.

Irasburg
Town
ZIP: 05845   **Lat:** 44-49-01 N **Long:** 72-17-00 W
Pop: 907 (1990); 870 (1980)   **Pop Density:** 22.3
Land: 40.7 sq. mi.; **Water:** 0.1 sq. mi.
Chartered Feb 23, 1781.
Name origin: For pioneer Ira Allen. The town of Ira in Rut-
land County is another town named for him.

Jay
Town
ZIP: 05859   **Lat:** 44-58-38 N **Long:** 72-28-45 W
Pop: 381 (1990); 302 (1980)   **Pop Density:** 11.2
Land: 33.9 sq. mi.; **Water:** 0.0 sq. mi.
Chartered Nov 7, 1792.
Name origin: For John Jay (1745–1829), U.S. jurist and
statesman.

Lowell
Town
ZIP: 05847   **Lat:** 44-47-50 N **Long:** 72-27-07 W
Pop: 594 (1990); 573 (1980)   **Pop Density:** 10.6
Land: 55.9 sq. mi.; **Water:** 0.1 sq. mi.
Chartered Mar 5, 1787.
Name origin: For John Lowell, a prominent manufacturer.
Previously named Kellyvale.

Morgan
Town
ZIP: 05853   **Lat:** 44-53-27 N **Long:** 71-58-16 W
Pop: 497 (1990); 460 (1980)   **Pop Density:** 16.2
Land: 30.7 sq. mi.; **Water:** 2.7 sq. mi.
Chartered Nov 8, 1780; organized Mar 25, 1807.
Name origin: Named in 1801 for John Morgan, a landowner.
Previously called Caldersburgh for another landowner.

Newport
City
ZIP: 05855   **Lat:** 44-56-13 N **Long:** 72-12-32 W
Pop: 4,434 (1990); 4,756 (1980)   **Pop Density:** 703.8
Land: 6.3 sq. mi.; **Water:** 1.6 sq. mi.   **Elev:** 723 ft.
Incorporated Mar 5, 1918. City is not coextensive with the
town of Newport.

*Newport
Town
ZIP: 05855   **Lat:** 44-56-00 N **Long:** 72-18-08 W
Pop: 1,367 (1990); 1,319 (1980)   **Pop Density:** 32.9
Land: 41.6 sq. mi.; **Water:** 1.5 sq. mi.
Granted Oct 26, 1781; chartered Oct 30, 1802.
Name origin: Possibly for Newport, RI. Originally called
Duncansborough for George Duncan, an original grantee.
Name changed Oct 30, 1816.

North Troy
Village
ZIP: 05859 **Lat:** 44-59-43 N **Long:** 72-24-17 W
Pop: 723 (1990); 717 (1980) **Pop Density:** 361.5
Land: 2.0 sq. mi.; **Water:** 0.0 sq. mi.
Incorporated 1876.
Name origin: For Troy, NY. Originally called Missisquoi.

Orleans
Village
ZIP: 05860 **Lat:** 44-48-38 N **Long:** 72-12-06 W
Pop: 806 (1990); 983 (1980) **Pop Density:** 1151.4
Land: 0.7 sq. mi.; **Water:** 0.0 sq. mi. **Elev:** 740 ft.
Name origin: For French Revolution hero Louis Phillipe
Joseph (1747–93), the Duke of Orleans.

Troy
Town
Lat: 44-55-24 N **Long:** 72-23-10 W
Pop: 1,609 (1990); 1,498 (1980) **Pop Density:** 44.8
Land: 35.9 sq. mi.; **Water:** 0.0 sq. mi.
Organized Oct 28, 1801.
Name origin: For Troy, NY.

Westfield
Town
ZIP: 05874 **Lat:** 44-52-48 N **Long:** 72-29-01 W
Pop: 422 (1990); 418 (1980) **Pop Density:** 10.6
Land: 39.8 sq. mi.; **Water:** 0.0 sq. mi.
Chartered May 15, 1780.
Name origin: For William West of RI.

Westmore
Town
ZIP: 05860 **Lat:** 44-45-25 N **Long:** 72-01-35 W
Pop: 305 (1990); 257 (1980) **Pop Density:** 8.8
Land: 34.7 sq. mi.; **Water:** 2.9 sq. mi.
Chartered Aug 17, 1781; organized Aug 16, 1804.
Name origin: For its location on the then western frontier.

Rutland County
County Seat: Rutland (ZIP: 05701)

Pop: 62,142 (1990); 58,347 (1980) **Pop Density:** 66.7
Land: 932.2 sq. mi.; **Water:** 12.2 sq. mi. **Area Code:** 802
On the central western border of VT, south of Middlebury; organized Feb 22, 1781
(prior to statehood) from Bennington County.
Name origin: For the town, its county seat.

Benson
Town
Lat: 43-42-32 N **Long:** 73-18-31 W
Pop: 847 (1990); 739 (1980) **Pop Density:** 19.3
Land: 44.0 sq. mi.; **Water:** 1.5 sq. mi.
Chartered May 5, 1780.
Name origin: For Egbert Benson (1746–1833), Revolutionary
War patriot.

Brandon
Town
ZIP: 05733 **Lat:** 43-47-51 N **Long:** 73-04-58 W
Pop: 4,223 (1990); 4,194 (1980) **Pop Density:** 105.3
Land: 40.1 sq. mi.; **Water:** 0.0 sq. mi.
Chartered Oct 20, 1761.
Name origin: For Brandon Bay in Ireland. Originally called
Neshobe.

Castleton
Town
ZIP: 05735 **Lat:** 43-38-04 N **Long:** 73-10-49 W
Pop: 4,278 (1990); 3,637 (1980) **Pop Density:** 109.7
Land: 39.0 sq. mi.; **Water:** 3.3 sq. mi.
Chartered Sep 22, 1761; settled late 1700s.
Name origin: For Castleton, England.

Chittenden
Town
ZIP: 05737 **Lat:** 43-43-48 N **Long:** 72-54-46 W
Pop: 1,102 (1990); 927 (1980) **Pop Density:** 15.1
Land: 73.0 sq. mi.; **Water:** 1.2 sq. mi.
Chartered Mar 16, 1780.
Name origin: For VT's first governor, Thomas Chittenden
(1730–97).

Clarendon
Town
ZIP: 05759 **Lat:** 43-31-33 N **Long:** 72-58-44 W
Pop: 2,835 (1990); 2,372 (1980) **Pop Density:** 89.7
Land: 31.6 sq. mi.; **Water:** 0.0 sq. mi.
Chartered Sep 5, 1761.
Name origin: Named by NH colonial Gov. Benning Went-
worth (1696–1770) for Clarendon, Wiltshire, England.

Danby
Town
ZIP: 05739 **Lat:** 43-21-28 N **Long:** 73-03-28 W
Pop: 1,193 (1990); 992 (1980) **Pop Density:** 28.8
Land: 41.4 sq. mi.; **Water:** 0.1 sq. mi.
Chartered Aug 27, 1761; organized Mar 14, 1769.
Name origin: Named by NH colonial Gov. Benning Went-
worth (1696–1770) for Basil Fielding, 6th Earl of Denbigh,
with spelling alteration.

Fair Haven
Town
ZIP: 05743 **Lat:** 43-37-07 N **Long:** 73-16-07 W
Pop: 2,887 (1990); 2,819 (1980) **Pop Density:** 164.0
Land: 17.6 sq. mi.; **Water:** 0.5 sq. mi.
Chartered Oct 27, 1779; settled 1780s.

Hubbardton
Town
Lat: 43-42-31 N **Long:** 73-10-50 W
Pop: 576 (1990); 490 (1980) **Pop Density:** 20.9
Land: 27.5 sq. mi.; **Water:** 1.3 sq. mi.
Chartered Jun 15, 1764. Site of a Revolutionary War battle
in 1777.
Name origin: For Thomas Hubbard, a prosperous Boston
merchant.

Ira
Town
ZIP: 05777 Lat: 43-32-40 N Long: 73-04-50 W
Pop: 426 (1990); 354 (1980) Pop Density: 20.0
Land: 21.3 sq. mi.; Water: 0.0 sq. mi.
Organized 1779; chartered Oct 12, 1780.
Name origin: For Ira Allen (1751–1814), the major land-owner. Irasburg in Orleans County is another town named for him.

Mendon
Town
Lat: 43-37-13 N Long: 72-52-33 W
Pop: 1,049 (1990); 1,056 (1980) Pop Density: 27.5
Land: 38.1 sq. mi.; Water: 0.0 sq. mi.
Chartered Feb 23, 1781.
Name origin: For Mendon, MA.

Middletown Springs
Town
ZIP: 05757 Lat: 43-28-59 N Long: 73-07-27 W
Pop: 686 (1990); 603 (1980) Pop Density: 30.1
Land: 22.8 sq. mi.; Water: 0.0 sq. mi.
Organized Oct 28, 1784.
Name origin: For Middletown, CT, and for a local mineral springs.

Mount Holly
Town
ZIP: 05758 Lat: 43-26-20 N Long: 72-48-40 W
Pop: 1,093 (1990); 938 (1980) Pop Density: 22.4
Land: 48.7 sq. mi.; Water: 0.4 sq. mi.
Organized Oct 31, 1792.
Name origin: For Mount Holly, NJ.

Mount Tabor
Town
ZIP: 05739 Lat: 43-21-35 N Long: 72-55-06 W
Pop: 214 (1990); 211 (1980) Pop Density: 4.9
Land: 43.7 sq. mi.; Water: 0.0 sq. mi.
Chartered Aug 28, 1761.
Name origin: For Gideon Tabor, a Revolutionary War veteran. Originally called Harwich.

Pawlet
Town
ZIP: 05761 Lat: 43-21-46 N Long: 73-11-14 W
Pop: 1,314 (1990); 1,244 (1980) Pop Density: 30.6
Land: 42.9 sq. mi.; Water: 0.0 sq. mi.
Chartered Aug 26, 1761.
Name origin: For Charles Paulet, Duke of Bolton, with an alternate spelling.

Pittsfield
Town
ZIP: 05762 Lat: 43-49-01 N Long: 72-50-33 W
Pop: 389 (1990); 396 (1980) Pop Density: 19.4
Land: 20.1 sq. mi.; Water: 0.0 sq. mi.
Chartered Jul 29, 1781; organized Mar 26, 1793.
Name origin: For Pittsfield, MA.

Pittsford
Town
ZIP: 05763 Lat: 43-43-03 N Long: 73-02-46 W
Pop: 2,919 (1990); 2,590 (1980) Pop Density: 66.9
Land: 43.6 sq. mi.; Water: 0.1 sq. mi.
Settled 1769; chartered Oct 12, 1761. Village and town are not coextensive.
Name origin: For William Pitt (1708–1778), 1st Earl of Chatham, and its location at a ford on Otter Creek.

Poultney
Town
ZIP: 05764 Lat: 43-31-42 N Long: 73-11-36 W
Pop: 3,498 (1990); 3,196 (1980) Pop Density: 79.7
Land: 43.9 sq. mi.; Water: 0.9 sq. mi.
Chartered Sep 21, 1761. Village and town are not coextensive.
Name origin: For William Poultney, 1st Earl of Bath.

*Poultney
Village
ZIP: 05764 Lat: 43-31-03 N Long: 73-14-09 W
Pop: 1,731 (1990); 1,554 (1980) Pop Density: 2885.0
Land: 0.6 sq. mi.; Water: 0.0 sq. mi. Elev: 432 ft.

Proctor
Town
ZIP: 05765 Lat: 43-39-07 N Long: 73-02-07 W
Pop: 1,979 (1990); 1,998 (1980) Pop Density: 263.9
Land: 7.5 sq. mi.; Water: 0.0 sq. mi.
Famous as a marble quarry area. Incorporated Nov 18, 1886.
Name origin: Named in 1882 for Redfield Proctor, president of the Vermont Marble Company.

Rutland
City
ZIP: 05701 Lat: 43-36-32 N Long: 72-58-46 W
Pop: 18,230 (1990); 18,436 (1980) Pop Density: 2398.7
Land: 7.6 sq. mi.; Water: 0.0 sq. mi. Elev: 648 ft.
In central-western VT, 35 mi. northwest of Brattleboro. Incorporated as a city Mar 7, 1893. Summer/ winter resort; industry includes marble finishing, stoneworking machinery. Town and city are not coextensive.
Name origin: Named by NH colonial Gov. Benning Wentworth (1696–1770) for John Manners (1696–1779), the 3rd Duke of Rutland.

*Rutland
Town
Lat: 43-37-49 N Long: 72-58-40 W
Pop: 3,781 (1990); 3,300 (1980) Pop Density: 194.9
Land: 19.4 sq. mi.; Water: 0.1 sq. mi.
Original charter Sep 7, 1761. Settled 1770.

Sherburne
Town
ZIP: 05751 Lat: 43-39-23 N Long: 72-47-24 W
Pop: 738 (1990); 891 (1980) Pop Density: 15.8
Land: 46.6 sq. mi.; Water: 0.2 sq. mi.
Chartered July 7, 1761.
Name origin: Named in 1800 for grantee Col. Benjamin Sherburne. Originally called Killington.

Shrewsbury
Town
ZIP: 05738 Lat: 43-32-10 N Long: 72-51-14 W
Pop: 1,107 (1990); 866 (1980) Pop Density: 22.1
Land: 50.1 sq. mi.; Water: 0.1 sq. mi.
Chartered Sep 4, 1761; organized Mar 20, 1781.
Name origin: For the Earldom of Shrewsbury.

Sudbury
Town
ZIP: 05733 Lat: 43-47-03 N Long: 73-10-48 W
Pop: 516 (1990); 380 (1980) Pop Density: 23.9
Land: 21.6 sq. mi.; Water: 0.7 sq. mi.
Granted 1763 by NH colonial Gov. Benning Wentworth (1696–1770).
Name origin: For Sudbury, Middlesex, England.

Tinmouth
Town
ZIP: 05773 **Lat:** 43-26-56 N **Long:** 73-03-19 W
Pop: 455 (1990); 406 (1980) **Pop Density:** 16.1
Land: 28.3 sq. mi.; **Water:** 0.1 sq. mi.
Chartered Sep 15, 1761.
Name origin: For Tynemouth, England, with a spelling variation.

Wallingford
Town
ZIP: 05773 **Lat:** 43-26-57 N **Long:** 72-55-49 W
Pop: 2,184 (1990); 1,893 (1980) **Pop Density:** 50.6
Land: 43.2 sq. mi.; **Water:** 0.2 sq. mi.
Chartered Nov 27, 1761; settled 1770s.
Name origin: For Wallingford, CT, which was named for Wallingford, England.

Wells
Town
ZIP: 05774 **Lat:** 43-26-00 N **Long:** 73-11-46 W
Pop: 902 (1990); 815 (1980) **Pop Density:** 39.9
Land: 22.6 sq. mi.; **Water:** 0.8 sq. mi.
Chartered Sep 15, 1761.
Name origin: For Wells, Somerset, England.

West Haven
Town
ZIP: 05743 **Lat:** 43-38-36 N **Long:** 73-21-50 W
Pop: 273 (1990); 253 (1980) **Pop Density:** 9.8
Land: 28.0 sq. mi.; **Water:** 0.5 sq. mi.
Originally part of Fair Haven. Chartered Oct 20, 1792.
Name origin: Renamed in 1792 for its location in relation to Fair Haven.

West Rutland
Town
ZIP: 05777 **Lat:** 43-36-44 N **Long:** 73-03-39 W
Pop: 2,448 (1990); 2,351 (1980) **Pop Density:** 137.5
Land: 17.8 sq. mi.; **Water:** 0.0 sq. mi.
Organized Nov 19, 1886.
Name origin: For its relation to Rutland, from which it was created.

Washington County
County Seat: Montpelier (ZIP: 05602)

Pop: 54,928 (1990); 52,393 (1980) **Pop Density:** 79.7
Land: 689.6 sq. mi.; **Water:** 6.3 sq. mi. **Area Code:** 802
In north-central VT, east of Burlington; organized as Jefferson County Nov 1, 1810 from Addison, Caledonia, Chittenden, and Orange counties.
Name origin: For George Washington (1732–99), U.S. patriot and first U.S. president. Originally named Jefferson; changed Nov 8, 1814, by newly elected Federalist majority in VT legislature.

Barre
City
ZIP: 05641 **Lat:** 44-12-00 N **Long:** 72-30-28 W
Pop: 9,482 (1990); 9,824 (1980) **Pop Density:** 2370.5
Land: 4.0 sq. mi.; **Water:** 0.0 sq. mi. **Elev:** 609 ft.
In north-central VT, 6 mi. southeast of Montpelier. Founded 1790s. Settled c. 1788; incorporated as city Mar 5, 1895. Not coextensive with the town of Barre.

*Barre
Town
ZIP: 05641 **Lat:** 44-11-11 N **Long:** 72-28-55 W
Pop: 7,411 (1990); 7,090 (1980) **Pop Density:** 242.2
Land: 30.6 sq. mi.; **Water:** 0.1 sq. mi.
In central VT, southeast of Montpelier. Founded 1793; chartered as Wildersburgh Aug 12, 1781; renamed Oct 18, 1793.
Name origin: For Barre, MA. The name caused a dispute between two former inhabitants of MA towns. After a town meeting they went behind a barn and settled the issue with their fists.

Berlin
Town
ZIP: 05641 **Lat:** 44-12-50 N **Long:** 72-36-54 W
Pop: 2,561 (1990); 2,454 (1980) **Pop Density:** 70.2
Land: 36.5 sq. mi.; **Water:** 0.5 sq. mi.
Chartered Jun 6, 1763.
Name origin: Origin uncertain: either for Berlin, MA or the capital of Germany.

Cabot
Town
ZIP: 05647 **Lat:** 44-24-12 N **Long:** 72-17-55 W
Pop: 1,043 (1990); 958 (1980) **Pop Density:** 28.1
Land: 37.1 sq. mi.; **Water:** 1.2 sq. mi.
Chartered Aug 17, 1781. Village and town are not coextensive.
Name origin: For Sophia Cabot, wife of Maj. Lyman Hitchcock, one of the largest land-holders.

*Cabot
Village
ZIP: 05647 **Lat:** 44-24-30 N **Long:** 72-18-39 W
Pop: 220 (1990); 259 (1980) **Pop Density:** 200.0
Land: 1.1 sq. mi.; **Water:** 0.0 sq. mi. **Elev:** 1064 ft.

Calais
Town
ZIP: 05648 **Lat:** 44-21-57 N **Long:** 72-27-58 W
Pop: 1,521 (1990); 1,207 (1980) **Pop Density:** 40.0
Land: 38.0 sq. mi.; **Water:** 0.6 sq. mi.
Chartered Aug 15, 1781.
Name origin: For Calais, France.

Duxbury
Town
ZIP: 05676 **Lat:** 44-17-18 N **Long:** 72-49-59 W
Pop: 976 (1990); 877 (1980) **Pop Density:** 22.8
Land: 42.9 sq. mi.; **Water:** 0.2 sq. mi.
Chartered Jun 7, 1763.
Name origin: For Duxbury, MA.

East Montpelier
Town
Lat: 44-17-13 N **Long:** 72-30-12 W
Pop: 2,239 (1990); 2,205 (1980)   **Pop Density:** 70.0
Land: 32.0 sq. mi.; **Water:** 0.1 sq. mi.
Organized Jan 1, 1849.
Name origin: Originally part of Montpelier.

Fayston
Town
ZIP: 05660   **Lat:** 44-13-45 N **Long:** 72-53-03 W
Pop: 846 (1990); 657 (1980)   **Pop Density:** 23.2
Land: 36.5 sq. mi.; **Water:** 0.0 sq. mi.
Chartered Feb 27, 1782.
Name origin: For a prominent 18th-century VT family.

Graniteville-East Barre
CDP
Lat: 44-09-28 N **Long:** 72-28-13 W
Pop: 2,189 (1990); 2,172 (1980)   **Pop Density:** 312.7
Land: 7.0 sq. mi.; **Water:** 0.0 sq. mi.

Marshfield
Town
ZIP: 05658   **Lat:** 44-18-44 N **Long:** 72-22-03 W
Pop: 1,331 (1990); 1,267 (1980)   **Pop Density:** 30.9
Land: 43.1 sq. mi.; **Water:** 0.3 sq. mi.
Chartered Oct 26, 1782; organized Mar 18, 1800. Village and town are not coextensive.
Name origin: For Col. Isaac Marsh, an early landowner.

*Marshfield
Village
ZIP: 05658   **Lat:** 44-21-02 N **Long:** 72-21-07 W
Pop: 257 (1990); 301 (1980)   **Pop Density:** 856.7
Land: 0.3 sq. mi.; **Water:** 0.0 sq. mi.   **Elev:** 857 ft.

Middlesex
Town
Lat: 44-18-53 N **Long:** 72-38-39 W
Pop: 1,514 (1990); 1,235 (1980)   **Pop Density:** 38.1
Land: 39.7 sq. mi.; **Water:** 0.2 sq. mi.
Chartered Jun 8, 1763.
Name origin: Named by NH colonial Gov. Benning Wentworth (1696–1770) for Middlesex, England.

Montpelier
City
ZIP: 05602   **Lat:** 44-15-59 N **Long:** 72-34-18 W
Pop: 8,247 (1990); 8,241 (1980)   **Pop Density:** 800.7
Land: 10.3 sq. mi.; **Water:** 0.0 sq. mi.   **Elev:** 525 ft.
In north-central VT, northwest of Barre. State capital; chartered Oct 21, 1780.
Name origin: For Montpelier, France, in gratitude for France's help during the American Revolution.

Moretown
Town
ZIP: 05660   **Lat:** 44-15-42 N **Long:** 72-43-48 W
Pop: 1,415 (1990); 1,221 (1980)   **Pop Density:** 35.3
Land: 40.1 sq. mi.; **Water:** 0.1 sq. mi.
Chartered Jun 7, 1763.
Name origin: For a local family.

Northfield
Town
ZIP: 05663   **Lat:** 44-09-10 N **Long:** 72-41-36 W
Pop: 5,610 (1990); 5,435 (1980)   **Pop Density:** 128.7
Land: 43.6 sq. mi.; **Water:** 0.0 sq. mi.
Chartered Aug 10, 1781. Village and town are not coextensive.
Name origin: For Northfield, MA.

*Northfield
Village
ZIP: 05663   **Lat:** 44-09-08 N **Long:** 72-39-23 W
Pop: 1,889 (1990); 2,033 (1980)   **Pop Density:** 1349.3
Land: 1.4 sq. mi.; **Water:** 0.0 sq. mi.   **Elev:** 7341 ft.

Plainfield
Town
ZIP: 05667   **Lat:** 44-14-46 N **Long:** 72-24-28 W
Pop: 1,302 (1990); 1,249 (1980)   **Pop Density:** 62.0
Land: 21.0 sq. mi.; **Water:** 0.0 sq. mi.
Chartered Oct 26, 1787; incorporated 1797.
Name origin: For Plainfield, CT, former home of its incorporator, John Chapman.

Roxbury
Town
Lat: 44-04-20 N **Long:** 72-43-43 W
Pop: 575 (1990); 452 (1980)   **Pop Density:** 13.8
Land: 41.8 sq. mi.; **Water:** 0.0 sq. mi.
Chartered Aug 6, 1781.
Name origin: For Roxbury, MA.

South Barre
CDP
Lat: 44-09-48 N **Long:** 72-30-23 W
Pop: 1,314 (1990); 1,301 (1980)   **Pop Density:** 625.7
Land: 2.1 sq. mi.; **Water:** 0.0 sq. mi.

Waitsfield
Town
ZIP: 05673   **Lat:** 44-10-50 N **Long:** 72-47-53 W
Pop: 1,422 (1990); 1,300 (1980)   **Pop Density:** 52.9
Land: 26.9 sq. mi.; **Water:** 0.0 sq. mi.
Chartered Feb 15, 1782.
Name origin: For prominent citizen Benjamin Wait.

Warren
Town
ZIP: 05674   **Lat:** 44-07-05 N **Long:** 72-51-27 W
Pop: 1,172 (1990); 956 (1980)   **Pop Density:** 29.3
Land: 40.0 sq. mi.; **Water:** 0.0 sq. mi.
Chartered Oct 20, 1789.
Name origin: For Dr. Joseph Warren (1741–75), Revolutionary War hero killed at the Battle of Bunker Hill.

Waterbury
Town
ZIP: 05676   **Lat:** 44-23-31 N **Long:** 72-44-58 W
Pop: 4,589 (1990); 4,465 (1980)   **Pop Density:** 95.0
Land: 48.3 sq. mi.; **Water:** 1.5 sq. mi.
Chartered Jun 7, 1763. Village and town are not coextensive.
Name origin: For Waterbury, CT, former home of many early settlers.

*Waterbury
Village
ZIP: 05676   **Lat:** 44-20-21 N **Long:** 72-45-09 W
Pop: 1,702 (1990); 1,892 (1980)   **Pop Density:** 1418.3
Land: 1.2 sq. mi.; **Water:** 0.0 sq. mi.   **Elev:** 428 ft.

Woodbury
Town
ZIP: 05681   **Lat:** 44-26-10 N **Long:** 72-24-18 W
Pop: 766 (1990); 573 (1980)   **Pop Density:** 20.3
Land: 37.7 sq. mi.; **Water:** 1.3 sq. mi.
Chartered Aug 16, 1781; organized 1805.
Name origin: For Col. Ebenezer Wood.

Worcester
Town
ZIP: 05682   **Lat:** 44-25-00 N **Long:** 72-34-06 W
Pop: 906 (1990); 727 (1980)   **Pop Density:** 23.0
Land: 39.4 sq. mi.; **Water:** 0.1 sq. mi.
Chartered Jun 8, 1763; organized 1803.
Name origin: For Worcester, MA.

Windham County
County Seat: Newfane (ZIP: 05345)

Pop: 41,588 (1990); 36,933 (1980)　　　　　　　　**Pop Density:** 52.7
Land: 788.8 sq. mi.; **Water:** 9.4 sq. mi.　　　　　**Area Code:** 802

At the southeastern corner of VT; organized Feb 11, 1781 (prior to statehood) from the former Cumberland County.
Name origin: For Windham, CT, former home of early settlers.

Athens
Town
Lat: 43-06-57 N **Long:** 72-36-04 W
Pop: 313 (1990); 250 (1980)　　　**Pop Density:** 24.1
Land: 13.0 sq. mi.; **Water:** 0.0 sq. mi.

Settled late 1700s. Chartered May 3, 1780; organized Mar 4, 1781.
Name origin: For Athens, Greece.

Bellows Falls
Village
ZIP: 05101　　　　　**Lat:** 43-08-10 N **Long:** 72-27-11 W
Pop: 3,313 (1990); 3,456 (1980)　　**Pop Density:** 2366.4
Land: 1.4 sq. mi.; **Water:** 0.0 sq. mi.　　**Elev:** 299 ft.

On the southeastern border of VT with NH.
Name origin: For an early settler and for nearby falls on the Connecticut River.

Brattleboro
Town
ZIP: 05351　　　　　**Lat:** 42-51-43 N **Long:** 72-37-08 W
Pop: 12,241 (1990); 11,886 (1980)　　**Pop Density:** 382.5
Land: 32.0 sq. mi.; **Water:** 0.5 sq. mi.

In southeastern VT, on NH border. Granted by NH colonial Gov. Benning Wentworth (1696–1770). Chartered Dec 26, 1753.
Name origin: For grantee Col. William Brattle (?–1776).

Brookline
Town
ZIP: 05345　　　　　**Lat:** 43-00-52 N **Long:** 72-36-26 W
Pop: 403 (1990); 310 (1980)　　　**Pop Density:** 31.2
Land: 12.9 sq. mi.; **Water:** 0.0 sq. mi.

Chartered Nov 30, 1794.
Name origin: For the Grassy Brook, which flows through the town in a nearly straight line.

Dover
Town
ZIP: 05341　　　　　**Lat:** 42-57-47 N **Long:** 72-50-22 W
Pop: 994 (1990); 666 (1980)　　　**Pop Density:** 28.2
Land: 35.3 sq. mi.; **Water:** 0.0 sq. mi.

Organized Oct 30, 1810.
Name origin: For Dover, NH.

Dummerston
Town
ZIP: 05346　　　　　**Lat:** 42-55-48 N **Long:** 72-35-49 W
Pop: 1,863 (1990); 1,574 (1980)　　**Pop Density:** 60.9
Land: 30.6 sq. mi.; **Water:** 0.2 sq. mi.

Chartered Dec 26, 1753.
Name origin: For William Dummer, 18th-century lieutenant governor of MA.

Grafton
Town
ZIP: 05146　　　　　**Lat:** 43-11-09 N **Long:** 72-37-01 W
Pop: 602 (1990); 604 (1980)　　　**Pop Density:** 15.7
Land: 38.4 sq. mi.; **Water:** 0.0 sq. mi.

Chartered Apr 8, 1754; settled 1790s.
Name origin: For Grafton, MA.

Guilford
Town
Lat: 42-47-28 N **Long:** 72-37-24 W
Pop: 1,941 (1990); 1,532 (1980)　　**Pop Density:** 48.6
Land: 39.9 sq. mi.; **Water:** 0.1 sq. mi.

Chartered Apr 2, 1754, just before the outbreak of the French and Indian War.
Name origin: Named by NH colonial Gov. Benning Wentworth (1696–1770) for one of the Earls of Guilford. Spelling altered to reflect pronunciation.

Halifax
Town
ZIP: 05358　　　　　**Lat:** 42-46-54 N **Long:** 72-44-59 W
Pop: 588 (1990); 488 (1980)　　　**Pop Density:** 14.8
Land: 39.8 sq. mi.; **Water:** 0.1 sq. mi.

Chartered May 11, 1750.
Name origin: For George Montagu-Dunk, 2nd Earl of Halifax, a prominent colonial administrator.

Jacksonville
Village
ZIP: 05342　　　　　**Lat:** 42-47-50 N **Long:** 72-49-14 W
Pop: 244 (1990); 252 (1980)　　　**Pop Density:** 271.1
Land: 0.9 sq. mi.; **Water:** 0.0 sq. mi.　　**Elev:** 1334 ft.

Name origin: For Andrew Jackson (1767–1845), seventh U.S. president.

Jamaica
Town
ZIP: 05343　　　　　**Lat:** 43-06-27 N **Long:** 72-47-52 W
Pop: 754 (1990); 681 (1980)　　　**Pop Density:** 15.3
Land: 49.4 sq. mi.; **Water:** 0.1 sq. mi.

Chartered Nov 7, 1780.
Name origin: Said to be from a Natick Indian word meaning 'beaver,' but may recall the prior use of the same name in MA and NY.

Londonderry
Town
ZIP: 05148　　　　　**Lat:** 43-12-21 N **Long:** 72-47-58 W
Pop: 1,506 (1990); 1,510 (1980)　　**Pop Density:** 42.2
Land: 35.7 sq. mi.; **Water:** 0.2 sq. mi.

Chartered Apr 20, 1780; settled late 1700s.
Name origin: For Londonderry, NH.

Marlboro
Town
Lat: 42-53-08 N **Long:** 72-44-41 W
Pop: 924 (1990); 695 (1980)　　　**Pop Density:** 22.9
Land: 40.3 sq. mi.; **Water:** 0.3 sq. mi.

Chartered Apr 19, 1751.
Name origin: For John Churchill, Duke of Marlborough, renowned 17th-century military commander; with spelling variation.

Newfane
Town

ZIP: 05345   **Lat:** 42-57-54 N **Long:** 72-42-04 W
Pop: 1,555 (1990); 1,129 (1980)   **Pop Density:** 38.7
Land: 40.2 sq. mi.; **Water:** 0.1 sq. mi.

Chartered Jun 19, 1753; organized 1774. Village and town are not coextensive.

Name origin: For John Fane, a favored relative of NH colonial Gov. Benning Wentworth (1696–1770).

*Newfane
Village

ZIP: 05345   **Lat:** 42-59-15 N **Long:** 72-39-22 W
Pop: 164 (1990); 119 (1980)   **Pop Density:** 820.0
Land: 0.2 sq. mi.; **Water:** 0.0 sq. mi.   **Elev:** 536 ft.

North Westminster
Village

ZIP: 05101   **Lat:** 43-07-11 N **Long:** 72-27-18 W
Pop: 268 (1990); 310 (1980)   **Pop Density:** 893.3
Land: 0.3 sq. mi.; **Water:** 0.0 sq. mi.

Name origin: For its location in the town of Westminster.

Putney
Town

ZIP: 05346   **Lat:** 42-59-28 N **Long:** 72-31-48 W
Pop: 2,352 (1990); 1,850 (1980)   **Pop Density:** 87.8
Land: 26.8 sq. mi.; **Water:** 0.0 sq. mi.

Chartered Dec 26, 1753; organized May 8, 1770.

Name origin: Named by NH colonial Gov. Benning Wentworth (1696–1770) for Putney, England.

Rockingham
Town

ZIP: 05101   **Lat:** 43-10-37 N **Long:** 72-30-22 W
Pop: 5,484 (1990); 5,538 (1980)   **Pop Density:** 130.9
Land: 41.9 sq. mi.; **Water:** 0.4 sq. mi.

Chartered Dec 28, 1752.

Name origin: For Charles Watson-Wentworth (1730–82), the 2nd Marquis of Rockingham.

Saxtons River
Village

ZIP: 05154   **Lat:** 43-08-20 N **Long:** 72-30-40 W
Pop: 541 (1990); 593 (1980)   **Pop Density:** 1082.0
Land: 0.5 sq. mi.; **Water:** 0.0 sq. mi.   **Elev:** 528 ft.

Name origin: For its location on the river.

Somerset
Town

Lat: 42-58-18 N **Long:** 72-56-56 W
Pop: 2 (1990); 2 (1980)   **Pop Density:** 0.1
Land: 26.1 sq. mi.; **Water:** 2.0 sq. mi.

Stratton
Town

ZIP: 05360   **Lat:** 43-04-47 N **Long:** 72-54-56 W
Pop: 121 (1990); 122 (1980)   **Pop Density:** 2.6
Land: 46.4 sq. mi.; **Water:** 0.5 sq. mi.

Chartered Jul 30, 1761.

Name origin: For Stratton, Cornwall, England.

Townshend
Town

Lat: 43-04-15 N **Long:** 72-39-52 W
Pop: 1,019 (1990); 849 (1980)   **Pop Density:** 23.9
Land: 42.7 sq. mi.; **Water:** 0.1 sq. mi.

Chartered Jun 20, 1753; organized 1771.

Name origin: Named by NH colonial Gov. Benning Wentworth (1696–1770) for a prominent British political family.

Vernon
Town

ZIP: 05354   **Lat:** 42-45-52 N **Long:** 72-31-25 W
Pop: 1,850 (1990); 1,175 (1980)   **Pop Density:** 95.4
Land: 19.4 sq. mi.; **Water:** 0.6 sq. mi.

Chartered Sep 3, 1753; organized 1802.

Name origin: For Mt. Vernon, the VA estate of George Washington (1732–99).

Wardsboro
Town

ZIP: 05355   **Lat:** 43-01-13 N **Long:** 72-49-04 W
Pop: 654 (1990); 505 (1980)   **Pop Density:** 22.3
Land: 29.3 sq. mi.; **Water:** 0.0 sq. mi.

Chartered Nov 7, 1780.

Name origin: For the original grantee, William Ward.

West Brattleboro
CDP

Lat: 42-51-05 N **Long:** 72-36-39 W
Pop: 3,135 (1990); 2,795 (1980)   **Pop Density:** 313.5
Land: 10.0 sq. mi.; **Water:** 0.0 sq. mi.

Westminster
Town

ZIP: 05158   **Lat:** 43-04-28 N **Long:** 72-30-30 W
Pop: 3,026 (1990); 2,493 (1980)   **Pop Density:** 65.6
Land: 46.1 sq. mi.; **Water:** 0.0 sq. mi.

Chartered Nov 9, 1752. Village and town are not coextensive.

Name origin: For Westminster, England.

*Westminster
Village

ZIP: 05158   **Lat:** 43-04-34 N **Long:** 72-27-21 W
Pop: 399 (1990); 319 (1980)   **Pop Density:** 234.7
Land: 1.7 sq. mi.; **Water:** 0.0 sq. mi.

Whitingham
Town

ZIP: 05361   **Lat:** 42-46-55 N **Long:** 72-52-12 W
Pop: 1,177 (1990); 1,043 (1980)   **Pop Density:** 32.1
Land: 36.7 sq. mi.; **Water:** 2.2 sq. mi.

Chartered Mar 12, 1780.

Name origin: For its first grantee, Nathan Whiting.

Wilmington
Town

ZIP: 05363   **Lat:** 42-52-28 N **Long:** 72-51-45 W
Pop: 1,968 (1990); 1,808 (1980)   **Pop Density:** 49.3
Land: 39.9 sq. mi.; **Water:** 1.9 sq. mi.

Chartered Apr 29, 1751.

Name origin: Named by NH colonial Gov. Benning Wentworth (1696–1770) for an old friend, Spencer Compton (1673?–1743), 1st Earl of Wilmington.

Windham
Town

Lat: 43-10-24 N **Long:** 72-43-28 W
Pop: 251 (1990); 223 (1980)   **Pop Density:** 9.6
Land: 26.1 sq. mi.; **Water:** 0.0 sq. mi.

Organized Oct 22, 1795.

Name origin: For Charles Wyndham, a close friend of NH colonial Gov. Benning Wentworth (1696–1770), with a spelling alteration.

Windsor County
County Seat: Woodstock (ZIP: 05091)

Pop: 54,055 (1990); 51,030 (1980)   **Pop Density:** 55.7
Land: 971.3 sq. mi.; **Water:** 4.8 sq. mi.   **Area Code:** 802
On the central eastern border of VT, east of Rutland; organized Feb 22, 1781 (prior to statehood) from the former Cumberland County.
Name origin: For the English town of Windsor.

Andover   Town
Lat: 43-17-01 N **Long:** 72-42-56 W
Pop: 373 (1990); 350 (1980)   **Pop Density:** 13.0
Land: 28.8 sq. mi.; **Water:** 0.0 sq. mi.
Chartered Oct 13, 1761.
Name origin: For Andover, Hampshire, England.

Baltimore   Town
Lat: 43-21-34 N **Long:** 72-33-57 W
Pop: 190 (1990); 181 (1980)   **Pop Density:** 40.4
Land: 4.7 sq. mi.; **Water:** 0.0 sq. mi.
Organized by legislative act Oct 19, 1793.
Name origin: Origin uncertain; possibly for Baltimore, MD.

Barnard   Town
Lat: 43-43-59 N **Long:** 72-37-28 W
Pop: 872 (1990); 790 (1980)   **Pop Density:** 17.9
Land: 48.7 sq. mi.; **Water:** 0.2 sq. mi.
Chartered Jul 17, 1761.
Name origin: For Francis Bernard (1712–79), governor of the Massachusetts Bay Colony 1760–69, with spelling alteration.

Bethel   Town
ZIP: 05032   Lat: 43-50-50 N **Long:** 72-40-16 W
Pop: 1,866 (1990); 1,715 (1980)   **Pop Density:** 41.3
Land: 45.2 sq. mi.; **Water:** 0.1 sq. mi.
Chartered Dec 23, 1779. The first town created by the then independent republic of VT.
Name origin: For the biblical site.

Bridgewater   Town
ZIP: 05034   Lat: 43-37-39 N **Long:** 72-39-52 W
Pop: 895 (1990); 867 (1980)   **Pop Density:** 18.0
Land: 49.6 sq. mi.; **Water:** 0.0 sq. mi.
Chartered Jul 10, 1761.
Name origin: For Francis Egerton (1736–1803), 3rd Duke of Bridgewater, famed for his construction of Britain's first canals.

Cavendish   Town
ZIP: 05142   Lat: 43-24-32 N **Long:** 72-36-14 W
Pop: 1,323 (1990); 1,355 (1980)   **Pop Density:** 33.4
Land: 39.6 sq. mi.; **Water:** 0.1 sq. mi.
Granted Oct 12, 1761.
Name origin: For William Cavendish (1720–64), the 4th Duke of Devonshire, and an influential British peer.

Chester   Town
Lat: 43-17-16 N **Long:** 72-36-55 W
Pop: 2,832 (1990); 2,791 (1980)   **Pop Density:** 50.7
Land: 55.9 sq. mi.; **Water:** 0.0 sq. mi.
Chartered Feb 22, 1754.
Name origin: Named in 1766 for Prince George Augustus Frederick (1762–1830), Earl of Chester and eldest son of King George III (1738–1820) of England. Originally called New Flamstead.

Hartford   Town
ZIP: 05047   Lat: 43-39-52 N **Long:** 72-23-12 W
Pop: 9,404 (1990); 7,963 (1980)   **Pop Density:** 208.1
Land: 45.2 sq. mi.; **Water:** 0.7 sq. mi.
Chartered Jul 4, 1761.
Name origin: For Hartford, CT.

Hartland   Town
ZIP: 05048   Lat: 43-33-59 N **Long:** 72-26-04 W
Pop: 2,988 (1990); 2,396 (1980)   **Pop Density:** 66.4
Land: 45.0 sq. mi.; **Water:** 0.2 sq. mi.
Chartered Jul 10, 1761, as Hertford by NH colonial Gov. Benning Wentworth (1696–1770).
Name origin: Present name adopted in 1782, for Hartland, CT. Changed to eliminate confusion with adjoining town of Hartford. Originally named for Hertford in England.

Ludlow   Town
ZIP: 05149   Lat: 43-23-46 N **Long:** 72-42-16 W
Pop: 2,302 (1990); 2,414 (1980)   **Pop Density:** 64.3
Land: 35.8 sq. mi.; **Water:** 0.4 sq. mi.
Chartered Sep 16, 1761. Village and town are not coextensive.
Name origin: For Henry Herbert, Viscount Ludlow.

*Ludlow   Village
ZIP: 05149   Lat: 43-23-46 N **Long:** 72-41-50 W
Pop: 1,123 (1990); 1,352 (1980)   **Pop Density:** 802.1
Land: 1.4 sq. mi.; **Water:** 0.0 sq. mi.   **Elev:** 1067 ft.

Norwich   Town
ZIP: 05055   Lat: 43-44-40 N **Long:** 72-19-06 W
Pop: 3,093 (1990); 2,398 (1980)   **Pop Density:** 69.2
Land: 44.7 sq. mi.; **Water:** 0.1 sq. mi.
Chartered Jul 4, 1761.
Name origin: For Norwich, CT, which is named for Norwich, England.

Perkinsville   Village
ZIP: 05151   Lat: 43-22-10 N **Long:** 72-30-58 W
Pop: 148 (1990); 187 (1980)   **Pop Density:** 740.0
Land: 0.2 sq. mi.; **Water:** 0.0 sq. mi.

Plymouth   Town
ZIP: 05056   Lat: 43-31-18 N **Long:** 72-43-19 W
Pop: 440 (1990); 405 (1980)   **Pop Density:** 9.1
Land: 48.2 sq. mi.; **Water:** 0.5 sq. mi.
Chartered Jul 6, 1761.
Name origin: For Plymouth, MA, site of the first Pilgrim colony.

Pomfret   Town
ZIP: 05053   Lat: 43-42-16 N **Long:** 72-30-31 W
Pop: 874 (1990); 856 (1980)   **Pop Density:** 22.2
Land: 39.4 sq. mi.; **Water:** 0.1 sq. mi.
Chartered Jul 8, 1761.
Name origin: For Thomas Fermor, the 1st Earl of Pomfret.

Proctorsville
Village
ZIP: 05153   **Lat:** 43-22-56 N **Long:** 07-23-82 W
Name origin: For an early settler.

Reading
Town
ZIP: 05062   **Lat:** 43-29-38 N **Long:** 72-35-48 W
Pop: 614 (1990); 647 (1980)   **Pop Density:** 14.8
Land: 41.5 sq. mi.; **Water:** 0.2 sq. mi.
Chartered Jul 6, 1761.
Name origin: For Reading, MA, which is named for Reading, England.

Rochester
Town
ZIP: 05767   **Lat:** 43-52-38 N **Long:** 72-49-58 W
Pop: 1,181 (1990); 1,054 (1980)   **Pop Density:** 21.1
Land: 56.0 sq. mi.; **Water:** 0.1 sq. mi.
Chartered Jul 30, 1781.
Name origin: For Rochester, MA.

Royalton
Town
ZIP: 05068   **Lat:** 43-48-50 N **Long:** 72-33-14 W
Pop: 2,389 (1990); 2,100 (1980)   **Pop Density:** 59.1
Land: 40.4 sq. mi.; **Water:** 0.5 sq. mi.
Chartered Dec 20, 1781.
Name origin: A contraction of "Royal Town"; named in 1769 by acting Gov. Cadwallader Colden (1688–1776) to honor King George III (1738–1820) of England.

Sharon
Town
ZIP: 05065   **Lat:** 43-47-18 N **Long:** 72-26-13 W
Pop: 1,211 (1990); 828 (1980)   **Pop Density:** 30.6
Land: 39.6 sq. mi.; **Water:** 0.5 sq. mi.
Chartered Aug 17, 1761.
Name origin: For Sharon, CT.

Springfield
Town
ZIP: 05156   **Lat:** 43-17-22 N **Long:** 72-28-45 W
Pop: 9,579 (1990); 10,190 (1980)   **Pop Density:** 194.3
Land: 49.3 sq. mi.; **Water:** 0.1 sq. mi.
In eastern VT on the Black River, 32 mi. southeast of Rutland. Chartered Aug 20, 1761.
Name origin: For Springfield, MA.

Stockbridge
Town
ZIP: 05772   **Lat:** 43-45-42 N **Long:** 72-44-14 W
Pop: 618 (1990); 508 (1980)   **Pop Density:** 13.4
Land: 46.1 sq. mi.; **Water:** 0.1 sq. mi.
Chartered July 21, 1761.
Name origin: For Stockbridge, MA, which was named for Stockbridge, England.

Weathersfield
Town
ZIP: 05151   **Lat:** 43-23-27 N **Long:** 72-28-34 W
Pop: 2,674 (1990); 2,534 (1980)   **Pop Density:** 61.1
Land: 43.8 sq. mi.; **Water:** 0.4 sq. mi.
Chartered Aug 20, 1761; organized 1768.
Name origin: Probably for Wethersfield, CT, with a spelling alteration.

Weston
Town
ZIP: 05161   **Lat:** 43-19-08 N **Long:** 72-48-04 W
Pop: 488 (1990); 627 (1980)   **Pop Density:** 13.9
Land: 35.1 sq. mi.; **Water:** 0.1 sq. mi.
Chartered Oct 26, 1779.
Name origin: Because it was created from the part of Andover referred to as West Town.

West Windsor
Town
ZIP: 05037   **Lat:** 43-29-10 N **Long:** 72-29-35 W
Pop: 923 (1990); 763 (1980)   **Pop Density:** 37.4
Land: 24.7 sq. mi.; **Water:** 0.0 sq. mi.
Chartered Jul 6, 1761; incorporated Nov 4, 1814.
Name origin: For its relation to Windsor, from which it was created.

White River Junction
CDP
Lat: 43-39-00 N **Long:** 72-19-24 W
Pop: 2,521 (1990); 2,582 (1980)   **Pop Density:** 1575.6
Land: 1.6 sq. mi.; **Water:** 0.0 sq. mi.

Wilder
CDP
Lat: 43-40-20 N **Long:** 72-18-40 W
Pop: 1,576 (1990); 1,461 (1980)   **Pop Density:** 1970.0
Land: 0.8 sq. mi.; **Water:** 0.0 sq. mi.

Windsor
Town
ZIP: 05089   **Lat:** 43-28-33 N **Long:** 72-25-26 W
Pop: 3,714 (1990); 4,084 (1980)   **Pop Density:** 189.5
Land: 19.6 sq. mi.; **Water:** 0.2 sq. mi.
Chartered Jul 6, 1761.
Name origin: Probably for Windsor, CT, itself named for Windsor, England; or possibly for Windsor Castle.

Woodstock
Town
ZIP: 05091   **Lat:** 43-35-46 N **Long:** 72-32-56 W
Pop: 3,212 (1990); 3,214 (1980)   **Pop Density:** 72.2
Land: 44.5 sq. mi.; **Water:** 0.1 sq. mi.
Chartered Jul 10, 1761. Village and town are not coextensive.
Name origin: Named by NH colonial Gov. Benning Wentworth (1696–1770) for Woodstock, Oxfordshire, England.

*Woodstock
Village
ZIP: 05091   **Lat:** 43-37-34 N **Long:** 72-31-01 W
Pop: 1,037 (1990); 1,178 (1980)   **Pop Density:** 1037.0
Land: 1.0 sq. mi.; **Water:** 0.0 sq. mi.   **Elev:** 705 ft.

Index to Places and Counties in Vermont